The Computer Package
STATCAT
Source Programs and User Manual

The Computer Package
STATCAT
Source Programs and User Manual

HUGH DAVID

1982

NORTH-HOLLAND PUBLISHING COMPANY
AMSTERDAM · NEW YORK · OXFORD

© NORTH-HOLLAND PUBLISHING COMPANY, 1982

All rights reserved. No part of this publication may be reproduced, stored in a retrieval system, or transmitted, in any form or by any means, electronic, mechanical, photocopying, recording or otherwise, without the prior permission of the copyright owner.

ISBN: 0 444 86453 9

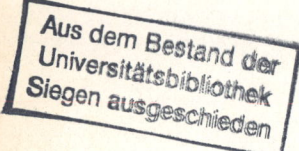

Publishers:

NORTH-HOLLAND PUBLISHING COMPANY
AMSTERDAM · NEW YORK · OXFORD

Sole distributors for the U.S.A. and Canada:

ELSEVIER SCIENCE PUBLISHING COMPANY, INC.
52 VANDERBILT AVENUE
NEW YORK, N.Y. 10017

```
Library of Congress Cataloging in Publication Data

David, Hugh, 1937-
   The statistical package STATCAT.

   Bibliography: p.
   Includes indexes.
   1. STATCAT (Computer programs)   I. Title.
II. Title: Statistical package S.T.A.T.C.A.T.
QA276.4.D38   1982      001.64'25      82-8215
ISBN 0-444-86453-9
```

PRINTED IN THE NETHERLANDS

The author wishes to thank the Director General of the European Commission for Safety in the Air (EUROCONTROL) for permission to publish this work.

The author wishes also to acknowledge the assistance and encouragement of his colleagues at Loughborough University of Technology and at EUROCONTROL Experimental Centre, Bretigny-sur-Orge, France.

TABLE OF CONTENTS

I. INTRODUCTION ... 1

    The STATCAT System ... 1
    Origins ... 1
    Scope ... 1
    Choice of Language ... 2
    System Tactics ... 2
    Computer facilities required ... 3
    Freedom to use STATCAT ... 3
    Computer Readable Source Modules ... 4
    Caveat ... 4

II. DATA ... 5

    Context ... 6
    STATCAT demonstration data ... 10
    Data Level 1 - DUMMY ... 10
    Data Level 2 - NOMINAL ... 11
    Data Level 3 - ORDINAL ... 12
    Data Level 4 - INTERVAL ... 14
    Data Level 5 - RATIO ... 16
    Choice of Data Level ... 17
    STATCAT Data Bank ... 18

III. STANDARD STATCAT INPUT MODULES ... 21

    General Input Conventions ... 21
    File Control Card ... 27
    Data Starter Card ... 35
    Data Description Module ... 41
    Sample Specification ... 49
    Subset Specification ... 57
    Variate Specification Module ... 65
    Data Handling Instruction ... 85
    Combination of Input Modules ... 92

IV. SETTING UP A STATCAT DATA BANK 95

Program STHEAD - Create empty STATCAT Data Bank 96
Program STLOAD - Load STATCAT Data Bank 101
Program STCHEK - Check STATCAT Data Bank 115
Program STCORR - Correct STATCAT Data Bank 133

V. DESCRIPTIVE STATISTICS 153

Program STLIST - List Entries 154
Program STDESC - Describe STATCAT Data Bank 174
Program STASTA - Large Cross-Tabulations 201

VI. COMPARING SAMPLES 225

Program ST2IND - Test Two Independent Samples 227
Program STKIND - Test Several Independent Samples 252
Program ST2REL - Test Two Related Samples 276
Program STKREL - Test Several Related Samples 301

VII. MODEL TESTING 323

Program STANOV - Analysis of Variance 324
Program STMULT - Multiple Regression 362
Program STFACT - Factor Analysis 391
Program STMDIS - Multiple Discriminant Analysis 418
Program STCANO - Canonical Analysis 441

VIII. DATA STUDY 466

Program STGRPS - Semi-Automatic Grouping of Entries 467
Program STAIAD - Automatic Interaction Detector 488
Program STCLUS - Clustering Correlation Matrix 523

IX. STATCAT PLAIN-LANGUAGE DATA BANKS 544

Program STLOAD - Plain-language Input 545
Program STLIST - Plain-language Output 554
Program STLOAD - Plain-language Cross-referencing 564
Program STWORD - Keyword and Soundex Codes 573

X. DATA MANIPULATION 593

    Program STMANI - Manipulating Single Entries   595
    Program STSORT - Sorting Entries into order   616
    Program STMERG - Merging/Matching STATCAT
       Data Banks   635
    Program STSYNC - Synchronising STATCAT Data   660
    Program STCOMB - Combining Entries   678

XI. AUXILIARY PROGRAMS AND SUBROUTINES 704

    Program STCOPY - Copying Entire STATCAT Data Bank   705
    Program STBANK - Verifying STATCAT Data Bank
       Contents   711
    Matrix Operations MINV, MOP, WMAT, MATM and ASEV   716
    Ordering Subroutines - PR, INSERT, POSN and POSCL   727
    CHI-squared Auxiliaries - REDROW, DICOLA and CHISQ   735
    Switching Auxiliaries - ISW, NEXY and NEXC   740
    Class Auxiliaries - CLASIF, CLIMS and PRTCLS   745
    Probability Evaluation - PRBF and GAUS   750
    Miscellaneous Auxiliaries - CHIKEN and FITIT   755

XII. STATISTICAL DIFFICULTIES AND DANGERS 758

INDEX 769

INDEX OF SOURCE MODULES 773

BIBLIOGRAPHY 775

SUBJECT / REFERENCE INDEX 780

Chapter I

INTRODUCTION

1.1 THE STATCAT SYSTEM

The STATCAT - STATistical Context Aided Testing - system is a system for the storage, retrieval and analysis of numerical data. The system is designed to cope with most types of statistical analyses, while being adaptable to more specialised tasks. (For example, it can be used to a limited extent for text handling.)

1.2 ORIGINS

STATCAT is the product of the author's experiences in scientific research and technical development over the past twenty-odd years. Initially, when digital computers were scarce and costly devices, the major problem was to find or construct methods for analysing particular sets of data. As the problem of computing power eased, and high-level languages became available, problems of data checking and system compatibility became more important. Recently computer program packages have become generally available. In principle, these solve many of the problems that faced earlier users, but they have some remaining drawbacks. It is not always easy to discover from the documentation exactly how exceptions and extreme cases have been treated, which corrections have been used or exactly where or why a malfunction occurred. Finally, there remains the problem of cost. Professionally written, marketed, serviced and maintained packages must be paid for at commercial rates. Usually this implies an annual cost of thousands of dollars - far beyond the resources of the individual researcher, and - perhaps more important - beyond the reach of many scientific teams and departments in poor countries.

The author is perhaps naive and perhaps old-fashioned, but feels very deeply that the tools of scientific research and communication ought to be freely available to all. This book is the result of that feeling. It is intended to provide the scientist or technologist with the means to use a digital computer carry out statistical processes, with a minimum of unnecessary effort, and with the minimum of mistakes.

1.3 SCOPE

THIS BOOK CONTAINS THE ENTIRE STATCAT SYSTEM.

This book describes the STATCAT system primarily from the point of view of the system user. It is aimed at the statistician who wants to use a computer to take over the donkey-work of statistical calculation, and at the computer user who wants to analyse data using statistical methods. Generally accepted computing techniques are applied to generally accepted statistical methods. The few innovations that have been found necessary have been introduced only where major gaps occur in common use. It is written as simply as the author's limited skill permits. Bibliographical references and discussions of statistical methods have been reduced to the minimum, and references given to generally available text-books rather than to original theses buried in the decent obscurity of university libraries.

1.4   CHOICE OF LANGUAGE

The STATCAT system consists of twenty-seven computer programs. These programs are all written in ASA FORTRAN IV - following the American Standards Association definition as closely as possible. The system should therefore work in its present form on any digital computer which has a FORTRAN IV compiler. FORTRAN IV was chosen for essentially the same reason that this book is written in the English language - because it is the most widely available language. FORTRAN IV has an additional advantage in that it is the most closely standardised generally available high-order language, and ought therefore to be the easiest to transfer from machine to machine. FORTRAN IV has been available since 1966, and would not now be recommended as an language for beginners. Most of its defects affect the writer of programs rather than the user - compiled FORTRAN programs are generally efficient. Finally, there are so many programs written in FORTRAN IV that compilers are written for new computers as a matter of course. (FORTRAN IV has been called the "Immortal Dinosaur" of computing.)

In general, the strategy of the system is to store data in a permanent computer-readable form in data banks of a simple but flexible standardised form. As much information as practically possible is stored with the data.

Because the available internal storage of a digital computer varies according to the size of the computer, all programs in the system are written to make the most of the available storage, to minimise the number of occasions that the system has to search through the bulk storage, while being adaptable to smaller working space at the cost of repeated reference to the bulk storage.

The programs are designed in modules to allow the overlaying of input subroutines or of statistical test routines. Dynamic storage allocation is employed throughout, to minimise the changes necessary to adapt the programs to larger or smaller working stores. A system flow-chart is provided for each module, designed to help the user to understand the way in which the module operates. Irrelevant detail is ignored and each program module is charted on at most one page. For large modules, the resultant flow-chart may vary from the epigrammatic to the enigmatic, and verbal supplements are therefore also provided. The listings of master programs contain detailed comments, specifying the required sizes of arrays, etc..

The author is fully aware that the programs listed in this book do not conform to current programming practice in structure or in style. If he could afford several further years of part-time effort, or a year of full-time work he would re-write many modules. Constraints of time, cost and increasing responsibilities make this impossible. If sufficient interest develops, a student text may be produced, and, possibly a "front-end" processor to provide an easier input format may be developed, but major revisions are unlikely.

1.5 SYSTEM TACTICS

As far as possible, the user is never asked to provide any information that the system can deduce, and what information he gives is checked for credibility, and repeated back to provide an opportunity for verification, or for post-mortems if required. Where choices of statistical method exist, the computer chooses an appropriate method on the basis of the stored description, although it can be over-ruled by the user. The path of statistical virtue is smoothed as far as possible at the expense of the (statistically speaking) wicked. The level of prolixity (detail) in the output can also be controlled by the user.

To help the user understand the output, effort has been devoted to making the output forms resemble as closely as possible those found in current textbooks, even at some cost in complexity. Wherever inferential statistics - such as values of chi-squared - are derived, they are accompanied by an estimate of the associated probability. Where the estimate is liable to be in error, a warning is given.

1.6 COMPUTER FACILITIES REQUIRED

The system has been designed to require the minimum possible equipment. In principle, what is necessary is an input device, an output device, a quantity of internal (random-access) storage and a serially organised bulk-storage medium. The input device is assumed to be a card-reader, the output a line-printer, and the bulk storage a magnetic tape unit in the written descriptions in this book, but input could be by magnetic tape, or by VDT keyboard, output could be via a VDT display (although the page and line control FORTRAN conventions would need to be revised to produce a professional output), and the bulk-storage medium could be a disk or cassette.

Some of the auxiliary data manipulation programs use two bulk-storage media, one for input and one for output. The program STMERG, which merges two input data banks, normally uses two input and one output medium, but can be run with only one input bulk-storage and an input device in place of the second input bulk-storage device. These auxiliary programs are not necessary for the running of the system, although they can save much routine drudgery.

1.7 FREEDOM TO USE STATCAT

The purchaser of this book may copy any or all of the STATCAT source modules into any computer system, and compile, link and use them for instruction, research, public service or entertainment without further formality.

Copies may not be made of other parts of this book (text, illustrations, etc.) which are subject to normal copyright restrictions in accordance with the copyright notice inserted in the title pages.

1.8 COMPUTER READABLE SOURCE MODULES

IBM Standard nine-track 800/1600/6250 bits per inch magnetic tapes containing all STATCAT source modules and demonstration input data are available at cost price (Eight Pounds Sterling or equivalent - until 1 January 1984 - subject to increase after that date) together with assistance in bringing STATCAT into operation, and general advice, from ; -

> Dr. H. David
> 7 High Wickham
> Hastings Old Town
> Sussex TN35 5PB
> ENGLAND

In fairness to his employers, the author can only undertake this work in his own time, outside normal working hours. As a matter of principle, he will accept no fees or rewards for doing so.

1.9 CAVEAT

Although all known errors have been eliminated, it is certain that some must remain. The author will be grateful, if not gratified, if these are brought to his attention, and will attempt to correct them. These corrections will be incorporated into the magnetic tapes, and into later editions of the text, if any.

Neither the author nor the publisher can accept responsibility for the consequences of programming or documentation errors.

Chapter II

DATA

The term 'data' is widely used in the computer world. It is a vague term, and seems to have no generally accepted definition. The original definitions, like those of many other terms in this field, are obsolete. The word appears in the dictionaries as the plural of ' datum ', defined as a reference point or a base for measurement. (Mean Sea Level or the International Date line are data in this sense.) In the computer world, the word is applied to information, facts or figures in bulk, as opposed to instructions, which tell the computer what to do with the data. In the earliest machines, the data and the instructions were completely separate; data appearing as punched holes in tapes or cards, and instructions as the positions of switches, or the presence of plugs in sockets. While to a certain extent this distinction remains valuable, most systems now accept both instructions and data from the same sources, what are instructions to the programmer will be data to the compiler writer, and so on. In addition to the mere physical confusion that can occur, as many a harassed programmer has discovered when his program has attempted to execute a datum as if it were an instruction, there are more profound philosophical problems, and for statisticians (among others) some very knotty problems of interpretation. Most statistical methods are very simple in their fundamental conceptions, not only because more elaborate models were too laborious to evaluate by hand, but because the conceptual framework in which they are set is usually an order of magnitude more complex. (Witness the prolonged and acrimonious debates about factor analysis.)

Most statistical methods are, or were, based on a scheme of hypothesis, test and comparison, making the minimal use of parameters derived from the data. The computer has made it possible to produce models fitted both qualitatively and quantitatively to the data, and theory has to a certain extent lagged behind. The methods touched on in Chapter 8 of this book are some of those at the 'growing edge' of statistics, and, in general, are described as 'empirical' - which is to say that theory has not caught up with practice.

While the computer has brought problems to the statistician, it has solved many more. In its role as obedient slave, it has taken over the very real drudgery of statistical analysis, as its little brothers have relieved students of many afternoons of cranking at handles, scraped knuckles and sore finger-tips. But this is not all that a computer can do. It is possible, (as this book demonstrates) to allocate to the computer much of the elementary decision making involved in routine statistical analysis. To do so, the system must be given information about the data on which it is to operate.

It became necessary to tell the computer something about the data it receives, implictly or explicitly, as soon as common input devices were devised. The distinction between information and data had to be made, and different types of data - integers, real numbers, complex numbers and ultimately non-numeric data had to be distinguished. In this system, a further step has been taken, by providing a means of informing the computer of the quality of data it will receive.

This has been done by incorporating in the system a coded representation of the context of the data.

2.1   CONTEXT

In Douglas Adams's "Hitch-hiker's Guide to the Galaxy" mention is made of a computer designed to calculate the answer to the Ultimate Question of Life, the Universe and Everything. After some seven and a half million years it announced the answer (forty-two), leaving the exquisite problem of what was the actual question. This is perhaps an extreme example of the importance of context.

The context of data is the information accompanying the data which tells the user what they mean. When human users receive numerical data these are almost always in an explicit or implicit context. Tables of numbers have headings, stating what is being measured, what units are being used and directly or indirectly what sort of data are represented by the numbers. A reading on an instrument is in a context. In ordinary human use, we do not need to define the context more precisely, since we know from our experience what sort of data can be expected in a given situation. The number given by the position of a certain pointer on a certain dial in our car indicates the speed of the car. We know that this reading is more or less reliable, that it is liable to be in a certain range of values, that the numbers are in terms of a certain defined unit, and that they are quantitative measurements on a continuous scale.

The digital computer does not have this implied background knowledge. It must be specifically told that a certain number is a speedometer reading in miles per hour, that this is a true measurement, that negative values are impossible, and that values exceeding 100 merit investigation. If the system is provided with all this information, and explicitly told to check the data, it will do so much more efficiently than a human being, within its specific instructions, because it is undistracted by lapses of attention, boredom, terror, hangover, falling in love or other causes of human error.

If the system can call on this context information, coded in a fashion it can understand, the user can give much more general orders. Instead of saying: "Take the following 17 values, and compare them by using a student's 't' test assuming uniformity of variance." he may say "Take all males over 17 and compare the logarithm of their weights with those of females over 19 - if the difference is statistically significant tell me how, what test you used, and why. Give me brief details. Otherwise say nothing" Figure 2.11 is an example of the sort of data that may be presented to a statistician. This is a two-way table in which the rows represent operators, and the columns working positions. The values in the cells represent the percentage of errors made by the operator while carrying out a series of drilling operations with the equipment at that working position. For example, operator Fred made 2.1 per cent of errors using the equipment at working position K.

Figure 2.12 shows the steps that might be taken by a systematic and conscientious statistician analysing this data. It shows that the analysis depends largely on the context, subject to modifications as knowledge is obtained during the analysis. Most of the decisions given in Figure 2.12 could equally well have been made by a suitably programmed computer. There are some points, such as the decision to use a variance-reducing transform, where different statisticians might make other decisions. In practice, this sort of decision is usually influenced by the resources available, the importance of the analysis, and other factors not strictly connected to the data.

Limitations of machine capacity and, more important, limitations of programming and testing capacity make it impractical to provide the computer system with the ability to handle all the decisions involved in statistical analysis. It is, however, possible to carry the process rather further than is normally done, by storing information about the context of the data and programming the system to make use of this information.

To show how this can be done, let us consider the data of Figure 2.11 again. Although the presentation of this table is (relatively) easy for the human to understand, unambiguous, and economical it requires that the whole of the table be visible for it to convey information, and it lacks generality - if we wished to add another datum to each cell, it would become complex and difficult to read. Figure 2.13 presents the same data in a more explicit form. In this form, each row gives all the information relating to the datum involved. Although this way of representing data is less compact, and is not so attractive to the human eye, it has considerable advantages for the computer system. Each line of the table is virtually self-contained, so that only one line need be held by the system at any time. In addition, the form is more flexible. Extra data can be added to the end of existing rows, or extra rows can be added. Each line of Figure 2.13 is an "ordered set", and the whole table forms an (unordered) set of ordered sets. Within the STATCAT system a single numerical value is called a 'datum', and normally forms, so to speak, the atom of the system. These data are not all the result of observation, but include numeric aspects of the context. The number of the operator, and the number of the working position, are parts of the data. In most real-life situations, there will be more than three data in the line, which is known as an 'entry', and some of these may not be numeric values. (In principle, all data subject to analysis are stored as numbers, although special techniques are available to handle non-numeric data.)

The collection of entries which contains the actual data is called the 'Data Storage Segment'. It is not necessary for entries to be in order, although it is often a help if they are.

In most statistical systems, and indeed in many computer applications applications, data files consist simply of strings or arrays of numbers stored in some form of computer storage. If this technique is adopted, several problems can arise, and some certainly will. To mention only a few ; -

The user forgets in which order he wrote down his data, and finds that he has analysed the number of the entry in terms of the operator, when he wished to analyse the productivity in terms of time of day.

The user loses a card, or the machine destroys a record, so that when an analysis is repeated, a different answer is produced.

The user decides to add some more data, from a further experiment, but forgets the order in which the original data were given, and finds that he has a file in which the second datum indicates the operator and the third the observer for half the entries, and vice versa for the rest.

Owing to a slight error in punching, the least significant digit of one datum is taken for the most-significant of the next datum.

The user forgets whether file 13458 contains the data from the July experiment, and 14358 that from the September experiment or the other way round. He discards the wrong one, and writes new data over his original. This can make life difficult, especially if the original data are no longer available.

To avoid all these possible disasters, we load and check some basic information about the data at the start of the file. The 'Data Starter' contains the title of the file, the number of data per entry, and other generally applicable information. This is followed by a 'Data Description Segment', containing descriptions of the data found in each position in the entries. By analogy with Figure 2.13, these are known as 'Data Column Descriptions'. Each Data Column Description contains a description in words of the datum, with a description of the data level. These data levels describe the quality of the data in the data column, and are defined, explained and illustrated in 2.3. The "Data Storage segment', containing the entries, follows the Data Description Segment, and is followed by the 'Data Terminator' - a blank entry used to signal the end of the file to the system.

Section 2.2, following, contains a description of a representative situation in which data might be collected. It has been put together to illustrate the use of STATCAT programs, and is used in examples in the rest of the book, including 2.3.

Figure 2.11

Example of Statistical Data

Percentage of Errors during Drilling Operations

Working Position		Operator Name		
	Eric	Fred	Gina	Hugh
I	1.93	0.06	3.00	1.30
J	0.28	3.00	0.42	1.30
K	2.80	0.20	0.26	0.57
L	0.12	2.10	1.73	0.47

Questions : -

Are some operators more precise than others?
Are there more errors in some working positions than in others?

Figure 2.12

Phase	Activity	Depends on	Solution
1.	Checking for errors in the data	Context	
1.1	Are any values negative?	Data	None
1.2	Are any values far from centre?	Data	None
1.3	Refer queries to originator of data		No errors
1.4	Repeat until visible anomalies corrected or explained		
2.	Choice of most appropriate test	Context	
2.1	What level is the row classification?	Context	Nominal
2.2	What level is the column classification	Context	Nominal
2.3	What level is the cell value?	Context	Ratio
2.4	What sort of difference is sought?	Context	Means
2.5	What test is appropriate?	Experience	Analysis of Variance
2.6	What is the required significance level	Experience	
3.	Execution of chosen test		
3.1	Reduction of data	Test	Sums and Sums of squares
3.2	Derive test statistic	Test	Calculate Anovar table
3.3	Accept/reject null hypothesis	Result	Compare
4.	Precautions against distortion.		
4.1	Consider possible causes of error	Experience	Non-linear Data
4.2	Determine if error cause is present	Inspection	Yes
4.3	Take action to reduce error	Experience	Use logs
4.4	Repeat analysis		

Figure 2.13 - Example 2.11 arranged as a list

Session	Operator	Working Position	Percentage Accuracy
1	Hugh	J	1.30
2	Gina	I	3.00
3	Fred	L	2.10
4	Eric	K	2.80
5	Gina	K	0.26
6	Hugh	L	0.47
7	Eric	I	1.93
8	Fred	J	3.00
9	Fred	I	0.06
10	Eric	J	0.28
11	Hugh	K	0.57
12	Gina	L	1.73
13	Eric	L	0.12
14	Fred	K	0.20
15	Gina	J	0.42
16	Hugh	I	1.30

2.2   STATCAT DEMONSTRATION DATA

Most people find it easier to grasp unfamiliar ideas and procedures if they are given a concrete example on which to practice. A set of artificial data has been made up, to illustrate the principles and practice of the STATCAT system. This situation is used to illustrate all STATCAT programs, except those using non-numeric data, for which a separate example is provided.

Imagine a light engineering workshop, containing machine tools, the people who work them, and people observing the workers. Four alternative positions for equipment have been worked out, and are installed in the shop. In the first, the equipment is arranged in a line against one wall. In the second, part of the equipment is laid out at the end of the line is laid out in a semi-circle around a stool. In the third, two rows of equipment are arranged at an angle to the backing wall, and in the fourth, the equipment is laid out in a corner of the building. These arrangements are coded I, J, K and L; the letter shapes representing the layout.

Four types of work are carried on at these positions. These are the assembling of various small components, the bending of sheet metal to form a chassis, cutting metal sheet to the right size, and drilling a number of fixing holes in the chassis. These tasks are considered to be in increasing order of difficulty.

Four operators, Eric, Fred, Gina and Hugh carry out each task at each working position. There are four observers, Mike, Noel, Oscar and Pete, who watch the operators, making notes and assessing their performance, and the environmental hazards.

A total of sixteen experimental sessions are carried out, two in the morning, and two in the afternoon for four successive days.

After each session, each observer assesses the efficiency of the operator, measures the time required to complete an allotted quantity of work, notes the percentage of defective products, and notes the operator's self-assessment of efficiency, and of the difficulty of the task.

The observers also recorded the temperature during the session, with any significant disturbing features of the environment - heat, noise etc. Finally, the operators wore small heart-rate recorders, from which their mean heart-rate during the session could be deduced.

In all sixteen items were recorded for each experimental session, for each working position. These are a planned mixture of data, such as observers, operators, working positions and tasks, measures of performance, such as efficiency ratings, and time taken, measures of physiological stress, such as heart-rate and possible interfering factors, such as ambient temperature and environmental stress.

This heterogeneous collection of measures in fact represents quite well the sorts of collections of data often found in real situations. In the following section, the classification of data is explained, and the consequences of error discussed.

(The actual values for the data are given in Figure 4.23b in the form in which they are given to the system.)

2.3 DATA LEVEL 1 - DUMMY

DUMMY data are data which are not primarily intended for statistical analysis.

2.3.1 Mathematical Properties

DUMMY data are simply stored information. They need not be numeric values, so that DUMMY data columns may be used to store such things as names and addresses or bibliographic references. Numeric data can be stored in DUMMY data columns where it would be wasteful to provide many separate classes.

2.3.2 Explanation

DUMMY data columns are not treated mathematically by the system - for example the checking routines do not attempt to form maxima or minima (see 4.2). They can therefore be used to handle information in non-numeric form, which might cause errors or overflows in arithmetic manipulation, provoking error messages, and even system failures on some computers. They may also be used to store numbers which need not be subject to statistical analysis and checking - questionnaire numbers, or identification codes. These numbers are not then restricted to a fixed number of alternative classes, but may be used to identify particular entries in the data bank.

2.3.3 Examples

A long-term study was being made of the changes in student attitudes during their university careers. Each student was assigned an identity number and a STATCAT data bank containing these numbers with the appropriate names was compiled (using a special method described in 9.2). The same number was given to a questionnaire filled in by each student, which was analysed using STATCAT programs. At the end of each year, the first file was used to match follow-up questionnaires with the original records.

The first item in each of the entries in Figure 2.13 is the line number. This could be coded as a DUMMY data column, and used to find any particular entry.

It is reasonable to suppose that the sixteen sessions (four on each of four days) may show individual differences which are not necessarily the effects of session and day added arithmetically. It is therefore useful to have the number of the session (1 - 16) stored with the entry. We will have only 10 classes, so we call this data column DUMMY, to save space, and avoid unnecessary checking.

2.4 DATA LEVEL 2 - NOMINAL

NOMINAL data are data for which the numbers serve only to identify which one of a finite number of alternative classes the data belong to. The alternative classes cannot be placed in a relevant order.

2.4.1 Mathematical Properties

NOMINAL data are said to be 'unique up to a one-to-one correspondance'. This is to say that the identifying numbers could be switched round, substituting any one number in the new coding for any one number in the old.

2.4.2 Explanation

When each datum belongs to exactly one of a finite number of classes, and the classes have no special order, then the data level of the variate is said to be NOMINAL (meaning that each class has a name). Multiple-choice questionnaires are often of this form, requiring the choice of one of a number of alternative answers. Because only one response may be made, the choice is mutually exclusive. If the respondent is allowed to choose several responses it is usually necessary to code each possible response separately as a two-way 'yes/no' choice. This sort of datum is usually the basis for counting statistics.

2.4.3 Examples

- In a survey, respondents are asked what is their main source of heating for their houses. They are asked to tick one of a series of boxes marked NONE, GAS, OIL, ELECTRICITY, OTHER. The responses are recorded by punching a number from 1 to 5.

- In an election count, voting papers are sorted into piles according to candidate. Each paper is placed on one of three heaps marked 1-SMITH, 2-JONES or 3-SPOILT PAPERS. The numbers assigned to these piles are purely labels, which could equally well be altered to 1-JONES, 2-SPOILT PAPERS and 3-SMITH. (Provided of course that the change was made for all papers, not half-way through the sorting process.)

- In our example data the name of an observer for a particular entry:
   1=MIKE   2=NOEL 3=OSCR 4=PETE

  or an operator : -

  1=ERIC   2=FRED 3=GINA 4=HUGH

  may each be coded from 1 - 4

- Finally, the observers were asked to note the presence of certain potential stress factors in the environment. These were excessive heat, excessive humidity, and distracting noise. Although these are not necessarily mutually exclusive, they can be made so by insisting that observers are limited to reporting the most serious of these - or none. These could be coded thus : -

  1 NONE   2 HEAT   3 DAMP   4 NOIS
  (No Stress) (Excessive Heat) (Excesssive Humidity) (Distracting Noise)

REFERENCES Veldman (ch 8), Siegel (ch 3)

2.5 DATA LEVEL 3 - ORDINAL

ORDINAL data are data for which the numbers indicate which one of a finite number of classes, arranged in a relevant order, the data belong to.

2.5.1 Mathematical Properties

ORDINAL data are said to be 'unique up to a monotonic transformation'. This means that the classes of data may be assigned numbers in any way that does not change their order - each class must end up between the same two neighbours as it had before the transform.

2.5.2 Explanation

ORDINAL data are similar to those described as NOMINAL data, (and in fact they are NOMINAL data, since they satisfy the definition of NOMINAL data), but with the additional information value that the order of classes provides information. This means that you cannot change the order of classes without losing this information. In general, the higher the data level, the more information each datum contains, and the more sensitive it is to manipulations.

If for example, you have three possible answers to an opinion survey question - favourable, neutral and hostile - you can code these as 1,2 and 3 on an ORDINAL scale. If you then arranged the data in number order and found the response with as many below as above you would have the median value, an indication of what the average feeling might be. If you coded the responses 1,77 and 392 you would arrive at exactly the same response as the median. If however you coded the responses 1,3 and 2 you would count the hostile before the neutral responses, and would get, probably, a different median value.

It is as well to make sure that the ordering relationship you have used is relevant. In the examples of NOMINAL scales provided, observers and operators were listed in alphabetical order. This could be considered as an ORDINAL scale, but we have no reason to suppose that it reflects anything except a traditional ordering of letters. If this ordering were included in the data bank, then the data would be tested for more specific differences than are justified, and more general differences might not be detected.

Sometimes partial ordering arrangements occur. In these some classes are definitely ordered above others, while others are more or less ambiguous. These may be dealt with in two ways. The doubtful cases may be combined, so that the reduced set of classes is fully ordered - in effect this is what is done whenever the number of choices is less than the number of data being ranked. Alternatively, if the disturbance of ordering is relatively minor, the classes may be specified in the data bank as being in NOMINAL order, but given in order as far as possible, and the ambiguous data eliminated from the data subset used when the user instructs the computer to make its test on an ORDINAL level. (Facilities for specifying which data are to be included, and for over-riding the original data level are provided throughout the system - although the system is inclined to talk back when its judgement is ignored.)

Ranking or ordering statistics are most frequently used with data at this level.

2.5.3 Examples

- In a survey of stress in hospital patients, the number of dependents of each patient was known. It was believed that the more dependents the more would be the stress, but there was no reason to expect the relationship to be linear, so that only ordinal tests would be considered relevant. (As an example of a partially ordered scale, the original data specified classes as NONE, Husband, wife, child, Husband and child, wife and child and so on. These were simplified by simply counting the number of dependents to form an ordered scale. Obviously this involves some loss of precision, but in the judgement of the statistician in charge, the loss was not important.)

- (A special case) Readings were taken by telemetry from an artificial satellite. These were supposed to be measurements of field strength in gauss. After the probe was launched, when it was no longer possible to make calibration measurements, it was discovered that the readings were subject to distortion. It was possible to be sure that readings were in the correct order, but the differences of successive readings were not comparable. The data could be placed in classes, and treated as ORDINAL level data.

- In the example, the four days of the investigation can be considered to form an ORDINAL scale, the classes being: -

1	2	3	4
Monday	Tuesday	Wednesday	Thursday

Similarly the time of the experimental session within the day can be considered as an ORDINAL scale, with the classes : -

1	2	3	4
First Morning	Second Morning	First Afternoon	Second Afternoon

The four tasks carried out can similarly be ranked in order of their technical complexity : -

1	2	3	4
Assembly	Bending	Cutting	Drilling

- The fourth ORDINAL data column in the example contains an assessment of the difficulty of the task given by the operator at the end of the session. This assessment is on a seven level scale, with classes : -

1	2	3	4	5	6	7
Very Easy	Easy	Rel. Easy	Normal	Rel. Hard	Hard	Very Hard

REFERENCES Veldman (ch 8), Siegel (ch 3)

2.6 DATA LEVEL 4 - INTERVAL

INTERVAL data are measurements. They do not necessarily have an absolute zero, and may be negative.

2.6.1 Mathematical Properties

INTERVAL data are defined as being 'unique up to the addition of a constant and multiplication by a positive constant'. If we add a constant to a datum on an INTERVAL scale we do not affect the results of statistical tests or comparisons of parameters between samples. Similarly, if we change our scale of measurement from, say, knots to metres per second, the statistical significance of the results will be unchanged. The name of the scale is based on its property that the ratio of the differences between pairs of numbers is always maintained.

2.6.2 Explanation

Practically, INTERVAL data are measurements on continuous scales, which may be negative.

The meaning of the mathematical conditions involved is not easy to grasp at first sight. A detailed example is perhaps the most useful form of explanation. Consider readings of temperature in normal environmental conditions (in Centigrade).

Reading A = -10 c : Reading B = 10 c : Reading C = 50 c

In Farenheit degrees these correspond to: -

Reading A = 14 f : Reading B = 50 f : Reading C = 122 f

The differences B - A and C - B are 20 and 40 Centigrade degrees respectively. The corresponding Farenheit differences are 36 and 72 Farenheit degrees. Although the ratio of actual values is changed (C/B = 4 in Centigrade or 2.44 in Farenheit) the ratio of differences is unchanged (C-B/B-A = 2 in Centigrade = 2 in Farenheit)

Most 'parametric' statistics are applied to data on this level. (The most important exception is the coefficient of variation, which requires data on a RATIO level - see 2.7)

2.6.3 Examples

- In the example of STATCAT data we have included a measure of operator speed which is the percentage difference between the time allowed for the task and the time actually taken. This percentage could be negative or zero, so that ratios of measurements would be practically meaningless.

- Similarly the efficiency of the operator as estimated by himself and as estimated by the observer can be considered as data on an INTERVAL level, since there is no true zero base-line. Theoretically either of these measures could be negative - although this does not in fact occur with the data employed.

- The mean temperature of the working position is a classic example of an INTERVAL datum. Negative temperatures on a Centigrade scale are quite possible,since the zero point is essentially arbitrary, and there is no reason to suppose that the ratio of measurements of temperature will correspond to a meaningful phenomenon.

REFERENCES Siegel (ch 3)

2.7 DATA LEVEL 5 - RATIO

RATIO level data are measurements on an absolute scale. Ratio level measures must not be negative.

2.7.1 Mathematical Properties

RATIO level data are 'unique up to multiplication by a positive constant'. We can alter our scale of measurement (from say pounds to kilograms) but we cannot add or subtract a constant without losing information, and reducing the data to an INTERVAL level.

2.7.2 Explanation

As for INTERVAL data, the best way of explaining RATIO data is by example. If we have measurements of masses, we can express these in pounds, ounces, kilograms or catties without altering the ratio of one value to another. For example : -

Mass A = 1 kg : Mass B = 2 kg : Mass C = 4 kg

Could equally well be expressed as : -

Mass A = 2.2 lb : Mass B = 4.4 lb : Mass C = 8.8 lb

The ratio of B to A in kilograms is 1 to 2.

The ratio of B to A in pounds is 2.2 to 4.4 = 1 to 2.

The ratio of the actual measurements is unchanged. (The ratio of differences of measurements is also unchanged - C - B to B - A is 2 to 1 whichever scale is used, so that any data on a RATIO level is also on an INTERVAL level).

In practice, there is very little that can be done on a RATIO level that cannot be done on an INTERVAL level. The Geometric Mean and the Coefficient of Variation are the most important items.

2.7.3 Examples

- In general, data for which negative values would be meaningless, such as speed (as against velocity), mass (as against weight), or duration (time from start to finish of an event) may be on ratio scales. Even where special tests are not available, it is possible to make an automatic check for the occurrence of negative values. This can be valuable where data have been derived by differencing methods.

- In the STATCAT example, the heart-rate of the operator may be considered a RATIO level measurement, since negative heart-rates are impossible by definition. Moreover, it seems probable that doubling the heart-rate indicates a doubling of something in the real world.

- The time taken by the operator to complete the task is a duration measurement. It cannot be negative since the operator cannot finish before he starts. It can be considered to be on a RATIO level.

- The time allowed as a norm for the experimental session can be considered to be on a RATIO level for the same reason.

- The percentage of errors produced by an operator can be considered to be on a RATIO level. Percentages are rather special measurements, because they are limited to a range from 0 to 100 per cent. Special methods are sometimes necessary to handle them.

REFERENCES Siegel (ch 3)

2.8   CHOICE OF DATA LEVEL

It is very important that data should be given the correct level. An error in allocation will cause the system to produce irrelevant and sometimes meaningless statistics. The previous sections have given definitions of the data levels in ascending order of information content but these may be found confusing by inexperienced and some other users. Accordingly, a decision procedure is given in the following paragraph, to assist in making this decision. (It should be noted that this decision procedure cannot be applied purely mechanically. The user must exercise his judgement about the relevance of the criteria he is using to the type of testing or description he wishes to carry out. For example, any set of class names can be arranged in alphabetical order. This makes for ease of reference in tables etc., but rarely justifies considering the data as being on an ORDINAL rather than a NOMINAL level.)

2.8.1   Decision process for choice of Data Level

The most important difference is whether the data are measurements or classifications into categories. Measurements are usually on a continuous scale, although large integer numbers can often be treated as if they are measurements. (For example - numbers of cars passing a point in an hour.) If any of the measurements are negative or zero, then the level must be INTERVAL. If it can be shown that negative values are logically impossible then the data are on a RATIO level. If there is any doubt, it is best to consider the data to be on an INTERVAL level. There are very few statistics or tests which are specific to RATIO level data - this level is more important as a means of providing an automatic error check.

If the data are not measurements but classifications, see if the classes into which they fall can be ranged in a relevant, unambiguous, order. It is not necessary that the data themselves should be so arranged, because many data may occupy the same class. If they can be so arranged, then they should be considered as on an ORDINAL level. If they are not really information-carrying data, but items added for ease of reference (For example - entry numbers or names) they should be coded as DUMMY and entered as four-character words. Otherwise they should be coded as NOMINAL level.

It will sometimes happen that most items in an entry can be coded using a small number of alternative classes, while one requires many alternatives. To avoid wasting computer storage space, this data column may be stored as class numbers and classified as DUMMY, the data level being over-ridden where required.

2.8.2 Effects of Overestimating Data Level

If the data level chosen is higher than the real level of the data, the tests applied to the data will make assumptions that are not necessarily valid, and may deduce significant differences which have no justification in reality. For example, if two samples are compared on the assumption that the data compared are on an INTERVAL level, a Student's "t" test will be used, which may detect a statistically significant difference. If the data are actually on a NOMINAL level (So that no 1 means Fred, Number 2 means Gina etc..) this difference will be meaningless. If the data had been on an ORDINAL level there might be some relation to the true situation, but it would be distorted, the associated probability completely incorrect and the derived statistics (arithmetic mean and standard deviation) meaningless.

2.8.3 Effects of Underestimating Data Level

If the data level used to describe the data is lower than the real level, then the tests used will make fewer assumptions than are justified by the true level of the data. These tests will not be invalid, but they will be less sensitive to differences, and they may not detect the specific difference for which you are searching. If for example, you are comparing two samples on what the computer has been told to consider a NOMINAL level, then a Chi-squared test will be used. If the data is actually on an ORDINAL level, then the computer could have used the Median test to test whether the average of one sample was higher than that of the other. This test, which works by grouping classes above or below the common median, is far more sensitive to such differences than is the chi-squared test, and will detect statistically significant differences where the chi-squared does not.

2.8.4 Over-riding the specified Data Level

Most programs in the STATCAT system allow the user to over-ride the judgement of the system, and to force the choice of a test not suited to the specified data level. This facility should be used with restraint. The system works much more efficiently if the user takes time to ponder over the data levels involved before he attempts to analyse them - or (better still) before he collects them. It is also easier to describe the data before one becomes emotionally involved with them.

One temptation should be resisted. If you have decided that certain data should be treated as on an ORDINAL level, on the basis of its properties, and find a difference between samples that does not quite attain statistical significance, you may be tempted to reconsider your definition and consider the data to be on an INTERVAL level.

DO NOT DO SO.

Such a procedure is as incorrect as altering the data to match the required result.

2.9 STATCAT DATA BANK

A STATCAT data bank is made up of four elements. These are the Data Starter, Data Description Segment, Data Storage Segment, and the Data Terminator. These are considered to be stored on a serial-access medium in an unformatted form - this being the most economic form of bulk storage.

2.9.1 Data Starter

The Data Starter is the first unformatted record stored in the STATCAT data bank. It contains 19 real words. These contain, in order, the number of items per entry in this data bank, the default number of alternative classes, the 'non-value' used for missing data, a ten four-character word title for the data bank, which is printed whenever the data bank is used, four spare words which may be put to use for elementary security precautions, a confidential security key word (see 5.1 and 3.2) and a public file name (four characters). The Data Starter serves to identify the STATCAT data bank, contains the information necessary to allow it to be read, and allows the user to maintain some elementary security precautions.

2.9.2 Data Description Segment

The Data Description Segment contains the 'context' information which allows the system to make its tactical decisions, and to identify the output in an easily comprehensible form. It contains as many records as there are items in an entry - given as the first word of the Data Starter. Each record is a 'Data Column Description' and describes the data in the corresponding position in each entry. (If the entries were written in a table like that of Figure 2.13 this record would describe a column of data - hence the title applied to it.) Each record consists of a four-character short title for the data column, one two-character plus 17 four-character words forming a detailed title for the data column, and including the data level name for the column, as many four-character class names as there are alternative classes specified in the Data Starter, an integer giving the numeric code for the data level, and two real values giving the maximum and minimum value for the column. Some of these items are normally redundant but are included, usually as default values, for use where the defined data level is over-ridden.

2.9.3 Data Storage Segment

The Data Storage Segment contains the information stored in the file. It consists of successive records each containing one entry, stored as unformatted real words. The number of records is limited only by the storage capacity available and the time taken to access them - STATCAT data banks have been employed with less than one hundred or more than one hundred thousand records. The Data Storage Segment need not necessarily be in any specific order, although it is often convenient to store data in order for ease of retrieval and subsequent processing. Auxiliary programs allow the selection, sorting, matching and merging of entries, where this is necessary or convenient.

2.9.4 Data Terminator

The Data Terminator is a record containing one entry consisting entirely of non-values. This is placed at the end of the STATCAT data bank to signal to programs that the end of the data bank has been reached, without requiring a (non-standard) end-of-file marker to be recognised.

Figure 2.91 - STATCAT data bank (schematic)

Element	records	words(each)	Contents
Data Starter	1	16	NQ,NALT,Q,title+Security key
Data Description Segment	NQ	19+NALT+3	Short+long Title,class names, data level,maximum+minimum
Data Storage Segment	not limited	NQ	one entry per record
Data Terminator	1	NQ	NQ non-values (Q)

Chapter III

STANDARD STATCAT INPUT MODULES

This chapter describes the standard input modules used by the STATCAT system, and the manner in which they are combined in the operation of the system. It begins with a description of the input conventions for the use of punched cards, as they are used in this system, with a technical note for programmers on how these conventions have been realised in ASA FORTRAN IV. (Some users who are not familiar with computers experience considerable difficulty in understanding how punched cards are used, and some experienced programmers do not remember that some types of format are machine-specific extensions of the standard.)

The remaining sections of the chapter describe the standard input modules in the order that they are most often encountered. Each description begins with a statement of the purpose of the module, followed by a card-by-card listing. This is followed by a field-by-field listing of the contents of each type of card, with a detailed description of the normal use of each field. This is followed by an example of card input for the module, with the corresponding output listing. Finally, any relevant service subroutines are described, with system flow-charts and card listings.

3.1 GENERAL INPUT CONVENTIONS

3.1.1 Punched Cards

The STATCAT system, as described here, receives its data and instructions from punched cards. (In practice, the punched cards may be replaced by successive lines on an interactive terminal, or by some other means of input.) Each card can be punched with rectangular holes in eighty columns, read from left to right. The holes in any column may be in any of twelve positions, but only certain combinations of holes have a defined meaning. Figure 3.12 shows the vocabulary of characters (letters, digits and special symbols used by ASA FORTRAN IV. It should be noted that the last symbol on the card is what is called the 'currency symbol'. Depending on their country of origin, different printers may produce a sterling, dollar, franc, yen or other symbol for this pattern of punched holes. Some computers use different patterns of punched holes, and almost all offer additional codes and symbols, but these need not concern the user.

3.1.2 Special Cards

Except for cards read by user-written subroutines (4.2.5) or by run-time formats (4.4.5) the following rules apply: -

- All blank cards will be ignored. (The system will read another card, without producing an echo-print.)

- A card having BACK in the first four columns will cause the program to step back to the previous input module.

- A card having END. , ENDb , .END or bEND (Where b is a blank column) in the first four columns, will cause the program to start reading the next input module (but see 3.7).

- A card having STOP in the first four columns will cause the program to stop. If an output STATCAT data bank is being constructed, a data terminator will be written to it at that time, unless a check program has been run on the output STATCAT data bank.

- If any END or BACK card occurs where the context implies that cards are disordered, an error message will be produced, and an error index set to prevent the execution of the program with garbled data.

3.1.3 Input Cards

Each card, when read by the computer, is divided into fields, defined by a column or columns on the card. (Most punched cards have a pre-printed field layout on them to aid the human eye in reading and checking what has been punched - this layout is not known to the computer and should be ignored by the user.) Each of these fields contains an 'item' as defined by the card layout.

The FORTRAN type listed in the card layout specifies what characters will be accepted in each field, according to the following rules:-

-I indicates that the digits 0 - 9 with a preceding minus sign if necessary, will be accepted. Any other characters will be ignored, including blanks and decimal points. The most significant digit will be the first punched - the leftmost on the card.

-F implies that the digits 0 - 9, with a preceding negative sign if necessary, and the first decimal point encountered will be accepted. If no decimal point is found, it is assumed to follow the least significant (rightmost) digit. Any other characters, blanks, letters, special symbols etc. will be ignored. Numbers need not be left or right justified.

- A implies that all characters will be read, and stored unchanged, including blanks, commas, special characters and so on. Only single character and four-character A formats are used in this system. Note that all four characters in a four-character format are used. Thus bABC is not the same as ABCb (where b represents a space), and would not be recognised as the same if used as a class name (see 4.1). Similarly using b for a blank, and reading a four-column A format, the five inputs b1b2 , bb12 , 12bb , 12.b , and b12. would all be considered different, although they would all represent the number 12 if read with an I or F format.

3.1.4 Programming Note

In general, all input to STATCAT programs - except inputs controlled by user-written subroutines (4.1.5) or run-time formats (4.2.5) - is actually read in A format. If the orthodox I or F formats were used, then the presence of a misplaced character or a disordered card deck would usually cause the program to fail without hope of recovery. (This may not be true of all compilers on all machines, but there are no ASA FORTRAN IV defined recovery procedures.)

The use of the A format allows the input process to be more flexible, and more tolerant of mistakes. Only two A formats are used. A4 is used to read titles, comments, and other plain-language information, and A1 for everything else. It is assumed that the A4 input can be stored in a single real variable, and that Hollerith constants are numerically identical to equivalent A formats with the same number of characters. No assumption is made about the way successive characters are stored in one word, or what the rest of the word may contain.

The FORTRAN functions COPYA and COMPA (Figure 3.11) are provided to allow the copying of characters from real variable to real variable, and for comparing characters stored in real variables. The versions provided after this chapter assume that arithmetic comparisons can be made on characters stored in real variables. If this is not possible on the user's machine, equivalent low-level functions should be produced.

The function ICH (Figure 3.11) is used to identify which one of a set of possible codes is present in an input cell. If the code is not one of the set of possibilities, it returns with the value 0.

The function IBL is used to identify the special cards described in 3.1.2. As can be seen from the summary flow-chart (Figure 3.11) this function will operate with data in A1 or A4 format - one or four characters per variable.

The function AN (Figure 3.11) is used to convert a string of A1 characters into a real variable. It is possible that, on some systems, rounding errors may occur so that values obtained by this function will differ slightly from similar numbers read directly from cards, or derived within the system. All possible precautions have been taken to avoid such annoyances, but some problems may still occur.

Figure 3.12 - FORTRAN Standard characters

Letters	ABCDEFGHIJKLMNOPQRSTUVWXYZ	Alphabetic	)
			) Alphanumeric
Digits	0123456789	Numeric	)
Special	b=+-*/(), .¢	Special characters	

(b indicates a blank column - ¢ is the currency symbol)

Figure 3.11 - System Flow-charts - AN, COMPA, COPYA, IBL+ICH

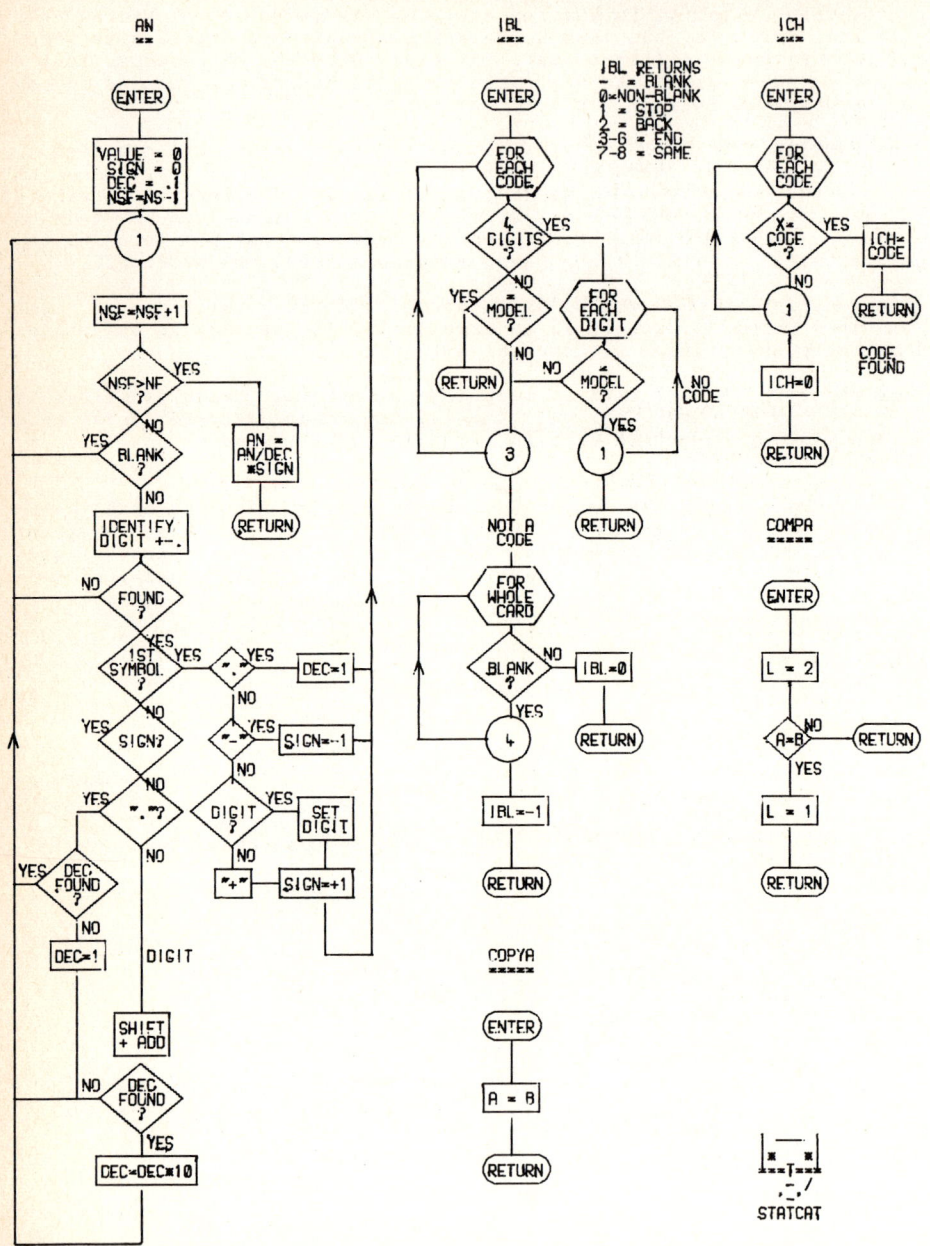

```
      FUNCTION AN(D,NQ,NS,NF)
C AN     (SEE  3.1 ) SERVICE    ALPHA  TO NUMERIC VALUE
      DIMENSION D(NQ),AB(14)
      DATA AB/1H1,1H2,1H3,1H4,1H5,1H6,1H7,1H8,1H9,1H0,1H ,1H+,1H-,1H./
      AN = 0.
      SIGN = 0.
      DEC = .1
      NSF = NS-1
    1 NSF = NSF + 1
C NEXT ALPHA - END IF END OF ARRAY
      IF(NSF.GT.NF) GO TO 30
      CALL COMPA(D(NSF),AB(11),L)
      IF(SIGN.EQ.0..AND.L.EQ.1) GO TO 1
C IDENTIFY DIGIT,SIGN OR POINT - IGNORE OTHERS
      J = 0
      DO 2 I = 1,14
      CALL COMPA(D(NSF),AB(I),L)
      IF(L.NE.1) GO TO 2
      J = I
      GO TO 3
    2 CONTINUE
    3 IF(J.EQ.0) GO TO 1
      IF(SIGN.NE.0.)GO TO 20
C LEADING CHARACTER
      GO TO (11,11,11,11,11,11,11,11,11,10,12,13,14,15),J
C ZERO START
   10 J = 0
C DIGIT START
   11 X = J
      AN = X
C + START
   13 SIGN = 1.
   12 GO TO 1
C -VE START
   14 SIGN = -1.
      GO TO 1
C DECIMAL POINT START
   15 DEC = DEC*10.
      GO TO 13
C TRAILING CHARACTERS
   20 GO TO (21,21,21,21,21,21,21,21,21,19,22,22,22,25),J
C TRAILING ZERO
   19 J = 0
C TRAILING DIGIT
   21 X=J
      AN = AN*10. + X
      IF(DEC.LT..9)GO TO 1
      DEC = DEC*10.
C REDUNDANT SIGNS AND BLANKS
   22 GO TO 1
C DECIMAL POINT - REDUNDANT IF NOT FIRST
   25 IF(DEC.LT..9) DEC = 1.
      GO TO 1
C ADJUST DECIMAL PLACES AND SIGN
   30 IF(DEC.LT..9) DEC = 1.
      AN = AN*SIGN/DEC
      RETURN
      END


      SUBROUTINE COMPA(A,B,L)
C COMPA (SEE  3.1) SERVICE      COMPARES ALPHAMERIC VALUES
      L = 2
```

```
      IF(A.NE.B) RETURN
      L = 1
      RETURN
      END


      SUBROUTINE COPYA(A,B)
C COPYA   (SEE  3.1 ) SERVICE     COPIES ALPHAMERIC VALUE
      A = B
      RETURN
      END


      FUNCTION IBL(A,N,ND)
C IBL    (SEE  3.1 ) SERVICE    DETECTS BLANK,END AND STOP CARDS
C IBL  NEG.    0      1     2     3     4     5     6     7     8
C BLANK NON-BLANK |STOP|BACK|END |END.|.END| END|STET|SAME|
      DIMENSION A(N),CODE(8),C1(4,8)
      DATA CODE/4HSTOP,4HBACK,4HEND ,4HEND.,4H.END,4H END,4HSTET,4HSAME/
      DATA C1/1HS,1HT,1HO,1HP,1HB,1HA,1HC,1HK,1HE,1HN,1HD,1H ,1HE,1HN,1H
     1D,1H.,1H.,1HE,1HN,1HD,1H ,1HE,1HN,1HD,1HS,1HT,1HE,1HT,1HS,1HA,1HM,
     21HE/,B1/1H /,B4/4H     /
      IBL = 1
C END CODING
      DO 3 I = 1,8
      IBL = I
      IF(ND.EQ.4) GO TO 2
      DO 1 J = 1,4
      IF(J.GT.N) GO TO 3
      CALL COMPA(C1(J,I),A(J),L)
      IF(L.NE.1) GO TO 3
    1 CONTINUE
      RETURN
    2 CALL COMPA(CODE(I),A(1),L)
      IF(L.EQ.1) RETURN
    3 CONTINUE
      IBL = 0
      DO 4 I = 1,N
      IF(ND.EQ.1) CALL COMPA(A(I),B1,L)
      IF(ND.EQ.4) CALL COMPA(A(I),B4,L)
      IF(L.NE.1) RETURN
    4 CONTINUE
C BLANK CARD TO N
      IBL = -1
      RETURN
      END


      FUNCTION ICH(X,CODE,N)
C ICH    (SEE  3.1 ) SERVICE    IDENTIFIES ALPHAMERIC CODES
C THIS FUNCTION IDENTIFIES X AS ONE OF THE CODES STORED IN  CODE
C ICH IS 0 IF CODE IS NOT FOUND
      DIMENSION CODE(N)
      ICH = 0
      DO 1 I = 1,N
      CALL COMPA(X,CODE(I),L)
      IF(L.NE.1) GO TO 1
      ICH = I
      GO TO 2
    1 CONTINUE
    2 RETURN
      END
```

3.2   FILE CONTROL CARD

3.2.1   Purpose

This card specifies the program in use and the STATCAT data banks to which it will be applied. It ensures that the correct set of input instructions is applied to the correct data bank or banks by the correct program. It also provides some very elementary file protection to discourage casual snooping. This protection will not last long under determined attack, and must never be trusted where security is important.

3.2.2   Card Layout

AAAABBBBCCCCDDDDEEEEFFFFGGGGHHHHIIIIIIIIIIIIIIII................

Columns on card	Item Code	FORTRAN Type	Function	See
1- 4	A	A	File Control Card Identifier	Below
5- 8	B	A	Program Identifier	Below
9- 12	C	A	) Input STATCAT (Name	Below
13- 16	D	A	) Data Bank (Key	Below
17- 20	E	A	) Output STATCAT (Name	Below
21- 24	F	A	) Data Bank (Key	Below
25- 28	G	A	) Second Input STATCAT (Name	Below
29- 32	H	A	) Data Bank (Key	Below
33- 80	I	A	Comment (NOT KEPT)	-

A - File Control Card Identifier

This is a four-character code which identifies the input card as a file control card. It must contain the four characters **ST. If any other code is read where a file control card is expected it will be listed with an appropriate error message. (If a blank card is read, it will be ignored, and a STOP card will cause the program to stop.)

B - Program Identifier

This is a four-character code which identifies the program to which the following input modules are to be applied. The name of any STATCAT program consists of six letters of which the first two are ST and the last four form the Program Identifier.

C, E, G - Data Bank Names

These are the four-character names used to identify the STATCAT data banks used by the program. These four characters must agree EXACTLY with those specified in the data starter (see 3.3) of the data bank required. If they do not agree, an error message will be printed, and the data bank will not be made available.

A special code facility may be used where a STATCAT data bank has already been specified on one of the three media. If the code SAME is given, then the system will leave that medium in its current state, without returning to the start of the file to check identity. This facility allows, for example, the input STATCAT data bank to be changed while an output STATCAT data bank is being constructed using STMERG, without the output STATCAT data bank being over-written at this point.

If the code SAME is used where there was no previous STATCAT data bank on the medium, or where the STATCAT data bank was not released, an error message will be produced, and the data bank will not be made available.

If a code consisting of four blanks is used, the system will assume that no data bank is required, and the peripheral number corresponding wil be set to zero.

D, F, H - Data Bank Keys

These are four-character names used to permit access to the STATCAT data banks specified by any program. They must agree EXACTLY with those specified in the data starter (see 3.3) of the STATCAT data banks named. These keys are never output by the system, and form an elementary security barrier. If a key is not correctly specified, the STATCAT data bank in question will not be released to the user, and a warning message must be passed to the operator. (The subroutine FIFI which reads and checks this module assumes that the peripheral MEDO is directly readable by the operator. Normally this will be a console typewriter or display screen - the user should check the required peripheral number for his system.)

A key consisting of four blanks will be treated exactly like any other key. It is normally used for free-access data banks.

C, D - Input STATCAT Data Bank

The input STATCAT data bank is the most frequently used. It must be a complete STATCAT data bank, and is not changed at any time by the system.

E, F - Output STATCAT Data Bank

The output STATCAT data bank is the only STATCAT data bank into which entries are written at any time. Before it is used, the data bank name and key are checked. Only if these are correct will the system permit the existing data bank to be over-written. The only exception to this limitation is the auxiliary program STHEAD, (4.1) which is used only to produce new (empty) STATCAT data banks, or to over-write obsolete files.

The task of opening new STATCAT data banks has been deliberately isolated into the program STHEAD to minimise the chance of the accidental destruction of data banks.

G, H - Second Input STATCAT Data Bank

The second input STATCAT data bank is, like the first, a read-only data bank, never over-written by the system. It is necessary only where large-scale merging or data-matching operations are being carried out using STMERG (10.4). STMERG may be used without this data bank in some circumstances.

3.2.3 Subroutine FIFI

The subroutine FIFI, of which a system flow-chart is given in Figure 3.21, serves three main purposes:

- It sets the numerical values for the standard system peripherals. The values shown on the listing are those used on IBM 360/50 systems, other systems may require different numbers.

- It verifies that the calling program is in fact the one for which the data were intended.

- It verifies that the STATCAT files called for have been correctly loaded, that the user has supplied the correct key for each file, and raises the alarm if he has not.

In the version given here, the numbers of the units assigned for second and subsequent calls in the same program are increased by 3 units units, so that the second input STATCAT data bank, for example, will be on unit 19 at the first call, and on unit 22 at the second. If the code SAME is used for the output STATCAT data bank, its number will not be incremented.

3.2.4 Examples

Figure 3.22 illustrates the file control cards used for one run of STDESC (5.2) and for two runs of STMERG. In the first example, which provides the output given in Figure 3.23, a single input file is specified - the most common form for this card.

In the second example three files are specified for the first pass, the second being an output STATCAT data bank, on which it must be possible for the system to write - the other two (input) STATCAT data banks should be in a 'read-only' state, as a precaution. For the second pass of STMERG, the unit numbers will be increased by three, so that the new first input becomes unit 20 in place of unit 17, and the new second input becomes unit 22 in place of unit 19. The use of SAME for the output unit means that it will not be disturbed, and will still be called unit 18. Figure 3.24 gives the corresponding output, omitting the intermediate outputs from the rest of the program.

Figure 3.21 - System Flow-chart - FIFI

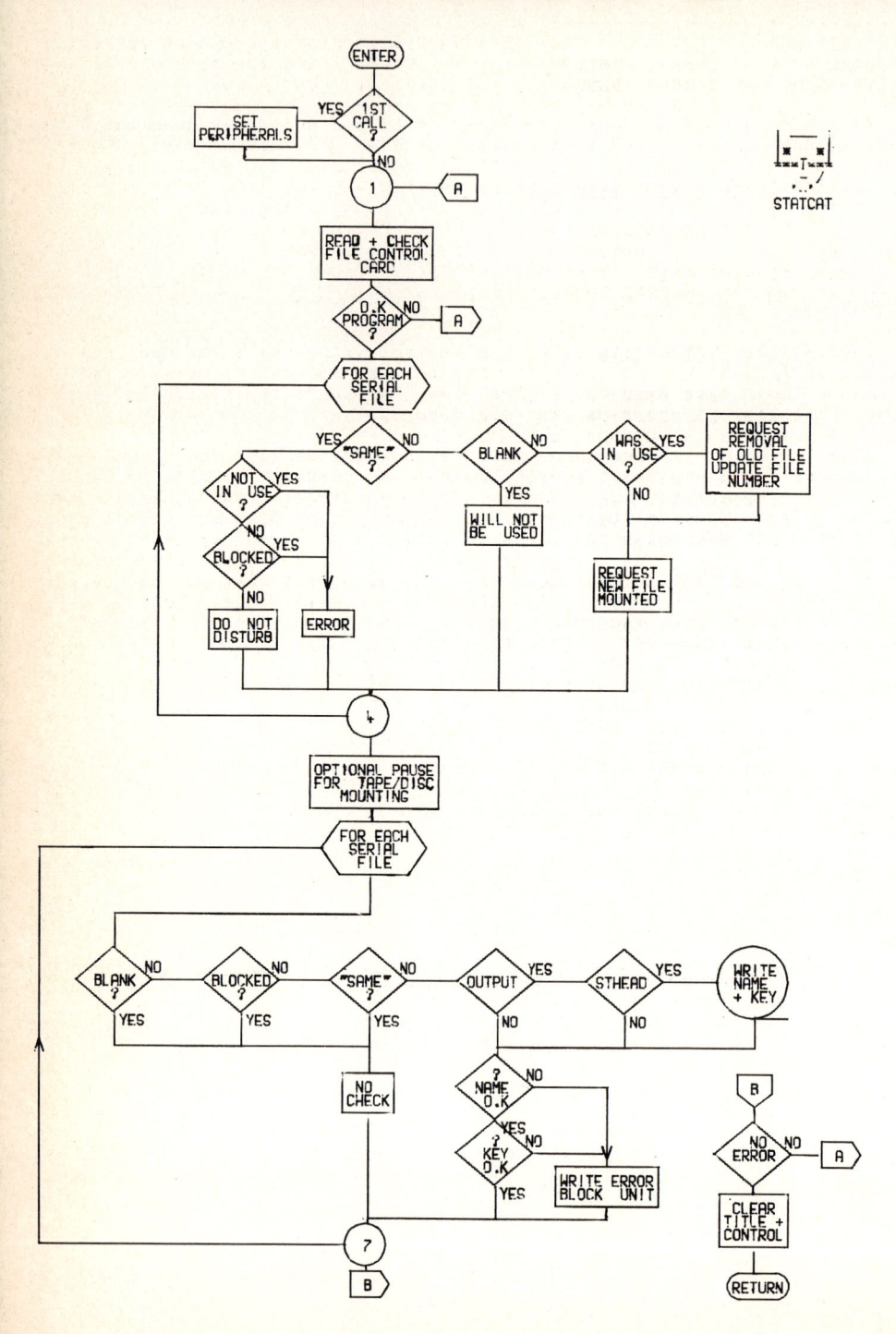

Figure 3.22 - File Control Cards - Examples

```
---------1---------2---------3---------4---------5---------6---------7--
**STDESCDEMO                                DEMONSTRATION STATCAT DATA BANK
**STMERGDEMO       DUFF      COPY           COMBINE DEMO AND COPY ON DUFF
**STMERGCOPY       SAME      DEMO           COMBINE COPY AND DEMO ON DUFF
---------1---------2---------3---------4---------5---------6---------7--
```

Figure 3.23 - File Control - Example of Output - STDESC

```
LOAD FILE DEMO ON UNIT  17 READ ONLY
         DEMONSTRATION STATCAT DATA BANK
FILE ON UNIT  17 IS DEMO (FREE)
SYSTEM RETURNS TO MAIN PROGRAM
```

Figure 3.24 - File Control - Examples of Output - STMERG

```
LOAD FILE DEMO ON UNIT  17 READ ONLY
LOAD FILE DUFF ON UNIT  18 READ/WRITE
LOAD FILE COPY ON UNIT  19 READ ONLY
         COMBINE DEMO AND COPY ON DUFF
FILE ON UNIT  17 IS DEMO (FREE)
FILE ON UNIT  18 IS DUFF (FREE)
FILE ON UNIT  19 IS COPY (FREE)
SYSTEM RETURNS TO MAIN PROGRAM
```

(Here follows the output for the first pass)

```
REMOVE FILE FROM UNIT  20
LOAD FILE COPY ON UNIT  20 READ ONLY
REMOVE FILE FROM UNIT  22
LOAD FILE DEMO ON UNIT  22 READ ONLY
         COMBINE COPY AND DEMO ON DUFF
FILE ON UNIT  20 IS COPY (FREE)
FILE ON UNIT  22 IS DEMO (FREE)
SYSTEM RETURNS TO MAIN PROGRAM
```

(Here follows the output for the second pass)

```
      SUBROUTINE FIFI
C FIFI     (SEE  3.2 ) SYSTEM      ALLOCATES PERIPHERALS-CHECKS FILES
C FOR USE WITH IBM HASP SYSTEM - FILES SPECIFIED BY JCL-CHECKED HERE
C BLOCKED FILE UNITS HAVE NEGATIVE UNIT NUMBERS
C UNIT      TYPE (USUAL)           FUNCTION IN STATCAT
C MED1      CARD READER            CONTROL INPUT
C MED2      LINE PRINTER           BULK OUTPUT
C MED3      MAG. TAPE/DISC READ    MAIN INPUT FILE
C MED4      MAG. TAPE/DISC WRITE   OUTPUT FILE
C MED5      CARD READER            BULK INPUT
C MED6      LINE PRINTER           CONTROL OUTPUT
C MED13     MAG.TAPE/DISC READ     AUXILIARY INPUT FILE
      COMMON /STCT/MED1,MED2,MED3,MED4,MED5,MED6,MED13,Q,V(20),TT(30)
      DATA BL/4H    /,SAME/4HSAME/,FILE/4H**ST/,STOP/4HSTOP/,HED/4HHEAD/
      IF(MED1.GT.0) GO TO 10
      MED1 = 5
      MED2 = 6
      MED3 = 0
      MED4 = 0
      MED5 = 5
      MED6 = 6
      MED13= 0
   10 CONTINUE
      WRITE(MED2,912) TT(1)
    1 READ(MED1,900)  V
      IF(IBL(V,20,4))1,2,2
C CHECK THIS IS FILE CARD
    2 CALL COMPA(V(1),FILE,L)
      IF(L.EQ.1) GO TO 3
      CALL COMPA(V(1),STOP,L)
      WRITE(MED2,901)  V
      IF(L.EQ.1) STOP
      WRITE(MED2,915)
      GO TO 1
C CHECK PROGRAM CORRESPONDS TO DATA
    3 CALL COMPA(TT(1),V(2),L)
      IF(L.NE.1) WRITE(MED2,914)  TT(1),V(2)
      IF(L.NE.1) GO TO 1
      IPAUSE = 0
      IFAULT = 0
C CALL FOR TAPES
      DO 5 I = 2,6,2
      IF(I.EQ.2)MED = MED3
      IF(I.EQ.4)MED = MED4
      IF(I.EQ.6)MED = MED13
C SAME TAPE REQUIRED (NO TAPE REWIND OR CHECK - IF IT EXISTS+ IS FREE
      CALL COMPA(V(I+1),SAME,LS)
      IF(LS.EQ.1.AND.MED.GT.0) GO TO 5
      IF(LS.NE.1) GO TO 4
      IFAULT = 1
      IF(MED.LT.0) ME = -MED
      IF(MED.EQ.0)                       WRITE(MED6,903)ME
      IF(MED.LT.0)                       WRITE(MED6,904)ME
      IF(MED.EQ.0.AND.MED2.NE.MED6) WRITE(MED2,903)ME
      IF(MED.LT.0.AND.MED2.NE.MED6) WRITE(MED2,904)ME
      GO TO 5
C NO TAPE REQUIRED
    4 CALL COMPA(V(I+1),BL,LB)
      IF(LB.EQ.1) GO TO 5
C CALL TO REMOVE PREVIOUS TAPE
      IF(MED.LT.0) MED = -MED
      IF(MED.GT.0) REWIND MED
      IF(MED.GT.0) WRITE(MED6,905)  MED
```

```
      IF(MED.GT.0.AND.MED2.NE.MED6) WRITE(MED2,905) MED
C NEXT UNIT NO ADVANCED BY THREE FOR SEPARATE PERIPHERAL
      IF(MED.GT.0) MED = MED + 3
      IF(MED.EQ.0) MED = I/2 + 16
      IF(I.NE.4) WRITE(MED6,910) V(I+1),MED
      IF(I.EQ.4) WRITE(MED6,911) V(I+1),MED
      IF(I.EQ.2) MED3 = MED
      IF(I.EQ.4) MED4 = MED
      IF(I.EQ.6) MED13= MED
      IF(MED.GT.0)IPAUSE = 1
    5 CONTINUE
      IF(IPAUSE.EQ.1) WRITE(MED6,902) (V(I),I=8,20)
C VERIFY NEW TAPES
      Y = -1.
      J = 1
      CALL COMPA(TT(1),HED,IH)
      DO 7 I = 2,6,2
      CALL COMPA(V(I+1),SAME,LS)
      IF(LS.EQ.1) GO TO 7
      IF(I.EQ.2) MED = MED3
      IF(I.EQ.4) MED = MED4
      IF(I.EQ.6) MED = MED13
      CALL COMPA(V(I+1),BL,LB)
      IF(MED.GT.0.AND.LB.EQ.1)MED = - MED
      IF(LB.EQ.1) GO TO 6
      IF(MED.LT.1) GO TO 7
      IF(I.EQ.4.AND.IH.EQ.1) REWIND MED
      IF(I.EQ.4.AND.IH.EQ.1) WRITE(MED) J,J,Y,(BL,K=1,14),V(6),V(5)
      REWIND MED
      READ(MED) NX,NX,X,(TT(K),K=2,17)
      REWIND MED
      CALL COMPA(TT(17),V(I+1),LB)
      IF(LB.NE.1.AND.MED2.NE.MED6) WRITE(MED2,906) MED,TT(17),V(I+1)
      IF(LB.NE.1) WRITE(MED6,906)MED,TT(17),V(I+1)
      CALL COMPA(TT(16),V(I+2),LS)
      IF(LS.NE.1) IFAULT = 1
      IF(LB.EQ.1.AND.LS.NE.1) WRITE(MED6,907)MED,TT(17)
      IF(LB.EQ.1.AND.LS.NE.1.AND.MED2.NE.MED6) WRITE(MED2,907) MED,TT(17)
      IF(LB.NE.1.OR.LS.NE.1) MED = -MED
      IF(LB.NE.1.OR.LS.NE.1) IFAULT = 1
      IF(LB.EQ.1.AND.LS.EQ.1.AND.MED2.NE.MED6)WRITE(MED2,908)MED,TT(17)
      IF(LB.EQ.1.AND.LS.EQ.1)WRITE(MED6,908) MED,TT(17)
    6 IF(I.EQ.2)MED3 = MED
      IF(I.EQ.4)MED4 = MED
      IF(I.EQ.6)MED13= MED
    7 CONTINUE
      IF(IFAULT.EQ.0) WRITE(MED2,913)
      IF(IFAULT.NE.0) WRITE(MED2,909)
      IF(IFAULT.NE.0) GO TO 1
C CLEAR STORAGE
      DO 8 I = 1,20
    8 V(I) = 0.
      DO 9 I = 1,30
    9 CALL COPYA(TT(I),BL)
      RETURN
  900 FORMAT(20A4)
  901 FORMAT(21X,20A4)
  902 FORMAT(21X,13A4,10H - COMMENT)
  903 FORMAT(21X,12HFILE ON UNIT,I4,28H SAME FILE NOT YET SPECIFIED )
  904 FORMAT(21X,12HFILE ON UNIT,I4,28H SAME FILE IS STILL BLOCKED  )
  905 FORMAT(21X,21HREMOVE FILE FROM UNIT,I4)
  906 FORMAT(21X,12HFILE ON UNIT,I4, 4H IS ,A4,11H SHOULD BE ,A4)
  907 FORMAT(21X,12HFILE ON UNIT,I4, 4H IS ,A4,10H (BLOCKED) )
```

```
  908 FORMAT(21X,12HFILE ON UNIT,I4, 4H IS ,A4,10H (FREE)    )
  909 FORMAT(21X,46HSYSTEM READS FORWARD TO NEXT FILE CONTROL CARD)
  910 FORMAT(21X,10HLOAD FILE ,A4,8H ON UNIT,I4,11H READ ONLY )
  911 FORMAT(21X,10HLOAD FILE ,A4,8H ON UNIT,I4,11H READ/WRITE)
  912 FORMAT(1H1,20X,46HRECORD OF FILE CONTROL OPERATIONS - PROGRAM ST,
     1A4/)
  913 FORMAT(21X,30HSYSTEM RETURNS TO MAIN PROGRAM )
  914 FORMAT(1H0,20X,13HPROGRAM IS ST,A4,17H - DATA IS FOR ST,A4/)
  915 FORMAT(1H+,101X,12H - DISCARDED)
      END
```

3.3 DATA STARTER CARD

3.3.1 Purpose

This card is used whenever a new STATCAT data bank is to be produced, directly (by loading the data with STLOAD), or indirectly (by correcting an existing STATCAT data bank or by one of the data handling programs described in Chapter 10). It provides the fundamental parameters of the STATCAT data bank, the name of the data bank (as a four-character code and in more detail as a forty-character title), the default value for the number of classes to be used, the 'non-value' used in place of missing data, and the security key. (This card contains the plaintext file title, the file name and the security key - it should therefore be treated with as much care as the most confidential information in the file itself.)

3.3.2 Card Layout

```
ABCCCDDDEEEEEEEEFFFFFFFFFFFFFFFFFFFFFFFFFFFFFF......GGGGHHHH
```

Columns on card	Item Code	FORTRAN Type	Function	See
1	A	I	Output Control Index (Normally) Below +	4.2
2	B	I	Checking Control Index Below +	4.3
3- 5	C	I	Number of items per entry	4.2
6- 8	D	I	Number of alternative classes (Default)	4.2
9-16	E	F	Non-value	4.2
17-56	F	A	Plain language title of data bank	4.2
57-72	.	A	NOT USED	-
73-76	G	A	STATCAT data bank Key	3.2
77-80	H	A	STATCAT data bank Name	3.2

A - Output Control Index

This index controls the degree of detail (if any) to which entries are printed during the construction of the data bank. In some programs (STMERG) it has been necessary to pre-empt this index for other purposes. It is therefore advisable to check the specific program documentation.

B - Checking Control Index

This index controls the extent of data checking carried out after the STATCAT data bank has been constructed. It more often appears in the same place on a Data Handling Instruction, when additional details may be specified. When it appears on a Data Starter card default values are used. This index may also be pre-empted for other purposes (STMERG) so that the specific program documentation should be checked.

3.3.3 Examples

Figure 3.32 lists a number of Data Starter Cards, used as examples in program descriptions. These examples show how some programs use only a few of the fields from the data starter, usually because the system can deduce the required values from the context - for example, when the program is copying or sorting entries into order, then the file parameters will be unchanged, although a new file name and key will be needed. Where the program STLOAD is used to load the plain-language STATCAT data banks described in Chapter 9, the file parameters are fixed, and in several cases, the indices A and B are used with other meanings than those given in the description of STLOAD. It is always wisest to check the specific documentation for a program before using it.

3.3.4 Subroutine LDAP

Figure 3.31 contains a system flow-chart for the subroutine LDAP, which is used to provide a display of the information stored on the Data Starter for a file, and to verify that it possible to treat the file stored within the limits of storage available to the program.

Three possible error conditions can be detected: -

If the unit on which the program expects to find a STATCAT data bank is not available, then the subroutine will produce an error message: -

UNIDENTIFIED PERIPHERAL FOR DATA BANK NNNN

where NNNN is the name of the STATCAT data bank, and return to the main program with a switch set to cause the program to read a new file control card.

If there are too many items per entry for the program to handle, the error index will be set to 1.

If there are too many alternative classes the error index will be set to 2.

If both conditions apply, the error index will be set to 3.

Appropriate warning messages will then be produced, the subroutine will return to the main program, and the system will continue to read input modules.

Figure 3.33 gives an example of the output of LDAP.

Figure 3.31 - System Flow-chart for LDAP

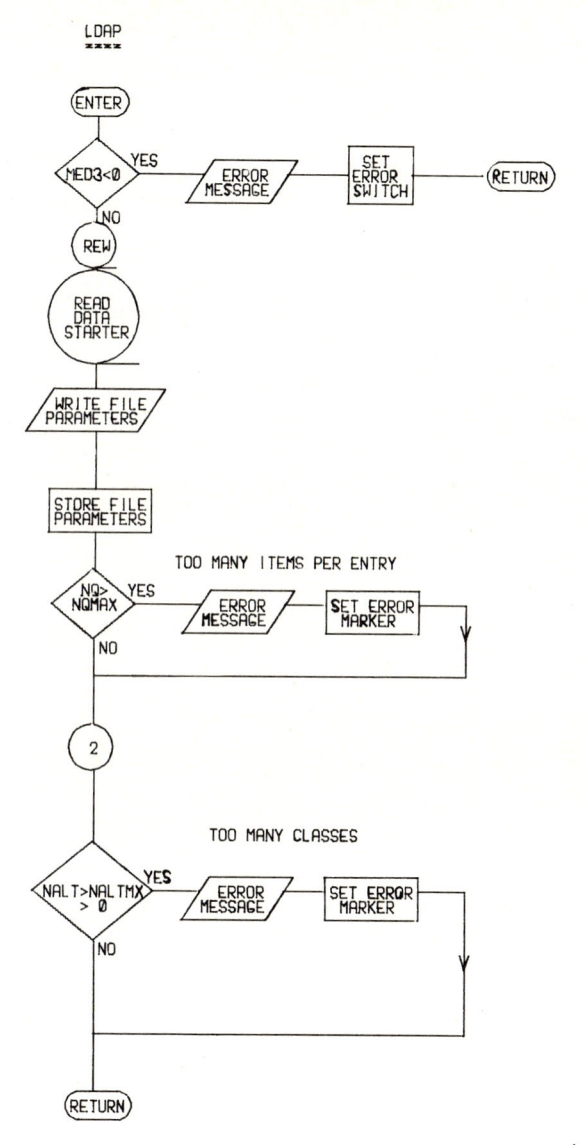

Figure 3.32 - Data Starter - Examples

```
        STLOAD (4.2)   Standard Form   (- = not used, * = fixed)
---------1---------2---------3---------4---------5------///-7---------8
ABCCCDDDEEEEEEEEFFFFFFFFFFFFFFFFFFFFFFFFFFFFFFFFFFF-///----GGGGHHHH
00 18 10    -1.   DEMONSTRATION STATCAT DATA BANK                 DEMO


        STLOAD (9.1,9.3) Plain-language (- = not used, * = fixed)
---------1---------2---------3---------4---------5------///-7---------8
*****************FFFFFFFFFFFFFFFFFFFFFFFFFFFFFFFFFFF-///----GGGGHHHH
40 21  5    -1.   PLAIN LANGUAGE DEMONSTRATION                    PLAN
40 21  5    -1.   CROSS-REFERENCE DEMONSTRATION                   DUFF


   STSORT(10.2), STCOPY(11.1) Title and Key only (- = not used)
---------1---------2---------3---------4---------5------///-7---------8
-----------------FFFFFFFFFFFFFFFFFFFFFFFFFFFFFFFFFFF-///----GGGGHHHH
                  RE-ORDERED STATCAT DATA BANK                    DUFF
                  COPY OF DEMO STATCAT DATA BANK                  COPY


   STMANI(10.1), STCOMB(10.5)  (-=not used, + = special meaning)
---------1---------2---------3---------4---------5------///-7---------8
+BCCCDDDEEEEEEEEFFFFFFFFFFFFFFFFFFFFFFFFFFFFFFFFFFF-///----GGGGHHHH
   2 22     -1.   TRANSFORMATION TO FACTOR WEIGHTS                DUFF
  11 10     -1.   DIFF + EFFICIENCY STCOMB                        DUFF


   STMERG(10.3) Output data Dank (-=not used, + = special meaning)
---------1---------2---------3---------4---------5------///-7---------8
+-CCCDDDEEEEEEEEFFFFFFFFFFFFFFFFFFFFFFFFFFFFFFFFFFF-///----GGGGHHHH
2  3 10     -1.   ADDING AGE TO OPERATOR                          DUFF


   STMERG(10.3) Direct Input    (-=not used)
---------1---------2---------3---------4---------5------///-7---------8
--CCCDDDEEEEEEEEFFFFFFFFFFFFFFFFFFFFFFFFFFFFFFFFFFF-///-------------
   2 10     -1.   AGE OF OPERATOR


        STSYNC(10.4)  (-=not used )
---------1---------2---------3---------4---------5------///-7---------8
--CCCDDDEEEEEEEEFFFFFFFFFFFFFFFFFFFFFFFFFFFFFFFFFFF-///----GGGGHHHH
   4 20     -1.   SYNCHRONISED STATCAT DATA BANK                  DUFF
```

Figure 3.33 - Example of Output - LDAP

```
DATA BANK PARAMETERS FOR COPY
( DUPLICATE STATCAT DATA BANK                    )

   16 DATA COLUMNS (=ITEMS PER ENTRY)
   10 CLASSES UNLESS OTHERWISE SPECIFIED
   -1.0000 = NON-VALUE (MISSING DATUM)




DATA BANK PARAMETERS FOR DUPE
( EMPTY STATCAT DATA BANK - READY FOR USE  )

    1 DATA COLUMNS (=ITEMS PER ENTRY)
    1 CLASSES UNLESS OTHERWISE SPECIFIED
   -1.0000 = NON-VALUE (MISSING DATUM)
```

```
      SUBROUTINE LDAP(MED2,MED3,V,TT,Q,NQ,NALT,NQMAX,NALTMX,IGO)
C LDAP     (SEE  3.3 ) SERVICE     LOAD/CHECK DATA BASE PARAMETERS
      DIMENSION V(20),TT(30)
      IGO = 0
      IF(MED3.LT.0) IGO = 1
      IF(MED3.LT.0) WRITE(MED2,900) MED3
      IF(MED3.LT.0) RETURN
      REWIND MED3
      READ(MED3) NQ,NALT,Q,(TT(I),I=1,16)
      WRITE(MED2,901)TT(16),(TT(I),I=1,10),NQ,NALT,Q
      V(4) = NQ
      V(14) = TT(14)
      IF(NQ.LE.NQMAX) GO TO 2
      WRITE(MED2,902) NQ,NQMAX
      V(10) = 1.
      NQ = NQMAX
    2 IF(NALT.LE.NALTMX.OR.NALTMX.EQ.0) RETURN
      WRITE(MED2,903) NALT,NALTMX
      V(10) = V(10) + 2.
      NALT = NALTMX
      RETURN
  900 FORMAT(38H UNIDENTIFIED PERIPHERAL FOR DATA BANK ,I4)
  901 FORMAT(1H0,20X,25HDATA BANK PARAMETERS FOR ,A4/
     121X,2H ( ,10A4,2H )/1H0,20X,I4,32H DATA COLUMNS (=ITEMS PER ENTRY)/
     2   21X,I4,35H CLASSES UNLESS OTHERWISE SPECIFIED /
     3   19X,F11.4,28H = NON-VALUE (MISSING DATUM) / )
  902 FORMAT(4H0THE,I4,29H ITEMS PER ENTRY EXCEED THE ,I4,34H AVAILABLE
     1STORAGE - FATAL ERROR 1,32X,13H** WARNING **)
  903 FORMAT(4H0THE,I4,30H CLASSES PER COLUMN EXCEED THE,I4,34H AVAILABL
     1E STORAGE - FATAL ERROR 2,32X,13H** WARNING **)
      END
```

3.4 DATA DESCRIPTION MODULE

3.4.1 Purpose

This module is used to provide the necessary information about the data which will follow it in the STATCAT data bank. It stores information in plain language which is later printed out as headings to tables, diagrams and tests, and as numerical information which is used by the computer to determine what tests and statistics should be produced.

Figure 3.41 contains flow-charts of LDDS, a system subroutine used to load, or read, a complete data description segment, and of the subroutines LCOM, which reads complementary information, and WDCD, which prints a data column description.

3.4.2 Module layout

```
DATA COLUMN TITLE CARD              )
COMPLEMENTARY INFORMATION CARD(S)   )  First Data Column
DATA COLUMN TITLE CARD              )
COMPLEMENTARY INFORMATION CARD(S)   )  Second Data Column

....................

DATA COLUMN TITLE CARD              )
COMPLEMENTARY INFORMATION CARD(S)   )  Final Data Column
'END' CARD
```

3.4.3 Card Layout - Data Column Title Card

AAAAABBBBCCCCCCCCCCCCCCCCCCC................DDDDDDD

Columns on Card	Item Code	FORTRAN Type	Function
1 - 6	A	I	Number of STATCAT data column
7 - 10	B	A	Short Title of data column
11 - 72	C	A	Full Title of data column
73 - 80	D	A	Data Level of data column

A - Number of STATCAT Data Column

This index identifies the data column to which the card refers. In most programs the data columns are numbered in order from 1 to NQ, where NQ is the number of data columns on the tape. This is not true for the data correction program STCORR nor for certain data manipulation programs, specific requirements should be checked with the individual program description.

B - Short Title of Data Column

This is a four character code used to identify the data column where it is inconvenient to use the full title. Any readable characters may be used, provided that the same combination is not used for two data columns on the same tape, and is not a blank or an 'END' code.

C - Full Title of Data Column

This is a total of sixty-two characters stored as sixteen words in the STATCAT data bank, and used as a title for tables, diagrams and tests in which this data column is involved. The computer itself does not have the capability of understanding this title, so that it can carry out no check that the data in the column are what the title says.

D - Data Level of Data Column

This is an eight letter word stored in two computer words in the STATCAT data bank. It states what is the level of the data (See Chapter 2 Data). It may be any one of the following:

```
     DUMMYbbb    Where b is a blank column
     NOMINALb
     ORDINALb
     INTERVAL
     RATIObbb
```

3.4.4 Complementary Information Card

The form of this card depends on the Data Level of the data column.

For DUMMY data, no card is used.

For NOMINAL or ORDINAL level data, the complementary information card is:

Card Layout - Complementary Information Card
                NOMINAL or ORDINAL data

AAAABBBBCCCCDDDDEEEEFFFFGGGGHHHHIIIIJJJJKKKKLLLLMMMMNNNN...

Columns on Card	Item Code	FORTRAN Type	Function
1 - 4	AAAA	A	
5 - 8	BBBB	A	Names of data classes
9 - 12	CCCC	A	
13 - 16	DDDD	A	
etc.			

A, B, C, D, etc.

The card contains up to 20 four character names for data classes. If the NALT parameter defining the maximum number of alternative classes for this data bank exceeds 20, a second and further cards must be provided after EACH nominal or ordinal Data Title Card, so that a title is available for each of the NALT classes, even if these titles are blank. A blank card read in as part of this list of titles will be accepted and 20 blank titles stored appropriately.

For INTERVAL and RATIO level data the complementary information is:

Card Layout - Complementary Information Card

AAAAAAAAAAAAAAAABBBBBBBBBBBB

Columns on Card	Item Code	FORTRAN Type	Function
1 - 10	A	F	Lower class limit
11 - 20	B	F	Class Interval

A - Lower Class Limit

This value is that taken as the lower limit of the second lowest class. The lowest class contains all values below this limit.

B - Class Interval

This value gives the width of each class. There will be one class containing all readings below the lower class limit, NALT-2 classes this wide, and one class containing all at or above the upper limit of the highest class. Thus if A is set to 1, and B is also 1, and NALT is 22, the lowest class will contain all values below 1, the second all values from 1 up to but not including 2, and the twenty-second class all values greater than or equal to 21.

If the value of B is zero, then the computer will determine the highest and lowest values in the Data Bank when programs are run, and adjust the class interval accordingly. This is a time consuming process and should be avoided whenever possible.

End of Module

The module must end with a standard 'END' card.

3.4.5 Examples

To avoid unnecessary duplication, an example of the loading of a data description segment is taken from the general STATCAT loading program STLOAD (4.2). Figure 4.23a lists the complete data description segment input for the standard demonstration STATCAT data bank. (Because only 72 characters can be produced across the printed page, columns 62-69 are omitted from this figure.)

Note that the units in which a number is measured should be included in the column title. Figure 4.26 gives the output corresponding to this data description segment.

The subroutine LDDS can also be used to read a data description segment from an input STATCAT data bank, or to read specific lines of a data description segment. LDDS also checks for missing, disordered or redundant titles.

The subroutine LCOM loads complementary information for a data column, given the title card, from card format. As well as its use in LDDS, it is used where column titles are not available in regular order - such as in STMERG. (LCOM checks for misplaced data level names.)

The subroutine WDCD simply writes a data column description in full, including line number, class names, and class limits as needed.

Figure 3.41 - System Flowcharts - LDDS, LCOM, WDCD

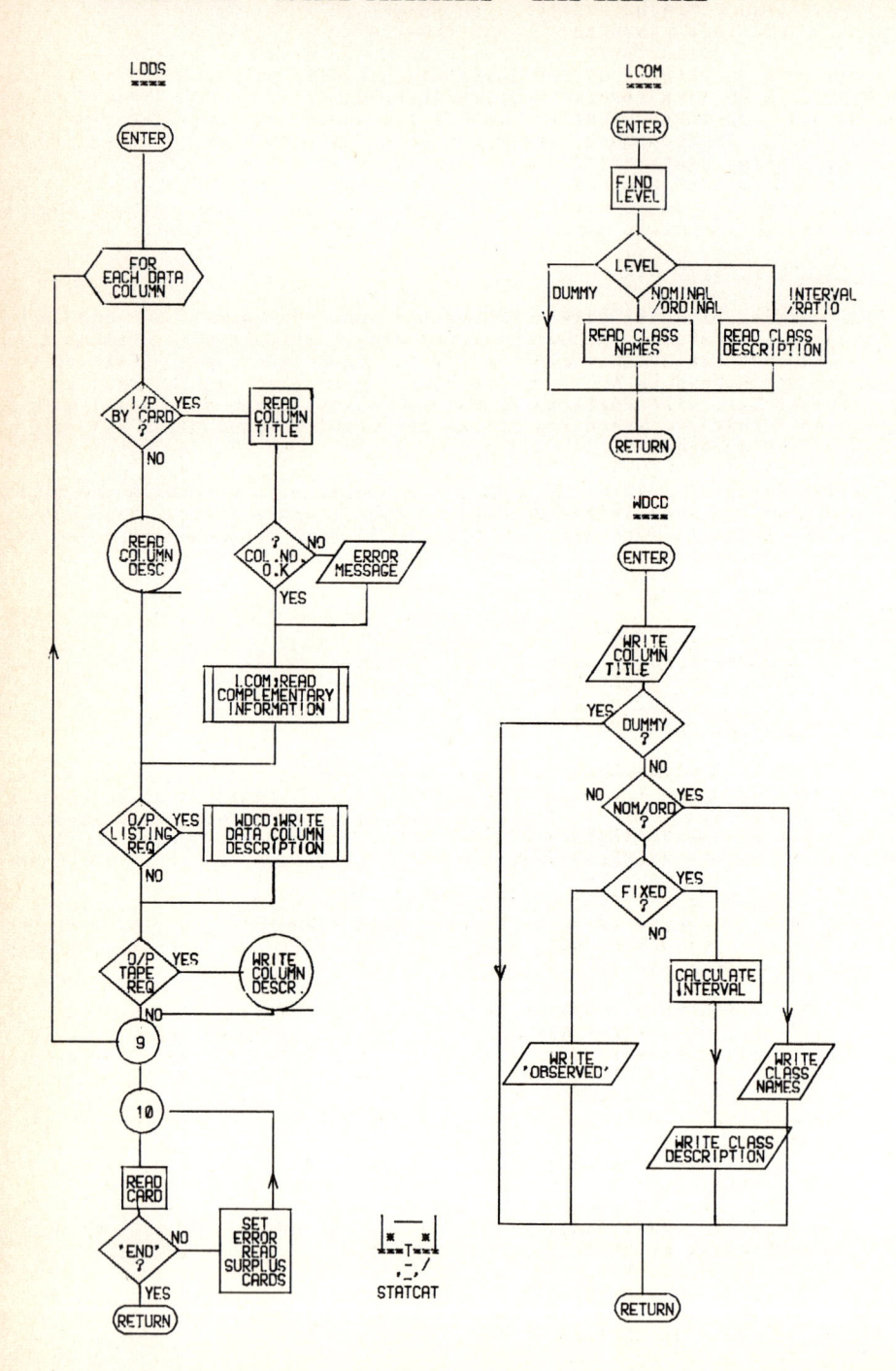

```
      SUBROUTINE LDDS(TRT,NALT,D,NQ,ST,NQS,IT,NQT,RT,NQR,DMIN,DMAX,NQM,
     1 LI,NSW,Q,VT,MED1,MED2,MED3,MED4,IGO)
C LDDS    (SEE  3.4 ) SYSTEM      LOADS DATA DESCRIPTION SEGMENT
C MED1 = 0 - NO CARD INPUT       NQR=0 NO CLASS NAMES   LI=LINES PRINTED
C MED2 = 0 - NO PRINTER OUTPUT   NQS=0 NO SHORT TITLES  NSW=0 NO SWEEP
C MED3 = 0 - NO TAPE INPUT       NQT=0 NO DATA LEVELS   VT=NTRYS IN D.B.
C MED4 = 0 - NO TAPE OUTPUT      NQM=0 NO CLASS LIMITS  LI=LINES PRINTED
C IGO 0=O.K., 1=DISORDERED, 2=NOT ENOUGH TITLES (TOO MANY=WARNING)
      DIMENSION D(NQ),ST(NQS),IT(NQT),RT(NQR,NALT),DMIN(NQM),DMAX(NQM)
      DIMENSION TRT(NALT),FORM(6),TX(19)
      IGO = 0
      ISW = 0
      ALT= NALT-2
      IF(NALT.LE.2) ALT = 1
      LR = (NALT+49)/10
      IF(MED2.GT.0) WRITE(MED2,900)
      DO 9 I = 1,NQ
      IF(IGO.EQ.2) GO TO 7
      IF(MED1.EQ.0) GO TO 5
    1 READ(MED1,901) FORM,TX
      IF(IBL(FORM,6,1)) 1,2,3
    2 J = AN(FORM,6,1,6)
      IF(I.EQ.J) GO TO 4
C DISORDERED INPUT
      IF(MED2.GT.0) WRITE(MED2,902) J,I
      IF(IGO.EQ.0) IGO = 1
      GO TO 4
C PREMATURE END ON INPUT CARDS
    3 IF(MED2.GT.0) WRITE(MED2,903)
      IGO = 2
      GO TO 7
    4 CALL LCOM(TX,TRT,NALT,NX,DMINX,DMAXX,MED1,MED2)
    5 IF(MED3.GT.0) READ(MED3) TX,TRT,NX,DMINX,DMAXX
C OUTPUT PHASE - PRINT IF REQUIRED
      IF(MED2.LE.0) GO TO 7
      IF(NX.EQ.1) LS = 2
      IF(NX.EQ.2.OR.NX.EQ.3) LS = LR
      IF(NX.GE.4) LS = 3
      LI = LI + LS
      IF(LI.GT.50) WRITE(MED2,904)
      IF(LI.GT.50) WRITE(MED2,900)
      IF(LI.GT.50) LI = LS + 3
      CALL WDCD(TX,TRT,NALT,NX,DMINX,DMAXX,I,MED2)
    7 IF(MED4.GT.0) WRITE(MED4) TX,TRT,NX,DMINX,DMAXX
C OUTPUT PHASE - STORE AS REQUIRED
      IF(I.LE.NQS) CALL COPYA(ST(I),TX(1))
      IF(I.LE.NQT) IT(I) = NX
      IF(I.LE.NQM) DMIN(I)=DMINX
      IF(I.LE.NQM) DMAX(I)=DMAXX
      IF(I.LE.NQM.AND.NX.GE.4.AND.NX.LE.5.AND.NSW.EQ.1) DMIN(I)=Q
      IF(I.LE.NQM.AND.NX.GE.4.AND.NX.LE.5.AND.NSW.EQ.1) DMAX(I)=Q
      IF(DMIN(I).EQ.Q) ISW=ISW+1
      IF(I.GT.NQR) GO TO 9
      DO 8 J=1,NALT
    8 CALL COPYA(RT(I,J),TRT(J))
    9 CONTINUE
C CORRECT END - REJECT SURPLUS
      IF(MED3.GT.0.OR.IGO.EQ.2) GO TO 12
   10 READ(MED1,901) FORM,TX
      IF(IBL(FORM,6,1)) 10,11,12
   11 IF(MED2.GT.0) WRITE(MED2,905) FORM,TX
      GO TO 10
   12 IF(NSW.EQ.0.OR.MED3.LE.0) GO TO 30
```

```
C SWEEP REQUIRED - PREPARE AND COUNT
      VX = 0.
   20 READ(MED3) D
      DO 21 I = 1,NQ
      IF(D(I).NE.Q) GO TO 40
   21 CONTINUE
C END OF COUNTING - OUTPUT NO,OUTPUT CLASS LIMITS IF ANY AND IF REQUIRED
      IF(MED2.GT.0) WRITE(MED2,906) VX
      IF(ISW.EQ.0.OR.NQM.EQ.0) GO TO 30
      REWIND MED3
      IF(MED2.LE.0) GO TO 22
      IF(LI+ISW*6+2.GT.50) WRITE(MED2,904)
      IF(LI+ISW*6+2.GT.50) WRITE(MED2,900)
      IF(LI+ISW*6+2.GT.50) WRITE(MED2,907)
      IF(LI+ISW*6+2.GT.50) LI = 4
   22 READ(MED3) NQ, NALT, (X,I=1,17)
C TIDY UP CLASS INTERVALS
      DO 25 I = 1,NQ
      READ(MED3) TX,TRT,NX,DMINX,DMAXX
      IF(NX.NE.4.AND.NX.NE.5) GO TO 25
      IF(MED2.LE.0) GO TO 23
      LI=LI+6
      IF(LI.GT.50) WRITE(MED2,904)
      IF(LI.GT.50) WRITE(MED2,900)
      IF(LI.GT.50) WRITE(MED2,907)
      IF(LI.GT.50) LI = 8
      WRITE(MED2,908) I,NX,TX
      WRITE(MED2,909) DMIN(I),DMAX(I)
   23 CALL CLIMS(DMIN(I),DMAX(I),NALT)
      DT =(DMAX(I)-DMIN(I))/ALT
      IF(MED2.GT.0) WRITE(MED2,910) DMIN(I),DT,DMAX(I)
   25 CONTINUE
C NORMAL END
   30 IF(MED3.GT.0) REWIND MED3
      IF(NQM.EQ.0.OR.ISW.EQ.0.OR.MED3.LE.0) RETURN
      DEL = 0.
      DO 35 I = 1,NQ
      IF(DMIN(I).NE.Q.OR.DMAX(I).NE.Q) GO TO 35
      DMIN(I) = 1.5
      DMAX(I) = ALT+ 1.5
      IF(MED2.LE.0) GO TO 35
      IF(DEL.EQ.0.) WRITE(MED2,911)
      DEL = 1.
      WRITE(MED2,910) DMIN(I),DEL,DMAX(I)
      WRITE(MED2,912) I,ST(I)
   35 CONTINUE
      RETURN
C DATA CUMULATION LOOP
   40 VX = VX + 1.
      IF(ISW.EQ.0) GO TO 20
      DO 41 I = 1,NQ
      IF(IT(I).LT.4.OR.IT(I).GT.5) GO TO 41
      IF(DMIN(I).EQ.Q.OR.D(I).LT.DMIN(I)) DMIN(I) = D(I)
      IF(DMAX(I).EQ.Q.OR.D(I).GT.DMAX(I)) DMAX(I) = D(I)
   41 CONTINUE
      GO TO 20
  900 FORMAT (1H0,20X,25H DATA DESCRIPTION SEGMENT /
     1 21H0COLUMN SCALE    SHORT,10X,10HFULL TITLE/
     2 21H NUMBER CODE    TITLE,65X,5HLEVEL    )
  901 FORMAT (6A1,A4,A2,17A4)
  902 FORMAT(37H0 NOT ENOUGH DATA COLUMN DESCRIPTIONS,73X,11H**WARNING**
     1)
  903 FORMAT(18H TITLES DISORDERED,I4,5H FOR ,I4,12H1H QUESTION.)
```

```
      904 FORMAT(1H1)
      905 FORMAT(14H SURPLUS CARD ,6A1,A4,A2,17A4)
      906 FORMAT(1H0,28HNUMBER OF ENTRIES ON FILE  -,2X,F8.0)
      907 FORMAT(1H0,20X,33HCLASS INTERVALS DERIVED FROM DATA)
      908 FORMAT(1H0,I5,I6,4X,A4,4X,A2,17A4)
      909 FORMAT(1H0,20X,30HOBSERVED MINIMUM AND MAXIMUM =,2F20.8)
      910 FORMAT(1H0,20X,18HCLASSES FROM BELOW,F12.2,14H BY CLASSES OF,F12.4
         1,3H TO,F12.2,9H AND OVER  )
      911 FORMAT(1H1,19X,45HNO DATA SWEEP - UNDEFINED LIMITS SET AS BELOW/
         1 19H0COLUMN NUMBER NAME//)
      912 FORMAT(1H+,8X,I4,2X,A4)
          END


          SUBROUTINE LCOM(TT,TRT,NALT,NX,DMIN,DMAX,MED1,MED2)
    C LCOM    (SEE  3.4 ) SYSTEM        LOADS COMPLEMENTARY INFORMATION
          DIMENSION TRT(NALT),P(23),CN(100),TT(19),FORM(20),PP(5)
          DATA P/4HDUMM,4HNOMI,4HORDI,4HINTE,4HRATI,4H DUM,4H  DU,4H   D,4H
         1NOM,4HNOM1,4HNOMI,4HNOM1,4H NOM,4H ORD,4HORD1,4HORDI,4HORD1,4H ORD
         1,4HINTE,4H RAT,4H  RA,4H    R,4HRAT1/
          DATA PP/4HY   ,4HINAL,4HINAL,4HRVAL,4HO    /
          DATA  CN/4HCLA1,4HCLA2,4HCLA3,4HCLA4,4HCLA5,4HCLA6,4HCLA7,4HCLA8,4
         1HCLA9,4HCL10,4HCL11,4HCL12,4HCL13,4HCL14,4HCL15,4HCL16,4HCL17,4HC
         218,4HCL19,4HCL20,4HCL21,4HCL22,4HCL23,4HCL24,4HCL25,4HCL26,4HCL27,
         34HCL28,4HCL29,4HCL30,4HCL31,4HCL32,4HCL33,4HCL34,4HCL35,4HCL36,4HC
         4L37,4HCL38,4HCL39,4HCL40,4HCL41,4HCL42,4HCL43,4HCL44,4HCL45,4HCL46
         5,4HCL47,4HCL48,4HCL49,4HCL50,4HCL51,4HCL52,4HCL53,4HCL54,4HCL55,4H
         6CL56,4HCL57,4HCL58,4HCL59,4HCL60,4HCL61,4HCL62,4HCL63,4HCL64,4HCL6
         75,4HCL66,4HCL67,4HCL68,4HCL69,4HCL70,4HCL71,4HCL72,4HCL73,4HCL74,4
         8HCL75,4HCL76,4HCL77,4HCL78,4HCL79,4HCL80,4HCL81,4HCL82,4HCL83,4HCL
         984,4HCL85,4HCL86,4HCL87,4HCL88,4HCL89,4HCL90,4HCL91,4HCL92,4HCL93,
         94HCL94,4HCL95,4HCL96,4HCL97,4HCL98,4HCL99,4HCL100/
          NX = ICH(TT(18),P,23)
          IF(NX.EQ.0) NX = 6
          IF(NX.GE.6.AND.NX.LE.8) WRITE(MED2,993)P(1),PP(1)
          IF(NX.GE.6.AND.NX.LE.8) NX = 1
          IF(NX.GE.9.AND.NX.LE.13) WRITE(MED2,993)P(2),PP(2)
          IF(NX.GE.9.AND.NX.LE.13) NX = 2
          IF(NX.GE.14.AND.NX.LE.18) WRITE(MED2,993)P(3),PP(3)
          IF(NX.GE.14.AND.NX.LE.18) NX = 3
          IF(NX.EQ.19) WRITE(MED2,993) P(4),PP(4)
          IF(NX.EQ.19) NX = 4
          IF(NX.GE.20) WRITE(MED2,993)P(5),PP(5)
          IF(NX.GE.20) NX = 5
          IF(NX.NE.2.AND.NX.NE.3) GO TO 3
          DO 2 I = 1,NALT,20
          J = I + 19
          IF(J.GT.NALT) J = NALT
        1 READ(MED1,990) (TRT(K),K=I,J)
          K = J-I + 1
          IF(IBL(TRT(I),K,4))8,2,2
        8 DO 9 K = J,NALT
        9 CALL COPYA(TRT(K),TRT(J))
          GO TO 3
        2 CONTINUE
        3 DMIN = 1.5
          DEL = 1.0
          IF(NX.EQ.2.OR.NX.EQ.3) GO TO 6
          DO 7 J = 1,NALT
          INDX = J - J/100*100
        7 CALL COPYA(TRT(J),CN(INDX))
          IF(NX.LE.3) GO TO 6
        4 READ(MED1,991) FORM
```

```
      IF(IBL(FORM,20,1))4,5,5
    5 DMIN = AN(FORM,10,1,10)
      DEL  = AN(FORM,20,11,20)
      IF(DEL.NE.0.) NX = NX + 2
    6 R = NALT - 2
      DMAX = DMIN + DEL*R
      RETURN
  990 FORMAT(20A4)
  991 FORMAT(20A1)
  993 FORMAT(39H NON-STANDARD DATA LEVEL ASSUMED TO BE ,2A4)
      END


      SUBROUTINE WDCD(TT,TRT,NALT,NX,DMIN,DMAX,I,MED2)
C WDCD    (SEE  3.4 ) SERVICE       WRITE DATA COLUMN DESCRIPTION
      DIMENSION TRT(NALT),TT(19)
      WRITE (MED2,999)I,NX,(TT(J),J=1,19)
      IF(NX.EQ.2.OR.NX.EQ.3) WRITE(MED2,990) (TRT(J),J = 1,NALT)
      IF(NX.EQ.4.OR.NX.EQ.5) WRITE(MED2,992)
      IF(NX.LE.5) RETURN
      ALT = NALT - 2
      DEL = (DMAX-DMIN)/ALT
      IF(NX.EQ.6.OR.NX.EQ.7) WRITE(MED2,993)DMIN,DEL,DMAX
      RETURN
  990 FORMAT(1H0,20X,10(A4,1H-)/(21X,10(A4,1H-)))
  992 FORMAT(21X,77HLOWEST CLASS LIMIT = OBSERVED MINIMUM, HIGHEST CLASS
     1 LIMIT = OBSERVED MAXIMUM          )
  993 FORMAT (21X,18HCLASSES FROM BELOW,F12.4,14H BY CLASSES OF,F12.6,3H
     1 TO,F12.4,9H AND OVER   )
  999 FORMAT(1H0,I4,I6,6X,A4,4X,A2,17A4)
      END
```

3.5 SAMPLE SPECIFICATION

3.5.1 Purpose

This module is employed to specify two or more independent samples, usually so that tests of the statistical significance of differences between them may be carried out.

3.5.2 Module layout

```
SAMPLE SET TITLE CARD
FIRST SAMPLE TITLE     )    First sample
FIRST SPECIFICATION    )
SECOND SAMPLE TITLE    )    Second sample
SECOND SPECIFICATION   )

................

FINAL SAMPLE TITLE     )    Final sample
FINAL SPECIFICATION    )
END CARD SIGNALLING END OF MODULE
```

3.5.3 Card Layout - Sample Set Title Card

AAAAAAAAAAAAAAAAAAAAAAAAAAAAAAAAAAAAAAAABBBBBBBBBBBBBB............

Columns on Card	Item Code	FORTRAN Type	Function
1 - 40	A	A	Title of set of samples
41 - 80	B	A	Comment (not kept)

A - Title of set of samples

This is a title consisting of 10 four-character words serving to identify the entire set of samples being used at a given time. Any readable characters may be used.

3.5.4 Card Layout - Sample Title

CCCCDDDDDDDDDDDDDDDDDDDD..........

Columns on Card	Item Code	FORTRAN Type	Function
1 - 4	C	A	Title of an individual sample
5 - 80	D	A	Comment (not kept)

A - Title of an Individual Sample

This is a title consisting of one four-character word. It serves to identify the sample defined in the immediately following specification. Any readable characters may be used.

3.5.5 Specification

The way in which a specification is defined is described in the following description of a Subset specification module.

End of Module

At the end of the module there must be an END card where the next title of an individual sample would be expected to appear. This will be in addition to the END card ending the specification of the final sample.

3.5.6 Examples

Figure 3.51 contains simplified flow-charts for the subroutines LSAMP, which is used to load the titles, sample names and sample specifications for a set of samples, and for LSET, which is used to define a set of conditions. (See section 3.6 for detailed discussion of how a set of conditions is applied.)

Figure 3.52 shows how sample sets may be specified and identified. Notice that in the first example the samples are specified by a single class name - the last of these conditions is strictly speaking redundant because there were only four possible classes. Figure 3.53 lists the output produced for this sample set.

A method of reducing wasted time is demonstrated in the second example. (Figure 3.54 lists the output corresponding to this input.) Here it will be noted that the earlier samples are the most simply defined and contain the largest numbers of entries. Within a definition, the conditions most likely to cause rejection should be tested first, and the alternatives most likely to lead to acceptance should be placed first. (Because, once an acceptable set of conditions has been found, the remaining conditions are not tested). Notice also that in the second example the last specification consists of a single END card, embracing all remaining conditions. Notice that both example modules have two final END cards. One of these signals the end of the last specification, the other the end of the set of samples. All sample sets end in this way.

Figure 3.51 - System flow-charts for LSAMP and LSET

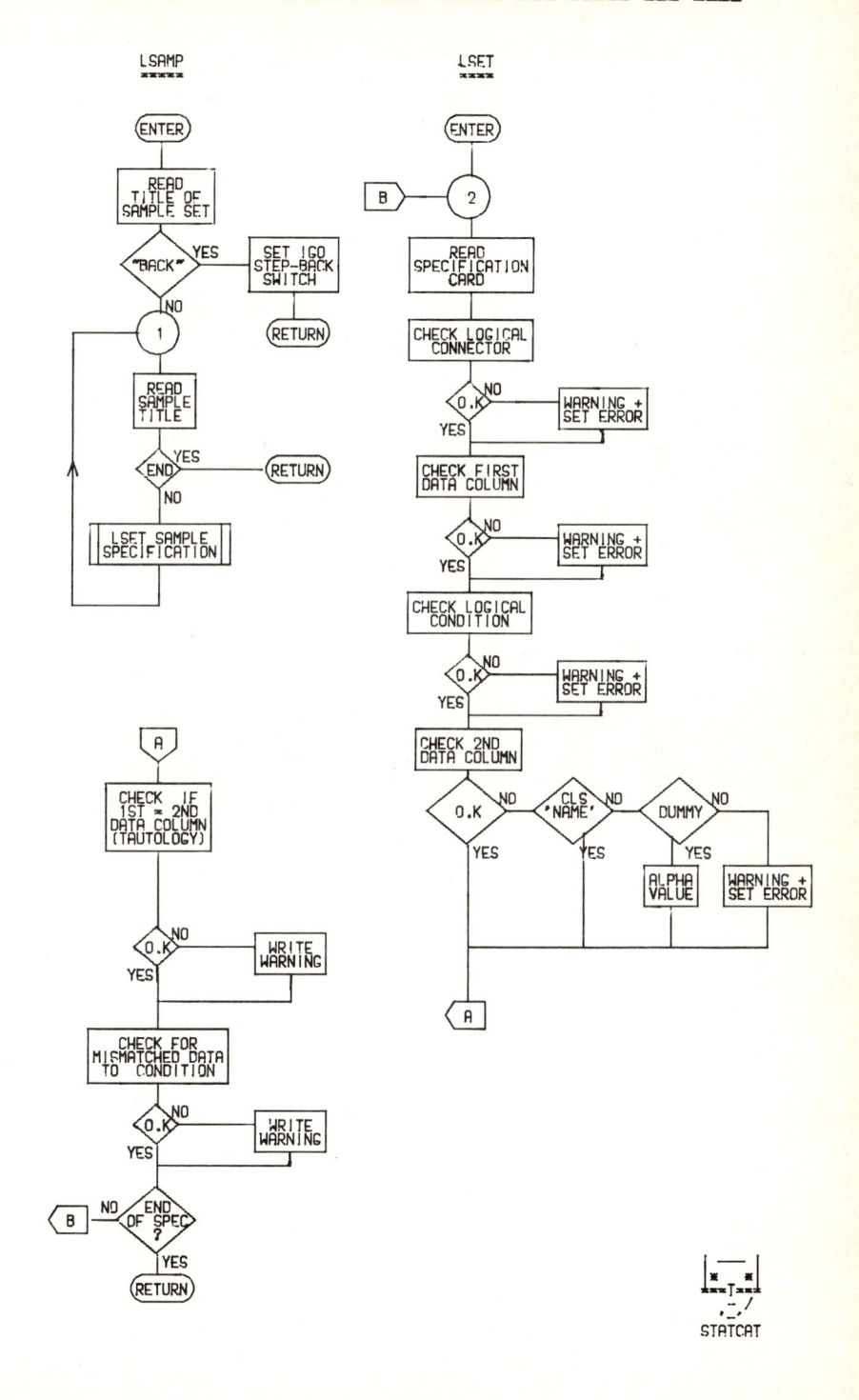

Figure 3.52 - Demonstration Input Cards for Two Sample Sets

```
---------1---------2---------3---------4---------5---------6---------7
OPERATOR                                FOUR INDEPENDENT SAMPLES
ERIC
.IF.OPER.EQ.ERIC
END OF SAMPLE ONE
FRED
.IF.OPER.EQ.FRED
END OF SAMPLE TWO
GINA
.IF.OPER.EQ.GINA
END OF SAMPLE THREE
HUGH
.IF.OPER.EQ.HUGH
END OF SAMPLE FOUR
END OF SAMPLE SET


ARBITRARY SELECTION
ONE
.IF.NTRY.GE.      33                    33 UPWARDS
END OF SAMPLE ONE
TWO
.IF.NTRY.GE.      27                    ENTRIES 0 TO 9 AND 27 TO 32
.OR.NTRY.LE.       9
END OF SAMPLE TWO
THREE
.IF.NTRY.GE.      15                    ENTRIES  15,16,17
AND.NTRY.LE.      17
END OF SAMPLE THREE
FOUR
.IF.NTRY.GE.      20                    ENTRIES 20,21,22,23,24
AND.NTRY.LE.      24
END OF SAMPLE FOUR
FIVE                                    ALL REMAINING VALUES
END OF SAMPLE FIVE
END OF SAMPLE SET
---------1---------2---------3---------4---------5---------6---------7
```

Figure 3.53 - Output for First Demonstration Sample Set

```
            SAMPLE SET TITLE - OPERATORS                           COMMENT   FOUR INDEPENDENT SAMPLES
SAMPLES ARE DEFINED AS BELOW - FIRST DEFINITION SATISFIED HAS PRIORITY.

SAMPLE NUMBER    1 NAME - ERIC                                     COMMENT
IS DEFINED AS BELOW -
.IF.  OPER  .EQ.  ERIC                                             COMMENT

END OF SAMPLE ONE                                                  COMMENT

SAMPLE NUMBER    2 NAME - FRED                                     COMMENT
IS DEFINED AS BELOW -
.IF.  OPER  .EQ.  FRED                                             COMMENT

END OF SAMPLE TWO                                                  COMMENT

SAMPLE NUMBER    3 NAME - GINA                                     COMMENT
IS DEFINED AS BELOW -
.IF.  OPER  .EQ.  GINA                                             COMMENT

END OF SAMPLE THREE                                                COMMENT

SAMPLE NUMBER    4 NAME - HUGH                                     COMMENT
IS DEFINED AS BELOW -
.IF.  OPER  .EQ.  HUGH                                             COMMENT

END OF SAMPLE FOUR                                                 COMMENT

BACK
```

Figure 3.54 - Output for Second Demonstration Sample Set

```
            SAMPLE SET TITLE - ARBITRARY SELECTION                 COMMENT
SAMPLES ARE DEFINED AS BELOW - FIRST DEFINITION SATISFIED HAS PRIORITY.

SAMPLE NUMBER    1 NAME - ONE                                      COMMENT
IS DEFINED AS BELOW -
.IF.  NTRY  .GE.       33.000000                                   COMMENT   33 UPWARDS

DATA USED ARE ON A DUMMY SCALE    THEY SHOULD BE ON AN ORDINAL SCALE    ARE EXTRA ASUMPTIONS VALID      **WARNING**
END OF SAMPLE ONE                                                  COMMENT

SAMPLE NUMBER    2 NAME - TWO                                      COMMENT
IS DEFINED AS BELOW -
.IF.  NTRY  .GE.       27.000000                                   COMMENT   ENTRIES 27 TO 32 AND

DATA USED ARE ON A DUMMY SCALE    THEY SHOULD BE ON AN ORDINAL SCALE    ARE EXTRA ASUMPTIONS VALID      **WARNING**
.OR.  NTRY  .LE.        9.000000                                   COMMENT   ENTRIES 1 TO 9

DATA USED ARE ON A DUMMY SCALE    THEY SHOULD BE ON AN ORDINAL SCALE    ARE EXTRA ASUMPTIONS VALID      **WARNING**
END OF SAMPLE TWO                                                  COMMENT

SAMPLE NUMBER    3 NAME - THREE                                    COMMENT
IS DEFINED AS BELOW -
.IF.  NTRY  .GE.       15.000000                                   COMMENT   ENTRIES 15,16 AND 17

DATA USED ARE ON A DUMMY SCALE    THEY SHOULD BE ON AN ORDINAL SCALE    ARE EXTRA ASUMPTIONS VALID      **WARNING**
.AND. NTRY  .LE.       17.000000                                   COMMENT

DATA USED ARE ON A DUMMY SCALE    THEY SHOULD BE ON AN ORDINAL SCALE    ARE EXTRA ASUMPTIONS VALID      **WARNING**
END OF SAMPLE THREE                                                COMMENT

SAMPLE NUMBER    4 NAME - FOUR                                     COMMENT
IS DEFINED AS BELOW -
.IF.  NTRY  .GE.       20.000000                                   COMMENT   ENTRIES 20, 21, 22, 23 AND 24

DATA USED ARE ON A DUMMY SCALE    THEY SHOULD BE ON AN ORDINAL SCALE    ARE EXTRA ASUMPTIONS VALID      **WARNING**
.IF.  NTRY  .LE.       24.000000                                   COMMENT

DATA USED ARE ON A DUMMY SCALE    THEY SHOULD BE ON AN ORDINAL SCALE    ARE EXTRA ASUMPTIONS VALID      **WARNING**
END OF SAMPLE FOUR                                                 COMMENT

SAMPLE NUMBER    5 NAME - FIVE                                     COMMENT   ALL REMAINING VALUES
IS DEFINED AS BELOW -

END OF SAMPLE FIVE                                                 COMMENT
                ALL REMAINING ENTRIES ARE INCLUDED IN THIS SAMPLE - FOLLOWING SAMPLES MUST BE EMPTY

STOP
```

```
      SUBROUTINE LSAMP(SCON,NCON,MAXSAC,TS,NS,NSMAX,CN,ST,IT,NQ,TRT,NALT
     1,IGO)
C LSAMP   (SEE  3.5 ) SYSTEM       LOADS SAMPLE SET DEFINITION
      DIMENSION SCON(5,MAXSAC),TS(NSMAX),CN(NQ),ST(NQ),IT(NQ),C(11)
      DIMENSION TRT(NALT)
      COMMON /STCT/MED1,MED2,MED3,MED4,MED5,MED6,MED13,Q,V(20),TT(30)
      NCON = 0
      NS = 0
      ISF = NQ + 1
    5 READ (MED1,905) (TT(J),J=11,20),(C(J),J=1,10)
      IGO = IBL(TT(11),10,4)
      IF(IGO) 5,7,6
    6 WRITE(MED2,906) (TT(J),J=11,20),(C(J),J=1,10)
      RETURN
    7 WRITE(MED2,907) (TT(J),J=11,20),(C(J),J=1,10)
      WRITE(MED2,900)
C  READ SAMPLE TITLE
    1 READ(MED1,901) C
      IF(IBL(C,1,4)) 1,2,4
    2 NS = NS + 1
      WRITE(MED2,902) NS,C
      IF(NS.GT.NSMAX) GO TO 3
      CALL COPYA(TS(NS),C(1))
      NSF = NCON
      CALL LSET(SCON,NCON,MAXSAC,CN,ST,IT,NQ,TRT,NALT,ISF)
      IF(NCON.EQ.NSF+1) WRITE(MED2,921)
      GO TO 1
    3 WRITE(MED2,903) NSMAX
      CALL LSET(SCON,NCON,NCON,CN,ST,IT,NQ,TRT,NALT,ISF)
      GO TO 1
    4 RETURN
  900 FORMAT (74H SAMPLES ARE DEFINED AS BELOW - FIRST DEFINITION SATISF
     1IED HAS PRIORITY.    )
  901 FORMAT(A4,36X,10A4)
  902 FORMAT(14H0SAMPLE NUMBER,I4,8H NAME - ,A4,41X,10H  COMMENT ,10A4/2
     12H IS DEFINED AS BELOW - )
  903 FORMAT (47H0NUMBER OF SAMPLES EXCEEDS AVAILABLE STORAGE - ,I6/47H
     1INCREASE NSMAX - PROGRAM DISCARDS THIS SAMPLE     )
  905 FORMAT(20A4)
  906 FORMAT(1H ,20A4)
  907 FORMAT (1H1,11X,19HSAMPLE SET TITLE - ,10A4,10H  COMMENT   ,10A4)
  921 FORMAT(1H0,30X,83HALL REMAINING ENTRIES ARE INCLUDED IN THIS SAMPL
     1E - FOLLOWING SAMPLES MUST BE EMPTY)
      END


      SUBROUTINE LSET(SCON,NCON,NCMAX,CN,ST,IT,NQ,TRT,NALT,ISF)
C LSET    (SEE  3.5 ) SYSTEM       LOADS DEFINING CONDITIONS
      DIMENSION SCON(5,NCMAX),CN(NQ),ST(NQ),IT(NQ),C(38),C1(4),C3(6)
      DIMENSION TRT(NALT)
      DATA C1/4H.IF.,4HAND.,4H.OR.,4H.OR./,BL/4H    /,XMIS/4HMISS/
      DATA C3/4H.EQ.,4H.NE.,4H.GT.,4H.GE.,4H.LT.,4H.LE./
      COMMON /STCT/MED1,MED2,MED3,MED4,MED5,MED6,MED13,Q,V(20),TT(30)
      NLIN = 5
    1 READ(MED1,900) (C(I),I=1,3),CX,(C(I),I=5,38)
      IF(IBL(C,3,4).LT.0.AND.IBL(C(5),24,1).LT.0.AND.IBL(C(29),10,4).LT.
     10) GO TO 1
  100 NOK = 1
      IF(IBL(C,3,4).GT.0) GO TO 17
      WRITE(MED2,901) (C(I),I=1,3),CX,(C(I),I=29,38)
      C(5) = AN(C,28,5,28)
      IF(C(5).NE.0..OR.ICH(CX,BL,1).EQ.1) WRITE(MED2,903) C(5)
      IF(C(5).GT.0..AND.ICH(CX,BL,1).NE.1) WRITE(MED2,902)
```

```
      C(1) = ICH(C(1),C1,4)
      IF(C(1).EQ.4.)C(1) = 3.
      IF(C(1).GT.0.) GO TO 2
      WRITE(MED2,911)
      NOK = NOK + 1
    2 X = ICH(C(2),ST,NQ)
      C(2) = ICH(C(2),CN,NQ)
      IF(C(2).EQ.0.) C(2) = X
      IF(C(2).NE.0.) GO TO 3
      WRITE(MED2,912)
      NOK = NOK + 1
    3 C(3) = ICH(C(3),C3,6)
      IF(C(3).NE.0.) GO TO 4
      WRITE(MED2,913)
      NOK = NOK + 1
    4 C(4) = 0.
      IF(ICH(CX,BL,1).EQ.1) GO TO 5
      IF(ICH(CX,XMIS,1).EQ.1) C(5) = C(5) + Q
      IF(ICH(CX,XMIS,1).EQ.1) GO TO 5
      C(4) = ICH(CX,ST,NQ)
      IF(C(4).GT.0.5) GO TO 5
      C(4) = ICH(CX,CN,NQ)
      IF(C(4).GT.0.5) GO TO 5
      K = C(2) + 0.1
      IF(K.LE.0) GO TO 44
   40 IF(ISF-K)42,43,41
   41 ISF = 0
      REWIND MED3
      READ(MED3)NX,NX,(X,I=1,17)
   42 ISF = ISF + 1
      READ(MED3)(X,I=1,19),TRT,NX,X,X
      GO TO 40
   43 X = ICH(CX,TRT,NALT)
      IF(X.GT. 0.5)C(5) = C(5) + X
      IF(X.GT. 0.5) GO TO 5
      IF(NX.GT.1) GO TO 44
      C(5) = CX
      GO TO 5
   44 WRITE(MED2,914)
      NOK = NOK + 1
    5 NLIN = NLIN + NOK
      IF(NLIN.LE.50) GO TO 6
      WRITE(MED2,915)
      NLIN = 0
    6 IF(NOK.GT.1) GO TO 1
      IF(NCON.LT.NCMAX) GO TO 9
      WRITE (MED2,916)
      NLIN = NLIN + 1
      GO TO 1
C READ-TIME CHECKING OF INDIVIDUAL CONDITIONS
C 1 FIRST = SECOND (TAUTOLOGY)
    9 IF(C(2).NE.C(4)) GO TO 14
      NB = C(3)
      NLIN = NLIN + 1
      IF(C(5).EQ.0.)GO TO 10
      IF(C(5).LT.0.)GO TO 11
      GO TO (12,13,12,12,13,13),NB
   10 GO TO (13,12,12,13,12,13),NB
   11 GO TO (12,13,13,13,12,12),NB
   12 WRITE(MED2,918)
      GO TO 14
   13 WRITE(MED2,919)
C 2 INADEQUATE DATA SCALE FOR CONDITION
```

```
   14 LR = 3
      IF(C(3).LE.2.) LR = 2
      DO 16 J = 2,4,2
      IF(C(2).EQ.C(4).AND.J.EQ.4) GO TO 16
      NA = C(J)
      IF(NA.EQ.0) GO TO 16
      NB = IT(NA)
      IF(NB.GE.LR) GO TO 16
      CALL CHIKEN(LR,NB)
      NLIN = NLIN + 2
   16 CONTINUE
      GO TO 19
   17 IF(NCON.LT.NCMAX) GO TO 18
      WRITE(MED2,917)
      NLIN = NLIN + 1
      NCON = NCON - 1
   18 WRITE(MED2,922) (C(I),I=1,3),CX,(C(I),I=5,38)
      C(1) = 4.
   19 NCON = NCON + 1
      DO 20 I = 1,5
   20 SCON(I,NCON) = C(I)
      IF(C(1).NE.4.) GO TO 1
      RETURN
  900 FORMAT (4A4,24A1,10A4)
  901 FORMAT(1H ,4(A4,2X),48X,8HCOMMENT ,10A4)
  902 FORMAT(1H+,24X,1H+)
  903 FORMAT(1H+,24X,F12.6)
  911 FORMAT (23H UNIDENTIFIED CONNECTOR)
  912 FORMAT (7X,24HUNIDENTIFIED DATA COLUMN)
  913 FORMAT (13X,22HUNIDENTIFIED CONDITION)
  914 FORMAT (19X,24HUNIDENTIFIED DATA COLUMN)
  915 FORMAT (1H1)
  916 FORMAT (25X,47HNOT ENOUGH STORAGE AVAILABLE FOR THIS CONDITION)
  917 FORMAT (25X,50HLAST CONDITION STORED IS OVER-WRITTEN TO STORE END)
  918 FORMAT (50H FIRST AND SECOND COLUMNS IDENTICAL - ALWAYS FALSE)
  919 FORMAT (50H FIRST AND SECOND COLUMNS IDENTICAL - ALWAYS TRUE )
  922 FORMAT(1H0,4A4,24A1,32X,8HCOMMENT ,10A4)
      END
```

3.6 SUBSET SPECIFICATION

3.6.1 Purpose

This module specifies the subset of the STATCAT data bank which will be included in the subsequent analyses. It is employed by all STATCAT programs except the basic data loading program and the auxiliary copying, verifying and heading programs.

3.6.2 Module layout

```
SUBSET TITLE CARD
SPECIFICATION CARDS
END OF MODULE CARD
```

3.6.3 Card Layout - Subset Title Card

```
AAAAAAAAA..........AAAAAABBBBBBB............BBBBBBBBBBBBBB
```

Columns on Card	Item Code	FORTRAN Type	Function
1 - 40	A	A	Title of STATCAT data bank subset
41 - 80	B	A	Comment

A - Title of STATCAT Data Bank Subset

This is a title consisting of 10 four-character words which identify the subset of the data bank which is being used for the given analysis. It is written in plain language, using any readable characters. The computer will reproduce this title at the head of each page of results, but it cannot use any information contained in the title.

B - Comment

This comment consists of 10 four-character words which provide additional comment on the STATCAT data bank subset title. It is printed out at the time the module is read in, but it is not kept for later use.

Special Cases

If this card is an END card, the program will step back to the previous input module. If this card is blank, the program will read another card using the same format until a non-blank card is found.

3.6.4 Card Layout - Specification Card

```
AAAABBBBCCCCDDDDEEEEEEEEEEEEEEEEEEEEEEFFFFFFFFFFFFFFFFFFF
```

Columns	Item	FORTRAN

on Card	Code	Type	Function
1 - 4	A	A	Logical Connector
5 - 8	B	A	Column Identification
9 - 12	C	A	Condition
13 - 16	D	A	Column Identification
17 - 40	E	F	Constant
41 - 80	F	A	Comment

A - Logical Connector

This is a four-letter code connecting the logical condition specified in this card with the previous conditions. It may be any of the following codes : .IF. .AND .OR.

The code .IF. means that the condition expressed on the card must be satisfied by entries to be included in the specification.

The code .AND has essentially the same significance, except that it is usually used with later cards of a set.

The code .OR. means that the condition on the card is an alternative, or the first of a set of alternative conditions. An entry is accepted as soon as it is found to satisfy any set of conditions, regardless of whether it also satisfies other conditions.

B - Column Identification

This is a four-letter code identifying the first data column involved in a given condition. It may be the short title of a data column, or a standard column number of the form given in section 3.7. (i.e. COL1 to COL9, CL10 - CL99, C100 upwards).

C - Condition

This is a logical condition, connecting the first data column with the remaining data column and constant. The six possible conditions are:

```
.EQ.  -  Equals
.NE.  -  Not equal to
.GT.  -  Greater than
.GE.  -  Greater than or equal to
.LT.  -  Less than
.LE.  -  Less than or equal to
```

D - Column Identification

This is a four-character code. It may be used to identify a second data column (by four-character name or number), in which case the numerical value found in that data column will be compared with the value in the first data column, or it may be a class name for the first data column - in which case the numerical value of the class will be used, or it may be blank, in which case the value stored in E will be compared with the value found in the first data column.

If it is none of these, and the first data column is on a DUMMY scale, and E is blank, then this four-character code will be compared with whatever was stored in the first data column, on the assumption that that was a four-letter code.

Strict ASA FORTRAN IV does not allow comparisons of strings of characters, but most computer systems will in fact allow comparisons to be made. The relations .EQ. and .NE. may be expected to operate normally, but other relations may produce unexpected results, depending on the way in which alphanumeric codings are stored within the machine.

E - Constant

This is a number of up to 24 digits (most computers will not be able to use all these digits, but will retain only a number of the most significant digits, and the total size of the number). It may contain a decimal point, and it may have a positive or negative sign - although none of these are necessary.

Blanks, non-numerical characters and signs or decimal points after the first will be discarded.

F - Comment

This comment consists of ten four-character words which may be used to provide an explanation of the condition given on the card. This comment is printed out at the time the module is read, but it is not kept.

Special Cases

If the specification card is an 'END' card, the program stops reading conditions and proceeds to the next input module. If the 'END' card is the first specification card, all entries will be included in the subset.

3.6.5   Error Messages

Certain input errors can be detected by the system and result in error messages.

      1 UNIDENTIFIABLE CONNECTOR

      2 UNIDENTIFIABLE DATA COLUMN

      3 UNIDENTIFIABLE CONDITION

The occurence of any of these error leads to the card on which they occur being discarded, but does not halt program execution.

      4 NOT ENOUGH STORAGE AVAILABLE FOR THIS CONDITION

If the number of conditions exceeds the available storage, the surplus conditions are read, checked and printed with this warning. They are then discarded.

      5 LAST CONDITION STORED IS OVER-WRITTEN TO STORE END

If there are too many conditions for the available storage, the last line of storage space must be used to store the 'END' code so that the last condition stored must be discarded.

Neither of these error causes execution to halt, although the data bank subset so defined may not be correct.

      6 FIRST AND SECOND COLUMNS IDENTICAL - ALWAYS FALSE

If the two specified columns are the same, and the conditions are such that the relation can never be satisfied - for instance - .EQ. with a non-zero constant, this message is printed. The condition is not discarded since it may be one of a group of alternatives.

7 FIRST AND SECOND COLUMNS IDENTICAL - ALWAYS TRUE

If the two specified columns are the same, and the conditions are such that they must always be satisfied - for instance - the relation .GT. with a positive constant, this message is printed. The condition is not discarded since it may be one of a group of combined conditions.

8 DATA USED ARE ON A NOMINAL SCALE
THEY SHOULD BE ON AN ORDINAL SCALE
ARE EXTRA ASSUMPTIONS JUSTIFIED

If the relationship involves a ranking of the data items from the two data columns (.GT.,.GE.,.LT.,.LE.) and at least one of the data columns is on a nominal scale, a warning is printed that the comparison may not be legitimate. It does not affect the running of the analysis. Similarly if a data column is on a dummy scale, the corresponding message is printed out (whatever the condition used).
The condition is not discarded and the analysis is carried out normally.

Non-values

Non-values (See 4.2) are treated in exactly the same way as ordinary values. They may be specified as constants or appear as values in data and will be included or discarded in accordance with their numerical value.

3.6.6   Examples

Figure 3.62 contains an example of a subset specification, deliberately designed to induce as many error messages as possible. Figure 3.63 contains the corresponding output. The various error messages are explained in the previous section.

3.6.7   AND vs OR

Sets of conditions defining subsets or samples are specified in 'minterm' form. This means that they consist of sets of conditions linked by AND which are themselves linked by OR. An entry is included if it satisfies any complete set of conditions linked by AND. Thus:

```
.IF.OPER.EQ.FRED
AND.TASK.EQ.BEND
.OR.TASK.EQ.CUT.
END OF SAMPLE
```

will accept the four entries for which the operator is FRED and the task is BEND, and the sixteen entries for which the task is CUT. To specify BEND or CUT for FRED only, we must specify:-

```
.IF.OPER.EQ.FRED
AND.TASK.EQ.BEND
.OR.OPER.EQ.FRED
AND.TASK.EQ.CUT.
END OF SAMPLE
```

Any set of conditions can be reduced to minterm form. Space does not permit a description of the methods used, (Truth Tables, Venn diagrams, Karnaugh Maps etc.) - consult any modern mathematics text, or the references below.

REFERENCES: - Selby and Sweet (Ch 5),Mosteller, Rourke and Thomas (Ch 3),Kemeny, Snell and Thompson (Ch 3),Stilson (Ch 4).

Figure 3.61 - System Flow-charts - LDBS + CLSAM

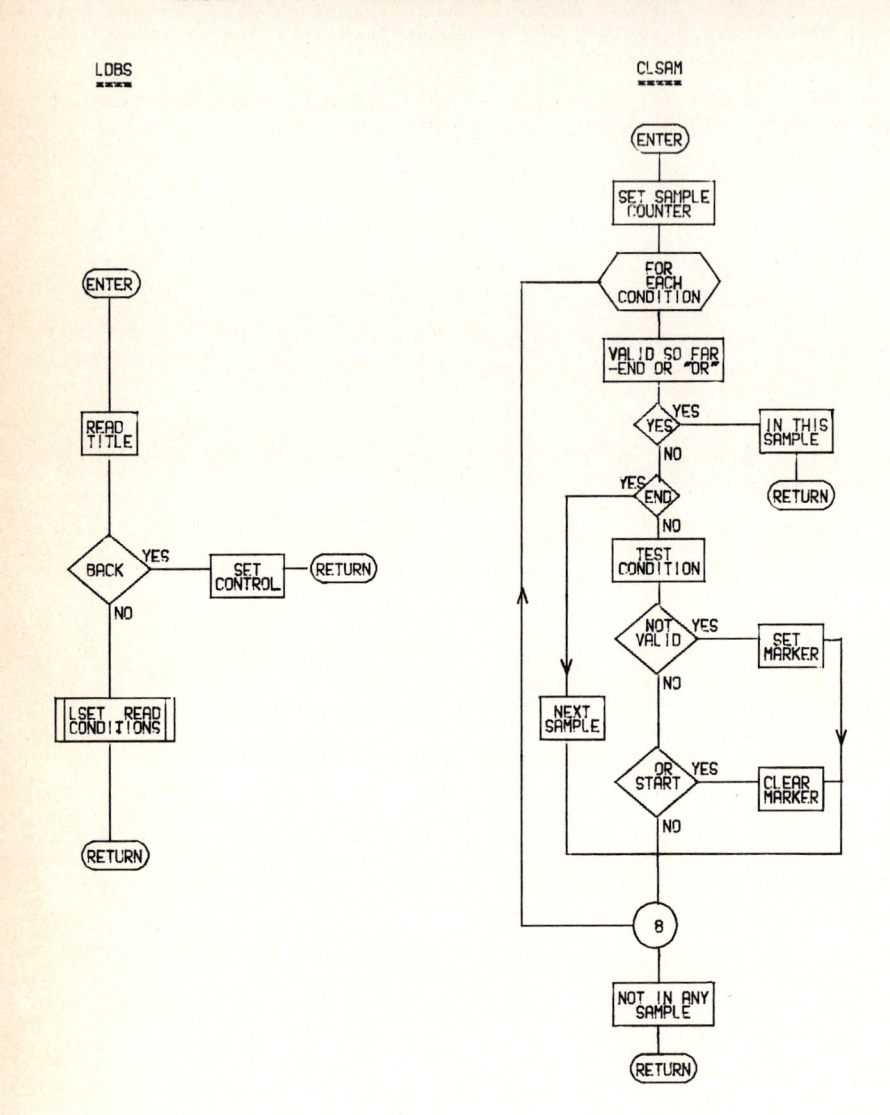

Figure 3.62 - Input example - LDBS

```
---------1---------2---------3---------4---------5---------6---------7-
SUBSET SPECIFICATION - ERRORS
.IF.DIFF.LE.DIFF
.OR.DIFF.LT.DIFF
AND.NTRY.GT.     1000
.OR ITEMis= 300
END OF SUBSET
---------1---------2---------3---------4---------5---------6---------7-
```

Figure 3.63 - Output Example - LDBS (Error messages)

```
        DATA BANK SUBSET TITLE - SUBSET SPECIFICATION - ERRORS        COMMENT
.IF.  DIFF  .LE.  DIFF                                                COMMENT
FIRST AND SECOND COLUMNS IDENTICAL - ALWAYS TRUE
.OR.  DIFF  .LT.  DIFF                                                COMMENT
FIRST AND SECOND COLUMNS IDENTICAL - ALWAYS FALSE
AND.  NTRY  .GT.         1000.000000                                  COMMENT

DATA USED ARE ON A DUMMY SCALE      THEY SHOULD BE ON AN ORDINAL SCALE      ARE EXTRA ASUMPTIONS VALID      **WARNING**
.OR   ITEM  IS=   300                                                 COMMENT
UNIDENTIFIED CONNECTOR
       UNIDENTIFIED DATA COLUMN
              UNIDENTIFIED CONDITION
                    UNIDENTIFIED DATA COLUMN

END OF SUBSET                                                         COMMENT
```

```
      SUBROUTINE LDBS(SCON,NCON,NCMAX,CN,ST,IT,NQ,TRT,NALT,IGO)
C LDBS    (SEE  3.6 ) SYSTEM        LOADS SUBSET DEFINITION
      DIMENSION SCON(5,NCMAX),CN(NQ),ST(NQ),IT(NQ),C(10),TRT(NALT)
      COMMON /STCT/MED1,MED2,MED3,MED4,MED5,MED6,MED13,Q,V(20),TT(30)
    1 READ(MED1,900) (TT(J),J=21,30),C
      IGO = IBL(TT(21),10,4)
      IF(IGO) 1,3,2
    2 WRITE(MED2,901) (TT(J),J=21,30),C
      RETURN
    3 NCON = 0
      ISF = NQ + 1
      WRITE(MED2,902) (TT(J),J=21,30),C
      CALL LSET(SCON,NCON,NCMAX,CN,ST,IT,NQ,TRT,NALT,ISF)
      IF(NCON.EQ.1) WRITE(MED2,903)
      RETURN
  900 FORMAT(20A4)
  901 FORMAT(1H0,20A4)
  902 FORMAT (1H1,5X,25HDATA BANK SUBSET TITLE - ,10A4,10H  COMMENT ,10A
     14)
  903 FORMAT(1H0,65X,48HSYSTEM COMMENT - SUBSET WILL CONTAIN ALL ENTRIES
     1)
      END


      SUBROUTINE CLSAM(D,NQ,SCON,NCON,NIN,NS)
C CLSAM   (SEE  3.5 ) SERVICE       ALLOTS ENTRY TO SAMPLE/SUBSET
C NIN RETURNS WITH SAMPLE NUMBER FOR FIRST CONDITIONS SATISFIED
      DIMENSION D(NQ),SCON(5,NCON)
      COMMON /STCT/MED1,MED2,MED3,MED4,MED5,MED6,MED13,Q,V(20),TT(30)
      NIN = 1
      IN  = 1
      IF(NCON.EQ.0) RETURN
      DO 8 J = 1,NCON
      I1 = SCON(1,J)
      IF(IN.EQ.1.AND.I1.GE.3) RETURN
      IF(IN.EQ.0.AND.I1.EQ.4) GO TO 5
      I2 = SCON(2,J)
      I3 = SCON(3,J)
      I4 = SCON(4,J)
      A  = SCON(5,J)
      IF(I4.GT.0) A = A + D(I4)
      IT = 1
      IF(D(I2).EQ.A) GO TO 1
      IF(D(I2).LT.A) GO TO 2
      GO TO  (3,4,4,4,3,3),I3
    1 GO TO  (4,3,3,4,3,4),I3
    2 GO TO  (3,4,3,3,4,4),I3
    3 IT = 0
    4 IF(IN.EQ.1.AND.IT.EQ.0)GO TO 7
      IF(IN.EQ.0.AND.IT.EQ.1.AND.I1.EQ.3) GO TO 6
      GO TO 8
    5 NIN = NIN + 1
      IF(NIN.GT.NS) GO TO 9
    6 IN  = 1
      GO TO 8
    7 IN = 0
    8 CONTINUE
    9 NIN = 0
      RETURN
      END
```

3.7 VARIATE SPECIFICATION MODULE

3.7.1 Purpose

This module is used to specify a series of data columns which may be used as variates in analyses or descriptive statistics. Depending on the particular program, the variates may be transformed, converted to representative statistics, or assigned a priority order for ranking. They may be delayed (that is to say that the value employed will be that for a previous entry in order in the STATCAT data bank) or they may be classified. Modified class intervals and/or number of classes may also be specified, where these are relevant. Where no specific values are required by the user, default values specified in the data description segment of the STATCAT data bank will be employed. In certain programs (STASTA -5.3 for example) a Variate Specification Module is initially called to specify the variates to be employed, with appropriate transforms, and separate Variate Specification Modules are called to chose which of these variates are used to assign priorities or define parameters of these variates.

Figure 3.71 contains a simplified flow-chart of the system subroutines LGEN (which loads, standardises and stores this module) and MEDIAT (which selects entries from the data bank according to the subset specification, and performs the necessary transforms and/or delays) and of the function TRANS (which carries out the transformation of a single datum).

3.7.2 Module layout

```
PARAMETRIC VARIATE CARD )
PARAMETRIC VARIATE CARD )
......................           One card per variate
PARAMETRIC VARIATE CARD )
END OF MODULE CARD
```

3.7.3 Card Layout - Parametric Variate Card

```
AAAABBBBCCCCDDDDEEEEEEEEFFFFFFFFGGGGGGGGHHHHHHHHHHHHH
HHHHHHHHHHHH................
```

Columns on Card	Item Code	FORTRAN Type	Function
1 - 4	A	A	Transform/Priority Code/Parameter Code
5 - 8	B	A	Data Column Name/Number
9 - 12	C	A	Delay/Classification Code
13 - 16	D	I	Number of alternative classes
17 - 24	E	F	Modified Lower Class Limit
25 - 32	F	F	Modified Class Interval
33 - 40	G	F	Modified Upper Class Limit
41 - 80	H	A	Comment

Note: Some of these parameters may not be employed by a specific program - check the description of the program.

A - <u>Transform Name/Priority Code/Parameter Code</u>

The transform name must be one of the four-letter codes specified in Figure 3.72, except if the module is being used for loading priority codes (See 11.4. - Ordering subroutines) or parameter codes (See 5.3. - Program STASTA). The operation specified by that four-letter code will be performed on the value of the data column specified by parameter B on the same card. If the value in the specified data column is a 'non-value' it will remain a 'non-value' after transformation, except for the special transform PRES (Table 3.72) which takes the value 1 if a data item is present, or 0 if a 'non-value' is present. Section 3.7.7. contains more detailed explanations of these transforms whose meaning is not immediately apparent.

B - <u>Data Column Name/Number</u>

The data column name is the four-character code specified as the 'short title' for the data column. It is originally specified in columns 7-10 of the data column title card (see 3.4) when the data description segment is loaded, and is printed out at the start of each program (See figure 5.17 for an example). As an alternative to the data column name, the data column number may be specified. This must be of the forms COL1 to COL9, CL10 to CL99 and C100 upwards.

C - <u>Delay/Classification Code</u>

Where the value of a variate may be affected by the value of the same or another variate at a previous stage, it is sometimes useful to carry out a correlation analysis between the variate and previous values of the same or other variates. This may be done by specifying a delay for the variate.

If any variate is delayed, the first variate specified by the module must correspond to the time variate. The system assumes that successive entries follow at unit time intervals, checking only that the first variate (which may be transformed) does not decrease. If the value of the first variate is found to be less than that in the previously read entry, the system assumes that a new time sequence begins - discarding all stored values of delayed variables. The system can therefore be used to perform time-series analyses where the time-series is incomplete or where it is repeated.

The actual value employed as a time variate need not necessarily be a direct measure of time, but may be a measure of distance, depth, age etc. If the STATCAT data bank is not in the required order, it may be possible to specify an order reversing transform (for example the transform NEG. will convert a descending series to an ascending one) or the program STSORT may be used to sort the STATCAT data bank into the required order. Where the intervals are not regular, the program STSYNC may be used to interpolate values at standard intervals.

In some programs where delay is not employed this parameter is used to indicate whether the program will operate on the transformed variate value or on the number of the class to which it belongs. If any characters other than blanks are found in these four columns on the data card, the number of the class will be employed. If these four columns are blank, the transformed value of the variate will be employed.

D - <u>Number of Alternative Classes</u>

Where the number of alternative classes required is not that specified in the data starter (for greater precision, or to economise on storage space) an alternative number may be inserted here. If this parameter is specified less than two, or it is not specified, then the number will be deduced from the class interval specified, or failing that, the number of classes specified in the data starter will be used.

E - <u>Modified Lower Class Limit</u>

G - <u>Modified Upper Class Limit</u>

The modified lower class limit is the lower limit of the lowest class but one; the lowest class contains all values below this limit. The modified upper class limit is the upper limit of the highest class but one; the highest class contains all values at or above this limit. If both these limits are zero, or unspecified, the lower class limit specified in the data description segment will be taken.

F - <u>Modified Class Interval</u>

If the number of alternative classes is not specified, it will be deduced from the specified class interval, which will define the width of one class.

The number of classes will be obtained by dividing the differences of the class limits by the class interval and adding two (for the classes outside the limits). The number of classes will be the nearest integer below this number, and the class interval will then be re-calculated to ensure compatibility. Where both the class interval and the number of classes are specified, the number of classes has priority if they conflict with the upper and lower class limits. The class interval will be adjusted to fit.

H - <u>Comment</u>

This forty-character field is printed at the time the card is read, but is not stored.

<u>Fields not in use</u>

Different programs use different parts of the general variate specification. Always consult the documentation of the specific program to determine which parts of the specification are in use. Unused parts of the parameter card should be left blank, but the program will in fact function correctly if they contain characters.

3.7.4   <u>Error Messages</u>

Certain input errors can be detected by the system and will result in error messages.

1 UNIDENTIFIABLE TRANSFORM CODING

The code in columns 1-4 is not one of those acceptable to this program at this point.

2 UNIDENTIFIABLE DATA COLUMN

The code in columns 5-8 is not the short title or number code for a data column in the current STATCAT data bank.

3 DELAY OUT OF RANGE

The specified delay is negative or exceeds the maximum storage capacity of the module at this point in this program.

4 NO FURTHER STORAGE AVAILABLE

The number of parametric variate cards exceeds the number acceptable at this point.

The previous and any following parameters are not stored - but the program may run for those parameters so far defined, if this is possible.

End of Module

The module is ended by a standard 'END OF MODULE' card. In most programs, if no variates are specified before the 'END' card, the program will step back to the previous input module.

3.7.5 Examples

Figure 3.73 is a listing of the input cards for the variates used in the example of program STASTA (5.3.). This program uses all the options specified on the variate card, including the possibility of delay, and the input data have been arranged to provide examples of the ways in which terms left blank on the input card are derived by the module.

Figure 3.75 is a listing of the input cards for the column specification and a parameter specification taken from the same program STASTA showing how these specifications refer back to the set of variates given in 3.73, using priority and parameter codes, as described for program STSORT (10.2.) and STASTA (5.3.) respectively.

3.7.6 Output

Figure 3.74 is the output corresponding to the input data of Figure 3.73 and Figure 3.76 is the output corresponding to Figure 3.75. (In each case the column headings are provided by the calling program - STASTA). The following points should be noted at this time since they relate to the input process - other points about this table are discussed in 5.3.4., since they relate to the specific program.

Variates A - D each lack one of the four terms defining classes. The lacking term is deduced from those present. Variates E to J lack two terms each. In this case, one term is derived from the original data column specification, taking in order of preference the number of classes, the class interval and the lower case limit. The remaining unknown term is then deduced from the three now present.

Variates K to N lack three of the four terms defining the classes. Two of the lacking terms are derived from the original data column specification, in the same order of preference, and the remaining term is deduced.

Variate O has no terms defining the classes - in this case they are copied directly from the original data column specification.

Variate P is included to illustrate the correction of a specification containing less than two classes, in which the number of classes is replaced by that from the original data bank.

The number of cycles delay is taken to be zero if it is not specified. LGEN verifies that sufficient storage is available to store the variates and the values held in intermediate storage for delayed terms.

Turning to the specification of row and parameter terms, we need only note at this point that they use the letter code or number referring to the variates in the set specified in 3.74, and that while the column specification offers an option of the class into which a value falls, or the value itself, the parameter specification allows only the parameter code and the variate code to be specified. Those parts of the input card which are not used by LGEN are not printed out. They may contain any character readable by the system but should preferably be left blank.

3.7.7 Transform Codes

Transform codes are four-character codes used to instruct the computer to transform the data items from a given data column so that they possess some more desirable property or present a more easily interpreted form. The original data item is unchanged so that one program may make use of several different transforms of a single data column. A program exists which can be used, among other things, to produce a new output STATCAT data bank containing transformed variates. (See STMANI - 10.1.). Transforms do not employ any fore-knowledge of the statistical properties of the data they operate upon.

The transforms provided in the STATCAT system fall into several groups.

There are five transforms (VALU, VAL., VALb, bVAL and bbbb) which are identity transforms, having no effect on the value of the data item.

There are eight transforms (SQAR, CUBE, 4PWR, 5PWR, 6PWR, 7PWR, 8PWR and 9PWR) which provide the second to ninth powers of the value of the data item. It should be noted that, although these values are produced by successive multiplication rather than exponentiation, they may be subject to rounding errors, particularly on machines having a short word length.

There are twelve classical trigonometric functions, representing transforms to and from radians or degrees denoted by R or D as the last character, with SIN for the sine, COS for the cosine, TAN for the tangent, ASI for the arcsine, ACO for the arccosine and ATA for the arctangent functions. In addition, there are three hyperbolic functions, SINH, COSH and TANH, and transforms from radians to degrees (RTOD), from degrees to radians (DTOR), from decimal hours to Hours(or degrees) minutes and seconds (H.MS) and from hours/degrees, minutes and seconds to hours and decimal hours(H.HH). (To make the datum easier to recognise hours are printed before the decimal point, and decimal hours or minutes, seconds and decimal seconds after.)

There are four rather complex transformations provided specifically as variance reducing transforms for the analysis of variance (PSNA, PSNB, BINO and LG+1). These are discussed in 7.1.7.

Two further transforms give the logarithm to the base e and to the base 10 of the value (LOGE and LG10). These transforms are useful, both as variance reducing transforms and as methods of producing multiplicative models using analysis of variance methods. EXPT produces the exponent of the value - this is e to the power X, where X is the value. EXPT(X) is also the natural anti-logarithm of X. 10** is ten to the power X - the anti-logarithm to base 10. If X is too large to allow EXPT(X) or 10**(X) to be stored in the system, then Y is set to a non-value. The user should check that the value of RANGE given in TRANS (representing the highest power of ten - positive or negative - that can be expressed as a real variable) is compatible with his machine.

Nine simple mathematical functions are provided. RECP provides the reciprocal of a value, SQRT, the square root (of the absolute value), ABSV provides the absolute value (discarding the sign), SIGN, on the other hand, gives the sign of the value only, having the values +1, 0 and -1. INTG provides the largest integer below the value, and FRAC, the difference between INTG and the value, the fractional part of the number. The transform PRES, which has already been mentioned, has the value 1 if the value of the data item is present, or zero if it is a non-value. The transform NEG. simply changes the sign of a value.

Finally, a group of test transformations is provided. These nine transforms maybe used to test the sensitivity of models based on observed data, or to estimate the effects of possible systematic or random errors in the measured data. The transforms ADD1, SUB1, ADDP and SUBP add or subtract one unit or one per cent to or from the data item. The transform +100 adds one hundred units to the data item. The transforms +/-1 and +/-P add or subtract randomly 1 unit or one per cent to or from the data item.

The transforms NOR1 and NORP add a value taken from a random normal distribution with zero mean and standard deviation of one unit or one per cent respectively.

The transform RM10 randomly suppresses one value in ten (a literal decimation of the data). This transform provides a useful means of examining empirically the effects of incomplete data on analytic techniques.

3.7.8   Random Number Control

The derivation and technical limitations of the random binary digits and random normal variates used in the system are discussed in Chapter 12.7.

From the user's point of view, the rules governing the system are:

i) If only the data handling instruction is changed, the same variate values will be obtained.

ii) If the variate specification is repeated - even if it is identical to the previous variate specification - a different set of variate values will be obtained.

iii) If the file specification is repeated - even if it is identical to the previous specification - the base for random numbers will be reset to the initial value.

In this case only, an identical variate specification will produce values identical to those obtained on a previous occasion with the same subset.

Figure 3.71 - System Flow-chart - LGEN

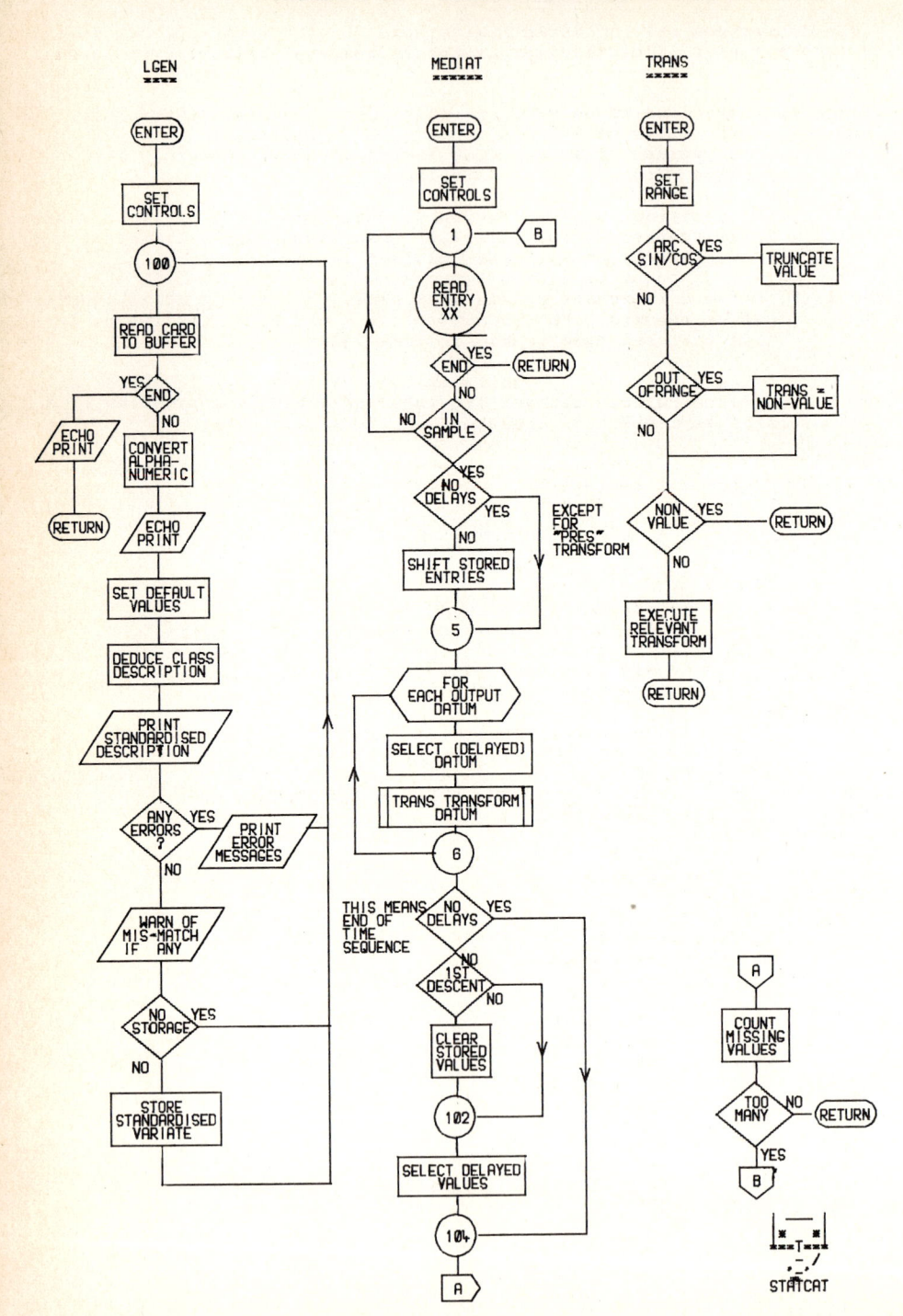

Figure 3.72 - Transform Codes

```
Code Note            Function (X = original value, Y = transformed value)
---------            --------

ABSV                 Absolute value of X
ACOD    A            Arccosine of X         (Y expressed in degrees)
ACOR    A            Arccosine of X         (Y expressed in radians)
ADD1    2            Y = X+1
ADDP    2            Y = X+1% of X
ASID    A            Arcsine of X           (Y expressed in degrees)
ASIR    A            Arcsine of X           (Y expressed in radians)
ATAD                 Arctangent of X        (Y expressed in degrees)
ATAR                 Arctangent of X        (Y expressed in radians)
BINO    1B           Y = 2 x Arcsine(Square root of X)
COSD                 Cosine of X            (X expressed in degrees)
COSH                 Hyperbolic cosine of X
COSR                 Cosine of X            (X expressed in radians)
CUBE                 Cube of X
DTOR                 X in degrees becomes Y in radians
EXPT    G            e to the X
FRAC                 Fractional part of X
H.HH                 Hours/degrees minutes and seconds to decimal hours/degrees
H.MS                 Decimal hours/degrees to hours/degrees minutes and seconds
INTG                 Integer part of X
LG+1    3C           Y = log(X+1) ( to base e)
LG10    D            Y = log   (X) (to base 10)
LOGE    D            Y = log   (X) (to base e)
NEG.                 Y = - X
NOR1    2            Y = X + random normal variate
NORP    2            Y = X (1+.01. random normal variate)
PRES    4            Y = 1 if X is present : Y = 0 if X is missing
PSNA    5E           Y = square root of X plus square root of (X+1)
PSNB    5E           Y = square root of (X+.5)
RECP    F            Y = 1/X
RMIS                 One value in ten set to non-value
RTOD                 X in radians becomes Y in degrees
SIGN                 Y = -1 if X is negative: Y = 0 if X = 0: Y = 1 if X positive
SIND                 Sine of X              (X expressed in degrees)
SINH                 Hyperbolic sine of X
SINR                 Sine of X              (X expressed in radians)
SQAR                 Square of X
SQRT    E            Square root of X
SUB1    2            Y = X-1
SUBP    2            Y = X-1% of X
TAND                 Tangent of X           (X expressed in degrees)
TANH                 Hyperbolic tangent of X
TANR                 Tangent of X           (X expressed in radians)
VAL.    6            Y = X
10**    H            Y = ten to the power X
4PWR    7            Fourth power of X
5PWR    7            Fifth power of X
6PWR    7            Sixth power of X
7PWR    7            Seventh power of X
8PWR    7            Eighth power of X
9PWR    7            Ninth power of X
+/-1    2            Y = X +/-1 (at random)
+/-P    2            Y = X +/-% of X (at random)
+100    2            Y = X+100
```

Explanatory Notes for Figure 3.72 - Transform Codes

Note
1 Reduces non-homogeneity of variances for binomially distributed data

2 May be used to test the sensitivity of models to data errors

3 Reduces non-homogeneity of positively skewed distributions

4 This is the only transformation for which if X is a non-value Y is not also a non-value

5 Reduces non-homogeneity of variance for poisson-distributed data

6 Codes VALb, bVAL, and VALU (where b is a blank column) will also be recognised as an identity transform

7 Equations involving high powers of X may become inaccurate because of rounding errors

LIMITATIONS ON RANGE OF X

A X must be between -0.999 and +0.999
X is set to nearest limit if out of range

B X must be between 0.002 and 0.998
X is set to nearest limit if out of range

C If X equals -1, Y is set to non-value
If (X+1) is negative sign is ignored

D If X equals 0, Y is set to non-value
If X is negative sign is ignored

E Sign of function to be square-rooted is ignored

F If X equals 0, Y is set to non-value

G If X is beyond +/- 2.3 x RANGE (=172.5 as set)
Y is set to non-value

H If X is beyond +/- RANGE (= 75 as set)
Y is set to non-value

Figure 3.73 - Input Example - LGEN (variates)

```
---------1---------2---------3---------4---------5---------6---------7--
VAL.SESS       16      1.5     1.0         TIME VARIATE - NOT USED
VAL.OBSR        4      1.5             3.5 THESE VARIATES
VAL.OPER        4              1.0     3.5 FORM A
VAL.TASK               1.5     1.0     3.5 FOUR LEVEL SIX WAY
VAL.DAY.        4      1.5                 HYPER-GRAECO-LATIN CUBE
VAL.TIME        4              1.0         WHICH FORMS
VAL.W.P.        4                       3.5 THE BASIC EXPERIMENTAL DESIGN
VAL.EFOB               0.0           100.0
VAL.EFOP                      10.0   100.0
VAL.H.R.               0.0    10.0         HEART RATE
+100SET.       64                          +100 MAKES THE ITEMS EASIER TO F
PRESH.R.               0.5                 = 1 IN ALL CASES
ABSVTEMP                       1.0         ABSV TRANSFORM IS REDUNDANT
VAL.W.P.                                3.5
VAL.SET.
VAL.TASK  4    2       1.5              3.5 NOTICE CORRECTIONS
END OF VARIATE SPECIFICATION
---------1---------2---------3---------4---------5---------6---------7--
```

Figure 3.74 - Output Example - LGEN (variates)

```
SET OF VARIATES FOR DATA SHEEP

NO.         TRANS  DATA  CYCLES  NUMBER OF  LOWER         CLASS      UPPER
CODE        -FORM  COLUMN DELAY  CLASSES USED CLASS LIMIT  INTERVAL   CLASS LIMIT   COMMENT

 1 ORIGINAL VAL.  SESS                                                              TIME VARIATE - NOT USED
 A STANDARD VAL.  COL2    0        10        1.5000       1.0000     9.5000

 2 ORIGINAL VAL.  OBSR                +       1.5                     3.5           THESE VARIATES
 B STANDARD VAL.  COL3    0         4        1.5000       1.0000     3.5000

 3 ORIGINAL VAL.  OPER                +                    1.0        3.5           FORM A
 C STANDARD VAL.  COL4    0         4        1.5000       1.0000     3.5000

 4 ORIGINAL VAL.  TASK                        1.5          1.0        3.5           FOUR LEVEL SIX WAY
 D STANDARD VAL.  COL9    0         +        1.5000       1.0000     3.5000

 5 ORIGINAL VAL.  DAY.                        4            1.5                      HYPER-GRAECO-LATIN CUBE
 E STANDARD VAL.  COL7    0         +        1.5000       1.0000     3.5000

 6 ORIGINAL VAL.  TIME                +                    1.0                      WHICH FORMS
 F STANDARD VAL.  COL8    0         +        1.5000       1.0000     3.5000

 7 ORIGINAL VAL.  W.P.                +                               3.5           THE BASIC EXPERIMENTAL DESIGN
 G STANDARD VAL.  COL5    0         +        1.5000       1.0000     3.5000

 8 ORIGINAL VAL.  EFOB                        0.0                    100.0
 H STANDARD VAL.  CL14    0        10        0.0         12.5000    100.0000

 9 ORIGINAL VAL.  EFOP                                    10.0       100.0
 I STANDARD VAL.  CL13    0        10       20.0000      10.0000    100.0000

10 ORIGINAL VAL.  H.R.                        0.0         10.0                      HEART RATE
 J STANDARD VAL.  CL15    0        10        0.0         10.0000     80.0000

11 ORIGINAL +100  NTRY              04                                              +100 MAKES ITEMS MORE VISIBLE
 K STANDARD +100  COL1    0        64        1.5000       1.0000     63.5000

DATA USED ARE ON A DUMMY SCALE    THEY SHOULD BE ON A NOMINAL SCALE    ARE EXTRA ASSUMPTIONS VALID      **WARNING**

12 ORIGINAL PRES  H.R.                        0.5                                   = 1 IN ALL CASES
 L STANDARD PRES  CL15    0        10        0.5000       5.0000     40.5000

13 ORIGINAL ABSV  TEMP                                     1.0                      ABSV TRANSFORM IS REDUNDANT
 M STANDARD ABSV  CL11    0        10       16.0000       1.0000     24.0000


             (CONTINUATION)

14 ORIGINAL VAL.  W.P.                                                3.5
 N STANDARD VAL.  COL5    0        10       -4.5000       1.0000     3.5000

15 ORIGINAL VAL.  NTRY
 O STANDARD VAL.  COL1    0        10        1.5000       1.0000     9.5000

16 ORIGINAL VAL.  TASK    +         2        1.5                      3.5           NOTICE CORRECTIONS
 P STANDARD VAL.  COL9    +         2        1.5000       0.0        3.5000

END OF VARIATE SPECIFICATION
```

Figure 3.75 - **Input Example** - **LGEN** (**priority** + **parameters**)

```
---------1---------2---------3---------4---------5---------6---------7--
2Q1.VARE CL                            TABULATION STARTS AT TOP OF PAGE
2Q1.VARF *                             AND WORKS DOWNWARDS
2Q1.VAR7                               HIGH VALUE FIRST GIVES LARGEST A
END OF ROW SPECIFICATION
1Q2.VARBCLAS                           TABULATION LEFT TO RIGHT
1Q2.VARC                               LOW VALUE FIRST - LARGEST ON RIG
1Q2.VAR4VAL.                           ANY CODE MEANS CLASS NOT VALUE
END OF COLUMN SPECIFICATION
IDENVARK
END OF PARAMETER SPECIFICATION
---------1---------2---------3---------4---------5---------6---------7--
```

Figure 3.76 - **Output Example** - **LGEN** (**priority** + **parameters**)

```
           ROW VARIATES IN ORDER

NUMBER    PRIOR   VARI CLASS/
CODE      -ITY    -ATE VALUE                       COMMENT

  1 ORIGINAL 2Q1.  VARE  CL                        TABULATION STARTS AT TOP OF PAGE
  A STANDARD 2Q1.  VAR5(CLASS)

  2 ORIGINAL 2Q1.  VARF  *                         AND WORKS DOWNWARDS
  B STANDARD 2Q1.  VAR6(CLASS)

  3 ORIGINAL 2Q1.  VAR7                            HIGH VALUE FIRST=LARGEST AT TOP
  C STANDARD 2Q1.  VARG(VALUE)

END OF ROW SPECIFICATION


           COLUMN VARIATES IN ORDER

NUMBER    PRIOR   VARI CLASS/
CODE      -ITY    -ATE VALUE                       COMMENT

  4 ORIGINAL 1Q2.  VARB  CLAS                      TABULATION LEFT TO RIGHT
  D STANDARD 1Q2.  VAR2(CLASS)

  5 ORIGINAL 1Q2.  VARC                            LOW VALUE FIRST=LARGEST ON RIGHT
  E STANDARD 1Q2.  VAR3(VALUE)

  6 ORIGINAL 1Q2.  VAR4  VAL.                      ANY CODE MEANS CLASS NOT VALUE
  F STANDARD 1Q2.  VARD(CLASS)

END OF COLUMN SPECIFICATION


           PARAMETERS TO BE TABULATED

NUMBER    PARAM   VARI
CODE      -ETER   -ATE

  1 ORIGINAL IDEN  VARK
  A STANDARD IDEN  VA11

END OF PARAMETER SPECIFICATION
```

```
      SUBROUTINE LGEN(T,NT1,LT,NT2,ST,IT,CN,NQ,NCL,M1,DMIN,DMAX,NQ1,TMIN
     1,TMAX,M2,MAXD,NALT,NA,NB,M,ISP,IFIN,NCHK,NCDF)
C LGEN    (SEE  3.7 ) SYSTEM       LOADS GENERALISED VARIATES
      DIMENSION T(NT1),LT(NT2),ST(NQ),IT(NQ),CN(NQ),NCL(M1),F(36),C1(32)
      DIMENSION DMIN(NQ1),DMAX(NQ1),TMIN(M2),TMAX(M2),NA(M),NB(M),C(17)
      DATA F/1HA,1HB,1HC,1HD,1HE,1HF,1HG,1HH,1HI,1HJ,1HK,1HL,1HM,1HN,1HO
     1,1HP,1HQ,1HR,1HS,1HT,1HU,1HV,1HW,1HX,1HY,1HZ,1E1,1H2,1H3,1H4,1H5,1
     2H6,1H7,1H8,1H9,1H0/
      DATA BL/4H    /,QU/4HQQQQ/,B1/1H /
      COMMON /STCT/MED1,MED2,MED3,MED4,MED5,MED6,MED13,Q,V(20),TT(30)
C IF NT1 = 0 NO TRANSFORMS READ
C IF NT2 = 0 NO CHECK ON SUITABILITY OF TRANSFORM
C IF NCHK EQUALS   0            1                2              3
C             NO CHECK     NOT JUSTIFIED   CONSERVATIVE      EITHER
C IF M1 = 0 NO INDIVIDUAL ALLOCATION OF CLASS NUMBERS OR WIDTHS
C IF M2 = 0 NO REVISED OR MINIMA
C IF NQ1 = 0 NO DEFAULT VALUES OF MAXIMA OR MINIMA AVAILABLE
C IF MAXD = 0 NO DELAYS ACCEPTED
C IF MAXD NEGATIVE ANY CODE IN COLS 9 - 12 IMPLIES CLASSES
C NALT = MAXIMUM NUMBER OF CLASSES ACCEPTABLE
C NCDF = DEFAULT NUMBER OF CLASSES (IF NONE SPECIFIED OR IMPLIED)
C NA CONTAINS DELAY PARAMETER
C NB CONTAINS TRANSFORM + COLUMN NUMBER
C V(11) RETURNS WITH NUMBER OF VARIATES ACCEPTED
C V(19) RETURNS WITH LINES USED ON THIS PAGE
C V(20) RETURNS WITH NUMBER OF VARIATES REJECTED (MAX=9)
      V(11) = 0.
      V(19) = 6.
      V(20) = 0.
      TST = 0
      IF(MAXD.GT.0) TST = MAXD
      DSF = 0.
      XM = M
  100 READ (MED1,900)C(1),C(2),C1,(C(J),J=8,17)
      IF(IBL(C,2,4))100,106,105
  105 WRITE(MED2,915)C(1),C(2),C1,(C(J),J=8,17)
      IF(V(20).GT.9.)V(20)=9.
      RETURN
  106 INEX = ISP + 1
      IF(V(19).GT.44.)WRITE(MED2,926)
      IF(V(19).GT.44.) V(19) = 6.
      V(19) = V(19) + 3.
      C(3) = AN(C1,4,1,4)
      ND = 0
      DO 107 J = 1,4
  107 IF(ICH(C1(J),B1,1).NE.1) ND = 1
      IF(MAXD.GT.0) ND = C(3) + .1
      C(4) = AN(C1,8,5,8)
      C(5) = AN(C1,16,9,16)
      C(6) = AN(C1,24,17,24)
      NH = 1
      IF(C(6).LT.0..AND.M1.GT.0) NH = 0
      IF(C(6).LT.0.) C(6) = -C(6)
      C(7) = AN(C1,32,25,32)
      N5 = 1
      IF(IBL(C1( 9),8,1).LT.0) N5 = 0
      N7 = 1
      IF(IBL(C1(25),8,1).LT.0) N7 = 0
      VLIM = TST/(DSF+3.)
      IF(VLIM.GT.XM) VLIM = XM
      LIMD = TST/(V(11)+1.) - 3.
C PRINT ORIGINAL INPUT VALUES
      WRITE(MED2,902)INEX,C(2),(C(J),J=8,17)
```

```
      IF(NT1.GT.0)WRITE(MED2,901)C(1)
      IF(MAXD.NE.0)WRITE(MED2,923) (C1(J),J=1,4)
      IF(M1.GT.0) WRITE(MED2,924) (C1(J),J= 5, 8),(C1(J),J=17,24)
      IF(M2.GT.0)WRITE(MED2,925) (C1(J),J= 9,16),(C1(J),J=25,32)
      IF(NT1.NE.0)C(1) = ICH(C(1),T,NT1)
      NCAL = 0
      X = ICH(C(2),CN,NQ)
      IF(X.NE.0.) NCAL = 2
      C(2) = ICH(C(2),ST,NQ)
      IF(C(2).NE.0.) NCAL = 1
      IF(C(2).EQ.0.) C(2) = X
      NC = C(2)
      NE = 1
      NF = 1
      NG = 1
      IF(MAXD.GT.0.AND.ND.LT.0.OR.MAXD.GT.0.AND.ND.GT.LIMD)NE = 0
C SET DEFAULT VALUES - BASIC
      DMINX = 1.5
      DEL = 1.0
      NCLX = NCDF
      CLX = NCLX
      IF(M1.EQ.0) GO TO 104
C DEFAULT VALUES OF LOWER LIMIT AND CLASS INTERVAL FROM D.D.S
      IF(M2.EQ.0) GO TO 102
      IF(NQ1.EQ.0)NF = 0
      IF(NQ1.EQ.0) GO TO 102
      IF(NC.EQ.0) GO TO 102
      DMINX = DMIN(NC)
      IF(NCLX.GT.2) DEL = (DMAX(NC)-DMIN(NC))/(CLX-2.)
C NUMBER OF CLASSES - SUBJECT TO MAXIMUM IMPOSED
  102 NCLX = NCDF
      IF(NCLX.GT.NALT.AND.M1.NE.0.AND.NALT.NE.0) NCLX = NALT
      CLX = NCLX
C SET NUMBER OF CLASSES FROM DATA IF POSSIBLE
      IF(C(4).LT.2..AND.N5*N7.GT.0.AND.C(6).NE.0.) C(4)=(C(7)-C(5))/C(6)
     1 + 2.
      IF(C(4).LT.2.) C(4) = CLX
      NCLX = C(4) + .0001
      IF(NCLX.GT.NALT) NG = 0
      C(4) = NCLX
C IF BOTH LIMITS MISSING SET LOWER TO DMINX
      IF(N5+N7.EQ.0) C(5) = DMINX
      IF(N5+N7.EQ.0) N5 = 1
C IF ONE LIMIT AND NO CLASS INTERVAL FIND CLASS INTERVAL
C NUMBER OF CLASSES MUST BE AN INTEGER
      IF(N5*N7.EQ.0.AND.C(6).EQ.0.) C(6) = DEL
      IF(N5.EQ.0) C(5) = C(7) - C(6)*(C(4)-2.)
      IF(N7.EQ.0) C(7) = C(5) + C(6)*(C(4)-2.)
C STANDARDISE CLASS INTERVAL TO LIMITS AND NUMBER OF CLASSES
      IF(C(4).GT.2.)C(6) = (C(7)-C(5))/(C(4)-2.)
      IF(C(4).LE.2.)C(6) = 0.
C PRINT STANDARDISED VALUES AS STORED
  104 IF(NC.EQ.0) WRITE(MED2,906)QU
      IF(NCAL.EQ.1)  WRITE(MED2,906)  CN(NC)
      IF(NCAL.EQ.2)  WRITE(MED2,906)  ST(NC)
      IF(INEX.LE.36)WRITE(MED2,913) F(INEX)
      NT = C(1)
      IF(NT.EQ.0.AND.NT1.NE.0)  WRITE(MED2,901) QU
      IF(NT.NE.0.AND.NT1.NE.0)  WRITE(MED2,901) T(NT)
      IF(MAXD.GT.0)              WRITE(MED2,903) ND
      IF(MAXD.LT.0.AND.ND.EQ.0)   WRITE(MED2,916)
      IF(MAXD.LT.0.AND.ND.EQ.1)   WRITE(MED2,917)
      IF(M1.GT.0)                WRITE(MED2,904)NCLX,C(6)
```

```
      IF(M2.GT.0)                 WRITE(MED2,905)C(5),C(7)
C PRINT ERROR MESSAGES
      V(20) = V(20) + 1.
      IF(NT.EQ.0.AND.NT1.NE.0) WRITE(MED2,907)
      IF(NT.EQ.0.AND.NT1.NE.0) V(19) = V(19) + 1.
      IF(NC.EQ.0)              WRITE(MED2,908)
      IF(NC.EQ.0)              V(19) = V(19) + 1.
      IF(NE.EQ.0)              WRITE(MED2,909)
      IF(NE.EQ.0)              V(19) = V(19) + 1.
      IF(NG.EQ.0)              WRITE(MED2,918)
      IF(NG.EQ.0)              V(19) = V(19) + 1.
      IF(NF.EQ.0)              WRITE(MED2,910)
      IF(NF.EQ.0)              V(19) = V(19) + 1.
      IF(NH.EQ.0)              WRITE(MED2,927)
      IF(NH.EQ.0)              V(19) = V(19) + 1.
      IF(NT.EQ.0.AND.NT1.NE.0.OR.NC*NE*NF*NG.EQ.0) GO TO 100
      IF(NT1.EQ.0.OR.NT2.EQ.0.OR.NCHK.EQ.0)GO TO 101
      IF(NCHK.EQ.1..AND.LT(NT).LE.IT(NC).OR.NCHK.EQ.2..AND.LT(NT).GE.IT(
     1NC).OR.LT(NT).EQ.IT(NC))GO TO 101
      V(19) = V(19) + 2.
      CALL CHIKEN(LT(NT),IT(NC))
  101 ISF = ISF + 1
C TEST FOR STORAGE AVAILABLE
      IF(ISF.GT.IFIN) WRITE(MED2,912)
      IF(ISF.GT.M) WRITE(MED2,911)
      IF(MAXD.GT.0.AND.V(11).GT.VLIM) WRITE(MED2,914)
      IF(ISF.GT.IFIN.OR.ISF.GT.M) GO TO 100
      IF(MAXD.GT.0.AND.V(11).GT.VLIM) GO TO 100
C STORE ACCEPTED VARIATE
      V(11) = V(11) + 1.
      V(20) = V(20) - 1.
      IF(MAXD.NE.0) NA(ISF) = ND
      IF(MAXD.GT.0.AND.DSF.LT.C(3)) DSF = C(3)
      NB(ISF) = NT*1000 + NC
      IF(M1.GT.0)NCL(ISF) = NCLX
      IF(M2.EQ.0) GO TO 100
      TMIN(ISF) = C(5)
      TMAX(ISF) = C(7)
      GO TO 100
  900 FORMAT (2A4,32A1,10A4)
  901 FORMAT (1H+,13X,A4)
  902 FORMAT (1H0,I3,10H ORIGINAL ,6X,A4,57X,10A4)
  903 FORMAT (1H+,23X,I6)
  904 FORMAT (1H+,34X,I6,13X,F13.4)
  905 FORMAT (1H+,40X,F13.4,13X,F13.4)
  906 FORMAT (1H ,4X,8HSTANDARD,7X,A4)
  907 FORMAT (14X,24HUNRECOGNISABLE TRANSFORM  )
  908 FORMAT (20X,26HUNRECOGNISABLE DATA COLUMN)
  909 FORMAT (25X,23HDELAY OUT OF RANGE        )
  910 FORMAT (40X,48HMAXIMUM AND MINIMUM DEFAULT VALUES NOT AVAILABLE )
  911 FORMAT (30H NO FURTHER STORAGE AVAILABLE  )
  912 FORMAT (54H NUMBER OF VARIATES EXCEEDS THAT ALLOWED AT THIS STEP )
  913 FORMAT(3H+  ,A1)
  914 FORMAT(50H NOT ENOUGH STORAGE AVAILABLE FOR DELAYED VARIATE )
  915 FORMAT(1H0,2A4,32A1,40X,10A4)
  916 FORMAT(1H+,23X,7H(VALUE))
  917 FORMAT(1H+,23X,7H(CLASS))
  918 FORMAT(35X,16HTOO MANY CLASSES)
  923 FORMAT(1H+,25X,4A1)
  924 FORMAT (1H+,36X,4A1,15X,8A1)
  925 FORMAT(1H+,42X,8A1,18X,8A1)
  926 FORMAT(1H1,10X,14H(CONTINUATION)/)
  927 FORMAT(1H ,53X,31HCLASS INTERVAL MUST BE POSITIVE)
```

```
      END

      SUBROUTINE MEDIAT(M,NAD,NBD,MN,D,XX,NQ,SCON,NCON)
C MEDIAT (SEE  3.7 ) SERVICE     FETCHES NEXT VARIATE SET
C READS IN ENTRY AND TRANSFORMS AND/OR DELAYS DATA AS REQUIRED
      DIMENSION D(MN),NAD(M),NBD(M),XX(NQ),SCON(5,NCON)
      COMMON /STCT/MED1,MED2,MED3,MED4,MED5,MED6,MED13,Q,V(20),TT(30)
C CONTROL INDICES
C VALUES V(6)          V(7)           V(8)             V(9)
C   NEG
C   0    NUMBER OF    NO CHANGE      NO CHECK LAST    ACCEPT UP TO
C   1    SETS WHEN    TRANSFORM      CHECK IF LAST    THIS NUMBER OF
C   2    V(2) = 2.    DELAY ONLY     V(6) IS TOTAL    MISSING VALUES
C   3                 TRANS+DELAY    NUMBER IN
C                                    DATA SUBSET
      IBASE = V(10)
      N = MN/M
      IF(V(6).NE.0.) GO TO 1
      DO 100 I = 1,MN
C SELECT DELAYED VALUES
  100 D(I) = Q
    1 READ(MED3) XX
      IF(V(8).EQ.0.)GO TO 3
      DO 2 I = 1,NQ
      IF(XX(I).NE.Q) GO TO 3
    2 CONTINUE
      V(8) = 2.
      RETURN
    3 CALL CLSAM(XX,NQ,SCON,NCON,NIN,1)
      IF(NIN.NE.1) GO TO 1
      IF(V(7).LE.1.)GO TO 5
C SHIFT ALONG LAST VALUES
      DO 4 J = 1,M
      DO 4 K = 3,N
      L = M*(N-K+2) + J
      LM = L-M
    4 D(L) = D(LM)
    5 DO 6 J = 1,M
      I = NBD(J) -NBD(J)/1000*1000
      JM = J
      IF(V(7).GE.2.)JM=J+M
      D(JM) = XX(I)
      IF(V(7).NE.1..AND.V(7).NE.3.) GO TO 6
      K = NBD(J)/1000
      D(JM) = TRANS(XX(I),Q,K,IBASE)
    6 CONTINUE
      V(10) = IBASE
      IF(V(7).LE.1.) GO TO 104
      I = M + 1
      J = I + M
      IF(D(I).EQ.Q.OR.D(J).EQ.Q.OR.D(I).GE.D(J)) GO TO 102
C END OF SEQUENCE - FIRST ITEM DESCENDS
      DO 101 I = J,MN
  101 D(I) = Q
  102 DO 103 J = 1,M
      K= NAD(J) -NAD(J)/1000*1000
      K=M*(K+1) + J
  103 D(J) = D(K)
C TEST FOR TOO MANY MISSING VALUES
  104 XMIS = 0.
      DO 105 J = 1,M
      IF(D(J).EQ.Q) XMIS = XMIS + 1.
```

```
      IF(XMIS.GT.V(9)) GO TO 1
  105 CONTINUE
      IF(V(8).EQ.1.)V(6) = V(6) + 1.
      RETURN
      END


      FUNCTION TRANS(D,Q,N,IBASE)
C TRANS  (SEE  3.7 ) SERVICE      CARRIES OUT REQUIRED TRANSFORM
C D = VALUE TO BE TRANSFORMED / Q = NON-VALUE / N = TRANSFORM
C IBASE = RANDOM NUMBER SEED / R = RANGE (POWERS OF TEN)
      RANGE = 75
      TRANS = D
      IF(N.NE.48.AND.TRANS.EQ.Q) GO TO 1
      IF(N.NE.14.AND.N.NE.15.AND.N.NE.24.AND.N.NE.25) GO TO 70
      IF(TRANS.LT.-.999) TRANS = -.999
      IF(TRANS.GT..999) TRANS = .999
   70 CONTINUE
      IF(N.EQ.34.AND.TRANS.EQ.-1.) TRANS = Q
      IF(N.GE.35.AND.N.LE.36.AND.TRANS.EQ.0.) TRANS = Q
      IF(N.EQ.41.AND.TRANS.EQ. 0.) TRANS = Q
      IF(N.EQ.47.AND.TRANS.GT.31.8) TRANS = Q
      IF(N.NE.48.AND.TRANS.EQ.Q) GO TO 1
      IF(N.LE.1.OR.N.GE.60) GO TO 1
      GO TO (1,2,3,4,5,6,7,8,9,1,11,12,13,14,15,16,17,18,19,
     120,21,22,23,24,25,26,27,28,29,1,31,32,33,34,35,36,37,1,1,
     21,41,42,43,44,45,46,47,48,49,51,51,52,53,54,51,56,57,54,59),N
    9 TRANS = TRANS * D
    8 TRANS = TRANS * D
    7 TRANS = TRANS * D
    6 TRANS = TRANS * D
    5 TRANS = TRANS * D
    4 TRANS = TRANS * D
    3 TRANS = TRANS * D
    2 TRANS = TRANS * D
    1 RETURN
   11 TRANS = SIN(D)
      GO TO 1
   12 TRANS = COS(D)
      GO TO 1
   13 TRANS = TAN(D)
      GO TO 1
   14 TRANS = ARSIN(TRANS)
      GO TO 1
   15 TRANS = ARCOS(TRANS)
      GO TO 1
   16 TRANS = ATAN(D)
      GO TO 1
   17 TRANS = SINH(D)
      GO TO 1
   18 TRANS = COSH(D)
      GO TO 1
   19 TRANS = TANH(D)
      GO TO 1
   20 K = D*60.
      TRANS = FLOAT(K + K/60*40)*0.01 + (D*60. - FLOAT(K))*0.006
      GO TO 1
   21 TRANS = SIN(D*0.017453278)
      GO TO 1
   22 TRANS = COS(D*0.017453278)
      GO TO 1
   23 TRANS = TAN(D*0.017453278)
      GO TO 1
```

```
   24 TRANS = 57.295827*ARSIN(TRANS)
      GO TO 1
   25 TRANS = 57.295827*ARCOS(TRANS)
      GO TO 1
   26 TRANS = 57.295827 * ATAN(D)
      GO TO 1
   27 TRANS = D*0.017453278
      GO TO 1
   28 TRANS = D*57.295827
      GO TO 1
   29 K = D*100. + .1
      TRANS =(FLOAT(K - K/100*40) + (D*100.- FLOAT(K))/0.6)/60.
      A = FLOAT(K-K/100*40)
      B = D*100.-FLOAT(K)
      C = A + B/0.6
      WRITE(6,666) A,B,C,D,TRANS
  666 FORMAT(5F12.4)
      GO TO 1
   31 TRANS = SQRT(ABS(D)) + SQRT(ABS(D+1.))
      GO TO 1
   32 TRANS = SQRT(ABS(D+0.5))
      GO TO 1
   33 TRANS = D
      IF(TRANS.GT..998)TRANS = .998
      IF(TRANS.LT..002)TRANS = .002
      TRANS = 2.*ARSIN(SQRT(TRANS))
      GO TO 1
   34 TRANS = ALOG(ABS(D+1.))
      GO TO 1
   35 TRANS = ALOG(ABS(D))
      GO TO 1
   36 TRANS = ALOG(ABS(D))*0.434294
      GO TO 1
   37 IF(TRANS.LT.-RANGE)  TRANS = -RANGE
      IF(TRANS.GT. RANGE)  TRANS =  RANGE
      TRANS = 10.**TRANS
      GO TO 1
   41 TRANS = 1./D
      GO TO 1
   42 TRANS = SQRT(ABS(D))
      GO TO 1
   43 TRANS = D
      IF(TRANS.LT.0.) TRANS = -D
      GO TO 1
   44 TRANS = 1
      IF(D.EQ.0.) TRANS = 0.
      IF(D.LT.0.) TRANS = -1.
      GO TO 1
   45 I = D
      TRANS = I
      GO TO 1
   46 I = D
      TRANS = I
      TRANS = D - TRANS
      GO TO 1
   47 IF(TRANS.LT.-RANGE*2.3) TRANS = -RANGE*2.3
      IF(TRANS.GT. RANGE*2.3) TRANS =  RANGE*2.3
      TRANS = EXP(TRANS)
      GO TO 1
   48 TRANS = 1
      IF(D.EQ.Q) TRANS = 0
      GO TO 1
   49 TRANS = -D
```

```
          GO TO 1
       50 IF(IBASE.LT.3277)TRANS = Q
          GO TO 1
C CONSTRUCT RANDOM BINARY VARIATE - SHIFT PRIME NO OF TIMES
       51 DO 151 I = 1,11
          IB = IBASE/64-IBASE/128*2
C EXTRACT BITS 7 AND 15 - SHIFT - ADD MOD2 SUM OF BITS AT BIT 1
          IC = IBASE/16384
          IBASE = (IBASE-IC*16384)*2
      151 IF(IB.NE.IC) IBASE = IBASE + 1
          IF(N.EQ.50) GO TO 50
          IF(N.EQ.55) GO TO 55
          IF(IB) 52,52,53
       52 TRANS = TRANS + 1.
          GO TO 1
       53 TRANS = TRANS - 1.
          GO TO 1
C CONSTRUCT RANDOM NORMAL VARIATE MEAN = 0 S.D. = 2
       54 V = -8.
          DO 154 I = 1,16
C EXTRACT BITS 7 AND 15 - SHIFT - ADD MOD2 SUM OF BITS AT BIT 1
          IB = IBASE/64-IBASE/128*2
          IC = IBASE/16384
          IBASE = (IBASE-IC*16384)*2
          IF(IB.NE.IC) IBASE = IBASE + 1
          X = IBASE
      154 V = V + X/32768.
          IF(N.EQ.58) GO TO 58
          TRANS = TRANS + 0.5*V
          GO TO 1
       55 IF(IB) 56,56,57
       56 TRANS = TRANS * 1.01
          GO TO 1
       57 TRANS = TRANS * 0.99
          GO TO 1
       58 TRANS = TRANS * (1. + .005 *V )
          GO TO 1
       59 TRANS = TRANS + 100.
          GO TO 1
          END
```

3.8 DATA HANDLING INSTRUCTION

3.8.1 Purpose

This card is employed by most programs as the last input module before the program is executed. It is used to give the computer instructions about the way in which it is to perform the tasks already specified and choices of overall strategy. Although the format is the same wherever it is used, it is used to convey different items of information to the system, according to the program in use. It is used to specify, among other things, the amount of detail to be output, the data checking to be undertaken, the maximum number of 'non-values' in any entry, the types of testing to be employed or the level of associated probability that is to be considered statistically significant.

It would be confusing, and a waste of space, to attempt to define all uses of the card in full detail at this point, but a general description is possible. The specific description of the program you intend to use should be consulted to find the exact use, and default values, for the variates drawn from this card.

Figure 3.81 gives a system flow-chart for the subroutine LDHI, which reads and checks data handling instructions, and writes the corrected control values derived from them.

3.8.2 Card Layout - Data Handling Instruction

ABBBBDDDEEEEEEEFFFFFFFGGGGGGGGGGHHHHHHHHHHHHHH..........

Columns on Card	Item Code	FORTRAN Type	Function
1	A	I	Output Control Index
2	B	I	Analysis Control Index
3 - 5	C	F	First Maximum
6 - 8	D	F	Second Maximum
9 - 16	E	F	Parameter Value
17 - 24	F	F	Second Parameter Value
25 - 40	G	F	Blind Space
41 - 80	H	A	Comment/Run Title

A - Output Control Index

This index controls the amount of output produced by the program, the output of intermediate results and the output of checking information obtained during the running of the program. In general, descriptive programs will produce the most detailed output unless otherwise instructed, and analytic programs the least.

B - Analysis Control Index

This index controls the strategic choices made by the program: for example, the choice of Factor Analysis method, the technique for the elimination or selection of variates in Multiple Linear Regression, the carrying out of tests at a specified level, or at that appropriate to the data and so on.

C,D - Maximum Values

These values are used to specify maximum, or sometimes minimum, values for analyses and descriptions, such as the number of factors to be extracted, the number of non-values to be accepted in any entry and so on.

E,F - Parameter Values

These values are used to specify quantitative values required in an analysis, for example the level of probability taken as statistically significant, the minimum eigenroot to be retained, and so on.

G - Blind Space

This is the only input to the STATCAT system which is not immediately output as an echo check (except for a part of the Data Starter - See 3.3.). It is not output because it is used only to specify the Auxiliary Security Key wherever this is used (5.1. and 9.4.). If this were to be echo-printed then anyone obtaining an output listing would be in possession of the key.

It follows that where the Auxiliary Security key is used, the data handling instruction card should be treated as confidential information. (The user will find a brief sermon on the subject of Security, Privacy and Freedom of Information in Chapter 12.4).

H - Comment/Run Title

This portion of the input card is reserved for plain-language comment. In some programs, where common storage space is available, this comment is stored as a Run Title and printed as part of the heading of each output page.

General

If the system finds non-numeric information, or blanks in any field on the card, it will use the appropriate default value for the corresponding item. Any plain-language message, such as GO, RUN or GET LOST, will cause the program to run with default values throughout. (The standard rules about blank, STOP or END cards apply).

3.8.3 Input Example

Figure 3.82 is an example of a data handling instruction. This data handling instruction concerns an analysis carried out by STCLUS (8.3.), which uses all input items normally reproduced. (It does not use the auxiliary security key). The non-numeric instruction "GO" causes default values to be used throughout.

3.8.4 Output Example

Figure 3.83 is the output corresponding to the data handling instruction specified in Figure 3.82. Notice that default values for the number of iterations and significance level for improvement have been substituted and that a warning message is printed. A deliberate mistake in earlier data caused the run to be cancelled - demonstrating the error warning message.

3.8.5 Subroutine LDHI

Figure 3.81 contains a system flow-chart for the subroutine LDHI which loads the data handling instruction, identifies special cards, makes an echo-print and converts the input fields into numeric values.

After the data handling instruction has been read, the system returns to the main program to carry out any necessary standardisation, (specific to each program) then calls subroutine LDHI again, to print the data handling instruction, warn of standardisation if any, and perform a check for remaining errors in the data, setting an error index where necessary.

Figure 3.81 - System Flow-chart - LDHI

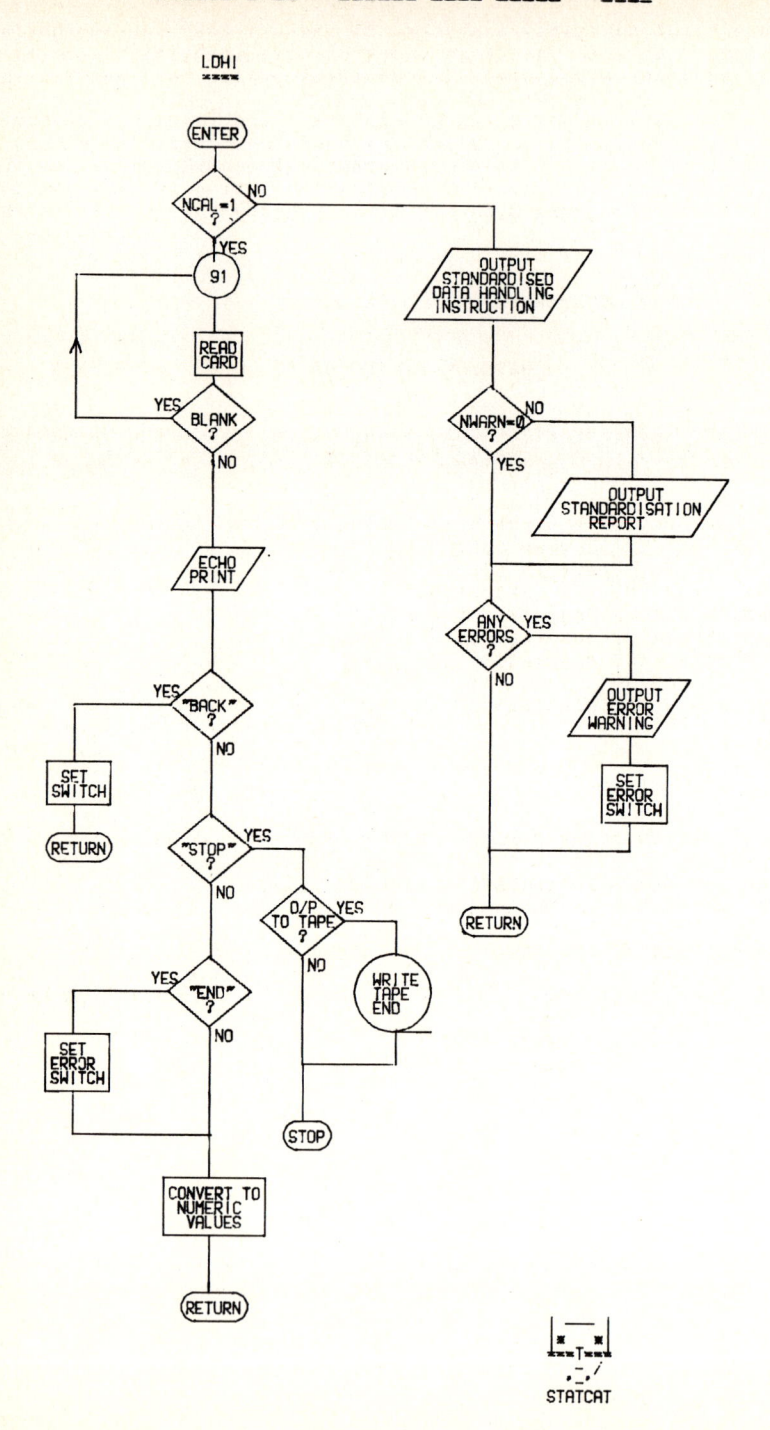

Figure 3.82 - LDHI - Input Example

```
---------1---------2---------3---------4---------5---------6---------7-
GO                                      DEFAULT OUTPUT
---------1---------2---------3---------4---------5---------6---------7-
```

Figure 3.83 - LDHI - Output Example

(first call output)
           STATCAT CLUSTERING CORRELATIONS

                    DATA HANDLING INSTRUCTION - ECHO PRINT

ABCCCDDDEEEEEEEEFFFFFFFFGGGGGGGGGGGGGGGGHHHHHHHHHHHHHHHHHHHHHHHHHHHHHH
GO   XXXXXXXXXXXXXXXXDEFAULT OUTPUT

(second call output - slightly compressed to 72 columns)
                    OUTPUT CONTROL INDEX =   0
                    ANALYSIS CONTROL INDEX =   0
MAXIMUM NUMBER OF NON-VALUES (MISSING) =   0   (ONLY COMPLETE ENTRIES)
MAXIMUM NUMBER OF VARIATES PERMUTED   =   7
MAXIMUM NUMBER OF NON-VALUES (MISSING) =   1000
MAXIMUM NUMBER OF NON-VALUES (MISSING) =   1.0000

THE SYSTEM HAS STANDARDISED 3 CONTROL VALUES FROM THE DATA HANDLING
                                   (INSTRUCTION   ** WARNING **

PLEASE VERIFY THAT THE ASSUMPTIONS IT HAS MADE ARE CORRECT AND
                                        (ADJUST STORAGE IF NECESSARY

HILL-CLIMBING APPROACH WILL BE ADOPTED FOR THE 8 VARIATES SPECIFIED

     1000. POSSIBLE ARRANGEMENTS WILL BE TRIED
   (UNLESS A MINIMUM IS REACHED EARLIER)

     MINIMUM PERCENTAGE IMPROVEMENT - 1.00

PROGRAM CANNOT OPERATE.   (** WARNING **

EARLIEST UNCORRECTED ERROR CODE = 51.

```
      SUBROUTINE LDHI(V1,NA,V2,NB,V3,NC,V4,ND,V5,NE,V6,NF,V7,V10,
     1 T,F,M1,M2,M4,Q,NQ,NWARN,NCALL,IGO)
C LDHI     (SEE  3.8 ) SERVICE    LOAD/LIST STANDARDISED D H I
      DIMENSION T(10),TIND(3,7),CAR(5,18),F(40)
C   NO   NA,NB (CONTROL INDEX)      NC,ND,NE,NF (PARAMETERS)
C   1    OUTPUT              NO. OF FIRST COLUMN OUTPUT
C   2    ANALYSIS                   LAST COLUMN OUTPUT
C   3    CHECKING                   OUTPUT DEVICE
C   4    GENERAL                    ARBITRARY SAMPLES
C   5    TESTING                    PREDICTORS PINNED
C   6    AUXILIARY           MIN.   ENTRIES PER SAMPLE
C   7    TEST CHOICE         MAX.   NON-VALUES
C   8      -                        ITERATIONS
C   9      -                        SAMPLES DERIVED
C   10     -                        FACTORS DERIVED
C   11     -                        DISCRIMINANTS
C   12     -                        VARIATES PERMUTED
C   13     -                        CANONICAL VARIATES
C   14     -                        HILL-CLIMBING TRIALS
C   15     -    MIN  PERCENTAGE     OF ITEMS IN CLASS
C   16     -                        SIGNIFICANCE LEVEL
C   17     -                        INITIAL IMPROVEMENT
C   18     -                   MIN  S.D. FROM A.M.
C   19     -                        MINIMUM EIGENVALUE RETAINED
      DATA TIND/4H    ,4H OUT,4HPUT ,4H   A,4HNALY,4HSIS ,4H   C,4HHECK,
     1 4HING ,   4H    ,4HGENE,4HRAL ,4H    ,4HTEST,4HING ,4H  AU,4HXILI,
     2 4HARY ,   4HTETS,4H CHO,4HICE /
      DATA CAR/4HFIRS,4HT CO,4HLUMN,4H OUT,4HPUT ,4HLAST,4H COL,4HUMN ,
     1 4HOUTP,4HUT .,4HOUTP,4HUT D,4HEVIC,4HE ..,4H....,4HARBI,4HTRAR,
     2 4HY SA,4HMPLE,4HS ..,4HPRED,4HICTO,4HRS P,4HINNE,4HD ..,4HENTR,
     3 4HIES ,4HPER ,4HSAMP,4HLE .,4HNON-,4HVALU,4HES (,4HMISS,4HING),
     4 4HITER,4HATIO,4HNS .,4H....,4H....,4HSAMP,4HLES ,4HDERI,4HVED ,
     5 4H....,4HFACT,4HORS ,4HDERI,4HVED ,4H....,4H....,4HDISC,4HRIMI,4HNANT,
     6 4HS ..,4H....,4HVARI,4HATES,4H PER,4HMUTE,4HD ..,4HCANO,4HNICA,
     74HL VA,4HRIAT,4HES .,4HHILL,4H-CLI,4HMBIN,4HG TR,4HIALS,4H OF ,4HI
     8TEM,4HS IN,4H CLA,4HSS .,4H SIG,4HNIFI,4HCANC,4HE LE,4HVEL ,4H INI
     9,4HTIAL,4H IMP,4HROVE,4HMENT,4HSTD.,4H DEV,4HN. F,4HROM ,4HA.M./
      IGO = 0
      IF(NCALL.NE.1) GO TO 95
C READ CARD,CHECK FOR BACK,STOP,END,RETURN FOR STANDARDISATION
   91 READ(M1,900)F,T
      IF(IBL(F,40,1))92,93,93
   92 IF(IBL(T,10,4))91,93,93
C ECHO-PRINT OF (NON-BLANK) DATA HANDLING INSTRUCTION
   93 WRITE(M2,901)(F(I),I=1,24),T
      NX = IBL(F,4,1)
      IF(NX.EQ.2) IGO = 1
      IF(NX.EQ.2) RETURN
      IF(NX.EQ.1.AND.M4.GT.0)WRITE(M4)(Q,I=1,NQ)
      IF(NX.EQ.1) STOP
      IF(NX.GT.2.AND.V10.LT.0.5) V10 = 91.
      V1 = AN(F,1,1,1)
      V2 = AN(F,2,2,2)
      V3 = AN(F,5,3,5)
      V4 = AN(F,8,6,8)
      V5 = AN(F,16,9,16)
      V6 = AN(F,24,17,24)
      V7 = AN(F,40,17,40)
      NWARN = 0
   95 IF(NCALL.NE.2) RETURN
C PRINT STANDARDISED DHI
      K = V1
      IF(NA.GT.0)WRITE(M2,910)(TIND(I,NA),I=1,3),K
```

```
            K = V2
            IF(NB.GT.0) WRITE(M2,910) (TIND(I,NB),I=1,3),K
C OUTPUT OF NAMED PARAMETERS - C TO F
            DO 100 KK = 1,4
            IF(KK.EQ.1) N = NC
            IF(KK.EQ.2) N = ND
            IF(KK.EQ.3) N = NE
            IF(KK.EQ.4) N = NF
            IF(N.LT.1.OR.N.GT.19) GO TO 100
            IF(KK.EQ.1) V = V3
            IF(KK.EQ.2) V = V4
            IF(KK.EQ.3) V = V5
            IF(KK.EQ.4) V = V6
            K = V + 0.01
            IF(N.LE.5)                WRITE(M2,911) (CAR(I,N),I=1,5),K
            IF(N.EQ.6)                WRITE(M2,912) (CAR(I,N),I=1,5),K
            IF(N.GE. 7.AND.N.LE.14)   WRITE(M2,913) (CAR(I,N),I=1,5),K
            IF(N.EQ. 7.AND.K.EQ. 0)   WRITE(M2,917)
            IF(N.GE.15.AND.N.LE.17)   WRITE(M2,914) (CAR(I,N),I=1,5),V
            IF(N.EQ.18)               WRITE(M2,915) (CAR(I,N),I=1,5),V
        100 IF(N.EQ.19)               WRITE(M2,916) V
C REPORT STANDARDISATION - IF ANY
            IF(NWARN.GT.0) WRITE(M2,920)
            IF(NWARN.EQ.1) WRITE(M2,921)
            IF(NWARN.GT.1) WRITE(M2,922) NWARN
            IF(NWARN.GT.0)  WRITE(M2,923)
C TEST FOR CONTINUING ERRORS
            IGO = 0
            IF(V10.LT.0.5) RETURN
            IGO = 1
            WRITE(M2,930) V10
            RETURN
        900 FORMAT (40A1,10A4)
        901 FORMAT (/1H0,34X,38HDATA HANDLING INSTRUCTION - ECHO PRINT //
           16X,8HABCCCDDD,2(4HEEEE),2(4HFFFF),4(4HGGGG),10(4HHHHH)/
           26X,24A1,4(4HXXX),10A4//)
        910 FORMAT(14X,3A4,15HCONTROL INDEX =,I6)
        911 FORMAT(9X,10HNUMBER OF ,5A4,2H =,I6)
        912 FORMAT(19H MINIMUM NUMBER OF ,5A4,2H =,I6)
        913 FORMAT(19H MAXIMUM NUMBER OF ,5A4,2H =,I6)
        914 FORMAT(19H MINIMUM PERCENTAGE,5A4,2H =,F11.4)
        915 FORMAT(19H MAXIMUM NUMBER OF ,5A4,2H =,F11.4)
        916 FORMAT(29H MINIMUM EIGENVALUE RETAINED ,10(1H.),2H =,F11.4)
        917 FORMAT(1H+,53X,23H(ONLY COMPLETE ENTRIES) )
        920 FORMAT(1H0,9X,27HTHE SYSTEM HAS STANDARDISED,19X,34HFROM THE DATA
           1HANDLING INSTRUCTION,18X,13H** WARNING **)
        921 FORMAT(1H+,37X,17HONE CONTROL VALUE)
        922 FORMAT(1H+,36X,I3,15H CONTROL VALUES)
        923 FORMAT(1H0,9X,90HPLEASE VERIFY THAT THE ASSUMPTIONS IT HAS MADE AR
           1E CORRECT AND ADJUST STORAGE IF NECESSABY)
            IF(NWARN.GT.0) WRITE(M2,923)
        930 FORMAT(1H0,9X,23HPROGRAM CANNOT OPERATE.,75X,13H** WARNING **/
           11H0,9X,33HEARLIEST UNCORRECTED ERROR CODE =,F4.0)
            END
```

3.9 COMBINATION OF INPUT MODULES

The data modules described in this chapter (with a few specialised modules described in the documentation of specific programs) are used to provide the necessary information - context, data and instructions - to STATCAT programs. Some programs require only two or three input modules, others as many as six. All programs require a File Control card as the first card, and most programs require a data handling instruction.

If the user had to start from scratch with each analysis, he would waste considerable time and effort in repeating sets of input data differing only in minor details. The system would have to sweep through the data bank for each analysis required, while it is often possible, by properly organising the input of instructions, to carry out a single data sweep on which a number of analyses can be based. (For example, the program STMULT, which carries out multiple regression analysis (7.2) can be made to collect the necessary data for a large correlation matrix, from which different sets of variates can be selected for analysis.)

To provide a relatively simple means of minimising input and optimising data collection, a convention has been adopted for input. Data modules are read on successive levels by the system, as required by the program, until the last module has been read. If there are no uncorrected errors in the data, the program will carry out the operation required, usually calling a an executive subroutine to do so. (If there are fatal errors the program will not attempt to run, but will provide a reminder message of the earliest uncorrected error.) After completing the run, the program will read a new data handling instruction, if appropriate. If this is a BACK card (see 3.0) the system will step back to read the previous input module. If this begins with a BACK card, the program steps back to the previous module, until either it reads a BACK card for the File Control Card and stops, or it reads a complete set of input modules and calls up the executive subroutine, or it encounters a STOP card and halts.

Figure 3.91 illustrates this process, for a typical program (ST2IND (6.1) - testing two independent samples). It is not always possible to forsee exactly how the system will react to some forms of garbling. It is possible for the system to get out of step with the input data stream, and some types of faulty input may provoke error routines from the computer's operating system before the FORTRAN system containing STATCAT is reached (mis-punched cards - defective remote input terminals etc..). Most common errors will be caught, without much waste of running time, because all possible checking is carried out before the main program hands over control to the executive subroutine, which uses the bulk of the computing time.

The order of the modules input is a compromise, based on experience, between the demands of standardisation to avoid confusion, consistency with a 'natural' order of data presentation, economy of effort, and the mutual checking sometimes necessary between modules. The descriptions of programs in the following chapters contain a summary of the input modules required by the program (in order) with a valid set of input data cards, which produces the demonstration output included with the program description.

Where the program is unable to correct data input errors, it provides error messages at the point of error, with an additional warning message when it refuses to call the executive subroutine. This message gives a reference number for the error encountered, which may be compared with Figure 3.92 to identify the location of the earliest uncorrected error. (There may be others later in the sequence.)

Figure 3.91

Example of Input Sequence - ST2IND

```
Data Input Levels(ST2IND)  Execution (C2IND)
```

A	D	E	F	G	Data Sweep	Testing	Comment	See
1	2	3	4	5				
A							File Control Card	3.2
	D						Sample Specification	3.5
		E					Subset Specification	3.6
			F				Variate Specification	3.7
				G			Data Handling Instruction	3.8
					H		Sweep for required data	6.1
						I	Test first variate	6.1
						I	Test second variate	6.1
					H		Sweep for remaining data	6.1
						I	Test third variate	6.1
			B				DHI - BACK to read variate	3.8
		F					Variate spec - in error	3.7
				G			DHI - running inhibited	3.8
				G			DHI - running inhibited	3.8
			B				DHI - BACK to read variate	3.8
			B				Variate Spec - BACK	3.7
		E					Subset Specification	3.6
			F				Variate Specification	3.7
				G			Data Handling Instruction	3.8
					H		Sweep for required data	6.1
						I	Test first variate	6.1
						I	Test second variate	6.1
				S			DHI - STOP (Close down)	3.8

Figure 3.92a - Error Message Codes (summary)

Code   Error

    1   Too many items per entry
    2   Too many classes per data column
    3   1 and 2 together
    5   Data description being loaded from cards is out of order
    6   Data description being loaded has not enough column descriptions
    7   STWORD requires 21 column plain-language STATCAT data bank.

    11 Error in sample specification
    12 Not enough samples defined
    13 Different no of columns for second STSORT Input
    14 Data manipulation cards out of order
    15 Data manipulation cards not recognised
    16 Too many items per entry (in output DDS)
    17 Too many classes per data column (in output DDS)
    18 ST2IND requires exactly two samples

N.B. Only the earliest uncorrected error code is normally given

N.B. Refer to output listing for exact details of error(s)

Figure 3.92b - Error Codes (summary)

Code	Error
21	Error in subset definition
23	Error in priority specification
24	Error in secondary priority specification
25	Error in parameter specification
26	Wrong number of data columns defined
27	Error in data description segment
28	Insufficient storage for data description segment
31	Error in variate specification
32	No recognisable variates
33	Error in time/variate pairs
34	Analysis of variance model out of order
35	Insufficient storage for analysis of variance model
36	Undefined variate in analysis of variance model
37	Too many variates in analysis of variance Model
38	Too many sub-totals required in analysis of variance
39	Error in priority specification
41	Error in row priority specification
42	No valid column variates
43	Error in variate set
44	Error in priority specification
45	Insufficient storage
46	Only one related sample in STKREL
47	No time variates
51	Error in column priority specification (STASTA)
52	No valid row variates (ST2REL)
53	No valid predicted variates (STMULT)
54	No valid criterion variates (STAIAD)
55	Error in selection of variates (STCLUS)
56	Fewer than 3 variates selected (STCLUS)
57	No merging specification
58	Columns not specified
59	Error in predicted variates
61	No valid parameters (STASTA)
62	No valid Predictors
63	Insufficient storage space
64	Error in primary priority specification
65	Different number of matching columns in primary and secondary I/P
66	Different direction of priority in primary and sceondary inputs
67	Error in predictor variates
71	Error in record specification (STWORD)
91	Insufficient storage to carry out analyses called for

N.B. Only the earliest uncorrected error code is normally given

N.B. Refer to output listing for exact details of error(s)

Chapter IV

SETTING UP A STATCAT DATA BANK

This chapter describes programs for loading, checking and correcting STATCAT data banks.

The program STHEAD prepares STATCAT data banks. As a safety measure, only the program STHEAD is allowed to write directly into a data bank, without having first checked its name. It is necessary that some program should have this capability, because the data starter has to be put into the file in the first place, and the system will crash if it tries to read a record which is not there. On the other hand, if all data loading programs could over-write the output STATCAT data bank without checking that it was the one expected, there would be no way of keeping STATCAT data banks safe from accidental destruction.

The program STLOAD loads complete STATCAT data banks (consisting of a Data Starter, Data Description Segment, Data Storage Segment and a Data Terminator) directly from an input medium, such as punched cards. It also performs routine checks of the STATCAT data bank produced.

The program STCHEK performs the same routine checks on complete STATCAT data banks, or on subsets of data banks. The user has more freedom to define what is considered abnormal when using STCHEK, and may test different subsets by different criteria.

The program STCORR may be used to delete single entries, or groups of entries, to interpolate new entries or to alter existing entries. It may also be used to correct the Data Description Segment, or to modify the Data Starter. This program produces a revised STATCAT data bank on the output storage unit, but leaves the original intact on the main input storage medium.

Several programs not specifically designed for the purpose can be useful in checking STATCAT data banks (STLIST, STMULT, STANOV). A brief discussion is available in 4.3.5.

STATCAT data banks may be produced by STLOAD, STCORR, or by the various data manipulation programs described in Chapter 10. All programs include routine data checking, which will be carried out unless explicitly cancelled, and all STATCAT data banks, however produced, may be checked and corrected using the programs STCHEK and STCORR.

4.1 PROGRAM STHEAD - CREATE EMPTY STATCAT DATA BANK

4.1.1 Purpose

This program creates STATCAT data banks from unlabelled tape or disk files. It writes the file name and security key given by a file control card onto the STATCAT output medium, adding enough dummy information - data starter, data description segment, data storage segment and data terminator - to allow the resultant STATCAT data bank to be used as an input for other programs (particularly for the next program STLOAD and for the auxiliary program STBANK (11.2) which is used to check the contents of existing STATCAT data banks). Figure 4.11 is a system flow-chart for STHEAD. There is no executive subroutine, in view of the simplicity of the program.

4.1.2 Input Data

Summary

Item	Level	Format	Function	See
1	0	A	File Control Card	Below + 3.2

1 - File Control Card

This must contain the file name and security key for the OUTPUT STATCAT data bank. If it is not a file control card, it will be ignored, except that END or STOP cards will cause the program to halt. FOR THIS PROGRAM ONLY, NO CHECK IS MADE OF THE IDENTITY OF THE OUTPUT STATCAT DATA BANK before it is over-written. Great care must be used to avoid accidental over-writing of data banks.

4.1.3 Input Example

Figure 4.12 is a listing of input modules for STHEAD, indented according to the program structure. Figure 4.13 is a listing of input cards for the creation of three STATCAT data banks which will be used in the rest of this book for examples and demonstrations. Because this is a simple repetitive program, the structure of the data is correspondingly simple.

4.1.4 Output Example

Figure 4.14 gives the general structure of the output of STHEAD. Figure 4.15 is a page-by-page summary of the output produced by the example run of 4.13. Figure 4.16 shows the complete output for one run. Note that the dummy STATCAT data bank contains only one data column, and ten single datum entries, plus a non-value as terminator. The last program in this book (STBANK - 11.2) lists the content of an empty STATCAT data bank.

4.1.5 Commentary

The sole and unique purpose of this program is to prepare STATCAT data banks that can be read and checked by other STATCAT programs. It inserts just enough information for that purpose and no more.

This program may be used to destroy STATCAT data banks for which the security key has been forgotten, or which are otherwise useless, but the user should remember that, although he is making it impossible to retrieve the data on the file using STATCAT programs, it may still be possible for some ingenious person to obtain access to the data by using a lower level language, or some peculiarity of the operating system. Only a physical over-writing of the data themselves is almost certain to make it irretrievable - and only physical destruction of the storage medium can make it absolutely certain.

Figure 4.11 - System Flow-chart - STHEAD

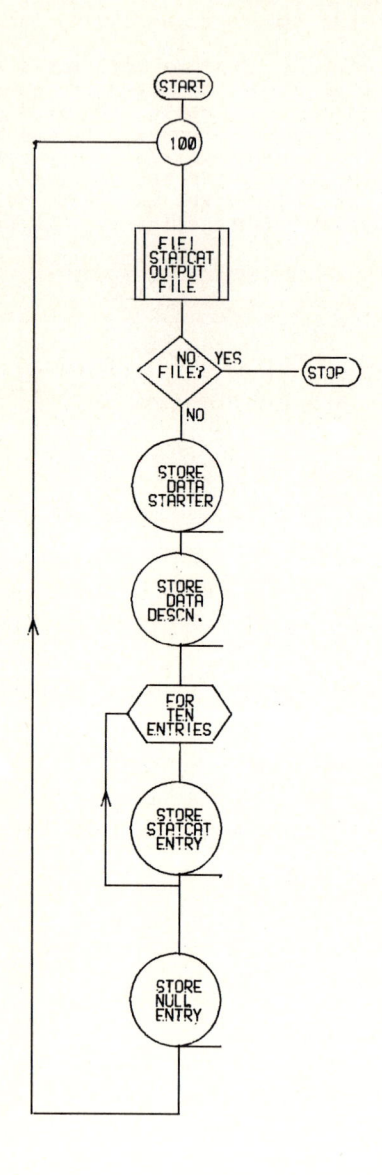

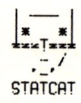

Figure 4.12 - STHEAD - Input Structure

```
          Level
 0   1    2    3    4    5    6    7    8    9
FILE CONTROL CARD
FILE CONTROL CARD
FILE CONTROL CARD
STOP
```

Figure 4.13 - STHEAD - Input Example

```
---------1----------2----------3----------4----------5----------6----------7--
**STHEAD      DEMO
**STHEAD      COPY
**STHEAD      DUFF
STOP
---------1----------2----------3----------4----------5----------6----------7--
```

Figure 4.14 - STHEAD - Output Structure

```
For each new file : File Control Record
                    File Title (dummy) + name
```

Figure 4.15 - STHEAD - Output Example page-by-page Listing

Page	Contents	Origin
1	File Control Record File Title (dummy) + name (DEMO)	FIFI STHEAD
2	File Control Record File Title (dummy) + name (COPY)	FIFI STHEAD
3	File Control Record File Title (dummy) + name (DUFF)	FIFI STHEAD

Figure 4.16 - STHEAD - Complete output for STHEAD

```
 RECORD OF FILE CONTROL OPERATIONS
LOAD FILE DEMO ON UNIT   18 READ/WRITE

FILE ON UNIT   18 IS DEMO (FREE)
SYSTEM RETURNS TO MAIN PROGRAM

STHEAD - SET UP NEW DATA BANK

FILE PARAMETERS

NUMBER OF DATA COLUMNS IS -         1

STORED NUMBER OF CLASSES IS         1

VALUE USED FOR MISSING DATA IS -           -1.00000000

FILE TITLE   EMPTY STATCAT DATA BANK - READY FOR USE   FILE REFERENCE DEMO
```

```
C MASTER STHEAD - CONSTRUCTS EMPTY DATA BANK WITHOUT CHECKING FIRST
C   SUBROUTINES AND FUNCTIONS REQUIRED
C NAME              TYPE              COMMENT
C COMPA   (SEE  3.1 )  SERVICE    COMPARES ALPHAMERIC VALUES
C COPYA   (SEE  3.1 )  SERVICE    COPIES ALPHAMERIC VALUE
C FIFI    (SEE  3.2 )  SYSTEM     ALLOCATES PERIPHERALS
C IBL     (SEE  3.1 )  SERVICE    DETECTS BLANK,END AND STOP CARDS
      DIMENSION TX(17)
      DATA TX/4HEMPT,4HY ST,4HATCA,4HT DA,4HTA B,4HANK ,4H- RE,4HADY ,4H
     1FOR ,4HUSE ,5*4H     ,4HDUMM,4HY   /
      DATA B2/2H  /,ULL/4HNULL/,PROG/4HHEAD/
      COMMON /STCT/MED1,MED2,MED3,MED4,MED5,MED6,MED13,Q,V(20),TT(30)
      MED1 = -1
      X = 0.
      Q = -1.
      NX = 1
    1 CALL COPYA(TT(1),PROG)
      CALL FIFI
      IF(MED4.LT.1) GO TO 1
      REWIND MED4
      READ(MED4) NQ,NALT,Y,(TT(I),I=1,16)
      REWIND MED4
      WRITE(MED4) NX,NX,Q,(TX(I),I=1,14),TT(15),TT(16)
      WRITE(MED4) ULL,B2,TX,ULL,NX,X,X
      DO 2 I = 1,10
    2 WRITE(MED4) X
      WRITE(MED4) Q
      REWIND MED4
      WRITE(MED2,900) NX,NX,Q,(TX(I),I=1,10),TT(16)
      GO TO 1
  900 FORMAT(30HOSTHEAD - SET UP NEW DATA BANK    ////16HOFILE PARAMETER
     2S/29HONUMBER OF DATA COLUMNS IS - ,I6/29HOSTORED NUMBER OF CLASSES
     3 IS ,I6/34HOVALUE USED FOR MISSING DATA IS - ,F20.8/13HOFILE TITLE
     4  ,10A4,10X,15HFILE REFERENCE ,A4)
      END
```

4.2   PROGRAM STLOAD - LOAD STATCAT DATA BANK

4.2.1   Purpose

This program loads STATCAT data banks. The data starter and data description segment are listed as the data bank is loaded. The data storage segment may be listed entry-by-entry as it is loaded, or check records may be output at regular intervals. A detailed check of the STATCAT data bank is carried out at completion, although this may be suppressed or reduced if not required.

This program does not use the nesting process described in 3.9., except that after loading and, if required, checking one STATCAT data bank, it returns to the start, to read in a new file control card, so that the user may produce another complete STATCAT data bank if he wishes.

Figure 4.21 contains system flow-charts for the main program STLOAD, the executive subroutine CLOAD, and the subroutine DATA, which is called by the executive subroutine to load an entry. Several different versions of the subroutine DATA are available. The example given with this program is a 'Free-Format' subroutine, which reads as many data as are required from cards, assuming that each entry begins on a new card, and that data are separated by blank spaces, or by the end of a card. Further details are given in 4.2.5. An alternative subroutine DATA is described in 4.4.5 and a third, more specialised, version in 9.1.5. The user will often find it useful to supply his own DATA subroutine, to allow for the peculiarities of his circumstances. Some guidance on how to do so is given in 4.2.6.

4.2.2   Input Data

Item	Level	Format	Function	See
1	0	A	File control	3.2
2	0	B	Data starter	3.3
3	0	C	Data description segment	3.4
4	1	-	Entries	Below

Data Starter

Card Layout - Data Starter - STLOAD

ABCCCDDDEEEEEEEEF..Cols 17-56..FG..Cols 57-72..GHHHHIIII

Columns	Item	Function	See
1	A	Output control index	Below
2	B	Data checking control index 4.3 +	Below
3 - 5	C	Number of data columns in this STATCAT data bank	Below
6 - 8	D	Default value for number of classes	Below
9 - 16	E	Numeric value used for missing values (non-value)	Below
17 - 56	F	Title of STATCAT data bank	Below
57 - 72	G	Not defined (used for auxiliary security key)	-
73 - 76	H	Security key	Below
77 - 80	I	Data bank name	Below

A - Output Control Index

This index controls the amount of information output as the entries are loaded into the data storage segment. It is usually advisable to have some check on what has been entered, although this may be ruled out by the bulk or nature of the data. Periodic checks of the number of entries accepted are useful to indicate the progress of the loading process if it may be stopped, by, for example, a datum that the computer cannot read.

ALTERNATIVES

A = 0   ; All entries printed as soon as read.

A = 1   ; Only the number of the entry is output.

A = 2   ; Only the number of every tenth entry is output.

A = 3   ; Only the number of every hundredth entry is output.

A = 4   ; No printing of entries during loading.

A = 5 - 9   ; As for A = 0

DEFAULT Value. A = 0, 5-9 and any non-numeric codes - entries printed in full.

B - Data Checking Control Index

As described in 4.3. Limits of five standard deviations from the arithmetic mean and less than one per cent in the class. Any missing values considered abnormal.

C - Number of Data Columns.

This value specifies the number of data columns in the STATCAT data bank to be constructed.

D - Number of Alternative Classes

This value specifies the number of alternative classes that will be found in any column of the STATCAT data bank. This number of alternative classes may be over-ruled by specific instructions in later input modules, but it is used a a general default value, and for data checking.

E - 'non-value'

This is the numerical value to be used wherever the datum does not exist. It should be chosen as a value which will not be found in the data 'in its own right' so to speak. In any subsequent analyses, the system will assume that any datum taking this value is non-existent, and calculate accordingly.

F - Title of STATCAT Data Bank

This string of ten four-character words is the plain-language title given to the STATCAT data bank to be constructed. It is output as a page header and as an initial check by practically every STATCAT program. It should therefore be as complete an indication of the content of the file as possible. If space permits, the data of creation of the file may be included as a reference.

G - STATCAT Data Bank Key

This four-character field is the confidential key to the STATCAT data
bank being constructed. It is never printed out, even during the construction of the data bank. If there is no need for confidentiality,
this field should be left blank. Note that the four-character key read
from this card replaces that existing on the output unit as soon as this
card has been read, standardised and accepted. If for any reason the
program fails or is deleted in such a way that the output unit must be
re-used it must then be addressed by the key and name defined on this
card, not by that used on the file control card for this task.

H - <u>STATCAT Data Bank Name</u>

This four-character field is the public name of the STATCAT file under construction. It is printed whenever the STATCAT data bank is called
into use by any STATCAT program. It may be chosen to integrate with an
operating system - as the name of a magnetic tape, or of a disk file. It
should be noted that, because this is an A format, the presence of
blanks in this name is important. If this field   e completely
blank the   e data bank
being constructed will be inaccessible to any other program- sometimes a
useful feature, as in 4.4, where a deliberately faulty output STATCAT
data bank is constructed. By giving it a blank name this data bank is
isolated from the system, and cannot be accessed by accident when working with other programs.

<u>Data Input Module</u>

This module contains the data cards required to provide the information to the program, using the subroutine DATA. The end of the data input segment is signalled to the system by a complete record of non-values, which cannot occur in normal data. Although the program is designed to employ a DATA subroutine that takes data entry-by-entry from
an input medium, other methods are possible, as described in 4.2.7 below.

4.2.3   <u>Input Example</u>

Figure 4.22 is a summary of the input structure for the demonstration
STATCAT data bank, showing the general layout of the input data modules.
Figure 4.23a shows the file control card, data starter card and data
description module, and Figures 4.23b and 4.23c the input cards for the
data storage segment for the demonstration STATCAT data bank. Notice
that the final input card, which consists of non-values only, forming
the data terminator, does not have the same layout of data fields as the
others. This is necessary to meet the requirement that values read by
the free-form input subroutine must be separated by at least one blank
card column.

4.2.4   <u>Output Example</u>

Figure 4.24 is a summary of the output structure corresponding to the
input structure of 4.22. Figure 4.25 is a page-by-page summary of the
output corresponding to the specific example given in 4.2.3. (Because of
the quantity of output involved, only a selection can be reproduced
here.) Figure 4.26 shows the listing of the data starter and the data
description segment. Figure 4.27 shows the start and end of the data
storage segment, including the report of the number of entries loaded,

made as a check by the executive subroutine CLOAD. The subroutine CHECK is called after the loading of the data bank is complete, to examine the data bank in detail, and call attention to abnormalities. This subroutine is described in detail in 4.3.5 following, and is therefore not discussed here.

4.2.5 Subroutine DATA (Free-format)

The subroutine DATA given here is designed to read one entry and prepare it to be added to the STATCAT data bank. (Other versions are given in 4.4.5 and 9.1.5) This is a free-format version, which reads data as a stream of real values, separated by at least one blank, or by the end of a card. Each entry is assumed to start on a new card.

The subroutine DATA has three input parameters, D, NQ and FORM. The parameter D is a vector containing NQ real values. (NQ is the number of data columns, supplied to the system by C on the data starter card.) FORM is an 80 value vector, used in this version of the subroutine to store the 80 characters read from an input card.

When the subroutine is called, it reads a card. It scans this card for groups of symbols separated by blanks, converting these to real numbers, and storing them in order in the vector D until either the vector D is full, or the card is exhausted. If the card is exhausted, a new card will be read, and the process of filling the vector D continued. When the vector D is filled, the subroutine returns to the executive subroutine CLOAD, which loads the entry onto the STATCAT data bank, adds one to the count, and prints any output called for.

4.2.6 User-Written Subroutine DATA

The user will often find it more convenient to write his own DATA subroutine, adapted to his own particular situation. He should then take note of the following points: -

- The vector D is completely filled with non-values when the subroutine DATA is first called. At subsequent calls it contains the last entry loaded.

- The COMMON statement labelled STCT defines the peripheral numbers for : -

MED1 - Control input medium   (usually console or card reader)

MED2 - Control output medium   (usually console or line printer)

MED3 - Input STATCAT data bank (if defined on file control card)

MED4 - Output STATCAT data bank (under construction - if defined)

MED5 - Bulk input medium (card reader usually)

MED6 - Bulk output medium (line printer usually)

MED13- Second Input STATCAT data bank (if defined on file control card.

Q - the non-value

- The user-written DATA subroutine may write entries directly onto the output STATCAT data bank on MED4, but these entries will not be counted by the subroutine CLOAD in totting up the number of entries, or in deciding when to make periodical outputs. They will, however, be counted by CHECK, included in all checks performed by that subroutine, and in all subsequent analyses.

- The values in the vector D when the subroutine returns to the main program are written to the output STATCAT data file as soon as the program returns to the executive subroutine. The user-written subroutine must return to the executive completely filled with non-values only when the data terminator has been recognised in the input information, and must do so then. The user-written subroutine may recognise the end of data in a more convenient way, then fill D with non-values.

The user-written subroutine DATA should ignore blank cards, to be compatible with the rest of the system.

4.2.7 Special DATA Subroutines

The experienced user of FORTRAN will soon find that he can save a good deal of time and effort by writing his own more elaborate input DATA subroutines. These need not be limited to reading a single entry - for example the version given in 9.1 reads a variable sized set of entries, and the version given in 9.3 reads in, treats and re-writes a complete data description segment. (The disadvantage of this is that the executive subroutine CLIST cannot state how many entries have been stored - it only indicates the number of calls to the subroutine DATA, from which a valid entry was returned. In the first example above the number of calls will be the number of entries, and in the second it will always be zero - since the call which returns with the data terminator is not included.)

Figure 4.21 - System Flow-charts - STLOAD, CLOAD and DATA(FREE)

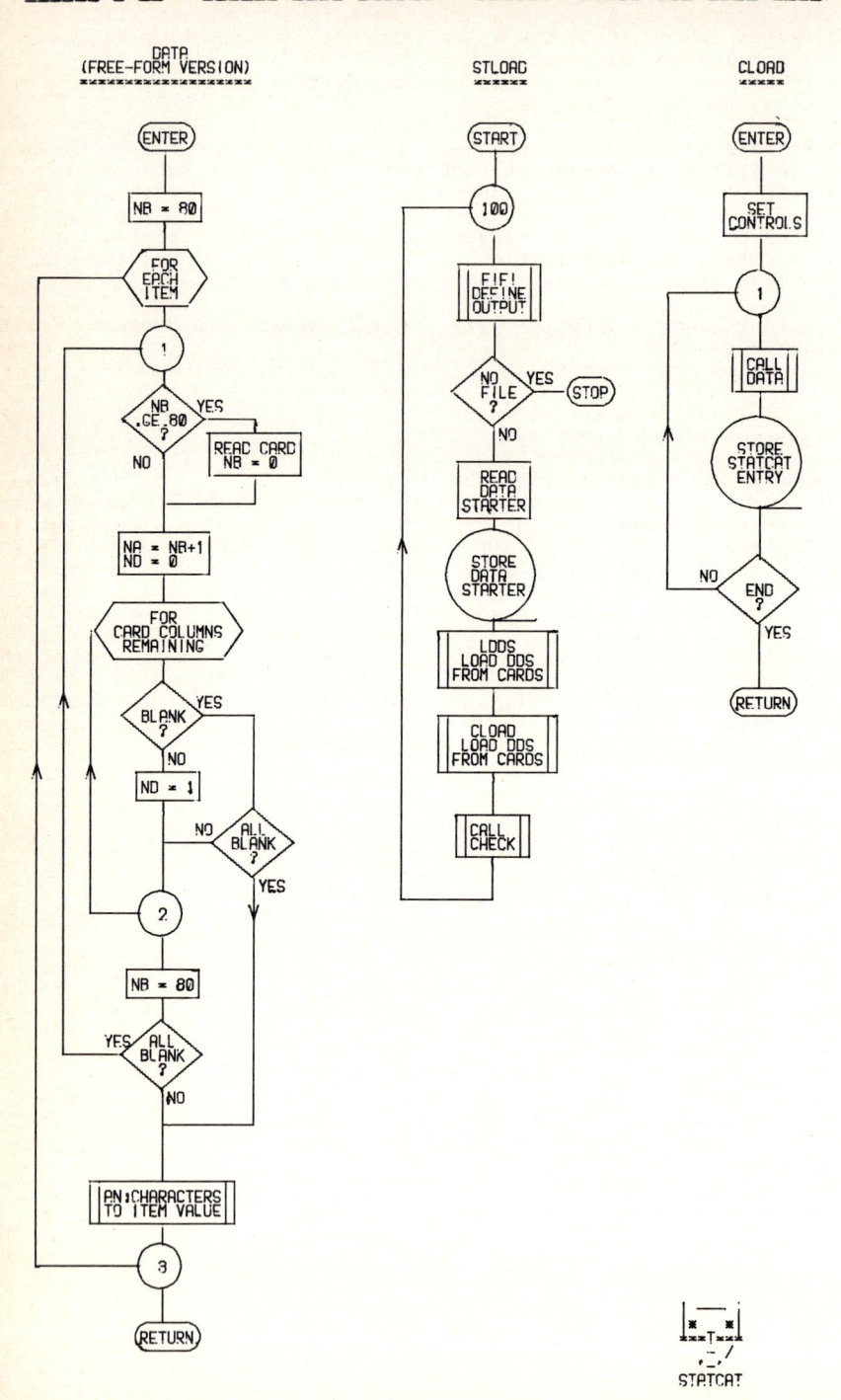

Figure 4.22 - STLOAD - Input Structure

```
        Level
 0    1    2    3    4    5    6    7    8    9
FILE CONTROL CARD
DATA STARTER
DATA DESCRIPTION SEGMENT
    |COLUMN TITLE                   |  FOR NO |
    |(COMPLEMENTARY INFORMATION)|   COLUMNS |
    |END CARD|
DATA STORAGE SEGMENT
    |ENTRIES|
    |ENTRY CONSISTING OF NON-VALUES|
STOP
```

Figure 4.23a - STLOAD - Input Example - Data Description

```
---------1---------2---------3---------4---------5-----////--7---------8
**STLOAD        DEMO                    DEMONSTRATION DATA BANK
00 18 10   -1.  DEMONSTRATION STATCAT DATA BANK                 DEMO
    1NTRY       ENTRY NUMBER                                    DUMMY
    2SESS       NUMBER OF TEST SESSION                          DUMMY
    3OBSR       OBSERVER                                        NOMINAL
MIKENOELOSCRPETE
    4OPER       OPERATOR                                        NOMINAL
ERICFREDGINAHUGH
    5W.P.       WORKING POSITION                                NOMINAL
  I   J   K   L
    6STRS       STRESS FACTOR - OBSERVED                        NOMINAL
NONEHEATDAMPNOIS
    7DAY.       DAY OF INVESTIGATION                            ORDINAL
MON.TUESWED.THUR
    8TIME       TIME WITHIN DAY                                 ORDINAL
AM1 AM2 PM1 PM2
    9TASK       TASKS (IN ORDER OF EXPECTED DIFFICULTY)         ORDINAL
ASSLBENDCUT.DRIL
    10DIFF      ASSESSMENT OF DIFFICULTY BY OPERATOR            ORDINAL
VEASEASYREASNULLRHARHARDVHAR
    11TEMP      TEMPERATURE OF WORKING POSITION (CENTIGRADE)    INTERVAL
    0.0    0.0
    12TPCT      TIME TO COMPLETE AS PERCENTAGE OF TIME ALLOWED  INTERVAL
    0.0    0.0
    13EFOP      EFFICIENCY RATING BY OPERATOR                   INTERVAL
    30.    10.
    14EFOB      EFFICIENCY RATING BY OBSERVER                   INTERVAL
    30.    10.
    15H.R.      MEAN HEART RATE DURING TEST   (BEATS/MINUTE)    RATIO
    0.0    0.0
    16TCOM      TIME TAKEN TO COMPLETE   (MINUTES)              RATIO
    0.0    0.0
    17TALL      TIME ALLOWED FOR EXPERIMENTAL SESSION (MINUTES) RATIO
    40.0   5.0
    18ERRP      PERCENTAGE OF ERRORS IN FINAL PRODUCTS          RATIO
    1.     1.
END OF DATA DESCRIPTION SEGMENT
---------1---------2---------3---------4---------5-----////--7---------8
```

Figure 4.23b - STLOAD - Input Example - Data Storage

```
---------1----------2---------3----------4---------5---------6---------7--
 1   1 1 1 1  1 1 1 1 1 22    0.62   13.31   91.59  35.52  48.30 48 0.5
 2   1 3 4 2  3 1 1 4 6 25  -12.50   95.99   84.13  54.45  63.00 72 1.3
 3   1 4 2 3  3 1 1 2 2 27   -5.96   27.24   78.82  40.07  43.26 46 1.3
 4   1 2 3 4  1 1 1 3 5 24   -8.71   80.96   79.73  62.19  46.56 51 0.5
 5   2 4 3 1  4 1 2 4 5 24   -5.69   71.28   63.01  49.50  67.90 72 3.0
 6   2 2 2 2  2 1 2 1 2 26   -1.29   26.13   77.89  41.28  47.38 48 1.4
 7   2 1 4 3  2 1 2 3 6 28  -15.29  101.42   68.85  56.10  43.20 51 1.4
 8   2 3 1 4  1 1 2 2 2 26   -4.13   26.92   94.28  43.33  44.10 46 1.0
 9   3 2 4 1  3 1 3 2 5 26  -17.83   84.35   43.13  45.41  37.80 46 3.9
10   3 4 1 2  2 1 3 3 2 28   -1.18   26.84   75.07  44.89  50.40 51 2.1
11   3 3 3 3  2 1 3 1 3 30   -7.04   44.93   61.44  39.77  44.62 48 2.1
12   3 1 2 4  2 1 3 4 4 28    0.14   51.22   75.11  60.38  72.10 72 2.1
13   4 3 2 1  4 1 4 3 4 25   -3.06   50.55   46.78  49.87  49.44 51 6.0
14   4 1 3 2  4 1 4 2 4 26  -11.43   61.79   31.43  41.59  40.74 46 6.0
15   4 2 1 3  2 1 4 4 2 28    2.08   24.17   66.50  44.55  73.50 72 2.8
16   4 4 4 4  3 1 4 1 6 26  -13.75   93.97   38.40  54.57  41.40 48 5.2
17   5 4 4 1  4 2 1 3 7 22  -15.29  116.40   79.16  56.10  43.20 51 0.3
18   5 2 1 2  3 2 1 2 1 24   -4.13   16.60   86.38  36.06  44.10 46 0.3
19   5 1 3 3  3 2 1 4 4 27   -5.69   59.89   87.85  49.87  67.90 72 0.3
20   5 3 2 4  1 2 1 1 2 25   -1.29   35.72  105.72  47.78  47.38 48 0.1
21   6 1 2 1  3 2 2 2 2 23   -5.96   26.49   81.89  39.47  43.26 46 0.9
22   6 3 3 2  3 2 2 3 4 26   -8.71   61.94   71.38  49.87  46.56 51 0.9
23   6 4 1 3  2 2 2 1 1 29    0.62   14.45   92.93  36.34  48.30 48 0.5
24   6 2 4 4  2 2 2 4 7 26  -12.50  114.18   76.42  65.42  63.00 72 0.5
25   7 3 1 1  4 2 3 4 3 27    2.08   39.10   90.40  45.22  73.50 72 1.9
26   7 1 4 2  2 2 3 1 5 28  -13.75   80.37   74.49  43.75  41.40 48 0.9
27   7 2 2 3  2 2 3 3 3 30   -3.06   41.24   81.22  51.00  49.44 51 0.9
28   7 4 3 4  2 2 3 2 4 28  -11.43   63.26   77.59  49.24  40.74 46 0.9
29   8 2 3 1  2 2 4 1 3 24   -7.04   46.15   72.94  40.38  44.62 48 1.4
30   8 4 2 2  4 2 4 4 4 25    0.14   50.56   67.10  50.25  72.10 72 3.0
31   8 3 4 3  2 2 4 2 5 28  -17.83   85.73   78.67  45.08  37.80 46 1.4
32   8 1 1 4  1 2 4 3 3 26   -1.18   39.35   84.94  53.52  50.40 51 1.0
33   9 2 2 1  1 3 1 4 2 19    0.14   37.18   92.58  49.50  72.10 72 0.1
34   9 4 3 2  1 3 1 1 3 22   -7.04   46.33   89.44  40.07  44.62 48 0.1
35   9 3 1 3  2 3 1 3 2 24   -1.18   27.56  106.05  44.89  50.40 51 0.1
36   9 1 4 4  4 3 1 2 7 22  -17.83  114.73   76.80  53.36  37.80 46 0.2
37  10 3 4 1  2 3 2 1 5 23  -13.75   81.35   91.84  44.08  41.40 48 0.3
38  10 1 1 2  3 3 2 4 2 24    2.08   27.31   95.22  46.23  73.50 72 0.3
39  10 2 3 3  2 3 2 2 3 26  -11.43   47.77   79.09  39.16  40.74 46 0.3
40  10 4 2 4  4 3 2 3 5 25   -3.06   68.75   88.12  60.38  49.44 51 0.6
41  11 1 3 1  3 3 3 3 4 24   -8.71   61.25   77.58  49.50  46.56 51 1.1
42  11 3 2 2  4 3 3 2 3 26   -5.96   42.88   90.50  41.28  43.26 46 1.2
43  11 4 4 3  2 3 3 4 6 26  -12.50   98.59   79.49  55.69  63.00 72 0.6
44  11 2 1 4  1 3 3 1 2 26    0.62   23.69   89.51  43.00  48.30 48 0.4
45  12 4 1 1  3 3 4 2 1 22   -4.13   17.02   76.25  36.61  44.10 46 1.7
46  12 2 4 2  3 3 4 3 6 24  -15.29   99.10   63.02  54.86  43.20 51 1.7
47  12 1 2 3  4 3 4 1 3 26   -1.29   39.24   74.97  40.98  47.38 48 2.0
48  12 3 3 4  3 3 4 4 5 24   -5.69   73.00   65.96  59.47  67.90 72 1.7
49  13 3 3 1  4 4 1 2 4 19  -11.43   64.71   75.54  40.98  40.74 46 0.1
50  13 1 2 2  4 4 1 3 4 22   -3.06   53.96   91.82  49.87  49.44 51 0.1
---------1----------2---------3----------4---------5---------6---------7--
```

Figure 4.23c - STLOAD - Input Example - Data Storage

```
---------1---------2---------3---------4---------5---------6---------7--
51 13 2 4 3 4 4 1 1 6 25 -13.75   94.91  78.25  43.75  41.40 48 0.1
52 13 4 1 4 4 4 1 4 4 22   2.08   52.45  97.91  54.34  73.50 72 0.1
53 14 2 1 1 4 4 2 3 3 22  -1.18   41.38  87.59  44.89  50.40 51 0.4
54 14 4 4 2 3 4 2 2 5 25 -17.83   85.38  76.12  44.41  37.80 46 0.4
55 14 3 2 3 2 4 2 4 2 26   0.14   36.60 106.14  49.13  72.10 72 0.2
56 14 1 3 4 2 4 2 1 4 25  -7.04   60.04  87.10  49.24  44.62 48 0.2
57 15 4 2 1 1 4 3 1 2 24  -1.29   24.75  92.75  40.07  47.38 48 0.3
58 15 2 3 2 2 4 3 4 4 26  -5.69   60.90  83.34  50.62  67.90 72 0.4
59 15 1 1 3 2 4 3 2 1 28  -4.13   16.56  87.84  36.06  44.10 46 0.4
60 15 3 4 4 2 4 3 3 7 26 -15.29  116.84  89.15  64.92  43.20 51 0.4
61 16 1 4 1 1 4 4 4 6 22 -12.50   97.34  79.13  54.86  63.00 72 0.5
62 16 3 1 2 3 4 4 1 1 25   0.62   15.01  95.54  36.88  48.30 48 1.3
63 16 4 3 3 4 4 4 3 5 26  -8.71   75.90  74.60  50.25  46.56 51 1.5
64 16 2 2 4 4 4 4 2 4 24  -5.96   55.49  72.94  49.97  43.26 46 1.5
-1 -1 -1 -1 -1 -1 -1 -1 -1 -1 -1  -1 -1 -1 -1 -1 -1 -1  EXTRA IGNORED
STOP                                      SYSTEM CLOSES DOWN
---------1---------2---------3---------4---------5---------6---------7--
```

Figure 4.24 - STLOAD - Output Structure

```
For each    )    : File Control Record
output file )      Data Starter Record
                   Data Description Record
                   for each     ) : Data Column Title
                   data column)   Complementary Information
                   Data Storage Record
                   <for each entry : standard listing>
                   <at intervals   : progress check>
                   Data Terminator Record
                   <Data Bank Checks: see 4.34>
```

Carated(<>) items are optional.

Figure 4.25 - STLOAD - Output Example page-by-page Listing

Page	Contents	Origin
1-2	File Control/Program Title	FIFI/LDAP/STLOAD
	Data Description record	LDDS
3- 7	Data Storage Segment	CLOAD
8	Limit Check	CHECK
9-17	Distribution Check	CHECK
18-39	All Entries	CHECK
40	Data Handling Instruction (STOP)	LDHI

Figure 4.26 - Program Heading and Data Description Segment

```
                    STATCAT GENERAL FILE LOADING PROGRAM

                    DATA BANK PARAMETERS FOR DEMO
                    ( DEMONSTRATION STATCAT DATA BANK

                       18 DATA COLUMNS (=ITEMS PER ENTRY)
                       10 CLASSES UNLESS OTHERWISE SPECIFIED
                       -1.0000 = NON-VALUE (MISSING DATUM)

                    OUTPUT CONTROL INDEX    =    0
                    CHECKING CONTROL INDEX  =    0
MAXIMUM NUMBER OF STD. DEVN. FROM A.M.  =    5.0000
MINIMUM PERCENTAGE OF ITEMS IN CLASS . =    1.0000

                         DATA DESCRIPTION SEGMENT

COLUMN  SCALE   SHORT         FULL TITLE
NUMBER  CODE    TITLE                                                    LEVEL

  1       1     NTRY          ENTRY NUMBER                               DUMMY

  2       1     SESS          NUMBER OF TEST SESSION                     DUMMY

  3       2     OBSR          OBSERVER                                   NOMINAL
                MIKE-NOEL-OSCR-PETE-  -  -  -  -  -  -

  4       2     OPER          OPERATOR                                   NOMINAL
                ERIC-FRED-GINA-HUGH-  -  -  -  -  -  -

  5       2     W.P.          WORKING POSITION                           NOMINAL
                 I  - J  - K  - L  -  -  -  -  -  -  -

  6       2     STRS          STRESS FACTOR - OBSERVED                   NOMINAL
                NONE-HEAT-DARP-NOIS-  -  -  -  -  -  -

  7       3     DAY.          DAY OF INVESTIGATION                       ORDINAL
                MON.-TUES-WED.-THUR-  -  -  -  -  -  -


                         DATA DESCRIPTION SEGMENT

COLUMN  SCALE   SHORT         FULL TITLE
NUMBER  CODE    TITLE                                                    LEVEL

  8       3     TIME          TIME WITHIN DAY                            ORDINAL
                A11 -A12 -P11 -P12 -  -  -  -  -  -  -

  9       3     TASK          TASKS (IN ORDER OF EXPECTED DIFFICULTY)    ORDINAL
                ASSL-BEND-CUT.-DRIL-  -  -  -  -  -  -

 10       3     DIFF          ASSESSMENT OF DIFFICULTY BY OPERATOR       ORDINAL
                VEAS-EASY-REAS-NULL-RHAR-HARD-VHAR-  -  -  -

 11       4     TEMP          MEAN TEMPERATURE OF WORKING POSITION DURING TEST (CENT.) INTERVAL
                  LOWEST CLASS LIMIT = OBSERVED MINIMUM, HIGHEST CLASS LIMIT = OBSERVED MAXIMUM
 12       4     TPCT          TIME TO COMPLETE AS PERCENTAGE OF TIME ALLOWED        INTERVAL
                  LOWEST CLASS LIMIT = OBSERVED MINIMUM, HIGHEST CLASS LIMIT = OBSERVED MAXIMUM
 13       6     EFOP          EFFICIENCY RATING BY OPERATOR                         INTERVAL
                  CLASSES FROM BELOW      30.0000 BY CLASSES OF    10.000000 TO   110.0000 AND OVER
 14       6     EFOB          EFFICIENCY RATING BY OBSERVER                         INTERVAL
                  CLASSES FROM BELOW      30.0000 BY CLASSES OF    10.000000 TO   110.0000 AND OVER
 15       5     H.R.          MEAN HEART RATE DURING TEST (BEATS/MINUTE)            RATIO
                  LOWEST CLASS LIMIT = OBSERVED MINIMUM, HIGHEST CLASS LIMIT = OBSERVED MAXIMUM
 16       5     TCOM          TIME TAKEN TO COMPLETE EXPERIMENTAL SESSION (MINUTES) RATIO
                  LOWEST CLASS LIMIT = OBSERVED MINIMUM, HIGHEST CLASS LIMIT = OBSERVED MAXIMUM
 17       7     TALL          TIME ALLOWED FOR EXPERIMENTAL SESSION     (MINUTES)   RATIO
                  CLASSES FROM BELOW      20.0000 BY CLASSES OF     5.000000 TO    60.0000 AND OVER
 18       7     ERRP          PERCENTAGE OF ERRORS IN FINAL PRODUCTS                RATIO
                  CLASSES FROM BELOW       1.0000 BY CLASSES OF     1.000000 TO     9.0000 AND OVER
```

Figure 4.27 - **STLOAD** - **Data Storage Segment** - **Start/End**

```
          DATA INPUT RECORD

ENTRY NUMBER    1
       1.00000000         1.00000000         1.00000000         1.00000000         1.00000000         1.00000000
       1.00000000         1.00000000         1.00000000         1.00000000        22.00000000         0.61999995
      13.30999947        91.58999634        35.51998901        48.29998779        48.00000000         0.50000000
ENTRY NUMBER    2
       2.00000000         1.00000000         3.00000000         4.00000000         2.00000000         3.00000000
       1.00000000         1.00000000         4.00000000         6.00000000        25.00000000       -12.50000000
      95.98999023        84.12998962        54.44999695        63.00000000        72.00000000         1.29999924
ENTRY NUMBER    3
       3.00000000         1.00000000         4.00000000         2.00000000         3.00000000         3.00000000
       1.00000000         1.00000000         2.00000000         2.00000000        27.00000000        -5.95999908
      27.23999023        78.81999207        40.06999207        43.25399451        46.00000000         1.29999924
ENTRY NUMBER    4
       4.00000000         1.00000000         2.00000000         3.00000000         4.00000000         1.00000000
       1.00000000         1.00000000         3.00000000         5.00000000        24.00000000        -8.70999908
      80.95999146        79.72999573        62.18998718        46.55999756        51.00000000         0.50000000
ENTRY NUMBER    5
       5.00000000         2.00000000         4.00000000         3.00000000         1.00000000         4.00000000
       1.00000000         2.00000000         4.00000000         5.00000000        24.00000000        -5.68999953
      71.27999878        83.00999451        49.50000000        67.89999390        72.00000000         3.00000000



ENTRY NUMBER   61
      61.00000000        16.00000000         1.00000000         4.00000000         1.00000000         1.00000000
       4.00000000         4.00000000         4.00000000         6.00000000        22.00000000       -12.50000000
      97.33999634        79.12998962        54.85998535        63.00000000        72.00000000         0.50000000
ENTRY NUMBER   62
      62.00000000        16.00000000         3.00000000         1.00000000         2.00000000         3.00000000
       4.00000000         4.00000000         1.00000000         1.00000000        25.00000000         0.61999995
      15.00999928        95.53999329        36.87998962        48.29998779        46.00000000         1.29999924
ENTRY NUMBER   63
      63.00000000        16.00000000         4.00000000         3.00000000         3.00000000         4.00000000
       4.00000000         4.00000000         3.00000000         5.00000000        25.00000000        -8.70999908
      75.89999390        74.59999084        50.25000000        46.55999756        51.00000000         1.50000000
ENTRY NUMBER   64
      64.00000000        16.00000000         2.00000000         2.00000000         1.00000000         4.00000000
       4.00000000         4.00000000         2.00000000         4.00000000        24.00000000        -5.95999908
      55.48999023        72.93999710        45.96998596        43.25999451        46.00000000         1.50000000

NULL ENTRY FOUND
TOTAL OF    64 ENTRIES (CALLS OF DATA SUBROUTINE)

LOADING COMPLETED - CHECKING STARTS
```

```
C MASTER STLOAD - LOADS STATCAT DATA BANKS
C   SUBROUTINES AND FUNCTIONS REQUIRED
C   NAME            TYPE            COMMENT
C   CHECK   (SEE 4.3 ) EXECUTIVE   CHECKS DATA BANK OR SUBSET
C   CLOAD   (SEE 4.2 ) EXECUTIVE   LOADS STATCAT DATA BANK
C   CLSAM   (SEE 3.5 ) SERVICE     ALLOTS ENTRY TO SAMPLE/SUBSET
C   COMPA   (SEE 3.1 ) SERVICE     COMPARES ALPHAMERIC VALUES
C   COPYA   (SEE 3.1 ) SERVICE     COPIES ALPHAMERIC VALUE
C   DATA    (SEE BELOW) SERVICE    LOADS ONE ENTRY (THREE VERSIONS)
C   DATA    (SEE 4.1 ) SERVICE     FREE-FORMAT INPUT     (VERSION DATA)
C   DATA    (SEE 4.3 ) SERVICE     RUN-TIME FORMAT       (VERSION DATB)
C   DATA    (SEE 9.4 ) SERVICE     PLAIN-LANGUAGE INPUT  (VERSION DATL)
C   FIFI    (SEE 3.2 ) SYSTEM      ALLOCATES PERIPHERALS
C   IBL     (SEE 3.1 ) SERVICE     DETECTS BLANK,END AND STOP CARDS
C   ICH     (SEE 3.1 ) SERVICE     IDENTIFIES ALPHAMERIC CODES
C   LCOM    (SEE 3.4 ) SYSTEM      LOADS COMPLEMENTARY INFORMATION
C   LDAP    (SEE 3.3 ) SYSTEM      LOADS/CHECKS DATA BASE PARAMETERS
C   LDDS    (SEE 3.4 ) SYSTEM      LOADS DATA DESCRIPTION SEGMENT
C   LDHI    (SEE 3.8 ) SYSTEM      LOADS/CHECKS DATA HANDLING INSTN
C   WDCD    (SEE 3.4 ) SERVICE     WRITE DATA COLUMN DESCRIPTION
C NQMAX = MAXIMUM NUMBER OF DATA COLUMNS
C DIMENSION D(NQMAX),DMAX(NQMAX),DMIN(NQMAX),IT(NQMAX),ST(NQMAX)
      NQMAX = 100
      DIMENSION D(100),DMAX(100),DMIN(100),IT(100),ST(100)
C DIMENSION TRT(NALTMX),(RT(NQMAX,NALTMX) = MAX NO. OF CLASSES ON TAPE
C DIMENSION RT(NQMAX,NALTMX)
      NALTMX = 50
      DIMENSION  TRT(50),RT(100,50)
C THE FOLLOWING DIMENSIONS ARE FIXED
      DIMENSION SCON(1,1),FORM(16),FORK(16)
      COMMON /STCT/MED1,MED2,MED3,MED4,MED5,MED6,MED13,Q,V(20),TT(30)
      DATA PROG/4HLOAD/,BL/4H    /
      MED1 = -1
C LEVEL 0 - ASSIGN PERIPHERALS
    1 CALL COPYA(TT(1),PROG)
      CALL FIFI
      IF(MED4.LE.0) GO TO 1
      REWIND MED4
C LEVEL 0 - LOAD DATA STARTER
      READ(MED1,900)FORM,(TT(J),J=1,10),FORK,TT(15),TT(16)
      V(1) = AN(FORM,1,1,1)
      V(2) = AN(FORM,2,2,2)
      NQ   = AN(FORM,5,3,5)
      NALT = AN(FORM,8,6,8)
      Q = AN(FORM,16,9,16)
      CALL COPYA(TT(11),BL)
      CALL COPYA(TT(12),BL)
      CALL COPYA(TT(13),BL)
      TT(14) = AN(FORK,16,1,16)
      WRITE(MED4) NQ,NALT,Q,(TT(I),I=1,16)
      WRITE(MED2,901)
      CALL LDAP(MED2,MED4,V,TT,Q,NQ,NALT,NQMAX,NALTMX,IGO)
      IF(IGO.GT.0) GO TO 1
      NWARN = 0
      APT = 1.
      ASDL = 5.
      NCON = 0.
      IF(V(1).GT.4.)NWARN = NWARN + 1
      IF(V(1).GT.4.)V(1)= -1.
      IF(V(2).GT.8.)NWARN = NWARN + 1
      IF(V(2).GT.8.)V(2)= -1.
      CALL LDHI(V(1),1,V(2),3,ASDL,18,APT,15,Z,0,Z,0,Z,V(10),
     1 Z,Z,MED1,MED2,MED4,Q,NQ,NWARN,2,IGO)
```

```
      IF(IGO.GT.0) GO TO 1
C RELOAD HEADER,THEN CALL LDDS TO LOAD DATA DESCRIPTION SEGMENT
      REWIND MED4
      WRITE(MED4) NQ,NALT,Q,(TT(J),J=1,16)
      LI = 18
      CALL LDDS(TRT,NALT,D,NQ,ST,NQ,IT,NQ,H,0,H,H,0,LI,0,Q,VX,
     1 MED1,MED2,0,MED4,IGO)
C TRY TO LOAD EVEN IF DDS IS WRONG - MAY YIELD CLUES WHY
C CALL EXECUTIVE TO LOAD DATA STORAGE SEGMENT AND TERMINATOR
      CALL CLOAD(D,NQ)
      IF(V(2).GE.0.) GO TO 99
      WRITE(MED6,907)
      GO TO 1
   99 WRITE(MED6,905)
C CARRY OUT PRELIMINARY CHECK OF DATA TAPE
      CALL CHECK (D,DMAX,DMIN,RT,IT,TRT,NQ,NALT,ASDL,APT,SCON,NCON,ST)
      WRITE(MED6,906)
      GO TO 1
  900 FORMAT(16A1,10A4,16A1,2A4)
  901 FORMAT (1H0,20X,36HSTATCAT GENERAL FILE LOADING PROGRAM)
  905 FORMAT(36HOLOADING COMPLETED - CHECKING STARTS)
  906 FORMAT(19HOCHECKING COMPLETED)
  907 FORMAT(40HOLOADING COMPLETED - CHECKING SUPPRESSED)
      END


      SUBROUTINE CLOAD(D,NQ)
C CLOAD  (SEE  4.2 ) EXECUTIVE   LOADS STATCAT DATA BANK
      DIMENSION D(NQ),FORM(80)
      COMMON /STCT/MED1,MED2,MED3,MED4,MED5,MED6,MED13,Q,V(20),TT(30)
C LOAD DATA STORAGE SEGMENT
      ND = V(1)
      NOP = 0
      NSUB = 0
      IF(ND.EQ.0.OR.ND.EQ.1) NOP = 1
      IF(ND.EQ.2) NOP = 10
      IF(ND.EQ.3) NOP = 100
      IF(ND.EQ.4) NOP = 1000
      WRITE(MED2,996)
      NL = 0
      DO 15 J = 1,NQ
   15 D(J) = Q
   16 CALL DATA (D,NQ,FORM)
      WRITE(MED4) D
      DO 17 J = 1,NQ
      IF(D(J).NE.Q) GO TO 18
   17 CONTINUE
      WRITE(MED2,999) NSUB
      V(6) = NSUB
      RETURN
   18 NSUB = NSUB + 1
      IF(NOP.EQ.0) GO TO 16
      IF(NSUB.NE.NSUB/NOP*NOP) GO TO 16
      NL = NL + 1
      IF(ND.EQ.0) NL = NL + (NQ+5)/6
      IF(NL.GE.50) WRITE(MED2,996)
      IF(NL.GE.50) NL = 0
      IF(ND.EQ.0)WRITE(MED2,998) NSUB,D
      IF(ND.NE.0)WRITE(MED2,997) NSUB,D(1)
      GO TO 16
  996 FORMAT (1H1,20X,17HDATA INPUT RECORD//)
  997 FORMAT (14H ENTRY NUMBER ,I6,17H FIRST DATA ITEM ,F20.8)
  998 FORMAT (14H ENTRY NUMBER ,I6/(1H ,6F20.8))
```

```
  999 FORMAT(17HONULL ENTRY FOUND/10H TOTAL OF ,I6,35H ENTRIES (CALLS OF
     1 DATA SUBROUTINE))
      END


      SUBROUTINE DATA (D,NQ,FORM)
C DATA    (SEE  4.2 ) SERVICE      FREE-FORMAT INPUT     (VERSION DATA)
C FREE-FORM DATA (DEFAULT) - STARTS EACH ENTRY ON NEW CARD - NO OVERLAP
      DIMENSION D(NQ),FORM(80)
      COMMON /STCT/MED1,MED2,MED3,MED4,MED5,MED6,MED13,Q,V(20),TT(30)
      DATA B1/1H /
  900 FORMAT (80A1)
      NB = 80
      DO 3 I = 1,NQ
    1 IF(NB.GE.80) READ(MED5,900) FORM
      IF(NB.GE.80) NB = 0
      NA = NB+1
      ND = 0
      DO 2 NB =NA,80
      CALL COMPA(B1,FORM(NB),L)
      IF(L.EQ.1.AND.ND.NE.0) GO TO 3
    2 IF(L.NE.1) ND = 1
      NB = 80
      IF(ND.EQ.0) GO TO 1
    3 D(I) = AN(FORM,80,NA,NB)
      RETURN
      END
```

4.3 PROGRAM STCHEK - CHECK STATCAT DATA BANK

4.3.1 Purpose

This program checks STATCAT data banks. It may be used to check a complete STATCAT data bank, or a specified subset. The extent of checking and the thresholds defining what is considered abnormal may be varied by the user.

Figure 4.31 contains system flow-charts for the main program STCHEK and the executive subroutine CHECK.

4.3.2 Input Data

Item	Level	Format	Function	See
1	0	A	File control	3.2
2	4	E	Subset specification	3.6
3	9	H	Data handling instruction	Below + 3.8

Data Handling Instruction

Card Layout - Data Handling Instruction - STCHEK

ABCCCDDDEEEEEEEEFFFFFFFFGGGGGGGGGGGGGGGGHHHHHHHHHH.....etc

Columns	Item	Function	See
1	A	Not used	-
2	B	Data checking control index	Below
3 - 5	C	Maximum number of 'non-values' accepted	Below
6 - 8	D	Minimum percentage in any class	Below
9 - 16	E	Maximum S.D. from A.M.	Below
17 - 24	F	Not used	-
25 - 40	G	Not used	-
41 - 80	H	Comment (NOT KEPT)	-

B - Data Checking Control Index

This index controls the extent of checking carried out by the system. Three types of checking are available : -

i) Limit Check

For all data columns except those on a DUMMY level, the maximum, minimum, mean, standard deviation and total number of data are printed.

ii) Distribution Check

for all data columns except those on a DUMMY level, the number of data in each class and the number of non-values are printed. For data on NOMINAL or ORDINAL levels, the numbers of data above or below the range 1-NALT (where NALT is the number of classes specified for this data bank) is also printed.

iii) Abnormality Check

All abnormal entries are printed. Abnormal entries are defined as follows ; -

a) OUT OF RANGE. Any datum on NOMINAL or ORDINAL levels outside the range 1 to NALT (Number of classes specified as a default) or any datum at or below zero on a RATIO level.

b) EXTREME Check. For data on INTERVAL or RATIO levels - any datum more than the specified number of standard deviations from the arithmetic mean (E)

c) RARE CLASS. For NOMINAL and ORDINAL data only, any datum in a class containing less than the minimum percentage D of data, or any unique datum.

d) RARE VALUE. For INTERVAL and RATIO data only, any datum in a class containing less than the minimum percentage D of data, or any unique datum.

e) EXCESS MISSING VALUES Any record containing more than the maximum number of 'non-values' (C).

ALTERNATIVES

B = 0 (Default) : Limit Check, Distribution Check and Abnormality Check (to level e) with full listing of all entries.

B = 1 : Limit Check, Distribution Check and Abnormality Check (to level e) with full listing of abnormal entries.

B = 2 : Limit Check, Distribution Check and Abnormality Check (to level d) with full listing of abnormal entries.

B = 3 : Limit Check, Distribution Check and Abnormality Check (to level c) with full listing of abnormal entries.

B = 4 : Limit Check, Distribution Check and Abnormality Check (to level b) with full listing of abnormal entries.

B = 5 : Limit Check, Distribution Check and Abnormality Check (to level a) with full listing of abnormal entries.

B = 6 : Limit Check and Distribution Check only

B = 7 : Limit Check only

B = 8 : Number of entries in data bank and subset only printed.

B = 9 : No checking

DEFAULT VALUE = 0 (Input as 0, blank or any non-numeric code)

C - Maximum Number of 'non-values'

This is the maximum number of non-values which will be tolerated in an entry before it is considered abnormal, on this account alone.

DEFAULT VALUE = 0 (Input as 0, blank or any non-numeric code)

SPECIAL CASE : Any negative value suppresses this check.

D - Minimum Percentage in any Class

This value specifies the percentage of data within any class below which a datum is considered abnormal.

DEFAULT VALUE = 1 (Input as 0, blank or any non-numeric code)

SPECIAL CASE : Any negative value suppresses this check.

E - Maximum Number of Standard Deviations from Arithmetic Mean

This is the number of standard deviations away from the arithmetic mean beyond which a datum is considered abnormal, for INTERVAL and RATIO level data columns.

DEFAULT VALUE = 5 (Input as 0, blank or any non-numeric code)

SPECIAL CASE : Any negative value suppresses this check.

4.3.3   Input Example

Figure 4.32 is a summary of the input data for two checks of the demonstration STATCAT data bank. In the first run, the complete data bank is checked for entries containing less than 7.5 per cent of the data bank, and in the second, a general check is made of all the occasions on which the operator classified the task as HARD or VHAR (=Very HARd). Figure 4.33 lists the input data for the two runs.

4.3.4   Output Example

Figure 4.34 is a summary of the output structure corresponding to the input structure of 4.32. Figure 4.35 is a page-by-page summary of the output corresponding to the specific example given in 4.3.3. Figure 4.36 provides a summary of the input checking information for the first run. Note that the negative value for E is standardised to 99999. Figure 4.37 shows some selected distribution checks. Figure 4.38 shows some of the output produced by the abnormality check for the first run. Figure 4.39 shows the limit check for the second run. Note that column 4 (OPER) is a constant at 4 (HUGH).

4.3.5   Commentary

It should be noted that this program detects abnormalities, in the literal sense, not errors. In practice most abnormal data are errors, but there can be abnormalities which are not errors and vice versa. Transcription or transposition errors in the least significant digits of data will often escape notice. Even where the transcription process has been carefully checked, it cannot detect errors made when the data were recorded.

Experience shows that the bulk of time and effort in computer statistical analysis (once the system is established) is spent in finding and correcting errors in the data bank. Although this program is the only one dedicated exclusively to error detection, there are several other programs in the system which may be used to detect errors.

The program STLIST (5.1) can be used to list any entries falling into impossible or improbable combinations of conditions. (The classic example - batchelors with five children - although not impossible, certainly merits further investigation.) Where, as often happens, data have some internal structure (successive positions of a ship, annual indices of economic activity etc.) plots and other specialised output subroutines (Subroutine WOWN - 5.1.5) are useful. In addition to making it easier to read the data, they can bring outliers to the eye. (It is often a good idea to plot your data before analysing it.)

Examinations of residuals, as provided in STMULT (7.2), will often bring to light smaller errors which were not visible before large systematic effects were compensated for. Similarly, the appearance of large standard deviations in a few cells of an analysis of variance (7.1) may indicate the presence of erratic entries.

Ideally, all errors should be corrected as soon as found, and all previous analyses repeated. Experienced statisticians may often be able to correct analyses for a few errors, or to show that their effects are negligible. (Any fool can use a cook-book, many can write one, but it takes an expert to put the cherries into the cake after it has been baked.)

Figure 4.31 - System Flow-charts - STCHEK and CHECK

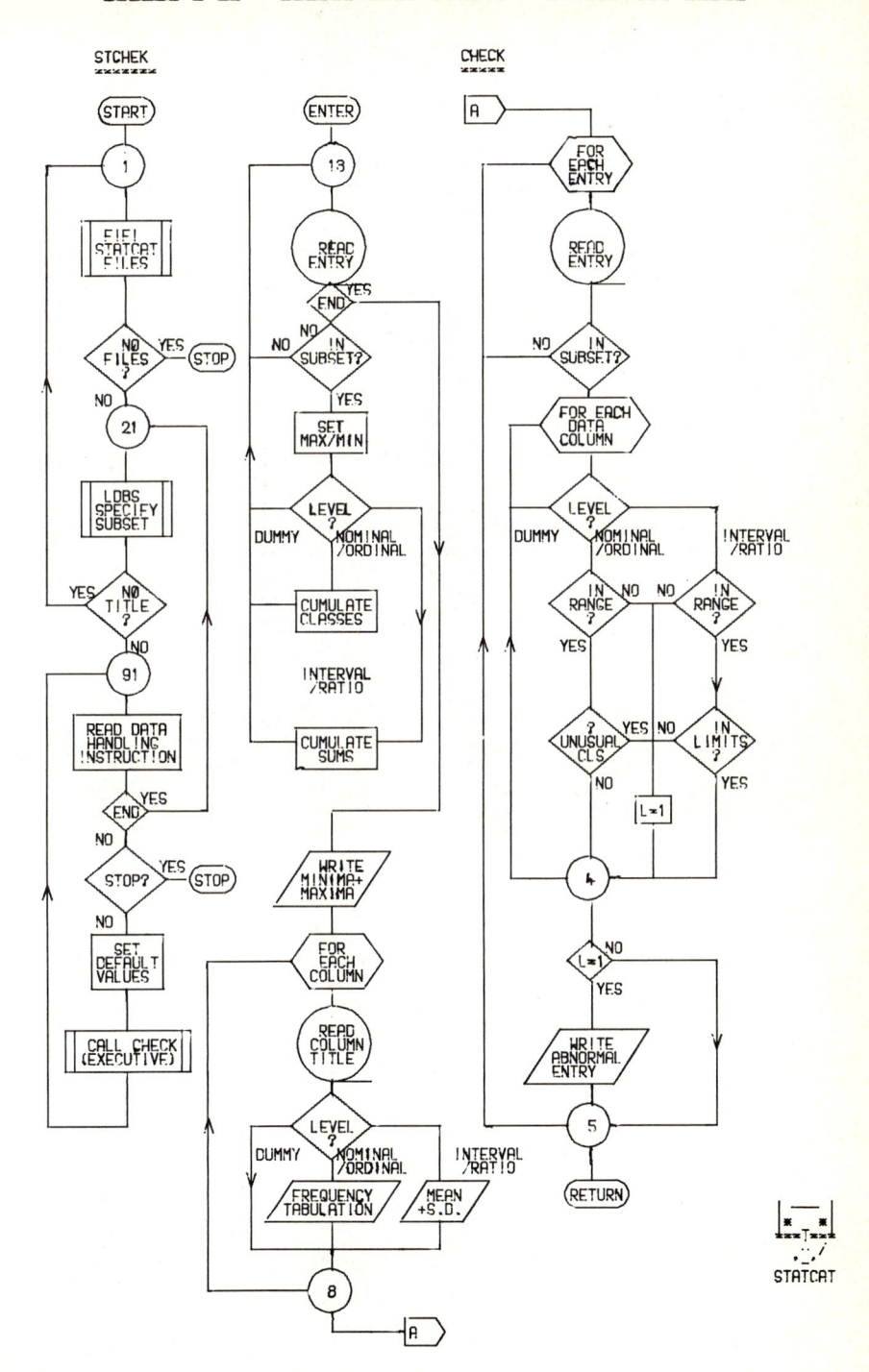

Figure 4.32 - STCHEK - Input Structure

```
       Level
0   1   2   3   4   5   6   7   8   9
FILE CONTROL CARD
    SUBSET SPECIFICATION
        DATA HANDLING INSTRUCTION
        BACK TO READ NEW SUBSET
    SUBSET SPECIFICATION
        DATA HANDLING INSTRUCTION
        'STOP' CARD
```

Figure 4.33 - STCHEK - Input Example

```
---------1---------2---------3---------4---------5---------6---------7--
**STCHEKDEMO                            DEMONSTRATION FILE IS INPUT
ALL DATA                                NO CONDITIONS ARE SPECIFIED
END OF SUBSET SPECIFICATION             ALL ENTRIES ARE INCLUDED
55   7.5   -1.0                         PARAMETRIC TESTING SUPPRESSED
BACK                                    READ NEW SUBSET DEFINITION
DIFFICULT WORK                          TITLE OF NEW DATA BANK SUBSET
.IF.DIFF.GE.     6.                     6 = HARD   7 = VERY HARD
END OF SUBSET SPECIFICATION             ONLY HARD AND VERY HARD WORK
GO                                      DEFAULT VALUES USED
STOP                                    SYSTEM CLOSES DOWN
---------1---------2---------3---------4---------5---------6---------7--
```

Figure 4.34 - STCHEK - Output Structure

```
For each    ) : File Control Record
output file )   File Parameters
                Data Description
                For each) :  Subset Input Record
                Subset  )    For each         )  Number of Entries
                             Data Handling    )  <Limit Check>
                             Instruction      )  <Distribution Check)   >
                                                 For each ) : Frequency
                                                 Column   )   Tabulation
                                                 <Abnormality Check>    >
                                                 For each ) : Number
                                                 <Abnormal>)  <Abnormality>
                                                 Entry     )  <Listing>
```

Carated(<>) items are optional.

Figure 4.35 - STCHEK - Page-by-page output summary

Page	Contents	Origin
1-2	File Control Record	FIFI
	Program Title	STCHECK
	File Parameters	LDAP
	Data Description record	LDDS
3	Subset record	LSAMP
	Data Handling Instruction	LDHI
4	Limit Check	CHECK
5-13	Distribution Check	CHECK
14-35	Entry Listing	CHECK
36	Data Handling Instruction (BACK)	LDHI
37	Subset record	LSAMP
	Data Handling Instruction	LDHI
38	Limit Check	CHECK
39-47	Distribution Check	CHECK
48-51	Entry Listing	CHECK
52	Data Handling Instruction (STOP)	LDHI

Figure 4.36 - STCHEK - Input checks - First Run

```
DATA BANK SUBSET TITLE - ALL DATA                    COMMENT NO CONDITIONS ARE SPECIFIED
END OF SUBSET SPECIFICATION                          COMMENT ALL ENTRIES ARE INCLUDED
                                                     SYSTEM COMMENT - SUBSET WILL CONTAIN ALL ENTRIES

                        DATA HANDLING INSTRUCTION - ECHO PRINT

ABCCCDDDEEEEEEEFFFFFFFGGGGGGGGGGGGGGHHHHHHHHHHHHHHHHHHHHHHHHHHHHHHHHH
00   7.5  -1.0           XXXXXXXXXXXXXXXXPARAMETRIC TESTING SUPPRESSED

             CHECKING CONTROL INDEX =      0
MAXIMUM NUMBER OF NON-VALUES (MISSING) =   0     (ONLY COMPLETE ENTRIES)
MINIMUM PERCENTAGE OF ITEMS IN CLASS . =   7.5000
MAXIMUM NUMBER OF STD. DEVS. FROM A.M. = 99999.0000

      THE SYSTEM HAS STANDARDISED ONE CONTROL VALUE FROM THE DATA HANDLING INSTRUCTION         ** WARNING **

      PLEASE VERIFY THAT THE ASSUMPTIONS IT HAS MADE ARE CORRECT AND ADJUST STORAGE IF NECESSARY
```

Figure 4.37 - STCHEK - Distribution checks- First run

```
STATCAT SUBROUTINE CHECK      -    CHECKING OUTPUT STATCAT DATA BANK
OUTPUT DATA BANK TITLE        -    DEMONSTRATION STATCAT DATA BANK
DATA BANK SUBSET TITLE        -    ALL DATA

COLUMN  SHORT                      FULL TITLE                                      DATA TYPE
NUMBER  TITLE

   1    NTRY                       ENTRY NUMBER                                    DUMMY

--------------------------------------------------------------------------------------------

COLUMN  SHORT                      FULL TITLE                                      DATA TYPE
NUMBER  TITLE

   3    OBSR                       OBSERVER                                        NOMINAL

        OUT OF RANGE - TOO HIGH        0
   4    PETE                          16
   3    OSCR                          16
   2    NOEL                          16
   1    MIKE                          16
        OUT OF RANGE - TOO LOW         0

                VALUES (PRESENT)     64
                NON-VALUES (MISSING)  0

--------------------------------------------------------------------------------------------

COLUMN  SHORT                      FULL TITLE                                      DATA TYPE
NUMBER  TITLE

  10    DIFF                       ASSESSMENT OF DIFFICULTY BY OPERATOR            ORDINAL

        OUT OF RANGE - TOO HIGH        0
   7    VHAR                           4
   6    HARD                           7
   5    RHAR                          10
   4    NULL                          14
   3    REAS                          10
   2    EASY                          13
   1    VEAS                           6
        OUT OF RANGE - TOO LOW         0

                VALUES (PRESENT)     64
                NON-VALUES (MISSING)  0

--------------------------------------------------------------------------------------------

COLUMN  SHORT                      FULL TITLE                                      DATA TYPE
NUMBER  TITLE

  11    TEMP                       MEAN TEMPERATURE OF WORKING POSITION DURING TEST (CENT.) INTERVAL

  10    30.00 +OVER                    2
   9    28.63 TO  30.00                1
   8    27.25 TO  28.63                9
   7    25.88 TO  27.25               19
   6    24.50 TO  25.88                9
   5    23.13 TO  24.50               11
   4    21.75 TO  23.13               11
   3    20.38 TO  21.75                0         EMPTY
   2    19.00 TO  20.38                2
   1    UNDER     19.00                0         EMPTY

                VALUES (PRESENT)     64
                NON-VALUES (MISSING)  0

--------------------------------------------------------------------------------------------

COLUMN  SHORT                      FULL TITLE                                      DATA TYPE
NUMBER  TITLE

  18    FRRP                       PERCENTAGE OF ERRORS IN FINAL PRODUCTS          RATIO

  10    9.00 +OVER                     0         EMPTY
   9    8.00 TO   9.00                 0         EMPTY
   8    7.00 TO   8.00                 0         EMPTY
   7    6.00 TO   7.00                 2
   6    5.00 TO   6.00                 1
   5    4.00 TO   5.00                 0         EMPTY
   4    3.00 TO   4.00                 3
   3    2.00 TO   3.00                 5
   2    1.00 TO   2.00                17
   1    UNDER     1.00                36

                VALUES (PRESENT)     64
                NON-VALUES (MISSING)  0

--------------------------------------------------------------------------------------------
```

Figure 4.38 - STCHEK - Abnormality Checks - First Run

```
STATCAT SUBROUTINE CHECK        -   CHECKING OUTPUT STATCAT DATA BANK
OUTPUT DATA BANK TITLE          -   DEMONSTRATION STATCAT DATA BANK
DATA BANK SUBSET TITLE          -   ALL DATA

        LISTING OF ALL ENTRIES      - ABNORMAL MEANS -

        A - ANY ITEMS OUT OF RANGE 1 - 10 FOR NOMINAL/ORDINAL OR NON-POSITIVE FOR RATIO LEVELS (OUT)
        B - ANY ITEMS MORE THAN***** S.D. FROM MEAN (HIGH/LOW)
        C/D ANY ITEMS IN CLASSES CONTAINING FEWER THAN  4.9 ENTRIES (RARE)
        E - MORE THAN   0 MISSING ITEMS PER ENTRY (MISS)

ENTRY NUMBER    22 (   22 IN SUBSET)      ABNORMAL ITEM

COLUMN          1        2        3        4        5        6        7        8        9       10
TITLE         NTRY     SESS     OBSR     OPER     W.P.     STRS     DAY.     TIME     TASK     DIFF
DATA         22.00     6.00     3.00     3.00     2.00     3.00     2.00     2.00     3.00     4.00
QUERY          B)       A-

COLUMN         11       12       13       14       15       16       17       18
TITLE         TEMP     TPCT     EFOP     EFOB     H.R.     TCOM     TALL     ERRP
DATA         26.00    -8.71    51.94    71.58    49.87    46.56    51.00     0.90
QUERY                  RARE

ENTRY NUMBER    23 (   23 IN SUBSET)      ABNORMAL ITEM

COLUMN          1        2        3        4        5        6        7        8        9       10
TITLE         NTRY     SESS     OBSR     OPER     W.P.     STRS     DAY.     TIME     TASK     DIFF
DATA         23.00     6.00     4.00     1.00     3.00     2.00     2.00     2.00     1.00     1.00
QUERY          B)       A-

COLUMN         11       12       13       14       15       16       17       18
TITLE         TEMP     TPCT     EFOP     EFOB     H.R.     TCOM     TALL     ERRP
DATA         29.00     0.62    14.45    92.93    36.34    48.30    48.00     0.50
QUERY                  RARE

ENTRY NUMBER    24 (   24 IN SUBSET)    2 ABNORMAL ITEMS

COLUMN          1        2        3        4        5        6        7        8        9       10
TITLE         NTRY     SESS     OBSR     OPER     W.P.     STRS     DAY.     TIME     TASK     DIFF
DATA         24.00     6.00     2.00     4.00     4.00     2.00     2.00     2.00     4.00     7.00
QUERY          B).      A-                                                                     RARE

COLUMN         11       12       13       14       15       16       17       18
TITLE         TEMP     TPCT     EFOP     EFOB     H.R.     TCOM     TALL     ERRP
DATA         26.00   -12.50   114.18    70.42    65.42    63.00    72.00     0.50
QUERY                                                     RARE
```

Figure 4.39 - STCHEK - Limit check - Second Run

```
STATCAT SUBROUTINE CHECK        -       CHECKING OUTPUT STATCAT DATA BANK
OUTPUT DATA BANK TITLE          -       DEMONSTRATION STATCAT DATA BANK
DATA BANK SUBSET TITLE          -       DIFFICULT WORK

TOTAL NUMBER OF ENTRIES   -      64 OF WHICH    11 ARE CONTAINED IN SUBSET

   COLUMN    OBSERVED    OBSERVED            ARITHMETIC   STANDARD
   NO NAME   MINIMUM     MAXIMUM    VALUES      MEAN      DEVIATION
    1 NTRY                                                            DUMMY
    2 SESS                                                            DUMMY
    3 OBSR    1.0000      4.0000      11       2.4545       1.2136
    4 OPER    4.0000      4.0000      11       4.0000       0.0      CONSTANT
    5 V.P.    1.0000      4.0000      11       2.8182       1.1678
    6 STRS    1.0000      4.0000      11       2.7273       1.0091
    7 DAY.    1.0000      4.0000      11       2.5455       1.2136
    8 TIME    1.0000      4.0000      11       2.3636       1.2863
    9 TASK    1.0000      4.0000      11       2.9091       1.1362
   10 DIFF    6.0000      7.0000      11       6.3636       0.5045
   11 TEMP   22.0000     28.0000      11      24.9091       2.2117
   12 TPCT  -17.8300    -12.5000      11     -14.2264       1.7288
   13 EFDP   93.9700    116.3400      11     103.9517       9.4293
   14 EFOB   38.4000     89.1500      11      73.6908      13.6434
   15 H.R.   43.7500     65.4200      11      55.8254       5.7638
   16 TCOM   37.8000     63.0000      11      49.5818      10.7509
   17 TALL   46.0000     72.0000      11      57.6364      11.5003
   18 ERRP    0.1000      5.2000      11       1.1091       1.4563
```

```
C MASTER STCHEK - CHECKS INPUT STATCAT DATA BANK (NOT OUTPUT AS NORMAL)
C   SUBROUTINES AND FUNCTIONS REQUIRED
C  NAME            TYPE              COMMENT
C  AN      (SEE  3.1 )  SERVICE    ALPHA - TO NUMERIC VALUE
C  CHIKEN  (SEE 11.9 )  SERVICE    WARNS OF MISMATCHED DATA LEVEL
C  CHECK   (SEE  4.3 )  EXECUTIVE  CHECKS DATA BANK OR SUBSET
C  CLSAM   (SEE  3.5 )  SERVICE    ALLOTS ENTRY TO SAMPLE/SUBSET
C  COMPA   (SEE  3.1 )  SERVICE    COMPARES ALPHAMERIC VALUES
C  COPYA   (SEE  3.1 )  SERVICE    COPIES ALPHAMERIC VALUE
C  FIFI    (SEE  3.2 )  SYSTEM     ALLOCATES PERIPHERALS
C  IBL     (SEE  3.1 )  SERVICE    DETECTS BLANK,END AND STOP CARDS
C  ICH     (SEE  3.1 )  SERVICE    IDENTIFIES ALPHAMERIC CODES
C  LDAP    (SEE  3.3 )  SYSTEM     LOADS/CHECKS DATA BANK PARAMETERS
C  LDBS    (SEE  3.6 )  SYSTEM     LOADS SUBSET DEFINITION
C  LDDS    (SEE  3.4 )  SYSTEM     LOADS DATA DESCRIPTION SEGMENT
C  LDHI    (SEE  3.8 )  SYSTEM     LOADS/CHECKS DATA HANDLING INSTN
C  LSET    (SEE  3.5 )  SYSTEM     LOADS DEFINING CONDITIONS
C IF NQMAX = MAX. NO. OF DATA COLS IS CHANGED , CHANGE CN DATA STATEMENT
C DIMENSION D(NQMAX),DMAX(NQMAX),DMIN(NQMAX),IT(NQMAX),ST(NQMAX)
C DIMENSION CN(NQMAX)
      NQMAX = 100
      DIMENSION D(100),DMAX(100),DMIN(100),IT(100),ST(100),CN(100)
      DATA  CN/4HCOL1,4HCOL2,4HCOL3,4HCOL4,4HCOL5,4HCOL6,4HCOL7,4HCOL8,4
     1HCOL9,4HCL10,4HCL11,4HCL12,4HCL13,4HCL14,4HCL15,4HCL16,4HCL17,4HCL
     218,4HCL19,4HCL20,4HCL21,4HCL22,4HCL23,4HCL24,4HCL25,4HCL26,4HCL27,
     34HCL28,4HCL29,4HCL30,4HCL31,4HCL32,4HCL33,4HCL34,4HCL35,4HCL36,4HC
     4L37,4HCL38,4HCL39,4HCL40,4HCL41,4HCL42,4HCL43,4HCL44,4HCL45,4HCL46
     5,4HCL47,4HCL48,4HCL49,4HCL50,4HCL51,4HCL52,4HCL53,4HCL54,4HCL55,4H
     6CL56,4HCL57,4HCL58,4HCL59,4HCL60,4HCL61,4HCL62,4HCL63,4HCL64,4HCL6
     75,4HCL66,4HCL67,4HCL68,4HCL69,4HCL70,4HCL71,4HCL72,4HCL73,4HCL74,4
     8HCL75,4HCL76,4HCL77,4HCL78,4HCL79,4HCL80,4HCL81,4HCL82,4HCL83,4HCL
     984,4HCL85,4HCL86,4HCL87,4HCL88,4HCL89,4HCL90,4HCL91,4HCL92,4HCL93,
     94HCL94,4HCL95,4HCL96,4HCL97,4HCL98,4HCL99,4HC100/
C DIMENSION TRT(NALTMX),RT(NQMAX,NALTMX)= MAX NO OF CLASSES IN DATA BANK
C DIMENSION RT(NQMAX,NALTMX)
      NALTMX = 50
      DIMENSION  TRT(50),RT(100,50)
C DIMENSION SCON(5,MAXDBC)=MAXIMUM NUMBER OF SUBSET CONDITIONS
      MAXDBC = 50
      DIMENSION SCON(5,50)
C THE FOLLOWING DIMENSION IS FIXED
      DIMENSION FORM(50)
      COMMON /STCT/MED1,MED2,MED3,MED4,MED5,MED6,MED13,Q,V(20),TT(30)
      DATA PROG/4HCHEK/,BL/4H    /
      MED1 = -1
C SETTING UP * LEVEL 0
    1 CALL COPYA(TT(1),PROG)
      CALL FIFI
      CALL LDAP(MED2,MED3,V,TT,Q,NQ,NALT,NQMAX,NALTMX,IGO)
      IF(IGO.GT.0) GO TO 1
C USE LDDS TO FIND COLUMN NAMES AND LEVELS IN ORIGINAL DATA BANK
      LI = 18
      CALL LDDS(TRT,NALT,D,NQ,ST,NQ,IT,NQ,H,0,H,H,0,LI,0,Q,VX,
     1 0,MED2,MED3,0,IGO)
C LEVEL 2 - READ DATA BANK SUBSET SPECIFICATION
   21 IF(V(10).GE.20.) V(10) = 0.
      CALL LDBS(SCON,NCON,MAXDBC,CN,ST,IT,NQ,TRT,NALT,IGO)
      IF(IGO.GT.0) GO TO 1
C LEVEL 9 - LOAD DATA HANDLING INSTRUCTION
   91 IF(V(10).GT.90.) V(10) = 0.
      CALL LDHI(V(1),0,V(2),3,V(9),7,APT,15,ASDL,18,2,0,Z,V(10),
     1FORM(41),FORM,MED1,MED2,0,Q,NQ,NWARN,1,IGO)
      IF(IGO.GT.0) GO TO 21
```

```
C STANDARDISATION
      IF(V(9).LT.0.) NWARN = NWARN + 1
      IF(V(9).LT.0.) V(9) = NQ
      IF(ASDL.LE.0.) NWARN = NWARN + 1
      IF(ASDL.EQ.0.) ASDL = 5.
      IF(ASDL.LT.0.) ASDL = 99999.
      IF(APT.LE.0.) NWARN = NWARN + 1
      IF(APT.EQ.0.) APT = 1.
      IF(APT.LT.0.) APT = 0.
      CALL LDHI(V(1),0,V(2),3,V(9),7,APT,15,ASDL,18,2,0,Z,V(10),
     1FORM(41),FORM,MED1,MED2,0,Q,NQ,NWARN,2,IGO)
      IF(IGO.GT.0) GO TO 91
      MED4 = MED3
      CALL CHECK (D,DMAX,DMIN,RT,IT,TRT,NQ,NALT,ASDL,APT,SCON,NCON,ST)
      V(10) = 0.
      WRITE(MED6,999)
      GO TO 91
  901 FORMAT (1H1,20X,33HSTATCAT CHECKING DATA BANK SUBSET/)
  999 FORMAT (36H1CHECKING COMPLETED - READ NEW INPUT)
      END


      SUBROUTINE CHECK (D,DMAX,DMIN,RT,IT,TRT,NQ,NALT,ASDL,APT,SCON,NCON
     1,ST)
C CHECK  (SEE  4.3 ) EXECUTIVE   CHECKS DATA BANK OR SUBSET
C NOP = V(2)                                       IT = DATA LEVEL
C - = NO OUTPUT                                       -
C 0 = TEST TO NO OF MISSING LIST ALL ENTRIES          -
C 1 = TEST TO NO OF MISSING LIST ABNORMAL ENTRIES  DUMMY
C 2 = TEST TO RARE INT/RAT   LIST ABNORMAL ENTRIES NOMINAL
C 3 = TEST TO RARE NOM/ORD   LIST ABNORMAL ENTRIES ORDINAL
C 4 = TEST EXTREME DEVN      LIST ABNORMAL ENTRIES INTERVAL
C 5 = TEST OUT-OF-RANGE      LIST ABNORMAL ENTRIES RATIO
C 6 = LIMIT + DISTN CHECK    NO LIST               FIXED INTERVAL
C 7 = LIMIT CHECK ONLY       NO LIST               FIXED RATIO
C 8 = ENTRIES IN SUBSET      NO LIST               NOT USED
C 9 = NOT USED                                     NOT USED
      DIMENSION D(NQ),DMAX(NQ),DMIN(NQ),IT(NQ),RT(NQ,NALT),TRT(NALT)
      DIMENSION SCON(5,NCON),ST(NQ),TTC(18)
      COMMON /STCT/MED1,MED2,MED3,MED4,MED5,MED6,MED13,Q,V(20),TT(30)
      DATA HI/4HHIGH/,BE/4HLOW /,RA/4HRARE/
      DATA BL/4H    /,XIS/4HMISS/,OUT/4H OUT/
      NOP = V(2)
      IF(NOP.LT.0.OR.NOP.GT.8) RETURN
      NINS = 0
      NSUB = 0
      REWIND MED4
      READ(MED4) NQ,NALT,Q,(TT(J),J = 1,16)
      WRITE(MED2,901) (TT(J),J=1,10)
      IF(NCON.GT.0) WRITE(MED2,902) (TT(J),J=21,30)
      ALT = NALT
      DO 1 I=1,NQ
      READ(MED4)ST(I),TTC,TRT,IT(I),X,X
      IF(NOP.EQ.8) GO TO 1
      DMIN(I) = Q
      DMAX(I) = Q
      IF(NOP.EQ.7) GO TO 1
      DO 1 J=1,NALT
      RT(I,J) = 0.
    1 CONTINUE
C MAXIMA,MINIMA MEAN AND S.D. IF REQUIRED
    9 READ(MED4) D
      DO 10 I=1,NQ
```

```
      IF(D(I).NE.Q) GO TO 11
   10 CONTINUE
      GO TO 12
   11 NSUB = NSUB + 1
      CALL CLSAM (D,NQ,SCON,NCON,NIN,1)
      IF(NIN.EQ.0) GO TO 9
      NINS = NINS + 1
      IF(NOP.EQ.8) GO TO 9
      DO 2 I=1,NQ
      IF (IT(I).LE.1) GO TO 2
      IF(D(I).EQ.Q ) GO TO 2
      IF(DMAX(I).EQ.Q)  DMAX(I) = D(I)
      IF(D(I).GT.DMAX(I))  DMAX(I) = D(I)
      IF(DMIN(I).EQ.Q)       DMIN(I) = D(I)
      IF(D(I).LT.DMIN(I))    DMIN(I) = D(I)
      IF(NOP.EQ.7) GO TO 2
      RT(I,1)=RT(I,1)+1.
      RT(I,2)=RT(I,2)+D(I)
      RT(I,3)=RT(I,3)+D(I)*D(I)
    2 CONTINUE
      GO TO 9
C NUMBER OF  ENTRIES IN SAMPLE COMPARED WITH COMPLETE TAPE
   12 WRITE(MED2,993) NSUB,NINS
      IF(NINS.EQ.0) WRITE(MED2,903)
      REWIND MED4
      IF(NOP.EQ.8.OR.NINS.LE.0) RETURN
C PRINT MINIMUM,MAXIMUM,MEAN,S.D.
      NLIN = 60
      DO 16 I = 1,NQ
      NLIN = NLIN + 1
      IF(NLIN.LE.50) GO TO 14
      IF(NLIN.LT.60) WRITE(MED2,901) (TT(J),J=1,10)
      IF(NLIN.LT.60.AND.NCON.GT.0) WRITE(MED2,902) (TT(J),J=21,30)
      IF(NOP.GT.6) WRITE(MED2,917)
      IF(NOP.LE.6) WRITE(MED2,917) BL
      IF(NOP.GT.6) WRITE(MED2,918)
      IF(NOP.LE.6) WRITE(MED2,918) BL
      NLIN = 10
   14 IF(IT(I).EQ.1) WRITE(MED2,910) I,ST(I)
      IF(IT(I).EQ.1) GO TO 16
      WRITE(MED2,911) I,ST(I),DMIN(I),DMAX(I)
      IF(DMIN(I).EQ.DMAX(I).AND.DMIN(I).NE.Q) WRITE(MED2,912)
      IF(DMIN(I).EQ.DMAX(I).AND.DMIN(I).EQ.Q) WRITE(MED2,913)
      IF(DMIN(I).EQ.DMAX(I)) GO TO 15
      IF(DMIN(I).LE.0.0.AND.IT(I).NE.4.AND.IT(I).NE.6) WRITE(MED2,914)
      IF(DMIN(I).GT.ALT.AND.IT(I).GT.1.AND.IT(I).LT.4) WRITE(MED2,915)
   15 IF(NOP.GT.6) GO TO 16
      IF(RT(I,1).LT.1.5)  RT(I,3) = 0.
      IF(RT(I,1).GT.1.5)  RT(I,2) = RT(I,2)/RT(I,1)
      IF(RT(I,1).GT.1.5)  RT(I,3) =
    1 SQRT(ABS(RT(I,3)-RT(I,2)*RT(I,2)*RT(I,1))/(RT(I,1)-1.))
      K=RT(I,1)
      IF(K.LT.1) WRITE(MED2,916) K
      IF(K.EQ.1) WRITE(MED2,916) K,RT(I,2)
      IF(K.GT.1) WRITE(MED2,916) K,RT(I,2),RT(I,3)
   16 CONTINUE
      IF(NOP.GE.7) GO TO 60
C COLLECT FREQUENCY TABLE DATA - SET UP CLASS LIMITS
      READ(MED4) NX,MX,(X,I=1,17)
      DO 17 I = 1,NQ
      READ(MED4) X,TTC,TRT,NX,DMINX,DMAXX
      IF(NX.LE.3) DMIN(I) = 0.
      IF(NX.LE.3) DMAX(I) = 0.
```

```
      IF(NX.GE.6)DMIN(I) = DMINX
      IF(NX.GE.6)DMAX(I) = DMAXX
      IF(NX.GE.4.AND.DMAX(I).EQ.DMIN(I))DMAX(I) = DMIN(I)+ALT-2.
      IF(NX.EQ.4.OR.NX.EQ.5)CALL CLIMS(DMIN(I),DMAX(I),NALT)
      DO 17 J = 1,NALT
   17 RT(I,J) = 0.
C COLLECT FREQUENCY TABLE DATA - COLLECT DATA
      DO 20 K = 1,NINS
   18 READ(MED4) D
      CALL CLSAM(D,NQ,SCON,NCON,NIN,1)
      IF(NIN.NE.1) GO TO 18
      DO 19 I = 1,NQ
      ITX = IT(I)
      DX = D(I)
      IF(ITX.EQ.1.OR.DX.EQ.Q) GO TO 19
      IF(ITX.LE.3.AND.DX.LT.1.) DMIN(I) = DMIN(I) + 1.
      IF(ITX.LE.3.AND.DX.LT.1.) GO TO 19
      IF(ITX.LE.3.AND.DX.GT.ALT)DMAX(I) = DMAX(I) + 1.
      IF(ITX.LE.3.AND.DX.GT.ALT)GO TO 19
      IF(ITX.LE.3) N = DX
      IF(ITX.GE.4)N = (DX-DMIN(I))/(DMAX(I)-DMIN(I))*(ALT-2.) + 2.
      IF(N.LT.1) N = 1
      IF(N.GT.NALT) N = NALT
      RT(I,N) = RT(I,N) + 1.
   19 CONTINUE
   20 CONTINUE
      REWIND MED4
C OUTPUT FREQUENCY TABLE - FIND LINES REQUIRED
      READ(MED4)NX,NX,(X,I=1,17)
      NLIN = 50
      DO 27 I = 1,NQ
      READ(MED4)X,TTC,TRT,NX,DMINX,DMAXX
      IF(NX.LE.1) NPS = 7
      IF(NX.GE.4) NPS = NALT + 11
      IF(NX.LE.1.OR.NX.GE.4) GO TO 22
      NPS = 0
      DO 21 J = 1,NALT
      CALL COMPA(TRT(J),BL,L)
   21 IF(L.NE.1.OR.RT(I,J).GT.0.5) NPS = J
      NPS = NPS + 13
   22 NLIN = NLIN + NPS
      IF(NLIN.LT.50) GO TO 23
C PRINT HEADER IF NO ROOM ON CURRENT PAGE
      WRITE(MED2,901) (TT(J),J=1,10)
      IF(NCON.GT.0) WRITE(MED2,902) (TT(J),J=21,30)
      NLIN = NPS + 2
C PRINT COLUMN TITLE,(OVER),TABLE,(UNDER),NON-VALUES
   23 WRITE(MED2,981)I,ST(I),TTC
      IF(NX.LE.1) GO TO 27
      NSUB = 0
      K = DMAX(I)
      IF(NX.LE.3) NSUB = K
      IF(NX.LE.3)WRITE(MED2,982) HI,K
      NMAX = NALT
      IF(NX.GT.1.AND.NX.LT.4.AND.NPS-13.LT.NALT) NMAX = NPS-13
      DO 25 JJ = 1,NMAX
      J = NMAX+1-JJ
      K = RT(I,J)
      NSUB = NSUB + K
      WRITE(MED2,983) K
      IF(K.EQ.0) WRITE(MED2,913)
      IF(NX.GE.4.AND.NX.LE.5) DMAXX = DMAX(I)
      IF(NX.GE.4.AND.NX.LE.5) DMINX = DMIN(I)
```

```
   25 CALL PRTCLS(DMAXX,DMINX,J,TRT(J),NALT,NX,MED2)
      K = DMIN(I)
      IF(NX.LE.3)WRITE(MED2,982) BE,K
      IF(NX.LE.3) NSUB = NSUB + K
      K = NINS - NSUB
      WRITE(MED2,984) NSUB
      WRITE(MED2,985) K
      IF(NX.LE.3) GO TO 27
      CI = (DMAX(I)-DMIN(I))/(ALT-2.)
      S = 0.
      SX = 0.
      SXX = 0.
      DO 26 J = 1,NALT
      X = J
      X = DMIN(I)+CI*(X-1.5)
      S = S + RT(I,J)
      SX = SX + RT(I,J)*X
   26 SXX = SXX + RT(I,J)*X*X
      IF(S.LT.0.5) SX = 0.
      IF(S.GT.0.5) SX = SX/S
      IF(S.LT.1.5) SXX = 0.
      IF(S.GT.1.5)SXX=SQRT(ABS(SXX-SX*S*SX)/(S-1.))*ASDL
      IF(SXX.LT.CI) SXX = 999.*CI
      RT(I,1) = SX - SXX
      RT(I,NALT) = SX + SXX
   27 WRITE(MED2,990)
      IF(NOP.GE.6) GO TO 60
C CHECK FOR ABNORMAL ITEMS
      X = NINS
      PT = APT*X*0.01
      IF(PT.LT.1.5) PT=1.5
      NLIN=50
      NPS=(NQ + 9)/10*5 + 2
      NSUB = 0
      MXMIS = V(9)
      DO 50 KIN = 1,NINS
   28 READ(MED4) D
      NSUB = NSUB + 1
      CALL CLSAM(D,NQ,SCON,NCON,NIN,1)
      IF(NIN.NE.1) GO TO 28
      L=0
      NMIS = 0
      DO 35 I = I,NQ
      ITX = IT(I)
      DX = D(I)
C COUNT NON-VALUES
      IF(DX.EQ.Q) NMIS = NMIS + 1
      IF(ITX.LE.1.OR.DX.EQ.Q) GO TO 35
C COUNT OUT-OF-RANGE ITEMS
      IF(ITX.LE.3.AND.DX.GT.ALT) L = L + 1
      IF(ITX.LE.3.AND.DX.GT.ALT) GO TO 35
      IF(ITX.NE.4.AND.ITX.NE.6.AND.DX.LE.0.) L = L + 1
      IF(ITX.NE.4.AND.ITX.NE.6.AND.DX.LE.0.) GO TO 35
      IF(ITX.LE.3) N = D(I)
      IF(ITX.LE.3) GO TO 33
      IF(NOP.EQ.5) GO TO 35
C COUNT EXTREME VALUES OF PARAMETRIC LEVELS
      IF(DX.GT.RT(I,NALT).OR.DX.LT.RT(I,1)) L = L + 1
      IF(DX.GT.RT(I,NALT).OR.DX.LT.RT(I,1)) GO TO 35
      N =(D(I)-DMIN(I))/(DMAX(I)-DMIN(I))*(ALT-2.) + 2.
      IF(N.EQ.1.OR.N.EQ.NALT) GO TO 35
   33 IF(N.LT.1.OR.N.GT.NALT) GO TO 35
      IF(NOP.EQ.4.OR.ITX.GT.3.AND.NOP.EQ.3)GO TO 35
```

```
C COUNT RARE VALUES
      IF(RT(I,N).LT.PT) L = L + 1
   35 CONTINUE
      IF(L.EQ.0.AND.NMIS.LE.MXMIS.AND.NOP.NE.0)GO TO 50
      NLIN= NLIN + NPS
      IF(NLIN.LE.50)GO TO 41
C PAGE HEADER
      WRITE(MED2,901) (TT(J),J=1,10)
      IF(NCON.GT.0) WRITE(MED2,902) (TT(J),J=21,30)
      IF(NOP.EQ.0)  WRITE(MED2,930)
      IF(NOP.GT.0)  WRITE(MED2,931)
      IF(NOP.LE.5)  WRITE(MED2,932) NALT
      IF(NOP.LE.4)  WRITE(MED2,933) ASDL
      IF(NOP.LE.3)  WRITE(MED2,934) PT
      IF(NOP.EQ.3)  WRITE(MED2,935)
      IF(NOP.LT.3)  WRITE(MED2,936)
      IF(NOP.LE.1)  WRITE(MED2,937) MXMIS
      NLIN=NPS + 6
   41 WRITE(MED2,920) NSUB,KIN
      IF(L.GT.1) WRITE(MED2,921) L
      IF(L.GE.1) WRITE(MED2,922)
      IF(NMIS.GT.1) WRITE(MED2,923) NMIS
      IF(NMIS.GE.1) WRITE(MED2,924)
      DO 49 II = 1,NQ,10
      JJ = II + 9
      IF(JJ.GT.NQ) JJ = NQ
      KK = JJ + 1 - II
      DO 45 I = II,JJ
      K = I + 1 - II
      ITX = IT(I)
      DX = D(I)
C MARK NON-VALUES AND ALPHA VALUES FOR DUMMIES
      IF(ITX.LE.1) TTC(K) = DX
      IF(DX.EQ.Q)  CALL COPYA(TTC(K),XIS)
      IF(ITX.LE.1.OR.DX.EQ.Q) GO TO 45
C MARK OUT-OF-RANGE ITEMS
      IF(ITX.LE.3.AND.DX.GT.ALT) CALL COPYA(TTC(K),OUT)
      IF(ITX.LE.3.AND.DX.GT.ALT) GO TO 45
      IF(ITX.NE.4.AND.ITX.NE.6.AND.DX.LE.0.) CALL COPYA(TTC(K),OUT)
      IF(ITX.NE.4.AND.ITX.NE.6.AND.DX.LE.0.) GO TO 45
      CALL COPYA(TTC(K),BL)
      IF(ITX.LE.3) N = D(I)
      IF(ITX.LE.3) GO TO 43
      IF(NOP.EQ.5) GO TO 45
C MARK EXTREME VALUES OF PARAMETRIC LEVELS
      IF(DX.GT.RT(I,NALT)) CALL COPYA(TTC(K),HI)
      IF(DX.LT.RT(I,1)) CALL COPYA(TTC(K),BE)
      IF(DX.GT.RT(I,NALT).OR.DX.LT.RT(I,1).OR.NOP.EQ.4) GO TO 45
      N =(D(I)-DMIN(I))/(DMAX(I)-DMIN(I))*(ALT-2.) + 2.
      IF(N.EQ.1.OR.N.EQ.NALT) GO TO 45
   43 IF(N.LT.1.OR.N.GT.NALT) GO TO 45
C MARK RARE VALUES
      IF(RT(I,N).LT.PT.AND.NOP.LE.2) CALL COPYA(TTC(K),RA)
      IF(NOP.EQ.3.AND.ITX.LE.3.AND.RT(I,N).LT.PT) CALL COPYA(TTC(K),RA)
   45 CONTINUE
      WRITE(MED2,996) (I,I=II,JJ)
      WRITE(MED2,989) (ST(I),I=II,JJ)
      WRITE(MED2,998) (D(I),I=II,JJ)
      WRITE(MED2,997) (TTC(I),I=1,KK)
   49 CONTINUE
   50 CONTINUE
   60 REWIND MED4
      RETURN
```

```
  901 FORMAT(25H1STATCAT SUBROUTINE CHECK,5X,1H-,4X,33HCHECKING OUTPUT S
     1TATCAT DATA BANK/23H OUTPUT DATA BANK TITLE,7X,1H-,4X,10A4)
  902 FORMAT(23H DATA BANK SUBSET TITLE,7X,1H-,4X,10A4)
  903 FORMAT(1H0,10X,12HNO ENTRIES    )
  910 FORMAT(I4,1X,A4,53X,5HDUMMY)
  911 FORMAT(I4,1X,A4,2F12.4)
  912 FORMAT(1H+,61X,8HCONSTANT)
  913 FORMAT(1H+,61X,5HEMPTY)
  914 FORMAT(1H+,61X,19HMINIMUM BELOW RANGE)
  915 FORMAT(1H+,81X,19HMAXIMUM ABOVE RANGE)
  916 FORMAT(1H+,32X,I6,F12.4,F10.4)
  917 FORMAT(7H0COLUMN,2(4X,8HOBSERVED),A4,5X,20HARITHMETIC   STANDARD)
  918 FORMAT(30H  NO NAME  MINIMUM       MAXIMUM,A3,28HVALUES      MEAN
     1DEVIATION)
  920 FORMAT(13H0ENTRY NUMBER,I6,2H (,I6,11H IN SUBSET))
  921 FORMAT(1H+,37X,I6,14X,1HS)
  922 FORMAT(1H+,44X,13HABNORMAL ITEM)
  923 FORMAT(1H+,58X,I6,13X,1HS)
  924 FORMAT(1H+,65X,12HMISSING ITEM)
  930 FORMAT(1H0,10X,46HLISTING OF ALL ENTRIES         - ABNORMAL MEANS -/)
  931 FORMAT(1H0,10X,46HLISTING OF ABNORMAL ENTRIES - ABNORMAL MEANS -/)
  932 FORMAT(11X,30HA - ANY ITEMS OUT OF RANGE 1 -,I4,59H FOR NOMINAL/OR
     1DINAL OR NON-POSITIVE FOR RATIO LEVELS (OUT) )
  933 FORMAT(11X,23HB - ANY ITEMS MORE THAN,F6.2,26H S.D. FROM MEAN (HIG
     1H/LOW) )
  934 FORMAT(11X,46HC    ANY ITEMS IN CLASSES CONTAINING FEWER THAN,F5.1,
     115H ENTRIES (RARE) )
  935 FORMAT(1H+,70X,29H(NOMINAL/ORDINAL LEVELS ONLY) )
  936 FORMAT(1H+,11X,2H/D)
  937 FORMAT(11X,13HE - MORE THAN,I4,31H MISSING ITEMS PER ENTRY (MISS))
  980 FORMAT (1H1)
  981 FORMAT (13H0COLUMN SHORT,20X,10HFULL TITLE,42X,9HDATA TYPE/
     113H NUMBER TITLE/1H0,I4,4X,A4,10X,A2,17A4/)
  982 FORMAT(7X,19HOUT OF RANGE - TOO ,A4,I6)
  983 FORMAT(30X,I6)
  984 FORMAT(1H0,13X,16HVALUES (PRESENT),I6)
  985 FORMAT(10X,20HNON-VALUES (MISSING),I6)
  989 FORMAT  (6H TITLE,10(6X,A4))
  990 FORMAT(1H0,23(4H----))
  992 FORMAT(1H+,75X,45HCONSTANT - CORRELATION IMPOSSIBLE **WARNING**)
  993 FORMAT(28H0TOTAL NUMBER OF ENTRIES   - ,I6,10H OF WHICH ,I6,24H ARE
     1 CONTAINED IN SUBSET)
  994 FORMAT (1H0,20X,26HOBSERVED MINIMA AND MAXIMA/)
  995 FORMAT(11X,6HCOLUMN,I4,13H SHORT TITLE ,A4,2F15.4)
  996 FORMAT (7H0COLUMN,10(5X,I4,1X))
  997 FORMAT (6H QUERY,10(6X,A4))
  998 FORMAT (6H DATA ,10F10.2)
 1000 FORMAT (1H0,I6,2X,A2,16A4,17H - DATA SCALE IS ,2A4)
      END
```

4.4 PROGRAM STCORR - CORRECT STATCAT DATA BANK

4.4.1 Purpose

This program produces revised STATCAT data banks, derived from existing STATCAT data banks by the omission of groups of entries, or of specific entries, by the revision of entries or by the addition of entries within or at the end of the existing STATCAT data bank. It may also be used to modify the data starter or the data description segment.

Figure 4.41a contains system flow-charts for the main program STCORR and for a different version of the input subroutine DATA. Figure 4.41b is a simplified flow-chart for the executive subroutine CRECT, which reconstructs the data description segment, data storage segment and data terminator for the revised STATCAT data bank. (The complexity of this flow-chart reflects the difficulty in designing genuinely flexible programs.) (This program does not employ the stepped input process described in 3.9 in the same way and for the same reasons that STLOAD(4.2) does not.)

4.4.2 Input Data

Item	Level	Format	Function	See
1	0	A	File control (Input and Output)	3.2
2	0	E	Subset specification	3.6
3	0	B	Data starter	Below + 3.3
4	1	C	Data column description	Below + 3.4
5	1	-	Correction Card	Below
6	1	-	Entry (if required)	Below

Card Layout - Data Starter - STCORR

ABCCCDDDEEEEEEEEF..COLS 17-56..FG..COLS 57-72..GHHHHIIII

Columns	Item	Function	See
1	A	Correction Record control Index	Below
2	B	Data checking control index	4.3
3 - 5	C	Revised number of data columns	Below
6 - 8	D	Revised number of classes	Below
9 - 16	E	Revised 'non-value'	Below
17 - 56	F	Revised title of STATCAT data bank	Below
57 - 72	G	Not defined (used for auxiliary security key)	-
73 - 76	H	Revised security key	Below
77 - 80	I	Revised data bank name	Below

A - Correction Record Control Index

This index controls the amount of information output as the entries are corrected. Depending on the size of the data bank, the user may wish to keep a detailed record of all actions, of corrections only, or of uncorrected records only.

ALTERNATIVES

A = 0 ; Disposal of all entries recorded -
all transferred entries listed

A = 1 ; Numbers of entries deleted, corrected or added listed -
all transferred entries listed

A = 2   ; Numbers of entries retained, corrected or added listed -
           all transferred entries listed

A = 3   ; Numbers of entries corrected or added listed -
           all transferred entries listed

A = 4   ; All transferred entries listed.

A = 5   ; Disposal of all entries recorded.

A = 6   ; Numbers of entries deleted, corrected or added listed.

A = 7   ; Numbers of entries corrected or added listed.

A = 8 - 9 ; No output during correction phase.

DEFAULT Value. A = 0, blank or any non-numeric codes - disposal of entries and transferred entries printed in full.

C - Revised Number of Data Columns.

This value specifies the number of data columns in the STATCAT data bank to be constructed.

DEFAULT value (C= blank, zero, or non-numeric characters) The original value is retained.

D - Revised number of Alternative Classes

This value specifies the number of alternative classes that will be found in any column of the STATCAT data bank.

DEFAULT value (D= blank, zero, or non-numeric characters) The original value is retained.

E - Revised 'non-value'

This is the numerical value to be used wherever the datum does not exist. It should be chosen as a value which will not be found in the data 'in its own right' so to speak. This number will replace the original 'non-value' wherever it is encountered in entries copied from the original STATCAT data bank (but not in entries read in at this time)

DEFAULT value (D= blank, zero, or non-numeric characters and the revised STATCAT data bank title blank) The original value is retained.

F - Revised Title of STATCAT Data Bank

This string of ten four-character words is the plain-language title given to the STATCAT data bank to be constructed.

DEFAULT value (F is blank throughout) The original title is retained.

G - Revised STATCAT Data Bank Key

If blank, is not replaced by the original, but remains blank.

H - Revised STATCAT Data Bank Name

If this field is blank, the STATCAT data bank being constructed will be inaccessible to any other program - as in the example, where a deliberately faulty output STATCAT data bank is constructed. By giving it a blank name this faulty data bank is isolated from the system, and cannot be accessed by accident when working with other programs.

4 - Revised Data Column Descriptions

If any data column descriptions are to be corrected, or if any data columns are added, the data column description, consisting of the data column title card, and the necessary complementary information must be supplied. The number of class names for NOMINAL or ORDINAL data levels must correspond to the number of alternative columns in the revised STATCAT data bank. The data column descriptions must be supplied in ascending numerical order, with any additional data column descriptions added at the end of the sequence. The sequence must terminate with an END card. If no data descriptions are changed, the END card alone is required. Where the number of classes is changed, the additional class names for unmodified data column descriptions are set to blanks, or the highest-numbered classes deleted. The lower class limit and class interval are maintained.

5 - Correction Card

Each correction of the data storage segment, except for the omission of entries not in the subset specified, is indicated by a correction card. These cards must be in increasing numerical order of entry number. They indicate the type of correction to be carried out and the point at which it is to be applied. Corrections introduced out of order will produce an error message and will not be applied.

Card Layout - Correction Card - STCORR

AAAAAABBBBBBBBBBBBBBBBBBBBBBBBBBBBBBBBBBBB

Columns on card	Item code	FORTRAN Type	Function
1 - 6	A	A	Correction Code
7 - 40	B	I	Original STATCAT entry number

A - Correction Code

   Four possible correction codes are available : -

DELETE - The entry B is deleted.

REVISE - The entry B is deleted, and replaced by an entry read by the subroutine DATA immediately following the correction card.

FOLLOW - The entry B is read from the original and written to the output STATCAT data bank, provided that it has not already been deleted, revised or otherwise transferred. A new entry is read by the subroutine DATA and written immediately after the entry B. Several entries may be inserted in this way, but each must be preceded by a FOLLOW correction card.

FINISH - All the remaining entries on the original STATCAT data bank contained in the subset are transferred to the output STATCAT data bank. After the last of these has been written, entries are read by the subroutine DATA until it returns to the executive subroutine with a null entry.

   In addition to these four correction cards, an END or STOP card will be recognised. This card will cause all remaining entries in the subset to be transferred to the output STATCAT data bank, without reading any more correction cards, and a data terminator placed after them.

A FINISH card is used where more entries are to be added to the data bank, and must be followed by at least a null entry from the DATA subroutine. An END or STOP card needs no further input. Non-values read by the subroutine DATA should be those for the output STATCAT data bank. Any non-values read from the input STATCAT data bank will be changed automatically by the system.

B - Number of Entry

This is the number of the entry referred to in the original STATCAT data bank. It may be placed anywhere between columns 7 to 40. Entry numbers should be in ascending numerical order, although several FOLLOW cards may have the same number. FINISH, END and STOP cards need not have an entry number.

6 - Entries

One complete entry must follow each REVISE or FOLLOW card. A FINISH card may be followed by as many complete entries as are required to be added to the output STATCAT data bank following the original entries. These entries will be read in using the subroutine DATA. Usually, it is convenient to use the same version of DATA as was used to load the original STATCAT data bank. If another subroutine is used, the user must take great care to ensure that it is compatible with the existing data.

The system will convert the original non-values to the revised non-value for all entries taken from the original STATCAT data bank, but the entries read by the subroutine DATA must use the revised non-value. If the number of data in an entry has been decreased, the system will delete the later data in each entry. If the number of data has been increased, the copied entries will be made up with non-values.

For interest's sake, a different DATA subroutine has been used here. This version uses a 'run-time format' and is described in 4.4.5. following.

4.4.3   Input Example

Figure 4.42 is a summary of the input data for two runs of STCORR. The first run produces a data bank containing a number of deliberate errors to demonstrate the detection of abnormalities in individual entries - and to demonstrate the construction of a STATCAT data bank with a blank name - inaccessible to any other program. (It seemed more considerate to construct a fault-free STATCAT data bank as an example in 4.2 (STLOAD) and add the errors afterwards, rather than impose the details of error-correction on all users at first sight.) The second run demonstrates a specialised use of STCORR to produce a copy of an existing STATCAT data bank.

Figure 4.43 lists the input data for these two runs of STCORR. The user may be interested to scan Figure 4.43 to detect three obvious errors in the "revised" input entries at this point.

4.4.4 Output Example

Figure 4.44 is a summary of the output structure corresponding to the input structure of 4.42. Figure 4.45 is a page-by-page summary of the output corresponding to the specific example given in 4.4.3. Because of the quantity of output generated, only a portion can be displayed here. The output begins with the input STATCAT data bank header and listing of the data description segment, provided by most programs as an aide-memoire and checking aid. This is followed by the subset record, then (Figure 4.46) by the original and revised (input and output) data starters with their file names (but not, of course, their security keys, which are never printed.) The values of the control indices are printed, with a warning where they have been standardised, and an acceptance/rejection message. (If the system rejects the job, it will attempt to read through the redundant information to reach the next job, but may well become confused on the way.)

This page continues with the revised data description segment, similar in layout to that produced when the original was loaded by STLOAD. Note that because the number of classes has been reduced from ten to eight the range of data column eleven has been reduced, while the class interval has been maintained. The data description for data column eighteen has been re-loaded, giving zero for the lower class limit and class interval. This causes the system to derive class interval and limits from the data bank subset selected for analysis. This may be justifiable where there is genuinely no way of knowing what range of data is likely to be encountered, but it requires at least one extra run through the data storage for any analysis, and is therefore not recommended. Data column nineteen, which has been added to the data bank to illustrate the addition of a data column, is simply a fake, and is titled accordingly.

After the completion of the revised data description segment, the revised data storage segment is printed out (Figure 4.47). In the interests of brevity, the entries loaded to the tape have not been listed. Note that the system is counting both the original and revised entry numbers. This often provides a useful check that the program is operating as required.

Immediately the file has been completed, the subroutine CHECK carries out standard checks of the output STATCAT data bank. These checks are the same as those given in 4.3. Figure 4.48 contains only the more interesting of these. The range check picks up the point that data column 19 is a constant zero. Note that only ten readings are present in this column - corresponding to the ten readings drawn from cards. All the entries transferred from the original data bank have a non-value in this column.

Finally, the abnormality check lists the first 56 entries, mostly because they contain a non-value. It also picks up two entries (5 and 18 in the revised STATCAT data bank containing abnormal items (Figure 4.48). In entry 5, the percentage of errors is given as 33 percent, some seven and a half standard deviations from the mean. A check with the corresponding line of Figure 4.23 suggests that this should be 3 - an accidental double strike being a common card-punching error. In entry 18, data column eighteen has a negative value, which is impossible for a datum on a RATIO level - a negative percentage of errors is meaningless. The system detects this only because it was told that the datum was on a RATIO scale - had it been classified as INTERVAL, no comment would have been made, since it is within five standard deviations of the mean. Examination of the original data suggests that the negative sign is a simple mistake. In the same entry, the code digit stored for Stress, in data column six, is zero. On examining the card, we find a blank in the appropriate cell, where the original card had a 3. If we were using the original 'free-form' input subroutine DATA, this would cause all the remaining data to be displaced one field forward and the next card to be read to fill the last cell of this entry, leaving one entry garbled, and one complete entry lost.

Because this is only an illustration, we can now delete the 'revised' output file, and continue to work on the original file 'DEMO'. In a normal working sequence, we would re-run STCORR with 'DUFF' as input to correct the errors in entries 5 and 18.

Figure 4.49 gives the start and end of the output for the second run of STCORR, in which a straightforward copy has been made of the original demonstration STATCAT data bank.

4.4.5 Subroutine DATA - Run-time Format

The version of the input subroutine DATA provided with this program uses a 'run-time format'. This is read on the first occasion that the subroutine is called, and determines how subsequent cards will be read.

(The way in which a format is specified in FORTRAN IV is defined in the ASA FORTRAN IV standard, and explained in all textbooks on FORTRAN programming. Many installations offer extra facilities, and some may lack some of the standard ones, so that an explanation at this point might be either redundant or misleading. The user is advised to check with his computer centre staff that the system he is using is capable of handling run-time formats normally.)

The subroutine effectively divides each data card that it reads into fields corresponding to the data columns. It requires that each data item should be in the same place on the card for successive entries, but it does not require that items should be separated by blanks, as did the subroutine described in 4.2.5. This subroutine will fail catastrophically if it finds alphabetic information where it expects numeric information, or if it finds a decimal point where it expects an integer. (The subroutine given in 4.2.5 would happily read a correction card as part of the data for an entry without observing any abnormality.) Because the failure occurs at the level of the FORTRAN system, there is no way of retrieving the error, and the program will halt leaving the output STATCAT data bank without a terminator, and therefore not not normally available to STATCAT programs. (The program STLIST (5.1) may be used to list entries, but will fail when it reaches the end of the information stored in the STATCAT data bank.)

Note in the listing of input cards (Figure 4.42) that the card used to supply the data terminator for the first run is not the same as that used when the original file was loaded (Figure 4.22b). Note also that a format appears in Figure 4.42 immediately before the first set of data cards loaded. This format is retained for the first passage of the program, but must be replaced or repeated if a second revised output STATCAT data bank is created.

REFERENCES McCracken (1972), ASA FORTRAN IV Standard (1972)

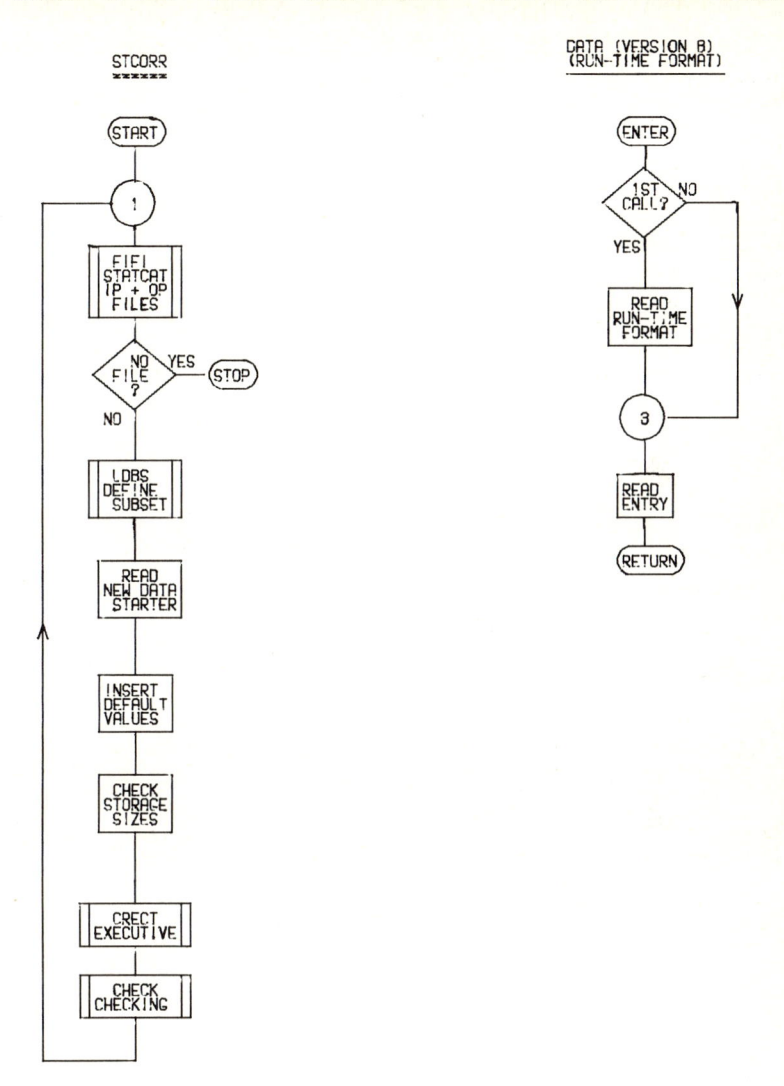

Figure 4.41a - System Flow-charts - STCORR and DATA (RUNTIM)

Figure 4.41b - System Flow-chart - CRECT

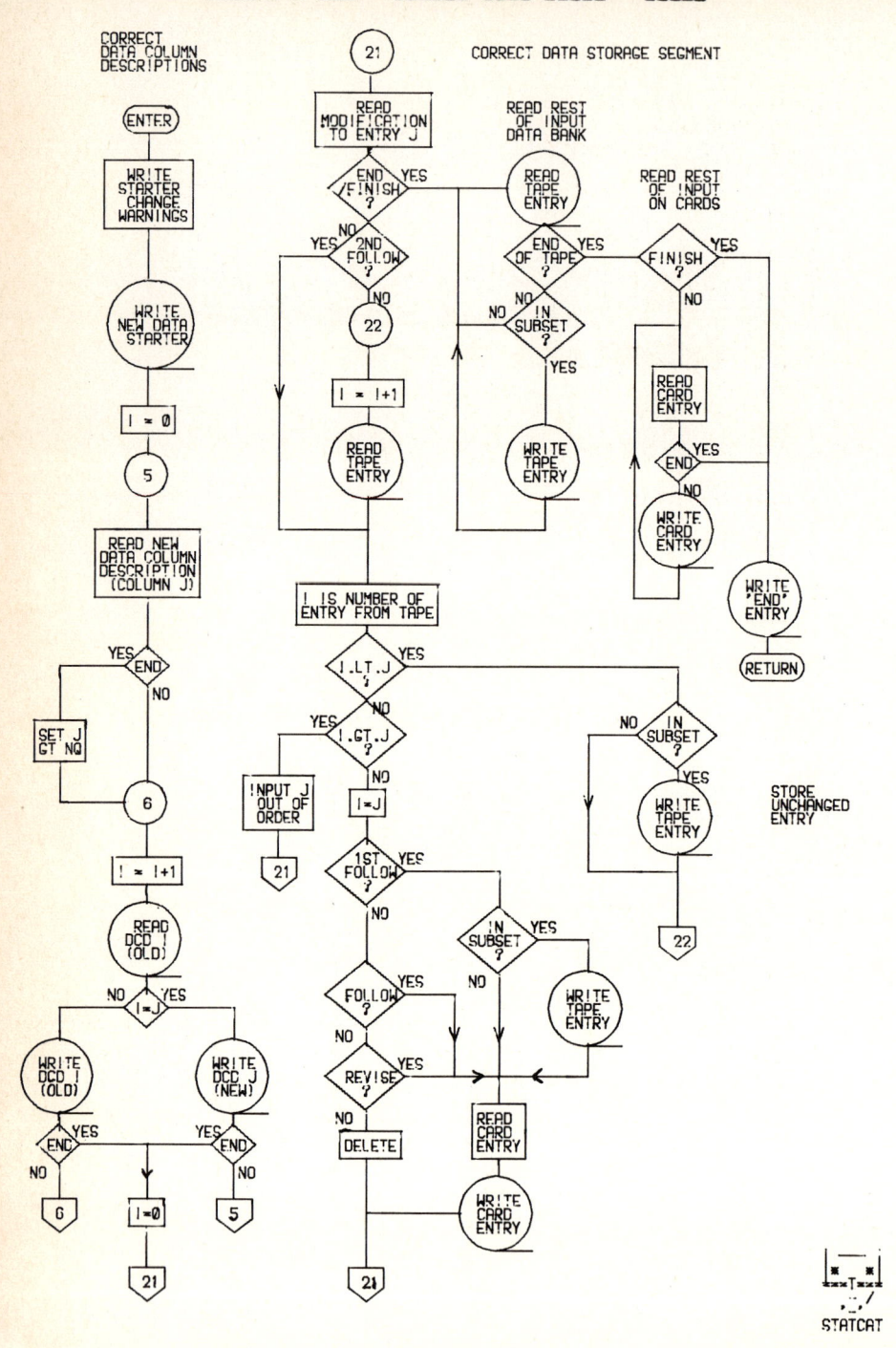

Figure 4.42 - STCORR - Input Structure

```
          Level
   0    1    2    3    4    5    6    7    8    9
FILE CONTROL CARD
     SUBSET SPECIFICATION
     DATA STARTER CARD
     DATA DESCRIPTION SEGMENT
         |COLUMN TITLE                   |  FOR CORRECTIONS IN ORDER    |
         |(COMPLEMENTARY INFORMATION)|  FOLLOWED BY NEW COLUMNS IF ANY |
         |END CARD|
     DATA CORRECTION SEGMENT
         |CORRECTION CARD                     |
         |(RUN-TIME FORMAT BEFORE FIRST ENTRY)|
         |(ENTRY IF REQUIRED)                 |
         |FINISH CARD|
         |ENTRIES IF REQUIRED                 |
         |ENTRY CONSISTING OF NON-VALUES      |
FILE CONTROL CARD
     SUBSET SPECIFICATION
     DATA STARTER CARD
     DATA DESCRIPTION SEGMENT (NO CHANGES)
     FINISH CARD
         |(RUN-TIME FORMAT BEFORE FIRST ENTRY)|
         |ENTRY CONSISTING OF NON-VALUES      |
STOP
```

Figure 4.43 - STCORR - Input Example

```
---------1----------2----------3----------4----------5----------6----------7--
**STCORRDEMO    DUFF                     DEMO IS INPUT OUTPUT FILE DUFF I
SETS 1 - 56
.IF.NTRY.LT.    57.
END OF SUBSET SPECIFICATION
62 19  8 -1.0    CORRECTED DATA BANK - DELIBERATE ERRORS
    18ERRP       PERCENTAGE OF ERRORS IN FINAL PRODUCTS
     0.0          0.0
    19FAKE       DUMMY COLUMN TO ILLUSTRATE CHANGE
     0.0     0.0
END OF REVISED DATA DESCRIPTION SEGMENT
DELETE    5
FOLLOW    5
(F2.0,F3.0,8F2.0,F3.0,5F7.2,F3.0,F4.1,F4.0)



 5  2 4 3 1 4 1 2 4 5 24   -5.69   71.28   63.01   49.50   67.90 72 33.0
REVISE   18
18  5 2 1 2 0 2 1 2 1 24   -4.13   16.60   86.38   36.06   44.10 46 -.3
FINISHED WITH TAPE
57 15 4 2 1 1 4 3 1 2 24   -1.29   24.75   92.75   40.07   47.38 48 0.3
58 15 2 3 2 2 4 3 4 4 26   -5.69   60.90   83.34   50.62   67.90 72 0.4
59 15 1 1 3 2 4 3 2 1 28   -4.13   16.56   87.84   36.06   44.10 46 0.4
60 15 3 4 4 2 4 3 3 7 26  -15.29  116.84   89.15   64.92   43.20 51 0.4
61 16 1 4 1 1 4 4 4 6 22  -12.50   97.34   79.13   54.86   63.00 72 0.5
62 16 3 1 2 3 4 4 1 1 25    0.62   15.01   95.54   36.88   48.30 48 1.3
63 16 4 3 3 4 4 4 3 5 26   -8.71   75.90   74.60   50.25   46.56 51 1.5
64 16 2 2 4 4 4 4 2 4 24   -5.96   55.49   72.94   49.97   43.26 46 1.5
-1 -1-1-1-1-1-1-1-1-1 -1   -1.00   -1.00   -1.00   -1.00   -1.00 -1 -1.  -1.
**STCORRSAME    COPY                     INPUT   DEMO OUTPUT COPY
ALL DATA
END OF DBS
99              COPY OF DEMO STATCAT DATA BANK
END OF DDS
END OF DSS
STOP
/*
---------1----------2----------3----------4----------5----------6----------7--
```

Figure 4.44 - STCORR - Output Structure

```
For each     ) : Input File Control Record
output file  )   Input File Parameters
                 Input Data Description
                 Subset Input Record
                 Input/Output File Parameters
                 Output/Checking Controls
                 Revised Data Description
                 Revised Data Storage Segment
                     <for each output entry: listing>
                     <for each input entry : disposal>
                     <for each alteration  : number of entry listed>
```

Carated(<>) items are optional.

Figure 4.45 - STCORR - Page-by-page output summary

Page	Contents	Origin
1- 2	File Control Record	FIFI
	Program Title	STCORR
	Input File Parameters	LDAP
	Input Data Description record	LDDS
3	Subset record	LDBS/LSET
4-6	Input/Output File Parameters	STCORR
	Output/Checking Controls	CRECT
	Revised Data Description Segment	CRECT
7	Alteration record	CRECT
8	Limit Check	CHECK
9-17	Distribution Check	CHECK
18-36	Abnormal Entries	CHECK
37-38	File Control Record	FIFI
	Program Title	STCORR
	Input File Parameters	LDAP
	Input Data Description record	LDDS
39	Subset record	LDBS/LSET
40-41	Input/Output File Parameters	STCORR
	Output/Checking Controls	CRECT
	Revised Data Description Segment	CRECT
42	Minimum DSS Record	CRECT
43	Data Handling Instruction (STOP)	LDHI

Figure 4.46 - STCORR - Original and revised Data Headers

```
STATCAT PROGRAM STCORR - REVISION OF DATA TAPE
NUMBER OF ITEMS PER ENTRY                        ORIGINAL -  18           REVISED -  19
MAXIMUM NUMBER OF ALTERNATIVE CLASSES            ORIGINAL -  10           REVISED -   8
NUMBER USED FOR MISSING VALUES                   ORIGINAL -     -1.0000   REVISED -     -1.0000
ORIGINAL FILE TITLE -DEMONSTRATION STATCAT DATA BANK          FILE REFERENCE DEMO
REVISED FILE TITLE -CORRECTED DATA BANK - DELIBERATE ERRORS   FILE REFERENCE


DATA OUTPUT CONTROL INDEX   -     6.
DATA CHECKING CONTROL INDEX -     2.
          OUTPUT FILE NAME IS NOW BLANK - CANNOT BE READ BY ANY OTHER STATCAT PROGRAM             **WARNING**
INPUT ACCEPTED - CORRECTION COMMENCES
    EXCEPT FOR ENTRIES READ IN FROM CARDS,EXTRA COLUMNS ARE SET TO THE MISSING VALUE
NAMES OF ORIGINAL EXTRA CLASSES ARE DISCARDED
                    REVISED DATA DESCRIPTION SEGMENT
COLUMN  SCALE   SHORT       FULL TITLE                                  DATA
NUMBER  CODE    TITLE                                                   LEVEL

  1       1     NTRY        ENTRY NUMBER                                DUMMY

  2       1     SESS        NUMBER OF TEST SESSION                      DUMMY

  3       2     OBSR        OBSERVER                                    NOMINAL
                    MIKE-NOEL-OSCR-PETE-  -  -  -

  4       2     OPER        OPERATOR                                    NOMINAL
                    ERIC-FRED-GINA-HUGH-  -  -  -

  5       2     W.P.        WORKING POSITION                            NOMINAL
                    I  -  J  -  K  -  L  -
```

Figure 4.47 - STCORR - Revised Data Storage Segment

```
                    REVISED DATA STORAGE SEGMENT
     ENTRY     5 DISCARDED - CORRECTION
     AFTER ENTRY     5 EXTRA ENTRY NO.    1 BECOMES ENTRY     5 ON NEW TAPE
     ENTRY    13 REPLACED BY REVISED ENTRY    13 ON NEW TAPE
     ENTRY    57 DISCARDED - NOT IN SUBSET
     ENTRY    58 DISCARDED - NOT IN SUBSET
     ENTRY    59 DISCARDED - NOT IN SUBSET
     ENTRY    60 DISCARDED - NOT IN SUBSET
     ENTRY    61 DISCARDED - NOT IN SUBSET
     ENTRY    62 DISCARDED - NOT IN SUBSET
     ENTRY    63 DISCARDED - NOT IN SUBSET
     ENTRY    64 DISCARDED - NOT IN SUBSET
     AFTER ENTRY    64 EXTRA ENTRY NO.    1 BECOMES ENTRY    57 ON NEW TAPE
     AFTER ENTRY    64 EXTRA ENTRY NO.    2 BECOMES ENTRY    58 ON NEW TAPE
     AFTER ENTRY    64 EXTRA ENTRY NO.    3 BECOMES ENTRY    59 ON NEW TAPE
     AFTER ENTRY    64 EXTRA ENTRY NO.    4 BECOMES ENTRY    60 ON NEW TAPE
     AFTER ENTRY    64 EXTRA ENTRY NO.    5 BECOMES ENTRY    61 ON NEW TAPE
     AFTER ENTRY    64 EXTRA ENTRY NO.    6 BECOMES ENTRY    62 ON NEW TAPE
     AFTER ENTRY    64 EXTRA ENTRY NO.    7 BECOMES ENTRY    63 ON NEW TAPE
     AFTER ENTRY    64 EXTRA ENTRY NO.    8 BECOMES ENTRY    64 ON NEW TAPE

     NUMBER OF ENTRIES IN ORIGINAL DATA BANK =     64
     NUMBER OF ENTRIES IN REVISED DATA BANK  =     64
     CORRECTION COMPLETED - CHECKING STARTS
```

Figure 4.48 - STCORR - Limit checks (Selected) and Abnormality Checks

```
STATCAT SUBROUTINE CHECK      -    CHECKING OUTPUT STATCAT DATA BANK
OUTPUT DATA BANK TITLE        -    CORRECTED DATA BANK - DELIBERATE ERRORS

TOTAL NUMBER OF ENTRIES  -      64 OF WHICH    64 ARE CONTAINED IN SUBSET

COLUMN       OBSERVED   OBSERVED              ARITHMETIC   STANDARD
NO NAME      MINIMUM    MAXIMUM    VALUES     MEAN         DEVIATION
  1 NTRY                                                              DUMMY
  2 SESS                                                              DUMMY
  3 OBSR      1.0000     4.0000     64         2.5000      1.1269
  4 OPER      1.0000     4.0000     64         2.5000      1.1269
  5 W.P.      1.0000     4.0000     64         2.5000      1.1269
  6 STRS      0.0        4.0000     64         2.5465      1.0573  MINIMUM BELOW RANGE

 17 TALL     46.0000    72.0000     64        54.2500     10.4835
 18 ERRP     -0.3000    33.0000     64         1.0484      4.1891  MINIMUM BELOW RANGE
 19 FAKE      0.0        0.0        10         0.0         0.0     CONSTANT


ENTRY NUMBER    5 (    5 IN SUBSET)       ABNORMAL ITEM

COLUMN      1       2       3       4       5       6       7       8       9       10
TITLE     NTRY    SESS    OBSR    OPER    W.P.    STRS    DAY.    TIME    TASK    DIFF
DATA      5.00    2.00    4.00    3.00    1.00    4.00    1.00    2.00    4.00    5.00
QUERY      AS      A-

COLUMN     11      12      13      14      15      16      17      18      19
TITLE     TEMP    TPCT    EFUP    EFUB    H.R.    TCOM    TALL    ERRP    FAKE
DATA     24.00   -5.69   71.28   63.01   49.50   67.90   72.00   33.00    0.0
QUERY                                                                    HIGH


ENTRY NUMBER   18 (   18 IN SUBSET)      2 ABNORMAL ITEMS

COLUMN      1       2       3       4       5       6       7       8       9       10
TITLE     NTRY    SESS    OBSR    OPER    W.P.    STRS    DAY.    TIME    TASK    DIFF
DATA     18.00    5.00    2.00    1.00    2.00    0.0     2.00    1.00    2.00    1.00
QUERY      BK      AS                                     OUT

COLUMN     11      12      13      14      15      16      17      18      19
TITLE     TEMP    TPCT    EFUP    EFUB    H.R.    TCOM    TALL    ERRP    FAKE
DATA     24.00   -4.13   16.60   86.38   36.06   44.10   46.00   -0.30    0.0
QUERY                                                                    OUT
```

Figure 4.49 - STCORR - Second Run (Start and End)

```
STATCAT PROGRAM STCORR - REVISION OF DATA TAPE

NUMBER OF ITEMS PER ENTRY                           ORIGINAL -  18            REVISED - 18

MAXIMUM NUMBER OF ALTERNATIVE CLASSES               ORIGINAL -  10            REVISED - 10

NUMBER USED FOR MISSING VALUES                      ORIGINAL -      -1.0000   REVISED -      -1.0000

ORIGINAL FILE TITLE - DEMONSTRATION STATCAT DATA BANK         FILE REFERENCE DEMO

REVISED FILE TITLE - COPY OF DEMO STATCAT DATA BANK           FILE REFERENCE


DATA OUTPUT CONTROL INDEX    -   -1.

DATA CHECKING CONTROL INDEX  -    9.

        OUTPUT FILE NAME IS NOW BLANK - CANNOT BE READ BY ANY OTHER STATCAT PROGRAM      **WARNING**
        THE SYSTEM HAS STANDARDISED  4 CONTROL VALUES FROM THE DATA HANDLING INSTRUCTION  **WARNING**
        PLEASE VERIFY THAT THE ASSUMPTIONS IT HAS MADE ARE CORRECT AND ADJUST STORAGE IF NECESSARY
INPUT ACCEPTED - CORRECTION COMMENCES
                    REVISED DATA DESCRIPTION SEGMENT

COLUMN  SCALE   SHORT       FULL TITLE                                       DATA
NUMBER  CODE    TITLE                                                        LEVEL

  1       1     NTRY        ENTRY NUMBER                                     DUMMY

  2       1     SESS        NUMBER OF TEST SESSION                           DUMMY



                    REVISED DATA STORAGE SEGMENT
NUMBER OF ENTRIES IN ORIGINAL DATA BANK =     64
NUMBER OF ENTRIES IN REVISED  DATA BANK =     64
CORRECTION COMPLETED - CHECKING STARTS
CHECKING COMPLETED - READ NEW INPUT/OUTPUT FILES
```

```
C MASTER STCORR - CORRECTS STATCAT DATA BANKS
C   SUBROUTINES AND FUNCTIONS REQUIRED
C NAME            TYPE              COMMENT
C AN      (SEE  3.1 ) SERVICE   ALPHA - TO NUMERIC VALUE
C CHECK   (SEE  4.3 ) EXECUTIVE CHECKS DATA BANK OR SUBSET
C CHIKEN  (SEE 11.9 ) SERVICE   WARNS OF MISMATCHED DATA LEVEL
C CLSAM   (SEE  3.5 ) SERVICE   ALLOTS ENTRY TO SAMPLE/SUBSET
C COMPA   (SEE  3.1 ) SERVICE   COMPARES ALPHAMERIC VALUES
C COPYA   (SEE  3.1 ) SERVICE   COPIES ALPHAMERIC VALUE
C CRECT   (SEE  4.4 ) EXECUTIVE CORRECTS STATCAT DATA BANK
C DATA    (SEE BELOW) SERVICE   LOADS ONE ENTRY (THREE VERSIONS)
C DATA    (SEE  4.2 ) SERVICE   FREE-FORMAT INPUT      (VERSION DATAFF)
C DATA    (SEE  4.3 ) SERVICE   RUN-TIME FORMAT        (VERSION DATART)
C DATA    (SEE  9.4 ) SERVICE   PLAIN-LANGUAGE INPUT   (VERSION DATAPL)
C FIFI    (SEE  3.2 ) SYSTEM    ALLOCATES PERIPHERALS-CHECKS FILES
C IBL     (SEE  3.1 ) SERVICE   DETECTS BLANK,END AND STOP CARDS
C ICH     (SEE  3.1 ) SERVICE   IDENTIFIES ALPHAMERIC CODES
C LCOM    (SEE  3.4 ) SYSTEM    LOADS COMPLEMENTARY INFORMATION
C LDAP    (SEE  3.3 ) SYSTEM    LOADS/CHECKS DATA BANK PARAMETERS
C LDBS    (SEE  3.6 ) SYSTEM    LOADS SUBSET DEFINITION
C LDDS    (SEE  3.4 ) SYSTEM    LOADS DATA DESCRIPTION SEGMENT
C LSET    (SEE  3.5 ) SYSTEM    LOADS DEFINING CONDITIONS
C WDCD    (SEE  3.4 ) SERVICE   WRITE DATA COLUMN DESCRIPTION
C IF NQMAX = MAXIMUM NO OF DATA COLS IS CHANGED CHANGE CN DATA ALSO
C DIMENSION D(NQMAX),DMAX(NQMAX),DMIN(NQMAX),IT(NQMAX),ST(NQMAX)
C DIMENSION CN(NQMAX)
      NQMAX = 100
      DIMENSION D(100),DMAX(100),DMIN(100),IT(100),ST(100),CN(100)
      DATA    CN/4HCOL1,4HCOL2,4HCOL3,4HCOL4,4HCOL5,4HCOL6,4HCOL7,4HCOL8,4
     1HCOL9,4HCL10,4HCL11,4HCL12,4HCL13,4HCL14,4HCL15,4HCL16,4HCL17,4HCL
     218,4HCL19,4HCL20,4HCL21,4HCL22,4HCL23,4HCL24,4HCL25,4HCL26,4HCL27,
     34HCL28,4HCL29,4HCL30,4HCL31,4HCL32,4HCL33,4HCL34,4HCL35,4HCL36,4HC
     4L37,4HCL38,4HCL39,4HCL40,4HCL41,4HCL42,4HCL43,4HCL44,4HCL45,4HCL46
     5,4HCL47,4HCL48,4HCL49,4HCL50,4HCL51,4HCL52,4HCL53,4HCL54,4HCL55,4H
     6CL56,4HCL57,4HCL58,4HCL59,4HCL60,4HCL61,4HCL62,4HCL63,4HCL64,4HCL6
     75,4HCL66,4HCL67,4HCL68,4HCL69,4HCL70,4HCL71,4HCL72,4HCL73,4HCL74,4
     8HCL75,4HCL76,4HCL77,4HCL78,4HCL79,4HCL80,4HCL81,4HCL82,4HCL83,4HCL
     984,4HCL85,4HCL86,4HCL87,4HCL88,4HCL89,4HCL90,4HCL91,4HCL92,4HCL93,
     94HCL94,4HCL95,4HCL96,4HCL97,4HCL98,4HCL99,4HC100/
C DIMENSION TRT(NALTMX),RT(NQMAX,NALTMX)=MAX.NO OF CLASSES IN DATA BANK
      NALTMX = 50
      DIMENSION TRT(50),RT(100,50)
C DIMENSION SCON(5,MAXDBC) = MAXIMUM NO OF SUBSET CONDITIONS
      MAXDBC = 50
      DIMENSION SCON(5,50)
C THE FOLLOWING DIMENSIONS ARE FIXED
      DIMENSION TTA(20),TTB(20),FORM(16)
      COMMON /STCT/MED1,MED2,MED3,MED4,MED5,MED6,MED13,Q,V(20),TT(30)
      DATA PROG/4HCORR/
      MED1 = -1
C LEVEL 0 - SETTING UP INPUT AND OUTPUT DATA BANKS
    1 CALL COPYA(TT(1),PROG)
      CALL FIFI
      IF(MED6.GT.0) WRITE(MED6,901)
      CALL LDAP(MED2,MED3,V,TTB,QB,NQB,NALTB,NQMAX,NALTMX,IGO)
      IF(IGO.GT.0) GO TO 1
      LI = 18
      CALL LDDS(TRT,NALTB,D,NQB,ST,NQB,IT,NQB,H,O,H,H,O,LI,O,Q,VX,
     1 O,MED2,MED3,O,IGO)
C READ DATA BANK SUBSET SPECIFICATION - LEVEL 2
   21 IF(V(10).GE.20.) V(10) = 0.
      CALL LDBS(SCON,NCON,MAXDBC,CN,ST,IT,NQB,TRT,NALTB,IGO)
      IF(IGO.GT.0) NCON = 0
```

```
    2 READ(MED1,900)FORM,(TTA(K),K=1,16)
      IF(IBL(FORM,16,1)) 3,4,4
    3 IF(IBL(TTA,16,4)) 2,4,4
    4 V(1) = AN(FORM,1,1,1)
      V(2) = AN(FORM,2,2,2)
      NQA = AN(FORM,5,3,5)
      NALTA = AN(FORM,8,6,8)
      QA = AN(FORM,16,9,16)
      NWARN = 0
C STANDARDISATION
C IF NQ,NALT OR Q FOR OUTPUT NOT SPECIFIED COPY FROM INPUT
      IF(NQA.EQ.0) NWARN = NWARN + 1
      IF(NQA.EQ.0) NQA = NQB
      IF(NALTA.EQ.0) NWARN = NWARN + 1
      IF(NALTA.EQ.0) NALTA = NALTB
      IF(IBL(FORM(9),8,1).LT.0) NWARN = NWARN + 1
      IF(IBL(FORM(9),8,1).LT.0) QA = QB
C IF REVISED TITLE IS BLANK COPY ORIGINAL
      IF(IBL(TTA,10,4)) 5,7,7
    5 DO 6 K = 1,10
    6 CALL COPYA(TTA(K),TTB(K))
      NWARN = NWARN + 1
    7 IF(V(1).GT.7.5) NWARN = NWARN + 1
      IF(V(1).GT.7.5) V(1) = -1.
      WRITE(MED6,931) NQB,NQA,NALTB,NALTA,QB,QA,(TTB(K),K=1,10),TTB(16),(
     1TTA(K),K=1,10),TTA(16),V(1),V(2)
      IF(IBL(TTA(16),1,4).LT.0) WRITE(MED6,904)
      IF(NWARN.GT.0) WRITE(MED6,996) NWARN
      V(10) = 0.
      IF(NQA.LE.NQMAX.AND.NQB.LE.NQMAX) GO TO 9
      V(10) = 1.
      IF(NQB.LE.NQMAX) GO TO 8
      WRITE(MED6,902) NQB,NQMAX
      WRITE(MED6,908)
    8 IF(NQA.LE.NQMAX) GO TO 9
      WRITE(MED6,902) NQA,NQMAX
      WRITE(MED6,909)
    9 IF(NALTA.LE.NALTMX.AND.NALTB.LE.NALTMX) GO TO 11
      V(10) = 2.
      IF(NALTB.LE.NALTMX) GO TO 10
      WRITE(MED6,903) NALTB,NALTMX
      WRITE(MED6,908)
   10 IF(NALTA.LE.NALTMX) GO TO 11
      WRITE(MED6,903) NALTA,NALTMX
      WRITE(MED6,909)
   11 CONTINUE
C TEST FOR ACCEPTED INPUT SPECIFICATION
  100 IF(V(10).EQ.0.) GO TO 101
      WRITE(MED6,997) V(10)
      GO TO 1
  101 WRITE(MED6,998)
C READ AND LOAD CORRECTED STATCAT DATA BANK
      CALL  CRECT(TTA,TTB,TRT,NALTA,NALTB,NALTMX,D,NQA,QA,DMIN,NQMAX,SCO
     1N,NCON)
C CHECK REVISED DATA TAPE
      NCON = 0
      ASDL = 5.
      APT = 1.0
      IF(V(2).GE.0.)GO TO 50
      WRITE(MED6,907)
      GO TO 1
   50 WRITE(MED6,905)
      CALL CHECK (D,DMAX,DMIN,RT,IT,TRT,NQA,NALTA,ASDL,APT,SCON,NCON,ST)
```

```
      V(10) = 0.
      WRITE(MED6,999)
      GO TO 1
  901 FORMAT (1H0,20X,28HSTATCAT CORRECTING DATA BANK )
  900 FORMAT (16A1,16A4)
  902 FORMAT (4H0THE,I6,40H ITEMS PER ENTRY EXCEED THE AVAILABLE   ,I6,1
     16H STORAGE COLUMNS)
  903 FORMAT (4H0THE,I6,40H CLASSES PER COLUMN EXCEED THE AVAILABLE,I6,1
     16H STORAGE COLUMNS)
  904 FORMAT(1H0,10X,75HOUTPUT FILE NAME IS NOW BLANK - CANNOT BE READ B
     1Y ANY OTHER STATCAT PROGRAM,23X,11H**WARNING**)
  905 FORMAT(39H0CORRECTION COMPLETED - CHECKING STARTS)
  907 FORMAT(43H0CORRECTION COMPLETED - CHECKING SUPPRESSED)
  908 FORMAT (1H+,80X,20H(ORIGINAL DATA BANK))
  909 FORMAT (1H+,80X,20H( REVISED DATA BANK))
  931 FORMAT(47H1STATCAT PROGRAM STCORR - REVISION OF DATA TAPE/29H0NUMB
     1ER OF ITEMS PER ENTRY     ,31X,10HORIGINAL -,I4,16X,9HREVISED -,I4/3
     28H0MAXIMUM NUMBER OF ALTERNATIVE CLASSES,22X,10HORIGINAL -,I4,16X,
     39HREVISED -,I4/31H0NUMBER USED FOR MISSING VALUES,29X,10HORIGINAL
     4-,F16.4,4X,9HREVISED -,F16.4/22H0ORIGINAL FILE TITLE -,10A4,10X,15
     5HFILE REFERENCE ,A4/22H0 REVISED FILE TITLE -,10A4,10X,15HFILE REF
     6ERENCE ,A4///31H0DATA OUTPUT CONTROL INDEX   - ,F6.0/
     731H0DATA CHECKING CONTROL INDEX - ,F6.0)
  996 FORMAT (1H0,9X,27HTHE SYSTEM HAS STANDARDISED,I3,50H CONTROL VALUE
     1S FROM THE DATA HANDLING INSTRUCTION,20X,11H**WARNING**
     2            /1H0,9X,90HPLEASE VERIFY THAT THE ASSUMPTIONS IT HAS MADE
     3 ARE CORRECT AND ADJUST STORAGE IF NECESSARY        )
  997 FORMAT (24H0PROGRAM CANNOT OPERATE.//37H    EARLIEST UNCORRECTED ER
     1ROR CODE = , F5.0)
  998 FORMAT(38H0INPUT ACCEPTED - CORRECTION COMMENCES)
  999 FORMAT(49H0CHECKING COMPLETED - READ NEW INPUT/OUTPUT FILES    )
      END


      SUBROUTINE CRECT(TTA,TTB,TRT,NALTA,NALTB,NALTMX,D,NQA,QA,DB,NQMAX,
     1SCON,NCON)
C CRECT   (SEE  4.4 ) EXECUTIVE    CORRECTS STATCAT DATA BANK
      DIMENSION P(5),TTA(20),TTB(20),TRT(NALTMX),FJ(6),DB(NQMAX)
      DIMENSION D(NQA  ),SCON(5,NCON),CODE(4),FORMB(47),FORM(80)
      COMMON /STCT/MED1,MED2,MED3,MED4,MED5,MED6,MED13,Q,V(20),TT(30)
      DATA P/4HNOMI,4HORDI,4HINTE,4HRATI,4HFIXE/
      DATA CODE/4HDELE,4HREVI,4HFOLL,4HFINI/
      DATA BL/4H    /
      REWIND MED3
      READ(MED3) NQB,NALTB,QB,(TTB(K),K=1,16)
C REMINDERS FOR CHANGED TAPE PARAMETERS
      IF(NQA.GT.NQB) WRITE(MED2,201)
      IF(NQA.LT.NQB) WRITE(MED2,202)
      IF(NALTA.GT.NALTB) WRITE(MED2,203)
      IF(NALTA.LT.NALTB) WRITE(MED2,204)
      IF(NALTA.LE.NALTB) GO TO 4
      DO 3 K = NALTB,NALTA
    3 CALL COPYA(TRT(K),BL)
    4 A = NALTA - 2
      B = NALTB - 2
      B = A/B
      REWIND MED4
      WRITE(MED4) NQA,NALTA,QA,(TTA(K),K=1,16)
      WRITE (MED2,200)
      I = 0
      NLIN = 30
    5 READ(MED1,205) FJ,(TTA(K),K = 1,19)
      J = AN(FJ,6,1,6)
```

```
      IF(IBL(FJ,6,1)) 5,6,2
C END CARD FOUND
    2 J = NQA + NQB
    6 I = I + 1
      IF(I.GT.NQA ) GO TO 8
      IF(I.GT.NQB ) GO TO 7
      READ(MED3) (TTB(K),K=1,19),(TRT(K),K=1,NALTB),NX,DMIN,DMAX
      IF(I.EQ.J) GO TO 7
      IF(NALTA.NE.NALTB) DMAX = DMIN +B*(DMAX-DMIN)
      WRITE(MED4) (TTB(K),K=1,19),(TRT(K),K=1,NALTA),NX,DMIN,DMAX
      IF(NX.EQ.1) NLIN = NLIN + 2
      IF(NX.EQ.2.OR.NX.EQ.3) NLIN = NLIN + (NALTA-1)/10 + 5
      IF(NX.GE.4) NLIN = NLIN + 3
      IF(NLIN.GT.50) WRITE(MED2,206)
      IF(NLIN.GT.50) WRITE(MED2,200)
      IF(NLIN.GT.50) NLIN = 5
      CALL WDCD(TTB,TRT,NALTA,NX,DMIN,DMAX,I,MED2)
      GO TO 6
C READ NEW DATA DESCRIPTION FROM CARDS
    7 CALL LCOM(TTA,TRT,NALTA,NX,DMIN,DMAX,MED1,MED2)
      WRITE(MED4) (TTA(K),K=1,19),(TRT(K),K=1,NALTA),NX,DMIN,DMAX
      IF(NX.EQ.1) NLIN = NLIN + 2
      IF(NX.EQ.2.OR.NX.EQ.3) NLIN = NLIN + (NALTA-1)/10 + 5
      IF(NX.GE.4) NLIN = NLIN + 3
      IF(NLIN.GT.50) WRITE(MED2,206)
      IF(NLIN.GT.50) WRITE(MED2,200)
      IF(NLIN.GT.50) NLIN = 5
      CALL WDCD(TTA,TRT,NALTA,NX,DMIN,DMAX,I,MED2)
      GO TO 5
C READ SURPLUS DATA DESCRIPTIONS FROM ORIGINAL TAPE
    8 IF(NQA.GE.NQB) GO TO 10
      L = NQA + 1
      DO 9 J = L,NQB
    9 READ(MED3) (TTB(K),K=1,19),(TRT(K),K=1,NALTB),NX,DMIN,DMAX
   10 CONTINUE
C READ IN DATA AS SPECIFIED
      WRITE(MED2,313)
      Q = QA
      NX = (NQA+19)/10
      L2 = 0
      IF(V(1).GT.-0.5.AND.V(1).LT.4.5) L2 = 1
      IF(V(1).GT.4.) V(1) = V(1) - 5.
      DO 19 I = 1,NQA
   19 D(I) = Q
      I = 0
      NSUBA = 0
   20 IGO = 1
      NSF = 1
   21 READ(MED1,300) FORMB
      IB=IBL(FORMB,1,4)
      IF(IB.GT.0) J=0
      IF(IB.LE.0) J=AN(FORMB,37,2,37)
      IF(IB.LT.0.AND.J.LE.0) GO TO 21
      NT = ICH(FORMB(1),CODE,4)
      IF(NT.EQ.0.AND.IB.LE.0) WRITE(MED2,314) FORMB
      IF(NT.EQ.0.AND.IB.LE.0) GO TO 21
      IF(NT.EQ.3) GO TO 25
      GO TO (22,25,153,170),IGO
   22 READ(MED3) (DB(K),K=1,NQB)
      CALL CLSAM(DB,NQB,SCON,NCON,NIN,1)
      I = I + 1
      IEND = 1
      NSF = 0
```

```
      DO 23 K = 1,NQA
      IF(K.GT.NQB)DB(K) = QA
      IF(DB(K).EQ.QB) DB(K) = QA
      IF(DB(K).NE.QA) IEND = 0
   23 CONTINUE
      IF(IEND.EQ.1) I = I - 1
   24 IF(IEND.EQ.1) GO TO 170
   25 IF(NT.EQ.4) J = 0
      IF(J.EQ.0)        GO TO 120
      IF(J.LT.I)        GO TO 110
      IF(J.GT.I)        GO TO 120
      IF(NT.EQ.1)       GO TO 130
      IF(NT.EQ.2)       GO TO 140
      IF(NT.EQ.3)       GO TO 150
      GO TO 120
  110 WRITE(MED2,301)J,I
C CORRECTION MESSAGE OUT OF ORDER
      IF(NT.EQ.2.OR.NT.EQ.3) CALL DATA(D,NQA,FORM)
      IGO = 2
      GO TO 21
  120 IF(NIN.NE.1) GO TO 121
C TRANSFER OF UNCHANGED DATA ITEM
      WRITE(MED4) (DB(K),K=1,NQA)
      NSUBA = NSUBA + 1
      IF(V(1).GE.0..AND.V(1).NE.1.) NLIN = NLIN + 1
      IF(L2.EQ.1) NLIN = NLIN + NX
      IF(NLIN.GT.50) WRITE(MED2,313)
      IF(NLIN.GT.50) NLIN = 0
      IF(V(1).GE.0..AND.V(1).NE.1.) WRITE(MED2,305)I,NSUBA
      IF(L2.EQ.1) WRITE(MED2,400) (DB(K),K=1,NQA)
      GO TO 22
  121 IF(V(1).GE.0..AND.V(1).NE.2.) NLIN = NLIN + 1
      IF(NLIN.GT.50) WRITE(MED2,313)
      IF(NLIN.GT.50) NLIN = 0
      IF(V(1).GE.0..AND.V(1).NE.2.) WRITE(MED2,302) I
      GO TO 22
C ENTRY DELETED
  130 IF(V(1).GE.0..AND.V(1).NE.2.) NLIN = NLIN + 1
      IF(NLIN.GT.50) WRITE(MED2,313)
      IF(NLIN.GT.50) NLIN = 0
      IF(V(1).GE.0..AND.V(1).NE.2.) WRITE(MED2,303)I
      GO TO 20
  140 CALL DATA (D,NQA,FORM)
C CHANGED ENTRY
      WRITE(MED4) (D(K),K=1,NQA)
      NSUBA = NSUBA + 1
      IF(V(1).GE.0.) NLIN = NLIN + 1
      IF(L2.EQ.1) NLIN = NLIN + NX
      IF(NLIN.GT.50) WRITE(MED2,313)
      IF(NLIN.GT.50) NLIN = 0
      IF(V(1).GE.0.) WRITE(MED2,306)I,NSUBA
      IF(L2.EQ.1) WRITE(MED2,400) ( D(K),K=1,NQA)
      GO TO 20
C ADDING DATA ITEMS FOLLOWING ITEM J
  150 IF(NSP.NE.0)GO TO 152
      IF(NIN.NE.1)GO TO 151
      WRITE(MED4) (D(K), K = 1,NQA)
      NSUBA = NSUBA + 1
      IF(V(1).GE.0..AND.V(1).NE.2.) NLIN = NLIN + 1
      IF(L2.EQ.1) NLIN = NLIN + NX
      IF(NLIN.GT.50) WRITE(MED2,313)
      IF(NLIN.GT.50) NLIN = 0
      IF(V(1).GE.0..AND.V(1).NE.2.) WRITE(MED2,302) I
```

```
      IF(L2.EQ.1) WRITE(MED2,400) ( D(K),K=1,NQA)
  151 NSF = 0
  152 CALL DATA (D,NQA,FORM)
      WRITE(MED4) (D(K),K=1,NQA)
      NSUBA = NSUBA + 1
      IF(V(1).GE.0.) NLIN = NLIN + 1
      IF(L2.EQ.1) NLIN = NLIN + NX
      IF(NLIN.GT.50) WRITE(MED2,313)
      IF(NLIN.GT.50) NLIN = 0
      IF(V(1).GE.0.)WRITE(MED2,309)I,NSF,NSUBA
      IF(L2.EQ.1) WRITE(MED2,400) ( D(K),K=1,NQA)
      NSF = NSF + 1
      IGO = 3
      GO TO 21
  153 IF(J.EQ.I.AND.NT.EQ.3) GO TO 152
      GO TO 22
C READ ANY REMAINING CORRECTIONS AFTER TAPE END
  170 NSF = 0
      IF(J.EQ.0.AND.NT.EQ.4) GO TO 195
      IF(J.EQ.0) GO TO 190
      IF(J.LT.I)WRITE(MED2,310)J,I,NT
      IF(J.GT.I)WRITE(MED2,311)J,NT
      IF(NT.EQ.1)GO TO 180
      CALL DATA (D,NQA,FORM)
      IF(NT.EQ.2)GO TO 180
  171 WRITE(MED4)(D(K), K = 1,NQA)
      NSUBA = NSUBA + 1
      NSF = NSF + 1
      IF(V(1).GE.0.) NLIN = NLIN + 1
      IF(L2.EQ.1) NLIN = NLIN + NX
      IF(NLIN.GT.50) WRITE(MED2,313)
      IF(NLIN.GT.50) NLIN = 0
      IF(V(1).GE.0.)WRITE(MED2,309) I,NSF,NSUBA
      IF(L2.EQ.1) WRITE(MED2,400) ( D(K),K=1,NQA)
      IF(J.EQ.0.AND.NT.EQ.4) GO TO 195
  180 IGO = 4
      GO TO 21
  195 CALL DATA (D,NQA,FORM)
      DO 196 K = 1,NQA
      IF(D(K).NE.QA) GO TO 171
  196 CONTINUE
  190 WRITE(MED2,312)I,NSUBA
      WRITE(MED4) (QA,K=1,NQA)
      REWIND MED4
      RETURN
  200 FORMAT(1H0,20X,32HREVISED DATA DESCRIPTION SEGMENT    /
     121H0COLUMN SCALE    SHORT,10X,10HFULL TITLE,45X,4HDATA/
     221H NUMBER CODE     TITLE,65X,5HLEVEL    )
  201 FORMAT (83H0   EXCEPT FOR ENTRIES READ IN FROM CARDS,EXTRA COLUMNS
     1ARE SET TO THE MISSING VALUE)
  202 FORMAT (47HOVALUES IN ORIGINAL EXTRA COLUMNS ARE DISCARDED)
  203 FORMAT (79H0EXCEPT FOR DATA COLUMNS READ IN FROM CARDS,EXTRA CLASS
     1 NAMES ARE SET TO BLANKS)
  204 FORMAT (47HONAMES OF ORIGINAL EXTRA CLASSES ARE DISCARDED )
  205 FORMAT(6A1,A4,A2,17A4)
  206 FORMAT (1H1)
  300 FORMAT(A4,36A1,10A4)
  301 FORMAT(30H CORRECTION MESSAGE FOR ENTRY ,I6,13H AFTER ENTRY ,I6)
  302 FORMAT(6H ENTRY,I6,26H DISCARDED - NOT IN SUBSET)
  303 FORMAT(6H ENTRY,I6,26H DISCARDED - CORRECTION   )
  305 FORMAT (6H ENTRY,I6,14H BECOMES ENTRY,I6,13H ON NEW TAPE )
  306 FORMAT (6H ENTRY,I6,26H REPLACED BY REVISED ENTRY,I6,12H ON NEW TA
     1PE)
```

```
  309 FORMAT (12H AFTER ENTRY,I6,17H EXTRA ENTRY NO. ,I4,14H BECOMES ENT
     1RY,I6,12H ON NEW TAPE)
  310 FORMAT (29H CORRECTION MESSAGE FOR ENTRY,I6,17H AFTER LAST ENTRY,I6
     1,6H (TYPE,I2,1H))
  311 FORMAT (29H CORRECTION MESSAGE FOR ENTRY,I6,21H WHICH IS NOT ON TA
     1PE,6H (TYPE,I2,1H))
  312 FORMAT(42HONUMBER OF ENTRIES IN ORIGINAL DATA BANK =,I6/
     142HONUMBER OF ENTRIES IN REVISED DATA BANK = ,I6)
  313 FORMAT (1H1,20X,28HREVISED DATA STORAGE SEGMENT)
  314 FORMAT(30HOUNIDENTIFIED CORRECTION CARD-,A4,36A1,10A4,11H**WARNING
     1**)
  400 FORMAT(1H0,10F12.3/(1H ,10F12.3))
      END


      SUBROUTINE DATA (D,NQ,FORM)
C DATA    (SEE  4.1 ) SERVICE      RUN-TIME FORMAT READ INITIALLY
      DIMENSION D(NQ),FORM(80)
      COMMON /STCT/MED1,MED2,MED3,MED4,MED5,MED6,MED13,Q,V(20),TT(30)
      DO 1 I = 1,NQ
      IF(D(I).NE.Q) GO TO 2
    1 CONTINUE
      READ(MED5,900) FORM
    2 READ(MED5,FORM) D
      RETURN
  900 FORMAT(20A4)
      END
```

Chapter V

DESCRIPTIVE STATISTICS

This chapter contains three programs for the description of samples of data from STATCAT data banks.

STLIST provides entry-by-entry listings of selections of data from STATCAT data banks. Numerical data may be printed with more or less detail, and with more or less space per datum. Several optional forms of output are provided, including one where the form of the output can be specified by the user, and another which may be used for output to a card or tape punch, or other machine readable medium. Details are provided to allow the user to write his own special purpose subroutine.

STDESC provides descriptive statistics for original or transformed data selected from specified columns. Parametric or 'non-parametric' statistics will be provided, appropriate to the data level. (It is possible to over-ride the originally specified data level, and to control the degree of detail produced.)

STASTA produces very large association tables, showing descriptive statistics for all possible combinations of several variates in both rows and columns.

5.1 PROGRAM STLIST - LIST ENTRIES

5.1.1 Purpose

This program lists entries drawn from a STATCAT data bank. Several alternative forms of listing are available including a special output form for plain-language data, and a form that may be used to punch cards or make other mechanical output from plain language or other STATCAT data banks. A flexible output format is also provided, which may be used to provide output more easily read by the user.

Figure 5.11a contains system flow-charts for the main program STLIST STLIST, the executive subroutine CLIST, and the output subroutine WCAR, which produces 'card-image' output. Figure 5.11b contains flow-charts for the subroutines WSET, which is the general output for numeric data, WFLEX, which uses a flexible run-time format (5.1.6), and WOWN(DFLT) (5.1.5), the default user-written output subroutine.

5.1.2 Input Data

Item	Level	Format	Function	See
1	0	A	File control	3.2
2	4	E	Subset specification	3.6
3	9	H	Data handling instruction	Below + 3.8

Data Handling Instruction

Card Layout - Data Handling Instruction - STLIST

ABCCCDDDEEEEEEEEEFFFFFFFFGGGGGGGGGGGGGGGGGHHHHHHHH.....etc

Columns	Item	Function	See
1	A	Output control index	Below
2	B	Auxiliary control index	Below
3 - 5	C	First data column output	Below
6 - 8	D	Last data column output	Below
9 - 16	E	Output Device	Below
17 - 24	F	Not used	-
25 - 40	G	Auxiliary Security Key	Below
41 - 80	H	Run Title (KEPT)	-

A - Output Control Index

This index controls the choice of the type of listing that will be produced.

ALTERNATIVES

A = 0,blank : Five data per line, with eight decimal places, in
(DEFAULT)   exponent notation (i.e. 0.23456789E 1 = 2.3456789)

A = 1   : Five data per line, in normal notation, with eight
             decimal places. (i.e. 2.34567890)

A = 2   : Ten data per line, with five decimal places.
             (i.e. 2.34568)

A = 3   : Fifteen data per line, with three decimal places
             (i.e. 2.346)

A = 4   : Twenty data per line, with two decimal places.

(i.e. 2.35)

A = 5   : Twenty-five data per line, with no decimal places
              (i.e. 2)

A = 6   : User-written output subroutine (5.1.5)

A = 7   : Flexible output format subroutine (5.1.6)

A = 8   : Output on Medium E of all entries in subset

A = 9   : Output on Medium E of all entries not in subset

DEFAULT value = 0 (0, blank or non-numeric character)

B - Auxiliary Control Index

This index controls the amount of detail included in an output listing,
Its exact meaning depends on the value of the Output control index A.

If A is non-numeric, blank or 0, the following alternatives apply

ALTERNATIVES

B = 0, blank : For each entry
    or non-numeric
              A) Number of entry in STATCAT data bank
              B) Value of first datum
              C) Number of first datum listed
              D) Value of first datum listed
           For each datum
              E) Item Number
              F) Numerical Value
              G) Class name for Nominal or Ordinal data
                 Value in A4 for DUMMY data
                 MISS for missing data
                 OUT for out of range data

B = 1   : As for B = 0, less G

B = 2   : As for B = 0, less E and G

B = 3   : Items A, B, C and D

B = 4   : Items A and B

B = 5   : Item A only

B = 6   : Item G only

B = 7 - 9   : No output

DEFAULT value = 0 (0, blank or non-numeric character)

If index A = 6 See Chapter 9 for an example of the use of B

If index A = 7 index B must be set to 0, and will be set to 0
                by the system if not so set.

If index A = 8 or 9 :-

ALTERNATIVES

B = 0   : Four data per card with eight decimal places, in exponent notation.

B = 1   : Four data per card in normal notation, with eight decimal places.

B = 2   : Eight data per card, with five decimal places.

B = 3   : Twelve data per card, with two decimal places.

B = 4   : Sixteen data per card, with two decimal places.

B = 5   : Twenty data per card, with no decimal places.

B = 6   : Twenty data per card, in A4 format

B = 7   : Forty data per card, in A2 format

B = 8   : Eighty data per card, in A1 format

B = 9   : Twenty data per card decoded from the plain-language format described in 9.1.

DEFAULT value = 0 (0 , blank or non-numeric character)

C - First Data Column to be Listed

This is the first data column that will be listed for each entry. If this value is set to zero or left blank, the listing will commence at the first data column in the STATCAT data bank. This column will not be standardised if the Data Output Control index is set to 6.

D - Last Data Column Listed

This specifies the last data column to be listed for each entry. If it is set to zero, or a non-numeric value, left blank or set to less than the first data column C, then it will be set equal to C and only one data column will be listed. If the first data column is also blank, then the whole entry will be listed. This field will not be standardised if the Data Listing Control index A is set to 6.

E - Output Device

This value gives the numerical code for the peripheral used by WCAR. Normally this will be a card punch, but other devices capable of handling eighty-character records without line controls may be used. This value is available to the user-written subroutine WOWN (5.1.5). If set to blank, zero, or a non-numeric value the value of MEDP set in the main program STLIST will be used.

G - Auxiliary Security Key

This value is an optional extra for the system, designed to prevent casual snooping. It is employed (in the standard version of the system) only in conjunction with the output subroutine for plain-language information. If this value is not correctly specified, the system will not release any information from the STATCAT plain-language file. The way in which it is employed is described in Chapter 9. This key, like the security key used on the file control card (3.2) is never printed on the output.

5.1.3 Input Example

Figure 5.12 is a summary of the input structure for two runs of STLIST. In the first run, the general purpose listing subroutine is used to list complete entries for which there is a considerable difference between the observer's and operator's estimates of efficiency. In the second, the flexible output subroutine is used to produce a short report of the trials found very difficult by the operator. Figure 5.13 is a listing of the input cards required to carry out these two runs.

5.1.4 Output Example

Figure 5.14 is a general summary of the output for this program, indented to correspond to the overall program structure. Figure 5.15 is a page-by-page summary of the output corresponding to the specific example given in 5.1.3. Figure 5.16 shows the subset definition and data handling instruction for the first run, and figure 5.17 shows the complete output listing. Figure 5.18 shows the run time format and variate definition for the second run, and Figure 5.19 the complete output for the second run. Notice that all the records in the first run concerned one operator (ERIC) carrying out very easy or easy tasks, at which he considered his efficiency to be low, while a consensus of observers held his performance to be average. In the second listing the operator (HUGH) consistently rated his efficiency higher than did the observers. These observations suggest that there are differences between operators in their self-assessments, and that there may well be differences in the way that operators and observers form their judgements.

5.1.5 User-written output Subroutine

The subroutine WOWN allows the user to define his own output layout to suit his special needs - graphics using a plotter, specialised forms of tabulation, transcriptions of encoded or encrypted data into plain language, specialised punched card formats to suit other systems, etc. Different versions of WOWN are usually given identifying names in columns 73-76 of the punched card, if they are used in that form, or otherwise identified if a more modern storage medium is available. This is for aid in storage, identification and discussion by the user, and makes no difference to the system.

Two versions of WOWN are provided in this book. The first is a simple version WOWN(DFLT) which is listed after this program, and should be used as the default version. A system flow-chart is provided in Figure 5.11b. A more elaborate version, WOWN(PLAN), is provided in Chapter 9.2 to provide plain-language listings of references.

The subroutine WOWN(DFLT) illustrates what is available to the user, and what is required of him. The subroutine header, the DIMENSION statement and the labelled COMMON statement should all appear in this form in all user-written versions of this subroutine.

At each entry to the subroutine, the vector D contains one entry, satisfying the conditions laid down in the subset specification. After all relevant entries have been read, a final call will be made to WOWN, with the vector D consisting entirely of non-values. This provides an opportunity to carry out any operations necessary at the end of an output - end of plotting, new page, output table, etc. A preliminary test should be carried out to identify this call to the subroutine and branch to the appropriate part of the subroutine.

The array FORM provides storage for 80 words of information. These may be cleared at the first call, and used to accumulate data for a final output, or at some intermediate point.

The array SCON contains the coded subset specification (see 3.4), and should not be altered by the user. If the subroutine WOWN is used conventionally - to read and output single entries - than this array will not be referred to. In some circumstances, however, it may be convenient to read entries directly from the STATCAT data bank, as is done in WOWN(PLAN), and to test them to see if they form part of the required subset before including them in the output. Care should be taken that this process does not read the data terminator, or if it does, that either a BACKSPACE operation is included to allow STLIST to read the terminator normally, (remembering that BACKSPACE may be treacherous on some computers), or two terminators are already present on the input STATCAT data bank.

The vector V contains control variates, most of which need not concern the user. V(1) will always be 6 when the subroutine WOWN is called, and must not be changed. V(2) is read in as B, the auxiliary control index, and may be used to specify options for output, as is done in WOWN(PLAN). V(4) contains the number of items per entry(NQ), and V(5) contains the default number of alternative classes. V(7) and V(8) contain the values of C and D from the data handling instruction, and may also be used to control the output subroutine. V(9) contains the number of the output device specified by the data handling instruction. This last value is also present in MED7 as an integer, being re-set from V(9) at the start of each run. V(10) may be used as a line counter, by accumulating the number of lines printed until a threshold is reached, and a new page header is printed, re-setting the value of V(10) to zero and repeating the process. At the first call to the subroutine WOWN, V(10) will be set to 100, so that, provided V(10) is not allowed to reach 100 again, this may be used as an indication of the first call, when any special initialisation work may be carried out. The rest of the vector V should not be used.

The vector TT contains the STATCAT data bank title, subset title and run title. These may be incorporated in the page header, as in WOWN(DFLT).

WOWN(DFLT) includes dummy orders using MED7, SCON and FORM to justify the appearance of these variates in the subroutine title. (Some FORTRAN IV compilers treat the presence of unused variates in a subroutine title as a fatal error).

5.1.6 Output by user-defined Run-time Format

Subroutine WFLEX allows the user to specify the way in which individual entries are to be output. He/she specifies the format into which the data are to be fitted, and provides a list of the data, transformed as required to be fitted into this format. The system flow-chart of Figure 5.11b and the comments provided in the listing of the subroutine indicate how the information is given to the system. (As the comments indicate, a difficulty may occur for machines of differing word-length. Normally, FORTRAN compilers assume, when storing a 'run-time format' that each word in the vector stores as many characters as it can hold. If this is not the case - because an A4 format has been used where words can store six characters for example - the trailing characters may be filled with gibberish, causing the system to fail, or with blanks, which will cause trouble only if 'Hollerith fields' (H formats) are used. The user should ensure that format 900 stores the maximum number of characters per word, and that sufficient cards are read to fill the input vector FORM. Additional blank cards will be ignored.)

Users who are unfamiliar with the definition of a FORTRAN format should consult any standard FORTRAN text (See the references below) or any computer programmer.

The run-time format, and its trailing blank cards should be followed by a variate specification (3.7). Only the transformation code and the data column code are used, the remaining items being discarded. In addition to the transform codes specified in Figure 3.72, a special code NAME is available for NOMINAL or ORDINAL level data, which causes the name of the class to be printed in place of its number (or MISS for non-values, or OUT if the class number is out of range).

It is up to the user to ensure that the run-time format, and the list of variates correspond - that there are the right variates, with appropriate formats in the right order.

The user should also ensure that the number of lines output by the system for one entry is an exact fraction of the number of lines per page produced by his printer, to avoid overlapping page endings.

The run-time format and variate specification are retained for one run through the STATCAT data bank, then discarded. If a second run is required, the format and variate specification must be repeated. If no entry satisfies the subset conditions, then the subroutine WFLEX will be called only when the data terminator is read - it will then print a record of the format and variate specification, with a message that the subset is empty.

REFERENCES : McCracken (1972), ASA FORTRAN IV (1966)

Figure 5.11a - System Flow-charts - STLIST, CLIST and WCAR

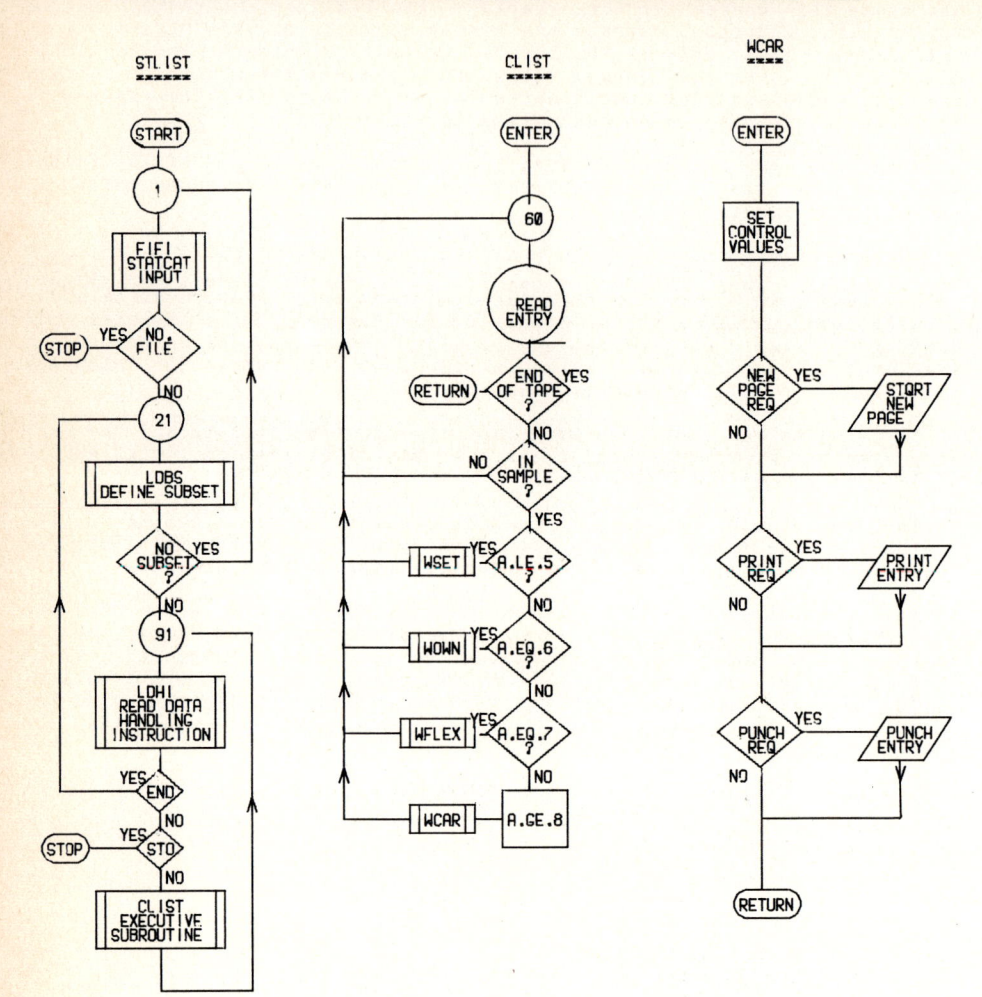

Figure 5.11b - System Flow-charts - WSET, WFLEX and WOWN

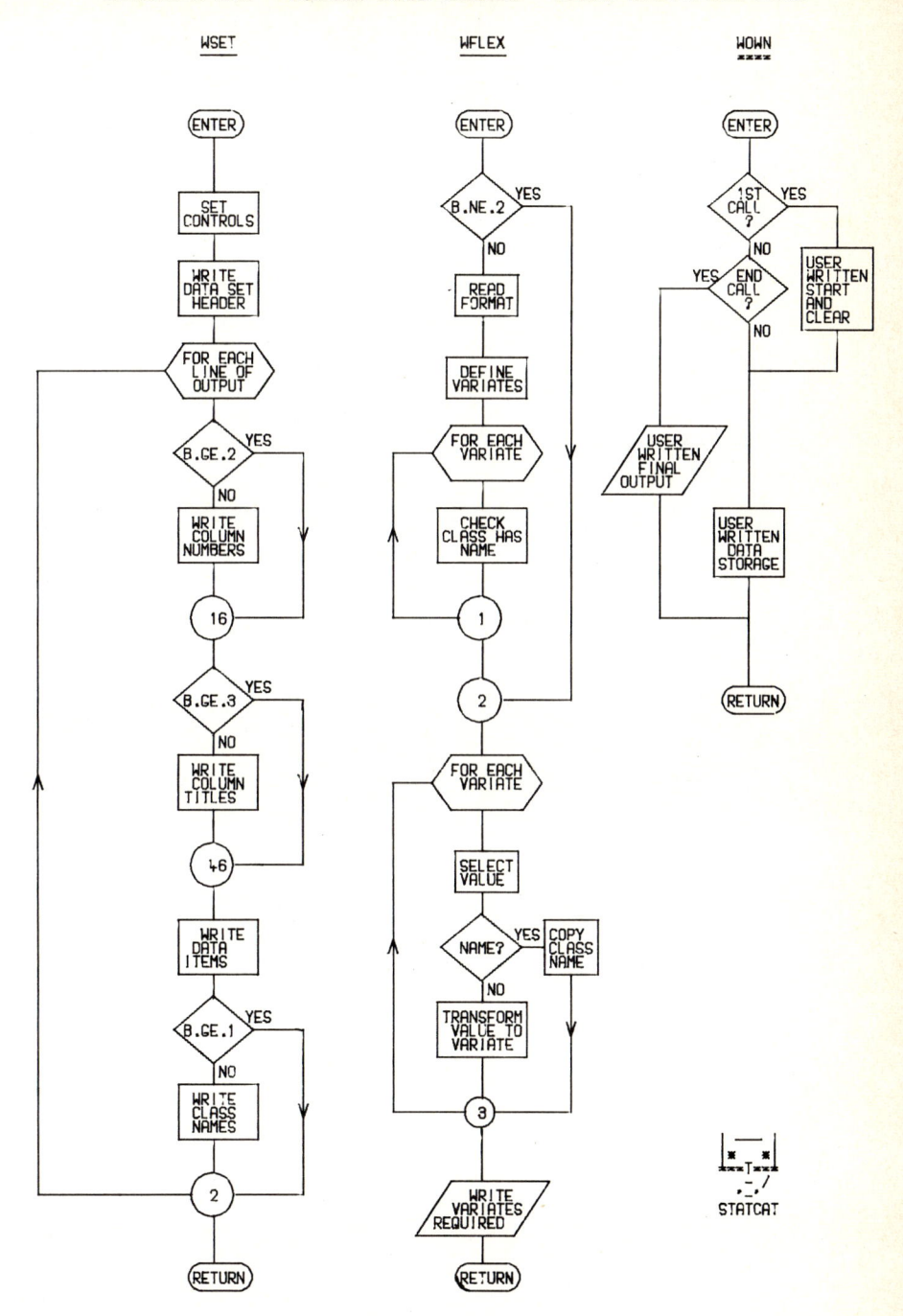

Figure 5.12 - STLIST - Input Structure

```
          Level
   0   1   2   3   4   5   6   7   8   9
FILE CONTROL CARD
    SUBSET SPECIFICATION
        DATA HANDLING INSTRUCTION
        BACK TO READ NEW SUBSET
    SUBSET SPECIFICATION
        DATA HANDLING INSTRUCTION
        |RUN-TIME FORMAT                   |
        |RUN-TIME VARIATE SPECIFICATION    |
        STOP
```

Figure 5.13 - STLIST - Input Example

```
---------1---------2---------3---------4---------5---------6---------7--
**STLISTDEMO                            DEMONSTRATION STATCAT DATA BANK
VERY DIFFERENT EFFICIENCY ESTIMATES
.IF.EFOB.LE.EFOP-75.                    OBSERVER LOWER THAN OPERATOR
.OR.EFOB.GT.EFOP+75.                    OBSERVER HIGHER THAN OPERATOR
END OF SUBSET SPECIFICATION

4                                       TWENTY ITEMS PER RUN
BACK                                    READ NEW DATA BANK SUBSET

ASSESSED AS VERY HARD                   BY OPERATOR
.IF.DIFF.EQ.VHAR
END OF SUBSET SPECIFICATION

7                                       FOLLOWED BY ADDITIONAL DATA
(12H0AT SESSION ,F4.0,4H ON ,A4,4HDAY ,A4,10H OPERATOR ,A4,
21H AT WORKING POSITION ,A4/
10X,20HFOUND THE OPERATION ,A4,21H VERY HARD (STRESS - ,A4,2H ))


VAL.SESS
NAMEDAY.
NAMETIME
NAMEOPER
NAMEW.P.
NAMETASK
NAMESTRS
END OF VARIATE SPECIFICATION
STOP
---------1---------2---------3---------4---------5---------6---------7--
```

Figure 5.14 - STLIST - Output Structure

```
For each    ) : File Control Record
output file )   File Parameters
                Data Description
                For each)  : Subset Input Record
                Subset  )    For each        ) Input Record
                             Data Handling   ) For each) Listing
                             Instruction     ) entry in) as
                                               subset  ) specified
```

Figure 5.15 - STLIST - Output Example page-by-page Listing

Page	Contents	Origin
1-2	File Control Record	FIFI
	Program Title	STLIST
	File Parameters	LDAP
	Data Description record	LDDS
3	Subset record	LSAMP
	Data Handling Instruction	LDHI
4	Listing of entries	CLIST/WSET
5	End of Run Message	CLIST
	Data Handling Instruction (BACK)	LDHI
6	Subset record	LSAMP
	Data Handling Instruction	LDHI
7	Run-time Format + Variates	WOWN/LGEN
8	Listing of Entries	WOWN
9	End of Run Message	CLIST
	Data Handling Instruction (STOP)	LDHI

Figure 5.16 - STLIST - Subset and DHI - First Run

```
    DATA BANK SUBSET TITLE - VERY DIFFERENT EFFICIENCY ESTIMATES    COMMENT
.IF.   EFOB   .LE.   EFOP   - 75.000000                              COMMENT OBSERVER MUCH LOWER THAN OPERATOR
.OR.   EFOB   .GT.   EFOP   + 75.000000                              COMMENT OBSERVER MUCH HIGHER THAN OPERATOR
END OF SUBSET SPECIFICATION                                          COMMENT

                        DATA HANDLING INSTRUCTION - ECFC PRINT

ABCCCDDDEFEEEEFEFFFFFFFGGGGGGGGGGGGGGGGHHHHHHHHHHHHHHHHHHHHHHHHHHHHHH
  4                         XXXXXXXXXXXXXXXXXTwENTY ITEMS PER RUN

            OUTPUT CONTROL INDEX   =    4
            AUXILIARY CONTROL INDEX =    0
       NUMBER OF FIRST COLUMN OUTPUT =    1
       NUMBER OF LAST COLUMN OUTPUT . =   18
       NUMBER OF OUTPUT DEVICE ...... =    0

    THE SYSTEM HAS STANDARDISED  2 CONTROL VALUES FROM THE DATA HANDLING INSTRUCTION        ** WARNING **
       PLEASE VERIFY THAT THE ASSUMPTIONS IT HAS MADE ARE CORRECT AND ADJUST STORAGE IF NECESSARY

INPUT ACCEPTED - LISTING COMMENCES
```

Figure 5.17 - STLIST - Output - First Run

```
        DATA BANK TITLE - DEMONSTRATION STATCNT DATA BANK
        DATA BANK SUBSET TITLE - TWENTY ITEMS PER RUN
            LISTED FROM COLUMN   1 TO COLUMN  18

        ENTRY NUMBER      1    FIRST DATA ITEM       1.00000

     1    2    3    4    5    6    7    8    9   10   11   12   13   14   15   16   17   18
  NTRY SESS OBSR OPER W.P. STRS DAY. TIME TASK DIFF TEMP TPCT EFCP EFOB H.R. TCOM TALL ERRP
  1.00 1.00 1.00 1.00 1.00 1.00 1.00 1.00 1.00 22.00 0.62 13.31 91.59 35.52 48.30 48.00 0.50
   A&   A&  MIKE ERIC   I   NONE MON. AM1  ASSL VFAS BO        ;BJ AM5R ESP  BTE; BO<<  BO

        ENTRY NUMBER     23    FIRST DATA ITEM      23.00000

     1    2    3    4    5    6    7    8    9   10   11   12   13   14   15   16   17   18
  NTRY SESS OBSR OPER W.P. STRS DAY. TIME TASK DIFF TEMP TPCT EFCP EFOB H.R. TCOM TALL ERRP
 23.00 6.00 4.00 1.00 3.00 2.00 2.00 2.00 1.00 29.00 0.62 14.45 92.93 36.34 48.30 48.00 0.50
   BP   A-  PETE ERIC   K   HEAT TUES AM2 ASSL VFAS BJ        ;BJ AX33 B*>M BUP  BO<< BO

        ENTRY NUMBER     35    FIRST DATA ITEM      35.00000

     1    2    3    4    5    6    7    8    9   10   11   12   13   14   15   16   17   18
  NTRY SESS OBSR OPER W.P. STRS DAY. TIME TASK DIFF TEMP TPCT EFCP EFOB H.R. TCOM TALL ERRP
 35.00 9.00 3.00 1.00 3.00 2.00 3.00 1.00 3.00 2.00 24.00 -1.18 27.56 106.05 44.84 50.40 51.00 0.10
   BT   A&  OSCR ERIC   K   HEAT WED. AM1  CUT. EASY BO  AK/G 9$!*  B <<  B.TP B2mm  B3   RRR

        ENTRY NUMBER     62    FIRST DATA ITEM      62.00000

     1    2    3    4    5    6    7    8    9   10   11   12   13   14   15   16   17   18
  NTRY SESS OBSR OPER W.P. STRS DAY. TIME TASK DIFF TEMP TPCT EFOP EFOB H.R. TCOM TALL ERRP
 62.00 16.00 3.00 1.00 2.00 3.00 4.00 4.00 1.00 1.00 25.00 0.62 15.01 55.54 36.00 48.30 48.00 1.30
   B=   B&  OSCR ERIC   J   DAMP THUR PA2  ASSL VFAS BR        ;BJ A0Y5 B- ' BU/G BO<<  BO   AM<<
```

Figure 5.18 - STLIST - Run-time Format / Variates - 2nd run

USING FORMAT :

```
(12H AT SESSION ,F4.0,4H ON ,A4,4HDAY ,A4,10H OPERATOR ,A4,
21H AT WORKING POSITION ,A4/
10X,20HFOUND THE OPERATION ,A4,2/H VERY DIFFICULT (STRESS - ,A4,2H ))
```

```
1 ORIGINAL VAL.    SESS
A STANDARD VAL.    COL2

2 ORIGINAL NAME    DAY.
B STANDARD NAME    COL7

3 ORIGINAL NAME    TIME
C STANDARD NAME    COL8

4 ORIGINAL NAME    OPER
D STANDARD NAME    COL4

5 ORIGINAL NAME    W.P.
E STANDARD NAME    COL5

6 ORIGINAL NAME    TASK
F STANDARD NAME    COL9

7 ORIGINAL NAME    STRS
G STANDARD NAME    COL6
```

END OF VARIATE SPECIFICATION

Figure 5.19 - STLIST - Output - Second Run

```
AT SESSION    5. ON TUESDAY AM1  OPERATOR HUGH AT WORKING POSITION  I
     FOUND THE OPERATION CUT. VERY HARD (STRESS - NOIS )

AT SESSION    6. ON TUESDAY AM2  OPERATOR HUGH AT WORKING POSITION  L
     FOUND THE OPERATION DRIL VERY HARD (STRESS - HEAT )

AT SESSION    9. ON WED.DAY AM1  OPERATOR HUGH AT WORKING POSITION  L
     FOUND THE OPERATION BEND VERY HARD (STRESS - NOIS )

AT SESSION   15. ON THURDAY PM1  OPERATOR HUGH AT WORKING POSITION  L
     FOUND THE OPERATION CUT. VERY HARD (STRESS - HEAT )
```

```
C MASTER STLIST - LISTS ENTRIES IN A DATA BANK SUBSET
C   SUBROUTINES AND FUNCTIONS REQUIRED
C  NAME            TYPE              COMMENT
C  AN      (SEE  3.1 ) SERVICE     ALPHA - TO NUMERIC VALUE
C  CHIKEN  (SEE 11.9 ) SERVICE     WARNS OF MISMATCHED DATA LEVEL
C  CLIST   (SEE  5.1 ) EXECUTIVE   LISTS DATA BANK OR SUBSET
C  CLSAM   (SEE  3.5 ) SERVICE     ALLOTS ENTRY TO SAMPLE/SUBSET
C  COMPA   (SEE  3.1 ) SERVICE     COMPARES ALPHAMERIC VALUES
C  COPYA   (SEE  3.1 ) SERVICE     COPIES ALPHAMERIC VALUE
C  FIFI    (SEE  3.2 ) SYSTEM      ALLOCATES PERIPHERALS
C  IBL     (SEE  3.1 ) SERVICE     DETECTS BLANK,END AND STOP CARDS
C  ICH     (SEE  3.1 ) SERVICE     IDENTIFIES ALPHAMERIC CODES
C  LDAP    (SEE  3.3 ) SYSTEM      LOADS/CHECKS DATA BANK PARAMETERS
C  LDBS    (SEE  3.6 ) SYSTEM      LOADS SUBSET DEFINITION
C  LDDS    (SEE  3.4 ) SYSTEM      LOADS DATA DESCRIPTION SEGMENT
C  LDHI    (SEE  3.8 ) SYSTEM      LOADS/CHECKS DATA HANDLING INSTN
C  LGEN    (SEE  3.7 ) SYSTEM      LOADS GENERALISED VARIATES
C  LSET    (SEE  3.5 ) SYSTEM      LOADS DEFINING CONDITIONS
C  TRANS   (SEE  3.7 ) SERVICE     CARRIES OUT REQUIRED TRANSFORM
C  WCAR    (SEE  5.1 ) SERVICE     OUTPUT PUNCHED CARDS
C  WFLEX   (SEE  5.1 ) SERVICE     WRITE WITH RUN-TIME FORMAT
C  WOWN    (SEE  9.4 ) SERVICE     WRITE AS DEFINED BY USER
C  WSET    (SEE  5.1 ) SERVICE     WRITE ENTRY - STANDARD FORM
C IF NQMAX=NO OF DATA COLUMNS IS ALTERED ALTER DATA CN STATEMENT
C DIMENSION D(NQMAX),IT(NQMAX),CN(NQMAX),ST(NQMAX)
      NQMAX = 100
      DIMENSION D(100),IT(100),CN(100),ST(100)
      DATA  CN/4HCOL1,4HCOL2,4HCOL3,4HCOL4,4HCOL5,4HCOL6,4HCOL7,4HCOL8,4
     1HCOL9,4HCL10,4HCL11,4HCL12,4HCL13,4HCL14,4HCL15,4HCL16,4HCL17,4HCL
     218,4HCL19,4HCL20,4HCL21,4HCL22,4HCL23,4HCL24,4HCL25,4HCL26,4HCL27,
     34HCL28,4HCL29,4HCL30,4HCL31,4HCL32,4HCL33,4HCL34,4HCL35,4HCL36,4HC
     4L37,4HCL38,4HCL39,4HCL40,4HCL41,4HCL42,4HCL43,4HCL44,4HCL45,4HCL46
     5,4HCL47,4HCL48,4HCL49,4HCL50,4HCL51,4HCL52,4HCL53,4HCL54,4HCL55,4H
     6CL56,4HCL57,4HCL58,4HCL59,4HCL60,4HCL61,4HCL62,4HCL63,4HCL64,4HCL6
     75,4HCL66,4HCL67,4HCL68,4HCL69,4HCL70,4HCL71,4HCL72,4HCL73,4HCL74,4
     8HCL75,4HCL76,4HCL77,4HCL78,4HCL79,4HCL80,4HCL81,4HCL82,4HCL83,4HCL
     984,4HCL85,4HCL86,4HCL87,4HCL88,4HCL89,4HCL90,4HCL91,4HCL92,4HCL93,
     94HCL94,4HCL95,4HCL96,4HCL97,4HCL98,4HCL99,4HC100/
C DIMENSION  TRT(NALTMX)=MAXIMUM NUMBER OF CLASSES ON TAPE
      NALTMX = 50
      DIMENSION  TRT(50)
C DIMENSION RT(MAXM) = NUMBER OF STORAGE CELLS AVAILABLE
      MAXM = 2000
      DIMENSION RT(2000)
C DIMENSION SCON(5,MAXDBC)= NUMBER OF SUBSET CONDITIONS
      MAXDBC=100
      DIMENSION SCON(5,100)
C THE FOLLOWING DIMENSIONS ARE FIXED
      NU = 60
      DIMENSION U(60),LU(60),FORM(50)
C TRANSFORMATION CODES
C UNITS                       BLOCKS
C        0 - 9  10 - 19   20 - 29   30 - 39   40 - 49   50 - 59
C       POWERS TRIG       TRIG      STATIST   MATHS     TEST
C              RADIANS    DEGREES   TRANSF    FUNCTS    FUNCTIONS
C  0      -       -       H.MS         -         -      RM10
C  1     VAL.    SINR     SIND       PSNA      RECP     +/-1
C  2     SQAR    COSR     COSD       PSNB      SQRT     ADD1
C  3     CUBE    TANR     TAND       BINO      ABSV     SUB1
C  4     4PWR    ASIR     ASID       LG+1      SIGN     NOR1
C  5     5PWR    ACOR     ACOD       LOGE      INTG     +/-P
C  6     6PWR    ATAR     ATAD       LG10      FRAC     ADDP
C  7     7PWR    SINH     DTOR       AL10      EXPT     SUBP
```

```
C     8    8PWR    COSH         RTOD         -           PRES    NORP
C     9    9PWR    TANH         H.HH         -           NEG.    +100
      DATA U/4HVAL.,4HSQAR,4HCUBE,4H4PWR,4H5PWR,4H6PWR,4H7PWR,4H8PWR,4H9
     1PWR,4HVAL ,4HSINR,4HCOSR,4HTANR,4HASIR,4HACOR,4HATAR,4HSINH,4HCOSH
     2,4HTANH,4HH.MS,4HSIND,4HCOSD,4HTAND,4HASID,4HACOD,4HATAD,4HDTOR,4H
     3RTOD,4HH.HH,4H VAL,4HPSNA,4HPSNB,4HBINO,4HLG+1,4HLOGE,4HLG10,4HAL1
     40,4H    ,4H    ,4H    ,4HRECP,4HSQRT,4HABSV,4HSIGN,4HINTG,4HFRAC,4
     5HEXPT,4HPRES,4HNEG.,4HRM10,4H+/-1,4HADD1,4HSUB1,4HNOR1,4H+/-P,4HAD
     6DP,4HSUBP,4HNORP,4H+100,4HNAME/
      DATA LU/1,8*5,1,9*5,1,9*5,1,6*5,4*1,2*5,2*3,3*5,7*2,4*5,2*2/
      COMMON /STCT/MED1,MED2,MED3,MED4,MED5,MED6,MED13,Q,V(20),TT(30)
      DATA PROG/4HLIST/,BL/4H    /
      MED1 = -1
C LEVEL 0 = SETTING UP (MEDP=OUTPUT MEDIUM,USUALLY CARD PUNCH)
      MEDP = 6
    1 CALL COPYA(TT(1),PROG)
      CALL FIFI
      IF(MED6.GT.0) WRITE(MED6,901)
      CALL LDAP(MED2,MED3,V,TT,Q,NQ,NALT,NQMAX,NALTMX,IGO)
      IF(IGO.GT.0) GO TO 1
      LI = 18
      CALL LDDS(TRT,NALT,D,NQ,ST,NQ,IT,NQ,H,0,H,H,0,LI,0,Q,VX,
     1 0,MED2,MED3,0,IGO)
C LEVEL 2 - LOAD SUBSET SPECIFICATION - MOVE SUBSET TITLE UP
   21 IF(V(10).GE.20.) V(10) = 0.
      CALL LDBS(SCON,NCON,MAXDBC,CM,ST,IT,NQ,TRT,NALT,IGO)
      DO 22 I = 11,20
   22 CALL COPYA(TT(I),TT(I+10))
      IF(IGO.GT.0) GO TO 1
C LEVEL 9 - DATA HANDLING INSTRUCTION
   91 IF(V(10).GT.90.) V(10) = 0.
      CALL LDHI(V(1),1,V(2),6,V(7),1,V(8),2,V(9),3,VX,0,V(14),V(10),
     1TT(21),FORM,MED1,MED2,0,Q,NQ,NWARN,1,IGO)
      IF(IGO.GT.0) GO TO 21
C STANDARDISATION   V(1)=6 USER OUTPUT - NO STANDARDISATION
      NT = V(1)
      IF(NT.EQ.6)WRITE (MED6,991)V(2),V(7),V(8),V(9)
      IF(NT.EQ.6) GO TO 100
C V(1) = 0-5,7-9 1 LE V(7) LE V(8) LE NQ  V(7)=V(8)=0 BECOMES 1-NQ
      IF(V(7).LT.0.5.AND.V(8).LT.0.5) NWARN = NWARN + 1
      IF(V(7).LT.0.5.AND.V(8).LT.0.5) V(8) = V(4)
      IF(V(7).GT.V(4)) NWARN = NWARN + 1
      IF(V(7).GT.V(4)) V(7) = V(4)
      IF(V(7).LT.0.5) NWARN = NWARN + 1
      IF(V(7).LT.0.5) V(7) = 1.
      IF(V(8).GT.V(4))NWARN = NWARN + 1
      IF(V(8).GT.V(4))V(8) = V(4)
      IF(V(8).LT.V(7)) NWARN = NWARN + 1
      IF(V(8).LT.V(7)) V(8) = V(7)
      IF(NT.LE.5) GO TO 98
      IF(NT.GE.8) GO TO 97
C V(1)=7 (RUN-TIME FORMAT) V(2) MUST BE 0
      IF(V(2).NE.0.) NWARN = NWARN + 1
      IF(V(2).NE.0.) V(2) = 0.
      GO TO 98
C V(1) = 8-9 OUTPUT MEDIUM (PUNCH,ETC.) = MEDP IF NOT SPECIFIED
   97 IF(IBL(FORM(9),8,1).GE.0) GO TO 98
      NWARN = NWARN + 1
      V(9) = MEDP
   98 CALL LDHI(V(1),1,V(2),6,V(7),1,V(8),2,V(9),3,VX,0,V(14),V(10),
     1TT(21),FORM,MED1,MED2,0,Q,NQ,NWARN,2,IGO)
      IF(IGO.GT.0) GO TO 91
C DETECT IMPOSSIBLE PARAMETERS
```

```
      NCAV = MAXM/NALT
      NQA = V(8) - V(7) + 1.
      IF(NQA.LE.NCAV) GO TO 100
      WRITE(MED2,994) NQA,NCAV
      GO TO 91
  100 WRITE(MED6,998)
C CALL EXECUTIVE
      V(10) = 100.
      CALL CLIST(D,IT,ST,RT,NQ,NALT,SCON,NCON,NCAV,CN,U,LU,NU)
      V(10) = 0.
      WRITE(MED6,999)
      GO TO 91
  901 FORMAT (1H0,20X,26HSTATCAT LISTING OF ENTRIES)
  991 FORMAT (1H0//35H USER-WRITTEN SUBROUTINE CALLED FOR /
     121X,34HNO STANDARDISATION OF INPUT VALUES/
     221X,11HV(1) =    6./21X,6HV(2) =,F5.1/21X,6HV(7) =,F5.1/
     321X,6HV(8) =,F20.8/21X,6HV(9) =,F20.8//)
  994 FORMAT (1H0,I6,24HCOLUMNS REQUIRED - ONLY ,I4,10H AVAILABLE)
  998 FORMAT(35H0INPUT ACCEPTED - LISTING COMMENCES)
  999 FORMAT (35H1LISTING COMPLETED - READ NEW INPUT)
      END
```

```
      SUBROUTINE CLIST(D,IT,ST,RT,NQ,NALT,SCON,NCON,NCAV,CN,TR,LT,NT)
C CLIST    (SEE  5.1 )  EXECUTIVE    LISTS DATA BANK OR SUBSET
C LISTS ALL   ENTRIES IN THE GIVEN DATA BANK SUBSET
C MED7 SHOULD BE CARD PUNCH OR OTHER OUTPUT DEVICE
      DIMENSION D(NQ),IT(NQ),ST(NQ),CN(NQ),RT(NCAV,NALT)
      DIMENSION TR(NT),LT(NT),IP(50),FORM(100),SCON(5,NCON)
      COMMON /STCT/MED1,MED2,MED3,MED4,MED5,MED6,MED13,Q,V(20),TT(30)
      NS = V(7)
      NF = V(8)
      MED7 = V(9)
      NZ = NF-NS+1
      V(6) = 0.
      REWIND MED3
      READ(MED3)NX,NX,X,(TT(J),J=1,10),(X,J=1,6)
      DO 1 J = 1,NQ
      M = J - NS + 1
      IF(J.LT.NS.OR.J.GT.NF) READ(MED3) (X,I=1,19),(X,I=1,NALT),NX,X,X
    1 IF(J.GE.NS.AND.J.LE.NF) READ(MED3) (X,I=1,19),(RT(M,I),I=1,NALT),NX,
     1X,X
C LIST   ENTRIES IN DATA BANK SUBSET
      NR = 0
      NA = V(1)
      V(10) = 100.
    2 NR = NR + 1
      READ(MED3) D
C CHECK FOR END OF TAPE -
      DO 3 I = 1,NQ
      IF(D(I).NE.Q) GO TO 4
    3 CONTINUE
      REWIND MED3
      IF(NA.EQ.7.AND.V(6).EQ.0.)
     1CALL WFLEX(D,NQ,RT,NALT,NCAV,IP,CN,ST,IT,FORM,TR,LT,NT)
      IF(NA.EQ.6) CALL WOWN(D,NQ,FORM,SCON,NCON,MED7)
      RETURN
C CHECK IF IN SAMPLE
    4 CALL CLSAM(D,NQ,SCON,NCON,NIN,1)
      IF(NIN.NE.1) GO TO 2
      V(6) = V(6) + 1.
C CALL APPROPRIATE OUTPUT SUBROUTINE
      IF(NA.LE.5) CALL WSET(D,NQ,RT,NCAV,NALT,IT,ST,NR,TT,V,MED2)
      IF(NA.EQ.6) CALL WOWN(D,NQ,FORM,SCON,NCON,MED7)
      IF(NA.EQ.7) CALL WFLEX(D,NQ,RT,NALT,NCAV,IP,CN,ST,IT,FORM,TR,LT,NT)
      IF(NA.GE.8) CALL WCAR(D(NS),NZ,V,MED2,MED7)
      GO TO 2
      END


      SUBROUTINE WSET(D,NQ,RT,NCAV,NALT,IT,ST,NR,TT,V,MED2)
C WSET     (SEE   5.1 ) SERVICE     WRITE ENTRY - STANDARD FORM
C PARAMETERS CONTROLLING OUTPUT
C V(1) = NA       V(2) = NB     V(7) = NS      V(8) = NF      V(10)
C  NEG NO OUTPUT
C  0  5E FORMAT        CLASS NAME    START         FINISH         COUNTS
C  1  5F24.8           COL NUMBER    COLUMN        COLUMN         LINES
C  2  10F12.5          COLUMN NAME                                OUTPUT
C  3  15F 8.3          DATA ITEMS
C  4  20F 6.2          ENTRY NO,ITEM 1,ITEM NS
C  5  25F 4.1          ENTRY NO,ITEM 1
C  6                   ENTRY NO ONLY
      DIMENSION D(NQ),RT(NCAV,NALT),IT(NCAV),V(20),TT(30),ST(NCAV)
      DIMENSION F1(6),F2(5),FA(5,5),TA(2),ER(4)
      DATA ER/4HMISS,4HNEG ,4HLOW ,4HHIGH/,TA/4H I4 ,4H A4 /
      DATA F1/4H(1H ,4H, 5(,4H11X,,4H I4 ,4H,9X ,4H)) /
```

```fortran
      DATA F2/4H(1H ,4H, 5(,4H   E,4H24.8,4H))   /
      DATA FA/4H, 5(,4H11X,,4H,9X ,4H    F,4H24.8,4H, 10(,4H 2X,,4H,6X  ,
     1 4H    F,4H12.4,4H,15(,4H    ,4H,4X ,4H    F,4H 8.3,4H,20(,4H    ,
     2 4H,2X ,4H    F,4H 6.2,4H,25(,4H    ,4H    ,4H    F,4H 4.1/
      IF(V(1).LT.0..OR.V(2).LT.0..OR.V(2).GE.7.) RETURN
      NA = V(1)
      NB = V(2)
      NS = V(7)
      NF = V(8)
C CALCULATE LINES REQUIRED - NEW PAGE IF REQUIRED - ADJUST FORMATS
      NINL = NA*5
      IF(NINL.LE.0) NINL = 5
      NLIN = (NF-NS)/NINL + 1
      IF(NB.GE.4) REQ = 1
      IF(NB.LE.3) REQ = 2 + (5-NB)*NLIN
      V(10) = V(10) + REQ
      IF(V(10).GT.50)
     1 WRITE(MED2,900) (TT(J),J=1,10),(TT(J),J=21,30),NS,NF
      IF(V(10).GT.50) V(10) = REQ + 3.
      IF(NA.EQ.0)GO TO 1
      CALL COPYA(F1(2),FA(1,NA))
      CALL COPYA(F1(3),FA(2,NA))
      CALL COPYA(F1(5),FA(3,NA))
      CALL COPYA(F2(2),FA(1,NA))
      CALL COPYA(F2(3),FA(4,NA))
      CALL COPYA(F2(4),FA(5,NA))
C ENTRY NUMBER ETC.
    1 IF(NB.LE.3) WRITE(MED2,904)
      WRITE(MED2,901) NR
      IF(NB.EQ.6) RETURN
      WRITE(MED2,902)D(1)
      IF(NB.EQ.5) RETURN
      IF(NS.GT.1)WRITE(MED2,903)NS,D(NS)
      IF(NB.EQ.4) RETURN
      DO 3 IST = NS,NF,NINL
      IF(NB.LE.3)WRITE(MED2,904)
      IFIN = IST + NINL - 1
      IF(IFIN.GT.NF) IFIN = NF
      IF(NB.LE.1)CALL COPYA(F1(4),TA(1))
C COLUMN NUMBER IF REQUIRED
      IF(NB.LE.1)WRITE(MED2,F1)  (I,I=IST,IFIN)
      L = IST-NS+ 1
      M = IFIN - NS + 1
      IF(NB.LE.2)CALL COPYA(F1(4),TA(2))
C COLUMN NAME IF REQUIRED
      IF(NB.LE.2)WRITE(MED2,F1)  (ST(I),I=L,M)
C DATA ITEM
      WRITE(MED2,F2) (D(I),I= IST,IFIN)
      IF(NB.EQ.3) GO TO 3
C CLASS NAMES IF REQUIRED - PLUS WARNINGS
      DO 2 I = IST,IFIN
      M = I-NS+1
      ITM = IT(M)
      N = D(I)
      IE=0
      IF(ITM.GE.5.AND.ITM.NE.6.AND.D(I).LE.0.) IE = 2
      IF(ITM.GE.2.AND.ITM.LE.3.AND.N.LT.1)     IE = 3
      IF(ITM.GE.2.AND.ITM.LE.3.AND.N.GT.NALT)  IE = 4
      IF(D(I).EQ.Q) IE = 1
      IF(ITM.GE.2.AND.ITM.LE.3.AND.IE.EQ.0) CALL COPYA(D(I),RT(M,N))
    2 IF(IE.NE.0) CALL COPYA(D(I),ER(IE))
      CALL COPYA(F1(4),TA(2))
      WRITE(MED2,F1)(D(I),I=IST,IFIN)
```

```
      3 CONTINUE
        RETURN
    900 FORMAT(1H1,10X,18HDATA BANK TITLE - ,10A4/1H ,10X,25HDATA BANK SUB
       1SET TITLE - ,10A4/1H ,15X,20H  LISTED FROM COLUMN,I4,3H TO,7H COLU
       2MN,I4)
    901 FORMAT(1H ,10X,13HENTRY NUMBER ,I6)
    902 FORMAT(1H+,33X,16HFIRST DATA ITEM ,F14.5)
    903 FORMAT(1H+,70X,10HDATA ITEM ,I6,F16.5)
    904 FORMAT(1H )
        END


        SUBROUTINE WFLEX(D,NQ,RT,NALT,NCAV,IP,CN,ST,IT,FORM,T,LT,NT)
C WFLEX   (SEE  5.1 ) SERVICE       WRITE WITH RUN-TIME FORMAT
        DIMENSION RT(NCAV,NALT),T(NT),LT(NT),H(1),IH(1)
        DIMENSION D(NQ),ST(NQ),CN(NQ),IT(NQ),IP(50),E(50),FORM(100)
        DATA XMIS/4HMISS/,OUT/4H OUT/
        COMMON /STCT/MED1,MED2,MED3,MED4,MED5,MED6,MED13,Q,V(20),TT(30)
C NOTE TO PROGRAMMERS
C SOME FORTRAN COMPILERS GIVE AN ERROR IF THE A UNIT IN FORMAT 900
C IS NOT THE LARGEST POSSIBLE,AND H FIELDS ARE USED. IF THIS HAPPENS,
C MODIFY THE FORMAT,AND INCREASE THE NUMBER OF CARDS USED TO SUIT THE
C THE NUMBER OF VALUES READ PER CARD. ADJUST FORMATS 900 AND 902 TO FIT
C I.E. FOR 20A4 USE        5 CARDS
C       FOR 16A5 USE    7 CARDS
C       FOR 13A6 USE    8 CARDS (IGNORE COLUMNS 79-80)
C       FOR 11A7 USE   10 CARDS (IGNORE COLUMNS 78-80)
C       FOR 10A8 USE   10 CARDS
C ADDITIONAL BLANKS WILL BE IGNORED
    900 FORMAT(20A4)
    901 FORMAT(8H0VARIATE,I4,35H USES THE CLASS NAME OF DATA COLUMN,I4,2H
       1(,A4,23H) WHICH IS NOT IN STORE,34X,11H**WARNING**)
    902 FORMAT(15H1USING FORMAT : /8(/10X,20A4)//14H WITH VARIATES/)
    903 FORMAT(1H1)
    904 FORMAT(1H0,10X,22HNO DATA IN THIS SAMPLE)
        XALT = NALT
        IBASE = V(19)
        NS = V(7)
        NF = V(8)
        IF(V(2).NE.0.) GO TO 3
        READ(MED1,900) FORM
        WRITE(MED2,902) FORM
        M = 50
        IFIN = M
        ISF = 0
        CALL LGEN(T,NT,LT,NT,ST,IT,CN,NQ,IH,0,H,H,0,H,H,0,0,0,IH,IP,M,ISF,
       1IFIN,1,NALT)
        V(2) = 1.
        DO 1 I = 1,ISF
        JT = IP(I)/1000
        IC = IP(I) - JT*1000
        IF(JT.LT.60) GO TO 1
        IF(IC.LT.NS.OR.IC.GT.NF)WRITE(MED2,901)I,IC,ST(IC)
      1 CONTINUE
        WRITE(MED2,903)
        DO 2 I = 1,NQ
        IF(D(I).NE.Q) GO TO 3
      2 CONTINUE
        WRITE(MED2,904)
        RETURN
      3 DO 4 I = 1,ISF
        JT = IP(I)/1000
        IC = IP(I) - JT*1000
```

```
      IF(JT.LT.60) E(I) = TRANS(D(IC),Q,JT,IBASE)
      IF(JT.LT.60) GO TO 4
      IF(D(IC).EQ.Q.OR.IC.LT.NS.OR.IC.GT.NF)CALL COPYA(E(I),XMIS)
      IF(D(IC).EQ.Q.OR.IC.LT.NS.OR.IC.GT.NF) GO TO 4
      IF(D(IC).LT.1..OR.D(IC).GT.XALT)CALL COPYA(E(I),OUT)
      IF(D(IC).EQ.Q.OR.D(IC).LT.1..OR.D(IC).GT.XALT) GO TO 4
      J = D(IC)
      IC2 = IC-NS+1
      CALL COPYA(E(I),RT(IC2,J))
    4 CONTINUE
      WRITE(MED2,FORM)(E(I),I = 1,ISP)
      V(19) = IBASE
      RETURN
      END
```

```
      SUBROUTINE WOWN(D,NQ,FORM,SCON,NCON,MED7)
C WOWN    (SEE  5.1 ) SERVICE     USER OUTPUT - DEFAULT VERSION
C V(2) = 1  NUMERIC ONLY     V(2) = 2 ALPHA ONLY    V(2)= OTHER BOTH
C D CONTAINS THE NQ ITEMS IN THE CURRENT ENTRY
C V(10) = 100. AT FIRST CALL - USED AS LINE COUNTER THEREAFTER
C TT(1-10) = DATA BANK TITLE    TT(11-20) = SUBSET TITLE
C TT(21-30) = RUN TITLE      MED7 = PUNCH -SPECIFIED ON D.H.I.
      DIMENSION D(NQ),FORM(80),SCON(5,NCON)
      COMMON /STCT/MED1,MED2,MED3,MED4,MED5,MED6,MED13,Q,V(20),TT(30)
C TEST FOR END OF DATA BANK
      DO 1 I = 1,NQ
      IF(D(I).NE.Q) GO TO 2
    1 CONTINUE
      RETURN
    2 NL = V(10)
      NC = V(2) + 0.01
      NNL = 0
      IF(NC.NE.1) NNL = NNL + (NQ+59)/30
      IF(NC.NE.2) NNL = NNL + (NQ+9)/5
      NL = NL + NNL
      IF(NL.GT.50) WRITE(MED2,900)     TT
      IF(NL.GT.50) NL =    NNL + 4
      V(10) = NL
      IF(NC.NE.2) WRITE(MED2,901) D
      IF(NC.NE.1) WRITE(MED2,902) D
C SOME COMPILERS CHECK THAT ALL DUMMY VARIABLES ARE USED  SO -
      FORM(1) = FORM(1)
      SCON(1,1) = SCON(1,1)
      MED7 = MED7
      RETURN
  900 FORMAT(23H1USER OUTPUT - DEFAULT ,7X,1H-,4X,18HLISTING OF ENTRIES/
     1         16H DATA BANK TITLE,14X,1H-,4X,10A4/23H DATA BANK SUBSET TI
     2TLE,7X,1H-,4X,10A4/10H RUN TITLE,20X,1H-,4X,10A4)
  901 FORMAT(1H0,5F24.8/(1H ,5F24.8))
  902 FORMAT(1H0,30A4/(1H ,30A4))
      END
```

5.2 PROGRAM STDESC - DESCRIBE STATCAT DATA BANK

5.2.1 Purpose

This program describes STATCAT data bank subsets. It will provide frequency tabulations of subsets of data, either in their stored form, or after transformation by any of the transforms given in 3.7. Statistics appropriate to the data level and simple graphical representations of the distribution of data will also be produced. In addition, statistics appropriate to other data levels, and listings of the data may be produced by varying the relevant control indices.

Figure 5.21a contains system flow-charts for the main program STDESC and the executive subroutine CDESC. Figure 5.21b contains system flow-charts for the subroutines DCFT (Frequency Tabulation - 5.2.5) and DCBC (Bar Charts - 5.2.7). Figure 5.21c contains system flow-charts for the subroutines DCDS (Descriptive Statistics - 5.2.6) and DCPS (Parametric Descriptive Statistics - 5.2.6).

5.2.2 Input Data

Item	Level	Format	Function	See
1	0	A	File control	3.2
2	2	E	Subset Specification	3.6
3	4	F	Variate specification (At least 1 - no delays)	3.7
4	9	H	Data handling instruction	Below + 3.8

Data Handling Instruction

Card Layout - Data Handling Instruction - STDESC

ABCCCDDDEEEEEEEEFFFFFFFFGGGGGGGGGGGGGGGGHHHHHHHH.....etc

Columns	Item	Function	See
1	A	Output control index	Below
2	B	General	Below
3 - 5	C	Not Used	-
6 - 8	D	Not Used	-
9 - 16	E	Not Used	-
17 - 24	F	Not used	-
25 - 40	G	Not used	-
41 - 80	H	Run Title (KEPT)	-

A - Output Control Index

This index controls the quantity of information output, and the production of statistics at the desired level or at all lower levels.

ALTERNATIVES

A = 0,blank: No descriptive statistics.(*see SPECIAL CASE below)

A = 1   : Frequency table and bar chart or positive and negative cumulative histogram as appropriate to data level.

A = 2   : Descriptive statistics at specified level only.

A = 3   : Frequency table and bar chart or positive and negative cumulative histogram as appropriate to data level. Descriptive statistics at specified level only.

A = 4   : Summary table only.

A = 5   : No descriptive statistics.

A = 6   : Frequency table and bar chart with positive/negative cumulative histogram if appropriate to data level.

A = 7   : Descriptive statistics up to specified level only.

A = 8   : Frequency table and bar chart with positive/negative cumulative histogram if appropriate to data level. Descriptive statistics up to specified level.

A = 9   : Summary table only.

DEFAULT value = 0 (0, blank or non-numeric characters)

B - General Control Index

This index controls the level at which the data are considered to be, and permits the user to list the transformed data items for all entries in the subset.

ALTERNATIVES

B = 0,blank: No listing, data level as specified in
(Default)   data description segment

B = 1   : No listing, NOMINAL level assumed

B = 2   : No listing, ORDINAL level assumed.

B = 3   : No listing, INTERVAL level assumed.

B = 4   : No listing, RATIO level assumed

B = 5   : Listing, data level as specified in data description segment

B = 6   : Listing, NOMINAL level assumed

B = 7   : Listing, ORDINAL level assumed.

B = 8   : Listing, INTERVAL level assumed.

B = 9   : Listing, RATIO level assumed

DEFAULT value = 0 (0, blank or non-numeric character)

SPECIAL CASE If A and B are both 0, blank or non-numeric then A is set to 3. (because the unchanged values would produce no output - an effect more economically achieved by not running the program.)

5.2.3   Input Example

Figure 5.22 is a summary of the input structure for three runs of STDESC. In the first run a standard description of an unchanged STATCAT data column on an ORDINAL level is given. In the section, the maximum output is obtained for a transformed variate. In the third a listing of the transformed variate, with a selection of unchanged data from the original subset is produced for inspection. Figure 5.23 is a listing of the input cards required to carry out these three runs.

5.2.4 Output Example

Figure 5.24 is a general summary of the output structure of this program indented according to the program structure. Figure 5.25 is a page-by-page summary of the output corresponding to the specific example given in 5.2.3. (There is too much output for it all to be reproduced here.) Figure 5.26 gives the complete output for the first run. Briefly, this consists of a frequency table, values for percentiles and order-based measures of dispersion and skewness, followed by the cumulative curves. The definitions and meanings of these parameters are given in 5.2.5 - 5.2.7 following.

Figure 5.27 contains the variate specification and data handling instruction for the second run. All possible output options are employed. The first variate is specified by column number, which is translated by the system to column name as a check. The transform +100 has been applied to the data column TPCT, which contained the percentage difference between the time to complete the experimental session and the time allowed. (By adding 100 we can return to the original ratio.) The change in the size of the values makes it necessary to modify the class description accordingly, and, for good measure, the number of alternative classes has been changed from 10 to 12. Class limits have been set at 75 and 125, and the class width has been set to 4 per cent. Because the last value is not compatible with the class limits and the specified number of classes, it is reset to 5 per cent by the system. The values given by the data handling instruction (84) produce all statistics up to RATIO level, with all auxiliary information. These statistics are described in detail in 5.2.6 following, but note that a warning is printed with the coefficient of variation, a statistic that would not be justified for data on an INTERVAL level, as this was before transformation. In this instance, the transform has returned the data to the original RATIO level, but the system has no way of knowing this, and plays safe by issuing a warning message, in case.

Figure 5.28 shows the complete output for this run, giving all possible descriptive statistics.

Figure 5.29 shows part of the listing for the third run of the program. Here the first two items serve to identify a particular entry, and the remaining three, the operator, working position and task itself, might affect the performance. Unexpected effects can often be found by scanning a listing of this type. Although not all ideas so generated stand up to examination, simply looking at data is an often neglected but very valuable statistical method. It is a fertile source for hypotheses, often neglected by number-crunchers, and provides a useful counterbalance to the standardising tendencies inherent in routine analytic methods.

5.2.5 Frequency Tabulation

The standard frequency table output by DCFT starts by giving the number of data, and the number of non-values for the (transformed) variate. (The proportion of non-values can sometimes - for example, in the analysis of a questionnaire - be a valuable piece of information in its own right.)

For each class of the data column, the number of the class, and its name (NOMINAL or ORDINAL) or class limits (INTERVAL or RATIO), are given. Any data falling exactly on the lower boundary of a class are included in that class. Any data falling on the upper boundary are included in the class above. For each class the actual number of readings falling in the class is given, followed (in brackets) by the percentage of the number of values present to which this corresponds and by estimates of the 95% confidence limits that can be attached to the percentage. These confidence limits define an interval into which the proportion could be expected to fall, for a sample of this size. For most practical purposes it is equivalent to saying that there is a 95% chance that the population value is within this range.

The formula employed for this calculation is:-

$$100 \cdot n(x/n + z^2/2n +/- z \cdot (x \cdot (n-x/n)^2 + z^2/4n)^{1/2})$$

Where n = number of data present
      x = number of data in class
      z = 1.96 = the number of standard deviations from the sample mean enclosing 95% of the normal distribution.

This formula becomes unreliable where the number of data in the class is less than five, or the number left outside is less than five.

Where the Data are on an ORDINAL or higher level, or where the the system has been instructed to treat it as if it were, the cumulative distributions are also listed.

The positive cumulative distribution gives, for each class, the number of readings falling below the upper class limit of the class, with the corresponding proportion and confidence limits.

The negative cumulative distribution gives for each class the number of data falling at or above the lower class limit of the class, with the corresponding proportion and confidence limits.

Empty classes above the observed data are not listed to avoid wasting space.

5.2.6 Descriptive Statistics

The standard descriptive statistics are produced by the subroutine DCDS (which calls the subroutine DCPS to produce parametric statistics). There are statistics appropriate to each data level, which will be produced unless the system has been instructed otherwise. When statistics not normally appropriate to a data level are produced, the system will print a warning message.

There are no appropriate statistics for data on a DUMMY level, so only a warning message will be produced, unless the system is overridden.

For data on a NOMINAL level, only the MODE is appropriate. The mode is the most frequent value of a datum. For NOMINAL or ORDINAL data it will be the class containing the most values. If there are several classes containing the same maximum number, the subroutine will produce the first, but note that there are several modal classes. If the data is in fact on an INTERVAL or RATIO level, a more precise estimate of the mode, corresponding to the peak of the distribution, by considering the frequencies in adjoining classes. This estimate is given as the estimated mode of the population. In Figure 5.27, the population mode is the boundary of two adjacent modal classes.

For data on an ORDINAL level, more elaborate statistics may be produced. Two series are presented. First, the classes containing the minimum, fifth percentile, twenty-fifth percentile (first quartile), fiftieth percentile (the MEDIAN), seventy-fifth percentile (third quartile), ninety-fifth percentile and maximum are listed, with, for INTERVAL or RATIO level data, estimates of the corresponding values in the population from which the sample was drawn, derived by interpolation from the class frequencies. (Because these values are estimated from the class frequencies, they are approximate for the sample, but the averaging inherent in the approximation may, in practice, produce a better estimate for the underlying population than an actual count would.)

From the estimated first, second (Median) and third quartiles a measure of the dispersion of the data is derived by halving the difference between the first and third quartiles, and a measure of skewness (lack of symmetry in the data -see below) can be found by the formula: -

$$\text{Quartile Skewness} = (2.Q2 - Q1 - Q3)/(Q3 - Q1)$$

where $Q1$, $Q2$, $Q3$ are the first second and third quartiles.

For INTERVAL or RATIO data, statistics may be derived from the sums of the powers of values of the data. The subroutine DCPS derives these statistics. It begins by producing the number of data on which it is operating. This is followed by the arithmetic mean, with its standard error. Roughly speaking, there is a 95% chance that the true value of the mean for the population is within 1.96 standard errors of the value for the mean of the sample.

The sample standard deviation is then given, with its standard error. Again there is roughly speaking a 95% chance that the population standard deviation is within 1.96 standard errors of the sample value. Note that the standard error of the standard deviation tends to be larger than the standard error of the arithmetic mean. This is because the former requires two estimated parameters from the sample, while the latter requires only one.

If the data is on a RATIO level, the coefficient of variation, (which is the standard deviation divided by the arithmetic mean, and expressed as a percentage) will be given. The system will also calculate this parameter if ordered to for data on lower levels, except that an error message will be produced if the arithmetic mean is not greater than zero (when the coefficient of variation is undefined).

The skewness and kurtosis of the data are also calculated, with their standard error. The skewness, derived from the third power of the data, measures the extent to which the distribution is assymetric, a positive skewness indicating that the data consists mainly of low values, with a few high ones forming a tail. (The distribution of ERRP, the percentage of errors, in the demonstration data bank is an example). A negative skewness implies the reverse, with the bulk of the data being high, and a few values forming a tail at the lower end. A high value for kurtosis implies that the distribution is more peaked than a normal distribution, while a low value implies that it is more or less rectangular. For example, the distribution of TPCT given in Figure 5.28 tends to be more square than would expected for a normal distribution. In our example, the differences are not sufficiently marked to be statistically significant. If either of these parameters has a probability of less than 2.5 per cent, the system prints a warning that the distribution of the data is not normal.

The standard error for skewness, which may also be used to assess the significance of kurtosis, is also given. This standard error depends only on the number of values, both skewness and kurtosis being dimensionless ratios.

If the number of data in the sample is N, and S1 to S4 are the sums of the first to fourth powers of their values, then the parametric statistics and their standard errors are derived as follows : -

Arithmetic Mean = AM = S1/N

Standard Deviation = S = $((S2 - AM.S1)/(N-1))^{1/2}$

Skewness = SK = $(S3/N - 3S2/N.AM + 2(AM)^3)/S^3$

Kurtosis = KU = $(S4/N - 4(S3/N).AM + 6(S2/N).AM^2 - 3(AM)^4) / S^4$

Standard error of the arithmetic mean = $S/N^{1/2}$

Standard error of the standard deviation = $S.((1+SeS.KU)/2S)^{1/2}$

(This expression contains a term taking into account the kurtosis of the distribution.)

Standard error for skewness = SeS = $(6/N)^{1/2}$

Skewness Ratio = SK/SeS

Kurtosis Ratio = KU/(2.SeS)

In general, to identify the distribution of INTERVAL level data, it is better to compare the skewness and kurtosis with those of the theoretical distribution (see Hastings and Peacock 1974) than to classify the data and perform a chi-squared test (see 6.1.5) as is sometimes suggested.

5.2.7 Bar Charts and Cumulative Frequency Curves

Bar charts and cumulative frequency curves are produced by the subroutine DCBC, employing a control parameter to determine which type of output is to be produced.

When a bar chart is plotted a scale from 0 to 100 is laid out across the page. If the maximum number of data in any class is more than 100,then percentages, rather than individual data will be plotted, with an appropriate heading, and each symbol will represent one per cent cent. Classes containing no readings will be printed only if they are above or between classes containing data. Classes are plotted in descending order,so that the highest values appear at the top of the plot.

Positive and negative cumulative frequencies are plotted in the same way, except that "+" signs are used for the positive cumulative, and "-" signs for the negative cumulative frequency. The positive cumulative curve takes in all data below the upper limit of the class, while the negative cumulative includes all data at or above the lower class limit of the class. Percentages will be plotted in place of actual frequencies if the total is greater than 100 data. In Figures 5.26 and 5.27 both curves are presented superimposed.

REFERENCES Spiegel (Ch 2-4), Dixon and Massey (ch 8-9), Veldman (Ch 8), Hastings and Peacock (1974)

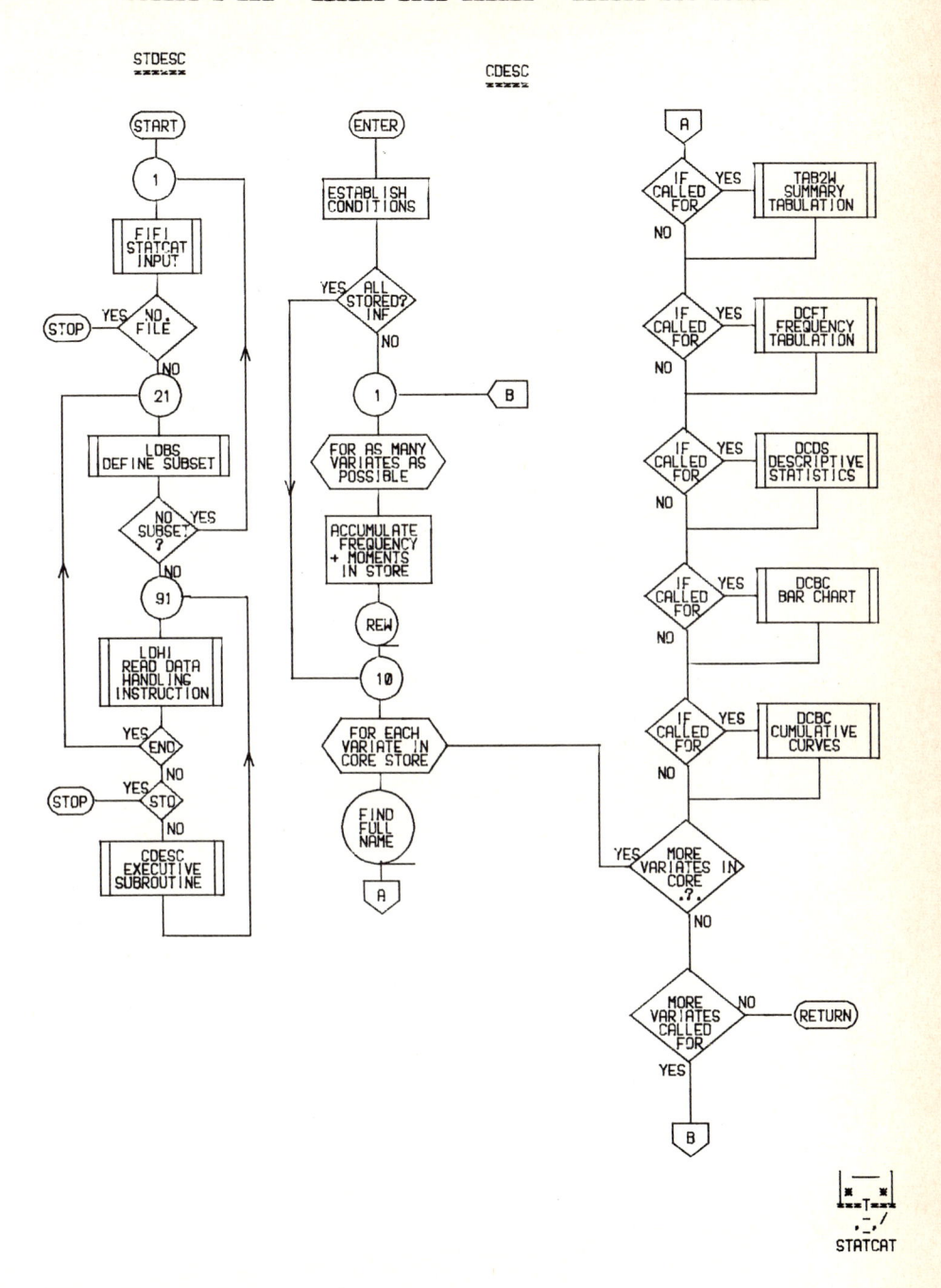

Figure 5.21a - System Flow-Charts - STDESC and CDESC

Figure 5.21b - System Flow-Charts - DCBC and DCFT

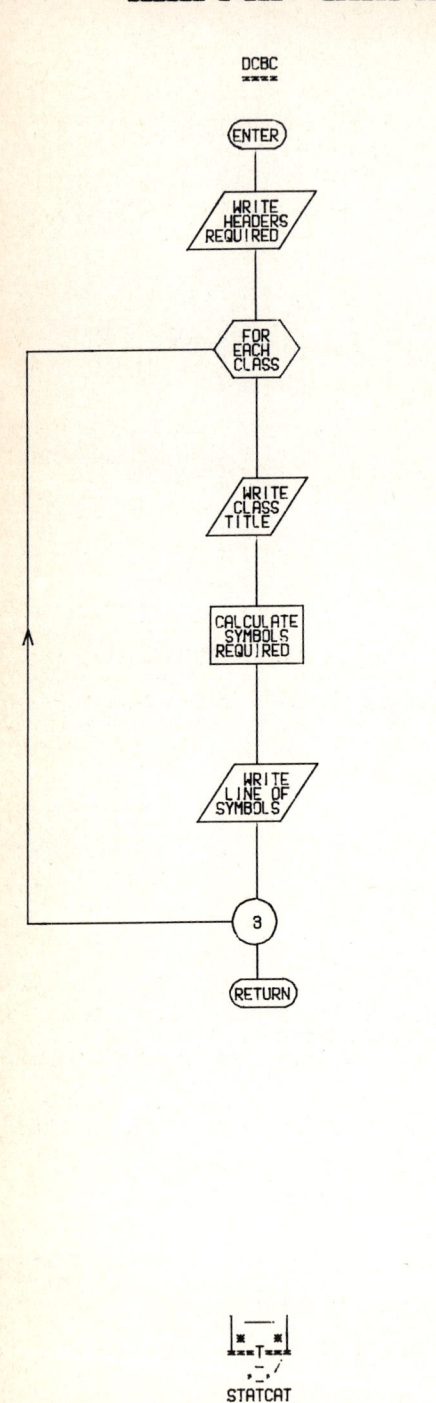

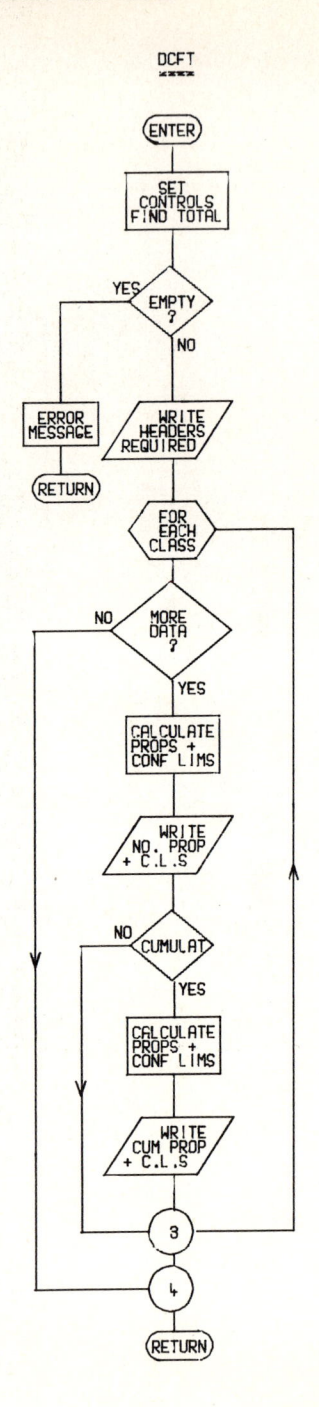

Figure 5.21c - System Flow-Charts - DCDS and DCPS

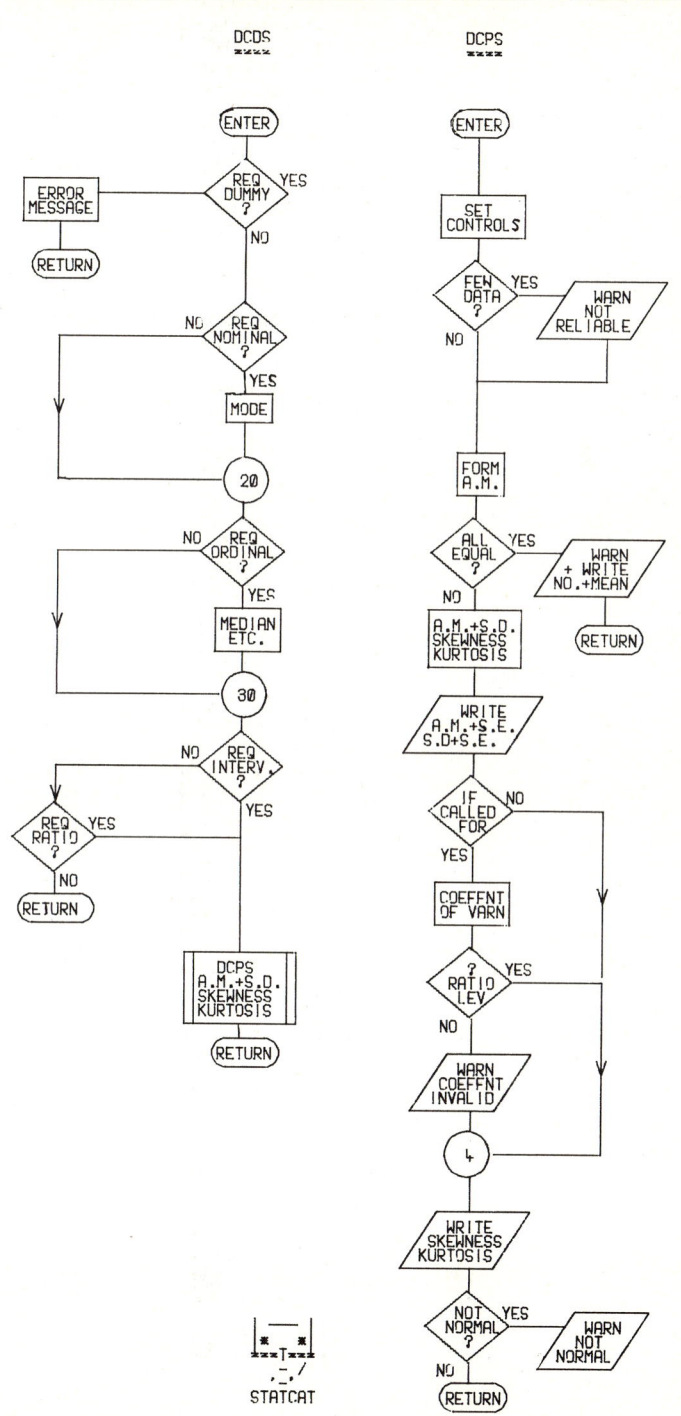

Figure 5.22 - STDESC - Input Structure

```
         Level
  0   1   2   3   4   5   6   7   8   9
FILE CONTROL CARD
    SUBSET SPECIFICATION
        VARIATE SPECIFICATION
            DATA HANDLING INSTRUCTION
            BACK TO READ NEW VARIATES
        VARIATE SPECIFICATION
            DATA HANDLING INSTRUCTION
            BACK TO READ NEW VARIATES
        VARIATE SPECIFICATION
            DATA HANDLING INSTRUCTION
            STOP
```

Figure 5.23 - STDESC - Input Example

```
---------1---------2---------3---------4---------5---------6---------7--
**STDESCDEMO                            DEMONSTRATION STATCAT DATA BANK
ALL DATA
END OF SUBSET SPECIFICATION

VAL.DIFF                                RUN ONE
END OF VARIATE SPECIFICATION

RUN WITH STANDARD VALUES                FREQ TABLE,DESC STAT,GRAPH AT LE
BACK TO READ NEW VARIATES

+100TPCT       12     75.0     4.0    125.0RUN 2
END OF VARIATE SPECIFICATION
84                                      FREQ TAB,DESC STAT,GRAPHICS UP T
BACK TO READ NEW VARIATES
VAL COL2                                RUN 3
VAL.OPER
VAL W.P.
VAL TASK
+100TPCT
END OF VARIATE SPECIFICATION

05                                      LISTING ONLY
STOP                                    END OF JOB
---------1---------2---------3---------4---------5---------6---------7--
```

Figure 5.24 - STDESC - Output Structure

```
For each    ) : File Control Record
output file )   File Parameters
                Data Description
                For each) : Subset Input Record
                Subset  )   For each Set) Variate Input Record
                            of Variates )  For each ) Input Record
                                           Data     )<Listing>
                                           Handling ) For each)<Freqncy
                                           Instrctn ) Variate)Table>
                                                                <Desc.
                                                                 Stats>
                                                                <Distn.
                                                                 Plot.>
```

Carated(<>) items are optional.

Figure 5.25 - STDESC - Output Example - Page-by-Page Listing

Page	Contents	Origin
1- 3	File Control Record	FIFI
	Program Title	STDESC
	File Parameters	LDAP
	Data Description record	LDDS
4	Subset record	LSAMP
5	Set of Variates	LGEN
	Data Handling Instruction	LDHI
6	Frequency Tabulation	DCFT
	Descriptive Statistics	DCDS
	Cumulative Distributions	DCBC
8	Data Handling Instruction (BACK)	LDHI
9	Set of Variates	LGEN
	Data Handling Instruction	LDHI
10	Frequency Tabulation	DCFT
	Descriptive Statistics	DCDS/DCPS
11	Bar Chart	DCBC
	Cumulative Distributions	DCBC
12	Data Handling Instruction (BACK)	LDHI
13	Set of Variates	LGEN
	Data Handling Instruction	LDHI
14-17	Listing of selected transformed data	CDESC
18	Data Handling Instruction (STOP)	LDHI

Figure 5.26 - STDESC - First run - Complete Output

```
DATA BANK TITLE              -    DEMONSTRATION STATCAT DATA BANK
DATA BANK SUBSET TITLE       -    ALL DATA
VAL. OF DATA COLUMN NUMBER   10   SHORT TITLE   DIFF
FULL TITLE                   -    ASSESSMENT OF DIFFICULTY BY OPERATOR              DATA LEVEL -ORDINAL

                    FREQUENCY TABLE.

NUMBER OF READINGS PRESENT -    64=(100.0PCT)
NUMBER OF READINGS MISSING -     0=(  0.0PCT)

                    ACTUAL DISTRIBUTION              POSITIVE CUMULATIVE              NEGATIVE CUMULATIVE
NO.   CLASS NAME    NUMBER PER CENT 95PCT CONF LIMITS  NUMBER PER CENT 95PCT CONF LIMITS  NUMBER PER CENT 95PCT CONF LIMITS
 7    VHAR           4 (  6.25   5.90 -  11.60)       64 (100.00  97.18 - 100.00)        4 (  6.25   5.90 -  11.60)
 6    HARD           7 ( 10.94   9.49 -  16.85)       60 ( 93.75  88.44 -  94.15)       11 ( 17.19  14.62 -  23.52)
 5    RHAR          10 ( 15.63  13.31 -  21.88)       53 ( 82.81  76.53 -  85.43)       21 ( 32.81  28.27 -  39.34)
 4    NULL          14 ( 21.88  18.01 -  28.36)       43 ( 67.19  60.70 -  71.77)       35 ( 54.69  48.57 -  60.31)
 3    REAS          10 ( 15.63  13.31 -  21.88)       29 ( 45.31  39.73 -  51.47)       45 ( 70.31  63.80 -  74.57)
 2    EASY          13 ( 20.31  17.27 -  26.76)       19 ( 29.69  25.47 -  36.25)       58 ( 90.63  84.91 -  91.78)
 1    VEAS           6 (  9.38   8.26 -  15.13)        6 (  9.38   8.26 -  15.13)       64 (100.00  97.19 - 100.00)

BASED ON OBSERVED CLASS FREQUENCIES

 1    VEAS          IS THE             MINIMUM CLASS
 1    VEAS          IS THE   5.TH PERCENTILE CLASS
 2    EASY          IS THE  25.TH PERCENTILE CLASS
 4    NULL          IS THE  50.TH PERCENTILE CLASS
 5    RHAR          IS THE  75.TH PERCENTILE CLASS
 7    VHAR          IS THE  95.TH PERCENTILE CLASS
 7    VHAR          IS THE             MAXIMUM CLASS

                MEDIAN =            4.0000

SEMI-INTERQUARTILE RANGE =          1.5000

    QUARTILE SKEWNESS =             0.3333

            POSITIVE CUMULATIVE DISTRIBUTION   NEGATIVE CUMULATIVE DISTRIBUTION

ACTUAL FREQUENCY (TOTAL =   64)
                      0     10    20    30    40    50    60    70    80    90   100
NO.   CLASS NAME      .     .     .     .     .     .     .     .     .     .     .
 7    VHAR          ****
 6    HARD          ***********------------------------------------------------
 5    RHAR          ****************-------------------------------
 4    NULL          ***********************+++++++++++++++-------
 3    REAS          ***************++++++++++++++++++++++++++
 2    EASY          ********************++++++++++++++++++++++++++++++++++++
 1    VEAS          *******+++++++++++++++++++++++++++++++++++++++++++++++++++
```

Figure 5.27 - STDESC - Second run - Variate Specification

```
            SET OF VARIATES FOR DATA SWEEP

NO.     TRANS  DATA      NUMBER OF    LOWER         CLASS      UPPER
CODE    -FORM  COLUMN    CLASSES USED CLASS LIMIT   INTERVAL   CLASS LIMIT

 1  ORIGINAL  +100  TPCT     12        75.0           4.0       125.0    RUN 2
 A  STANDARD  +100  CL12     12        75.0000        5.0000    125.0000

END OF VARIATE SPECIFICATION

                DATA HANDLING INSTRUCTION - FCFC PRINT

ABCCCDDDEEEEEEEEFFFFFFFGGGGGGGGGGGGGHHHHHHHHHHHHHHHHHHHHHHHHHHHHHH
 8+                    AAXXXXXXXXXXXXXXXFREQ TAB,DESC STAT,GRAPH    ICS JP T

INPUT ACCEPTED - DESCRIPTION COMMENCES
                OUTPUT CONTROL INDEX  =     6
                GENERAL CONTROL INDEX =     4
```

Figure 5.28 - STDESC - Second run - Complete Output

```
DATA BANK TITLE              -   DEMONSTRATION STATCAT DATA BANK
DATA BANK SUBSET TITLE       -   ALL DATA
+100 OF DATA COLUMN NUMBER   12 SHORT TITLE   TPCT
FULL TITLE                   -       TIME TO COMPLETE AS PERCENTAGE OF TIME ALLOWED          DATA LEVEL -INTERVAL

                    FREQUENCY TABLE.

NUMBER OF READINGS PRESENT -   64=(100.0PCT)
NUMBER OF READINGS MISSING -    0=(  0.0PCT)
                         ACTUAL DISTRIBUTION                   POSITIVE CUMULATIVE                    NEGATIVE CUMULATIVE
NO.   CLASS NAME    NUMBER PER CENT 95PCT CONF LIMITS  NUMBER PER CENT 95PCT CONF LIMITS  NUMBER PER CENT 95PCT CONF LIMITS
 7 100.00 TO 105.00    12 ( 18.75   15.99 -  25.14)     64 (100.00   97.18 - 100.00)      12 ( 18.75   15.94 -  25.14)
 6  95.00 TO 100.00    16 ( 25.00   21.33 -  31.54)     52 ( 81.25   74.90 -  84.11)      28 ( 43.75   38.28 -  49.96)
 5  90.00 TO  95.00    16 ( 25.00   21.33 -  31.54)     36 ( 56.25   50.37 -  61.77)      44 ( 68.75   62.24 -  73.18)
 4  85.00 TO  90.00    12 ( 18.75   15.99 -  25.14)     20 ( 31.25   26.87 -  37.80)      56 ( 87.50   81.50 -  85.30)
 3  80.00 TO  85.00     8 ( 12.50   10.75 -  18.55)      8 ( 12.50   10.75 -  18.55)      64 (100.00   97.18 - 100.00)

 5  90.00 TO  95.00     IS THE MODAL CLASS                     95.0000 IS ESTIMATED MODE OF POPULATION FIRST OF   2 MODES

BASED ON OBSERVED CLASS FREQUENCIES

 3  80.00 TO  85.00     IS THE         MINIMUM CLASS           82.1700 IS THE EXACT MINIMUM VALUE
 3  80.00 TO  85.00     IS THE  5.TH PERCENTILE CLASS          82.3000 IS THE  5.TH PERCENTILE ESTIMATE
 4  85.00 TO  90.00     IS THE 25.TH PERCENTILE CLASS          88.3333 IS THE 25.TH PERCENTILE ESTIMATE
 5  90.00 TO  95.00     IS THE 50.TH PERCENTILE CLASS          93.7500 IS THE 50.TH PERCENTILE ESTIMATE
 6  95.00 TO 100.00     IS THE 75.TH PERCENTILE CLASS          98.7500 IS THE 75.TH PERCENTILE ESTIMATE
 7 100.00 TO 105.00     IS THE 95.TH PERCENTILE CLASS         103.6667 IS THE 95.TH PERCENTILE ESTIMATE
 7 100.00 TO 105.00     IS THE         MAXIMUM CLASS          102.0800 IS THE EXACT MAXIMUM VALUE

              MEDIAN =                    93.7500

SEMI-INTERQUARTILE RANGE =                5.2083

           QUARTILE SKEWNESS =            0.0400

NUMBER OF READINGS=            64.

ARITHMETIC MEAN =              93.435425       S.E. OF MEAN =       0.750630

STANDARD DEVIATION=             6.005040       S.E. OF S.D. =       0.695047

COEF. OF VARIATION=             6.426938   NOT JUSTIFIED BY ORIGINAL DATA LEVEL                         **WARNING**

        SKEWNESS =             -0.415618  SKEWNESS RATIO =         -1.357404 PROBABILITY=     0.171399

        KURTOSIS =              0.714772  KURTOSIS RATIO =          2.334435 PROBABILITY=     0.018662

S.E. FOR SKEWNESS =             0.306185   DISTRIBUTION IS PROBABLY NOT NORMAL                          **WARNING**


DATA BANK TITLE              -   DEMONSTRATION STATCAT DATA BANK
DATA BANK SUBSET TITLE       -   ALL DATA
+100 OF DATA COLUMN NUMBER   12 SHORT TITLE   TPCT
FULL TITLE                   -       TIME TO COMPLETE AS PERCENTAGE OF TIME ALLOWED          DATA LEVEL -INTERVAL

BAR CHART

ACTUAL FREQUENCY (TOTAL =    64)
                    0        10        20        30        40        50        60        70        80        90       100
NO.   CLASS NAME    .    .    .    .    .    .    .    .    .    .    .    .    .    .    .    .    .    .    .    .    .
 7 100.00 TO 105.00 XXXXXXXXXXXX
 6  95.00 TO 100.00 XXXXXXXXXXXXXXXX
 5  90.00 TO  95.00 XXXXXXXXXXXXXXXX
 4  85.00 TO  90.00 XXXXXXXXXXXX
 3  80.00 TO  85.00 XXXXXXXX

                POSITIVE CUMULATIVE DISTRIBUTION   NEGATIVE CUMULATIVE DISTRIBUTION

ACTUAL FREQUENCY (TOTAL =    64)
                    0        10        20        30        40        50        60        70        80        90       100
NO.   CLASS NAME    .    .    .    .    .    .    .    .    .    .    .    .    .    .    .    .    .    .    .    .    .
 7 100.00 TO 105.00 ************----------------------------------------------------------------------------
 6  95.00 TO 100.00 ****************----------------------------------------------------
 5  90.00 TO  95.00 ********************************++++++++++++++++++++++++++++
 4  85.00 TO  90.00 ********************++++++++++++++++++++++++++++++++++++
 3  80.00 TO  85.00 ********+++++++++++++++++++++++++++++++++++++++++++++++++++++++++
```

187

Figure 5.29 - STDESC - Third run - Partial Output

		ENTRIES IN SUBSET		
1 VAL OF SESS	2 VAL. OF OPER	3 VAL OF W.P.	4 VAL OF TASK	5 +100 CF TPCT
	ENTRY NUMBER	1.		
1.0000	1.0000	1.0000	1.0000	100.6200
	ENTRY NUMBER	2.		
1.0000	4.0000	2.0000	4.0000	87.5000
	ENTRY NUMBER	3.		
1.0000	2.0000	3.0000	2.0000	94.0400
	ENTRY NUMBER	4.		
1.0000	3.0000	4.0000	3.0000	91.2900
	ENTRY NUMBER	5.		
2.0000	3.0000	1.0000	4.0000	94.3100
	ENTRY NUMBER	6.		
2.0000	2.0000	2.0000	1.0000	98.7100
	ENTRY NUMBER	7.		
2.0000	4.0000	3.0000	3.0000	84.7100
	ENTRY NUMBER	8.		
2.0000	1.0000	4.0000	2.0000	95.8700
	ENTRY NUMBER	9.		
3.0000	4.0000	1.0000	2.0000	82.1700
	ENTRY NUMBER	10.		
3.0000	1.0000	2.0000	3.0000	98.8200
	ENTRY NUMBER	11.		
3.0000	3.0000	3.0000	1.0000	92.9600
	ENTRY NUMBER	12.		
3.0000	2.0000	4.0000	4.0000	100.1400
	ENTRY NUMBER	13.		
4.0000	2.0000	1.0000	3.0000	96.9400
	ENTRY NUMBER	14.		
4.0000	3.0000	2.0000	2.0000	88.5700
	ENTRY NUMBER	15.		
4.0000	1.0000	3.0000	4.0000	102.0800
	ENTRY NUMBER	16.		
4.0000	4.0000	4.0000	1.0000	86.2500

```
C  MASTER STDESC - DESCRIBES SELECTED SUBSETS OF DATA BANKS
C    SUBROUTINES AND FUNCTIONS REQUIRED
C  NAME              TYPE               COMMENT
C  AN      (SEE  3.1 )  SERVICE     ALPHA - TO NUMERIC VALUE
C  CH      (SEE 11.6 )  SERVICE     CHOOSES TEST/DESCRIPTION REQUIRED
C  CHIKEN  (SEE 11.9 )  SERVICE     WARNS OF MISMATCHED DATA LEVEL
C  CDESC   (SEE  5.2 )  EXECUTIVE   DESCRIBES DATA BANK OR SUBSET
C  CLASIF  (SEE 11.7 )  SERVICE     CLASSIFIES DATA ITEM
C  CLSAM   (SEE  3.5 )  SERVICE     ALLOTS ENTRY TO SAMPLE/SUBSET
C  COMPA   (SEE  3.1 )  SERVICE     COMPARES ALPHAMERIC VALUES
C  COPYA   (SEE  3.1 )  SERVICE     COPIES ALPHAMERIC VALUE
C  DCBC    (SEE  5.2 )  STATISTICAL CONSTRUCTS BAR-CHARTS
C  DCDS    (SEE  5.2 )  STATISTICAL DESCRIPTIVE STATISTICS
C  DCFT    (SEE  5.2 )  STATISTICAL FREQUENCY TABULATION
C  DCPS    (SEE  5.2 )  STATISTICAL MOMENT(PARAMETRIC) STATISTICS
C  FIFI    (SEE  3.2 )  SYSTEM      ALLOCATES PERIPHERALS
C  GAUS    (SEE 11.8 )  STATISTICAL FINDS ASS. PROB. OF N VALUE
C  IBL     (SEE  3.1 )  SERVICE     DETECTS BLANK,END AND STOP CARDS
C  ICH     (SEE  3.1 )  SERVICE     IDENTIFIES ALPHAMERIC CODES
C  LDAP    (SEE  3.3 )  SYSTEM      LOADS/CHECKS DATA BANK PARAMETERS
C  LDBS    (SEE  3.6 )  SYSTEM      LOADS SUBSET DEFINITION
C  LDDS    (SEE  3.4 )  SYSTEM      LOADS DATA DESCRIPTION SEGMENT
C  LDHI    (SEE  3.8 )  SYSTEM      LOADS/CHECKS DATA HANLDING INSTN
C  LGEN    (SEE  3.7 )  SYSTEM      LOADS GENERALISED VARIATES
C  LSET    (SEE  3.5 )  SYSTEM      LOADS DEFINING CONDITIONS
C  MEDIAT  (SEE  3.7 )  SERVICE     FETCHES NEXT VARIATE SET
C  PRBF    (SEE 11.8 )  STATISTICAL FINDS PROBABILITY OF F-RATIO
C  PRTCLS  (SEE 11.7 )  SERVICE     PRINTS CLASS NAME/LIMITS
C  TRANS   (SEE  3.7 )  SERVICE     CARRIES OUT REQUIRED TRANSFORM
C  IF NQMAX = MAXIMUM NO. OF DATA COLUMNS IS CHANGED, CHANGE CN DATA ALSO
C  DIMENSION D(NQMAX),DMAX(NQMAX),DMIN(NQMAX),IT(NQMAX),ST(NQMAX)
C  DIMENSION CN(NQMAX)
      NQMAX = 100
      DIMENSION D(100),DMAX(100),DMIN(100),IT(100),ST(100),CN(100)
      DATA  CN/4HCOL1,4HCOL2,4HCOL3,4HCOL4,4HCOL5,4HCOL6,4HCOL7,4HCOL8,4
     1HCOL9,4HCL10,4HCL11,4HCL12,4HCL13,4HCL14,4HCL15,4HCL16,4HCL17,4HCL
     218,4HCL19,4HCL20,4HCL21,4HCL22,4HCL23,4HCL24,4HCL25,4HCL26,4HCL27,
     34HCL28,4HCL29,4HCL30,4HCL31,4HCL32,4HCL33,4HCL34,4HCL35,4HCL36,4HC
     4L37,4HCL38,4HCL39,4HCL40,4HCL41,4HCL42,4HCL43,4HCL44,4HCL45,4HCL46
     5,4HCL47,4HCL48,4HCL49,4HCL50,4HCL51,4HCL52,4HCL53,4HCL54,4HCL55,4H
     6CL56,4HCL57,4HCL58,4HCL59,4HCL60,4HCL61,4HCL62,4HCL63,4HCL64,4HCL6
     75,4HCL66,4HCL67,4HCL68,4HCL69,4HCL70,4HCL71,4HCL72,4HCL73,4HCL74,4
     8HCL75,4HCL76,4HCL77,4HCL78,4HCL79,4HCL80,4HCL81,4HCL82,4HCL83,4HCL
     984,4HCL85,4HCL86,4HCL87,4HCL88,4HCL89,4HCL90,4HCL91,4HCL92,4HCL93,
     94HCL94,4HCL95,4HCL96,4HCL97,4HCL98,4HCL99,4HC100/
C  DIMENSION TRT(MALTMX)=MAXIMUM NUMBER OF STORED CLASSES
      MALTMX = 50
      DIMENSION  TRT(50)
C  DIMENSION TRTR(NRMAX)=MAXIMUM NO OF CLASSES USED
      DIMENSION TRTR(102)
      NRMAX = 102
C  NRAV = MAXIMUM AVAILABLE WORKING STORAGE
C  RT(NRAV) CONTAINS ALL FREE STORAGE USED FOR FREQUENCY TABLES
C  AND MOMENTS - MUST BE AT LEAST NCL(J) + 5
C  WHERE NCL(J) IS THE LARGEST NUMBER OF CLASSES USED
      NRAV = 1000
      DIMENSION RT(1000)
C  MAXM = MAXIMUM NUMBER OF VARIATES ACCEPTED FOR ANY DATA SWEEP
C  DIMENSION TMAX(MAXM),TMIN(MAXM),NCL(MAXM),T(MAXM),NP(MAXM)
      MAXM = 60
      DIMENSION TMAX(60),TMIN(60),NCL(60),T(60),NP(60)
C  DIMENSION SCON(5,MAXDBC)=MAXIMUM NUMBER OF SUBSET CONDITIONS
      MAXDBC = 50
```

```
              DIMENSION SCON(5,50)
C THE FOLLOWING DIMENSIONS ARE FIXED
              DIMENSION U(60),LU(60)
              NU = 60
C TRANSFORMATION CODES
C UNITS                          BLOCKS
C       0 - 9   10 - 19   20 - 29   30 - 39   40 - 49   50 - 59
C       POWERS  TRIG      TRIG      STATIST   MATHS     TEST
C               RADIANS   DEGREES   TRANSF    FUNCTS    FUNCTIONS
C   0     -                H.MS        -         -      RM10
C   1   VAL.    SINR      SIND      PSNA      RECP      +/-1
C   2   SQAR    COSR      COSD      PSNB      SQRT      ADD1
C   3   CUBE    TANR      TAND      BINO      ABSV      SUB1
C   4   4PWR    ASIR      ASID      LG+1      SIGN      NOR1
C   5   5PWR    ACOR      ACOD      LOGE      INTG      +/-P
C   6   6PWR    ATAR      ATAD      LG10      FRAC      ADDP
C   7   7PWR    SINH      DTOR      AL10      EXPT      SUBP
C   8   8PWR    COSH      RTOD        -       PRES      NORP
C   9   9PWR    TANH      H.HH        -       NEG.      +100
      DATA U/4HVAL.,4HSQAR,4HCUBE,4H4PWR,4H5PWR,4H6PWR,4H7PWR,4H8PWR,4H9
     1PWR,4HVAL ,4HSINR,4HCOSR,4HTANR,4HASIR,4HACOR,4HATAR,4HSINH,4HCOSH
     2,4HTANH,4HH.MS,4HSIND,4HCOSD,4HTAND,4HASID,4HACOD,4HATAD,4HDTOR,4H
     3RTOD,4HH.HH,4H VAL,4HPSNA,4HPSNB,4HBINO,4HLG+1,4HLOGE,4HLG10,4HAL1
     40,4H     ,4H    ,4H    ,4HRECP,4HSQRT,4HABSV,4HSIGN,4HINTG,4HFRAC,4
     5HEXPT,4HPRES,4HNEG.,4HRM10,4H+/-1,4HADD1,4HSUB1,4HNOR1,4H+/-P,4HAD
     6DP,4HSUBP,4HNORP,4H+100,4H    /
      DATA LU/1,8*5,1,9*5,1,9*5,1,6*5,4*1,2*5,2*3,3*5,7*2,4*5,2*2/
C THE FOLLOWING DIMENSIONS ARE FIXED
      DIMENSION TTA(20),TTB(20),TTC(20),FORM(50),IH(1),H(1),C(10)
      COMMON /STCT/MED1,MED2,MED3,MED4,MED5,MED6,MED13,Q,V(20),TT(30)
      DATA PROG/4HDESC/,BL/4H    /
      MED1 = -1
C LEVEL 0 - SETTING UP DATA BANK
    1 CALL COPYA(TT(1),PROG)
      CALL FIFI
      WRITE(MED6,901)
      CALL LDAP(MED2,MED3,V,TT,Q,NQ,NALT,NQMAX,NALTMX,IGO)
      IF(IGO.GT.0) GO TO 1
      LIMC = NRMAX
      IF(LIMC.GT.NRAV-7) LIMC = NRAV - 7
      LI = 18
      CALL LDDS(TRT,NALT,D,NQ,ST,NQ,IT,NQ,H,0,DMIN,DMAX,NQ,LI,1,Q,VX,
     1 0,MED2,MED3,0,IGO)
   21 IF(V(10).GE.20.) V(10) = 0.
      CALL LDBS(SCON,NCON,MAXDBC,CN,ST,IT,NQ,TRT,NALT,IGO)
      IF(IGO.GT.0) GO TO 1
      ARAN = 5236.
C LEVEL 3 - SET OF VARIATES FOR DATA SWEEP
   31 IF(V(10).GE.30.) V(10) = 0.
      IFIN = MAXM
      M = 0
      WRITE(MED6,931)
      WRITE(MED6,935)
      CALL LGEN(U,NU,LU,NU,ST,IT,CN,NQ,NCL,MAXM,DMIN,DMAX,NQ,TMIN,TMAX,M
     1AXM,0,LIMC,IH,NP,MAXM,M,MAXM,1,NALT)
      IF(V(11).LT.0.5.AND.V(20).LT.0.5) GO TO 21
      IF(V(11).LT.0.5.AND.V(20).GT.0.5.AND.V(10).LT.0.5) V(10)= 32.
      BRAN = ARAN
      V(19) = 0.
C LEVEL 9 - DATA HANDLING INSTRUCTION
   91 IF(V(10).GT.90.) V(10) = 0.
      CALL LDHI(V(1),1,V(2),4,H,0,H,0,H,0,H,0,H,V(10),
     1FORM(41),FORM,MED1,MED2,0,Q,NQ,NWARN,1,IGO)
```

```
      IF(IGO.GT.0) GO TO 31
C STANDARDISATION
      IF(V(1).LE.0..AND.V(2).LE.0.) NWARN = NWARN + 1
      IF(V(1).LE.0..AND.V(2).LE.0.) V(1) = 3.
      WRITE(MED6,998)
      CALL LDHI(V(1),1,V(2),4,H,0,H,0,H,0,H,0,H,V(10),
     1FORM(41),FORM,MED1,MED2,0,Q,NQ,NWARN,2,IGO)
      IF(IGO.GT.0) GO TO 31
      V(19) = V(19) + 1.
C CALL EXECUTIVE SUBROUTINE
      V(10) = BRAN
      CALL CDESC(D,IT,NQ,TRT,NALT,T,TMIN,TMAX,NP,M,TRTR,NRMAX,RT,NRAV,SC
     10N,NCON,NCL,U,NU,ST)
      ARAN = V(10)
      V(10) = 0.
      WRITE(MED6,999)
      GO TO 91
  901 FORMAT (1H0,20X,36HSTATCAT DATA BANK SUBSET DESCRIPTION)
  931 FORMAT (1H1,10X,30HSET OF VARIATES FOR DATA SWEEP/)
  935 FORMAT (4HONO.,9X,30HTRANS    DATA            NUMBER OF,7X,5HLOWER,6X,
     15HCLASS,7X,5HUPPER/5H CODE,8X,68H-FORM COLUMN           CLASSES USED
     2 CLASS LIMIT   INTERVAL   CLASS LIMIT)
  998 FORMAT(40H0INPUT ACCEPTED - DESCRIPTION COMMENCES )
  999 FORMAT(40H1DESCRIPTION COMPLETED - READ NEW INPUT )
      END


      SUBROUTINE CDESC(X,IT,NQ,TRT,NALT,D,DMIN,DMAX,NP,M,TRTR,NRMAX,RT,N
     1RAV,SCON,NCON,NCL,U,NU,ST)
C CDESC   (SEE  5.2 ) EXECUTIVE    DESCRIBES DATA BANK OR SUBSET
      DIMENSION X(NQ),IT(NQ),TRT(NALT),D(M),DMIN(M),DMAX(M),NP(M),NCL(M)
      DIMENSION RT(NRAV),SCON(5,NCON),TRTC(1),TTR(19),U(NU),TRTR(NRMAX)
      DIMENSION ST(NQ),TEM(10)
      COMMON /STCT/MED1,MED2,MED3,MED4,MED5,MED6,MED13,Q,V(20),TT(30)
      DATA B4/4H    /,TRTC/4H NO./
C STARTING CONDITIONS
      NALTC = 1
      V10 = V(10)
      V19 = V(19)
      LB = V(1)
      LC = V(2)
      LDB = LC-LC/5*5
      LD = LDB + 1
      JFIN = 0
C ESTABLISH CAPACITY FOR PARAMETRIC AND NON PARAMETRIC DATA
    1 JST = JFIN + 1
      NR = NRAV
    2 JFIN = JFIN + 1
      NR = NR - NCL(JFIN) - 7
    3 IF(NR)  5,4,4
    4 IF(JFIN-M)2,6,6
    5 JFIN = JFIN - 1
    6 KAP = JFIN-JST + 1
      REWIND MED3
      NLIN = 60
      IF (V19.GT.1.5) GO TO 10
C CLEAR STORAGE ARRAY
      J = 0
      DO 9 ICX = JST,JFIN
      N = NCL(ICX)+5
      DO 7 J2 = 1,N
      J = J+1
    7 RT(J) = 0.
```

```
      DO 9 J2 =1,2
      J = J+ 1
    9 RT(J) = Q
      V(6) = 0.
      V(7) = 1.
      V(8) = 1.
      V(9) = M
      V(10) = V10
      READ(MED3) NX,NX,Y,(TT(I),I=1,10),(Y,I=1,6)
      DO 13 I = 1,NQ
   13 READ(MED3)TTR,TRT,NX,Y,Y
C READ DATA FOR DESCRIPTION
    8 CALL MEDIAT(M,NP,NP,M,D,X,NQ,SCON,NCON)
      IF(V(8).EQ.2.) GO TO 10
      IF(LC.LE.4.) GO TO 32
      NLIN = NLIN + (KAP+29)/10
      IF(NLIN.LE.50) GO TO 31
      NLIN = (KAP+9)/10*3 + 2
      WRITE(MED2,991)
      DO 30 J = JST,JFIN,10
      IMAX = JFIN - J + 1
      IF(IMAX.GT.10) IMAX = 10
      JMAX = IMAX + J - 1
      WRITE(MED2,993) (JX,JX=J,JMAX)
      DO 28 IX = 1,IMAX
      JTR = J + IX - 1
      INDX = NP(JTR)/1000
   28 CALL COPYA(TEM(IX),U(INDX))
      WRITE(MED2,994) (TEM(I),I=1,IMAX)
      DO 29 IX = 1,IMAX
      JTR = J + IX - 1
      INDX = NP(JTR) -NP(JTR)/1000*1000
   29 CALL COPYA(TEM(IX),ST(INDX))
      WRITE(MED2,995) (TEM(I),I=1,IMAX)
   30 CONTINUE
   31 WRITE(MED2,992) V(6)
      WRITE(MED2,996) (D(J),J=JST,JFIN)
   32 IF(LB.EQ.0.OR.LB.EQ.5) GO TO 8
      JBASE = 0
      JTR = JST
      DO 24 J = 1,KAP
      XR = D(JTR)
      IF(XR.EQ.Q) GO TO 23
      INDX = NP(JTR)-NP(JTR)/1000*1000
      CALL CLASIF  (XR,DMAX(JTR),DMIN(JTR),IT(INDX),NCL(JTR),JR)
      JR = JBASE + JR
      RT(JR) = RT(JR) + 1.
      JR = JBASE + NCL(JTR)
      RT(JR + 1) = RT(JR + 1) + 1.
      RT(JR + 2) = RT(JR + 2) + XR
      RT(JR + 3) = RT(JR + 3) + XR*XR
      RT(JR + 4) = RT(JR + 4) + XR*XR*XR
      RT(JR + 5) = RT(JR + 5) + XR*XR*XR*XR
      IF(RT(JR+6).EQ.Q.OR.RT(JR+6).GT.XR) RT(JR+6) = XR
      IF(RT(JR+7).EQ.Q.OR.RT(JR+7).LT.XR) RT(JR+7) = XR
   23 JBASE = JBASE + NCL(JTR) + 7
   24 JTR = JTR + 1
      GO TO 8
   10 REWIND MED3
      IF(LB.EQ.0.OR.LB.EQ.5) V(19) = V19-1.
      IF(LB.EQ.0.OR.LB.EQ.5) RETURN
C OUTPUT PHASE
      INOW = NQ + 1
```

```
      JBASE = 1
      ICX = JST
      DO 400 IC = 1,KAP
      V(10) = 0.
      NC = NP(ICX) - NP(ICX)/1000*1000
      NTR= NP(ICX)/1000
      IF(LDB.EQ.0) LD = IT(NC)
      IF(LDB.NE.0) LD = LDB+ 1
      V(7) = IT(NC)
      V(2) = LC
      IF(INOW.LE.NC) GO TO 11
      REWIND MED3
      INOW = 0
      READ(MED3) NX,NX,(Y,I=1,17)
   11 IF(INOW.EQ.NC) GO TO 12
      INOW = INOW + 1
      READ(MED3) TTR,TRT,NX,Y,Y
      GO TO 11
   12 NALTR = NCL(ICX)
      DO 14 J = 1,NALTR
      IF(J.LE.NALT) CALL COPYA(TRTR(J),TRT(J))
   14 IF(J.GT.NALT) CALL COPYA(TRTR(J),B4)
      JR = JBASE + NALTR
      IF(ISW(LB,LC,LD,8).LT.0) GO TO 101
C SUMMARY TABULATION
  100 WRITE(MED2,999) (TT(J),J=1,10),(TT(J),J=21,30),U(NTR),NC,TTR
      V(8) = 6.
      CALL TAB2W   (RT(JBASE),NALTC,NALTR,TRTC,TRTC,TRTR,2,IT(NC),0.,DMIN
     1(ICX),0.,DMAX(ICX),V,MED2)
  101 V(8) = 60.
      NLIN = 0
      DO 102 J = 1,NALTR
      JQ = J+JBASE - 1
  102 IF(RT(JQ).GT.0.) NLIN = J
      VX = NLIN
      IF(RT(JR).LE.0.)
     1WRITE(MED2,999) (TT(J),J=1,10),(TT(J),J=21,30),U(NTR),NC,TTR
      IF(RT(JR).LE.0.) WRITE(MED2,997)
      IF(RT(JR).LE.0.) GO TO 390
      IF(ISW(LB,LC,LD,6).LE.0) GO TO 120
      IF(V(8).GE.(44.-VX))
     1WRITE(MED2,999) (TT(J),J=1,10),(TT(J),J=21,30),U(NTR),NC,TTR
      IF(V(8).GE.(44.-VX))  V(8) = 4.
C FREQUENCY TABULATION
      CALL DCFT (RT(JR),DMAX(ICX),DMIN(ICX),RT(JBASE),TRTR,NALTR,V,MED2)
  120 IF(ISW(LB,LC,LD,7).LE.0) GO TO 130
      IF(V(8).GE.20.)
     1WRITE(MED2,999) (TT(J),J=1,10),(TT(J),J=21,30),U(NTR),NC,TTR
      IF(V(8).GE.20.)  V(8) = 4.
C DESCRIPTIVE STATISTICS
  122 CALL DCDS(DMAX(ICX),DMIN(ICX),RT(JBASE),TRTR,NALTR,RT(JR),RT(JR+1)
     1,RT(JR+2),RT(JR+3),RT(JR+4),RT(JR+5),RT(JR+6),V,MED2)
  130 IF(ISW(LB,LC,LD,6).LE.0) GO TO 145
      V(1) = 3.
      IF(ISW(LB,LC,LD,2).LT.0) GO TO 142
      V(2) = 1.
      IF(V(8).GE.(56.-VX))
     1WRITE(MED2,999) (TT(J),J=1,10),(TT(J),J=21,30),U(NTR),NC,TTR
      IF(V(8).GE.(56.-VX))  V(8) = 4.
C BAR CHART
      CALL DCBC(DMAX(ICX),DMIN(ICX),RT(JBASE),TRTR,NALTR,V,MED2)
  142 IF(ISW(LB,LC,LD,3).LT.0) GO TO 145
      IF(V(8).GE.(56.-VX))
```

```
      1WRITE(MED2,999) (TT(J),J=1,10),(TT(J),J=21,30),U(NTR),NC,TTR
       IF(V(8).GE.(56.-VX))   V(8) = 4.
C CUMULATIVE FREQUENCY CURVES
       V(2) = 6.
       CALL DCBC(DMAX(ICX),DMIN(ICX),RT(JBASE),TRTR,NALTR,V,MED2)
  145  V(1) = LB
       V(2) = LC
  390  JBASE = JBASE + NALTR + 7
  400  ICX = ICX + 1
       IF(JFIN.LT.M) GO TO 1
       REWIND MED3
       V(19) = V19
       IF(JST.NE.1) V(19) = 0.
       RETURN
  991  FORMAT(1H1,20X,18H ENTRIES IN SUBSET )
  992  FORMAT(1H0,15X,13HENTRY NUMBER ,F8.0)
  993  FORMAT(1H ,10(I4,8X))
  994  FORMAT(1H+,10(5X,A4,3H OF))
  995  FORMAT(1H ,10(4X,A4,4X))
  996  FORMAT(1H ,10F12.4)
  997  FORMAT(1H0,20X,37HSUBSET IS EMPTY - CANNOT BE DESCRIBED)
  999  FORMAT(16H1DATA BANK TITLE,14X,1H-,4X,10A4/23H DATA BANK SUBSET TI
      1TLE,7X,1H-,4X,10A4/1H ,A4,22H OF DATA COLUMN NUMBER,I4,12H SHORT T
      2ITLE,4X,A4/11H FULL TITLE,19X,1H-,4X,A2,15A4,13H DATA LEVEL -,2A4)
       END


       SUBROUTINE DCBC(DMAX,DMIN,X,TRT,NALT,V,MED2)
C DCBC    (SEE  5.2 ) STATISTICAL CONSTRUCTS BAR-CHARTS
C PRODUCES BAR CHART + CUMULATIVE FREQUENCY CURVES
       DIMENSION X(NALT),TRT(NALT),V(20),AC(6),PE(6)
C VALUE OF V1-RESULT      VALUE OF V2 - BAR CHART   POS CUM    NEG CUM
C   1    ACTUAL              1         YES            NO         NO
C   2    PERCENTAGE          2         NO             YES        NO
C   3    PC IF OVER 100      3         NO             NO         YES
C                            4         YES            YES        NO
C                            5         YES            NO         YES
C                            6         NO             YES        YES
C                            7         YES            YES        YES
C NEGATIVE CUMULATIVE FREQUENCY IS ALWAYS CALCULATED TO TERMINATE
C PLOTTING WITHOUT UNNECESSARY EXTRA LINES
       DATA Y/1HX/,P/1H+/,M/1H-/,S/1H*/
       DATA AC/4H0ACT,4HUAL ,4HFREQ,4HUENC,4HY (T,4HOTAL/
       DATA PE/4H0PER,4HCENT,4HAGE ,4H(100,4H PER,4HCENT/
       V1 = V(1)
       V2 = V(2)
       IT= V(7)
       TR = 0.
       TM = 0.
       JMIN = NALT
       DO 4 J = 1,NALT
       IF(X(J).LT.0.5) GO TO 4
       IF(X(J).GT.TM) TM = X(J)
       JMAX = J
       IF(JMIN.GT.J) JMIN = J
    4  TR = TR + X(J)
       IF(TR.LE.0.)RETURN
       IF(V(2).NE.1.)TM = TR
       CSP = 0.
       CGP = TR
       NTT = TR
       V(8) = V(8) + 4.
       WRITE(MED2,997)
```

```
      WRITE(MED2,997)
      IF(V2.NE.2..AND.V2.NE.3..AND.V2.NE.6.) WRITE(MED2,994)
      IF(V2.NE.1..AND.V2.NE.3..AND.V2.NE.5.) WRITE(MED2,998)
      IF(V2.NE.1..AND.V2.NE.2..AND.V2.NE.4.) WRITE(MED2,999)
      IF(V1.EQ.1.) WRITE(MED2,992) AC,NTT,(K,K = 1,10)
      IF(V1.EQ.2.) WRITE(MED2,992) PE,NTT,(K,K = 1,10)
      IF(V1.EQ.3..AND.TM.LE.100.) WRITE(MED2,992) AC,NTT,(K,K = 1,10)
      IF(V1.EQ.3..AND.TM.GT.100.) WRITE(MED2,992) PE,NTT,(K,K = 1,10)
      IF(V1.EQ.1..OR.V1.EQ.3..AND.TM.LE.100.) TR = 100.
      DO 3 JJ = JMIN,JMAX
      J = JMAX-JJ+JMIN
      IF(CGF.LE.0.) RETURN
      WRITE(MED2,997)
      CALL PRTCLS(DMAX,DMIN,J,TRT(J),NALT,IT,MED2)
      V(8) = V(8) + 1.
      NF = X(J)*100./TR  + 0.5
      CSF = CSF + X(J)
      NP = CSF*100./TR + 0.5
      NM = CGF*100./TR + 0.5
      IF(V2.EQ.1..OR.V2.EQ.2..OR.V2.EQ.4.) NM = 0
      IF(V2.EQ.1..OR.V2.EQ.3..OR.V2.EQ.5.) NP = 0
      IF(V2.EQ.2..OR.V2.EQ.3..OR.V2.EQ.6.) NF = 0
      NS = NP
      IF(NM.LT.NP) NS = NM
      NP = NP-NS
      NM = NM-NS
      NS = NS-NF
      I = 0
      IF(NP.GT.0) I = 1
      IF(NM.GT.0) I = 2
      IF(NS.GT.0) I = I+3
      IF(NF.GT.0) I = I+6
      IF(I.EQ. 1) WRITE(MED2,996)                           (P,K=1,NP)
      IF(I.EQ. 2) WRITE(MED2,996)                           (M,K=1,NM)
      IF(I.EQ. 3) WRITE(MED2,996)              (S,K=1,NS)
      IF(I.EQ. 4) WRITE(MED2,996)              (S,K=1,NS),(P,K=1,NP)
      IF(I.EQ. 5) WRITE(MED2,996)              (S,K=1,NS),(M,K=1,NM)
      IF(I.EQ. 6) WRITE(MED2,996) (Y,K=1,NF)
      IF(I.EQ. 7) WRITE(MED2,996) (Y,K=1,NF),              (P,K=1,NP)
      IF(I.EQ. 8) WRITE(MED2,996) (Y,K=1,NF),              (M,K=1,NM)
      IF(I.EQ. 9) WRITE(MED2,996) (Y,K=1,NF),(S,K=1,NS)
      IF(I.EQ.11) WRITE(MED2,996) (Y,K=1,NF),(S,K=1,NS),(M,K=1,NM)
      IF(I.EQ.10) WRITE(MED2,996) (Y,K=1,NF),(S,K=1,NS),(P,K=1,NP)
      Z = (NF+NS+NP+NM-1)/100
      V(8) = V(8) + Z
    2 CGF = CGF - X(J)
      IF(V(8).GT.50.) WRITE(MED2,991)
    3 IF(V(8).GT.50.) V(8) = 0.
      RETURN
  991 FORMAT(1H1)
  992 FORMAT(6A4,3H = ,I4,1H)/20X,1H0,10(7X,I2,1H0)/4H NO.,3X,10HCLASS N
     1AME,3X,1H.,20(4X,1H.))
  994 FORMAT(10H+BAR CHART)
  996 FORMAT(1H+,20X,100A1)
  997 FORMAT(1H )
  998 FORMAT (1H+,12X,32HPOSITIVE CUMULATIVE DISTRIBUTION)
  999 FORMAT (1H+,47X,32HNEGATIVE CUMULATIVE DISTRIBUTION)
      END


      SUBROUTINE DCFT(TOT,DMAX,DMIN,X,TRT,NALT,V,MED2)
C DCFT    (SEE  5.2 ) STATISTICAL FREQUENCY TABULATION
      DIMENSION X(NALT),TRT(NALT),V(20)
```

```
C PRINT FREQUENCY TABLE FOR VECTOR X
      IS = V(7)
      IT = V(7)
      LB = V(1)
      IF(LB.LE.4) LB = LB + 5
      LC = V(2)
      IF(IT.GT.3) IT = 3
      WRITE(MED2,998)
      V(8) = V(8) + 2.
      TR=0.
      JMIN = NALT
      DO 1 J=1,NALT
      IF(X(J).LT.0.5) GO TO 1
      IF(JMIN.GT.J) JMIN = J
      JMAX = J
    1 TR = TR+ X(J)
      NTT=TR
      V(11) = TR
      W = TR/(TR+3.8416)*100.
      IF(NTT.GT.0) GO TO 2
      WRITE(MED2,990)
      V(8) = V(8) + 2.
      RETURN
    2 Z= TR/TOT*100.
      Y = 1.9208/TR + 0.9604/TR/TR
      WRITE(MED2,995) NTT,Z
      V(8) = V(8) + 2.
      J=TOT - TR
      Z=(TOT-TR)/TOT*100.
      WRITE(MED2,999) J,Z
      IF(ISW(LB,LC,IT,3).GE.0.AND.IT.LE.2) CALL CHIKEN(3,IT)
      IF(ISW(LB,LC,IT,3).GE.0.AND.IT.LE.2) V(8) = V(8) + 2.
      IF(ISW(LB,LC,IT,3).GE.0) WRITE(MED2,994)
      IF(ISW(LB,LC,IT,3).GE.0) V(8) = V(8) + 1.
      WRITE(MED2,992)
      V(8) = V(8) + 1.
      IF(ISW(LB,LC,IT,3).GE.0) WRITE(MED2,993)
      NSF =0
C FREQUENCY TABULATION
      DO 3 JJ = JMIN,JMAX
      J = JMAX-JJ+JMIN
      IF(NSF.GE.NTT) GO TO 4
      IF(V(8).LE.50.) GO TO 5
      WRITE(MED2,991)
      IF(ISW(LB,LC,IT,3).GE.0) WRITE(MED2,994)
      WRITE(MED2,992)
      V(8) = 2.
      IF(ISW(LB,LC,IT,3).GE.0) WRITE(MED2,993)
      IF(ISW(LB,LC,IT,3).GE.0) V(8) = V(8) + 1.
    5 V(8) = V(8) + 1.
      KK = X(J)
      PR = X(J)/TR*100.
      Z = SQRT(ABS(X(J)*(TR-X(J))/TR))/TR
      CL1 = W*(Y+PR*.01-Z)
      CL2 = W*(Y+PR*.01+Z)
      IF(CL1.GT.PR) CL1= PR
      IF(CL2.LT.PR) CL2 = PR
      WRITE(MED2,996) KK,PR,CL1,CL2
      CALL PRTCLS(DMAX,DMIN,J,TRT(J),NALT,IS,MED2)
C CUMULATIVE FREQUENCY TABULATION
      NSF=NSF+KK
      IF(ISW(LB,LC,IT,3).LT.0) GO TO 3
      CSF=NSF
```

```
      NSG = MTT-NSF+KK
      Z = SQRT(ABS(CSF*(TR-CSF)/TR))/TR
      CSF = CSF/TR
      CL3 = W*(Y+CSF-Z)
      CL4 = W*(Y+CSF+Z)
      CSF = CSF*100.
      IF(CL3.GT.CSF) CL3 = CSF
      IF(CL4.LT.CSF) CL4 = CSF
      CSG = 100.-CSF + PR
      Z = CSG*TR*.01
      Z = SQRT(ABS(Z*(TR-Z)/TR))/TR
      CL5 = W*(Y+CSG*.01-Z)
      CL6 = W*(Y+CSG*.01+Z)
      IF(CL5.GT.CSG) CL5 = CSG
      IF(CL6.LT.CSG) CL6 = CSG
      WRITE(MED2,997) NSG,CSG,CL5,CL6,NSF,CSF,CL3,CL4
    3 CONTINUE
    4 RETURN
  990 FORMAT (23HONO DATA IN THIS SAMPLE)
  991 FORMAT(1H1)
  992 FORMAT(53H NO.      CLASS NAME    NUMBER PER CENT 95PCT CONF LIMITS)
  993 FORMAT(1H+,52X,2(34H NUMBER PER CENT 95PCT CONF LIMITS))
  994 FORMAT(1H0,26X,19HACTUAL DISTRIBUTION,15X,19HPOSITIVE CUMULATIVE,
     115X,19HNEGATIVE CUMULATIVE)
  995 FORMAT (30HONUMBER OF READINGS PRESENT - ,I4,2H=(,F5.1,4HPCT))
  996 FORMAT(21X,I6,2H  (,F6.2,F8.2,3H - ,F6.2,1H))
  997 FORMAT(1H+,53X,2(I6,2H  (,F6.2,F8.2,3H - ,F6.2,1H)))
  998 FORMAT(1H0,20X,16HFREQUENCY TABLE.)
  999 FORMAT (30H NUMBER OF READINGS MISSING - ,I4,2H=(,F5.1,4HPCT))
      END


      SUBROUTINE DCDS(DMAX,DMIN,X,TRT,NALT,S,SX,S2,S3,S4,S5,S6,V,MED2)
C DCDS    (SEE  5.2 ) STATISTICAL DESCRIPTIVE STATISTICS
      DIMENSION X(NALT),TRT(NALT),V(20),P(7),Q(5)
      DATA P/5.,25.,50.,75.,95.,4HMINI,4HMAXI/
      LB = V(1)
      LC = V(2)
      IT = V(7)
      AJ = NALT - 2
      IF(NALT.GT.2) DEL=(DMAX-DMIN)/AJ
      IF(NALT.LE.2) DEL= 0
      IF(IT.EQ.1.AND.LC.LT.4) WRITE(MED2,92)
C MODE
    4 IF(ISW(LB,LC,IT,2).LT.0) GO TO 20
      IF(IT.LT.2) CALL CHIKEN(2,IT)
      IF(IT.LT.2) V(8) = V(8) + 2.
      NMOD=1
      FL=0.
      FU=0.
      N = 1
      DO 11 J=2,NALT
      IF(X(J).EQ.X(NMOD)) N = N+1
      IF(X(J).LE.X(NMOD)) GO TO 11
      NMOD=J
      N = 1
   11 CONTINUE
      V(8) = V(8) + 2.
      WRITE (MED2,95)
      CALL PRTCLS(DMAX,DMIN,NMOD,TRT(NMOD),NALT,IT,MED2)
      V(20) = NMOD
      IF(N.GT.1) WRITE(MED2,91) N
      IF(ISW(LB,LC,IT,4).LT.0.AND.ISW(LB,LC,IT,5).LT.0)GO TO 20
```

```
C MODAL ESTIMATE
      IF(NMOD.GT.1) FL = X(NMOD-1)
      IF(NMOD.LT.NALT) FU = X(NMOD+1)
   16 A = NMOD - 2
      A = DMIN + A*DEL +DEL*(X(NMOD)-FL)/(2.*X(NMOD) - FL -FU)
      WRITE (MED2,94) A
      V(20) = A
C PERCENTILES
   20 IF(ISW(LB,LC,IT,3).LT.0) GO TO 30
      IF(IT.LT.3) V(8) = V(8) + 2.
      IF(IT.LT.3) CALL CHIKEN(3,IT)
      WRITE(MED2,93)
      V(8) = V(8) + 5.
      CALL CLASIF(S5,DMAX,DMIN,IT,NALT,J)
      WRITE(MED2,89) P(6)
      CALL PRTCLS(DMAX,DMIN,J,TRT(J),NALT,IT,MED2)
      IF(ISW(LB,LC,IT,4).GE.0.OR.ISW(LB,LC,IT,5).GE.0)
     1WRITE(MED2,90)S5,P(6)
      SUM = 0.
      N = 1.
      TR = 0.
      DO 10 J = 1,NALT
   10 TR = TR + X(J)
      DO 15 J=1,NALT
      SUM = SUM + X(J)
   13 Y=P(N)*TR*.01
      IF(Y.GT.SUM)GOTO 15
      WRITE(MED2,97)P(N)
      V(8) = V(8) + 1.
      CALL PRTCLS(DMAX,DMIN,J,TRT(J),NALT,IT,MED2)
      Q(N) = J
      IF(ISW(LB,LC,IT,4).LT.0.AND.ISW(LB,LC,IT,5).LT.0) GO TO 14
C PERCENTILE ESTIMATES
      AJ = J - 2
      A = DMIN + DEL*AJ + (Y-SUM+X(J))/X(J)*DEL
      WRITE (MED2,96)A,P(N)
      Q(N) = A
   14 N=N+1
      IF(N-5) 13,13,17
   15 CONTINUE
   17 V(17) = Q(3)
      V(18) = (Q(4)-Q(2))*0.5
      V(19) = 0.
      IF(Q(2).NE.Q(4))V(19) =(Q(2)+Q(4)-2.*Q(3))/(Q(2)-Q(4))
      CALL CLASIF(S6,DMAX,DMIN,IT,NALT,J)
      WRITE(MED2,89) P(7)
      CALL PRTCLS(DMAX,DMIN,J,TRT(J),NALT,IT,MED2)
      IF(ISW(LB,LC,IT,4).GE.0.OR.ISW(LB,LC,IT,5).GE.0)
     1WRITE(MED2,90)S6,P(7)
      WRITE(MED2,98)V(17),V(18),V(19)
      V(8) = V(8) + 6.
   30 IF(ISW(LB,LC,IT,4).LT.0.AND.ISW(LB,LC,IT,5).LT.0) RETURN
      IF(IT.LE.4) CALL CHIKEN(4,IT)
      IF(IT.LE.4) V(8) = V(8) + 2.
C PARAMETRIC STATISTICS
      CALL DCPS(S,SX,S2,S3,S4,V,MED2)
   40 RETURN
   89 FORMAT(1H ,25X,7HIS THE ,9X,A4,9HMUM CLASS)
   90 FORMAT (1H+,57X,F12.4,14H IS THE EXACT ,A4,9HMUM VALUE)
   91 FORMAT (1H+,101X,9H FIRST OF,I4,6H MODES)
   92 FORMAT(45HONO STATISTICS ARE APPROPRIATE FOR DUMMY DATA)
   93 FORMAT(36HOBASED ON OBSERVED CLASS FREQUENCIES/)
   94 FORMAT (1H+,57X,F12.4,32H IS ESTIMATED MODE OF POPULATION)
```

```
   95 FORMAT (1H0,25X,19H IS THE MODAL CLASS)
   96 FORMAT (1H+,57X,F12.4,8H IS THE ,F3.0,22HTH PERCENTILE ESTIMATE)
   97 FORMAT (1H ,25X,7HIS THE ,F3.0,19HTH PERCENTILE CLASS)
   98 FORMAT (1H0,18X,9HMEDIAN = ,F20.4/28H0SEMI-INTERQUARTILE RANGE = ,F
     120.4/1H0,7X,20HQUARTILE SKEWNESS = ,F20.4)
      END


      SUBROUTINE DCPS(S,SX,SXX,SXXX,SXXXX,V,MED2)
C DCPS     (SEE  5.2 ) STATISTICAL MOMENT (PARAMETRIC) STATISTICS
C THIS SUBROUTINE TAKES SUMS OF POWERS AND CALCULATES MOMENTS
C IF MED2 IS SET NEGATIVE NO PRINTOUT EVEN FOR ERRORS
      DIMENSION V(20)
      LB = V(1)
      IF(LB.LT.0) LB = -LB
      LC = V(2)
      LD = V(7)
      IF(MED2.GE.0) V(8) = V(8) + 6.
      VKURT=0.
      SKEW=0.
      SD=0.
      IF(MED2.GE.0.AND.S.LT.10.) WRITE(MED2,95) S
      AM = SX
      IF(S.GT.0.) AM = SX/S
      IF(SXX.GT.AM*SX) GO TO 2
      IF(MED2.GE.0) WRITE(MED2,96) S,AM
      RETURN
    2 SES = SQRT(6./S)
      V(11) = AM
      SD =SQRT((SXX-AM*SX)/(S-1.))
      SIGMA=SD/SQRT(S)
      V(12) = SIGMA
      IF(V(1).LE.0.) GO TO 5
      U1=AM
      U2=SD*SD
      U3=SXXX/S-3.*SXX/S*AM+2.*AM*AM*AM
      U4=SXXXX/S-4.*SXXX/S*AM+6.*SXX/S*AM*AM-3.*AM*AM*AM*AM
      SES=SQRT(6./S)
      IF(SD*U2*SES.GE..00001) SKEW = U3/(U2*SD*SES)
      IF(SD.GE..00001) VKURT = (U4/(U2*U2)-3.)/(2.*SES)
      PS=PRBF(1.0,1000.0,SKEW*SKEW)
      PK=PRBF(1.0,1000.0,VKURT*VKURT)
      U1=SES*SKEW
      U2=SES*VKURT
    5 SESD = SD*SQRT(ABS((1.+VKURT*SES)/(2.*S)))
      V(13) = SD
      V(14) = SESD
      V(15) = SKEW
      V(16) = VKURT
      V(17) = SES
      IF(MED2.LT.0) RETURN
      WRITE(MED2,90) S,AM,SIGMA,SD,SESD
      IF(ISW(LB,LC,LD,5).LT.0) GO TO 4
      COV = -1.
      IF(AM.GT.0.) COV = SD/AM*100.
      V(8) = V(8) + 2.
      IF(COV.GE.0.) WRITE(MED2,91) COV
      IF(COV.LT.0.) WRITE(MED2,98)
      IF(LD.NE.5.AND.LD.NE.7) WRITE(MED2,99)
    4 IF(V(1).LE.0.) RETURN
      WRITE(MED2,92) U1,SKEW,PS
      WRITE(MED2,93) U2,VKURT,PK
      WRITE(MED2,94) SES
```

```
      IF(PS.LT..025.OR.PK.LT..025) WRITE(MED2,97)
      V(8) = V(8) + 6.
      RETURN
   90 FORMAT (20HONUMBER OF READINGS=,F12.0/20H0ARITHMETIC MEAN =   ,F18.
     16,20H       S.E. OF MEAN =,F18.6/20H0STANDARD DEVIATION=,F18.6,20H
     2      S.E. OF S.D. =,F18.6)
   91 FORMAT (20H0COEF. OF VARIATION=,F18.6)
   92 FORMAT (1H0,8X,11HSKEWNESS = ,F18.6,20H SKEWNESS RATIO =   ,F18.6,
     113H PROBABILITY=,F18.6)
   93 FORMAT (1H0,8X,11HKURTOSIS = ,F18.6,20H KURTOSIS RATIO =   ,F18.6,
     113H PROBABILITY=,F18.6)
   94 FORMAT (20H0S.E. FOR SKEWNESS =,F18.6)
   95 FORMAT (5H0ONLY,F4.0,45H READINGS -PARAMETRIC STATISTICS NOT RELIAB
     1LE,56X,11H**WARNING**)
   96 FORMAT (20H0NUMBER OF READINGS=,F12.0/20H0ARITHMETIC MEAN =   ,F18.
     16/20H0 READINGS CONSTANT.)
   97 FORMAT(1H+,40X,35HDISTRIBUTION IS PROBABLY NOT NORMAL,35X,11H**WAR
     1NING**)
   98 FORMAT(35H0COEFFICIENT OF VARIATION UNDEFINED)
   99 FORMAT(1H+,40X,36HNOT JUSTIFIED BY ORIGINAL DATA LEVEL,33X,11H**WA
     1RNING**)
      END
```

5.3 PROGRAM STASTA - LARGE CROSS-TABULATIONS

5.3.1 Purpose

This program produces large cross-tabulations of descriptive statistics for STATCAT data banks, subdivided for all possible combinations of values of several data columns. The size of table that can be produced is virtually unlimited, but, because the program makes extremely economical use of storage, information to allow statistical testing is not available. The user may specify up to 25 variates, according to the format laid down in 3.7, which may be transformed and delayed as required. From this set of transformed variates, he then selects up to five row, and up to five column variates, specifying ascending or descending order, and whether actual values, or classes are to be used in the tabulation. Next, he specifies the variates he wishes to tabulate, and what parameters of each are to be tabulated. Finally, the data handling instruction enables him to choose how the results are to be presented, and to what accuracy.

Figure 5.31a contains system flow-charts for the main program STASTA and the executive subroutine CASTA. Figure 5.31b contains system flow charts for the subroutines FORMTI, FORMAS and WASTA which are used to construct the lists of rows and columns containing data, to derive the actual tables, and to produce the required outputs. Certain special features of these subroutines are noted in COMMENT statements at the heads of the listings following this section, which may serve to aid the user who wishes to follow the sorting logic in detail.

5.3.2 Input Data

Item	Level	Format	Function	See
1	0	A	File control	3.2
2	2	E	Subset Specification	3.6
3	3	F	Variate specification (Transform, column, delay)	3.7
4	4	F	Row specification (Priority, Variate, Class)	below+3.7
5	5	F	Column Specification ditto	below+3.7
6	6	F	Parameter specification (Parameter, variate)	below+3.7
7	9	H	Data handling instruction	below+3.8

4, 5 - Row and Column Specifications

These are of the standard form given in 3.7, but with differences in the way that the fields on the card are used. In place of the transform code in field A, priority codes (Figure 11.42) are employed, and in place of data column names or numbers, variate names or numbers are employed. These are names from VARA to VARY, or number codes from VAR1 to VAR9 and VA10 to VA25. The presence of anything other than blanks in the third field (columns 9-12), causes the program to assume that the row or column variate to be used is to be grouped into classes, according to the class description of the original data column, or the class description provided on this card.

DEFAULT VALUES. For priority - numeric ascending order, including non-values at their arithmetic place. For variate, no default is possible - input is discarded, with error message. For field C, actual values, not grouped in classes.

Parameter Variates

This is also of the standard form specified in 3.7, but with important modifications in the meanings of the fields. The first field (A - columns 1-4) contains a parameter code (Figure 5.36, and 5.3.5 following). The second field (B - columns 5-8) contains a variate name or number, as described in the preceding paragraph. Any non-blank value in the third field causes the class to be used in place of the variate. The rest of the card is not used.

Data Handling Instruction

Card Layout - Data Handling Instruction - STASTA

ABCCCDDDEEEEEEEEFFFFFFFFGGGGGGGGGGGGGGGGGHHHHHHHH......etc

Columns	Item	Function	See
1	A	Output control index	Below
2	B	General control index	Below
3 - 5	C	Not Used	-
6 - 8	D	Not Used	-
9 - 16	E	Not Used	-
17 - 24	F	Not used	-
25 - 40	G	Not used	-
41 - 80	H	Run Title (KEPT)	-

A - Output Control Index

This index controls the space allotted to the values of row variates, and of parameters within the association table. Column headings are allowed the same space as the parameters within the table. If there are too many columns to get them all onto one page, the system will print appropriately titled extra pages.

Four sizes of output space are available : -
8 characters - values from -9999.99 to 99999.99 (Two decimal places)
10 characters - values from -99999.999 to 999999.99 (3 decimals)
13 characters - values from -9999999.9999 to 99999999.9999 (4 decimals)
20 characters - values from -9999999999.99999999 to 99999999999.99999999 (8 decimals)

ALTERNATIVES

A = 0 : Up to five 8-character row values, with ten 8-character table values

A = 1 : Up to five 8-character row values, with eight 10-character table values

A = 2 : Up to five 8-character row values, with six 13-character table values

A = 3 : Up to four 10-character row values, with ten 8-character table values

A = 4 : Up to four 10-character row values, with eight 10-character table values

A = 5 : Up to four 10-character row values, with six 13-character table values

A = 6 : Up to three 13-character row values, with ten 8-character table values

A = 7 : Up to three 13-character row values, with eight 10-character table values

A = 8 : Up to three 13-character row values, with six 13-character table values

A = 9 : Up to two 20-character row values, with four 20-character table values

DEFAULT value = 0 (0, blank or non-numeric characters)

B - General Control Index

This index controls the general form of the output table, and the overall output strategy, whether empty lines are printed, and how the output is arranged

ALTERNATIVES

B = 0 : Specified parameters only, parameters separately, for non-empty lines

B = 1 : Specified parameters, columns separately, for non-empty lines

B = 2 : Specified parameters, parameters separately, for all lines

B = 3 : Specified parameters, columns separately, for all lines

B = 4 : All parameters, parameters separately, for non-empty lines

B = 5 : All parameters, columns separately, for non-empty lines

B = 6 : All parameters, parameters separately, for all lines

B = 7 : All parameters, columns separately, for all lines

B = 8 : Parameters and sums, for each parameter separately, for non-empty lines.

B = 9 : Parameters and sums, for each column separately, for non-empty lines.

DEFAULT value = 0 (0, blank or non-numeric character)

5.3.3 Input Example

Figure 5.32 is a summary of the input structure for three runs of STASTA. The first produces a large association table, the other two relatively small tables. Each table includes the whole of the demonstration STATCAT data bank, using the same file control and subset specification. The first association table shows how the sixty-four entries are drawn from the 4096 possible combinations of six variates each at four levels. The second table gives the observed temperature at each working position for each session, and the third shows a selection of descriptive parameters for each session.

Figure 5.33 is a listing of the input cards required to carry out these three runs.

5.3.4 Output Example

Figure 5.34 is a summary of the output structure indented according to the program structure. Figure 5.35 is a page-by-page summary of the output corresponding to the specific example given in 5.3.3. Because of the volume of output produced, only small samples are reproduced here. The checking information is generally standard, and the variate specification is listed as an example in Figure 3.73. Figure 5.36 shows the parameter codes employed to define what is tabulated. Figure 5.37 shows part of the output of the first run. Figure 5.38 shows the whole of the second association table, and figure 5.39 shows the whole of the third table.

5.3.5 Parameter Codes

Figure 5.36 starts with the parameter codes normally employed in their own right. These produce the number of values present in the cell (which may be different for different variates, because non-values are not counted), the arithmetic mean, sample standard deviation, sample variance (dividing by one less than the number of values for both standard deviation and variance), skewness and kurtosis. The Geometric Mean (anti-log of the arithmetic mean of logarithms), and the Harmonic Mean (reciprocal of the arithmetic mean of the reciprocals) are also provided. (These require Ratio level measurement - a warning will be printed if they are not justified, and non-values produced if they are not computable owing to the presence of zero or negative values.)

In addition, the minimum and maximum values in any cell may be obtained, and a special parameter IDEN will give the value in the cell if all values in the cell are identical or a non-value if they are not identical.

When these parameters are being assembled, other, possibly useful, values are obtained in the process. TOT., SSQ., SCUB, and S4TH are the sums of successive powers of the variate, and SLOG and SREC are sums of logarithms and of reciprocals respectively - any of which may be useful, if only for data checking.

Figure 5.36 indicates which additional parameters and summations will be added if the general control index B is set appropriately.

Figure 5.31a - System Flow-chart - STASTA and CASTA

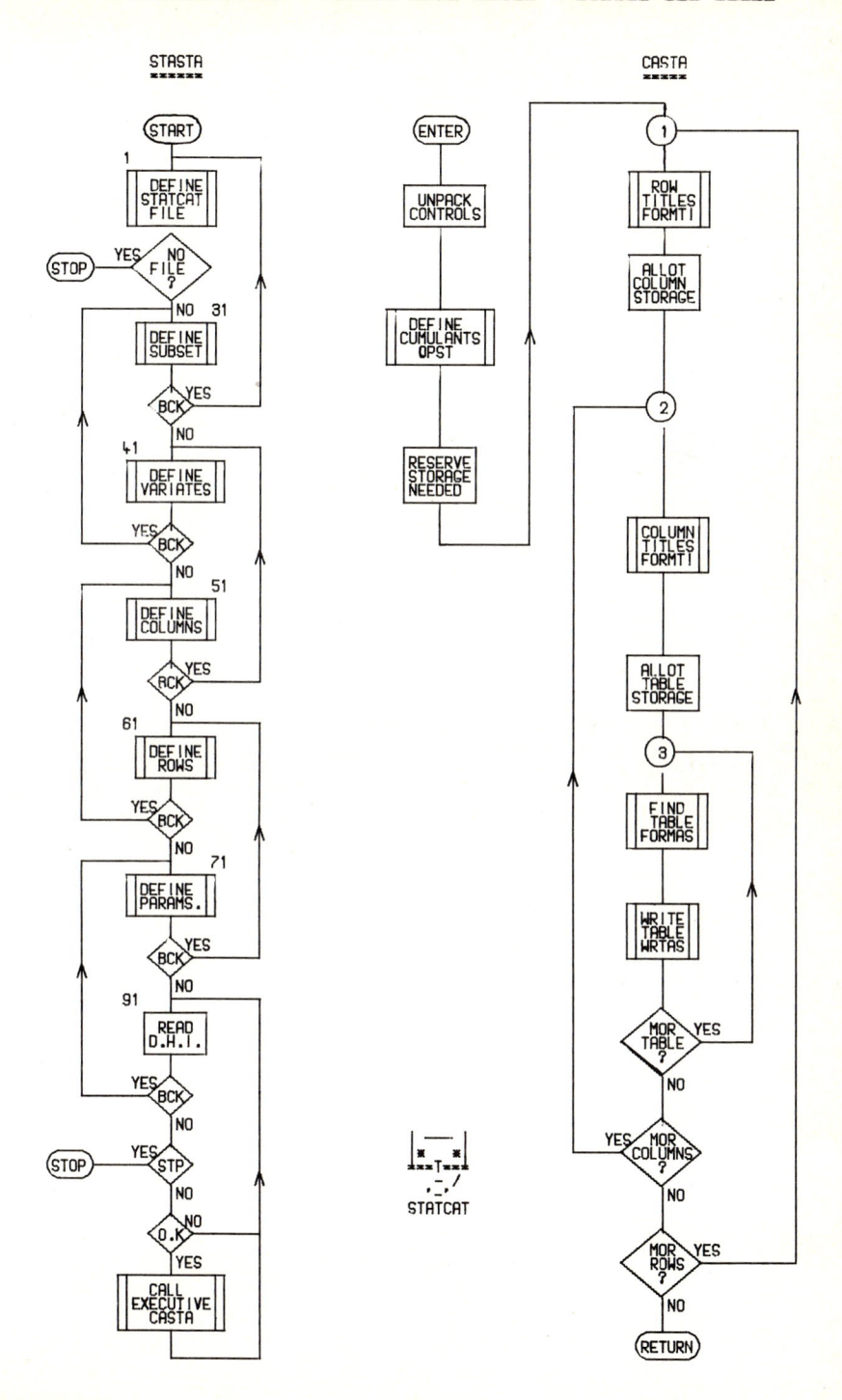

Figure 5.31b - System Flow-chart - FORMTI, FORMAS and WASTA

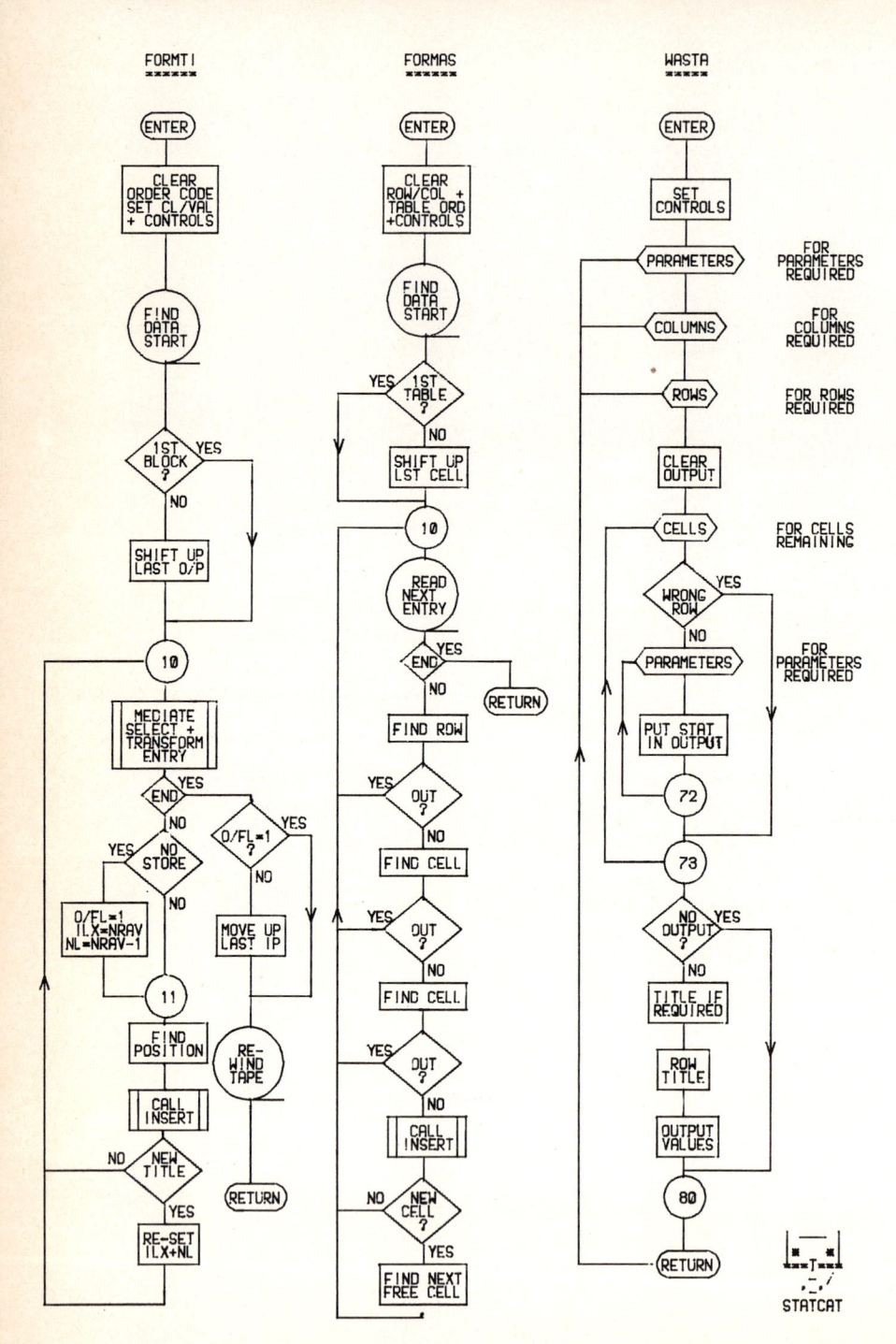

Figure 5.32 - STASTA - Input Structure

```
         Level
0    1    2    3    4    5    6    7    8    9
FILE CONTROL CARD
    SUBSET SPECIFICATION
        VARIATE SPECIFICATION
            ROW SPECIFICATION
                COLUMN SPECIFICATION
                    PARAMETER SPECIFICATION
                        DATA HANDLING INSTRUCTION
                        BACK TO READ NEW PARAMETERS
                    BACK TO READ NEW COLUMNS
                BACK TO READ NEW ROWS
            ROW SPECIFICATION
                COLUMN SPECIFICATION
                    PARAMETER SPECIFICATION
                        DATA HANDLING INSTRUCTION
                        BACK TO READ NEW PARAMETERS
                    BACK TO READ NEW COLUMNS
                COLUMN SPECIFICATION
                    PARAMETER SPECIFICATION
                        DATA HANDLING INSTRUCTION
                        STOP
```

Figure 5.34 - STASTA - Output Structure

```
For each     ) : File Control Record
output file  )   File Parameters
                 Data Description
                 For each) : Subset Input Record
                 Subset  )   For each) Input Record
                             set of  ) For each) Input Record
                             Variates) Row spec) For each) Input Record
                                                 Column ) For each ) See
                                                 Spec   ) Parameter) Left
                                                                   Spec    )

For each          ) Input Record
Parameter         ) For Each   ) Input Record
Specification) Data Handling) For each  ) Column Titles
               Instruction  ) n* columns) For each  ) Row Title
                                          fifty rows) Parameter Values
```

* n depends on data handling instruction

Carated(<>) items are optional.

Figure 5.33 - STASTA - Input Example

```
---------1---------2---------3---------4---------5---------6---------7--
**STASTADEMO                            DEMONSTRATION STATCAT DATA BANK
ALL DATA                                DATA BANK SUBSET TITLE
END OF DATA BANK SUBSET SPECIFICATION   ALL ENTRIES ARE INCLUDED
VAL.SESS        16      1.5     1.0     TIME VARIATE - NOT USED
VAL.OBSR        4       1.5             3.5 THESE VARIATES
VAL.OPER        4               1.0     3.5 FORM A
VAL.TASK                1.5     1.0     3.5 FOUR LEVEL SIX WAY
VAL.DAY.        4       1.5             HYPER-GRAECO-LATIN CUBE
VAL.TIME        4               1.0     WHICH FORMS
VAL.W.P.        4                       3.5 THE BASIC EXPERIMENTAL DESIGN
VAL.EFOB                0.0     100.0
VAL.EFOP                        10.0   100.0
VAL.H.R.                0.0     10.0    HEART RATE
+100SET.        64                      +100 MAKES THE ITEMS EASIER TO F
PRESH.R.                0.5             = 1 IN ALL CASES
ABSVTEMP                        1.0     ABSV TRANSFORM IS REDUNDANT
VAL.W.P.                                3.5
VAL.SET.
VAL.TASK        4    2  1.5             3.5 NOTICE CORRECTIONS
END OF VARIATE SPECIFICATION
2Q1.VARE CL                             TABULATION STARTS AT TOP OF PAGE
2Q1.VARF *                              AND WORKS DOWNWARDS
2Q1.VAR7                                HIGH VALUE FIRST GIVES LARGEST A
END OF ROW SPECIFICATION
1Q2.VARBCLAS                            TABULATION LEFT TO RIGHT
1Q2.VARC                                LOW VALUE FIRST - LARGEST ON RIG
1Q2.VAR4VAL.                            ANY CODE MEANS CLASS NOT VALUE
END OF COLUMN SPECIFICATION
IDENVARK
END OF PARAMETER SPECIFICATION
28                                      COLUMNS ACROSS PAGE - 3 ROW 6 TA
BACK TO READ PARAMETERS
BACK TO READ COLUMNS
BACK TO READ ROWS
1Q2.VARA                                A - SESSION SUFFICIENT FOR SORTI
1Q2.VAR5                                DAY     REDUNDANT BUT
1Q2.VAR6                                TIME    USEFUL FOR REFERENCE
END OF ROW SPECIFICATION
1Q2.VAR7                                WORKING POSITION
END OF COLUMN SPECIFICATION
TOT.VARM                                FOR 1 VALUE TOT = MEAN USES LESS
END OF PARAMETER SPECIFICATION
GO
BACK TO READ PARAMETERS
BACK TO READ COLUMNS
1Q2.VARL                                ALWAYS 1 FOR DEMO DATA BANK
END OF COLUMN SPECIFICATION
NUMBVARJ
G.M.VARJ
H.M.VARJ
MAXIVARJ
MINIVARJ
KURTVARJ
END OF PARAMETER SPECIFICATION
GO
STOP
---------1---------2---------3---------4---------5---------6---------7--
```

Figure 5.35 - STASTA - Output Example Page-by-Page listing

Page	Contents	Origin
1- 3	File Control Record	FIFI
	Program Title	STASTA
	File Parameters	LDAP
	Data Description record	LDDS
4	Subset record	LSAMP
5- 6	Set of Variates record	LGEN
7	Row Variates record	LGEN
8	Column Variates record	LGEN
9	Parameter Variates record	LGEN
	Data Handling Instruction	LDHI
10-31	Tabulation	WASTA
32	Data Handling Instruction (BACK)	LDHI
33	Parameter record (BACK)	LGEN
34	Column record (BACK)	LGEN
35	Row Variates record	LGEN
36	Column Variates record	LGEN
37	Parameter Variates record	LGEN
	Data Handling Instruction	LDHI
38	Tabulation	WASTA
39	Data Handling Instruction (BACK)	LDHI
40	Parameter record (BACK)	LGEN
41	Column Variates record	LGEN
42	Parameter Variates record	LGEN
	Data Handling Instruction	LDHI
43	Tabulation	WASTA
44	Data Handling Instruction (STOP)	LDHI

Figure 5.36 - Parameter Codes

Code	Parameter	Extra Parameters	Sums
NUMB	Number of Values		
A.M.	Arithmetic Mean	NUMB	TOT.
S.D.	Standard Deviation	NUMB, A.M., VAR.	TOT., SSQ.
VAR.	Variance	NUMB, A.M., S.D.	As Above
SKEW	Skewness	As above + VAR.	As Above + SCUB
KURT	Kurtosis	As above + SKEW	As Above + S4TH
G.M.	Geometric Mean	NUMB	SLOG
H.M.	Harmonic Mean	NUMB	SREC
IDEN	Identity		
MINI	Minimum Value		
MAXI	Maximum Value		
TOT.	Total of Values		
SSQ.	Sum of Squares		
SCUB	Sum of Cubes		
S4TH	Sum of fourth powers		
SLOG	Sum of Logarithms		
SREC	Sum of Reciprocals		

211

Figure 5.37 - SPASTA - Large table (part)

```
DATA BANK TITLE - DEMONSTRATION STATCAT DATA BANK
DATA BANK SUBSET TITLE - ALL DATA

PARAMETER TABULATED - IDEN OF +100 OF DATA COLUMN    1 (NTRY)

        COLUMN TITLES              COLUMN VALUES
CLAS OF VAL. OF OBSR=   3          1.0000    1.0000    1.0000    1.0000    1.0000    1.0000
VAL. OF VAL. OF OPER=   4          1.0000    1.0000    1.0000    1.0000    2.0000    2.0000
CLAS OF VAL. OF TASK=   9          1.0000    2.0000    3.0000    4.0000    1.0000    2.0000

          ROW TITLES AND VALUES
  CLAS OF     CLAS OF      VAL. OF
  VAL. OF     VAL. OF      VAL. OF
  DAY. 7.     TIME  8.      A.P. 5.
   4.0000      4.0000       4.0000      0.0       0.0       0.0       0.0       0.0       0.0
   4.0000      4.0000       3.0000      0.0       0.0       0.0       0.0       0.0       0.0
   4.0000      4.0000       2.0000      0.0       0.0       0.0       0.0       0.0       0.0
   4.0000      4.0000       1.0000      0.0       0.0       0.0       0.0       0.0       0.0
   4.0000      3.0000       4.0000      0.0       0.0       0.0       0.0       0.0       0.0
   4.0000      3.0000       3.0000      0.0     155.0000    0.0       0.0       0.0       0.0
   4.0000      3.0000       2.0000      0.0       0.0       0.0       0.0       0.0       0.0
   4.0000      3.0000       1.0000      0.0       0.0       0.0       0.0       0.0       0.0
   4.0000      2.0000       4.0000      0.0       0.0       0.0       0.0       0.0       0.0
   4.0000      2.0000       3.0000      0.0       0.0       0.0       0.0       0.0       0.0
   4.0000      2.0000       2.0000      0.0       0.0       0.0       0.0       0.0       0.0
   4.0000      2.0000       1.0000      0.0       0.0       0.0       0.0       0.0       0.0
   4.0000      1.0000       4.0000      0.0       0.0       0.0       0.0       0.0       0.0
   4.0000      1.0000       3.0000      0.0       0.0       0.0       0.0       0.0       0.0
   4.0000      1.0000       2.0000      0.0       0.0       0.0       0.0       0.0       0.0
   4.0000      1.0000       1.0000      0.0       0.0       0.0       0.0       0.0       0.0
   3.0000      4.0000       4.0000      0.0       0.0       0.0       0.0       0.0       0.0
   3.0000      4.0000       3.0000      0.0       0.0       0.0       0.0     147.0000    0.0
   3.0000      4.0000       2.0000      0.0       0.0       0.0       0.0       0.0       0.0
   3.0000      4.0000       1.0000      0.0       0.0       0.0       0.0       0.0       0.0
   3.0000      3.0000       4.0000      0.0       0.0       0.0       0.0       0.0       0.0
   3.0000      3.0000       3.0000      0.0       0.0       0.0       0.0       0.0       0.0
   3.0000      3.0000       2.0000      0.0       0.0       0.0       0.0       0.0       0.0
   3.0000      3.0000       1.0000      0.0       0.0       0.0       0.0       0.0       0.0
   3.0000      2.0000       4.0000      0.0       0.0       0.0       0.0       0.0       0.0
   3.0000      2.0000       3.0000      0.0       0.0       0.0       0.0       0.0       0.0
   3.0000      2.0000       2.0000      0.0       0.0       0.0     135.0000    0.0       0.0
   3.0000      2.0000       1.0000      0.0       0.0       0.0       0.0       0.0       0.0
   3.0000      1.0000       4.0000      0.0       0.0       0.0       0.0       0.0       0.0
   3.0000      1.0000       3.0000      0.0       0.0       0.0       0.0       0.0       0.0
   3.0000      1.0000       2.0000      0.0       0.0       0.0       0.0       0.0       0.0
   3.0000      1.0000       1.0000      0.0       0.0       0.0       0.0       0.0       0.0
   2.0000      4.0000       4.0000      0.0       0.0     132.0000    0.0       0.0       0.0
   2.0000      4.0000       3.0000      0.0       0.0       0.0       0.0       0.0       0.0
   2.0000      4.0000       2.0000      0.0       0.0       0.0       0.0       0.0       0.0
   2.0000      4.0000       1.0000      0.0       0.0       0.0       0.0       0.0       0.0
   2.0000      3.0000       4.0000      0.0       0.0       0.0       0.0       0.0       0.0
   2.0000      3.0000       3.0000      0.0       0.0       0.0       0.0       0.0       0.0
   2.0000      3.0000       2.0000      0.0       0.0       0.0       0.0       0.0       0.0
   2.0000      3.0000       1.0000      0.0       0.0       0.0       0.0       0.0       0.0
   2.0000      2.0000       4.0000      0.0       0.0       0.0       0.0       0.0       0.0
   2.0000      2.0000       3.0000      0.0       0.0       0.0       0.0       0.0       0.0
   2.0000      2.0000       2.0000      0.0       0.0       0.0       0.0       0.0       0.0
   2.0000      2.0000       1.0000      0.0       0.0       0.0       0.0       0.0     121.0000
   2.0000      1.0000       4.0000      0.0       0.0       0.0       0.0       0.0       0.0


DATA BANK TITLE - DEMONSTRATION STATCAT DATA BANK
DATA BANK SUBSET TITLE - ALL DATA

PARAMETER TABULATED - IDEN OF +100 OF DATA COLUMN    1 (NTRY)

        COLUMN TITLES              COLUMN VALUES
CLAS OF VAL. OF OBSR=   3          1.0000    1.0000    1.0000    1.0000    1.0000    1.0000
VAL. OF VAL. OF OPER=   4          1.0000    1.0000    1.0000    1.0000    2.0000    2.0000
CLAS OF VAL. OF TASK=   9          1.0000    2.0000    3.0000    4.0000    1.0000    2.0000

          ROW TITLES AND VALUES
  CLAS OF     CLAS OF      VAL. OF
  VAL. OF     VAL. OF      VAL. OF
  DAY. 7.     TIME  8.      A.P. 5.
   2.0000      1.0000       3.0000      0.0       0.0       0.0       0.0       0.0       0.0
   2.0000      1.0000       2.0000      0.0       0.0       0.0       0.0       0.0       0.0
   2.0000      1.0000       1.0000      0.0       0.0       0.0       0.0       0.0       0.0
   1.0000      4.0000       4.0000      0.0       0.0       0.0       0.0       0.0       0.0
   1.0000      4.0000       3.0000      0.0       0.0       0.0       0.0       0.0       0.0
   1.0000      4.0000       2.0000      0.0       0.0       0.0       0.0       0.0       0.0
   1.0000      4.0000       1.0000      0.0       0.0       0.0       0.0       0.0       0.0
   1.0000      3.0000       4.0000      0.0       0.0       0.0       0.0       0.0       0.0
   1.0000      3.0000       3.0000      0.0       0.0       0.0       0.0       0.0       0.0
   1.0000      3.0000       2.0000      0.0       0.0       0.0       0.0       0.0       0.0
   1.0000      3.0000       1.0000      0.0       0.0       0.0       0.0       0.0       0.0
   1.0000      2.0000       4.0000      0.0       0.0       0.0       0.0       0.0       0.0
   1.0000      2.0000       3.0000      0.0       0.0       0.0       0.0       0.0       0.0
   1.0000      2.0000       2.0000      0.0       0.0       0.0       0.0       0.0       0.0
   1.0000      2.0000       1.0000      0.0       0.0       0.0       0.0       0.0       0.0
   1.0000      1.0000       4.0000      0.0       0.0       0.0       0.0       0.0       0.0
   1.0000      1.0000       3.0000      0.0       0.0       0.0       0.0       0.0       0.0
   1.0000      1.0000       2.0000      0.0       0.0       0.0       0.0       0.0       0.0
   1.0000      1.0000       1.0000    101.0000    0.0       0.0       0.0       0.0       0.0
```

Figure 5.38 - STASTA - Small two-way table

```
         DATA BANK TITLE - DEMONSTRATION STATCAT DATA BANK
         DATA BANK SUBSET TITLE - ALL DATA

         PARAMETER TABULATED - TOT. OF ABSV OF DATA COLUMN   11 (TEMP)

             COLUMN TITLES              COLUMN VALUES
  VAL. OF VAL. OF W.P.= 5                 1.00    2.00    3.00    4.00

             ROW TITLES AND VALUES
  VAL. OF VAL. OF VAL. OF
  VAL. OF VAL. OF VAL. OF
  SESS  2.DAY.  7.TIME 8.
    1.00    1.00    1.00              22.00   25.00   27.00   24.00
    2.00    1.00    2.00              24.00   26.00   28.00   26.00
    3.00    1.00    3.00              26.00   28.00   30.00   28.00
    4.00    1.00    4.00              25.00   26.00   28.00   26.00
    5.00    2.00    1.00              22.00   24.00   27.00   25.00
    6.00    2.00    2.00              23.00   26.00   29.00   26.00
    7.00    2.00    3.00              27.00   28.00   30.00   28.00
    8.00    2.00    4.00              24.00   25.00   28.00   26.00
    9.00    3.00    1.00              19.00   22.00   24.00   22.00
   10.00    3.00    2.00              23.00   24.00   26.00   25.00
   11.00    3.00    3.00              24.00   26.00   28.00   26.00
   12.00    3.00    4.00              22.00   24.00   26.00   24.00
   13.00    4.00    1.00              19.00   22.00   25.00   22.00
   14.00    4.00    2.00              22.00   25.00   26.00   25.00
   15.00    4.00    3.00              24.00   26.00   28.00   26.00
   16.00    4.00    4.00              22.00   25.00   26.00   24.00
```

Figure 5.39 - STASTA - One-way tabulation of parameters

```
DATA BANK TITLE - DEMONSTRATION STATCAT DATA BANK
DATA BANK SUBSET TITLE - ALL DATA
```

COLUMN TITLES	COLUMN VALUES
VAL. OF PRES OF H.R.= 15	1.00

ROW TITLES AND VALUES			PARAMETER TITLES					
VAL. OF SESS 2.	VAL. OF DAY 7.	VAL. OF TIME 8.	NUMB OF VAL. OF H.R. 15.	G.M. OF VAL. OF H.R. 15.	H.M. OF VAL. OF H.R. 15.	MAXI OF VAL. OF H.R. 15.	MINI OF VAL. OF H.R. 15.	KURT OF VAL. OF H.R. 15.
1.00	1.00	1.00	4.00	46.85	45.65	62.19	35.52	0.74
2.00	1.00	2.00	4.00	47.21	46.88	56.10	41.28	0.90
3.00	1.00	3.00	4.00	47.04	46.51	60.38	39.77	1.22
4.00	1.00	4.00	4.00	47.39	47.13	54.57	41.59	0.86
5.00	2.00	1.00	4.00	46.86	46.22	56.10	36.06	1.14
6.00	2.00	2.00	4.00	46.51	45.36	65.42	36.34	1.01
7.00	2.00	3.00	4.00	47.21	47.12	51.00	43.75	0.78
8.00	2.00	4.00	4.00	47.04	46.77	53.52	40.38	0.86
9.00	3.00	1.00	4.00	46.69	46.42	53.36	40.07	0.92
10.00	3.00	2.00	4.00	46.85	46.29	60.38	39.16	1.19
11.00	3.00	3.00	4.00	47.03	46.71	55.69	41.28	0.87
12.00	3.00	4.00	4.00	47.04	46.10	59.47	36.61	0.68
13.00	4.00	1.00	4.00	46.95	46.67	54.34	40.98	0.82
14.00	4.00	2.00	4.00	46.86	46.81	49.24	44.41	0.86
15.00	4.00	3.00	4.00	46.68	45.53	64.92	36.06	0.97
16.00	4.00	4.00	4.00	47.48	46.92	54.86	36.88	1.22

```
C     MASTER STASTA - CONSTRUCTS AND PRINTS LARGE ASSOCIATION TABLES
C        SUBROUTINES AND FUNCTIONS REQUIRED
C        NAME             TYPE              COMMENT
C        AN      (SEE  3.1 ) SERVICE     ALPHA - TO NUMERIC VALUE
C        CASTA   (SEE  5.3 ) EXECUTIVE   LARGE ASSOCIATION TABLES
C        CHIKEN  (SEE 11.9 ) SERVICE     WARNS OF MISMATCHED DATA LEVEL
C        CLASIF  (SEE 11.7 ) SERVICE     CLASSIFIES DATA ITEM
C        CLSAM   (SEE  3.5 ) SERVICE     ALLOTS ENTRY TO SAMPLE/SUBSET
C        COMPA   (SEE  3.1 ) SERVICE     COMPARES ALPHAMERIC VALUES
C        COPYA   (SEE  3.1 ) SERVICE     COPIES ALPHAMERIC VALUE
C        FIFI    (SEE  3.2 ) SYSTEM      ALLOCATES PERIPHERALS
C        FORMPT  (SEE  5.3 ) SYSTEM      FORMS LARGE ASSOCIATION TABLE
C        FORMTI  (SEE  5.3 ) SYSTEM      FORMS TITLE LISTS FOR ASSOCN TABLES
C        IBL     (SEE  3.1 ) SERVICE     DETECTS BLANK,END AND STOP CARDS
C        ICH     (SEE  3.1 ) SERVICE     IDENTIFIES ALPHAMERIC CODES
C        INSERT  (SEE 11.4 ) SERVICE     INSERTS ENTRY INTO ARRAY
C        LCOM    (SEE  3.4 )   SERVICE   LOADS COMPLEMENTARY INFORMATION
C        LDAP    (SEE  3.3 ) SYSTEM      LOADS/CHECKS DATA BANK PARAMETERS
C        LDBS    (SEE  3.6 ) SYSTEM      LOADS SUBSET DEFINITION
C        LDDS    (SEE  3.4 ) SYSTEM      LOADS DATA DESCRIPTION SEGMENT
C        LDHI    (SEE  3.8 ) SYSTEM      LOADS/CHECKS DATA HANDLING INSTN
C        LGEN    (SEE  3.7 ) SYSTEM      LOADS GENERALISED VARIATES
C        LSET    (SEE  3.5 ) SYSTEM      LOADS DEFINING CONDITIONS
C        MEDIAT  (SEE  3.7 ) SERVICE     FETCHES NEXT VARIATE SET
C        OPST    (SEE 10.5 ) SERVICE     DEDUCES SUMS REQUIRED FOR STATISTIC
C        POSCL   (SEE 11.4 ) SERVICE     FINDS POSITION - CLASSIFIED IF REQD
C        POSN    (SEE 11.4 ) SERVICE     FINDS POSITION OF ENTRY IN ORDER
C        PR      (SEE 10.2 ) SERVICE     DETERMINES PRIORITY IN SORTING
C        STAT    (SEE 10.5 ) SERVICE     CONVERTS SUMS TO STATISTICS
C        TRANS   (SEE  3.7 ) SERVICE     CARRIES OUT REQUIRED TRANSFORM
C        WASTA   (SEE  5.3 ) SYSTEM      WRITES LARGE ASSOCIATION TABLE
C        WDCD    (SEE  3.4 ) SYSTEM      WRITES DATA COLUMN DESCRIPTION
C     IF NQMAX = MAXIMUM NO OF DATA COLUMNS IS CHANGED UPDATE CN DATA
C     DIMENSION CN(NQMAX),DMAX(NQMAX),DMIN(NQMAX),IT(NQMAX),ST(NQMAX)
C     DIMENSION XX(NQMAX)
      NQMAX = 100
      DIMENSION CN(100),DMAX(100),DMIN(100),IT(100),ST(100),XX(100)
      DATA   CN/4HCOL1,4HCOL2,4HCOL3,4HCOL4,4HCOL5,4HCOL6,4HCOL7,4HCOL8,4
     1HCOL9,4HCL10,4HCL11,4HCL12,4HCL13,4HCL14,4HCL15,4HCL16,4HCL17,4HC
     2L18,4HCL19,4HCL20,4HCL21,4HCL22,4HCL23,4HCL24,4HCL25,4HCL26,4HCL27,
     34HCL28,4HCL29,4HCL30,4HCL31,4HCL32,4HCL33,4HCL34,4HCL35,4HCL36,4HC
     4L37,4HCL38,4HCL39,4HCL40,4HCL41,4HCL42,4HCL43,4HCL44,4HCL45,4HCL46
     5,4HCL47,4HCL48,4HCL49,4HCL50,4HCL51,4HCL52,4HCL53,4HCL54,4HCL55,4H
     6CL56,4HCL57,4HCL58,4HCL59,4HCL60,4HCL61,4HCL62,4HCL63,4HCL64,4HCL6
     75,4HCL66,4HCL67,4HCL68,4HCL69,4HCL70,4HCL71,4HCL72,4HCL73,4HCL74,4
     8HCL75,4HCL76,4HCL77,4HCL78,4HCL79,4HCL80,4HCL81,4HCL82,4HCL83,4HCL
     984,4HCL85,4HCL86,4HCL87,4HCL88,4HCL89,4HCL90,4HCL91,4HCL92,4HCL93,
     94HCL94,4HCL95,4HCL96,4HCL97,4HCL98,4HCL99,4HC100/
C     NIL = MAXIMUM NUMBER OF INDEX LINES AVAILABLE
C     NIL SHOULD BE AT LEAST (ROWS+2) + (COLUMNS+2) + (CELLS+1)
C     FOR ONE PAGE 47 + 12 + 251 = 310 (VERY SLOW)
C     ABSOLUTE MINIMUM = 3+6+6 = 15 (VERY,VERY SLOW)
      NIL = 1000
      DIMENSION IL(1000)
C     DIMENSION TRT(NALTMX) = MAXIMUM NO OF CLASSES IN DATA BANK
      NALTMX = 50
      DIMENSION TRT(50)
C     MAXM = MAXIMUM NUMBER OF VARIATES THAT CAN BE STORED FOR USE AS ROW,
C     COLUMN OR PARAMETER VARIATES AT ONE TIME
C     DIMENSION TMAX(MAXM),TMIN(MAXM),NCL(MAXM),NP(MAXM),NDP(MAXM)
C     DIMENSION VNA(MAXM),VNO(MAXM),JT(MAXM)
      MAXM = 25
      DIMENSION TMAX(25),TMIN(25),NCL(25),NP(25),NDP(25)
```

```
      DIMENSION VNA(25),VNO(25),JT(25)
      DATA VNO/4HVAR1,4HVAR2,4HVAR3,4HVAR4,4HVAR5,4HVAR6,4HVAR7,4HVAR8,4
     1HVAR9,4HVA10,4HVA11,4HVA12,4HVA13,4HVA14,4HVA15,4HVA16,4HVA17,4HVA
     218,4HVA19,4HVA20,4HVA21,4HVA22,4HVA23,4HVA24,4HVA25/
      DATA VNA/4HVARA,4HVARB,4HVARC,4HVARD,4HVARE,4HVARF,4HVARG,4HVARH,4
     1HVARI,4HVARJ,4HVARK,4HVARL,4HVARM,4HVARN,4HVARO,4HVARP,4HVARQ,4HVA
     2RR,4HVARS,4HVART,4HVARU,4HVARV,4HVARW,4HVARX,4HVARY/
C MAXD = STORAGE AVAILABLE FOR DELAYED   ENTRIES
C (MAXIMUM DELAY + 3.) * M MUST NOT EXCEED MAXD
C DIMENSION IPQ(NPMAX)= MAXIMUM NO OF PARAMETERS DEFINED
      NPMAX = 25
      DIMENSION IPQ(25)
C MNPQ = MAXIMUM NUMBER OF STORED VARIATES IN A DATA SWEEP
C DIMENSION IE(MNPQ),IG(MNPQ),IX(MNPQ),IY(MNPQ)
      MNPQ = 25
      DIMENSION IE(25),IG(25),IX(25),IY(25)
C NLAV = NUMBER OF LINES OF 100 AVAILABLE AS WORKING STORE
      NLAV = 25
      DIMENSION RT(100,25)
C DIMENSION D(MAXD) IF MAXD NOT ZERO
      MAXD = 250
      DIMENSION D(250)
C DIMENSION SCON(5,MAXDBC)= MAXIMUM NUMBER OF SUBSET CONDITIONS
      MAXDBC = 50
      DIMENSION SCON(5,50)
C THE FOLLOWING DIMENSIONS ARE FIXED
      DIMENSION U(60),LU(60),FORM(50),H(1),IH(1),C(10)
      NU = 60
C TRANSFORMATION CODES
C UNITS                   BLOCKS
C   0 - 9   10 - 19   20 - 29   30 - 39   40 - 49   50 - 59
C   POWERS TRIG        TRIG      STATIST   MATHS     TEST
C          RADIANS     DEGREES   TRANSF    FUNCTS    FUNCTIONS
C   0       -           -        H.MS         -        -         RM10
C   1     VAL.  SINR   SIND      PSNA      RECP      +/-1
C   2     SQAR  COSR   COSD      PSNB      SQRT      ADD1
C   3     CUBE  TANR   TAND      BINO      ABSV      SUB1
C   4     4PWR  ASIR   ASID      LG+1      SIGN      NOR1
C   5     5PWR  ACOR   ACOD      LOGE      INTG      +/-P
C   6     6PWR  ATAR   ATAD      LG10      FRAC      ADDP
C   7     7PWR  SINH   DTOR      AL10      EXPT      SUBP
C   8     8PWR  COSH   RTOD       -        PRES      NORP
C   9     9PWR  TANH   H. HH      -        NEG.      +100
      DATA U/4HVAL.,4HSQAR,4HCUBE,4H4PWR,4H5PWR,4H6PWR,4H7PWR,4H8PWR,4H9
     1PWR,4HVAL ,4HSINR,4HCOSR,4HTANR,4HASIR,4HACOR,4HATAR,4HSINH,4HCOSH
     2,4HTANH,4HH.MS,4HSIND,4HCOSD,4HTAND,4HASID,4HACOD,4HATAD,4HDTOR,4H
     3RTOD,4HH.HH,4H VAL,4HPSNA,4HPSNB,4HBINO,4HLG+1,4HLOGE,4HLG10,4HAL1
     40,4H   ,4H   ,4HRECP,4HSQRT,4HABSV,4HSIGN,4HINTG,4HFRAC,4
     5HEXPT,4HPRES,4HNEG.,4HRM10,4H+/-1,4HADD1,4HSUB1,4HNOR1,4H+/-P,4HAD
     6DP,4HSUBP,4HNORP,4H+100,4H    /
      DATA LU/1,8*5,1,9*5,1,9*5,1,6*5,4*1,2*5,2*3,3*5,7*2,4*5,2*2/
      DIMENSION W(8),PC(17),LC(17)
C PRIORITY RULES
C RULES      1      2       3       4       5       6       7       8
      DATA W/4H1Q2.,4H2Q1.,4HQ12.,4HQ21.,4H12Q.,4H21Q.,4H12-.,4H21-./
      NPC = 17
C STANDARD PARAMETERS
      DATA PC/4HA.M.,4HS.D.,4HVAR.,4HSKEW,4HKURT,4HG.M.,4HH.M.,4HMINI,4H
     1MAXI,4HNUMB,4HTOT.,4HSSQ.,4HSCUB,4HS4TH,4HSLOG,4HSREC,4HIDEN/
C REQUIRED DATA LEVELS FOR STANDARD DESCRIPTIVE PARAMETERS
      DATA LC/5*4,2*5,2*3,1,4*4,2*5,1/
      COMMON /STCT/MED1,MED2,MED3,MED4,MED5,MED6,MED13,Q,V(20),TT(30)
      DATA PROG/4HASTA/
```

```
      MED1 = -1
C LEVEL 0 - SETTING UP DATA BANK
    1 CALL COPYA(TT(1),PROG)
      CALL FIFI
      WRITE(MED6,901)
      CALL LDAP(MED2,MED3,V,TT,Q,NQ,NALT,NQMAX,NALTMX,IGO)
      IF(IGO.GT.0) GO TO 1
      LI=18
      CALL LDDS(TRT,NALT,D,NQ,ST,NQ,IT,NQ,RT,NQ,DMIN,DMAX,NQ,LI,1,Q,VX,
     1 0,MED2,MED3,0,IGO)
      IF(IGO.GT.0) GO TO 1
C LEVEL 2 - SPECIFY DATA BANK SUBSET
   21 IF(V(10).GE.20.)  V(10) = 0.
      CALL LDBS(SCON,NCON,MAXDBC,CN,ST,IT,NQ,TRT,NALT,IGO)
      IF(IGO.GT.0) GO TO 1
C LEVEL 3 - READ SET OF VARIATES FOR DATA SWEEP
   31 IF(V(10).GE.30.) V(10) = 0.
      IFIN = MAXM
      M = 0
      V(6) = 0.
      WRITE(MED6,931)
      WRITE(MED6,932)
      CALL LGEN(U,NU,LU,NU,ST,IT,CN,NQ,NCL,MAXM,DMIN,DMAX,NQ,TMIN,TMAX,M
     1AXM,MAXD,NIL,NDP,NP,MAXM,M,IFIN,1,NALT)
      IF(V(20).LT.0.5.AND.V(11).LT.0.5) GO TO 21
      IF(V(20).GT.0.5.AND.V(10).LT.0.5) V(10) = 32.
      IF(M.LT.1) GO TO 41
C STORE LEVEL ASSUMED IN JT
      DO 32 I = 1,M
      NTR = NP(I)/1000
      NCOL = NP(I)-NTR*1000
      IF(IT(NCOL).GE.LU(NTR)) JT(I) = IT(NCOL)
   32 IF(IT(NCOL).LT.LU(NTR)) JT(I) = LU(NTR)
C LEVEL 4 - SPECIFY ROW VARIATES WITH PRIORITY CODES
   41 IF(V(10).GT.40.) V(10) = 0.
      WRITE(MED6,941)
      WRITE(MED6,952)
      MX = 5
      ISF = 0
      IFIN = M
      CALL LGEN(W,8,H,0,VNA,JT,VNO,M,IH,0,H,H,0,H,H,0,-1,0,IY,IX,MX,ISF
     1,IFIN,1,0)
      IF(V(20).LT.0.5.AND.V(11).LT.0.5) GO TO 31
      IF(V(20).GT.0.5.AND.V(10).LT.0.5) V(10) = 41.
      NR = ISF
C LEVEL 5 - SPECIFY COLUMN VARIATES WITH PRIORITY CODES
   51 IF(V(10).GE.50.)V(10) = 0.
      WRITE(MED6,951)
      WRITE(MED6,952)
      MX = M
      ISF = NR
      CALL LGEN(W,8,H,0,VNA,JT,VNO,M,IH,0,H,H,0,H,H,0,-1,0,IY,IX,MX,ISF
     1,IFIN,1,0)
      IF(V(20).LT.0.5.AND.V(11).LT.0.5) GO TO 41
      IF(V(20).GT.0.5.AND.V(10).LT.0.5) V(10) = 51.
      NC = ISF-NR
C LEVEL 6 - SPECIFY PARAMETER VARIATES WITH PARAMETER CODES
   61 IF(V(10).GE.60.) V(10) = 0.
      WRITE(MED2,961)
      WRITE(MED6,962)
      NPAR = 0
      CALL LGEN(PC,NPC,LC,NPC,VNA,JT,VNO,M,IH,0,H,H,0,H,H,0,0,0,IH,IPQ,N
     1PMAX,NPAR,NPMAX,1,0)
```

```
      IF(V(20).LT.0.5.AND.V(11).LT.0.5) GO TO 51
      IF(V(11).LT.0.5.AND.V(10).LT.0.5) V(10) = 61.
C LEVEL 9 - DATA HANDLING INSTRUCTION
   91 IF(V(10).GT.90.) V(10) = 0.
      CALL LDHI(V(1),1,V(2),4,V(9),7,H,0,H,0,H,0,H,V(10),
     1FORM(41),FORM,MED1,MED2,0,Q,NQ,NWARN,1,IGO)
      IF(IGO.GT.0) GO TO 61
C STANDARDISATION
      N4 = V(2) + .01
      N3 = N4/3
      IF(N3+NR.GT.5)NWARN = NWARN + 1
      IF(N3+NR.GT.5)V(2) = N4 - (N3+NR-5)*3
      CALL LDHI(V(1),1,V(2),4,V(9),7,H,0,H,0,H,0,H,V(10),
     1FORM(41),FORM,MED1,MED2,0,Q,NQ,NWARN,2,IGO)
      IF(IGO.GT.0) GO TO 91
      WRITE(MED6,998)
C CALL EXECUTIVE
      V(10) = 5326.
      CALL CASTA(IE,IG,IX,IY,MNPQ,IPQ,NPAR,RT,NLAV,D,MAXD,XX,ST,NQ,NDP,N
     1P,TMAX,TMIN,JT,NCL,M,SCON,NCON,U,NU,PC,NPC,IL,NIL,NC,NR,NPMAX)
      V(10) = 0.
      WRITE(MED6,999)
      GO TO 91
  901 FORMAT (1H0,20X,58HSTATCAT PROGRAM STASTA - PRODUCES LARGE ASSOCIA
     1TION TABLES)
  931 FORMAT (1H1,10X,30HSET OF VARIATES FOR DATA SWEEP/)
  932 FORMAT (4H0NO.,9X,30HTRANS  DATA  CYCLES  NUMBER OF,7X,5HLOWER,6X,
     15HCLASS,7X,5HUPPER/5H CODE,8X,68H-FORM COLUMN DELAY  CLASSES USED
     2 CLASS LIMIT  INTERVAL  CLASS LIMIT,5X,7HCOMMENT)
  941 FORMAT(1H1,10X,21HROW VARIATES IN ORDER/)
  951 FORMAT(1H1,10X,24HCOLUMN VARIATES IN ORDER/)
  952 FORMAT (7H0NUMBER,6X,18HPRIOR  VARI CLASS//5H CODE,9X,16H-ITY  -AT
     1E VALUE,54X,7HCOMMENT)
  961 FORMAT(1H1,10X,26HPARAMETERS TO BE TABULATED/)
  962 FORMAT (7H0NUMBER,6X,11HPARAM  VARI/5H CODE,8X,11H-ETER  -ATE,60X,
     17HCOMMENT)
  998 FORMAT (36H0INPUT ACCEPTED - ANALYSIS COMMENCES)
  999 FORMAT (36H1ANALYSIS COMPLETED - READ NEW INPUT)
      END


      SUBROUTINE CASTA(IE,IG,IX,IY,MNPQ,IPQ,NP1 ,RT,NLAV,D,MAXD,XX,ST,NQ
     1,NDP,NP,TMAX,TMIN,JT,NCL,M,SCON,NCON,U,NU,PC,NPC,IL,NIL,NC,NR,NPMA
     2X)
C CASTA   (SEE  5.3 ) EXECUTIVE   LARGE ASSOCIATION TABLES
C EXECUTIVE OF STAST,FINDS ROW AND COLUMN CODES,FORMS AND LISTS
      DIMENSION IE(MNPQ),IG(MNPQ),IX(MNPQ),IY(MNPQ),IPQ(NPMAX)
      DIMENSION RT(100,NLAV),D(MAXD),XX(NQ),ST(NQ)
      DIMENSION NP(M),NDP(M),TMAX(M),TMIN(M),JT(M),NCL(M)
      DIMENSION SCON(5,NCON),U(NU),PC(NPC),IL(NIL)
      COMMON /STCT/MED1,MED2,MED3,MED4,MED5,MED6,MED13,Q,V(20),TT(30)
      N2 = V(1) + .01
      N5 = N2 - N2/2*2
      N5 = (48+2*N5-NC)/5*5
      N2 = N2/2 -N2/4*2
      N4 = V(2) + .01
      N4 = 10-2*(N4-N4/3*3)
      ISF = NC + NR
      JSF = ISF
      ISF = ISF + 2
      CALL OPST(IX,IY,MNPQ,ISF,IST,IPQ,NPMAX,NP1,NPAR)
      NPA = IST-JSF
C NPMIN = PAGE PLUS 1 IF ROOM FOR ROWS+COLUMNS
```

```
C IF NOT AS MUCH AS POSSIBLE
    5 NPMIN = (NLAV*100-(N4+2)*NC - (N5+2)*NR)/NPA
      IF(NPMIN.GT.NIL-N4-N5 - 4) NPMIN = NIL-N4-N5-4
      IF(NPMIN.GT.N5*N4+1) NPMIN = N5*N4 + 1
      IF(NPMIN.GE.N5*N4 + 1) GO TO 6
      IF(N5.GT.10) N5 = N5 - 4
      IF(N5.GT. 0) N5 = N5 - 1
      IF(N5.GT. 0) GO TO 5
      WRITE(MED2,900)
  900 FORMAT(74H0NOT ENOUGH STORAGE FOR EVEN ONE LINE OF TABLE - JOB WIL
     1L NOT BE ATTEMPTED)
      RETURN
C FIND ROW CODES
    6 NRAX = (NLAV*100 - (N4+2)*NC - NPMIN*NPA)/NR
      NRAV = NIL - (N4+2) - NPMIN
      IF(NRAV.GT.NRAX) NRAV = NRAX
      IF(NRAX.GT.NRAV) NRAX = NRAV
      JST = 0
    1 NRAV = (NRAX-2)/N5*N5 + 1 + JST
      CALL FORMTI(RT,IL,NRAV,IX,IY,IE,IG,NR,NDP,NP,TMAX,TMIN,JT,NCL,M,D,
     1MAXD,XX,NQ,SCON,NCON,JST,JOFL,NLR)
C FIND COLUMN CODES
      NUSED = NR*NLR
      JA = NUSED/100 + 1
      IA = NUSED - JA*100 + 101
      ILS = NLR + 1
      IXS = NR + 1
      NCAX = (NLAV*100 - NUSED - NPMIN*NPA)/NC
      NCAV = NIL - NPMIN - NLR
      IF(NCAX.GT.NCAV) NCAX = NCAV
      IF(NCAV.GT.NCAX) NCAV = NCAX
      IST = 0
    2 NCAV = (NCAX-2)/N4*N4 + 1 + IST
      CALL FORMTI ( RT(IA,JA),IL(ILS),NCAV,IX(IXS),IY(IXS),IE,IG,NC,NDP,
     1NP,TMAX,TMIN,JT,NCL,M,D,MAXD,XX,NQ,SCON,NCON,IST,IOFL,NLC)
      NUSET = NUSED + NLC*NC
      JB = NUSET/100 + 1
      IB = NUSET - JB*100 + 101
      ILT = NLR + NLC + 1
      IXT = NR + NC + 1
      NPAX = (NLAV*100-NUSET)/NPA
      NPAV = NIL - NLR - NLC
      IF(NPAV.GT.NPAX) NPAV = NPAX
      IF(NPAX.GT.NPAV) NPAX = NPAV
      KSF = 0
    3 CALL FORMAS(RT,IL,IX,IY,IE,IG,NR,NLR,
     1RT(IA,JA),IL(ILS),IX(IXS),IY(IXS),IE(IXS),IG(IXS),NC,NLC,
     2RT(IB,JB),IL(ILT),IX(IXT),IE(IXT),IY(IXT)   ,NPA,NPAV,NDP,NP,
     3TMAX,TMIN,JT,NCL,M,D,MAXD,XX,NQ,SCON,NCON,KSF,KOFL,IST,JST,NLP)
      IF(NLP.EQ.0.AND.N2.EQ.0) GO TO 4
      CALL WASTA(RF,IL,IX,IY,NR,NLR,RT(IA,JA),IL(ILS),IX(IXS),IY(IXS),NC
     1,NLC,RT(IB,JB),IL(ILT),IX(IXT),NPA,NPAV,NDP,NP,M,KSF,NLP,IPQ,NPAR,
     2ST,NQ,U,NU,PC,MPC,IST,JST)
    4 KSF = 1
      IF(KOFL.NE.0) GO TO 3
      IST = 1
      IF(IOFL.NE.0) GO TO 2
      JST = 1
      IF(JOFL.NE.0) GO TO 1
      RETURN
      END
```

```
      SUBROUTINE FORMTI(RT,IL,NRAV,ID,IDP,IE,IG,NC,NA,NB,DMAX,DMIN,IT,NC
     1L,M,D,MN,XX,NQ,SCON,NCON,IST,IOFL,NL)
C FORMTI (SEE  5.3 ) SYSTEM       FORMS TITLE LISTS FOR ASSOCN TABLES
C CONSTRUCTS ORDERED ARRAY OF TITLES   IL(1) IS FIRST IN ORDER
C IF IST = 0 THIS IS FIRST RUN IF NOT IL(1) IS LAST OF PREVIOUS
C IF IOFL = 0 ON RETURN THERE IS NO OVERFLOW
      DIMENSION RT(NC,NRAV),IL(NRAV),ID(NC),IDP(NC),IE(NC),IG(NC)
      DIMENSION NA(M),NB(M),DMAX(M),DMIN(M),IT(M),NCL(M),D(MN)
      DIMENSION XX(NQ),SCON(5,NCON)
      COMMON /STCT/MED1,MED2,MED3,MED4,MED5,MED6,MED13,Q,V(20),TT(30)
      REWIND MED3
      DO 1 I = 1,NC
      IE(I) = I
    1 IG(I) = ID(I)/1000
      IF(IST.NE.0) ILY = IL(NL-1)
      DO 2 J = 1,NRAV
    2 IL(J) = J
      READ(MED3) NQ,NALT,Q,(X,I = 1,16)
      DO 3 K = 1,NQ
    3 READ(MED3) (X,I= 1,19),(X,I=1,NALT),MX,X,X
      V(6) = 0.
      V(7) = 3.
      V(8) = 1.
      V(9) = M
      NL = 0
      ILX = 1
      IOFL = 0
      IF(IST.EQ.0) GO TO 10
      DO 4 I = 1,NC
    4 RT(I,1) = RT(I,ILY)
      NL = 1
      ILX = 2
C DATA COLLECTION SWEEP
   10 CALL MEDIAT(M,NA,NB,MN,D,XX,NQ,SCON,NCON)
      IF(V(8).EQ.2.) GO TO 30
C ILX.EQ.0 MEANS ALL STORE IS IN USE
      IF(ILX.NE.0) GO TO 11
      IOFL = 1
      ILX = NRAV
      NL= NRAV-1
   11 POS=POSCL(RT,NC,NRAV,IL,D,DMAX,DMIN,NCL,IT,M,IDP,ID,IE,IG,NL,ILX)
      CALL INSERT(RT,NC,NRAV,IL,IG,IE,ILX,NL,Q,1,IST,POS)
C IF(ILX.EQ.0) NEW STORAGE LINE IS REQUIRED
      IF(ILX.NE.0) GO TO 10
      IF(NL.GE.NRAV-1) GO TO 10
      NL = NL + 1
      ILX= NL + 1
      GO TO 10
   30 REWIND MED3
      IF(IOFL.EQ.0.AND.ILX.NE.0) GO TO 37
      DO 35 J = 1,NL
   35 IF(IL(J).EQ.NL+1) ILX = J
      IF(ILX.EQ.NL+1) GO TO 37
      IF(ILX.EQ.0)GO TO 37
      ILY = IL(NL+1)
      IL(ILX) = ILY
      DO 36 I = 1,NC
   36 RT(I,ILY) = RT(I,NL+1)
   37 NL = NL + 1
      RETURN
      END
```

```
      SUBROUTINE FORMAS (QT,JL,JD,JDP,JE,JG,NR,NRAV,PT,IL,ID,IDP,IE,IG,N
     1C,NCAV,RT,KL,KD,     KE,KG,NP,NPAV,NA,NB,DMAX,DMIN,IT,NCL,M,D,MN,XX
     2,NQ,SCON,NCON,KST,KOFL,ISP,JSP,NL)
C CONSTRUCTS ORDERED ASSOCIATION TABLE
C PT,IL,ID,IDP,IE,IG,NC,NCAV CONTAIN COLUMN IDENTIFICATION
C QT,JL,JD,JDP,JE,JG,NR,NRAV CONTAIN ROW IDENTIFICATION
C RT,KL,KD,    KE,KG,NP,NPAV CONTAIN CELL IDENTIFICATION
C D,DMAX,DMIN,IT,NCL,M,MN,SCON,NCON,NA,NB TRANSFORM BASIC DATA
C KST = 0 IF THIS IS FIRST PASS   KOFL RETURNS AS 1 IF OVERFLOW
C IF KST = 1 KL(1) CONTAINS LAST ITEM OF PREVIOUS PASS
C NL = LAST PARAMETER SORTAGE LINE USED
      DIMENSION PT(NC,NCAV),IL(NCAV),IE(NC),IG(NC),ID(NC),IDP(NC)
      DIMENSION QT(NR,NRAV),JL(NRAV),JE(NR),JG(NR),JD(NR),JDP(NR)
      DIMENSION RT(NP,NPAV),KL(NPAV),KE(NP),KG(NP),KD(NP)
      DIMENSION XX(NQ),D(MN),SCON(5,NCON)
      DIMENSION DMAX(M),DMIN(M),NA(M),NB(M),IT(M),NCL(M)
      COMMON /STCT/MED1,MED2,MED3,MED4,MED5,MED6,MED13,Q,V(20),TT(30)
      REWIND MED3
      DO 1 I = 1,NC
      IE(I) = I
    1 IG(I) = ID(I)/1000
      DO 2 I = 1,NR
      JE(I) = I
    2 JG(I) = JD(I)/1000
      IF(KST.NE.0)KLY = KL(NL-1)
      DO 3 J = 1,NPAV
    3 KL(J) = J
      DO 4 I = 1,NP
    4 KE(I) = I
      KG(1) = 1
      KG(2) = 1
      XM = ISP + 1
      YM = JSP + 1
      NCA1=NCAV-1
      NRA1=NRAV-1
      VCAV = NCA1
      VRAV = NRA1
      V(6) = 0.
      V(7) = 3.
      V(8) = 1.
      V(9) = M
      NL = 0
      IL(NCAV) = NCAV
      JL(NRAV) = NRAV
      READ(MED3) NQ,NALT,Q,(TT(J),J=1,16)
      DO 5 K = 1,NQ
    5 READ(MED3) (X,I=1,19),(X,I=1,NALT),NX,X,X
      KOFL= 0
      ILX = 1
      IF(KST.EQ.0) GO TO 10
      NL = 1
      ILX = 2
      DO 6 I = 1,3
    6 RT(I,1) = RT(I,KLY)
C DATA COLLECTION SWEEP
   10 CALL MEDIAT(M,NA,NB,MN,D,XX,NQ,SCON,NCON)
      IF(V(8).EQ.2.) GO TO 30
      IF(KOFL.EQ.1.AND.V(1).GE.3.) WRITE(MED2,901)
      X=POSCL(PT,NC,NCAV,IL,D,DMAX,DMIN,NCL,IT,M,IDP,ID,IE,IG,NCA1,NCAV)
      IF(X.LT.XM.OR.X.GT.VCAV+.3)GO TO 10
      Y=POSCL(QT,NR,NRAV,JL,D,DMAX,DMIN,NCL,IT,M,JDP,JD,JE,JG,NRA1,NRAV)
      IF(Y.LT.YM.OR.Y.GT.VRAV+.3) GO TO 10
      X = X + 0.6
```

```
      Y = Y + 0.6
      KLX = KL(ILX)
      RT(1,KLX) = X
      RT(2,KLX) = Y
      DO 20 I = 3,NP
      ILY = KD(I)/1000
      ILZ = KD(I) - ILY*1000
   20 RT(I,KLX) = TRANS(D(ILZ),Q,ILY,IBASE)
      IF(NL.EQ.0) GO TO 25
      POS = -1
      CALL INSERT(RT,NP,NPAV,KL,KG,KE,ILX,NL,Q,1,KST,POS)
      IF(ILX.NE.0) GO TO 10
   25 IF(NL.LT.NPAV) NL = NL + 1
      IF(NL.LT.NPAV) ILX = NL + 1
      IF(ILX.NE.0) GO TO 10
      KOFL = KOFL + 1
      ILX = NL
      GO TO 10
   30 REWIND MED3
      IF(NL.EQ.0) RETURN
      RETURN
  901 FORMAT (20H STORAGE OVERFLOW 2   )
      END

      SUBROUTINE WASTA(QT,JL,JD,JDP,NR,NRAV,PT,IL,ID,IDP,NC,NCAV,RT,KL,K
     1D,NP,NPAV,MA,NB,M,KST,NL,IPQ,NPAR,ST,NQ,U,NU,PC,NPC,IST,JST)
C WASTA    (SEE  5.3 ) SYSTEM      WRITES LARGE ASSOCIATION TABLE
C WRITES OUT BLOCK OF ASSOCIATION TABLE WITH HEADERS
      DIMENSION PT(NC,NCAV),IL(NCAV),ID(NC),IDP(NC)
      DIMENSION QT(NR,NRAV),JL(NRAV),JD(NR),JDP(NR)
      DIMENSION RT(NP,NPAV),KL(NPAV),KD(NP),IPQ(NPAR)
      DIMENSION ST(NQ),U(NU),PC(NPC),CV(2),W(20),NA(M),NB(M),A(10)
      DIMENSION A1(8),B1(4),A2(9),B2(5),F78(4),FA(6,3)
      DATA A1/4H(1H ,4H ,5 ,4H    (  ,4H A4,,4HF4.0,4H     ,4H ) ,4H  ) /
      DATA B1/4H(1H ,4H, 5 ,4HF 8.,4H2 ) /
      DATA A2/4H(1H+,4H,40X,4H,10 ,4H    (  ,4H A4,,4HF4.0,4H     ,4H  )
     1,4H  ) /
      DATA B2/4H(1H+,4H,40X,4H,10 ,4HF 8.,4H2 ) /
      DATA F78/4HF4.0,4H     ,4H4H 0,4HF    /
      DATA FA/4H,  4 ,4H(1X,,4H,1X),4HF10.,4H3)   ,4H, 8 ,4H, 3 ,4H(3X,,
     1 4H,2X),4HF13.,4H4)   ,4H, 6 ,4H, 2 ,4H(6X,,4H,6X),4HF20.,4H8)   ,
     2 4H, 4 /
      COMMON /STCT/MED1,MED2,MED3,MED4,MED5,MED6,MED13,Q,V(20),TT(30)
      DATA CV/4HVAL.,4HCLAS/
      NCS = IST + 1
      NRS = JST + 1
      NCA1 = NCAV - 1
      NRA1 = NRAV - 1
C UNPACK V(1) AND V(2) CONTROL INDICES
      N1 = V(1) + .01
      N1 = N1-N1/4*4
      N2 = N1/2
      N1 = N1 - N2*2
      N4 = V(2) + .01
      N3 = N4/3
      N4 = N4 - N3*3
      IF(N3.EQ.3) N4 = 3
      N5 = (48+2*N1-NC)/5*5
      IF(N2.EQ.0.AND.NPAV.EQ.0) RETURN
C SET MASTER FORMATS
      IF(N3.GT.0)CALL COPYA(A1(2),FA(1,N3))
      IF(N3.GT.0)CALL COPYA(A1(3),FA(2,N3))
```

```
      IF(N3.GT.0)CALL COPYA(A1(7),FA(3,N3))
      IF(N3.GT.0)CALL COPYA(B1(2),FA(1,N3))
      IF(N3.GT.0)CALL COPYA(B1(3),FA(4,N3))
      IF(N3.GT.0)CALL COPYA(B1(4),FA(5,N3))
      IF(N4.GT.0)CALL COPYA(A2(3),FA(6,N4))
      IF(N4.GT.0)CALL COPYA(A2(4),FA(2,N4))
      IF(N4.GT.0)CALL COPYA(A2(8),FA(3,N4))
      IF(N4.GT.0)CALL COPYA(B2(3),FA(6,N4))
      IF(N4.GT.0)CALL COPYA(B2(4),FA(4,N4))
      IF(N4.GT.0)CALL COPYA(B2(5),FA(5,N4))
      NCOL = 10-2*N4
      NPIN = 1
      IF(N1.EQ.1) NPIN = NCOL
      NCIN = NCOL/NPIN
      DO 80 KS = 1,NPAR,NPIN
      KF = KS+NPIN-1
      IF(KF.GT.NPAR) KF = NPAR
      JTX = KF-KS+1
      LF = KST
      DO 80 IS = NCS,NCA1,NCIN
      IF = IS + NCIN -1
      IF(IF.GT.NCA1) IF = NCA1
      ITX = IF - IS + 1
      IJTX = ITX*JTX
      LS = LF + 1
      NLIN = 0
      DO 80 JA = NRS,NRA1
      JLA = JL(JA)
      IPR = N2
      DO 71 I = 1,IJTX
   71 A(I) = 0.
      IF(LS.GT.NL) GO TO 74
      DO 73 L = LS,NL
      KLL = KL(L)
      IB = RT(1,KLL)
      IF(IB.GT.IF)GO TO 74
      JB = RT(2,KLL)
      IF(JA.NE.JB)GO TO 73
      IF(LF.LT.L)LF = L
      DO 72 K = KS,KF
      IX = (IB-IS)*JTX + (K-KS) + 1
      IF(IX.LT.1.OR.IX.GT.IJTX) GO TO 72
      A(IX) = STAT(IPQ(K),RT(3,KLL), KD(3),NP-2)
      IF(A(IX).NE.0..AND.A(IX).NE.-999.99)IPR = 1
   72 CONTINUE
   73 CONTINUE
   74 IF(IPR.EQ.0) GO TO 80
      IF(NLIN.NE.0) GO TO 70
      WRITE(MED2,911) (TT(I),I=1,10),(TT(I),I=21,30)
      IF(NPIN.NE.1) GO TO 51
C SINGLE PARAMETER - MULTIPLE COLUMN
      IPQK = IPQ(KS)
      IPK = IPQK/1000
      IQK = IPQK - IPK*1000
      ITK = NB(IQK)/1000
      ICK = NB(IQK) - ITK*1000
      WRITE(MED2,912) PC(IPK),U(ITK),ICK,ST(ICK)
      IF(NA(IQK).NE.0)WRITE(MED2,9121)NA(IQK)
   51 WRITE(MED2,913)
      DO 62 I = 1,NC
      ICL = 1
      IF(IDP(I).NE.0)ICL = 2
      IDI = ID(I) - ID(I)/1000*1000
```

```
      ITI = NB(IDI)/1000
      ICI = NB(IDI) - ITI*1000
      WRITE(MED2,914) CV(ICL),U(ITI),ST(ICI),ICI
      IF(NA(IDI).GT.0)WRITE(MED2,9141) NA(IDI)
      IF(ITI.EQ.48.AND.NC.EQ.1.AND.NCA1.EQ.2) GO TO 62
      ISP = 0
      DO 61 IX = IS,IF
      ISP = ISP + 1
      J = IL(IX)
   61 W(ISP) = PT(I,J)
      WRITE(MED2,B2) (W(J),J=1,ISP)
   62 CONTINUE
   60 WRITE(MED2,916)
      IF(NPIN.NE.1) WRITE(MED2,9161)
      DO 63 J = 1,NR
      IF(JDP(J).EQ.0) CALL COPYA(W(J),CV(1))
   63 IF(JDP(J).NE.0) CALL COPYA(W(J),CV(2))
      CALL COPYA(A1(5),F78(3))
      CALL COPYA(A1(6),F78(4))
      WRITE(MED2,A1) (W(J),J=1,NR)
      IF(NPIN.EQ.1) GO TO 53
      ISP = 0
      DO 52 K = KS,KF
      ISP = ISP + 1
      IPK = IPQ(K)/1000
   52 CALL COPYA(W(ISP),PC(IPK))
      CALL COPYA(A2(6),F78(3))
      CALL COPYA(A2(7),F78(4))
      WRITE(MED2,A2) (W(I),I=1,ISP)
   53 DO 64 J = 1,NR
      JDJ = JD(J) - JD(J)/1000*1000
      JTJ = NB(JDJ)/1000
   64 CALL COPYA(W(J),U(JTJ))
      WRITE(MED2,A1) (W(J),J=1,NR)
      IF(NPIN.EQ.1) GO TO 55
      ISP = 0
      DO 54 K = KS,KF
      ISP = ISP + 1
      IQK = IPQ(K) - IPQ(K)/1000*1000
      ITK = NB(IQK)/1000
   54 CALL COPYA(W(ISP),U(ITK))
      WRITE(MED2,A2) (W(I),I=1,ISP)
   55 ISP = 0
      IDL = 0
      JDL = 0
      DO 65 J = 1,NR
      JDJ = JD(J) - JD(J)/1000*1000
      JCJ = NB(JDJ)-NB(JDJ)/1000*1000
      IF(NA(JDJ).NE.0) IDL = 1
      ISP = ISP + 1
      CALL COPYA(W(ISP),ST(JCJ))
      ISP = ISP + 1
   65 W(ISP) = JCJ
      CALL COPYA(A1(5),F78(1))
      CALL COPYA(A1(6),F78(2))
      WRITE(MED2,A1) (W(J),J=1,ISP)
      IF(NPIN.EQ.1) GO TO 57
      ISP = 0
      DO 56 K = KS,KF
      ISP = ISP + 1
      IQK = IPQ(K) - IPQ(K)/1000*1000
      ICK = NB(IQK) - NB(IQK)/1000*1000
      CALL COPYA(W(ISP),ST(ICK))
```

```
      IF(NA(IQK).NE.0) JDL = 1
      ISF = ISF + 1
   56 W(ISF) = ICK
      CALL COPYA(A2(6),F78(1))
      CALL COPYA(A2(7),F78(2))
      WRITE(MED2,A2) (W(K),K=1,ISF)
   57 IF(IDL.EQ.0.AND.JDL.EQ.0) GO TO 70
      WRITE(MED2,920)
      IF(IDL.EQ.0) GO TO 58
      DO 66 J = 1,NR
      JDJ = JD(J) - JD(J)/1000*1000
   66 W(J) = NA(JDJ)
      WRITE(MED2,B1) (W(J),J=1,NR)
   58 IF(JDL.EQ.0) GO TO 70
      ISF = 0
      DO 59 K = KS,KF
      ISF = ISF + 1
      IQK = IPQ(K) - IPQ(K)/1000*1000
   59 W(ISF) = NA(IQK)
      WRITE(MED2,B2) (W(J),J=1,ISF)
   70 NLIN = NLIN + 1
      IF(NLIN.EQ.N5) NLIN = 0
      WRITE(MED2,B1) (QT(J,JLA),J=1,NR)
      WRITE(MED2,B2) (A(I),I=1,IJTX)
   80 CONTINUE
      RETURN
  911 FORMAT(1H1,10X,18HDATA BANK TITLE - ,10A4/11X,25HDATA BANK SUBSET
     1TITLE - ,10A4)
  912 FORMAT(1H0,10X,22HPARAMETER TABULATED - ,A4,4H OF ,A4,4H OF ,12HDA
     1TA COLUMN ,I4,2H (,A4,1H))
  913 FORMAT(1H0,10X,13HCOLUMN TITLES,20X,13HCOLUMN VALUES)
  914 FORMAT(1H ,A4,2(4H OF ,A4),1H=,I3)
  916 FORMAT(1H0,10X,21HROW TITLES AND VALUES)
  920 FORMAT (25H DELAY ( IN ENTRY UNITS )   /)
 9121 FORMAT(1H+,70X,14H - DELAYED BY ,I3,7H CYCLES)
 9141 FORMAT(1H+,24X,I3,13H CYCLES DELAY)
 9161 FORMAT (1H+,40X,16HPARAMETER TITLES)
```

Chapter VI

COMPARING SAMPLES

This chapter describes four programs for comparing samples. The types of tests used to determine whether samples differ significantly depend on the data level, the number of samples involved, and on knowledge about relationships between data within the samples.

Section 3.5 shows how a number of samples can be defined within a data bank subset. The samples so defined are known as 'independent' samples, so defined that no entry appears in two samples. (It is not necessary that every entry should be in a sample - unwanted entries are simply discarded.) Samples need not contain the same numbers of entries, and it is assumed that there is no significant systematic relationship between individual entries in one sample and those in another. Examples of such samples might be the temperature at different workplaces, or the assessed efficiencies of different operators. (In our data it is not true that there are no systematic relationships between entries in different samples, but in a preliminary analysis we may assume this to be so.)

The other type of sample is a "Related" sample. In related samples, each datum in a given sample has something in common with one datum in each other sample, and testing is based on the differences between the data. Any systematic variations will be cancelled out. For example, the operator's assessment of his own efficiency is likely to be affected by some of the factors in the situation in the same way as is the observer's estimate. If we wish to compare the observers' estimates with the operators' estimates, we will find that the overall averages tend to be generally similar, but that individual data are very variable. If, however, we analyse the difference between the observer's and the operator's estimates for a given situation, all the systematic difference differences between days, times of day, types of work and so on are cancelled out, and any genuine effects will appear more clearly when the 'background noise' is suppressed. To be able to make comparisons this way we must be able to match each item in each sample to exactly one in any other sample. In the STATCAT system, this decision is made when we set up the data bank, since each entry is considered to consist of related items, and we specify our related samples by choosing data columns (or transforms thereof) from the data description segment.

In general, we investigate differences in "Central Tendency" (is one sample bigger than another?) and "Dispersion" (Is one sample more spread out than another?) for independent samples. We investigate "Central Difference" (is the datum from one sample consistently bigger than that from another?) and "Correlation" (Do the variables really have something in common?) for related samples. It is sometimes also possible to carry out tests of "Dispersion" on related samples if extra assumptions are made.

In the STATCAT system, independent samples are defined by the method given in 3.5, for a subset defined by the method of 3.6, and tested in terms of variates defined by the method of 3.7. Related samples are defined, after specifying a subset by the method of 3.6, in terms of variates defined by the method of 3.7.

Because the methods appropriate for two samples are often not applicable to three or more samples, two programs are provided for each type of sample. The first program (ST2IND - 6.1 or ST2REL - 6.3) is designed to handle two samples, and the second (STKIND - 6.2 or STKREL - 6.4) to handle multiple samples. The second program will treat two samples, if required to do so, but will provide a warning that another program is perferable. Each program will carry out tests appropriate to the level of data being tested (the lowest level for related samples) unless over-ruled. The user may instruct the system to carry out all tests appropriate to data levels at or below the appropriate or a specified level, change the level of statistical significance, or call for more detailed descriptive output.

These programs are designed to provide the widest practical variety of sample testing methods. The user should realise that simply because it is possible, and hopefully easy, to carry out a test it is not necessarily true that the test should be made. Tests should only be made to investigate defined hypotheses - 'fishing expeditions' should be avoided, for reasons discussed in 12.1. He/she should also take to heart the discussion of statistical significance in that chapter.

REFERENCES : Siegel (Ch 3)

6.1 PROGRAM ST2IND - TEST TWO INDEPENDENT SAMPLES

6.1.1 Purpose

This program compares two independent samples of data drawn from a STATCAT data bank. The tests employed will be those appropriate to the level of the data being tested, unless the system is over-ridden. The choice of tests made by the system may be over-ridden to make tests on a specfic level, or to make tests on all levels up to the appropriate or a specific level. The level of significance below which results are not reported may be varied, and more or less detailed descriptive statistics produced. Variates tested may be transformed by any of the transforms given in Figure 3.72, but delayed variates may not be used. Class definitions may be specified, or the default values given in the data description segment may be used.

Figure 6.11a contains system flow-charts for the main program ST2IND and the executive subroutine C2IND. Figure 6.11b contains system flow-charts for the subroutines CHISQD (Self-adjusting Chi-Squared test - 6.1.5) and KS2SA (Kolmogorov-Smirnov Two-sample test - 6.1.6) Figure 6.11c contains system flow-charts for the subroutines MANWIT (Mann-Whitney "U" test - 6.1.7), and TFIND (Student's "t" and Snedecor's "F" tests - 6.1.8)

6.1.2 Input Data

Item	Level	Format	Function	See
1	0	A	File control	3.2
2	3	B	Sample specification (exactly two samples)	3.5
5	4	E	Subset specification	3.6
6	5	F	Variate specification (At least 1 - no delays)	3.7
7	9	H	Data handling instruction Below +	3.8

Data Handling Instruction

Card Layout - Data Handling Instruction - ST2IND

ABCCCDDDEEEEEEEEFFFFFFFFGGGGGGGGGGGGGGGGHHHHHHH.....etc

Columns	Item	Function	See
1	A	Output control index	Below
2	B	Analysis control index	Below
3 - 5	C	Significance level for reporting (per cent)	Below
6 - 8	D	Not used	-
9 - 16	E	Not used	-
17 - 24	F	Not used	-
25 - 40	G	Not used	-
41 - 80	H	Comment (NOT KEPT)	-

A - Output Control Index

This index controls the quantity of information output, and the application of testing at the desired level or at all lower levels.

ALTERNATIVES

A = 0 : No descriptive statistics. Tests at specified level only.

A = 1 : Frequency table and bar chart with positive and negative cumulative histogram if appropriate to data level. Tests at specified level only.

A = 2   : Descriptive statistics at specified level only. Tests
          at specified level only.

A = 3   : Frequency table and bar chart with positive and negative
          cumulative histogram if appropriate to data level.
          Descriptive statistics at specified level only. Tests
          at specified level only.

A = 4   : Summary table. Tests at specified level only.

A = 5   : No descriptive statistics. Tests up to specified level.

A = 6   : Frequency table and bar chart with positive and negative
          cumulative histogram if appropriate to data level. Tests
          up to specified level.

A = 7   : Descriptive statistics up to specified level only. Tests
          up to specified level.

A = 8   : Frequency table and bar chart with positive and negative
          cumulative histogram if appropriate to data level.
          Descriptive statistics up to specified level. Tests
          up to specified level.

A = 9   : Summary table. Tests up to specified level .

DEFAULT value = 0 (0, blank or non-numeric characters)

B - Analysis Control Index

This index controls the level at which testing is carried out, and the conditions under which the results are printed.

ALTERNATIVES

B = 0,blank: Tests at data level
(Default)   Print results if statistically significant.

B = 1   : Tests for NOMINAL level only (Chi-squared)
            Print results if statistically significant.

B = 2   : Tests for ORDINAL level only (Kolmogorov-Smirnov
            two sample test, Median Test, Quartile Test)
            Print results if statistically significant.

B = 3   : Tests for INTERVAL level(Mann-Whitney "U" Test,
            Student's "t" Test, "t-like" Test, Snedecor's "F" Test)
            Print results if statistically significant

B = 4   : Tests for RATIO level (as for INTERVAL)
            Print results if statistically significant.

B = 5   : Tests at data level - print all results.

B = 6   : Tests at NOMINAL level - print all results.

B = 7   : Tests at ORDINAL level - print all results.

B = 8   : Tests at INTERVAL level - print all results.

B = 9   : Tests at RATIO level - print all results.

DEFAULT value = 0 (0, blank or non-numeric character)

C - Significance Level

The significance level is the level of probability, expressed as a percentage, at or below which test results will be printed. The probability associated with a statistical test is the probability of observing a result as extreme as, or more extreme than that observed if in fact there were no difference between the populations from which the samples were drawn. The smaller the numerical value of this probability, the more significant a result must be to be reported.

DEFAULT value = 1 per cent (o, blank or non-numeric characters)

SPECIAL CASE : if B is negative and A is set to 4 or less, then testing is suppressed. (The program can then be used to produce purely descriptive statistics for the column variates.)

6.1.3 Input Example

Figure 6.12 is a summary of the input structure for two runs of ST2IND, using first the default values, then the full output available. Two independent samples are employed, which are the morning and afternoon sessions. All entries are included in the subset, and four variates are specified for testing. Although no transforms are used, the class definitions of the first two variates have been modified to reduce the number of classes used, saving time and storage space. The first data handling instruction employs default values throughout, producing only the results of statistically significant tests appropriate to the data level, where these have a probability of less than one per cent. The second data handling instruction produces the most detailed output possible. Figure 6.13 is a listing of the input cards required to carry out these two runs.

6.1.4 Output Example

Figure 6.14 is a summary of the output structure corresponding to the input structure of 6.12. Figure 6.15 is a page-by-page summary of the output corresponding to the specific example given in 6.1.3.

6.1.5 Statistical Tests - NOMINAL Level

A - CHISQD - Chi-squared Test for Two Independent Samples

This is a standard chi-squared test in which the rows correspond to classes of the variate and the columns to samples. The test requires only that the data used should be at least on a NOMINAL level, and that data should be mutually independent. (Practically, the latter requirement means that entries should not appear in several samples, which is impossible in the STATCAT system, and that entries should not be repetitions, or near repetitions of each other. If this is the situation, the statistical significance of calculated chi-squared values may be over-estimated.)

As the test is used here, it tests whether the probability of a datum being in a specific class depends on the sample from which it is drawn. If a statistically significant result is reported, this implies that a difference of some sort exists between the samples, but the exact nature of the difference must be determined by inspection.

The chi-squared test is usually considered unreliable if more than one fifth of the cells have an expected frequency less than 5, or if any one cell has an expected frequency less than one. If this happens, the program will print a warning message that the value obtained is not reliable, and procede to combine adjacent classes until the requirement is satisfied, or there are only two classes left. If the value so obtained is still not reliable, a further warning message will be provided.

Figure 6.16 illustrates the output of a chi-squared test.

REFERENCES : Siegel (Ch 6), Spiegel (Ch 12),

               Kendall and Stuart (Ch 33)

6.1.6 Statistical Tests - ORDINAL Level

A - KS2SA - Kolmogorov-Smirnov Two-sample Test

The Kolmogorov-Smirnov test can be used as either a test for difference in central tendency, or as a test of general difference. The test compares the relative cumulative frequency distributions of the two samples, and finds their maximum difference. If the test is for general difference, the maximum absolute difference is required, while if the test is whether one sample is from a population generally larger than the other, the maximum difference in the required direction is used. The basic assumptions underlying the two uses are different, so that apparently contradictory results may be obtained from time to time.

Unlike the chi-squared test, and its derivatives, the more classes the better the test works. It is neither necessary nor desirable to combine classes for this test.

Figure 6.17 illustrates the output of a Kolmogorov-Smirnov test.

REFERENCES : Siegel (Ch 6), Hollander and Wolfe (Ch 10)
               Kendall and Stuart (Ch 30)

B - MANWIT - Mann-Whitney "U" Test

The Mann-Whitney "U" test is a test for difference in central tendency. It operates, in essence, by counting, for each value in one sample, the number of data in the other sample that are in a lower class than it is. It forms the total of these scores, then calculates the probability of observing a total as great, or greater than that observed, if the values had been assigned at random to either sample.

This test is particularly useful because it can be applied to data on an INTERVAL scale where the user does not wish to make the assumption of normality required by normal parametric statistics (6.1.7) and is practically as sensitive.

Figure 6.17 also contains the output of a Mann-Whitney test.

REFERENCES : Siegel (Ch 6), Hollander and Wolfe (Ch 4)

6.1.7 Statistical Tests - INTERVAL Level

A - TFIND - Student's "t" Test

Student's "t" test is a test for difference in central tendency. It operates by assuming that the two samples have a common variance, and calculating the probability of observing a difference in sample means as great as or greater than that observed. In principle, the test assumes that the distribution of the data is normal (Gaussian), but it can be shown that this assumption is not critical, and that the test may be used where the data are not normally distributed.

Figure 6.18 (second paragraph) contains the output of a Student t test.

REFERENCES : Dixon and Massey (Ch 9), Kendall and Stuart (ch 31)

B - TFIND - The "t-like" Test

The "t-like" test is a test for difference in central tendency. It operates, like the "t" test, by estimating the probability of observing a difference of two sample means as great as or greater than that observed. It does not assume that the variance of the two samples is equal, so that it can produce different results from the "t" test applied to the same data. This test is more appropriate where the standard error is expected to be proportional to the mean, or where one sample is known to have a much greater variance than the other. It is called "t-like" because it uses an approximation to estimate degrees of freedom for the statistic derived, rather than using a value derived directly from the number of data. The number of degrees of freedom so derived is not necessarily an integer, and the theoretical justification is not entirely clear. However, for all but the smallest and most eccentric samples, the normal approximation holds.

Figure 6.18 (third paragraph) contains the output of a t-like test.

REFERENCES : Dixon and Massey (Ch 9), Kendall and Stuart (ch 31)

C - TFIND - Snedecor's "F" Test

Snedecor's "F" test is a test for the difference of dispersion of samples. It operates by calculating the ratio of the variances of two samples, and comparing this with the theoretical distribution of this ratio for samples of the same sizes drawn from normal populations. This test, like the "t" and "t-like" tests assumes that the underlying populations are normal (gaussian), but it is considered to be rather more sensitive to departures from that assumption.

Figure 6.19 (first paragraph) contains the output of a Snedecor's "F" test.

REFERENCES : Dixon and Massey (Ch 8), Kendall and Stuart (ch 31)

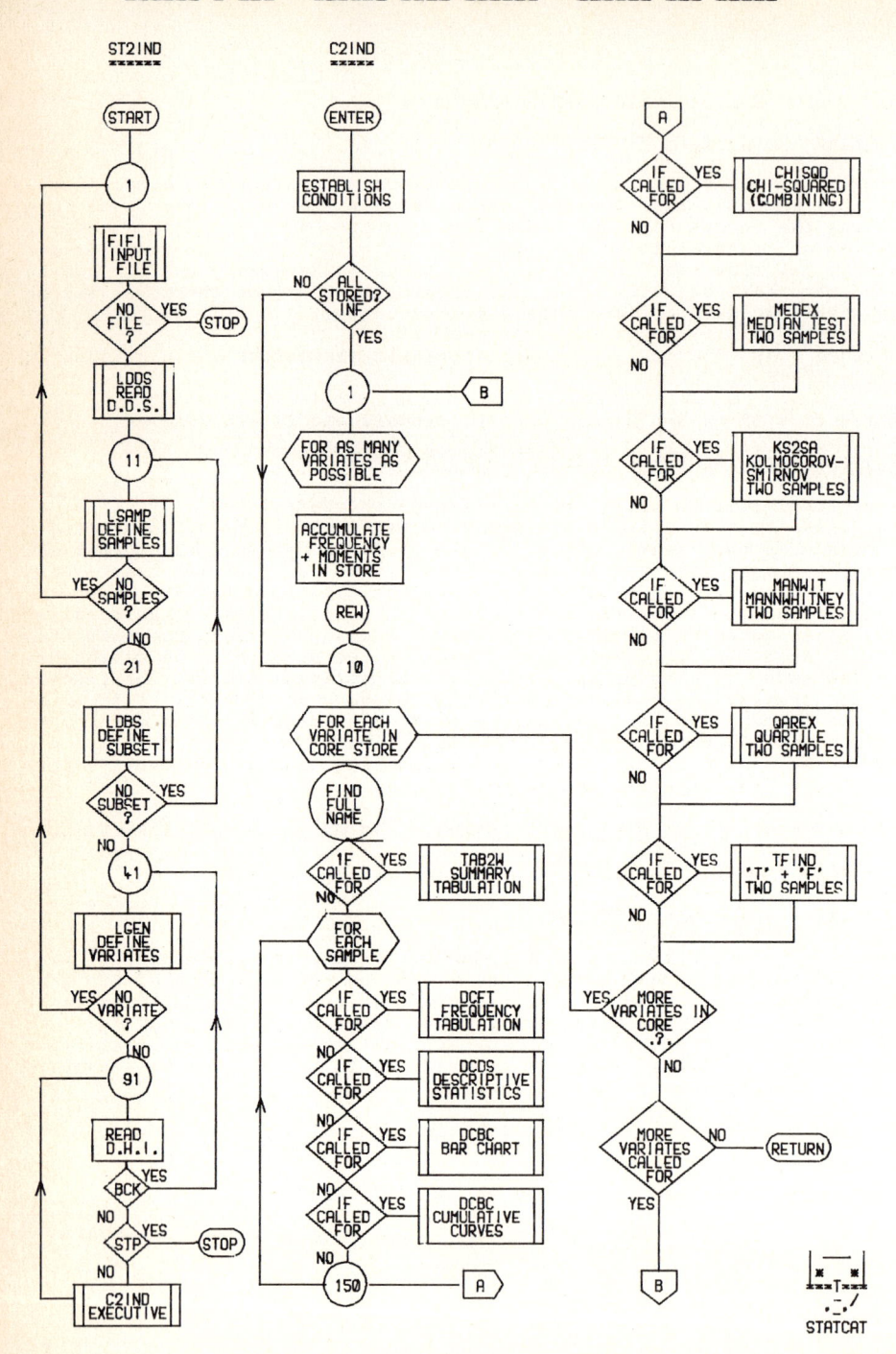

Figure 6.11a - System Flow-charts - ST2IND and C2IND

233

Figure 6.11b - System Flow-charts - CHISQD and KS2S

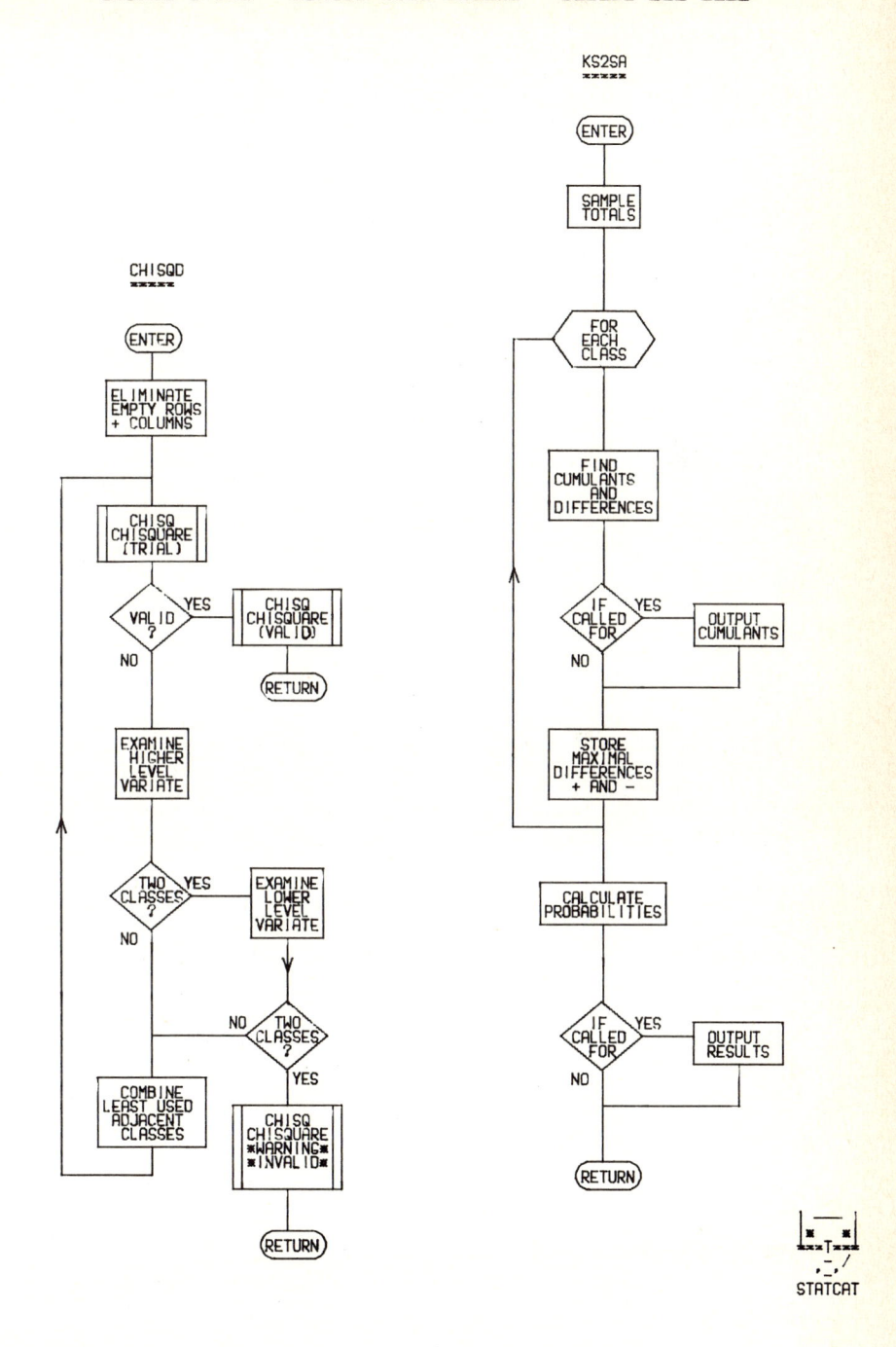

Figure 6.11c - System Flow-charts - MANWIT and TFIND

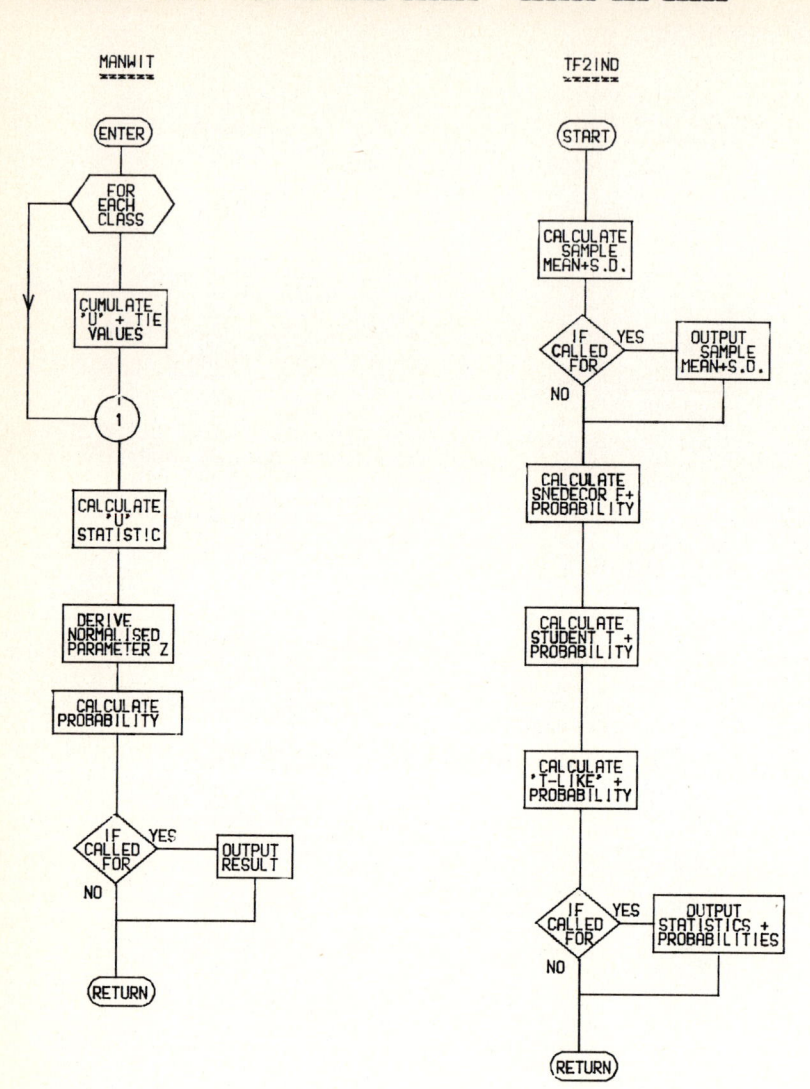

MANWIT

ENTER → FOR EACH CLASS → CUMULATE 'U' + TIE VALUES → (1) → CALCULATE 'U' STATISTIC → DERIVE NORMALISED PARAMETER Z → CALCULATE PROBABILITY → IF CALLED FOR — YES → OUTPUT RESULT ; NO → RETURN

TF2IND

START → CALCULATE SAMPLE MEAN+S.D. → IF CALLED FOR — YES → OUTPUT SAMPLE MEAN+S.D. ; NO → CALCULATE SNEDECOR F + PROBABILITY → CALCULATE STUDENT T + PROBABILITY → CALCULATE 'T-LIKE' + PROBABILITY → IF CALLED FOR — YES → OUTPUT STATISTICS + PROBABILITIES ; NO → RETURN

STATCAT

Figure 6.12 - ST2IND - Input Structure

```
         Level
 0    1    2    3    4    5    6    7    8    9
FILE CONTROL CARD
     SAMPLE SPECIFICATION
          SUBSET SPECIFICATION
               VARIATE SPECIFICATION
                    DATA HANDLING INSTRUCTION
                    DATA HANDLING INSTRUCTION
                    STOP
```

Figure 6.13 - ST2IND - Input Example

```
---------1----------2----------3----------4----------5----------6----------7--
**ST2INDDEMO
MORNING/AFTERNOON
A.M.
.IF.TIME.EQ.AM1
.OR.TIME.EQ.AM2
END OF SAMPLE ONE
P.M.
.IF.TIME.EQ.PM1
.OR.TIME.EQ.PM2
END OF SAMPLE TWO
END OF SAMPLE SET SPECIFICATION
ALL DATA                                 ALL DATA ARE INCLUDED
END OF SUBSET SPECIFICATION
VAL.STRS         4      1.5      1.0    3.5 NOMINAL LEVEL VARIATE
VAL.DIFF         7      1.5      1.0    6.5 ORDINAL LEVEL VARIATE
VAL.TEMP                                    INTERVAL LEVEL VARIATE
VAL.H.R.                                    RATIO    LEVEL VARIATE
END OF VARIATE SPECIFICATION
GO                                       SIG RESULTS ONLY (P LE 1 PCT) AT
88                                       MAXIMUM OUTPUT - FULL TESTS + DE
STOP
---------1----------2----------3----------4----------5----------6----------7--
```

Figure 6.14 - ST2IND - Output Structure

```
For each     ) : File Control Record
output file  )   File Parameters
                 Data Description
                 For each) :  Sample Input Record
                 Sample  )    For each) Subset Input Record
                 Specifn )    Subset  ) For each)Input Record
                                         Set of  )For each)   See
                                         Variates Variate )   Left
For each) <Cross-tabulation>
Variate )  For Each)<FrequencyTable>
           Sample  )<Descriptive Statistics>
                    <Frequency Curves/Bar Chart>

           NOMINAL   <Chi-squared>
           ORDINAL   <Median Test>
                     <Quartile Test>
                     <Kolmogorov-Smirnov 2 sample Test>
                     <Mann-Whitney  2 sample Test>
           INTERVAL) <Student's "t" or "t-like" test>
           /RATIO  ) <Snedecor's "F" test>
```

Carated(<>) items are optional.

Figure 6.15 - ST2IND - Output Example Page-by-Page listing

Page	Contents	Origin
1- 3	File Control Record	FIFI
	Program Title	ST2IND
	File Parameters	LDAP
	Data Description record	LDDS
4	Sample record	LSAMP/LSET
5	Subset record	LDBS/LSET
6	Set of Variates record	LGEN
	Data Handling Instruction	LDHI
7	Kolmogorov-Smirnov 2 Sample test (Difficulty)	KS2SA
8	T and F tests (Temperature)	TFIND
9	Data Handling Instruction (Detailed output)	LDHI
10-13	Sample Descriptions (Stress)	DCFT/DCDS/DCPS/DCBC
14	Chi-squared test (Stress)	CHISQD
15	Median Test (Stress)	MEDEX
16	Kolmogorov-Smirnov 2 Sample test (Stress)	KS2SA
17	Mann-Whitney 2 sample test (Stress)	MANWIT
18	Quartile Test (Stress)	QAREX
19	T and F tests (Stress)	TFIND
26-35	Sample Descriptions/ Test Reports (Difficulty)	As above
36-45	Sample Descriptions/ Test Reports (Temperature)	As above
46-55	Sample Descriptions/ Test Reports (Heart Rate)	As above
56	Data Handling Instruction (STOP)	LDHI

Figure 6.16 - ST2IND - Chi-squared 2 Sample test - Stress

```
DATA BANK TITLE              -   DEMONSTRATION STATCAT DATA BANK
SAMPLE SET TITLE             -   MORNING/AFTERNOON
DATA BANK SUBSET TITLE       -   ALL DATA
VAL. OF DATA COLUMN NUMBER   6   SHORT TITLE    STRS
FULL TITLE                   -          STRESS FACTOR - OBSERVED                    DATA SCALE -NOMINAL

CHI-SQUARED - WITHOUT COMBINING CELLS    COMBINATION NOT REQUIRED

ROW  1
OBSERVED          6.0000        4.0000
EXPECTED          5.0000        5.0000
CHI-SQUARE        0.2000        0.2000

ROW  2
OBSERVED         10.0000       13.0000
EXPECTED         11.5000       11.5000
CHI-SQUARE        0.1957        0.1957

ROW  3
OBSERVED          7.0000        7.0000
EXPECTED          7.0000        7.0000
CHI-SQUARE        0.0           0.0

ROW  4
OBSERVED          9.0000        8.0000
EXPECTED          8.5000        8.5000
CHI-SQUARE        0.0294        0.0294

     CHI-SQUARED IS       0.85 WITH      3 DEGREES OF FREEDOM PROBABILITY OF 0.83903873

NUMBER OF CELLS LESS THAN ONE    0
NUMBER OF CELLS LESS THAN FIVE   0
```

Figure 6.17 - ST2IND - Kolmogorov-Smirnov + Mann-Whitney tests

```
DATA BANK TITLE              -   DEMONSTRATION STATCAT DATA BANK
SAMPLE SET TITLE             -   MORNING/AFTERNOON
DATA BANK SUBSET TITLE       -   ALL DATA
VAL. OF DATA COLUMN NUMBER  10   SHORT TITLE    DIFF
FULL TITLE                   -          ASSESSMENT OF DIFFICULTY BY OPERATOR         DATA SCALE -ORDINAL

KOLMOGOROV-SMIRNOV TWO-SAMPLE TEST

              RELATIVE CUMULATIVE FREQUENCY

  CLASS INTERVAL    SAMPLE A.M.    SAMPLE P.M.    DIFFERENCE

        1             0.094          0.094          0.0
        2             0.375          0.219          0.156
        3             0.469          0.438          0.031
        4             0.656          0.688         -0.031
        5             0.813          0.844         -0.031
        6             0.938          0.969         -0.063 (?)... 0.997
        7             1.000          1.000          0.0

KOLMOGOROV-SMIRNOV TWO-SAMPLE TEST

PROBABILITY THAT A.M. IS NOT GREATER THAN P.M. =    0.882442   D =   -0.0625
PROBABILITY THAT A.M. IS NOT LESS THAN P.M.    =    0.538121   D =    0.1563
PROBABILITY THAT A.M. IS NOT THE SAME AS P.M.  =    0.0        D =    0.1563

(PROBABILITIES ARE INDEPENDENTLY DERIVED)
LARGE SAMPLE APPROXIMATION DOES NOT HOLD.

SAMPLE A.M. CONTAINS       32. READINGS AND SAMPLE P.M. CONTAINS     32. READINGS
FOR MORE EXACT PROBABILITY CONSULT SIEGEL TABLE L P 278


DATA BANK TITLE              -   DEMONSTRATION STATCAT DATA BANK
SAMPLE SET TITLE             -   MORNING/AFTERNOON
DATA BANK SUBSET TITLE       -   ALL DATA
VAL. OF DATA COLUMN NUMBER  10   SHORT TITLE    DIFF
FULL TITLE                   -          ASSESSMENT OF DIFFICULTY BY OPERATOR         DATA SCALE -ORDINAL

MANN-WHITNEY TWO-SAMPLE TEST      T

PROBABILITY THAT A.M. IS NOT GREATER THAN P.M. =    0.355867   U =    531.0000
PROBABILITY THAT A.M. IS NOT LESS THAN P.M.    =    0.604133   U =    493.0000
PROBABILITY THAT A.M. IS NOT THE SAME AS P.M.  =    0.791734


SAMPLE A.M. CONTAINS       32. READINGS AND SAMPLE P.M. CONTAINS     32. READINGS
```

Figure 6.18 - ST2IND - Student "t" and Snedecor "F" tests

```
DATA BANK TITLE            -      DEMONSTRATION STATCAT DATA BANK
SAMPLE SET TITLE           -      MORNING/AFTERNOON
DATA BANK SUBSET TITLE     -      ALL DATA
VAL. OF DATA COLUMN NUMBER  15 SHORT TITLE    H.R.
FULL TITLE                 -      MEAN HEART RATE DURING TEST  (BEATS/MINUTE)             DATA SCALE -RATIO

TESTS OF TWO UNRELATED SAMPLES

FOR EQUALITY OF VARIANCE

SNEDECOR F TEST =        1.100255 WITH        31. OVER         31. DEGREES OF FREEDOM

PROBABILITY THAT S.D. OF POPULATION A.M. IS GREATER THAN S.D. OF POPULATION P.M. =   0.604106
PROBABILITY THAT S.D. OF POPULATION A.M. IS LESS THAN    S.D. OF POPULATION P.M. =   0.395894
PROBABILITY THAT S.D. OF POPULATION A.M. IS EQUAL TO     S.D. OF POPULATION P.M. =   0.791787

    SAMPLE   NO OF READINGS   ARITHMETIC MEAN   STANDARD DEVIATION

    A.M.         32.              47.4258            7.6269

    P.M.         32.              47.6402            7.2711

ASSUMING VARIANCES DO NOT DIFFER

FOR EQUALITY OF MEANS

STUDENT T TEST =       -0.115089 WITH        62. DEGREES OF FREEDOM

PROBABILITY THAT MEAN OF POPULATION A.M. IS GREATER THAN MEAN OF POPULATION P.M. =   0.452372
PROBABILITY THAT MEAN OF POPULATION A.M. IS LESS THAN    MEAN OF POPULATION P.M. =   0.547628
PROBABILITY THAT MEAN OF POPULATION A.M. IS EQUAL TO     MEAN OF POPULATION P.M. =   0.904745

ASSUMING VARIANCES DIFFER

FOR EQUALITY OF MEANS

T-LIKE STATISTIC =     -0.115089 WITH        62. DEGREES OF FREEDOM

PROBABILITY THAT MEAN OF POPULATION A.M. IS GREATER THAN MEAN OF POPULATION P.M. =   0.452373
PROBABILITY THAT MEAN OF POPULATION A.M. IS LESS THAN    MEAN OF POPULATION P.M. =   0.547627
PROBABILITY THAT MEAN OF POPULATION A.M. IS EQUAL TO     MEAN OF POPULATION P.M. =   0.904745
```

```
C MASTER ST2IND - THIS PROGRAM TESTS EXACTLY TWO INDEP. SAMPLES OF DATA
C   SUBROUTINES AND FUNCTIONS REQUIRED
C   NAME            TYPE                 COMMENT
C   AN       (SEE  3.1 ) SERVICE     ALPHA - TO NUMERIC VALUE
C   CH       (SEE 11.6 ) SERVICE     CHOOSES TEST/DESCRIPTION REQUIRED
C   CHIKEN   (SEE 11.9 ) SERVICE     WARNS OF MISMATCHED DATA LEVEL
C   CHISQ    (SEE 11.5 ) STATISTICAL BASIC CHI-SQUARED CALCULATION
C   CHISQD   (SEE  6.1 ) STATISTICAL SELF-STABILISED CHI-SQUARED
C   C2IND    (SEE  6.1 ) EXECUTIVE   TESTS TWO INDEPENDENT SAMPLES
C   CLASIF   (SEE 11.7 ) SERVICE     CLASSIFIES DATA ITEM
C   CLSAM    (SEE  3.5 ) SERVICE     ALLOTS ENTRY TO SAMPLE/SUBSET
C   COMPA    (SEE  3.1 ) SERVICE     COMPARES ALPHAMERIC VALUES
C   COPYA    (SEE  3.1 ) SERVICE     COPIES ALPHAMERIC VALUE
C   DCBC     (SEE  5.2 ) STATISTICAL CONSTRUCTS BAR-CHARTS
C   DCDS     (SEE  5.2 ) STATISTICAL DESCRIPTIVE STATISTICS
C   DCFT     (SEE  5.2 ) STATISTICAL FREQUENCY TABULATION
C   DCPS     (SEE  5.2 ) STATISTICAL MOMENT(PARAMETRIC) STATISTICS
C   DICOLA   (SEE 11.5 ) STATISTICAL DESCRIBES ROW/COLUMN COMBINATION
C   FIFI     (SEE  3.2 ) SYSTEM      ALLOCATES PERIPHERALS
C   GAUS     (SEE 11.8 ) STATISTICAL FINDS ASS. PROB. OF N VALUE
C   IBL      (SEE  3.1 ) SERVICE     DETECTS BLANK,END AND STOP CARDS
C   ICH      (SEE  3.1 ) SERVICE     IDENTIFIES ALPHAMERIC CODES
C   KS2SA    (SEE  6.1 ) STATISTICAL KOLMOGOROV-SMIRNOV TWO-SAMPLE TEST
C   LDAP     (SEE  3.3 ) SYSTEM      LOADS/CHECKS DATA BANK PARAMETERS
C   LDBS     (SEE  3.6 ) SYSTEM      LOADS SUBSET DEFINITION
C   LDDS     (SEE  3.4 ) SYSTEM      LOADS DATA DESCRIPTION SEGMENT
C   LDHI     (SEE  3.8 ) SYSTEM      LOADS/CHECKS DATA HANDLING INSTN
C   LGEN     (SEE  3.7 ) SYSTEM      LOADS GENERALISED VARIATES
C   LSAMP    (SEE  3.5 ) SYSTEM      LOADS SAMPLE SET DEFINITION
C   LSET     (SEE  3.5 ) SYSTEM      LOADS DEFINING CONDITIONS
C   MANWIT   (SEE  6.1 ) STATISTICAL MANN-WHITNEY TEST (TWO SAMPLES)
C   MEDEX    (SEE  6.1 ) STATISTICAL MEDIAN TEST (EXTENDED)
C   MEDIAT   (SEE  3.7 ) SERVICE     FETCHES NEXT VARIATE SET
C   PRBF     (SEE 11.8 ) STATISTICAL FINDS PROBABILITY OF F-RATIO
C   PRTCLS   (SEE 11.7 ) SERVICE     PRINTS CLASS NAME/LIMITS
C   QAREX    (SEE  6.1 ) STATISTICAL QUARTILE TEST (EXTENDED)
C   REDROW   (SEE 11.5 ) STATISTICAL CHOOSES ROW/COLUMN FOR COMBINATION
C   TAB2W    (SEE  6.4 ) STATISTICAL TABULATES WITH VARIATE NAMES ETC
C   TFIND    (SEE  6.1 ) STATISTICAL T AND F TESTS - INDEPENDENT SAMPLES
C   TRANS    (SEE  3.7 ) SERVICE     CARRIES OUT REQUIRED TRANSFORM
C IF NQMAX= MAXIMUM NO OF DATA COLS IS INCREASED INCREASE CN DATA
C DIMENSION D(NQMAX),DMAX(NQMAX),DMIN(NQMAX),IT(NQMAX),ST(NQMAX)
C DIMENSION CN(NQMAX)
      NQMAX = 100
      DIMENSION D(100),DMAX(100),DMIN(100),IT(100),ST(100),CN(100)
      DATA CN/4HCOL1,4HCOL2,4HCOL3,4HCOL4,4HCOL5,4HCOL6,4HCOL7,4HCOL8,4
     1HCOL9,4HCL10,4HCL11,4HCL12,4HCL13,4HCL14,4HCL15,4HCL16,4HCL17,4HC
     218,4HCL19,4HCL20,4HCL21,4HCL22,4HCL23,4HCL24,4HCL25,4HCL26,4HCL27,
     34HCL28,4HCL29,4HCL30,4HCL31,4HCL32,4HCL33,4HCL34,4HCL35,4HCL36,4HC
     4L37,4HCL38,4HCL39,4HCL40,4HCL41,4HCL42,4HCL43,4HCL44,4HCL45,4HCL46
     5,4HCL47,4HCL48,4HCL49,4HCL50,4HCL51,4HCL52,4HCL53,4HCL54,4HCL55,4H
     6CL56,4HCL57,4HCL58,4HCL59,4HCL60,4HCL61,4HCL62,4HCL63,4HCL64,4HCL6
     75,4HCL66,4HCL67,4HCL68,4HCL69,4HCL70,4HCL71,4HCL72,4HCL73,4HCL74,4
     8HCL75,4HCL76,4HCL77,4HCL78,4HCL79,4HCL80,4HCL81,4HCL82,4HCL83,4HCL
     984,4HCL85,4HCL86,4HCL87,4HCL88,4HCL89,4HCL90,4HCL91,4HCL92,4HCL93,
     94HCL94,4HCL95,4HCL96,4HCL97,4HCL98,4HCL99,4HCL100/
C DIMENSION TRT(NALTMX)= MAXIMUM NUMBER OF CLASSES IN DATA BANK
      NALTMX = 50
      DIMENSION TRT(50)
C DIMENSION RX(NRMAX),KR(NRMAX),TRTR(NRMAX)=MAXIMUM NO OF CLASSES USED
      NRMAX = 52
      DIMENSION RX(52),KR(52),TRTR(52)
C MAXST = FREE STORAGE FOR TABLES AND MOMENTS MUST BE AT LEAST
```

```
C     2*(NCL(J) + 7) WHERE NCL(J) IS LARGEST NO OF CLASSES USED
C     DIMENSION RT(MAXST)
      MAXST=2000
      DIMENSION RT(2000)
C     MAXM = MAXIMUM NUMBER OF VARIATES ACCEPTED FOR ANY DATA SWEEP
C     DIMENSION NCL(MAXM),NP(MAXM),T(MAXM),TMIN(MAXM),TMAX(MAXM)
      MAXM=20
      DIMENSION NCL(20),NP(20),T(20),TMIN(20),TMAX(20)
C     DIMENSION SCON(5,MAXDBC)= MAXIMUM NUMBER OF COND (SUBSET+SAMPLE)
      MAXDBC = 50
      DIMENSION SCON(5,50)
C     THE FOLLOWING DIMENSIONS STORE NAMES OF DATA TRANSFORMS, ACCEPTABLE
C     LEVELS FOR TRANSFORMATIONS,FIXED SIZE AND DUMMY ARRAYS
      DIMENSION U(60),LU(60),H(1),IH(1),FORM(50),CX(2),KC(2),TRTC(2)
      NU = 60
C     TRANSFORMATION CODES
C     UNITS                         BLOCKS
C           0 - 9   10 - 19  20 - 29   30 - 39   40 - 49   50 - 59
C           POWERS  TRIG     TRIG      STATIST   MATHS     TEST
C                   RADIANS  DEGREES   TRANSF    FUNCTS    FUNCTIONS
C     0     -       -        H.MS      -         -         RM10
C     1     VAL.    SINR     SIND      PSNA      RECP      +/-1
C     2     SQAR    COSR     COSD      PSNB      SQRT      ADD1
C     3     CUBE    TANR     TAND      BINO      ABSV      SUB1
C     4     4PWR    ASIR     ASID      LG+1      SIGN      NOE1
C     5     5PWR    ACOR     ACOD      LOGE      INTG      +/-P
C     6     6PWR    ATAR     ATAD      LG10      FRAC      ADDP
C     7     7PWR    SINH     DTOR      AL10      EXPT      SUBP
C     8     8PWR    COSH     RTOD      -         PRES      NORP
C     9     9PWR    TANH     H.HH      -         NEG.      +100
      DATA U/4HVAL.,4HSQAR,4HCUBE,4H4PWR,4H5PWR,4H6PWR,4H7PWR,4H8PWR,4H9
     1PWR,4HVAL ,4HSINR,4HCOSR,4HTANR,4HASIR,4HACOR,4HATAR,4HSINH,4HCOSH
     2,4HTANH,4HH.MS,4HSIND,4HCOSD,4HTAND,4HASID,4HACOD,4HATAD,4HDTOR,4H
     3RTOD,4HH.HH,4H VAL,4HPSNA,4HPSNB,4HBINO,4HLG+1,4HLOGE,4HLG10,4HAL1
     40,4H   ,4H   ,4HRECP,4HSQRT,4HABSV,4HSIGN,4HINTG,4HFRAC,4
     5HEXPT,4HPRES,4HNEG.,4HRM10,4H+/-1,4HADD1,4HSUB1,4HNOR1,4H+/-P,4HAD
     6DP,4HSUBP,4HNORP,4H+100,4H    /
      DATA LU/1,8*5,1,9*5,1,9*5,1,6*5,4*1,2*5,2*3,3*5,7*2,4*5,2*2/
      COMMON /STCT/MED1,MED2,MED3,MED4,MED5,MED6,MED13,Q,V(20),TT(30)
      DATA PROG/4H2IND/
      MED1 = -1
C     LEVEL 0 - SETTING UP
    1 CALL COPYA(TT(1),PROG)
      CALL FIFI
      IF(MED2.GT.0) WRITE(MED2,901)
      CALL LDAP(MED2,MED3,V,TT,Q,NQ,NALT,NQMAX,NALTMX,IGO)
      IF(IGO.GT.0) GO TO 1
      LI = 18
      CALL LDDS(TRT,NALT,D,NQ,ST,NQ,IT,MQ,H,0,DMIN,DMAX,NQ,LI,1,Q,VX,
     1 0,MED2,MED3,0,IGO)
C     LEVEL 1 - READ SAMPLE SPECIFICATION
   11 IF(V(10).GE.10.) V(10) = 0.
      CALL LSAMP(SCON,NCON,MAXDBC,TRTC,NS,2,CN,ST,IT,NQ,TRT,NALT,IGO
     1)
      IF(NS.NE.2) WRITE(MED2,924)
      IF(NS.NE.2.AND.V(10).EQ.0.)V(10) = 18.
      IF(IGO.GT.0) GO TO 1
      MAXLEF = MAXDBC-NCON
      NCON1 = NCON+1
C     NRAV - LINES AVAILABLE/LIMC-MAXIMUM FOR ONE VARIATE
      NRAV = MAXST/NS
      LIMC = NRAV - 7
      IF(LIMC.GT.NRMAX ) LIMC = NRMAX
```

```
C LEVEL 2 - READ SUBSET SPECIFICATION
   21 IF(V(10).GE.20.) V(10) = 0.
      CALL LDBS(SCON(1,NCON1),NCONB,MAXLEF,CN,ST,IT,NQ,TRT,NALT,IGO)
      IF(IGO.GT.0) GO TO 11
      ARAN = 5236.
C LEVEL 3 - READ SET OF VARIATES FOR DATA SWEEP
   31 IF(V(10).GE.30.) V(10) = 0.
      IFIN = MAXM
      M = 0
      WRITE(MED6,931)
      WRITE(MED6,935)
      CALL LGEN(U,NU,LU,NU,ST,IT,CN,NQ,NCL,MAXM,DMIN,DMAX,NQ,TMIN,TMAX,M
     1AXM,0,LIMC,IH,NP,MAXM,M,MAXM,1,NALT)
      IF(V(11).LT.0.5.AND.V(20).LT.0.5) GO TO 21
      IF(V(11).LT.0.5.AND.V(20).GT.0.5.AND.V(10).LT.0.5) V(10)= 32.
      V(19) = 0.
      BRAN = ARAN
C LEVEL 9 - READ DATA HANDLING INSTRUCTION
   91 IF(V(10).GT.90.) V(10) = 0.
      CALL LDHI(V(1),1,V(2),4,V(3),16,H,0,H,0,H,0,H,V(10),
     1 FORM(41),FORM,MED1,MED2,0,Q,NQ,NWARN,1,IGO)
      IF(IGO.GT.0) GO TO 31
C STANDARDISATION
      IF(V(3).LE.0.) NWARN = NWARN + 1
      IF(V(3).EQ.0.) V(3) = 1.
      IF(V(3).LT.0.) V(3) = 0.
      CALL LDHI(V(1),1,V(2),4,V(3),16,H,0,H,0,H,0,H,V(10),
     1 FORM(41),FORM,MED1,MED2,0,Q,NQ,NWARN,2,IGO)
      IF(IGO.GT.0) GO TO 91
      V(19) = V(19) + 1.
      V(10) = BRAN
      V(3) = V(3)*0.01
      CALL C2IND(D,IT,NQ,TRT,NALT,T,TMIN,TMAX,NP,M,TRTC,CX,KC,TRTR,RX
     1,KR,NRMAX,RT,NRAV,SCON(1,NCON1),NCONB,SCON,NCON,NCL,U,NU)
      ARAN = V(10)
      V(10) = 0.
      WRITE(MED6,999)
      GO TO 91
  901 FORMAT (1H0,20X,40HSTATCAT TESTS OF TWO INDEPENDENT SAMPLES/)
  924 FORMAT (1H0,9X,41HTHIS PROGRAM REQUIRES EXACTLY TWO SAMPLES,59X,
     111H**WARNING**/10X,57H USE STDESC FOR ONE, OR STKIND FOR THREE OR
     2MORE SAMPLES.//)
  931 FORMAT (1H1,10X,30HSET OF VARIATES FOR DATA SWEEP/)
  935 FORMAT (4H0NO.,9X,30HTRANS  DATA            NUMBER OF,7X,5HLOWER,6X,
     15HCLASS,7X,5HUPPER/5H CODE,8X,68H-FORM COLUMN            CLASSES USED
     2 CLASS LIMIT   INTERVAL   CLASS LIMIT )
  999 FORMAT (36H1ANALYSIS COMPLETED - READ NEW INPUT)
      END


      SUBROUTINE C2IND(X,IT,NQ,TRT,NALT,D,DMIN,DMAX,NP,M,TRTC,CX,KC,TRTR
     1,RX,KR,NRMAX,RT,NRAV,SCON,NCON,SACON,NACON,NCL,U,NU)
C TESTS EXACTLY TWO INDEPENDENT SAMPLES
      DIMENSION X(NQ),IT(NQ),TRT(NALT),D(M),DMIN(M),DMAX(M),NP(M),NCL(M)
      DIMENSION TRTR(NRMAX),RX(NRMAX),KR(NRMAX),TRTC(2),CX(2),KC(2)
      DIMENSION RT(2,NRAV),SCON(5,NCON),SACON(5,NACON),TTR(19),U(NU)
      COMMON /STCT/MED1,MED2,MED3,MED4,MED5,MED6,MED13,Q,V(20),TT(30)
      DATA B4/4H   /
C STARTING CONDITIONS
      V1 = V(1)
      V2 = V(2)
      V10 = V(10)
      V19 = V(19)
```

```
      LB = V1
      LC = V2
      LDB = LC-LC/5*5
      LD = LDB + 1
      JFIN = 0
C ESTABLISH CAPACITY FOR PARAMETRIC AND NON PARAMETRIC DATA
    1 JST = JFIN + 1
      NR = NRAV
    2 JFIN = JFIN + 1
      NR = NR - NCL(JFIN) - 7
    3 IF(NR) 5,4,4
    4 IF(JFIN-M)2,6,6
    5 JFIN = JFIN - 1
    6 KAP = JFIN-JST + 1
C CLEAR STORAGE ARRAY
      IF(V19.GT.1.5) GO TO 10
      V(10) = V10
      REWIND MED3
      J = 0
      DO 9 ICX = JST,JFIN
      N = NCL(ICX) + 5
      DO 7 J2 = 1,N
      J = J+1
      DO 7 I = 1,2
    7 RT(I,J) = 0.
      DO 9 J2=1,2
      J = J+ 1
      DO 9 I =1,2
    9 RT(I,J) = Q
      V(6) = 0.
      V(7) = 1.
      V(8) = 1.
      V(9) = M
      READ(MED3)NX,NX,Y,(TT(I),I=1,10),(Y,I=1,6)
      DO 13 I = 1,NQ
   13 READ(MED3)TTR,TRT,NX,Y,Y
C READ DATA FOR TESTS
    8 CALL MEDIAT(M,NP,NP,M,D,X,NQ,SCON,NCON)
      IF(V(8).EQ.2.) GO TO 10
      CALL CLSAM(X,NQ,SACON,NACON,I,2)
      IF(I.LE.0.OR.I.GT.2) GO TO 8
      JBASE = 0
      JTR = JST
      DO 24 J = 1,KAP
      XR = D(JTR)
      IF(XR.EQ.Q) GO TO 23
      INDX = NP(JTR)-NP(JTR)/1000*1000
      IF(LDB.EQ.0) LD = IT(INDX)
      CALL CLASIF   (XR,DMAX(JTR),DMIN(JTR),IT(INDX),NCL(JTR),JR)
      JR = JBASE + JR
      RT(I,JR) = RT(I,JR) + 1.
      JR = JBASE + NCL(JTR)
      RT(I,JR+1) = RT(I,JR+1) + 1.
      RT(I,JR+2) = RT(I,JR+2) + XR
      RT(I,JR+3) = RT(I,JR+3) +XR*XR
      RT(I,JR+4) = RT(I,JR+4) +XR*XR*XR
      RT(I,JR+5) = RT(I,JR+5) + XR*XR*XR*XR
      IF(RT(I,JR+6).EQ.Q.OR.RT(I,JR+6).GT.XR)RT(I,JR+6) = XR
      IF(RT(I,JR+7).EQ.Q.OR.RT(I,JR+7).LT.XR)RT(I,JR+7) = XR
   23 JBASE = JBASE + NCL(JTR) + 7
   24 JTR = JTR + 1
      GO TO 8
   10 REWIND MED3
```

```
C OUTPUT PHASE
      INOW = NQ + 1
      JBASE = 1
      DO 400 IC = 1,KAP
      V(10) = 0.
      ICX = JST+IC-1
      NC = NP(ICX) - NP(ICX)/1000*1000
      NTR= NP(ICX)/1000
      IF(LDB.EQ.0) LD = IT(NC)
      IF(LDB.NE.0) LD = LDB+ 1
      V(7) = IT(NC)
      V(2) = V2
      IF(INOW.LE.NC) GO TO 11
      REWIND MED3
      INOW = 0
      READ(MED3)NX,NX,(Y,I=1,17)
   11 IF(INOW.EQ.NC) GO TO 12
      INOW = INOW + 1
      READ(MED3)TTR,TRT,NX,Y,Y
      GO TO 11
   12 NALTR = NCL(ICX)
      DO 14 J = 1,NALTR
      IF(J.LE.NALT) CALL COPYA(TRTR(J),TRT(J))
   14 IF(J.GT.NALT) CALL COPYA(TRTR(J),B4)
      JR = JBASE + NALTR
      IF(ISW(LB,LC,LD,8).LE.0) GO TO 101
C SUMMARY TABULATION
      WRITE(MED2,999)TT,U(NTR),NC,TTR
      V(8) = 6.
      CALL TAB2W(RT(1,JBASE),2,NALTR,TRTC,TRTC,TRTR,2,IT(NC),0.,DMIN(ICX
     1 ),0.,DMAX(ICX),V,MED2)
      GO TO 200
  101 MIS = 0
      DO 150 I = 1,2
      V(8) = 60.
      NLIN = 0
      DO 102 J = 1,NALTR
      JQ = J+JBASE - 1
      IF(RT(I,JQ).GT.0.)NLIN = J
  102 RX(J) = RT(I,JQ)
      VX = NLIN
      IF(RT(I,JR).EQ.0.) MIS = MIS + 1
      IF(RT(I,JR).GT.0.) GO TO 110
      WRITE(MED2,999)TT,U(NTR),NC,TTR,B4,I,TRTC(I)
      WRITE(MED2,997)
      GO TO 150
  110 IF(ISW(LB,LC,LD,6).LT.0) GO TO 120
      IF(V(8).GE.(44.-VX)) WRITE(MED2,999)TT,U(NTR),NC,TTR,B4,I,TRTC(I)
      IF(V(8).GE.(44.-VX)) V(8) = 8.
C FREQUENCY TABULATION
      CALL DCFT (RT(I,JR),DMAX(ICX),DMIN(ICX),RX,TRTR,NALTR,V,MED2)
  120 IF(ISW(LB,LC,LD,7).LT.0)GO TO 130
      IF(V(8).GT.20.) WRITE(MED2,999)TT,U(NTR),NC,TTR,B4,I,TRTC(I)
      IF(V(8).GT.20.) V(8) = 8.
C DESCRIPTIVE STATISTICS
      CALL DCDS(DMAX(ICX),DMIN(ICX),RX,TRTR,NALTR,RT(I,JR),RT(I,JR+1),RT
     1(I,JR+2),RT(I,JR+3),RT(I,JR+4),RT(I,JR+5),RT(I,JR+6),V,MED2)
  130 IF(ISW(LB,LC,LD,6).LT.0) GO TO 150
      IF(V(8).GE.(56.-VX)) WRITE(MED2,999)TT,U(NTR),NC,TTR,B4,I,TRTC(I)
      IF(V(8).GE.(56.-VX)) V(8) = 8.
      V(1) = 3.
      V(2) = 1.
C BAR CHART
```

```
              CALL DCBC(DMAX(ICX),DMIN(ICX),RX,TRTR,NALTR,V,MED2)
    140 IF(LD.LE.3) GO TO 145
              IF(V(8).GE.(56.-VX)) WRITE(MED2,999)TT,U(NTR),NC,TTR,B4,I,TRTC(I)
              IF(V(8).GE.(56.-VX)) V(8) = 8.
C CUMULATIVE FREQUENCY CURVES
              V(2) = 6.
              V(1) = 3.
              CALL DCBC   (DMAX(ICX),DMIN(ICX),RX,TRTR,NALTR,V,MED2)
    145 V(1) = V1
              V(2) = V2
    150 CONTINUE
    200 IF(MIS.GE.1.OR.V(3).LE.0.) GO TO 390
    320 IF(ISW(LB,LC,LD,2)) 330,321,322
C NOMINAL DATA LEVEL TESTS
    321 V(1) = -1.
              CALL CHISQD(RT(1,JBASE),2,NALTR,CX,RX,KC,KR,2,NX,TRTC,TRTR,0.,
             1DMIN(ICX),0.,DMAX(ICX),V,MED2)
              IF(V(11).GT.V(3)) GO TO 330
    322 WRITE(MED2,999)TT,U(NTR),NC,TTR
              V(1) = 3.
              CALL CHIKEN(2,NX)
              CALL CHISQD(RT(1,JBASE),2,NALTR,CX,RX,KC,KR,2,NX,TRTC,TRTR,0.,
             1DMIN(ICX),0.,DMAX(ICX),V,MED2)
    330 IF(ISW(LB,LC,LD,3)) 349,331,332
C ORDINAL DATA LEVEL TESTS
    331 V(1) = -1.
              CALL MEDEX (RT(1,JBASE),2,NALTR,CX,RX,KC,KR,2,NX,TRTC,TRTR,0.,
             1DMIN(ICX),0.,DMAX(ICX),V,MED2)
              IF(V(11).GT.V(3)) GO TO 333
    332 WRITE(MED2,999)TT,U(NTR),NC,TTR
              V(1) = 3.
              CALL CHIKEN(3,NX)
              CALL MEDEX  (RT(1,JBASE),2,NALTR,CX,RX,KC,KR,2,NX,TRTC,TRTR,0.,
             1DMIN(ICX),0.,DMAX(ICX),V,MED2)
    333 IF(ISW(LB,LC,LD,3)) 349,334,335
    334 V(1) = -1.
              CALL KS2SA (RT(1,JBASE),2,NALTR,TRTC,V,MED2)
              IF(V(11).GT.V(3)) GO TO 336
    335 WRITE(MED2,999)TT,U(NTR),NC,TTR
              V(1) = 3.
              CALL CHIKEN(3,NX)
              CALL KS2SA  (RT(1,JBASE),2,NALTR,TRTC,V,MED2)
    336 IF(ISW(LB,LC,LD,3)) 349,337,338
    337 V(1) = -1.
              CALL MANWIT(RT(1,JBASE),2,NALTR,TRTC,V,MED2)
              IF(V(11).GT.V(3)) GO TO 339
    338 WRITE(MED2,999)TT,U(NTR),NC,TTR
              V(1) = 3.
              CALL CHIKEN(3,NX)
              CALL MANWIT(RT(1,JBASE),2,NALTR,TRTC,V,MED2)
    339 IF(ISW(LB,LC,LD,3)) 349,340,341
    340 V(1) = -1.
              CALL QAREX  (RT(1,JBASE),2,NALTR,CX,KC,KR,2,NX,TRTC,TRTR,0.,DMIN
             1 (ICX),0.,DMAX(ICX),V,MED2)
              IF(V(11).GT.V(3)) GO TO 349
    341 WRITE(MED2,999)TT,U(NTR),NC,TTR
              V(1) = 3.
              CALL CHIKEN(3,NX)
              CALL QAREX  (RT(1,JBASE),2,NALTR,CX,KC,KR,2,NX,TRTC,TRTR,0.,DMIN
             1 (ICX),0.,DMAX(ICX),V,MED2)
C INTERVAL DATA LEVEL TESTS
    349 IF(ISW(LB,LC,LD,4)) 350,351,352
    350 IF(ISW(LB,LC,LD,5)) 390,351,352
```

```
      351 V(1) = -1.
          CALL TFIND(RT(1,JR),RT(1,JR+1),RT(1,JR+2),RT(2,JR),RT(2,JR+1),RT(2
         1,JR+2),V,TRTC,MED2)
          IF(V(11).GT.V(3)) GO TO 390
      352 WRITE(MED2,999)TT,U(NTR),NC,TTR
          V(1) = 1.
          IF(LD.NE.4.AND.LD.NE.7) CALL CHIKEN(4,NX)
          IF(LD.EQ.5.OR.LD.EQ.7) WRITE(MED2,992)
          CALL TFIND(RT(1,JR),RT(1,JR+1),RT(1,JR+2),RT(2,JR),RT(2,JR+1),RT(2
         1,JR+2),V,TRTC,MED2)
      390 CONTINUE
      400 JBASE = JBASE + NALTR + 7
          IF(JFIN.LT.M) GO TO 1
          REWIND MED3
          V(19) = V19
          IF(JST.NE.1) V(19) = 0.
          RETURN
      992 FORMAT (62HONO PURELY RATIO SCALE TESTS AVAILABLE - INTERVAL USED
         1INSTEAD)
      997 FORMAT(1H+,50X,39H IS EMPTY - SAMPLE SET CANNOT BE TESTED)
      999 FORMAT(16H1DATA BANK TITLE,14X,1H-,4X,10A4/17H SAMPLE SET TITLE,13
         1X,1H-,4X,10A4/23H DATA BANK SUBSET TITLE,7X,1H-,4X,10A4/
         2 1H ,4X,22H OF DATA COLUMN NUMBER,I4,12H SHORT TITLE,4X,A4/
         311H FULL TITLE,19X,1H-,4X,A2,15A4,13H DATA SCALE - ,2A4,A1/
         410HOSAMPLE NO,I4,6H TITLE,10X,1H-,14X,A4)
          END


          SUBROUTINE CHISQD(RT,NC,NR,CX,RX,KC,KR,ITC,ITR,TRTC,TRTR,DMINC,DMI
         1NR,DMAXC,DMAXR,V,MED2)
C CHISQD (SEE  6.1 ) STATISTICAL SELF-STABILISED CHI-SQUARED
C CHI-SQUARED TEST WITH AUTOMATIC ELIMINATION OF SMALL CELL VALUES
          DIMENSION RT(NC,NR),RX(NR),KR(NR),CX(NC),KC(NC)
          DIMENSION TRTR(NR),TRTC(NC)
          DIMENSION V(20)
          V(11) = 1.0
          DO 3 I=1,NC
          CX(I)=0.
        3 KC(I)=I
          DO 4 J=1,NR
          RX(J)=0.
        4 KR(J)=J
          TT=0.
          NSC = 0
          NSR = 0
          MSC = NC
          MSR = NR
          DO 1 I=1,NC
          DO 6 J=1,NR
          IF(RT(I,J).EQ.0.) GO TO 6
          CX(I)=CX(I)+RT(I,J)
          RX(J)=RX(J)+RT(I,J)
          IF(I.GT.NSC) NSC= I
          IF(I.LT.MSC) MSC = I
          IF(J.GT.NSR) NSR = J
          IF(J.LT.MSR) MSR = J
        6 CONTINUE
        1 TT=TT+CX(I)
          NXC = NSC
          NXR = NSR
          IF(TT.LT.0.5.AND.V(1).GT.0.) WRITE(MED2,97)
          IF(MSC.EQ.NSC.AND.V(1).GT.0.) WRITE(MED2,98)NSC
          IF(MSR.EQ.NSR.AND.V(1).GT.0.) WRITE(MED2,99)NSR
```

```
      IF(NSC.GE.NSC.OR.NSR.GE.NSR) V(11) = 1.1
      IF(V(11).GT.1.05) RETURN
      NUND1=0
      NUND5=0
      DO 5 I=1,NSC
      DO 5 J=1,NSR
      E=CX(I)*RX(J)/TT
      IF(E.GE.5.)GO TO 5
      NUND5=NUND5+5
      IF(E.GE.1.)GO TO 5
      NUND1=NUND1+1
    5 CONTINUE
      N=NSR*NSC
      VX=V(1)
      IF(V(1).GT.0.)WRITE (MED2,95)
      IF(NUND1.LT.1.AND.NUND5.LT.N)GO TO 40
      IF(V(1).GT.0.)WRITE(MED2,93)
      IF(V(1).LE.1.)GO TO 2
      CALL CHISQ (RT,NC,NR,KC,KR,NSC,NSR,NUND5,NUND1,V,MED2)
    2 IF(NSR.EQ.2.AND.NSC.EQ.2)GO TO 30
      IF(ITR.GT.ITC)GO TO 10
      IF(ITR.LT.ITC)GO TO 20
      IF(NSC.GT.NSR)GO TO 20
   10 IF(NSR.LE.2.AND.NSC.GT.2)GO TO 20
C REDUCE ROWS
      CALL REDROW(RX,KR,NR,NSR,CX,KC,NC,NSC,NUND5,NUND1)
      N=NSR*NSC
      IF(NUND1.LT.1.AND.NUND5.LT.N)GO TO 30
      GO TO 2
   20 IF(NSC.LE.2.AND.NSR.GT.2)GO TO 10
C REDUCE COLUMNS
      CALL REDROW(CX,KC,NC,NSC,RX,KR,NR,NSR,NUND5,NUND1)
      N=NSR*NSC
      IF(NUND1.LT.1.AND.NUND5.LT.N)GO TO 30
      GO TO 2
   30 IF(V(1).GT.0.)GO TO 31
      V(1)=0.-1.
      CALL CHISQ (RT,NC,NR,KC,KR,NSC,NSR,NUND5,NUND1,V,MED2)
      V(1)=VX
      IF(V(1).LT.0.)RETURN
      IF(V(1).EQ.0..AND.V(2).LT.V(11))RETURN
      WRITE (MED2,93)
   31 CONTINUE
      WRITE(MED2,94)
      CALL DICOLA (TRTC,TRTR,KC,KR,NC,NR,ITC,ITR,DMINC,DMINR,DMAXC,DMAXR
     1,NXC,NXR,MED2)
   33 IF(NXC+NXR.GE.20) WRITE(MED2,94)
      WRITE (MED2,96)
      IF(V(1).EQ.0.)V(1)=1.
      CALL CHISQ (RT,NC,NR,KC,KR,NSC,NSR,NUND5,NUND1,V,MED2)
      V(1)=VX
      RETURN
   40 CONTINUE
      IF(V(1).GT.0.)GO TO 41
      V(1)=0.-1.
      CALL CHISQ (RT,NC,NR,KC,KR,NSC,NSR,NUND5,NUND1,V,MED2)
      V(1)=VX
      IF(V(1).LT.0.)RETURN
      IF(V(1).EQ.0..AND.V(2).LT.V(11))RETURN
   41 WRITE(MED2,92)
      IF(V(1).EQ.0.)V(1)=1.
      CALL CHISQ (RT,NC,NR,KC,KR,NSC,NSR,NUND5,NUND1,V,MED2)
      V(1)=VX
```

```
      RETURN
   92 FORMAT(1H+,40X,24HCOMBINATION NOT REQUIRED)
   93 FORMAT(1H+,40X,20HCOMBINATION REQUIRED)
   94 FORMAT(1H1)
   95 FORMAT (38HOCHI-SQUARED - WITHOUT COMBINING CELLS)
   96 FORMAT (55HOCHI-SQUARED COMBINED TO GIVE ADEQUATE CELL FREQUENCIES
     1)
   97 FORMAT (22HOCHI-SQUARED - NO DATA)
   98 FORMAT(33HOCHI-SQUARED - ALL DATA IN COLUMN      ,I4)
   99 FORMAT(30HOCHI-SQUARED - ALL DATA IN ROW         ,I4)
      END


      SUBROUTINE KS2SA(RT,NC,NR,TS,V,MED2)
C KS2SA   (SEE 6.1 ) STATISTICAL KOLMOGOROV-SMIRNOV TWO SAMPLE
      DIMENSION RT(NC,NR),V(20),TS(2)
      TA=0.
      TB=0.
      DO 1 J=1,NR
      TA=TA+RT(1,J)
    1 TB=TB+RT(2,J)
      CUA=0.
      CUB=0.
      DPOS=0.
      DNEG=0.
      IF(V(1).GT.1.)WRITE(MED2,97) TS
      DO 2 J=1,NR
      CUA=CUA+RT(1,J)/TA
      CUB=CUB+RT(2,J)/TB
      DX=CUA-CUB
      IF(V(1).GT.1.)WRITE(MED2,98) J,CUA,CUB,DX
      IF(DPOS.GT.DX)GO TO 3
      DPOS=DX
    3 IF(DNEG.LT.DX)GO TO 2
      DNEG=DX
    2 CONTINUE
      DX=DPOS
      IF(DPOS.GT.(0.-DNEG))GO TO 4
      DX=0.-DNEG
    4 TF=TA*TB/(TA+TB)
      PB=4.*DNEG*DNEG*TF
      PA=4.*DPOS*DPOS*TF
      PA=PRBF(2.,10000.,PA/2.)
      PB=PRBF(2.,10000.,PB/2.)
      PC=EXP(5.7-6.3154*(DX*SQRT(TF)))
      IF(PC.GT.1.)PC=1.
      PC = 1. - PC
      V(11)=PA
      V(12)=PA
      V(13)=PB
      V(14)=PC
      IF(V(11).GT.PB)  V(11) = PB
      IF(V(11).GT.PC)  V(11) = PC
      IF(V(1).LT.0.)RETURN
      IF(V(11).GT.V(3).AND.V(1).LE.0.) RETURN
      WRITE(MED2,99)TS,PB,DNEG,TS,PA,DPOS,TS,PC,DX
      IF(TA.GT.40..AND.TB.GT.40.)RETURN
      WRITE(MED2,991)TS(1),TA,TS(2),TB
      IF(TA.EQ.TB)WRITE(MED2,992)
      IF(TA.EQ.TB)RETURN
      WRITE(MED2,993)
      RETURN
   97 FORMAT (35HOKOLMOGOROV-SMIRNOV TWO-SAMPLE TEST//1H0,20X,30HRELATIV
```

```
      1E CUMULATIVE FREQUENCY /1H0,2X,14HCLASS INTERVAL,5X,7HSAMPLE ,A4,5
     2X,7HSAMPLE ,A4,5X,10HDIFFERENCE/)
   98 FORMAT(1H ,5X,I5,10X,3(F8.3,7X))
   99 FORMAT (35H0KOLMOGOROV-SMIRNOV TWO-SAMPLE TEST//18H PROBABILITY TH
     1AT ,A4,21H IS NOT GREATER THAN ,A4,3H = ,F12.6,5H D = ,F12.4/18H P
     2ROBABILITY THAT ,A4,18H IS NOT LESS THAN ,A4,2H =,4X,F12.6,5H D =
     3,F12.4/18H PROBABILITY THAT ,A4,20H IS NOT THE SAME AS ,A4,4H =  ,
     4F12.6,5H D = ,F12.4/42H0(PROBABILITIES ARE INDEPENDENTLY DERIVED))
  991 FORMAT(42H LARGE SAMPLE APPROXIMATION DOES NOT HOLD./8H0SAMPLE ,A4
     1,10H CONTAINS ,F8.0,21H READINGS AND SAMPLE ,A4,10H CONTAINS ,F8.0
     2,9H READINGS)
  992 FORMAT(56H FOR MORE EXACT PROBABILITY CONSULT SIEGEL TABLE L P 278
     1)
  993 FORMAT(39H PROBABILITIES DERIVED ARE CONSERVATIVE)
      END


      SUBROUTINE MANWIT(RT,NC,NR,TS,V,MED2)
C MANWIT (SEE   6.1 ) STATISTICAL MANN-WHITNEY TEST
      DIMENSION RT(NC,NR),V(20),TS(2)
      TS(1) = TS(1)
      T=0.
      R1=0.
      R2=0.
      S1=0.
      S2=0.
      RSF=0.
      DO 1 J=1,NR
      RL=RT(1,J)+RT(2,J)
      IF(RL.EQ.0.) GO TO 1
      S1=S1+RT(1,J)
      S2=S2+RT(2,J)
      RAN=RSF+(RL+1.)*0.5
      R1=R1+RAN*RT(1,J)
      T=T+(RL*RL-1.)*RL/12.
    1 RSF=RSF+RL
      R1=S1*S2+S1*(S1+1.)*0.5-R1
      R2=S1*S2-R1
      Z=SQRT((S1*S2/(RSF*(RSF-1.)))*(RSF*(RSF*RSF-1.)/12.-T))
      Z=(R1-S1*S2*0.5)/Z
      PA=PRBF(1.,10000.,Z*Z)*0.5
      IF(Z.GT.1.) PA=1.-PA
      PB=1.-PA
      PC=2.*PA
      IF(PC.GT.1.) PC=2.*PB
      NMAX=S1
      IF(S2.GT.S1)NMAX=S2
      V(11)=PA
      IF(PB.LT.PA) V(11) = PB
      V(12)=Z
      V(13)=R1
      V(14)=S1
      V(15)=S2
      IF(V(1).LT.0.)RETURN
      IF(V(1).EQ.0..AND.V(2).LT.V(11)) RETURN
      WRITE(MED2,999)TS,PA,R1,TS,PB,R2,TS,PC
      WRITE(MED2,991) TS(1),S1,TS(2),S2
      IF(NMAX.LT.8) WRITE(MED2,998)
      IF(NMAX.LT.8) RETURN
      IF(NMAX.LT.20)WRITE(MED2,997)
      RETURN
  991 FORMAT(8H0SAMPLE ,A4,10H CONTAINS ,F8.0,21H READINGS AND SAMPLE ,A
     14,10H CONTAINS ,F8.0,9H READINGS)
```

```
      997 FORMAT(56HOFOR MORE EXACT PROBABILITY CONSULT SIEGEL TABLE K P274)
      998 FORMAT(56HOFOR MORE EXACT PROBABILITY CONSULT SIEGEL TABLE J P271)
      999 FORMAT (35HOMANN-WHITNEY TWO-SAMPLE TEST       T//18H PROBABILITY TH
     1AT ,A4,21H IS NOT GREATER THAN ,A4,3H = ,F12.6,5H U = ,F12.4/18H P
     2ROBABILITY THAT ,A4,18H IS NOT LESS THAN ,A4,2H =,4X,F12.6,5H U =
     3,F12.4/18H PROBABILITY THAT ,A4,20H IS NOT THE SAME AS ,A4,4H =  ,
     4F12.6/)
      END


      SUBROUTINE TFIND(S1,SX1,SXX1,S2,SX2,SXX2,V,TS,MED2)
C TFIND  (SEE  6.1 ) STATISTICAL T AND F TESTS - INDEPENDENT SAMPLES
C V(1) = -1 NO O/P = 0 SIG ONLY = 1 FULL OUTPUT
      DIMENSION V(20),TS(2),QS(2),RS(3,3)
      DATA RS/4HGREA,4HTER ,4HTHAN,4H LE,4HSS T,4HHAN ,4H  EQ,4HUAL ,4H
     1 TO /,QS/4HS. D.,4HMEAN/
      IF(S1.LT.3..OR.S2.LT.3.AND.V(1).GE.0.) WRITE(MED2,999)S1,S2
      IF(S1.LT.3..OR.S2.LT.3.) RETURN
      XBAR=SX1/S1
      YBAR=SX2/S2
      SX=(SXX1-SX1*XBAR)/(S1-1.)
      SY=(SXX2-SX2*YBAR)/(S2-1.)
      FR=SX/SY
      SX = SQRT(SX)
      SY = SQRT(SY)
      DFX=S1-1.
      DFY=S2-1.
      XA=PRBF(DFX,DFY,FR)
      XB=1.-XA
      XC=2.*XA
      IF(XC.GT.1.)XC=2.*XB
      VX=SX*SX/S1
      VY=SY*SY/S2
      TU=(XBAR-YBAR)/SQRT(VX+VY)
      C= VX/(VX+VY)
      DFU = DFY*DFX/(DFY*C*C + DFX*(1.-C)*(1.-C))
      XD=PRBF(1.,DFU,TU*TU)*0.5
      IF(XBAR.LT.YBAR)XD = 1.- XD
      XE=1.-XD
      XF=2.*XD
      IF(XF.GT.1.)XF=2.*XE
      SP=((S1-1.)*SX*SX+(S2-1.)*SY*SY)/(S1+S2-2.)
      TV=(XBAR-YBAR)/SQRT(SP*(1./S1+1./S2))
      DFV=S1+S2-2.
      XG=PRBF(1.,DFV,TV*TV)*0.5
      IF(XBAR.LT.YBAR)XG= 1. - XG
      XH=1.-XG
      XI=2.*XG
      IF(XI.GT.1.)XI=2.*XH
      V(11) = XA
      V(12) = XC
      V(13) = XF
      V(14) = XI
      IF(V(11).GT.V(13)) V(11) = V(13)
      IF(V(11).GT.V(14)) V(11) = V(14)
      V(11) = V(11)*.5
C V(11) IS NOW SMALLEST ONE-TAILED PROBABILITY
      V(15) = XBAR
      V(16) = SX
      V(17) = YBAR
      V(18) = SY
      IF(V(1).LT.0..OR.V(1).EQ.0..AND.V(11).GT.V(3)) RETURN
      WRITE(MED2,990)FR,DFX,DFY
```

```
     1,QS(1),TS(1),(RS(I,1),I=1,3),QS(1),TS(2),XB
     2,QS(1),TS(1),(RS(I,2),I=1,3),QS(1),TS(2),XA
     3,QS(1),TS(1),(RS(I,3),I=1,3),QS(1),TS(2),XC
      IF(V(1).GT.0.)WRITE(MED2,997)TS(1),S1,XBAR,SX,TS(2),S2,YBAR,SY
      IF(V(1).GT.0..OR.V(3)*2..LE.XA.AND.V(3)*2..GE.XG)
     1 WRITE(MED2,992)TV,DFV
     2,QS(2),TS(1),(RS(I,1),I=1,3),QS(2),TS(2),XH
     3,QS(2),TS(1),(RS(I,2),I=1,3),QS(2),TS(2),XG
     4,QS(2),TS(1),(RS(I,3),I=1,3),QS(2),TS(2),XI
      IF(V(1).GT.0..OR.V(3)*2..GT.XA.AND.V(3)*2..GE.XD)
     1 WRITE(MED2,994) TU,DFU
     2,QS(2),TS(1),(RS(I,1),I=1,3),QS(2),TS(2),XE
     3,QS(2),TS(1),(RS(I,2),I=1,3),QS(2),TS(2),XD
     4,QS(2),TS(1),(RS(I,3),I=1,3),QS(2),TS(2),XF
      RETURN
  990 FORMAT (31H0TESTS OF TWO UNRELATED SAMPLES/25H0FOR EQUALITY OF VAR
     1IANCE/19H0SNEDECOR F TEST = ,F15.6,6H WITH ,F10.0,6H OVER ,F10.0,1
     29H DEGREES OF FREEDOM//(18H PROBABILITY THAT ,A4,15H OF POPULATION
     3 ,A4,4H IS ,3A4,1X,A4,15H OF POPULATION ,A4,3H = ,F10.6))
  992 FORMAT (33H0ASSUMING VARIANCES DO NOT DIFFER/22H0FOR EQUALITY OF M
     1EANS/18H0STUDENT T TEST = ,F15.6,6H WITH ,              F10.0,1
     29H DEGREES OF FREEDOM//(18H PROBABILITY THAT ,A4,15H OF POPULATION
     3 ,A4,4H IS ,3A4,1X,A4,15H OF POPULATION ,A4,3H = ,F10.6))
  994 FORMAT (26H0ASSUMING VARIANCES DIFFER/22H0FOR EQUALITY OF MEANS/19
     1H0T-LIKE STATISTIC =,F16.6,6H WITH ,                    F10.0,1
     29H DEGREES OF FREEDOM//(18H PROBABILITY THAT ,A4,15H OF POPULATION
     3 ,A4,4H IS ,3A4,1X,A4,15H OF POPULATION ,A4,3H = ,F10.6))
  997 FORMAT (63H0    SAMPLE    NO OF READINGS   ARITHMETIC MEAN   STANDARD D
     1EVIATION/(1H0,4X,A4,6X,F6.0,2F20.4))
  999 FORMAT(5H ONLY,F6.0,5H AND ,F6.0,33H  READINGS - NOT SUFFICIENT DA
     1TA.)
      END
```

6.2 PROGRAM STKIND - TEST SEVERAL INDEPENDENT SAMPLES

6.2.1 Purpose

This program compares several independent samples of data drawn from a STATCAT data bank. It may be applied to two samples, but will than produce a warning message recommending the use of ST2IND before running. The tests employed will be those appropriate to the level of the data being tested, unless the system is over-ridden. The choice of tests made by the system may be over-ridden to make tests on a specific level, or to make tests on all levels up to the appropriate or a specific level. The level of significance below which results are not reported may be varied, and more or less detailed descriptive statistics produced. Variates tested may be transformed by any of the transforms given in Figure 3.72, but delayed variates may not be used. Class definitions may be specified, or the default values given in the data description segment may be used.

Figure 6.21a contains system flow-charts for the main program STKIND and the executive subroutine CKIND. Figure 6.21b contains system flow-charts for the subroutines MEDEX (Extension of the Median test - 6.2.5) and QAREX (Extension of the Quartile test - 6.2.5) Figure 6.21c contains system flow-charts for the subroutines KW1W (Kruskall-Wallis one-way analysis of variance by ranks -6.2.5) and PAR1W (Parametric one-way analysis of variance with Bartlett's test of equality of variance).

6.2.2 Input Data

Item	Level	Format	Function	SEE
1	0	A	File control	3.2
2	1	B	Sample specification (2/preferably more samples)	3.5
3	2	E	Subset specification	3.6
4	5	F	Variate specification (At least 1 - no delays)	3.7
5	9	G	Data handling instruction	Below + 3.8

Data Handling Instruction

Card Layout - Data Handling Instruction - STKIND

```
ABCCCDDDEEEEEEEEFFFFFFFFGGGGGGGGGGGGGGGGHHHHHHHHHHHHHHHHH.....etc
```

Columns	Item	Function	See
1	A	Output control index	6.1
2	B	Analysis control index	Below
3 - 5	C	Significance level for reporting (per cent)	6.1
6 - 8	D	Not used	-
9 - 16	E	Not used	-
17 - 24	F	Not used	-
25 - 40	G	Not used	-
41 - 80	H	Comment (NOT KEPT)	-

B - Analysis Control Index

This index controls the level at which testing is carried out, and the conditions under which the results are printed.

ALTERNATIVES

B = 0,blank: Tests at data level
(Default)   Print results if statistically significant.

B = 1   : Tests for NOMINAL level only (Chi-squared)
              Print results if statistically significant.

B = 2   : Tests for ORDINAL level only (Kruskal-Wallis
              one way analysis of variance by rank, Extension
              of the Median Test, Extension of the Quartile
              Test) - print results if statistically significant.

B = 3   : Tests for INTERVAL level (One-way Analysis of
              variance, Bartlett's test for homogenity of
              variance) - print results if statistically
              significant.

B = 4   : Tests for RATIO level (as for INTERVAL)
              Print results if statistically significant.

B = 5   : Tests at data level - print all results.

B = 6   : Tests at NOMINAL level - print all results.

B = 7   : Tests at ORDINAL level - print all results.

B = 8   : Tests at INTERVAL level - print all results.

B = 9   : Tests at RATIO level - print all results.

DEFAULT value = 0 (0, blank or non-numeric character)

6.2.3 Input Example

Figure 6.22 is a summary of the input structure for two runs of STKIND, using first the default values, then the full output available. Two independent samples are employed, which are the morning and afternoon sessions. All entries are included in the subset, and four variates are specified for testing. Although no transforms are used, the class definitions of the first two variates have been modified to reduce the number of classes used, saving time and storage space. The first data handling instruction employs default values throughout, producing only the results of statistically significant tests appropriate to the data level, where these have a probability of less than one per cent. The second data handling instruction produces the most detailed output possible. Figure 6.23 is a listing of the input cards required to carry out these two runs.

6.2.4 Output Example

Figure 6.24 is a summary of the output structure corresponding to the input structure of 6.22. Figure 6.25 is a page-by-page summary of the output corresponding to the specific example given in 6.2.3. Figure 6.26 shows the two statistical tests that reach a one per cent statistical significance level for the second variate, which is the value of Column 10, the operator's assessment of the difficulty of the task. The extension of the Median test (6.2.5) involves generalising that test to several samples, in place of two, dividing them at the common median. In this case the classes VEAS (Very easy) to REAS (Rather easy) are included in one half, and the classes NULL (neither hard nor easy) to VHAR

(Very hard) are included in the other. Examination of the table of chi-squared values suggest a steady progression in assessment from operators ERIC to HUGH, the later finding the task more difficult.

The Kruskal-Wallis one-way analysis of variance by ranks is discussed in more detail in section 6.2.5, but it should be noted here that the probability associated with the observed statistic "H" is smaller (more significant) than that associated with the chi-squared statistic obtained in the extension of the median test. The Kruskal-Wallis test is more sensitive because it uses more of the information available in the data.

Figure 6.27 shows an analysis of variance for the variate in Column 15 - the operator's heart rate, showing a statistically significant difference between operators. Bartlett's test shows that the variances do not differ significantly for the different operators. The figures suggest that Eric's heart rate is low and Hugh's is high, while the other two are intermediate.

It should be noted that Columns 6 (STRS) and 11 (TEMP) show no significant differences between operators - as might be expected, since they are both external, environmental, factors. If significant differences had been found, then further investigation would be needed urgently.

6.2.5 Statistical Tests - ORDINAL Level

A - MEDEX - Extension of the Median Test

The median test is a test for difference in central tendency. It requires data on at least an ORDINAL level, and tests whether the two samples have come from populations having the same median. It operates by finding the median of the combined samples, then by finding how many data in each sample fall above or below the combined median. It then applies a classic chi-squared test to determine whether the frequencies in each cell are evenly distributed or not. If they are not, then it concludes that the samples do not have the same median.

The chi-squared test generated is subject to the same constraints, as far as cell numbers are concerned, as any other chi-squared test (6.1.5). Each sample should have at least ten entries if the test is to be reliable. The subroutine MEDEX operates by finding the median class, in a frequency tabulation, which is slightly less efficient, but far faster, than a strict determination of the common median. If most of the samples concentrate in one class, the Median test will not be able to produce a reliable output. (The remedy is to use an explicit class definition in the variate specification - 3.7.)

The extension of this test lies in its extension from two to several samples.

Figure 6.26 contains an example of the Median test output.

REFERENCES : Siegel (Ch 7)

B - QAREX - Extension of the Quartile Test

The quartile test is a test for differences in dispersion. It requires data on at least an ORDINAL scale, with (except when the median classes of all samples are identical) equal intervals between classes. g It operates by finding the median class for each sample, and calculatingg the number of data falling in successive clases above or below the median class for each sample, and forming a total for each successive class. Having determined the relative position (in classes) of the first quartile (25th percentile) and third quartile (75th percentile) of the combined samples, it determines how many of each sample fall outside and inside these quartiles. It performs a classical chi-squared test to determine whether there are significant differences between samples in the number of readings falling outside the common adjusted quartiles.

This test is subject to the same restrictions in validity as the traditional chi-squared test (6.1.5). In practice it requires at least fifteen entries per sample, even with very small class intervals. In addition, it is liable to fail where the numbers of classes containing data for a sample is small, so that the allocation to quartiles is impractical - this may happen even when the overall distribution is reasonable, if the median classes are widely separated. The allocation of classes reported in the full test report should be checked if the test is used.

The extension of this test lies in its extension from two to several samples.

Figure 6.28 contains an example of the Quartile test output.

REFERENCES - none (The author has not found a suitable non-parametric test for dispersion in the literature, and has been constrained, in this instance only, to be original.)

C - KW1W - Kruskall-Wallis One way analysis of Variance by Ranks

This test calculates the probability that samples are drawn from populations having the same average. It is a test of central tendency, and does not detect differences in dispersion. It requires that the data should be on a continuous scale, although they are used as ordinal class frequencies. The test operates, in principle, by ranking all the data from all the samples in one consecutive ranking, and finding the average rank of each sample. It then estimates the probability that these ranks would be as different as they are, were they drawn from populations with the same average.

Figure 6.26 also contains an example of the Kruskall-Wallis test output.

REFERENCES : Siegel (Ch 7)

6.2.6 Statistical Tests - INTERVAL Level

A - PAR1W - One-way Analysis of variance

The classical one-way analysis of variance calculates the probability that the samples are drawn from populations having the same average. It is a test of central tendency, and does not detect differences in dispersion. It requires data on an INTERVAL scale at least, and that the samples should be drawn from normally distributed populations, of equal variance. It operates by making two estimates of the underlying population variance (dispersion), one by comparing the means of the samples (Between Samples) and the other by comparing the data with the mean of the sample to which they belong (Within Samples). It then forms the ratio of these two variance estimates, and estimates, from parametric statistical theory, the probability of obtaining as large a ratio by chance if there were no difference in population means.

Although the analysis of variance makes parametric asumptions, it is known to be very little affected by unequal population variances or non-normal distributions. (It benefits from the observation that if you average enough of anything, the distribution of the result will resemble a normal distribution.)

Figure 6.27 includes an example of the analysis of variance as produced by this program.

REFERENCES - See Chapter 7.1 - STANOV.

B - PAR1W - Bartlett's Test for difference of Variance

Bartlett's test for 'homoscedasticity'(equality of dispersion) calculates the probability that the samples are drawn from populations having the same variance. It is a pure test of dispersion, and is not affected by differences in central tendency. It requires that the data are on an INTERVAL level, and that the distributions of data from which samples are drawn should be normal.

It operates, in priniciple, by comparing a variance estimate for all the data with an estimate made by averaging the variances of the samples, and estimating the probability of a ratio so extreme occurring when the samples come from populations with the same variance.

A significant result from Bartlett's test should be interpreted as meaning that the samples do not have the same variance, but need not imply that the analysis of variance accompanying it in PAR1W is invalid, although it may be a useful warning sign. (Practically, it is often an indication that a data error has crept through the checking processes.) Bartlett's test becomes more sensitive to the relative sizes of variances as the sample sizes increase. For very large samples it will detect 'significant' differences that are obviously of no practical importance. It should be intuitively obvious that taking larger samples should not impede our chances of detecting differences by analysis of variance.

Should the user be disturbed by the inequality of his samples' variances, he should consult 7.1.6, where he will find a discussion, with illustrations and references, of the use of variance stabilising transforms.

Bartlett's test produces a statistic distributed like Snedecor's "F" statistic - in certain circumstances the degrees of freedom for the denominator of this statistic may appear very high - this is not a computer error. In fact, Bartlett's Test is often evaluated like a chi-squared statistic - see Chapter 7.1.

Figure 6.27 also contains an example of Bartlett's test output.

REFERENCES - Winer (Ch 3), Dixon and Massey (Ch 10)

257

Figure 6.21a - System Flow-Charts - STKIND and CKIND

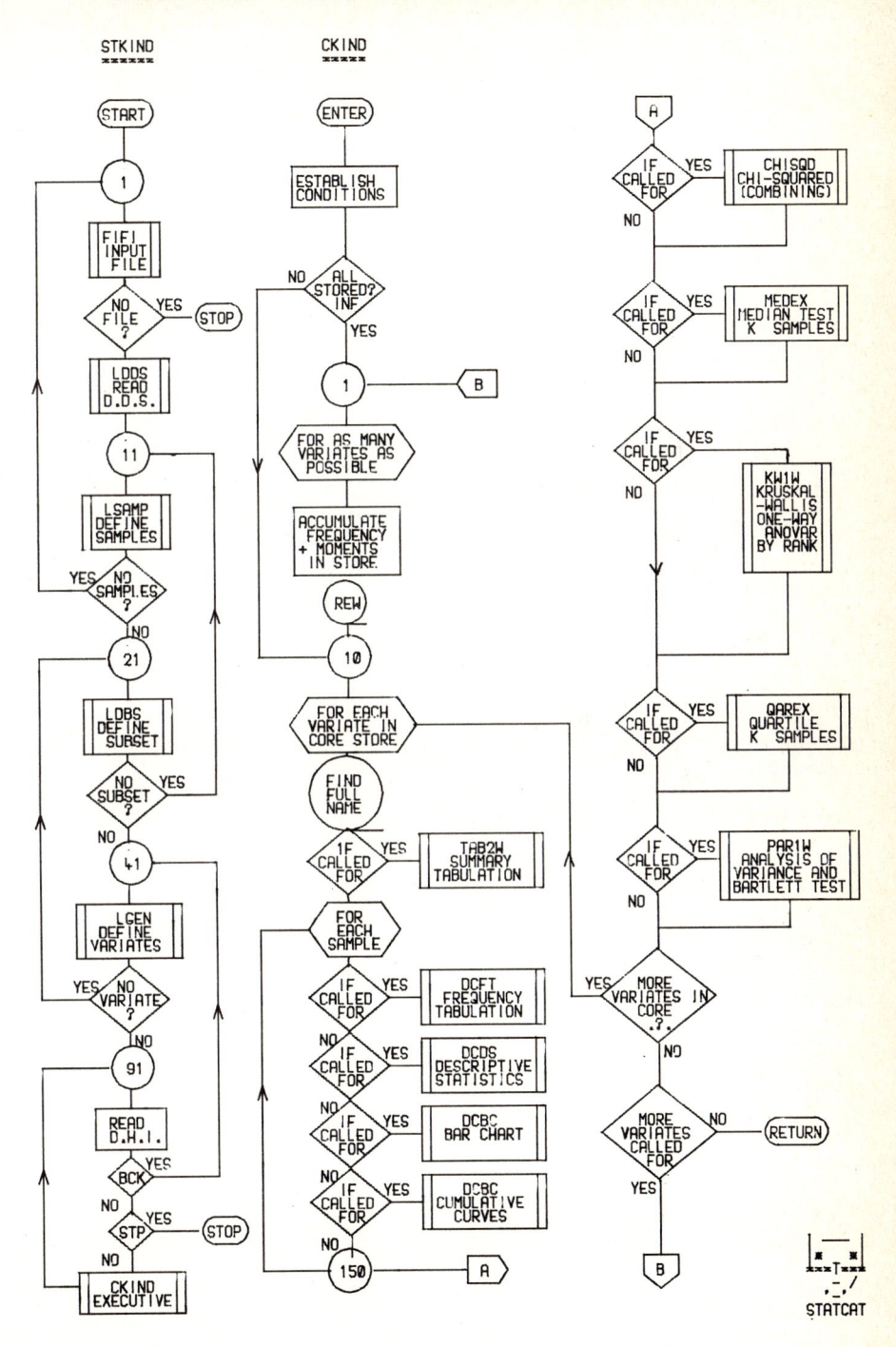

Figure 6.21b - System Flow-Charts - MEDEX and QAREX

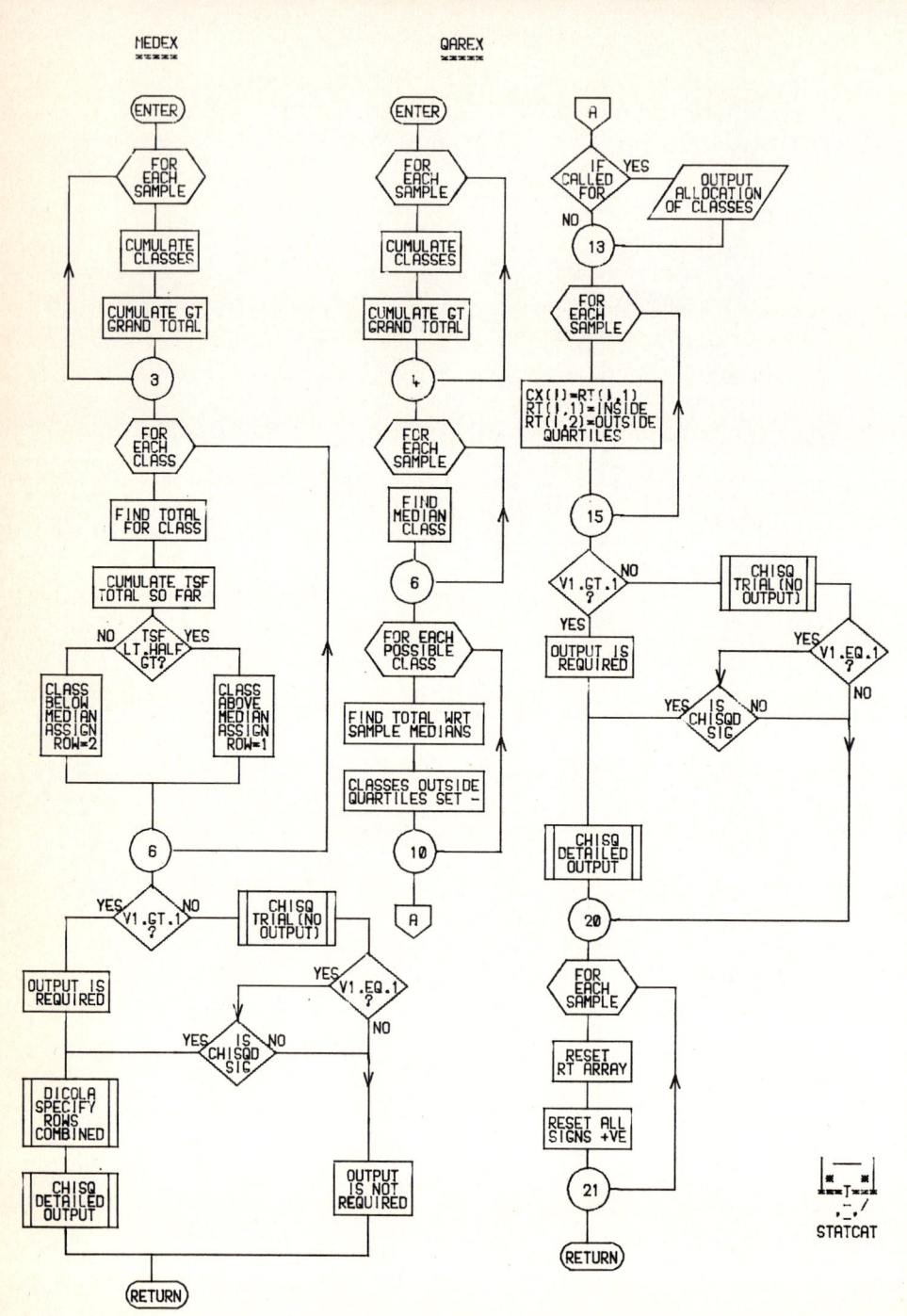

Figure 6.21c - System Flow-Charts - KW1W and PAR1W

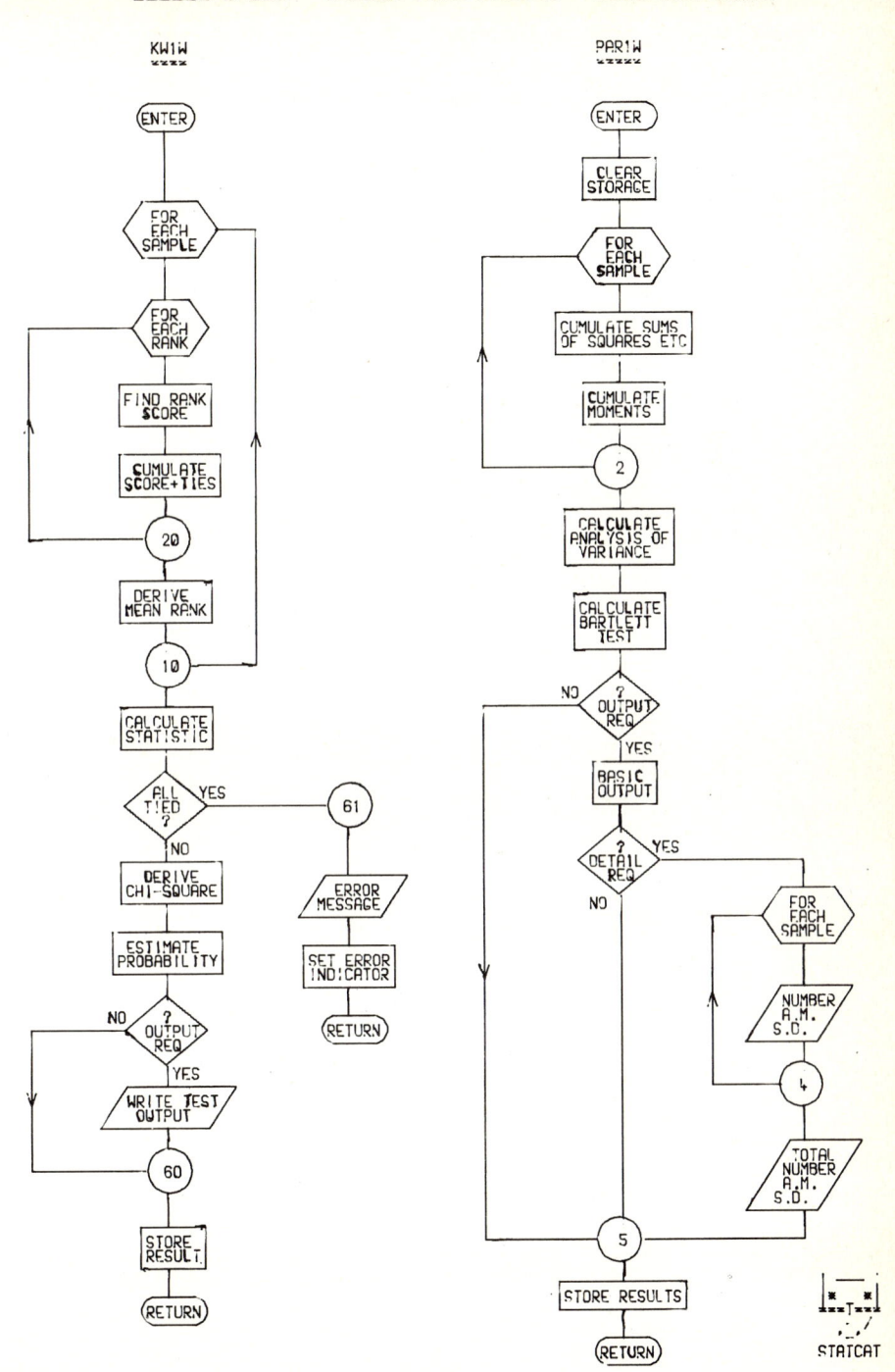

KW1W

ENTER → FOR EACH SAMPLE → FOR EACH RANK → FIND RANK SCORE → CUMULATE SCORE+TIES → (20) → DERIVE MEAN RANK → (10) → CALCULATE STATISTIC → ALL TIED?
- YES → (61) → ERROR MESSAGE → SET ERROR INDICATOR → RETURN
- NO → DERIVE CHI-SQUARE → ESTIMATE PROBABILITY → OUTPUT REQ?
  - YES → WRITE TEST OUTPUT → (60)
  - NO → (60) → STORE RESULT → RETURN

PAR1W

ENTER → CLEAR STORAGE → FOR EACH SAMPLE → CUMULATE SUMS OF SQUARES ETC → CUMULATE MOMENTS → (2) → CALCULATE ANALYSIS OF VARIANCE → CALCULATE BARTLETT TEST → OUTPUT REQ?
- NO → (5)
- YES → BASIC OUTPUT → DETAIL REQ?
  - YES → FOR EACH SAMPLE → NUMBER A.M. S.D. → (4) → TOTAL NUMBER A.M. S.D. → (5)
  - NO → (5)
- (5) → STORE RESULTS → RETURN

STATCAT

<u>Figure 6.22 - STKIND - Input Structure</u>

```
        Level
  0   1   2   3   4   5   6   7   8   9
FILE CONTROL CARD
    SAMPLE SPECIFICATION
        SUBSET SPECIFICATION
            VARIATE SPECIFICATION
                DATA HANDLING INSTRUCTION
                DATA HANDLING INSTRUCTION
                STOP
```

<u>Figure 6.23 - STKIND - Input Example</u>

```
---------1---------2---------3---------4---------5---------6---------7--
**STKINDDEMO                          DEMO TAPE IS NO 22
OPERATORS                             FOUR INDEPENDENT SAMPLES
ERIC
.IF.OPER.EQ.ERIC
END OF SAMPLE ONE
FRED
.IF.OPER.EQ.FRED
END OF SAMPLE TWO
GINA
.IF.OPER.EQ.GINA
END OF SAMPLE THREE
HUGH
.IF.OPER.EQ.HUGH
END OF SAMPLE FOUR
END OF SAMPLE SET SPECIFICATION
ALL DATA
END OF SUBSET
VAL.STRS       4      1.5     1.0     3.5 NOMINAL LEVEL VARIATE
VAL.DIFF       7      1.5     1.0     6.5 ORDINAL LEVEL VARIATE
VAL.TEMP                                  INTERVAL LEVEL VARIATE
VAL.H.R.                                  RATIO LEVEL VARIATE
END OF SET OF VARIATES
GO                   DEFAULT VALUES   SIG ( 1 PCT) RESULTS ONLY AT DA
88                                    MAXIMUM DESCRIPTIVE OUTPUT AND T
STOP
---------1---------2---------3---------4---------5---------6---------7--
```

                    Figure 6.24 - STKIND - Output Structure

For each   ) : File Control Record
output file)   File Parameters
                 Data Description
                 For each) : Sample Input Record
                 Sample)   For each) Subset Input Record
                 Specifn)   Subset) For each) Input Record
                                        Set of   ) For each) See
                                                 Variates Variate) Left
For each) <Cross-tabulation>
Variate)   For Each)<FrequencyTable>
            Sample)<Descriptive Statistics>
                    <Frequency Curves/Bar Chart>

         NOMINAL   <Chi-squared>
         ORDINAL   <Extension of the Median Test>
                    <Kruskal-Wallis one-way Anovar by ranks>
                    <Extension of the Quartile Test>
         INTERVAL) <Classical one-way Analysis of Variance>
         /RATIO) <Bartlett's Test for Homeoscedasticity>

 Carated(<>) items are optional.

Figure 6.25 - STKIND - Output Example Page-by-Page listing

Page	Contents	Origin
1	File Control Record	FIFI
2	Program Title File Parameters	STKIND LDAP
3- 4	Data Description record	LDDS
5	Sample record	LSAMP/LSET
6	Subset record	LDBS/LSET
7	Set of Variates record Data Handling Instruction	LGEN LDHI
8	Extension of the Median test (Difficulty)	MEDEX
9	Kruskal-Wallis one-way Anovar (Difficulty)	KW1WA
10	Analysis of Variance + Bartlett's Test	PAR1W
11	Data Handling Instruction	LDHI
12-19	Sample Descriptions (Stress) DCFT/DCDS/DCPS/DCBC	
20-26	Test Reports (Stress)	As above
27-41	Sample Descriptions/ Test Reports(Difficulty)	As above
32-56	Sample Descriptions/ Test Reports(Temperature)	As above
47-71	Sample Descriptions/ Test Reports(Heart Rate)	As above
72	Data Handling Instruction (STOP)	LDHI

Figure 6.26 - Extension of the Median and Kruskall-Wallis Tests

```
DATA BANK TITLE              -    DEMONSTRATION STATCAT DATA BANK
SAMPLE SET TITLE             -    OPERATORS
DATA BANK SUBSET TITLE       -    ALL DATA
VAL. OF DATA COLUMN NUMBER   10 SHORT TITLE   DIFF
FULL TITLE                   -    ASSESSMENT OF DIFFICULTY BY OPERATOR

EXTENSION OF THE MEDIAN TEST.

COMBINATIONS OF COLUMNS

COLUMN TITLE        ORIGINAL COMBINED

  1     ERIC            1        1
  2     FRED            2        2
  3     GINA            3        3
  4     HUGH            4        4

COMBINATIONS OF ROWS

ROW TITLE           ORIGINAL COMBINED

  1     VEAS            1        1
  2     EASY            2        1
  3     REAS            3        1
  4     NULL            4        2
  5     RHAR            5        2
  6     HARD            6        2
  7     VHAR            7        2

ROW  1
OBSERVED      15.0000   10.0000    4.0000    0.0
EXPECTED       7.2500    7.2500    7.2500    7.2500
CHI-SQUARE     8.2845    1.0431    1.4569    7.2500

ROW  2
OBSERVED       1.0000    6.0000   12.0000   16.0000
EXPECTED       8.7500    8.7500    8.7500    8.7500
CHI-SQUARE     6.8643    0.8643    1.2071    6.0071

     CHI-SQUARED IS    32.98 WITH    3 DEGREES OF FREEDOM PROBABILITY OF 0.00001187

NUMBER OF CELLS LESS THAN ONE      0
NUMBER OF CELLS LESS THAN FIVE     0




DATA BANK TITLE              -    DEMONSTRATION STATCAT DATA BANK
SAMPLE SET TITLE             -    OPERATORS
DATA BANK SUBSET TITLE       -    ALL DATA
VAL. OF DATA COLUMN NUMBER   10 SHORT TITLE   DIFF
FULL TITLE                   -    ASSESSMENT OF DIFFICULTY BY OPERATOR

KRUSKAL-WALLIS ONE-WAY ANALYSIS OF VARIANCE BY RANKS

         SAMPLE  1 ERIC  MEAN RANK =   13.0625 FOR    16.ENTRIES
         SAMPLE  2 FRED  MEAN RANK =   24.7188 FOR    16.ENTRIES
         SAMPLE  3 GINA  MEAN RANK =   36.5000 FOR    16.ENTRIES
         SAMPLE  4 HUGH  MEAN RANK =   55.7188 FOR    16.ENTRIES

H. (DISTRIBUTED AS CHI-SQUARED) =       47.2034 WITH    3. DEGREES OF FREEDOM.
ASSOCIATED PROBABILITY =          0.0
```

Figure 6.27 - Analysis of Variance and Bartlett's Tests

```
DATA BANK TITLE              -    DEMONSTRATION STATCAT DATA BANK
SAMPLE SET TITLE             -    OPERATORS
DATA BANK SUBSET TITLE       -    ALL DATA
VAL. OF DATA COLUMN NUMBER  15  SHORT TITLE    H.R.
FULL TITLE                   -    MEAN HEART RATE DURING TEST  (BEATS/MINUTE)           DATA SCALE -RATIO

DATA USED ARE ON A RATIO SCALE    THEY SHOULD BE ON AN INTERVAL SCALE   SIGNIFICANCE MAY BE REDUCED    **WARNING**

NO PURELY RATIO SCALE TESTS AVAILABLE - INTERVAL USED INSTEAD

ANALYSIS OF VARIANCE

SOURCE OF VARIATION TOTAL SUM OF SQUARES   D.F.  MEAN SUM OF SQUARES  VARIANCE RATIO   PROBABILITY
BETWEEN SAMPLES        746.0000           3.         248.6667            5.5325           0.0024
 WITHIN SAMPLES       2696.8125          60.          44.9469
TOTAL                 3442.8125          63.

BARTLETT CHI-SQUARED TEST FOR HOMOGENEITY OF VARIANCE

CHI-SQUARED          1.0259

PROBABILITY          0.370656

SAMPLE    1 (ERIC)         16. READINGS  -  MEAN =   42.6456  S.D. =    6.0046
SAMPLE    2 (FRED)         16. READINGS  -  MEAN =   47.5799  S.D. =    6.6854
SAMPLE    3 (GINA)         16. READINGS  -  MEAN =   47.6062  S.D. =    6.9001
SAMPLE    4 (HUGH)         16. READINGS  -  MEAN =   52.3006  S.D. =    7.1716
ALL SAMPLES                64. READINGS  -  MEAN =   47.5331  S.D. =    7.3924
```

Figure 6.28 - Extension of the Quartile Test

```
DATA BANK TITLE              -    DEMONSTRATION STATCAT DATA BANK
SAMPLE SET TITLE             -    OPERATORS
DATA BANK SUBSET TITLE       -    ALL DATA
VAL. OF DATA COLUMN NUMBER  10  SHORT TITLE    DIFF
FULL TITLE                   -    ASSESSMENT OF DIFFICULTY BY OPERATOR         DATA SCALE -ORDINAL

EXTENSION OF THE QUARTILE TEST

ALLOCATION OF CLASSES

SAMPLE NUMBER           1        2        3        4
  1     VEAS            1        0        0        0
  2     EASY            1        1        0        0
  3     REAS            2        1        1        0
  4     NULL            2        2        1        0
  5     RHAR            0        2        2        1
  6     HARD            0        0        0        1
  7     VHAR            0        0        0        2

COMBINATIONS OF COLUMNS

COLUMN TITLE         ORIGINAL  COMBINED

  1     ERIC            1        1
  2     FRED            2        2
  3     GINA            3        3
  4     HUGH            4        4

EXTENSION OF THE QUARTILE TEST

ROW   1
OBSERVED       12.0000   10.0000   12.0000   12.0000
EXPECTED       11.5000   11.5000   11.5000   11.5000
CHI-SQUARE      0.0217    0.1957    0.0217    0.0217

ROW   2
OBSERVED        4.0000    6.0000    4.0000    4.0000
EXPECTED        4.5000    4.5000    4.5000    4.5000
CHI-SQUARE      0.0556    0.5000    0.0556    0.0556

     CHI-SQUARED IS       0.93  WITH    3 DEGREES OF FREEDOM  PROBABILITY OF 0.82088941   THIS CHI-SQUARED IS NOT RELIABLE

NUMBER OF CELLS LESS THAN ONE      0
NUMBER OF CELLS LESS THAN FIVE     4
```

```
C MASTER STKIND - TESTS THREE OR MORE INDEPENDENT SAMPLES OF DATA
C  SUBROUTINES AND FUNCTIONS REQUIRED
C  NAME            TYPE          COMMENT
C  AN      (SEE  3.1 ) SERVICE      ALPHA - TO NUMERIC VALUE
C  CH      (SEE 11.6 ) SERVICE      CHOOSES TEST/DESCRIPTION REQUIRED
C  CHIKEN  (SEE 11.9 ) SERVICE      WARNS OF MISMATCHED DATA LEVEL
C  CHISQ   (SEE 11.5 ) STATISTICAL  BASIC CHI-SQUARED CALCULATION
C  CHISQD  (SEE  6.1 ) STATISTICAL  SELF-STABILISED CHI-SQUARED
C  CKIND   (SEE  6.2 ) EXECUTIVE    TESTS SEVERAL INDEPENDENT SAMPLES
C  CLASIF  (SEE 11.7 ) SERVICE      CLASSIFIES DATA ITEM
C  CLSAM   (SEE  3.5 ) SERVICE      ALLOTS ENTRY TO SAMPLE/SUBSET
C  COMPA   (SEE  3.1 ) SERVICE      COMPARES ALPHAMERIC VALUES
C  COPYA   (SEE  3.1 ) SERVICE      COPIES ALPHAMERIC VALUE
C  DCBC    (SEE  5.2 ) STATISTICAL  CONSTRUCTS BAR-CHARTS
C  DCDS    (SEE  5.2 ) STATISTICAL  DESCRIPTIVE STATISTICS
C  DCFT    (SEE  5.2 ) STATISTICAL  FREQUENCY TABULATION
C  DCPS    (SEE  5.2 ) STATISTICAL  MOMENT(PARAMETRIC) STATISTICS
C  DICOLA  (SEE 11.5 ) STATISTICAL  DESCRIBES ROW/COLUMN COMBINATION
C  FIPI    (SEE  3.2 ) SYSTEM       ALLOCATES PERIPHERALS
C  GAUS    (SEE 11.8 ) STATISTICAL  FINDS ASS. PROB. OF N VALUE
C  IBL     (SEE  3.1 ) SERVICE      DETECTS BLANK,END AND STOP CARDS
C  ICH     (SEE  3.1 ) SERVICE      IDENTIFIES ALPHAMERIC CODES
C  KW1W    (SEE  6.2 ) STATISTICAL  KRUSKAL-WALLIS 1-WAY ANOVAR BY RANK
C  LDAP    (SEE  3.3 ) SYSTEM       LOADS/CHECKS DATA BANK PARAMETERS
C  LDBS    (SEE  3.6 ) SYSTEM       LOADS SUBSET DEFINITION
C  LDDS    (SEE  3.4 ) SYSTEM       LOADS DATA DESCRIPTION SEGMENT
C  LDHI    (SEE  3.8 ) SYSTEM       LOADS/CHECKS DATA HANDLING INSTN
C  LGEN    (SEE  3.7 ) SYSTEM       LOADS GENERALISED VARIATES
C  LSAMP   (SEE  3.5 ) SYSTEM       LOADS SAMPLE SET DEFINITION
C  LSET    (SEE  3.5 ) SYSTEM       LOADS DEFINING CONDITIONS
C  MEDEX   (SEE  6.1 ) STATISTICAL  MEDIAN TEST (EXTENDED)
C  MEDIAT  (SEE  3.7 ) SERVICE      FETCHES NEXT VARIATE SET
C  PAR1W   (SEE  6.2 ) STATISTICAL  1-WAY ANOVAR + BARTLETT TEST
C  PRBF    (SEE 11.8 ) STATISTICAL  FINDS PROBABILITY OF F-RATIO
C  PRTCLS  (SEE 11.7 ) SERVICE      PRINTS CLASS NAME/LIMITS
C  QAREX   (SEE  6.1 ) STATISTICAL  QUARTILE TEST (EXTENDED)
C  REDROW  (SEE 11.5 ) STATISTICAL  CHOOSES ROW/COLUMN FOR COMBINATION
C  TAB2W   (SEE  6.4 ) STATISTICAL  TABULATES WITH VARIATE NAMES ETC
C  TPIND   (SEE  6.1 ) STATISTICAL  T AND F TESTS - INDEPENDENT SAMPLES
C  TRANS   (SEE  3.7 ) SERVICE      CARRIES OUT REQUIRED TRANSFORM
C  IF NQMAX= MAXIMUM NO OF DATA COLS IS INCREASED INCREASE CN DATA
C  DIMENSION D(NQMAX),DMAX(NQMAX),DMIN(NQMAX),IT(NQMAX),ST(NQMAX)
C  DIMENSION CN(NQMAX)
      NQMAX = 100
      DIMENSION D(100),DMAX(100),DMIN(100),IT(100),ST(100),CN(100)
      DATA  CN/4HCOL1,4HCOL2,4HCOL3,4HCOL4,4HCOL5,4HCOL6,4HCOL7,4HCOL8,4
     1HCOL9,4HCL10,4HCL11,4HCL12,4HCL13,4HCL14,4HCL15,4HCL16,4HCL17,4HC
     218,4HCL19,4HCL20,4HCL21,4HCL22,4HCL23,4HCL24,4HCL25,4HCL26,4HCL27,
     34HCL28,4HCL29,4HCL30,4HCL31,4HCL32,4HCL33,4HCL34,4HCL35,4HCL36,4HC
     4L37,4HCL38,4HCL39,4HCL40,4HCL41,4HCL42,4HCL43,4HCL44,4HCL45,4HCL46
     5,4HCL47,4HCL48,4HCL49,4HCL50,4HCL51,4HCL52,4HCL53,4HCL54,4HCL55,4H
     6CL56,4HCL57,4HCL58,4HCL59,4HCL60,4HCL61,4HCL62,4HCL63,4HCL64,4HCL6
     75,4HCL66,4HCL67,4HCL68,4HCL69,4HCL70,4HCL71,4HCL72,4HCL73,4HCL74,4
     8HCL75,4HCL76,4HCL77,4HCL78,4HCL79,4HCL80,4HCL81,4HCL82,4HCL83,4HCL
     984,4HCL85,4HCL86,4HCL87,4HCL88,4HCL89,4HCL90,4HCL91,4HCL92,4HCL93,
     94HCL94,4HCL95,4HCL96,4HCL97,4HCL98,4HCL99,4HC100/
C  DIMENSION TRT(NALTMX)= MAXIMUM NUMBER OF CLASSES IN DATA BANK
      NALTMX = 50
      DIMENSION TRT(50)
C  DIMENSION CX(NSMAX),KC(NSMAX),TRTC(NSMAX)= MAXIMUM NO OF SAMPLES
      NSMAX = 20
      DIMENSION CX(20),KC(20),TRTC(20)
C  DIMENSION RX(NRMAX),KR(NRMAX),TRTR(NRMAX)=MAXIMUM NO OF CLASSES USED
```

```
      NRMAX = 52
      DIMENSION RX(52),KR(52),TRTR(52)
C MAXST = FREE STORAGE FOR TABLES AND MOMENTS MUST BE AT LEAST
C 2*(NCL(J) + 7) WHERE NCL(J) IS LARGEST NO OF CLASSES USED
C DIMENSION RT(MAXST)
      MAXST=2000
      DIMENSION RT(2000)
C MAXM = MAXIMUM NUMBER OF VARIATES ACCEPTED FOR ANY DATA SWEEP
C DIMENSION NCL(MAXM),NP(MAXM),T(MAXM),TMIN(MAXM),TMAX(MAXM)
      MAXM=20
      DIMENSION NCL(20),NP(20),T(20),TMIN(20),TMAX(20)
C DIMENSION SCON(5,MAXDBC)= MAXIMUM NUMBER OF COND (SUBSET+SAMPLE)
      MAXDBC = 50
      DIMENSION SCON(5,50)
C THE FOLLOWING DIMENSION STORES THE NAMES OF THE DATA TRANSFORMS
C AND THE ACCEPTABLE LEVELS FOR TRANSFORMATIONS
      DIMENSION U(60),LU(60),H(1),IH(1),FORM(50)
      NU = 60
C TRANSFORMATION CODES
C UNITS                    BLOCKS
C       0 - 9   10 - 19   20 - 29   30 - 39   40 - 49   50 - 59
C       POWERS TRIG       TRIG      STATIST   MATHS     TEST
C              RADIANS    DEGREES   TRANSF    FUNCTS    FUNCTIONS
C  0     -       -        H.MS        -         -       RM10
C  1    VAL.    SINR      SIND      PSNA      RECP      +/-1
C  2    SQAR    COSR      COSD      PSNB      SQRT      ADD1
C  3    CUBE    TANR      TAND      BINO      ABSV      SUB1
C  4    4PWR    ASIR      ASID      LG+1      SIGN      NOR1
C  5    5PWR    ACOR      ACOD      LOGE      INTG      +/-P
C  6    6PWR    ATAR      ATAD      LG10      FRAC      ADDP
C  7    7PWR    SINH      DTOR      AL10      EXPT      SUBP
C  8    8PWR    COSH      RTOD        -       PRES      NORP
C  9    9PWR    TANH      H.HH        -       NEG.      +100
      DATA U/4HVAL.,4HSQAR,4HCUBE,4H4PWR,4H5PWR,4H6PWR,4H7PWR,4H8PWR,4H9
     1PWR,4HVAL ,4HSINR,4HCOSR,4HTANR,4HASIR,4HACOR,4HATAR,4HSINH,4HCOSH
     2,4HTANH,4HH.MS,4HSIND,4HCOSD,4HTAND,4HASID,4HACOD,4HATAD,4HDTOR,4H
     3RTOD,4HH.HH,4H VAL,4HPSNA,4HPSNB,4HBINO,4HLG+1,4HLOGE,4HLG10,4HAL1
     40   ,4H    ,4H    ,4H    ,4HRECP,4HSQRT,4HABSV,4HSIGN,4HINTG,4HFRAC,4
     5HEXPT,4HPRES,4HNEG.,4HRM10,4H+/-1,4HADD1,4HSUB1,4HNOR1,4H+/-P,4HAD
     6DP,4HSUBP,4HNORP,4H+100,4H     /
      DATA LU/1,8*5,1,9*5,1,9*5,1,6*5,4*1,2*5,2*3,3*5,7*2,4*5,2*2/
      COMMON /STCT/MED1,MED2,MED3,MED4,MED5,MED6,MED13,Q,V(20),TT(30)
      DATA PROG/4HKIND/
      MED1 = -1
C LEVEL 0 - SETTING UP
    1 CALL COPYA(TT(1),PROG)
      CALL FIFI
      IF(MED2.GT.0) WRITE(MED2,901)
      CALL LDAP(MED2,MED3,V,TT,Q,NQ,NALT,NQMAX,NALTMX,IGO)
      IF(IGO.GT.0) GO TO 1
      LI = 18
      CALL LDDS(TRT,NALT,D,NQ,ST,NQ,IT,NQ,H,0,DMIN,DMAX,NQ,LI,1,Q,VX,
     1 0,MED2,MED3,0,IGO)
C LEVEL 1 - READ SAMPLE SPECIFICATION
   11 IF(V(10).GE.10.) V(10) = 0.
      CALL LSAMP(SCON,NCON,MAXDBC,TRTC,NS,NSMAX,CN,ST,IT,NQ,TRT,NALT,IGO
     1)
      IF(NS.EQ.2)WRITE(MED2,924)
      IF(IGO.GT.0) GO TO 1
      MAXLEF = MAXDBC-NCON
      NCON1 = NCON+1
C NRAV - LINES AVAILABLE/LIMC-MAXIMUM FOR ONE VARIATE
      NRAV = MAXST/NS
```

```
      LIMC = NRAV - 7
      IF(LIMC.GT.NRMAX ) LIMC = NRMAX
C LEVEL 2 - READ SUBSET SPECIFICATION
   21 IF(V(10).GE.20.) V(10) = 0.
      CALL LDBS(SCON(1,NCON1),NCONB,MAXLEF,CN,ST,IT,NQ,TRT,NALT,IGO)
      IF(IGO.GT.0) GO TO 11
      ARAN = 5236.
C LEVEL 3 - READ SET OF VARIATES FOR DATA SWEEP
   31 IF(V(10).GE.30.) V(10) = 0.
      IPIN = MAXM
      M = 0
      WRITE(MED6,931)
      WRITE(MED6,935)
      CALL LGEN(U,NU,LU,NU,ST,IT,CN,NQ,NCL,MAXM,DMIN,DMAX,NQ,TMIN,TMAX,M
     1AXM,0,LIMC,IH,NP,MAXM,M,MAXM,1,NALT)
      IF(V(11).LT.0.5.AND.V(20).LT.0.5) GO TO 21
      IF(V(11).LT.0.5.AND.V(20).GT.0.5.AND.V(10).LT.0.5) V(10)= 31.
      V(19) = 0.
      BRAN = ARAN
C LEVEL 9 - READ DATA HANDLING INSTRUCTION
   91 IF(V(10).GT.90.) V(10) = 0.
      CALL LDHI(V(1),1,V(2),4,V(3),16,H,0,H,0,H,0,H,V(10),
     1 FORM(41),FORM,MED1,MED2,0,Q,NQ,NWARN,1,IGO)
      IF(IGO.GT.0) GO TO 31
C STANDARDISATION
      IF(V(3).LE.0.) NWARN = NWARN + 1
      IF(V(3).EQ.0.) V(3) = 1.
      IF(V(3).LT.0.) V(3) = 0.
      CALL LDHI(V(1),1,V(2),4,V(3),16,H,0,H,0,H,0,H,V(10),
     1 FORM(41),FORM,MED1,MED2,0,Q,NQ,NWARN,2,IGO)
      IF(IGO.GT.0) GO TO 91
      V(19) = V(19) + 1.
      V(10) = BRAN
      V(3) = V(3)*0.01
      CALL CKIND(D,IT,NQ,TRT,NALT,T,TMIN,TMAX,NP,M,TBTC,CX,KC,NS,TBTR,RX
     1,KR,NRMAX,RT,NRAV,SCON(1,NCON1),NCONB,SCON,NCON,NCL,U,NU)
      ARAN = V(10)
      V(10) = 0.
      WRITE(MED6,999)
      GO TO 91
  901 FORMAT (1H0,20X,46HSTATCAT TESTS OF 3 OR MORE INDEPENDENT SAMPLES)
  924 FORMAT (1H0,9X,55HTHIS PROGRAM IS DESIGNED TO TEST THREE OR MORE S
     1AMPLES.,45X,11H**WARNING**              /10X,74HWHILE IT IS NO
     2T INCORRECT FOR TWO SAMPLES PROGRAM ST2IND IS MORE POWERFUL.)
  931 FORMAT (1H1,10X,30HSET OF VARIATES FOR DATA SWEEP/)
  935 FORMAT (4HONO.,9X,30HTRANS DATA        NUMBER OF,7X,5HLOWER,6X,
     15HCLASS,7X,5HUPPER/5H CODE,8X,68H-FORM COLUMN           CLASSES USED
     2 CLASS LIMIT  INTERVAL   CLASS LIMIT )
  999 FORMAT (36H1ANALYSIS COMPLETED - READ NEW INPUT)
      END


      SUBROUTINE CKIND(X,IT,NQ,TRT,NALT,D,DMIN,DMAX,NP,M,TRTC,CX,KC,NALT
     1C,TRTR,RX,KR,NRMAX,RT,NRAV,SCON,NCON,SACON,NACON,NCL,U,NU)
C CKIND  (SEE  6.2 ) EXECUTIVE    TESTS SEVERAL INDEPENDENT SAMPLES
      DIMENSION X(NQ),IT(NQ),TRT(NALT),D(M),DMIN(M),DMAX(M),NP(M),NCL(M)
      DIMENSION TRTC(NALTC),CX(NALTC),KC(NALTC)
      DIMENSION TRTR(NRMAX),RX(NRMAX),KR(NRMAX)
      DIMENSION RT(NALTC,NRAV),SCON(5,NCON),SACON(5,NACON),TTR(19),U(NU)
      COMMON /STCT/MED1,MED2,MED3,MED4,MED5,MED6,MED13,Q,V(20),TT(30)
      DATA B4/4H    /
  997 FORMAT(1H+,50X,39H IS EMPTY - SAMPLE SET CANNOT BE TESTED)
  998 FORMAT (62HONO PURELY RATIO SCALE TESTS AVAILABLE - INTERVAL USED
```

```
       1INSTEAD)
   999 FORMAT(16H1DATA BANK TITLE,14X,1H-,4X,10A4/17H SAMPLE SET TITLE,13
      1X,1H-,4X,10A4/23H DATA BANK SUBSET TITLE,7X,1H-,4X,10A4/
      21H ,A4,22H OF DATA COLUMN NUMBER,I4,12H SHORT TITLE,4X,A4/
      311H FULL TITLE,19X,1H-,4X,A2,15A4,13H DATA SCALE - ,2A4,A1/
      4 10H0SAMPLE NO,I4,6H TITLE,10X,1H-,14X,A4)
C STARTING CONDITIONS
       V10 = V(10)
       V19 = V(19)
       LB = V(1)
       LC = V(2)
       LDB = LC-LC/5*5
       LD = LDB + 1
       JFIN = 0
C ESTABLISH CAPACITY FOR PARAMETRIC AND NON PARAMETRIC DATA
     1 JST = JFIN + 1
       NR = NRAV
     2 JFIN = JFIN + 1
       NR = NR - NCL(JFIN) - 7
     3 IF(NR) 5,4,4
     4 IF(JFIN-M)2,6,6
     5 JFIN = JFIN - 1
     6 KAP = JFIN-JST + 1
C CLEAR STORAGE ARRAY
       IF(V19.GT.1.5) GO TO 10
       V(10) = V10
       REWIND MED3
       J = 0
       DO 9 ICX = JST,JFIN
       N = NCL(ICX) + 5
       DO 7 J2 = 1,N
       J = J+1
       DO 7 I = 1,NALTC
     7 RT(I,J) = 0.
       DO 9 J2 = 1,2
       J = J+1
       DO 9 I = 1,NALTC
     9 RT(I,J) = Q
       V(6) = 0.
       V(7) = 1.
       V(8) = 1.
       V(9) = M
       READ(MED3)NX,NX,Y,(TT(I),I=1,10),(Y,I=1,6)
       DO 13 I = 1,NQ
    13 READ(MED3)TTR,TRT,NX,Y,Y
C READ DATA FOR TESTS
     8 CALL MEDIAT(M,NP,NP,M,D,X,NQ,SCON,NCON)
       IF(V(8).EQ.2.) GO TO 10
       CALL CLSAM(X,NQ,SACON,NACON,I,NALTC)
       IF(I.LE.0.OR.I.GT.NALTC) GO TO 8
       JBASE = 0
       JTR = JST
       DO 24 J = 1,KAP
       XR = D(JTR)
       IF(XR.EQ.Q) GO TO 23
       INDX = NP(JTR)-NP(JTR)/1000*1000
       CALL CLASIF   (XR,DMAX(JTR),DMIN(JTR),IT(INDX),NCL(JTR),JR)
       JR = JBASE + JR
       RT(I,JR) = RT(I,JR) + 1.
       JR = JBASE + NCL(JTR)
       RT(I,JR+1) = RT(I,JR+1) + 1.
       RT(I,JR+2) = RT(I,JR+2) + XR
       RT(I,JR+3) = RT(I,JR+3) +XR*XR
```

```
      RT(I,JR+4) = RT(I,JR+4) +XR*XR*XR
      RT(I,JR+5) = RT(I,JR+5) + XR*XR*XR*XR
      IF(RT(I,JR+6).EQ.Q.OR.RT(I,JR+6).GT.XR)RT(I,JR+6) = XR
      IF(RT(I,JR+7).EQ.Q.OR.RT(I,JR+7).LT.XR)RT(I,JR+7) = XR
   23 JBASE = JBASE + NCL(JTR) + 7
   24 JTR = JTR + 1
      GO TO 8
   10 REWIND MED3
C OUTPUT PHASE
      INOW = NQ + 1
      JBASE = 1
      DO 400 IC = 1,KAP
      V(1) = LB
      V(10) = 0.
      ICX = JST+IC-1
      NC = NP(ICX) - NP(ICX)/1000*1000
      NTR= NP(ICX)/1000
      IF(LDB.EQ.0) LD = IT(NC)
      IF(LDB.NE.0) LD = LDB+ 1
      V(7) = IT(NC)
      IF(INOW.LE.NC) GO TO 11
      REWIND MED3
      INOW = 0
      READ(MED3)NX,NX,(Y,I=1,17)
   11 IF(INOW.EQ.NC) GO TO 12
      INOW = INOW + 1
      READ(MED3)TTR,TRT,NX,Y,Y
      GO TO 11
   12 NALTR = NCL(ICX)
      JX = DMIN(ICX)-1.499
      DO 14 K = 1,NALTR
      J = K + JX
      IF(J.LE.NALT) CALL COPYA(TRTR(K),TRT(J))
   14 IF(J.GT.NALT) CALL COPYA(TRTR(K),B4)
      JR = JBASE + NALTR
      IF(ISW(LB,LC,LD,8).LE.0.) GO TO 101
C SUMMARY TABULATION
      WRITE(MED2,999)TT,U(NTR),NC,TTR
      V(8) = 6.
      CALL TAB2W(RT(1,JBASE),NALTC,NALTR,TRTC,TRTC,TRTR,2,IT(NC),0.,DMIN
     1(ICX),0.,DMAX(ICX),V,MED2)
  101 MIS = 0
      DO 150 I = 1,NALTC
      V(8) = 60.
      NLIN = 0
      DO 102 J = 1,NALTR
      JQ = J+JBASE - 1
      IF(RT(I,JQ).GT.0.)NLIN = J
  102 RX(J) = RT(I,JQ)
      VX = NLIN
      IF(RT(I,JR).EQ.0.) MIS = MIS + 1
      IF(RT(I,JR).EQ.0.) WRITE(MED2,999)TT,U(NTR),NC,TTR,B4,I,TRTC(I)
      IF(RT(I,JR).EQ.0.) WRITE(MED2,997)
      IF(RT(I,JR).EQ.0.) GO TO 150
      IF(ISW(LB,LC,LD,6).LE.0.) GO TO 120
      IF(V(8).GE.(43.-VX)) WRITE(MED2,999)TT,U(NTR),NC,TTR,B4,I,TRTC(I)
      IF(V(8).GE.(43.-VX)) V(8) = 8.
C FREQUENCY TABULATION
      CALL DCFT(RT(I,JR),DMAX(ICX),DMIN(ICX),RX,TRTR,NALTR,V,MED2)
  120 IF(ISW(LB,LC,LD,7).LE.0.) GO TO 130
      IF(V(8).GE.23.) WRITE(MED2,999)TT,U(NTR),NC,TTR,B4,I,TRTC(I)
      IF(V(8).GE.23.) V(8) = 8.
C DESCRIPTIVE STATISTICS
```

```
      CALL DCDS(DMAX(ICX),DMIN(ICX),RX,TRTR,NALTR,RT(I,JR),RT(I,JR+1),RT
     1(I,JR+2),RT(I,JR+3),RT(I,JR+4),RT(I,JR+5),RT(I,JR+6),V,MED2)
  130 IF(ISW(LB,LC,LD,6).LE.0.) GO TO 150
      IF(V(8).GE.(40.-VX)) WRITE(MED2,999)TT,U(NTR),NC,TTR,B4,I,TRTC(I)
      IF(V(8).GE.(40.-VX)) V(8) = 8.
  132 V(1) = 3.
      V(2) = 1.
C BAR CHART
      CALL DCBC(DMAX(ICX),DMIN(ICX),RX,TRTR,NALTR,V,MED2)
  140 IF(LD.LE.3) GO TO 145
      IF(V(8).GE.(54.-VX)) WRITE(MED2,999)TT,U(NTR),NC,TTR,B4,I,TRTC(I)
      IF(V(8).GE.(54.-VX)) V(8) = 8.
C CUMULATIVE FREQUENCY CURVES
      V(2) = 6.
      CALL DCBC (DMAX(ICX),DMIN(ICX),RX,TRTR,NALTR,V,MED2)
  145 V(1) = LB
      V(2) = LC
  150 CONTINUE
  200 IF(MIS.GT.0.OR.V(3).LE.0.) GO TO 390
  320 IF(ISW(LB,LC,LD,2)) 330,321,322
C NOMINAL DATA LEVEL TESTS
  321 V(1) = -1.
      CALL CHISQD(RT(1,JBASE),NALTC,NALTR,CX,RX,KC,KR,2,NX,TRTC,TRTR,0.,
     1DMIN(ICX),0.,DMAX(ICX),V,MED2)
      IF(V(11).GT.V(3)) GO TO 330
  322 WRITE(MED2,999)TT,U(NTR),NC,TTR
      V(1) = 3.
      CALL CHIKEN(2,NX)
      CALL CHISQD(RT(1,JBASE),NALTC,NALTR,CX,RX,KC,KR,2,NX,TRTC,TRTR,0.,
     1DMIN(ICX),0.,DMAX(ICX),V,MED2)
  330 IF(ISW(LB,LC,LD,3)) 340,331,332
C ORDINAL DATA LEVEL TESTS
  331 V(1) = -1.
      CALL MEDEX (RT(1,JBASE),NALTC,NALTR,CX,RX,KC,KR,2,NX,TRTC,TRTR,0.,
     1DMIN(ICX),0.,DMAX(ICX),V,MED2)
      IF(V(11).GT.V(3)) GO TO 333
  332 WRITE(MED2,999)TT,U(NTR),NC,TTR
      V(1) = 3.
      CALL CHIKEN(3,NX)
      CALL MEDEX (RT(1,JBASE),NALTC,NALTR,CX,RX,KC,KR,2,NX,TRTC,TRTR,0.,
     1DMIN(ICX),0.,DMAX(ICX),V,MED2)
  333 IF(ISW(LB,LC,LD,3)) 340,334,335
  334 V(1) = -1.
      CALL KW1W(RT(1,JBASE),TRTC,NALTC,NALTR,V,MED2)
      IF(V(11).GT.V(3)) GO TO 336
  335 WRITE(MED2,999)TT,U(NTR),NC,TTR
      V(1) = 3.
      CALL CHIKEN(3,NX)
      CALL KW1W(RT(1,JBASE),TRTC,NALTC,NALTR,V,MED2)
  336 IF(ISW(LB,LC,LD,3)) 340,337,338
  337 V(1) = -1.
      CALL QAREX (RT(1,JBASE),NALTC,NALTR,CX,KC,KR,2,NX,TRTC,TRTR,0.,DMI
     1N(ICX),0.,DMAX(ICX),V,MED2)
      IF(V(11).GT.V(3)) GO TO 340
  338 WRITE(MED2,999)TT,U(NTR),NC,TTR
      V(1) = 3.
      CALL CHIKEN(3,NX)
      CALL QAREX (RT(1,JBASE),NALTC,NALTR,CX,KC,KR,2,NX,TRTC,TRTR,0.,DMI
     1N(ICX),0.,DMAX(ICX),V,MED2)
C INTERVAL DATA LEVEL TESTS
  340 IF(ISW(LB,LC,LD,4)) 350,351,352
  350 IF(ISW(LB,LC,LD,5)) 390,351,352
  351 V(1) = -1.
```

```
      CALL PAR1W(RT(1,JR),TRTC,NALTC,V,0.,0.,2,MED2)
      IF(V(11).GT.V(3).AND.V(13).GT.V(3)) GO TO 390
  352 WRITE(MED2,999)TT,U(NTB),NC,TTR
      V(1) = 3.
      IF(LD.NE.4.AND.LD.NE.7) CALL CHIKEN(4,NX)
      IF(LD.EQ.5.OR.LD.EQ.7) WRITE(MED2,998)
      CALL PAR1W(RT(1,JR),TRTC,NALTC,V,0.,0.,2,MED2)
  390 ICX = ICX + 1
  400 JBASE = JBASE + NALTR + 7
      IF(JFIN.LT.M) GO TO 1
      REWIND MED3
      V(19) = V19
      IF(JST.NE.1) V(19) = 0.
      RETURN
      END


      SUBROUTINE MEDEX (RT,NC,NR,CX,RX,KC,KR,ITC,ITR,TRTC,TRTR,DMINC,DMI
     1NR,DMAXC,DMAXR,V,MED2)
C MEDEX   (SEE  6.1 ) STATISTICAL MEDIAN TEST (EXTENDED)
C MEDIAN TEST (CENTRAL DIFFERENCE)
      DIMENSION RT(NC,NR),RX(NR),KR(NR),CX(NC),KC(NC)
      DIMENSION TRTR(NR),TRTC(NC)
      DIMENSION V(20)
   95 FORMAT(30H0EXTENSION OF THE MEDIAN TEST.)
   96 FORMAT(13H0MEDIAN TEST.)
      TT=0.
      DO 3 I=1,NC
      CX(I)=0.
      KC(I)=I
      DO 3 J=1,NR
      CX(I)=CX(I)+RT(I,J)
    3 TT=TT+RT(I,J)
      TSF=0.
      DO 6 J=1,NR
      KR(J)=2
      RX(J)=0.
      DO 1 I=1,NC
    1 RX(J)=RX(J)+RT(I,J)
      IF(RX(J).GT.0.) NXR = J
      TSF=TSF+RX(J)/TT
      IF(TSF.GT..5)GO TO 6
      KR(J)=1
    6 CONTINUE
      NSR=2
      NSC=NC
      VX=V(1)
      IF(V(1).GT.1.)GO TO 5
      V(1)=0.-1.
      CALL CHISQ (RT,NC,NR,KC,KR,NSC,NSR,NUND5,NUND1,V,MED2)
      V(1)=VX
      IF(V(1).LT.0.)RETURN
      IF(V(1).EQ.0..AND.V(2).LT.V(11))RETURN
    5 V(1)=2.
      IF(NC.EQ.2) WRITE(MED2,96)
      IF(NC.NE.2) WRITE(MED2,95)
      CALL DICOLA (TRTC,TRTR,KC,KR,NC,NR,ITC,ITR,DMINC,DMINR,DMAXC,DMAXR
     1,NC,NXR,MED2)
      CALL CHISQ (RT,NC,NR,KC,KR,NSC,NSR,NUND5,NUND1,V,MED2)
      V(1)=VX
      RETURN
      END
```

```
      SUBROUTINE QAREX (RT,NC,NR,CX,KC,KR,ITC,ITR,TRTC,TRTR,DMINC,DMINR,
     1DMAXC,DMAXR,V,MED2)
C QAREX   (SEE  6.1 ) STATISTICAL QUARTILE TEST (EXTENDED)
      DIMENSION RT(NC,NR),KR(NR),CX(NC),KC(NC)
      DIMENSION TRTR(NR),TRTC(NC),V(20)
      TT = 0.
      MR = 0
      DO 4 I = 1,NC
      CX(I) = 0.
      DO 3 J = 1,NR
      IF(RT(I,J).GT.0..AND.J.GT.MR) MR = J
    3 CX(I) = CX(I) + RT(I,J)
    4 TT = TT + CX(I)
      DO 6 I = 1,NC
      TSF = 0.
      DO 5 J = 1,NR
      TSF = TSF + RT(I,J) + RT(I,J)
      KC(I) = J
      IF(TSF.GT.CX(I)) GO TO 6
    5 CONTINUE
    6 CONTINUE
      TSF = 0.
      A = TT*0.25
      B = TT*0.75
      LIM = 2*NR - 1
      DO 10 K = 1,LIM
      DO  8 I = 1,NC
      J = K + KC(I) - NR
      IF(J.LT.1.OR.J.GT.NR) GO TO 8
      TSF = TSF + RT(I,J)
    8 CONTINUE
      IF(TSF.GT.A.AND.TSF.LT.B) GO TO 10
      DO 9 I = 1,NC
      J = K + KC(I) - NR
      IF(J.LT.1.OR.J.GT.NR) GO TO 9
      RT(I,J) = 0. - RT(I,J)
    9 CONTINUE
   10 CONTINUE
      IF(V(1).LT.2.) GO TO 13
      IF(NC.EQ.2) WRITE(MED2,96)
      IF(NC.NE.2) WRITE(MED2,95)
      WRITE(MED2,97)(I,I=1,NC)
      DO 12 J = 1,NR
      KR(J) = 0
      IF(J.GT.MR) GO TO 12
      DO 11 I = 1,NC
      KC(I) = 0
      IF(RT(I,J).LT.0.)KC(I) = 2
      IF(RT(I,J).GT.0.)KC(I) = 1
   11 CONTINUE
      WRITE(MED2,98)KC
      CALL PRTCLS(DMAXR,DMINR,J,TRTR(J),NR,ITR,MED2)
      IF(J.EQ.J/50*50) WRITE(MED2,91)
   12 CONTINUE
   13 DO 15 I = 1,NC
      A = 0.
      B = 0.
      CX(I) = RT(I,1)
      KC(I) = I
      DO 14 J = 1,NR
      IF(RT(I,J).LT.0.) B = B - RT(I,J)
      IF(RT(I,J).GT.0.) A = A + RT(I,J)
   14 CONTINUE
```

```
      RT(I,1) = A
   15 RT(I,2) = B
      IF(NR-NR/50*50+NC.GT.30) WRITE(MED2,91)
      IF(V(1).GE.2.)CALL DICOLA(TRTC,TRTR,KC,KR,NC,NR,ITC,ITR,DMINC,DMIN
     1R,DMAXC,DMAXR,NC,0,MED2)
      KR(1) = 1
      KR(2) = 2
      NSR=2
      NSC=NC
      VX=V(1)
      IF(V(1).GT.1.)GO TO 16
      V(1)=0.-1.
      CALL CHISQ (RT,NC, 2,KC,KR,NSC,NSR,NUND5,NUND1,V,MED2)
      V(1)=VX
      IF(V(1).LT.0.) GO TO 20
      IF(V(1).EQ.0..AND.V(2).LT.V(11))   GO TO 20
   16 V(1)=2.
      IF(NC.EQ.2) WRITE(MED2,96)
      IF(NC.NE.2) WRITE(MED2,95)
      CALL CHISQ (RT,NC, 2,KC,KR,NSC,NSR,NUND5,NUND1,V,MED2)
      V(1)=VX
   20 DO 21 I = 1,NC
      RT(I,2) = RT(I,1) + RT(I,2)
      RT(I,1) = CX(I)
      DO 21 J = 1,NR
      IF(RT(I,J).LT.0.)RT(I,J) = 0. - RT(I,J)
      IF(J.NE.2) RT(I,2) = RT(I,2) - RT(I,J)
   21 CONTINUE
      RETURN
   91 FORMAT(1H1)
   95 FORMAT(31HOEXTENSION OF THE QUARTILE TEST)
   96 FORMAT (14HOQUARTILE TEST)
   97 FORMAT (22HOALLOCATION OF CLASSES/14HOSAMPLE NUMBER,6X,10(4X,I4,2X
     1)/13H NO     CLASS)
   98 FORMAT (21X,10(4X,I4,2X))
      END


      SUBROUTINE KW1W(RT,TS,NC,NR,V,MED2)
C KW1W      (SEE   6.2 ) STATISTICAL KRUSKAL-WALLIS 1-WAY ANOVAR BY RANK
      DIMENSION RT(NC,NR),V(20),TS(NC)
   73 FORMAT(11X,6HSAMPLE,I3,1X,A4,13H  MEAN RANK =,F10.4,5H FOR ,F6.0,7
     1HENTRIES)
   72 FORMAT (43HOALL READINGS TIED - NO CONCLUSION POSSIBLE)
   71 FORMAT(53HOKRUSKAL-WALLIS ONE-WAY ANALYSIS OF VARIANCE BY RANKS//)
   70 FORMAT(34HOH. (DISTRIBUTED AS CHI-SQUARED)= ,F12.4,6H WITH ,F6.0,2
     10H DEGREES OF FREEDOM./26H ASSOCIATED PROBABILITY = ,F12.6)
      XNB=0.
      TNI=0.
      TRI=0.
      IF(V(1).GT.1.5)WRITE(MED2,71)
      DO 10 I=1,NC
      RNI=0.
      RTI=0.
      XNA=0.
      DO 20 J=1,NR
      XRT=0.
      DO 30 IX=1,NC
   30 XRT=XRT+RT(IX,J)
      XNB=XNA+(XRT+1.)/2.
      XNA=XNA+XRT
      RNI=RNI+RT(I,J)
   20 RTI=RTI+RT(I,J)*XNB
```

```
      TNI=TNI+RNI
      TRI=RTI*RTI/RNI+TRI
      RTI=RTI/RNI
      IF(V(1).LT.1.5)GO TO 10
      WRITE(MED2,73)I,TS(I),RTI,RNI
   10 CONTINUE
      TTT=0.
      DO 40 J=1,NR
      XNB=0.
      DO 50 I=1,NC
   50 XNB=XNB+RT(I,J)
   40 TTT=TTT+XNB*(XNB+1.)*(XNB-1.)
      TTT=TTT/(TNI*(TNI+1.)*(TNI-1.))
      XNA = NC - 1
      TRI=12.*TRI/(TNI*(TNI+1.))-3.*(TNI+1.)
      IF(TTT.EQ.1.) GO TO 61
      TRI=TRI/(1.-TTT)
      CHI=PRBF(XNA,10000.,TRI/XNA)
      IF(V(1).LT.0.)GO TO 60
      IF(V(1).EQ.0..AND.V(2).LT.CHI)GO TO 60
      IF(V(1).LT.1.5) WRITE(MED2,71)
      WRITE(MED2,70)TRI,XNA,CHI
   60 V(11)=CHI
      V(12)=TRI
      V(13)=XNA
      RETURN
   61 IF(V(1).LE.1.5.AND.V(1).GT.0.5) WRITE(MED2,71)
      IF(V(1).GT.0.5) WRITE(MED2,72)
      V(11) = 1.1
      RETURN
      END


      SUBROUTINE PAR1W(DT,TTS,NC,V,DMAX,DMIN,ITX,MED2)
C PAR1W  (SEE  6.2 ) STATISTICAL 1-WAY ANOVAR + BARTLETT TEST
C 1 WAY ANALYSIS OF VARIANCE  + BARTLETT TEST FOR HOMOSCEDASTICITY
      DIMENSION DT(NC,5),TTS(NC),V(20),T(5)
      DO 1 I = 1,5
    1 T(I) = 0.
      DFS = -1.
      REC = 0.
      SSQ = 0.
      SLG = 0.
      PR  = 1.1
      PBT = 1.1
      VR  = 0.
      BT  = 0.
C CUMULATE SUMS OF SQUARES ETC
      DO 2 I = 1,NC
      IF(DT(I,1).EQ.0.) GO TO 2
      DFS = DFS + 1.
      X = DT(I,2)*DT(I,2)/DT(I,1)
      SSQ = SSQ + X
      REC = REC + 1./DT(I,1)
      IF(DT(I,1).LE.1.) GO TO 2
      DTX=(DT(I,3)-X)/    (DT(I,1)-1.)
      IF(DTX.GT.0.) SLG=SLG+(DT(I,1)-1.)*ALOG(DTX)
      DO 3 L = 1,5
    3 T(L) = T(L)+DT(I,L)
    2 CONTINUE
C CALCULATE ANALYSIS OF VARIANCE
      CF = T(2)*T(2)/T(1)
      SSQ = SSQ - CF
```

```
      D = T(3) - CF
      E = T(1) -1.
      A = D - SSQ
      SSM = SSQ/DFS
      B = E - DFS
      C = A/B
      IF(C.GT.0..AND.SSM.GT.0.) VR = SSM/C
      IF(C.GT.0..AND.SSM.GE.0.) PR = PRBF(DFS,B,VR)
      IF(C.EQ.0..AND.SSM.GT.0.)PR = 0.
C CALCULATE BARTLETTS TEST
      BT = 1.+(REC-1./B)/(3.*DFS)
      IF(C.GT.0.) BT=1./BT*(B*ALOG(C)-SLG)
      IF(C.GT.0.) BT = 1. + (REC-1./B)/(3.*DFS)
      IF(C.GT.0.) PBT= PRBF(B,1000.,BT*BT)
      V(11) = PR
      V(12) = PR
      V(13) = PBT
      V(14) = VR
      IF(V(11).GT.V(13))V(11)=V(13)
      IF(V(1).LT.0..OR.V(11).LT.V(3).AND.V(1).EQ.0.) RETURN
C BASIC OUTPUT
      WRITE(MED2,93)SSQ,DFS,SSM,VR,PR,A,B,C,D,E
      WRITE(MED2,94)
      IF(PBT.GE.0.) WRITE(MED2,95) BT,PBT
      IF(PBT.LT.0.) WRITE(MED2,96)
      IF(V(1).LT.0.5) RETURN
C DETAILED OUTPUT
      DO 5 I = 1,NC
      X=DT(I,1)
      Y=DT(I,2)
      Z = 0.
      IF(X.LE.1.)GO TO 4
      Y = DT(I,2)/X
      Z = SQRT(ABS((DT(I,3)-Y*Y*X)/(X-1.)))
    4 WRITE(MED2,97)I,TTS(I)
    5 WRITE(MED2,98)X,Y,Z
      IF(T(1).LE.1) RETURN
      Y = T(2)/T(1)
      Z = SQRT(ABS(D/E))
      WRITE(MED2,99)
      WRITE(MED2,98)T(1),Y,Z
      RETURN
   93 FORMAT(21H0ANALYSIS OF VARIANCE/93H0SOURCE OF VARIATION TOTAL SUM
     1OF SQUARES D.F. MEAN SUM OF SQUARES VARIANCE RATIO PROBABILITY/16H
     2 BETWEEN SAMPLES,13X,F12.4,F5.0,8X,F12.4,3X,2F12.4/16H   WITHIN SAM
     3PLES,13X,F12.4,F5.0,8X,F12.4/7H TOTAL ,22X,F12.4,F5.0)
   94 FORMAT(54H0BARTLETT CHI-SQUARED TEST FOR HOMOGENEITY OF VARIANCE/)
   95 FORMAT(12H0CHI-SQUARED,F20.4/12H0PROBABILITY ,F22.6)
   96 FORMAT(20H CANNOT BE EMPLOYED.)
   97 FORMAT(8H0SAMPLE ,I4,2H (,A4,2H) )
   98 FORMAT(1H+,24X,F8.0,20H READINGS  -   MEAN =,F12.4,7H S.D. =,F12.4)
   99 FORMAT(12H0ALL SAMPLES)
      END
```

6.3 PROGRAM ST2REL - TEST TWO RELATED SAMPLES

6.3.1 Purpose

This program compares two related samples of data drawn from a STATCAT data bank. It will use the tests appropriate to the lower of the two data levels, unless it is over-ridden to make tests at all levels up to that level, or at or up to a specified level. The level of statistical significance below which results are not reported may be varied and more or less detailed descriptive statistics may be produced. The variates tested may be transformed by any of the transforms given in Figure 3.72, but delayed values of variates may not be used. The class definitions assumed by the data description segment will be used, unless over-ridden by revised specifications.

Figure 6.31a contains system flow-charts for the main program ST2REL and the executive subroutine C2REL. Figure 6.31b contains simplified flow-charts for the subroutines KENTAU (Kendall's "tau" coefficient - 6.3.5), SIGN (Sign Test - 6.3.5) and WILCOX (Wilcoxon's Test - 6.3.5). Figure 6.31c contains system flow-charts for the subroutines COREG (Correlation and Regression for two related variates - 6.3.6) and TFREL (Student's "t" test for the differences of two related samples, and for the difference of standard deviations of two related samples.)

6.3.2 Input Data

Item	Level	Format	Function	SEE
1	0	A	File control	3.2
2	2	E	Subset specification	3.6
3	4	F	Column Variate Specification) (At least one each	3.7
4	5	F	Row Variate Specification) (no delays	3.7
5	9	H	Data handling instruction	Below + 3.8

Data Handling Instruction

Card Layout - Data Handling Instruction - ST2REL
ABCCCDDDEEEEEEEEEFFFFFFFFGGGGGGGGGGGGGGGGHHHHHHHHHHHHHHHHH.....etc

Columns	Item	Function	See
1	A	Output control index	6.1
2	B	Analysis control index	Below
3 - 5	C	Significance level for reporting (per cent)	6.1
6 - 8	D	Not used	-
9 - 16	E	Not used	-
17 - 24	F	Not used	-
25 - 40	G	Not used	-
41 - 80	H	Comment (NOT KEPT)	-

B - Analysis Control Index
This index controls the level at which testing is carried out, and the conditions under which the results are printed.

ALTERNATIVES

B = 0,blank: Test at lower of row/column data level.
 (Default)   Print results if statistically significant.

B = 1   : Tests for NOMINAL level only (Chi-squared).
              Print results if statistically significant.

B = 2   : Tests for ORDINAL level only (Freidmann's
               Two-way analysis of variance by ranks)
               print results if statistically significant.

B = 3   : Tests for INTERVAL level(Two-way Analysis of
               variance, Bartlett's test for homogenity of
               variance) - print results if statistically
               significant.

B = 4   : Tests for RATIO level (as for INTERVAL) -
               print results if statistically significant.

B = 5   : Tests at lower of row/column level - print all results.

B = 6   : Tests at NOMINAL level - print all results.

B = 7   : Tests at ORDINAL level - print all results.

B = 8   : Tests at INTERVAL level - print all results.

B = 9   : Tests at RATIO level - print all results.

DEFAULT value = 0 (0, blank or non-numeric character)

6.3.3 Input Example

Figure 6.32 is a summary of the input structure for two runs of STREL using first the default values, then the full output available. The two related variates compared are the efficiency of the operator as assessed by himself, and by the observer. All entries are included in the subset, and no transforms or modifications of class definitions were used. The first data handling instruction employs the default values throughout, producing only the results of tests where these are statistically significant at a probability of 1 per cent. The second data handling instruction produces all test results, and full descriptive output. Figure 6.33 lists the input data cards required to produce the two runs described above.

6.3.4 Output Example

Figure 6.34 is a general summary of the output structure of this program indented according to the program structure. Figure 6.35 is a summary of the output corresponding to the specific example given in 6.3.3. The input checking information is essentially standard and is not therefore reproduced here. Figure 6.36 illustrates the statistically significant results produced by the first data handling instruction. These results are produced by the subroutines TPREL and COREG (6.3.7). When the program is run with the second data handling instruction, the system produces statistical descriptions of each class of the column variate, in terms of the row variate. The descriptions, being practically identical to those for independent samples, are not reproduced here. Similarly the test for NOMINAL level data - the chi-squared test for two related variates - is similar in appearance to that for several independent samples, and is also not shown, though it is discussed below (6.3.5). Figure 6.37 illustrates the results of the sign test, the Wilcoxon Matched-pairs signed-ranks test and Kendall's "tau" statistic, as produced by the second data handling instruction. These tests are discussed in 6.3.6. Notice that the system has printed a warning that these tests are not appropriate to this data level.

An examination of the test results will show that the mean value of the efficiency as estimated by the operator is significantly higher than that estimated by the observer. The most interesting result is that there is a significant negative correlation between the two estimates. This means, as the regression equations imply, that the higher is the operator's estimate of his efficiency, the lower is the observer's estimate. Although this may appear paradoxical, such results are by no means infrequent, and often suggest that different criteria are being used by different respondents.

6.3.5 Statistical Tests - NOMINAL Level

A - Chi-squared Test for Two Related Samples

This is a standard two-way chi-squared test, in which the rows and columns correspond to classes of the row and column variates. This test calculates the frequency in each cell of the two-way table that would be expected if the two marginal distributions were produced by chance, and estimates the probability of observing a distribution as different as that observed, if in fact there were no interaction between the variates. The test requires data on a NOMINAL or higher level, and is subject to the usual limitations of a chi-squared test (not more than one fifth of the cells with an expected value below 5, and no cell with an expected frequency less than one). If the value of chi-squared obtained is not reliable, the system will chose the smallest class of the variate on the higher data level and combine this with its neighbour, repeating the calculation of chi-squared. This process is repeated until either a reliable result is produced, or there are only two classes of this variate left. In the latter case, classes of the lower level variate are combined until the reliability conditions are met, or only two classes are left for each variate. The chi-squared test for the combined classes is carried out, with a warning if it is not reliable.

The chi-squared test works from a two-way frequency table. It is most efficient when the data are evenly distributed throughout the table, and is unable to work if all the data are in one class of row or column variate. Excessively uneven distributions will lead to significant differences being ignored, so the user should be prepared to re-define the class definition, if necessary, in such a way as to provide a more even spread of data through the classes.

REFERENCES : Siegel (Ch 9), Kendal and Stuart (Ch 31)

6.3.6 Statistical tests - ORDINAL Level

A - SIGN - Sign Test

The sign test requires data for which both the row and column variates are on at least an ordinal scale, with the same meanings to the classes. It is a test of central tendency, and draws a conclusion on the hypotheses that the mean of one sample is higher than, lower than, or different from that of the other. It operates by counting the number of pairs of data where the first is higher than the second, and vice-versa, and provides estimates of the probability of such a result occurring by chance. The associated probability is calculated by the subroutine by a conversion from the binary to the normal distribution, with a correction for continuity.

Figure 6.37 contains the output for a Sign test.

REFERENCES : Siegel (Ch 5), Kendall and Stuart (Ch 32)

B - **WILCOX** - Wilcoxon's Matched-pairs Signed-ranks Test

Wilcoxon's matched-pairs signed-ranks test is a test of central difference, and requires data on at least an ordinal scale. In addition, it requires that the magnitude as well as the direction of the difference between the two variates for each entry should be known. (The classes must be known to be at equal intervals - on both scales).

In general, the Wilcoxon test operates by ranking the differences without regard to their direction, then applying the sign of the difference to the rank and summing. On the basis of the number of entries, the probability of observing as extreme a value is then calculated. In the subroutine WILCOX, the size of the difference is derived from the distance of the cell from the diagonal of the frequency table, and its sign from the position above or below the diagonal, and the resultant statistic is evaluated using a normalising transform.

Figure 6.37 also contains the output for a Wilcoxon test.

REFERENCES : Siegel (Ch 5), Hollander and Wolfe (Ch 3)
Kendall and Stuart (Ch 31)

C - **KENTAU** - Kendall's Tau Statistic

Kendall's "Tau" coefficient measures the extent to which row and column variates are assocciated. It requires that the data for each variate be on at least an ORDINAL scale. In principle, it is calculated by placing the entries in rank order for one variate, then measuring the extent to which the other variate is also ranked. This is done by comparing the ranks of all pairs of items on the other variate, and noting the proportion of these which are in the same order as the first variate. The STATCAT system uses an adaptation of the test for large samples, in which the comparisons are carried out on a cell-by-cell basis for a two-way frequency table, all data in a given cell being considered tied.

The statistical significance of Kendall's "Tau" statistic can be derived, for samples of at least ten data, by a normalising transform. For ten or fewer data, tables should be consulted.

Kendall's "Tau" cannot be calculated if all the data for one variate fall into one class, or of there are no data - in these cases an error message will be produced.

Figure 6.37 also contains the output of a Kendall tau statistic

REFERENCES : Siegel (Ch 9), Hollander and Wolfe (Ch 8)
Kendall (1955)

6.3.7 Statistical Tests - INTERVAL Level

A - TFREL - Student's "t" test for means of related samples

This test is similar to the classic Student's "t" test for two independent samples, except that it operates on the differences between pairs of data. This test requires that both variates be on at least an INTERVAL level, and that the differences between pairs pairs of data should be normally distributed.

It operates by calculating the mean of the differences between data, and the corresponding variance, then deriving an estimate for the probability of observing a sample mean as large as or larger than that observed forthe given number of data, with the given sample variance. The statistical significance, as with the classic "t" test, will depend on whether the test is being used as a 'one-tailed' or a 'two-tailed' test, and the direction of the expected difference. The STATCAT system does not require that the class definitions should be the same for row and column variates, because it works directly using sums of powers and cross-products for the original data.

Figure 6.36 contains an example of the output of a "t" test for related samples.

REFERENCES : Dixon and Massey (Ch 9)

B - TFREL - Student's "t" test for variances of related samples

This test is an adaptation of the classic Student's "t" test, as applied to two independent samples, to the variances of two related samples. It requires that the data should be on at least INTERVAL scales for both variates, that the sampling distribution of variances should be more or less normal - a fairly robust assumption - and that the distributions of the two variates should also be approximately normal. If the latter condition is violated, the product-moment correlation coefficient "r" calculated may be inaccurate. (this assumption is probably more sensitive than the first, but is generally acceptable.)

The test operates, in principle, by calculating the difference of variances, and dividing by the estimated standard error of the difference, corrected for the correlation of the variates. The statistic resulting from these operations is distributed like Student's 't', and may be tested in the same way.

The STATCAT system does not require that the class definitions should be the same for row and column variates, because it works directly using sums of powers and cross-products for the original data.

Figure 6.36 contains, among other items, a "t" test for the variance of related samples.

C - COREG - Product-moment Correlation Coefficient

This coefficient is the classic correlation coefficient. It requires data for both row and column variates that are on at least an INTERVAL scale. The measure of statistical significance for this coefficient assumes that the data are also normally distributed on each axis. If this is not so, then the associated probability will be incorrect.

The measure is derived, in principle, by correcting each scale to zero mean and unit standard deviation, then forming the cross-product of the variates. The measure is tested by applying a transform to normality, and calculating the associated probability of the resultant normalised variate. In practice, the statistic is derived directly from the successive moments and cross product of the sample data.

The statistic cannot be calculated when one or other variate has no variability (is a constant). The STATCAT system will identify this state, and print a warning message.

Figure 6.36 contains, among other items, a correlation coefficient

REFERENCES : Dixon and Massey (Ch 11), Kendall and Stuart (Ch 26)
Spiegel (Ch 14)

D - COREG - Regression Equations

The two regression equations given here are the least-squares best-fit regression equations for the row variate in terms of the column variate, and vice versa. These two equations are not equivalent - substituting in one equation will not produce the same row/column pairs as for the other, except for the arithmetic means of the two samples, which correspond to the crossing point of the two regression lines. The cosine of the angle between the regression lines corresponds to the correlation coefficient. If the correlation coefficient is one, then the correlation accounts for all the variation present, there will be no remaining deviation, and all points will lie on the common regression line. If the correlation coefficient is zero, then the regression lines will be at right angles, and there will be no variation accounted for by the regression line. (This is not to say that there is no relation between the two variates - if, for example, the underlying relation were that the sum of the squares of the variates was constant, then there would be no linear correlation, but (because all points would lie on a circle centred at the origin) there would be a very high non-linear correlation.

Correlation and regression are discussed in more detail in 7.2, in the context of multiple linear regression.

Figure 6.36 also contains the two regression equations.

REFERENCES : Dixon and Massey (Ch 11), Kendall and Stuart (ch26)
Spiegel (Ch 14), Draper and Smith.

Figure 6.31a - System Flow-Charts - ST2REL and C2REL

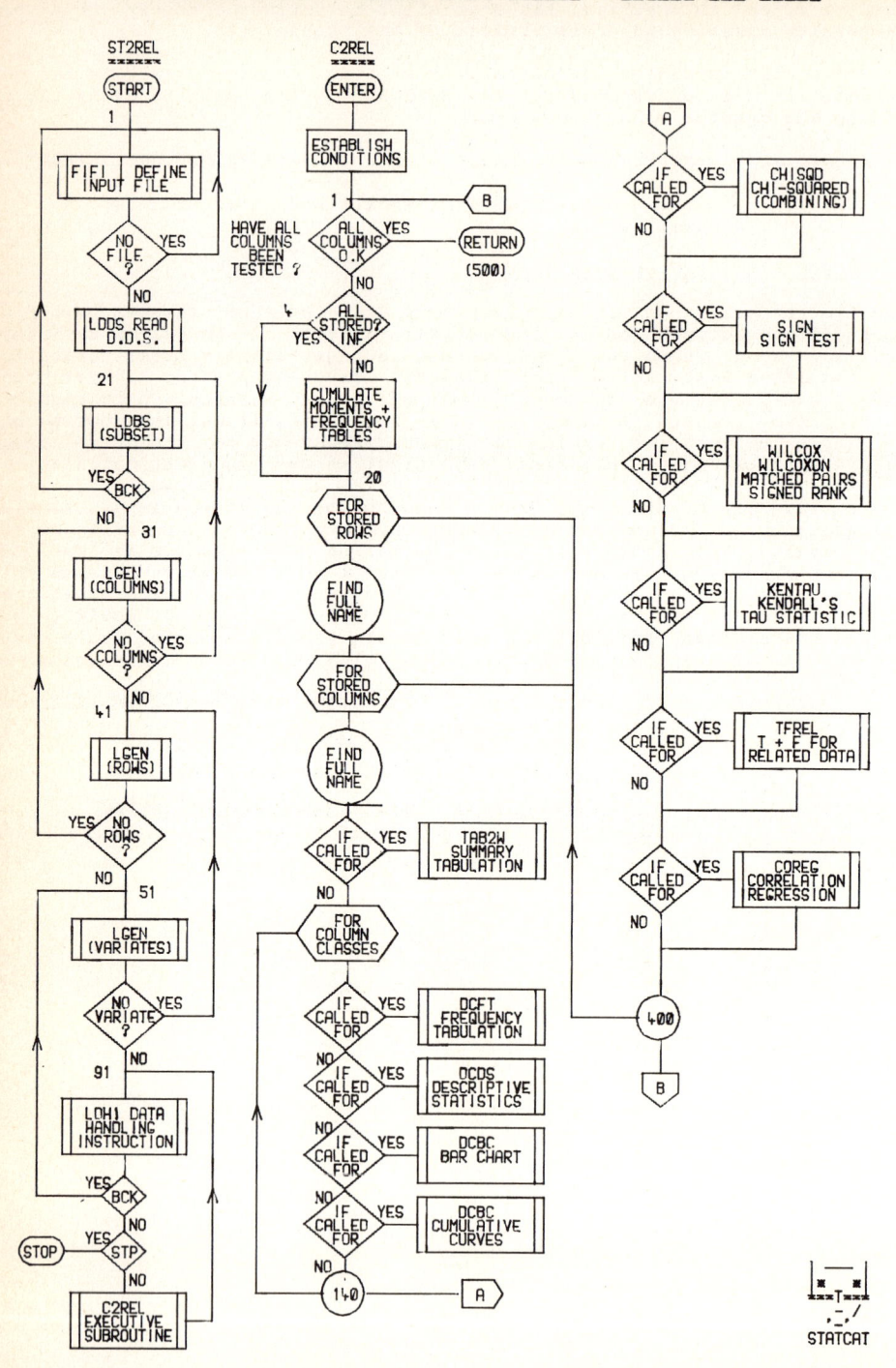

283

Figure 6.31b - System Flow-Charts - KENTAU and WILCOX

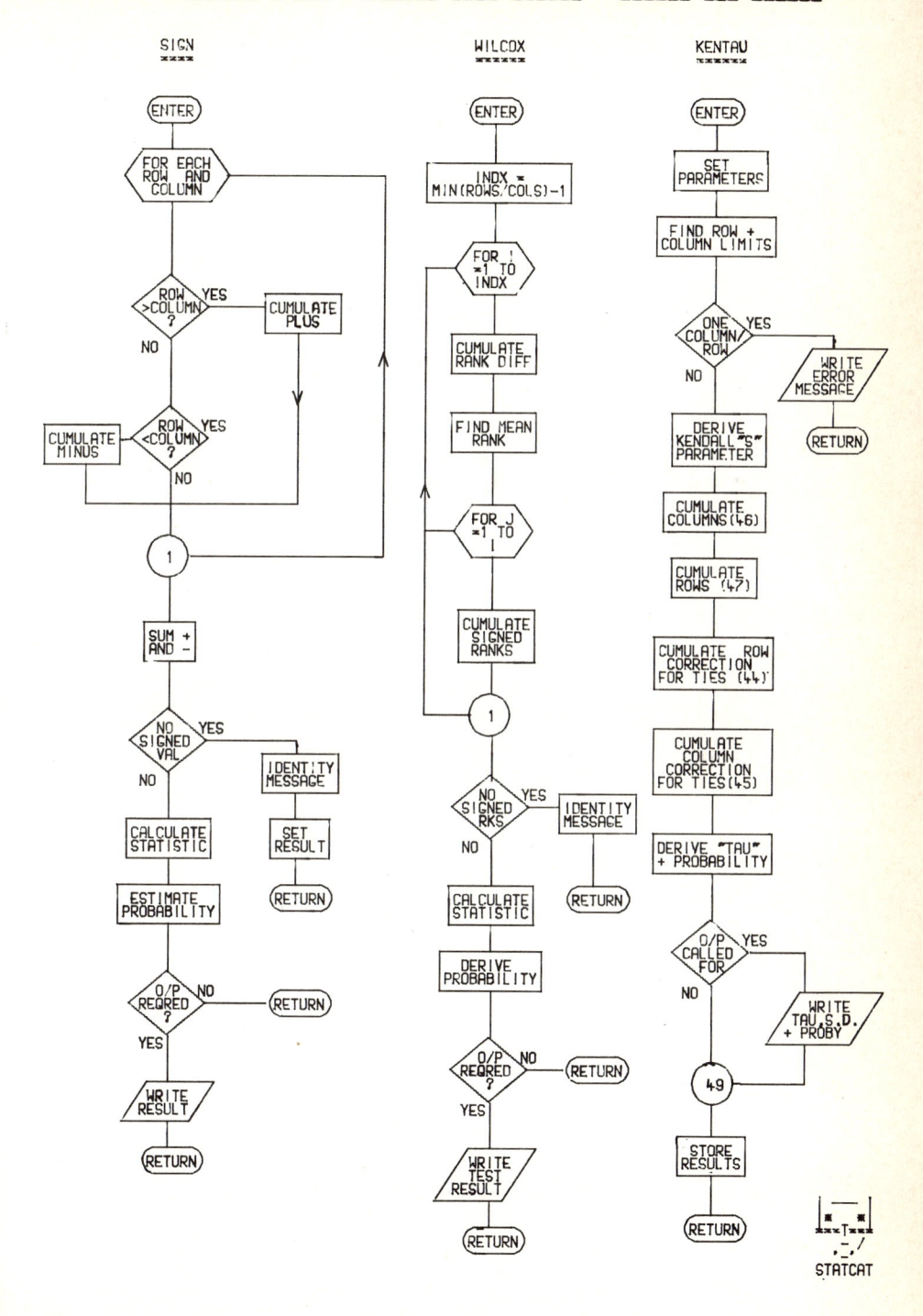

SIGN

```
ENTER
  │
  ▼
FOR EACH ROW AND COLUMN
  │
  ▼
ROW > COLUMN ? ──YES──► CUMULATE PLUS
  │ NO                      │
  ▼                         │
ROW < COLUMN ? ──YES──► CUMULATE MINUS
  │ NO
  ▼
 (1)
  │
  ▼
SUM + AND -
  │
  ▼
NO SIGNED VAL ──YES──► IDENTITY MESSAGE ──► SET RESULT ──► RETURN
  │ NO
  ▼
CALCULATE STATISTIC
  │
  ▼
ESTIMATE PROBABILITY
  │
  ▼
O/P REQRED ? ──NO──► RETURN
  │ YES
  ▼
WRITE RESULT
  │
  ▼
RETURN
```

WILCOX

```
ENTER
  │
  ▼
INDX = MIN(ROWS,COLS)-1
  │
  ▼
FOR I = 1 TO INDX
  │
  ▼
CUMULATE RANK DIFF
  │
  ▼
FIND MEAN RANK
  │
  ▼
FOR J = 1 TO I
  │
  ▼
CUMULATE SIGNED RANKS
  │
  ▼
 (1)
  │
  ▼
NO SIGNED RKS ──YES──► IDENTITY MESSAGE ──► RETURN
  │ NO
  ▼
CALCULATE STATISTIC
  │
  ▼
DERIVE PROBABILITY
  │
  ▼
O/P REQRED ? ──NO──► RETURN
  │ YES
  ▼
WRITE TEST RESULT
  │
  ▼
RETURN
```

KENTAU

```
ENTER
  │
  ▼
SET PARAMETERS
  │
  ▼
FIND ROW + COLUMN LIMITS
  │
  ▼
ONE COLUMN/ROW ──YES──► WRITE ERROR MESSAGE ──► RETURN
  │ NO
  ▼
DERIVE KENDALL "S" PARAMETER
  │
  ▼
CUMULATE COLUMNS (46)
  │
  ▼
CUMULATE ROWS (47)
  │
  ▼
CUMULATE ROW CORRECTION FOR TIES (44)
  │
  ▼
CUMULATE COLUMN CORRECTION FOR TIES (45)
  │
  ▼
DERIVE "TAU" + PROBABILITY
  │
  ▼
O/P CALLED FOR ──YES──► WRITE TAU, S.D. + PROBY
  │ NO                      │
  ▼◄─────────────────────── ┘
 (49)
  │
  ▼
STORE RESULTS
  │
  ▼
RETURN
```

STATCAT

Figure 6.31c - System Flow-Charts - COREG and TFREL

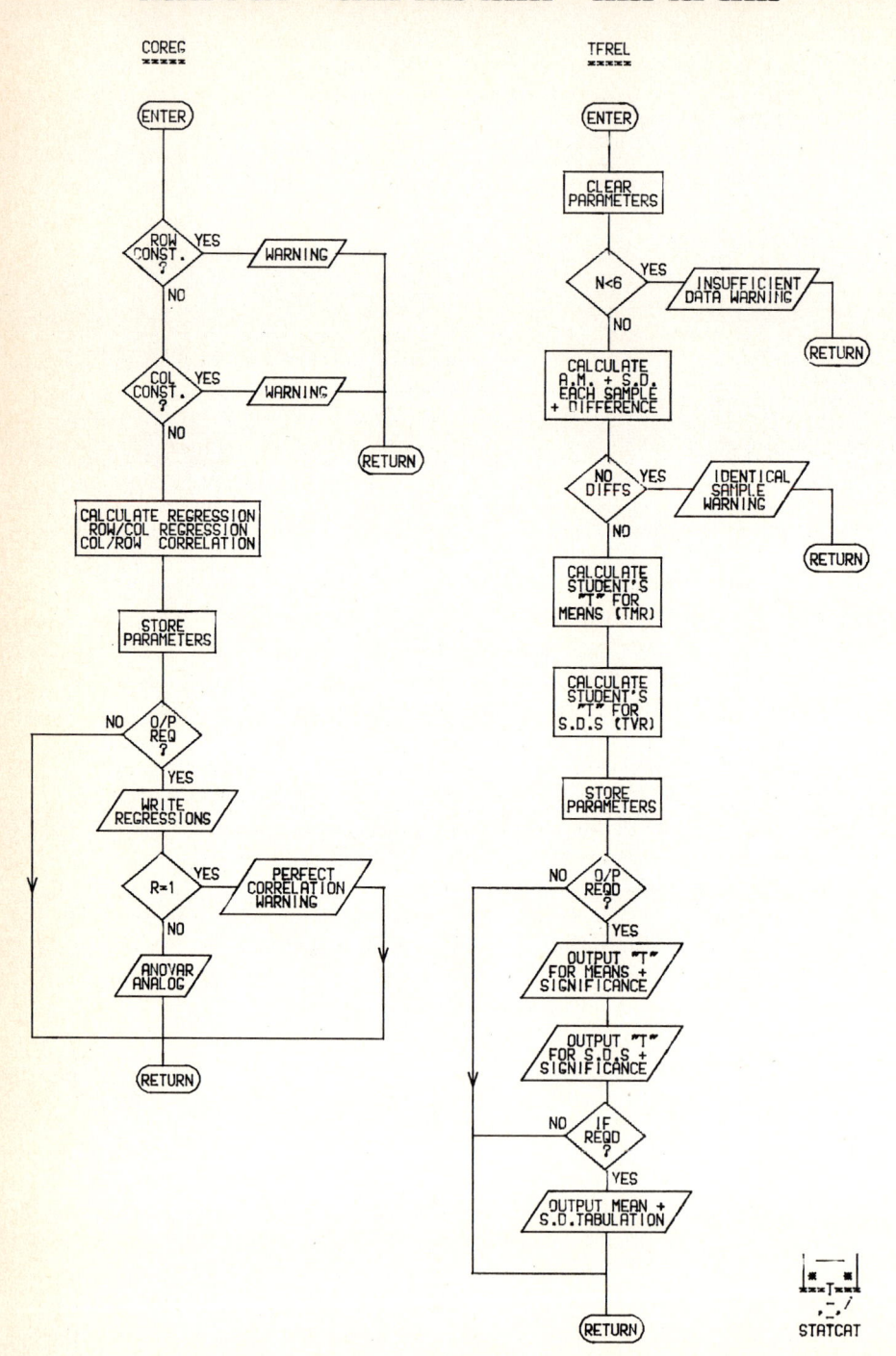

285

Figure 6.32 - ST2REL - Input Structure

```
            Level
  0   1   2   3   4   5   6   7   8   9
FILE CONTROL CARD
    SUBSET SPECIFICATION
        COLUMN SPECIFICATION
            ROW SPECIFICATION
                DATA HANDLING INSTRUCTION
                DATA HANDLING INSTRUCTION
                STOP
```

Figure 6.33 - ST2REL - Input Example

```
---------1---------2---------3---------4---------5---------6---------7--
**ST2RELDEMO                              DEMONSTRATION STATCAT DATA BANK
ALL DATA                                  ALL DATA ARE INCLUDED
END OF SUBSET SPECIFICATION               NO CONDITIONS SPECIFIED
VAL.EFOB
END OF COLUMN SPECIFICATION
VAL.EFOP
END OF ROW SPECIFICATION
GO                      DEFAULT VALUES    SIG RESULTS ONLY AT DATA LEVEL
89                      MAXIMUM OUTPUT    ALL TESTS AND DESCR STATISTICS
STOP
---------1---------2---------3---------4---------5---------6---------7--
```

Figure 6.34 - ST2REL - Output Structure

```
For each     ) : File Control Record
output file  )   File Parameters
                 Data Description
                 For each) : Subset Input Record
                 Subset  )   For each) Variate Input Record
                 Specifn )   Set of  ) For each) Input Record
                             Columns ) Set of  ) For each)  See
                                       Rows      Column/ )  Left
For each) <Cross-tabulation>                     Row pair
Column/ )  For Each)<FrequencyTable>
Row pair   Column  )<Descriptive Statistics>
           Class    <Frequency Curves/Bar Chart>

           NOMINAL   <Chi-squared>
           ORDINAL   <Sign Test>
                     <Wilcoxon Matched-pairs Signed-ranks Test>
                     <Kendall's "tau" statistic >
           INTERVAL) <Student's "t" or "t-like" test + Snedecor's
           /RATIO  ) < "F" test for related samples>
                     <Correlation and regression formulae>
```

Carated(<>) items are optional.

Figure 6.35 - ST2REL - Output Example Page-by-Page listing

Page	Contents	Origin
1- 3	File Control Record	FIFI
	Program Title	ST2REL
	File Parameters	LDAP
	Data Description record	LDDS
4	Subset record	LDBS/LSET
5	Column Variates Record	LGEN
6	Row Variates record	LGEN
	Data Handling Instruction	LDHI
7	Differences in A.M. and S.D.	TFREL
	Correlation and Regression	COREG
8	Data Handling Instruction	LDHI
9-18	Column Class Descriptions	DCBC,DCFT,DCDS
19-20	Chi-squared test for independence	CHISQD
21	Sign test	SIGN
	Wilcoxon test	WILCOX
	Kendall's Tau coefficient	KENTAU
22	Differences in A.M. and S.D.	TFREL
	Correlation and Regression	COREG
23	Data Handling Instruction (STOP)	LDHI

Figure 6.36 - ST2REL - Significant results - First run

```
            STATCAT DATA BANK - DEMONSTRATION STATCAT DATA BANK
             DATA BANK SUBSET -  ALL TESTS AND DESCR STATISTICS

COLUMNS = VAL. OF EFOB (COL. 14.) =       EFFICIENCY RATING BY OBSERVER               INTERVAL
   ROWS = VAL. OF EFOP (COL. 13.) =       EFFICIENCY RATING BY OPERATOR               INTERVAL

FOR DIFFERENCE OF MEANS OF RELATED SAMPLES

           STUDENTS T =     4.7526 WITH    63. DEGREES OF FREEDOM

           PROBABILITY THAT MEAN OF ROWS IS GREATER THAN MEAN OF COLUMNS = 0.000024
           PROBABILITY THAT MEAN OF ROWS IS LESS THAN MEAN OF COLUMNS = 0.999976
           PROBABILITY THAT MEAN OF ROWS IS EQUAL TO MEAN OF COLUMNS = 0.000048

FOR DIFFERENCE OF S.D.S OF RELATED SAMPLES

           STUDENTS T =    -5.0998 WITH    62. DEGREES OF FREEDOM

           PROBABILITY THAT S.D. OF ROWS IS GREATER THAN S.D. OF COLUMNS = 0.999982
           PROBABILITY THAT S.D. OF ROWS IS LESS THAN S.D. OF COLUMNS = 0.000018
           PROBABILITY THAT S.D. OF ROWS IS EQUAL TO S.D. OF COLUMNS = 0.000037

           VARIATE  ARITHMETIC MEAN   STANDARD DEVIATION
           COLUMN       79.646750        14.553200
           ROW          56.725983        29.221832
           DIFFERENCE   22.920807        37.024521

FOR RELATED SAMPLES - CORRELATION AND REGRESSION

CORRELATION COEFFICIENT =  -0.358727

REGRESSION EQUATIONS

          COLUMN =  114.0958 +   -0.7205 ROW
             ROW =   89.7811 +   -0.1787 COLUMN

ANALYSIS OF VARIANCE ANALOGUE

SOURCE OF VARIANCE  TOTAL SUM OF SQUARES DF  MEAN SUM OF SQUARES  VARIANCE RATIO  PROBABILITY

REGRESSION               6922.82813   1.       6922.82813         9.15683         0.0038900
RESIDUAL                46873.79688  62.        756.02881
TOTAL                   53796.62500  63.
```

Figure 6.37 - ST2REL - Sign, Wilcoxon and Kendall tau

```
            STATCAT DATA BANK - DEMONSTRATION STATCAT DATA BANK
             DATA BANK SUBSET -  ALL TESTS AND DESCR STATISTICS

COLUMNS = VAL. OF EFOB (COL. 14.) =       EFFICIENCY RATING BY OBSERVER               INTERVAL
   ROWS = VAL. OF EFOP (COL. 13.) =       EFFICIENCY RATING BY OPERATOR               INTERVAL

DATA USED ARE ON AN INTERVAL SCALE THEY SHOULD BE ON AN ORDINAL SCALE     SIGNIFICANCE MAY BE REDUCED    **WARNING**

SIGN TEST FOR MATCHED PAIRS

TESTS CENTRAL DIFFERENCE OF RELATED ROW AND COLUMN VARIATES

NORMALISED Z = -174.619583         20. PLUS AND     43. MINUS SIGNS

PROBABILITY THAT ROW IS GREATER THAN COLUMN =    0.0
   PROBABILITY THAT ROW IS LESS THAN COLUMN =    1.000000
   PROBABILITY THAT ROW IS EQUAL TO COLUMN =     0.0

 IF LESS THAN 25 PAIRS CONSULT SIEGEL TABLE D P250

DATA USED ARE ON AN INTERVAL SCALE THEY SHOULD BE ON AN ORDINAL SCALE     SIGNIFICANCE MAY BE REDUCED    **WARNING**

WILCOXON MATCHED PAIRS SIGNED-RANKS TEST

TESTS CENTRAL DIFFERENCE OF RELATED ROW AND COLUMN VARIATES

NORMALISED Z =    -1.047454  U =   855.000000 NUMBER OF PAIRS =    63.

PROBABILITY THAT ROW IS GREATER THAN COLUMN =    0.147548
   PROBABILITY THAT ROW IS LESS THAN COLUMN =    0.852452
   PROBABILITY THAT ROW IS EQUAL TO COLUMN =     0.295095

 IF LESS THAN 25 PAIRS CONSULT SIEGEL TABLE G P254

DATA USED ARE ON AN INTERVAL SCALE THEY SHOULD BE ON AN ORDINAL SCALE     SIGNIFICANCE MAY BE REDUCED    **WARNING**

KENDALL TAU MEASURE OF RANK CORRELATION
TAU =       -0.3672  S.D. OF TAU =     0.0988  ASSOCIATED PROBABILITY =   0.000458
```

```
C MASTER ST2REL - TESTS OF TWO RELATED SAMPLES (PAIRS OF DATA COLUMNS)
C SUBROUTINES AND FUNCTIONS REQUIRED
C NAME              TYPE            COMMENT
C AN      (SEE  3.1 )  SERVICE       ALPHA - TO NUMERIC VALUE
C CH      (SEE 11.6 )  SERVICE       CHOOSES TEST/DESCRIPTION REQUIRED
C CHIKEN  (SEE 11.9 )  SERVICE       WARNS OF MISMATCHED DATA LEVEL
C CHISQ   (SEE 11.5 )  STATISTICAL   BASIC CHI-SQUARED CALCULATION
C CHISQD  (SEE  6.1 )  STATISTICAL   SELF-STABILISED CHI-SQUARED
C CLASIF  (SEE 11.7 )  SERVICE       CLASSIFIES DATA ITEM
C CLSAM   (SEE  3.5 )  SERVICE       ALLOTS ENTRY TO SAMPLE/SUBSET
C COMPA   (SEE  3.1 )  SERVICE       COMPARES ALPHAMERIC VALUES
C COPYA   (SEE  3.1 )  SERVICE       COPIES ALPHAMERIC VALUE
C COREG   (SEE  6.3 )  STATISTICAL   SINGLE CORRELATION/REGRESSION
C C2REL   (SEE  6.3 )  EXECUTIVE     TESTS TWO RELATED SAMPLES
C DCBC    (SEE  5.2 )  STATISTICAL   CONSTRUCTS BAR-CHARTS
C DCDS    (SEE  5.2 )  STATISTICAL   DESCRIPTIVE STATISTICS
C DCFT    (SEE  5.2 )  STATISTICAL   FREQUENCY TABULATION
C DCPS    (SEE  5.2 )  STATISTICAL   MOMENT(PARAMETRIC) STATISTICS
C DICOLA  (SEE 11.5 )  STATISTICAL   DESCRIBES ROW/COLUMN COMBINATION
C FIFI    (SEE  3.2 )  SYSTEM        ALLOCATES PERIPHERALS
C FITIT   (SEE 11.9 )  SERVICE       FINDS COLUMN TITLE + DESCRIPTION
C GAUS    (SEE 11.8 )  STATISTICAL   FINDS ASS. PROB. OF N VALUE
C IBL     (SEE  3.1 )  SERVICE       DETECTS BLANK,END AND STOP CARDS
C ICH     (SEE  3.1 )  SERVICE       IDENTIFIES ALPHAMERIC CODES
C KENTAU  (SEE  6.3 )  STATISTICAL   KENDALL TAU - LARGE SAMPLES
C LDAP    (SEE  3.3 )  SYSTEM        LOADS/CHECKS DATA BANK PARAMETERS
C LDBS    (SEE  3.6 )  SYSTEM        LOADS SUBSET DEFINITION
C LDDS    (SEE  3.4 )  SYSTEM        LOADS DATA DESCRIPTION SEGMENT
C LDHI    (SEE  3.8 )  SYSTEM        LOADS/CHECKS DATA HANDLING INSTN
C LGEN    (SEE  3.7 )  SYSTEM        LOADS GENERALISED VARIATES
C LSET    (SEE  3.5 )  SYSTEM        LOADS DEFINING CONDITIONS
C MEDIAT  (SEE  3.7 )  SERVICE       FETCHES NEXT VARIATE SET
C NEXY    (SEE  6.3 )  SERVICE       FINDS NEXT ARRAY COORDS
C PRBF    (SEE 11.8 )  STATISTICAL   FINDS PROBABILITY OF F-RATIO
C PRTCLS  (SEE 11.7 )  SERVICE       PRINTS CLASS NAME/LIMITS
C REDROW  (SEE 11.5 )  STATISTICAL   CHOOSES ROW/COLUMN FOR COMBINATIONS
C SIGN    (SEE  6.3 )  STATISTICAL   SIGN TEST
C TAB2W   (SEE  6.4 )  STATISTICAL   TABULATES WITH VARIATE NAMES ETC
C TFREL   (SEE  6.3 )  STATISTICAL   T AND F TESTS - RELATED SAMPLES
C TRANS   (SEE  3.7 )  SERVICE       CARRIES OUT REQUIRED TRANSFORM
C WILCOX  (SEE  6.3 )  STATISTICAL   WILCOXON TEST
C IF NQMAX = MAX NO OF DATA COLUMNS IS INCREASED INCREASE CN DATA ALSO
C DIMENSION D(NQMAX),DMAX(NQMAX),DMIN(NQMAX),IT(NQMAX),ST(NQMAX)
C DIMENSION CN(NQMAX)
      NQMAX = 100
      DIMENSION D(100),DMAX(100),DMIN(100),IT(100),ST(100),CN(100)
      DATA   CN/4HCOL1,4HCOL2,4HCOL3,4HCOL4,4HCOL5,4HCOL6,4HCOL7,4HCOL8,4
     1HCOL9,4HCL10,4HCL11,4HCL12,4HCL13,4HCL14,4HCL15,4HCL16,4HCL17,4HC
     218,4HCL19,4HCL20,4HCL21,4HCL22,4HCL23,4HCL24,4HCL25,4HCL26,4HCL27,
     34HCL28,4HCL29,4HCL30,4HCL31,4HCL32,4HCL33,4HCL34,4HCL35,4HCL36,4HC
     4L37,4HCL38,4HCL39,4HCL40,4HCL41,4HCL42,4HCL43,4HCL44,4HCL45,4HCL46
     5,4HCL47,4HCL48,4HCL49,4HCL50,4HCL51,4HCL52,4HCL53,4HCL54,4HCL55,4H
     6CL56,4HCL57,4HCL58,4HCL59,4HCL60,4HCL61,4HCL62,4HCL63,4HCL64,4HCL6
     75,4HCL66,4HCL67,4HCL68,4HCL69,4HCL70,4HCL71,4HCL72,4HCL73,4HCL74,4
     8HCL75,4HCL76,4HCL77,4HCL78,4HCL79,4HCL80,4HCL81,4HCL82,4HCL83,4HCL
     984,4HCL85,4HCL86,4HCL87,4HCL88,4HCL89,4HCL90,4HCL91,4HCL92,4HCL93,
     94HCL94,4HCL95,4HCL96,4HCL97,4HCL98,4HCL99,4HC100/
C DIMENSION TRT(NALTMX) = MAXIMUM NUMBER OF CLASSES IN DATA BANK
      NALTMX = 50
      DIMENSION TRT(50)
C NCMAX = MAXIMUM NUMBER OF CLASSES ACTUALLY USED FOR COLUMNS
C DIMENSION CX(NCMAX),KC(NCMAX),TRTC(NCMAX)
      NCMAX = 100
```

```
      DIMENSION CX(100),KC(100),TRTC(100)
C NRMAX= MAXIMUM NUMBER OF CLASSES ACTUALLY USED FOR ROWS
C DIMENSION RX(NRMAX),KR(NRMAX),TRTR(NRMAX)
      NRMAX = 100
      DIMENSION RX(100),KR(100),TRTR(100)
C MAXST = MAXIMUM AVAILABLE WORKING STORAGE MUST CONTAIN ALL FREE
C STORAGE FOR FREQUENCY TABLES AND MOMENTS AT LEAST NCMAX*NRMAX+6
C BUT NEED ONLY BE MAXIMA ACTUALLY USED TOGETHER PLUS 6
C DIMENSION RT(MAXST *100)
      MAXST = 10
      DIMENSION RT(1000)
C MAXM = MAXIMUM NUMBER OF VARIATES ACCEPTED FOR ANY DATA SWEEP
C DIMENSION TMAX(MAXM),TMIN(MAXM),NCL(MAXM),NP(MAXM),T(MAXM)
      MAXM = 10
      DIMENSION TMAX(10),TMIN(10),NCL(10),NP(10),T(10)
C DIMENSION SCON(5,MAXDBC)= MAX NUMBER OF DATA BANK SUBSET CONDITIONS
      MAXDBC = 50
      DIMENSION SCON(5,50)
C THE FOLLOWING DIMENSIONS STORE NAMES AND LEVELS OF TRANSFORMS ETC.
      DIMENSION U(60),LU(60),FORM(50),IH(1)
      NU = 60
C TRANSFORMATION CODES
C UNITS                        BLOCKS
C      0 - 9   10 - 19   20 - 29   30 - 39   40 - 49   50 - 59
C      POWERS  TRIG      TRIG      STATIST   MATHS     TEST
C              RADIANS   DEGREES   TRANSF    FUNCTS    FUNCTIONS
C  0    -        -       H.MS        -         -       RM10
C  1    VAL.   SINR      SIND      PSNA      RECP      +/-1
C  2    SQAR   COSR      COSD      PSNB      SQRT      ADD1
C  3    CUBE   TANR      TAND      BINO      ABSV      SUB1
C  4    4PWR   ASIR      ASID      LG+1      SIGN      NOR1
C  5    5PWR   ACOR      ACOD      LOGE      INTG      +/-P
C  6    6PWR   ATAR      ATAD      LG10      FRAC      ADDP
C  7    7PWR   SINH      DTOR      AL10      EXPT      SUBP
C  8    8PWR   COSH      RTOD        -       PRES      NORP
C  9    9PWR   TANH      H.HH        -       NEG.      +100
      DATA U/4HVAL.,4HSQAR,4HCUBE,4H4PWR,4H5PWR,4H6PWR,4H7PWR,4H8PWR,4H9
     1PWR,4HVAL ,4HSINR,4HCOSR,4HTANR,4HASIR,4HACOR,4HATAR,4HSINH,4HCOSH
     2,4HTANH,4HH.MS,4HSIND,4HCOSD,4HTAND,4HASID,4HACOD,4HATAD,4HDTOR,4H
     3RTOD,4HH.HH,4H VAL,4HPSNA,4HPSNB,4HBINO,4HLG+1,4HLOGE,4HLG10,4HAL1
     40,4H    ,4H    ,4H    ,4HRECP,4HSQRT,4HABSV,4HSIGN,4HINTG,4HFRAC,4
     5HEXPT,4HPRES,4HNEG.,4HRM10,4H+/-1,4HADD1,4HSUB1,4HNOR1,4H+/-P,4HAD
     6DP,4HSUBP,4HNORP,4H+100,4H    /
      DATA LU/1,8*5,1,9*5,1,9*5,1,6*5,4*1,2*5,2*3,3*5,7*2,4*5,2*2/
      COMMON /STCT/MED1,MED2,MED3,MED4,MED5,MED6,MED13,Q,V(20),TT(30)
      DATA PROG/4H2REL/
      MED1 = -1
C LEVEL 0 - SETTING UP
    1 CALL COPYA(TT(1),PROG)
      CALL FIFI
      IF(MED3.GT.0) WRITE(MED2,901)
      CALL LDAP(MED2,MED3,V,TT,Q,NQ,NALT,NQMAX,NALTMX,IGO)
      IF(IGO.GT.0) GO TO 1
      LI = 18
      CALL LDDS(TRT,NALT,D,NQ,ST,NQ,IT,NQ,H,0,DMIN,DMAX,NQ,LI,1,Q,VX,
     1 0,MED2,MED3,0,IGO)
C LEVEL 2 - DEFINE SUBSET
   21 IF(V(10).GE.20.)V(10) = 0.
      CALL LDBS(SCON,NCON,MAXDBC,CN,ST,IT,NQ,TRT,NALT,IGO)
      IF(IGO.GT.0) GO TO 1
      ARAN = 5236.
C LEVEL 4 - READ COLUMN VARIATES
   41 IF(V(10).GE.40.) V(10) = 0.
```

```
      IFIN = MAXM - 1
      M = 0
      WRITE(MED6,941)
      WRITE(MED6,945)
  845 CALL LGEN(U,NU,LU,NU,ST,IT,CN,NQ,NCL,MAXM,DMIN,DMAX,NQ,TMIN,TMAX,M
     1AXM,0,NCMAX,IH,NP,MAXM,M,MAXM,1,NALT)
      IF(V(11).LT.0.5.AND.V(20).LT.0.5) GO TO 21
      IF(V(10).LT.0.5.AND.V(20).GT.0.5.AND.V(11).LT.0.5) V(10)= 42.
      K = M
C LEVEL 5 - READ ROW VARIATES
   51 IF(V(10).GT.50.) V(10) = 0.
      WRITE(MED6,951)
      WRITE(MED6,945)
      M = K
      J = 0
      IF(M.EQ.0) GO TO 53
      DO 52 I = 1,M
   52 IF(NCL(I).GT.J) J = NCL(I)
   53 IF(J.EQ.0) LIMR=NRMAX
      IF(J.NE.0) LIMR = MAXST*100/J
      IF(LIMR.GT.NRMAX) LIMR = NRMAX
      CALL LGEN(U,NU,LU,NU,ST,IT,CN,NQ,NCL,MAXM,DMIN,DMAX,NQ,TMIN,TMAX,M
     1AXM,0,LIMR,IH,NP,IFIN,M,MAXM,1,NALT)
      IF(V(11).LT.0.5.AND.V(20).LT.0.5) GO TO 41
      IF(V(10).LT.0.5.AND.V(20).GT.0.5.AND.V(11).LT.0.5) V(10)= 52.
      V(19) = 0.
      BRAN = ARAN
C LEVEL 9 - DATA HANDLING INSTRUCTION
   91 IF(V(10).GE.90.) V(10) = 0.
      CALL LDHI(V(1),1,V(2),2,V(3),16,H,0,H,0,H,0,H,V(10),
     1 TT(21),FORM,MED1,MED2,MED4,Q,NQ,NWARN,1,IGO)
      IF(IGO.GE.1) GO TO 51
      V(19) = V(19) + 1.
C IF V(19) IS GREATER THAN 1 THIS IS A SECOND RUN OF SAME DATA
C STANDARDISATION
      IF(V(3).LE.0.) NWARN = NWARN + 1
      IF(V(3).EQ.0.) V(3) = 1.
      IF(V(3).LT.0.) V(3) = 0.
      CALL LDHI(V(1),1,V(2),2,V(3),16,H,0,H,0,H,0,H,V(10),
     1 TT(21),FORM,MED1,MED2,MED4,Q,NQ,NWARN,2,IGO)
      IF(IGO.GE.1) GO TO 91
      V(10) = BRAN
      V(3) = V(3)*0.01
      CALL C2REL(D,IT,NQ,TRT,NALT,T,TMIN,TMAX,NP,M,TRTC,CX,KC,NCMAX,TRTR
     1,RX,KR,NRMAX,RT,MAXST,SCON,NCON,NCL,U,NU,K)
      ARAN = V(10)
      V(10) = 0.
      WRITE(MED6,999)
      GO TO 91
  901 FORMAT (1H0,20X,36HSTATCAT TESTS OF TWO RELATED SAMPLES  )
  941 FORMAT(30H1  COLUMN VARIABLES SELECTED         /)
  945 FORMAT (4H0NO..,9X,30HTRANS   DATA             NUMBER OF,7X,5HLOWER,6X,
     15HCLASS,7X,5HUPPER/5H CODE,8X,68H-FORM COLUMN            CLASSES USED
     2 CLASS LIMIT  INTERVAL   CLASS LIMIT)
  951 FORMAT(30H1   ROW VARIABLES SELECTED          /)
  999 FORMAT (36H1ANALYSIS COMPLETED - READ NEW INPUT)
      END


      SUBROUTINE C2REL(XX,IT,NQ,TRT,NALT,D,DMIN,DMAX,NP,M,TRTC,CX,KC,NCM
     1AX,TRTR,RX,KR,NRMAX,RT,MAXST,SCON,NCON,NCL,U,NU,K)
C C2REL   (SEE  6.3 ) EXECUTIVE   TESTS TWO RELATED SAMPLES
      DIMENSION TRTC(NCMAX),CX(NCMAX),KC(NCMAX),TTC(21)
```

```
      DIMENSION TRTR(NRMAX),RX(NRMAX),KR(NRMAX),TTR(21)
      DIMENSION RT(100,MAXST),SCON(5,NCON),U(NU)
      DIMENSION D(M),DMIN(M),DMAX(M),NP(M),NCL(M)
      DIMENSION XX(NQ),IT(NQ),TRT(NALT)
      DATA BL/4H    /
      COMMON /STCT/MED1,MED2,MED3,MED4,MED5,MED6,MED13,Q,V(20),TT(30)
C STARTING CONDITIONS
      LB = V(1)
      LC = V(2)
      SIG= V(3)
      V10 = V(10)
      V19 = V(19)
      INOW = 0
C START POINT
      IF = 0
      JF = 1
C NEXT DATA SWEEP - BEGIN CAPACITY CALCULATION
    1 REWIND MED3
      L = M-K
      CALL NEXY(IF,IF,K,JF,JF,1)
      IF(JF.GT.L) GO TO 500
      IR = 0
      JR = 1
      JBK = JF+K
      JBK = NCL(IF)*NCL(JBK)+6
      CALL NEXY(IR,IR,100,JR,JR,JBK)
      CALL NEXY(IF,IS,K,JF,JS,0)
      CALL NEXY(IF,IB,K,JF,JB,0)
C FIND NEXT PAIR OF VARIATES REQUIRED
    3 CALL NEXY(IB,IB,K,JB,JB,1)
      IF(JB.GT.L)  GO TO 4
C NO MORE PAIRS OF VARIATES TO BE TESTED
      JBK = JB+K
      JBK = NCL(IB)*NCL(JBK) + 6
      CALL NEXY(IR,IR,100,JR,JR,JBK)
      IF(JR.GT.MAXST)GO TO 4
C THIS PAIR OF VARIATES WOULD EXCEED THE STORAGE CAPACITY AVAILABLE
      CALL NEXY(IB,IF,K,JB,JF,0)
      GO TO 3
C DATA SWEEP (IF NECESSARY)
    4 INOW = 0
      V(10) = V10
C IF(V(19).GT.1) DATA ARE STILL IN CORE
      IF(V19.GT.1.5) GO TO 20
      V(6) = 0.
      V(7) = 1.
      V(8) = 1.
      V(9) = M
      DO 2 I = 1,100
      DO 2 J = 1,MAXST
    2 RT(I,J) = 0.
      READ(MED3)NX,NX,X,(TT(J),J=1,10),(X,J=1,6)
      DO 5 I = 1,NQ
    5 READ(MED3)(X,J=1,19),TRT,NX,X,X
   10 CALL MEDIAT(M,NP,NP,M,D,XX,NQ,SCON,NCON)
      IF(V(8).EQ.2.) GO TO 20
      IA = 0
      JA = 1
      DO 12 J1 = JS,JF
      J = J1+K
      Y = D(J)
      INDJ = NP(J) - NP(J)/1000*1000
      CALL CLASIF(D(J),DMAX(J),DMIN(J),IT(INDJ),NCL(J),JR)
```

```
      DO 12 I = 1,K
      IF(I.LT.IS.AND.J1.EQ.JS) GO TO 12
      IF(I.GT.IF.AND.J1.EQ.JF) GO TO 12
      X = D(I)
      JBK = 0
      IF(X.EQ.Q.OR.Y.EQ.Q)       GO TO 11
      INDI = NP(I) - NP(I)/1000*1000
      CALL CLASIF(D(I),DMAX(I),DMIN(I),IT(INDI),NCL(I),IC)
      JBK = IC + (JR-1)*NCL(I)
      CALL NEXY(IA,IA,100,JA,JA,JBK)
      RT(IA,JA) = RT(IA,JA) + 1.
   11 JBK = NCL(I)*NCL(J) -JBK
      IF(X.EQ.Q.OR.Y.EQ.Q)  JBK = NCL(I)*NCL(J) +6
      CALL NEXY(IA,IA,100,JA,JA,JBK)
      IF(X.EQ.Q.OR.Y.EQ.Q)       GO TO 12
      CALL NEXY(IA,IA,100,JA,JA,1)
      RT(IA,JA) = RT(IA,JA) + 1.
      CALL NEXY(IA,IA,100,JA,JA,1)
      RT(IA,JA) = RT(IA,JA) + X
      CALL NEXY(IA,IA,100,JA,JA,1)
      RT(IA,JA) = RT(IA,JA) + Y
      CALL NEXY(IA,IA,100,JA,JA,1)
      RT(IA,JA) = RT(IA,JA) + X*X
      CALL NEXY(IA,IA,100,JA,JA,1)
      RT(IA,JA) = RT(IA,JA) + Y*Y
      CALL NEXY(IA,IA,100,JA,JA,1)
      RT(IA,JA) = RT(IA,JA) + X*Y
   12 CONTINUE
      GO TO 10
   20 REWIND MED3
      INOW = 0
C ANALYSIS OF DATA
      IA = 1
      JA = 1
      DO 400 JX1= JS,JF
      JX = JX1+ K
      NR = NP(JX)/1000
      CALL COPYA(TTR(1),U(NR))
      NR = NP(JX) - NR*1000
      CALL FITIT(INOW,NR-1,NQ,NALT)
      INOW = INOW + 1
C IDENTIFICATION OF ROW TITLES
      NALTR = NCL(JX)
      ALTR = NALTR
      DMINR = DMIN(JX)
      DMAXR = DMAX(JX)
      ITR = IT(NR)
      TTR(3) = NR
      READ(MED3)TTR(2),(TTR(L),L=4,21),TRT,NX,X,X
      DO 8 L = 1,NALTR
      CALL COPYA(TRTR(L),BL)
    8 IF(L.LE.NALT) CALL COPYA(TRTR(L),TRT(L))
      DO 400 IX = 1,K
      IF(JX1.EQ.JS.AND.IX.LT.IS) GO TO 400
      IF(JX1.EQ.JF.AND.IX.GT.IF) GO TO 400
C IDENTIFICATION OF COLUMN TITLES
      NC = NP(IX)/1000
      CALL COPYA(TTC(1),U(NC))
      NC = NP(IX) - NC*1000
      CALL FITIT(INOW,NC-1,NQ,NALT)
      INOW = INOW+ 1
      NALTC = NCL(IX)
      ALTC = NALTC
```

```
      DMINC = DMIN(IX)
      DMAXC = DMAX(IX)
      TTC(3) = NC
      ITC = IT(NC)
      READ(MED3) TTC(2),(TTC(L),L=4,21),TRT,NX,X,X
      DO 9 L = 1,NALTC
      CALL COPYA(TRTC(L),BL)
    9 IF(L.LE.NALT) CALL COPYA(TRTC(L),TRT(L))
C DESCRIPTION OF DATA COLUMNS AS REQUIRED
      LD = ITC
      V(7) = LD
      V(8) = 6.
      V(2) = LC
      IF(ISW(LB,LC,LD,8).LE.0) GO TO 120
C TABULATION ONLY REQUIRED
      WRITE(MED2,999) (TT(I),I=1,10),(TT(I),I=21,30),TTC,TTR
      CALL TAB2W(RT(IA,JA),NALTC,NALTR,TRTC,TRTC,TRTR,ITC,ITR,DMINC,DMIN
     1R,DMAXC,DMAXR,V,MED2)
      GO TO 200
  120 IF(LB.LT.1.OR.LB.EQ.5) GO TO 200
C DESCRIPTIONS OF INDIVIDUAL CLASSES OF THE COLUMN VARIATE ONLY
      CALL NEXY(IA,IB,100,JA,JB,0)
      DO 140 JY = 1,NALTR
      V(1) = LB
      V(8) = 60.
      CALL NEXY(IB,IC,100,JB,JC,0)
      ALT = 0.
      DO 121 I = 1,NALTC
      IF(RT(IC,JC).GT.0.) ALT = I
  121 CALL NEXY(IC,IC,100,JC,JC,1)
      IF(ISW(LB,LC,LD,6).LE.0.OR.ALT.EQ.0.) GO TO 130
      V(8) = 6.
      WRITE(MED2,998) (TT(I),I=1,10),(TT(I),I=21,30),TTC,TTR
      CALL PRTCLS(DMAXR,DMINR,JY,TRTR(JY),NALTR,ITR,MED2)
      CALL DCFT(V(6),DMAXC,DMINC,RT(IB,JB),TRTC,NALTC,V,MED2)
      V(1) = 3.
      V(2) = 1.
      IF(V(8).LT.54.-ALT ) GO TO   123
      V(8) = 6.
      WRITE(MED2,998) (TT(I),I=1,10),(TT(I),I=21,30),TTC,TTR
      CALL PRTCLS(DMAXR,DMINR,JY,TRTR(JY),NALTR,ITR,MED2)
  123 CALL DCBC(DMAXC,DMINC,RT(IB,JB),TRTC,NALTC,V,MED2)
      IF(LD.LT.3) GO TO 130
      V(2) = 6.
      IF(V(8).LT.54.-ALT ) GO TO   124
      V(8) = 6.
      WRITE(MED2,998) (TT(I),I=1,10),(TT(I),I=21,30),TTC,TTR
      CALL PRTCLS(DMAXR,DMINR,JY,TRTR(JY),NALTR,ITR,MED2)
  124 CALL DCBC(DMAXC,DMINC,RT(IB,JB),TRTC,NALTC,V,MED2)
  130 V(1) = LB
      V(2) = LC
  140 CONTINUE
  200 CONTINUE
C TESTING OF DATA AS REQUIRED
      IF(SIG.LE.0.) GO TO 370
      V(3) = SIG
      V(8) = 60.
      LD = ITR
      IF(ITC.LT.ITR.AND.ITC.NE.5) LD = ITC
C NOMINAL SCALE TESTS
  320 IF(ISW(LB,LC,LD,2)) 330,321,322
  321 V(1) = -1
      CALL CHISQD(RT(IA,JA),NALTC,NALTR,CX,RX,KC,KR,ITC,ITR,TRTC,TRTR,DM
```

```
      1INC,DMINR,DMAXC,DMAXR,V,MED2)
       IF(V(11).GT.V(3)) GO TO 330
  322 V(1) = 2
       WRITE(MED2,999) (TT(I),I=1,10),(TT(I),I=21,30),TTC,TTR
       CALL CHIKEN(2,LD)
       CALL CHISQD(RT(IA,JA),NALTC,NALTR,CX,RX,KC,KR,ITC,ITR,TRTC,TRTR,DM
      1INC,DMINR,DMAXC,DMAXR,V,MED2)
C ORDINAL SCALE TESTS
  330 IF(ISW(LB,LC,LD,3)) 340,331,332
  331 V(1) = -1
       CALL SIGN(RT(IA,JA),NALTC,NALTR,V,MED2)
       IF(V(14).GT.V(3)*2.) GO TO 333
  332 V(1) = 2
       WRITE(MED2,999) (TT(I),I=1,10),(TT(I),I=21,30),TTC,TTR
       CALL CHIKEN(3,LD)
       CALL SIGN(RT(IA,JA),NALTC,NALTR,V,MED2)
       V(8) = 18.
  333 IF(ISW(LB,LC,LD,3)) 340,334,335
  334 V(1) = -1
       CALL WILCOX(RT(IA,JA),NALTC,NALTR,V,MED2)
       IF(V(14).GT.V(3)*2.) GO TO 336
  335 V(1) = 2
       IF(V(8).GE.45.)
      1WRITE(MED2,999) (TT(I),I=1,10),(TT(I),I=21,30),TTC,TTR
       IF(V(8).GE.45.) V(8) = 6.
       V(8) = V(8) + 12.
       CALL CHIKEN(3,LD)
       CALL WILCOX(RT(IA,JA),NALTC,NALTR,V,MED2)
  336 IF(ISW(LB,LC,LD,3)) 340,337,338
  337 V(1) = -1
       CALL KENTAU(RT(IA,JA),CX,RX,NALTC,NALTR,V,MED2)
       IF(V(11).GT.V(3)) GO TO 340
  338 V(1) = 2
       IF(V(8).GE.55.)
      1WRITE(MED2,999) (TT(I),I=1,10),(TT(I),I=21,30),TTC,TTR
       IF(V(8).GE.55.) V(8) = 6.
       CALL CHIKEN(3,LD)
       CALL KENTAU(RT(IA,JA),CX,RX,NALTC,NALTR,V,MED2)
C INTERVAL SCALE TESTS
  340 CALL NEXY(IA,IB,100,JA,JB,NALTC*NALTR)
       IF(ISW(LB,LC,LD,4)) 350,351,352
C RATIO SCALE TESTS
  350 IF(ISW(LB,LC,LD,5)) 360,351,352
  351 V(1) = -1.
       CALL TPREL(RT(IB,JB),V,MED2)
       IF(V(11)*(1.-V(11)).LT.V(3)*(1.-V(3))) GO TO 352
       CALL COREG(RT(IB,JB),V,MED2)
       IF(V(11).GT.V(3)) GO TO 360
  352 V(1) = 2.
  353 CONTINUE
       V(8) = 6.
       WRITE(MED2,999) (TT(I),I=1,10),(TT(I),I=21,30),TTC,TTR
       CALL CHIKEN(4,LD)
       CALL TPREL(RT(IB,JB),V,MED2)
       CALL COREG(RT(IB,JB),V,MED2)
  360 CONTINUE
       IF(V(8).EQ.60.) WRITE(MED2,999) (TT(I),I=1,10),(TT(I),I=21,30),TTC,T
      1TR
       WRITE(MED2,996)
  370 V(1) = LB
       V(2) = LC
       CALL NEXY(IA,IA,100,JA,JA,NALTC*NALTR+6)
  400 CONTINUE
```

```
      GO TO 1
C RESET CONTROLS - SET V(19) = 0 IF ANY DATA HAVE BEEN OVERWRITTEN
  500 V(1) = LB
      V(2) = LC
      V(19) = V19
      IF(IS.NE.1.OR.JS.NE.1)V(19) = 0.
      RETURN
  992 FORMAT (62HONO PURELY RATIO SCALE TESTS AVAILABLE - INTERVAL USED
     1INSTEAD)
  996 FORMAT(1H0,10X,20HEND OF TEST SEQUENCE         )
  998 FORMAT(1H1,15X,20HSTATCAT DATA BANK - ,10A4/16X,20H DATA BANK SUBS
     1ET - ,10A4/
     21H0,15X,10HVARIATE = ,A4,4H OF ,A4,6H (COL.,F4.0,4H ) = ,A2,17A4/
     312H FOR CLASS -    /
     41H0,21X,2(4H OF ,A4),6H (COL.,F4.0,4H) = ,A2,17A4)
  999 FORMAT(1H1,15X,20HSTATCAT DATA BANK - ,10A4/16X,20H DATA BANK SUBS
     1ET - ,10A4/
     211HOCOLUMNS = ,A4,4H OF ,A4,6H (COL.,F4.0,4H) = ,A2,17A4/
     311H0  ROWS  = ,A4,4H OF ,A4,6H (COL.,F4.0,4H) = ,A2,17A4/)
      END



      SUBROUTINE SIGN(RT,NC,NR,V,MED2)
C SIGN    (SEE  6.3 ) STATISTICAL SIGN TEST
      DIMENSION RT(NC,NR),V(20)
      XPL=0.
      XMI=0.
      DO 1 I=1,NC
      DO 1 J = 1,NR
      IF(I.LT.J) XPL = XPL + RT(I,J)
    1 IF(I.GT.J) XMI = XMI + RT(I,J)
      XT=XPL+XMI
      IF(XT.GT.0.5) GO TO 4
      WRITE(MED2,98)
      V(14) = 1.
      RETURN
    4 V(11)=XPL-XT*0.5
      IF(V(11).EQ.0.)GO TO 5
      IF(V(11).GT.0.)GO TO 2
      V(11)=V(11)+1.
    2 V(11)=V(11)-0.5
    5 V(11) = 2.*V(11) * SQRT(XT)
      V(12)=PRBF(1.,10000.,V(11)*V(11))*0.5
      IF(V(11).GT.0.) GO TO 3
      V(12)=1.-V(12)
    3 V(13)=1.-V(12)
      V(14)=V(12)*2.
      IF(V(14).GT.1.)V(14)=V(13)*2.
      IF(V(1).LT.0.) RETURN
      IF(V(1).LT.1..AND.V(14).GT.V(2)*2.) RETURN
      WRITE(MED2,99) V(11),XPL,XMI,V(13),V(12),V(14)
      RETURN
   98 FORMAT (30HOSIGN TEST FOR MATCHED PAIRS                          /
     160H0  NO MATCHED PAIRS UNEQUALLY RANKED - ROW IS SAME AS COLUMN/)
   99 FORMAT (30HOSIGN TEST FOR MATCHED PAIRS                          /
     160HOTESTS CENTRAL DIFFERENCE OF RELATED ROW AND COLUMN VARIATES  /
     215HONORMALISED Z =,F12.6,F12.0,9H PLUS AND,F6.0,12H MINUS SIGNS  /
     346HOPROBABILITY THAT ROW IS GREATER THAN COLUMN =,F12.6          /
     446H     PROBABILITY THAT ROW IS LESS THAN COLUMN =,F12.6          /
     546H     PROBABILITY THAT ROW IS EQUAL TO COLUMN =,F12.6          /
     652H0  IF LESS THAN 25 PAIRS CONSULT SIEGEL TABLE D P250          )
      END
```

```
      SUBROUTINE WILCOX(RT,NC,NR,V,MED2)
C WILCOX (SEE  6.3 ) STATISTICAL WILCOXON TEST
      DIMENSION RT(NC,NR)  ,V(20)
      TRPL=0.
      TRMI=0.
      XNA=0.
      INDX = NC - 1
      IF(NR.GT.NC)INDX = NR-1
      DO 1 I = 1,INDX
      XNB=0.
      L = INDX - I + 1
      DO 2 J=1,I
      IX=L+J
      IF(J.LE.NR.AND.IX.LE.NC) XNB = XNB + RT(IX,J)
    2 IF(J.LE.NC.AND.IX.LE.NR) XNB = XNB + RT(J,IX)
      XR=XNA+(XNB+1.)*0.5
      XNA=XNA+XNB
      DO 1 J=1,I
      IX=L+J
      IF(J.LE.NR.AND.IX.LE.NC) TRPL = TRPL + RT(IX,J)*XR
    1 IF(J.LE.NC.AND.IX.LE.NR) TRMI = TRMI + RT(J,IX)*XR
      IF(XNA.GT.0.5) GO TO 5
      WRITE(MED2,98)
      V(14) = 1.
      RETURN
    5 TR=TRPL
      V(11)=(TR-XNA*(XNA+1.)*.25)/SQRT(XNA*(XNA+1.)*(2.*XNA+1.)/24.)
      V(12)=PRBF(1.0,10000.0,V(11)*V(11))*0.5
      IF(TRPL.LT.TRMI)GO TO 3
      IF(TRPL.GT.TRMI)TR=TRMI
      V(12)=1.-V(12)
      V(11)=0.-V(11)
    3 V(13)=1.-V(12)
      V(14)=2.*V(12)
      IF(V(14).GT.1.)V(14)=V(13)*2.
      IF(V(1).LT.0.) RETURN
      IF(V(1).LT.1..AND.V(14).GT.V(2)*2.) RETURN
      WRITE(MED2,99)   V(11),TR,XNA,V(13),V(12),V(14)
      RETURN
   98 FORMAT (41H0WILCOXON MATCHED PAIRS SIGNED-RANKS TEST          /
     160H0  NO MATCHED PAIRS UNEQUALLY RANKED - ROW IS SAME AS COLUMN/)
   99 FORMAT (41H0WILCOXON MATCHED PAIRS SIGNED-RANKS TEST          /
     160H0TESTS CENTRAL DIFFERENCE OF RELATED ROW AND COLUMN VARIATES/
     215H0NORMALISED Z =,F12.6,4H U =,F12.6,18H NUMBER OF PAIRS =,F7.0/
     346H0PROBABILITY THAT ROW IS GREATER THAN COLUMN =,F12.6        /
     446H     PROBABILITY THAT ROW IS LESS THAN COLUMN =,F12.6       /
     546H        PROBABILITY THAT ROW IS EQUAL TO COLUMN =,F12.6     /
     652H0   IF LESS THAN 25 PAIRS CONSULT SIEGEL TABLE G P254       )
      END



      SUBROUTINE KENTAU(CR,CT,RT,NALTC,NALTR,V,MED2)
C KENTAU (SEE  6.3 ) STATISTICAL KENDALL TAU - LARGE SAMPLES
C CALCULATES KENDALLS TAU FOR ASSOCIATION TABLE
      DIMENSION CR(NALTC,NALTR),CT(NALTC),RT(NALTR),V(20)
      T=0
      NMAX = 0
      MMAX = 0
      V(11) = 999.
      NMIN = NALTC
      MMIN = NALTR
C FIND LIMITS OF ROWS AND COLUMNS IN USE
      DO 48 I=1,NALTC
```

```
      DO 48 J=1,NALTR
      IF(CR(I,J).EQ.0.)GO TO 48
      IF(I.GT.NMAX) NMAX = I
      IF(J.GT.MMAX) MMAX = J
      IF(I.LT.NMIN) NMIN = I
      IF(J.LT.MMIN) MMIN = J
      T = T + CR(I,J)
   48 CONTINUE
      IF(T.LT.1..AND.V(1).GT.0.) WRITE(MED2,990)
      IF(T.LT.1.) RETURN
      IF(NMIN.GE.NMAX.AND.V(1).GT.0.) WRITE(MED2,991)NMAX
      IF(MMIN.GE.MMAX.AND.V(1).GT.0.) WRITE(MED2,992)MMAX
      IF(MMIN.GE.MMAX.OR.NMIN.EQ.NMAX) RETURN
C CALCULATE S
      S=0.
      MMAX1 = MMAX - 1
      DO 40 M = MMIN,MMAX1
      M1 = M+1
      DO 40 N = NMIN,NMAX
      IF(CR(N,M).LE..1) GO TO 40
      DO 40 NX = NMIN,NMAX
      IF(NX.EQ.N) GO TO 40
      DO 41 MX = M1,MMAX
      IF(NX.LT.N)S = S - CR(N,M)*CR(NX,MX)
   41 IF(NX.GT.N)S = S + CR(N,M)*CR(NX,MX)
   40 CONTINUE
C CORRECT FOR TIES
      TCA=0.
      TCB=0.
      TCC=0.
      TRA=0.
      TRB=0.
      TRC=0.
      DO 46 N=1,NMAX
      CT(N)=0.
      DO 46 M=1,MMAX
   46 CT(N)=CT(N)+CR(N,M)
      DO 47 M=1,MMAX
      RT(M)=0.
      DO 47 N=1,NMAX
   47 RT(M)=RT(M)+CR(N,M)
      DO 44 N=1,NMAX
      IF(CT(N).LE.1.)GO TO 44
      TCA=TCA+CT(N)*(CT(N)-1.)
      TCB=TCB+CT(N)*(CT(N)-1.)*(CT(N)*2.+5.)
      TCC=TCC+CT(N)*(CT(N)-1.)*(CT(N)-2.)
   44 CONTINUE
      DO 45 M=1,MMAX
      IF(RT(M).LE.1.)GO TO 45
      TRA=TRA+RT(M)*(RT(M)-1.)
      TRB=TRB+RT(M)*(RT(M)-1.)*(RT(M)*2.+5.)
      TRC=TRC+RT(M)*(RT(M)-1.)*(RT(M)-2.)
   45 CONTINUE
C FORM TAU AND DERIVE PROBABILITY
      STAU=(T*(T-1.)*(2.*T+5.)-TRB-TCB)/18.
      STAU=STAU+TRC*TCC/(9.*T*(T-1.)*(T-2.))
      STAU=STAU+TRA*TCA/(2.*T*(T-1.))
      TRA=.5*T*(T-1.)-.5*TRA
      TCA=.5*T*(T-1.)-.5*TCA
      TAU=S/(SQRT(TRA)*SQRT(TCA))
      STAU=SQRT(STAU/TRA/TCA)
      S=TAU/STAU
      TRA=PRBF(1.0,1000.0,S*S)
```

```
C     OUTPUT IF REQUIRED
      IF(V(1).LT.0.)GO TO 49
      IF(V(1).EQ.0..AND.V(2).LT.TRA)GO TO 49
      WRITE(MED2,993)TAU,STAU,TRA
   49 V(11)=TRA
      V(12)=TAU
      V(13)=STAU
      RETURN
  990 FORMAT(38HONO DATA - KENDALLS TAU NOT CALCULATED)
  991 FORMAT(19HOALL DATA IN COLUMN,I4,28H KENDALLS TAU NOT CALCULATED)
  992 FORMAT(19HOALL DATA IN ROW    ,I4,28H KENDALLS TAU NOT CALCULATED)
  993 FORMAT(40HOKENDALL TAU MEASURE OF RANK CORRELATION/ 6H TAU =,F14.4
     1,14H S.D. OF TAU =,F10.4,25H ASSOCIATED PROBABILITY =,F10.6)
      END


      SUBROUTINE COREG(P,V,MED2)
C COREG   (SEE  6.3 ) STATISTICAL SINGLE CORRELATION/REGRESSION
C CALCULATES + TESTS CORRELATION AND REGRESSION FOR TWO RELATED SAMPLES
C VECTOR P CONTAINS N,SX,SY,SXX,SYY,SXY
C SET V(1) TO -1 FOR NO O/P,0 FOR SIG ONLY ,1 FOR FULL DETAILS
C V(11) = ASSOCIATED PROBABILITY - V(12) = CORRELATION COEFFICIENT
C COLUMN = V(13) + V(14)*ROW       - ROW = V(15) + V(16)*COLUMN
      DIMENSION P(6),V(20)
      IF(P(1).LE.5.) V(11) = 999.
      IF(V(1).GE.0..AND.P(1).LE.5.)WRITE(MED2,999)P(1)
      IF(V(1).GE.0..AND.P(4)*P(1).LE.P(2)*P(2)) WRITE(MED2,991)
      IF(V(1).GE.0..AND.P(5)*P(1).LE.P(3)*P(3))  WRITE(MED2,992)
      IF(P(4)*P(1).LE.P(2)*P(2).OR.P(5)*P(1).LE.P(3)*P(3))V(11) = 999.
      IF(V(11).EQ.999.) RETURN
      B=(P(1)*P(6)-P(2)*P(3))/(P(1)*P(4)-P(2)*P(2))
      A=(P(3)-B*P(2))/P(1)
      BDASH=(P(1)*P(6)-P(2)*P(3))/(P(1)*P(5)-P(3)*P(3))
      ADASH=(P(2)-BDASH*P(3))/P(1)
      R=SQRT(B*BDASH)
      IF(B.LT.0.) R = 0. - R
      XA=P(5)-P(3)*P(3)/P(1)
      XB=R*R*XA
      XC=1.
      XD=XB
      XG=XA-XB
      XH=P(1)-2.
      XI=XG/XH
      XJ=P(1)-1.
      IF(XI.GT.0.)XE = XD/XI
      XF = 0.
      IF(XI.GT.0.)XF = PRBF(XC,XH,XE)
      V(11)=XF
      V(12)=R
      V(13)=A
      V(14)=B
      V(15)=ADASH
      V(16)=BDASH
      IF(V(1).LT.0.)RETURN
      IF(V(1).EQ.0..AND.V(2).LT.XF)RETURN
      WRITE(MED2,990)R,A,B,ADASH,BDASH
      IF(R.GE.1.)WRITE(MED2,993)
      IF(R.GE.1.)RETURN
      WRITE(MED2,998)XB,XC,XD,XE,XF,XG,XH,XI,XA,XJ
      RETURN
  990 FORMAT(50HOFOR RELATED SAMPLES - CORRELATION AND REGRESSION      /
     1 27HOCORRELATION COEFFICIENT = ,F10.6/21HOREGRESSION EQUATIONS   /
     2 1H0,9X,8HCOLUMN =,F10.4,2H +,F10.4,4H ROW/1H ,12X,5HROW =,F10.4,2H
```

```
      3 +,F10.4,7H COLUMN   )
  991 FORMAT(50H0FOR RELATED SAMPLES - CORRELATION AND REGRESSION     /
     150H0COLUMN VALUES CONSTANT - NO CORRELATION POSSIBLE            )
  992 FORMAT(50H0FOR RELATED SAMPLES - CORRELATION AND REGRESSION     /
     150H    ROW VALUES CONSTANT - NO CORRELATION POSSIBLE            )
  993 FORMAT(46H0   PERFECT CORRELATION - NO RESIDUAL VARIATION      /)
  998 FORMAT (30H0ANALYSIS OF VARIANCE ANALOGUE/91H0SOURCE OF VARIANCE
     1TOTAL SUM OF SQUARES DF MEAN SUM OF SQUARES VARIANCE RATIO PROBAB!
     2LITY/11H0REGRESSION,10X,F18.5,F6.0,F17.5,F15.5,F14.7/9H RESIDUAL,1
     32X,F18.5,F6.0,F17.5/6H TOTAL,15X,F18.5,F6.0////)
  999 FORMAT(50H0FOR RELATED SAMPLES - CORRELATION AND REGRESSION     /
     1    40X,5H ONLY,F6.0,33H READINGS - NOT SUFFICIENT DATA.)
      END


      SUBROUTINE TFREL(P,V,MED2)
C TFREL   (SEE  6.3 ) STATISTICAL T AND F TESTS - RELATED SAMPLES
C PARAMETRIC TESTS OF DIFFERENCE AND DISPERSION       - 2 RELATED SAMPLES
C VECTOR P CONTAINS N,SX,SY,SXX,SYY,SXY
C SET V(1) TO -1 FOR NO O/P,0 FOR SIG ONLY ,1 FOR FULL DETAILS
C OUTPUT PARAMETERS
C V(11) = PROBABILITY THAT COLUMN MEAN IS GREATER THAN ROW MEAN
C V(12) = PROBABILITY THAT COLUMN S.D. IS GREATER THAN ROW S.D.
C V(13) = MEAN OF DIFFERENCES        (ROW - COLUMN)
C V(14) = S.D. OF DIFFERENCES        (ROW - COLUMN)
C V(15) = CORRELATION COEFFICIENT
      DIMENSION P(6),V(20)
      DATA SD/4HS.D./,EAN/4HMEAN/
  995 FORMAT(25H0    SAMPLES ARE IDENTICAL)
  996 FORMAT (19H0FOR DIFFERENCE OF ,A4,20H S OF RELATED SAMPLES/1H0,10X,
     112HSTUDENTS T =,F10.4,5H WITH,F6.0,19H DEGREES OF FREEDOM    )
  997 FORMAT (1H0,9X,45HVARIATE   ARITHMETIC MEAN   STANDARD DEVIATION //
     110X,10H COLUMN   ,2(F14.6,4X)/10X,10H   ROW    ,2(F14.6,4X)/
     210X,10HDIFFERENCE,2(F14.6,4X))
  998 FORMAT                    (1H0,10X,17HPROBABILITY THAT ,A4,25
     1H OF ROWS IS GREATER THAN ,A4,13H OF COLUMNS =,F9.6/14X,17HPROBABI
     2LITY THAT ,A4,22H OF ROWS IS LESS THAN ,A4,13H OF COLUMNS =,F9.6/1
     35X,17HPROBABILITY THAT ,A4,21H OF ROWS IS EQUAL TO ,A4,13H OF COLU
     4MNS =,F9.6)
  999 FORMAT(50H0FOR RELATED SAMPLES - COMPARING MEAN AND S.D.        /
     1    40X,5H ONLY,F6.0,33H READINGS - NOT SUFFICIENT DATA.)
      V(11) = 999.
      V(12) = 999.
      V(13) = 0.
      V(14) = 0.
      V(15) = 1.
      IF(P(1).GT.5.)GO TO 1
      IF(V(1).GE.0.)WRITE(MED2,999) P(1)
      RETURN
    1 XBAR=P(2)/P(1)
      YBAR=P(3)/P(1)
      SX=SQRT((P(4)-XBAR*P(2))/(P(1)-1.))
      SY=SQRT((P(5)-YBAR*P(3))/(P(1)-1.))
      XDIF=XBAR-YBAR
      SDIF=     ((P(1)*P(4)-2.*P(1)*P(6)+P(1)*P(5)-P(2)*P(2)+2.*P(2)*P(3)
     1-P(3)*P(3))/(P(1)*P(1)-P(1)))
      SDIF = SQRT(ABS(SDIF))
      IF(XDIF.EQ.0..AND.SDIF.EQ.0.) WRITE(MED2,995)
      IF(XDIF.EQ.0..AND.SDIF.EQ.0.) RETURN
      TMR = 999.
      IF(SDIF.NE.0.)   TMR = (XBAR-YBAR)*SQRT(P(1))/SDIF
      DFM=P(1)-1.
      XA=PRBF(1.,DFM,TMR*TMR)*0.5
```

```
      IF(XBAR.LT.YBAR) XA = 1. - XA
      XB = 1. - XA
      XC=2.*XA
      IF(XC.GT.1.)XC=2.*XB
      R = 0.
      IF(SX.LE.0..OR.SY.LE.0.) TVR = 1./SQRT(2.*P(1)-2.)
      IF(SX.LE.0..OR.SY.LE.0.) GO TO 2
      R=(P(1)*P(6)-P(2)*P(3))/SQRT((P(1)*P(4)-P(2)*P(2))*(P(1)*P(5)-P(3)
     1*P(3)))
      TVR = 999.
      IF(R.LT.1.)TVR =SQRT((SX*SX-SY*SY)*(SX*SX-SY*SY)*(P(1)-2.)/(4.*(1.
     1-R)*SX*SX*SY*SY))
    2 DFV=P(1)-2.
      XD=PRBF(1.,DFV,TVR*TVR)*0.5
      IF(SX.EQ.SY)XD = 0.5
      IF(SX.GT.SY)GO TO 3
      TVR=0.-TVR
      XD=1.-XD
    3 XE=1.-XD
      XF=2.*XD
      IF(XF.GT.1.)XF=2.*XE
      V(11)=XA
      V(12)=XD
      V(13)=XDIF
      V(14)=SDIF
      V(15)=R
      IF(V(1).LT.0.)RETURN
      IF(V(1).EQ.0..AND.XA.GT.V(2).AND.XB.GT.V(2).AND.XD.GT.V(2).AND.XE.
     1GT.V(2))RETURN
      WRITE(MED2,996)EAN,TMR,DFM
      WRITE(MED2,998)EAN,EAN,XA,EAN,EAN,XB,EAN,EAN,XC
      WRITE(MED2,996)SD,TVR,DFV
      WRITE(MED2,998) SD, SD,XD, SD, SD,XE, SD, SD,XF
      IF(V(1).GT.1.)WRITE (MED2,997)XBAR,SX,YBAR,SY,XDIF,SDIF
      RETURN
      END
```

6.4 PROGRAM STKREL - TEST SEVERAL RELATED SAMPLES

6.4.1 Purpose

This program compares several related samples of data drawn from a STATCAT data bank. It will normally use the non-parametric or parametric tests appropriate to the lowest data level being used. The user may over-ride the choice of test to make tests on a specified level, or on all levels up to a specified level, or that chosen by the system. If tests are made which are not appropriate to the data level, the system will print warning messages. The amount of accompanying detail may be controlled by the user, and descriptions of the data in each sample may be obtained. The system will accept any number of related samples from two upwards, but will print a warning message, for two samples, advising the use of ST2REL (6.3). The variates tested may be transformed by any of the transforms given in Figure 3.72, but delayed values may not be used. The class definitions given in the data description will be used unless overridden.

Figure 6.41a contains system flow-charts for the main program STKREL and the executive subroutine CKREL. Figure 6.41b contains system flow-charts for CHISQ1 (Chi-squared test for proportion of modal class - 6.4.5) and FREID2 (Freidmann's two-way analysis of variance by ranks - 6.4.6). Figure 6.41c contains system flow-charts for PAR2W (Parametric two-way analysis of variance with Bartlett's test for equality of variance -6.4.7) and TAB2W (Two-way Frequency tabulation - 6.4.8).

6.4.2 Input Data

Item	Level	Format	Function	See
1	0	A	File control	3.2
5	4	E	Subset specification	3.6
6	5	F	Variate specification (At least 2 - no delays)	3.7
7	9	G	Data handling instruction	Below + 3.8

Data Handling Instruction

Card Layout - Data Handling Instruction - STKREL

A BCCCDDDEEEEEEEEFFFFFFFFGGGGGGGGGGGGGGGGHHHHHHHHHHHHHHHH......etc

Columns	Item	Function	See
1	A	Output control index	6.1
2	B	Analysis control index	Below
3 - 5	C	Significance level for reporting (per cent)	6.1
6 - 8	D	Not used	-
9 - 16	E	Not used	-
17 - 24	F	Not used	-
25 - 40	G	Not used	-
41 - 80	H	Comment (NOT KEPT)	-

B - Analysis Control Index

This index controls the level at which testing is carried out, and the conditions under which the results are printed.

ALTERNATIVES

B = 0,blank: Test at lowest data level - print results if
(Default)   statistically significant.

B = 1   : Tests for NOMINAL level only (Chi-squared)

	Print results if statistically significant.
B = 2	: Tests for ORDINAL level only (Freidmann's Two-way analysis of variance by ranks). Print results if statistically significant.
B = 3	: Tests for INTERVAL level (Two-way Analysis of variance, Bartlett's test for homogenity of variance). Print results if statistically significant.
B = 4	: Tests for RATIO level (as for INTERVAL). Print results if statistically significant.
B = 5	: Tests at lowest data level - print all results.
B = 6	: Tests at NOMINAL level - print all results.
B = 7	: Tests at ORDINAL level - print all results.
B = 8	: Tests at INTERVAL level - print all results.
B = 9	: Tests at RATIO level - print all results.

DEFAULT value = 0 (0, or blank, or non-numeric character)

6.4.3 Input Example

Figure 6.42 is a summary of the input structure for two runs of STKREL using first the default values, then the full output available. The five related variates compared are the value of the heart-rate of the operator, and the same datum subjected to the transforms +/-1, +/-P, NOR1 and NORP. These four transforms respectively add or subtract one unit at random, add or subtract one per cent of the observed value at random, add a unit random normal variate, or multiply by one plus or minus one humndredth of a unit random normal variate. The first data handling instruction produces only the result of statistically significant tests, while the second produces all possible results.

Figure 6.43 lists the input cards required.

6.4.4 Output Example

Figure 6.44 is a summary of the output structure corresponding to the input structure of 6.42. Figure 6.45 is a page-by-page summary of the output corresponding to the specific example given in 6.4.3. Figure 6.46 shows the output generated by the first data handling instruction. The only significant result here is the difference between successive entries, found by the classical analysis of variance. Figure 6.47 shows the output of a Chi-squared one sample test for equal distribution of means, and of a Freidmann two-way analysis of variance by ranks, as described in 6.4.5 and 6.4.6 respectively. Note that the system prints a warning that these tests are not on the appropriate data level.

6.4.5 Statistical Tests - NOMINAL Level

A - CHISQ1 - Chi-squared One-Sample Test

There is no generally accepted test for comparisons of related data on a nominal scale. This test is an adaptation of the general chi-squared test for equal frequencies. It requires that the data should be on at least a nominal scale, with the same class names.

The number of occasions that a datum falls into a modal class for the set of data drawn from one entry is accumulated for all entries, for each related sample. A test is then made against the hypothesis that these numbers are equally distributed among the various samples. If a statistically significant probability is returned by the test carried out by CHISQ1, then it appears that some data columns are more likely to be in the modal class for their entry than others.

Figure 6.47 includes an example of the output of CHISQ1.

6.4.6 Statistical Tests - ORDINAL Level

A - FREID2 - Freidmann Two-way A.o.V. by Ranks

This is test of central difference applied to related variates, where the data within each entry can be ranked. The total rank is accumulated, and tested against the assumption that the mean ranks for each variate are the same. If the average ranks are not the same, then some variates have consistently higher rankings than others in the same entry. The subroutine takes into account the possibility of tied rankings.

The test is called a "two-way" analysis of variance, although only one result is produced, by analogy with the classical two-way analysis of variance, where also the systematic differences between entries are eliminated so that differences within entries can be observed.

Figure 6.47 includes an example of the output of FREID2.

REFERENCES : Siegel (Ch 7)

6.4.7 Statistical Tests - INTERVAL Level

A - PAR2W - Parametric Two-way Analysis of Variance

This is a test for central difference, requiring at least INTERVAL level measurements, for several related variates. In principle, this test operates by dividing the variation observed into three parts, one corresponding to the difference betwen means of the related variates, one to the differences betwen means of successive entries, and a third part, not related to either sample or entry, which is usually used as an estimate of residual error. This unexplained error is usually taken as a measure of the 'noise level' of the system, and the ratios of the other two quantities to this one indicate the probability of obtaining such results if there are no systematic differences between entries or between data columns. We would expect there to be a substantial difference between mean values for each entry - it is usually for this reason that related samples are employed. If the variance ratio for a subset is less than 1, it is worth examining the data to see if there is some particular reason that the means should be the same, or similar.

REFERENCES : See Chapter 7.1

B - PAR2W - Bartlett's Test for Equality of Variance

In addition to the parametric analysis of variance, which tests the differences between mean values, a test may be made of the dispersions of related variates. This test, Bartlett's test, tests whether the variances of the differences of related samples from the mean of the entry are the same. It requires data on at least an Interval scale for all variates. If the result of Bartlett's test is statistically significant, then some variates are more variable than others.

Because this test compares the additional variance from the mean value for each entry, it eliminates the effect of the differences between the means of successive entries. It is possible for relatively small differences between the standard deviations of related variates to be highly significant, when the variation due to differences between entries has been eliminated.

REFERENCES : See Chapter 7.1

6.4.8   Subroutine TAB2W - Two-way Frequency Tabulation

The subroutine TAB2W is a general subroutine for output of two-way tabulations. It may be used to display data in labelled classes, or from different samples, according to the program from which it is called. It presents no particular theoretical or practical difficulties, and is presented here mainly because it was most conveniently fitted into the sequence of flow-charts at this point.

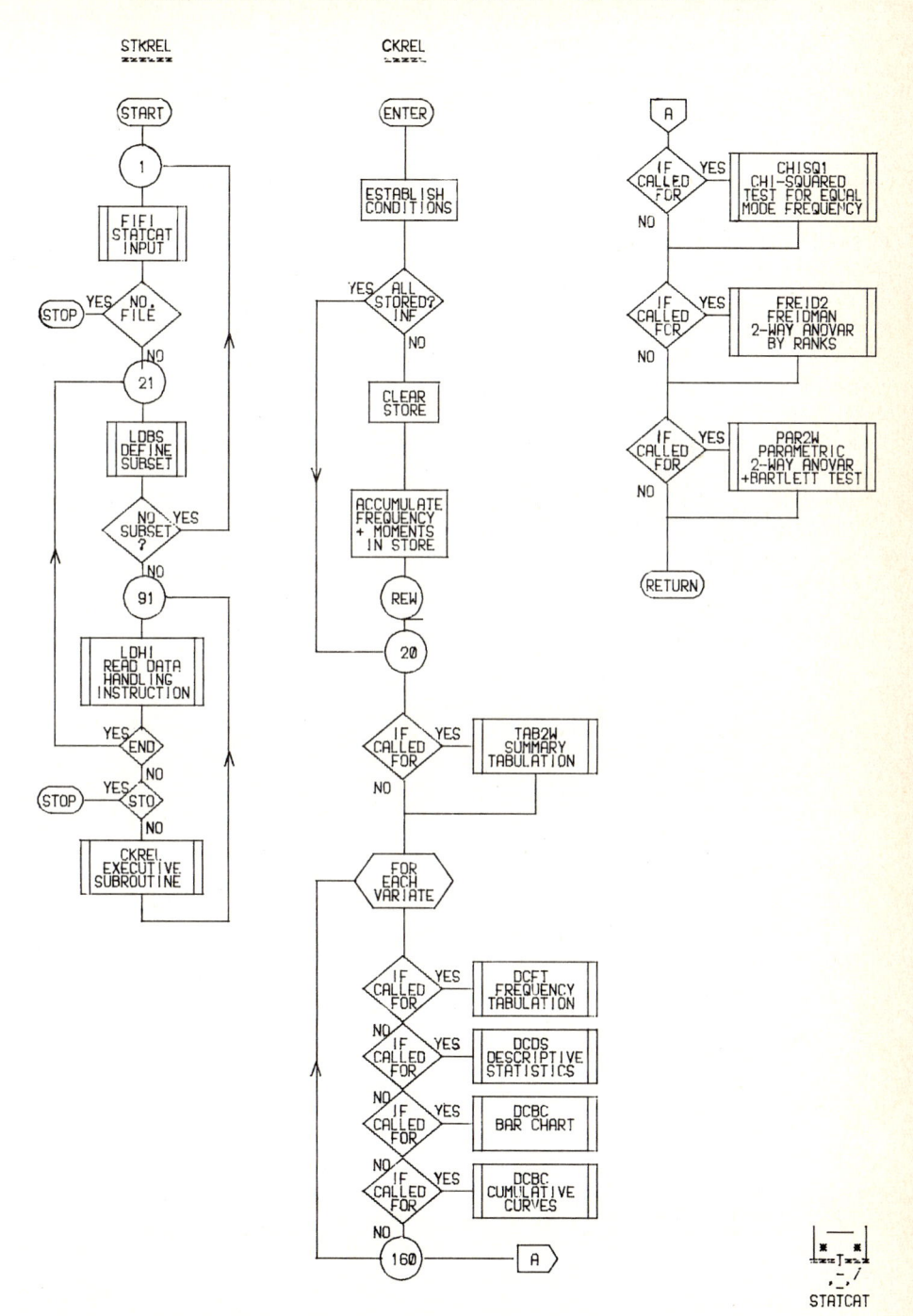

Figure 6.41a - System Flow-Charts - STKREL and CKREL

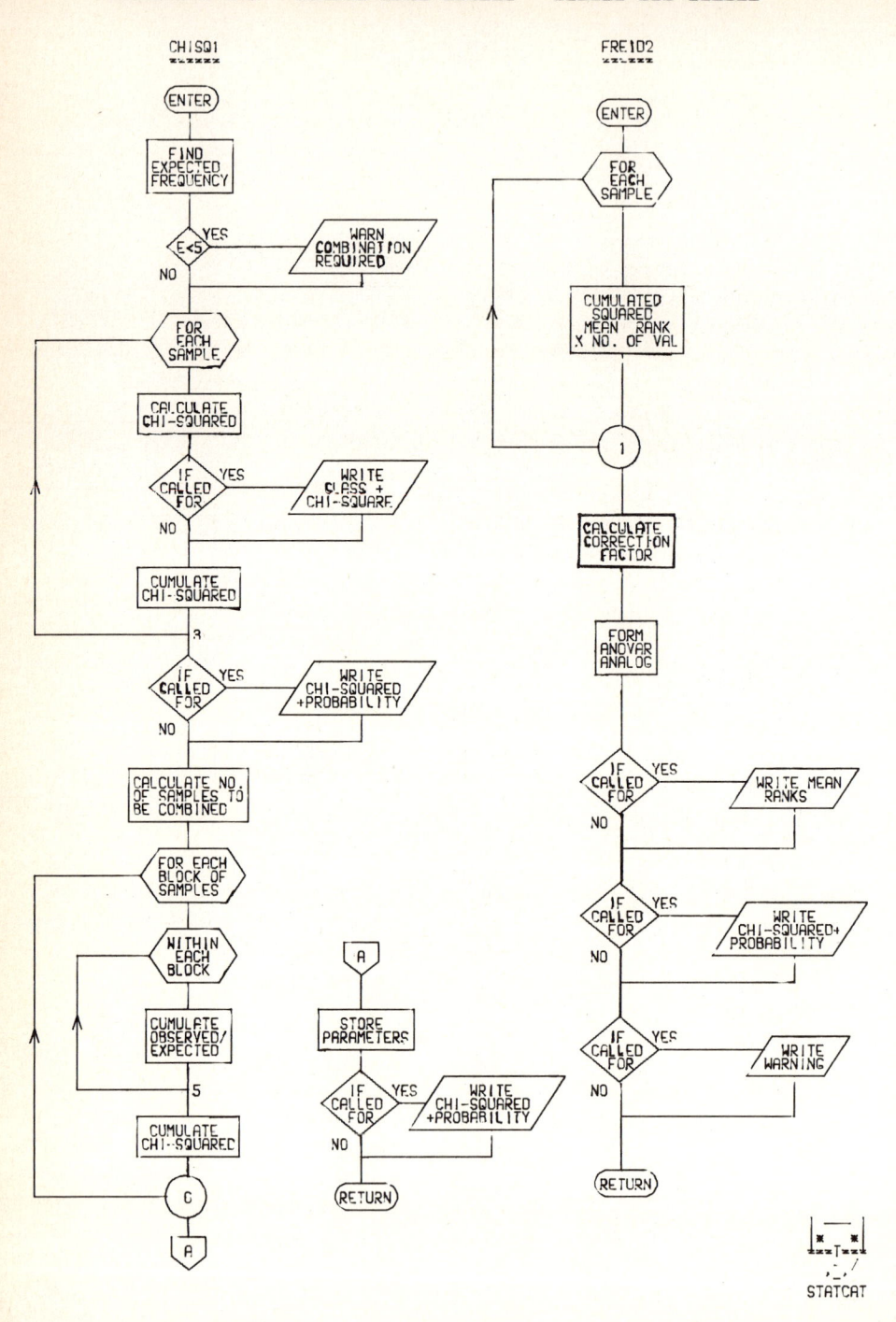

Figure 6.41b - System Flow-Charts - CHISQ1 and FREID2

307

Figure 6.41c - System Flow-Charts - PAR2W and TAB2W

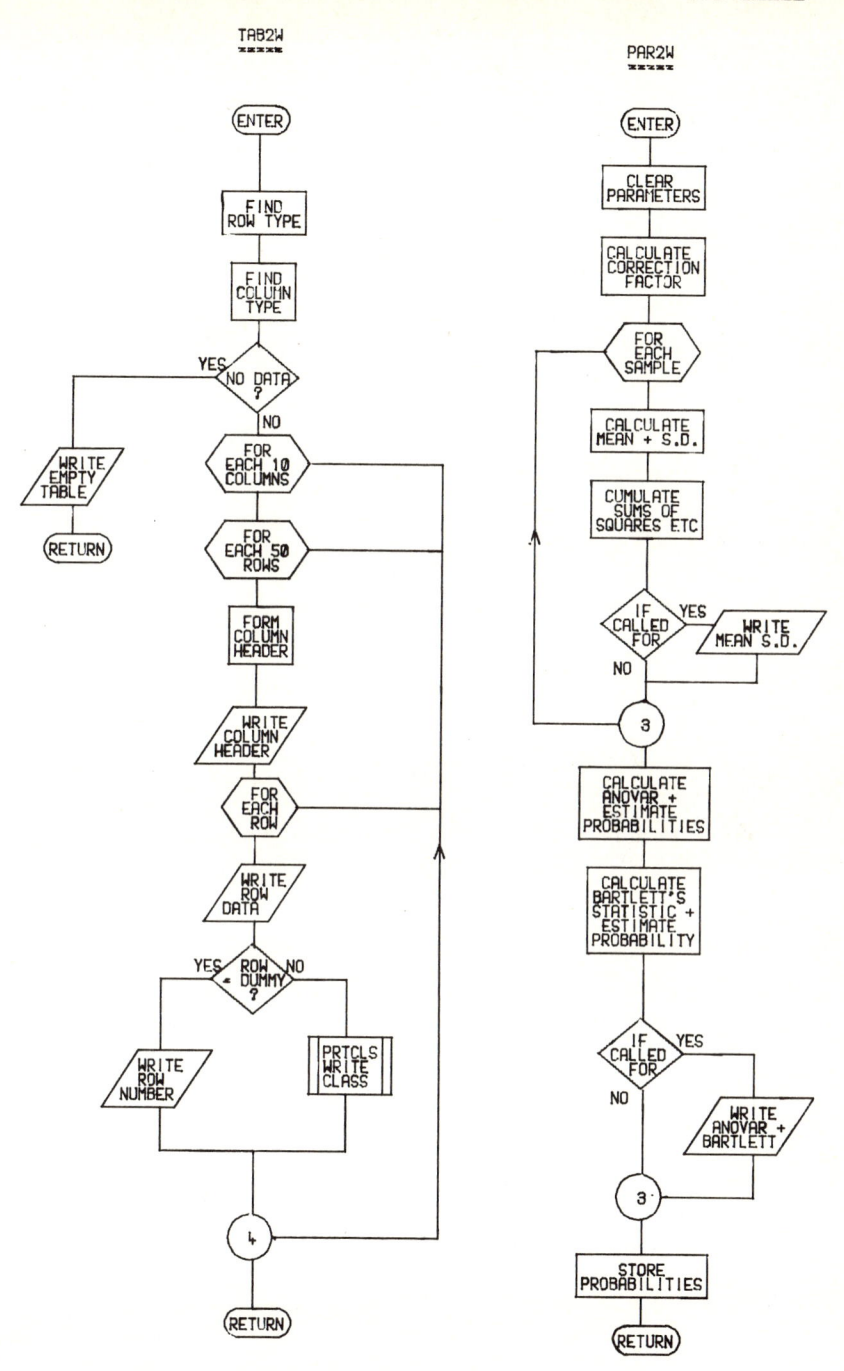

Figure 6.42 - STKREL - Input Structure

```
        Level
   0   1   2   3   4   5   6   7   8   9
FILE CONTROL CARD
    SUBSET SPECIFICATION
        VARIATE SPECIFICATION
            DATA HANDLING INSTRUCTION
            DATA HANDLING INSTRUCTION
            STOP
```

Figure 6.43 - STKREL - Input Example

```
---------1----------2----------3----------4----------5----------6----------7--
**STKRELDEMO                            DEMONSTRATION STATCAT DATA BANK
ALL DATA
END OF SUBSET DEFINITION
VAL.H.R.
+/-1H.R.
+/-PH.R.
NOR1H.R.
NORPH.R.
END OF SET OF RELATED VARIATES
GO                                      DEFAULT OUTPUT
89                                      DETAILED OUTPUT
STOP
---------1----------2----------3----------4----------5----------6----------7--
```

Figure 6.44 - STKREL - Output Structure

```
For each    ) : File Control Record
output file )   File Parameters
                Data Description
                For each) Subset Input Record
                Subset  ) For each)Input Record
                          Set of  )   See
                          Variates)   Left
For each) <Cross-tabulation>
Subset  )  For Each)<FrequencyTable>
           Variate )<Descriptive Statistics>
                    <Frequency Curves/Bar Chart>

        NOMINAL    <Chi-squared>
        ORDINAL    <Freidmann's Two-way Anovar by ranks>
        INTERVAL)  <Classical Two-way Analysis of Vaiance>
        /RATIO  )  <Bartlett's Test for Homoscedasticity>
```

Carated(<>) items are optional.

Figure 6.45 - STKREL - Output Example Page-by-Page listing

Page	Contents	Origin
1- 3	File Control Record	FIFI
	Program Title	STKREL
	File Parameters	LDAP
	Data Description record	LDDS
4	Subset record	LDBS/LSET
5	Set of Variates record	LGEN
	Data Handling Instruction	LDHI
6	Analysis of Variance and Bartlett test	PAR2W
7	Data Handling Instruction	LDHI
8-17	Sample Descriptions	DCFT/DCDS/DCPS/DCBC
18	Chi-squared One-sample test	CHISQ1
19	Freidmann Two way analysis of Variance by Rank	FREID2
20	Analysis of Varriance and Bartlett test	PAR2W
21	Data Handling Instruction (STOP)	LDHI

Figure 6.46 - STKREL - Output Example - Default Output

```
            STATCAT DATA BANK - DEMONSTRATION STATCAT DATA BANK
                  DATA BANK SUBSET - ALL DATA

VARIATES -VAL. OF.+/-1 OF.+/-P OF.NOR1 OF.NORP OF.
          H.R.     H.R.    H.R.    H.R.    H.R.

DATA USED ARE ON A RATIO SCALE    THEY SHOULD BE ON AN INTERVAL SCALE    SIGNIFICANCE MAY BE REDUCED        **WARNING**

CLASSICAL TWO-WAY ANALYSIS OF VARIANCE

  VARIATE      VALUE OF VARIATE           DIFFERENCE FROM ENTRY MEAN
               ARITHMETIC   STANDARD      ARITHMETIC    STANDARD
                 MEAN       DEVIATION       MEAN        DEVIATION
 VAL. OF H.R.   47.5330      7.3917        -0.0135        0.2370
 +/-1 OF H.R.   47.4705      7.3824        -0.0760        0.8959
 +/-P OF H.R.   47.5561      7.3830         0.0096        0.5055
 NOR1 OF H.R.   47.6046      7.3311         0.0581        0.5535
 NORP OF H.R.   47.5683      7.8050         0.0218        0.4714
 ENTRY MEAN     47.5465      7.3989

 SOURCE OF     TOTAL SUM    DEGREES OF    MEAN SUM      VARIANCE    ASSOCIATED
 VARIATION     OF SQUARES    FREEDOM      OF SQUARES    RATIO       PROBABILITY

 VARIATES       0.7500         4.          0.1875       0.3342       0.8555
 ENTRIES    17244.5625        63.        273.7231     487.9097       0.0
 RESIDUAL     141.3750       252.          0.5610


BARTLETT TEST FOR EQUALITY OF VARIANCE BETWEEN VARIATES

F-LIKE STATISTIC =     32.2830 WITH          4. AND       148838. DEGREES OF FREEDOM

ASSOCIATED PROBABILITY =      0.0

       END OF TEST SEQUENCE
```

Figure 6.47 - STKREL - Output Example - CHISQ1 and FREID2

```
            STATCAT DATA BANK - DEMONSTRATION STATCAT DATA BANK
                  DATA BANK SUBSET - ALL DATA

VARIATES -VAL. OF.+/-1 OF.+/-P OF.NOR1 OF.NORP OF.
          H.R.     H.R.    H.R.    H.R.    H.R.

DATA USED ARE ON A RATIO SCALE    THEY SHOULD BE ON A NOMINAL SCALE    SIGNIFICANCE MAY BE REDUCED        **WARNING**

      CHI-SQUARED ONE-SAMPLE TEST - COMBINATION REQUIRED

 CLASS OR SAMPLE    OBSERVED   EXPECTED   CHI-SQUARE
 1  VAL. OF H.R.     57.00      52.00       0.48
 2  +/-1 OF H.R.     44.00      52.00       1.23
 3  +/-P OF H.R.     56.00      52.00       0.31
 4  NOR1 OF H.R.     45.00      52.00       0.94
 5  NORP OF H.R.     58.00      52.00       0.69


      CHI-SQUARED =       3.6538 WITH   4. DEGREES OF FREEDOM

         ASSOCIATED PROBABILITY =  0.656787



            STATCAT DATA BANK - DEMONSTRATION STATCAT DATA BANK
                  DATA BANK SUBSET - ALL DATA

VARIATES -VAL. OF.+/-1 OF.+/-P OF.NOR1 OF.NORP OF.
          H.R.     H.R.    H.R.    H.R.    H.R.

DATA USED ARE ON A RATIO SCALE    THEY SHOULD BE ON AN ORDINAL SCALE    SIGNIFICANCE MAY BE REDUCED        **WARNING**

FRIEDMAN TWO-WAY ANALYSIS OF VARIANCE BY RANKS

RELATED VARIATE  MEAN RANK
  VAL. OF H.R.     2.97
  +/-1 OF H.R.     3.11
  +/-P OF H.R.     2.89
  NOR1 OF H.R.     3.02
  NORP OF H.R.     3.02

FRIEDMAN TWO-WAY ANALYSIS OF VARIANCE BY RANKS

        CHI-SQUARED(R) =        0.6500 WITH     4. DEGREES OF FREEDOM
        ASSOCIATED PROBABILITY =       0.9548
```

```
C MASTER STKREL - TESTS (TWO) THREE OR MORE RELATED SAMPLES
C   SUBROUTINES AND FUNCTIONS REQUIRED
C  NAME              TYPE           COMMENT
C  AN     (SEE  3.1 ) SERVICE      ALPHA - TO NUMERIC VALUE
C  CH     (SEE 11.6 ) SERVICE      CHOOSES TEST/DESCRIPTION REQUIRED
C  CHIKEN (SEE 11.9 ) SERVICE      WARNS OF MISMATCHED DATA LEVEL
C  CHISQ  (SEE 11.5 ) STATISTICAL  BASIC CHI-SQUARED CALCULATION
C  CKREL  (SEE  6.4 ) EXECUTIVE    TESTS SEVERAL RELATED SAMPLES
C  CLASIF (SEE 11.7 ) SERVICE      CLASSIFIES DATA ITEM
C  CLSAM  (SEE  3.5 ) SERVICE      ALLOTS ENTRY TO SAMPLE/SUBSET
C  COMPA  (SEE  3.1 ) SERVICE      COMPARES ALPHAMERIC VALUES
C  COPYA  (SEE  3.1 ) SERVICE      COPIES ALPHAMERIC VALUE
C  DCBC   (SEE  5.2 ) STATISTICAL  CONSTRUCTS BAR-CHARTS
C  DCDS   (SEE  5.2 ) STATISTICAL  DESCRIPTIVE STATISTICS
C  DCFT   (SEE  5.2 ) STATISTICAL  FREQUENCY TABULATION
C  DCPS   (SEE  5.2 ) STATISTICAL  MOMENT(PARAMETRIC) STATISTICS
C  FIFI   (SEE  3.2 ) SYSTEM       ALLOCATES PERIPHERALS
C  FITIT  (SEE 11.9 ) SERVICE      FINDS COLUMN TITLE + DESCRIPTION
C  FREID2 (SEE  6.4 ) STATISTICAL  FREIDMAN 2-WAY ANOVAR BY RANKS
C  GAUS   (SEE 11.8 ) STATISTICAL  FINDS ASS. PROB. OF N VALUE
C  IBL    (SEE  3.1 ) SERVICE      DETECTS BLANK,END AND STOP CARDS
C  ICH    (SEE  3.1 ) SERVICE      IDENTIFIES ALPHAMERIC CODES
C  LDAP   (SEE  3.3 ) SYSTEM       LOADS/CHECKS DATA BANK PARAMETERS
C  LDBS   (SEE  3.6 ) SYSTEM       LOADS SUBSET DEFINITION
C  LDDS   (SEE  3.4 ) SYSTEM       LOADS DATA DESCRIPTION SEGMENT
C  LDHI   (SEE  3.8 ) SYSTEM       LOADS/CHECKS DATA HANDLING INSTN
C  LGEN   (SEE  3.7 ) SYSTEM       LOADS GENERALISED VARIATES
C  LSET   (SEE  3.5 ) SYSTEM       LOADS DEFINING CONDITIONS
C  MEDIAT (SEE  3.7 ) SERVICE      FETCHES NEXT VARIATE SET
C  PAR2W  (SEE  6.4 ) STATISTICAL  2-WAY ANOVAR + BARTLETT TEST
C  PRBF   (SEE 11.8 ) STATISTICAL  FINDS PROBABILITY OF F-RATIO
C  PRTCLS (SEE 11.7 ) SERVICE      PRINTS CLASS NAME/LIMITS
C  TAB2W  (SEE  6.4 ) STATISTICAL  TABULATES WITH VARIATE NAMES ETC
C  TRANS  (SEE  3.7 ) SERVICE      CARRIES OUT REQUIRED TRANSFORM
C SETTING OF ARRAY DIMENSIONS
C THE FOLLOWING DIMENSIONS MUST BE AT LEAST AS BIG AS THOSE
C SPECIFIED BY THE DATA TAPE,SAMPLE SPECIFICATIONS,ETC.
C NQMAX = MAXIMUM NUMBER OF DATA COLUMNS
C IF NQMAX AND ARRAYS ARE CHANGED,CHANGE DATA STATEMENT FOR CN
C DIMENSION D(NQMAX),DMAX(NQMAX),DMIN(NQMAX),IT(NQMAX),ST(NQMAX)
C DIMENSION CN(NQMAX)
      NQMAX = 100
      DIMENSION D(100  ),DMAX(100  ),DMIN(100  ),IT(100  ),ST(100  )
      DIMENSION CN(100)
      DATA  CN/4HCOL1,4HCOL2,4HCOL3,4HCOL4,4HCOL5,4HCOL6,4HCOL7,4HCOL8,4
     1HCOL9,4HCL10,4HCL11,4HCL12,4HCL13,4HCL14,4HCL15,4HCL16,4HCL17,4HCL
     218,4HCL19,4HCL20,4HCL21,4HCL22,4HCL23,4HCL24,4HCL25,4HCL26,4HCL27,
     34HCL28,4HCL29,4HCL30,4HCL31,4HCL32,4HCL33,4HCL34,4HCL35,4HCL36,4HC
     4L37,4HCL38,4HCL39,4HCL40,4HCL41,4HCL42,4HCL43,4HCL44,4HCL45,4HCL46
     5,4HCL47,4HCL48,4HCL49,4HCL50,4HCL51,4HCL52,4HCL53,4HCL54,4HCL55,4H
     6CL56,4HCL57,4HCL58,4HCL59,4HCL60,4HCL61,4HCL62,4HCL63,4HCL64,4HCL6
     75,4HCL66,4HCL67,4HCL68,4HCL69,4HCL70,4HCL71,4HCL72,4HCL73,4HCL74,4
     8HCL75,4HCL76,4HCL77,4HCL78,4HCL79,4HCL80,4HCL81,4HCL82,4HCL83,4HCL
     984,4HCL85,4HCL86,4HCL87,4HCL88,4HCL89,4HCL90,4HCL91,4HCL92,4HCL93,
     94HCL94,4HCL95,4HCL96,4HCL97,4HCL98,4HCL99,4HC100/
C NALTMX = MAXIMUM NUMBER OF CLASSES ON TAPE
C DIMENSION     TRT(NALTMX)
      NALTMX = 50
      DIMENSION TRT(50)
C MAXM = MAXIMUM NUMBER OF CELLS AVAILABLE IN STORAGE - IN 100S
C DIMENSION NP(MAXM),CX(MAXM),KC(MAXM),TRTC(MAXM),CRTC(MAXM)
C  DIMENSION TMAX(MAXM),TMIN(MAXM),NCL(MAXM)
      MAXM = 25
```

```
      DIMENSION NP(   25),CX(   25),KC(   25),TRTC(   25),CRTC(   25)
      DIMENSION TMAX(   25),TMIN(   25),NCL(   25)
C NRMAX= MAXIMUM NUMBER OF CLASSES ACTUALLY USED FOR ROWS
C DIMENSION RX(NRMAX),KR(NRMAX),TRTR(NRMAX)
      NRMAX = 50
      DIMENSION RX(   50),KR(   50),TRTR(   50)
C NLAV = MAXIMUM NUMBER OF CELLS AVAILABLE IN STORAGE - IN 100S
C RT(NLAV,100) CONTAINS ALL WORKING STORAGE
C MUST BE AT LEAST(NALTC*(NALTR+10))
C WHERE NALTC = ACTUAL NUMBER OF VARIATES
C AND NALTR = LARGEST NUMBER OF ALTERNATE CLASSES ACTUALLY USED
      NLAV = 10
      DIMENSION RT(10,100)
C MAXDBC = MAXIMUM NUMBER OF DATA BANK SUBSET CONDITIONS
C DIMENSION SCON(5,MAXDBC)
      MAXDBC = 50
      DIMENSION SCON(5,50)
C THE FOLLOWING DIMENSION STORES THE NAMES OF THE DATA TRANSFORMS
C AND THE ACCEPTABLE LEVELS FOR TRANSFORMATIONS
      DIMENSION U(60),LU(60)
      NU = 60
C TRANSFORMATION CODES
C UNITS                        BLOCKS
C       0 - 9   10 - 19   20 - 29   30 - 39   40 - 49   50 - 59
C       POWERS  TRIG      TRIG      STATIST   MATHS     TEST
C               RADIANS   DEGREES   TRANSF    FUNCTS    FUNCTIONS
C   0    -       -         H.MS      -         -         RM10
C   1   VAL.    SINR      SIND      PSNA      RECP      +/-1
C   2   SQAR    COSR      COSD      PSNB      SQRT      ADD1
C   3   CUBE    TANR      TAND      BINO      ABSV      SUB1
C   4   4PWR    ASIR      ASID      LG+1      SIGN      NOR1
C   5   5PWR    ACOR      ACOD      LOGE      INTG      +/-P
C   6   6PWR    ATAR      ATAD      LG10      FRAC      ADDP
C   7   7PWR    SINH      DTOR      AL10      EXPT      SUBP
C   8   8PWR    COSH      RTOD       -        PRES      NORP
C   9   9PWR    TANH      H.HH       -        NEG.      +100
      DATA U/4HVAL.,4HSQAR,4HCUBE,4H4PWR,4H5PWR,4H6PWR,4H7PWR,4H8PWR,4H9
     1PWR,4HVAL ,4HSINR,4HCOSR,4HTANR,4HASIR,4HACOR,4HATAR,4HSINH,4HCOSH
     2,4HTANH,4HH.MS,4HSIND,4HCOSD,4HTAND,4HASID,4HACOD,4HATAD,4HDTOR,4H
     3RTOD,4HH.HH,4H VAL,4HPSNA,4HPSNB,4HBINO,4HLG+1,4HLOGE,4HLG10,4HAL1
     40,4H    ,4H    ,4H    ,4HRECP,4HSQRT,4HABSV,4HSIGN,4HINTG,4HFRAC,4
     5HEXPT,4HPRES,4HNEG.,4HRM10,4H+/-1,4HADD1,4HSUB1,4HNOR1,4H+/-P,4HAD
     6DP,4HSUBP,4HNORP,4H+100,4H    /
      DATA LU/1,8*5,1,9*5,1,9*5,1,6*5,4*1,2*5,2*3,3*5,7*2,4*5,2*2/
C DUMMY ARRAYS USED IN CALLS OF LGEN
      DIMENSION IH(1),H(1),C(10)
      DIMENSION FORM(50)
C THE FOLLOWING DIMENSIONS ARE FIXED
      DIMENSION TTA(20),TTB(20),TTC(20)
      DATA BL/1H /
      COMMON /STCT/MED1,MED2,MED3,MED4,MED5,MED6,MED13,Q,V(20),TT(30)
      DATA PROG/4HKREL/
      MED1 = -1
C SETTING UP * LEVEL 0
    1 CALL COPYA(TT(1),PROG)
      CALL FIFI
      IF(MED3.GT.0) WRITE(MED2,901)
      CALL LDAP(MED2,MED3,V,TT,Q,NQ,NALT,NQMAX,NALTMX,IGO)
      IF(IGO.GT.0) GO TO 1
      LIMC = NRMAX
      LI = 18
      CALL LDDS(TRT,NALT,D,NQ,ST,NQ,IT,NQ,H,0,DMIN,DMAX,NQ,LI,1,Q,VX,
     1 0,MED2,MED3,0,IGO)
```

```
      21 IF(V(10).GE.20.) V(10) = 0.
         CALL LDBS(SCON,NCON,MAXDBC,CN,ST,IT,NQ,TRT,NALT,IGO)
         IF(IGO.GT.0) GO TO 1
         ARAN = 5326.
C LEVEL 4 - SET OF VARIATES FOR DATA SWEEP
      41 IF(V(10).GE.40.) V(10) = 0.
         IFIN = MAXM
         M = 0
         WRITE(MED6,941)
         WRITE(MED6,945)
         CALL LGEN(U,NU,LU,NU,ST,IT,CN,NQ,NCL,MAXM,DMIN,DMAX,NQ,TMIN,TMAX,M
        1AXM,0,LIMC,IH,NP,MAXM,M,MAXM,0,NALT)
         IF(V(11).LT.0.5.AND.V(20).LT.0.5) GO TO 21
         IF(V(10).LT.0.5.AND.V(20).GT.0.5) V(10) = 43.
         NALTC = V(11) + .5
         IF(NALTC.EQ.1) WRITE(MED6,942)
         IF(NALTC.EQ.1.AND.V(10).LT.0.5)V(10) = 46.
         IF(NALTC.EQ.2) WRITE(MED2,943)
         NALTR = 3
         IF(NALTC.LE.0) GO TO 43
         DO 42 I = 1,NALTC
         J = NP(I)/1000
         TRTC(I) = U(J)
         J = NP(I) - 1000*J
         CRTC(I)=ST(J)
      42 IF(NCL(I).GT.NALTR) NALTR = NCL(I)
      43 V(19) = 0.
         BRAN = ARAN
         X = NLAV
         TST = X*100.
         SREQ = NALTR + 8
         X = NALTC
         SREQ = SREQ*X
         IF(SREQ.LE.TST) GO TO 49
         WRITE(MED6,944)SREQ,TST
         IF(V(10).EQ.0.)V(10) = 45.
      49 CONTINUE
C LEVEL 8 - NOT AT PRESENT IN USE
C LEVEL 9 - DATA HANDLING INSTRUCTION
      91 IF(V(10).GT.90.) V(10) = 0.
         CALL LDHI(V(1),1,V(2),4,V(3),16,H,0,H,0,H,0,H,V(10),
        1 FORM(41),FORM,MED1,MED2,MED4,Q,NQ,NWARN,1,IGO)
         IF(IGO.GT.0) GO TO 41
C STANDARDISATION
         IF(V(3).LE.0.) NWARN = NWARN + 1
         IF(V(3).EQ.0.) V(3) = 1.
         IF(V(3).LT.0.) V(3) = 0.
         CALL LDHI(V(1),1,V(2),4,V(3),16,H,0,H,0,H,0,H,V(10),
        1 FORM(41),FORM,MED1,MED2,MED4,Q,NQ,NWARN,2,IGO)
         IF(IGO.GT.0) GO TO 91
         INDR = NALTC*10/100 + 1
         INDC = NALTC*10 - 100*INDR + 101
         V(10) = BRAN
         V(19) = V(19) + 1.
         CALL CKREL(TMIN,TMAX,CRTC,TRTC,CX,KC,NP,NALTC,TRTR,RX,KR,NALTR,D,
        1IT,NQ,TRT,NALT,SCON,NCON,RT,RT(INDC,INDR),U,NU,NCL)
         ARAN = V(10)
         V(10) = 0.
         WRITE(MED6,999)
         GO TO 91
     901 FORMAT (1H0,20X,40HSTATCAT TESTS OF SEVERAL RELATED SAMPLES   )
     941 FORMAT (1H1,10X,30HSET OF RELATED VARIATES         /)
     942 FORMAT(1H0,10X,36HONLY ONE SAMPLE - PROGRAM CANNOT RUN,63X,11H**WA
```

```
      1RNING**)
  943 FORMAT(1H0,10X,47HONLY TWO SAMPLES - PROGRAM ST2REL IS PREFERABLE,
     152X,11H**WARNING**)
  944 FORMAT(4H0THE,F6.0,34H STORAGE CELLS REQUIRED EXCEED THE   ,F6.0,
     110H AVAILABLE    )
  945 FORMAT (4H0NO.,9X,30HTRANS  DATA            NUMBER OF,7X,5HLOWER,6X,
     15HCLASS,7X,5HUPPER/5H CODE,8X,68H-FORM COLUMN         CLASSES USED
     2 CLASS LIMIT    INTERVAL    CLASS LIMIT)
  999 FORMAT (36H1ANALYSIS COMPLETED - READ NEW INPUT)
      END


      SUBROUTINE CKREL(DMIN,DMAX,CRTC,TRTC,CX,KC,NP,NALTC,TRTR,RX,KR,NAL
     1TR,D,IT,NQ,TRT,NALT,SCON,NCON,PD,RT,U,NU,NCL)
C CKREL  (SEE  6.4 ) EXECUTIVE     TESTS SEVERAL RELATED SAMPLES
      DIMENSION TRTC(NALTC),CX(NALTC),KC(NALTC),NP(NALTC)
      DIMENSION DMIN(NALTC),DMAX(NALTC),CRTC(NALTC),NCL(NALTC)
      DIMENSION TRTR(NALTR),RX(NALTR),KR(NALTR)
      DIMENSION D(NQ),IT(NQ),TRT(NALT),SCON(5,NCON),TTA(10),TTR(21)
      DIMENSION PD(NALTC,10),RT(NALTC,NALTR),U(NU)
      DATA BL/4H    /
      COMMON /STCT/MED1,MED2,MED3,MED4,MED5,MED6,MED13,Q,V(20),TT(30)
  996 FORMAT(1H0,10X,20HEND OF TEST SEQUENCE      )
  997 FORMAT(12X,10(2X,A4,2X))
  998 FORMAT(1H1,15X,20HSTATCAT DATA BANK - ,10A4/16X,20H DATA BANK SUBS
     1ET - ,10A4/
     21H0,15X,10HVARIATE = ,A4,4H OF ,A4,6H (COL.,F4.0,4H ) = ,A2,17A4)
  999 FORMAT(1H1,15X,20HSTATCAT DATA BANK - ,10A4/
     1         16X,20H DATA BANK SUBSET - ,10A4/
     212H0 VARIATES -,10(A4,4H OF.)/(12X,10(A4,4H OF.)))
      INOW = 0
      LB = V(1)
      LC = V(2)
      SIG = V(3)
      V10 = V(10)
      V19 = V(19)
      LD = 2
      ALTR = NALTR
      ALTC = NALTC
      RSS = V(17)
      SSR = V(18)
      REWIND MED3
      READ(MED3) NQ,NALT,Q,TTA,(X,K=1,6)
C IF(V(19).GT.1) DATA ARE STILL IN CORE
      IF(V19.GT.1.5) GO TO 20
C CLEAR STORAGE ARRAYS
      DO 2 I = 1,NALTC
      DO 3 J = 1,8
    3 PD(I,J) = 0.
      PD(I,9) = Q
      PD(I,10) = Q
      DO 2 J = 1,NALTR
    2 RT(I,J) = 0.
      V(6) = 0.
      REWIND MED3
      CALL FITIT(INOW,NQ,NQ,NALT)
      SSR = 0.
      RSS = 0.
C DATA COLLECTION SWEEP
      V(6) = 0.
      V(7) = 1.
      V(8) = 1.
      V(9) = 0.
```

```
    4 CALL MEDIAT(NALTC,NP,NP,NALTC,CX,D,NQ,SCON,NCON)
      IF(V(8).EQ.2.) GO TO 20
      SR = 0.
      DO 8 I = 1,NALTC
      X = CX(I)
      SR = SR + X
      PD(I,1) = PD(I,1) + 1.
      PD(I,2) = PD(I,2) + X
      PD(I,3) = PD(I,3) + X*X
      PD(I,4) = PD(I,4) + X*X*X
      PD(I,5) = PD(I,5) + X*X*X*X
      IF(PD(I,9).EQ.Q.OR.PD(I,9).GT.X) PD(I,9) = X
      IF(PD(I,10).EQ.Q.OR.PD(I,10).LT.X) PD(I,10) = X
    8 KC(I) = -1
      SSR = SSR + SR*SR
      SR = SR/ALTC
      DO 10 I = 1,NALTC
      X = CX(I)-SR
   10 PD(I,8) = PD(I,8) + X*X
      DO 12 J = 1,NALTR
   12 KR(J) = 0
      DO 13 I = 1,NALTC
      X = 0.5
      DO 9 J = 1,NALTC
      IF(CX(I).LT.CX(J))X = X + 1.
    9 IF(CX(I).EQ.CX(J))X = X + 0.5
      PD(I,6) = PD(I,6) + X
      RSS = RSS+ X*X
      NC = NP(I)-NP(I)/1000*1000
      CALL CLASIF(CX(I),DMIN(I),DMAX(I),IT(NC),NCL(I),KC(I))
      J = KC(I)
      KR(J) = KR(J) + 1
   13 RT(I,J) = RT(I,J) + 1.
      JSF = 1
      DO 14 J = 2,NALTR
   14 IF(KR(J).GT.KR(JSF))JSF = J
      DO 15 I = 1,NALTC
      J = KC(I)
   15 IF(KR(J).EQ.KR(JSF))PD(I,7) = PD(I,7) + 1.
      GO TO 4
C END OF DATA SWEEP
   20 REWIND MED3
      INOW = 0
C DESCRIPTION OF DATA COLUMNS IF REQUIRED
      IF(ISW(LB,LC,LD,8).LE.0) GO TO 120
      WRITE(MED2,999)TTA,(TT(J),J=21,30),TRTC
      WRITE(MED2,997)CRTC
      CALL TAB2W(RT,NALTC,NALTR,TRTC,CRTC,TRTR,-1,-1,X,X,X,X,V,MED2)
      GO TO 200
  120 IF(LB.LT.1.OR.LB.EQ.5) GO TO 200
      DO 150 I = 1,NALTC
      V(1) = LB
      ALTR = 1
      DO 121 J = 1,NALTR
      IF(RT(I,J).GT.0.5) ALTR = J
  121 RX(J) = RT(I,J)
C IDENTIFICATION OF ROW TITLES
      NALTX = NCL(I)
      DMINR = DMIN(I)
      DMAXR = DMAX(I)
      NR = NP(I)/1000
      CALL COPYA(TTR(1),U(NR))
      NR = NP(I) - NR*1000
```

```
      ITR = IT(NR)
      CALL FITIT(INOW,NR-1,NQ,NALT)
      INOW = INOW + 1
      TTR(3) = NR
      READ(MED3) TTR(2),(TTR(L),L=4,21),TRT,NX,X,X
      DO 122 L = 1,NALTX
      CALL COPYA(TRTR(L),BL)
  122 IF(L.LE.NALT) CALL COPYA(TRTR(L),TRT(L))
      LD = ITR
      V(7) = LD
      V(8) = 60.
      IF(ISW(LB,LC,LD,6).LE.0) GO TO 130
      WRITE(MED2,998) TTA,(TT(J),J=21,30),TTR
      V(8) = 6.
      CALL DCFT(V(6),DMAXR,DMINR,RX,TRTR,NALTX,V,MED2)
      IF(V(11).EQ.0.) GO TO 150
  130 IF(ISW(LB,LC,LD,7).LE.0) GO TO 140
      IF(V(8).GE.20.) WRITE(MED2,998) TTA,(TT(J),J=21,30),TTR
      IF(V(8).GE.20.) V(8) = 6.
      V(1) = LB
      CALL DCDS(DMAXR,DMINR,RX,TRTR,NALTX,PD(I,1),PD(I,2),PD(I,3),PD(I,4
     1),PD(I,5),PD(I,9),PD(I,10),V,MED2)
  140 IF(ISW(LB,LC,LD,6).LE.0) GO TO 150
      IF(V(8).GE.40.-ALTR) WRITE(MED2,998) TTA,(TT(J),J=21,30),TTR
      IF(V(8).GE.40.-ALTR) V(8) = 6.
      V(2) = 1.
      V(1) = 3.
      CALL DCBC(DMAXR,DMINR,RX,TRTR,NALTX,V,MED2)
      IF(V(8).GE.54.-ALTR) WRITE(MED2,998) TTA,(TT(J),J=21,30),TTR
      IF(V(8).GE.54.-ALTR) V(8) = 6.
      V(2) = 6.
      CALL DCBC(DMAXR,DMINR,RX,TRTR,NALTX,V,MED2)
      V(1) = LB
      V(2) = LC
  150 CONTINUE
  200 CONTINUE
C TESTING OF DATA AS REQUIRED BY MINIMUM VALUE OF LEVEL OF DATA LD
      LD = 5
      DO 180 I = 1,NALTC
      J = NP(I) - NP(I)/1000*1000
      IF(LD.EQ.5.AND.IT(J).EQ.6) LD = 4
      IF(LD.GT.IT(J))   LD = IT(J)
  180 CONTINUE
      V(3) = SIG
      IF(SIG.LE.0.) GO TO 370
      V(8) = 60.
C NOMINAL SCALE TESTS
  320 IF(ISW(LB,LC,LD,2)) 330,321,322
  321 V(1) = -1
      CALL CHISQ1(PD(1,7),TRTC,CRTC,NALTC,V,X,X,-1,MED2)
      IF(V(11).GT.V(2)) GO TO 330
  322 V(1) = 2
      WRITE(MED2,999) TTA,(TT(J),J=21,30),TRTC
      WRITE(MED2,997) CRTC
      CALL CHIKEN(2,LD)
      CALL CHISQ1(PD(1,7),TRTC,CRTC,NALTC,V,X,X,-1,MED2)
C ORDINAL SCALE TESTS
  330 IF(ISW(LB,LC,LD,3)) 340,331,332
  331 V(1) = -1
      CALL FREID2(PD(1,6),TRTC,CRTC,NALTC,RSS,V,MED2)
      IF(V(11).GT.V(3)) GO TO 340
  332 V(1) = 2
      WRITE(MED2,999) TTA,(TT(J),J=21,30),TRTC
```

```
      WRITE(MED2,997) CRTC
      CALL CHIKEN(3,LD)
      CALL FRIED2(PD(1,6),TRTC,CRTC,NALTC,RSS,V,MED2)
      V(8) = 18.
C INTERVAL SCALE TESTS
  340 IF(ISW(LB,LC,LD,4)) 350,351,352
C RATIO SCALE TESTS
  350 IF(ISW(LB,LC,LD,5)) 360,351,352
  351 V(1) = -1.
      CALL PAR2W(PD(1,2),PD(1,3),PD(1,8),TRTC,CRTC,NALTC,SSR,V,MED2)
      IF(V(11).GT.V(3).AND.V(12).GT.V(3).AND.V(13).GT.V(3)) GO TO 360
  352 V(1) = 2.
      WRITE(MED2,999) TTA,(TT(J),J=21,30),TRTC
      WRITE(MED2,997) CRTC
      V(8) = 6.
      CALL CHIKEN(4,LD)
      CALL PAR2W(PD(1,2),PD(1,3),PD(1,8),TRTC,CRTC,NALTC,SSR,V,MED2)
  360 CONTINUE
      IF(V(8).EQ.60.) WRITE(MED2,999) TTA,(TT(J),J=21,30),TRTC
      IF(V(8).EQ.60.) WRITE(MED2,997) CRTC
      WRITE(MED2,996)
  370 V(1) = LB
      V(2) = LC
  400 CONTINUE
      V(10) = V10
      V(17) = RSS
      V(18) = SSR
      V(19) = V19
      RETURN
      END


      SUBROUTINE CHISQ1(S,TRTC,CRTC,NALTC,V,DMAX,DMIN,IT,MED2)
C ONE-WAY CHI-SQUARED TEST FOR EQUAL FREQUENCIES
      DIMENSION S(NALTC),V(20),TRTC(NALTC),CRTC(NALTC)
C V(1) CONTROLS PRINTOUT       V(2) SIGNIFICANCE LEVEL
C NEG  NO PRINTOUT              V(8) LINES ON PAGE SO FAR
C  0   SIGNIFICANT RESULT       V(11) PROBABILITY
C  1   RESULT                   V(12) CHI-SQUARED VALUE
C  2   FULL DETAILS             V(13) DEG OF FREEDOM
C NALTC = NUMBER OF SAMPLES
C TRTC  = TITLES OF CLASSES/SAMPLES
C S     = READINGS IN SAMPLES
      ALTC = NALTC
      T = 0.
      DO 1 I = 1,NALTC
    1 T = T + S(I)
      E = T/ALTC
      IF(V(1).LT.2.) GO TO 2
      IF(E.GE.5.) WRITE(MED2,900)
      IF(E.LT.5.) WRITE(MED2,901)
      WRITE(MED2,902)
      V(8) = V(8) + 3.
    2 CHISQ = 0.
      DO 3 I = 1,NALTC
      CHI = (S(I) - E)*(S(I) - E)/E
      CHISQ = CHISQ + CHI
      IF(V(1).LT.2.) GO TO 3
      WRITE(MED2,903) S(I),E,CHI
      IF(IT.GE.0) CALL PRTCLS(DMAX,DMIN,I,TRTC(I),NALTC,IT,MED2)
      IF(IT.LT.0) WRITE(MED2,909) I,TRTC(I),CRTC(I)
    3 CONTINUE
      V(12) = CHISQ
```

```
      V(13) = ALTC - 1.
      V(11) = PRBF(1.,1000.,V(12)/V(13))
      IF(V(1).LT.0..OR.V(1).EQ.0..AND.V(2).LT.V(11)) GO TO 4
      WRITE(MED2,904) V(12),V(13),V(11)
      V(8) = V(8) + 5.
    4 IF(E.GE.5.) RETURN
      IF(V(1).GE.2..AND.V(8).GT.50.-ALTC) WRITE(MED2,905)
      IF(V(1).GE.2..AND.V(8).GT.50.-ALTC) V(8) = 5.
      IF(V(1).GE.2.) WRITE(MED2,906)
      J = (E-.00001)/5. + 1.
      NCL = (NALTC-1)/J +1
      IF(NCL*J.GT.NALTC.AND.NCL.LT.5) NCL = NCL - 1
      CHISQ = 0.
      NSF = 0.
      DO 6 IS = 1,NALTC,J
      IF = IS + J - 1
      NSF = NSF + 1
      IF(NSF.EQ.NCL) IF = NALTC
      OB = 0.
      EX = 0.
      DO 5 I = IS,IF
      OB = OB + S(I)
      EX = EX + E
      IF(V(1).LT.2.) GO TO 5
      WRITE(MED2,907)
      V(8) = V(8) + 1.
    5 CONTINUE
      CHI = (OB-EX)*(OB-EX)/EX
      CHISQ = CHISQ + CHI
      IF(V(1).LT.2.) GO TO 6
      WRITE(MED2,907)
      WRITE(MED2,903) OB,EX,CHI
      V(8) = V(8) + 1.
    6 CONTINUE
      V(12) = CHISQ
      V(13) = NCL - 1
      V(11) = PRBF(V(13),1000.,V(12)/V(13))
      IF(V(1).EQ.0..AND.V(11).GT.V(2).OR.V(1).LT.0.) RETURN
      WRITE(MED2,904) V(12),V(13),V(11)
      WRITE(MED2,908)
      RETURN
  900 FORMAT (1H0,52X,8HREQUIRED)
  901 FORMAT (1H0,52X,13H NOT REQUIRED)
  902 FORMAT (1H+,10X,42HCHI-SQUARED ONE-SAMPLE TEST - COMBINATION   ,/
     151H0 CLASS OR SAMPLE     OBSERVED   EXPECTED CHI-SQUARE)
  903 FORMAT (21X,3F10.2)
  904 FORMAT (///11X,13HCHI-SQUARED = ,F12.4,5H WITH,F4.0,19HDEGREES OF
     1FREEDOM // 11X,24HASSOCIATED PROBABILITY =,F10.6)
  905 FORMAT (1H1)
  906 FORMAT (1H0,10X,50HCHI-SQUARED ONE-SAMPLE TEST - COMBINATION REQUI
     1RED   /51H0 CLASS OR SAMPLE     OBSERVED   EXPECTED CHI-SQUARE)
  907 FORMAT (22X,4HPLUS)
  908 FORMAT (80H0      ADJACENT CLASSES OR SAMPLES COMBINED TO OBTAIN ST
     1ABLE CHI-SQUARED ESTIMATE)
  909 FORMAT (1H+,I2,2X,A4,4H OF ,A4)
      END


      SUBROUTINE FREID2(SR,TRTR,CNTR,NS,SSR,V,MED2)
C FREID2 (SEE  6.4 ) STATISTICAL FRIEDMAN 2-WAY ANOVAR BY RANKS
      DIMENSION SR(NS),TRTR(NS),CNTR(NS),V(20)
C SR CONTAINS SUM OF RANKS
C SSR CONTAINS SUM OF SQUARES OF RANKS
```

```
      C V(6) CONTAINS NUMBER OF   ENTRIES
      C V(1) CONTAINS OUTPUT CONTROL
      C V(2) CONTAINS SIGNIFICANCE LEVEL
            SN=NS
            TR=0.
            TS=V(6)
            DO 1 I=1,NS
          1 TR = TR + SR(I)/TS*SR(I)
            CF = NS*(NS+1)*(NS+1)
            CF = CF*0.25*TS
            V(13)=SN-1.
            V(12) = 0.
            IF(SSR.GT.CF) V(12) = V(6)*V(13)*(TR-CF)/(SSR-CF)
            V(11)=PRBF(V(13),1000.,V(12)/V(13))
            IF(V(1).LT.0.)GO TO 4
            IF(V(1).EQ.0..AND.V(2).LT.V(11))GO TO 4
            IF(V(1).LT.2.)GO TO 3
            WRITE(MED2,900)
            DO 2 I=1,NS
            TS=SR(I)/V(6)
          2 WRITE(MED2,901)TRTR(I),CNTR(I),TS
          3 WRITE(MED2,902) V(12),V(13),V(11)
            IF(SSR.LE.CF) WRITE(MED2,903)
          4 RETURN
        900 FORMAT(50H0 FRIEDMAN TWO-WAY ANALYSIS OF VARIANCE BY RANKS   /
           126H0RELATED VARIATE MEAN RANK)
        901 FORMAT(5X,A4,4H OF ,A4,F12.2)
        902 FORMAT(50H0 FRIEDMAN TWO-WAY ANALYSIS OF VARIANCE BY RANKS           /
           11H0,9X,16HCHI-SQUARED(R) =,F12.4,5H WITH,F8.0,20H DEGREES OF FREED
           20M  /10X,24HASSOCIATED PROBABILITY =,F12.4)
        903 FORMAT(35H0ALL RANKS ARE TIED FOR ALL ENTRIES)
            END


            SUBROUTINE TAB2W(RT,NC,NR,TRTC,CRTC,TRTR,JTC,JTR,DMINC,DMINR,DMAXC
           1,DMAXR,V,MED2)
      C TAB2W  (SEE   6.4 ) STATISTICAL TABLES WITH VARIATE NAMES ETC
            DIMENSION RT(NC,NR),TRTC(NC),CRTC(NC),TRTR(NR)
            DIMENSION V(20),XX(10),ABO(2),BEL(2),DUM(2)
            DATA ABO/4HAT/A,4HBOVE/
            DATA BEL/4H BEL,4HOW  /
            DATA DUM/4H (DUM,4HMY) /
            IC = 1
            ITR = JTR
            DEL = NR-2
            IF(DMAXR.GT.DMINR+DEL+0.1.OR.DMAXR.LT.DMINR+DEL-0.1) IC = 0
            IF(DMAXR.EQ.DMINR) IC = 1
            IF(ITR.GE.2.AND.ITR.LE.3.AND.IC.EQ.0) ITR = 4
            IC = 1
            ITC = JTC
            DEL = NC-2
            IF(DMAXC.GT.DMINC+DEL+0.1.OR.DMAXC.LT.DMINC+DEL-0.1) IC = 0
            IF(DMAXC.EQ.DMINC) IC = 1
            IF(ITC.GE.2.AND.ITC.LE.3.AND.IC.EQ.0)  ITC = 4
            IF(ITC.GT.3) DEL = (DMAXC-DMINC)/DEL
            NSC = NC
            NSR = NR
            NFC = 0
            NFR = 0
            DO 1 I = 1,NC
            DO 1 J = 1,NR
            IF(RT(I,J).LE.0.) GO TO 1
            IF(NSC.GT.I) NSC = I
```

```
      IF(NSR.GT.J) NSR = J
      IF(NFC.LT.I) NFC = I
      IF(NFR.LT.J) NFR = J
    1 CONTINUE
      IF(NFC.GT.0) GO TO 2
      WRITE(MED2,906)
      RETURN
    2 DO 4 IS = NSC,NFC,10
      IF = IS + 9
      IF(IF.GT.NFC) IF = NFC
      IF(ITC.LT.4) GO TO 7
      IL = IF - IS + 1
      DO 6 I = 1,IL
      X = IS + I - 2
    6 XX(I) = DMINC + DEL*X
      IF(IF.EQ.NC)XX(IL) = DMAXC
    7 MINUS = IF-1
      DO 4 JS = NSR,NFR,50
      JF = JS + 49
      IF(JF.GT.NFR) JF = NFR
      X = JF - JS + 1
      V(8) = V(8) + X
      IF(V(8).LT.60.) GO TO 3
      V(8) = X + 4.
      WRITE(MED2,905)
    3 WRITE(MED2,900) (I,I= IS,IF)
      IF(ITC.LE.0)WRITE(MED2,909) (TRTC(I),I=IS,IF)
      IF(ITC.LE.0)WRITE(MED2,908) (CRTC(I),I=IS,IF)
      IF(ITC.EQ.1)WRITE(MED2,902) (DUM,I=IS,IF)
      IF(ITC.EQ.2.OR.ITC.EQ.3) WRITE(MED2,901) (TRTC(I),I=IS,IF)
      IF(ITC.LT.4) GO TO 5
      IF(IF.NE.NC)              WRITE(MED2,902) (BEL,I = IS,IF)
      IF(IF.EQ.NC.AND.IS.NE.IF)WRITE(MED2,902) (BEL,I=IS,MINUS),ABO
      IF(IF.EQ.NC.AND.IS.EQ.IF) WRITE(MED2,902) ABO
      WRITE(MED2,903) (XX(I),I=1,IL)
    5 DO 4 JJ = JS,JF
      J = JF+JS-JJ
      WRITE(MED2,904) (RT(I,J),I = IS,IF)
      IF(ITR.LE.0)WRITE(MED2,907) J
    4 IF(ITR.GT.0) CALL PRTCLS(DMAXR,DMINR,J,TRTR(J),NR,ITR,MED2)
      RETURN
  900 FORMAT (1H0,10X,10HCOLUMN NO.,10(2X,I4,4X))
  901 FORMAT (4H ROW,17X,13HCOLUMN TITLES/16H NO.  ROW TITLES,6X,10(3X,A
     14,3X))
  902 FORMAT (2(5H ROW ),4X,7HCOLUMN ,10(2X,2A4))
  903 FORMAT (21H NO. TITLES    TITLES ,10(F9.2,1X))
  904 FORMAT (21X,10(F9.2,1X))
  905 FORMAT(1H1)
  906 FORMAT(1H0,10X,16HNO DATA IN TABLE    )
  907 FORMAT(8H+  CLASS,I6)
  908 FORMAT(18X,10(6X,A4))
  909 FORMAT (4H ROW,17X,13HCOLUMN TITLES/16H NO.  ROW TITLES,6X,10(A4,3
     1H OF,3X))
      END


      SUBROUTINE PAR2W(SX,SXX,SXD,TRTC,CRTC,NS,RSS,V,MED2)
C TWO-WAY TESTS OF  K PARAMETRIC  RELATED DATA COLUMNS
      DIMENSION SX(NS),SXX(NS),SXD(NS),TRTC(NS),CRTC(NS),V(20)
C SX CONTAINS COLUMN SUMS
C SXX CONTAINS COLUMN SUMS OF SQUARES
C V(6) CONTAINS NUMBER OF  ENTRIES
C V(1) CONTROLS OUTPUT
```

```
C V(2) IS SIGNIFICANCE LEVEL
C SSR CONTAINS SUMS OF SQUARES OF ROWS
      SSR = RSS
      SN = NS
      CF = 0.
      SSC = 0.
      TSS = 0.
      TSQ = 0.
      TLOG = 0.
      IF(V(1).GE.2.) WRITE (MED2,900)
      IF(V(1).GE.2.) WRITE (MED2,901)
    1 DO 2 I = 1,NS
    2 CF = CF + SX(I)
      E = CF/SN/V(6)
      F = SQRT(ABS((SSR/SN/SN-E*CF/SN)/(V(6)-1.)))
      DO 3 I = 1,NS
      SSC = SSC + SX(I)*SX(I)
      TSS = TSS + SXX(I)
      A = SX(I)/V(6)
      B = SQRT(ABS((SXX(I)-A*SX(I))/(V(6)-1.)))
      C = A-E
      D = SXD(I)-C*C*V(6)
      TSQ = TSQ + D
      D = SQRT(ABS(D/(V(6)-1.)))
      TLOG = TLOG + ALOG(D*D)*(V(6)-1.)
    3 IF(V(1).GE.2.) WRITE(MED2,902)TRTC(I),CRTC(I),A,B,C,D
      IF(V(1).GE.2.)WRITE(MED2,909)E,F
      CF = CF/V(6)*CF/SN
      TSS = TSS -CF
      SSC = SSC/V(6) - CF
      SSR = SSR/SN -CF
      TSS = TSS - SSC - SSR
      DFC = SN-1.
      DFR = V(6) - 1.
      DFRES = DFC*DFR
      SMC = SSC/DFC
      SMR = SSR/DFR
      VC = 0.
      VR = 0.
      PC = 0.
      PR = 0.
      SRES= TSS/DFRES
      IF(SRES.GT.0..AND.SMC.GT.0.) VC = SMC/SRES
      IF(SRES.GT.0..AND.SMR.GT.0.) VR = SMR/SRES
      PC = PRBF(DFC,DFRES,VC)
      PR = PRBF(DFR,DFRES,VR)
      V1 = SN-1.
      A = (SN+1.)/SN/3./(V(6)-1.)
      V2 = (SN+1.)/A/A
      B = V2/(1.-A+2./V2)
      SP = TSQ/(V(6)-1.)/SN
      AM = 0.
      IF(SP.GT.0.)AM = (V(6)-1.)*SN*ALOG(SP)-TLOG
      BAR = 0.
      PV = 1.
      IF(AM.LE.0.) GO TO 4
      BAR = V2*AM/(V1*(B-AM))
      PV = PRBF(V1,V2,BAR)
    4 V(11) = PC
      V(12) = PR
      V(13) = PV
      IF(V(1).LT.0.) RETURN
      IF(PC.GT.V(2).AND.PR.GT.V(2).AND.PV.GT.V(2).AND.V(1).LE.0.) RETURN
```

```
      IF(V(1).LE.1.) WRITE(MED2,900)
      WRITE(MED2,903) SSC,DFC,SMC,VC,PC,SSR,DFR,SMR,VR,PR,TSS,DFRES,SRES
      IF(VC.EQ.0.) WRITE(MED2,907)
      IF(VR.EQ.0.) WRITE(MED2,908)
      IF(SRES.LE.0.) WRITE(MED2,905)
      WRITE(MED2,904) BAR,V1,V2,PV
      IF(AM.LE.0.) WRITE(MED2,906)
      RETURN
  900 FORMAT (40H0CLASSICAL TWO-WAY ANALYSIS OF VARIANCE    )
  901 FORMAT(11H0    VARIATE,8X,16HVALUE OF VARIATE,12X,26HDIFFERENCE FRO
     1M ENTRY MEAN/12X,2(5X,10HARITHMETIC,5X,8HSTANDARD)/13X,2(7X,4HMEAN
     2,8X,9HDEVIATION))
  902 FORMAT (2X,A4,4H OF ,A4,F13.4,3F14.4)
  903 FORMAT (80H0SOURCE OF             TOTAL SUM         DEGREES OF   MEAN SUM
     1     VARIANCE   ASSOCIATED   /80H VARIATION                       OF SQUARES      F
     2REEDOM    OF SQUARES  RATIO         PROBABILITY      /
     311H0VARIATES   ,F18.4,F9.0,F18.4,2F10.4/
     411H ENTRIES    ,F18.4,F9.0,F18.4,2F10.4/
     511H RESIDUAL   ,F18.4,F9.0,F18.4//)
  904 FORMAT (57H0BARTLETT TEST FOR EQUALITY OF VARIANCE BETWEEN VARIATE
     1S     /20H0F-LIKE STATISTIC = ,F12.4,5H WITH,F12.0,4H AND,F12.0,20
     2H DEGREES OF FREEDOM    /26H0ASSOCIATED PROBABILITY =     ,F12.6)
  905 FORMAT(45H0NO RESIDUAL VARIATION - TESTING NOT POSSIBLE)
  906 FORMAT(31HS.D.S OF VARIATES ARE IDENTICAL)
  907 FORMAT(33H0MEANS FOR VARIATES ARE IDENTICAL)
  908 FORMAT(33H0MEANS FOR ENTRIES ARE IDENTICAL )
  909 FORMAT(2X,10HENTRY MEAN,F15.4,F14.4)
      END
```

Chapter VII

MODEL TESTING

Where data were gathered under controlled conditions, so that several variables have been systematically varied - the choice of work task, work position, operator and observer - and other possible intervening factors have been measured - working temperature and disturbing factors for example - a good deal more can be done than simple testing of differences between samples of results. Over the last half-century techniques have been developed for the design of experiments, and the analysis of results in many fields, some highly specialised, others of more general application. It is impossible for a solitary worker to summarise this vast body of work in a single volume, let alone digest it into easily-usable forms. The writer has therefore been forced to make a rather arbitrary choice of available techniques, concentrating on techniques generally known and accepted. The five programs described in this chapter may be used to carry out most of the better known types of statistical analysis. In the interests of clarity, the explanations given are deliberately simplified. Interested users should consult the sources quoted for further details, for mathematical analyses of techniques, for examples and for awful warnings of what can happen if methods are used without sufficient thought.

The first program (7.1. - STANOV) is a general purpose analysis of variance program. It has been written to accomodate most normal analysis of variance designs. The user is required to specify his analysis in a more-or-less conventional analysis of variance table.

The second program (7.2. - STMULT) is a general purpose multiple regression program. The user may specify transforms of data columns, and may use delayed values of variates to carry out auto-correlation and lag-correlation analyses. Powers of variables are available, and random perturbations may be used to test the sensitivity of results.

The program for factor analysis (7.3. - STFACT) contains options allowing the user to perform a principal components analysis, with a Varimax rotation of the components. The Guttman technique for estimating covariance may be employed as an alternative, and different methods of cut-off are available. Factor scores may also be produced.

The program for Multiple Discriminant analysis (7.4. - STMDIS) uses the entries in specified samples to form discriminant functions, but all entries in the specified STATCAT data bank subset are classified into the most probable group, if individual discriminants are calculated.

Finally a program for Canonical Correlation analysis is provided (7.5. - STCANO). This technique is useful where a set of predictor variates is used to predict a number of criterion variates, rather than a single one as is done in multiple regression.

The discussion of each program contains warnings of ways in which these techniques may be misleading. The user is advised to bear these in mind, and to follow up any points relevant to his interests.

7.1 PROGRAM STANOV - ANALYSIS OF VARIANCE

7.1.1 Purpose

This program is a general purpose analysis of variance program. Because the analysis of variance model is read in as part of the input data, most analysis of variance designs can be handled by this program. Options are provided to allow the printing of individual values of the dependent variate, numbers of readings, arithmetic means and standard deviations of the data at each level of each variate, and for any combination of variates used in the analysis. The possibility that the variances of component terms are significantly different from each other is checked using Bartlett's Test for homoscedasticity of variance, if required. Because this program is sometimes useful to produce numbers, means and standard deviations where analysis of variance is not applicable, the analysis of variance table itself can be suppressed. If it is produced, the table is initially printed in the form specified, even if some terms have no available degree of freedom. It is then reprinted with these terms combined appropriately, as described below, and then with any terms not significant at a defined threshold level pooled. This process is repeated until all remaining terms are significant at the defined level.

Figure 7.11a contains simplified flow-charts of the main program STANOV, the executive subroutine CANOV and the analysis of variance model loading subroutine LANOV. Figure 7.11b contains simplified flow-charts of the model interpreting and checking subroutine SIGSUM, the data collecting subroutine CASIGS and the output subroutine AOVOUT.

7.1.2 Input Data

Summary

Item	Level	Format	Function	Section
1	1	A	File Control Card (Input only)	3.2
2	2	E	Subset Specification	3.6
3	3	F	Independent Variates Specification	3.7 and below
4	4	-	Analysis of Variance Model Spec.	Below
5	5	F	Dependent Variates Specification	3.7 and below
6	6	G	Data Handling Instruction	3.8 and below

3 - Independent Variate Specification

This module specifies the independent variates of the following analyses of variance. It is a standard variate specification as described in 3.7.

The variates may be transformed, but not delayed. Unless otherwise specified they will be clasified into the number of classes given in the Data Starter. The number of classes, lower class limit, class interval and upper class limit may be specified. Entries which contain missing values for any of the independent variates employed in a specific analysis will be discarded.

4 - Analysis of Variance Model Specification

Purpose

This module specifies an analysis of variance model, with relationships between the parameters employed and adds any necessary terms.

Module Layout

```
ANOVAR SPECIFICATION CARD
ANOVAR SPECIFICATION CARD
ANOVAR SPECIFICATION CARD
........................
'END' CARD
```

Card Layout - Anovar Specification Card

AABBBBBBBBBBBBB BBBB BCCCCCCCC CCCCCCCCC CCCCCCCCCCCCCCCCCCCCC......

Columns on Card	Item Code	FORTRAN Type	Function
1 - 2	AA	I	Card Number - verifies order
2 - 20	BBB..	A	Analysis of Variance Model
21 - 80	C	A	Comment

A - Card Number

The successive cards of an analysis of variance model must be numbered in consecutive order from 1 upwards. If the number on the card does not correspond to the number expected, the card will be rejected, and more cards will be read until the corresponding number is found, or until an 'END' card is read. If a card is missing from the model, all subsequent cards will be rejected, but any necessary residuals will be inserted and an attempt will be made to run the analysis if no other, fatal, error is present.

B - Analysis of Variance Model

The analysis of variance model is specified in terms of the letters assigned to the independent variates specified in the preceding stage of data input. These variates are given letters in order of entry from A to Z. A simple effect is specified by a single letter and an interaction by the letters of the variates involved. The sequence of letters may be terminated by an = sign. All letters after the = sign are retained for printing in the analysis of variance output, but are not included in the definitions of the term for the given line. They may therefore be used to expand the letter code to provide a more directly readable output.

Blanks at the start of the line are used to indicate 'nested variates'. If we wish to analyse data for which the variate A represents one of sixteen days, and the variate B represents one of four weeks, each containing four of the days, a model of the form given below could be used (assuming that there are several data for each day).

```
1 A = DAY OF EXPERIMENT
```

```
 2    B = WEEK
END OF ANOVAR MODEL
```

The module would then automatically add the necessary residual terms, producing an output of the form:

```
              ANALYSIS OF VARIANCE MODEL

   CARD LINE          MODEL

    1    1      A = DAY OF EXPERIMENT
    2    2        B = WEEK
         3        RES
         4      RES
                END OF ANOVAR MODEL
```

The system would interpret the last line of the model as an instruction to obtain the residual variation after the 'A' effect has been isolated and the third line of the model as an instruction to obtain the residual variation between days, after the variation between weeks has been isolated. The user may insert the RESIDUAL order himself. The module will recognise any card for which the first three characters following any leading blanks are RES as a residual card, and will not insert a second residual. The system tests any terms against the residual on the same level next following. The system will detect, but cannot rectify, cases where an interaction term requires terms not yet specified in the model. It will take account of missing values and of cases where the degrees of freedom of a line of the analysis of variance have become insufficient.

The order of the letters defining an interaction term is not important and blank columns may be left between or after these letters. (Should the interaction of terms lettered E, S and R be required, the order RES should not be used, since this will be taken for a residual term.)

C - <u>Comment</u>

The remainder of the Anovar Specification card may be used for any comment to be printed out at the loading stage.

<u>Error Messages</u>

Certain input errors can be detected by the input module and result in error messages. These error messages will be printed next to the user's comment for the appropriate line of the analysis of variance model.

DISORDERED - SHOULD BE XXX

This message is produced when an ANOVAR card is read which does not have the expected number (NX). The card (which has been printed out), is discarded and further cards are read until either a card with the correct number is read, or the end of the model is found. This is a fatal error, and will, if no previous error has been found, cause the error index to be set to 34.

NO MORE STORAGE AVAILABLE - INCREASE NDMAX

This message is produced when the number of ANOVAR cards required for a model exceeds the available storage. It is a fatal error, and will, if no previous error has been found, cause the error index to be set to 35. The module will continue to read cards until an 'END OF MODULE' card is found.

RESIDUAL ADDED BY SYSTEM

This message, not strictly an error message, is produced wherever a residual term is required for the analysis of variance, but is not provided by the user. It is followed by other ANOVAR cards. The error index is not altered.

REDUNDANT RESIDUAL

This message is printed out wherever a residual term is read in, if no simple or interaction term has been specified at that level (with the same number of leading blanks), or if a residual term has already been provided at the given level. The residual term is discarded, but the error index is not altered.

NOT USED - MODEL COMPLETE

This message is printed out if an ANOVAR specification card is read in after a residual has been stored at the lowest level at which there are any simple or interaction terms. The ANOVAR line is discarded, but the error index is not altered.

End of Analysis-of-Variance Module

The end of the module is identified by any standard 'END OF MODULE' card. When this card is read, the module will insert any necessary residual terms, provided that there is room for them, and will record that a model containing so many lines has been read. The message takes the form

NN LINE MODEL ACCEPTED

Where NN is the number of valid lines (including residuals added by the system).

Empty Analysis-of-Variance Module

If there are no acceptable terms in the model at the time that the 'END OF MODULE' card is read, the program will step back to the previous input module and read in a new set of independent variates. The module will print a message :

NO NEW MODEL - STEP BACK

Tests of Model outside loading Module

Certain tests are applied to the analysis of variance module which require knowledge of the characteristics of the independent variates, which may be changed (See below) without reading in a new analysis of variance model. These tests are applied by the main program - immediately after loading the model or a new set of independent variates, or in the model interpreting subroutine SIGSUM. The following errors, all fatal, can be detected.

UNDEFINED VARIATE IN COLUMN xx OF LINE yy OF MODEL = z

The symbol z found in the xxth column of the card corresponding to the yth line of the analysis of variance model is not one of the letters for which an independent variate has been defined. This may be either because some independent variates were rejected, or because the symbol itself is incorrectly punched (1 for I,0 for O for example). The error index will be set to 36 if not already set.

www VARIATES ALREADY IN MODEL - z IN COLUMN xx OF LINE yy
CANNOT BE ACCEPTED - INCREASE NLMAX

The arrays used for storing the model, sums of squares definitions, and working vectors have been assigned www cells only, in the main program STANOV. The analysis as defined requires more than this number. The analysis of variance model should, however, be checked to ensure that no unintended variates have crept in - through omitting an = sign for example. The error index will be set to 37 if not already set.

The subroutine SIGSUM detects two further errors.

TOO MANY SUBTOTALS REQUIRED IN THE FOLLOWING LINE
(xxx) WHILE ONLY xxx ARE AVAILABLE

The analysis of variance term for which the sum of squares term is being calculated will need more space to store subtotals than is available. Check that the numbers of classes for the variates are correctly defined, and, if possible, increase the array SIG and the index NDATX in the main program. The error index will be set to 38 if not already set.

NEXT LINE REQUIRES AN UNEVALUATED SIGMA TERM

The next line in the analysis of variance table is an interaction term, of which one component interaction at least has not been defined. The system is not, at present, capable of deciding at what level this term should be placed, and accordingly registers a fatal error.

5 - Dependent Variates

This module specifies the dependent variates. It is a standard variate specification as described in 3.7. Only the transform name and data column name or number are used. Variates may not be delayed. Class definitions are not employed. Entries which contain missing values will be included in those analyses for which the values are present. If the first card of the specification is an 'END' card, the program will step back to the previous level and read a new Anovar model.

6 - Data Handling Instruction

This is a standard data handling instruction as described in 3.8. Because it is often necessary to run the same analysis of variance model with a number of different data bank subsets, or with different independent or dependent variates, a special feature has been incorporated in this program. If this card contains the following code words, revised input data are read accordingly. (All code words are of four characters, starting in column 1 of the card).

LDBS - Program reads new data bank subset module

LIND - Program reads new independent variates

LAOV - Program reads new analysis of variance model

LDEP - Program reads new dependent variates

In addition any 'END' card will cause the program to step back to read a new set of dependent variates and a 'STOP' card will cause the program to terminate. If the data handling instruction is not a four-letter word of this sort, it is interpreted as below:

Card Layout - Data Handling Instruction - STANOV

ABCCCDDDDDDDDDDDDDDDDD..........

Columns on Card	Item Code	FORTRAN Type	Function
1	A	I	Output Control Index
2	B	I	Test Control Index
3 - 5	C	F	Probability Limit for Pooling
6 - 80	D	A	Comment

A - Output Control Index

This index controls the amount of detail output in the course of calculation and data collection.

Unless otherwise specified, only error messages and analysis results are printed.

Alternatives

A = 0 or blank : Only error messages and analyses required.

A = 1   : Number of readings in each subset is also printed.

A = 2   : Arithmetic mean of readings is also printed.

A = 3   : Standard deviations of sub-totals also printed.

A = 4   : Individual readings also printed out.

A = 5 - 9   : As for A = 0

B - Test Control Index

This index controls what tests are carried out.

Unless otherwise specified, only an analysis of variance is output.

B = 0 or blank : Analysis of variance only.

B = 1   : Analysis of variance only.

B = 2   : Analysis of variance + Bartlett's Test for last line.

B = 3   : Analysis of variance + Bartlett's Test for all lines.

B = 4   : Bartlett's Test for last line only.

B = 5   : Bartlett's Test for all lines.

B = 6 - 9   : No tests are carried out.

(Where the main interest is in mean values and standard deviations for defined groups and sub-groups, it is often possible to use this program to provide these statistics in one data sweep.)

C - Percentage Limit for Pooling

This index specifies the percentage probability level at or below which terms will not be pooled. At the first output of the analysis of variance program, all terms are printed, even if they have no remaining degrees of freedom, or are negative through rounding or because the design is not orthogonal.

A second output of the analysis of variance table is produced, in which all incorrect terms are combined with appropriate residuals and the previous term to any zero residual is added to the residual. (If there are no faults of this type, this output is suppressed).

A third output suppresses all terms for which the probability is above this limit, adding them to their respective residuals. In the process of doing so, some further terms may become non-significant. These will be suppressed until a table is output in which all terms are statistically significant, or all terms have been suppressed. Where a term is suppressed which contains one or more nested variates, the first level of nested variate is brought down to the level of the suppressed term and tested against the residual at that level.

7.1.3   Input Example

Figure 7.12 is a summary of the input data for four analyses of variance. The analyses all treat the whole demonstration STATCAT data bank, and have a common set of independent variates. In the first analysis of variance model the six independent variates make up a hyper-greco-latin cube, in which each value of each variate occurs exactly once in association with each possible pair of any other two variates, giving a total of 64 combinations, corresponding to the 64 entries in the demonstration STATCAT data bank. The two dependent variates are the value of the heart rate of the operator and the logarithm to the base 10 of this value, for reasons which will be explained when the output is discussed. In the second analysis, the factors C (working position) and H (session) in fact determine the value of G (the entry number), and the factors D (day of experiment) and E (time within day) determine the value of H. The interaction terms DE and GH therefore leave no degrees of freedom for the nested analyses. Similarly, the term G has only one value at each of its 64 levels, so that there are no degrees of freedom for its residual at the basic level. The output will show how the program solves these problems.

The two dependent variates shown here are the temperature and the '+/-1' transform of temperature, in which one unit is added or subtracted randomly from each value.

Figure 7.13 lists the complete input data required to produce these four analyses of variance, including the specification of the input file and the final 'STOP' instruction.

7.1.4 Output Example

Figure 7.14 is a general summary of the output structure of this program, indented according to the structure of the program. Figure 7.15 is a page-by-page summary of the output produced by the input data given below.

Because of the quantity of output produced, only a selection of examples can be given. The program identification, data description segment, and data bank subset specifications are not shown, as these are, with the exception of the program name, identical to the examples given earlier. Figure 7.16 shows the checking output for the independent variate definition, the first analysis of variance model, the first two dependent variates and the first data handling instruction. Figure 7.17 shows the tabulation of sigma and sum matrices for this model. The first of these tables defines which terms are required to be calculated to provide the sums of squares terms for the analysis of variance model. Each term is calculated by identifying the variate letters in a given line. A check is made that all required component terms have already been specified. (For example :- if the term ABC is required, that A,B,C,AB,AC and BC are already specified. An error message will be printed if this is not the case. The 'Formation of Analysis of Variance' table shows how the sigma terms are combined to form the analysis of variance table. Figure 7.17 also shows a part of the listing of individual data values and the overall number of readings, arithmetic mean and standard deviation for all readings. Figure 7.18 is the standardised analysis of variance table for this analysis with and without pooling non-significant terms. Figure 7.19 shows the input record for the second analysis of variance model, the formation of sigma terms and the sum matrix controlling their combination and the analysis of variance for the first variate. This is first shown in the form specified, then with incorrect terms merged, and finally with non-significant terms merged into the appropriate residuals.

7.1.5 Discussion

Analysis of variance is one of the oldest and most widely used methods of statistical analysis. In its simplest form it looks at several samples of data and tries to determine if their arithmetic means are more widely dispersed than they could be expected to be if all the samples were drawn from a population having the same overall mean and a variance estimated from the variation around the mean. In essence, the technique makes use of convenient mathematical proporties of the sums of squares of deviations to partition the variance into components representing the variation between samples and the variation within samples. (Space does not permit a detailed explation here, but Li (1964) provides a convincing non-mathematical explanation of why the method works.)

Although analysis of variance works, in principle, by comparing mean values, it has been the custom to work largely in terms of total squares of sums divided by the number of values on which they are based, rather than on squares of means multiplied by the number of values on which they are based. Until the advent of the digital computer it was more convenient to work in this way since it required fewer division operations. The digital computer is less concerned to avoid division, but is more likely to suffer from difficulties with too-large numbers, so that the calculations involved are rearranged accordingly, and do not exactly correspond to those laid out in many textbooks.

From the simple one-way analysis of variance (as carried out by PAR1W - see 6.2) it is reasonable to progress to a two-way analysis, in which the effects of rows and columns are extracted separately, and compared with the variation remaining after both have been extracted (as in PAR2W - see 6.4 - which does this in a restricted sense, since the two ways must be comparisons between samples and between entries). This is the fundamental two-way analysis of variance. Provided that the numbers in all cells are proportional this analysis can be performed by the simple method of forming sums of squares, and sums of squares of mean values. In doing so, we assume that there is no 'interaction' between the two factors represented by rows and columns. If we have several readings in each cell of our analysis, we can form an estimate of the 'residual error' - which we assume to be a measure of the 'noise' in the system, and by comparing the variation of cell means (after extracting the systematic effects of rows and columns) we can estimate the significance of the 'interaction'. The process can be generalised to several classifications. For four classifications we can extract not only the four basic classifications A,B,C and D say, but the two-way interactions AB,AC,AD,BC,BD and Cd, the three-way interactions ABC, ABD, ACD and BCD, and the four-way interaction ABCD. (What exactly a four-way interaction means in practice is left to the reader.) The number of entries needed, however, is at least the product of the number of alternatives for each classification, or a multiple of this if we wish to have a 'residual' to test the highest-order interaction against. Often this is an excessive or impossible number of entries, or we may simply be willing to assume that there is no interaction above a certain order. The sets of combinations of conditions that should be tested can be arranged to provide acceptable estimations for the main factors and some interaction terms by a suitable experimental design. Unfortunately, experimental design is far too large and complex subject for treatment here - see Winer, Kendall and Stuart or Dixon and Massey for detailed examples.

A second point of difficulty in the analysis of variance is the choice of what term to use as an estimate of residual error. Two types of 'analysis of variance model' exist. In one, we know that the levels of the classification we are testing cover all possible cases - for example left-handed versus right-handed. In the other our levels are simply samples from a population - subjects drawn from a panel of volunteers for example. Depending on the type of model, we may or may not be able to combine non-significant terms, and should test main terms directly against the overall residual or against higher-order interaction terms. Unfortunately, in practice, most analyses involve mixed models, in which some classifications are exhaustive and others random samples. The correct choice of residual, and pooling procedure is very much a matter of judgement, and an expert should be consulted if there is any doubt.

7.1.6   Non-orthogonality

Practically, the major problem with analysis of variance is that it requires that the classifications employed should be 'orthogonal'. This means that each cell of the analysis should contain a number of readings proportional to the overall frequencies of the conditions on which it is based. Section 12.5 gives an example of what can happen if this condition is not observed.

The program STANOV checks for proportionality for each interaction term evaluated. (It assumes that unevaluated higher-order terms are proportional.) Warning messages are printed out when disproportionate subtotals are found.

Even when an analysis of variance has been properly designed and specified, data may be lost for one reason or another, resulting in non-orthogonality. In analyses based on thousands of readings, the loss of a few values may not lead to any significant inaccuracy - see Winer (1970) for a complete treatment of this approach.

If non-orthogonality cannot be ignored, several approaches are possible. If, in a two-way analysis, one factor is considered more important than the other, an initial analysis may be made of that factor alone, then separate analyses made of the minor factor within each level of the major. These analyses can then be combined to provide a hierachical model.

If there are plenty of data, the program STCOMB may be used to form mean values for each cell, with the numbers of data on which they are based and the within-cell variance. An analysis of variance can be carried out on the cell means, adjusted (according to Winer) by multiplication by the harmonic mean of the cell numbers, and compared with the pooled cell means.

As a penultimate measure, missing values can be estimated by successive approximation or interpolation from row and column means. This process can be very laborious, and where a substantial proportion of data is missing can lead to instabilities. It is subject to the fundamental problem that the best estimate of the missing value can never substitute for reality - which may in fact be very different.

As a last resort, if we are prepared to abandon interaction terms, we can analyse the data using multiple linear regression. Here we do not assume orthogonality, but we do assume linearity of predictors. (So that level 2 of a predictor has twice the effect of level 1, and half the effect of level 4.) If we cannot, or do not want to, make this assumption (for example when one of our variates was on a NOMINAL level), we can re-write our data bank, using STMANI, or a user-written DATA subroutine, to turn each NOMINAL or ORDINAL variate into a series of yes/no classifications (one less than the number of alternative classes). The resultant multiple regression tends to be very large if there more than a few variates with several classes, and risks becoming singular (see STMULT - 7.2) if there are too few data or some conditions are always linked.

Methods for handling non-orthogonal analysis of variance do exist, but it appears that their complexity is rarely justified in practice - either because a simpler method is more appropriate, or better data should be found. Searle (1971) provides a detailed investigation of the problem, reaching generally pessimistic conclusions.

REFERENCES : Li (1964), Winer (Chs. 3-10), Dixon and Massey (Ch 10) Searle (1971)

7.1.7 Transformations before analysis of variance

Transformations of the data before analysis of variance is carried out may be undertaken for three reasons : -

- to ensure that the error variance is evenly distributed, so that the pooled error term is homogeneous.

- to ensure that within-cell variance is normal, so that the F test assumptions are satisfied.

- to produce a simple additive model.

The concensus of contemporary opinion is that the first two reasons are probably not very important, since it has been shown that the distribution of the F ratio is not very sensitive to moderate departures from equality of variance in pooling, or from normality within cells. If the experimental design requires a strictly additive model, or if it is to be incorporated into some further analysis, the use of an appropriate transform will reduce the proportion of variance not allocated to main effects and increase the 'visibility' of the main efects. The use of the logarithmic transform in the accompanying example shows how this works.

Certain specialised transforms are often used for any or all of the three reasons given above. The choice of transform is guided in part by the sort of theoretical model we suspect underlies our data (if we expect a multiplicative relation we would probably use a logarithmic transform, for example), and in part by the observed relation between cell mean and cell variance (before transformation). Common sense is occasionally also involved.

If the cell variance is proportional to the cell mean, then the within-cell distribution is often Poissonian in shape. If cell means are relatively large a simple square root transform is adequate. If they are small (less than ten) then PSNA (square root plus square root of value plus one) or PSNB (square root of value plus one half) are recommended.

If the data are drawn from a binomial distribution then the mean will be betwen 0 and 1 and the variance largest near a mean of 0.5. The BINO transform is recommended - twice the arcsine of the square root of the x value. (If x is within 0.02 of the limits 0 and 1 the transform clips the extreme values.)

If the variance is proportional to the square of the mean cell value (standard deviation proportional to mean) then the logarithmic transform (LOGE or LG10 - the difference is simply a scale factor) will normally stabilise variances. If original values are close to zero, the transform LG+1 gives the log of the original value plus one.

If the data are percentages between 20% and 80% no transform may be necessary. If they range forther, than they should be expressed as fractions (by dividing by 100) and treated as if binomial. If they are all close to zero, then LG+1 should be used. If they are close to 100% then LG+1 should be used on the difference from 100%. STMANI (10.1) is the best way of manipulating the data.

If the original data units are dichotomised, as say 0 or 1, then no transformation of this original data can affect the analysis of variance, except to alter its units. The total variation within the analysis will be determined by the proportion of zeros to units, and the part not assigned to differences between cell means will not be a valid residual. Special methods exist for such data.

REFERENCES : Winer (Ch 5)

Figure 7.11a - System Flow-Charts - STANOV, CANOV + LANOV

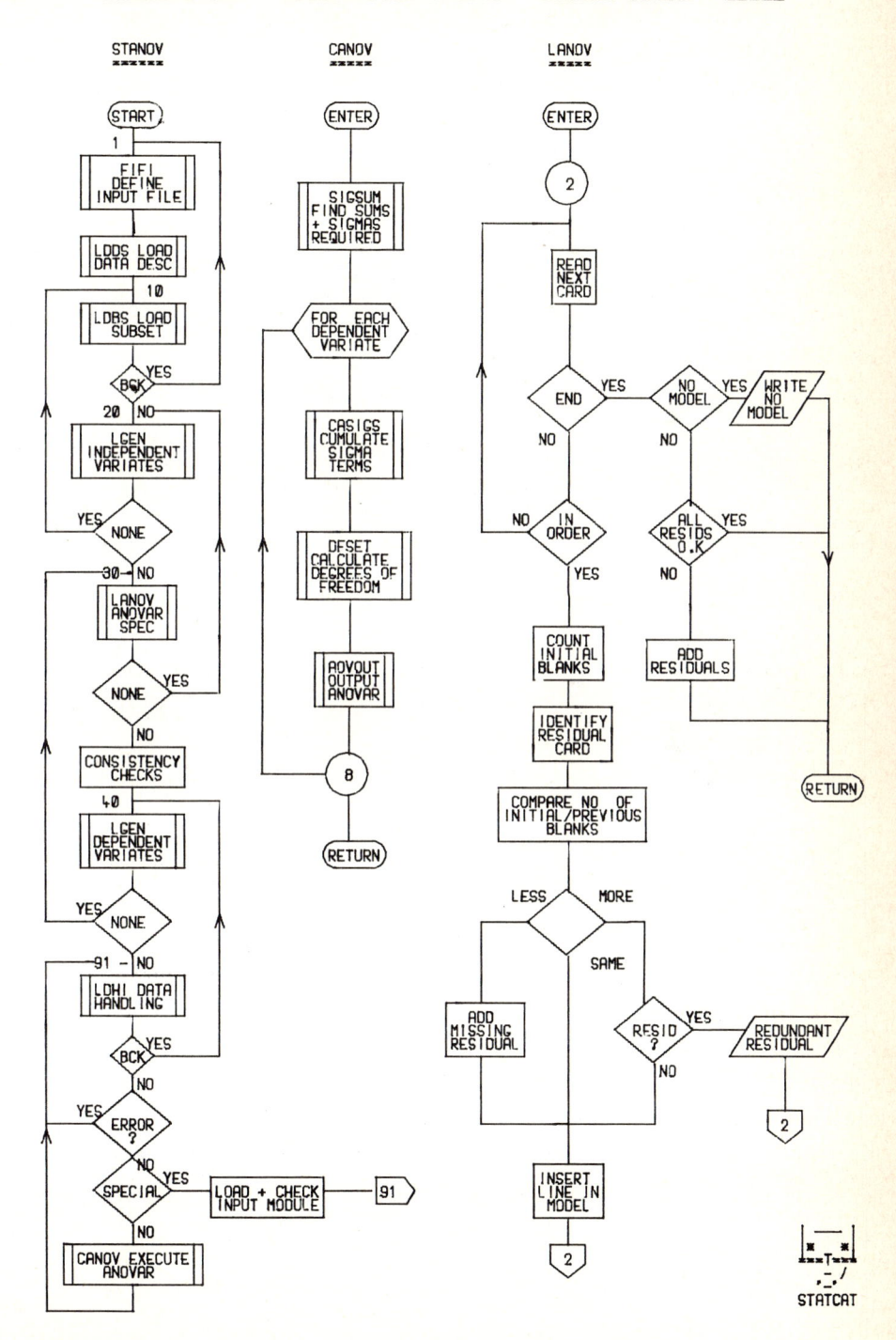

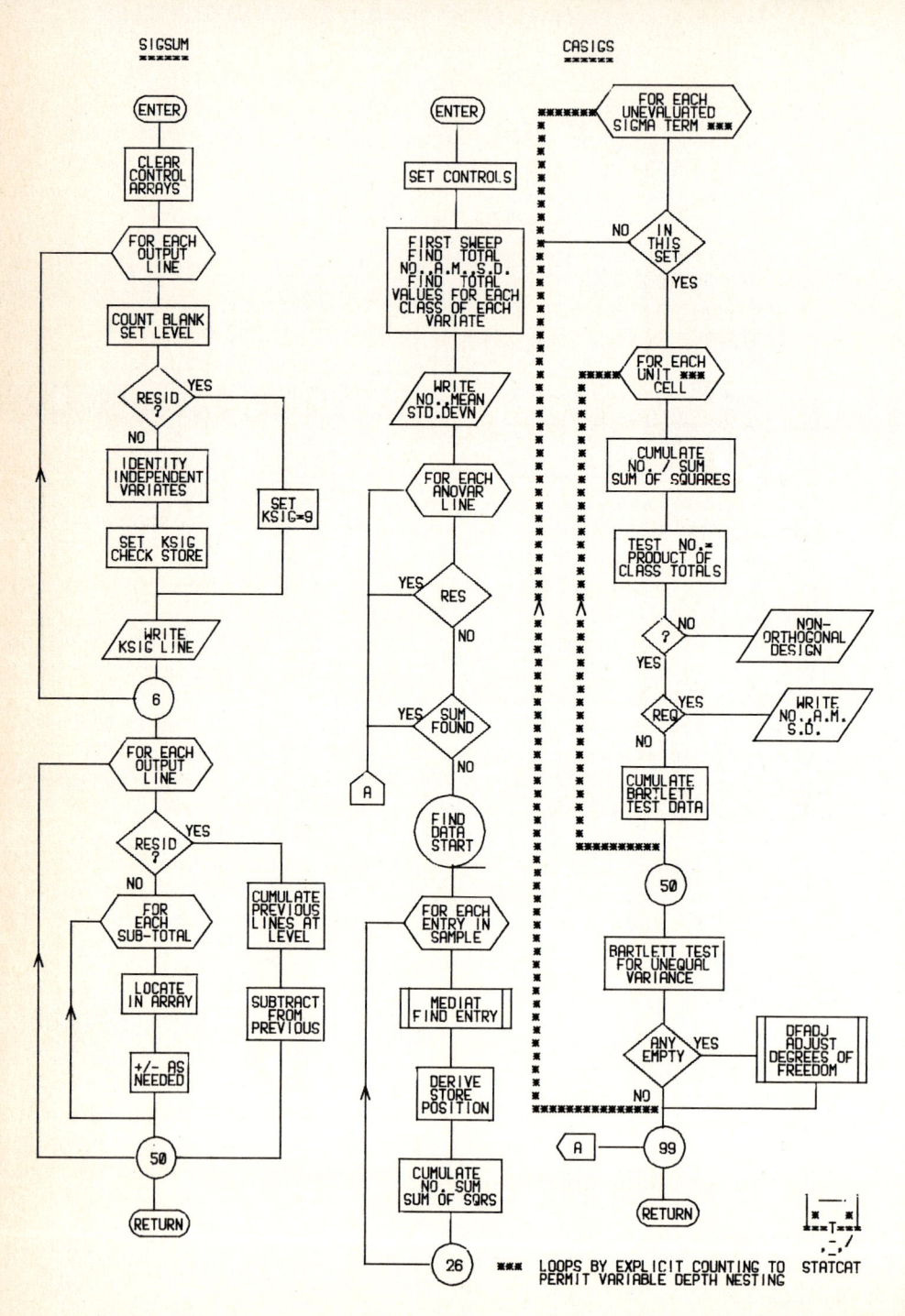

Figure 7.11b - System Flow-Charts - SIGSUM, CASIGS + AOVOUT

FIGURE 7.11C - SYSTEM FLOW-CHARTS - AOVOUT, DFADJ, DFSET

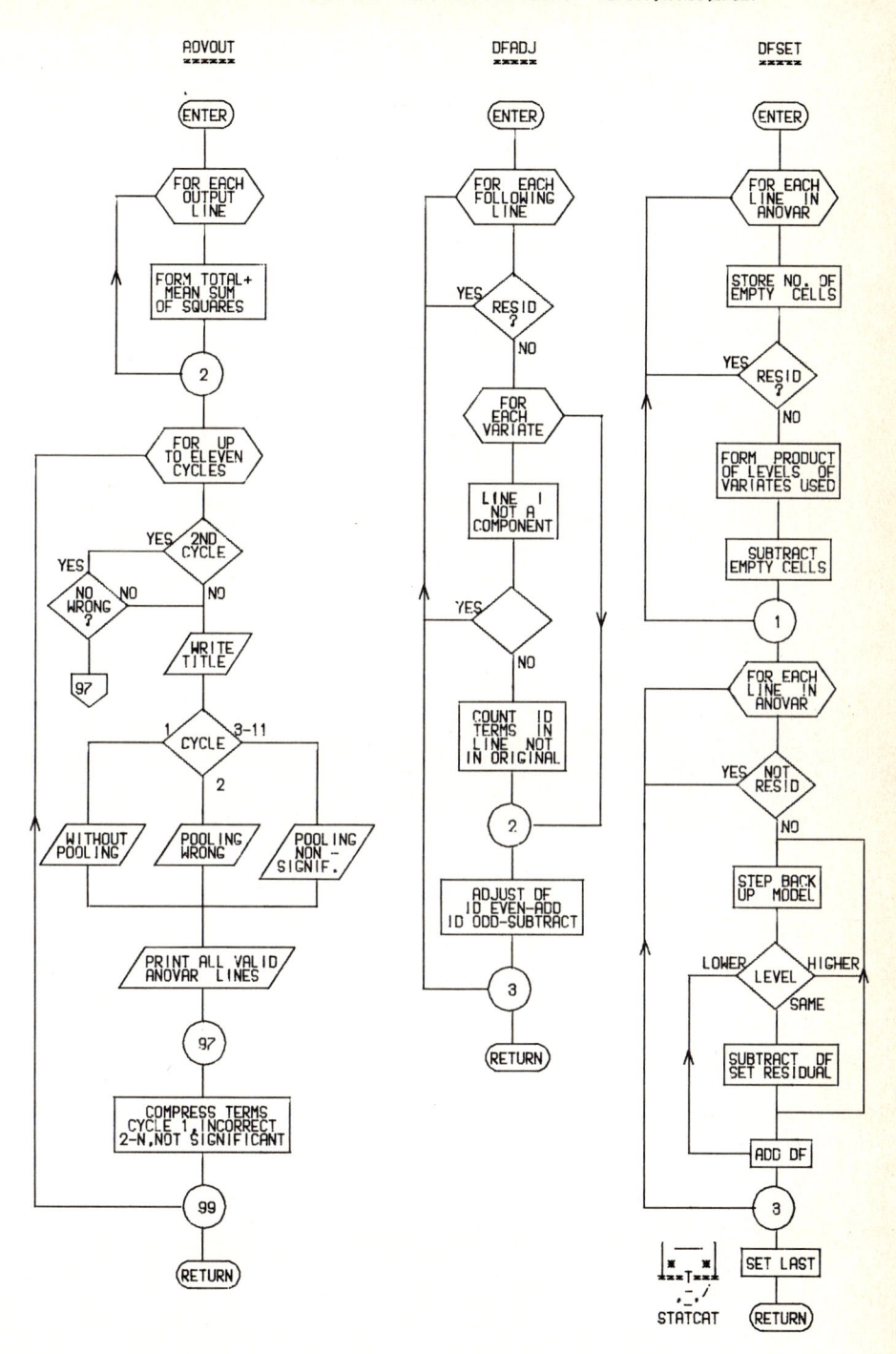

Figure 7.12 - <u>STANOV</u> - <u>Input Structure</u>

```
         Level
  0    1    2    3    4    5    6    7    8    9
FILE CONTROL CARD
    SUBSET SPECIFICATION
        INDEPENDENT VARIATE SPECIFICATION
            ANALYSIS OF VARIANCE MODEL
                DEPENDENT VARIATE SPECIFICATION
                    DATA HANDLING INSTRUCTION
                    LAOV - LOAD NEW ANALYSIS OF VARIANCE MODEL
            ANALYSIS OF VARIANCE MODEL
                LDEP - LOAD NEW DEPENDENT VARIATES
                DEPENDENT VARIATE SPECIFICATION
                DATA HANDLING INSTRUCTION
                STOP
```

Figure 7.13 - <u>STANOV</u> - <u>Input Example</u>

```
---------1---------2---------3---------4---------5---------6---------7--
**STANOVDEMO                            DEMONSTRATION STATCAT DATA BANK
ALL DATA                                TITLE OF DATA BANK SUBSET
END OF DATA BANK SUBSET                 NO CONDITIONS APPLIED TO DATA
VAL.OBSR        4    1.5    1.0    3.5  NUMBER OF CLASSES
VAL.OPER        4    1.5    1.0    3.5  SET TO FOUR
VAL.W.P.        4    1.5    1.0    3.5  AND LIMITS ADJUSTED
VAL.DAY.        4    1.5    1.0    3.5  TO AVOID WASTING STORAGE
VAL.TIME        4    1.5    1.0    3.5
VAL.TASK        4    1.5    1.0    3.5
VAL.SET.       64    1.5    1.0   63.5  64 CLASSES REQUIRED
VAL.SESS       16    1.5    1.0   15.5  16 CLASSES REQUIRED
END OF INDEPENDENT VARIATE SPECIFICATION
 1A=OBSERVER         THESE SIX TERMS
 2B=OPERATOR         FORM A
 3C=WORK POSITION    FOUR LEVEL
 4D=DAY OF WEEK      SIX WAY
 5E=TIME OF DAY      HYPER-GRECO-LATIN CUBE
 6F=WORK TASK        ANALYSIS OF VARIANCE MODEL
END OF ANOVAR MODEL
VAL.ERRP                                ADDITIVE MODEL
LG10ERRP                                MULTIPLICATIVE MODEL
END OF SET OF DEPENDENT VARIATES
43                                      FULL OUTPUT WITH ALL POSSIBLE TE
LAOV                                    LOAD NEW MODEL FOR ANALYSIS
 1G=ENTRY                               LEAVES NO DF FOR RESIDUAL
 2 H = SESSION
 3  D=DAY OF WEEK
 4  E=TIME IN DAY
 5  DE=DAY/TIME IA                      LEAVES NO DF INSIDE H TERM
 6  C=WORK POSITION
 7  HC=W.P./SESSION IA                  LEAVES NO DF INSIDE G TERM
 8  DC=DAY/W.P.
 9  EC=TIME/W.P.
10  DEC=DAY/TIME/W.P                    LEAVES NO DF INSIDE HC TERM
END OF ANOVAR MODEL
LDEP                                    LOAD NEW SET OF DEPENDENT VARIAT
VAL.TEMP
+/-1TEMP                                RANDOM DIGIT + OR MINUS 1 ADDED
END OF DEPENDENT VARIATES
GO                                      DEFAULT OUTPUT - ANOVAR ONLY
STOP
---------1---------2---------3---------4---------5---------6---------7--
```

Figure 7.14 - STANOV - Output Structure

```
For each      ) : File Control Record
output file )     File Parameters
                  Data Description
                  For each) : Subset Input Record
                  Subset  )   For each set of) : Input Record
                              Independent    )   For each      ) : Input
                              Variates       )   Analysis of)      Record
                                                 Variance   )
                                                 Model      )

For each set) : Input Record
of dependent)   For each Data) : Input Record
Variates    )   Handling     )   For Each     ) See left
                Instruction  )   dependent    )
                                 Variate      )

For each    ) Sigma term definition                          ) First Variate
dependent   ) Formation of Analysis of Variance Table)  Only
variate     ) <Individual data>
    .         <Non-Values>
    .         <Overall N,a.m. and s.d.>
    .         <For each line:Page Title>
    .         <of ANOV table  For each cell ) Number
    .                .              in ANOV line ) Mean
    .                .                                s.d.
    .         <Bartlett test for uneven variance>
Analysis of variance table
Analysis of variance table  (Pooling Incorrect terms)
Analysis of variance table  (Pooling non-significant terms)

Carated(<>) items are optional.
```

Figure 7.15 - STANOV - Page-by-page output summary

Page	Contents	Origin
1-3	File Control/Program title Data Description record	FIFI/LDAP/STANOV LDDS
4	Subset record	LDBS/LSAMP
5	Independent Variate record Analysis of Variance Model record	LGEN LANOV
6	Dependent Variate record Data Handling Instruction	LGEN LDHI
7	Sigma Term definition	SIGSUM
8	Formation of Analysis of Variance Table	SIGSUM
9-10	Individual data	CASIGS
11	Number/Mean/s.d. overall	CASIGS
12-17	No./Mean/s.d. for each line of A.o.V. table	CASIGS
18	Analysis of Variance tables	AOVOUT
19-28	As pp 9-18 for new dependent variate	CASIGS/AOVOUT
29	Data Handling Instruction (LAOV) Analysis of Variance Model record Data Handling Instruction (LDEP)	LDHI LANOV LDHI
30	Dependent Variate record Data Handling Instruction	LGEN LDHI
31	Sigma Term definition	SIGSUM
32	Formation of Analysis of Variance Table	SIGSUM
33	Analysis of Variance tables (first variate)	AOVOUT
34	Analysis of Variance tables (second variate)	AOVOUT
35	Data Handling Instruction (STOP)	LDHI

Figure 7.16 - STANOV - Output Example - Checking output

```
INDEPENDENT VARIATES

NO.         TRANS   DATA    CLASS/ NUMBER OF    LOWER        CLASS     UPPER
CODE        -FORM   COLUMN  VALUE  CLASSES USED CLASS LIMIT  INTERVAL  CLASS LIMIT

 1 ORIGINAL VAL.    OBSR              4          1.5          1.0       3.5       NUMBER OF CLASSES
 A STANDARD VAL.    COL3(VALUE)       4          1.5000       1.0000    3.5000

 2 ORIGINAL VAL.    OPER              4          1.5          1.0       3.5       SET TO FOUR
 B STANDARD VAL.    COL4(VALUE)       4          1.5000       1.0000    3.5000

 3 ORIGINAL VAL.    W.P.              4          1.5          1.0       3.5       AND LIMITS ADJUSTED
 C STANDARD VAL.    COL5(VALUE)       4          1.5000       1.0000    3.5000

 4 ORIGINAL VAL.    DAY.              4          1.5          1.0       3.5       TO AVOID WASTING STORAGE
 D STANDARD VAL.    COL7(VALUE)       4          1.5000       1.0000    3.5000

 5 ORIGINAL VAL.    TIME              4          1.5          1.0       3.5
 E STANDARD VAL.    COL8(VALUE)       4          1.5000       1.0000    3.5000

 6 ORIGINAL VAL.    TASK              4          1.5          1.0       3.5
 F STANDARD VAL.    COL9(VALUE)       4          1.5000       1.0000    3.5000

 7 ORIGINAL VAL.    NTRY             64          1.5          1.0
 G STANDARD VAL.    COL1(VALUE)      64          1.5000       1.0000   63.5000

 8 ORIGINAL VAL.    SESS             16          1.5          1.0
 H STANDARD VAL.    COL2(VALUE)      16          1.5000       1.0000   15.5000

END OF INDEPENDENT VARIATE SPECIFICATION

        ANALYSIS OF VARIANCE MODEL
CARD LINE     MODEL                  USER COMMENT                             SYSTEM COMMENT
  1        1 A=OBSERVER           THESE SIX TERMS
  2        2 B=OPERATOR           FORM A
  3        3 C=WORK POSITION      FOUR LEVEL
  4        4 D=DAY OF WEEK        SIX WAY
  5        5 E=TIME OF DAY        HYPER-GRECO-LATIN CUBE
  6        6 F=WORK TASK          ANALYSIS OF VARIANCE MODEL
           7 RES                                                        RESIDUAL ADDED BY SYSTEM

    END OF ANOVAR MODEL                                                 7 LINE MODEL ACCEPTED




DEPENDENT VARIATES

NO.         TRANS   DATA
CODE        -FORM   COLUMN

 1 ORIGINAL VAL.    ERRP                                        ADDITIVE MODEL
 A STANDARD VAL.    C 18

 2 ORIGINAL LG10    ERRP                                        MULTIPLICATIVE MODEL
 B STANDARD LG10    C 18

END OF SET OF DEPENDENT VARIATES

                    DATA HANDLING INSTRUCTION - ECHO PRINT

ABCCCDDDEEEEEEEEFFFFFFFGGGGGGGGGGGGGGGGGGHHHHHHHHHHHHHHHHHHHHHHHHHHHHHHHHHHH
43                   XXXXXXXXXXXXXXXXFULL OUTPUT WITH ALL TESTS


            OUTPUT CONTROL INDEX =     4
            TESTING CONTROL INDEX =    3
MINIMUM PERCENTAGE SIGNIFICANCE LEVEL =   5.0000

    THE SYSTEM HAS STANDARDISED ONE CONTROL VALUE FROM THE DATA HANDLING INSTRUCTION    ** WARNING **
    PLEASE VERIFY THAT THE ASSUMPTIONS IT HAS MADE ARE CORRECT AND ADJUST STORAGE IF NECESSARY

INPUT ACCEPTED - ANALYSIS COMMENCES
```

Figure 7.17 - STANOV - Output Example - Partial output

SIGMA TERMS

1=SUM BEFORE SQUARING
2=SQUARE BEFORE SUMMING
9 IN COL 1 - RESIDUAL TERM

```
NO  A  B  C  D  E  F
1   2  1  1  1  1  1
2   1  2  1  1  1  1
3   1  1  2  1  1  1
4   1  1  1  2  1  1
5   1  1  1  1  2  1
6   1  1  1  1  1  2
7   9  1  1  1  1  1
```

FORMATION OF ANALYSIS OF VARIANCE TABLE

```
                              SUM  O    SIGMA TERMS
NO      SOURCE         OF LEVEL RESID SYS F  1  2  3  4  5  6
1   A=OBSERVER          1           0 -1   1  0  0  0  0  0
2   B=OPERATOR          1           0 -1   0  1  0  0  0  0
3   C=WORK POSITION     1           0 -1   0  0  1  0  0  0
4   D=DAY OF WEEK       1           0 -1   0  0  0  1  0  0
5   E=TIME OF DAY       1           0 -1   0  0  0  0  1  0
6   F=WORK TASK         1           0 -1   0  0  0  0  0  1
7   RES                 1           1  9  -1 -1 -1 -1 -1 -1
8       TOTAL                       1 -1   0  0  0  0  0  0
```

DATA BANK TITLE - DEMONSTRATION STATCAT DATA BANK   INDEPENDENT VARIATES
       SUBSET TITLE - ALL DATA   A   B   C   D   E   F
                                                           VAL. VAL. VAL. VAL. VAL. VAL.
DEPENDENT VARIATE - VAL. OF EXP.   VAL. VAL. VAL. VAL. VAL. VAL.
                                                           OBSR OPER W.P. DAY. TIME TASK
FULL TITLE OF VARIABLE -   PERCENTAGE OF ERRORS IN FINAL PRODUCTS   DATA LEVEL - RATIO

```
                                 INDIVIDUAL READINGS
                                      0.5000          1  1  1  1  1  1
                                      1.3000          3  4  2  1  1  4
                                      1.3000          4  2  3  1  1  2
                                      0.5000          2  3  4  1  1  3
                                      3.0000          4  3  1  1  2  4
                                      1.4000          2  2  2  1  2  1
                                      1.4000          1  4  3  1  2  3
                                      1.0000          3  1  4  1  2  2
                                      3.5000          2  4  1  1  3  2
                                      2.1000          4  1  2  1  3  3
                                      2.1000          3  3  3  1  3  1
                                      2.1000          1  2  4  1  3  4
                                      6.0000          3  2  1  1  4  3
                                      6.0000          1  3  2  1  4  2
                                      2.3000          2  1  3  1  4  4
                                      5.2000          4  4  4  1  4  1
                                      0.3000          4  4  1  2  1  3
                                      0.3000          2  1  2  2  1  2
                                      0.3000          1  3  3  2  1  4
                                      0.1000          3  2  4  2  1  1
                                      0.5000          1  2  1  2  2  2
                                      0.5000          3  3  2  2  2  3
                                      0.5000          4  1  3  2  2  1
                                      0.5000          2  4  4  2  2  4
                                      1.9000          3  1  1  2  3  4
                                      0.6000          1  4  2  2  3  1
                                      0.5000          2  2  3  2  3  3
                                      0.0000          4  3  4  2  3  2
                                      1.4000          2  3  1  2  4  1
                                      3.0000          4  2  2  2  4  4
                                      1.4000          3  4  3  2  4  2
                                      1.0000          1  1  4  2  4  3
                                      0.1000          2  2  1  3  1  4
                                      0.1000          4  3  2  3  1  1
                                      0.1000          3  1  3  3  1  3
                                      0.2000          1  4  4  3  1  2
                                      0.3000          3  4  1  3  2  1
                                      0.3000          1  1  2  3  2  4
                                      0.3000          2  3  3  3  2  2
                                      0.6000          4  2  4  3  2  3
                                      1.1000          1  3  1  3  3  3
                                      1.2000          3  2  2  3  3  2
                                      0.6000          4  4  3  3  3  4
                                      0.4000          2  1  4  3  3  1
                                      1.7000          4  1  1  3  4  2
                                      1.7000          2  4  2  3  4  3
                                      2.0000          1  2  3  3  4  1
                                      1.7000          3  3  4  3  4  4
                                      0.1000          3  3  1  4  1  2
                                      0.1000          1  2  2  4  1  3
```

Figure 7.18 - STANOV - Output Example - Analysis of Variance

```
        DATA BANK TITLE - DEMONSTRATION STATCAT DATA BANK        INDEPENDENT VARIATES
             SUBSET TITLE - ALL DATA                              A    B    C    D    E    F
                                                                 VAL. VAL. VAL. VAL. VAL. VAL.
        DEPENDENT VARIATE - VAL. OF ERRP                         VAL. VAL. VAL. VAL. VAL. VAL.
                                                                 OBSR OPER W.P. DAY. TIME TASK
   FULL TITLE OF VARIATE -     PERCENTAGE OF ERRORS IN FINAL PRODUCTS                    DATA LEVEL - RATIO

        ANALYSIS OF VARIANCE - WITHOUT POOLING TERMS
        SOURCE OF VARIATION SUM OF SQUARES DF MEAN SUM OF SQS VAR RATIO WRT PROBABILITY
1       A=OBSERVER           0.9209      3      0.3070      0.5815     7 0.64721     -
2       B=OPERATOR           1.6996      3      0.5665      1.0364     7 0.38638     -
3       C=WORK POSITION      2.1059      3      0.7020      1.2841     7 0.29076     -
4       D=DAY OF WEEK       40.4858      3     13.4953     24.6367     7 0.0         ***
5       E=TIME OF DAY       38.4745      3     12.8248     23.4693     7 0.0         ***
6       F=WORK TASK          0.6959      3      0.2320      0.4243     7 0.74004     -
7       RES                 24.5957     45      0.5467
8          TOTAL           108.9824     63

        ANALYSIS OF VARIANCE - POOLING NON-SIGNIFICANT TERMS
        SOURCE OF VARIATION SUM OF SQUARES DF MEAN SUM OF SQS VAR RATIO WRT PROBABILITY
4       D=DAY OF WEEK       40.4858      3     13.4953     25.6222     7 0.0         ***
5       E=TIME OF DAY       38.4745      3     12.8248     24.3493     7 0.0         ***
7       RES                 30.0220     57      0.5267
8.         TOTAL           108.9824     63
```

Figure 7.19 - STANOV - Output Example - Over-specified Model

```
               ANALYSIS OF VARIANCE MODEL
CARD LINE     MODEL                    USER COMMENT                                              SYSTEM COMMENT
  1     1  G=ENTRY                                    LEAVES NC DF FOR RESIDUAL      00640013
  2     2  H = SESSION                                                               00650013
  3     3  D=DAY OF WEEK                                                             00660013
  4     4  E=TIME IN DAY                                                             00670013
  5     5  DE=DAY/TIME IA                             LEAVES NC DF INSIDE H TERM     00680013
        6  RES                                                                                    RESIDUAL ADDED BY SYSTEM
  6     7  C=WORK POSITION                                                           00690013
  7     8  HC=W.P./SESSION I         A                LEAVES NC DF INSIDE G TERM     00700013
  8     9  DC=DAY/W.P.                                                               00710013
  9    10  EC=TIME/W.P.                                                              00720013
 10    11  DEC=DAY/TIME/W.P                           LEAVES NC DF INSIDE HC TERM    00730013
       12  RES                                                                                    RESIDUAL ADDED BY SYSTEM
       13  RES                                                                                    RESIDUAL ADDED BY SYSTEM
       14  RES                                                                                    RESIDUAL ADDED BY SYSTEM

          END OF ANOVAR MODEL                                                        00740013    14 LINE MODEL ACCEPTED
```

```
SIGMA TERMS                        FORMATION OF ANALYSIS OF VARIANCE TABLE
                                                                      SUM  C   SIGMA TERMS
1=SUM BEFORE SQUARING                                                                                                       
2=SQUARE BEFORE SUMMING             NC    SOURCE         OF LEVEL RESID SQS F   1  2  3  4  5  6  7  8  9 10 11 12 13
9 IN COL 1 - RESIDUAL TERM           1  G=ENTRY                        0 -1   1  0  0  0  0  0  0  0  0  0  0  0  0
                                     2  H = SESSION          2         0 -1   0  1  0  0  0  0  0  0  0  0  0  0  0
NO  G  H  C  F  C                    3  D=DAY OF WEEK        3         0 -1   0  0  1  0  0  0  0  0  0  0  0  0  0
 1  2  1  1  1  1                    4  E=TIME IN DAY        3         0 -1   0  0  0  1  0  0  0  0  0  0  0  0  0
 2  1  2  1  1  1                    5  DE=DAY/TIME IA       3         0  0  0  0 -1 -1  1  0  0  0  0  0  0  0  0
 3  1  1  2  1  1                   -6  RES                             0  0  0  1  0  0 -1  0  0  0  0  0  0  0  0
 4  1  1  1  2  1                    7  C=WORK POSITION      2         0 -1   0  0  0  0  0  1  0  0  0  0  0  0  0
 5  1  1  2  2  1                    8  HC=W.P./SESSION I    2         0  1  0 -1  0  0  0 -1  1  0  0  0  0  0  0
 6  9  1  1  1  1                    9  DC=DAY/W.P.          3         0  1  0  0 -1  0  0 -1  0  1  0  0  0  0  0
 7  1  1  1  1  2                   10  EC=TIME/W.P.         3         0 -1   0  0  0 -1  0 -1  0  0  1  0  0  0  0
 8  1  2  1  1  2                   11  DEC=DAY/TIME/W.P     3         0  0  0 -1  0  0  1  0  0  1  0 -1 -1  1  0  0
 9  1  1  2  1  2                   12  RES                             0  0  1  0  0  0  0  0  0 -1  0  0 -1  0  0
10  1  1  1  2  2                   13  RES                   2         0  0 -1  0  0  0  0  0  0  0  0  0  0  0  0
11  1  1  1  2  2                   14  RES                   1         1  0 -1  0  0  0  0  0  0  0  0  0  0  0  0
12  9  1  1  1  1                   15     TOTAL                        1 -1  0  0  0  0  0  0  0  0  0  0  0  0  0
13  9  1  1  1  1
14  9  1  1  1  1
```

```
     DATA BANK TITLE - DEMONSTRATION STATCAT DATA BANK           INDEPENDENT VARIATES
              SUBSET TITLE - ALL DATA                            G    H    D    E    C
                                                                 VAL. VAL. VAL. VAL. VAL.
        DEPENDENT VARIATE - VAL. OF TEMP                         VAL. VAL. VAL. VAL. VAL.
                                                                 NTRY SESS DAY  TIME W.P.
        FULL TITLE OF VARIABLE -      MEAN TEMPERATURE OF WORKING POSITION DURING TEST (CENT.)   DATA LEVEL - INTERVAL

        ANALYSIS OF VARIANCE - WITHOUT POOLING TERMS

        SOURCE OF VARIATION SUM OF SQUARES DF MEAN SUM OF SQS VAR RATIO WRT PROBABILITY
 1      G=ENTRY               345.7344   63     5.4878       EXCESSIVE NON-ORTHOGONALITY                  NO RESIDUAL
 2      H = SESSION           189.9844   15    12.6656       EXCESSIVE NON-ORTHOGONALITY                  NO RESIDUAL
 3      D=DAY OF WEEK          66.1719    3    22.0573       EXCESSIVE NON-ORTHOGONALITY                  NO RESIDUAL
 4      E=TIME IN DAY         120.4219    3    40.1406       EXCESSIVE NON-ORTHOGONALITY                  NO RESIDUAL
 5      DE=DAY/TIME IA          3.3906    9     0.3767       EXCESSIVE NON-ORTHOGONALITY                  NO RESIDUAL
 6      RES                     0.0       0    -1.0000
 7      C=WORK POSITION       144.5469    3    48.1823       EXCESSIVE NON-ORTHOGONALITY                  NO RESIDUAL
 8      HC=W.P./SESSION I      11.2031   45     0.2490       EXCESSIVE NON-ORTHOGONALITY                  NO RESIDUAL
 9      DC=DAY/W.P.             2.2656    9     0.2517       EXCESSIVE NON-ORTHOGONALITY                  NO RESIDUAL
10      EC=TIME/W.P.            3.5156    9     0.3906       EXCESSIVE NON-ORTHOGONALITY                  NO RESIDUAL
11      DEC=DAY/TIME/W.P        5.4219   27     0.2008       EXCESSIVE NON-ORTHOGONALITY                  NO RESIDUAL
12      RES                     0.0       0    -1.0000
13      RES                     0.0       0    -1.0000
14      RES                     0.0       0    -1.0000
15         TOTAL              345.7344   63

        ANALYSIS OF VARIANCE - POOLING INCORRECT TERMS

        SOURCE OF VARIATION SUM OF SQUARES DF MEAN SUM OF SCS VAR RATIO WRT PROBABILITY
 2      H = SESSION           189.9844   15    12.6656       63.0726   14 0.0          ***
 3      D=DAY OF WEEK          66.1719    3    22.0573       58.5484    6 0.00004      ***
 4      E=TIME IN DAY         120.4219    3    40.1406      106.5484    6 0.00001      ***
 6      RES                     3.3906    9     0.3767
 7      C=WORK POSITION       144.5469    3    48.1823      239.9395   14 0.0          ***
 9      DC=DAY/W.P.             2.2656    9     0.2517        1.2536   14 0.30542       -
10      EC=TIME/W.P.            3.5156    9     0.3906        1.9452   14 0.08754       -
14      RES                     5.4219   27     0.2008
15         TOTAL              345.7344   63

        ANALYSIS OF VARIANCE - POOLING NON-SIGNIFICANT TERMS

        SOURCE OF VARIATION SUM OF SQUARES DF MEAN SUM OF SCS VAR RATIO WRT PROBABILITY
 2      H = SESSION           189.9844   15    12.6656       50.8745   14 0.0          ***
 3      D=DAY OF WEEK          66.1719    3    22.0573       58.5484    6 0.00004      *** °
 4      E=TIME IN DAY         120.4219    3    40.1406      106.5484    6 0.00001      ***
 6      RES                     3.3906    9     0.3767
 7      C=WORK POSITION       144.5469    3    48.1823      193.5356   14 0.0          ***
14      RES                    11.2031   45     0.2490
15         TOTAL              345.7344   63
```

```
C MASTER STANOV - GENERAL ANALYSIS OF VARIANCE
C   SUBROUTINES AND FUNCTIONS REQUIRED
C  NAME         TYPE                 COMMENT
C  AN      (SEE  3.1 ) SERVICE     ALPHA - TO NUMERIC VALUE
C  AOVOUT  (SEE  7.1 ) SYSTEM      OUTPUT ANALYSIS OF VARIANCE
C  CANOV   (SEE  7.1 ) EXECUTIVE   ANALYSIS OF VARIANCE
C  CASIGS  (SEE  7.1 ) SYSTEM      SUMS OF SQUARES FOR ANOVAR
C  CHIKEN  (SEE 11.9 ) SERVICE     WARNS OF MISMATCHED DATA LEVEL
C  CLSAM   (SEE  3.5 ) SERVICE     ALLOTS ENTRY TO SAMPLE/SUBSET
C  COMPA   (SEE  3.1 ) SERVICE     COMPARES ALPHAMERIC VALUES
C  COPYA   (SEE  3.1 ) SERVICE     COPIES ALPHAMERIC VALUE
C  DFADJ   (SEE  7.1 ) SERVICE     ADJUSTS ANOVAR DEG. FREEDOM
C  DFSET   (SEE  7.1 ) SERVICE     CALCULATES DEG FREEDOM INITIALLY
C  FIFI    (SEE  3.2 ) SYSTEM      ALLOCATES PERIPHERALS
C  GAUS    (SEE 11.8 ) STATISTICAL FINDS ASS. PROB. OF N VALUE
C  IBL     (SEE  3.1 ) SERVICE     DETECTS BLANK,END AND STOP CARDS
C  ICH     (SEE  3.1 ) SERVICE     IDENTIFIES ALPHAMERIC CODES
C  LANOV   (SEE  7.1 ) SYSTEM      LOADS ANALYSIS OF VARIANCE MODEL
C  LDAP    (SEE  3.3 ) SYSTEM      LOADS/CHECKS DATA BANK PARAMETERS
C  LDBS    (SEE  3.6 ) SYSTEM      LOADS SUBSET DEFINITION
C  LDDS    (SEE  3.4 ) SYSTEM      LOADS DATA DESCRIPTION SEGMENT
C  LDHI    (SEE  3.8 ) SYSTEM      LOADS/CHECKS DATA HANDLING INSTN
C  LGEN    (SEE  3.7 ) SYSTEM      LOADS GENERALISED VARIATES
C  LSET    (SEE  3.5 ) SYSTEM      LOADS DEFINING CONDITIONS
C  MEDIAT  (SEE  3.7 ) SERVICE     FETCHES NEXT VARIATE SET
C  PRBF    (SEE 11.8 ) STATISTICAL FINDS PROBABILITY OF F-RATIO
C  SIGSUM  (SEE  7.1 ) SYSTEM      CALCULATES SUM TERMS FOR ANOVAR
C  TRANS   (SEE  3.7 ) SERVICE     CARRIES OUT REQUIRED TRANSFORM
C SETTING OF DIMENSIONS OF STORAGE ARRAYS
C DIMENSIONS MUST BE SET TO THE NUMERICAL VALUES OF THE PARAMETERS
C GIVEN IN BRACKETS IN THE COMMENT STATEMENT - IF THE VALUE IS
C CHANGED SO MUST BE THAT OF THE PARAMETER ASSIGNED IN THE PROGRAM
C THE PROGRAM CAN HANDLE ANY CASES WHERE THE DIMENSIONS NEEDED ARE
C SMALLER. CHANGES SHOULD ONLY BE MADE IF DIMENSIONS ARE TOO SMALL
C NQMAX = MAXIMUM NUMBER OF DATA COLUMNS
C DIMENSION XX(NQMAX),DMAX(NQMAX),DMIN(NQMAX),IT(NQMAX),ST(NQMAX)
C  DIMENSION CN(NQMAX)
      NQMAX = 100
      DIMENSION XX(100),DMAX(100),DMIN(100),IT(100),ST(100),CN(100)
      DATA   CN/4HCOL1,4HCOL2,4HCOL3,4HCOL4,4HCOL5,4HCOL6,4HCOL7,4HCOL8,4
     1HCOL9,4HCL10,4HCL11,4HCL12,4HCL13,4HCL14,4HCL15,4HCL16,4HCL17,4HC
     2L18,4HCL19,4HCL20,4HCL21,4HCL22,4HCL23,4HCL24,4HCL25,4HCL26,4HCL27,
     3 4HCL28,4HCL29,4HCL30,4HCL31,4HCL32,4HCL33,4HCL34,4HCL35,4HCL36,4HC
     4L37,4HCL38,4HCL39,4HCL40,4HCL41,4HCL42,4HCL43,4HCL44,4HCL45,4HCL46
     5,4HCL47,4HCL48,4HCL49,4HCL50,4HCL51,4HCL52,4HCL53,4HCL54,4HCL55,4H
     6CL56,4HCL57,4HCL58,4HCL59,4HCL60,4HCL61,4HCL62,4HCL63,4HCL64,4HCL6
     75,4HCL66,4HCL67,4HCL68,4HCL69,4HCL70,4HCL71,4HCL72,4HCL73,4HCL74,4
     8HCL75,4HCL76,4HCL77,4HCL78,4HCL79,4HCL80,4HCL81,4HCL82,4HCL83,4HCL
     984,4HCL85,4HCL86,4HCL87,4HCL88,4HCL89,4HCL90,4HCL91,4HCL92,4HCL93,
     94HCL94,4HCL95,4HCL96,4HCL97,4HCL98,4HCL99,4HC100/
C NALTMX = MAXIMUM NUMBER OF CLASSES FROM TAPE
C DIMENSION TRT(NALTMX)
      NALTMX = 90
      DIMENSION TRT(90      )
C MAXM = MAXIMUM NUMBER OF INDEPENDENT VARIABLES IN STORE
C DIMENSION FNAME(MAXM),MCL(MAXM),SMAX(MAXM),SMIN(MAXM)
C DIMENSION MDP(MAXM),MP(MAXM)
C FNAME MUST CONTAIN THE LETTERS IN ORDER AT LEAST UP TO V
C DIMENSION OF FNAME MUST BE AT LEAST 22 WITH A DATA STATEMENT TO
C CORRESPOND TO THE DIMENSION.
      MAXM = 26
      DIMENSION FNAME(26),MCL(26),SMAX(26),SMIN(26),MDP(26),MP(26)
      DATA FNAME/1HA,1HB,1HC,1HD,1HE,1HF,1HG,1HH,1HI,1HJ,1HK,1HL,1HM,1HN
```

```
      1,1HO,1HP,1HQ,1HR,1HS,1HT,1HU,1HV,1HW,1HX,1HY,1HZ/
C NLMAX = MAXIMUM NUMBER OF INDEPENDENT VARIABLES IN ONE ANALYSIS
C DIMENSION NCL(NLMAX),NTL(NLMAX),NINL(NLMAX),NDP(NLMAX),TMIN(NLMAX)
C DIMENSION TMAX(NLMAX),NP(NLMAX+1),D(NLMAX+1)
C DIMENSION TMAX(NLMAX),NP(NLMAX+1),D(NLMAX+1),TST(NLMAX,4)
      NLMAX = 10
      DIMENSION NCL(10),NTL(10),NINL(10),TMAX(10),TMIN(10),NDP(10)
      DIMENSION NP(11),D(11),TST(10,4)
C NDMAX = MAXIMUM NO OF LINES IN A.O.V. TABLE PLUS THREE   (NOUT+3)
C DIMENSIONS NF(NDMAX),NR(NDMAX),NL(NDMAX),SUM(NDMAX)
C DIMENSION NLX(NDMAX),NRX(NDMAX)
C DIMENSION TITL(18,NDMAX),KSUM(NDMAX,NDMAX),KSIG(NDMAX,NLMAX)
      NDMAX = 28
      DIMENSION NF(28),NR(28),NL(28),SUM(28)
      DIMENSION NLX(28),NRX(28)
      DIMENSION TITL(18,28),KSUM(28,28),KSIG(28,10)
C NRPMX = MAXIMUM NO. OF DEPENDENT VARIABLES
C DIMENSION IPQ(NRPMX)
      NRPMX = 20
      DIMENSION IPQ(20)
C DIMENSION STO(NCAV) = TOTAL STORE FOR SUB-TOTALS AND PROPORTIONS
      NCAV = 3600
      DIMENSION STO(3600)
C DIMENSION SCON(5,MAXDBC)= MAXIMUM NO OF SUBSET CONDITIONS
      MAXDBC = 50
      DIMENSION SCON(5,50)
C THE FOLLOWING DIMENSIONS STORE THE NAMES OF THE DATA TRANSFORMS
C AND THE ACCEPTABLE LEVELS FOR TRANSFORMATIONS
      DIMENSION U(60),LU(60)
      NU = 60
C TRANSFORMATION CODES
C UNITS               BLOCKS
C   0 - 9   10 - 19   20 - 29   30 - 39   40 - 49   50 - 59
C   POWERS  TRIG      TRIG      STATIST   MATHS     TEST
C           RADIANS   DEGREES   TRANSF    FUNCTS    FUNCTIONS
C   0       -         -         H.MS      -         -         RM10
C   1       VAL.      SINR      SIND      PSNA      RECP      +/-1
C   2       SQAR      COSR      COSD      PSNB      SQRT      ADD1
C   3       CUBE      TANR      TAND      BINO      ABSV      SUB1
C   4       4PWR      ASIR      ASID      LG+1      SIGN      NOR1
C   5       5PWR      ACOR      ACOD      LOGE      INTG      +/-P
C   6       6PWR      ATAR      ATAD      LG10      FRAC      ADDP
C   7       7PWR      SINH      DTOR      AL10      EXPT      SUBP
C   8       8PWR      COSH      RTOD      -         PRES      NOBP
C   9       9PWR      TANH      H.HH      -         NEG.      +100
      DATA U/4HVAL.,4HSQAR,4HCUBE,4H4PWR,4H5PWR,4H6PWR,4H7PWR,4H8PWR,4H9
     1PWR,4HVAL,4HSINR,4HCOSR,4HTANR,4HASIR,4HACOR,4HATAR,4HSINH,4HCOSH
     2,4HTANH,4HH.MS,4HSIND,4HCOSD,4HTAND,4HASID,4HACOD,4HATAD,4HDTOR,4H
     3RTOD,4HH.HH,4H VAL,4HPSNA,4HPSNB,4HBINO,4HLG+1,4HLOGE,4HLG10,4HAL1
     40,4H    ,4H    ,4H    ,4HRECP,4HSQRT,4HABSV,4HSIGN,4HINTG,4HFRAC,4
     5HEXPT,4HPRES,4HNEG.,4HRM10,4H+/-1,4HADD1,4HSUB1,4HNOR1,4H+/-P,4HAD
     6DP,4HSUBP,4HNORP,4H+100,4H      /
      DATA LU/1,8*5,1,9*5,1,9*5,1,6*5,4*1,2*5,2*3,3*5,7*2,4*5,2*2/
C ARRAYS USED IN STANOV DUMMIES + CHECKING
      DIMENSION IH(1),H(1),RT(1,1),FORM(50),AOVE(5)
      DATA BL/1H /,EQ/1H=/,VA/4HVAL./,CL/4HCLAS/
      COMMON /STCT/MED1,MED2,MED3,MED4,MED5,MED6,MED13,Q,V(20),TT(30)
      DATA PROG/4HANOV/
      MED1 = -1
C SETTING UP * LEVEL 0
      ISM = 0
    1 CALL COPYA(TT(1),PROG)
      CALL FIFI
```

```
      WRITE(MED2,901)
      CALL LDAP(MED2,MED3,V,TT,Q,NQ,NALT,MQMAX,NALTMX,IGO)
      IF(IGO.GT.0) AOVE(1) = 1.
      IF(IGO.LE.0) AOVE(1) = 0.
      LI = 18
      CALL LDDS(TRT,NALT,D,NQ,ST,NQ,IT,MQ,H,0,DMIN,DMAX,NQ,LI,1,Q,VX,
     1 0,MED2,MED3,0,IGO)
C READ DATA BANK SUBSET SPECIFICATION - LEVEL 2
   10 IF(ISM.NE.0.AND.ISM.NE.2) GO TO 20
      V(10) = 0.
      AOVE(2) = 0
      CALL LDBS(SCON,NCON,MAXDBC,CN,ST,IT,NQ,TRT,NALT,IGO)
      IF(V(10).NE.0.)AOVE(2) = 1.
      IF(IGO.GT.0) GO TO 1
C INDEPENDENT VARIABLES - CODING AND LIMITS
   20 IF(ISM.NE.0.AND.ISM.NE.3) GO TO 30
      AOVE(3) = 0.
      V(9) = 0.
      WRITE(MED6,945)
      NVAR = 0
      CALL LGEN(U,NU,LU,NU,ST,IT,CN,NQ,MCL,MAXM,DMIN,DMAX,NQ,SMIN,SMAX,M
     1AXM,-1,NALTMX,MDP,MP,MAXM,NVAR,MAXM,0,NALT)
      V10 = 5326.
      IF(V(10).NE.0.)AOVE(3) = 1.
      IF(ISM.NE.0)GO TO 31
   30 IF(ISM.NE.0.AND.ISM.NE.4) GO TO 40
      V(10) = 0.
      AOVE(4) = 0.
C MODEL  LOADING
      V(9) = 0.
      NMOD = NDMAX -2
      CALL LANOV(TITL,NMOD,NOUT)
      ND3 = NOUT+ 3
      IF(V(10).NE.0.)AOVE(4) = 1.
   31 NLEV = 0
      DO 36 J = 1,NOUT
      DO 35 I = 1,18
      CALL COMPA(TITL(I,J),EQ,L)
      IF(L.EQ.1) GO TO 36
      CALL COMPA(TITL(I,J),BL,L)
      IF(L.EQ.1) GO TO 35
      IF(I.GT.16)GO TO 32
      CALL COMPA(TITL(I,J),FNAME(18),L)
      IF(L.NE.1) GO TO 32
      CALL COMPA(TITL(I+1,J),FNAME(5),L)
      IF(L.NE.1) GO TO 32
      CALL COMPA(TITL(I+2,J),FNAME(19),L)
      IF(L.EQ.1)GO TO 36
   32 IF(ICH(TITL(I,J),FNAME,NVAR).NE.0)GO TO 33
      WRITE(MED2,931)I,J,TITL(I,J)
      V(10) = 36.
      GO TO 35
   33 IF(NLEV.EQ.0) GO TO 34
      IF(ICH(TITL(I,J),TST,NLEV).NE.0) GO TO 35
      IF(NLEV.LT.NLMAX) GO TO 34
      WRITE(MED2,932)NLMAX,TITL(I,J),I,J
      V(10) = 37.
      GO TO 35
   34 NLEV = NLEV + 1
      CALL COPYA(TST(NLEV,1),TITL(I,J))
   35 CONTINUE
   36 CONTINUE
      NLEV1= NLEV +1
```

```
      NCT = 0
      DO 37 I = 1,NLEV
      J = ICH(TST(I,1),FNAME,NVAR)
      NDP(I) = MDP(J)
      IF(NDP(I).EQ.0) CALL COPYA(TST(I,2),VA)
      IF(NDP(I).NE.0) CALL COPYA(TST(I,2),CL)
      NP(I) = MP(J)
      NINL(I) = MCL(J)
      TMIN(I) = SMIN(J)
      TMAX(I) = SMAX(J)
      NCT = NCT + MCL(J)
      NTR = NP(I)/1000
      NCR = NP(I) - NTR*1000
      CALL COPYA(TST(I,3),U(NTR))
   37 CALL COPYA(TST(I,4),ST(NCR))
      NCT1 = NCT+1
      NCP = (NCAV-NCT)/3
      IF (NCP.LE.0) WRITE(MED2,933)
      IF (NCP.LE.0.AND.V(10).EQ.0.) V(10) = 38.
      IF(V(10).NE.0.)AOVE(4) = 1.
C     DEPENDENT VARIABLES - CODING AND TITLES
   40 IF(ISM.NE.0.AND.ISM.NE.5) GO TO 50
      V(10) = 0.
      AOVE(5) = 0.
      WRITE(MED6,947)
      NREP = 0
      CALL LGEN(U,NU,LU,NU,ST,IT,CN,NQ,IH,0,H,H,0,H,H,0,0,0,IH,IPQ,NRPMX
     1,NREP,NRPMX,1,0)
      IF(V(11).LT.0.5) AOVE(5) = 1.
C     OUTPUT AND TESTING INDICES
   49 CONTINUE
   50 CONTINUE
C LEVEL 9 - READ DATA HANDLING INSTRUCTION
   91 IF(V(10).GT.90.) V(10) = 0.
      CALL LDHI(V(1),1,V(2),5,V(7),16,H,0,H,0,H,0,H,V(10),
     1 FORM(41),FORM,MED1,MED2,0,Q,NQ,NWARN,1,IGO)
      IF(IGO.GT.0) GO TO 40
C STANDARDISATION  - AND STEPPING TO SPECIFIED LEVELS
      I=0
      DO 92 J=1,4
      K = ICH(FORM(J),FNAME,26)
      IF(K.EQ.0) GO TO 93
   92 I = K-1 + 26*I
      ISM=0
      IF(I.EQ. 93426)ISM=1
      IF(I.EQ.195408)ISM=2
      IF(I.EQ.199085)ISM=3
      IF(I.EQ.193721)ISM=4
      IF(I.EQ.195483)ISM=5
      GO TO (1,10,20,30,40),ISM
   93 IF(V(1).GT.4.) NWARN = NWARN + 1
      IF(V(1).GT.4.)V(1) = 0.
      IF(V(2).GT.5.) NWARN = NWARN + 1
      IF(V(2).GT.5.)V(2) = - 1.
      IF(V(7).EQ.0.) NWARN = NWARN + 1
      IF(V(7).EQ.0.) V(7) = 5.
      CALL LDHI(V(1),1,V(2),5,V(7),16,H,0,H,0,H,0,H,V(10),
     1 FORM(41),FORM,MED1,MED2,0,Q,NQ,NWARN,2,IGO)
      IF(IGO.GT.0) GO TO 91
      V(7) = V(7)*.01
C TEST FOR ACCEPTED DATA
  100 V(10) = 0.
      DO 101 I = 1,5
```

```
      IF(AOVE(I).EQ.0.) GO TO 101
      IF(V(10).EQ.0.) WRITE(MED6,997)
      V(10) = 1.
      J = I - 1
      WRITE(MED6,989) J
  101 CONTINUE
      IF(V(10).NE.0.) GO TO 91
      WRITE(MED6,998)
      V(10) = V10
      CALL CANOV (NF,NR,NL,SUM,TITL,KSIG,KSUM,ND3,XX,NQ,SCON,NCON,NTL,
     1NINL,NCL,NDP,TMIN,TMAX,NLEV,NP,D,NLEV1,TST,NLMAX,IPQ,NREP,STO,
     2NCT,STO(NCT1),NCP,NOUT,U,NU,NLX,NRX)
      V10 = V(10)
      V(10) = 0.
      WRITE(MED6,999)
      GO TO 91
  901 FORMAT (1H0,20X,36HSTATCAT GENERAL ANALYSIS OF VARIANCE)
  922 FORMAT (1H1,9X,21HINDEPENDENT VARIABLES/38H0COLUMN COLUMN MINIMUM
     1MAXIMUM OVERALL,15X,7HCOMMENT/38H    CODE NUMBER  VALUE    VALUE   R
     2ANGE )
  923 FORMAT (1H ,2X,A1,5X,4(I4,4X),16A4,A3)
  924 FORMAT (1H ,2X,A1,5X,I4,4X,40H- DISCARDED - NOT ENOUGH STORAGE (NL
     17AX))
  931 FORMAT (28H UNDEFINED VARIATE IN COLUMN,I3,8H OF LINE,I3,12H OF MO
     1DEL = ,A1)
  932 FORMAT (I4,29H VARIATES ALREADY IN MODEL - ,A1,11H IN COLUMN ,I3,
     1 18H OF LINE ,I3,35H CANNOT BE LOADED - INCREASE NLMAX )
  933 FORMAT (42H NO STORAGE FOR SUB-TITLES - INCREASE NCAV)
  945 FORMAT(21H1INDEPENDENT VARIATES       //
     1            4H0NO.,9X,30HTRANS   DATA     CLASS/ NUMBER OF,7X,5HLOWER,6X,
     1 15HCLASS,7X,5HUPPER/5H CODE,8X,68H-FORM COLUMN VALUE    CLASSES USED
     2 CLASS LIMIT   INTERVAL   CLASS LIMIT)
  947 FORMAT(21H1  DEPENDENT VARIATES       //
     1            4H0NO.,9X,11HTRANS   DATA/5H CODE,8X,12H-FORM COLUMN)
  989 FORMAT (21H FATAL ERROR AT LEVEL,I4)
  997 FORMAT (24H0PROGRAM CANNOT OPERATE.//)
  998 FORMAT (36H0INPUT ACCEPTED - ANALYSIS COMMENCES)
  999 FORMAT (36H1ANALYSIS COMPLETED - READ NEW INPUT)
      END


      SUBROUTINE CANOV (NF,NR,NL,SUM,TITL,KSIG,KSUM,ND3,XX    ,NQ,SCON,NC
     1ON,NTL,NINL,NCL,NDP,TMIN,TMAX,NLEV,NP,D,NLEV1,TST,NLMAX,IPQ,NREP,S
     2TO,NCT,SIG,NDATX,NOUT,U,NU,NLX,NRX)
C CANOV (SEE 7.1 ) EXECUTIVE     ANALYSIS OF VARIANCE
      DIMENSION TITL(18,ND3),KSUM(ND3,ND3),KSIG(ND3,NLEV),CV(2)
      DIMENSION NTL(NLEV),NINL(NLEV),NCL(NLEV),NDP(NLEV),NP(NLEV1)
      DIMENSION NF(ND3),NR(ND3),NL(ND3),SUM(ND3),U(NU),STO(NCT)
      DIMENSION NLX(ND3),NRX(ND3)
      DIMENSION TMIN(NLEV),TMAX(NLEV),D(NLEV1),TST(NLMAX,4)
      DIMENSION TSP(20),IPQ(NREP),SIG(NDATX,3),XX(NQ),SCON(5,NCON)
      COMMON /STCT/MED1,MED2,MED3,MED4,MED5,MED6,MED13,Q,V(20),TT(30)
      REWIND MED3
      V9 = V(9)
      V7 = V(7)
      IF(V9.EQ.1.) GO TO 1
C CALCULATE WHAT SUMMATION TERMS WILL BE NEEDED + HOW MODEL IS REALISED
      CALL SIGSUM(TITL,KSIG,KSUM,NL,TST,NINL,NTL,NR,ND3,NLEV,NOUT,NDATX)
      V9 = 1.
    1 IF(V(20).NE.0.) RETURN
    3 DO 8 J = 1,NREP
      REWIND MED3
C PREPARE FOR DEPENDENT VARIATE J
```

```
      DO 4 I = 1,ND3
    4 NF(I) = 0
      NP(NLEV1) = IPQ(J)
      NTR = IPQ(J)/1000
      NCR = IPQ(J) - NTR*1000
      READ(MED3) NQ,NALT,Q,(TT(I),I=1,10),(X,I=1,6)
      DO 5 K = 1,NCR
    5 READ(MED3) (TSP(I),I=2,20),(X,I=1,NALT),NX,X,X
      CALL COPYA(TSP(1),U(NTR))
      IF(NCR.EQ.NQ) GO TO 7
      NTR = NCR+1
      DO 6 K = NTR,NQ
    6 READ(MED3) (X,I=1,19),(X,I=1,NALT),NX,X,X
C CALCULATE ACTUAL SIGMA TERMS
    7 CALL CASIGS(NF,SUM,TITL,KSIG,TST,TSP,SIG,STO,NCT,NTL,NINL,NCL,TMIN
     1,TMAX,ND3,NLEV,NLEV1,NDATX,NOUT,XX,NQ,NP,NDP,D,SCON,NCON,NLMAX)
      NDATA = V(6)
      IF(NDATA.EQ.0) GO TO 8
C CALCULATE DEGREES OF FREEDOM
      CALL DFSET(NF,NL,NR,ND3,KSIG,NINL,NLEV,NOUT,NDATA)
      DO 9 II = 1,NOUT
      NLX(II) = NL(II+2)
    9 NRX(II) = NR(II)
C OUTPUT ANALYSIS OF VARIANCE
      IF(V(2).GT.3..OR.V(2).LT.0.) GO TO 8
      V(7) = V7
      CALL AOVOUT(NF,NRX,SUM,TITL,KSUM,TST,TSP,SIG,NL3,NDATX,NOUT,NLEV,
     1NLMAX,NLX)
    8 CONTINUE
      V(9) = V9
      V(20) = 0.
      RETURN
      END


      SUBROUTINE LANOV(TITL,NDMAX,INDR)
C LANOV   (SEE 7.1 ) SYSTEM     LOADS ANALYSIS OF VARIANCE MODEL
      DIMENSION TITL(18,NDMAX),C(35),TRES(3),LEVIN(18)
      DATA TRES/1HR,1HE,1HS/,B1/1H /
      COMMON /STCT/MED1,MED2,MED3,MED4,MED5,MED6,MED13,Q,V(20),TT(30)
C SETTING-UP
      CARD = 0.
      IDONE = 0
      INDR = 0
      NBL = 0
      NBN = 1
      NRES = 1
      DO 1 I = 1,18
    1 LEVIN(I) = 0
    2 CARD = CARD + 1.
    3 READ(MED1,900) C
      IF(IBL(C,20,1)) 3,4,55
    4 IF(CARD.EQ.1.) WRITE(MED2,901)
      IF(CARD.EQ.AN(C,2,1,2)) GO TO 5
      IF(V(10).EQ.0.) V(10) = 34.
      WRITE(MED2,903) C,CARD
      GO TO 2
    5 IF(IDONE.LT.0) GO TO 50
      NBN = 1
      DO 6 I = 3,20
      CALL COMPA(C(I),B1,L)
      IF(L.NE.1) GO TO 7
    6 NBN = NBN + 1
```

```
      7 NRES = 1
        DO 8 I = 1,3
        INDC = I + NBN + 1
        CALL COMPA(C(INDC),TRES(I),L)
        IF(L.NE.1) GO TO 10
      8 CONTINUE
      9 NRES = 0
     10 ICH = 10
        IF(NBN-NBL) 20,30,40
C FEWER BLANKS THAN PREVIOUS LINE
     20 IF(NBL.LE.0) GO TO 25
        IF(LEVIN(NBL)) 25,25,21
     21 IF(INDR.LT.NDMAX) GO TO 22
        WRITE(MED2,904)
        IF(V(10).EQ.0.) V(10) = 35.
        INDR = INDR - 1
     22 INDR = INDR + 1
        DO 23 I = 1,18
     23 CALL COPYA(TITL(I,INDR),B1)
        DO 24 I = 1,3
        INDC = I + NBL - 1
     24 CALL COPYA(TITL(INDC,INDR),TRES(I))
        WRITE(MED2,905)INDR,(TITL(I,INDR),I=1,18)
        LEVIN(NBL) = 0
     25 NBL = NBL - 1
        IF(NBL.LE.0) GO TO 57
        GO TO 10
C SAME BLANKS AS PREVIOUS LINE
     30 IF(NBL.LE.0) GO TO 57
        IF(LEVIN(NBL))31,31,32
     31 IF(NRES)35,35,32
     35 WRITE(MED2,908) C
        GO TO 2
     32 IF(INDR.LT.NDMAX) GO TO 33
        WRITE(MED2,904)
        IF(V(10).EQ.0.) V(10) = 35.
        INDR = INDR -1
     33 INDR = INDR + 1
        DO 34 I = 1,18
     34 CALL COPYA(TITL(I,INDR),C(I+2))
        WRITE(MED2,902) C(1),C(2),INDR,(C(I),I=3,35)
C IF MODEL IS COMPLETE SET WARNING INDICATOR
        IF(IDONE.EQ.-1) GO TO 57
        IF(NBL .EQ.1.AND.NRES.EQ.0) IDONE = -1
        LEVIN(NBN) = NRES
        NBL = NBN
        GO TO 2
C MORE BLANKS THAN PREVIOUS LINE
     40 IF(NRES) 41,41,32
     41 WRITE(MED2,908) C
        NBL = NBN
        GO TO 2
C CARDS AFTER COMPLETE MODEL READ IN - BEFORE END CARD
     50 WRITE(MED2,909) C
        GO TO 2
C END FOUND
     55 IF(IDONE) 57,56,56
C MODEL NOT STARTED
     56 IF(INDR.EQ.0) GO TO 58
C MODEL NOT ENDED
        NBN = 0
        NRES = 0
        GO TO 10
```

```
C MODEL COMPLETED AND END FOUND
   57 IF(CARD.EQ.1.) GO TO 58
C MODEL CORRECTLY READ
      WRITE(MED2,907) C,INDR
      RETURN
C NO MODEL READ
   58 WRITE(MED2,906) C
      RETURN
  900 FORMAT(20A1,15A4)
  901 FORMAT(1H0,10X,26HANALYSIS OF VARIANCE MODEL/10H0CARD LINE,5X,5HMO
     1DEL,20X,12HUSER COMMENT,50X,14HSYSTEM COMMENT)
  902 FORMAT (1H ,2A1,2X,I4,1X,18A1,5X,15A4)
  903 FORMAT(1H ,2A1,7X,18A1,5X,15A4,24H DISORDERED - SHOULD BE ,F4.0)
  904 FORMAT(43H NO MORE STORAGE AVAILABLE - INCREASE NDMAX)
  905 FORMAT(5X,I4,1X,18A1,66X,24HRESIDUAL ADDED BY SYSTEM)
  906 FORMAT(1H0,9X,20A1,15A4,3X,25H NO NEW MODEL - STEP BACK)
  907 FORMAT(1H0,9X,20A1,15A4,3X,I4,20H LINE MODEL ACCEPTED)
  908 FORMAT(1H ,2A1,7X,18A1,5X,15A4,19H REDUNDANT RESIDUAL)
  909 FORMAT(1H ,2A1,7X,18A1,5X,15A4,26H NOT USED - MODEL COMPLETE)
      END


      SUBROUTINE SIGSUM(TITL,KSIG,KSUM,NL,FN,NINL,NTL,NR,ND3,NLEV,NOUT,N
     1DATX)
C SIGSUM (SEE  7.1 ) SYSTEM        CALCULATES SUM TERMS FOR ANOVAR
C CALCULATE SIGMA AND SUM TERMS FOR GIVEN MODEL
      DIMENSION TITL(18,ND3),KSIG(ND3,NLEV),KSUM(ND3,ND3),NL(ND3)
      DIMENSION NR(ND3),FN(NLEV),NINL(NLEV),NTL(NLEV),R(3)
      COMMON /STCT/MED1,MED2,MED3,MED4,MED5,MED6,MED13,Q,V(20),TT(30)
      DATA BL/1H /,EQ/1H=/,R/1HR,1HE,1HS/
C CONSTRUCT LIST OF REQUIRED SIGMA TERMS
      V(20) = 0.
      NOUT2 = NOUT + 2
      DO 1 K=1,NOUT2
      NL(K)=1
      DO 1 L=1,NLEV
    1 KSIG(K,L)=1
      WRITE (MED2,901) (FN(KK),KK=1,NLEV)
      KSIG(1,1)=9
      DO 6 K=1,NOUT
      KS=K+2
      NX=1
      KK=0
      DO 4 L=1,18
      CALL COMPA(TITL(L,K),BL,LTEST)
      IF(LTEST.EQ.2)GO TO 2
      IF(KK.NE.0)GO TO 4
      NL(KS)=NL(KS)+1
      GO TO 4
    2 CONTINUE
      CALL COMPA(TITL(L,K),EQ,LTEST)
      IF(LTEST.EQ.1)GO TO 6
      IF(L.GT.16) GO TO 3
      IF(ICH(TITL(L,K),R,1).NE.1)   GO TO 3
      IF(ICH(TITL(L+1,K),R,2).NE.2) GO TO 3
      IF(ICH(TITL(L+2,K),R,3).EQ.3) GO TO 5
    3 KK=1
      DO 4 M=1,NLEV
      CALL COMPA(TITL(L,K),FN(M),LTEST)
      IF(LTEST.EQ.2)GO TO 4
      KSIG(KS,M)=2
      NX=NX*NINL(M)
    4 CONTINUE
```

```
      IF(NDATX.GE.NX)GO TO 6
      WRITE(MED2,902)NX,NDATX
      V(20) = 1.
      GO TO 6
    5 KSIG(KS,1)=9
    6 WRITE (MED2,903)K,(KSIG(KS,L),L=1,NLEV)
      NOUT1 = NOUT - 1
      WRITE(MED2,904)(L,L=1,NOUT1)
      NOUT1 = NOUT + 1
      DO 10 K = 1,NOUT1
      DO 10 L = 1,NOUT1
   10 KSUM(K,L)=0
      KSUM(NOUT+1,1)=1
      KSUM(NOUT+1,2)=0-1
      KSUM(NOUT,1)=1
      KSUM(NOUT,2)=0-1
      M=NOUT+2
      DO 50 K=1,NOUT
      MOUT=NOUT+1
      KS=K+2
      IF (KSIG(KS,1).GT.3)GO TO 20
      NX=0
      NVAR=0
      DO 11 L=1,NLEV
      NTL(L)=1
   11 NX=NX+KSIG(KS,L)-1
      GO TO 14
   12 NVAR=0
   13 NVAR=NVAR+1
      IF(NVAR.GT.NLEV)GO TO 30
      IF(KSIG(KS,NVAR).NE.2)GO TO 13
      NTL(NVAR)=NTL(NVAR)+1
      IF(NTL(NVAR).LE.2)GO TO 14
      NTL(NVAR)=1
      GO TO 13
   14 INSTOR=0
      DO 15 L=1,NLEV
   15 INSTOR=INSTOR+NTL(L)-1
      DO 17 N=1,M
      DO 16 L=1,NLEV
      IF(NTL(L).NE.KSIG(N,L))GO TO 17
   16 CONTINUE
      INSTOR=NX-INSTOR
      KSUM(K,N)=(0-1)**INSTOR
      GO TO 12
   17 CONTINUE
      WRITE (MED2,905)
      V(20) = 2.
      GO TO 30
   20 KSX=KS
   21 KSX=KSX-1
      IF(KSX.LE.2)GO TO 30
      IF(NL(KSX).GT.NL(KS))GO TO 21
      IF(NL(KSX).LT.NL(KS))GO TO 23
C CONSTRUCT EXPRESSIONS FOR SUMS OF SQUARES
      DO 22 N=1,MOUT
   22 KSUM(K,N)=KSUM(K,N)-KSUM(KSX-2,N)
      GO TO 21
   23 CONTINUE
      DO 24 N=1,MOUT
   24 KSUM(K,N)=KSUM(K,N)+KSUM(KSX-2,N)
   30 CONTINUE
      NR(K)=0
```

```
      IF (KSIG(K+2,1).GT.3)GO TO 50
      DO 40 L=K,NOUT
      IF (KSIG(L+2,1).NE.9)GO TO 40
      IF(NL(L+2).NE.NL(K+2))GO TO 40
      NR(K)=L
      GO TO 20
   40 CONTINUE
   50 WRITE(MED2,906)K,(TITL(L,K),L=1,18),NL(K+2),(KSUM(K,L),L=1,MOUT)
      WRITE(MED2,907)MOUT,(KSUM(MOUT,L),L = 1,MOUT)
  901 FORMAT(12H1SIGMA TERMS/22H01=SUM BEFORE SQUARING/24H 2=SQUARE BEFO
     1RE SUMMING/27H 9 IN COL 1 - RESIDUAL TERM/3HONO,20(1X,A1))
  902 FORMAT (53H TOO MANY SUB-TOTALS REQUIRED IN THE FOLLOWING LINE (,I
     14,12H WHILE ONLY ,I4,14H ARE AVAILABLE)
  903 FORMAT (1H ,21I2)
  904 FORMAT (40H1FORMATION OF ANALYSIS OF VARIANCE TABLE/1H0,39X,20HSUM
     1  C    SIGMA TERMS/3H NO,5X,6HSOURCE,11X,21HDF LEVEL RESID SQS  F,2
     25I3/(1H ,39X,27I3))
  905 FORMAT (45H NEXT LINE REQUIRES AN UNEVALUATED SIGMA TERM)
  906 FORMAT(1H ,I2,2X,18A1,4X,I4,9X,27I3/(1H ,39X,27I3))
  907 FORMAT(1H ,I2,7X,5HTOTAL,12X,13X,27I3/(1H ,39X,27I3))
      RETURN
      END


      SUBROUTINE CASIGS(NP,SUM,TITL,KSIG,TST,TSP,SIG,STO,NCT,NTL,NINL
     1,NCL,TMIN,TMAX,ND3,NLEV,NLEV1,NDATX,NOUT,XX,NQ,MP,NDP,D,SCON
     2,NCON,NLMAX)
C CASIGS (SEE  7.1 ) SYSTEM        SUMS OF SQUARES FOR ANOVAR
      DIMENSION NF(ND3),SUM(ND3),TITL(18,ND3),KSIG(ND3,NLEV),NTL(NLEV)
      DIMENSION TMIN(NLEV),TMAX(NLEV),XX(NQ),D(NLEV1),NP(NLEV1),STO(NCT)
      DIMENSION TST(NLMAX,4),TSP(20),SIG(NDATX,3),NCL(NLEV),NINL(NLEV)
      DIMENSION SCON(5,NCON),NDP(NLEV)
      COMMON /STCT/MED1,MED2,MED3,MED4,MED5,MED6,MED13,Q,V(20),TT(30)
      NOUT=NOUT+1
      NSUM=NOUT+1
      NSIG = V(1)
C FIND MEAN AND TOTAL SUM OF SQUARES
      Y=0.
      Z=0.
      SUM(1)=0.
      SUM(2)=0.
      SUM(3)=0.
      LI = 50
      IGO = 1
      XBAR = Q
      V(6) = 0.
      V(7) = 1.
      V(8) = 1.
      V(9) = NLEV1
      V10 = V(10)
      V(20) = 0.
      DO 6 I = 1,NCT
    6 STO(I) = 0.
   10 CALL MEDIAT(NLEV1,NDP,MP,NLEV1,D,XX,NQ,SCON,NCON)
      IF(V(8).EQ.2.) GO TO 11
      INDX = 0
      DO 2 L = 1,NLEV
      NTL(L) = D(L)
      IF(D(L).EQ.Q)V(6) = V(6) - 1.
      IF(D(L).EQ.Q) GO TO 10
      IF(NDP(L).EQ.0)GO TO 1
      DEL = NINL(L)-2
      IF(DEL.LT.0.5.AND.D(L).GE.TMIN(L))NTL(L)= 2
```

```
      IF(DEL.LT.0.5.AND.D(L).LT.TMIN(L))NTL(L) = 1
      IF(DEL.GT.0.5)NTL(L)=(D(L)-TMIN(L))/(TMAX(L)-TMIN(L))*DEL + 2.
    1 IF(NTL(L).LT.1) NTL(L) = 1
      IF(NTL(L).GT.NINL(L))NTL(L) = NINL(L)
      IND1 = INDX +NTL(L)
      STO(IND1) = STO(IND1) + 1.
    2 INDX = INDX + NINL(L)
      X = D(NLEV1)
C SET XBAR TO FIRST NON-MISSING VALUE OF VARIATE
      IF(XBAR.EQ.Q.AND.X.NE.Q)XBAR=X
      IF(X.NE.Q) GO TO 4
      LI = LI + 1
      IGO = 1
      IF(LI.GE.50) GO TO 100
    3 NOUT = NOUT + 1
      WRITE (MED2,909 )(NTL(L),L=1,NLEV)
      GO TO 10
    4 SUM(1) = SUM(1) +(X-XBAR)*(X-XBAR)
      SUM(2) = SUM(2) +X-XBAR
      SUM(3) =SUM(3) +1.
      IF(NSIG.LT.4) GO TO 10
      LI = LI + 1
      IGO = 2
      IF(LI.GE.50) GO TO 100
    5 WRITE(MED2,906)X,(NTL(L),L = 1,NLEV)
      GO TO 10
C END OF INITIAL DATA SWEEP - OVERALL TOTALS ETC
   11 CONTINUE
      REWIND MED3
      V(10) = V10
      NDATA = V(6)
      V(9) = 0.
      X=SUM(3)
      IGO = 3
      IF(NSIG.GE.1) GO TO 100
   12 IF(X.EQ.0.) WRITE(MED2,910)
      IF(X.EQ.0.) RETURN
      SUM(2) = SUM(2)/X
      SUM(3)=SQRT((SUM(1)-SUM(2)*SUM(2)*X)/(X-1.))
      IF(NSIG.EQ.0) GO TO 13
      SUM(2) = SUM(2) + XBAR
      WRITE (MED2,905)X,SUM(2),SUM(3)
      SUM(2) = SUM(2) - XBAR
   13 SUM(2) = SUM(2)*SUM(2)*X
C FIND SUCCESSIVE SIGMA VALUES
      DO 20 I = 3,NSUM
   20 SUM(I)=0.
      DO 28 I = 1,NCT
   28 STO(I) = STO(I)/V(6)
      DO 99 IJ=3,NSUM
      J=NSUM+3-IJ
      IF(SUM(J).NE.0..OR.KSIG(J,1).EQ.9)GO TO 99
C FIND SMALLEST SETS OF SUB-TOTALS - FOR HIGHEST ORDER INTERACTION
      DO 21 MM = 1,NDATX
      DO 21 N=1,3
   21 SIG(MM,N) = 0.
      READ(MED3) NQ,NALT,Q,(X,I=1,16)
      DO 22 N = 1,NQ
   22 READ(MED3) (X,I=1,19),(X,I=1,NALT),NX,X,X
      DO 26 LL=1,NDATA
      CALL MEDIAT(NLEV1,NDP,NP,NLEV1,D,XX,NQ,SCON,NCON)
      DO 24 L = 1,NLEV
      NTL(L) = D(L)
```

```
      IF(NDP(L).EQ.0) GO TO 23
      DEL = NINL(L)-2
      IF(DEL.LT.0.5.AND.D(L).GE.TMIN(L))NTL(L)= 2
      IF(DEL.LT.0.5.AND.D(L).LT.TMIN(L))NTL(L) = 1
      IF(DEL.GT.0.5)NTL(L)=(D(L)-TMIN(L))/(TMAX(L)-TMIN(L))*DEL + 2.
   23 IF(NTL(L).LT.1) NTL(L) = 1
   24 IF(NTL(L).GT.NINL(L))NTL(L) = NINL(L)
      X = D(NLEV1)
      IF(X.EQ.Q)GO TO 26
C REDUCE VALUE OF VARIATE BY FIRST READING (REDUCE SIZE)
      X=X-XBAR
      INSTOR=0
      DO 25 L=1,NLEV
      IF(KSIG(J,L).NE.2)GO TO 25
      INSTOR=INSTOR*NINL(L)+NTL(L)-1
   25 CONTINUE
      INSTOR=INSTOR+1
      SIG(INSTOR,1)=SIG(INSTOR,1)+1.
      SIG(INSTOR,2)=SIG(INSTOR,2)+X
      SIG(INSTOR,3)=SIG(INSTOR,3)+X*X
   26 CONTINUE
      REWIND MED3
      V(10) = V10
C NCL=SPECIFICATION OF THIS SUBSET,NTL=SPECIFICATION OF HIGHEST ORDE
C COMBINE SUB-SETS TO FORM LOWER ORDER INTERACTION TERMS
      DO 99 I=3,J
      IF(SUM(I).NE.0..OR.KSIG(I,1).EQ.9)GO TO 99
      DO 27 L=1,NLEV
      IF(KSIG(I,L).GT.KSIG(J,L))GO TO 99
   27 CONTINUE
      I2 = I-2
      MIS=0
      X=0
      Y=0
      Z=0
      CELLS = 0.
      DFBAR = 0.
      ERRMS = 0.
      FLOGS = 0.
      RECIP = 0.
      DO 30 L=1,NLEV
      NCL(L)=0
      NTL(L)=0
      IF(KSIG(I,L).EQ.2)NCL(L)=1
      IF(KSIG(J,L).EQ.2)NTL(L)=1
   30 CONTINUE
      NVAR=0
      IF (NSIG.EQ.0)GO TO 43
      KS=I-2
      LI = 50
      GO TO 43
   31 NVAR=NLEV+1
   32 NVAR=NVAR-1
      IF(NVAR.LE.0) GO TO 50
      IF (KSIG(I,NVAR).NE.2) GO TO 32
      NCL(NVAR)=NCL(NVAR)+1
      IF(NCL(NVAR).LE.NINL(NVAR))GO TO 33
      NCL(NVAR)=1.
      GO TO 32
   33 X=0.
      Y=0.
      Z=0.
      DO 40 L=1,NLEV
```

```
          NTL(L)=0
          IF(KSIG(I,L).EQ.2)NTL(L)=NCL(L)
          IF(KSIG(J,L).EQ.2.AND.KSIG(I,L).EQ.1)NTL(L)=1
   40 CONTINUE
          GO TO 43
   41 NVARX=0
   42 NVARX=NVARX+1
          IF(NVARX.GT.NLEV)GO TO 45
          IF(KSIG(J,NVARX).NE.2.OR.KSIG(I,NVARX).NE.1)GO TO 42
          NTL(NVARX)=NTL(NVARX)+1
          IF(NTL(NVARX).LE.NINL(NVARX))GO TO 43
          NTL(NVARX)=1
          GO TO 42
   43 INSTOR=0
          DO 44 L=1,NLEV
          IF(KSIG(J,L).NE.2)GO TO 44
          INSTOR=INSTOR*NINL(L)+NTL(L)-1
   44 CONTINUE
          INSTOR=INSTOR+1
          X=X+SIG(INSTOR,1)
          Y=Y+SIG(INSTOR,2)
          Z=Z+SIG(INSTOR,3)
          GO TO 41
   45 NS=1
          IF(X.NE.0.) GO TO 47
          MIS=MIS+1
          IF(NSIG.EQ.0)GO TO 31
          LI = LI + 1
          IGO = 4
          IF(LI.GE.50) GO TO 100
   46 WRITE (MED2,909 )(NCL(L),L=1,NLEV)
          GO TO 31
   47 Y=Y/X
          W=V(6)
          INDX = 0
          NONO = 0
          DO 51 L = 1,NLEV
          IF(NCL(L).EQ.0) GO TO 51
          IND1 = INDX+NCL(L)
          W = W*STO(IND1)
   51 INDX = INDX + NINL(L)
          IF (ABS(W-X).GT.0.00001) NONO=1
          IF (ABS(W-X).GT.0.00001) LI = LI + 1
          IF (NONO.EQ.1) V(20) = V(20) + 1.
          W = Y*Y*X
          IF(X.LE.1.) GO TO 48
          X1 = X - 1.
          Z=ABS(Z-W)/X1
          IF(V(2).LT.2..OR.Z.LE.0.) GO TO 48
          IF(V(2).EQ.2..AND.I.NE.NOUT) GO TO 48
          IF(V(2).EQ.4..AND.I.NE.NOUT) GO TO 48
C COLLECT DATA FOR BARTLETT TEST
          CELLS = CELLS + 1.
          DFBAR = DFBAR + X1
          ERRMS = ERRMS + Z*X1
          FLOGS = FLOGS + X1*ALOG(Z)
          RECIP = RECIP + 1./X1
C FORM SIGMA VALUES
   48 SUM(I) = SUM(I) + W
          IF (NSIG.EQ.0.AND.NONO.EQ.0)GO TO 31
          Y=Y+ XBAR
          LI = LI + 1
          IGO = 5
```

```
          IF(LI.GE.50) GO TO 100
       49 IF(NONO.GT.0) WRITE(MED2,912)
          WRITE(MED2,900) X,(NCL(L),L = 1,NLEV)
          IF(NSIG.GE.2) WRITE(MED2,901) Y
          IF(NSIG.GE.3.AND.X.GT.1.) Z = SQRT(Z)
          IF(NSIG.GE.3.AND.X.GT.1.) WRITE(MED2,902) Z
          GO TO 31
       50 IF(V(2).LT.2.) GO TO 60
          IF(V(2).EQ.2..AND.I.NE.NOUT) GO TO 60
          IF(V(2).EQ.4..AND.I.NE.NOUT) GO TO 60
          IF(NSIG.NE.0) GO TO 55
          KS = I-2
          WRITE(MED2,911 ) KS,(TITL(L,KS),L=1,18)
       55 WRITE(MED2,907)
C BARTLETT TEST FOR NON-HOMOGENEITY OF VARIANCE
          CELLS = CELLS - 1.
          IF(DFBAR.LE.0..OR.CELLS.LE.0.)  WRITE(MED2,924)
          IF(DFBAR.LE.0..OR.CELLS.LE.0.)  GO TO 60
          RECIP = 1.+(RECIP - 1./DFBAR)/3./CELLS
          ERRMS=(DFBAR*ALOG(ERRMS/DFBAR)  - FLOGS)/RECIP
          IF(ERRMS.LT.0.) ERRMS = 0.
          RECIP = PRBF(CELLS,9999.,ERRMS/CELLS)
          WRITE(MED2,908) ERRMS,CELLS,RECIP
       60 IF(MIS.EQ.0) GO TO 99
          CALL DFADJ(NF,KSIG,MIS,ND3,NLEV,I,NOUT)
       99 CONTINUE
          NOUT=NOUT-1
          V(10) = V10
          RETURN
C IN-CORE SUBROUTINE TO WRITE HEADER WITH APPROPRIATE SUB-TITLE
      100 WRITE(MED2,920) (TT(L),L=1,10),(TT(L),L=21,30),(TST(L,1),L=1,NLEV)
          WRITE(MED2,923) (TST(L,2),L=1,NLEV)
          WRITE(MED2,921) TSP(1),TSP(2),(TST(L,3),L=1,NLEV)
          WRITE(MED2,923) (TST(L,4),L=1,NLEV)
          WRITE(MED2,922)  (TSP(L),L=3,20)
          IF(IGO.LE.2)WRITE(MED2,903)
          IF(IGO.EQ.3)WRITE(MED2,913)
          IF(IGO.GE.4)WRITE(MED2,911) I2,(TITL(L,I2),L=1,18)
          LI = 0
          GO TO (3,5,12,46,49),IGO
      900 FORMAT (F19.0,50X,10I5/69X,10I5)
      901 FORMAT (1H+,22X,F22.4)
      902 FORMAT (1H+,44X,F22.4)
      903 FORMAT(1H0,50X,19HINDIVIDUAL READINGS)
      904 FORMAT(1H0,50X,14HMISSING VALUES)
      905 FORMAT(1H ,F18.0,4X,2F22.4,4X,10I5/71X,10I5)
      906 FORMAT (1H ,44X,F22.4,4X,10I5/71X,10I5)
      907 FORMAT(46H0BARTLETT TEST FOR NON-HOMOGENEITY OF VARIANCE)
      908 FORMAT (32H0BARTLETTS CHI-LIKE STATISTIC = ,F20.6/
         1           32H0WITH DEGREES OF FREEDOM       = ,F20.6/
         2           32H0ASSOCIATED PROBABILITY        = ,F20.6)
      909 FORMAT(51X,19HTHIS CELL IS EMPTY ,10I5/71X,10I5)
      910 FORMAT(51X,25HNO DATA FOR THIS ANALYSIS)
      911 FORMAT(1H0,10X,4HLINE,I4,4X,18A1/
         11H0,12X,6HNUMBER,11X,15HARITHMETIC MEAN,4X,18HSTANDARD DEVIATION)
      912 FORMAT(12H **WARNING**,20X,32HTHIS PARTITION IS NOT ORTHOGONAL,36X
         1,11H**WARNING**)
      913 FORMAT(1H0,10X,16HFOR ALL READINGS/
         11H0,12X,6HNUMBER,11X,15HARITHMETIC MEAN,4X,18HSTANDARD DEVIATION)
      920 FORMAT(1H1,12X,18HDATA BANK TITLE - ,10A4,     20HINDEPENDENT VARI
         1ATES/16X,15HSUBSET TITLE - ,10A4,10(2X,A1,2X)/(71X,10(2X,A1,2X)))
      921 FORMAT(11X,20HDEPENDENT VARIATE - ,A4,4H OF ,A4,28X,10(A4,1X)/71X,
         110(A4,1X))
```

```
  922 FORMAT(1H ,5X,25HFULL TITLE OF VARIABLE - ,A2,15A4,14H DATA LEVEL
     1- ,2A4)
  923 FORMAT(71X,10(A4,1X))
  924 FORMAT(1H0,10X,17HCANNOT BE APPLIED)
      END


      SUBROUTINE AOVOUT(NF,NR,SUM,TITL,KSUM,TST,TSP,SIG,ND3,NDATX,NOUT,N
     1LEV,NLMAX,NL)
C AOVOUT (SEE  7.1 ) SYSTEM       OUTPUT ANALYSIS OF VARIANCE
      DIMENSION NF(ND3),NR(ND3),SUM(ND3),TITL(18,ND3),KSUM(ND3,ND3)
      DIMENSION TSP(20),TST(NLMAX,4),SIG(NDATX,3)  ,NL(ND3)
      COMMON /STCT/MED1,MED2,MED3,MED4,MED5,MED6,MED13,Q,V(20),TT(30)
      NOUT1 = NOUT + 1
      NOUT2 = NOUT + 2
      DO 2 K = 1,NOUT1
      SIG(K,1) = 0.
      SIG(K,2) = -1.
      SIG(K,3) = 1.
      DO 1 I = 1,NOUT2
      X =KSUM(K,I)
    1 SIG(K,1) = SIG(K,1) + X*SUM(I)
      X = NF(K)
    2 IF(X.GT.0.)SIG(K,2) = SIG(K,1)/X
      NLIN = 60
      NOP = 0
      DO 100 M = 1,11
      IF(M.EQ.2.AND.NCH.EQ.0) GO TO 97
      IF(NLIN+NOP+4.LT.60) GO TO 5
      NLIN = 6
      WRITE(MED2,920) (TT(L),L=1,10),(TT(L),L=21,30),(TST(L,1),L=1,NLEV)
      WRITE(MED2,923) (TST(L,2),L=1,NLEV)
      WRITE(MED2,921) TSP(1),TSP(2),(TST(L,3),L=1,NLEV)
      WRITE(MED2,923) (TST(L,4),L=1,NLEV)
      WRITE(MED2,922)  (TSP(L),L=3,20)
    5 NOP = 0
      IF(M.EQ.1) WRITE(MED2,931)
      IF(M.EQ.2) WRITE(MED2,932)
      IF(M.GT.2) WRITE(MED2,933)
      IF(V(20).GT.0.) WRITE(MED2,934)
      WRITE (MED2,906)
      DO 4 K = 1,NOUT
      IF(NL(K).LT.0) GO TO 4
      WRITE (MED2,908)K,(TITL(L,K),L=1,18),SIG(K,1),NF(K),SIG(K,2)
      NOP = NOP + 1
      I = NR(K)
      IF(I.EQ.0) GO TO 4
      X = 2.
      IF(SIG(K,1).LT.0..OR.SIG(I,1).LE.0.)WRITE(MED2,905)
      IF(NF(K).LE.0)  WRITE(MED2,912)
      IF(NF(I).LE.0)  WRITE(MED2,913)
      IF(SIG(I,1).LE.0..OR.NF(I).LE.0) X = 1.3
      IF(NF(I).LE.0.OR.NF(K).LT.0.OR.SIG(K,1).LT.0..OR.SIG(I,1).LE.0.)
     1GO TO 3
      A = NF(K)
      B = NF(I)
      Y = SIG(K,2)/SIG(I,2)
      X = PRBF(A,B,Y)
      WRITE(MED2,909) Y,NR(K) ,X
      IF(X.GT.0.05)  WRITE(MED2,901)
      IF(X.LE.0.05)  WRITE(MED2,902)
      IF(X.LE.0.01)  WRITE(MED2,903)
      IF(X.LE.0.001) WRITE(MED2,904)
```

```
    3 SIG(K,3) = X
    4 CONTINUE
      IF(NOP.EQ.0)WRITE(MED2,914)
      WRITE(MED2,911) NOUT1,SIG(NOUT1,1),NF(NOUT1)
      IF(NOP.EQ.0) RETURN
      NLIN = NLIN+ NOP + 4
      NCH = 0
   97 DO 99 K = 1,NOUT
   98 IF(NL(K).LT.0) GO TO 99
      IF(NR(K).EQ.0.AND.NF(K).GT.0) GO TO 99
      IF(NR(K).EQ.0) GO TO 7
      IF(M.EQ.1.AND.SIG(K,3).LT.1.5) GO TO 99
      IF(M.GT.1.AND.SIG(K,3).LE.V(7)) GO TO 99
      IF(M.GT.1.AND.SIG(K,3).GT.1.1) GO TO 99
      I = K
      J = I
    6 J = J + 1
      IF(NL(I).NE.NL(J)) GO TO 6
      IF(NR(J).NE.0) GO TO 6
      GO TO 10
    7 J = K
      I = J
    8 I = I - 1
      IF(I.EQ.0) GO TO 9
      IF(NL(I).LT.0.OR.NL(I).GT.NL(J)) GO TO 8
      IF(NL(I).EQ.NL(J)) GO TO 10
    9 NL(K) = -1
      GO TO 98
   10 SIG(J,1) = SIG(J,1) + SIG(I,1)
      NF(J) = NF(J) + NF(I)
      NL(I) = -1
      NCH = NCH + 1
      IX = I
   11 IX = IX + 1
      IF(NL(IX).LT.0) GO TO 11
      IF(NL(IX).EQ.NL(J)) GO TO 14
      NLIX = NL(IX)
      DO 13 JX = IX,J
      IF(NL(JX).NE.NLIX) GO TO 13
      IF(NR(JX).EQ.0) GO TO 12
      SIG(J,1) = SIG(J,1) - SIG(JX,1)
      NF(J) = NF(J) - NF(JX)
      NR(JX) = J
      NL(JX) = NL(J)
      GO TO 13
   12 NL(JX) = -1
      GO TO 14
   13 CONTINUE
   14 X = NF(J)
      IF(X.GT.0.) SIG(J,2) = SIG(J,1)/X
      GO TO 98
   99 CONTINUE
      IF(M.GT.1.AND.NCH.EQ.0) RETURN
  100 CONTINUE
      RETURN
  666 FORMAT(5H AOVO,3F10.4,2I6)
  667 FORMAT(10I6)
  901 FORMAT (1H+,89X,1H-)
  902 FORMAT (1H+,89X,1H*)
  903 FORMAT (1H+,88X,1H*)
  904 FORMAT (1H+,87X,1H*)
  905 FORMAT (1H+,60X,27HEXCESSIVE NON-ORTHOGONALITY)
  906 FORMAT (1H0,7X,79HSOURCE OF VARIATION SUM OF SQUARES DF MEAN SUM O
```

```
     1F SQS VAR RATIO WRT PROBABILITY)
 908 FORMAT (1H ,I2,6X,18A1,F13.4,I4,F14.4,F10.3,I6)
 909 FORMAT (1H+,57X,F12.4,I5,F8.5)
 911 FORMAT (1H ,I2,10X,5HTOTAL,6X,F16.4,I4)
 912 FORMAT(1H+,88X,21HNO DEGREES OF FREEDOM)
 913 FORMAT(1H+,109X,11HNO RESIDUAL)
 914 FORMAT(1H0,10X,20HNO SIGNIFICANT TERMS)
 920 FORMAT( 1H1,12X,18HDATA BANK TITLE - ,10A4,    20HINDEPENDENT VARI
    1ATES/16X,15HSUBSET TITLE - ,10A4,10(2X,A1,2X)/(71X,10(2X,A1,2X)))
 921 FORMAT(11X,20HDEPENDENT VARIATE - ,A4,4H OF ,A4,28X,10(A4,1X)/71X,
    110(A4,1X))
 922 FORMAT(1H ,5X,25HFULL TITLE OF VARIABLE - ,A2,15A4,14H DATA LEVEL
    1- ,2A4)
 923 FORMAT(71X,10 (A4,1X))
 931 FORMAT(1H0,9X,44HANALYSIS OF VARIANCE - WITHOUT POOLING TERMS)
 932 FORMAT(1H0,9X,46HANALYSIS OF VARIANCE - POOLING INCORRECT TERMS)
 933 FORMAT(1H0,9X,52HANALYSIS OF VARIANCE - POOLING NON-SIGNIFICANT TE
    1RMS)
 934 FORMAT(1H0,9X,25HNON-ORTHOGONALITY PRESENT,70X,11H**WARNING**)
     END


     SUBROUTINE DFADJ(NF,KSIG,MIS,ND3,NLEV,I,NOUT)
C DFADJ   (SEE 7.1 ) SERVICE       ADJUSTS ANOVAR DEG. FREEDOM
C ADJUST DEGREES OF FREEDOM FOR MISSING VALUES
     DIMENSION NF(ND3),KSIG(ND3,NLEV)
     NOUT1 = NOUT + 1
     DO 3 IX = I,NOUT1
     IF(KSIG(IX,1).EQ.9)GO TO 3
     ID=1
     DO 2 L=1,NLEV
     IF(KSIG(IX,L).LT.KSIG(I,L))GO TO 3
     IF(KSIG(I,L).LT.KSIG(IX,L))ID=0-ID
   2 CONTINUE
     NF(IX-2)=NF(IX-2)-MIS*ID
   3 CONTINUE
     RETURN
     END


     SUBROUTINE DFSET(NF,NL,NR,ND3,KSIG,NINL,NLEV,NOUT,NDATA)
C DFSET   (SEE 7.1 ) SERVICE       CALCULATES DEG FREEDOM INITIALLY
C CALCULATE DEGREES OF FREEDOM FOR GIVEN TERMS
     DIMENSION NF(ND3),NL(ND3),NR(ND3),KSIG(ND3,NLEV),NINL(NLEV)
     NF(NOUT+1) = NF(NOUT+1) + NDATA - 1
     DO 1 K=1,NOUT
     MIS = NF(K)
     NF(K)=1
     KS=K+2
     IF(KSIG(KS,1).EQ.9)GO TO 1
     DO 2 L=1,NLEV
   2 IF(KSIG(KS,L).EQ.2) NF(K)=NF(K)*(NINL(L)-1)
   1 NF(K)  = NF(K)+MIS
C CALCULATE DEGREES OF FREEDOM FOR GIVEN RESIDUAL TERM
     DO 3 K=1,NOUT
     KS=K+2
     IF(KSIG(KS,1).NE.9)GO TO 3
     KSX=KS
     NF(K)=0
     NR(K)=0
   4 KSX=KSX - 1
     IF(KSX.LE.2)GO TO 3
     IF(NL(KSX).GT.NL(KS)) GO TO 4
```

```
      IF(NL(KSX).LT.NL(KS)) GO TO 5
      NF(K)=NF(K)-NF(KSX-2)
      NR(KSX-2)=K
      GO TO 4
    5 NF(K)=NF(K)+NF(KSX-2)
    3 CONTINUE
      NF(NOUT)=NF(NOUT)+NF(NOUT+1)
      NR(NOUT+1)=0
      RETURN
      END
```

7.2   PROGRAM STMULT - MULTIPLE REGRESSION

7.2.1   Purpose

This program is a general multiple regression program. The program includes facilities for transforming data before they are included in the regression, for selecting and transforming data from previous entries, and for selecting only a subset of the STATCAT data bank in use. The program may be used for orthodox single or multiple linear regression, for polynomial regression, for auto-correlation and for lag-correlation studies. Where auto-correlation and lag-correlation are used the program assumes that entries are presented in regular time sequence, although data may be missing from the sequence. (See, however, 7.2.8 for some warnings on this topic.) Control options permit forced inclusion of 'pinned variates', testing all possible singles, pairs or n-tuples of variates, systematic elimination of variates, successive inclusion or elimination of variates, printing of observed and expected values and residual terms and certain tests for sequential dependence and normality of residual terms.

Figure 7.21a contains simplified flow-charts of the main program STMULT and the executive subroutine CMULT. Figure 7.21b contains simplified flow-charts of the subroutines MULTR and WMULT which carry out multiple regression and report the results of a regression analysis respectively.

7.2.2   Input Data

Item	Level	Format	Function	See
1	0	A	File Control Card (Input only)	3.2
2	1	E	Subset specification	3.6
3	2	F	Set of Variates	Below + 3.7
4	3	F	Predicted Variates Specification	Below + 3.7
5	4	F	Predictor Variates Specification	Below + 3.7
6	5	F	Data Handling Instruction	Below + 3.8

3 - Set of Variates

This is a standard set of variates, as defined in 3.7. Only the transform code, the data column name or number and the number of entries delay are employed by this program, although any comment provided will be printed when the card is read. If delays are employed, the first variate specified here (which must not be delayed itself) will be taken as the time scale. If this variate is less than its previous value, all 'delayed' values will be lost and the 'time' sequence will be considered to re-start. If several analyses are to be carried out, it will be more economic in time to specify all variates at this stage, but if only one analysis or group of analyses is planned it is equally eficient to specify the variates as they are required, specifying only the 'time variate' at this stage. If no variates are specified (i.e. the first card of the module is an 'END' card) the program will step back to level 2 to read a new subset specification.

4 - Predicted Variates Specification

This is a standard set of variates, as defined in 3.7. Only the transform code, the column name or number and the number of entries delay are used, although the comment given on the card will be printed when the card is read. The variates specified should preferably be part of the set specified at the previous level, unless this is the first run with that set of variates, to avoid unnecessary data sweeps. If variates are specified which are not part of the original set of variates, they will be added to the set of variates, but a new data sweep will be required. If no predicted variates are specified (i.e. the first card of the module is an 'END' card) the program will step back to level 3 to read a new set of variates.

5 - Predictor Variates Specification

This is a standard set of variates, as defined in 3.7. Only the transform code, the data column name or number and the number of entries delay are used, although the comment given on the card will be printed when the card is read. The variates specified should preferably be part of the set specified at level 3, unless this is the first run with that set of variates. If variates are specified which are not part of that set, they will be added to the set of variates, but a new data sweep will be required. If no predictor variates are specified (i.e. the first card of the module is an 'END' card) the program will step back to level 4 to read a new set of predicted variates.

A predicted variate may appear as a predictor variate, but will, in that case, be used only to predict different predicted variates - all predictor variates having a perfect correlation with the predicted variate will be eliminated

6 - Data Handling Instruction

This is a standard data handling instruction as defined in 3.8. It is used to specify the degree of detail output, the number of 'non-values' that will be accepted in the set of variates, the strategy of the analysis, the minimum number of predictors to be retained and the cut-off level for statistical significance, where these are relevant.

Card Layout - Data Handling Instruction - STMULT

A BCCCDDDEEEEEEEEFFFFFFFFFFFFFFFFFFFFFGGGGGGGGGGGGGGGGGGGGGG...

Columns on Card	Item Code	FORTRAN Type	Function	See
1	A	I	Output control index	Below
2	B	I	Analysis control index	Below
3 - 5	C	I	Acceptable Number of 'Non-Values'	Below
6 - 8	D	I	Number of Predictors Retained ("pinned")	Below
9 - 16	E	F	Significance Level (per cent)	Below
17 - 40	F	A	Comment (printed with instruction)	-
41 - 80	G	A	Analysis Run Title	-

A - Output Control Index

This index controls the degree of detail output. **Unless otherwise specified** only the basic regression analysis and analysis of variance analogue are printed.

Alternatives

A = 0 or blank : Basic regression parameters and analysis of variance analogue are printed out for final (B=0-5) or best sets of variates (B= 6-9) - (Standard Output)

A = 1 : In addition, multiple correlation and variate selection for intermediate analyses are printed.(Reduced Output)

A = 2 : In addition to default output (A=0) standard output for intermediate analyses is also printed.

A = 3 : Overall means and standard deviations and correlation matrices for predictors/predicted variate are also printed.

A = 4 : Component means and standard deviations, and correlation coefficients for all variates in the complete set are also printed out.

A = 5 : Tests of the normal distribution and sequential independence of residual differences between predictors and predicted variate are also printed out.

A = 6 : Individual predicted variate values, estimates and residuals are also printed out.

A = 7 : Individual predictor variate values are also printed out.

A = 8 : The complete set of variate values is also printed out.

A = 9 : Individual data items are also printed out.

B - <u>Analysis Control Index</u>

This index controls the strategy of the program,in determining which predictors are to be considered, what type of cut-off criterion should be applied and which sets of possible predictors should be tried. The first D predictors will be retained at all times. (These are the "pinned" predictors.) <u>Unless otherwise specified</u> only the specified combination of predictors is used.

<u>Alternatives</u>

B = 0 or blank : Only the specified combination of predictors is used.

B = 1 : Least significant predictors are eliminated as long as the overall probability remains below E.

B = 2 : Least significant predictors are eliminated as long as the loss in overall probability remains below E.

B = 3 : Least significant predictors are eliminated as long as their individual probability is greater than E.

B = 4 : Least significant predictors are eliminated as long as the total unexplained portion of the variance is less than E.

B = 5 : Least significant predictors are eliminated as long as the increase in the unexplained portion of variance is less than E.

B = 6   : Best single predictor added to the D "pinned".

B = 7   : Successive Best single predictors added to the D "pinned".

B = 8   : Best sets of one, two etc. predictors added to the D "pinned".

B = 9   : Best sets of all, all but one, all but two etc predictors added to the D "pinned".

C - <u>Acceptable Number of 'Non-Values'</u>

This index specifies the number of 'non-values' which will be accepted in a set of transformed variates derived from an entry. (Non-values may occur because a value is not present in the entry, because the transform specified has no value for the given data item, or because not enough entries have been read for 'delayed' values to have been sufficiently delayed.) If this number of non-values is exceeded, the set of values will not be included in the analysis, but will count towards any required delays. <u>Unless otherwise specified</u> this value will be taken to be zero. If this value is left blank or set to zero for a run which is not the first with a given set of variates and requires no new variates, the previously specified value of this parameter will be retained. If the value is a non-zero value different from that for the previous data sweep a new data sweep will be carried out.

D - <u>Number of Predictors Retained ("pinned")</u>

This is the number of predictors (starting from the first) which will be retained in all analyses, whether or not they satisfy the conditions laid down by the Analysis Control Index. <u>Unless otherwise specified</u> or if set to 0, no predictor will be retained.

E - <u>Significance Level</u>

This number gives the significance level for individual or overall probability, or the proportion of variance used according to the condition laid down by B. <u>Unless otherwise specified</u>, or if set to zero, it will be considered to be one per cent. If a zero value is required, this level should be set to a negative value.

F - <u>Comment (printed with instruction)</u>

This comment is printed with the first half of data handling instruction card on entry, but is not kept.

G - <u>Analysis Run Title</u>

This forty-character title occupies the part of the data handling instruction normally used for comment. It is kept and is printed with the STATCAT data bank and subset titles to identify the run of the system.

<u>General</u>

If the data handling instruction is a 'STOP' card, the system will halt. If the data handling instruction is an 'END' card, the system steps back to level 5 to read a new set of predictor variates. If the data handling instruction card has no numerical values in card columns 1 - 16 default values are used throughout. - a multiple regression analysis is run for each predicted variate with all the predictor variates, using only complete sets of variates and only the basic regression analyses with analysis of variance analogues are printed out.

7.2.3 Input Example

Figure 7.22 is a summary of the input structure for five runs of STMULT. For the first two pairs of runs, two different predicted variates are used, with the same four predictors. In the first two runs the default values for the output and analysis control indices are employed. In the second pair of runs, only statistically significant individual predictors are employed, non-significant predictors being successfully discarded. In the final run only one predicted variate is retained, and fully detailed output is required. Figure 7.23 is a listing of the input cards required to produce this output.

7.2.4 Output Example

Figure 7.24 is a general summary of the output produced by this program, indented according to the program structure. Figure 7.25 is a page-by-page summary of the output corresponding to the specific input of Figure 7.23. The input checking information is essentially standard. Figures 7.26 and 7.27 illustrate the default output for the first two runs. (Note that LG10 H.R. is discarded as a predictor where it is the predicted variate, but is kept as a predictor otherwise. An appropriate error message is printed.) The output for the second pair of runs is similar, except that more detail is given. Numbers of readings, arithmetic means and standard deviations for all variates, and for those retained are provided, with the correlation matrices for predictors and the correlations between predictors and the predicted variate. Predictors are discarded until only statistically significant predictors remain, the least significant individual predictor being discarded at each stage. The standard multiple regression output is described in 7.2.5.

Figure 7.28 gives part of the output for the final run. The best set of predictors was called for, and all three were retained. The arithmetic means, standard deviations and correlation matrix for these, and their correlations to LG10 DIFF are printed first, then full details for each entry are printed, and finally an analysis of the distribution of the residuals is provided. Figure 7.28 shows an example of a complete residual entry and the residual analysis. These are described in more detail in 7.2.6. and 7.2.7.

7.2.5 Multiple Regression Output

Figure 7.26 illustrates the normal output for a multiple regression. Below the normal titles of the STATCAT data bank, the subset and the specific run, a table gives for each predictor variate in use, its title, its mean and standard deviation, its correlation with the predicted variate (See 6.3.7.), the regression coefficient for the variate and its standard error, the Student's value and its associated probability for that variate. (Strictly speaking the statistic used here is not Student's t, but it is distributed in the same way).

The regression coefficient is the multiplying factor to be applied to the value of a predictor variate. The standard error of this coefficient is an estimate of the accuracy of the value given - being the standard deviation of the distribution that would be expected in many runs with samples of data form the same population. From the regression coefficient and its standard error, the t value is obtained which represents the significance of the difference of the regression coefficient from zero. The associated probability is the probability of obtaining so large a value of t if the true value of the regression coefficient were zero. If this probability is sufficiently small, we may assume that that predictor variate is present.

Following the table of predictors, we have the mean and standard deviation of the predicted variate.

These are followed by the intercept. This is the constant term in the equation

$$\bar{Y} = A + B_1 X_1 + B_2 X_2 + B_3 X_3 + \ldots$$

which produce the best estimate of the predicted variate for a given set of values of the predictors (X) and the calculated regression coefficients (B). In our example the prediction equations are:

```
Log H.R.  = 0.83229 + 0.13207 Log OPER
                   + 0.10221 Log W.P.
                   + 0.17816 Log TASK
```

And

```
Log DIFF  = -2.65513 + 0.61510 Log OPER
                    - 0.04541 Log W.P.
                    + 0.00618 Log TASK
                    + 1.77700 Log H.R.
```

(In the latter equation the second and third predictors make no significant contribution to the prediction.) The multiple correlation is the correlation between the best estimate Y and the actual value Y. It acounts for an amount of variation proportional to the square of the regression coefficient. Usually, this proportion is less than the sums of the squares of the individual correlations given in the table above, because the predictors are themselves correlated. In our first example, the three predictors are in fact not correlated, and the square of the multiple correlation is the sum of the squares of the individual correlations.

The standard error of the estimate is the standard deviation of the estimated variation left when all systematic effects have been deducted.

The analysis of variance analogue is an estimate of the statistical significance of the prediction taken as a whole. The variation is divided into a systematic part, which coresponds to as many degrees of freedom as there are predictors, and a residual of unexplained variation, which may be used to estimate a variance ratio as in a simple analysis of variance (See 7.2.5.).

It should be noted that a high correlation between predictor and predicted variate need not imply a high regression coefficient. If another predictor in the regression is more highly correlated, it may render the first redundant. (This explains the unimportance of W.P. and TASK in estimating DIFF - their effects are better represented by H.R.). Similarly, a relatively uncorrelated variate may have a high regression coefficient if no other variate in the regression accounts for the same variation, or if the difference between this and another variate is an important factor in the regression equation. In the latter case, the two variates will have opposing weights, and when one is removed, the other will be reduced in significance.

The choice of the transform LG10 (logarithm to the base 10) was made to illustrate the use of a linear model to represent a multiplicative function. The first equation produced here might be converted to a form

$$H.R. = 6.796 \times OPER^{0.13207} \times W.P.^{0.10221} \times TASK^{0.1786}$$

In this form the predictors are multiplied rather than added. This type of equation has the property that the error is proportional to the size of the estimate - and is not therefore minimal, but where such a form is appropriate this property is often also appropriate.

7.2.6   Entry (Regression Analysis)

Figure 7.27 shows a complete output for one entry, with the appropriate headings. The page begins with the STATCAT data bank, subset and run titles. The predicted variate is then specified, with a note that individual entries are being considered. This is followed by headings corresponding to the lines of information provided for each entry. The actual amount of information output is controlled by the output control index, the first value drawn from the data handling instruction. (This example shows the maximum output.) The predictor variates retained in use are first listed, then the set of all variates, including those discarded by the system, and those excluded from the selection defined for this run. Finally, the names of all the data columns in the STATCAT data bank are given.

For each entry, the number of the entry in the STATCAT data bank is first given, with the actual value of the predicted variate (Y), its predicted value, and their difference.

The first line is followed by the values of the predictors used to calculate the predicted value, according to the equation specified in the Multiple Regression output (7.2.5.).

A warning message will be provided if any of these values are 'non-values' - and the 'non-value' in question will be replaced by the means of the variates concerned in calculating the predicted value. (This process tends to underestimate the variation present, but has the merit of simplicity and directness.)

The values of predictors used are followed by the values of all the variates, which will include the predictor variates and the predicted

variate, in addition to any other variates not used. Finally, the values
of each item in the entry are listed (without any transforms specified
in the variate specification, and without any delays). These values are
sometimes useful in the investigation of abnormally large residual values - providing an opportunity of verifying that the transforms used
have behaved as required, and of identifying mistakes in transcription
of data. It is also sometimes possible, by reviewing the individual reports to define the conditions under which a particular prediction equation becomes invalid.

7.2.7 Residual Analysis - Regression

If the analysis control index is set to 3 or higher, the system will
make an analysis of the distribution of residuals. This analysis consists of a parametric description, provided by the subroutine DCPS (See
5.2.6.), and a test of the sequential dependence of residuals.

The parametric description is of the standard type, with the following additional characteristics. The arithmetic mean should always be
equal in principle to zero, because the estimates should have the same
mean as the actual values. If entries containing 'non-values' have been
included in the analysis, the arithmetic mean may differ from zero.
There will, in any case, be minor rounding errors in the analysis, which
may lead to minor differences even in the absence of 'non-values'. The
standard deviation obtained should be similar to the calculated standard
error of the estimate, but will not be identical, for the same reason,
and in addition because the subroutine, assuming that the data is drawn
from a sample, rather than from a population, will apply slightly different calculation formulae to those used by the specific multiple regression analysis subroutine (MULTR).

The values of skewness and kurtosis are important as indicators of
the normality of the distribution of residuals. In general, abnormal values of skewness tend to suggest that some actual values were either incorrect or influenced by unconsidered factors, and abnormal kurtosis
that the predicted variate is not normally distributed. If it is on an
originally NOMINAL or ORDINAL level of measurement, this may well be the
case.

The test used for sequential dependency operates by comparing the estimate of the standard error of the residual derived from DCPS with an
estimate based on the differences between the value of the residual.
This test is useful for the detection of short term trends in the residuals, and also for the detection of systematic time-dependency effects.
If there are short-term cyclic effects present in data, then the mean-
square successive difference statistic will be larger than the standard
deviation of the residuals. If there are long-term slow non-linear variations (or linear variations where time is not a parameter of the equations) then the mean-square successive differences will be smaller than
the standard deviation of the residuals. If both effects occur at the
same time, they may not be detected by this test. (See Dixon and Massey
- ch 17)

In general, if irregularities are shown up by the analysis of residuals - and indeed as a precaution if they are not - it is advisable to
plot the residuals against the more important variates, and against the
preceding residual. The latter graph is particularly useful for the
identification of periodic variations.

Where irregularities have been detected in individual values, and their causes can be identified, the analyses may be repeated excluding the rejected entries. It is not wise to reject abnormally high residuals automatically, since this will lead to under-estimates of prediction error and to consequent over-estimation of the value of predictions. In addition, a fertile source of new hypotheses is lost, since the cases where a prediction fails to work are perhaps the most informative in research work.

The STATCAT subroutine RESID, which is used for the analysis of residuals is listed following Chapter 7.3. Figure 7.31b contains a system flow-chart of RESID, which is also used to examine canonical residuals in STCANO (7.5) and Factor Scores in STPACT (7.3).

7.2.8 Restrictions and reservations

The power and flexibility of multiple linear regresion are balanced by a number of drawbacks.

The technique, particularly if used iteratively without sufficient care, is vulnerable to the phenomenom of 'Constructed Significance' (See 12.1).

The technique employs linear prediction, so that it cannot be used to fit any inherently non-linear formula. Many apparently complex formulae can be reduced to a linear form, if suitable transformations are employes, but some cannot.
For example the equation

$$Y = A + Be^{-C.X} + error$$

cannot be transformed to a linear prediction, so that values for A,B and C can only be found by cut-and-try methods. There is nothing wrong with intelligent and judicious guessing at parameters, based on knowledge of the mechanisms involved, although it can make it difficult to establish the statistical significance of deviations.

Where transforms are used, as in our example, the assumptions of the multiple linear regresion apply to the transformed equation in its linear form, not to the form into which it is transformed back. The error term in our prediction is a multiplicative term in the final equation calculated in 7.2.5., not an additive one, and it is the logarithm of this term which should be normally distributed.

Although this program permits the use of delayed variates, the user should be aware that the analysis of time-series presents many theoretical and practical problems. These arise mainly from the fact that successive values of a time-series are not independent, in the relevant statistical sense. Kendall (1973) gives a readable account of the recent state of the art, and Box and Jenkins (1976) give more technical detail.

Practically important restrictions concern the area to which the regression is applicable. In many situations the experimenter has access only to conditions at one end, or at the centre of the potential range of variation. Since many phenomena tend to show differences at the extremes of their range, it is extremely dangerous to attempt to extrapolate using a multiple regression formula.

It should also be remembered that the multiple regression equation, like a simple regression equation of the type described in 6.3.7. must not be treated as an algebraic equation. It cannot be transformed to predict the operator from the heart-rate and the difficulty reported by simple manipulation.

Finally, it should be remembered that the use of the product-moment correlation implies that the variates are on an interval level of measurement. If they are not, there will always be a certain possible element of error. Where the predicted variate is on an ordinal level, and there are sufficient ranks available, the differences may be negligible. Where the predicted variate is on a nominal scale, and this scale has only two values (YES/NO,TRUE/FALSE,ACCEPT/REJECT) it is usually possible to produce a threshold level for the 'predicted value' above which it is accepted. Where there are a number of possible nominal responses, the linear predictor is usually meaningless. In such a situation, it may be possible to rank the nominal classes in some meaningful order, or it may be possible to convert the single nominal into a series of binary variates, each corresponding to one class of the original variate, using the program STRANS, or a special DATA subroutine. Multiple discriminant analysis (7.4.) or data splitting (8.2.) may be more appropriate in many cases.

REFERENCES Veldman (Ch 11), Searle (1966 - Ch 9)
            Box and Jenkins (1976),Kendall (1973) (Time Series)
            Kendall (1975 - ch7)
            Kendall and Stuart (Ch 28 + later)
            Draper and Smith (Choice of predictors and residuals)
            Dixon and Massey (Ch 17 - test of sequential dependency)

Figure 7.21a - System Flow-Charts - STMULT and CMULT

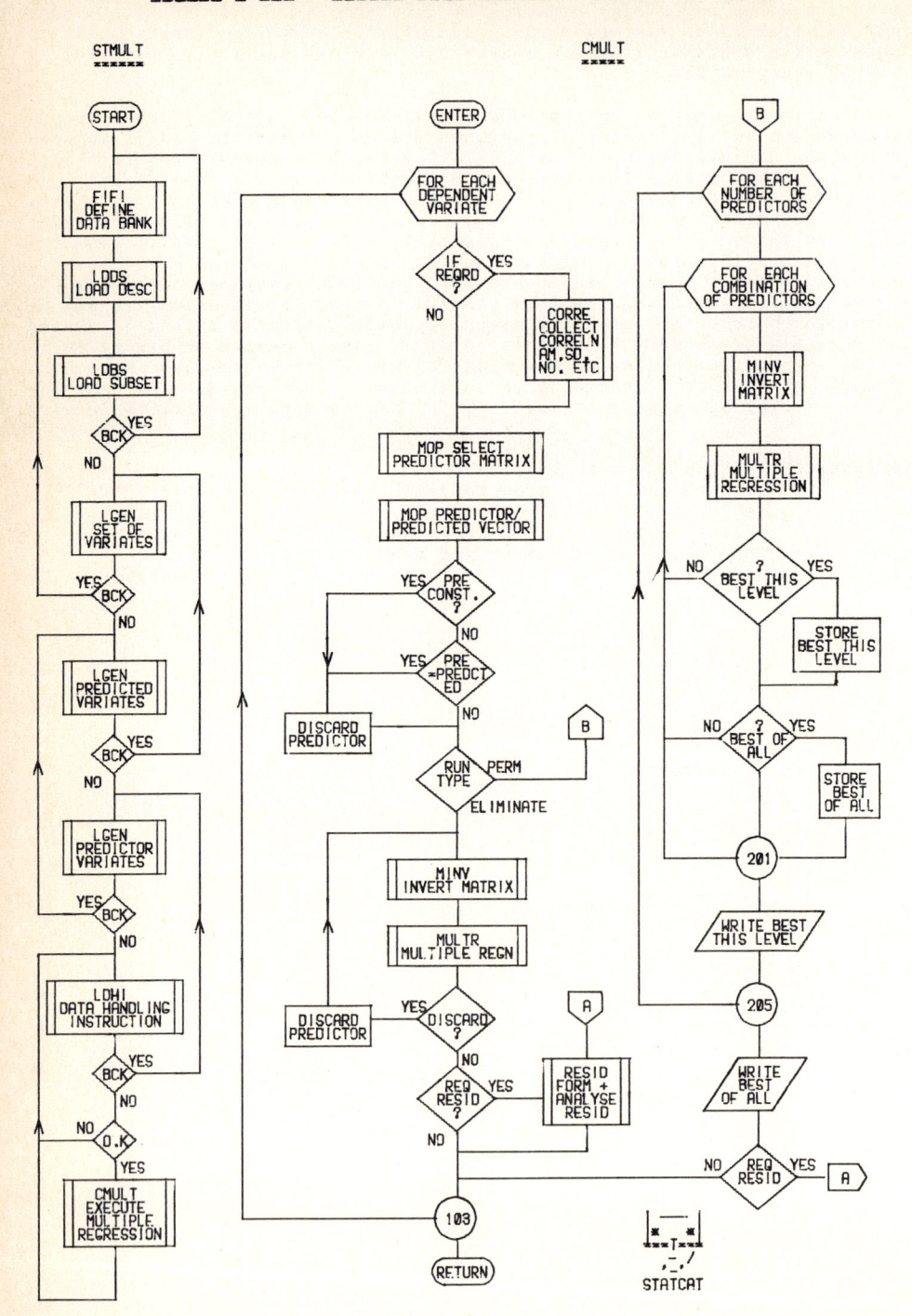

Figure 7.21b - System Flow-Charts - **MULTR** and **WMULT**

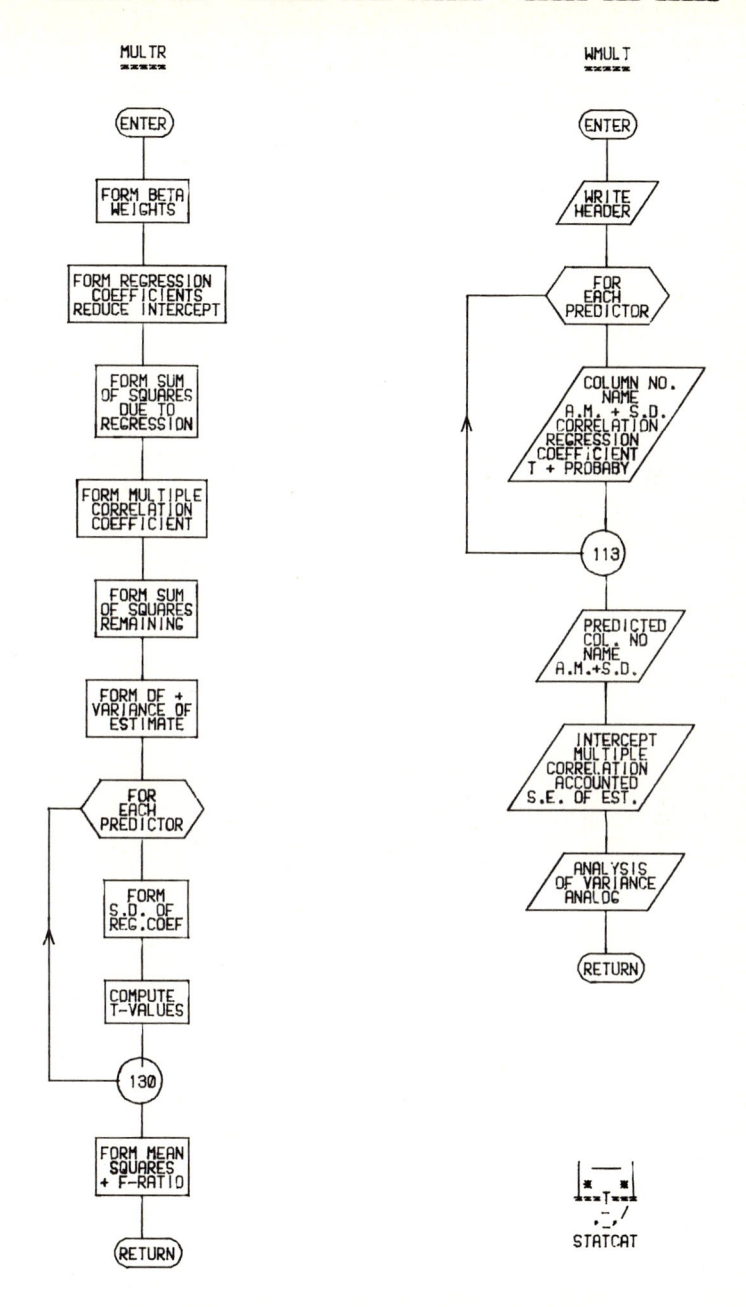

MULTR

```
ENTER
  │
FORM BETA
WEIGHTS
  │
FORM REGRESSION
COEFFICIENTS
REDUCE INTERCEPT
  │
FORM SUM
OF SQUARES
DUE TO
REGRESSION
  │
FORM MULTIPLE
CORRELATION
COEFFICIENT
  │
FORM SUM
OF SQUARES
REMAINING
  │
FORM DF +
VARIANCE OF
ESTIMATE
  │
FOR
EACH
PREDICTOR
  │
FORM
S.D. OF
REG.COEF
  │
COMPUTE
T-VALUES
  │
(130)
  │
FORM MEAN
SQUARES
+ F-RATIO
  │
RETURN
```

WMULT

```
ENTER
  │
WRITE
HEADER
  │
FOR
EACH
PREDICTOR
  │
COLUMN NO.
NAME
A.M. + S.D.
CORRELATION
REGRESSION
COEFFICIENT
T + PROBABY
  │
(113)
  │
PREDICTED
COL. NO
NAME
A.M.+S.D.
  │
INTERCEPT
MULTIPLE
CORRELATION
ACCOUNTED
S.E. OF EST.
  │
ANALYSIS
OF VARIANCE
ANALOG
  │
RETURN
```

STATCAT

373

Figure 7.22 - STMULT - Input Structure

```
         Level
  0    1    2    3    4    5    6    7    8    9
FILE CONTROL CARD
    SUBSET SPECIFICATION
        VARIATE SPECIFICATION
            PREDICTED VARIATES
                PREDICTOR VARIATES
                    DATA HANDLING INSTRUCTION
                    DATA HANDLING INSTRUCTION
                    BACK TO READ NEW PREDICTOR VARIATES
                BACK TO READ NEW PREDICTED VARIATES
            PREDICTED VARIATES
                PREDICTOR VARIATES
                    DATA HANDLING INSTRUCTION
                    STOP
```

Figure 7.23 - STMULT - Input Example

```
---------1---------2---------3---------4---------5---------6---------7--
**STMULTDEMO                            DEMONSTRATION STATCAT DATA BANK
ALL DATA                                WHOLE DATA BANK TO BE INCLUDED
END OF SUBSET DEFINITION
LG10OPER
LG10W.P.
LG10TASK
LG10H.R.
LG10DIFF
END OF SET OF VARIATES
LG10H.R.
LG10DIFF
END OF PREDICTED VARIATES
LG10OPER
LG10W.P.
LG10TASK
LG10H.R.
END OF PREDICTOR VARIATES
GO                                      DEFAULT RESPONSE
23                                      SIGNIFICANT PREDICTORS ONLY
BACK TO READ NEW PREDICTORS
BACK TO READ NEW PREDICTED VARIATES
LOG.H.R.
END OF SET OF PREDICTED VARIATES
LOG.TASK
LOG.W.P.
LOG.OPER
END OF PREDICTORS
73                                      DETAILED DESCRIPTIVE OUTPUT
STOP
---------1---------2---------3---------4---------5---------6---------7--
```

Figure 7.24 - STMULT - Output Structure

```
For each    ) : File Control Record
output file )   File Parameters
                Data Description
                For each) : Subset Input Record
                Subset  )   For each set) : Input Record
                            of Variates )   For each set ) : Input
                                        )   of Predicted )   Record
                                                Variates )
                                                Model    )
For each set) : Input Record
of Predictor)   For each Data) : Input Record
Variates    )   Handling     )   For Each    )  See left
                Instruction  )   Predicted   )
                                 Variate     )
For each  )  <No.,a.m. and s.d. for variates used>
Predicted )  <No.,a.m. and s.d. for all variates in store>
variate   )  <Correlation Matrix - all variates>
             <No.,a.m. and s.d. for each cell - if non-values present>
             <Correlation Matrix - Predictors>
             <Correlation Vector - Predictors/Predicted>
             .        For intermediate sets of variates : -
             .          <Standard/summary Multiple Regression report>
             Final Standard Multiple Regression report
             <Residual Analysis>
             .          For Each Entry : -
             .          <Prediction/Actual/Residual>
             .          <Predictor Values>
             .          <Variate Values>
             .          <Data Items>
             <Parametric Description of Residuals>
             <Test for Sequential Dependency>

Carated(<>) items are optional.
```

Figure 7.25 - STMULT - Page-by-page output summary

Page	Contents	Origin
1-2	File Control/Program title	FIPI/LDAP/STMULT
	Data Description record	LDDS
3	Subset record	LDBS/LSAMP
4	Set of Variates record	LGEN
5	Predicted Variate record	LGEN
6	Predictor Variate record	LGEN
	Data Handling Instruction	LDHI
7	Error - (Predictor = Predicted)	CMULT
8-9	Multiple Regression Reports	WMULT
10	Data Handling Instruction	LDHI
11	Error - (Predictor = Predicted)	CMULT
12	Multiple Regression Report (Lg10 H.R.)	WMULT
13-15	Multiple Regression Report (Lg10 DIFF)	WMULT
16	Data Handling Instruction (BACK)	LDHI
17	Predictor Variate record (BACK)	LGEN
18	Predicted Variate record	LGEN
19	Predictor Variate record	LGEN
	Data Handling Instruction	LDHI
20-22	Descriptive output	WBASE
23	Selected Predictors/predicted variate	WMAT/CMULT
24-34	Multiple regression reports	WMULT
35-56	Detailed Residual analysis	RESID
57	Statistical Summary	DCPS
58	Data Handling Instruction (STOP)	LDHI

Figure 7.26 - STMULT - Basic Output - First Run

```
STATCAT PROGRAM STMULT      -   MULTIPLE LINEAR REGRESSION
DATA BANK TITLE             -   DEMONSTRATION STATCAT DATA BANK
DATA BANK SUBSET TITLE      -   ALL DATA
RUN TITLE                   -   DEFAULT RESPONSE


LG10 OF COL  15 H.R. PREDICTOR=PREDICTED - DISCARDED



STATCAT PROGRAM STMULT      -   MULTIPLE LINEAR REGRESSION
DATA BANK TITLE             -   DEMONSTRATION STATCAT DATA BANK
DATA BANK SUBSET TITLE      -   ALL DATA
RUN TITLE                   -   DEFAULT RESPONSE
```

PREDICTOR VARIATE	MEAN	STANDARD DEVIATION	CORRELATION X VERSUS Y	REGRESSION COEFFICIENT	STD. ERROR OF REGRESSION	COMPUTED T VALUE	ASSOCIATED PROBABILITY
LG10 OF COL 4 OPER	0.34505	0.22611	0.45013	0.13206	0.02100	6.28924	0.0
LG10 OF COL 5 W.P.	0.34505	0.22611	0.34837	0.10220	0.02100	4.86744	0.00006
LG10 OF COL 9 TASK	0.34505	0.22611	0.60723	0.17815	0.02100	8.48447	0.0
PREDICTED VARIATE							
LG10 OF COL 15 H.R.	1.67190	0.06634					

```
INTERCEPT                   1.52960

MULTIPLE CORRELATION        0.83228     ACCOUNTING FOR  69.263 PER CENT OF OBSERVED VARIANCE

STD. ERROR OF ESTIMATE      0.03766
```

ANALYSIS OF VARIANCE ANALOG REGRESSION

SOURCE OF VARIATION	DEGREES OF FREEDOM	SUM OF SQUARES	MEAN SQUARES	F VALUE	PROBABILITY
ATTRIBUTABLE TO REGRESSION	3	0.19204	0.06401	45.07916	0.0
DEVIATION FROM REGRESSION	60	0.08520	0.00142		
TOTAL	63	0.27725			

Figure 7.27 - STMULT - Basic Output - Second Run

```
STATCAT PROGRAM STMULT      -   MULTIPLE LINEAR REGRESSION
DATA BANK TITLE             -   DEMONSTRATION STATCAT DATA BANK
DATA BANK SUBSET TITLE      -   ALL DATA
RUN TITLE                   -   DEFAULT RESPONSE
```

PREDICTOR VARIATE	MEAN	STANDARD DEVIATION	CORRELATION X VERSUS Y	REGRESSION COEFFICIENT	STD. ERROR OF REGRESSION	COMPUTED T VALUE	ASSOCIATED PROBABILITY
LG10 OF COL 4 OPER	0.34505	0.22611	0.81359	0.61515	0.06739	9.12778	0.0
LG10 OF COL 5 W.P.	0.34505	0.22611	0.13051	-0.04537	0.06179	-0.73418	0.52753
LG10 OF COL 9 TASK	0.34505	0.22611	0.30920	0.00625	0.07760	0.08051	0.93393
LG10 OF COL 15 H.R.	1.67190	0.06634	0.75305	1.77680	0.32168	5.52356	0.00002
PREDICTED VARIATE							
LG10 OF COL 10 DIFF	0.51454	0.23605					

```
INTERCEPT                   -2.65486

MULTIPLE CORRELATION        0.92294     ACCOUNTING FOR  85.182 PER CENT OF OBSERVED VARIANCE

STD. ERROR OF ESTIMATE      0.09390
```

ANALYSIS OF VARIANCE ANALOG REGRESSION

SOURCE OF VARIATION	DEGREES OF FREEDOM	SUM OF SQUARES	MEAN SQUARES	F VALUE	PROBABILITY
ATTRIBUTABLE TO REGRESSION	4	2.99030	0.74758	84.79381	0.0
DEVIATION FROM REGRESSION	59	0.52017	0.00882		
TOTAL	63	3.51047			

Figure 7.28 - STMULT - Correlation Matrix etc.

```
SYSTEM SUBROUTINE WBASE      -   CORRELATION MATRIX ETC.
DATA BANK TITLE              -   DEMONSTRATION STATCAT DATA BANK
DATA BANK SUBSET TITLE       -   ALL DATA
RUN TITLE                    -   DETAILED DESCRIPTIVE OUTPUT

FOR ALL ENTRIES FOR ALL VARIATES IN STORE

TRANSFORM COLUMN             NUMBER OF READINGS    ARITHMETIC MEAN    STANDARD DEVIATION
LG10 OF   4(OPER)                64.0000000           0.34505057         0.22610641
LG10 OF   5(W.P.)                64.0000000           0.34505057         0.22610641
LG10 OF   9(TASK)                64.0000000           0.34505057         0.22610635
LG10 OF  15(H.R.)                64.0000000           1.67190361         0.06633794
LG10 OF  10(DIFF)                64.0000000           0.51453590         0.23605460



SYSTEM SUBROUTINE WBASE      -   CORRELATION MATRIX ETC.
DATA BANK TITLE              -   DEMONSTRATION STATCAT DATA BANK
DATA BANK SUBSET TITLE       -   ALL DATA
RUN TITLE                    -   DETAILED DESCRIPTIVE OUTPUT

FOR ALL ENTRIES FOR ALL VARIATES IN THIS ANALYSIS

TRANSFORM COLUMN             NUMBER OF READINGS    ARITHMETIC MEAN    STANDARD DEVIATION
LG10 OF   9(TASK)                64.0000000           0.34505057         0.22610635
LG10 OF   5(W.P.)                64.0000000           0.34505057         0.22610641
LG10 OF   4(OPER)                64.0000000           0.34505057         0.22610641
LG10 OF  15(H.R.)                64.0000000           1.67190361         0.06633794



SYSTEM SUBROUTINE WBASE      -   CORRELATION MATRIX ETC.
DATA BANK TITLE              -   DEMONSTRATION STATCAT DATA BANK
DATA BANK SUBSET TITLE       -   ALL DATA
RUN TITLE                    -   DETAILED DESCRIPTIVE OUTPUT

                             CORRELATIONS BETWEEN ALL VARIATES DEFINED
         1         2         3         4         5
  1   1.0000    0.0000    0.0000    0.4501    0.8140
  2   0.0000    1.0000    0.0000    0.3434    0.1305
  3   0.0000    0.0000    1.0000    0.6072    0.3092
  4   0.4501    0.3434    0.6072    1.0000    0.7531
  5   0.8140    0.1305    0.3092    0.7531    1.0000

            ONLY COMPLETE ENTRIES USED IN THIS SET OF VARIATES



STATCAT PROGRAM STMULT       -   MULTIPLE LINEAR REGRESSION
DATA BANK TITLE              -   DEMONSTRATION STATCAT DATA BANK
DATA BANK SUBSET TITLE       -   ALL DATA
RUN TITLE                    -   DETAILED DESCRIPTIVE OUTPUT

        CORRELATIONS BETWEEN PREDICTORS SELECTED FOR THIS ANALYSIS

  TRANSFORM            LG10 OF    LG10 OF    LG10 OF
  COLUMN (NAME)        9.=TASK    5.=W.P.    4.=OPER
  TRANSFORM COLUMN
  LG10 OF   9(TASK)    1.0000     0.0000     0.0000
  LG10 OF   5(W.P.)    0.0000     1.0000     0.0000
  LG10 OF   4(OPER)    0.0000     0.0000     1.0000

        CORRELATIONS BETWEEN PREDICTORS AND PREDICTED VARIATE

  TRANSFORM            LG10 OF
  COLUMN (NAME)        15.=H.R.
  TRANSFORM COLUMN
  LG10 OF   9(TASK)    0.6072
  LG10 OF   5(W.P.)    0.3434
  LG10 OF   4(OPER)    0.4501
```

Figure 7.29 - STMULT - Entry and Residual Analysis

```
MULTIPLE LINEAR REGRESSION

DATA BANK TITLE            -    DEMONSTRATION STATCAT DATA BANK
DATA BANK SUBSET TITLE     -    ALL DATA
RUN TITLE                  -    DETAILED DESCRIPTIVE OUTPUT

INDIVIDUAL ENTRIES

PREDICTED VARIATES    LG10 OF
    SELECTED          H.R.( 15)

PREDICTOR VARIATES    LG10 OF    LG10 OF    LG10 OF
    SELECTED          OPER(  4)N.P.( 5)TASK(  5)

SET OF VARIATES       LG10 OF    LG10 OF    LG10 OF    LG10 OF    LG10 OF
    SELECTED          OPER(  4)N.P.( 5)TASK( 5)H.R.( 15)DIFF( 10)

    DATA COLUMN       1 = NTRY  2 = SESS  3 = OBSR  4 = OPER  5 = N.P.  6 = STRS  7 = DAY  8 = TIME  9 = TASK 10 = DIFF
                     11 = TEMP 12 = TPUT 13 = LFCF 14 = FFCF 15 = H.R. 16 = TCCM 17 = FALL 18 = SP20

ENTRY   63

    ACTUAL            1.7011
    PREDICTED         1.7264
    RESIDUAL         -0.0252

    PREDICTED VALUE   1.7011

    PREDICTOR VALUES  0.4771     0.4771     0.4771

    VARIATE VALUES    0.4771     0.4771     0.4771     1.7011     0.6990

    DATA ITEM VALUES  63.0000   16.0000     4.0000     3.0000     2.0000     4.0000     4.0000     4.0000     3.0000     5.0000
                      25.0000   -8.7100    73.9000    74.6000    50.2500    46.5600    51.0000     1.5000


MULTIPLE LINEAR REGRESSION

DATA BANK TITLE            -    DEMONSTRATION STATCAT DATA BANK
DATA BANK SUBSET TITLE     -    ALL DATA
RUN TITLE                  -    DETAILED DESCRIPTIVE OUTPUT


EXAMINATION OF RESIDUAL DIFFERENCES

NUMBER OF READINGS=        64.

ARITHMETIC MEAN =         -0.000000    S.E. OF MEAN =         0.004633

STANDARD DEVIATION=        0.037065    S.E. OF S.D. =         0.002969

COEFFICIENT OF VARIATION UNDEFINED     NOT JUSTIFIED BY ORIGINAL DATA LEVEL                              **WARNING**

        SKEWNESS =        -0.321539   SKEWNESS RATIO =       -1.050142  PROBABILITY=        0.294047

        KURTOSIS =        -0.178900   KURTOSIS RATIO =       -0.584286  PROBABILITY=        0.566376

S.E. FOR SKEWNESS =        0.306186

ROOT-MEAN-SQUARE SUCCESSIVE DEVIATION =  0.05769988

NORMALISED VALUE =  1.72049236

ASSOCIATED PROBABILITY =  0.08640587
```

```
C     GENERALISED MULTIPLE REGRESSION PROGRAM - INCLUDING
C     TRANSFORMED,POLYNOMIAL AND LAGGED REGRESSION
C         SUBROUTINES AND FUNCTIONS REQUIRED
C     NAME              TYPE           COMMENT
C     AN      (SEE  3.1 ) SERVICE      ALPHA - TO NUMERIC VALUE
C     CHIKEN  (SEE 11.9 ) SERVICE      WARNS OF MISMATCHED DATA LEVEL
C     CLSAM   (SEE  3.5 ) SERVICE      ALLOTS ENTRY TO SAMPLE/SUBSET
C     CMULT   (SEE  7.2 ) EXECUTIVE    MULTIPLE REGRESSION
C     COMPA   (SEE  3.1 ) SERVICE      COMPARES ALPHAMERIC VALUES
C     COPYA   (SEE  3.1 ) SERVICE      COPIES ALPHAMERIC VALUE
C     CORRE   (SEE  7.5 ) SYSTEM       MULTIPLE CORRELATION DATA
C     DCPS    (SEE  5.2 ) STATISTICAL  MOMENT(PARAMETRIC) STATISTICS
C     FIFI    (SEE  3.2 ) SYSTEM       ALLOCATES PERIPHERALS
C     GAUS    (SEE 11.8 ) STATISTICAL  FINDS ASS. PROB. OF N VALUE
C     IBL     (SEE  3.1 ) SERVICE      DETECTS BLANK,END AND STOP CARDS
C     ICH     (SEE  3.1 ) SERVICE      IDENTIFIES ALPHAMERIC CODES
C     LDAP    (SEE  3.3 ) SYSTEM       LOADS/CHECKS DATA BANK PARAMETERS
C     LDBS    (SEE  3.6 ) SYSTEM       LOADS SUBSET DEFINITION
C     LDDS    (SEE  3.4 ) SYSTEM       LOADS DATA DESCRIPTION SEGMENT
C     LDHI    (SEE  3.8 ) SYSTEM       LOADS/CHECKS DATA HANDLING INSTN
C     LGEN    (SEE  3.7 ) SYSTEM       LOADS GENERALISED VARIATES
C     LSET    (SEE  3.5 ) SYSTEM       LOADS DEFINING CONDITIONS
C     MEDIAT  (SEE  3.7 ) SERVICE      FETCHES NEXT VARIATE SET
C     MINV    (SEE 11.3 ) SERVICE      INVERTS MATRIX
C     MOP     (SEE 11.3 ) SERVICE      SELECTS/CONVERTS STORED MATRIX
C     MULTR   (SEE  7.2 ) STATISTICAL  CARRIES OUT SPECIFIC MULTIPLE REG
C     NEXC    (SEE 11.6 ) SERVICE      NEXT COMBINATION OF PREDICTORS
C     PRBF    (SEE 11.8 ) STATISTICAL  FINDS PROBABILITY OF F-RATIO
C     RESID   (SEE  7.3 ) SERVICE      EXAMINE RESIDUALS
C     TRANS   (SEE  3.7 ) SERVICE      CARRIES OUT REQUIRED TRANSFORM
C     WBASE   (SEE  7.5 ) SYSTEM       WRITE CORRELATION MATRIX ETC.
C     WMAT    (SEE 11.3 ) SERVICE      WRITE MATRIX WITH VARIATE TITLES
C     WMULT   (SEE  7.2 ) SYSTEM       WRITE MULTIPLE REGRESSION OUTPUT
C     SETTING OF ARRAY DIMENSIONS
C     THE FOLLOWING DIMENSIONS MUST BE AT LEAST AS BIG AS THOSE
C     SPECIFIED BY THE DATA TAPE,SAMPLE SPECIFICATIONS, ETC.
C     NQMAX = MAXIMUM NUMBER OF DATA COLUMNS
C     DIMENSION X(NQMAX),ST(NQMAX) ,IT(NQMAX),CN(NQMAX)
      NQMAX = 100
      DIMENSION X(100),ST(100),IT(100),CN(100)
      DATA  CN/4HCOL1,4HCOL2,4HCOL3,4HCOL4,4HCOL5,4HCOL6,4HCOL7,4HCOL8,4
     1HCOL9,4HCL10,4HCL11,4HCL12,4HCL13,4HCL14,4HCL15,4HCL16,4HCL17,4HCL
     218,4HCL19,4HCL20,4HCL21,4HCL22,4HCL23,4HCL24,4HCL25,4HCL26,4HCL27,
     34HCL28,4HCL29,4HCL30,4HCL31,4HCL32,4HCL33,4HCL34,4HCL35,4HCL36,4HC
     4L37,4HCL38,4HCL39,4HCL40,4HCL41,4HCL42,4HCL43,4HCL44,4HCL45,4HCL46
     5,4HCL47,4HCL48,4HCL49,4HCL50,4HCL51,4HCL52,4HCL53,4HCL54,4HCL55,4H
     6CL56,4HCL57,4HCL58,4HCL59,4HCL60,4HCL61,4HCL62,4HCL63,4HCL64,4HCL6
     75,4HCL66,4HCL67,4HCL68,4HCL69,4HCL70,4HCL71,4HCL72,4HCL73,4HCL74,4
     8HCL75,4HCL76,4HCL77,4HCL78,4HCL79,4HCL80,4HCL81,4HCL82,4HCL83,4HCL
     984,4HCL85,4HCL86,4HCL87,4HCL88,4HCL89,4HCL90,4HCL91,4HCL92,4HCL93,
     94HCL94,4HCL95,4HCL96,4HCL97,4HCL98,4HCL99,4HC100/
C     MAXM = MAXIMUM NUMBER OF DIFFERENT VARIATES SPECIFIED
C     DIMENSION XBAR(MAXM),STD(MAXM),RY(MAXM),W(MAXM),B(MAXM),JX(MAXM)
C     DIMENSION SB(MAXM),T(MAXM),NDP(MAXM),NP(MAXM),IX(MAXM),IY(MAXM)
C     DIMENSION ITEST(MAXM),IBEST(MAXM),IREST(MAXM)
      MAXM = 50
      DIMENSION XBAR(50),STD(50),RY(50),W(50),B(50),JX(50)
      DIMENSION SB(50),T(50),NP(50),NDP(50),IX(50),IY(50)
      DIMENSION ITEST(50),IBEST(50),IREST(50)
C     MAXAV = STORE FOR REGRESSION AND CORRELATION MATRICES
C     MAXAV MUST BE AT LEAST K*K + M*(M+1)*3 IF MISSING VALUES ALLOWED
C     MAXAV MUST BE AT LEAST K*K + M*(M+1)/2 IF NO MISSING VALUES
C     WHERE K = NUMBER OF PREDICTOR VARIATES
```

```
C AND M = NUMBER OF DIFFERENT VARIATES IN STORE
C DIMENSION R(MAXAV)
      MAXAV = 2500
      DIMENSION R(2500)
C MAXKPV = MAXIMUM OF PREDICTORS AND PREDICTED AT ANY RUN
C DIMENSION ISAVE(MAXKPV)
      MAXKPV = 50
      DIMENSION ISAVE(50)
C MAXD = STORAGE AVAILABLE FOR DELAYED ENTRIES
C      (MAXIMUM DELAY + 3.) * M MUST NOT EXCEED MAXD
C DIMENSION D(MAXD) IF MAXD NOT ZERO
C DIMENSION D(MAXD)
      MAXD = 500
      DIMENSION D(500)
C IF ALL 60 PREDICTORS USED,THE MAXIMUM DELAY WOULD BE 8 CYCLES
C IF ONLY 2 VARIABLES     USED,THE MAXIMUM DELAY WOULD BE 298 CYCLES
C DIMENSION TRT(NALTMX)  WHERE NALTMX = MAX NO OF CLASSES ON TAPE
      NALTMX = 50
      DIMENSION TRT(50)
C DIMENSION SCON(5,MAXDBC) = MAX NO OF DATA BANK SUBSET CONDITIONS
      MAXDBC = 50
      DIMENSION SCON(5,50)
C THE FOLLOWING DIMENSIONS STORE THE NAMES OF THE DATA TRANSFORMS
C AND THE ACCEPTABLE LEVELS FOR TRANSFORMATIONS
      DIMENSION U(60),LU(60)
      NU = 60
C TRANSFORMATION CODES
C UNITS                          BLOCKS
C         0 - 9   10 - 19   20 - 29   30 - 39   40 - 49   50 - 59
C         POWERS  TRIG      TRIG      STATIST   MATHS     TEST
C                 RADIANS   DEGREES   TRANSF    FUNCTS    FUNCTIONS
C  0       -       -        H.MS      -          -         RM10
C  1      VAL.    SINR      SIND      PSNA      RECP      +/-1
C  2      SQAR    COSR      COSD      PSNB      SQRT      ADD1
C  3      CUBE    TANR      TAND      BINO      ABSV      SUB1
C  4      4PWR    ASIR      ASID      LG+1      SIGN      NOR1
C  5      5PWR    ACOR      ACOD      LOGE      INTG      +/-P
C  6      6PWR    ATAR      ATAD      LG10      FRAC      ADDP
C  7      7PWR    SINH      DTOR      AL10      EXPT      SUBP
C  8      8PWR    COSH      RTOD       -        PRES      NOBP
C  9      9PWR    TANH      H.HH       -        NEG.      +100
      DATA U/4HVAL.,4HSQAR,4HCUBE,4H4PWR,4H5PWR,4H6PWR,4H7PWR,4H8PWR,4H9
     1PWR,4HVAL ,4HSINR,4HCOSR,4HTANR,4HASIR,4HACOR,4HATAR,4HSINH,4HCOSH
     2,4HTANH,4HH.MS,4HSIND,4HCOSD,4HTAND,4HASID,4HACOD,4HATAD,4HDTOR,4H
     3RTOD,4HH.HH,4H VAL,4HPSNA,4HPSNB,4HBINO,4HLG+1,4HLOGE,4HLG10,4HAL1
     40,4H    ,4H    ,4H    ,4HRECP,4HSQRT,4HABSV,4HSIGN,4HINTG,4HFRAC,4
     5HEXPT,4HPRES,4HNEG.,4HRM10,4H+/-1,4HADD1,4HSUB1,4HNOR1,4H+/-P,4HAD
     6DP,4HSUBP,4HNORP,4H+100,4H    /
C ACCEPTABLE CODE LEVELS
      DATA LU/60*4/
C DUMMY ARRAYS USED IN LGEN + D.H.I INPUT ARRAY
      DIMENSION IH(1),H(1),FORM(40)
      COMMON /STCT/MED1,MED2,MED3,MED4,MED5,MED6,MED13,Q,V(20),TT(30)
      DATA PROG/4HMULT/
      MED1 = -1
C LEVEL 0 - SETTING UP
    1 CALL COPYA(TT(1),PROG)
      CALL FIFI
      IF(MED2.GT.0) WRITE(MED2,901)
      CALL LDAP(MED2,MED3,V,TT,Q,NQ,NALT,NQMAX,NALTMX,IGO)
      IF(IGO.GT.0) GO TO 1
      LI = 18
      CALL LDDS(TRT,NALT,D,NQ,ST,NQ,IT,NQ,H,0,H,H,0,LI,0,Q,VX,
```

```
      1 0,MED2,MED3,0,IGO)
C LEVEL 2  - READ DATA BANK SUBSET
   21 IF(V(10).GE.20.) V(10) = 0.
      CALL LDBS(SCON,NCON,MAXDBC,CN,ST,IT,NQ,TRT,NALT,IGO)
      IF(IGO.GT.0) GO TO 1
      DO 22 I = 11,20
   22 CALL COPYA(TT(I),TT(I+10))
      ARAN = 5236.
C LEVEL 4  - READ SET OF VARIATES FOR DATA SWEEP
   41 IF(V(10).GE.40.) V(10) = 0.
      M = 0
      WRITE(MED6,941)
      WRITE(MED6,944)
      CALL LGEN(U,NU,LU,NU,ST,IT,CN,NQ,IH,0,H,H,0,H,H,0,MAXD,NALT,NDP,NP
     1,MAXM,M,MAXM,1,NALT)
      IF(V(11).LT.0.5.AND.V(20).LT.0.5)GO TO 21
      BRAN = ARAN
C LEVEL 5 - READ PREDICTED VARIATES
   51 IF(V(10).GT.50.) V(10) = 0.
      WRITE(MED6,951)
      WRITE(MED6,944)
      NPV = 0
      MX = MAXM
      CALL LGEN(U,NU,LU,NU,ST,IT,CN,NQ,IH,0,H,H,0,H,H,0,MAXD,0,IX,IY,MX,
     1NPV,MX,1,NALT)
      IF(V(11).LT.0.5.AND.V(20).LT.0.5)GO TO 41
      IF(NPV.LT.1) GO TO 54
C STORE AS NUMBERS IN VARIATE SET - ADD IF MISSING
      KM = 0
      DO 53 J = 1,NPV
      DO 52 L = 1,M
      IF(IX(J).NE.NDP(L).OR.IY(J).NE.NP(L)) GO TO 52
      ISAVE(J) = L
      GO TO 53
   52 CONTINUE
      V(19) = V(19) + 2.
      IF(V(19).GT.50.) WRITE(MED2,950)
      IF(V(19).GT.50.) V(19) = 2.
      WRITE(MED2,952) J
      IF(MAXM.EQ.M) WRITE(MED6,954)
      IF(MAXM.EQ.M) KM = KM + 1
      IF(MAXM.EQ.M) GO TO 53
      WRITE(MED2,953)
      M = M + 1
      NDP(M) = IX(J)
      NP(M) = IY(J)
      ISAVE(J) = M
      V(6) = 0.
      BRAN = ARAN
   53 CONTINUE
      NPV = NPV - KM
   54 IF(NPV.EQ.0.AND.V(10).LT.0.5) V(10) = 53.
C LEVEL 6 - READ PREDICTOR SET
   61 IF(V(10).GE.60.)V(10) = 0.
      WRITE(MED6,961)
      WRITE(MED6,944)
      K = 0
      MX = MAXM
      CALL LGEN(U,NU,LU,NU,ST,IT,CN,NQ,IH,0,H,H,0,H,H,0,MAXD,0,IX,IY,MX,
     1K,MX,1,NALT)
      IF(V(11).LT.0.5.AND.V(20).LT.0.5)GO TO 51
      ISP = NPV
      IF(K.EQ.0.OR.NPV.EQ.0) GO TO 91
```

```
      DO 65 J = 1,K
C TEST IF PREDICTOR = PREDICTED
      DO 62 N = 1,NPV
      L = ISAVE(N)
      IF(IX(J).NE.NDP(L).OR.IY(J).NE.NP(L)) GO TO 62
      V(19) = V(19) + 2.
      IF(V(19).GT.50.) WRITE(MED2,963)
      IF(V(19).GT.50.) V(19) = 2.
      WRITE(MED6,962)J,N
   62 CONTINUE
      DO 63 L = 1,M
      IF(IX(J).NE.NDP(L).OR.IY(J).NE.NP(L)) GO TO 63
      ISP = ISP + 1
      ISAVE(ISP) = L
      GO TO 65
   63 CONTINUE
C IF NOT IN SET - NOTE/ADD/UPDATE CONTROL VALUES
      V(19) = V(19) + 2.
      IF(V(19).GT.50.) WRITE(MED2,960)
      IF(V(19).GT.50.) V(19) = 2.
      WRITE(MED2,952) J
      IF(M.LT.MAXM) GO TO 64
      WRITE(MED6,954)
      IF(V(10).EQ.0.) V(10) = 63.
      GO TO 65
   64 M = M + 1
      WRITE(MED6,953)
      NDP(M) = IX(J)
      NP(M) = IY(J)
      ISP = ISP + 1
      ISAVE(ISP) = M
      V(6) = 0.
      BRAN = ARAN
   65 CONTINUE
      KBASE = K
      IF(K.EQ.0.AND.V(10).EQ.0.) V(10) = 62.
C LEVEL 9 - READ DATA HANDLING INSTRUCTION
   91 IF(V(10).GT.90.) V(10) = 0.
      CALL LDHI(V(1),1,V(2),2,VX,7,V(3),5,V(4),16,H,0,H,V(10),
     1 TT(21),FORM,MED1,MED2,0,Q,NQ,NWARN,1,IGO)
      IF(IGO.GT.0) GO TO 61
C STANDARDISATION
      IF(V(4).LE.0.) NWARN = NWARN + 1
      IF(V(4).EQ.0.) V(4) = 1.
      IF(V(4).LT.0.) V(4) = 0.
C MAXIMUM NUMBER OF MISSING VALUES
      IF(V(6).EQ.0.) V(9) = VX
      IF(VX.NE.V(9).AND.VX.NE.0.) V(6) = 0.
      IF(VX.NE.V(9).AND.VX.NE.0.) V(9) = VX
      MXM = K*K
      MDIAG = M*(M+1)/2
      IF(V(9).GT.0.5) MDIAG = MDIAG*6
      IF(MXM+MDIAG.LE.MAXAV) GO TO 92
      WRITE(MED6,992)MDIAG,MXM,MAXAV
      IF(V(10).LT.0.5) V(10) = 91.
   92 CALL LDHI(V(1),1,V(2),2,V(9),7,V(3),5,V(4),16,H,0,H,V(10),
     1 TT(21),FORM,MED1,MED2,0,Q,NQ,NWARN,2,IGO)
      IF(IGO.GT.0) GO TO 91
  101 WRITE(MED6,998)
      V(4) = V(4)*0.01
      V(10) = BRAN
      L = MDIAG + 1
      CALL CMULT(M,MXM,MDIAG,MAXD,XBAR,STD,D,RY,JX,B,SB,T,W,R(L),R,X,NQ,
```

```
     1NP,NDP,SCON,NCON,IX,IY,K,NPV,ISAVE,ST,U,NU,ISP,ITEST,IBEST,IREST)
      ARAN = V(10)
      V(10) = 0.
      WRITE(MED6,999)
      GO TO 91
  901 FORMAT (1H0,20X,42HSTATCAT GENERAL MULTIPLE LINEAR REGRESSION)
  941 FORMAT (1H1,10X,30HSET OF VARIATES FOR DATA SWEEP/)
  944 FORMAT(7H0NUMBER,6X,19HTRANS    DATA  CYCLES/5H CODE,8X,18H-FORM COL
     1UMN DELAY,66X,7HCOMMENT)
  950 FORMAT (42H1PREDICTED VARIATES NOT IN SET OF VARIATES)
  951 FORMAT (1H1,10X,18HPREDICTED VARIATES/)
  952 FORMAT (15H0VARIATE NUMBER,I4,30H IS NOT IN THE SET OF VARIATES)
  953 FORMAT (1H+,50X,33H- ADDED (NEW DATA SWEEP REQUIRED))
  954 FORMAT (1H+,50X,26H-NOT ADDED - NO MORE SPACE)
  960 FORMAT (42H1PREDICTOR VARIATES NOT IN SET OF VARIATES)
  961 FORMAT (1H1,10X,18HPREDICTOR VARIATES/)
  962 FORMAT (10H0PREDICTOR,I4,33H IS THE SAME AS PREDICTED VARIATE,I4)
  963 FORMAT (50H1 PREDICTOR VARIATES ALSO IN PREDICTED VARIATE SET)
  992 FORMAT (29H0 CORRELATION MATRIX REQUIRES,I6,6H CELLS/21H   REGRESSIO
     1N REQUIRES,I6,6H CELLS/6H0 ONLY,I6,27H AVAILABLE - INCREASE MAXAV)
  998 FORMAT (36H0INPUT ACCEPTED - ANALYSIS COMMENCES)
  999 FORMAT (36H1ANALYSIS COMPLETED - READ NEW INPUT)
      END


      SUBROUTINE CMULT(M,MXM,MDIAG,MN,XBAR,STD,D,RY,ISAVE,B,SB,T,W,RX,R,
     1X,NQ,NP,NDP,SCON,NCON,LW,MW,KBASE,NPV,JX,ST,U,NU,ISP,IT,IB,IS)
C CMULT   (SEE 7.2 ) EXECUTIVE    MULTIPLE REGRESSION
      DIMENSION XBAR(M),STD(M),RY(M),ISAVE(M),B(M),SB(M),T(M),W(M),LW(M)
      DIMENSION MW(M),NP(M),NDP(M),D(MN),RX(MXM),R(MDIAG),X(NQ),ST(NQ)
      DIMENSION SCON(5,NCON),U(NU),JX(ISP),IT(M),IB(M),IS(M),XT(8,5)
      DIMENSION RA(7,1)
      DATA XT/4H    ,4H    ,4H    ,4H    ,4H TO,4HTAL ,4HABIL,4HITY ,
     1         4H    ,4H    ,4H LO,4HSS O,4HF TO,4HTAL ,4HABIL,4HITY ,
     2         4H    ,4H    ,4H IND,4HIVID,4HUAL ,4HPROB,4HABIL,4HITY ,
     3         4H    ,4H    ,4H TO,4HTAL ,4HUNEX,4HPLAI,4HNED ,4HVARI,4HANCE,
     4         4HINCR,4HEASE,4H IN ,4HUNEX,4HPLAI,4HNED ,4HVARI,4HANCE/
      COMMON /STCT/MED1,MED2,MED3,MED4,MED5,MED6,MED13,Q,V(20),TT(30)
      KP = V(1)
      KMIN = V(3)
      VP = V(4)*100.
      DO 103 IBASE = 1,NPV
      KST = V(2)
      NDEP = JX(IBASE)
      K = KBASE
      NDEL = 0
      DO 102 J = 1,K
      L = NPV+J
      I = JX(L)
      IF(NDP(I).GT.0) NDEL = 1
  102 ISAVE(J) = I
      K1 = K + 1
      ISAVE(K+1) = NDEP
      PLAST = 1.0
      KR = 0
      BRAN = V(10)
      IF(V(6).GT.0.5) GO TO 104
      REWIND MED3
      READ(MED3) NQ,NALT,Q,(TT(J),J = 1,10),(Y,I=1,6)
      DO 29 J = 1,NQ
   29 READ(MED3)(Y,I=1,19),(Y,I=1,NALT),MX,Y,Y
      V(6) = 0.
      V(7) = 3.
```

```
      CALL CORRE(M,XBAR,STD,R,B,D,W,MDIAG,NP,NDP,X,NC,SCON,NCON,MN)
      IF(V(6).GT.0.5) GO TO 104
      WRITE(MED2,902) TT
      WRITE(MED2,923)
      GO TO 103
  104 N= V(6)
      IF(KP.EQ.3)CALL WBASE(ISAVE,NP,NDP,W,XBAR,STD,U,NU,ST,NQ,R,MDIAG,M
     1,NDEL,K1,1)
      IF(KP.GE.4)CALL WBASE(ISAVE,NP,NDP,W,XBAR,STD,U,NU,ST,NQ,R,MDIAG,M
     1,NDEL,K1,2)
      L = -M
      DO 101 I = 1,M
      L = L + M - I + 2
  101 D(I) = R(L)*STD(I)*STD(I)*(W(I)-1.)
  110 CONTINUE
      CALL MOP(R,3,M,M,MDIAG,RX,2,K,K,MXM,ISAVE,3,K,ISAVE,3,K,2,MED2)
      CALL MOP(R,3,M,M,MDIAG,RY,1,K,1,K,ISAVE,3,K,ISAVE(K1),3,1,2,MED2)
      IF(KP.LT.3.OR.K.LT.KBASE.AND.KR.EQ.0) GO TO 105
      WRITE(MED2,902) TT
      WRITE(MED2,937)
      CALL WMAT (RX,K,K,MXM,NP,NDP,M,ST,NQ,ISAVE,ISAVE,U,NU,MED2)
      WRITE(MED2,938)
      CALL WMAT (RY,1,K,K,NP,NDP,M,ST,NQ,ISAVE(K+1),ISAVE,U,NU,MED2)
  105 L = 0
C TEST FOR CONSTANT PREDICTORS AND PREDICTED PREDICTOR
      DO 115 J = 1,K
      L = ISAVE(J)
      IF(L.NE.NDEP.AND.STD(L).GT.0.) GO TO 115
      WRITE(MED2,902) TT
      JMIN = J
      II = NP(L)/1000
      JMAXA = NP(L)-II*1000
      IF(STD(L).LE.0.)WRITE(MED2,915)JMAXA,ST(JMAXA)
      IF(STD(L).GT.0..AND.L.EQ.NDEP) WRITE(MED2,925) JMAXA,ST(JMAXA)
      IF(II.GT.0)WRITE(MED2,919)U(II)
      IF(NDP(L).NE.0)WRITE(MED2,916) NDP(L)
      IF(K-1) 103,103,117
  115 CONTINUE
      IF(KST.GE.6) GO TO 200
      CALL MINV (RX,K,DET,LW,MW,MXM)
C TEST FOR SINGULAR MATRIX
      IF(DET) 112,111,112
  111 WRITE(MED2,902) TT
      WRITE(MED2,914)
      GO TO 103
  112 CALL MULTR(K,XBAR,STD,D,RX,RY,ISAVE,B,SB,T,M,MXM,V)
      PNOW = V(12)*V(12)
      IF(KST.EQ.1) PNOW = 0.0
      IF(KST.EQ.2) PNOW = PLAST
      IF(KST.EQ.1.AND.V(15).GT.0..AND.V(18).GT.0..AND.V(20).GE.0.)
     1PNOW = PRBF(V(15),V(18),V(20))
      IF(KST.EQ.2.AND.V(15).GT.0..AND.V(18).GT.0..AND.V(20).GE.0.)
     1PNOW = PRBF(V(15),V(18),V(20))
      IF(KST.EQ.1.AND.PNOW.GT.V(4).AND.PLAST.LT.1.) GO TO 119
      IF(KST.EQ.1.AND.PNOW.GT.V(4)) KST = 0
      IF(KST.EQ.2.AND.PLAST.GE.1.) PLAST = PNOW
      IF(KST.EQ.2.AND.PLAST-PNOW.GT.V(4)) GO TO 119
      IF(KST.EQ.4.AND.PNOW.LT.1.-V(4).AND.PLAST.LT.1.) GO TO 119
      IF(KST.EQ.4.AND.PNOW.LT.1.-V(4)) KST = 0
      IF(KST.EQ.5.AND.PLAST.GE.1.) PLAST = PNOW
      IF(KST.EQ.5.AND.PLAST-PNOW.GT.V(4)) GO TO 119
      IF(K.LE.1) KST = 0
      PLAST = PNOW
```

```
      WRITE(MED2,902) TT
      IF(KST.GT.0) WRITE(MED2,941) (XT(I,KST),I=1,8),VP
      CALL WMULT(ISAVE,NP,NDP,XBAR,STD,RY,B,SE,T,M,ST,NQ,U,NU,JMIN,
     1PMIN,K)
C STEP-DOWN / OUTPUT DECISION
      IF(KST.EQ.0.OR.KST.EQ.3.AND.PMIN.LT.V(4)) GO TO 119
C ELIMINATE LEAST SIGNIFICANT TERM - BUT STORE IT
  117 JLAST = JMIN
      ILAST = ISAVE(JMIN)
      LLAST = LW(JMIN)
      DO 118 J = 1,K
      IF(J.LT.JMIN) GO TO 118
      ISAVE(J) = ISAVE(J+1)
      LW(J) = LW(J+1)
  118 CONTINUE
      K = K - 1
      GO TO 110
C OUTPUT/NO OUTPUT DECISION
  119 CONTINUE
      IF(KP.LT.5) GO TO 103
      IF(KST.EQ.0.OR.KST.EQ.3) CALL RESID(RA,1,D,MN,ISAVE,K+1,NP,NDP,LW,
     1MW,SB,T,XBAR,STD,M,U,NU,ST,X,NQ,SCON,NCON,B,K,D,1,1,K+1,K,K+1,5)
      IF (KST.EQ.0.OR.KST.EQ.3) GO TO 103
C RESTORE LAST TERM DISCARDED
      DO 132 JJ = 1,K
      J = K + 1 - JJ
      ISAVE(J+1) = ISAVE(J)
      LW(J+1) = LW(J)
      IF(J.GT.JLAST) GO TO 132
      ISAVE(J) = ILAST
      LW(J) = LLAST
      GO TO 133
  132 CONTINUE
  133 K = K + 1
      KST = 0
      GO TO 110
C MULTIPLE COMBINATIONS OF VARIATES
  200 NREQ=1
      FBEST = 0.
      K3 = KMIN + 1
      K1 = K3
      NPOS = K - K3 + 1
      DO 205 K2 = K3,K
      IF(KST.EQ.6.AND.K2.GT.K3) GO TO 206
      IF(KST.EQ.7.AND.K2.GT.K3) K1 = K1+ 1
      IF(KST.EQ.8) NREQ = K2 - K3 + 1
      IF(KST.EQ.9) NREQ = K - K2 + 1
      IF(KST.EQ.7) NPOS = K - K1 + 1
      KPR = K1+NREQ
      IT(KPR) = NDEP
      IB(KPR) = NDEP
      KPR = KPR - 1
      FLAST = 0.
      NC = 0
      LI = 50
      IF(KP.EQ.0) LI=0
  201 CALL NEXC(ISAVE(K1),NPOS,NREQ,NC)
      IF(NC.EQ.0) GO TO 204
      DO 202 I = 1,KPR
  202 IT(I) = ISAVE(I)
      CALL MOP(R,3,M,M,MDIAG,RX,2,KPR,KPR,MXM,IT,3,KPR,IT,3,KPR,2,MED2)
      CALL MOP(R,3,M,M,MDIAG,RY,1,KPR,1,KPR,IT,3,KPR,IT(KPR+1),3,1,2,
     1MED2)
```

```
      CALL MINV(RX,KPR,DET,LW,MW,MXM)
      IF(KP.EQ.1) LI=LI+1
      IF(LI.GE.50)WRITE(MED2,902) TT
      IF(LI.GE.50)WRITE(MED2,903) NREQ
      IF(LI.GT.50) LI = 0
      IF(DET.EQ.0.) PNOW = 999.
      IF(DET.EQ.0.) WRITE(MED2,940) PNOW,(IT(I),I=1,KER)
      IF(DET.EQ.0.) WRITE(MED2,914)
      IF(DET.EQ.0.) GO TO 201
      CALL MULTR(KPR,XBAR,STD,D,RX,RY,IT,B,SB,T,M,MXM,V)
      IF(KP.EQ.1) WRITE(MED2,940)V(12),(IT(I),I= 1,KPR)
      IF(KP.GE.2) CALL WMULT(IT,NP,NDP,XBAR,STD,RY,B,SB,T,M,ST,NQ,U,NU,
     1JMIN,PMIN,KPR)
      IF(FLAST.GT.V(20))GO TO 201
      FLAST = V(20)
      DO 203 I = 1,KPR
  203 IB(I) = IT(I)
      IF(FBEST.GT.FLAST) GO TO 201
      FBEST = FLAST
      KBR = KPR
      DO 207 I = 1,KBR
  207 IS(I) = IT(I)
      IS(KBR+1) = IT(KBR+1)
      GO TO 201
  204 CALL MOP(R,3,M,M,MDIAG,RX,2,KPR,KPR,MXM,IB,3,KPR,IB,3,KPR,2,MED2)
      CALL MOP(R,3,M,M,MDIAG,RY,1,KPR,1,KPR,IB,3,KPR,IB(KPR+1),3,1,2,
     1MED2)
      CALL MINV(RX,KPR,DET,LW,MW,MXM)
      CALL MULTR(KPR,XBAR,STD,D,RX,RY,IB,B,SB,T,M,MXM,V)
      WRITE(MED2,902) TT
      WRITE(MED2,904) NREQ
      CALL WMULT(IB,NP,NDP,XBAR,STD,RY,B,SB,T,M,ST,NC,U,NU,JMIN,PMIN,
     1KPR)
  205 CONTINUE
  206 CALL MOP(R,3,M,M,MDIAG,RX,2,KBR,KBR,MXM,IS,3,KER,IS,3,KBR,2,MED2)
      CALL MOP(R,3,M,M,MDIAG,RY,1,KBR,1,KBR,IS,3,KBR,IS(KBR+1),3,1,2,
     1MED2)
      CALL MINV(RX,KBR,DET,LW,MW,MXM)
      CALL MULTR(KBR,XBAR,STD,D,RX,RY,IS,B,SB,T,M,MXM,V)
      WRITE(MED2,902) TT
      WRITE(MED2,905)
      CALL WMULT(IS,NP,NDP,XBAR,STD,RY,B,SB,T,M,ST,NC,U,NU,JMIN,PMIN,KBR
     1)
C RESIDUALS FOR BEST SET OF PREDICTORS
      IF(KP.GE.5) CALL RESID(RA,1,D,MN,IS,KBR+1,NP,NDP,LW,MW,SB,T,
     1 XBAR,STD,M,U,NU,ST,X,NQ,SCON,NCON,B,K,D,1,1,KBR+1,KBR,KBR+1,5)
  103 CONTINUE
      RETURN
  902 FORMAT(23H1STATCAT PROGRAM STMULT,7X,1H-,4X,26HMULTIPLE LINEAR REG
     1RESSION/16H DATA BANK TITLE,14X,1H-,4X,10A4/23H DATA BANK SUBSET T
     2ITLE,7X,1H-,4X,10A4/10H RUN TITLE,20X,1H-,4X,10A4/)
  903 FORMAT(1H0,20X,21HTESTING POSSIBLE LAST,I3,9H VARIATES)
  904 FORMAT(1H0,30X,9HBEST LAST,I3,9H VARIATES)
  905 FORMAT(1H0,20X,27HBEST SET OF VARIATES TESTED)
  913 FORMAT(53H1NUMBER OF SELECTIONS NOT SPECIFIED.   JOB TERMINATED.)
  914 FORMAT(52H0THE MATRIX IS SINGULAR.   THIS SELECTION IS SKIPPED.)
  915 FORMAT(1H0,8X,3HCOL,I4,1X,A4,24H IS CONSTANT - DISCARDED         )
  916 FORMAT (9H (DELAYED,I3,8H CYCLES))
  919 FORMAT(1H+,A4,4H OF )
  923 FORMAT(///19H0 NO DATA IN SAMPLE)
  925 FORMAT(1H0,8X,3HCOL,I4,1X,A4,32H PREDICTOR=PREDICTED - DISCARDED)
  937 FORMAT (1H0,5X,58HCORRELATIONS BETWEEN PREDICTORS SELECTED FOR THI
     1S ANALYSIS)
```

```
  938 FORMAT (1H0,5X,58HCORRELATIONS BETWEEN PREDICTORS AND PREDICTED VA
     1RIATE             )
  940 FORMAT(1H ,F6.4,34H MULTIPLE CORRELATION FOR VARIATES,20I4/
     1 (41X,20I4))
  941 FORMAT(1H0,20X,29HELIMINATING PREDICTORS WHILE ,8A4,9H IS BELOW,
     1 F7.2,9H PER CENT)
      END


      SUBROUTINE MULTR (K,XBAR,STD,D,RX,RY,ISAVE,B,SB,T,M,MXM,V)
C MULTR   (SEE  7.2 ) STATISTICAL CARRIES OUT SPECIFIC MULTIPLE REG
      DIMENSION XBAR(M),STD(M),D(M),RY(M),ISAVE(M),B(M),SB(M),T(M)
      DIMENSION RX(MXM),V(20)
      MM = K + 1
C BETA WEIGHTS
      DO 100 J = 1,K
  100 B(J) = 0.
      DO 110 J = 1,K
      L1 = K *(J-1)
      DO 110 I = 1,K
      L = L1 + I
  110 B(J) = B(J) + RY(I) * RX(L)
      RM = 0.
      BO = 0.
      L1 = ISAVE(MM)
C COEFFICIENT OF DETERMINATION
      DO 120 I = 1,K
      RM = RM + B(I)*RY(I)
C REGRESSION COEFFICIENTS
      L = ISAVE(I)
      B(I) = B(I) * (STD(L1)/STD(L))
C INTERCEPT
  120 BO = BO + B(I)*XBAR(L)
      V(11) = XBAR(L1) - BO
C SUM OF SQUARES ATTRIBUTABLE TO REGRESSION
      V(14) =    RM * D(L1)
C MULTIPLE CORRELATION COEFFICIENT
      V(12) = SQRT( ABS(RM))
C SUM OF SQUARES OF DEVIATIONS FROM REGRESSION
      V(17) = D(L1) - V(14)
C DEGREES OF FREEDOM ASSOCIATED WITH REGRESSION
      V(15) = K
C VARIANCE OF ESTIMATE
      V(18) = V(6) - V(15) - 1.
      V(13) = V(17)/V(18)
C S.D.S OF REGRESSION COEFFICIENTS
      DO 130 J = 1,K
      L1 = K*(J-1) + J
      L = ISAVE(J)
      SB(J) = SQRT(ABS((RX(L1)/D(L))*V(13)))
C COMPUTED T-VALUES
  130 T(J) = B(J)/SB(J)
C STANDARD ERROR OF ESTIMATE
      V(13) = SQRT( ABS(V(13)))
C MEAN SQUARE ATTRIBUTABLE TO REGRESSION
      V(16) = V(14)/V(15)
C MEAN SQUARE ATTRIBUTABLE TO DEVIATION FROM REGRESSION
      V(19) = V(17)/V(18)
C COMBINED F-RATIO
      V(20) = V(16)/V(19)
      RETURN
      END
```

```
      SUBROUTINE WMULT(ISAVE,NP,NDP,XBAR,STD,RY,B,SB,T,M,ST,NQ,U,NU,
     1JMIN,PMIN,K)
C WMULT    (SEE   7.2 ) SYSTEM      WRITE MULTIPLE REGRESSION OUTPUT
      DIMENSION XBAR(M),STD(M),RY(M),ISAVE(M),B(M),SB(M),T(M)
      DIMENSION NP(M),NDP(M),ST(NQ),U(NU)
      COMMON /STCT/MED1,MED2,MED3,MED4,MED5,MED6,MED13,Q,V(20),TT(30)
      WRITE(MED2,903)
      JMIN = 1
      KMIN = V(3)
      PMIN = 0.
      DO 113 J = 1,K
      L = ISAVE(J)
      P= 1.
      IF(V(18).GT.0.) P=PRBF(1.,V(18),T(J)*T(J))
      IF(P.GT.PMIN.AND.J.GT.KMIN) JMIN = J
      IF(P.GT.PMIN.AND.J.GT.KMIN) PMIN = P
      II = NP(L)/1000
      JMAXA = NP(L) - II*1000
      WRITE(MED2,904) JMAXA,ST(JMAXA),XBAR(L),STD(L),RY(J),B(J),SB(J),T(J
     1),P
      IF(II.GT.0) WRITE(MED2,919) U(II)
  113 IF(NDP(L).NE.0) WRITE(MED2,916) NDP(L)
      WRITE(MED2,905)
      L = ISAVE(K + 1)
      II = NP(L)/1000
      JMAXA = NP(L) - II*1000
      WRITE(MED2,904) JMAXA,ST(JMAXA),XBAR(L),STD(L)
      IF(II.GT.0) WRITE(MED2,919) U(II)
      IF(NDP(L).NE.0) WRITE(MED2,916) NDP(L)
C PRINT INTERCEPT,MULTIPLE CORRELATION,AND STANDARD ERROR OF
C ESTIMATE
      P = V(12)*V(12)*100.
      WRITE(MED2,906) V(11),V(12),P,V(13)
C ANALYSIS OF VARIANCE ANALOG
      WRITE(MED2,907)
      L = V(18)
      P = 999.99999
      IF(V(15).GT.0..AND.V(18).GT.0..AND.V(20).GE.0.) P = PRBF(V(15),V(1
     18),V(20))
      WRITE(MED2,908) K,V(14),V(16),V(20),P,L,V(17),V(19)
      L = K + L
      SUM = V(14) + V(17)
      WRITE(MED2,909) L,SUM
      IF(P.EQ.999.99999.OR.V(12).GT.1.0) WRITE(MED2,920)
      RETURN
  903 FORMAT(19H0PREDICTOR VARIATE  ,9X,4HMEAN,9X,8HSTANDARD,5X,38HCORREL
     2ATION    REGRESSION    STD. ERROR,5X,8HCOMPUTED,5X,10HASSOCIATED/
     21H ,40X,9HDEVIATION,5X,49HX VERSUS Y    COEFFICIENT   OF REGRESSION
     3  T VALUE,6X,11HPROBABILITY)
  904 FORMAT (1H ,8X,3HCOL,I4,1X,A4,7F14.5)
  905 FORMAT(19H PREDICTED VARIATE          )
  906 FORMAT(1H0/10H INTERCEPT,13X,F13.5//23H MULTIPLE CORRELATION   ,F13
     1.5,10X,15HACCOUNTING FOR ,F7.3,30H PER CENT OF OBSERVED VARIANCE
     2 //23H STD. ERROR OF ESTIMATE,F13.5//)
  907 FORMAT(1H0,21X,39HANALYSIS OF VARIANCE ANALOG  REGRESSION//5X,19HS
     1OURCE OF VARIATION,7X,7HDEGREES,7X,6HSUM OF,10X,4HMEAN,12X,7HF VAL
     2UE,3X,11HPROBABILITY/30X,10HOF FREEDOM,4X,7HSQUARES,9X,7HSQUARES)
  908 FORMAT(30H ATTRIBUTABLE TO REGRESSION    ,I6,4F16.5/30H DEVIATION F
     1ROM REGRESSION    ,I6,2F16.5)
  909 FORMAT(1H ,5X,5HTOTAL,19X,I6,F16.5)
  916 FORMAT (9H (DELAYED,I3,8H CYCLES))
  919 FORMAT(1H+,A4,4H OF )
  920 FORMAT(40H0ROUNDING ERRORS IN NEAR-SINGULAR MATRIX,67X,13H** WARNI
```

1NG **)
 END

7.3 PROGRAM STFACT - FACTOR ANALYSIS

7.3.1 Purpose

This program is a general factor analysis program. It includes facilities for transforming or delaying data, and for selecting a subset of the STATCAT data bank. The analysis may be a straightforward principal-components analysis, or a Guttman Image analysis, and a Varimax rotation of the factors retained may be performed. The number of factors to be retained may be pre-set, or a 'cut-off' level may be set. Factor scores, with the original variate values and the entire entry may be reproduced if necessary.

Figure 7.31a contains system flow-charts for the main program STFACT and the executive subroutine CFACT. Figure 7.31b contains system flow-charts for the subroutines VARMX (which carries out Varimax rotation) and RESID (which evaluates residuals or, in this program, factor scores).

7.3.2 Input Data

Item	Level	Format	Function	See
1	0	A	File control (Input only)	3.2
2	1	E	Subset specification	3.6
3	2	F	Variate Set (Transforms/delays)	3.7
4	3	F	Selected variates from set	3.7
5	4	G	Data handling instruction	Below + 3.8

Data Handling Instruction

Card Layout - Data Handling Instruction - STFACT

A BCCC DDD EEEEEEEE EFFF FFFFFFFFFF FFFFFFF FFFFFFGGGGGGGGG...etc

Columns	Item	Type	Function	
1	A	I	Output control index	Below
2	B	I	Analysis control index	Below
3 - 5	C	I	Acceptable number of non-values	Below
6 - 8	D	I	Maximum number of factors	Below
9 - 16	E	F	Cut-off value	Below
17 - 40	F	A	Comment (NOT KEPT)	-
41 - 80	H	A	Analysis run title (KEPT)	-

A - Output Control Index

This index controls the quantity of information output.

ALTERNATIVES

A = 0,blank: Eigenvalues, Factor scores and factor weights only.

A = 1   : In addition;correlation matrix for the selected
              variates with their arithmetic means and
              standard deviations.

A = 2   : In addition;correlation matrix for set of variates,
              with their means and standard deviations, and, if
              non-values are accepted, the means and standard deviations
              used in calculating individual correlation coefficients.

A = 3 - 4 : In addition, factor scores for each entry.

A = 5   : In addition; selected variate values for each entry.

A = 6   : In addition; set of variate values.

A = 7   : In addition; the complete entry.

A = 8 - 9 : As for A=1

DEFAULT value = 0 (0, blank or non-numeric characters)

B - <u>Analysis Control Index</u>

This index controls the strategy of the program. It defines which type of factor analysis is carried out, and whether Varimax rotation is to be used.

ALTERNATIVES

B = 0, blank: Principal components analysis only.

B = 1   : Principal Components Analysis, with Varimax Rotation of the factors retained.

B = 2   : Guttman Image analysis only.

B = 3   : Guttman Image analysis, with Varimax Rotation of the factors retained.

B = 4 - 9 : As for B = 0

DEFAULT value = 0 (0, blank or non-numeric character)

C - <u>Acceptable Number of Non-values</u>

This is the maximum number of non-values which will be accepted in a set of transformed delayed variates derived from an entry. (Non-values may occur because the original datum is not present, because the transform specified has no value for the given datum, or because insufficient entries have been read for values of delayed variates to be available. If this value is exceeded, then the entry concerned will not be included in the analysis, but will count towards the required delays.

DEFAULT value = 0 (0, blank or non-numeric characters)

SPECIAL CASE : if C is left blank or set to zero for a run which is not the first with a given set of variates, and which requires no new variates, the previously specified value will be retained. If a non-zero value different from that for the previous data sweep is read in, a new data sweep will be carried out.

D - <u>Maximum number of factors retained</u>

This is the maximum number of factors that will be extracted from the correlation matrix, provided that each factor has an eigenvalue exceeding E (defined below).

DEFAULT VALUE - (0, blank or non-numeric characters) will be set to the number of variates selected.

SPECIAL CASE - If there is insufficient storage space, D will be set to the maximum that can be stored.

E - Cut-off Value

Only factors having an eigen-value greater than this value will be retained.

DEFAULT VALUE = 1.0   (0, blank or non-numeric characters)

SPECIAL CASE - If D is specified then the default value of E will be set to 0.0 (the cut-off will not be used).

7.3.3   Input Example

Figure 7.32 is a summary of the input structure for three runs of STFACT, using first the default values, then a more detailed output (although not the most detailed output possible). The entire STATCAT data bank is included, and all the data columns are specified as variates. Eight variates are selected for the analysis. The first data handling instruction employs default values throughout, producing only a principal components analysis. The second data handling instruction calls for a Guttman Image analysis followed by Varimax rotation. The final data handling instruction causes the extraction of the single principal component and the calculation of factor scores for each entry.

Figure 7.33 is a listing of the input cards required to carry out these three runs.

7.3.4   Output Example

Figure 7.34 is a general summary of the output produced by this program, indented according to the program structure. Figure 7.35 is a page-by-page summary of the output corresponding to the specific example of Figure 7.33. The input checking information is essentially standard, and is not given here. Figure 7.36 gives the complete default output - principal components analysis, eigenvalues, factor loadings and factor score weights. (7.3.5)

Figure 7.37 gives the output for the second run of the program, providing the same parameters for the Guttman Image analysis (7.3.6) plus the result of Varimax rotation of the resultant factors (7.3.7). Figure 7.38 gives part of the output of factor scores obtained by the third data handling instruction.

7.3.5   Principal Components Analysis

Principal Components analysis is the most commonly employed method of 'factor analysis', and is generally what is intended when the term is used without further qualification. Factor analysis is used where a set of measurements have been made on a number of subjects or situations, and the experimenter wishes to get an idea of what the various measurements have in common. In, say, personality testing the experimenter may believe that the human personality can be described economically by values on a number of scales (for example Introversion or Neuroticism) and that the responses made on a questionnaire will be determined by the subject's position on these scales. If the experimenter could make exactly two measurements, one of Introversion, and one of Neuroticism, he would do so and have no further problem. In practice he cannot do so, but has to content himself with asking a number of questions, and deducing from them what are the values on the underlying scales. Exactly how the questions are chosen is a moot point, but not one which concerns us here. A form of weighted mean is required, and the problem is to determine the optimum weights.

Principal Components analysis begins by determining the matrix of correlation coefficients between all the variables employed. Mathematical techniques are then used to deduce the single linear combination of the variates which is most closely correlated with all the variates. The effect of this single linear combination is then removed by further mathematical processes, and the process repeated to obtain the next most important combination of variates, and so on. This process can be carried on until as many components have been extracted as there were variates initially. (Except if some of the variates originally used were linear combinations of others, or if there were fewer subjects than there were variates - in which case a suitable error message will be produced.)

The components obtained by Principal Components Analysis will be an economic description of the variates, but do not necessarily correspond to a well-defined phenomenon in the real world.

A measure of the relative importance of each component is given by the eigenvalues for the successive factors. In Figure 7.36 it appears that the first factor accounts for 46 per cent of the observed variation, the second for 19 per cent and the third for 15 per cent. In principle a further five factors could be obtained, which would between them account for all the variation present. Some of these factors must represent pure noise. There seems to be no agreed procedure for determining which factors should be kept.

Three methods have been provided for this program. These are (as explained in 7.3.2) a limit to the total number of factors, a proportion of the total variation to be explained and a minimum size of eigenvalue. Kaiser(1960) recommended the use of a cut-off at 1.0.

Having decided how many factors to retain, the user will wish to know how the factors relate to the original variates. The table of factor loadings provides this information. The factor loading of an original variate for a factor can be looked at as a correlation between them.

The user may often be interested in the scores allocated to the original entries in terms of the new factors. The factor score weights which are derived from the factor loadings will produce these scores. Figure 7.38 shows part of a listing of factor scores for the demonstration STATCAT data bank. It will be found that the factor scores have zero arithmetic mean and unit standard deviation, and that the first and second factors are uncorrelated. (Strictly this applies to the population of entries from which the factor scores were derived. If some entries are left out and others included, there will be some deviation from the ideal picture.)

7.3.6 Guttman Image Analysis

One of the fundamental problems of factor analysis is that the correlation coefficients on which the analysis is based may contain, in addition to random error, some systematic variation not related to the underlying factor structure - specific to the correlation itself.

An accepted method for dealing with this phenomenon is that developed by Guttman and others in which only variation shared with other variates is retained. The total shared variation for a specific variate is placed in the diagonal cells, in place of the value 1.0 which normally appears on the diagonal of a correlation matrix.

This value is the square of the multiple correlation obtained by predicting the variate using all other variates as predictors. A similar adjustment is made to off-diagonal elements of the correlation matrix. The resultant matrix is conventionally called the 'G' matrix, and can be analysed as if it were a normal correlation matrix. Fewer factors will be derived, if the same cut-off is used, and each will have a smaller eigenvalue. Kaiser(1963) suggests using half as many factors as there were original variates, but as was the case in principal components analysis there is no generally accepted test for which factors to discard.

Image analysis is particularly useful when the user wishes to reduce a large number of variates into a few factors representing the things they have in common. If some aspect of the data is represented by only one variate, this aspect will be lost in image analysis.

7.3.7 Varimax Rotation

The method used for the extraction of factors in factor analysis (Principal Components or Guttman Image analysis) is designed to extract the largest possible single factor first, followed by the next largest and so on. Although this method is often useful it sometimes produces factors which have no clear relation to anything in the outside world. If several factors have been extracted from a correlation matrix, it may be valuable to re-arrange the weighting of the factors in such a way that, as far as possible, each factor corresponds to some of the original variates, while the rest are nearly independent of it. If the user keeps all the factors, he will find that a Varimax rotation brings him back to the original set of variates, one per factor. It is usual to keep only the factors found worth retaining by the first factor analysis. Figure 7.37 shows the rotation of the two factors obtained by Guttman Image analysis of the selected variates. The relative positions of the points produced by plotting the original factor loadings as horizontal and vertical coordinates are unchanged when they are plotted in terms of the Varimax rotated axes.

Other forms of rotation are possible, and may be appropriate in special circumstances. Varimax rotation is, however, the best known and most generally accepted.

7.3.8 Restrictions and reservations

The techniques of factor analysis described and programmed in this chapter are essentially descriptive techniques. They perform mathematical manipulations of a correlation matrix, and describe only the matrix on which they are based. It will be found that factor weightings derived from one set of entries is usually not the most economical when applied to a different set of entries. Factors derived from one set of entries will usually account for less of the variation in another set of entries. (This phenomenon is sufficiently common to be known as 'shrinkage' among experimental psychologists.)

In addition, the technique, being based as it is on the product-moment correlation coefficient, suffers from the limitations of that measure. These limitations have been discussed in some detail in 6.3.5 and in 7.2.8.

A further problem in the use of factor analysis is the choice of variates to be included. If the user happens to include a number of variates which measure more or less the same characteristics of whatever he is measuring, then this characteristic will be heavily weighted in the final factors. If only one or two measurements involve an underlying characteristic, then this characteristic will not appear as an important factor. (In the extreme, of course, if no measurement is relevant to a characteristic, it will not appear at all - but it is hard to see how this can be avoided.) It is often the case that the phenomena subject to scientific study show differing patterns of correlation under different circumstances - because the underlying systems are subject to different constraints. The correlation coefficient is particularly useful when the changes of variates are relatively small, so that the resultant perturbations are nearly linear. Approaching the limits of operation of a system, the correlations of measurements may be very different.

REFERENCES : Veldman (Ch 9), Kendall (1975 - Chs 2 and 4)
               Morrison (Chs 7 and 8)
               Kelley (1960) for cut-off criteria

397

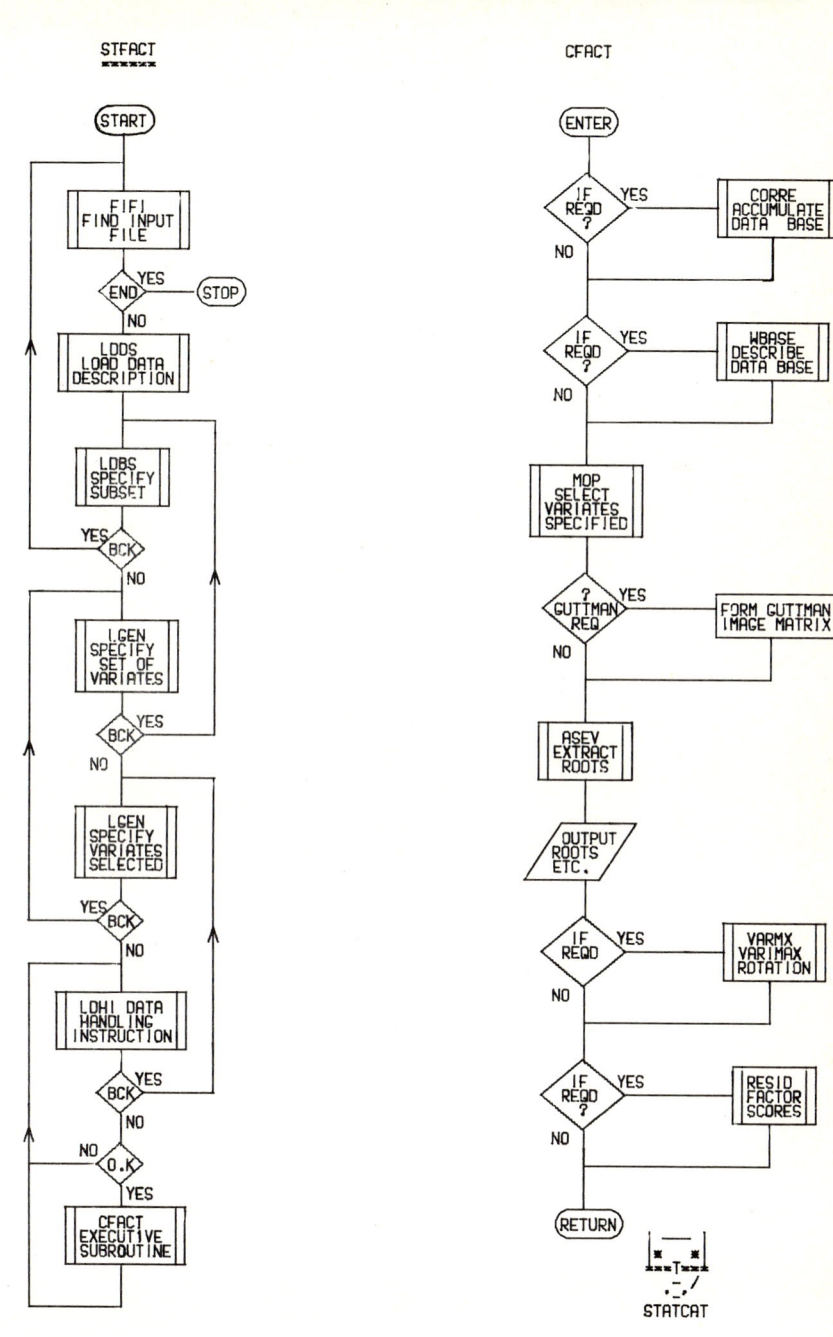

Figure 7.31a - System Flow-Charts - STFACT and CFACT

Figure 7.31b - System Flow-Charts - VARMX and RESID

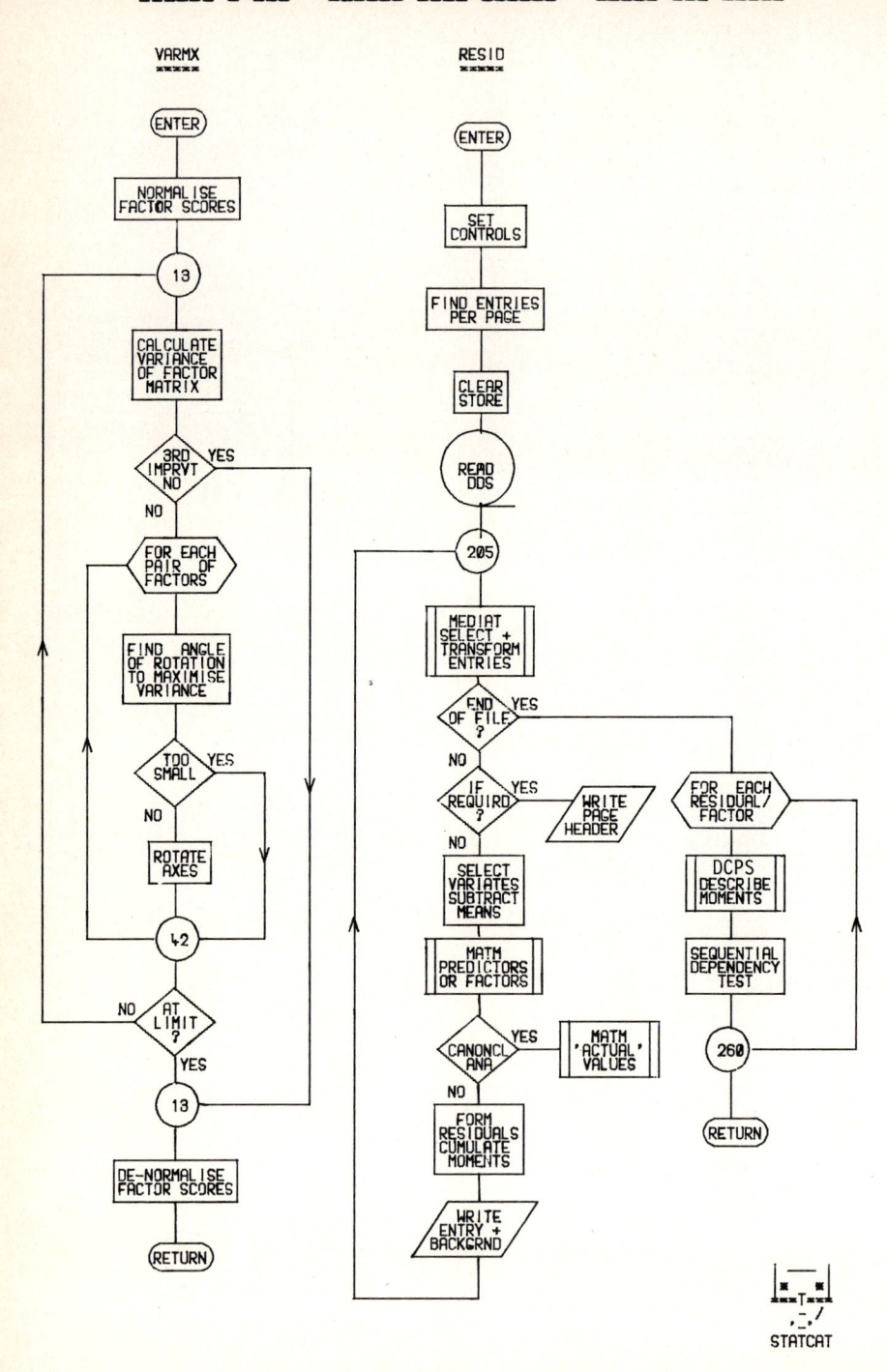

Figure 7.32 - STFACT - Input Structure

```
          Level
 0    1    2    3    4    5    6    7    8    9
FILE CONTROL CARD
     SUBSET SPECIFICATION
          VARIATE SPECIFICATION
               SELECTED VARIATES
                    DATA HANDLING INSTRUCTION
                    DATA HANDLING INSTRUCTION
                    DATA HANDLING INSTRUCTION
                    STOP
```

Figure 7.33 - STFACT - Input Example

```
---------1---------2---------3---------4---------5---------6---------7--
**STFACTDEMO                            DEMONSTRATION STATCAT DATA BANK
ALL DATA                                WHOLE DATA BANK TO BE INCLUDED
END OF SUBSET DEFINITION
VAL.NTRY
VAL.SESS
VAL.OBSR
VAL.DAY.
VAL.TIME
VAL.TEMP
VAL.TPCT
VAL.TCOM
VAL.TALL
VAL.ERRP
END OF SET OF VARIATES
VAL.OPER
VAL.W.P.
VAL.STRS
VAL.TASK
VAL.DIFF
VAL.EFOP
VAL.H.R.
VAL.EFOB
END OF VARIATES SELECTED                FOR FACTOR ANALYSIS
GO                                      DEFAULT OPTION
13                                      GUTTMAN IMAGE ANALYSIS/VARIMAX R
60       1                              PRINCIPAL COMPONENT ONLY
STOP
---------1---------2---------3---------4---------5---------6---------7--
```

Figure 7.34 - STFACT - Output Structure

```
For each     ) : File Control Record
output file  )   File Parameters
                 Data Description
                 For each) :  Subset Input Record
                 Subset  )    For each set) : Input Record
                              of Variates )   For each set ) : Input
                                          )   of Selected  )   Record
                                              Variates     )

For each     ) <No.,a.m. and s.d. for variates used>
Data         ) <No.,a.m. and s.d. for all variates in store>
Handling     ) <Correlation Matrix - all variates>
Instruction) ) <No.,a.m. and s.d. for each cell - if non-values present>
               <Correlation Matrix - Selected Variates>
               Eigenvalues
               Factor Loadings
               Factor Score Weights
               <Factor Evaluation>
               .        For Each Entry : -
               .           <Factor Score>
               .           <Predictor Values>
               .           <Variate Values>
               .           <Data Items>
```

Carated(<>) items are optional.

Figure 7.35 - STFACT - Page-by-page output summary

Page	Contents	Origin
1-2	File Control/Program title	FIFI/LDAP/STFACT
	Data Description record	LDDS
3	Subset record	LDBS/LSAMP
4-5	Set of Variates record	LGEN
6	Selected Variate record	LGEN
	Data Handling Instruction	LDHI
7	Principal Components Analysis	CFACT
8	Data Handling Instruction	LDHI
9	No.,a.m. and s.d. (this analysis)	WBASE
10	Correlation matrix/Guttman Image matrix	CFACT
11	Guttman Image analysis	CFACT
12	Varimax Rotation report	CFACT
13	Data Handling Instruction	LDHI
14-17	Descriptive output	WBASE
18	Principal Components Analysis	CFACT
19-25	Factor Scores	RESID
26	Data Handling Instruction (STOP)	LDHI

Figure 7.36 - STFACT - Output Example - Default Output

```
STATCAT PROGRAM STFACT        -    FACTOR ANALYSIS
DATA BANK TITLE               -    DEMONSTRATION STATCAT DATA BANK
DATA BANK SUBSET TITLE        -    ALL DATA
RUN TITLE                     -    DEFAULT OPTION

              PRINCIPAL COMPONENTS ANALYSIS                      EIGENVALUES

         NUMBER         VALUE       PERCENT OF TRACE
            1          3.71018         46.37723
            2          1.54451         19.30637
            3          1.17683         14.71033
         TOTAL         6.43152         80.39397

         TOTAL TRACE =                  8.00000

              PRINCIPAL COMPONENTS ANALYSIS                      FACTOR LOADINGS

FACTOR NUMBER                 1             2             3
TRANSFORM COLUMN
VAL. OF  4(OPER)           0.8398       -0.2485       -0.3835
VAL. OF  5(W.P.)           0.1968        0.6555       -0.5447
VAL. OF  6(STRS)           0.2854       -0.4947        0.5645
VAL. OF  9(TASK)           0.3779        0.4557        0.7454
VAL. OF 10(DIFF)           0.9814       -0.0575       -0.0675
VAL. OF 13(EFOP)           0.9869       -0.0483       -0.1422
VAL. OF 15(H.R.)           0.7954        0.5178        0.1636
VAL. OF 14(EFOB)          -0.4596        0.5910       -0.0085

              PRINCIPAL COMPONENTS ANALYSIS                      FACTOR SCORE WEIGHTS

FACTOR NUMBER                 1             2             3
TRANSFORM COLUMN
VAL. OF  4(OPER)           0.2263       -0.1609       -0.3089
VAL. OF  5(W.P.)           0.0530        0.4231       -0.2529
VAL. OF  6(STRS)           0.0769       -0.3203        0.4797
VAL. OF  9(TASK)           0.1019        0.2821        0.6334
VAL. OF 10(DIFF)           0.2645       -0.0244       -0.0574
VAL. OF 13(EFOP)           0.2606       -0.0313       -0.1208
VAL. OF 15(H.R.)           0.2144        0.3353        0.1390
VAL. OF 14(EFOB)          -0.1239        0.3826       -0.0072
```

Figure 7.37 - STFACT - Output Example - Guttman Image

```
STATCAT PROGRAM STFACT      -   FACTOR ANALYSIS
DATA BANK TITLE             -   DEMONSTRATION STATCAT DATA BANK
DATA BANK SUBSET TITLE      -   ALL DATA
RUN TITLE                   -   GUTTMAN IMAGE ANALYSIS/VARIMAX ROTATION


          GUTTMAN IMAGE ANALYSIS                      EIGENVALUES

       NUMBER       VALUE      PERCENT OF TRACE
          1        3.58623        62.67920
          2        1.06625        18.63559
        TOTAL      4.65248        81.51479

          TOTAL TRACE =           5.72157

          GUTTMAN IMAGE ANALYSIS                      FACTOR LOADINGS

FACTOR NUMBER                1          2
TRANSFORM COLUMN
VAL. OF  4(OPER)          0.8449    -0.3302
VAL. OF  5(W.P.)          0.1739     0.4698
VAL. OF  6(STRS)          0.2672    -0.2499
VAL. OF  9(TASK)          0.3219     0.5767
VAL. OF 10(DIFF)          0.9851    -0.0445
VAL. OF 13(EFOP)          0.9906    -0.1132
VAL. OF 15(H.R.)          0.7739     0.4447
VAL. OF 14(EFOB)         -0.3621     0.3186

          GUTTMAN IMAGE ANALYSIS                      FACTOR SCORE WEIGHTS

FACTOR NUMBER                1          2
TRANSFORM COLUMN
VAL. OF  4(OPER)          0.2337    -0.2360
VAL. OF  5(W.P.)          0.0510     0.2309
VAL. OF  6(STRS)          0.0648    -0.0486
VAL. OF  9(TASK)          0.0904     0.3333
VAL. OF 10(DIFF)          0.2741    -0.0725
VAL. OF 13(EFOP)          0.2711    -0.0365
VAL. OF 15(H.R.)          0.2093     0.4498
VAL. OF 14(EFOB)         -0.1030     0.2122




STATCAT PROGRAM STFACT      -   FACTOR ANALYSIS
DATA BANK TITLE             -   DEMONSTRATION STATCAT DATA BANK
DATA BANK SUBSET TITLE      -   ALL DATA
RUN TITLE                   -   GUTTMAN IMAGE ANALYSIS/VARIMAX ROTATION


          GUTTMAN IMAGE ANALYSIS                      VARIMAX ROTATION ANALYSIS

COMMUNALITY CHECK - AFTER   3 ROTATIONS

TRANSFORM COLUMN           BEFORE ROTATION    AFTER ROTATION    DIFFERENCE
VAL. OF  4(OPER)              0.82652655        0.82652555      0.00000107
VAL. OF  5(W.P.)              0.25268552        0.25268624      0.00000030
VAL. OF  6(STRS)              0.13388747        0.13389723      0.00000024
VAL. OF  9(TASK)              0.45967066        0.45967001      0.00000066
VAL. OF 10(DIFF)              0.97247920        0.97247809      0.00000119
VAL. OF 13(EFOP)              0.97447234        0.97447115      0.00000119
VAL. OF 15(H.R.)              0.79971210        0.79974107      0.00000107
VAL. OF 14(EFOB)              0.23261529        0.23261499      0.00000030

          GUTTMAN IMAGE ANALYSIS         VARIMAX ROTATION   FACTOR LOADINGS

FACTOR NUMBER                1          2
TRANSFORM COLUMN
VAL. OF  4(OPER)          0.9022     0.1136
VAL. OF  5(W.P.)         -0.0702     0.4978
VAL. OF  6(STRS)          0.3547    -0.0898
VAL. OF  9(TASK)         -0.0052     0.6780
VAL. OF 10(DIFF)          0.8842     0.4307
VAL. OF 13(EFOP)          0.9134     0.3744
VAL. OF 15(H.R.)          0.4647     0.7041
VAL. OF 14(EFOB)         -0.4709     0.1042

          GUTTMAN IMAGE ANALYSIS         VARIMAX ROTATION   FACTOR SCORE WEIGHTS

FACTOR NUMBER                1          2
TRANSFORM COLUMN
VAL. OF  4(OPER)          0.3423    -0.1370
VAL. OF  5(W.P.)         -0.0666     0.2268
VAL. OF  6(STRS)          0.0802    -0.0113
VAL. OF  9(TASK)         -0.0818     0.3355
VAL. OF 10(DIFF)          0.2751     0.0569
VAL. OF 13(EFOP)          0.2763     0.0004
VAL. OF 15(H.R.)         -0.0340     0.4950
VAL. OF 14(EFOB)         -0.1901     0.1375
```

Figure 7.38 - STFACT - Output Example - Factor Scores

PRINCIPAL COMPONENTS ANALYSIS

DATA BANK TITLE   -   DEMONSTRATION STATCAT DATA BANK
DATA BANK SUBSET TITLE   -   ALL DATA
RUN TITLE   -   PRINCIPAL COMPONENT ONLY

INDIVIDUAL ENTRIES

```
              FACTOR NUMBER    1
------------------------------------------------------------------------------------
ENTRY   61                    13.11
------------------------------------------------------------------------------------
ENTRY   62                   -16.33
------------------------------------------------------------------------------------
ENTRY   63                     6.84
------------------------------------------------------------------------------------
ENTRY   64                     1.13
```

PRINCIPAL COMPONENTS ANALYSIS

DATA BANK TITLE   -   DEMONSTRATION STATCAT DATA BANK
DATA BANK SUBSET TITLE   -   ALL DATA
RUN TITLE   -   PRINCIPAL COMPONENT ONLY

EXAMINATION OF FACTOR SCORES - FACTOR NUMBER   1

NUMBER OF READINGS=   64.

ARITHMETIC MEAN =   0.000057   S.E. OF MEAN =   1.284625

STANDARD DEVIATION=   10.277004   S.E. OF S.D. =   0.643963

    SKEWNESS =   0.245485 SKEWNESS RATIO =   0.801750 PROBABILITY=   0.571414

    KURTOSIS =   -0.497428 KURTOSIS RATIO =   -1.624593 PROBABILITY=   0.100439

S.E. FOR SKEWNESS =   0.306186

ROOT-MEAN-SQUARE SUCCESSIVE DEVIATION = 17.10134888

NORMALISED VALUE = 3.12498093

ASSOCIATED PROBABILITY = 0.00301186

```
C     MASTER STFACT - GENERALISED FACTOR ANALYSIS - TRANSFORMS AND POWERS
C          SUBROUTINES AND FUNCTIONS REQUIRED
C     NAME            TYPE           COMMENT
C     AN       (SEE  3.1 ) SERVICE     ALPHA - TO NUMERIC VALUE
C     ASEV     (SEE 11.3 ) SERVICE     EIGEN ROOTS ETC ASYMMETRIC MATRIX
C     CFACT    (SEE  7.3 ) EXECUTIVE   FACTOR ANALYSIS
C     CHIKEN   (SEE 11.9 ) SERVICE     WARNS OF MISMATCHED DATA LEVEL
C     CLSAM    (SEE  3.5 ) SERVICE     ALLOTS ENTRY TO SAMPLE/SUBSET
C     COMPA    (SEE  3.1 ) SERVICE     COMPARES ALPHAMERIC VALUES
C     COPYA    (SEE  3.1 ) SERVICE     COPIES ALPHAMERIC VALUE
C     CORRE    (SEE  7.5 ) SYSTEM      MULTIPLE CORRELATION DATA
C     DCPS     (SEE  5.2 ) STATISTICAL MOMENT(PARAMETRIC) STATISTICS
C     FIFI     (SEE  3.2 ) SYSTEM      ALLOCATES PERIPHERALS
C     GAUS     (SEE 11.8 ) STATISTICAL FINDS ASS. PROB. OF N VALUE
C     IBL      (SEE  3.1 ) SERVICE     DETECTS BLANK,END AND STOP CARDS
C     ICH      (SEE  3.1 ) SERVICE     IDENTIFIES ALPHAMERIC CODES
C     LDAP     (SEE  3.3 ) SYSTEM      LOADS/CHECKS DATA BANK PARAMETERS
C     LDBS     (SEE  3.6 ) SYSTEM      LOADS SUBSET DEFINITION
C     LDDS     (SEE  3.4 ) SYSTEM      LOADS DATA DESCRIPTION SEGMENT
C     LGEN     (SEE  3.7 ) SYSTEM      LOADS GENERALISED VARIATES
C     LDHI     (SEE  3.8 ) SYSTEM      LOADS/CHECKS DATA HANDLING INSTN
C     LSET     (SEE  3.5 ) SYSTEM      LOADS DEFINING CONDITIONS
C     MATM     (SEE 11.3 ) SERVICE     MULTIPLIES MATRICES
C     MEDIAT   (SEE  3.7 ) SERVICE     SELECTS NEXT VARIATE SET
C     MINV     (SEE 11.3 ) SERVICE     INVERTS MATRIX
C     MOP      (SEE 11.3 ) SERVICE     SELECTS/CONVERTS STORED MATRIX
C     PRBF     (SEE 11.8 ) STATISTICAL FINDS PROBABILITY OF F-RATIO
C     RESID    (SEE  7.5 ) SERVICE     EVALUATES RESIDUALS/FACTOR SCORES
C     TRANS    (SEE  3.7 ) SERVICE     CARRIES OUT REQUIRED TRANSFORM
C     WBASE    (SEE  7.5 ) SERVICE     WRITES CORRELATION MATRIX ETC.
C     WMAT     (SEE 11.3 ) SERVICE     WRITE MATRIX WITH VARIATE TITLES
C     VARMX    (SEE  7.3 ) SYSTEM      VARIMAX ROTATION
C     SETTING OF ARRAY DIMENSIONS
C     THE FOLLOWING DIMENSIONS MUST BE AT LEAST AS BIG AS THOSE
C     SPECIFIED BY THE DATA TAPE,SAMPLE SPECIFICATIONS, ETC.
C     NQMAX = MAXIMUM NUMBER OF DATA COLUMNS
C     DIMENSION X(NQMAX),ST(NQMAX) ,IT(NQMAX),CN(NQMAX)
      NQMAX = 100
      DIMENSION X(100),ST(100),IT(100),CN(100)
      DATA  CN/4HCOL1,4HCOL2,4HCOL3,4HCOL4,4HCOL5,4HCOL6,4HCOL7,4HCOL8,4
     1HCOL9,4HCL10,4HCL11,4HCL12,4HCL13,4HCL14,4HCL15,4HCL16,4HCL17,4HCL
     218,4HCL19,4HCL20,4HCL21,4HCL22,4HCL23,4HCL24,4HCL25,4HCL26,4HCL27,
     34HCL28,4HCL29,4HCL30,4HCL31,4HCL32,4HCL33,4HCL34,4HCL35,4HCL36,4HC
     4L37,4HCL38,4HCL39,4HCL40,4HCL41,4HCL42,4HCL43,4HCL44,4HCL45,4HCL46
     5,4HCL47,4HCL48,4HCL49,4HCL50,4HCL51,4HCL52,4HCL53,4HCL54,4HCL55,4H
     6CL56,4HCL57,4HCL58,4HCL59,4HCL60,4HCL61,4HCL62,4HCL63,4HCL64,4HCL6
     75,4HCL66,4HCL67,4HCL68,4HCL69,4HCL70,4HCL71,4HCL72,4HCL73,4HCL74,4
     8HCL75,4HCL76,4HCL77,4HCL78,4HCL79,4HCL80,4HCL81,4HCL82,4HCL83,4HCL
     984,4HCL85,4HCL86,4HCL87,4HCL88,4HCL89,4HCL90,4HCL91,4HCL92,4HCL93,
     94HCL94,4HCL95,4HCL96,4HCL97,4HCL98,4HCL99,4HC100/
C     MI = MAXIMUM NUMBER OF DIFFERENT VARIATES
C     DIMENSION ISAVE(MI),NP(MI),NDP(MI),LW(MI),MW(MI),IX(MI),IY(MI)
      MI = 50
      DIMENSION ISAVE(50),NP(50),NDP(50),LW(50),MW(50),IX(50),IY(50)
C     MAXAV = GENERAL STORE FOR CORRELATION AND ANALYSIS MATRICES
C     MAXAV MUST BE AT LEAST MDIAG + 7*M + 2*K*K + K*F
C     WHERE MDIAG = M*(M+1)/2 IF NO MISSING VALUES
C                 = M*(M+1) *3 IF MISSING VALUES ALLOWED
C           M = NUMBER OF DIFFERENT VARIATES IN STORE
C           K = NUMBER OF VARIATES SELECTED FOR THIS ANALYSIS
C           F = NUMBER OF FACTORS TO BE EXTRACTED
C     DIMENSION R(MAXAV)
      MAXAV = 3775
```

```
      DIMENSION R(3775)
C MAXD = STORAGE AVAILABLE FOR DELAYED         ENTRIES
C      (MAXIMUM DELAY + 3.) * M MUST NOT EXCEED MAXD
C DIMENSION D(MAXD) IF MAXD NOT ZERO
C DIMENSION D(MAXD)
      MAXD = 500
      DIMENSION D(500)
C IF ALL 50 VARIATES ARE USED MAXIMUM DELAY = 8
C IF ONLY 2 ARE USED MAXIMUM DELAY = 248
C FIRST VARIATE MUST BE TIME VARIATE
C NALTMX = MAXIMUM NUMBER OF CLASSES ON TAPE
C DIMENSION      TRT(NALTMX)
      NALTMX = 50
      DIMENSION  TRT(50)
C MAXDBC = MAXIMUM NUMBER OF DATA BANK SUBSET CONDITIONS
C DIMENSION SCON(5,MAXDBC)
      MAXDBC = 50
      DIMENSION SCON(5,50)
C THE FOLLOWING DIMENSION STORES THE NAMES OF THE DATA TRANSFORMS
C AND THE ACCEPTABLE LEVELS FOR TRANSFORMATIONS
      DIMENSION U(60),LU(60)
      NU = 60
C TRANSFORMATION CODES
C UNITS                          BLOCKS
C        0 - 9   10 - 19  20 - 29  30 - 39  40 - 49  50 - 59
C        POWERS  TRIG     TRIG     STATIST  MATHS    TEST
C                RADIANS  DEGREES  TRANSF   FUNCTS   FUNCTIONS
C   0    -        -       H.MS     -         -       RM10
C   1    VAL.    SINR     SIND     PSNA     RECP     +/-1
C   2    SQAR    COSR     COSD     PSNB     SQRT     ADD1
C   3    CUBE    TANR     TAND     BINO     ABSV     SUB1
C   4    4PWR    ASIR     ASID     LG+1     SIGN     NOR1
C   5    5PWR    ACOR     ACOD     LOGE     INTG     +/-P
C   6    6PWR    ATAR     ATAD     LG10     FRAC     ADDP
C   7    7PWR    SINH     DTOR     AL10     EXPT     SUBP
C   8    8PWR    COSH     RTOD     -        PRES     NORP
C   9    9PWR    TANH     H.HH     -        NEG.     +100
      DATA U/4HVAL.,4HSQAR,4HCUBE,4H4PWR,4H5PWR,4H6PWR,4H7PWR,4H8PWR,4H9
     1PWR,4HVAL ,4HSINR,4HCOSR,4HTANR,4HASIR,4HACOR,4HATAR,4HSINH,4HCOSH
     2,4HTANH,4HH.MS,4HSIND,4HCOSD,4HTAND,4HASID,4HACOD,4HATAD,4HDTOR,4H
     3RTOD,4HH.HH,4H VAL,4HPSNA,4HPSNB,4HBINO,4HLG+1,4HLOGE,4HLG10,4HAL1
     40,4H    ,4H    ,4H    ,4HRECP,4HSQRT,4HABSV,4HSIGN,4HINTG,4HFRAC,4
     5HEXPT,4HPRES,4HNEG.,4HRM10,4H+/-1,4HADD1,4HSUB1,4HNOR1,4H+/-P,4HAD
     6DP,4HSUBP,4HNORP,4H+100,4H    /
C ACCEPTABLE CODE LEVELS
      DATA LU/60*4/
C DUMMY ARRAYS USED IN LGEN + D.H.I INPUT ARRAY
      DIMENSION IH(1),H(1),FORM(40)
      COMMON /STCT/MED1,MED2,MED3,MED4,MED5,MED6,MED13,Q,V(20),TT(30)
      DATA PROG/4HFACT/
      MED1 = -1
C LEVEL 0 - SETTING UP
    1 CALL COPYA(TT(1),PROG)
      CALL FIFI
      IF(MED3.GT.0) WRITE(MED2,901)
      CALL LDAP(MED2,MED3,V,TT,Q,NQ,NALT,NQMAX,NALTMX,IGO)
      IF(IGO.GT.0) GO TO 1
      LI = 18
      CALL LDDS(TRT,NALT,D,NQ,ST,NQ,IT,NQ,H,O,H,H,O,LI,O,Q,VX,
     1 0,MED2,MED3,0,IGO)
      IF(IGO.GT.0) GO TO 1
   21 IF(V(10).GE.20.) V(10) = 0.
      CALL LDBS(SCON,NCON,MAXDBC,CN,ST,IT,NQ,TRT,NALT,IGO)
```

```
            IF(IGO.GT.0) GO TO 1
            DO 22 I = 11,20
         22 CALL COPYA(TT(I),TT(I+10))
            ARAN = 5236.
C     READ SET OF VARIATES FOR DATA SWEEP      - LEVEL 4
         41 IF(V(10).GE.40.) V(10) = 0.
            M = 0
            C = MAXAV - 5
            MAXM = (SQRT(7.5*7.5+2.*C) - 7.5)*0.25
            IF(MAXM.GT.MI) MAXM = MI
            WRITE(MED6,941)
            WRITE(MED6,944)
            CALL LGEN(U,NU,LU,NU,ST,IT,CN,NQ,IH,0,H,H,0,H,H,0,MAXD,NALT,NDP,NP
           1,MAXM,M,MAXM,1,NALT)
            IF(V(11).LT.0.5.AND.V(20).LT.0.5)GO TO 21
            BRAN = ARAN
C     READ PREDICTED VARIATES - LEVEL 5
         51 IF(V(10).GT.50.) V(10) = 0.
            WRITE(MED6,951)
            WRITE(MED6,944)
            NPV = 0
            C = MAXAV -M*(M+1)/2 - 7*M
            MX = (SQRT(1.+2.*C)-1.)*0.25
            IF(MX.GT.MI) MX = MI
            CALL LGEN(U,NU,LU,NU,ST,IT,CN,NQ,IH,0,H,H,0,H,H,0,MAXD,0,IX,IY,MX,
           1NPV,MX,1,NALT)
            IF(V(11).LT.0.5.AND.V(20).LT.0.5)GO TO 41
            IF(V(10).LT.0.5.AND.V(20).GT.0.5) V(10) = 55.
            IF(NPV.LT.1) GO TO 54
C     STORE AS NUMBERS IN VARIATE SET - ADD IF MISSING
            C = MAXAV - NPV*(2*NPV+1)
            MAXM = (SQRT(7.5*7.5+2.*C) - 7.5)*0.25
            IF(MAXM.GT.MI) MAXM = MI
            KM = 0
            DO 53 J = 1,NPV
            DO 52 L = 1,M
            IF(IX(J).NE.NDP(L).OR.IY(J).NE.NP(L)) GO TO 52
            ISAVE(J) = L
            GO TO 53
         52 CONTINUE
            V(19) = V(19) + 2.
            IF(V(19).GT.50.) V(19) = 2.
            IF(V(19).GT.50.) WRITE(MED2,950)
            WRITE(MED2,952) J
            IF(MAXM.EQ.M) WRITE(MED6,954)
            IF(MAXM.EQ.M) KM = KM + 1
            IF(MAXM.EQ.M) GO TO 53
            WRITE(MED2,953)
            M = M + 1
            NDP(M) = IX(J)
            NP(M) = IY(J)
            ISAVE(J) = M
            V(6) = 0.
            BRAN = ARAN
         53 CONTINUE
            NPV = NPV - KM
         54 IF(NPV.EQ.0.AND.V(10).LT.0.5) V(10) = 53.
C     LEVEL 9 - READ DATA HANDLING INSTRUCTION
         91 IF(V(10).GT.90.) V(10) = 0.
            CALL LDHI(V(1),1,V(2),2,VX,7,V(3),10,V(4),19,H,0,H,V(10),
           1 TT(21),FORM,MED1,MED2,0,Q,NQ,NWARN,1,IGO)
            IF(IGO.GT.0) GO TO 51
C     STANDARDISATION
```

```
      FMAX = NPV
      IF(V(2).GT.3.) NWARN = NWARN + 1
      IF(V(2).GT.3.) V(2) = 0.
      IF(V(3).EQ.0..AND.V(4).EQ.0.) NWARN = NWARN + 1
      IF(V(3).EQ.0..AND.V(4).EQ.0.) V(4) = 1.
      IF(V(3).GT.FMAX.OR.V(3).EQ.0.) NWARN = NWARN + 1
      IF(V(3).GT.FMAX.OR.V(3).EQ.0.) V(3) = FMAX
C MAXIMUM NUMBER OF MISSING VALUES
      IF(V(6).EQ.0.) V(9) = VX
      IF(VX.NE.V(9).AND.VX.NE.0.) V(6) = 0.
      IF(VX.NE.V(9).AND.VX.NE.0.) V(9) = VX
      NF = V(3)
      MXM = 7*M + 2*NPV*NPV + NPV*NF
      MDIAG = M*(M+1)/2
      IF(V(9).GT.0.5) MDIAG = MDIAG*6
      IF(MXM+MDIAG.LE.MAXAV) GO TO 97
      IF(V(9).LT.0.5) GO TO 96
      WRITE(MED6,980)
      V(9) = 0.
      MDIAG = M*(M+1)/2
   96 IF(MXM+MDIAG.LE.MAXAV) GO TO 97
      V(3) = (MAXAV-MDIAG-7*M-2*NPV*NPV)/NPV
      WRITE(MED6,981) V(3)
   97 CALL LDHI(V(1),1,V(2),2,V(9),7,V(3),10,V(4),19,H,0,H,V(10),
     1 TT(21),FORM,MED1,MED2,0,Q,NQ,NWARN,2,IGO)
      IF(IGO.GT.0) GO TO 91
      WRITE(MED6,998)
      NF = V(3)
      MXM = NPV*NPV
      MAXKF = NF*NPV
      IF(MAXKF.LT.7*NF) MAXKF = 7*NF
      IXB = MDIAG + 1
      IST = IXB + M
      IRY = IST + M
      IB = IRY + M
      JT = IB + M
      JY = JT + M
      IZ = JY + M
      IRX = IZ + M
      IW = IRX + MXM
      IS = IW + MXM
      V(10) = BRAN
      CALL CFACT(M,MXM,MDIAG,MAXD,R(IXB),R(IST),D,R(IRY),ISAVE,R(IB),R(I
     1S),R(JT),R(IRX),R,X,MQ,NP,NDP,SCON,NCON,NPV,R(IW),R(JY),R(IZ),MAXK
     2F,IX,IY,U,NU,ST)
      ARAN = V(10)
      V(10) = 0.
      WRITE(MED6,999)
      GO TO 91
  901 FORMAT (1H0,20X,23HSTATCAT FACTOR ANALYSIS/)
  941 FORMAT (1H1,10X,30HSET OF VARIATES FOR DATA SWEEP/)
  944 FORMAT(7H0NUMBER,6X,19HTRANS   DATA   CYCLES/5H CODE,8X,18H-FORM COL
     1UMN DELAY,66X,7HCOMMENT)
  950 FORMAT (41H1SELECTED VARIATES NOT IN SET OF VARIATES)
  951 FORMAT (1H1,10X,18H SELECTED VARIATES/)
  952 FORMAT (15H0VARIATE NUMBER,I4,30H IS NOT IN THE SET OF VARIATES)
  953 FORMAT(1H+,50X,33H- ADDED (NEW DATA SWEEP REQUIRED))
  954 FORMAT (1H+,50X,26H-NOT ADDED - NO MORE SPACE)
  980 FORMAT(46H0 NOT ENOUGH STORAGE TO INCLUDE MISSING VALUES)
  981 FORMAT(16H0 ONLY SPACE FOR,F6.0,8H FACTORS)
  998 FORMAT (36H0INPUT ACCEPTED - ANALYSIS COMMENCES)
  999 FORMAT (36H1ANALYSIS COMPLETED - READ NEW INPUT)
      END
```

```
      SUBROUTINE CFACT(M,MXM,MDIAG,MN,XBAR,STD,D,RY,ISAVE,B,S,T,RX,R,X,N
     1Q,NP,NDP,SCON,NCON,K,W,Y,Z,MAXKF,IX,IY,U,NU,ST)
C CFACT     (SEE   7.3 ) EXECUTIVE    FACTOR ANALYSIS
      DIMENSION XBAR(M),STD(M),RY(M),ISAVE(M),B(M),T(M),Y(M),Z(M),ST(NQ)
      DIMENSION NP(M),NDP(M),D(MN),RX(MXM),R(MDIAG),X(NQ),S(MAXKF)
      DIMENSION IX(M),IY(M),SCON(5,NCON),U(NU),W(MXM),TV(51)
      COMMON /STCT/MED1,MED2,MED3,MED4,MED5,MED6,MED13,Q,V(20),TT(30)
C V:1=ND = OUTPUT :2 = ANALYSIS :3=NF = MAX FACTORS :4 = MIN EIGENVALUE
      NB = V(2) + .001
      NA = NB/2
      NB = NB - 2*NA
      ND = V(1) + .001
      NF = V(3)
      KXK = K*K
      KF= K*NF
      NDEL = 0
      DO 28 I = 1,M
   28 IF(NDP(I).GT.NDEL)NDEL = NDP(I)
      IF(NDEL.EQ.0)  V(7) = 1.
      IF(NDEL.GT.0)  V(7) = 3.
C NA = 1 GUTTMAN IMAGE TRANSFORM IS APPLIED   NB = 1 VARIMAX ROTATION
      IF(V(6).GT.0.5) GO TO 1
      REWIND MED3
      READ(MED3) NQ,NALT,Q,(TT(J),J=1,10),(P,J=1,6)
      DO 29 I = 1,NQ
   29 READ(MED3) (P,J=1,19),(P,J=1,NALT),J,P,P
      V(6) = 0.
      CALL CORRE(M,XBAR,STD,R,B,D,T,MDIAG,NP,NDP,X,NQ,SCON,NCON,MN)
      IF(V(6).GT.0.5) GO TO 1
      WRITE(MED2,902)  TT
      WRITE(MED2,923)
    1 N= V(6)
      IF(ND.EQ.1) CALL WBASE(ISAVE,NP,NDP,T,XBAR,STD,U,NU,ST,NQ,R,MDIAG,
     1M,NDEL,K,1)
      IF(ND.GE.2) CALL WBASE(ISAVE,NP,NDP,T,XBAR,STD,U,NU,ST,NQ,R,MDIAG,
     1M,NDEL,K,2)
      NE = 2
      CALL MOP(R,3,M,M,MDIAG,RX,2,K,K,MXM,ISAVE,3,K,ISAVE,3,K,NE,MED2)
      IF(ND.LT.1) GO TO 50
      WRITE(MED2,902) TT
      WRITE(MED2,921)
      CALL WHAT(RX,K,K,KXK,NP,NDP,M,ST,NQ,ISAVE,ISAVE,U,NU,MED2)
   50 IF(NA.EQ.0) GO TO 77
C CONSTRUCT GUTTMAN IMAGE TRANSFORMED MATRIX
      CALL MOP(R,3,M,M,MDIAG,W,2,K,K,MXM,ISAVE,3,K,ISAVE,3,K, 2,MED2)
      CALL MINV(W,K,DET,IX,IY,MXM)
      INDX = -K
      DO 55 I = 1,K
      INDX = INDX + K + 1
   55 Y(I) = 1./W(INDX)
      INDX = - K
      INDY = 0
      DO 65 I = 1,K
      INDX = INDX + K + 1
      DO 60 J = 1,K
      INDY = INDY + 1
   60 RX(INDY) = RX(INDY) + Y(I)*W(INDY)*Y(J)
   65 RX(INDX) = RX(INDX) - 2.*Y(I)
      INDY = 0
      INDX = -K
      DO 75 I = 1,K
      INDX = INDX + K + 1
      DO 70 J = 1,K
```

```
          INDY = INDY + 1
       70 W(INDY) = -W(INDY)*Y(J)
          W(INDX) = W(INDX) + 1.
       75 RY(I) = RX(INDX)*100.
          CV = 0.
          DO 76 I = 1,K
       76 CV = CV + RY(I)
          IF(ND.LT.1) GO TO 77
          IF(K.GT.10) WRITE(MED2,902) TT
          WRITE(MED2,922)
          CALL WMAT(RX,K,K,KXK,NP,NDP,M,ST,NQ,ISAVE,ISAVE,U,NU,MED2)
       77 IX(1) = -1
          ISAVE(1) = 0 - ISAVE(1)
C FIND EIGEN VALUES
          CALL ASEV(RX,V(4),RY,K,KF,KXK,NP,S,B,Y,Z)
          WRITE(MED2,902) TT
          IF(NA.EQ.0) WRITE(MED2,950)
          IF(NA.EQ.1) WRITE(MED2,960)
          IF(NF.EQ.0) WRITE(MED2,924)
          IF(NF.EQ.0) RETURN
          WRITE(MED2,903) (J,RY(J),B(J),J=1,NF)
       78 P = 0.
          PT = 0.
          DO 104 J = 1,NF
          P = P + B(J)
      104 PT = PT + RY(J)
          TR = PT/P*100.
          WRITE(MED2,904) PT,P,TR
C FACTOR LOADINGS
          NLIN = 16 + NF + K
          IF(NLIN.GT.50) WRITE(MED2,902) TT
          IF(NLIN.GT.50) NLIN = K + 9
          IF(NA.EQ.0) WRITE(MED2,950)
          IF(NA.EQ.1) WRITE(MED2,960)
          WRITE(MED2,905)
          CALL WMAT( S,NF,K,KF,NP,NDP,M,ST,NQ,IX,ISAVE,U,NU,MED2)
          INDX = 0
          IF(NA.EQ.1) GO TO 109
          DO 108 J = 1,NF
          DO 108 I = 1,K
          INDX = INDX + 1
      108 RX(INDX) = S(INDX)/RY(J)
          GO TO 110
      109 CONTINUE
          CALL MATM(W,S,RX,K,K,NF,KXK,KF,KF)
          DO 105 J = 1,NF
          DO 105 I = 1,K
          INDX = INDX + 1
      105 RX(INDX) = RX(INDX)/RY(J)
      110 CONTINUE
C FACTOR SCORE WEIGHTS
          NLIN = NLIN + K + 5
          IF(NLIN.GT.50) WRITE(MED2,902) TT
          IF(NA.EQ.0) WRITE(MED2,950)
          IF(NA.EQ.1) WRITE(MED2,960)
          WRITE(MED2,906)
          CALL WMAT(RX,NF,K,KF,NP,NDP,M,ST,NQ,IX,ISAVE,U,NU,MED2)
          IF(NB.EQ.0.AND.ND.GT.2) GO TO 140
      201 INDX = 0
          IF(NF.LE.1) WRITE(MED2,910)
          IF(NF.LE.1) NB = 0
          IF(NB.LE.0) GO TO 140
C VARIMAX ROTATION - FORM WEIGHTING MATRIX
```

```
          DO 135 J = 1,NF
          DO 135 I = 1,K
          INDX = INDX + 1
      135 RX(INDX) = RX(INDX)/RY(J)
          CALL MATM(RX,S,W,K,-NF,K,KF,KF,KXK)
          DO 138 I = 1,K
          B(I) = 0.
          DO 138 J = 1,NF
          L = K*(J-1) + I
      138 B(I) = B(I) + S(L)*S(L)
          NIT = 50
          CALL VARMX(S,Y,K,NF,KF,NIT)
          DO 139 I = 1,K
      139 Z(I) = B(I) - Y(I)
          WRITE(MED2,902) TT
          IF(NA.EQ.0) WRITE(MED2,950)
          IF(NA.EQ.1) WRITE(MED2,960)
          WRITE(MED2,907) NIT
          IF(NDEL.GT.0) WRITE(MED2,943)
          DO 136 L = 1,K
          I = ISAVE(L)
          IF(I.LT.0) I = -I
          JT = NP(I)/1000
          JC = NP(I)-JT*1000
          WRITE(MED2,944) U(JT),JC,ST(JC),B(L),Y(L),Z(L)
          IF(NDEL.GT.0) WRITE(MED2,943)
      136 CONTINUE
    C FACTOR LOADINGS
          NLIN = 15 + 2*K
          IF(NLIN.GT.50) WRITE(MED2,902) TT
          IF(NLIN.GT.50) NLIN = K + 9
          IF(NA.EQ.0) WRITE(MED2,950)
          IF(NA.EQ.1) WRITE(MED2,960)
          IF(NB.EQ.1) WRITE(MED2,970)
          WRITE(MED2,905)
          CALL WMAT( S,NF,K,KF,NP,NDP,M,ST,NQ,IX,ISAVE,U,NU,MED2)
          CALL MATM(W,S,RX,K,K,NF,KXK,KF,KF)
    C FACTOR SCORE WEIGHTS    AFTER VARIMAX ROTATION
          NLIN = NLIN + K + 5
          IF(NLIN.GT.50) WRITE(MED2,902) TT
          IF(NA.EQ.0) WRITE(MED2,950)
          IF(NA.EQ.1) WRITE(MED2,960)
          IF(NB.EQ.1) WRITE(MED2,970)
          WRITE(MED2,906)
          CALL WMAT(RX,NF,K,KF,NP,NDP,M,ST,NQ,IX,ISAVE,U,NU,MED2)
      140 ISAVE(1) = 0 - ISAVE(1)
          IF(ND.LT.3) RETURN
          ND = 1 + NB + 2*NA
          CALL RESID(S,NF,D,MN,ISAVE,K,NP,NDP,IX,IY,RY,B,XBAR,STD,M,U,NU,
         1 ST,X,NQ,SCON,NCON,RX,MXM,D,1,1,1,K,0,ND)
          RETURN
      902 FORMAT(23H1STATCAT PROGRAM STFACT,7X,1H-,4X,15HFACTOR ANALYSIS/
         1           16H DATA BANK TITLE,14X,1H-,4X,10A4/23H DATA BANK SUBSET TI
         2TLE,7X,1H-,4X,10A4/10H RUN TITLE,20X,1H-,4X,10A4/)
      903 FORMAT(1H+,60X,11HEIGENVALUES/1H0,8X,6HNUMBER,8X,5HVALUE,5X,16HPER
         1CENT OF TRACE/(10X,I3,2F15.5))
      904 FORMAT(10X,5HTOTAL,F13.5,F15.5/1H0,9X,14HTOTAL TRACE = ,F19.5)
      905 FORMAT(1H+,60X,15HFACTOR LOADINGS/)
      906 FORMAT(1H+,60X,20HFACTOR SCORE WEIGHTS/)
      907 FORMAT(1H+,60X,25HVARIMAX ROTATION ANALYSIS/26H0COMMUNALITY CHECK
         1- AFTER,I4,10H ROTATIONS/17H0TRANSFORM COLUMN,16X,15HBEFORE ROTATI
         2ON,6X,14HAFTER ROTATION,8X,10HDIFFERENCE)
      910 FORMAT (47H0VARIMAX ROTATION REQUIRES AT LEAST TWO FACTORS            )
```

```
    921 FORMAT(1H0,5X,36HCORRELATION MATRIX FOR THIS ANALYSIS/)
    922 FORMAT(1H0,5X,31HGUTTMAN IMAGE COVARIANCE MATRIX/)
    923 FORMAT(///19H0 NO DATA IN SAMPLE)
    924 FORMAT(////12H0 NO FACTORS)
    943 FORMAT(1H+,17X,5HDELAY)
    944 FORMAT(1H ,A4,3H OF,I3,1H(,A4,1H),9X,3F20.8)
    950 FORMAT(1H0,10X,30HPRINCIPAL COMPONENTS ANALYSIS  )
    960 FORMAT(1H0,10X,30HGUTTMAN IMAGE ANALYSIS         )
    970 FORMAT(1H+,40X,16HVARIMAX ROTATION)
        END


        SUBROUTINE VARMX (A,H,M,K,MK,NIT)
C VARMX   (SEE 7.3 ) SYSTEM          VARIMAX ROTATION
        DIMENSION A(MK),H(M)
C A = FACTOR MATRIX (M BY K)   H = COMMUNALITIES (M)
C M = NO OF VARIATES  K = NO OF FACTORS    MK = M*K
C NIT = ITERATIONS   (IN = MAXIMUM, OUT = NO ACTUALLY USED)
        EPS=0.00116
        VARN = 0.0
        LL=K-1
        NV = 0
        NC=0
        FN=M
        FFN=FN*FN
        CONS=0.7071066
C CALCULATE ORIGINAL COMMUNALITIES
        DO 11 I=1,M
        H(I)=0.0
        DO 11 J=1,K
        L=M*(J-1)+I
     11 H(I)=H(I)+A(L)*A(L)
C CALCULATE NORMALIZED FACTOR MATRIX
        DO 12 I=1,M
        H(I)= SQRT(H(I))
        DO 12 J=1,K
        L=M*(J-1)+I
     12 A(L)=A(L)/H(I)
C CALCULATE VARIANCE FOR FACTOR MATRIX
     13 NV=NV+1
        VARL = VARN
        VARN = 0.
        DO 15 J=1,K
        AA=0.0
        BB=0.0
        LB=M*(J-1)
        DO 14 I=1,M
        L=LB+I
        CC=A(L)*A(L)
        AA=AA+CC
     14 BB=BB+CC*CC
     15 VARN = VARN +(FN*BB-AA*AA)/FFN
C TEST FOR NO MEASURABLE IMPROVEMENT ON THREE ITERATIONS
        IF(VARN-VARL-.000001.GT.0.) GO TO 19
     17 NC=NC+1
        IF(NC.EQ.3) GO TO 43
C ROTATION OF TWO FACTORS CONTINUES UP TO 42
     19 DO 42 J=1,LL
        L1=M*(J-1)
        II=J+1
C CALCULATE NUM AND DEN
        DO 42 K1=II,K
        L2=M*(K1-1)
```

```
      AA=0.0
      BB=0.0
      CC=0.0
      DD=0.0
      DO 23 I=1,M
      L3=L1+I
      L4=L2+I
      U=(A(L3)+A(L4))*(A(L3)-A(L4))
      T=A(L3)*A(L4)
      T=T+T
      CC=CC+(U+T)*(U-T)
      DD=DD+2.0*U*T
      AA=AA+U
   23 BB=BB+T
      T=DD-2.0*AA*BB/FN
      B=CC-(AA*AA-BB*BB)/FN
C COMPARE NUM AND DEN
      IF(T-B) 28,24,32
   24 IF((T+B)-EPS) 42,25,25
C NUM + DEN IS GREATER THAN OR EQUAL TO THE TOLERANCE EPS
   25 COS4T=CONS
      SIN4T=CONS
      GO TO 35
C NUM IS LESS THAN DEN
   28 TAN4T= ABS(T)/ ABS(B)
      IF(TAN4T-EPS) 30,29,29
   29 COS4T=1.0/ SQRT(1.0+TAN4T*TAN4T)
      SIN4T=TAN4T*COS4T
      GO TO 35
   30 IF(B) 31,42,42
   31 SINP=CONS
      COSP=CONS
      GO TO 40
C NUM IS GREATER THAN DEN
   32 CTN4T= ABS(T/B)
      IF(CTN4T-EPS) 34,33,33
   33 SIN4T=1.0/ SQRT(1.0+CTN4T*CTN4T)
      COS4T=CTN4T*SIN4T
      GO TO 35
   34 COS4T=0.0
      SIN4T=1.0
C DETERMINE COS THETA AND SIN THETA
   35 COS2T= SQRT((1.0+COS4T)/2.0)
      SIN2T=SIN4T/(2.0*COS2T)
      COST= SQRT((1.0+COS2T)/2.0)
      SINT=SIN2T/(2.0*COST)
C DETERMINE COS PHI AND SIN PHI
      IF(B) 37,37,36
   36 COSP=COST
      SINP=SINT
      GO TO 38
   37 COSP=CONS*COST+CONS*SINT
      SINP= ABS(CONS*COST-CONS*SINT)
   38 IF(T) 39,39,40
   39 SINP=-SINP
C PERFORM ROTATION
   40 DO 41 I=1,M
      L3=L1+I
      L4=L2+I
      AA=A(L3)*COSP+A(L4)*SINP
      A(L4)=-A(L3)*SINP+A(L4)*COSP
   41 A(L3)=AA
   42 CONTINUE
```

```
      IF(NV.LT.NIT) GO TO 13
C DENORMALIZE VARIMAX LOADINGS
   43 DO 44 I=1,M
      DO 44 J=1,K
      L=M*(J-1)+I
   44 A(L)=A(L)*H(I)
C CALCULATE FINAL COMMUNALITY
      DO 46 I = 1,M
      H(I) = 0.0
      DO 46 J = 1,K
      L = M*(J-1) + I
   46 H(I) = H(I) + A(L)*A(L)
      NIT = NV
      RETURN
      END


      SUBROUTINE RESID(RA,L,F,MN,ISAVE,K,NP,NDP,LW,NW,Y,Z,XBAR,STD,M,
     1U,NU,ST,X,NQ,SCON,NCON,C,NAB,D,NB2,N1,N2,N3,N4,N5)
C RESID   (SEE 7.2 ) SYSTEM          LIST AND DESCRIBE RESIDUALS/FACTORS
      DIMENSION RA(7,L),F(MN),ISAVE(K),U(NU),ST(NQ),X(NQ),C(NAB),D(NB2)
      DIMENSION NP(M),NDP(M),LW(M),NW(M),Y(M),Z(M),XBAR(M),STD(M)
      DIMENSION SCON(5,NCON),VA(2),ER(2),SC(2),VS(2),FAC(3)
      DIMENSION ACT(3),PED(3),POR(3),VAR(3),DAI(3),ORI(3),RES(3),SET(3)
      DATA VA/3HVAL,3HUE /,ER/3HERR,3HOR /,SC/3HSCO,3HRE /
      DATA VS/3HVAL,3HUES/,ACT/3H   ,3HACT,3HUAL/,PED/3HPRE,3HDIC,3HTED/
      DATA POR/3HPRE,3HDIC,3HTOR/,VAR/3H  V,3HARI,3HATE/
      DATA DAI/3HDAT,3HA I,3HTEM/,ORI/3H OR,3HIGI,3HNAL/
      DATA RES/3H RE,3HSID,3HUAL/,SET/3H   ,3HSET,3H OF/,B/3H   /
      DATA FAC/3H   ,3HFAC,3HTOR/
      COMMON /STCT/MED1,MED2,MED3,MED4,MED5,MED6,MED13,Q,V(20),TT(30)
C NA= N3-N1+1 = LARGER SET NC= 0 PRIN COMP   ND= 0,1 NO VARMX N5=5   MREG
C NB= N4-N2+1 =SMALLER SET NC= 1 GUTT IMAG   ND=2 VARIMAX ROT N5=6 CANON
      V10 = V(10)
      KP = V(1)
      L1 = L+1
      L2 = L+L
      NA = N3-N1 + 1
      NB = N4-N2 + 1
      NDEL = 0
      DO 100 I = 1,K
      IS = ISAVE(I)
  100 IF(NDP(IS).GT.0) NDEL = 1
      IF(NDEL.EQ.0) V(7) = 1.
      IF(NDEL.EQ.1) V(7) = 3.
      NC =(N5-1)/2
      ND = N5 - 2*NC
      IF(N5.GT.4) ND = 0
      NE = (L+2)/3
      NH = 8
      IF(KP.LT.4) GO TO 201
      IF(KP.EQ.4) GO TO 200
C CALCULATE ENTRIES PER PAGE FOR INDIVIDUAL LISTING
      LL = (L+9)/10
      NH = 8 + LL
      NE = 4 + LL*3
      IF(KP.EQ.5) GO TO 200
      LL = (NB+9)/10
      NH = NH + LL*3
      NE = NE + LL
      IF(NDEL.GT.0) NH = NH + LL
      IF(KP.EQ.6) GO TO 200
      LL = (NA+9)/10
```

```
      NH = NH + LL*3
      NE = NE + LL
      IF(NDEL.GT.0) NH = NH + LL
      IF(KP.EQ.7) GO TO 200
      LL = (M+9)/10
      NH = NH + LL*3
      NE = NE + LL
      IF(KP.EQ.8) GO TO 200
      LL = (NQ+19)/10
      NH = NH + LL
      NE = NE + LL
  200 NH = (50-NH)/NE
      NE = NH + 1
  201 DO 202 J = 1,L
      RA(7,J) = Q
      DO 202 I = 1,6
  202 RA(I,J) = 0.
      V(6) = 0.
      V(8) = 1.
      DO 203 I = 1,MN
  203 P(I) = Q
      READ(MED3) NQ,NALT,Q,(P,I=1,16)
      DO 204 J = 1,NQ
  204 READ(MED3) (P,I=1,19),(P,I=1,NALT),NN,P,P
  205 CALL MEDIAT(M,NDP,NP,MN,P,X,NQ,SCON,NCON)
      IF(V(8).GT.1.5) GO TO 250
      IF(NH.GE.NE.OR.KP.EQ.3) GO TO 211
C PRINT PAGE HEADER
      NE = 1
      IF(NC.EQ.0) WRITE(MED2,900)
      IF(NC.EQ.1) WRITE(MED2,901)
      IF(ND.EQ.2) WRITE(MED2,902)
      IF(N5.EQ.5) WRITE(MED2,905)
      IF(N5.EQ.6) WRITE(MED2,906)
      WRITE(MED2,907) TT
      WRITE(MED2,908)
      IF(KP.GE.4.AND.N5.LE.4)WRITE(MED2,910) (I,I=1,L)
      IF(KP.EQ.4.AND.N5.GE.5)WRITE(MED2,919) (I,I=1,L)
      IF(KP.GE.5.AND.N5.EQ.6)WRITE(MED2,920) (I,I=1,L)
      IF(KP.LE.5) GO TO 211
      DO 206 J = 1,K
      I = ISAVE(J)
      NT = NP(I)/1000
      NG = NP(I)-1000*NT
      LW(J) = NG
      CALL COPYA(Y(J),U(NT))
      CALL COPYA(Z(J),ST(NG))
  206 IF(NDEL.GT.0) NW(J)=NDP(I)
      IF(NB.EQ.0) GO TO 217
      DO 207 JS = N2,N4,10
      JF = JS + 9
      IF(JF.GT.N4) JF = N4
      WRITE(MED2,960) PED,(Y(J),J=JS,JF)
      WRITE(MED2,973) (Z(J),LW(J),J=JS,JF)
  207 IF(NDEL.GT.0) WRITE(MED2,974) (NW(J),J=JS,JF)
  217 IF(KP.EQ.6) GO TO 211
      DO 208 JS = N1,N3,10
      JF = JS + 9
      IF(JF.GT.N3) JF = N3
      IF(N5.LE.4) WRITE(MED2,960) ORI,(Y(J),J=JS,JF)
      IF(N5.GE.5) WRITE(MED2,960) POR,(Y(J),J=JS,JF)
      WRITE(MED2,973) (Z(J),LW(J),J=JS,JF)
  208 IF(NDEL.GT.0) WRITE(MED2,974) (NW(J),J=JS,JF)
```

```
      IF(KP.EQ.7) GO TO 211
      DO 209 J = 1,M
      NT = NP(J)/1000
      NG = NP(J)-1000*NT
      LW(J) = NG
      CALL COPYA(Y(J),U(NT))
  209 CALL COPYA(Z(J),ST(NG))
      DO 210 JS = 1,M,10
      JF = JS + 9
      IF(JF.GT.M) JF = M
      WRITE(MED2,960) SET,(Y(J),J=JS,JF)
      WRITE(MED2,973) (Z(J),LW(J),J=JS,JF)
  210 IF(NDEL.GT.0) WRITE(MED2,974) (NDP(J),J=JS,JF)
      IF(KP.EQ.8) GO TO 211
      WRITE(MED2,975) (I,ST(I),I=1,NQ)
  211 IF(KP.GT.3) NE = NE + 1
      NMIS = 0
      DO 212 J = 1,K
      I = ISAVE(J)
      Y(J) = F(I) - XBAR(I)
      IF(F(I).NE.Q) GO TO 212
      NMIS = NMIS + 1
      Y(J) = 0.
  212 CONTINUE
      CALL MATM(Y(N1),C,Z    ,1,NA,L,NA,NAB,L)
      IF(NB.GE.2) CALL MATM(Y(N2),D,Z(L1),1,NB,L,NB,NB2,L)
      IF(NB.EQ.1) Z(L1) = Y(N2)
      DO 213 J = 1,L
      JS = J + L
      IF(NB.EQ.0) P = Z(J)
      IF(NB.GE.1) P = Z(JS) - Z(J)
      Y(J) = P
      IF(NMIS.EQ.0.AND.RA(7,J).NE.Q)
     1 RA(6,J) = RA(6,J) + (RA(7,J)-P)*(RA(7,J)-P)
      IF(NMIS.EQ.0) RA(7,J) = P
      PP = 1
      DO 213 I = 1,5
      RA(I,J) = RA(I,J) + PP
  213 PP = PP*P
      IF(KP.LT.4) GO TO 205
      IF(N5.EQ.5) Z(1) = Z(1) + XBAR(N2)
      IF(N5.EQ.5) Z(2) = Z(2) + XBAR(N2)
      IF(KP.GT.4) WRITE(MED2,903)
      J = V(6)
      WRITE(MED2,911) J
      IF(NMIS.GT.0) WRITE(MED2,912) NMIS
      IF(KP.EQ.4.AND.N5.GE.5) WRITE(MED2,913)   (Z(J),Z(J+L),Y(J),J=1,L)
      IF(KP.GE.4.AND.N5.LE.4) WRITE(MED2,913)   (Z(J),J=1,L)
      IF(KP.EQ.4) GO TO 205
      IF(N5.LE.4) GO TO 216
      WRITE(MED2,904)
      WRITE(MED2,950) ACT,B,B,(Z(J),J=L1,L2)
      WRITE(MED2,950) PED,B,B,(Z(J),J=1,L)
      WRITE(MED2,950) RES,B,B,(Y(J),J=1,L)
  216 IF(KP.EQ.5) GO TO 205
      DO 215 J = 1,K
      I = ISAVE(J)
  215 Y(J) = F(I)
      IF(N2.LE.N4) WRITE(MED2,904)
      IF(N2.LT.N4) WRITE(MED2,950) PED,VS,(Y(J),J=N2,N4)
      IF(N2.EQ.N4) WRITE(MED2,950) PED,VA,Y(N2)
      IF(KP.EQ.6) GO TO 205
      WRITE(MED2,904)
```

```
      IF(N5.GE.5) WRITE(MED2,950)POR,VS,(Y(J),J=N1,N3)
      IF(N5.LE.4) WRITE(MED2,950)ORI,VS,(Y(J),J=N1,N3)
      IF(KP.EQ.7) GO TO 205
      WRITE(MED2,904)
      WRITE(MED2,950) VAR,VS,(F(J),J=1,M)
      IF(KP.EQ.8) GO TO 205
      WRITE(MED2,904)
      WRITE(MED2,950) DAI,VS,(X(J),J=1,NQ)
      GO TO 205
  250 REWIND MED3
      V(10) = V10
C STATISTICAL DESCRIPTION OF RESIDUALS
      DO 260 J = 1,L
      IF(J.NE.J/2*2+1)GO TO 255
      IF(NC.EQ.0) WRITE(MED2,900)
      IF(NC.EQ.1) WRITE(MED2,901)
      IF(ND.EQ.2) WRITE(MED2,902)
      IF(N5.EQ.5) WRITE(MED2,905)
      IF(N5.EQ.6) WRITE(MED2,906)
      WRITE(MED2,907) TT
  255 WRITE(MED2,903)
      IF(N5.LE.4) WRITE(MED2,970) J
      IF(N5.GE.5) WRITE(MED2,971)
      IF(N5.EQ.6) WRITE(MED2,972) J
      CALL DCPS(RA(1,J),RA(2,J),RA(3,J),RA(4,J),RA(5,J),V,MED2)
      S = RA(1,J)
      IF(S.LE.2.) GO TO 260
      RMS = SQRT(RA(6,J)/(S-1.))
      ZZ= RA(6,J)/(V(13)*V(13)*(S-1.))
      ZZ= (ZZ*0.5 -1.)/SQRT((S-2.)/(S*S-1.))
      PR = PRBF(1.,S,ZZ*ZZ)
  260 WRITE(MED2,922) RMS,ZZ,PR
      RETURN
  900 FORMAT(30H1PRINCIPAL COMPONENTS ANALYSIS)
  901 FORMAT(30H1       GUTTMANN IMAGE ANALYSIS)
  902 FORMAT(1H+,30X,21HWITH VARIMAX ROTATION)
  903 FORMAT(1H ,30(4H----)/)
  904 FORMAT(1H )
  905 FORMAT(30H1     MULTIPLE LINEAR REGRESSION)
  906 FORMAT(30H1            CANONICAL ANALYSIS)
  907 FORMAT(16H0DATA BANK TITLE,14X,1H-,4X,10A4/23H DATA BANK SUBSET TI
     1TLE,7X,1H-,4X,10A4/10H RUN TITLE,20X,1H-,4X,10A4)
  908 FORMAT(21H0INDIVIDUAL ENTRIES     )
  910 FORMAT (1H0,17X,13HFACTOR NUMBER,9(I6,4X)/(31X,9(I6,4X)))
  911 FORMAT(6H ENTRY,I6)
  912 FORMAT (1H+,12X,I3,15H MISSING VALUES)
  913 FORMAT (1H+,30X,9F10.2/(31X,9F10.2))
  919 FORMAT(1H+,30X,3(I2,28H ACTUAL PREDICTED RESIDUAL   )/
     1         (31X,3(I2,28H ACTUAL PREDICTED RESIDUAL   )))
  920 FORMAT (1H0,12X,18HCANONICAL VARIATES,9(I6,4X))
  922 FORMAT(40H0ROOT-MEAN-SQUARE SUCCESSIVE DEVIATION =,F12.8/
     119H0NORMALISED VALUE =,F12.8/25H0ASSOCIATED PROBABILITY =,F12.8)
  950 FORMAT  (5X,3A3,1X,2A3,10F10.4/(21X,10F10.4))
  960 FORMAT  (1H0,3A3,9H VARIATES,10(3X,A4,3H OF))
  970 FORMAT  (45H0EXAMINATION OF FACTOR SCORES - FACTOR NUMBER,I4)
  971 FORMAT  (36H0EXAMINATION OF RESIDUAL DIFFERENCES)
  972 FORMAT  (1H+,36X,27H - CANONICAL VARIATE NUMBER,I4)
  973 FORMAT(4X,8HSELECTED,9X,10(A4,1H(,I4,1H))
  974 FORMAT(4X,7HDELAYED,10X,10(I3,7H CYCLES))
  975 FORMAT  (21H0    DATA COLUMN          ,10(I3,3H = ,A4)/
     1(21X,10(I3,3H = ,A4)))
      END
```

7.4   PROGRAM STMDIS - MULTIPLE DISCRIMINANT ANALYSIS

7.4.1   Purpose

This program carries out multiple discriminant analyses for a set of independent samples drawn form a STATCAT data bank. The discriminant variates are derived from variates selected from a set of delayed and/or transformed variates. The program constructs a series of discriminant variates from the selected variates, which maximises the differences between the specified samples. The statistical significance of the differences between samples in terms of the discriminant variates and of the original selected variates is given, and, if required, individual entries may be classified according to their discriminant scores.

Figure 7.41a contains system flow-charts for the main program STMDIS and the executive subroutine CMDIS. Figure 7.41b contains a system flow-chart for the system subroutine MDISC, which carries out the multiple discriminant analysis.

7.4.2   Input Data

Item	Level	Format	Function	See
1	0	A	File control (Input Only)	3.2
2	3	B	Sample specification	3.5
3	4	E	Subset specification	3.6
4	5	F	Set of Variates (Transform/Delay)	3.7
5	6	F	Selected Variates (Transform/Delay)	3.7
6	9	H	Data handling instruction	Below + 3.8

Data Handling Instruction

Card Layout - Data Handling Instruction - STMDIS

A BCCCCDDDEEEEEEEE EFFFFFFFFFGGGGGGGGGGGGGGGGGGHHHHHHHH.....etc

Columns	Item	Function	See
1	A	Output control index	Below
2	B	Analysis control index	Below
3 - 5	C	Acceptable number of 'non-values'	7.2
6 - 8	D	Maximum Number of discriminants	Below
9 - 16	E	Cut-off for Significance	Below
17 - 24	F	Not used	-
25 - 40	G	Not used	-
41 - 80	H	Comment (NOT KEPT)	-

A - Output Control Index

This index controls the quantity of information output by the program.

ALTERNATIVES

A = 0, blank: Discriminant score weights, correlations with the selected variates, Wilk's Lambda test, chi-squared tests of individual discriminants, and analyses of variance for the selected variates, with sample means for the original and discriminant variates.

A = 1   : In addition, covariance, among-sample and within-sample matrices.

A = 2   : In addition, original means, standard deviations and correlation matrices.

A = 3   : For each changed entry (including entries in the subset, but not contained in any sample, and any entries containing non-values) original sample and most probable sample.

A = 4   : In addition, for each changed entry, probabilities of belonging to each sample in terms of discriminant variates.

A = 5   : In addition, for each changed entry, discriminant scores.

A = 6   : In addition, for each changed entry, values of selected variates.

A = 7   : In addition, for each changed entry, values of original data.

A = 8   : As for A = 3, but for all entries, including those remaining in their original sample.

A = 9   : As for A = 7, but for all entries, including those remaining in their original sample.

DEFAULT value = 0 (0, blank or non-numeric character)

B - Analysis Control Index

This index controls the program strategy. In this program it determines which discriminant variates are retained.

ALTERNATIVES

B = 0 or blank : All discriminant variates up to a maximum of D (Default) retained.

B = 1   : Discriminant variates eliminated as long as the overall associated probability remains below E.

B = 2   : Discriminant variables eliminated as long as the loss in overall associated probability remains below E.

B = 3   : Discriminant variates are eliminated as long as their individual probability remains below E.

B = 4   : Discriminant variates are eliminated as long as the total unexplained part of the variance remains below E.

B = 5   : Discriminant variates are eliminated as long as the increase in the unexplained portion of the variation remains below E.

B = 6   : All discriminant variates up to a maximum of D will be retained. Euclidian distance used in calculation of discriminants, and re-allocation of entries to samples.

B = 7   : Discriminant variates are eliminated as long as their individual probability remains above E. Euclidian dis-

                        tance is used in the calculation of discriminants, and
                        re-allocation of entries to samples.

B = 8   : All discriminant variates up to a maximum of D will be
                        retained. Euclidian distance used in calculation of
                        discriminants, but re-allocation of entries to samples
                        is on basis of "city-block" distance (total absolute
                        difference).

B = 9   : Discriminant variates are eliminated as long as their
                        individual probability remains above E. Euclidian dis-
                        tance is used in the calculation of discriminants, but
                        re-allocation of entries to samples is on the basis of
                        "city-block" distance. (total absolute difference.)

DEFAULT value = 0 (0, blank or non-numeric character)

D - Maximum Number of Discriminants

This value determines the maximum number of discriminant variates that will be produced by the program, subject to the control of the analysis control index. The maximum number of discriminants cannot exceed the number of variates selected, or one less than the number of samples specified. If it exceeds either of these two numbers it will be set to the lower of the two.

DEFAULT value = 0 (0, blank or non-numeric characters) set to number of variates selected, or one less than the number of samples, whichever is the less.

E - Cut-off for Significance

This value is used, subject to the analysis control index, to determine the number of discriminant variates that will be retained.

DEFAULT value = 0 (0, blank or non-numeric characters) set to 1.0 per cent if D is also originally 0.

7.4.3 Input Example

Figure 7.42 is a summary of the input structure for two runs of STMDIS. Two samples are specified, one containing all entries classified as 'very easy', the other containing all entries classified as 'difficult' or 'very difficult'. All entries are included in the subset to be analysied. Eleven variates are defined, all of which are included in the first selection of variates. For the first run, only the default output is produced. For the second run, only the four variates that were individually statistically significant have been retained. For this run a detailed output is called for for any entry not assigned to a sample.

Figure 7.43 is a listing of the input cards required to carry out these two runs.

7.4.4 Output Example

Figure 7.44 is a general summary of the output produced by this program, indented according to the program structure. Figure 7.45 is a page-by-page summary of the output corresponding to the input of Figure 7.43. The input checking information is essentially standard, and is therefore not repeated here. Figure 7.46 and 7.47 give the default output for this program. This information appears on four successive pages, and consists of (Figure 7.46) a summary of statistical significance for the discriminants retained, and (figure 7.47) the discriminant weights, correlations of original variates and discriminants, a table of the sample means and standard deviations in terms of the original and discriminant variates, and a note of the number of entries most resembling a sample other than their original one.

7.4.5 Basic Output

Figure 7.46 illustrates the basic output for multiple discriminant analysis. This begins with a summary of the statistical significance of the analysis. The overall significance of the discriminants retained is given by Wilks's "lambda" measure, which is transformed into a F-ratio and evaluated in the usual way. The associated probability is that of observing a difference as large as (or larger than) that observed if the samples were drawn from the same underlying population. If the value observed is statistically significant, then the samples are significantly different.

This is followed by an analysis, for the roots retained, of the proportion of the variation that they account for and of their individual significance, using a statistic which has a distribution similar to chi-squared. The probability associated with each root is that of observing a value as extreme (or more extreme) if there were no significant differences between samples.

Finally, an analysis of variance is carried out between samples using each original variate. It is not true that an original variate which is not statistically significant individually should be discarded, because it sometimes happens, as it does in multiple regression analysis, that two variates which are neither important in themself provide a valuable contribution to the discriminant function by their difference.

It should be noted that there can never be more discriminants than there were original variates, and there must always be less than the number of samples.

7.4.6 General Information Output

Figure 7.47 includes tables showing the discriminant weights for the one discriminant retained. These values are the multiplying factors to be applied to the values for each original variate to obtain the discriminant scores for each entry. The weights are followed by the correlations between the discriminants and the original variates. These may be used to give some idea of the nature of the distinction made by each discriminant.

In this example, there is a relatively high correlation with the number of the operator, and with the heart rate, and a relatively high negative correlation with the time taken as an excess over the time allowed. This suggests that one sample will contain entries from a high-numbered operator with an elevated heart-rate who completes the task within the time scheduled.

Finally a tabulation of means and standard deviations for each sample, for the original variates and the discriminant. Note that the sample 'difficult' is drawn entirely from ent_ies concerning operator no.4 (HUGH) - the variate OPER has mean 4 and standard deviation 0. The heart-rate for this operator is higher, and the excess time taken is less than for the other cases. Note that the two samples account for 30 out of 64 entries - the remaining 34 are included in the subset, but not in either sample. The mean of the discriminant variate is far higher for the sample labelled 'Hard' than for the other, and its standard deviation is less - reflecting the more uniform nature of the sample (in which all entries relate to one operator).

7.4.7 Individual Entries

Figure 7.48 contains examples of the output produced for entries when the fully detailed output is used. Each page, of course, commences with the STATCAT data bank, subset and run titles, with an indication that individual entries are being examined. The numbers of the discriminants retained are followed by the titles of the selected variates and the names of the data columns.

An initial summary is given for each entry. This gives the entry number, the original allocation of the entry to a sample (if any), the probability of that association on the basis of the discriminants retained, the sample it most resembles, with the associated probability (if this is not the same sample as it originally belonged to) and the forced-choice probability for the sample finally chosen. The latter, forced-choice probability, is derived on the assumption that the independent probabilities established on the basis of the means and standard deviations of each sample are in the correct ratio, but that the entry must belong to one and only one sample, and the total of probabilities must therefore add up to 1.0.

Following this summary, the system gives for each entry, the independent and forced-choice probabilities that it belongs to each sample. This is followed by the value of each discriminant for the entry, then by the values of each variate, then by the values of each datum. Where any value is missing the non-value is replaced by the sample mean from the original sample, if any, or by the overall mean of the subset if the entry was not included in any sample.

7.4.8 Discussion

Multiple Discriminant analysis can be considered as an extension of simple analysis of variance into multiple dimensions. If we assume that the entries in the samples we have defined have something in common in terms of the variates we have chosen, then we can visualise, instead of the sphere we considered in our discussion of factor analysis, several spheres (which may overlap) and think of our discriminants as a set of axes that maximise the differences between the centres of the spheres.

There is (at least) one objection to this picture. In the course of our analysis we separate the "Within Samples" variation from the "Between Samples" variation, and use the "Within Samples" as a measure of the significance of differences between samples. Kendall(1975) points out that the variation within one sample need not have anything in common with the variation within another - or with the between samples variation. For this reason, he doubts the value of using the "Mahalanobis" distance, and suggests assuming that the variates are in fact independent. (To reduce the size of the program, this option has been incorporated by setting off-diagonal elements in the matrix of correlation coefficients to zero - admittedly not efficient in crude processing time.)

Kendall suggested some further modifications, which will be discussed in Chapter 8.1 (Program STGRPS).

If a multiple discriminant analysis is taken as far as the examination of residuals, it will often appear that some entries in the samples are more like another sample than the one to which they were allocated 'a priori'. If they can be transferred to the preferred sample for good reason, then there is no objection to doing so. If however the only reason is that they are more like that sample, then we are in danger of "Constructed Significance" (See Chapter 12.1.) The use of 'a posteriori' information changes the technique to a form of Data Study, rather than of Model Testing. STGRPS (8.1), which shares the main system subroutines of STMDISC is in fact a program for automatic re-allocation of entries, starting from specified or arbitrary samples.

REFERENCES : Veldman (Ch 10)
             Kendall (1975 - Ch 10)
             Morrison (Ch 4)

Figure 7.41a - System Flow-Charts - STMDIS and CMDIS

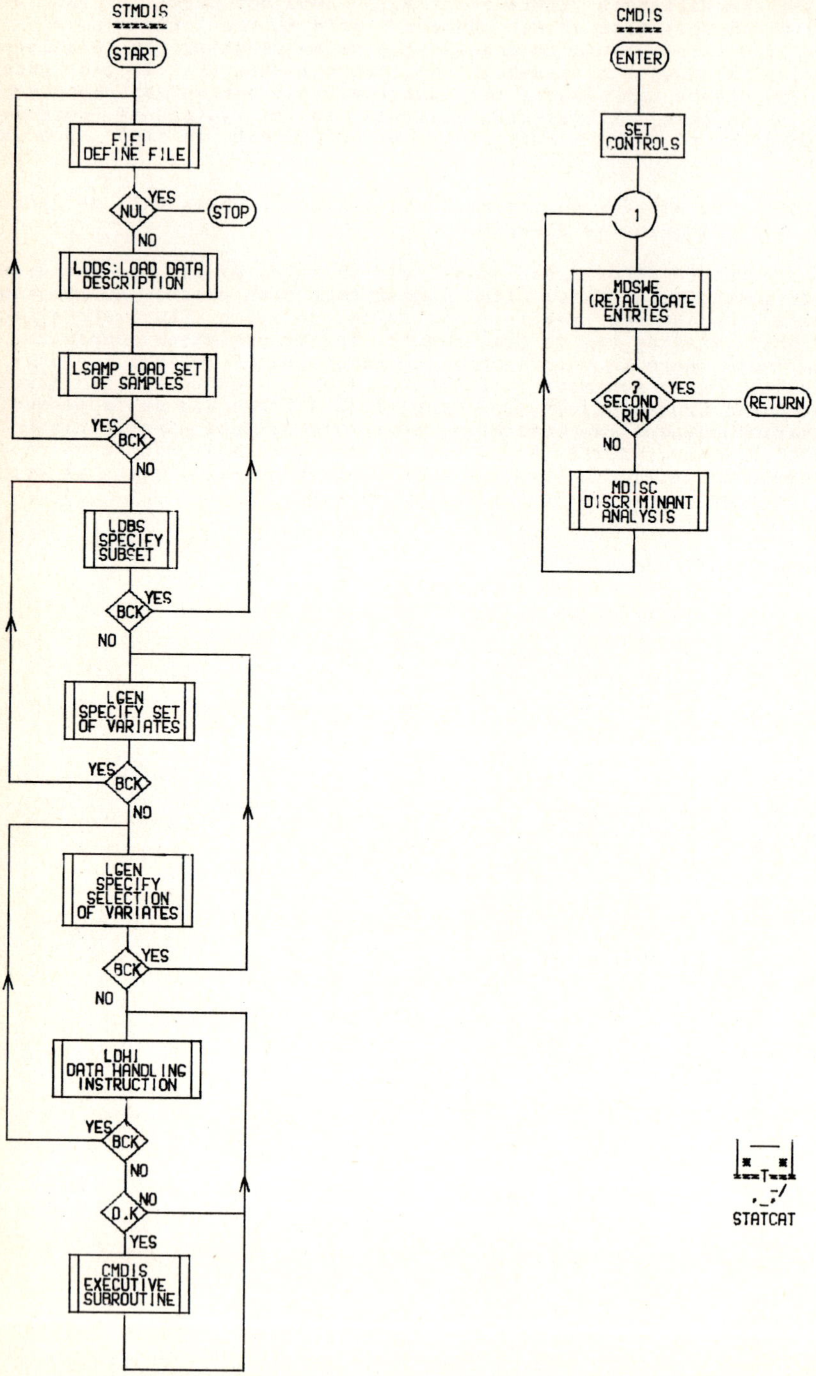

Figure 7.41b - System Flow-Chart - MDISC

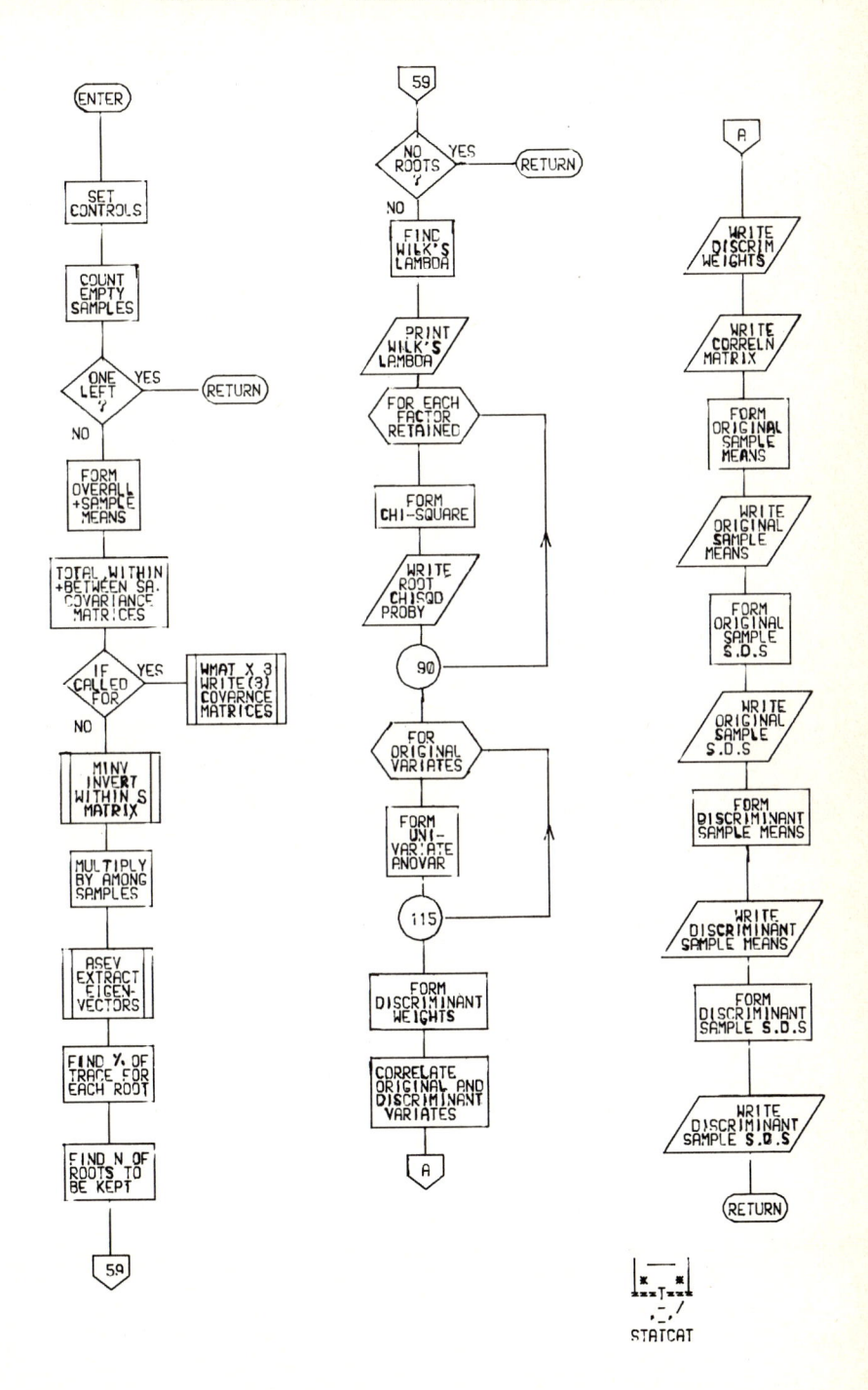

Figure 7.42 - STMDIS - Input Structure

```
        Level
 0   1   2   3   4   5   6   7   8   9
FILE CONTROL CARD
    SAMPLE SPECIFICATION
        SUBSET SPECIFICATION
            VARIATE SPECIFICATION
                SELECTED VARIATES
                    DATA HANDLING INSTRUCTION
                    BACK TO READ NEW SELECTED VARIATES
                SELECTED VARIATES
                    DATA HANDLING INSTRUCTION
                    STOP
```

Figure 7.43 - STMDIS - Input Example

```
---------1---------2---------3---------4---------5---------6---------7--
**STMDISDEMO                             DEMONSTRATION STATCAT DATA BANK
EASY VS HARD                             ALL EASY COMPARED WITH ALL DIFFI
EASY
.IF.DIFF.LT.      3.5                    RATHER EASY/EASY/VERY EASY
END OF SAMPLE ONE
HARD
.IF.DIFF.GT.      4.5                    RATHER DIFFICULT/DIFFICULT/VERY
END OF SAMPLE TWO
END OF SAMPLE SET
ALL DATA                                 WHOLE DATA BANK TO BE INCLUDED
END OF SUBSET DEFINITION
VAL.OPER
END OF SET OF VARIATES FOR DATA SWEEP
VAL.OPER
VAL.STRS
VAL.DAY.
VAL.TIME
VAL.TEMP
VAL.H.R.
VAL.TPCT
VAL.TCOM
VAL.TALL
VAL.ERRP
END OF SET OF VARIATES - FIRST RUN
GO                                       DEFAULT OPTION
BACK
VAL.OPER
VAL.STRS
VAL.TPCT
VAL.H.R.
END OF SET OF VARIATES - SECOND RUN      INDIVIDUALLY SIGNIFICANT ONLY
73                                       DETAILED OUTPUT
STOP
---------1---------2---------3---------4---------5---------6---------7--
```

Figure 7.44 - STMDIS - Output Structure

```
For each      ) : File Control Record
output file   )   File Parameters
                  Data Description
                  For each) :  Sample Input Record
                  Set of )        For each ) : Input Record
                  Samples         Subset   )    For each set ) : Input
                                           )    of Original  )   Record
                                                Variates     )   see left
For each Data) : Input Record
Handling      )  <Covariance matrix - Original Variates>
Instruction   )  <Among Samples matrix - Original Variates>
                 <Within Samples Matrix- Original Variates>
                 Wilkes Lambda Test
                 Univariate F tests
                 Discriminant Weights
                 Correlations original/discriminant variates
                 No,a.m and sd for original and discriminant variates
                 for each sample
                 <Attribution Record>
                     For Each <Changed> Entry : -
                     <Original/Revised sample/Proby : Forced choice>
                     <Prediscriminant Values>
                     <Variate Values>
                     <Data Items>
                 Total number of changed attributions
```

Carated(<>) items are optional.

Figure 7.45 - STMDIS - Page-by-page output summary

Page	Contents	Origin
1-2	File Control/Program title	FIFI/LDAP/STMDIS
	Data Description record	LDDS
3	Sample record	LSAMP/LSET
4	Subset record	LDBS/LSET
5	Original Variates record	LGEN
	Data Handling Instruction	LDHI
6	Covariance/among/within Samples Matrices	MDISC
7	Wilks Lambda /Univariate F tests	MDISC
8	Discriminant Weights/Correlations	MDISC
9	Sample no,a.m. and s.d.(Original+Discriminant)	MDISC
10-32	Reallocation - Samples to Discriminant set 1	MDSWE
33	Data Handling Instruction (STOP)	LDHI

Figure 7.46 - STMDIS - Output Example - Default Output

```
SYSTEM SUBROUTINE MDISC      -   DERIVE DESCRIMINANTS
DATA BANK TITLE              -   DEMONSTRATION STATCAT DATA BANK
DATA BANK SAMPLE SET         -   EASY VS HARD
DATA BANK SUBSET             -   ALL DATA
                             -   SAMPLES AS ORIGINALLY DEFINED

WILKS LAMBDA =    0.151

D.F. = 10. AND    39.

F-RATIO = 21.928     PROBABILITY = 0.0

ROOT 1    100.00PCT. VARIANCE  CHI-SQUARE =    83.181    D.F. = 10.    PROBABILITY = 0.0

UNIVARIATE F-TESTS. DFB = 1. DFN =   48.

   VARIATE        F RATIO  ASSOCIATED PROBABILITY

   VAL. OF    4(OPER)    121.3701    0.0
   VAL. OF    6(STRS)      4.2373    0.0424
   VAL. OF    7(DAY.)      0.0390    0.8385
   VAL. OF    8(TIME)      0.0553    0.8180
   VAL. OF   11(TEMP)      0.1393    0.7117
   VAL. OF   15(H.R.)     42.6748    0.0
   VAL. OF   12(TPCT)     93.1551    0.0
   VAL. OF   16(TCCM)      0.6355    0.5650
   VAL. OF   17(TALL)      1.3784    0.2450
   VAL. OF   18(FRRP)      1.2353    0.2713
```

Figure 7.47 - STMDIS - Output Example - Detailed Output

```
SYSTEM SUBROUTINE MDISC      -   DERIVE DESCRIMINANTS
DATA BANK TITLE              -   DEMONSTRATION STATCAT DATA BANK
DATA BANK SAMPLE SET         -   EASY VS HARD
DATA BANK SUBSET             -   ALL DATA
                             -   SAMPLES AS ORIGINALLY DEFINED
```

DISCRIMINANT SET 1

DISCRIMINANT WEIGHTS

	1
TRANSFORM COLUMN	
VAL. OF 4(OPER)	0.6647
VAL. OF 6(STRS)	0.4851
VAL. OF 7(DAY.)	0.1551
VAL. OF 8(TIME)	-0.0637
VAL. OF 11(TEMP)	-0.0399
VAL. OF 15(H.R.)	0.1750
VAL. OF 12(TPCT)	-0.1617
VAL. OF 16(TCOM)	-0.2551
VAL. OF 17(TALL)	0.2722
VAL. OF 18(ERRP)	0.3115

CORRELATIONS BETWEEN ORIGINAL VARIATES AND DISCRIMINANTS

	1
TRANSFORM COLUMN	
VAL. OF 4(OPER)	0.9137
VAL. OF 6(STRS)	0.3091
VAL. OF 7(DAY.)	0.0309
VAL. OF 8(TIME)	0.0368
VAL. OF 11(TEMP)	-0.0533
VAL. OF 15(H.R.)	0.7455
VAL. OF 12(TPCT)	-0.8817
VAL. OF 16(TCOM)	-0.1241
VAL. OF 17(TALL)	0.1312
VAL. OF 18(ERRP)	0.1719

```
SYSTEM SUBROUTINE MDISC      -   DERIVE DESCRIMINANTS
DATA BANK TITLE              -   DEMONSTRATION STATCAT DATA BANK
DATA BANK SAMPLE SET         -   EASY VS HARD
DATA BANK SUBSET             -   ALL DATA
```

ENTRIES IN SAMPLE

	EASY	HARD
	29.0000	21.0000

SAMPLE MEANS OF ORIGINAL VARIATES

	EASY	HARD
	1	2
TRANSFORM COLUMN		
VAL. OF 4(OPER)	1.6207	3.7143
VAL. OF 6(STRS)	2.1724	2.7619
VAL. OF 7(DAY.)	2.4138	2.4762
VAL. OF 8(TIME)	2.4483	2.5238
VAL. OF 11(TEMP)	25.3448	25.0952
VAL. OF 15(H.R.)	42.3425	53.2666
VAL. OF 12(TPCT)	-2.4445	-12.8257
VAL. OF 16(TCOM)	51.0082	48.5654
VAL. OF 17(TALL)	52.1034	55.4762
VAL. OF 18(ERRP)	0.9310	1.2571

SAMPLE S.D.S OF ORIGINAL VARIATES

	EASY	HARD
	1	2
TRANSFORM COLUMN		
VAL. OF 4(OPER)	0.7277	0.5606
VAL. OF 6(STRS)	1.0025	0.9952
VAL. OF 7(DAY.)	1.0528	1.1670
VAL. OF 8(TIME)	1.0885	1.1670
VAL. OF 11(TEMP)	2.5813	1.9471
VAL. OF 15(H.R.)	4.8135	6.9945
VAL. OF 12(TPCT)	3.3646	4.2350
VAL. OF 16(TCOM)	10.5089	10.8952
VAL. OF 17(TALL)	9.3899	10.8657
VAL. OF 18(ERRP)	0.7512	1.3140

DISCRIMINANT SET 1

SAMPLE MEANS OF DISCRIMINANTS

	EASY	HARD
DISCRIMINANT 1	10.6237	17.5545

SAMPLE S.D.S OF DISCRIMINANTS

	EASY	HARD
DISCRIMINANT 1	1.4190	1.5438

```
SYSTEM SUBROUTINE MDSWE      -   (RE-)ALLOCATE ENTRIES
DATA BANK TITLE              -   DEMONSTRATION STATCAT DATA BANK
DATA BANK SAMPLE SET         -   EASY VS HARD
DATA BANK SUBSET             -   ALL DATA
```

CHANGES FROM SAMPLES AS DEFINED TO DISCRIMINANT SET 1

TOTAL NUMBER OF CHANGES =   14

Figure 7.48 - STMDIS - Output Example - Typical Entries

```
SYSTEM SUBROUTINE MDSWE       -    (RE-)ALLOCATE ENTRIES
DATA BANK TITLE               -    DEMONSTRATION STATCAT DATA BANK
DATA BANK SAMPLE SET          -    EASY VS HARD
DATA BANK SUBSET              -    ALL DATA

CHANGES FROM SAMPLES AS DEFINED  TO DISCRIMINANT SET  1

DISCRIMINANT NUMBER      1

   VARIATES           VAL. OF    VAL. OF    VAL. OF    VAL. OF
   SELECTED           OPER(  4)STKS(  6)TPCT( 12)H.R.( 15)

   DATA COLUMN         1 = NTRY   2 = SESS   3 = OBSR   4 = OPER   5 = W.P.   6 = STRS   7 = DAY.   8 = TIME   9 = TASK  10 = DIFF
                      11 = TEMP  12 = TPCT  13 = EFOP  14 = EFCB  15 = H.R.  16 = TCCM  17 = TALL  18 = ERRP
----------------------------------------------------------------------------------------------------------------------------------
ENTRY     58 NOT IN ANY SAMPLE                           MOVED TO SAMPLE  2 (HARD) P = 0.026345 FORCED CHOICE P=  0.621854

SAMPLE PROBABILITY    EASY       HARD
   INDEPENDENT      0.016020   0.026345
   FORCED CHOICE    0.378145   0.621854

DISCRIMINANT SCORES    12.0771

       VARIATE VALUES    3.0000     2.0000    -5.8900    50.6200

       DATA ITEMS       58.0000    15.0000     2.0000     3.0000     2.0000     2.0000     4.0000     3.0000     4.0000     4.0000
                        26.0000    -5.8900    60.9000    83.3400    50.6200    67.9000    72.0000     0.4000
----------------------------------------------------------------------------------------------------------------------------------
ENTRY     64 NOT IN ANY SAMPLE                           MOVED TO SAMPLE  2 (HARD) P = 0.031596 FORCED CHOICE P=  0.704113

SAMPLE PROBABILITY    EASY       HARD
   INDEPENDENT      0.013278   0.031596
   FORCED CHOICE    0.295887   0.704113

DISCRIMINANT SCORES    12.7669

       VARIATE VALUES    2.0000     4.0000    -5.9800    49.9700

       DATA ITEMS       64.0000    16.0000     2.0000     2.0000     4.0000     4.0000     4.0000     4.0000     2.0000     4.0000
                        24.0000    -5.9800    55.4900    72.9400    49.9700    43.2600    48.0000     1.5000

       TOTAL NUMBER OF CHANGES =    14
```

```
C     MASTER STMDIS - GENERALISED MULTIPLE DISCRIMINANT ANALYSIS
C          SUBROUTINES AND FUNCTIONS REQUIRED
C    AN      (SEE  3.1 ) SERVICE      ALPHA - TO NUMERIC VALUE
C    ASEV    (SEE  7.5 ) SERVICE      EIGEN ROOTS ETC ASYMMETRIC MATRIX
C    CHIKEN  (SEE 11.9 ) SERVICE      WARNS OF MISMATCHED DATA LEVEL
C    CLENT   (SEE  8.1 ) SERVICE      FINDS PROB. ENTRY IS IN SAMPLES
C    CLSAM   (SEE  3.5 ) SERVICE      ALLOTS ENTRY TO SAMPLE/SUBSET
C    CMDIS   (SEE  7.4 ) EXECUTIVE    MULTIPLE DISCRIMINANT ANALYSIS
C    COMPA   (SEE  3.1 ) SERVICE      COMPARES ALPHAMERIC VALUES
C    COPYA   (SEE  3.1 ) SERVICE      COPIES ALPHAMERIC VALUE
C    FIFI    (SEE  3.2 ) SYSTEM       ALLOCATES PERIPHERALS
C    GAUS    (SEE 11.8 ) STATISTICAL  FINDS ASS. PROB. OF N VALUE
C    IBL     (SEE  3.1 ) SERVICE      DETECTS BLANK,END AND STOP CARDS
C    ICH     (SEE  3.1 ) SERVICE      IDENTIFIES ALPHAMERIC CODES
C    LCOM    (SEE  3.4 ) SERVICE      LOADS COMPLEMENTARY INFORMATION
C    LDAP    (SEE  3.3 ) SYSTEM       LOADS/CHECKS DATA BANK PARAMETERS
C    LDBS    (SEE  3.6 ) SYSTEM       LOADS SUBSET DEFINITION
C    LDDS    (SEE  3.4 ) SYSTEM       LOADS DATA DESCRIPTION SEGMENT
C    LDHI    (SEE  3.8 ) SYSTEM       LOADS/CHECKS DATA HANDLING INSTN
C    LGEN    (SEE  3.7 ) SYSTEM       LOADS GENERALISED VARIATES
C    LSAMP   (SEE  3.5 ) SYSTEM       LOADS SAMPLE SET DEFINITION
C    LSET    (SEE  3.5 ) SYSTEM       LOADS DEFINING CONDITIONS
C    MATM    (SEE 11.3 ) SERVICE      MULTIPLIES MATRICES
C    MDISC   (SEE  7.4 ) SYSTEM       MULTIPLE DISCRIMINANT ANALYSIS
C    MDSWE   (SEE  7.4 ) SYSTEM       CLASSIFIES ENTRIES IN MULT DISC  ANAL
C    MEDIAT  (SEE  3.7 ) SERVICE      FETCHES NEXT VARIATE SET
C    MINV    (SEE 11.3 ) SERVICE      INVERTS MATRIX
C    MOP     (SEE 11.3 ) SERVICE      SELECTS/CONVERTS STORED MATRIX
C    PRBF    (SEE 11.8 ) STATISTICAL  FINDS PROBABILITY OF F-RATIO
C    TRANS   (SEE  3.7 ) SERVICE      CARRIES OUT REQUIRED TRANSFORM
C    WDCD    (SEE  3.4 ) SERVICE      WRITES DATA COLUMN DESCRIPTION
C    WMAT    (SEE 11.3 ) SERVICE      WRITE MATRIX WITH VARIATE TITLES
C     SETTING OF ARRAY DIMENSIONS
C     THE FOLLOWING DIMENSIONS MUST BE AT LEAST AS BIG AS THOSE
C     SPECIFIED BY THE DATA TAPE,SAMPLE SPECIFICATIONS,ETC.
C     NQMAX = MAXIMUM NUMBER OF DATA COLUMNS
C     IF NQMAX AND ARRAYS ARE CHANGED,CHANGE DATA STATEMENT FOR CN
C     DIMENSION XX(NQMAX),IT(NQMAX),ST(NQMAX),CN(NQMAX)
      NQMAX = 100
      DIMENSION XX( 100),IT( 100),ST( 100),CN( 100)
      DATA  CN/4HCOL1,4HCOL2,4HCOL3,4HCOL4,4HCOL5,4HCOL6,4HCOL7,4HCOL8,4
     1HCOL9,4HCL10,4HCL11,4HCL12,4HCL13,4HCL14,4HCL15,4HCL16,4HCL17,4HC
     2L18,4HCL19,4HCL20,4HCL21,4HCL22,4HCL23,4HCL24,4HCL25,4HCL26,4HCL27,
     34HCL28,4HCL29,4HCL30,4HCL31,4HCL32,4HCL33,4HCL34,4HCL35,4HCL36,4HC
     4L37,4HCL38,4HCL39,4HCL40,4HCL41,4HCL42,4HCL43,4HCL44,4HCL45,4HCL46
     5,4HCL47,4HCL48,4HCL49,4HCL50,4HCL51,4HCL52,4HCL53,4HCL54,4HCL55,4H
     6CL56,4HCL57,4HCL58,4HCL59,4HCL60,4HCL61,4HCL62,4HCL63,4HCL64,4HCL6
     75,4HCL66,4HCL67,4HCL68,4HCL69,4HCL70,4HCL71,4HCL72,4HCL73,4HCL74,4
     8HCL75,4HCL76,4HCL77,4HCL78,4HCL79,4HCL80,4HCL81,4HCL82,4HCL83,4HCL
     984,4HCL85,4HCL86,4HCL87,4HCL88,4HCL89,4HCL90,4HCL91,4HCL92,4HCL93,
     94HCL94,4HCL95,4HCL96,4HCL97,4HCL98,4HCL99,4HC100/
C     DIMENSION NDP(MAXMI),NP(MAXMI) MAXMI = MAX VARIATES IN ANY SWEEP
      MAXMI = 50
      DIMENSION NDP(50),NP(50)
C     DIMENSION ISAVE(MAXKI),IX(MAXKI),IY(MAXKI)= MAX VARIATES IN ANALYSIS
      MAXKI = 50
      DIMENSION ISAVE( 50),IX( 50),IY( 50)
C     MAXAV = GENERAL STORE FOR CORRELATION MATRIX AND ANALYSIS
C     MUST BE AT LEAST NS*(M+2) + (NS+1)*(M+1)*M/2 + K*(4+3*K)
C     WHERE K = NUMBER OF VARIATES IN ANY ANALYSIS       MINIMUM = 1
C     WHERE M = NUMBER OF VARIATES IN STORE              MINIMUM = 1
C     WHERE NS= NUMBER OF SAMPLES IN USE                 MINIMUM = 2
C     DIMENSION R(MAXAV)
```

```
      MAXAV = 2000
      DIMENSION R(2000)
C DIMENSION D(MAXD) WHERE MAXD = STORAGE FOR DELAYED ENTRIES
C     (MAXIMUM DELAY + 3.) * M MUST NOT EXCEED MAXD
C DIMENSION D(MAXD) IF MAXD NOT ZERO
      MAXD = 500
      DIMENSION D(500)
C DIMENSION TRT(NALTMX) WHERE NALTMX = MAXIMUM NUMBER OF CLS FROM INPUT
      NALTMX = 50
      DIMENSION TRT(50)
C DIMENSION SCON(5,MAXDBC) MAXDBC= MAXIMUM CONDITIONS (SAMPLE + SUBSET)
      MAXDBC = 100
      DIMENSION SCON(5,100)
C THE FOLLOWING DIMENSION STORES THE NAMES OF THE DATA TRANSFORMS
C AND THE ACCEPTABLE LEVELS FOR TRANSFORMATIONS
      DIMENSION U(60),LU(60)
      NU = 60
C TRANSFORMATION CODES
C UNITS                       BLOCKS
C       0 - 9   10 - 19   20 - 29   30 - 39   40 - 49   50 - 59
C       POWERS  TRIG      TRIG      STATIST   MATHS     TEST
C               RADIANS   DEGREES   TRANSF    FUNCTS    FUNCTIONS
C  0     -       -         H.MS      -         -         RM10
C  1    VAL.    SINR      SIND      PSNA      RECP      +/-1
C  2    SQAR    COSR      COSD      PSNB      SQRT      ADD1
C  3    CUBE    TANR      TAND      BINO      ABSV      SUB1
C  4    4PWR    ASIR      ASID      LG+1      SIGN      NOR1
C  5    5PWR    ACOR      ACOD      LOGE      INTG      +/-P
C  6    6PWR    ATAR      ATAD      LG10      FRAC      ADDP
C  7    7PWR    SINH      DTOR      AL10      EXPT      SUBP
C  8    8PWR    COSH      RTOD      -         PRES      NORP
C  9    9PWR    TANH      H.HH      -         NEG.      +100
      DATA U/4HVAL.,4HSQAR,4HCUBE,4H4PWR,4H5PWR,4H6PWR,4H7PWR,4H8PWR,4H9
     1PWR,4HVAL ,4HSINR,4HCOSR,4HTANR,4HASIR,4HACOR,4HATAR,4HSINH,4HCOSH
     2,4HTANH,4HH.MS,4HSIND,4HCOSD,4HTAND,4HASID,4HACOD,4HATAD,4HDTOR,4H
     3RTOD,4HH.HH,4H VAL,4HPSNA,4HPSNB,4HBINO,4HLG+1,4HLOGE,4HLG10,4HAL1
     40,4HPWR   ,4H    ,4H    ,4HRECP,4HSQRT,4HABSV,4HSIGN,4HINTG,4HFRAC,4
     5HEXPT,4HPRES,4HNEG.,4HRM10,4H+/-1,4HADD1,4HSUB1,4HNOR1,4H+/-P,4HAD
     6DP,4HSUBP,4HNORP,4H+100,4H    /
C ACCEPTABLE CODE LEVELS
      DATA LU/60*4/
C DUMMY ARRAYS USED IN LGEN + D.H.I INPUT ARRAY
      DIMENSION FORM(80)
      COMMON /STCT/MED1,MED2,MED3,MED4,MED5,MED6,MED13,Q,V(20),TT(30)
      DATA PROG/4HMDIS/
      MED1 = -1
C LEVEL 0 - SETTING UP
    1 CALL COPYA(TT(1),PROG)
      CALL FIFI
      IF(MED3.GT.0) WRITE(MED2,901)
      CALL LDAP(MED2,MED3,V,TT,Q,NQ,NALT,NQMAX,NALTMX,IGO)
      IF(IGO.GT.0) GO TO 1
      LI = 18
      CALL LDDS(TRT,NALT,D,NQ,ST,NQ,IT,NQ,H,0,H,H,0,LI,0,Q,VX,
     1 0,MED2,MED3,0,IGO)
      IF(IGO.GT.0) GO TO 1
C LEVEL 1 - READ SAMPLE SPECIFICATION
   11 IF(V(10).GE.10.) V(10) = 0.
      NSMAX = (2*MAXAV-17)/5
      CALL LSAMP(SCON,NCON,MAXDBC,R,NS,NSMAX,CM,ST,IT,NQ,TRT,NALT,IGO)
      IF(IGO.GT.0) GO TO 1
      IF(V(10).LT.0.5.AND.V(20).GT.0.5) V(10) = 11.
      IF(V(10).LT.0.5.AND.NS.LT.2)      V(10) = 12.
```

```
      IF(NS.LT.2) WRITE(MED2,911)
C LEVEL 2 - READ DATA BANK SUBSET
   21 IF(V(10).GE.20.) V(10) = 0.
      MAXLEF = MAXDBC-NCON
      NCON1 = NCON+1
      CALL LDBS(SCON(1,NCON1),NCONB,MAXLEF,CN,ST,IT,NQ,TRT,NALT,IGO)
      IF(IGO.GT.0) GO TO 11
      ARAN = 5236.
C LEVEL 4 - READ SET OF VARIATES FOR DATA SWEEP
   41 IF(V(10).GE.40.) V(10) = 0.
      M = 0
      WRITE(MED6,941)
      WRITE(MED6,944)
      A = NS + 1
      B = NS + 5
      C = 4*NS+14-2*MAXAV
      MAXM = (SQRT(B*B-4.*A*C)-B)/A*0.5
      IF(MAXM.GT.MAXMI) MAXM = MAXMI
      CALL LGEN(U,NU,LU,NU,ST,IT,CN,NQ,IH,0,H,H,0,H,H,0,MAXD,NALT,NDP,NP
     1,MAXM,M,MAXM,1,NALT)
      IF(V(11).LT.0.5.AND.V(20).LT.0.5)GO TO 21
      BRAN = ARAN
C LEVEL 5 - READ PREDICTOR VARIATES
   51 IF(V(10).GT.50.) V(10) = 0.
      WRITE(MED6,951)
      WRITE(MED6,944)
      NPV = 0
      C = 2*M + (NS+1)*(M+1)*M/2 + 2*(M+NS) - MAXAV
         MX = (SQRT(4.-3.*C)-1.)/3.
      IF(MX.GT.MAXKI)MX = MAXKI
      CALL LGEN(U,NU,LU,NU,ST,IT,CN,NQ,IH,0,H,H,0,H,H,0,MAXD,0,IX,IY,MX,
     1NPV,MX,1,NALT)
      IF(V(11).LT.0.5.AND.V(20).LT.0.5)GO TO 41
      IF(V(10).LT.0.5.AND.V(20).GT.0.5) V(10) = 55.
      IF(NPV.LT.1) GO TO 54
C STORE AS NUMBERS IN VARIATE SET - ADD IF MISSING
      KM = 0
      C = J*NS + (3*K+4)*K - MAXAV
      IF(MAXM.GT.MAXMI) MAXM = MAXMI
      DO 53 J = 1,NPV
      DO 52 L = 1,M
      IF(IX(J).NE.NDP(L).OR.IY(J).NE.NP(L)) GO TO 52
      ISAVE(J) = L
      GO TO 53
   52 CONTINUE
      V(19) = V(19) + 2.
      IF(V(19).GT.50.) WRITE(MED2,950)
      IF(V(19).GT.50.) V(19) = 2.
      WRITE(MED2,952) J
      IF(MAXM.EQ.M) WRITE(MED6,954)
      IF(MAXM.EQ.M) KM = KM + 1
      IF(MAXM.EQ.M) GO TO 53
      WRITE(MED2,953)
      M = M + 1
      NDP(M) = IX(J)
      NP(M) = IY(J)
      ISAVE(J) = M
      V(6) = 0.
      BRAN = ARAN
   53 CONTINUE
      NPV = NPV - KM
   54 IF(NPV.EQ.0.AND.V(10).LT.0.5) V(10) = 53.
C LEVEL 9 - READ DATA HANDLING INSTRUCTION
```

```
   91 IF(V(10).GT.90.) V(10) = 0.
      IF(V(19).GT.30.) WRITE(MED6,991) TT
      CALL LDHI(V(1),1,V(2),2,VX,7,V(3),11,V(4),16,H,0,V7,V(10),
     1 FORM(41),FORM,MED1,MED2,0,Q,NQ,NWARN,1,IGO)
      IF(IGO.GT.0) GO TO 51
C STANDARDISATION
      NWARN = 0
      FMAX = NPV
      IF(NS.LE.NPV) FMAX = NS - 1
      IF(V(3).EQ.0..AND.V(4).EQ.0.) NWARN = NWARN + 1
      IF(V(3).EQ.0..AND.V(4).EQ.0.) V(4) = 1.
      IF(V(3).EQ.0.) NWARN = NWARN + 1
      IF(V(3).GT.FMAX) NWARN = NWARN + 1
      IF(V(3).EQ.0.) V(3) = FMAX
      IF(V(3).GT.FMAX) V(3) = FMAX
C MAXIMUM NUMBER OF MISSING VALUES
      IF(V(6).EQ.0.) V(9) = VX
      IF(VX.NE.V(9).AND.VX.NE.0.) V(6) = 0.
      IF(VX.NE.V(9).AND.VX.NE.0.) V(9) = VX
C CHECK STORAGE AVAILABLE
      MDIAG = (NS+1)*(M+1)*M/2 + NS*(M+2)
      MXM = NPV*(4+3*NPV)
      IF(MXM+MDIAG.LE.MAXAV) GO TO 92
      WRITE(MED6,992) MDIAG,MXM,MAXAV
      IF(V(10).LT.0.5) V(10) = 91.
   92 CALL LDHI(V(1),1,V(2),2,V(9),7,V(3),11,V(4),16,H,0,V7,V(10),
     1 FORM(41),FORM,MED1,MED2,0,Q,NQ,NWARN,2,IGO)
      IF(IGO.GT.0) GO TO 91
      V(4) = V(4)*.01
      WRITE(MED6,998)
      MDIAG = M*(M+1)/2
      MDNS = MDIAG*NS
      MNS = M*NS
      K1 = NS
      IF(K1.LT.NPV) K1 = NPV
      KXK = K1*NPV
      IT1 = NS+1
      IC = IT1 + NS
      IA = IC + MDIAG
      IXS = IA + MDNS
      IXB = IXS + MNS
      IE = IXB + M
      IX1 = IE + NPV
      JY = IX1 + K1
      IZ = JY + NPV
      IRA = IZ + NPV
      IRW = IRA + KXK
      IRC = IRW + KXK
      V(10) = BRAN
      CALL CMDIS(R(IA),R(IC),D,ISAVE,IX,IY,NDP,NP,R(IRA),R(IRC),R(IRW),S
     1CON,SCON(1,NCON1),R(IP1),R(IX1),R(IXB),R(IXS),XX,R(JY),R(IZ),NPV,K
     2XK,M,MDIAG,MAXD,NCON,NCONB,NQ,NS,R(IE),ST,B,U,NU,K1)
      ARAN = V(10)
      V(10) = 0.
      WRITE(MED6,999)
      GO TO 91
  901 FORMAT (1H0,20X,46HSTATCAT GENERAL MULTIPLE DISCRIMINANT ANALYSIS)
  911 FORMAT(31H0 AT LEAST TWO SAMPLES REQUIRED)
  941 FORMAT (1H1,10X,30HSET OF VARIATES FOR DATA SWEEP/)
  944 FORMAT(7H0NUMBER,6X,19HTRANS   DATA   CYCLES/5H CODE,8X,18H-FORM COL
     1UMN DELAY,66X,7HCOMMENT)
  950 FORMAT (41H1ORIGINAL VARIATES NOT IN SET OF VARIATES)
  951 FORMAT(44H1ORIGINAL VARIATES FOR DISCRIMINANT ANALYSIS/)
```

```
      952 FORMAT (15H0VARIATE NUMBER,I4,30H IS NOT IN THE SET OF VARIATES)
      953 FORMAT(1H+,50X,33H- ADDED (NEW DATA SWEEP REQUIRED))
      954 FORMAT (1H+,50X,26H-NOT ADDED - NO MORE SPACE)
      961 FORMAT (1H1,10X,18HPREDICTOR VARIATES/)
      962 FORMAT (10H0PREDICTOR,I4,33H IS THE SAME AS PREDICTED VARIATE,I4)
      963 FORMAT (8H0WARNING/35H THE CURRENT NUMBER OF PREDICTORS ( ,I4,51H
         1) IS LESS THAN THE NUMBER OF PREDICTED VARIABLES ( ,I4,2H )/
         277H THEY WILL BE INTERCHANGED FOR COMPUTATION - THIS WILL NOT AFFE
         2CT THE RESULTS)
      991 FORMAT(23H1STATCAT PROGRAM STMDIS,7X,1H-,4X,30HMULTIPLE DISCRIMINA
         1NT ANALYSIS/16H DATA BANK TITLE,14X,1H-,4X,10A4/21H DATA BANK SAMP
         2LE SET,9X,1H-,4X,10A4/17H DATA BANK SUBSET,13X,1H-,4X,10A4)
      992 FORMAT(29H0 CORRELATION MATRIX REQUIRES,I6,6H CELLS/21H       ANALYSI
         1S REQUIRES,I6,6H CELLS/6H0 ONLY,I6,27H AVAILABLE - INCREASE MAXAV)
      998 FORMAT (36H0INPUT ACCEPTED - ANALYSIS COMMENCES)
      999 FORMAT (36H1ANALYSIS COMPLETED - READ NEW INPUT)
          END



          SUBROUTINE CMDIS(A,C,D,ISAVE,IX,IY,NDP,NP,RA,RC,RW,SACON,SCON,T,X,
         1XBAR,XSAM,XX,Y,Z,K,KXK,M,MDIAG,MN,NACON,NCON,NQ,NS,E,ST,TRTC,U,NU,
         2K1)
    C CMDIS   (SEE  7.4 ) EXECUTIVE    MULTIPLE DISCRIMINANT ANALYSIS
          DIMENSION XBAR(M),T(NS),XSAM(M,NS),C(MDIAG),A(MDIAG,NS),TRTC(NS)
          DIMENSION XX(NQ),NDP(M),NP(M),D(MN),ST(NQ)
          DIMENSION SCON(5,NCON),SACON(5,NACON),U(NU)
          DIMENSION RW(KXK),RA(KXK),RC(KXK),X(K1),H(1)
          DIMENSION IX(M),ISAVE(M),IY(M),E(M),Y(M),Z(M)
          COMMON /STCT/MED1,MED2,MED3,MED4,MED5,MED6,MED13,Q,V(20),TT(30)
          REWIND MED3
          V(19) = NS
          NRUN = -1
          NT = 0
        1 CALL MDSWE(A,C,D,ISAVE,IX,IY,NDP,NP,RA,RC,RW,SACON,SCON,T,X,XBAR,
         1XSAM,XX,Y,Z,H,H,H,H,H,K,KXK,M,MDIAG,MN,NACON,NCON,NQ,NS,E,ST,TRTC,
         2U,NU,K1,NRUN,NXO,NP,KP,NSP,1,1,1,NT)
          IF(NRUN.EQ.NT) RETURN
          CALL MDISC(A,C,D,ISAVE,IX,IY,NDP,NP,RA,RC,RW,T,X,XBAR,XSAM,XX,Y,Z,
         1K,KXK,M,MDIAG,MN,NQ,NS,E,ST,TRTC,U,NU,K1,NRUN,NMT,NP,KP,NSP)
          IF(NMT.GE.NS-1.OR.NP.EQ.0) RETURN
          NRUN = NRUN + 1
          GO TO 1
          END



          SUBROUTINE MDISC(A,C,D,ISAVE,IX,IY,NDP,NP,RA,RC,RW,T,X,XBAR,XSAM,X
         1X,Y,Z,K,KXK,M,MDIAG,MN,NQ,NS,E,ST,TRTC,U,NU,K1,NRUN,NMT,NP,KP,NSP)
    C MDISC   (SEE  7.4 ) SYSTEM      CARRIES OUT MULTIPLE DISCRIMINANT ANAL.
          DIMENSION XBAR(M),T(NS),XSAM(M,NS),C(MDIAG),A(MDIAG,NS),TRTC(NS)
          DIMENSION XX(NQ),NDP(M),NP(M),D(MN),ST(NQ),U(NU)
          DIMENSION RW(KXK),RA(KXK),RC(KXK),X(K1)
          DIMENSION IX(M),ISAVE(M),IY(M),E(M),Y(M),Z(M)
          COMMON /STCT/MED1,MED2,MED3,MED4,MED5,MED6,MED13,Q,V(20),TT(30)
          KB = V(2)
          IF(KB.LE.5)KC = 0
          IF(KB.GE.6)KC = 1
          IF(KB.GE.8)KC = 2
          IF(KB.EQ.6.OR.KB.EQ.8) KB = 0
          IF(KB.EQ.7.OR.KB.EQ.9) KB = 3
          KA = V(1)
          IF(KA .EQ.8) KA = 3
          IF(KA .EQ.9) KA = 7
          NPMAX = V(3)
```

```
      NF = NFMAX
      KF = K*NF
      NSF = NS*NF
      NR1 = NRUN + 1
      NR2 = NRUN + 2
C SAMPLE MEANS AND OVERALL MEANS
      V(6) = 0.
      NMT = 0
      DO 5 I = 1,NS
      IF(T(I).GT.0.5) GO TO 5
      NMT = NMT + 1
      IF(NMT.EQ.1)WRITE(MED2,901) TT
      IF(KC.GE.1) WRITE(MED2,909)
      IF(KC.EQ.2) WRITE(MED2,910)
      WRITE(MED2,905)I,TRTC(I)
    5 V(6) = V(6) + T(I)
C   RETURN IF ONLY ONE SAMPLE LEFT
      IF(NMT.GE.NS-1) WRITE(MED2,915)
      IF(NMT.GE.NS-1) RETURN
      DO 15 I = 1,M
      XBAR(I) = 0.
      DO 10 KS = 1,NS
      XBAR(I) = XBAR(I) + XSAM(I,KS)
      IF(T(KS).LT.0.5) GO TO 10
      XSAM(I,KS) = XSAM(I,KS)/T(KS)
   10 CONTINUE
   15 IF(V(6).GT.0.5) XBAR(I) = XBAR(I)/V(6)
C FORM SQUARE COVARIANCE MATRICES
      NDEL = 0
      DO 25 INDX = 1,K
      I = ISAVE(INDX)
      IF(NDP(I).GT.0) NDEL = 1
      DO 25 INDY = INDX,K
      J = ISAVE(INDY)
      IF(I.GE.J) IJ = I + (J-1)*(2*M-J)/2
      IF(I.LT.J) IJ = J + (I-1)*(2*M-I)/2
      IJ1 = (INDX-1)*K + INDY
      IJ2 = (INDY-1)*K + INDX
      RC(IJ1) = 0.
      RW(IJ1) = 0.
      DO 20 KS = 1,NS
      RC(IJ1) = RC(IJ1) + A(IJ,KS)
   20 RW(IJ1) = RW(IJ1) -XSAM(I,KS)*XSAM(J,KS)*T(KS)
      RW(IJ1) = RW(IJ1) + RC(IJ1)
      RC(IJ1) = RC(IJ1)/V(6) - XBAR(I)*XBAR(J)
      RA(IJ1) = RC(IJ1)*V(6) - RW(IJ1)
      RA(IJ2) = RA(IJ1)
      RC(IJ2) = RC(IJ1)
   25 RW(IJ2) = RW(IJ1)
      IF(KC.EQ.0) GO TO 28
      L = 0
      DO 26 I = 1,K
      DO 26 J = 1,K
      L = L + 1
   26 IF(I.NE.J)RC(L) = 0.
   28 IF(KA.LT.2) GO TO 30
      WRITE(MED2,901) TT
      IF(KC.GE.1) WRITE(MED2,909)
      IF(KC.EQ.2) WRITE(MED2,910)
      IF(NRUN.LT.0) WRITE(MED2,906)
      IF(NRUN.GE.0) WRITE(MED2,907) NR1
      WRITE(MED2,902)
      CALL WMAT(RC,K,K,KXK,NP,NDP,M,ST,NQ,ISAVE,ISAVE,U,NU,MED2)
```

```
      IF(K.GT.19) WRITE(MED2,901) TT
      IF(KC.GE.1.AND.K.GT.19) WRITE(MED2,909)
      IF(KC.EQ.2.AND.K.GT.19) WRITE(MED2,910)
      WRITE(MED2,903)
      CALL WMAT(RA,K,K,KXK,NP,NDP,M,ST,NQ,ISAVE,ISAVE,U,NU,MED2)
      IF(K.GT.10) WRITE(MED2,901) TT
      IF(KC.GE.1.AND.K.GT.10) WRITE(MED2,909)
      IF(KC.EQ.2.AND.K.GT.10) WRITE(MED2,910)
      WRITE(MED2,904)
      CALL WMAT(RW,K,K,KXK,NP,NDP,M,ST,NQ,ISAVE,ISAVE,U,NU,MED2)
   30 KS = K*NS
      TN = V(6)
C COMPUTE AND FACTOR W-1 A
      CALL MINV   (RW,K,DET,IX,IY,KXK)
      DO 40 I = 1,K
      DO 35 J = 1,K
      INDX = (J-1)*K + I
   35 X(J) = RW(INDX)
      DO 40 J = 1,K
      INDX = (J-1)*K + I
      RW(INDX) = 0.
      DO 40 L = 1,K
      INDY = (J-1)*K + L
   40 RW(INDX) = RW(INDX) + X(L)*RA(INDY)
      NF = NS-1-NMT
      IF(NF.GT.K) NF = K
      KF = K*NF
      CALL ASEV(RW,0.,E,K,KF,KXK,NF,RA,X,Y,Z)
      VN = K
      SN = NS-NMT
      SM = SN -1.
      SS = SQRT((VN*VN*SM*SM-4.)/(VN*VN+SM*SM-5.))
      FA = VN*SM
      FB =((TN-1.)-(VN+SN)/2.)*SS - (VN*SM-2.)/2.
      TR = 0.
      DO 45 I = 1,NF
   45 TR = TR + E(I)
      XL = 1.
      DO 50 I = 1,NF
      XL = XL/(1.+E(I))
   50 X(I) = E(I)/TR*100.
      NFX = NF
      IF(KB.EQ.0) GO TO 75
      IF(KB.GT.2) GO TO 65
C WILKS LAMBDA FOR OVERALL SIGNIFICANCE OF DIFFERENCES
   55 PLAST = 1.
      DO 60 I1 = 1,NF
      YY = XL**(1./SS)
      F = (FB*(1.-YY))/(YY*FA)
      P = PRBF(FA,FB,F)
      IF(KB.EQ.1.AND.P.GT.V(4)) GO TO 75
      IF(KB.EQ.2.AND.PLAST.LT.1.0.AND.PLAST-P.GT.V(4)) GO TO 75
      PLAST = P
      XL = XL*(1.+E(NFX))
   60 NFX = NFX - 1
      GO TO 75
C INDIVIDUAL PROBABILITIES AND VARIANCE
   65 DF = VN + SN
      CC = TN - DF/2.
      VL = 0.
      DO 70 I1 = 1,NF
      I = NF + 1 - I1
      CS = CC*ALOG(1.+E(I))
```

```
              DF = DF-2.
              P = PRBF(DF,1000.,CS/DF)
              VL = VL + X(I)
              IF(KB.EQ.3.AND.P.LT.V(4)) GO TO 75
              IF(KB.EQ.4.AND.VL.GT.V(4)*100.) GO TO 75
              IF(KB.EQ.5.AND.X(I).GT.V(4)*100.) GO TO 75
           70 NFX = NFX - 1
           75 NF = NFX
              IF(NF.GT.NFMAX) NF = NFMAX
              IF(NF.EQ.0) WRITE(MED2,999)
              IF(NF.EQ.0) RETURN
C COMPUTE WILK'S LAMBDA
              WRITE(MED2,901) TT
              IF(KC.GE.1) WRITE(MED2,909)
              IF(KC.EQ.2) WRITE(MED2,910)
              IF(NRUN.LT.0) WRITE(MED2,906)
              IF(NRUN.GE.0) WRITE(MED2,907) NR1
              XL = 1.
              DO 80 I = 1,NF
           80 XL = XL/(1.+E(I))
              YY = XL**(1./SS)
              F = (FB*(1.-YY))/(YY*FA)
              P = PRBF(FA,FB,F)
              WRITE(MED2,985) XL,FA,FB,F,P
C COMPUTE CHI-SQUARED TESTS AND PROBABILITIES
              DF = VM + SN
              CC = TN - DF/2.
              DO 85 I = 1,NF
              CS = CC*ALOG(1.+E(I))
              DF = DF-2.
              P = PRBF(DF,1000.,CS/DF)
           85 WRITE(MED2,990) I,X(I),CS,DF,P
C UNIVARIATE ANALYSIS OF VARIANCE
              DFW = V(6) - SN
              WRITE(MED2,986) SM,DFW
              DO 95 L = 1,K
              I = ISAVE(L)
              INDX = I + (2*M-I)*(I-1)/2
              B = 0.
              FB = 0.
              DO 90 J = 1,NS
              FB = FB + A(INDX,J)
           90 B = B + XSAM(I,J)*XSAM(I,J)*T(J)
              CF = XBAR(I)*XBAR(I)*V(6)
              FB = (B-CF)/(FB-B)*DFW/SM
              P = PRBF(SM,DFW,FB)
              INDS = NP(I)/1000
              INDF = NP(I)-INDS*1000
              IF(INDS.EQ.0) INDS = 25
           95 WRITE(MED2,920) U(INDS),INDF,ST(INDF),FB,P
C CALCULATE DISCRIMINANT WEIGHTS
              INDX = 0.
              DO 100 J = 1,NF
              X1 = 1./SQRT(E(J))
              DO 100 I = 1,K
              INDX = INDX + 1
          100 RA(INDX) = RA(INDX)*X1
C CALCULATE CORRELATIONS BETWEEN DISCRIMINANT AND ORIGINAL VARIATES
              INDX = -K
              DO 105 I = 1,K
              INDX = INDX + K + 1
          105 X(I) = SQRT(RC(INDX))
              CALL MATM(RC,RA,RW,K,K,NF,KXK,KF,KF)
```

```
      DO 115 I = 1,NF
      Y(I) = 0.
      DO 110 J = 1,K
      INDX = (I-1)*K + J
  110 Y(I) = Y(I) +RA(INDX)*RW(INDX)
  115 Y(I) = SQRT(Y(I))
      INDX = 0
      DO 120 J = 1,NF
      DO 120 I = 1,K
      INDX = INDX + 1
  120 RC(INDX) = RW(INDX)/(X(I)*Y(J))
C OUTPUT DISCRIMINANT WEIGHTS
      IX(1) = 0
      WRITE(MED2,901) TT
      IF(KC.GE.1) WRITE(MED2,909)
      IF(KC.EQ.2) WRITE(MED2,910)
      IF(NRUN.LT.0) WRITE(MED2,906)
      IF(NRUN.GE.0) WRITE(MED2,907) NR1
      WRITE(MED2,908) NR2
      WRITE(MED2,950)
      ISAVE(1) = - ISAVE(1)
      CALL WMAT(RA,NF,K,KF,NP,NDP,M,ST,NQ,IX,ISAVE,U,NU,MED2)
C OUTPUT CORRELATION MATRIX
      WRITE(MED2,951)
      CALL WMAT (RC,NF,K,KF,NP,NDP,M,ST,NQ,IX,ISAVE,U,NU,MED2)
      ISAVE(1) =-ISAVE(1)
C COMPUTE MEANS AND S.D.S OF SAMPLES FOR ORIGINAL VARIATES
      WRITE(MED2,901) TT
      IF(KC.GE.1) WRITE(MED2,909)
      IF(KC.EQ.2) WRITE(MED2,910)
      WRITE(MED2,996)
      WRITE(MED2,995) TRTC
      WRITE(MED2,998) T
      INDX = 0
      DO 125 L = 1,K
      I = ISAVE(L)
      DO 125 J = 1,NS
      INDX = INDX + 1
      INDS = I + (I-1)*(2*M-I)/2
      RW(INDX) = 0.00001
      IF(T(J).GT.1.)
     1RW(INDX)=SQRT(ABS((A(INDS,J)-XSAM(I,J)*XSAM(I,J)*T(J))/(T(J)-1.)))
  125 RC(INDX) = XSAM(I,J)
      WRITE(MED2,991)
      WRITE(MED2,993)
      WRITE(MED2,995) TRTC
      CALL WMAT (RC,NS,K,KS,NP,NDP,M,ST,NQ,IX,ISAVE,U,NU,MED2)
      WRITE(MED2,992)
      WRITE(MED2,993)
      WRITE(MED2,995) TRTC
      CALL WMAT (RW,NS,K,KS,NP,NDP,M,ST,NQ,IX,ISAVE,U,NU,MED2)
C COMPUTE MEANS AND S.D.S OF SAMPLES FOR DISCRIMINANTS
      IF(NS+K.GT.20)WRITE(MED2,901) TT
      IF(KC.GE.1.AND.NS+K.GT.20) WRITE(MED2,909)
      IF(KC.EQ.2.AND.NS+K.GT.20) WRITE(MED2,910)
      WRITE(MED2,908) NR2
      NSF = NS*NF
      CALL MATM(RC,RA,RW, NS, K, NF,KS,KF,NSF)
      WRITE(MED2,991)
      WRITE(MED2,994)
      WRITE(MED2,995) TRTC
      INDF = 0
      DO 130 J = 1,NF
```

```
      INDS = INDF + 1
      INDF = INDF + NS
  130 WRITE(MED2,997)J,(RW(INDX),INDX=INDS,INDF)
      WRITE(MED2,992)
      WRITE(MED2,994)
      WRITE(MED2,995) TRTC
      INDX = 0
      DO 145 J = 1,NF
      DO 140 I = 1,NS
      INDX = INDX + 1
      RC(INDX) = 0.
      DO 135 JY = 1,K
      KY = ISAVE(JY)
      INDS = JY + (J-1)*K
      DO 135 JX = 1,K
      KX = ISAVE(JX)
      INDF = JX + (J-1)*K
      IF(KX.GE.KY) IJ = KX + (KY-1)*(2*M-KY)/2
      IF(KX.LT.KY) IJ = KY + (KX-1)*(2*M-KX)/2
  135 RC(INDX) = RC(INDX)
     1      + (A(IJ,I) - XSAM(KY,I)*XSAM(KX,I)*T(I))*RA(INDS)*RA(INDF)
      IF(T(I).LE.1.5) RC(INDX) = 0.00001
  140 IF(T(I).GT.1.5)RC(INDX) = SQRT(ABS(RC(INDX)/(T(I)-1.)))
      INDS = INDX+1-NS
  145 WRITE(MED2,997)J,(RC(I),I=INDS,INDX)
      RETURN
  901 FORMAT(24H1SYSTEM SUBROUTINE MDISC,6X,1H-,4X,20HDERIVE DESCRIMINAN
     1TS      /16H DATA BANK TITLE,14X,1H-,4X,10A4/21H DATA BANK SAMPLE SE
     2T,9X,1H-,4X,10A4/17H DATA BANK SUBSET,13X,1H-,4X,10A4)
  902 FORMAT(40HOCOVARIANCE MATRIX FOR ORIGINAL VARIATES/)
  903 FORMAT(43HOAMONG SAMPLES MATRIX FOR ORIGINAL VARIATES/)
  904 FORMAT(44HOWITHIN SAMPLES MATRIX FOR ORIGINAL VARIATES/)
  905 FORMAT(7HOSAMPLE,I4,2X,A4,10H IS EMPTY )
  906 FORMAT(30X,34H-      SAMPLES AS ORIGINALLY DEFINED)
  907 FORMAT(30X,49H-      SAMPLES AS CHANGED TO MATCH DISCRIMINANT SET,I
     13)
  908 FORMAT(17HODISCRIMINANT SET,I3)
  909 FORMAT(39HOASSUMING INDEPENDENT ORIGINAL VARIATES)
  910 FORMAT(1H+,39X,28HAND USING CITY-BLOCK METRIC.)
  915 FORMAT(43HOALL ENTRIES IN ONE SAMPLE - RUN TERMINATES)
  920 FORMAT(1H ,A4,4H OF ,I3,1H(,A4,1H),2P12.4)
  950 FORMAT(21HODISCRIMINANT WEIGHTS /)
  951 FORMAT(57HOCORRELATIONS BETWEEN ORIGINAL VARIATES AND DISCRIMINANT
     1S/)
  985 FORMAT(15HOWILKS LAMBDA = ,F10.3/7HOD.F. =,F5.0,4H AND,F7.0/
     110HOF-RATIO =,F8.3,5X,13HPROBABILITY =,F7.4)
  986 FORMAT (26HOUNIVARIATE F-TESTS. DFB =,F3.0,6H DFN =,F6.0/
     19HO VARIATE,9X,31HF RATIO   ASSOCIATED PROBABILITY      /)
  990 FORMAT (5HOROOT,I2,F10.2,14HPCT. VARIANCE ,
     113H CHI-SQUARE =,F10.3,5X,6HD.F. =,F5.0,5X,13HPROBABILITY =,F7.4)
  991 FORMAT(16HOSAMPLE MEANS OF)
  995 FORMAT(21X,10(3X,A4,3X))
  992 FORMAT(16HOSAMPLE S.D.S OF)
  993 FORMAT(1H+,16X,17HORIGINAL VARIATES)
  994 FORMAT(1H+,16X,13HDISCRIMINANTS)
  996 FORMAT(18HOENTRIES IN SAMPLE)
  997 FORMAT(3X,12HDISCRIMINANT,I3,3X,10F10.4/21X,10F10.4)
  998 FORMAT(21X,10F10.4)
  999 FORMAT(28HO   NO DISCRIMINANTS RETAINED)
      END
```

7.5 PROGRAM STCANO - CANONICAL ANALYSIS

7.5.1 Purpose

This program carries out multiple canonical analyses for a subset of a STATCAT data bank. The canonical variates are derived from variates selected from a set of delayed and/or transformed variates. The user may select any number of variates from the selected variates as predictor or predicted variates. Although the program will employ the larger set as predictor and the smaller as predicted variates, the results produced will not be affected by the change of name. The amount of detail output and the number of canonical variates retained may be varied by the user.

Figure 7.51a contains system flow-charts for the main program STCANO and the executive subroutine CANON. Figure 7.51b contains system flow-charts for the subroutines CORRE, (which collects data and forms correlation matrices) and WBASE (which writes the details of the correlation matrices, with the means and standard deviations on which they are based).

7.5.2 Input Data

Item	Level	Format	Function	See
1	0	A	File control (Input Only)	3.2
2	4	E	Subset specification	3.6
3	5	F	Set of Variates (Transform/Delay)	3.7
4	6	F	Predicted Variates (Transform/Delay)	3.7
5	7	F	Predictor Variates (Trans/Delay) (Not = to # 4)	3.7
6	9	H	Data handling instruction Below +	3.8

Data Handling Instruction

Card Layout - Data Handling Instruction - STCANO

ABCCCDDDEEEEEEEEFFFFFFFFGGGGGGGGGGGGGGGGGHHHHHHH.....etc

Columns	Item	Function	See
1	A	Output control index	Below
2	B	Analysis control index	Below
3 - 5	C	Acceptable number of 'non-values'	7.2
6 - 8	D	Maximum Number of canonical variates	Below
9 - 16	E	Cut-off for Significance	Below
17 - 24	F	Not used	-
25 - 40	G	Analysis Run Title	-
41 - 80	H	Comment (NOT KEPT)	-

A - Output Control Index

This index controls the quantity of information output by the program.

ALTERNATIVES

A = 0, blank: Correlations between the original and canonical variates, with factor weights, for variates retained.

A = 1   : In addition, summary information for intermediate analyses printed out.

A = 2   : In addition complete analysis reports for intermediate analyses printed out.

A = 3   : In addition, correlation matrices within and between
                 the predictor and predicted variates, with their means and
                 standard deviations.

A = 4   : In addition, correlation matrix for the set of variates,
                 with their means and standard deviations is printed out.
                 (If non-values are accepted, the means and standard
                 deviations used in deriving individual correlation
                 coefficients are also produced.)

A = 5   : In addition, tests of the normal distribution and
                 sequential independence of residual difference between
                 predicted and actual values of canonical variates (based
                 on predictor and predicted variates respectively)

A = 6   : In addition, for each entry, values of predicted and
                 actual canonical variates.

A = 7   : In addition, predictor and predicted variates
                 for each entry

A = 8   : In addition, values of selected variates for each entry.

A = 9   : In addition, values of original data for each entry.
DEFAULT value = 0 (0, blank or non-numeric character)

B - Analysis Control Index

This index controls the program strategy. In this program it
determines which canonical variates are retained.

ALTERNATIVES

B = 0 or blank : All canonical variates up to a maximum of D
(Default)   retained.

B = 1   : Discriminant variates eliminated as long as the
                 overall associated probability remains below E.

B = 2   : Discriminant variables eliminated as long as the
                 loss in overall associated probability remains
                 below E.

B = 3   : Discriminant variates are eliminated as long as
                 their individual probability remains below E.

B = 4   : Discriminant variates are eliminated as long as
                 the total unexplained part of the variance remains
                 below E.

B = 5   : Discriminant variates are eliminated as long as the
                 increase in the unexplained portion of the variation
                 remains below E.

B = 4 - 9   : As for B = 0

DEFAULT value = 0 (0, blank or non-numeric character)

D - Maximum Number of Canonical Variates

This value determines the maximum number of canonical variates that
will be produced by the program , subject to the control of the analysis

control index. The maximum number of canonicals cannot exceed the number of predicted variates, which will be the smaller of the two sets of variates selected.

DEFAULT value = 0 (0, blank or non-numeric characters) set to number of predictor variates selected, or the number of predictors, whichever is the less.

E - Cut-off for Significance

This value is used, subject to the analysis control index, to determine the number of canonical variates that will be retained.

DEFAULT value = 0 (0, blank or non-numeric characters) set to 1.0 per cent if D is also originally 0.

7.5.3 Input Example

Figure 7.52 is a summary of the input structure for two runs of STCANO. Only one variate was defined in item 3, but two predicted and four predictor variates are defined in items 4 and 5 respectively. All entries are included in the subset to be analysed. For the first run, only the default output is produced. For the second run, a more detailed output is produced, the program retaining only those canonical variates significant at the 1 per cent level, and calculating actual and predicted values of these variates. This is not the maximum output, but is sufficient to permit checking of individual entries.

Figure 7.53 is a listing of the input cards required to carry out these two runs.

7.5.4 Output Example

Figure 7.54 is a general summary of the output produced by this program, indented according to the program structure. Figure 7.55 is a page-by-page summary of the output corresponding to the input of Figure 7.53. The input checking information is essentially standard, and is therefore not repeated here. Figure 7.56 gives the default output for this program. This information appears on three successive pages, and consists of a summary of statistical significance for the canonicals retained (7.5.5), the correlations of the original predictor and predicted variates with canonicals, and a table of the weights to be applied to the predictor and predicted variates to obtain predicted and actual values of the canonical variates (7.5.6). Figure 7.57 gives part of the detailed output for the second run (7.5.7). This detailed output consists of a table of the number of entries, the arithmetic mean and standard deviation for all variates in store, and for those selected for this analysis, the correlation matrix for all variates in store, (Figure 7.57) tables of correlation between predictor variates, between predicted variates and between predictor and predicted variates. This is followed by the basic output given in Figure 7.56 and described above, and is followed by detailed output for each entry (Figure 7.58) - described in 7.5.6.

Figure 7.59 shows the examination of residual differences for canonical variates, as described in 7.5.7 following.

7.5.5 Basic Output

Figure 7.56 illustrates the basic output for canonical analysis. This output begins with a summary of the statistical significance of the canonical variates retained in accordance with the data handling instruction. The successive canonical variates are given in order of importance, the most statistically significant first. Each variate is associated with a root which gives an indication of its importance. This root can be transformed into a variate which is distributed like chi-squared, and can be assigned a probability. This is the probability of obtaining a root as large as, or larger than, that observed if the correlations between predictor and predicted variates are purely random. The successive canonical variates are mutually independent.

This table is followed by a table of the correlations between the predictor and canonical variates, and between the predicted and canonical variates. In our example the first canonical variate is highly correlated with the difficulty (LG10DIFF), with the heart-rate, and with the time taken as a percentage of that allowed, among the predictors, and with the efficiency as assessed by the operator among the predicted variates. It seems that the operator judges his efficiency by the difficulty of the task, the physical effort he exerts (as reflected by the heart-rate) and the extra time required to complete the task. Rather surprisingly, the latter measure is positively correlated with the operator's assessment of efficiency. One might expect that the longer it took him to do a job, the less well he would feel he was doing it. The measure employed is the excess of the time taken over the time allowed, so that it may well be that the original assessment was at fault.

The second variate correlates highly with the proportion of errors (as a predictor) and with the efficiency of the operator as assessed by the observer. Apparently the observer goes primarily by the amount of error, making an allowance for speed relative to the time allowed.

Finally, a table of the weights to be applied to the predictor and predicted variates to form the predicted and actual values of the canonical variates is produced. This table of weights is normalised to produce comparable canonical scores when they are applied to an entry. Note that the predictor variates are used to form a predicted value for each canonical variate, while the predicted values are used to form an actual value for the same canonical variates.

This table of weights indicates the contribution of each of the original variates to the calculation of variates, but it would be wrong to interpret these weights as an indication of the nature of the canonical variates - the previous matrix of correlation coefficients is a much better indication.

It should be noted that the maximum number of canonical variates that can be derived is the number of predicted variates, and that if there are more predicted than predictor variates the two sets will be interchanged. This will not affect the calculation, since the canonical correlation process is inherently symmetrical.

7.5.6 Entry

Figure 7.58 shows the part of the record for individual entries for one run of STCANO. Each page of output is headed by the normal program name, STATCAT data bank and subset titles, and a run title. This is followed by a heading giving the numbers of the canonical variates retained, the identities of the predictor variates, the identities of the predicted variates, the set of variates selected and the data columns of the STATCAT data bank, if all of these have been called for. In our example, the output control index was set to 5 so that the last two items were suppressed.

For each entry, a first line gives the entry number. This is followed by a tabulation of the predicted and actual values of each canonical variate, with their differences. The values of predictor and predicted variates, the complete set of variates, and the complete entry are then listed if required. (The last four items were not called for in our example, and therefore do not appear)

7.5.7 Residuals

If the output control index is set to 3 or higher, the system will make an analysis of the distributions of residuals for each canonical variate retained. This analysis consists of a parametric description presented by the subroutine DCPS(5.2.6) and a test for sequential dependency. (See 7.2.7)

These descriptions are of the standard type, with the following additional features. The arithmetic mean of each residual should be zero, because the average estimate should be equal to the actual mean for each canonical variate, which should be zero because the canonical weights are standardised for this purpose. If entries containing non-values are included, this will not be true, since these non-values will be replaced by the arithmetic means of the appropriate variates. The standard deviations of successive canonical variate residuals tend to be progressively larger, and consequently so do the standard errors of the 'mean residuals'. In general, except in extreme cases, the standard deviation of the residuals will be less than one, and the 'mean residuals' will be very small.

The skewness and kurtosis terms are valuable indicators of abnormality in the distributions of residuals. If a warning of non-normality is printed, it is usually advisable to examine the individual residuals, and examine the circumstances under which extreme residuals occur.

7.5.8 Restrictions and reservations

Canonical correlation is subject to most of the restrictions and reservations applicable to multiple regression (which can be considered to be a special case of canonical analysis, with only one predicted variate) Because it is based on a correlation matrix, it is subject to the assumptions involved in the calculation of correlation by the product-moment method. (Briefly these imply that the variates should be normally distributed, and that they should be on an INTERVAL or RATIO scale. If sufficient classes are employed, and a certain freedom allowed, ORDINAL variates may be employed, but NOMINAL variates should not be included in this type of analysis.)

The problem of the choice of variates to include applies to this type of analysis, as to factor analysis, but with the added problem that the inclusion of unimportant predicted variates may distort the primary canonical analysis, since the system applies equal weight to each predicted variate. There are no accepted rules for defining which variates should be retained - the user should either adopt a set of variates for his own reasons, or he should consult a statistical expert.

The problems of unrepresentative data apply as much to canonical analysis as they do to multiple linear regression, with the additional difficulty that the ranges of the predicted variates must be related to those of the actual canonical variates, and the ranges of the predictor variates to the predicted canonical variates. The systematic analysis of residuals in canonical analysis is an extremely complex and laborious task. Some reduction of the workload may be obtained by constructing a revised STATCAT data bank containing the original variates, the canonical variates and the residuals by means of STMANI, and applying descriptive and inferential statistics to the STATCAT data bank so constructed.

A final disadvantage of canonical analysis is that the technique produces results that are not intuitively related to the real world. The method of applying names to the canonical variates may be employed, as it is in factor analysis and subject to the same reservations, but the unfamiliarity of the method detracts from its usefulness in many situations to which it might be applied.

REFERENCES : Veldman (Ch 11), Morrison (Ch 6), Kendall (1975 Ch 6)

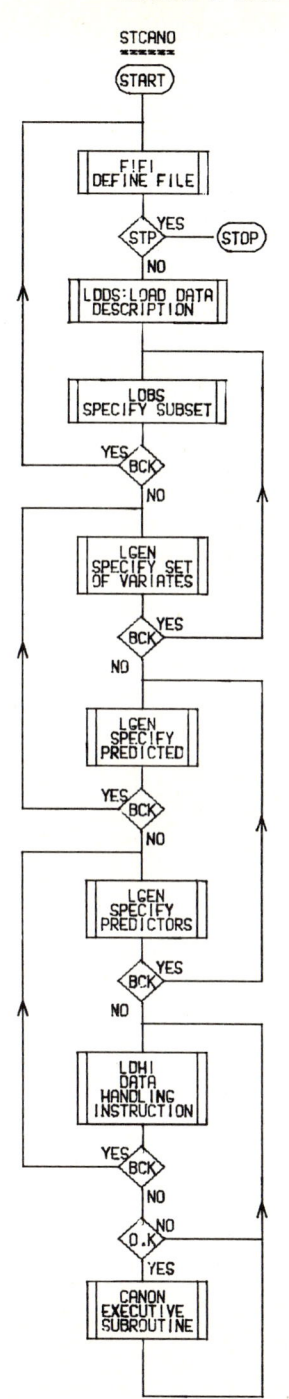

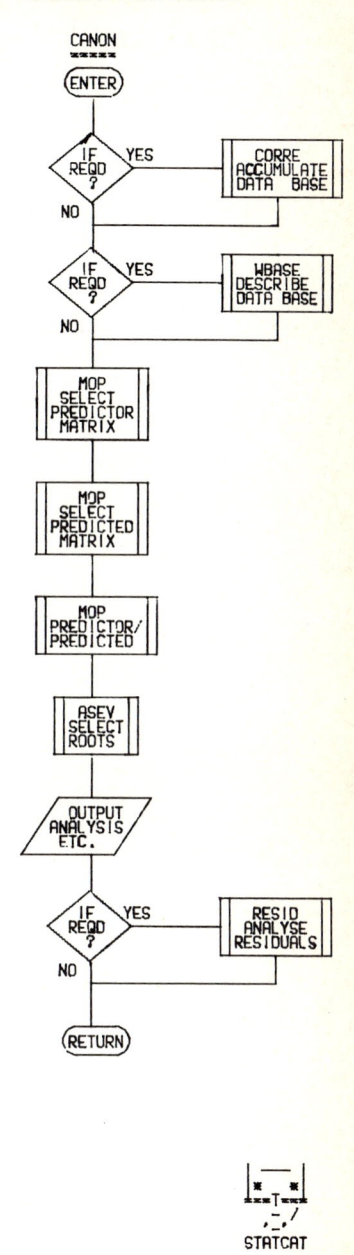

Figure 7.51a - System Flow-Charts - STCANO and CANON

Figure 7.51b - System Flow-Charts - CORRE and WBASE

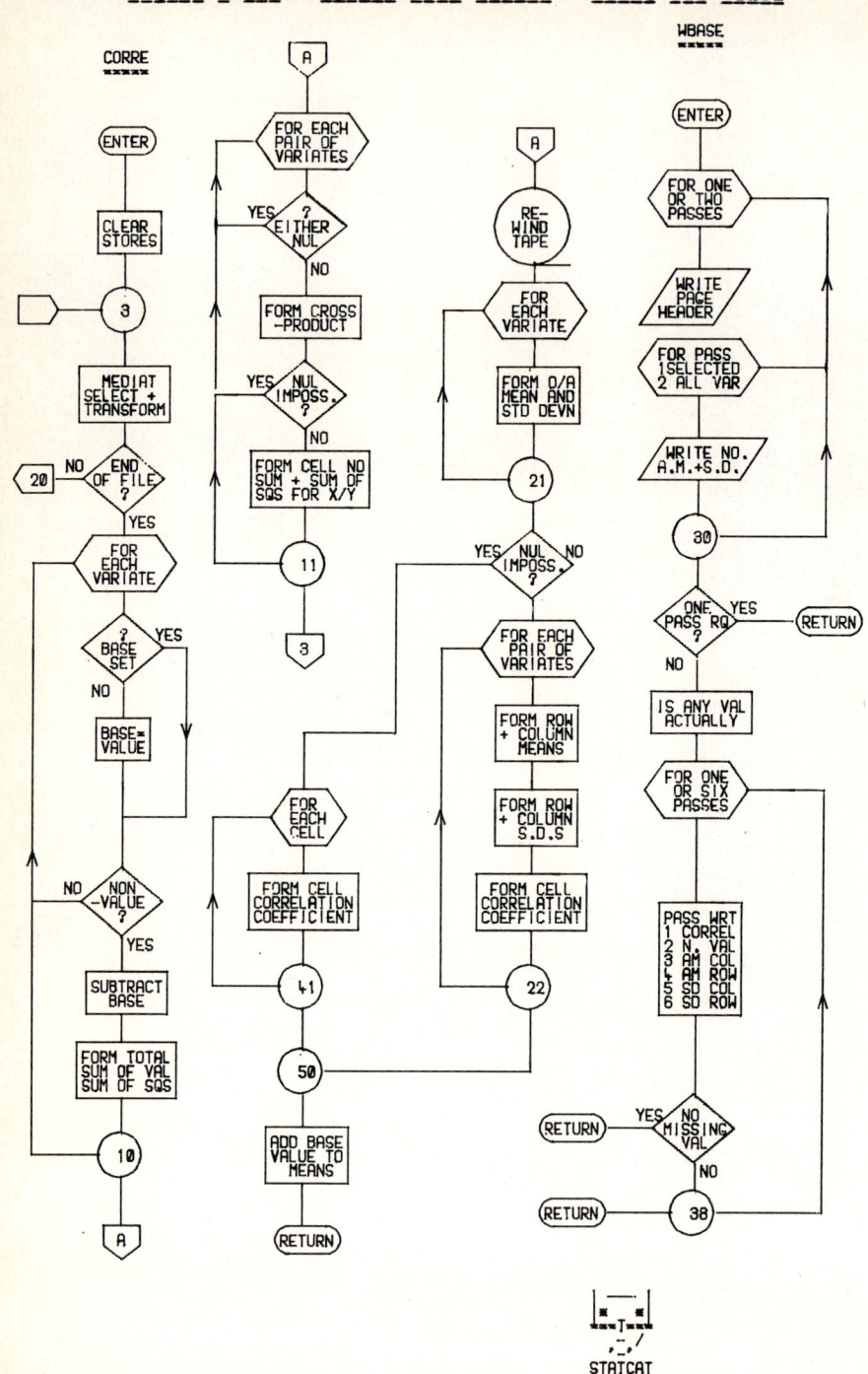

Figure 7.52 - STCANO - Input Structure

```
        Level
0   1   2   3   4   5   6   7   8   9
FILE CONTROL CARD
    SUBSET SPECIFICATION
        VARIATE SPECIFICATION
            PREDICTED VARIATES
                PREDICTOR VARIATES
                    DATA HANDLING INSTRUCTION
                    DATA HANDLING INSTRUCTION
                    STOP
```

Figure 7.53 - STCANO - Input Example

```
---------1---------2---------3---------4---------5---------6---------7--
**STCANODEMO                            DEMONSTRATION STATCAT DATA BANK
ALL DATA                                WHOLE DATA BANK TO BE INCLUDED
END OF SUBSET DEFINITION
LG10EFOP
LG10DIFF
LG10TPCT
LG10H.R.
LG10ERRP
LG10EFOB
END OF SET OF VARIATES
LG10EFOB
LG10EFOP
END OF PREDICTED VARIATES
LG10H.R.
LG10DIFF
LG10TPCT
LG10ERRP
END OF PREDICTOR VARIATES
GO                                      DEFAULT OPTION
63                                      DETAILED OUTPUT
STOP
---------1---------2---------3---------4---------5---------6---------7--
```

Figure 7.54 - STCANO - Output Structure

```
For each     ) : File Control Record
output file  )   File Parameters
                 Data Description
                 For each) : Subset Input Record
                 Subset )    For each set) : Input Record
                             of Variates )   For each set ) : Input
                                         )   of Predicted )   Record
                                                 Variates )   See Left
For each set) : Input Record
of Predictor)   For each Data) : Input Record
Variates    )   Handling    )   See left
                Instruction )

For each     ) <No.,a.m. and s.d. for variates used>
Data         ) <No.,a.m. and s.d. for all variates in store>
Handling     ) <Correlation Matrix - all variates>
Instruction) <No.,a.m. and s.d. for each cell - if non-values present>
             <Correlation Matrix - Predictors>
             <Correlation Vector - Predictors/Predicted>
             .        For intermediate sets of variates : -
             .        Multiple Canonical analysis Report
             Final Multiple Canonical analysis Report
             <Residual Analysis>
             .        For Each Entry : -
             .             <Prediction/Actual/Residual Canonical Variates>
             .             <Predicted Values>
             .             <Predictor Values>
             .             <Variate Values>
             .             <Data Items>
             <Parametric Description of Residuals>
```

Carated(<>) items are optional.

Figure 7.55 - STCANO - Page-by-page output summary

Page	Contents	Origin
1-2	File Control/Program title Data Description record	FIFI/LDAP/STCANO LDDS
3	Subset record	LDBS/LSAMP
4	Set of Variates record	LGEN
5	Predicted Variates record	LGEN
6	Predictor Variates record Data Handling Instruction	LGEN LDHI
7	Canonical Tests of Significance	CANON
8	Correlations with Canonical variates	CANON
9	Weights for Canonical Variates	CANON
10	Data Handling Instruction	LDHI
11-14	Detailed Description	WBASE/CANON
15-17	Canonical Tests/Correlations/Weights	CANON
18-30	Canonical Scores	CANON
31	Statistical Summary for residuals	DCPS
32	Data Handling Instruction (STOP)	LDHI

Figure 7.56 - STCANO - Output Example - Default output

```
STATCAT PROGRAM STCANO        -    MULTIPLE CANONICAL ANALYSIS
DATA BANK TITLE               -    DEMONSTRATION STATCAT DATA BANK
DATA BANK SUBSET TITLE        -    ALL DATA
RUN TITLE                     -    DEFAULT OPTION


STATISTICAL TESTS OF INDIVIDUAL CANONICAL VARIATES
NUMBER ROOT CHISQUARED DEGREES OF FREEDOM PROBABILITY
   1   0.9752   223.6910          5.              0.0
   2   0.5958    54.7978          3.              0.0




STATCAT PROGRAM STCANO        -    MULTIPLE CANONICAL ANALYSIS
DATA BANK TITLE               -    DEMONSTRATION STATCAT DATA BANK
DATA BANK SUBSET TITLE        -    ALL DATA
RUN TITLE                     -    DEFAULT OPTION


CORRELATIONS BETWEEN PREDICTOR AND CANONICAL VARIATES

                                  1          2
TRANSFORM COLUMN
LG10 OF 15(H.R.)               0.7459     0.1857
LG10 OF 10(DIFF)               0.9547    -0.3055
LG10 OF 12(TPCT)               0.6370    -0.2055
LG10 OF 16(ERRP)               0.0157    -0.9954

CORRELATIONS BETWEEN PREDICTED AND CANONICAL VARIATES

                                  1          2
TRANSFORM COLUMN
LG10 OF 14(EFOR)              -0.3211     0.9470
LG10 OF 13(EFOP)               0.9996    -0.0275




STATCAT PROGRAM STCANO        -    MULTIPLE CANONICAL ANALYSIS
DATA BANK TITLE               -    DEMONSTRATION STATCAT DATA BANK
DATA BANK SUBSET TITLE        -    ALL DATA
RUN TITLE                     -    DEFAULT OPTION


WEIGHTS FOR CANONICAL VARIATES RETAINED

PREDICTOR VARIATES                 ROOT NUMBER

                                  1          2
TRANSFORM COLUMN
LG10 OF 15(H.R.)               0.0463     0.3875
LG10 OF 10(DIFF)               0.9547    -0.2438
LG10 OF 12(TPCT)               0.1076    -0.0327
LG10 OF 18(ERRP)              -0.0324    -0.8875

PREDICTED VARIATES                 ROOT NUMBER

                                  1          2
TRANSFORM COLUMN
LG10 OF 14(EFOR)               0.0290     0.9521
LG10 OF 13(EFOP)               0.9996     0.3058
```

Figure 7.57 - STCANO - Output Example - Detailed Output

```
STATCAT PROGRAM STCANO        -     MULTIPLE CANONICAL ANALYSIS
DATA BANK TITLE               -     DEMONSTRATION STATCAT DATA BANK
DATA BANK SUBSET TITLE        -     ALL DATA
RUN TITLE                     -     DETAILED OUTPUT

CORRELATIONS BETWEEN PREDICTOR VARIATES


    TRANSFORM             LG10 OF      LG10 OF      LG10 OF     LG10 OF
    COLUMN (NAME)         15.=H.R.    10.=DIFF     12.=TPCT    18.=ERRP
TRANSFORM COLUMN
LG10 OF 15(H.R.)          1.0000       0.7531       0.1702      0.0236
LG10 OF 10(DIFF)          0.7531       1.0000       0.9390      0.0899
LG10 OF 12(TPCT)          0.1702       0.9390       1.0000      0.0764
LG10 OF 18(ERRP)          0.0236       0.0899       0.0764      1.0000

CORRELATIONS BETWEEN PREDICTED VARIATES


    TRANSFORM             LG10 OF      LG10 OF
    COLUMN (NAME)         14.=EFOB    13.=EFOP
TRANSFORM COLUMN
LG10 OF 14(EFOB)          1.0000      -0.3470
LG10 OF 13(EFOP)         -0.3470       1.0000

CORRELATIONS BETWEEN PREDICTOR AND PREDICTED VARIATES


    TRANSFORM             LG10 OF      LG10 OF      LG10 OF     LG10 OF
    COLUMN (NAME)         15.=H.R.    10.=DIFF     12.=TPCT    18.=ERRP
TRANSFORM COLUMN
LG10 OF 14(EFOB)         -0.1616      -0.3635      -0.3351     -0.7027
LG10 OF 13(EFOP)          0.7305       0.7333       0.6332      0.0336
```

Figure 7.58 - STCANO - Output Example - Entries

```
          CANONICAL ANALYSIS

DATA BANK TITLE               -     DEMONSTRATION STATCAT DATA BANK
DATA BANK SUBSET TITLE        -     ALL DATA
RUN TITLE                     -     DETAILED OUTPUT

INDIVIDUAL ENTRIES

            CANONICAL VARIATES       1            2
-----------------------------------------------------------------------
ENTRY   61

        ACTUAL              0.3003       0.0977
        PREDICTED           0.3290       0.0582
        RESIDUAL           -0.0287       0.0394
-----------------------------------------------------------------------
ENTRY   62

        ACTUAL             -0.5089      -0.0727
        PREDICTED          -0.6236      -0.1184
        RESIDUAL            0.1149       0.0456
-----------------------------------------------------------------------
ENTRY   63

        ACTUAL              0.1915       0.0402
        PREDICTED           0.1927      -0.3524
        RESIDUAL           -0.0011       0.3926
-----------------------------------------------------------------------
ENTRY   64

        ACTUAL              0.0553      -0.0107
        PREDICTED           0.0789      -0.3210
        RESIDUAL           -0.0236       0.3104
```

Figure 7.59 - STCANO - Output Example - Residual Analysis

```
        CANONICAL ANALYSIS
DATA BANK TITLE              -    DEMONSTRATION STATCAT DATA BANK
DATA BANK SUBSET TITLE       -    ALL DATA
RUN TITLE                    -    DETAILED OUTPUT
-----------------------------------------------------------------------------------------------------------------

EXAMINATION OF RESIDUAL DIFFERENCES - CANONICAL VARIATE NUMBER   1

NUMBER OF READINGS=          64.
ARITHMETIC MEAN =            -0.000001       S.E. OF MEAN =        0.007498
STANDARD DEVIATION=          0.059986        S.E. OF S.D. =        0.007402
     SKEWNESS =              1.179056  SKEWNESS RATIO =            3.850784 PROBABILITY=       0.000324
     KURTOSIS =              0.949211  KURTOSIS RATIO =            3.100110 PROBABILITY=       0.002397
S.E. FOR SKEWNESS =          0.306186   DISTRIBUTION IS PROBABLY NOT NORMAL                               **WARNING**
ROOT-MEAN-SQUARE SUCCESSIVE DEVIATION =  0.08307523
NORMALISED VALUE = -0.33343824
ASSOCIATED PROBABILITY = 0.73915255
-----------------------------------------------------------------------------------------------------------------

EXAMINATION OF RESIDUAL DIFFERENCES - CANONICAL VARIATE NUMBER   2

NUMBER OF READINGS=          64.
ARITHMETIC MEAN =            0.000003        S.E. OF MEAN =        0.049261
STANDARD DEVIATION=          0.394067        S.E. OF S.D. =        0.023765
     SKEWNESS =              -0.383500  SKEWNESS RATIO =           -1.252531 PROBABILITY=       0.207927
     KURTOSIS =              -0.452673  KURTOSIS RATIO =           -1.479077 PROBABILITY=       0.139385
S.E. FOR SKEWNESS =          0.306186
ROOT-MEAN-SQUARE SUCCESSIVE DEVIATION =  0.36130108
NORMALISED VALUE = -4.70659685
ASSOCIATED PROBABILITY = 0.00007056
```

```
C MASTER STCANO - MULTIPLE CANONICAL ANALYSIS
C       SUBROUTINES AND FUNCTIONS REQUIRED
C AN      (SEE  3.1 )  SERVICE     ALPHA - TO NUMERIC VALUE
C ASEV    (SEE 11.3 )  SERVICE     EIGEN ROOTS ETC ASYMMETRIC MATRIX
C CANON   (SEE  7.5 )  EXECUTIVE   CANONICAL CORRELATION ANALYSIS
C CHIKEN  (SEE 11.9 )  SERVICE     WARNS OF MISMATCHED DATA LEVEL
C CLSAM   (SEE  3.5 )  SERVICE     ALLOTS ENTRY TO SAMPLE/SUBSET
C COMPA   (SEE  3.1 )  SERVICE     COMPARES ALPHAMERIC VALUES
C COPYA   (SEE  3.1 )  SERVICE     COPIES ALPHAMERIC VALUE
C CORRE   (SEE  7.5 )  SYSTEM      MULTIPLE CORRELATION DATA
C DCPS    (SEE  5.2 )  STATISTICAL MOMENT(PARAMETRIC) STATISTICS
C FIFI    (SEE  3.2 )  SYSTEM      ALLOCATES PERIPHERALS
C GAUS    (SEE 11.8 )  STATISTICAL FINDS ASS. PROB. OF M VALUE
C IBL     (SEE  3.1 )  SERVICE     DETECTS BLANK,END AND STOP CARDS
C ICH     (SEE  3.1 )  SERVICE     IDENTIFIES ALPHAMERIC CODES
C LCOM    (SEE  3.4 )  SERVICE     LOADS COMPLEMENTARY INFORMATION
C LDAP    (SEE  3.3 )  SYSTEM      LOADS/CHECKS DATA BANK PARAMETERS
C LDBS    (SEE  3.6 )  SYSTEM      LOADS SUBSET DEFINITION
C LDDS    (SEE  3.4 )  SYSTEM      LOADS DATA DESCRIPTION SEGMENT
C LDHI    (SEE  3.8 )  SYSTEM      LOADS/CHECKS DATA HANDLING INSTN
C LGEN    (SEE  3.7 )  SYSTEM      LOADS GENERALISED VARIATES
C LSET    (SEE  3.5 )  SYSTEM      LOADS DEFINING CONDITIONS
C MATM    (SEE 11.3 )  SERVICE     MULTIPLIES MATRICES
C MEDIAT  (SEE  3.7 )  SERVICE     FETCHES NEXT VARIATE SET
C MINV    (SEE 11.3 )  SERVICE     INVERTS MATRIX
C MOP     (SEE 11.3 )  SERVICE     SELECTS/CONVERTS STORED MATRIX
C PRBF    (SEE 11.8 )  STATISTICAL FINDS PROBABILITY OF F-RATIO
C RESID   (SEE  7.2 )  SYSTEM      LIST AND DESCRIBE RESIDUALS/FACTORS
C TRANS   (SEE  3.7 )  SERVICE     CARRIES OUT REQUIRED TRANSFORM
C WBASE   (SEE  7.5 )  SYSTEM      WRITES CORRELATION MATRIX ETC
C WDCD    (SEE  3.4 )  SERVICE     WRITES DATA COLUMN DESCRIPTION
C WMAT    (SEE 11.3 )  SERVICE     WRITE MATRIX WITH VARIATE TITLES
C SETTING OF ARRAY DIMENSIONS
C THE FOLLOWING DIMENSIONS MUST BE AT LEAST AS BIG AS THOSE
C SPECIFIED BY THE DATA TAPE,SAMPLE SPECIFICATIONS, ETC.
C NQMAX = MAXIMUM NUMBER OF DATA COLUMNS
C DIMENSION X(NQMAX),ST(NQMAX) ,IT(NQMAX),CN(NQMAX)
      NQMAX = 100
      DIMENSION X(100),ST(100),IT(100),CN(100)
      DATA  CN/4HCOL1,4HCOL2,4HCOL3,4HCOL4,4HCOL5,4HCOL6,4HCOL7,4HCOL8,4
     1HCOL9,4HCL10,4HCL11,4HCL12,4HCL13,4HCL14,4HCL15,4HCL16,4HCL17,4HCL
     218,4HCL19,4HCL20,4HCL21,4HCL22,4HCL23,4HCL24,4HCL25,4HCL26,4HCL27,
     34HCL28,4HCL29,4HCL30,4HCL31,4HCL32,4HCL33,4HCL34,4HCL35,4HCL36,4HC
     4L37,4HCL38,4HCL39,4HCL40,4HCL41,4HCL42,4HCL43,4HCL44,4HCL45,4HCL46
     5,4HCL47,4HCL48,4HCL49,4HCL50,4HCL51,4HCL52,4HCL53,4HCL54,4HCL55,4H
     6CL56,4HCL57,4HCL58,4HCL59,4HCL60,4HCL61,4HCL62,4HCL63,4HCL64,4HCL6
     75,4HCL66,4HCL67,4HCL68,4HCL69,4HCL70,4HCL71,4HCL72,4HCL73,4HCL74,4
     8HCL75,4HCL76,4HCL77,4HCL78,4HCL79,4HCL80,4HCL81,4HCL82,4HCL83,4HCL
     984,4HCL85,4HCL86,4HCL87,4HCL88,4HCL89,4HCL90,4HCL91,4HCL92,4HCL93,
     94HCL94,4HCL95,4HCL96,4HCL97,4HCL98,4HCL99,4HC100/
C MAXM = MAXIMUM NUMBER OF DIFFERENT VARIATES SPECIFIED
C DIMENSION XBAR(MAXM),STD(MAXM),RY(MAXM),W(MAXM),T(MAXM),Y(MAXM)
C DIMENSION LW(MAXM),NDP(MAXM),NP(MAXM),IX(MAXM),IY(MAXM),ISAVE(MAXMSCNN
      MAXM = 50
      DIMENSION XBAR(50),STD(50),RY(50),W(50),T(50),Y(50)
      DIMENSION LW(50),NDP(50),NP(50),IX(50),IY(50),ISAVE(50)
C MAXAV = GENERAL STORE FOR CORRELATION AND ANALYSIS MATRICES
C MAXAV =(2*A+B)*(A+B) + B + (M*(M+1)/2 IF NO MISSING VALUES
C MAXAV =(2*A+B)*(A+B) + B + (M*(M+1)*3 IF MISSING VALUES ALLOWED
C WHERE M = NUMBER OF DIFFERENT VARIATES IN STORE
C    A = NUMBER OF PREDICTOR VARIATES - LARGER GROUP
C    B = NUMBER OF PREDICTED VARIATES - SMALLER GROUP
C  DIMENSION R(MAXAV)
```

```
      MAXAV = 1000
      DIMENSION R(1000)
C MAXD = STORAGE AVAILABLE FOR DELAYED ENTRIES
C (MAXIMUM DELAY + 3.) * M MUST NOT EXCEED MAXD
C DIMENSION D(MAXD) IF MAXD NOT ZERO
      MAXD = 500
      DIMENSION D(500)
C IF ALL 60 PREDICTORS USED,THE MAXIMUM DELAY WOULD BE 8 CYCLES
C IF ONLY 2 VARIABLES USED,THE MAXIMUM DELAY WOULD BE 298 CYCLES
C DIMENSION TRT(NALTMX) = MAX NO OF CLASSES ON TAPE
      NALTMX = 50
      DIMENSION  TRT(50)
C DIMENSION SCON(5,MAXDBC) = MAXIMUM NO. OF DATA BANK SUBSET CONDITIONS
      MAXDBC = 50
      DIMENSION SCON(5,50)
C THE FOLLOWING DIMENSION STORES THE NAMES OF THE DATA TRANSFORMS
C AND THE ACCEPTABLE LEVELS FOR TRANSFORMATIONS
      DIMENSION U(60),LU(60)
      NU = 60
C TRANSFORMATION CODES
C UNITS                      BLOCKS
C      0 - 9   10 - 19   20 - 29   30 - 39   40 - 49   50 - 59
C      POWERS  TRIG      TRIG      STATIST   MATHS     TEST
C              RADIANS   DEGREES   TRANSF    FUNCTS    FUNCTIONS
C  0    -       -        H.MS       -         -        RM10
C  1   VAL.    SINR      SIND      PSNA      RECP      +/-1
C  2   SQAR    COSR      COSD      PSNB      SQRT      ADD1
C  3   CUBE    TANR      TAND      BINO      ABSV      SUB1
C  4   4PWR    ASIR      ASID      LG+1      SIGN      NOR1
C  5   5PWR    ACOR      ACOD      LOGE      INTG      +/-P
C  6   6PWR    ATAR      ATAD      LG10      FRAC      ADDP
C  7   7PWR    SINH      DTOR      AL10      EXPT      SUBP
C  8   8PWR    COSH      RTOD       -        PRES      NORP
C  9   9PWR    TANH      H.HH       -        NEG.      +100
      DATA U/4HVAL. ,4HSQAR,4HCUBE,4H4PWR,4H5PWR,4H6PWR,4H7PWR,4H8PWR,4H9
     1PWR,4HVAL ,4HSINR,4HCOSR,4HTANR,4HASIR,4HACOR,4HATAR,4HSINH,4HCOSH
     2,4HTANH,4HH.MS,4HSIND,4HCOSD,4HTAND,4HASID,4HACOD,4HATAD,4HDTOR,4H
     3RTOD,4HH.HH,4H VAL ,4HPSNA,4HPSNB,4HBINO,4HLG+1,4HLOGE,4HLG10,4HAL1
     40,4H    ,4H    ,4H        ,4HRECP,4HSQRT,4HABSV,4HSIGN,4HINTG,4HFRAC,4
     5HEXPT,4HPRES,4HNEG. ,4HRM10,4H+/-1,4HADD1,4HSUB1,4HNOR1,4H+/-P,4HAD
     6DP,4HSUBP,4HNORP,4H+100,4H        /
C ACCEPTABLE CODE LEVELS
      DATA LU/60*4/
C DUMMY ARRAYS USED IN LGEN + D.H.I INPUT ARRAY
      DIMENSION IH(1),H(1),FORM(40)
      COMMON /STCT/MED1,MED2,MED3,MED4,MED5,MED6,MED13,Q,V(20),TT(30)
      DATA PROG/4HCANO/
      MED1 = -1
C SETTING UP * LEVEL 0
    1 CALL COPYA(TT(1),PROG)
      CALL FIFI
      WRITE(MED2,901)
      CALL LDAP(MED2,MED3,V,TT,Q,NQ,NALT,NQMAX,NALTMX,IGO)
      IF(IGO.GT.0) GO TO 1
      LI = 18
      CALL LDDS(TRT,NALT,D,NQ,ST,NQ,IT,NQ,H,0,H,H,0,LI,0,Q,VX,
     1 0,MED2,MED3,0,IGO)
      IF(IGO.GT.0) GO TO 1
   21 IF(V(10).GE.20.) V(10) = 0.
      CALL LDBS(SCON,NCON,MAXDBC,CN,ST,IT,NQ,TRT,NALT,IGO)
      IF(IGO.GT.0) GO TO 1
      DO 22 I = 11,20
   22 CALL COPYA(TT(I),TT(I+10))
```

```
      ARAN = 5236.
C READ SET OF VARIATES FOR DATA SWEEP         - LEVEL 4
   41 IF(V(10).GE.40.) V(10) = 0.
      M = 0
      WRITE(MED6,941)
      WRITE(MED6,944)
      CALL LGEN(U,NU,LU,NU,ST,IT,CN,NQ,IH,0,H,H,0,H,H,0,MAXD,NALT,NDP,NP
     1,MAXM,M,MAXM,1,0)
      IF(V(11).LT.0.5.AND.V(20).LT.0.5)GO TO 21
      BRAN = ARAN
C READ PREDICTED VARIATES - LEVEL 5
   51 IF(V(10).GT.50.) V(10) = 0.
      WRITE(MED6,951)
      WRITE(MED6,944)
      NPV = 0
      MX = MAXM
      CALL LGEN(U,NU,LU,NU,ST,IT,CN,NQ,IH,0,H,H,0,H,H,0,MAXD,0,IX,IY,MX,
     1NPV,MX,1,NALT)
      IF(V(11).LT.0.5.AND.V(20).LT.0.5)GO TO 41
      IF(V(10).LT.0.5.AND.V(20).GT.0.5) V(10) = 59.
      IF(NPV.LT.1) GO TO 54
C STORE AS NUMBERS IN VARIATE SET - ADD IF MISSING
      KM = 0
      DO 53 J = 1,NPV
      DO 52 L = 1,M
      IF(IX(J).NE.NDP(L).OR.IY(J).NE.NP(L)) GO TO 52
      ISAVE(J) = L
      GO TO 53
   52 CONTINUE
      V(19) = V(19) + 2.
      IF(V(19).GT.50.) WRITE(MED2,950)
      IF(V(19).GT.50.) V(19) = 2.
      WRITE(MED2,952) J
      IF(MAXM.EQ.M) WRITE(MED6,954)
      IF(MAXM.EQ.M) KM = KM + 1
      IF(MAXM.EQ.M) GO TO 53
      WRITE(MED2,953)
      M = M + 1
      NDP(M) = IX(J)
      NP(M) = IY(J)
      ISAVE(J) = M
      V(6) = 0.
      BRAN = ARAN
   53 CONTINUE
      NPV = NPV - KM
   54 IF(NPV.EQ.0.AND.V(10).LT.0.5) V(10) = 53.
C READ PREDICTOR (SET) - LEVEL 6
   61 IF(V(10).GE.60.)V(10) = 0.
      WRITE(MED6,961)
      WRITE(MED6,944)
      K = 0
      MX = MAXM
      CALL LGEN(U,NU,LU,NU,ST,IT,CN,NQ,IH,0,H,H,0,H,H,0,MAXD,0,IX,IY,MX,
     1K,MX,1,NALT)
      IF(V(11).LT.0.5.AND.V(20).LT.0.5)GO TO 51
      IF(V(10).LT.0.5.AND.V(20).GT.0.5) V(10) = 67.
      ISP = NPV
      IF(K.EQ.0.OR.NPV.EQ.0) GO TO 91
      DO 65 J = 1,K
C TEST IF PREDICTOR = PREDICTED
      DO 62 N = 1,NPV
      L = ISAVE(N)
      IF(IX(J).NE.NDP(L).OR.IY(J).NE.NP(L)) GO TO 62
```

```
          V(19) = V(19) + 2.
          IF(V(19).GT.50.) WRITE(MED2,964)
          IF(V(19).GT.50.) V(19) = 2.
          WRITE(MED6,962)J,M
       62 CONTINUE
          DO 63 L = 1,M
          IF(IX(J).NE.NDP(L).OR.IY(J).NE.NP(L)) GO TO 63
          ISF = ISF + 1
          ISAVE(ISF) = L
          GO TO 65
       63 CONTINUE
C IF NOT IN SET - NOTE/ADD/UPDATE CONTROL VALUES
          V(19) = V(19) + 2.
          IF(V(19).GT.50.) WRITE(MED2,960)
          IF(V(19).GT.50.) V(19) = 2.
          WRITE(MED2,952) J
          IF(M.LT.MAXM) GO TO 64
          WRITE(MED6,954)
          IF(V(10).EQ.0.) V(10) = 63.
          GO TO 65
       64 M = M + 1
          WRITE(MED6,953)
          NDP(M) = IX(J)
          NP(M) = IY(J)
          ISF = ISF + 1
          ISAVE(ISF) = M
          V(6) = 0.
          BRAN = ARAN
       65 CONTINUE
          IF(K.EQ.0.AND.V(10).EQ.0.) V(10) = 62.
C LEVEL 9 - DATA HANDLING INSTRUCTION
       91 IF(V(10).GT.90.) V(10) = 0.
          CALL LDHI(V(1),1,V(2),2,VX   ,7,V(7),5,V(3),16,V6,0,V7,V(10),
         1 TT(21),FORM,MED1,MED2,MED4,Q,NQ,NWARN,1,IGO)
          IF(IGO.GT.0) GO TO 61
C STANDARDISATION
          IF(V(2).GT.3.) NWARN = NWARN + 1
          IF(V(2).GT.3.) V(2) = 0.
          IF(V(7).EQ.0.) NWARN = NWARN + 1
          IF(V(7).EQ.0.) V(7) = NPV
          IF(V(3).EQ.0.) V(3) = 5.
C MAXIMUM NUMBER OF MISSING VALUES
          IF(V(6).EQ.0.) V(9) = VX
          IF(VX.NE.V(9).AND.VX.NE.0.) V(6) = 0.
          IF(VX.NE.V(9).AND.VX.NE.0.) V(9) = VX
          NA = K
          NB = NPV
          IF(K.LT.NPV) WRITE(MED2,963)K,NPV
          IF(K.LT.NPV) NA = NPV
          IF(K.LT.NPV) NB = K
          MXM = (2*NB+NA)*(NA+NB)+NA
          IF(NA*NB.LT.M) MXM = MXM -NA*NB + M
          MDIAG = M*(M+1)/2
          IF(V(9).GT.0.5) MDIAG = MDIAG*6
          IF(MXM+MDIAG.LE.MAXAV) GO TO 92
          WRITE(MED6,992)MDIAG,MXM,MAXAV
          IF(V(10).LT.0.5) V(10) = 91.
       92 CALL LDHI(V(1),1,V(2),2,V(9),7,V(7),5,V(3),16,V6,0,V7,V(10),
         1 TT(21),FORM,MED1,MED2,MED4,Q,NQ,NWARN,2,IGO)
          IF(IGO.GT.0) GO TO 91
          V(3) = V(3)*0.01
          WRITE(MED6,998)
          NA2 = NA*NA
```

```
      IF(NA2.LT.NB*7) NA2 = NB*7
      NB2 = NB*NB
      NAB = NA*NB
      IA = MDIAG + 1
      IB = IA+NAB
      IC = IB+NAB
      IF(NA*NB.LT.M) IC = IB + M
      ID = IC+NAB
      IRA = ID + NA2
      IRB = IRA + NA2
      IE = IRB + NB2
      V(10) = BRAN
      CALL CANON(ISAVE,LW,NDP,NP,STD,T,XBAR,M,R,MDIAG,X,ST,NQ,SCON,NCON,
     1R(IA),R(IB),R(IC),NAB,R(ID),R(IRA),NA2,R(IRB),NB2,R(IE),NPV,U,NU,D
     2,MAXD,Y,RY,IX)
      ARAN = V(10)
      V(10) = 0.
      WRITE(MED6,999)
      GO TO 91
  901 FORMAT (1H0,20X,38HSTATCAT MULTIPLE CANONICAL CORRELATION)
  941 FORMAT (1H1,10X,30HSET OF VARIATES FOR DATA SWEEP/)
  944 FORMAT(7H0NUMBER,6X,19HTRANS   DATA   CYCLES/5H CODE,8X,18H-FORM COL
     1UMN DELAY,66X,7HCOMMENT)
  950 FORMAT (42H1PREDICTED VARIATES NOT IN SET OF VARIATES)
  951 FORMAT (1H1,10X,18HPREDICTED VARIATES/)
  952 FORMAT (15H0VARIATE NUMBER,I4,30H IS NOT IN THE SET OF VARIATES)
  953 FORMAT(1H+,50X,33H- ADDED (NEW DATA SWEEP REQUIRED))
  954 FORMAT (1H+,50X,26H-NOT ADDED - NO MORE SPACE)
  960 FORMAT (42H1PREDICTOR VARIATES NOT IN SET OF VARIATES)
  961 FORMAT (1H1,10X,18HPREDICTOR VARIATES/)
  962 FORMAT (10H0PREDICTOR,I4,33H IS THE SAME AS PREDICTED VARIATE,I4)
  963 FORMAT (8H0WARNING/35H THE CURRENT NUMBER OF PREDICTORS ( ,I4,51H
     1) IS LESS THAN THE NUMBER OF PREDICTED VARIABLES ( ,I4,2H )/
     277H THEY WILL BE INTERCHANGED FOR COMPUTATION - THIS WILL NOT AFFE
     2CT THE RESULTS)
  964 FORMAT(50H1 PREDICTOR VARIATES ALSO IN PREDICTED VARIATE SET)
  992 FORMAT(29H0 CORRELATION MATRIX REQUIRES,I6,6H CELLS/21H     ANALYSI
     1S REQUIRES,I6,6H CELLS/6H0 ONLY,I6,27H AVAILABLE - INCREASE MAXAV)
  998 FORMAT (36H0INPUT ACCEPTED - ANALYSIS COMMENCES)
  999 FORMAT (36H1ANALYSIS COMPLETED - READ NEW INPUT)
      END


      SUBROUTINE CANON(ISAVE,LW,NDP,NP,STD,T,XBAR,M,R,MDIAG,X,ST,NQ,SCON
     1,NCON,A,B,C,NAB,D,RA,NA2,RB,NB2,E,NDEP,U,NU,F,MN,Y,Z,NW)
C CANON   (SEE  7.5 ) EXECUTIVE   CANONICAL CORRELATION ANALYSIS
      DIMENSION ISAVE(M),LW(M),NDP(M),NP(M),STD(M),T(M),XBAR(M),R(MDIAG)
      DIMENSION A(NAB),B(NAB),C(NAB),D(NA2),RA(NA2),RB(NB2),U(NU)
      DIMENSION X(NQ),ST(NQ),SCON(5,NCON),E(NDEP),F(MN),Y(M),Z(M),NW(M)
      COMMON /STCT/MED1,MED2,MED3,MED4,MED5,MED6,MED13,Q,V(20),TT(30)
      V10 = V(10)
      V11 = V(11)
      KP = V(1) + 0.01
      KA = V(2) + 0.01
      NPMAX = V(7) + 0.01
      V(7) = 3.
      NDEL = 0
      DO 28 I = 1,M
   28 IF(NDP(I).GT.NDEL)NDEL = NDP(I)
      IF(V(6).GT.0.5) GO TO 104
      REWIND MED3
      READ(MED3) NQ,NALT,Q,(TT(J),J=1,10),(P,J=1,6)
      DO 29 I = 1,NQ
```

```
   29 READ(MED3) (P,J=1,19),(P,J=1,NALT),J,P,P
      V(6) = 0.
      CALL CORRE(M,XBAR,STD,R,B,F,T,MDIAG,NP,NDP,X,NQ,SCON,NCON,MN)
      IF(V(6).GT.0.5) GO TO 104
      WRITE(MED2,902) TT
      WRITE(MED2,923)
      GO TO 300
  104 N= V(6)
      L = -M
  110 ISWAP = 0
      NE = 2
      NF = NFMAX
C NDEP IS SIZE OF FIRST OF THE TWO SETS IN ISAVE
      NA = V(11)
      NB = NDEP
      N1 = NB + 1
      N2 = 1
      N3 = NA+ NB
      N4 = NB
      IF(NA.GE.NB) GO TO 40
      ISWAP = 1
      NA = NDEP
      NB = V(11)
      N1 = 1
      N2 = NA + 1
      N3 = NA
      N4 = NA + NB
   40 K = NA + NB
C N1 TO N3 ARE THE NA COLUMNS OF THE LARGER PREDICTOR ARRAY RA
C N2 TO N4 ARE THE NB COLUMNS OF THE SMALLER PREDICTED ARRAY RB
      IF(KP.EQ.1)CALL WBASE(ISAVE,NP,NDP,T,XBAR,STD,U,NU,ST,NQ,R,MDIAG,
     1 M,NDEL,K,1)
      IF(KP.GE.2)CALL WBASE(ISAVE,NP,NDP,T,XBAR,STD,U,NU,ST,NQ,R,MDIAG,
     1 M,NDEL,K,2)
      CALL MOP(R,3,M,M,MDIAG,RA,2,NA,NA,NA2,ISAVE(N1),3,NA,ISAVE(N1),3,N
     1A,NE,MED2)
      CALL MOP(R,3,M,M,MDIAG,RB,2,NB,NB,NB2,ISAVE(N2),3,NB,ISAVE(N2),3,N
     1B,NE,MED2)
      CALL MOP(R,3,M,M,MDIAG,C ,1,NA,NB,NAB,ISAVE(N1),3,NA,ISAVE(N2),3,N
     1B,NE,MED2)
      CALL MOP(RA,2,NA,NA,NA2,D,2,NA,NA,NA2,ISAVE,1,NA,ISAVE,1,NA,2,MED
     1)
      IF(KP.LT.1) GO TO 41
      WRITE(MED2,902) TT
      WRITE(MED2,950)
      CALL WMAT(RA,NA,NA,NA2,NP,NDP,M,ST,NQ,ISAVE(N1),ISAVE(N1),U,NU,MED
     12)
      WRITE(MED2,951)
      CALL WMAT(RB,NB,NB,NB2,NP,NDP,M,ST,NQ,ISAVE(N2),ISAVE(N2),U,NU,MED
     12)
      WRITE(MED2,952)
      CALL WMAT(C ,NA,NB,NAB,NP,NDP,M,ST,NQ,ISAVE(N1),ISAVE(N2),U,NU,MED
     12)
   41 CALL MINV(D,NA,DET,LW,NW,NA2)
      CALL MATM(D,C,A,NA,NA,NB,NA2,NAB,NAB)
      CALL MOP(RB,2,NB,NB,NB2,D,2,NB,NB,NB2,ISAVE,1,NB,ISAVE,1,NB,2,MED
     1)
      CALL MINV(D,NB,DET,LW,NW,NB2)
      CALL MATM(D,C,B,NB,NA,NB2,NAB,NAB)
      CALL MATM(B,A,C,NB,NA,NB,NAB,NAB,NB2)
      CALL ASEV(C,0.0,E,NB,NB2,NB2,NB,D,X,Y,Z)
      NDX = 0
      DO 55 J = 1,NB
```

```
      P = 1./SQRT(E(J))
      DO 55 I = 1,NB
      NDX = NDX + 1
   55 D(NDX) = D(NDX) * P
      CALL MATM(A,D,C,NA,NB,NB,NAB,NA2,NAB)
C COMPUTE A SIDE WEIGHTS
      NDX = 0
      DO 61 J = 1,NB
      P = 0.
      NDY = NDX
      DO 60 I = 1,NA
      NDY = NDY + 1
   60 P = P + C(NDY)*C(NDY)
      P = 1./SQRT(P)
      DO 61 I = 1,NA
      NDX = NDX + 1
   61 C(NDX) = C(NDX)*P
C COMPUTE CORRELATIONS OF RAW AND CANONICAL VARIATES
      CALL MATM(RA,C,A,NA,NA,NB,NA2,NAB,NAB)
      NDX = 0
      DO 66 J = 1,NB
      P = 0.
      NDY = NDX
      DO 65 I = 1,NA
      NDY = NDY + 1
   65 P = P + C(NDY)*A(NDY)
      P = 1./SQRT(P)
      DO 66 I = 1,NA
      NDX = NDX + 1
   66 A(NDX) = A(NDX)*P
      CALL MATM(RB,D,B,NB,NB,NB,NB2,NB2,NB2)
      NDX = 0
      DO 71 J = 1,NB
      P = 0.
      NDY = NDX
      DO 70 I = 1,NB
      NDY = NDY + 1
   70 P = P + D(NDY)*B(NDY)
      P = 1./SQRT(P)
      DO 71 I = 1,NB
      NDX = NDX + 1
   71 B(NDX) = B(NDX)*P
C COMPUTE STATISTICAL TESTS OF INDIVIDUAL ROOTS
      P = NA + NB + 1
      P = P*.5 - V(6)
      W = 1.
      DO 75 I = 1,NB
   75 W = W*(1.-E(I))
      CS = P*ALOG(W)
      KDF = NAB
      PTOT = 1.
      IF(KA.NE.2) GO TO 79
      WX = W
      CSX = CS
      DO 78 I = 1,NB
      WX = WX/(1.-E(I))
      X1 = CSX - P*ALOG(WX)
      Y1 = KDF - (NA-I)*(NB-I)
      Z1 = PRBF(Y1,1000.,X1/Y1)
      KDF = (NA-I)*(NB-I)
      PTOT = PTOT*Z1
   78 CSX = CSX - X1
      KDF = NAB
```

```
   79 PALL = 1.
      L = 0
      WRITE(MED2,902) TT
      WRITE(MED2,982)
      DO 80 I = 1,NB
      W = W/(1.-E(I))
      X1 = CS - P*ALOG(W)
      Y1 = KDF - (NA-I)*(NB-I)
      Z1 = PRBF(Y1,1000.,X1/Y1)
      IF(KA.EQ.3.AND.Z1.GT.V(3)) GO TO 81
      PALL = PALL*Z1
      L = L + 1
      KDF = (NA-I)*(NB-I)
      CS = CS - X1
      WRITE(MED2,983) I,E(I),X1,Y1,Z1
      IF(KA.EQ.1.AND.PALL.LT.V(3)) GO TO 81
      IF(KA.EQ.2.AND.PALL*V(3).LT.PTOT) GO TO 81
   80 CONTINUE
   81 IF(L.GT.0) GO TO 82
      WRITE(MED2,984)
      GO TO 300
   82 L1 = L + 1
      L2 = L + L
C REDUCE MATRICES
      IA = 0
      DO 85 J = 1,NA
      IB = (J-1)*NB
      DO 85 I = 1,L
      IA = IA + 1
      IB = IB + 1
      A(IA) = A(IB)
   85 C(IA) = C(IB)
      IA = 0
      DO 90 J = 1,NB
      IB = (J-1)*NB
      DO 90 I = 1,L
      IA = IA + 1
      IB = IB + 1
      B(IA) = B(IB)
   90 D(IA) = D(IB)
      WRITE(MED2,902) TT
      WRITE(MED2,953)
      LW(1) = 0
      ISAVE(N1) = -ISAVE(N1)
      ISAVE(N2) = - ISAVE(N2)
      CALL WMAT(A, L,NA,NAB,NP,NDP,M,ST,NQ,LW,ISAVE(N1),U,NU,MED2)
      WRITE(MED2,954)
      CALL WMAT(B, L,NB,NB2,NP,NDP,M,ST,NQ,LW,ISAVE(N2),U,NU,MED2)
      WRITE(MED2,902) TT
      WRITE(MED2,985)
      CALL WMAT (C,L ,NA,NAB,NP,NDP,M,ST,NQ,LW,ISAVE(N1),U,NU,MED2)
      WRITE(MED2,986)
      CALL WMAT (D,L ,NB,NB2,NP,NDP,M,ST,NQ,LW,ISAVE(N2),U,NU,MED2)
      ISAVE(N1) = -ISAVE(N1)
      ISAVE(N2) = -ISAVE(N2)
      V(10) =V10
      IF(KP.GE.3) CALL RESID (RA,L,P,MN,ISAVE,K,NP,NDP,LW,NW,Y,Z,
     1XBAR,STD,M,U,NU,ST,X,NQ,SCON,NCON,C,NAB,D,NB2,N1,N2,N3,N4,6)
  300 CONTINUE
  301 V(11) = V11
      RETURN
  902 FORMAT(23H1STATCAT PROGRAM STCANO,7X,1H-,4X,27HMULTIPLE CANONICAL
     1ANALYSIS/16H DATA BANK TITLE,14X,1H-,4X,10A4/23H DATA BANK SUBSET
```

```
      2TITLE,7X,1H-,4X,10A4/10H RUN TITLE,20X,1H-,4X,10A4/)
  923 FORMAT(///19H0 NO DATA IN SAMPLE)
  950 FORMAT(54H0CORRELATIONS BETWEEN PREDICTOR VARIATES              /)
  951 FORMAT(54H0CORRELATIONS BETWEEN PREDICTED VARIATES              /)
  952 FORMAT(54H0CORRELATIONS BETWEEN PREDICTOR AND PREDICTED VARIATES/)
  953 FORMAT(54H0CORRELATIONS BETWEEN PREDICTOR AND CANONICAL VARIATES/)
  954 FORMAT(54H0CORRELATIONS BETWEEN PREDICTED AND CANONICAL VARIATES/)
  982 FORMAT(55H0STATISTICAL TESTS OF INDIVIDUAL CANONICAL VARIATES   /
     154H NUMBER ROOT CHISQUARED DEGREES OF FREEDOM PROBABILITY)
  983 FORMAT(I5,F8.4,F10.4,F12.0,F18.6)
  984 FORMAT (37H0NO SIGNIFICANT ROOTS - READ NEXT JOB)
  985 FORMAT(40H0WEIGHTS FOR CANONICAL VARIATES RETAINED /19H0PREDICTOR
     1VARIATES,10X,11HROOT NUMBER/)
  986 FORMAT(19H0PREDICTED VARIATES,10X,11HROOT NUMBER/)
      END


      SUBROUTINE CORRE(M,XBAR,STD,R,B,D,T,MD,NP,NDP,XX,NQ,SCON,NCON,MN)
C CORRE   (SEE  7.5 ) SYSTEM      MULTIPLE CORRELATION DATA
      DIMENSION NP(M),NDP(M),XBAR(M),STD(M),B(M),T(M)
      DIMENSION XX(NQ),SCON(5,NCON),R(MD),D(MN)
      COMMON /STCT/MED1,MED2,MED3,MED4,MED5,MED6,MED13,Q,V(20),TT(30)
      DO 1 I = 1,M
      B(I) = Q
      T(I) = 0.
      XBAR(I) = 0.
    1 STD(I) = 0.
      DO 2 I = 1,MD
    2 R(I) = 0.
      V(6) = 0.
      V(8) = 1.
    3 CALL MEDIAT(M,NDP,NP,MN,D,XX,NQ,SCON,NCON)
      IF(V(8).EQ.2.) GO TO 20
      DO 10 I = 1,M
      IF(D(I).EQ.Q) GO TO 10
      IF(B(I).EQ.Q) B(I) = D(I)
      D(I) = D(I) - B(I)
      T(I) = T(I) + 1.
      XBAR(I) = XBAR(I)+D(I)
      STD(I) = STD(I) + D(I)*D(I)
   10 CONTINUE
      IDIAG = M*(M+1)/2
      L = 0
      DO 11 J = 1,M
      DO 11 I = J,M
      L = L + 1
      IF((B(I)+D(I)).EQ.Q.OR.(B(J)+D(J)).EQ.Q) GO TO 11
      R(L)=R(L)+D(I)*D(J)
      IF(V(9).EQ.0.) GO TO 11
      IQ = IDIAG + L
      R(IQ) = R(IQ) + 1.
      IQ = IQ + IDIAG
      R(IQ) = R(IQ) + D(I)
      IQ = IQ + IDIAG
      R(IQ) = R(IQ) + D(J)
      IQ = IQ + IDIAG
      R(IQ) = R(IQ) + D(I)*D(I)
      IQ = IQ + IDIAG
      R(IQ) = R(IQ) + D(J)*D(J)
   11 CONTINUE
      GO TO 3
C COMPILE OVERALL MEANS AND STANDARD DEVIATIONS
   20 REWIND MED3
```

```
      DO 21 I = 1,M
      IF(T(I).LE.1.) GO TO 21
      XBAR(I) = XBAR(I)/T(I)
      STD(I) = SQRT(ABS((STD(I)-XBAR(I)*XBAR(I)*T(I))/(T(I))))
   21 CONTINUE
      IF(V(9).EQ.0.) GO TO 40
C WITH POSSIBLE MISSING VALUES
      L = 0
      DO 22 J = 1,M
      DO 22 I = J,M
      L = L + 1
      L1 = L + IDIAG
      IF(R(L1).EQ.0.) GO TO 22
      L2 = L1+ IDIAG
      L3 = L2+ IDIAG
      L4 = L3+ IDIAG
      L5 = L4+ IDIAG
      R(L2) = R(L2)/R(L1)
      R(L3) = R(L3)/R(L1)
      IF(R(L1).GT.1.) GO TO 23
      R(L4) = 0.
      R(L5) = 0.
      R(L ) = 0.
      GO TO 22
   23 R(L4) = SQRT(ABS((R(L4)-R(L1)*R(L2)*R(L2))/(R(L1))))
      R(L5) = SQRT(ABS((R(L5)-R(L1)*R(L3)*R(L3))/(R(L1))))
      IF(R(L4).GT.0..AND.R(L5).GT.0.) R(L)=(R(L)/R(L1)-R(L2)*R(L3))/(R(L4
     1)*R(L5))
      R(L2) = R(L2) + B(I)
      R(L3) = R(L3) +B(J)
   22 CONTINUE
      GO TO 50
C ASSUMING NO MISSING VALUES
   40 L = 0
      DO 41 J = 1,M
      DO 41 I = J,M
      L = L + 1
      IF(V(6).EQ.0..OR.STD(I).EQ.0..OR.STD(J).EQ.0.) GO TO 41
      R(L) = (R(L)/V(6)-XBAR(I)*XBAR(J))/(STD(I)*STD(J))
   41 CONTINUE
   50 DO 51 I = 1,M
   51 IF(T(I).GT.0.)XBAR(I) = XBAR(I)+B(I)
      RETURN
      END


      SUBROUTINE WBASE(ISAVE,NP,NDP,W,XBAR,STD,U,NU,ST,NQ,R,MDIAG,M,NDEL
     1,K,NX)
C WBASE   (SEE  7.5 ) SYSTEM       WRITE CORRELATION MATRIX ETC.
      DIMENSION XBAR(M),STD(M),ISAVE(M),W(M),NP(M),NDP(M),R(MDIAG)
      DIMENSION ST(NQ),U(NU),TM(4,5),USED(4)
      DATA USED/4H USE,4HD IN,4H FOR,4HMING/,B4/4H    /
      DATA TM/4HNUMB,4HER O,4HF VA,4HLUES,4H    ,4HCOLU,4HMN M,4HEANS,
     1       4H    ,4H    R,4HOW M,4HEANS,4H    ,4HCOLU,4HMN S,4H.D.S,
     2       4H    ,4H    R,4HOW S,4H.D.S/
      COMMON /STCT/MED1,MED2,MED3,MED4,MED5,MED6,MED13,Q,V(20),TT(30)
      DO 30 J = 1,NX
      WRITE(MED2,902) TT
      IF(J.EQ.1) WRITE(MED2,940)
      IF(J.EQ.2) WRITE(MED2,941)
      WRITE(MED2,942)
      IF(NDEL.GT.0) WRITE(MED2,943)
      IF(J.EQ.1)KM = K
```

```
      IF(J.EQ.2)KM = M
      DO 30 L = 1,KM
      IF(J.EQ.1)I = ISAVE(L)
      IF(J.EQ.2) I = L
      JT = NP(I)/1000
      JC = NP(I)-JT*1000
      WRITE(MED2,944)U(JT),JC,ST(JC),W(I),XBAR(I),STD(I)
      IF(NDEL.GT.0) WRITE(MED2,945)NDP(I)
   30 CONTINUE
      IF(NX.EQ.1) RETURN
      IDIAG = M*(M+1)/2
      MIS = 0
      IF(IDIAG.EQ.MDIAG) GO TO 36
      X = R(IDIAG+1)
      DO 32 I = 1,IDIAG
   32 IF(X.NE.R(IDIAG+I)) MIS = 1
   36 DO 38 I = 1,6
      L = (I-1)*IDIAG + 1
      WRITE(MED2,902) TT
      IF(I.EQ.1)WRITE(MED2,931)(B4,J=1,8)
      IF(I.GT.1)WRITE(MED2,931)(TM(J,I-1),J=1,4),USED
   37 CALL MOP (R(L),3,M,M,IDIAG,R(L),3,M,M,IDIAG,ISAVE,1,M,ISAVE,1,M,1,
     1MED2)
      IF(MIS.EQ.0) WRITE(MED2,932)
      IF(MIS.EQ.0) RETURN
   38 CONTINUE
      RETURN
  902 FORMAT(24H1SYSTEM SUBROUTINE WBASE,7X,1H-,4X,23HCORRELATION MATRIX
     1 ETC.   /16H DATA BANK TITLE,14X,1H-,4X,10A4/23H DATA BANK SUBSET T
     2ITLE,7X,1H-,4X,10A4/10H RUN TITLE,20X,1H-,4X,10A4/)
  931 FORMAT(1H0,5X,8A4,42H CORRELATIONS BETWEEN ALL VARIATES DEFINED)
  932 FORMAT(1H0,20X,50HONLY COMPLETE ENTRIES USED IN THIS SET OF VARIAT
     1ES)
  940 FORMAT(50H0FOR ALL ENTRIES FOR ALL VARIATES IN THIS ANALYSIS)
  941 FORMAT(42H0FOR ALL ENTRIES FOR ALL VARIATES IN STORE)
  942 FORMAT(17H0TRANSFORM COLUMN,12X,57HNUMBER OF READINGS   ARITHMETIC
     1MEAN     STANDARD DEVIATION)
  943 FORMAT(1H+,17X,5HDELAY)
  944 FORMAT(1H ,A4,3H OF,I3,1H(,A4,1H),9X,3F20.8)
  945 FORMAT(1H+,16X,I4)
      END
```

Chapter VIII

DATA STUDY

This chapter contains three programs designed to provide ideas of methods which may be used in the study of data. The rapid growth of this field has not yet led to any general agreement on the most useful and efficient methods such as exists (more or less) for the more traditional methods. At present, much of the work in this field must be treated with considerable reserve. The assumptions of many methods are not always explicit, and the problems of 'Constructed Significance' must necessarily play a large part in future argument in this field. The user who wishes only to obtain some sort of clues as to what is actually going on within a vast bulk of data may find that these techniques will help to draw his attention to regularities or abnormalities of data which might otherwise be overlooked.

The program STGRPS operates on a STATCAT data bank subset. It divides this subset into groups, using a set of criterion variates, such that the groups are as different as possible. The program is iterative and will continue until stable groups are formed, so that no further entries change groups, or until a limit is reached. It is, in fact, an iterative multiple discriminant analysis with automatic re-allocation of unassigned or aberrant entries.

The program STAIAD operates on a STATCAT data bank subset, in a more or less complementary way. It divides the subset into samples, using a set of predictor variables, in such a way that the samples are maximally different from each other in terms of a criterion variate. At each iteration, it selects the most significant subdivision of the largest remaining sample until either the maximum number of samples is reached, or no sample exceeds a given limit, or no further division is statistically significant.

The program STGRPS and STAIAD are, in a sense, complementary. If a data bank contains marked systematic effects, they should tend to produce the same result. Both programs can be considered as robot data analysers, and both programs, because they draw heavily on the actual values of data to control their strategy, may lead to problems of 'Constructed Significance'.

The program STCLUS performs a simple clustering operation on a large array of correlation coefficients, or on a selection from such an array. Where the array is relatively small, all possible orderings are tried, but because the number of possible orderings increases as the factorial of the number of variates, for medium and large sized arrays a hill-climbing technique is applied. This technique may lead to false peaks, since it has the ability to interchange only two variates at any time. The process is most likely to fail where the relationships present are weak or ambiguous. It may best be regarded as an auxiliary technique to the Factor Analysis described in the previous chapter. It is particularly useful where certain variates correspond closely to specific factors. The technique, unlike the two previously mentioned data analysers, requires data to be at least on an INTERVAL scale of measurement.

8.1   PROGRAM STGRPS - SEMI-AUTOMATIC GROUPING OF ENTRIES

8.1.1   Purpose

   This program divides a specified subset of a STATCAT data bank into samples which are as different from each other in terms of variates drawn from the STATCAT data bank as they can be made. The program may commence with an initially specified set of samples or it may be instructed to allocate the entries arbitrarily. On the basis of this initial allocation to samples, the program will construct discriminant axes on which the entries are again specified. This process is repeated until all entries are allocated to the same sample in two successive runs or until the limit to the number of runs is reached. A final run is then carried out comparing the initial and final allocations of each entry.

   Figure 8.11a contains system flow-charts for the main program STGRPS and the executive subroutine CGRPS. Figure 8.11b contains system flow-charts for the system subroutine MDSWE, and the service subroutine CLENT. The subroutine MDSWE runs through the data bank, classifying entries into groups according to one set of discriminants (or the initial definition), accumulating sums of squares for the next set, and comparing with the previous set. (This subroutine is also used by the program STMDIS (7.4) - although it is not there used iteratively.) CLENT identifies the group to which an entry is most closely related and calculates the probability that the entry belongs to each of the samples specified in terms of the discriminant axes.

8.1.2   Input Data

Item	Level	Format	Function	Section
1	0	A	File control Card	3.2
2	1	D	Sample specification	3.5
3	2	E	Subset specification	3.6
4	3	F	Set of Variates (DELAY)	3.7
5	4	G	Data Handling Instruction (below)	3.8

Data Handling Instruction

Card Layout - Data Handling Instruction - STGRPS

A BCCCDDDEEEEEEEEEFFFFFFFFGGGGGGGGGGGGGGGGHHHHHHHH.....etc

Columns on Card	Item Code	FORTRAN Type	Function	See
1	A	I	Output control index	below
2	B	I	Analysis control index	"
3 - 5	C	F	Maximum Number of Iterations without Convergence	"
6 - 8	D	F	Maximum number of discriminants	"
9 - 16	E	F	Cut-Off for significance	"
17 - 24	F	I	Number of Arbitrary Samples	"
25 - 40	G	A		
41 - 80	H	A	Comment (printed separately)	"

A - Output Control Index

This index controls the amount of detail output by the program. Unless otherwise specified, the program will produce the discriminant score weights, the correlations of the discriminant and original variates, the Wilk's Lambda test of overall significance, the chi-squared test of individual significance for the discriminant variates, univariate analyses of variance for the original variates and sample means for each original and discriminant variate.

<u>Alternatives</u>

A = 0 or blank : Discriminant score weights, correlations with original variates, Wilk's Lambda test, chi-squared tests of individual discriminants and analyses of variance for the original variates, with sample means for the original and discriminant variates.

A = 1 : In addition, covariance, among sample and within sample matrices.

A = 2 : In addition, original means, standard deviations and correlation matrices.

A = 3 : For each changed entry for each iteration (including entries in the subset but not included in any sample, and entries containing non-values) previous sample and new sample.

A = 4 : For each changed entry for each iteration, in addition to the above, probabilities of belonging to each sample in terms of discriminant variates.

A = 5 : For each changed entry for each iteration, in addition, discriminant scores.

A = 6 : For each changed entry for each iteration, in addition, values of variates selected.

A = 7 : For each changed entry for each iteration, in addition, values of original data items.

A = 8 : As for A = 3, but in the final iteration for all entries, including those remaining in their original sample.

A = 9 : As for A = 7, but in the final iteration for all entries, including those remaining in their original sample.

B - <u>Analysis Control Index</u>

This index controls the program strategy. In this program it controls the decision which discriminant variates are to be retained. <u>Unless otherwise specified</u>, all discriminant variates will be retained, up to the maximum number D.

<u>Alternatives</u>

B = 0 or blank : All discriminant variates up to a maximum of D will be retained.

B = 1   : Discriminant variates are eliminated as long as the overall probability remains below E.

B = 2   : Discriminant variates are eliminated as long as the loss in overall probability remains below E.

B = 3   : Discriminant variates are eliminated as long as their individual probability remains above E.

B = 4   : Discriminant variates are eliminated as long as the total unexplained portion of the variance remains below E.

B = 5   : Discriminant variates are eliminated as long as the increase in the unexplained portion of the variance remains below E.

B = 6   : All discriminant variates up to a maximum of D will be retained. Euclidian distance used in calculation of discriminants, and re-allocation of entries to samples.

B = 7   : Discriminant variates are eliminated as long as their individual probability remains above E. Euclidian distance is used in the calculation of discriminants, and re-allocation of entries to samples.

B = 8   : All discriminant variates up to a maximum of D will be retained. Euclidian distance used in calculation of discriminants, but re-allocation of entries to samples is on basis of "city-block" distance (total absolute difference).

B = 9   : Discriminant variates are eliminated as long as their individual probability remains above E. Euclidian distance is used in the calculation of discriminants, but re-allocation of entries to samples is on the basis of "city-block" distance. (total absolute difference.)

C - **Maximum Number of Iterations without Convergence**

This index determines the maximum number of iterations that will be carried out if the allocation of at least one entry is changed at each iteration. If an iteration occurs in which all entries remain in the same samples as for the previous iteration then the system has reached a stable position and no further iterations are required. <u>Unless otherwise specified</u> this value will be taken to be 100.

D - **Maximum Number of Discriminants**

This value determines the number of discriminant variates which will be produced by the program, subject to the requirements of the analysis control index. The maximum number of discriminant variates cannot exceed the number of variates selected, or one less than the number of samples. If the number specified is zero, or is greater than either of these quantities, it will be set to the lesser of the two.

E - <u>Cut-Off Significance</u>

This value is used, as specified by the analysis control index, in association with the value D, to determine the number of discriminant variates that will be retained. If the value D is originally zero, and the value of E is also zero, the value of E will be set to 1.0 per cent.

F - Number of Arbitrary Samples

If one or no sample is specified, the system will initially allocate the entries in rotation to form arbitrary samples. The maximum possible number of arbitrary samples will be calculated following step 3 - and will be printed at that time. This index, if it is greater than zero and less than the maximum, will determine the number of samples used. It may be varied to obtain other starting states.

8.1.3 Input Example

Figure 8.12 is a summary of the input structure for two runs of STGRPS. In the first run, the same two samples as were used in STMDIS (7.4) are defined (Easy versus Hard). The four predictors found individually significant are retained, and the system is set to continue cross-classification until two stable groups have been formed. In the second run no samples are defined, and the system is instructed to form ten arbitrary groups, and to move entries from group to group until a stable set of samples is obtained.

Figure 8.13 is a listing of the input cards required to carry out these two runs.

8.1.4 Output Example

Figure 8.14 is a general summary of the output produced by this program, indented according to the output structure. Figure 8.15 is a page-by-page summary of the output corresponding to the input of Figure 8.13. The input checking information is standard, and the multiple discriminant analysis information is identical to that for STMDIS (7.4). Figure 8.16 gives an example of the intermediate output for the second run, reporting which entries have changed their allocation. The final sweep through the data bank compares the initial and final allocations of entries. Figure 8.17 illustrates the evolution of four arbitrarily formed groups.

8.1.5 Discussion

This program is very similar to STMDIS(7.4), and represents a very minor step towards generality. Nevertheless, it poses some problems in interpretation. Suppose, for example, that we begin with randomly allocated entries, and end up, after a substantial number of changes, with a few coherent groups of entries. In this case, we can claim to have isolated some sort of internal structure in the data, although it would not be easy to assess the statistical significance of such groups. If on the other hand, we repeatedly end up with one group containing all but a few stragglers of our data, we could reasonably assert that there was no 'group' structure in our data - at least in terms of the variates we were examining. In the intermediate cases - stable groups without much difference between them - we are less well placed. Probably the best procedure in such cases is to note the groups so derived for further examination or future experimentation, but not to claim that they are statistically significantly different without a confirmatory experiment.

Empirical tests suggest that it is rare for the arbitrary allocation method to form stable groups, because one widely dispersed group tends to absorb all the others.

As was mentioned in the discussion of STMDIS (7.4) Kendall (1975) has suggested several alternatives to the "classical" multiple discriminant analysis. As well as the suggestion that the original variates may be treated as if they were independent (orthogonal), he has suggested the use of the 'city-block metric'. This is defined by analogy with the measurement of distances in (American) cities, laid out in squares, and is defined as the sum of the absolute differences along each axis (as opposed to the Euclidian root of the sum of squares, or the Mahalonobis measure which takes account of the mutual correlations of axes.) This possibility is included as an option for the re-allocation of entries in this program, although only the Euclidian or Mahalonobis distance can be used in the multiple discriminant section.

REFERENCES: See Chapter 7.4 (Especially Kendall (1975))

472

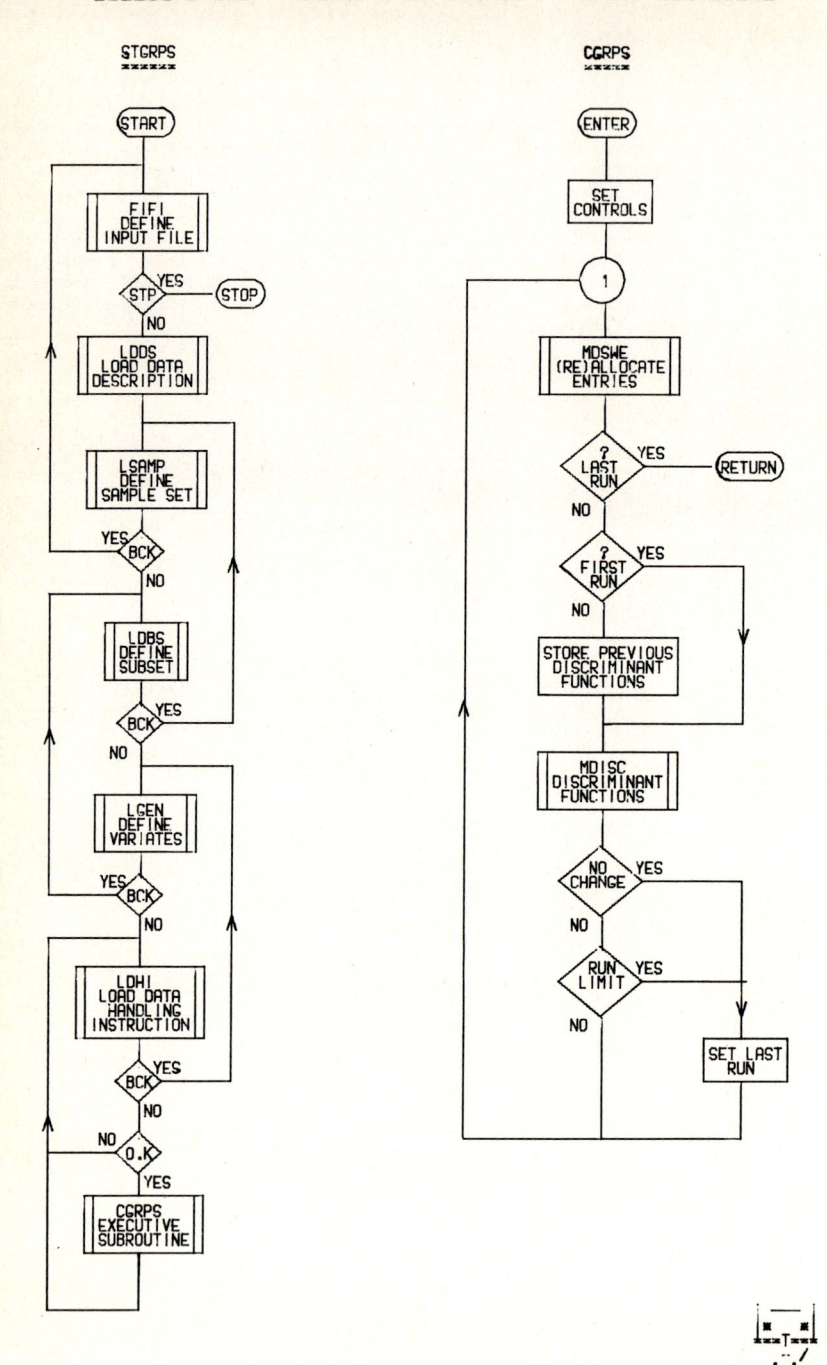

Figure 8.11a – System Flow-Charts – STGRPS and CGRPS

473

Figure 8.11b - System Flow-Charts - MDSWE and CLENT

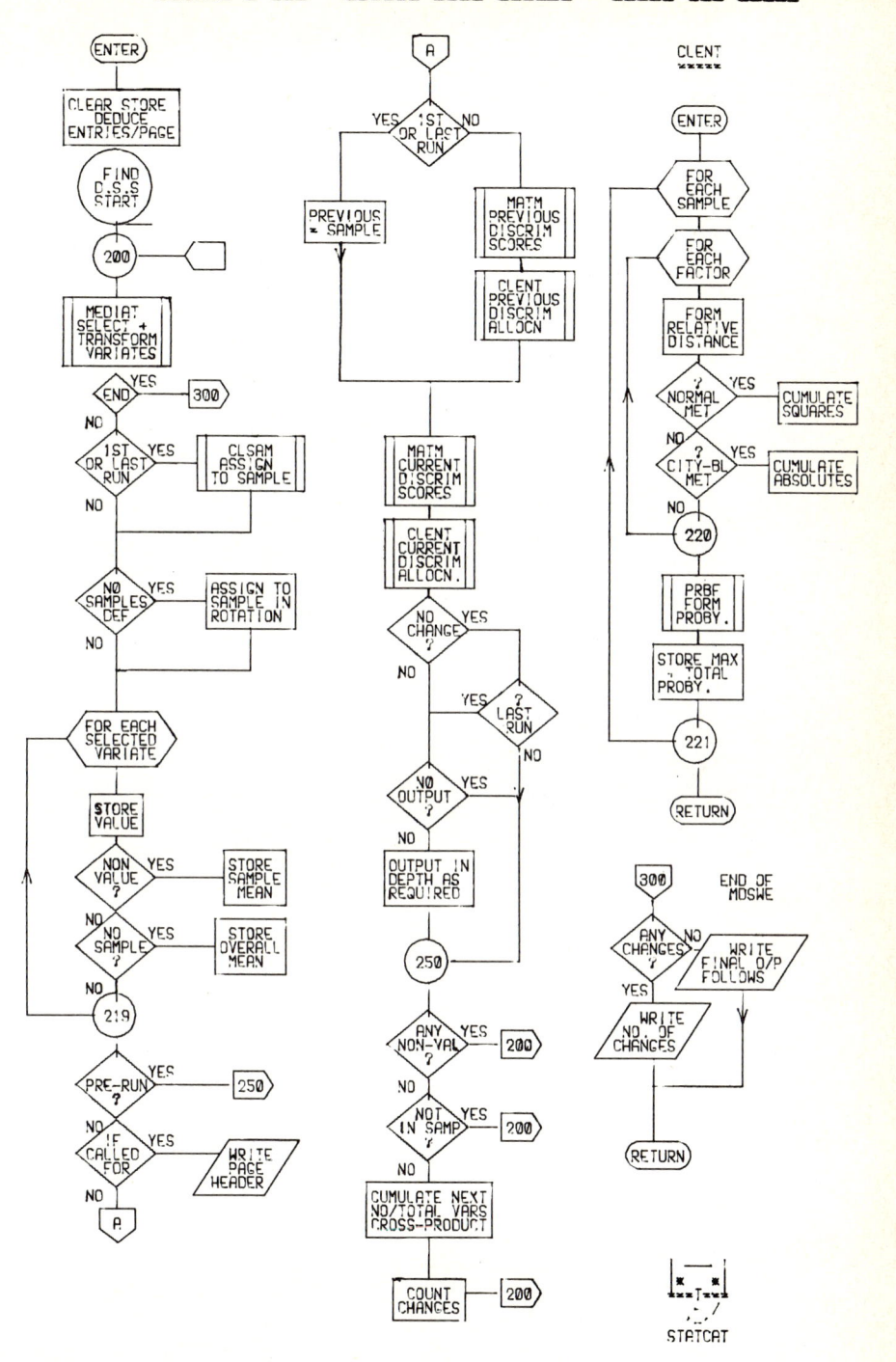

Figure 8.12 - STGRPS - Input Structure

```
         Level
 0   1   2   3   4   5   6   7   8   9
FILE CONTROL CARD
    SAMPLE SPECIFICATION
        SUBSET SPECIFICATION
            VARIATE SPECIFICATION
                DATA HANDLING INSTRUCTION
                BACK TO READ VARIATES
            BACK TO READ SUBSET
        BACK TO READ SAMPLES
    SAMPLE SPECIFICATION
        SUBSET SPECIFICATION
            VARIATE SPECIFICATION
                DATA HANDLING INSTRUCTION
                STOP
```

Figure 8.13 - STGRPS - Input Example

```
---------1---------2---------3---------4---------5---------6---------7--
**STGRPSDEMO                            DEMONSTRATION STATCAT DATA BANK
EASY VS HARD                            ALL EASY COMPARED WITH ALL DIFFI
EASY
.IF.DIFF.LT.       3.5                  RATHER EASY/EASY/VERY EASY
END OF SAMPLE ONE
HARD
.IF.DIFF.GT.       4.5                  RATHER DIFFICULT/DIFFICULT/VERY
END OF SAMPLE TWO
END OF SAMPLE SET
ALL DATA                                WHOLE DATA BANK TO BE INCLUDED
END OF SUBSET DEFINITION
VAL.OPER
VAL.STRS
VAL.TPCT
VAL.H.R.
END OF SET OF VARIATES
8 ONE LINE RECORD OF CHANGE
BACK TO READ VARIATES
BACK TO READ SUBSET
BACK TO READ SAMPLES
ARBITRARY SAMPLES
END OF EMPTY SAMPLE SPECIFICATION       NO SAMPLES SPECIFIED
ALL DATA
END OF SUBSET SPECIFICATION
VAL.OPER
VAL.STRS
VAL.TPCT
VAL.H.R.
END OF VARIATE SET
84           5.         4.
STOP
---------1---------2---------3---------4---------5---------6---------7--
```

Figure 8.14 - STGRPS - Output Structure

```
For each     ) : File Control Record
output file  )   File Parameters
                 Data Description
                 For each) :  Sample Input Record
                 Set of  )   For each ) : Input Record
                 Samples     Subset   )   For each set ) : Input
                                      )   of Original  )   Record
                                                Variates )   see left
For each Data) : Input Record
Handling     )   For Each Run *
Instruction  )   . <Covariance matrix - Original Variates>
variate      )   . <Among Samples matrix - Original Variates>
                 . <Within Samples Matrix- Original Variates>
                 . Wilkes Lambda Test
                 . Univariate F tests
                 . Discriminant Weights
                 . Correlations original/discriminant variates
                 . No,a.m and sd for original and discriminant variates
                   for each sample
                 . <Attribution Record>
                     . For Each <Changed> Entry : -
                     . <Original/Revised sample/Proby : Forced choice>
                     . <Prediscriminant Values>
                     . <Variate Values>
                     . <Data Items>
                 Total number of changed attributions
```

Carated(<>) items are optional.

* Until no further changes occur

Figure 8.15 - STGRPS - Page-by-page output summary

Page	Contents	Origin
1-2	File Control/Program title	FIFI/LDAP/STGRPS
	Data Description record	LDDS
3	Sample record	LSAMP/LSET
4	Subset record	LDBS/LSET
5	Original Variates record	LGEN
	Data Handling Instruction	LDHI
6	Covariance/among/within Samples Matrices	MDISC
7	Wilks Lambda /Univariate F tests	MDISC
8	Discriminant Weights/Correlations	MDISC
9	Sample no,a.m. and s.d. (Original+Discriminant)	MDISC
10	Reallocation - Samples to Discriminant set 1	MDSWE
11-14	Discriminant Analysis Discriminant set 2	MDISC
15	Reallocation - Discriminant sets 1 to 2	MDSWE
16-19	Discriminant Analysis Discriminant set 3	MDISC
20	Reallocation - Discriminant sets 2 to 3 (NONE)	MDSWE
21-22	Reallocation - Samples to Discriminant set 3	MDSWE
23	Data Handling Instruction (BACK)	LDHI
24	BACK to Subset/BACK to Samples	LGEN/LDBS
25	Arbitrary Sample Specification	LSAMP/STGRPS
26	Subset record	LDBS/LSET
27	Original Variates record	LGEN
	Data Handling Instruction	LDHI
28-31	Discriminant Analysis - Arbitrary Samples	MDISC
32-97	Discriminant Analysis + Reallocation (Discriminant sets 1 to 5)	MDISC/MDSWE
98-99	Reallocation - Samples to Discriminant set 5	MDSWE
100	Data Handling Instruction (STOP)	LDHI

Figure 8.16 - STGRPS - Partial Output - changed allocations

```
SYSTEM SUBROUTINE MDSWF       -    (RE-)ALLOCATE ENTRIES
DATA BANK TITLE               -    DEMONSTRATION STATCAT DATA BANK
DATA BANK SAMPLE SET          -    EASY VS HARD
DATA BANK SUBSET              -    ALL DATA

CHANGES FROM SAMPLES AS DEFINED  TO DISCRIMINANT SET  1

  ENTRY     12 NOT IN ANY SAMPLE                              MOVED TO SAMPLE  2 (HARD) P = 0.511201 FORCED CHOICE P= 0.996572
  ENTRY     13 NOT IN ANY SAMPLE                              MOVED TO SAMPLE  2 (HARD) P = 0.977509 FORCED CHOICE P= 0.585272
  ENTRY     14 NOT IN ANY SAMPLE                              MOVED TO SAMPLE  1 (EASY) P = 0.629294 FORCED CHOICE P= 0.720297
  ENTRY     19 NOT IN ANY SAMPLE                              MOVED TO SAMPLE  2 (HARD) P = 0.700194 FORCED CHOICE P= 0.536766
  ENTRY     22 NOT IN ANY SAMPLE                              MOVED TO SAMPLE  2 (HARD) P = 0.700194 FORCED CHOICE P= 0.538766
  ENTRY     25   DEFINED IN SAMPLE  1 (EASY) P = 0.100453 MOVED TO SAMPLE  2 (HARD) P = 0.529310 FORCED CHOICE P= 0.840437
  ENTRY     26   DEFINED IN SAMPLE  2 (HARD) P = 0.085319 MOVED TO SAMPLE  1 (EASY) P = 0.650655 FORCED CHOICE P= 0.504977
  ENTRY     27   DEFINED IN SAMPLE  1 (EASY) P = 0.100487 MOVED TO SAMPLE  2 (HARD) P = 0.529323 FORCED CHOICE P= 0.840448
  ENTRY     28 NOT IN ANY SAMPLE                              MOVED TO SAMPLE  2 (HARD) P = 0.624264 FORCED CHOICE P= 0.757341
  ENTRY     30 NOT IN ANY SAMPLE                              MOVED TO SAMPLE  2 (HARD) P = 0.933693 FORCED CHOICE P= 0.990807
  ENTRY     31   DEFINED IN SAMPLE  2 (HARD) P = 0.132752 MOVED TO SAMPLE  1 (EASY) P = 0.660435 FORCED CHOICE P= 0.832634
  ENTRY     32   DEFINED IN SAMPLE  1 (EASY) P = 0.117138 MOVED TO SAMPLE  2 (HARD) P = 0.504599 FORCED CHOICE P= 0.811596
  ENTRY     37   DEFINED IN SAMPLE  2 (HARD) P = 0.058826 MOVED TO SAMPLE  1 (EASY) P = 0.800671 FORCED CHOICE P= 0.890132
  ENTRY     41 NOT IN ANY SAMPLE                              MOVED TO SAMPLE  2 (HARD) P = 0.663553 FORCED CHOICE P= 0.924334
  ENTRY     49 NOT IN ANY SAMPLE                              MOVED TO SAMPLE  1 (EASY) P = 0.598428 FORCED CHOICE P= 0.727125
  ENTRY     50 NOT IN ANY SAMPLE                              MOVED TO SAMPLE  2 (HARD) P = 0.977509 FORCED CHOICE P= 0.989272
  ENTRY     52 NOT IN ANY SAMPLE                              MOVED TO SAMPLE  2 (HARD) P = 0.512391 FORCED CHOICE P= 0.996136
  ENTRY     53   DEFINED IN SAMPLE  1 (EASY) P = 0.115247 MOVED TO SAMPLE  2 (HARD) P = 0.501002 FORCED CHOICE P= 0.812987
  ENTRY     54   DEFINED IN SAMPLE  2 (HARD) P = 0.240177 MOVED TO SAMPLE  1 (EASY) P = 0.621467 FORCED CHOICE P= 0.721264
  ENTRY     55   DEFINED IN SAMPLE  1 (EASY) P = 0.208091 MOVED TO SAMPLE  2 (HARD) P = 0.633060 FORCED CHOICE P= 0.752611
  ENTRY     56 NOT IN ANY SAMPLE                              MOVED TO SAMPLE  2 (HARD) P = 0.624264 FORCED CHOICE P= 0.757341
  ENTRY     58 NOT IN ANY SAMPLE                              MOVED TO SAMPLE  2 (HARD) P = 0.505508 FORCED CHOICE P= 0.811242
  ENTRY     64 NOT IN ANY SAMPLE                              MOVED TO SAMPLE  2 (HARD) P = 0.966716 FORCED CHOICE P= 0.989707

            TOTAL NUMBER OF CHANGES =    23
```

Figure 8.17 - STGRPS - Evolution of arbitrary groups

Original Allocation (in rotation)

Second Pass	1	2	3	4	Total
1	8	6	4	0	18
2	1	0	4	3	8
3	3	7	4	5	19
4	4	3	4	8	19
Total	16	16	16	16	64

Second Pass

Third Pass	1	2	3	4	Total
1	11	4	0	0	15
2	7	3	10	0	20
3	0	0	7	3	10
4	0	1	2	16	19
Total	18	8	19	19	64

Third Pass

Fourth Pass	1	2	3	4	Total
1	0	0	0	0	0
2	0	0	0	0	0
3	0	4	9	0	13
4	15	16	1	19	51
Total	15	20	10	19	64

Fourth Pass

Fifth Pass	1	2	3	4	Total
1	0	0	0	0	0
2	0	0	0	0	0
3	0	0	9	18	27
4	0	0	4	33	37
Total	0	0	13	51	64

Original Allocation (in rotation)

Fifth Pass	1	2	3	4	Total
1	0	0	0	0	0
2	0	0	0	0	0
3	7	7	4	9	27
4	9	9	12	7	37
Total	16	16	16	16	64

```
C MASTER STGRPS - GENERAL MULTI-PASS GROUPING BY DISCRIMINANTS
C       SUBROUTINES AND FUNCTIONS REQUIRED
C AN      (SEE  3.1 ) SERVICE     ALPHA - TO NUMERIC VALUE
C ASEV    (SEE 11.3 ) SERVICE     EIGEN ROOTS ETC ASYMMETRIC MATRIX
C CHIKEN  (SEE 11.9 ) SERVICE     WARNS OF MISMATCHED DATA LEVEL
C CLENT   (SEE  8.1 ) SERVICE     FINDS PROB. ENTRY IS IN SAMPLES
C CLSAM   (SEE  3.5 ) SERVICE     ALLOTS ENTRY TO SAMPLE/SUBSET
C CGRPS   (SEE  8.1 ) EXECUTIVE   FORMS GROUPS OF ENTRIES
C COMPA   (SEE  3.1 ) SERVICE     COMPARES ALPHAMERIC VALUES
C COPYA   (SEE  3.1 ) SERVICE     COPIES ALPHAMERIC VALUE
C FIFI    (SEE  3.2 ) SYSTEM      ALLOCATES PERIPHERALS
C GAUS    (SEE 11.8 ) STATISTICAL FINDS ASS. PROB. OF N VALUE
C IBL     (SEE  3.1 ) SERVICE     DETECTS BLANK,END AND STOP CARDS
C ICH     (SEE  3.1 ) SERVICE     IDENTIFIES ALPHAMERIC CODES
C LCOM    (SEE  3.4 ) SERVICE     LOADS COMPLEMENTARY INFORMATION
C LDAP    (SEE  3.3 ) SYSTEM      LOADS/CHECKS DATA BANK PARAMETERS
C LDBS    (SEE  3.6 ) SYSTEM      LOADS SUBSET DEFINITION
C LDDS    (SEE  3.4 ) SYSTEM      LOADS DATA DESCRIPTION SEGMENT
C LDHI    (SEE  3.8 ) SYSTEM      LOADS/CHECKS DATA HANDLING INSTN
C LGEN    (SEE  3.7 ) SYSTEM      LOADS GENERALISED VARIATES
C LSAMP   (SEE  3.5 ) SYSTEM      LOADS SAMPLE SET DEFINITION
C LSET    (SEE  3.5 ) SYSTEM      LOADS DEFINING CONDITIONS
C MATM    (SEE 11.3 ) SERVICE     MULTIPLIES MATRICES
C MEDIAT  (SEE  3.7 ) SERVICE     FETCHES NEXT VARIATE SET
C MINV    (SEE 11.3 ) SERVICE     INVERTS MATRIX
C MOP     (SEE 11.3 ) SERVICE     SELECTS/CONVERTS STORED MATRIX
C PRBF    (SEE 11.8 ) STATISTICAL FINDS PROBABILITY OF F-RATIO
C TRANS   (SEE  3.7 ) SERVICE     CARRIES OUT REQUIRED TRANSFORM
C WBASE   (SEE  7.5 ) SYSTEM      WRITES CORRELATION MATRIX ETC
C WDCD    (SEE  3.4 ) SERVICE     WRITES DATA COLUMN DESCRIPTION
C WMAT    (SEE 11.3 ) SERVICE     WRITE MATRIX WITH VARIATE TITLES
C SETTING OF ARRAY DIMENSIONS
C THE FOLLOWING DIMENSIONS MUST BE AT LEAST AS BIG AS THOSE
C SPECIFIED BY THE DATA TAPE,SAMPLE SPECIFICATIONS,ETC.
C NQMAX = MAXIMUM NUMBER OF DATA COLUMNS
C IF NQMAX AND ARRAYS ARE CHANGED,CHANGE DATA STATEMENT FOR CN
C DIMENSION XX(NQMAX),IT(NQMAX),ST(NQMAX),CN(NQMAX)
      NQMAX = 100
      DIMENSION XX( 100),IT( 100),ST( 100),CN( 100)
      DATA  CN/4HCOL1,4HCOL2,4HCOL3,4HCOL4,4HCOL5,4HCOL6,4HCOL7,4HCOL8,4
     1HCOL9,4HCL10,4HCL11,4HCL12,4HCL13,4HCL14,4HCL15,4HCL16,4HCL17,4HC
     218,4HCL19,4HCL20,4HCL21,4HCL22,4HCL23,4HCL24,4HCL25,4HCL26,4HCL27,
     34HCL28,4HCL29,4HCL30,4HCL31,4HCL32,4HCL33,4HCL34,4HCL35,4HCL36,4HC
     4L37,4HCL38,4HCL39,4HCL40,4HCL41,4HCL42,4HCL43,4HCL44,4HCL45,4HCL46
     5,4HCL47,4HCL48,4HCL49,4HCL50,4HCL51,4HCL52,4HCL53,4HCL54,4HCL55,4H
     6CL56,4HCL57,4HCL58,4HCL59,4HCL60,4HCL61,4HCL62,4HCL63,4HCL64,4HCL6
     75,4HCL66,4HCL67,4HCL68,4HCL69,4HCL70,4HCL71,4HCL72,4HCL73,4HCL74,4
     8HCL75,4HCL76,4HCL77,4HCL78,4HCL79,4HCL80,4HCL81,4HCL82,4HCL83,4HCL
     984,4HCL85,4HCL86,4HCL87,4HCL88,4HCL89,4HCL90,4HCL91,4HCL92,4HCL93,
     94HCL94,4HCL95,4HCL96,4HCL97,4HCL98,4HCL99,4HC100/
C MAXMI = MAXIMUM NUMBER OF VARIATES IN ANY DATA SWEEP
C DIMENSION ISAVE(MAXMI),IX(MAXMI),IY(MAXMI),NDP(MAXMI),NP(MAXMI)
      MAXMI = 50
      DIMENSION ISAVE( 50),IX( 50),IY( 50),NDP( 50),NP( 50)
C MAXAV = GENERAL STORE FOR CORRELATION MATRIX AND ANALYSIS
C MUST BE AT LEAST NS*(M+2) + (NS+1)*(M+1)*M/2 + M*(5+6*M)
C WHERE M = NUMBER OF VARIATES IN STORE                    MINIMUM = 1
C WHERE NS= NUMBER OF SAMPLES IN USE                       MINIMUM = 2
C   DIMENSION R(MAXAV)
      MAXAV = 2000
      DIMENSION R(2000)
C MAXD = STORAGE AVAILABLE FOR DELAYED       ENTRIES
C   (MAXIMUM DELAY. + 3.) * M MUST NOT EXCEED MAXD
```

```
C DIMENSION D(MAXD) IF MAXD NOT ZERO
C DIMENSION D(MAXD)
      MAXD = 500
      DIMENSION D(500)
C NALTMX = MAXIMUM NUMBER OF CLASSES ON TAPE
C DIMENSION       TRT(NALTMX)
      NALTMX = 50
      DIMENSION  TRT(50)
C MAXDBC=MAXIMUM NUMBER OF CONDITIONS (SUBSET+SAMPLE)
C DIMENSION SCON(5,MAXDBC)
      MAXDBC = 100
      DIMENSION SCON(5,100)
C MAXSAC = MAXIMUM NUMBER OF SAMPLE DEFINITION CONDITIONS
C DIMENSION SACON(5,MAXSAC)
      DIMENSION SACON(5,150)
      MAXSAC = 150
C THE FOLLOWING DIMENSION STORES THE NAMES OF THE DATA TRANSFORMS
C AND THE ACCEPTABLE LEVELS FOR TRANSFORMATIONS
      DIMENSION U(60),LU(60)
      NU = 60
C TRANSFORMATION CODES
C UNITS                          BLOCKS
C      0 - 9   10 - 19   20 - 29   30 - 39   40 - 49   50 - 59
C      POWERS TRIG       TRIG      STATIST   MATHS     TEST
C             RADIANS    DEGREES   TRANSF    FUNCTS    FUNCTIONS
C  0    -       -        H.MS       -          -       RM10
C  1    VAL.    SINR     SIND      PSNA       RECP    +/-1
C  2    SQAR    COSR     COSD      PSNB       SQRT    ADD1
C  3    CUBE    TANR     TAND      BINO       ABSV    SUB1
C  4    4PWR    ASIR     ASID      LG+1       SIGN    NOR1
C  5    5PWR    ACOR     ACOD      LOGE       INTG    +/-P
C  6    6PWR    ATAR     ATAD      LG10       FRAC    ADDP
C  7    7PWR    SINH     DTOR      AL10       EXPT    SUBP
C  8    8PWR    COSH     RTOD       -         PRES    NORP
C  9    9PWR    TANH     H.HH                 NEG.    +100
      DATA U/4HVAL.,4HSQAR,4HCUBE,4H4PWR,4H5PWR,4H6PWR,4H7PWR,4H8PWR,4H9
     1PWR,4HVAL ,4HSINR,4HCOSR,4HTANR,4HASIR,4HACOR,4HATAR,4HSINH,4HCOSH
     2,4HTANH,4HH.MS,4HSIND,4HCOSD,4HTAND,4HASID,4HACOD,4HATAD,4HDTOR,4H
     3RTOD,4HH.HH,4H VAL,4HPSNA,4HPSNB,4HBINO,4HLG+1,4HLOGE,4HLG10,4HAL1
     40    ,4H   ,4H   ,4H      ,4HRECP,4HSQRT,4HABSV,4HSIGN,4HINTG,4HFRAC,4
     5HEXPT,4HPRES,4HNEG.,4HRM10,4H+/-1,4HADD1,4HSUB1,4HNOR1,4H+/-P,4HAD
     6DP,4HSUBP,4HNORP,4H+100,4H       /
C ACCEPTABLE CODE LEVELS
      DATA LU/60*4/
C DUMMY ARRAYS USED IN LGEN + D.H.I INPUT ARRAY
      DIMENSION FORM(50)
      COMMON /STCT/MED1,MED2,MED3,MED4,MED5,MED6,MED13,Q,V(20),TT(30)
      DATA PROG/4HGRPS/
      MED1 = -1
C LEVEL 0 - SETTING UP
    1 CALL COPYA(TT(1),PROG)
      CALL FIFI
      IF(MED3.GT.0) WRITE(MED2,901)
      CALL LDAP(MED2,MED3,V,TT,Q,NQ,NALT,NQMAX,NALTMX,IGO)
      IF(IGO.GT.0) GO TO 1
      CALL LDDS(TRT,NALT,D,NQ,ST,NQ,IT,NQ,H,0,H,H,0,LI,0,Q,VX,
     1 0,MED2,MED3,0,IGO)
      IF(IGO.GT.0) GO TO 1
C READ SAMPLE SPECIFICATION - LEVEL 1
   11 IF(V(10).GE.10.) V(10) = 0.
      NSMAX = (MAXAV-3)/26
      CALL LSAMP(SCON,NCON,MAXDBC,R,NS,NSMAX,CN,ST,IT,NQ,TRT,NALT,IGO)
      IF(IGO.GT.0) GO TO 1
```

```
      IF(V(10).LT.0.5.AND.V(20).GT.0.5) V(10) = 11.
      IF(NS.LT.2) V(19) = -1.
      IF(NS.GE.2) V(19) = NS
      IF(NS.EQ.0) WRITE(MED2,910)
      IF(NS.EQ.1) WRITE(MED2,911)
      IF(NS.LT.2) NS = 2
      NSB = NS
C READ DATA BANK SUBSET - LEVEL 2
   21 IF(V(10).GE.20.) V(10) = 0.
      MAXLEF = MAXDBC-NCON
      NCON1 = NCON+1
      CALL LDBS(SCON(1,NCON1),NCONB,MAXLEF,CN,ST,IT,NQ,TRT,NALT,IGO)
      IF(IGO.GT.0) GO TO 11
      IF(V(10).LT.0.5.AND.V(20).GT.0.5) V(10) = 21.
      ARAN = 5236.
C READ SET OF VARIATES FOR DATA SWEEP       - LEVEL 4
   41 IF(V(10).GE.40.) V(10) = 0.
      V19 = V(19)
      M = 0
      V(6) = 0.
      WRITE(MED6,941)
      WRITE(MED6,944)
      A = NS + 13
      B = 3*NS+15
      C = 4*NS - 2*MAXAV
      MAXM = (SQRT(B*B-4.*A*C)-B)/A*0.5
      IF(MAXM.LT.NS) A = NS + 1
      IF(MAXM.LT.NS) B = 15*NS + 1
      IF(MAXM.LT.NS) C = 18*NS - 2*MAXAV
      IF(MAXM.LT.NS) MAXM = (SQRT(B*B-4.*A*C)-B)/A*0.5
      IF(MAXM.GT.MAXMI) MAXM = MAXMI
      CALL LGEN(U,NU,LU,MU,ST,IT,CN,NQ,IH,0,H,H,0,H,H,0,MAXD,NALT,NDP,NP
     1,MAXM,M,MAXM,1,NALT)
      IF(V(11).LT.0.5.AND.V(20).LT.0.5)GO TO 21
      IF(V(10).LT.0.5.AND.V(20).GT.0.5) V(10) = 43.
      BRAN = ARAN
      V(19) = V19
      IF(V(19).GT.-0.5) GO TO 91
      NS = 2*MAXAV/(18+M*(15+M))
      IF(NS.LT.M) NS = (2*MAXAV-M*(14+12*M))/(2 + M*(M+3))
      IF(NS.GT.NQMAX) NS = NQMAX
      WRITE(MED2,942) NS
      NSB = NS
C LEVEL 9 - READ DATA HANDLING INSTRUCTION
   91 IF(V(10).GT.90.) V(10) = 0.
      CALL LDHI(V(1),1,V(2),2,V(9),8,V(3),11,V(4),16,VX,0,H,V(10),
     1 FORM(41),FORM,MED1,MED2,0,Q,NQ,NWARN,1,IGO)
      IF(IGO.GT.0) GO TO 41
C STANDARDISATION - IF V(19) NEGATIVE ARBITRARY SAMPLES
      NX = 0
      IF(V(19).GT.-0.5) GO TO 93
      NX = NSB
      NS = VX
      IF(NX.LT.NS.AND.NX.GT.0) NWARN = NWARN + 1
      IF(NX.LT.NS.AND.NX.GT.0) NS = NX
      DO 92 I = 1,NS
   92 CALL COPYA(R(I),CN(I))
      VX=NS
      NX=4
   93 FMAX = M
      IF(NS.LE.M ) FMAX = NS - 1
      IF(V(9).LE.0.5) NWARN = NWARN + 1
      IF(V(9).LE.0.5) V(9) = 100.
```

```
      IF(V(3).EQ.O..AND.V(4).EQ.0.) NWARN = NWARN + 1
      IF(V(3).EQ.O..AND.V(4).EQ.0.) V(4) = 1.
      IF(V(3).GT.FMAX.OR.V(3).EQ.0.) NWARN = NWARN + 1
      IF(V(3).GT.FMAX.OR.V(3).EQ.0.) V(3) = FMAX
      MDIAG = (NS+1)*(M+1)*M/2 + NS*(M+2)
      IF(M.GT.NS) MXM = (2+6*M)*M + 5*M
      IF(M.LE.NS) MXM = (2+6*M)*NS+ 5*M
      IF(MXM+MDIAG.LE.MAXAV) GO TO 100
      WRITE(MED6,992) MDIAG,MXM,MAXAV
      IF(V(10).EQ.0.)V(10) = 91.
  100 CALL LDHI(V(1),1,V(2),2,V(9),8,V(3),11,V(4),16,VX,NX,H,V(10),
     1 FORM(41),FORM,MED1,MED2,0,Q,NQ,NWARN,2,IGO)
      IF(IGO.GT.0) GO TO 91
C TEST FOR ACCEPTED DATA
  101 WRITE(MED6,998)
      V(4) = V(4)*.01
      MDIAG = M*(M+1)/2
      MDNS = MDIAG*NS
      MNS = M*NS
      K1 = NS
      IF(K1.LT.M) K1 = M
      NPV = K1
      KXK = K1*M
      IT1 = NS+1
      IC = IT1 + NS
      IA = IC + MDIAG
      IXS = IA + MDNS
      IXB = IXS + MNS
      IE = IXB + M
      IX1 = IE + NPV
      JY = IX1 + K1
      IZ  = JY + NPV
      IRA = IZ + NPV
      IRW = IRA + KXK
      IRC = IRW + KXK
      IW2 = IRC + KXK
      IA2 = IW2 + KXK
      IC2 = IA2 + KXK
      IX2 = IC2 + KXK
      IZ2 = IX2 + K1
      V(10) = BRAN
      CALL CGRPS(R(IA),R(IC),D,ISAVE,IX,IY,NDP,NP,R(IRA),R(IRC),R(IRW),S
     1CON,SCOM(1,NCON1),R(IT1),R(IX1),R(IXB),R(IXS),XX,R(JY),R(IZ),R(IA2
     2),R(IC2),R(IW2),R(IX2),R(IZ2),KXK,M,MDIAG,MAXD,NCON,NCONB,NQ,NS,R(
     3IE),ST,R,U,NU,K1)
      ARAN = V(10)
      V(10) = 0.
      WRITE(MED6,999)
      GO TO 91
  901 FORMAT (1H0,20X,32HSTATCAT GENERAL GROUPING PROGRAM )
  910 FORMAT(50H0NO SAMPLES SPECIFIED - SUBSET DIVIDED BY ROTATION/)
  911 FORMAT(48H0ONLY ONE SAMPLE SPECIFIED - DIVIDED BY ROTATION/)
  941 FORMAT(44H1ORIGINAL VARIATES FOR DISCRIMINANT ANALYSIS/)
  942 FORMAT(6H0UP TO ,I4,27H ARBITRARY SAMPLES EMPLOYED)
  944 FORMAT(7H0NUMBER,6X,19HTRANS   DATA   CYCLES/5H CODE,8X,18H-FORM COL
     1UMN DELAY,66X,7HCOMMENT)
  992 FORMAT(29H0 CORRELATION MATRIX REQUIRES,I6,6H CELLS/21H     ANALYSI
     1S REQUIRES,I6,6H CELLS/6H0 ONLY,I6,27H AVAILABLE - INCREASE MAXAV)
  998 FORMAT (36H0INPUT ACCEPTED - ANALYSIS COMMENCES)
  999 FORMAT (36H1ANALYSIS COMPLETED - READ NEW INPUT)
      END
```

```
      SUBROUTINE CGRPS(A,C,D,ISAVE,IX,IY,NDP,NP,RA,RC,RW,SACON,SCON,T,X,
     1XBAR,XSAM,XX,Y,Z,RA2,RC2,RW2,X2,Z2,KXK,M,MDIAG,MN,NACON,NCON,NQ,NS
     2,E,ST,TRTC,U,NU,K1)
C CGRPS  (SEE  8.1 ) EXECUTIVE    FORMS GROUPS OF ENTRIES
      DIMENSION XBAR(M),T(NS),XSAM(M,NS),C(MDIAG),A(MDIAG,NS),TRTC(NS)
      DIMENSION XX(NQ),NDP(M),NP(M),D(MN),ST(NQ)
      DIMENSION SCON(5,NCON),SACON(5,NACON),U(NU)
      DIMENSION RW(KXK),RA(KXK),RC(KXK),X(K1)
      DIMENSION RW2(KXK),RA2(KXK),RC2(KXK),X2(K1),Z2(M)
      DIMENSION IX(M),ISAVE(M),IY(M),E(M),Y(M),Z(M)
      COMMON /STCT/MED1,MED2,MED3,MED4,MED5,MED6,MED13,Q,V(20),TT(30)
      REWIND MED3
      DO 1 I = 1,M
    1 ISAVE(I) = I
      NRUN = -1
      NT = V(9)
      V(9) = 0.
      K = M
    2 CALL MDSWE(A,C,D,ISAVE,IX,IY,NDP,NP,RA,RC,RW,SACON,SCON,T,X,XBAR,
     1XSAM,XX,Y,Z,RA2,RC2,RW2,X2,Z2,K,KXK,M,MDIAG,MN,NACON,NCON,NQ,NS,E
     2,ST,TRTC,U,NU,K1,NRUN,NXO,NF,KF,NSF,NF2,KF2,NSF2,NT)
      IF(NRUN.EQ.NT) RETURN
      IF(NXO.EQ.0.AND.NRUN.GE.0) NT = NRUN
      IF(NRUN.EQ.NT) GO TO 2
      IF(NRUN.LT.0) GO TO 4
      DO 3 I = 1,KXK
      RA2(I) = RA(I)
      RW2(I) = RW(I)
    3 RC2(I) = RC(I)
      NF2 = NF
      KF2 = KF
      NSF2 = NSF
    4 CALL MDISC(A,C,D,ISAVE,IX,IY,NDP,NP,RA,RC,RW,T,X,XBAR,XSAM,XX,Y,Z,
     1K,KXK,M,MDIAG,MN,NQ,NS,E,ST,TRTC,U,NU,K1,NRUN,NMT,NF,KF,NSF)
      IF(NMT.GE.NS-1.OR.NF.EQ.0) RETURN
      NRUN = NRUN + 1
      GO TO 2
      END


      SUBROUTINE MDSWE(A,C,D,ISAVE,IX,IY,NDP,NP,RA,RC,RW,SACON,SCON,T,X,
     1XBAR,XSAM,XX,Y,Z,RA2,RC2,RW2,X2,Z2,K,KXK,M,MDIAG,MN,NACON,NCON,NQ,
     2NS,E,ST,TRTC,U,NU,K1,NRUN,NXO,NF,KF,NSF,NF2,KF2,NSF2,NT)
C MDSWE  (SEE  8.1 ) EXECUTIVE    (RE)ALLOCATES ENTRIES TO GROUPS
      DIMENSION XBAR(M),T(NS),XSAM(M,NS),C(MDIAG),A(MDIAG,NS),TRTC(NS)
      DIMENSION XX(NQ),NDP(M),NP(M),D(MN),ST(NQ)
      DIMENSION SCON(5,NCON),SACON(5,NACON),U(NU)
      DIMENSION RW(KXK),RA(KXK),RC(KXK),X(K1)
      DIMENSION RW2(KXK),RA2(KXK),RC2(KXK),X2(K1),Z2(M)
      DIMENSION IX(M),ISAVE(M),IY(M),E(M),Y(M),Z(M)
      COMMON /STCT/MED1,MED2,MED3,MED4,MED5,MED6,MED13,Q,V(20),TT(30)
      VBASE = V(10)
      V(7) = 3.
      MS= V(19)
      KA = V(1)
      KB = V(2)
      KAT= 0
      IF(KA.GT.7) KAT = 1
      IF(KA .EQ.8) KA = 3
      IF(KA .EQ.9) KA = 7
      NDEL = 0
      DO 10 I = 1,K
      IS = ISAVE(I)
```

```
   10 IF(NDP(IS).GT.0)NDEL = 1
C FIND LINES PER HEADER/ENTRY + DEDUCE ENTRIES/PAGE OUTPUT (NH)
      NH = 5
      IF(KA.GE.7) NH = NH + (NQ+19)/10
      IF(KA.GE.5) NH = NH + (NP+19)/10
      NE = NH - 4
      IF(KA.GE.4) NE = NE + (NS+9)/10*4 + 1
      IF(KA.GE.6) NE = NE + (M+9)/10
      IF(KA.GE.6) NH = NH + (M+9)/10*3
      IF(KA.GE.6.AND.NDEL.GT.0) NH = NH + (M+9)/10
      NH = (50-NH)/NE
      NE = NH + 1
C DATA COLLECTION SWEEP
      NR1 = NRUN + 1
      NR2 = NRUN + 2
      V(6) = 0.
      V(8) = 1.
      IF(NRUN.EQ.NT) GO TO 40
      DO 20 I = 1,M
      XBAR(I) = 0.
      DO 20 J = 1,NS
      T(J) = 0.
   20 XSAM(I,J) = 0.
      DO 30 I = 1,MDIAG
      C(I) = 0.
      DO 30 J = 1,NS
   30 A(I,J) = 0.
   40 NXO = 0
      READ(MED3) NQ,NALT,Q,(TT(I),I=1,10),(P,I=1,6)
      DO 100 J = 1,NQ
  100 READ(MED3) (P,I=1,19),(P,I=1,NALT),NX,P,P
  200 CALL MEDIAT(M,NDP,NP,MN,D,XX,NQ,SCON,NCON)
      IF(V(8).EQ.2.) GO TO 300
      J = V(6)
      IF(NRUN.EQ.NT.AND.MS.GE.1) CALL CLSAM(XX,NQ,SACON,NACON,NIN,NS)
      IF(NRUN.LE.0 .AND.MS.GE.1) CALL CLSAM(XX,NQ,SACON,NACON,NIN,NS)
      IF(MS.LE.0) NIN = J - (J-1)/NS*NS
      NMIS = 0
      DO 210 I = 1,K
      IS = ISAVE(I)
      Y(I) = D(IS)
      IF(D(IS).EQ.Q) NMIS = NMIS + 1
      IF(D(IS).EQ.Q.AND.NIN.EQ.0) Y(I) = XBAR(IS)
  210 IF(D(IS).EQ.Q.AND.NIN.NE.0) Y(I) = XSAM(IS,NIN)
      IF(NRUN.LT.0) GO TO 270
      IF(NE.LE.NH) GO TO 240
C PRINT PAGE HEADER
      NE = 1
      WRITE(MED2,901) TT
      IF(KB.GE.6)WRITE(MED2,902)
      IF(KB.GE.8)WRITE(MED2,903)
      WRITE(MED2,910) NR1
      IF(NRUN.EQ.NT.AND.KAT.EQ.1) WRITE(MED2,909)
      IF(NRUN.EQ.0.OR.NRUN.EQ.NT) WRITE(MED2,911)
      IF(NRUN.GT.0.AND.NRUN.LT.NT) WRITE(MED2,912) NRUN
      IF(KA.GE.5) WRITE(MED2,971) (I,I=1,NP)
      IF(KA.LT.6) GO TO 240
      DO 220 I = 1,K
      IS = ISAVE(I)
      L = NP(IS)/1000
      N = NP(IS)-L*1000
      IY(I) = N
      CALL COPYA(X(I),U(L))
```

```
      CALL COPYA(Z(I),ST(N))
  220 IF(NDEL.GT.0) IX(I) = NDP(IS)
      DO 230 IS = 1,K,10
      IE = IS + 9
      IF(IE.GT.K) IE = K
      WRITE(MED2,972) (X(I),I=IS,IE)
      WRITE(MED2,973) (Z(I),IY(I),I=IS,IE)
  230 IF(NDEL.GT.0) WRITE(MED2,974) (IX(I),I=IS,IE)
      IF(KA.EQ.7) WRITE(MED2,975) (I,ST(I),I=1,NQ)
  240 CONTINUE
C FIND PREVIOUS ALLOCATION (SAMPLE OR DISCRIMINANT)
      IF(NRUN.GT.0) CALL MATM (Y,RA2,Z2,1,M,NF2,M,KF2,NF2)
      IF(NRUN.GT.0) CALL CLENT(Z2,NF2,X2,NS,RW2,RC2,NSF2,NOLD,PT)
      IF(NRUN.LE.0.OR.NRUN.EQ.NT) NOLD = NIN
      J = V(6)
      CALL MATM(Y,RA,Z,1,K,NF,K,KF,NF)
      CALL CLENT (Z,NF,X,NS,RW,RC,NSF,NIN,PT)
      IF(PT.GT.0.) PMAX = X(NIN)/PT
      IF(PT.LE.0.) PMAX = 1.
      IF(NRUN.LT.NT.AND.NOLD.EQ.NIN) GO TO 270
      IF(NIN.EQ.NOLD.AND.KAT.EQ.0) GO TO 270
      IF(KA.EQ.0) GO TO 270
      NE = NE + 1
      IF(KA.GE.4) WRITE(MED2,956)
      IF(NRUN.LE.0.AND.NOLD.NE.0.OR.NRUN.EQ.NT.AND.NOLD.NE.0)
     1 WRITE (MED2,951) J,NOLD,TRTC(NOLD),X(NOLD)
      IF(NRUN.LE.0.AND.NOLD.EQ.0.OR.NRUN.EQ.NT.AND.NOLD.EQ.0)
     1 WRITE(MED2,952) J
      IF(NRUN.GT.0.AND.NRUN.LT.NT) WRITE(MED2,950)J,NOLD,TRTC(NOLD),X(NO
     1LD)
      IF(NOLD.EQ.NIN) WRITE(MED2,954)
      IF(NOLD.NE.NIN) WRITE(MED2,953) NIN,TRTC(NIN),X(NIN)
      IF(NMIS.GT.0.AND.NIN.EQ.0) WRITE(MED2,966)
      IF(NMIS.GT.0.AND.NIN.NE.0) WRITE(MED2,965)
      WRITE(MED2,955) PMAX
      IF(NMIS.GT.0) WRITE(MED2,967) NMIS
      IF(KA.LT.4) GO TO 270
      DO 260 JS = 1,NS,10
      JF = JS + 9
      IF(JF.GT.NS) JF = NS
      WRITE(MED2,968) (TRTC(J),J=JS,JF)
      IF(NRUN.LT.NT.AND.NRUN.GT.0) WRITE(MED2,959) (X2(J),J=JS,JF)
      WRITE(MED2,969) (X(J),J=JS,JF)
      DO 250 J = JS,JF
  250 IF(PT.GT.0.)X(J) = X(J)/PT
  260 WRITE(MED2,970) (X(J),J=JS,JF)
      IF(KA.GE.5) WRITE(MED2,978) (Z(J),J = 1,NF)
      IF(KA.GE.6) WRITE(MED2,979) (Y(J),J = 1,K)
      IF(KA.GE.7) WRITE(MED2,980) (XX(J),J = 1,NQ)
  270 CONTINUE
      IF(NIN.EQ.0.OR.NMIS.GT.0) GO TO 200
      T(NIN) = T(NIN) + 1.
      DO 280 I = 1,M
  280 XSAM(I,NIN) = XSAM(I,NIN) + D(I)
      L = 0
      DO 290 J = 1,M
      DO 290 I = J,M
      L = L + 1
  290 A(L,NIN) = A(L,NIN) + D(I)*D(J)
      IF(NIN.NE.NOLD) NXO = NXO + 1
      GO TO 200
  300 REWIND MED3
      V(10) = VBASE
```

```
      IF(NXO.GT.0.AND.NRUN.GE.0) WRITE(MED2,913) NXO
      IF(NXO.EQ.0.AND.NRUN.LT.NT) WRITE(MED2,914)
      RETURN
  901 FORMAT(24H1SYSTEM SUBROUTINE MDSWE,6X,1H-,4X,21H(RE-)ALLOCATE ENTR
     1IES    /16H DATA BANK TITLE,14X,1H-,4X,10A4/21H DATA BANK SAMPLE SE
     2T,9X,1H-,4X,10A4/17H DATA BANK SUBSET,13X,1H-,4X,10A4)
  902 FORMAT(39H0ASSUMING INDEPENDENT ORIGINAL VARIATES)
  903 FORMAT(1H+,39X,28HAND USING CITY-BLOCK METRIC.)
  909 FORMAT(1H+,60X,24H- PLUS UNCHANGED ENTRIES)
  910 FORMAT (13H0CHANGES FROM,21X,19HTO DISCRIMINANT SET,I3)
  911 FORMAT (1H+,13X,18HSAMPLES AS DEFINED /)
  912 FORMAT(1H+,13X,16HDISCRIMINANT SET,I3/)
  913 FORMAT(1H0,10X,25HTOTAL NUMBER OF CHANGES =,I5)
  914 FORMAT(1H0,10X,41HNO FURTHER CHANGES - FINAL OUTPUT FOLLOWS)
  950 FORMAT(6H ENTRY,I7,19H ASSIGNED TO SAMPLE,I3,2H (,A4,5H) P =,F9.6)
  951 FORMAT(6H ENTRY,I7,19H  DEFINED IN SAMPLE,I3,2H (,A4,5H) P =,F9.6)
  952 FORMAT(6H ENTRY,I7,18H NOT IN ANY SAMPLE)
  953 FORMAT(1H+,55X,15HMOVED TO SAMPLE,I3,2H (,A4,5H) P =,F9.6)
  954 FORMAT(1H+,55X,12HIS NOT MOVED)
  955 FORMAT(1H+,94X,17HFORCED CHOICE P= ,F9.6)
  956 FORMAT(1H ,30(4H----))
  959 FORMAT(5X,8HPREVIOUS,8X,10F10.6)
  965 FORMAT(26H+ (SAMPLE MEANS USED FOR ))
  966 FORMAT(26H+ (OVERALL MEANS USED FOR))
  967 FORMAT(3H+ (,I4,19H MISSING VARIATES ))
  968 FORMAT(21H0 SAMPLE PROBABILITY ,10(3X,A4,3X))
  969 FORMAT(5X,11HINDEPENDENT,5X,   10F10.6)
  970 FORMAT(5X,13HFORCED CHOICE,3X,10F10.6)
  971 FORMAT(21H0DISCRIMINANT NUMBER ,10(I6,4X))
  972 FORMAT(1H0,20H    VARIATES        ,10(1X,A4,5H OF  ))
  973 FORMAT(4X,8HSELECTED,9X,10(A4,1H(,I4,1H)))
  974 FORMAT(4X,7HDELAYED,10X,10(I3,7H CYCLES))
  975 FORMAT (21H0    DATA COLUMN     ,10(I3,3H = ,A4)/
     1(21X,10(I3,3H = ,A4)))
  978 FORMAT(21H0DISCRIMINANT SCORES ,10F10.4/(21X,10F10.4))
  979 FORMAT(1H0,6X,14HVARIATE VALUES,10F10.4/(21X,10F10.4))
  980 FORMAT(1H0,10X,10HDATA ITEMS    ,10F10.4/(21X,10F10.4))
      END
```

```
      SUBROUTINE CLENT(Z,NF,X,NS,RW,RC,NSF,N,PT)
C CLENT   (SEE  8.1 ) SERVICE     FINDS PROB. ENTRY IS IN SAMPLES
      DIMENSION RC(NSF),RW(NSF),Z(NF),X(NS)
      COMMON /STCT/MED1,MED2,MED3,MED4,MED5,MED6,MED13,Q,V(20),TT(30)
C Z = SCORE VECTOR (INDEPENDENT) - NF = NO INDEPENDENT FACTORS
C X = PROBABILITY VECTOR         - NS = NUMBER OF SAMPLES
C N = MOST PROBABLE SAMPLE
C PT= TOTAL OF INDEPENDENT PROBABILITIES
C RW = MEANS OF SAMPLES          - NSF = NS X NF
C RC = S.D.S OF SAMPLES
      F = NF
      N = 1
      PMAX = -1.
      PT = 0.
      DO 221 J = 1,NS
      X(J) = 0.
      INDX = J
      DO 220 I = 1,NF
      D = Z(I)-RW(INDX)
      IF(RC(INDX).GT.0.)P = D/RC(INDX)
      IF(RC(INDX).LE.0.)P = 9999.
      IF(D.EQ.0.)P = 0.
      INDX = INDX + NF
      IF(V(2).LE.7.)X(J) = X(J) + P*P
  220 IF(V(2).GE.8.)X(J) = X(J) + ABS(P)
      X(J) = PRBF(F,1000.,X(J)/F)
      IF(X(J).LE.PMAX) GO TO 221
      PMAX = X(J)
      N = J
  221 PT = PT + X(J)
      RETURN
      END
```

8.2 PROGRAM STAIAD - AUTOMATIC INTERACTION DETECTOR

8.2.1 Purpose

This program divides a specified subset of a STATCAT data bank into samples which are as different from each other in terms of a criterion variate as they can be made.

The program starts by considering all splits of the subset for the specified classes of a set of predictor values. The split which has the least 'pseudo-probability' associated with it is taken as the defining condition for two separate samples. The larger of the two samples is then divided in the same way, and the process repeated until no more storage is available, or the maximum number of samples required has been found, or no further split produces a statistically significant difference, or no split containing a minimum number of entries can be found. The user may specify whether the samples produced by splitting are to be re-combined with other samples if they are found not to be significantly different, and he may over-ride the data level specified for the criterion.

Figure 8.21a contains system flow-charts for the main program STAIAD and the executive subroutine CAIAD. Figure 8.21b contains system flow-charts for the system subroutines BSPLIT (which finds the condition which splits a sample into the most different parts) and RECOMB (which finds the samples which, when re-combined, reduce the statistical significance of differences least - or even sometimes increase this significance.) Figure 8.21c contains system flow-charts for the subroutines ISPLIT (which inserts the split found by BSPLIT into the list of sample definitions), IJOIN (which combines samples as required by RECOMB) and ITIDY (which puts samples in order and suppresses redundant conditions). Figure 8.21d contains a system flow-chart for WSAMP (which lists the samples defined with their appropriate mean, median or mode and the no of entries in them) and WSPLIT (which draws a tree showing how the samples are derived and re-combined.

8.2.2 Input Data

Item	Level	Format	Function	Section
1	0	A	File Control Card	3.2
2	1	E	Subset Specification	3.2
3	2	F	Set of Criteria (No delay)	Below + 3.7
4	3	F	Set of Predictors (No delay)	Below + 3.7
5	4	G	Data handling instruction	Below + 3.8

3 - Set of Criteria

This is a standard set of variates, as defined in 3.7. The transform code, the data column name or number and the class definition are employed, although any comment provided will be printed when the card is read. Delays may not be employed.

4 - Set of Predictors

This is a standard set of variates, as defined in 3.7. The transform code, the data column name or number and the class definition are employed, although any comment provided will be printed when the card is read. Delays may not be employed.

Data Handling Instruction

Card Layout - Data Handling Instruction - STAIAD

`A BCCCDDDEEEEEEEEFFFFFFFFFGGGGGGGGGGGGGGGGGGGG............`

Columns	Item	Function	See
1	A	Output Control Index	Below
2	B	Analysis Control Index	Below
3 - 5	C	Maximum Number of Samples	Below
6 - 8	D	Minimum Number of Entries	Below
9 - 16	E	Cut-Off Significance	Below
17 - 40	F	Not used	-
41 - 80	G	Run Title	3.7

A - Output Control Index

This index controls the amount of detail output by the program. <u>Unless otherwise specified</u>, the program will produce only the final sample definition and description.

Alternatives

A = 0 or blank : Only the final set of sample definitions, with their numbers of entries and appropriate descriptive parameter, splitting tree and cause of ending message are produced.

A = 1 : In addition, a frequency tabulation or mean and standard deviation for final samples (before recombination) is produced.

A = 2 : In addition, the sample definitions and splitting tree are produced for each step, with the result of the step, and the next sample chosen for analysis.

A = 3 : In addition, a frequency tabulation or mean and standard deviation for samples (before recombination) at each step is produced.

A = 4 : In addition, each potential combination resulting in an improvement in discrimination for the subset being tested is listed.

A = 5 : In addition, each potential partition resulting in an improvement in discrimination for the sample being tested is listed.

A = 6 : In addition, the result of each potential combination for the subset being tested is listed.

A = 7 : In addition, the result of each potential partition for the subset being tested is listed.

A = 8 : In addition, allocation of entries to final samples.

A = 9 : In addition, full test information on splitting.

B - Analysis Control Index

This index controls the control strategy of the program. **Unless otherwise specified**, the program will apply the test appropriate to the data level and will re-combine samples only after splitting is completed.

Alternatives

B = 0 or blank : Data level as in Data Description Segment, re-combination only after splitting completed.

B = 1 : Data level assumed Nominal, (Chi-squared test), re-combination only after splitting completed.

B = 2 : Data level assumed Ordinal, (Kruskall-Wallis one-way analysis of variance by rank), re-combination only after splitting completed.

B = 3 : Data level assumed Interval, (Standard Analysis of Variance), re-combination only after splitting completed.

B = 4 : Data level assumed Ratio, (Standard Analysis of Variance), re-combination only after splitting completed.

B = 5 : Data level as in Data Description Segment, samples combined if statistically significance improved thereby.

B = 6 : Data level assumed Nominal, (Chi-squared test) samples re-combined if statistical significance improved thereby.

B = 7 : Data level assumed to be Ordinal (Kruskall-Wallis one-way analysis of variance by rank), samples re-combined if statistical significance improved thereby.

B = 8 : Data level assumed to be Interval (Standard Analysis of Variance), samples re-combined if statistical significance improved thereby.

B = 9 : Data level assumed to be Ratio (Standard Analysis of Variance), samples re-combined if statistical significance improved thereby.

C - **Maximum Number of Samples**

This parameter specifies the maximum number of separate samples to be produced. If it is blank or zero, the maximum number for which space is provided will be employed. **Unless otherwise specified** 25 samples will be obtained at most.

D - **Minimum Number of Entries**

This parameter specifies the minimum number of entries per sample. Splits of the sample involving fewer than this number of readings will be rejected without testing. **Unless otherwise specified** a minimum of 5 will be required. (As a consequence of this requirement, the program will not attempt to split samples containing less than twice this number.)

E - **Cut-Off for Significance**

This value is used to determine whether the most significant split is accepted, and whether samples are to be re-combined if this option is used. Unless otherwise specified a value of 5 per cent is employed. It should be noted (See 8.2.5.) that the probabilities obtained in this analysis are subject to over-estimation by the nature of the technique. They are therefore described as 'pseudo-probabilities' throughout.

8.2.3 Input Example

Figure 8.22 is a summary of the input data for two runs of STAIAD, with default and maximum output respectively. Figure 8.23 lists the corresponding input data cards.

8.2.4 Output Example

Figure 8.24 is a summary of the output structure corresponding to the input structure of Figure 8.22. Figure 8.25 is a page-by-page summary of the output corresponding to the specific example given in Figure 8.23. Figure 8.26 gives the default output produced by the first run - consisting of the final subdivision of data into samples according to the constraints set by default. Figure 8.27 is an example of the more detailed en-route output produced in the second run, showing the cross-tabulation of the first predictor and the criterion for all data. Figure 8.28 shows the first page of the detailed running report of successive trial splits - because this is a NOMINAL level predictor each class is compared with the others, and because the criterion is on an INTERVAL level a parametric analysis of variance is employed (See 6.2 for a general description of this test.) Figure 8.29 shows part of the record of the re-combination of samples at the end of the run.

8.2.5 Discussion

The development of this type of 'Robot Data Analyser' is arousing considerable interest among statisticians and computer scientists. The potential of such methods is evidently enormous, but there are as yet no generally accepted generally applicable methods. The version presented here is a compromise between generality and simplicity of programming.

Most 'Robot Data Analysers' of the sample-splitting type assume that the criterion is on an INTERVAL scale of measurement at least. By using parametric tests, it is possible to use less space, fewer data sweeps, and hence less time. (Parametric tests require totals, sums and sums of squares - non-parametric - in this context - require cross-tabulations.)

The major problem is to decide which is the most promising sample to split next. If parametric methods are used, it is probably best to use the sample having the largest total sum of squares. For NOMINAL or ORDINAL data levels, it is harder to find a reasonable and convenient indicator. In the event, the largest sample was chosen as the next for splitting, regardless of criterion and data level. This method has the merits of simplicity and economy. (The choice of next sample to split can be made on the basis of the data available after each split, and samples with less than twice the minimum number need not be examined.) It does, however, imply that the initial order in which the sample is split will not necessarily be the order of importance of the splits. (The pseudo-probability of a later split may be greater than the first.)

As an indication of the relative importance of splits, the re-combination option is provided to provide insight into the relative values of successive differences. It is relatively rare for the orders of splitting and re-combination to be the same. (Consider two two-way splits, each affecting the criterion to the same extent. The first split will be on one criterion, then the two samples produced will be split according to the other. The samples with both or neither condition will be the most extreme, but the samples with one condition each may well have nearly identical criterion values, and will be combined first.) In fact, the first few re-combinations tend to decrease the 'pseudo-probability', producing the same explanatory power from fewer splits.

A fundamental problem shared with multiple linear regression, is the choice between highly correlated predictors. If we have two predictors which measure virtually the same thing except for noise, then the best split may be chosen practically at random. In STAIAD some splits will be in terms of one predictor, and some in terms of the other. For, example, if our criterion is the salary of an employee, and most employees join the organisation in their twenties and remain till retiring age, then successive splits may use age or years of service more or less at random. (In multiple regression, one or other predictor would be discarded, more or less at random.) The pragmatic 'cure' is to run the program twice, dropping first one then the other predictor.

If the automatic re-combination option is used, under certain circumstances a curious 'looping' pattern may be produced. This may occur when a set of very well-defined samples has been derived, for which the probability is practically zero. Two samples may be combined, giving a set of samples for which the probability is still practically zero. To determine whether this split is an improvement, the value of chi-squared or the 'F' ratio is compared with that from the previous level. Since this is based on more degrees of freedom, it will often be lower - causing the samples to be combined. The program performs, and reports, a test to ensure that samples previously split from each other will not be re-combined unless another sample has been added to or split from at least one of the original pair. It is not, however, practical to test for all possible forms of recombination, and it may be possible to split, say, sample 3 from 2, then 4 from 3, then recombine 2 and 4 and 2 and 3. The tree structure shows clearly what has happened in such cases. Pragmatically, the best remedy is to use an analysis control index below five, avoiding 'en-route' recombining.

The Automatic Interaction Detector is explicitly programmed to select the most different pairs of samples at each step. This is a classic example of constructed significance. The probabilities obtained by the statistical tests are based on the assumption that the test was made on an previously laid-down hypothesis, and are therefore inflated. They should therefore be regarded with some reserve.

REFERENCES : COMPSTAT 80, Kendall (1975)

493

Figure 8.21a - System Flow-Charts - STAIAD and CAIAD

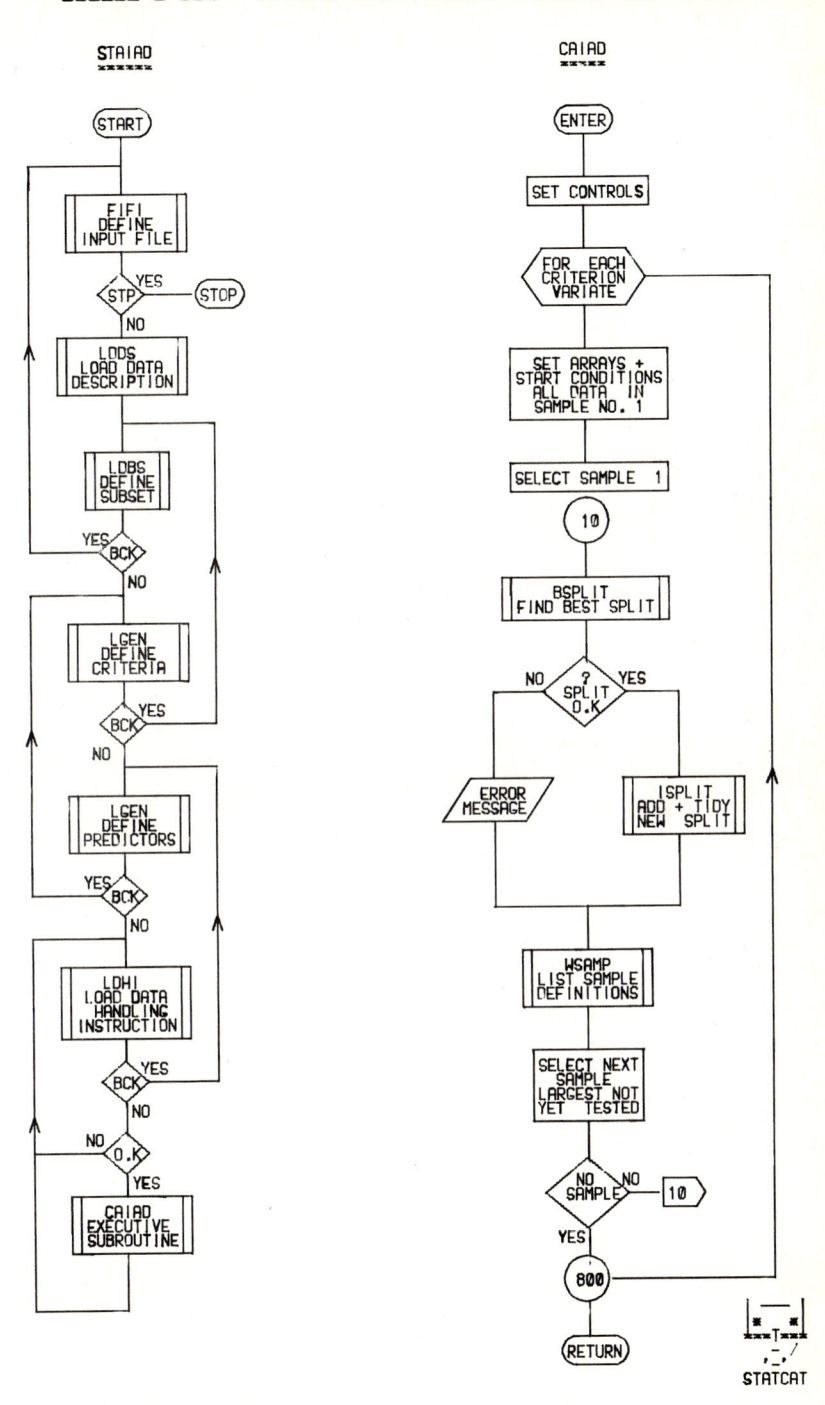

Figure 8.21b - System Flow-Charts - BSPLIT and RECOMB

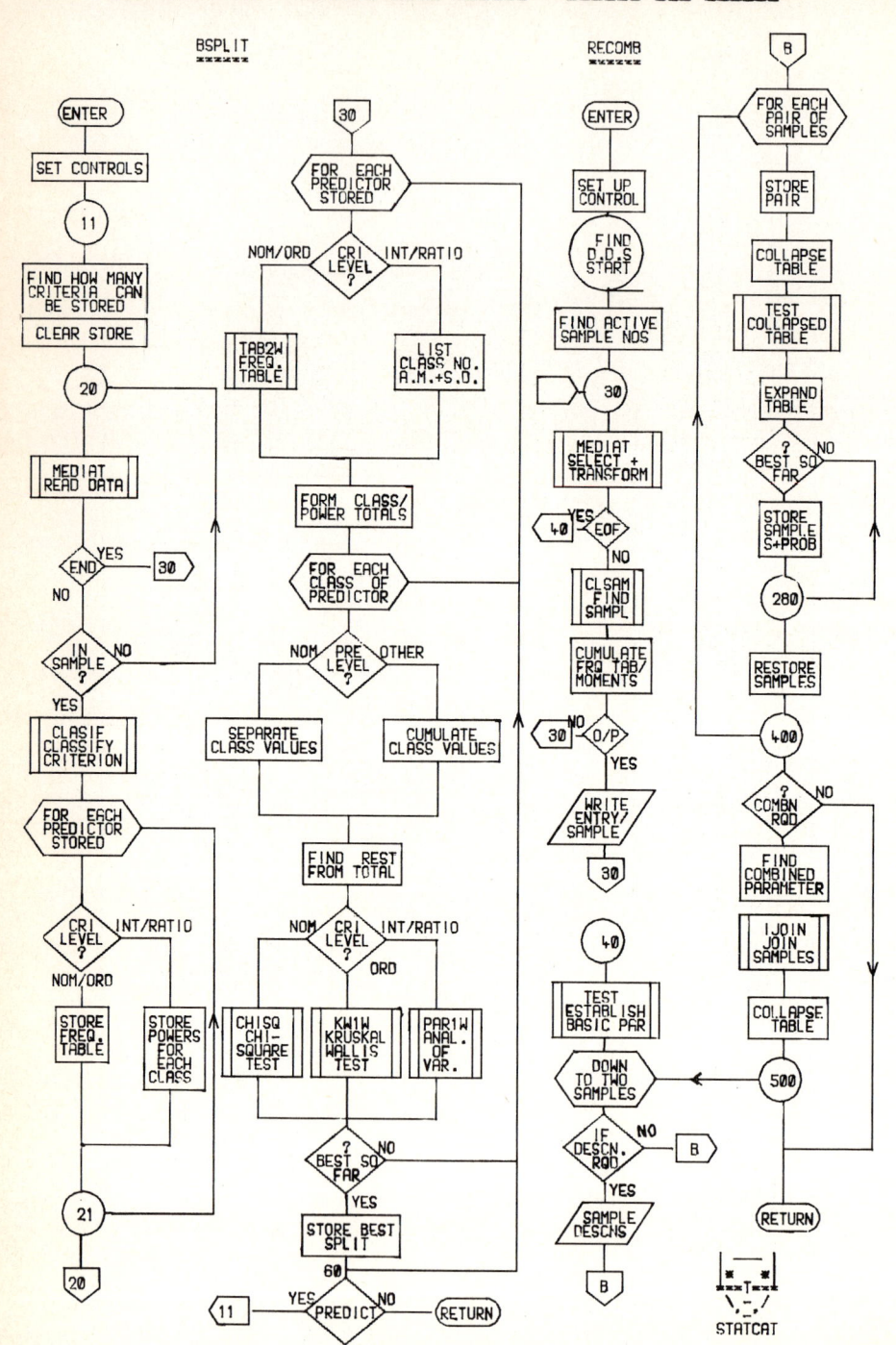

495

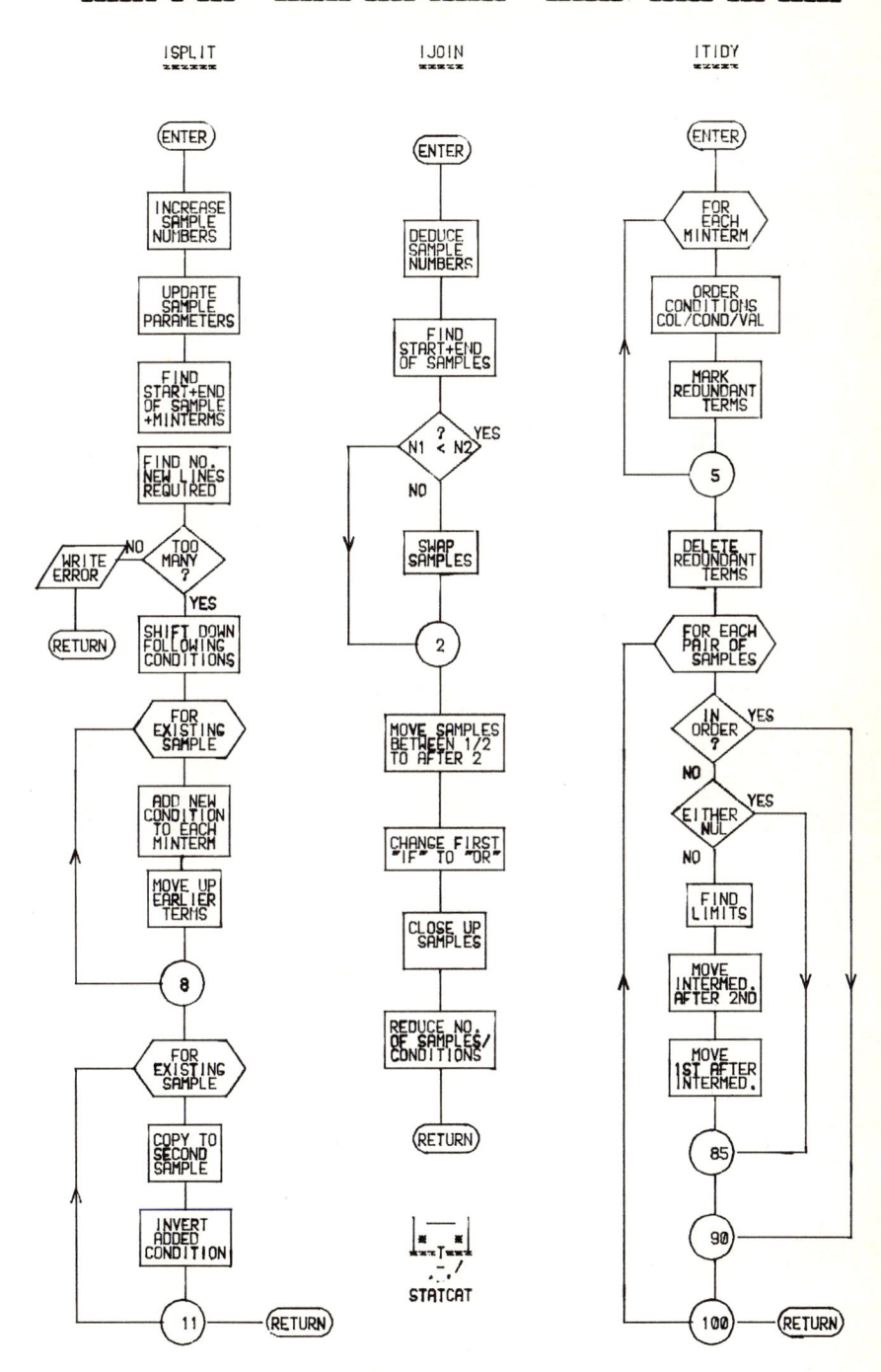

Figure 8.21c - System Flow-Charts - ISPLIT, IJOIN and ITIDY

Figure 8.21d - System Flow-Charts - WSAMP and WSPLIT

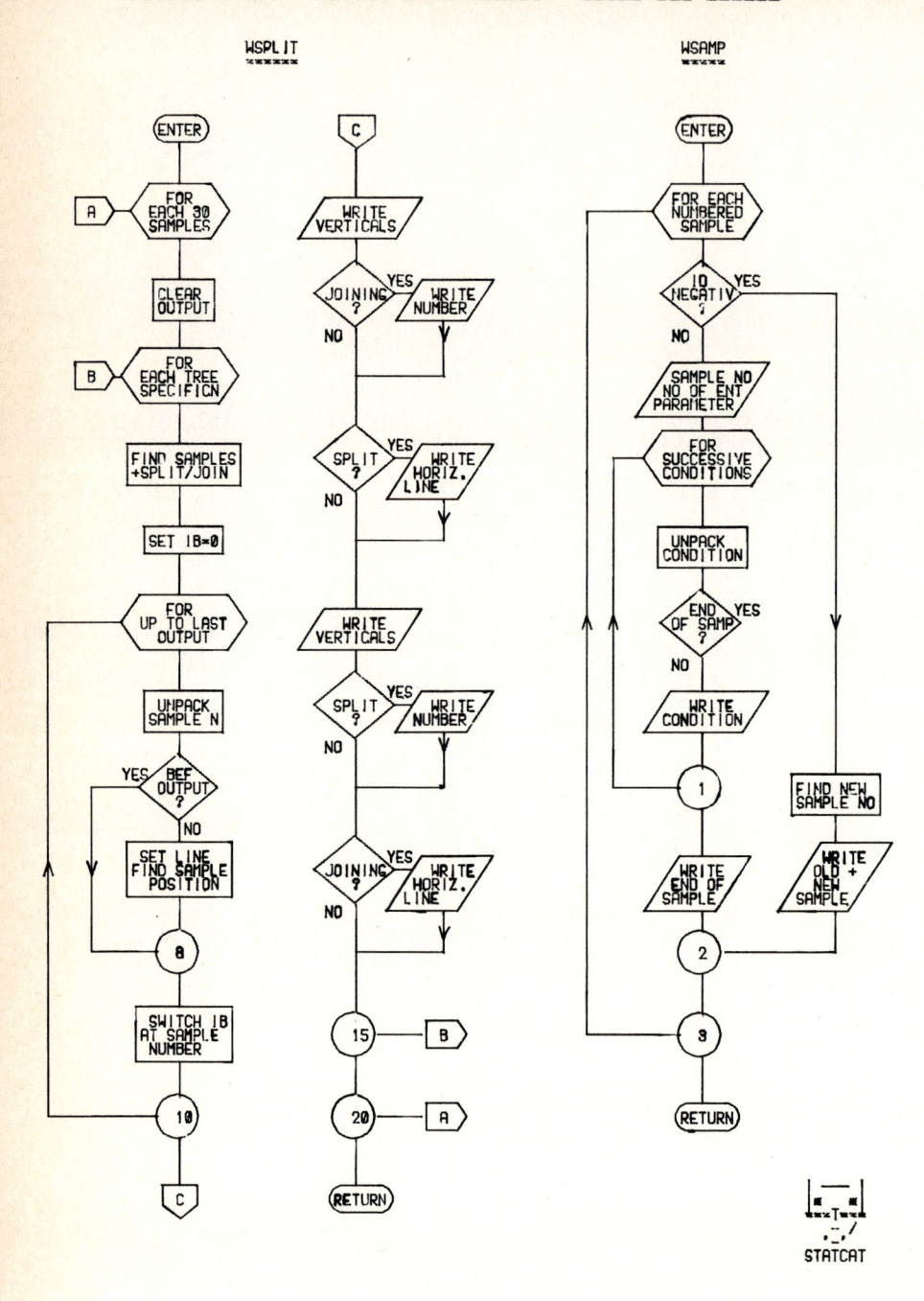

Figure 8.22 - STAIAD - Input Structure

```
          Level
  0   1   2   3   4   5   6   7   8   9
FILE CONTROL CARD
    SUBSET SPECIFICATION
        SET OF CRITERIA
            SET OF PREDICTORS
                DATA HANDLING INSTRUCTION
                DATA HANDLING INSTRUCTION
                DATA HANDLING INSTRUCTION
                STOP
```

Figure 8.23 - STAIAD - Input Example

```
---------1---------2---------3---------4---------5---------6---------7--
**STAIADDEMO                   DEMONSTRATION STATCAT DATA BANK
ALL DATA
END OF SUBSET
VAL.ERRP
END OF CRITERIA
VAL.OBSR           4    1.5      1.0      3.5
VAL.OPER           4    1.5      1.0      3.5
VAL.W.P.           4    1.5      1.0      3.5
VAL.DAY.           4    1.5      1.0      3.5
VAL.TIME           4    1.5      1.0      3.5
VAL.TASK           4    1.5      1.0      3.5
END OF PREDICTORS
GO                                      DEFAULT OUTPUT
8                                       ALL DECISIONS -FINAL ALLOCATION
---------1---------2---------3---------4---------5---------6---------7--
```

Figure 8.24 - STAIAD - Output Structure

```
For each      ) : File Control Record
output file   )   File Parameters
                  Data Description
                  For each) : Subset Input Record
                  Subset  )   For Set of   ) : Input Record
                              Criteria     )   For Each ) : Input
For Each  )                                )   Set of   )   Record
Criterion )      For Each )                    Predictors)  See Left
    .        Split       )   For Each )
    .            .           Predictor) <Cross-tabulation>
    .            .                        For Each  )  <Test Report>
    .            .                        Potential)   <Best so Far?>
    .            .                        Split     )
    .            .           <Listing of Samples so far>
    .            .           <Splitting Diagram>
    .            .           <Re-Combining Diagram>
    .
    .        Listing of Final Set of Samples
             Splitting Diagram
             Re-Combining Diagram

  Carated(<>) items are optional.
```

Figure 8.25 - STAIAD - Page-by-page output summary

Page	Contents	Origin
1-3	File Control/Program title/File Parameters	FIFI/LDAP
	Data Description record	LDDS
4	Subset record	LDBS
5	Criterion Record	LGEN
6	Predictor Record	LGEN
	Data Handling Instruction	LDHI
7-10	Default Output	CAIAD/WSAMP/WSPLIT
11	Data Handling Instruction	LDHI
12	Cross-Tabulation (First predictor)	BSPLIT
13-14	Tests for Nominal Classes	PAR1W
	Best Split Choices	BSPLIT
15-17	Tabulation/Testing (Second predictor)	CAIAD
18-29	Tabulation/Testing (Third to sixth predictors)	CAIAD etc
30	First Split Sample definition	WSAMP
31	First Split Diagram	WSPLIT
32-48	Tests to split Sample 1	CAIAD etc
49-50	Second Split Report	WSAMP/WSPLIT
52-153	Successive Splits and Reports	CAIAD etc
154-156	Final Split Report	WSAMP/WSPLIT
157-159	Allocation of entries to final samples	RECOMB
159-163	Recombining to leave most different samples	RECOMB
164	Final Recombination diagram	WSPLIT
165	Data Handling Instruction (STOP)	LDHI

Figure 8.26 - STAIAD - Output Example - Default Output

```
STATCAT PROGRAM STAIAD         -    AUTOMATIC INTERACTION DETECTOR
DATA BANK TITLE                -    DEMONSTRATION STATCAT DATA BANK
DATA BANK SUBSET TITLE         -    ALL DATA
RUN TITLE                      -    DEFAULT OUTPUT
CRITERION - VAL. OF ERR?= 18.-      PERCENTAGE OF ERRORS IN FINAL PRODUCTS              RATIO

     NO UNTESTED SAMPLE WITH AT LEAST   10. ENTRIES

SAMPLE NUMBER  5 CONTAINING    12 ENTRIES    MEAN =          0.158333

        .IF.DAY..GE.TUES
        AND.TIME.LT.AM2
        END OF SAMPLE NUMBER  5

SAMPLE NUMBER  4 CONTAINING    12 ENTRIES    MEAN =          0.458333

        .IF.DAY..GE.TUES
        AND.TIME.GE.AM2
        AND.TIME.LT.PM1
        END OF SAMPLE NUMBER  4

SAMPLE NUMBER  3 CONTAINING    12 ENTRIES    MEAN =          0.783332

        .IF.DAY..GE.TUES
        AND.TIME.GE.PM1
        AND.TIME.LT.PM2
        END OF SAMPLE NUMBER  3

SAMPLE NUMBER  6 CONTAINING     8 ENTRIES    MEAN =          1.299999

        .IF.DAY..LT.TUES
        AND.TIME.LT.PM1
        END OF SAMPLE NUMBER  6

SAMPLE NUMBER  1 CONTAINING    12 ENTRIES    MEAN =          1.558331

        .IF.DAY..GE.TUES
        AND.TIME.GE.PM2
        END OF SAMPLE NUMBER  1



STATCAT PROGRAM STAIAD         -    AUTOMATIC INTERACTION DETECTOR
DATA BANK TITLE                -    DEMONSTRATION STATCAT DATA BANK
DATA BANK SUBSET TITLE         -    ALL DATA
RUN TITLE                      -    DEFAULT OUTPUT
CRITERION - VAL. OF ERR?= 18.-      PERCENTAGE OF ERRORS IN FINAL PRODUCTS              RATIO

SAMPLE NUMBER  2 CONTAINING     8 ENTRIES    MEAN =          3.774994

        .IF.DAY..LT.TUES
        AND.TIME.GE.PM1
        END OF SAMPLE NUMBER  2




             SPLITTING LARGEST UNTESTED SAMPLE - COMBINING TO MAXIMISE SIGNIFICANCE OF DIFFERENCE
                         ,
                         1
                         |---,
                         |   2
                ,--------|   |
                    3    |   |
               ,---|     |   |
                 4 |     |   |
            ,---|  |     |   |
              5 |  |     |   |
              | |  |  ,---+---,
              | |  |  6 |     |
              | |  |  6 |     |
              | |  |  '---|   |
              5 |  |     |   |
              '---|     |   |
                 4 |     |   |
                 '---|   |   |
                    3    |   |
                    '--------|   |
                             |   2
                             |---'
```

Figure 8.27 - STAIAD - Output Example - Cross-Tabulation

```
STATCAT PROGRAM STAIAD      -   AUTOMATIC INTERACTION DETECTOR
DATA BANK TITLE             -   DEMONSTRATION STATCAT DATA BANK
DATA BANK SUBSET TITLE      -   ALL DATA
RUN TITLE                   -   MAXIMUM OUTPUT
CRITERION - VAL. OF ERRP= 18.-      PERCENTAGE OF ERRORS IN FINAL PRODUCTS          RATIO
PREDICTOR - VAL. OF DAY.=  7.-      DAY OF INVESTIGATION                            ORDINAL
    SAMPLE -  1. OF  1

        CLASS           NUMBER          ARITHMETIC MEAN     STANDARD DEVIATION

  1     MON.          16.000000             2.537498             1.827523
  2     TUES          16.000000             0.950000             0.726635
  3     WED.          16.000000             0.775000             0.679705
  4     THUR          16.000000             0.493750             0.486441
```

Figure 8.28 - STAIAD - Output Example - Tests of Splits

```
STATCAT PROGRAM STAIAD      -   AUTOMATIC INTERACTION DETECTOR
DATA BANK TITLE             -   DEMONSTRATION STATCAT DATA BANK
DATA BANK SUBSET TITLE      -   ALL DATA
RUN TITLE                   -   MAXIMUM OUTPUT
CRITERION - VAL. OF ERRP= 18.-      PERCENTAGE OF ERRORS IN FINAL PRODUCTS          RATIO
PREDICTOR - VAL. OF DAY.=  7.-      DAY OF INVESTIGATION                            ORDINAL
    SAMPLE -  1. OF  1

            CLASS MON. AND BELOW

ANALYSIS OF VARIANCE

SOURCE OF VARIATION TOTAL SUM OF SQUARES  D.F.  MEAN SUM OF SQUARES  VARIANCE RATIO  PROBABILITY
BETWEEN SAMPLES                38.7900    1.            38.7900          34.2627        0.0000
  WITHIN SAMPLES               70.1924   62.             1.1321
TOTAL                         108.9824   63.

BARTLETT CHI-SQUARED TEST FOR HOMOGENEITY OF VARIANCE

CHI-SQUARED            1.0224

PROBABILITY            0.383823

SAMPLE   1 (MON.)         16. READINGS  -  MEAN =   2.5375   S.D. =   1.8275

SAMPLE   2 (OVER)         48. READINGS  -  MEAN =   0.7396   S.D. =   0.6539

ALL SAMPLES               64. READINGS  -  MEAN =   1.1891   S.D. =   1.3152

        CLASS MON. AND BELOW IS THE BEST SPLIT SO FAR  - PSEUDO-PROBABILITY =  0.00000933

            CLASS TUES AND BELOW

ANALYSIS OF VARIANCE

SOURCE OF VARIATION TOTAL SUM OF SQUARES  D.F.  MEAN SUM OF SQUARES  VARIANCE RATIO  PROBABILITY
BETWEEN SAMPLES                19.6914    1.            19.6914          13.6729        0.0008
  WITHIN SAMPLES               89.2910   62.             1.4402
TOTAL                         108.9824   63.

BARTLETT CHI-SQUARED TEST FOR HOMOGENEITY OF VARIANCE

CHI-SQUARED            1.0155

PROBABILITY            0.412678

SAMPLE   1 (TUES)         32. READINGS  -  MEAN =   1.7437   S.D. =   1.5880

SAMPLE   2 (OVER)         32. READINGS  -  MEAN =   0.6344   S.D. =   0.5987

ALL SAMPLES               64. READINGS  -  MEAN =   1.1891   S.D. =   1.3152

        CLASS TUES AND BELOW IS NOT AN IMPROVEMENT     - PSEUDO-PROBABILITY =  0.00075409
```

Figure 8.29 - STAIAD - Output Example - Recombination

```
STATCAT PROGRAM STAIAD        -   AUTOMATIC INTERACTION DETECTOR
DATA BANK TITLE               -   DEMONSTRATION STATCAT DATA BANK
DATA BANK SUBSET TITLE        -   ALL DATA
RUN TITLE                     -   MAXIMUM OUTPUT
CRITERION - VAL. OF ERRP= 18.-        PERCENTAGE OF ERRORS IN FINAL PRODUCTS                          RATIO

         SAMPLE NUMBER     5.          4.          3.          6.          1.          2.
                  NO.      12.0000     12.0000     12.0000     8.0000      12.0000     8.0000
                  A.M.     0.1583      0.4583      0.7833      1.3000      1.5583      3.7750
                  S.D.     0.0900      0.2392      0.4687      0.7819      0.5946      1.7450

    WITHOUT COMBINING SAMPLES            ASSOCIATED PROBABILITY =    0.0         "F" VALUE =     27.1562

SAMPLE  5. COMBINED WITH SAMPLE  4. ASSOCIATED PROBABILITY =    0.0         "F" VALUE =     33.7279   BEST SO FAR
SAMPLE  5. COMBINED WITH SAMPLE  3. ASSOCIATED PROBABILITY =    0.0         "F" VALUE =     31.2269   NO IMPROVEMENT
SAMPLE  5. COMBINED WITH SAMPLE  6. ASSOCIATED PROBABILITY =    0.0         "F" VALUE =     26.5996   NO IMPROVEMENT
SAMPLE  5. COMBINED WITH SAMPLE  1. ASSOCIATED PROBABILITY =    0.0         "F" VALUE =     21.4716   NO IMPROVEMENT
SAMPLE  5. COMBINED WITH SAMPLE  2. ASSOCIATED PROBABILITY =    0.09137857  "F" VALUE =      2.0992   NO IMPROVEMENT
SAMPLE  4. COMBINED WITH SAMPLE  3. ASSOCIATED PROBABILITY =    0.0         "F" VALUE =     33.5912   NO IMPROVEMENT
SAMPLE  4. COMBINED WITH SAMPLE  6. ASSOCIATED PROBABILITY =    0.0         "F" VALUE =     29.8782   NO IMPROVEMENT
SAMPLE  4. COMBINED WITH SAMPLE  1. ASSOCIATED PROBABILITY =    0.0         "F" VALUE =     25.5589   NO IMPROVEMENT
SAMPLE  4. COMBINED WITH SAMPLE  2. ASSOCIATED PROBABILITY =    0.00583639  "F" VALUE =      4.0685   NO IMPROVEMENT
SAMPLE  3. COMBINED WITH SAMPLE  6. ASSOCIATED PROBABILITY =    0.0         "F" VALUE =     32.6678   NO IMPROVEMENT
SAMPLE  3. COMBINED WITH SAMPLE  1. ASSOCIATED PROBABILITY =    0.0         "F" VALUE =     29.6276   NO IMPROVEMENT
SAMPLE  3. COMBINED WITH SAMPLE  2. ASSOCIATED PROBABILITY =    0.00037769  "F" VALUE =      6.5189   NO IMPROVEMENT
SAMPLE  6. COMBINED WITH SAMPLE  1. ASSOCIATED PROBABILITY =    0.0         "F" VALUE =     34.0511   BEST SO FAR
SAMPLE  6. COMBINED WITH SAMPLE  2. ASSOCIATED PROBABILITY =    0.0         "F" VALUE =     13.3915   NO IMPROVEMENT
SAMPLE  1. COMBINED WITH SAMPLE  2. ASSOCIATED PROBABILITY =    0.0         "F" VALUE =     13.8507   NO IMPROVEMENT
SAMPLE  6. COMBINED WITH SAMPLE  1. ASSOCIATED PROBABILITY =    0.0         "F" VALUE =     34.0511   ADOPTED
```

```
C PROGRAM STAIAD - GENERAL AUTOMATIC INTERACTION DETECTOR
C   SUBROUTINES AND FUNCTIONS REQUIRED
C  NAME        TYPE              COMMENT
C  AN     (SEE  3.1 ) SERVICE     ALPHA - TO NUMERIC VALUE
C  BSPLIT (SEE  8.2 ) SYSTEM      SELECT NEXT SPLIT FOR SAMPLE ISSF
C  CAIAD  (SEE  8.2 ) EXECUTIVE   AUTOMATIC INTERACTION DETECTOR
C  ISW    (SEE 11.6 ) SERVICE     CHOOSES TEST/DESCRIPTION REQUIRED
C  CHIKEN (SEE 11.9 ) SERVICE     WARNS OF MISMATCHED DATA LEVEL
C  CHISQ  (SEE 11.5 ) STATISTICAL BASIC CHI-SQUARED CALCULATION
C  CHISQD (SEE  6.1 ) STATISTICAL SELF-STABILISED CHI-SQUARED
C  CLASIF (SEE 11.7 ) SERVICE     CLASSIFIES DATA ITEM
C  CLSAM  (SEE  3.5 ) SERVICE     ALLOTS ENTRY TO SAMPLE/SUBSET
C  COMPA  (SEE  3.1 ) SERVICE     COMPARES ALPHAMERIC VALUES
C  COPYA  (SEE  3.1 ) SERVICE     COPIES ALPHAMERIC VALUE
C  DICOLA (SEE 11.5 ) STATISTICAL DESCRIBES ROW/COLUMN COMBINATION
C  FIFI   (SEE  3.2 ) SYSTEM      ALLOCATES PERIPHERALS
C  GAUS   (SEE 11.8 ) STATISTICAL FINDS ASS. PROB. OF N VALUE
C  IBL    (SEE  3.1 ) SERVICE     DETECTS BLANK,END AND STOP CARDS
C  ICH    (SEE  3.1 ) SERVICE     IDENTIFIES ALPHAMERIC CODES
C  IJOIN  (SEE  8.2 ) SYSTEM      COMBINES SAMPLES
C  ISPLIT (SEE  8.2 ) SYSTEM      SPLITS SAMPLE INTO TWO
C  ITIDY  (SEE  8.2 ) SYSTEM      ARRANGES SAMPLES IN ORDER OF PARAMETER
C  KW1W   (SEE  6.2 ) STATISTICAL KRUSKAL-WALLIS 1-WAY ANOVAR RANK
C  LCOM   (SEE  3.4 ) SERVICE     LOADS COMPLEMENTARY INFORMATION
C  LDAP   (SEE  3.3 ) SYSTEM      LOADS/CHECKS DATA BANK PARAMETERS
C  LDBS   (SEE  3.6 ) SYSTEM      LOADS SUBSET DEFINITION
C  LDDS   (SEE  3.4 ) SYSTEM      LOADS DATA DESCRIPTION SEGMENT
C  LDHI   (SEE  3.8 ) SYSTEM      LOADS/CHECKS DATA HANDLING INSTN
C  LGEN   (SEE  3.7 ) SYSTEM      LOADS GENERALISED VARIATES
C  LSET   (SEE  3.5 ) SYSTEM      LOADS DEFINING CONDITIONS
C  MEDIAT (SEE  3.7 ) SERVICE     FETCHES NEXT VARIATE SET
C  NEXY   (SEE  6.3 ) SERVICE     FINDS NEXT ARRAY COORDS
C  PAR1W  (SEE  6.2 ) STATISTICAL 1-WAY ANOVAR + BARTLETT TEST
C  PRBF   (SEE 11.8 ) STATISTICAL FINDS PROBABILITY OF F-RATIO
C  PRTCLS (SEE 11.7 ) SERVICE     PRINTS CLASS NAME/LIMITS
C  REDROW (SEE 11.5 ) STATISTICAL CHOOSES ROW/COLUMN FOR COMBINATION
C  TAB2W  (SEE  6.4 ) STATISTICAL TABULATES WITH VARIATE NAMES ETC
C  TRANS  (SEE  3.7 ) SERVICE     CARRIES OUT REQUIRED TRANSFORM
C  WDCD   (SEE  3.4 ) SERVICE     WRITES DATA COLUMN DESCRIPTION
C  WSAMP  (SEE  8.2 ) SYSTEM      WRITES SAMPLE DEFINITION
C  WSPLIT (SEE  8.2 ) SYSTEM      PRODUCES DIAGRAM OF SPLITTING RECORD
C SETTING OF ARRAY DIMENSIONS
C THE FOLLOWING DIMENSIONS MUST BE AT LEAST AS BIG AS THOSE
C SPECIFIED BY THE DATA TAPE,SAMPLE SPECIFICATIONS,ETC.
C NQMAX = MAXIMUM NUMBER OF DATA COLUMNS
C IF NQMAX AND ARRAYS ARE CHANGED,CHANGE DATA STATEMENT FOR CN
C DIMENSION D(NQMAX),DMAX(NQMAX),DMIN(NQMAX),IT(NQMAX),ST(NQMAX)
C DIMENSION CN(NQMAX)
      NQMAX = 100
      DIMENSION D(100  ),DMAX(100  ),DMIN(100  ),IT(100  ),ST(100  )
      DIMENSION CN(100)
      DATA  CN/4HCOL1,4HCOL2,4HCOL3,4HCOL4,4HCOL5,4HCOL6,4HCOL7,4HCOL8,4
     1HCOL9,4HCL10,4HCL11,4HCL12,4HCL13,4HCL14,4HCL15,4HCL16,4HCL17,4HC
     218,4HCL19,4HCL20,4HCL21,4HCL22,4HCL23,4HCL24,4HCL25,4HCL26,4HCL27,
     34HCL28,4HCL29,4HCL30,4HCL31,4HCL32,4HCL33,4HCL34,4HCL35,4HCL36,4HC
     4L37,4HCL38,4HCL39,4HCL40,4HCL41,4HCL42,4HCL43,4HCL44,4HCL45,4HCL46
     5,4HCL47,4HCL48,4HCL49,4HCL50,4HCL51,4HCL52,4HCL53,4HCL54,4HCL55,4H
     6CL56,4HCL57,4HCL58,4HCL59,4HCL60,4HCL61,4HCL62,4HCL63,4HCL64,4HCL6
     75,4HCL66,4HCL67,4HCL68,4HCL69,4HCL70,4HCL71,4HCL72,4HCL73,4HCL74,4
     8HCL75,4HCL76,4HCL77,4HCL78,4HCL79,4HCL80,4HCL81,4HCL82,4HCL83,4HCL
     984,4HCL85,4HCL86,4HCL87,4HCL88,4HCL89,4HCL90,4HCL91,4HCL92,4HCL93,
     94HCL94,4HCL95,4HCL96,4HCL97,4HCL98,4HCL99,4HC100/
C NALTMX = MAXIMUM NUMBER OF CLASSES ON TAPE
```

```
C DIMENSION  TRT(NALTMX)
      NALTMX = 50
      DIMENSION  TRT(50)
C NCMAX = MAXIMUM NUMBER OF CLASSES ACTUALLY USED FOR CRITERIA
C  DIMENSION CX(NCMAX),KC(NCMAX),TRTC(NCMAX)
      NCMAX=30
      DIMENSION CX(30),KC(30),TRTC(30)
C NRMAX = MAXIMUM NUMBER OF CLASSES ACTUALLY USED FOR PREDICTORS
C DIMENSION RX(NRMAX),KR(NRMAX),TRTR(NRMAX)
      NRMAX=30
      DIMENSION RX(30),KR(30),TRTR(30)
C MAXST = MAXIMUM AVAILABLE WORKING STORAGE IN HUNDREDS
C RT CONTAINS ALL FREE STORAGE USED FOR FREQUENCY TABLES, MOMENTS,
C SUBSET AND SAMPLE CONDITIONS -
C DIMENSION RT(MAXST,100)
      MAXST=25
      DIMENSION RT(25,100)
C MAXM = MAXIMUM NUMBER OF VARIATES ACCEPTED FOR ANY DATA SWEEP
C DIMENSION TMAX(MAXM),TMIN(MAXM),NCL(MAXM),NP(MAXM),T(MAXM)
      MAXM = 50
      DIMENSION TMAX( 50),TMIN( 50),NCL( 50),NP( 50),T( 50)
C NSMAX = MAXIMUM NUMBER OF SAMPLES
C DIMENSION SN(NSMAX),SID(NSMAX),SP(NSMAX),S2(NSMAX*2),S3(NSMAX*2)
      NSMAX = 25
      DIMENSION SN(25),SID(25),SP(25),S2(50),S3(50)
C THE FOLLOWING DIMENSION STORES THE NAMES OF THE DATA TRANSFORMS
C AND THE ACCEPTABLE LEVELS FOR TRANSFORMATIONS
      DIMENSION U(60),LU(60)
      NU = 60
C TRANSFORMATION CODES
C UNITS                     BLOCKS
C  0 - 9   10 - 19   20 - 29   30 - 39   40 - 49   50 - 59
C  POWERS TRIG       TRIG      STATIST   MATHS     TEST
C         RADIANS    DEGREES   TRANSF    FUNCTS    FUNCTIONS
C  0       -          -         H.MS      -         RM10
C  1      VAL.       SINR       SIND      PSNA      RECP      +/-1
C  2      SQAR       COSR       COSD      PSNB      SQRT      ADD1
C  3      CUBE       TANR       TAND      BINO      ABSV      SUB1
C  4      4PWR       ASIR       ASID      LG+1      SIGN      NOR1
C  5      5PWR       ACOR       ACOD      LOGE      INTG      +/-P
C  6      6PWR       ATAR       ATAD      LG10      FRAC      ADDP
C  7      7PWR       SINH       DTOR      AL10      EXPT      SUBP
C  8      8PWR       COSH       RTOD       -        PRES      NORP
C  9      9PWR       TANH       H.HH       -        NEG.      +100
      DATA U/4HVAL.,4HSQAR,4HCUBE,4H4PWR,4H5PWR,4H6PWR,4H7PWR,4H8PWR,4H9
     1PWR,4HVAL ,4HSINR,4HCOSR,4HTANR,4HASIR,4HACOR,4HATAR,4HSINH,4HCOSH
     2,4HTANH,4HH.MS,4HSIND,4HCOSD,4HTAND,4HASID,4HACOD,4HATAD,4HDTOR,4H
     3RTOD,4HH.HH,4H VAL,4HPSNA,4HPSNB,4HBINO,4HLG+1,4HLOGE,4HLG10,4HAL1
     40,4H    ,4H    ,4H    ,4HRECP,4HSQRT,4HABSV,4HSIGN,4HINTG,4HFRAC,4
     5HEXPT,4HPRES,4HNEG.,4HRM10,4H+/-1,4HADD1,4HSUB1,4HNOR1,4H+/-P,4HAD
     6DP,4HSUBP,4HNORP,4H+100,4H     /
      DATA LU/1,8*5,1,9*5,1,9*5,1,6*5,4*1,2*5,2*3,3*5,7*2,4*5,2*2/
C FIXED ARRAYS (INCLUDING DUMMY FOR CALLS OF LGEN)
      DIMENSION FORM(40),IH(1),H(1)
      COMMON /STCT/MED1,MED2,MED3,MED4,MED5,MED6,MED13,Q,V(20),TT(30)
      DATA PROG/4HAIAD/
      MED1 = -1
C SETTING UP * LEVEL 0
    1 CALL COPYA(TT(1),PROG)
      CALL FIFI
      WRITE(MED2,901)
      CALL LDAP(MED2,MED3,V,TT,Q,NQ,NALT,NQMAX,NALTMX,IGO)
      IF(IGO.GT.0) GO TO 1
```

```
      LI = 18
      CALL LDDS(TRT,NALT,D,NQ,ST,NQ,IT,NQ,RT,NQ,DMIN,DMAX,NQ,LI,1,Q,VX,
     1 0,MED2,MED3,0,IGO)
      IF(IGO.GT.0) GO TO 1
C LEVEL 2 - READ SUBSET
   21 IF(V(10).GE.20.)V(10) = 0.
      MAXDBC = MAXST*4
      CALL LDBS(SCON,NCON,MAXDBC,CN,ST,IT,NQ,TRT,NALT,IGO)
      IF(IGO.GT.0) GO TO 1
      DO 22 I = 11,20
   22 CALL COPYA(TT(I),TT(I+10))
      ARAN = 5236.
      MAXAV = MAXST - (NCON+3)/4
      MS1 = NCON + 1
C LEVEL 5 - READ CRITERIA
   51 IF(V(10).GE.50.) V(10) = 0.
      IFIN = MAXM - 1
      M = 0
      WRITE(MED6,941)
      WRITE(MED6,945)
  845 CALL LGEN(U,NU,LU,NU,ST,IT,CN,NQ,NCL,MAXM,DMIN,DMAX,NQ,TMIN,TMAX,M
     1AXM,0,NCMAX,IH,NP,MAXM,M,MAXM,1,NALT)
      IF(V(11).LT.0.5.AND.V(20).LT.0.5) GO TO 21
      IF(V(10).LT.0.5.AND.V(20).GT.0.5.AND.V(11).LT.0.5) V(10)= 54.
      K = M
C LEVEL 6 - READ PREDICTORS
   61 IF(V(10).GT.60.) V(10) = 0.
      WRITE(MED6,951)
      WRITE(MED6,955)
      IFIN = MAXM
      M = K
      J = 0
      IF(M.EQ.0) GO TO 63
      DO 62 I = 1,M
   62 IF(NCL(I).GT.J) J = NCL(I)
   63 Y = J
      X = MAXAV
      IF(J.EQ.0) LIMR=NRMAX
      IF(J.NE.0) LIMR = X*100./Y
      IF(LIMR.GT.NRMAX) LIMR = NRMAX
      CALL LGEN(H,0,IH,0,ST,IT,CN,NQ,NCL,MAXM,DMIN,DMAX,NQ,TMIN,TMAX,M
     1AXM,0,LIMR,IH,NP,IFIN,M,MAXM,1,NALT)
      IF(V(11).LT.0.5.AND.V(20).LT.0.5) GO TO 51
      IF(V(10).LT.0.5.AND.V(20).GT.0.5.AND.V(11).LT.0.5) V(10)= 64.
      BRAN = ARAN
C LEVEL 9 - DATA HANDLING INSTRUCTION
   91 IF(V(10).GE.90.) V(10) = 0.
      CALL LDHI(V(1),1,V(2),2,V(7),9,V(8),6,V(3),16,V6,0,V7,V(10),
     1    TT(21),FORM,MED1,MED2,MED4,Q,NQ,NWARN,1,IGO)
      IF(IGO.GT.0) GO TO 61
C STANDARDISATION
      SMAX = NSMAX
      IF(V(7).LT.0.5.OR.V(7).GT.SMAX) NWARN = NWARN + 1
      IF(V(7).LT.0.5) V(7) = SMAX
      IF(V(7).GT.SMAX) V(7) = SMAX
      NSS = V(7)
      NSS2 = NSS*2
      IF(V(8).LE.0.5) NWARN = NWARN + 1
      IF(V(8).LE.0.5) V(8) = 5.
      IF(V(3).LE.0.) NWARN = NWARN + 1
      IF(V(3).EQ.0.) V(3) = 5.
      IF(V(3).LT.0.) V(3) = 0.
      CALL LDHI(V(1),1,V(2),2,V(7),9,V(8),6,V(3),16,V6,0,V7,V(10),
```

```
    1   TT(21),FORM,MED1,MED2,MED4,Q,NQ,NWARN,2,IGO)
        IF(IGO.GT.0) GO TO 91
        V(3) = V(3)*.01
        CALL CAIAD(D,IT,ST,NQ,TRT,NALT,T,TMIN,TMAX,NP,NCL,M,TRTC,CX,KC,NCM
       1AX,TRTR,RX,KR,NRMAX,RT,MAXAV,SCON,NCON,SN,SID,SP,S2,S3,NSS,NSS2,U,
       2NU,K)
        ARAN = V(10)
        V(10) = 0.
        WRITE(MED6,999)
        GO TO 91
    901 FORMAT (1H0,20X,38HSTATCAT AUTOMATIC INTERACTION DETECTOR)
    941 FORMAT(21H1    CRITERIA SELECTED   /)
    945 FORMAT (4H0NO.,9X,30HTRANS DATA              NUMBER OF,7X,5HLOWER,6X,
       15HCLASS,7X,5HUPPER/5H CODE,8X,68H-FORM COLUMN        CLASSES USED
       2 CLASS LIMIT   INTERVAL    CLASS LIMIT)
    951 FORMAT(21H1 PREDICTORS SELECTED   /)
    955 FORMAT (4H0NO.,9X,30H       DATA              NUMBER OF,7X,5HLOWER,6X,
       15HCLASS,7X,5HUPPER/5H CODE,8X,68H        COLUMN        CLASSES USED
       2 CLASS LIMIT   INTERVAL    CLASS LIMIT)
    998 FORMAT (36H0INPUT ACCEPTED - ANALYSIS COMMENCES)
    999 FORMAT (36H1ANALYSIS COMPLETED - READ NEW INPUT)
        END


        SUBROUTINE CAIAD(XX,IT,SH,NQ,TRT,NALT,D,DMIN,DMAX,NP,NCL,M,TRTC,CX
       1,KC,NCMAX,TRTR,RX,KR,NRMAX,RT,MAXST,SCON,NCON,SN,SID,SP,S2,S3
       2,NSMAX,NS2,U,NU,K)
C CAIAD  (SEE 8.2 ) EXECUTIVE   AUTOMATIC INTERACTION DETECTOR
C SETTING UP
        DIMENSION RT(100,MAXST),SCON(5,NCON),U(NU),SN(NSMAX),SID(NSMAX)
        DIMENSION S2(NS2),S3(NS2),SP(NSMAX),XX(BQ),IT(BQ)
        DIMENSION TRTC(NCMAX),CX(NCMAX),KC(NCMAX),TTC(21),TRT(NALT)
        DIMENSION TRTR(NRMAX),RX(NRMAX),KR(NRMAX),TTR(21)
        DIMENSION D(M),DMIN(M),DMAX(M),NP(M),NCL(M),SH(NQ)
        DATA BL/4H    /,RST/4HREST/,ABO/4HOVER/
        COMMON /STCT/MED1,MED2,MED3,MED4,MED5,MED6,MED13,Q,V(20),TT(30)
        V1 = V(1)
        V2 = V(2) + .01
        NST = V2
        IF(NST.GE.5) NST = NST - 5
        V3 = V(3)
        NSMAX = V(7) + .01
        SMIN2 = V(8)*2. -0.1
C CRITERIA = COLUMNS
        KK = K + 1
        DO 300 NCR = 1,K
        REWIND MED3
        IFAULT = 0
        NSAM = 1
        NALL = 1
        NSP = 0
        INOW = 0
        ISSP = 1
        JSSP = 1
        NACON = 1
        RT(1,1) = 4.
        SID(1) = 1.
        N1 = 1
        NC = 1
        S2(1) = 1
        S3(1) = 1
C INITIALLY SAMPLE 1 CONTAINS ALL THE SUBSET
        NTCR = NP(NCR)/1000
```

```
      NCCR = NP(NCR)-1000*NTCR
      ITCR = IT(NCCR)
      IF(NST.GT.0)ITCR = NST + 1
      IF(ITCR.LE.3) NALTC = NCL(NCR)
      IF(ITCR.GE.4) NALTC = 3.
      READ(MED3) NQ,NALT,X,(TT(I),I=1,10),(X,I=1,6)
      DO 10 J = 1,NQ
      IF(J.NE.NCCR) READ(MED3) (X,I=1,19),(X,I=1,NALT),NX,X,X
   10 IF(J.EQ.NCCR) READ(MED3) TTC(2),(TTC(I),I=4,21),TRT,NX,X,X
      TTC(3) = NCCR
      CALL COPYA(TTC(1),U(NTCR))
      DO 20 J = 1,NALTC
      IF(J.LE.NALT)  CALL COPYA(TRTC(J),TRT(J))
   20 IF(J.GT.NALT)  CALL COPYA(TRTC(J),BL)
C START SEARCH FOR BEST SPLIT OF SAMPLE ISSF
   30 CALL NEXY(1,I1,100,1,J1,5*NACON)
      CALL NEXY(I1,I2,100,J1,J2,2*NALTC)
      NRAV =(MAXST*100-5*NACON)/NALTC - 2
      CALL BSPLIT(SCON,RT,XX,IT,D,NCL,NP,DMIN,DMAX,RT(I1,J1),RT(I2,J2),
     1SID,SN,TRT,U,TRTR,TRTC,CX,KC,TTC,TTR,NCON,NACON,NQ,M,NALT,NALTC,
     2 NRAV,NSAM,NRMAX,NU,K,ISSF,NCR,NCPL,BSSF,CB,PB,TB,VB,PY,PZ,PN,
     3 JSSF,NALL)
C IF(BSSF.LE.V3) THERE IS A STATISTICALLY SIGNIFICANT SPLIT
      IF(BSSF.GT.V3)SN(JSSF) = - SN(JSSF)
      IF(BSSF.GT.V3) GO TO 50
C INSERT NEW SPLIT IN SEQUENCE OF SAMPLES + UPDATE HISTORY (WSPLIT)
      MAXSAC = MAXST*20 - (NSAM+2)*NALTC/5 - 2
      CALL ISPLIT(SN,SP,SID,RT,MAXSAC,NSMAX,PY,PZ,TB,VB,CB,PB,PN,ISSF,
     1 NSAM,NALL,NACON,IFAULT)
      NC = NC + 1
      S2(NC) = SID(JSSF+1)
      S3(NC) = NALL
      MAXSAC = MAXSAC + 1
      CALL ITIDY (SN,SP,SID,RT,NSMAX,NSAM,NALL,NACON,MAXSAC)
C OUTPUT SAMPLE DEFINITIONS WITH THEIR TOTALS
   50 IF(V1.LT.0.5.AND.IFAULT.EQ.0.AND.NSAM.GT.1) GO TO 70
      IF(BSSF.LE.V3.OR.V1.GT.0.5.OR.NSAM.EQ.1.OR.IFAULT.NE.0)
     1WRITE(MED2,999)TT,TTC
      IF(BSSF.LE.V3.OR.V1.GT.0.5.OR.NSAM.EQ.1.OR.IFAULT.NE.0)
     1CALL CHIKEN(ITCR,IT(NCCR))
      IF(BSSF.LE.V3.OR.V1.GT.0.5.OR.NSAM.EQ.1.OR.IFAULT.NE.0)
     1 NL = 8
      IF(BSSF.GT.V3.AND.NSAM.EQ.1) WRITE(MED2,918)
      IF(BSSF.GT.V3.AND.NSAM.EQ.1) GO TO 300
      IF(IFAULT.NE.0) GO TO 60
      IF(BSSF.GT.1.5)WRITE(MED2,913) N1
      IF(BSSF.LT.1.5.AND.BSSF.GT.V3) WRITE(MED2,914) N1,BSSF
      IF(BSSF.LE.V3) WRITE(MED2,916) NALL,N1,BSSF
   60 IF(IFAULT.EQ.1) WRITE(MED2,915)
      IF(IFAULT.EQ.2) WRITE(MED2,925) NALL
      IF(IFAULT.EQ.3) WRITE(MED2,926) SMIN2
      CALL WSAMP(RT,SID,SN,SP,TRTC,TTC,SH,NALL,NALTC,NACON,NQ,ITCR)
      CALL NEXY(1,I1,100,1,J1,5*NACON)
      CALL NEXY(I1,I2,100,J1,J2,NALL)
      CALL WSPLIT (SID,RT(I1,J1),RT(I2,J2),NALL,S2,S3,NC,MED2)
      IF(BSSF.GT.V3) GO TO 70
      CALL NEXY(I1,I2,100,J1,J2,2*NALTC)
      CALL NEXY(I2,I3,100,J2,J3,NSAM*NALTC)
      CALL NEXY(I3,I4,100,J3,J4,NSAM)
      IF(J4.GT.MAXST) WRITE(MED2,912)
      IF(J4.GT.MAXST.OR.V2.LT.5.OR.NSAM.LE.2) GO TO 70
      V(1) = V1
      V(2) = V2
```

```
      CALL RECOMB(RT(I2,J2),RT(I3,J3),SID,SN,SP,S2,S3,RT(I1,J1),
     1 NSAM,NALL,NS2,NC,NALTC,SCON,NCON,RT,NACON,D,NP,NCL,DMIN,DMAX,M,
     2 TTC,TRTC,XX,IT,SH,NQ,U,NU,NCR,RX,CX,KR,KC)
      CALL ITIDY (SN,SP,SID,RT,NSMAX,NSAM,NALL,NACON,MAXSAC)
      WRITE(MED2,999) TT,TTC
      CALL WSAMP(RT,SID,SN,SP,TRTC,TTC,SH,NALL,NALTC,NACON,NQ,ITCR)
      NCPL = 0
      CALL NEXY(1,I1,100,1,J1,5*NACON)
      CALL NEXY(I1,I2,100,J1,J2,NALL)
      CALL WSPLIT (SID,RT(I1,J1),RT(I2,J2),NALL,S2,S3,NC,MED2)
C CHOOSE NEXT SAMPLE TO BE SPLIT
   70 IF(IFAULT.GT.0) GO TO 200
      IF(NALL.EQ.NSMAX.AND.V1.LT.0.5) IFAULT = 2
      IF(NALL.EQ.NSMAX.AND.V1.LT.0.5) GO TO 50
      IF(NALL.EQ.NSMAX) WRITE(MED2,925) NSAM
      IF(NALL.EQ.NSMAX) GO TO 200
      ISSF = 0
      SMIN = SMIN2-0.5
      I = 0
      DO 80 J = 1,NALL
      IF(SID(J).LT.0.) GO TO 80
      I = I + 1
      IF(SN(J).LT.SMIN) GO TO 80
      SMIN = SN(J)
      ISSF = I
      JSSF = J
   80 CONTINUE
      IF(ISSF.EQ.0.AND.V1.LT.0.5) IFAULT = 3
      IF(ISSF.EQ.0.AND.V1.LT.0.5) GO TO 50
      IF(ISSF.EQ.0) WRITE(MED2,926) SMIN2
      IF(ISSF.EQ.0) GO TO 200
      N1 = SID(JSSF)
      IF(V1.LT.0.5) GO TO 100
      WRITE(MED2,927) N1,SN(JSSF)
      NL = NL + 2
  100 IF(NCPL.EQ.NQ) GO TO 30
      IF(NCPL.EQ.0) READ (MED3) NX,NX,(X,I=1,17)
      NCPL = NCPL + 1
      DO 110 J = NCPL,NQ
  110 READ(MED3) (X,I=1,19),(X,I=1,NALT),NX,X,X
      GO TO 30
  200 WRITE(MED2,930)
      CALL NEXY(1,I1,100,1,J1,5*NACON)
      CALL NEXY(I1,I2,100,J1,J2,2*NALTC)
      CALL NEXY(I2,I3,100,J2,J3,NSAM*NALTC)
      CALL NEXY(I3,I4,100,J3,J4,NSAM)
      IF(J4.GT.MAXST) WRITE(MED2,912)
      IF(J4.GT.MAXST) GO TO 300
      V(1) = V1
      V(2) = NST+10
      CALL RECOMB(RT(I2,J2),RT(I3,J3),SID,SN,SP,S2,S3,RT(I1,J1),
     1 NSAM,NALL,NS2,NC,NALTC,SCON,NCON,RT,NACON,D,NP,NCL,DMIN,DMAX,M,
     2 TTC,TRTC,XX,IT,SH,NQ,U,NU,NCR,RX,CX,KR,KC)
      CALL NEXY(I1,I2,100,J1,J2,NALL)
      CALL WSPLIT (SID,RT(I1,J1),RT(I2,J2),NALL,S2,S3,NC,MED2)
  300 CONTINUE
      RETURN
  912 FORMAT(27HONO SPACE FOR RECOMBINATION)
  913 FORMAT(1H0,10X,6HSAMPLE,I4,18H NO BALANCED SPLIT)
  914 FORMAT(1H0,10X,6HSAMPLE,I4,64H NO STATISTICALLY SIGNIFICANT SPLIT
     1- BEST PSEUDO-PROBABILITY = ,F10.6)
  915 FORMAT(1H0,5X,28HNO MORE SPACE FOR CONDITIONS)
  916 FORMAT(1H0,10X,6HSAMPLE,I4,25H IS SEPARATED FROM SAMPLE,I4,22H PSE
```

```
      1UDO-PROBABILITY = ,F10.6)
  918 FORMAT(1H0,10X,44HNO STATISTICALLY SIGNIFICANT SPLIT OF SUBSET)
  925 FORMAT(1H0,5X,25HNO MORE SPACE FOR SAMPLES,I4,9H IN STORE)
  926 FORMAT(1H0,5X,32HNO UNTESTED SAMPLE WITH AT LEAST,F6.0,8H ENTRIES)
  927 FORMAT(1H0,5X,13HSAMPLE NUMBER,I4,11H CONTAINING,F8.0,30HENTRIES S
     1ELECTED FOR SPLITTING)
  928 FORMAT(1H+,31X,22HCRITERION IS INVARIANT)
  930 FORMAT(1H0,5X,34HNO FURTHER SUB-DIVISION ACCEPTABLE)
  999 FORMAT(23H1STATCAT PROGRAM STAIAD,7X,1H-,4X,35HAUTOMATIC INTERACTI
     1ON DETECTOR       /16H DATA BANK TITLE,14X,1H-,4X,10A4/23H DATA BANK
     2 SUBSET TITLE,7X,1H-,4X,10A4/10H RUN TITLE,20X,1H-,4X,10A4/
     313H CRITERION - ,A4,4H OF ,A4,1H=,F4.0,1H-,4X,A2,18A4)
      END


      SUBROUTINE BSPLIT(SCON,SACON,XX,IT,D,NCL,NP,DMIN,DMAX,ST,RT,SID,
     1SN,TRT,U,TRTR,TRTC,CX,KC,TTC,TTR,NCON,NACON,NQ,M,NALT,NALTC,NRAV,
     2NSAM,NRMAX,NU,K,ISSF,NCR,NCPL,BSSF,CB,PB,TB,VB,PY,PZ,PN,JSSF,NALL)
C BSPLIT (SEE  8.2 ) SYSTEM        SELECT NEXT SPLIT FOR SAMPLE ISSF
      DIMENSION SCON(5,NCON),SACON(5,NACON),RT(NALTC,NRAV),ST(2,NALTC)
      DIMENSION D(M),NCL(M),NP(M),DMIN(M),DMAX(M),TTC(21),TTR(21)
      DIMENSION SID(NALL),SN(NALL),TRTR(NRMAX),TRTC(NALTC),TRT(NALT)
      DIMENSION XX(NQ),IT(NQ),U(NU)
      DIMENSION TS(2),RX(2),KR(2),CX(NALTC),KC(NALTC)
      DATA BL/4H    /,RST/4HREST/,ABO/4HOVER/
      COMMON /STCT/MED1,MED2,MED3,MED4,MED5,MED6,MED13,Q,V(20),TT(30)
      V1 = V(1)
      NST= V(2)
      NST = NST - NST/5*5
      SMIN = V(8)
      NTCR = NP(NCR)/1000
      NCCR = NP(NCR)-1000*NTCR
      ITCR = IT(NCCR)
      IF(NST.GT.0)ITCR = NST + 1
      DMINC = DMIN(NCR)
      DMAXC = DMAX(NCR)
      V10 = V(10)
   10 BSSF = 2.
C FIND STORAGE LIMIT FOR PREDICTORS
      KF = K
   11 KS = KF + 1
      KF = KS
      J = NRAV
   14 IF(KF.EQ.M) GO TO 12
      IF(J.LT.NCL(KF+1)) GO TO 12
      J = J - NCL(KF+1)
      KF = KF + 1
      GO TO 14
C DATA SWEEP FOR KS TO KF
   12 DO 13 I = 1,NALTC
      DO 13 J = 1,NRAV
   13 RT(I,J) = 0.
      V(6) = 0.
      V(7) = 1.
      V(8) = 1.
      V(9) = M
   20 CALL MEDIAT(M,NP,NP,M,D,XX,NQ,SCON,NCON)
      IF(V(8).EQ.2.) GO TO 30
      CALL CLSAM(XX,NQ,SACON,NACON,NIN,NSAM)
      IF(NIN.NE.ISSF) GO TO 20
      IF(D(NCR).EQ.Q) GO TO 20
      IF(ITCR.LE.3) CALL CLASIF(D(NCR),DMAXC,DMINC,IT(NCCR),NCL(NCR),IR)
      IF(ITCR.GT.3) IR = 1
```

```
              JC = 0
              Y = D(NCR)
              DO 21 K1 = KS,KF
              NCPR = NP(K1)-NP(K1)/1000*1000
              X = D(K1)
              IF(X.EQ.Q) GO TO 21
              CALL CLASIF(X,DMAX(K1),DMIN(K1),IT(NCPR),NCL(K1),JR)
              JR = JR + JC
              RT(IR,JR) = RT(IR,JR) + 1.
              IF(ITCR.GE.4) RT(2,JR) = RT(2,JR) + Y
              IF(ITCR.GE.4) RT(3,JR) = RT(3,JR) + Y*Y
           21 JC = JC + NCL(K1)
              GO TO 20
C ARRAY RT NOW CONTAINS SPLITS FOR PREDICTORS KS TO KF
           30 REWIND MED3
              V(10) = V10
              NCPL = 0
              JC = 1
              DO 60 K1 = KS,KF
              NTPR = NP(K1)/1000
              NCPR = NP(K1)-1000*NTPR
              IF(NTPR.EQ.0) NTPR = 1
              NALTR = NCL(K1)
              ITPR = IT(NCPR)
              ALTR = NALTR
              DMINR = DMIN(K1)
              DMAXR = DMAX(K1)
              IF(ITPR.LT.3) CALL COPYA(TS(2),RST)
              IF(ITPR.GE.3) CALL COPYA(TS(2),ABO)
              IF(V1.LT.1.5.AND.K1.NE.KS) GO TO 35
              IF(NCPR.LT.NCPL) REWIND MED3
              IF(NCPR.LT.NCPL) NCPL = 0
              IF(NCPL.EQ.0) READ(MED3) NX,NX,(X,I=1,17)
           31 IF(NCPL.EQ.NCPR) GO TO 32
              READ(MED3) TTR(2),(TTR(L),L=4,21),TRT,NX,X,X
              NCPL = NCPL + 1
              GO TO 31
           32 TTR(3) = NCPR
              CALL COPYA(TTR(1),U(NTPR))
              DO 33 I = 1,NALTR
              IF(I.LE.NALT) CALL COPYA(TRTR(I),TRT(I))
           33 IF(I.GT.NALT) CALL COPYA(TRTR(I),BL)
              IF(V1.LT.4.5) GO TO 35
              WRITE(MED2,999) TT,TTC,BL,TTR,SID(JSSF),NALL
              IF(ITCR.LE.3) CALL TAB2W(RT(1,JC),NALTC,NALTR,TRTC,TRTC,TRTR,
             1IT(NCCR),ITPR,DMINC,DMINR,DMAXC,DMAXR,V,MED2)
              IF(ITCR.LE.3) GO TO 35
              JD = JC
              WRITE(MED2,900)
              DO 34 J = 1,NALTR
              A = RT(1,JD)
              B = RT(2,JD)
              C = RT(3,JD)
              IF(A.LT.0.5) WRITE(MED2,901)
              IF(A.GT.0.5) B = B/A
              IF(A.GT.0.5.AND.A.LT.1.5) WRITE(MED2,902) B
              IF(A.GT.1.5) C = SQRT(ABS((C-B*B*A)/(A-1.)))
              IF(A.GT.1.5) WRITE(MED2,903) A,B,C
              JD = JD + 1
           34 CALL PRTCLS(DMAXR,DMINR,J,TRTR(J),NALTR,ITPR,MED2)
           35 CONTINUE
C CALCULATION OF BEST SPLIT - ROW AND COLUMN TOTALS FIRST
              JD = JC
```

```
      GT = 0.
      DO 50 I = 1,NALTC
      DO 50 J = 1,2
   50 ST(J,I) = 0.
C ACCUMULATE TOTAL NUMBERS IN EACH CLASS/POWER
      DO 52 J = 1,NALTR
      DO 51 I = 1,NALTC
      ST(2,I) = ST(2,I) + RT(I,JD)
   51 IF(I.EQ.1.OR.ITCR.LE.3)GT = GT + RT(I,JD)
   52 JD = JD + 1
      IF(NSAM.EQ.1) SN(1) = GT
      IF(V1.LT.4.5) NL = 0
      IF(V1.GT.4.5) NL = 60
      DO 60 J = 1,NALTR
      CALL COPYA(TS(1),TRTR(J))
      PX = J
      IF(ITPR.EQ.3) PX = PX + 1.
      IF(ITPR.GT.3) PX = DMINR+(PX-1.)*(DMAXR-DMINR)/(ALTR-2.)
      IF(J.EQ.1.OR.ITPR.LT.3) TX = 0.
C DIVIDE UP DATA BY SPLIT
      DO 53 I = 1,NALTC
      ST(2,I) =ST(2,I)+ST(1,I)
      IF(ITPR.LT.3) ST(1,I) = 0.
      ST(1,I) = ST(1,I) + RT(I,JC)
      ST(2,I) = ST(2,I) - ST(1,I)
   53 IF(I.EQ.1.OR.ITCR.LT.4)TX = TX + RT(I,JC)
      IF(TX.LT.0.5.OR.TX.GT.GT-0.5) GO TO 60
      IF(TX.LT.SMIN.OR.GT-TX.LT.SMIN) GO TO 55
      IF(V1.LT.1.5) GO TO 54
      IF(V1.GT.8.5.AND.ITCR.LT.3) NL = 50
      IF(V1.GT.8.5.AND.ITCR.EQ.3) NL = NL + 12
      IF(V1.GT.8.5.AND.ITCR.GT.3) NL = NL + 25
      IF(NL.GE.40) WRITE(MED2,999)TT,TTC,BL,TTR,SID(JSSF),NALL
      IF(NL.GE.40) CALL CHIKEN(ITCR,IT(NCCR))
      IF(NL.GE.40)NL = 0
      IF(V1.LT.8.5) GO TO 54
      IF(ITPR.LT.3) WRITE(MED2,904) TRTR(J)
      IF(ITPR.EQ.3) WRITE(MED2,905) TRTR(J)
      IF(ITPR.GT.3) WRITE(MED2,906) PX
   54 V(1) = -1.
      IF(V1.GT.8.5) V(1) = 3.
      V(11) = 2.
      IF(V1.GT.8.5.AND.ITCR.GT.3) V(1) = 1.
      IF(ITCR.GT.3) CALL PAR1W(ST,TS,2,V,DMAXC,DMINC,2,MED2)
      IF(ITCR.EQ.3) CALL KW1W (ST,TS,2,NALTC,V,MED2)
      IF(ITCR.EQ.2) CALL CHISQD(ST,2,NALTC,RX,CX,KR,KC,2,ITCR,TS,TRTC,DMI
     1NR,DMINC,DMAXR,DMAXC,V,MED2)
      IF(ITCR.GT.3) V(11) = V(12)
      IF(ITCR.GT.3) V(12) = V(14)
   55 IF(V1.LT.4.5) GO TO 56
      IF(V1.LT.6.5.AND.V(11).GT.BSSF) GO TO 56
      IF(V1.LT.6.5.AND.V(11).EQ.BSSF.AND.V(12).LT.SB) GO TO 56
      NL = NL + 2
      IF(TX.LT.SMIN.AND.NL.GT.40.OR.GT-TX.LT.SMIN.AND.NL.GT.40)
     1WRITE(MED2,999) TT,TTC,BL,TTR,SID(JSSF),NALL
      IF(TX.LT.SMIN.AND.NL.GT.40.OR.GT-TX.LT.SMIN.AND.NL.GT.40)
     1CALL CHIKEN(ITCR,IT(NCCR))
      IF(TX.LT.SMIN.AND.NL.GT.40.OR.GT-TX.LT.SMIN.AND.NL.GT.40)    NL = 2
      IF(ITPR.GT.3) WRITE(MED2,906) PX
      IF(ITPR.EQ.3) WRITE(MED2,905) TRTR(J)
      IF(ITPR.LT.3) WRITE(MED2,904) TRTR(J)
      IF(TX.LT.SMIN) WRITE(MED2,912) SMIN
      IF(GT-TX.LT.SMIN) WRITE(MED2,922) SMIN
```

```
      IF(TX.LT.SMIN.OR.GT-TX.LT.SMIN) GO TO 60
      IF(V(11).GT.1.05) WRITE(MED2,928)
      IF(V(11).GT.BSSF.AND.V(11).LE.1.0) WRITE(MED2,910) V(11)
      IF(V(11).EQ.BSSF.AND.V(12).LE.SB)  WRITE(MED2,910) V(11)
      IF(V(11).EQ.BSSF.AND.V(12).GT.SB)  WRITE(MED2,911) V(11)
      IF(V(11).LT.BSSF) WRITE(MED2,911) V(11)
   56 IF(TX.LT.SMIN.OR.GT-TX.LT.SMIN)GO TO 60
      IF(V(11).GT.BSSF.OR.V(11).GT.1.0)GO TO 60
      IF(V(11).EQ.BSSF.AND.V(12).LE.SB) GO TO 60
      BSSF = V(11)
      SB = V(12)
      VB = NCPR
      CB = 1.
      PB = PX
      TB = TX
      KB = K1
      IF(ITPR.GE.3) CB = 5.
C FIND ESTIMATED MODE,MEDIAN OR MEAN OF BOTH PARTS OF SPLIT SAMPLE
      DO 59 I =1,2
      IF(ITCR.GT.3) PZ = ST(I,2)/ST(I,1)
      IF(ITCR.GT.3) GO TO 59
      IF(I.EQ.1) TZ = TB
      IF(I.EQ.2) TZ = GT-TB
      TY = 0.
      DO 58 L = 1,NALTC
      B = ST(I,L)
      IF(ITCR.LT.3.AND.TY.GE.B) GO TO 58
      IF(ITCR.EQ.3.AND.TY+B+B.LT.TZ) GO TO 58
      PZ = L
      IF(ITCR.EQ.3) PZ = PZ + (TZ-TY)/B*0.5
      IF(ITCR.EQ.3) GO TO 59
      IF(L.EQ.0) A = 0
      IF(L.EQ.NALTC) C = 0.
      IF(L.GT.0) A = ST(I,L-1)
      IF(L.LT.NALTC) C =ST(I,L+1)
      IF(A+C.NE.B+B) PZ = PZ + (B-A)/(B+B-A-C)
      TY = B
   58 IF(ITCR.EQ.3) TY = TY + B + B
   59 IF(I.EQ.1) PY = PZ
   60 JC = JC + 1
      IF(KF.LT.M) GO TO 11
      V(1) = V1
      V(2) = MST
      V(8) = SMIN
      N = VB
      CALL COPYA(PN,BL)
      IF(IT(M).NE.2.AND.IT(M).NE.3) GO TO 75
      IF(ABS(DMAX(KB)-DMIN(KB)-FLOAT(NCL(KB)-2)).GT.0.1)GO TO 75
      REWIND MED3
      READ (MED3)NX,NX,(X,I=1,17)
      DO 70 J = 1,N
   70 READ(MED3) (X,I=1,19),TRT,NX,X,X
      NCPL = N
      J =PB
      CALL COPYA(PN,TRT(J))
   75 V(1) = V1
      RETURN
  900 FORMAT(1H0,5X,5HCLASS,17X,6HNUMBER,10X,15HARITHMETIC MEAN, 3X,18HS
     1TANDARD DEVIATION/)
  901 FORMAT(25X, 8HIS EMPTY )
  902 FORMAT(25X,14HONE READING = , F22.6)
  903 FORMAT(21X,3F20.6)
  904 FORMAT(1H0,10X,6HCLASS ,A4)
```

```
      905 FORMAT(1H0,10X,6HCLASS ,A4,10H AND BELOW)
      906 FORMAT(1H0,5X,10HALL BELOW ,F15.6)
      910 FORMAT(1H+,31X,47HIS NOT AN IMPROVEMENT      - PSEUDO-PROBABILITY =,
         1F12.8)
      911 FORMAT(1H+,31X,47HIS THE BEST SPLIT SO FAR - PSEUDO-PROBABILITY =,
         1F12.8)
      912 FORMAT(1H+,31X,38HIS DISCARDED - SAMPLE IS LESS THAN      ,F6.0,
         18H ENTRIES)
      922 FORMAT(1H+,31X,38HIS DISCARDED - REMAINDER IS LESS THAN   ,F6.0,
         18H ENTRIES)
      924 FORMAT(1H+,35X,32H- CONTAINS ALL REMAINING ENTRIES)
      925 FORMAT(1H0,5X,25HNO MORE SPACE FOR SAMPLES,I4,9H IN STORE)
      926 FORMAT(1H0,5X,32HNO UNTESTED SAMPLE WITH AT LEAST,F6.0,8H ENTRIES)
      927 FORMAT(1H0,5X,13HSAMPLE NUMBER,I4,11H CONTAINING,F8.0,30HENTRIES S
         1ELECTED FOR SPLITTING)
      928 FORMAT(1H+,31X,22HCRITERION IS INVARIANT)
      999 FORMAT(23H1STATCAT PROGRAM STAIAD,7X,1H-,4X,35HAUTOMATIC INTERACTI
         1ON DETECTOR      /16H DATA BANK TITLE,14X,1H-,4X,10A4/23H DATA BANK
         2 SUBSET TITLE,7X,1H-,4X,10A4/10H RUN TITLE,20X,1H-,4X,10A4/
         313H CRITERION  - ,A4,4H OF ,A4,1H=,F4.0,1H-,4X,A2,18A4/
         413H PREDICTOR  - ,A4,4H OF ,A4,1H=,F4.0,1H-,4X,A2,17A4/
         513H    SAMPLE  - ,F4.0,4H OF ,I4)
          END


          SUBROUTINE RECOMB(RT,SID,S1,SN,SP,S2,S3,ST,NSAM,NALL,NS2,NC,NALTC,
         1 SCON,NCON,SACON,NACON,D,NP,NCL,DMIN,DMAX,M,TTC,TRTC,XX,IT,SH,
         2 NQ,U,NU,NCR,RX,CX,KR,KC)
    C RECOMB  (SEE 8.2 ) SYSTEM          RECOMBINES SAMPLES
          DIMENSION RT(NSAM,NALTC),ST(2,NALTC),SCON(5,NCON),SACON(5,NACON)
          DIMENSION D(M),NP(M),NCL(M),DMIN(M),DMAX(M),TTC(21)
          DIMENSION SID(NSAM),KC(NSAM),CX(NSAM)
          DIMENSION RX(NALTC),KR(NALTC),TRTC(NALTC)
          DIMENSION S1(NALL),SN(NALL),SP(NALL),S2(NS2),S3(NS2)
          DIMENSION XX(NQ),IT(NQ),SH(NQ),U(NU)
          DATA XN/4HNO. /,AM/4HA.M./,SD/4HS.D./
          COMMON /STCT/MED1,MED2,MED3,MED4,MED5,MED6,MED13,Q,V(20),TT(30)
    C SET CONTROLS
          V1 =V(1)
          V(1) = -1.
          NOP = V1 + 0.1
          V2 =V(2)
          NST = V2 + 0.1
          LC = NST/5
          NST = NST - LC*5
          V8 = V(8)
          NTCR = NP(NCR)/1000
          NCCR = NP(NCR) - NTCR*1000
          ITCR =IT(NCCR)
          IF(NST.GT.0)ITCR = NST + 1
          DMAXC= DMAX(NCR)
          DMINC= DMIN(NCR)
    C DATA COLLECTION SWEEP
          REWIND MED3
          V10 = V(10)
          K = 0
          DO 10 I = 1,NSAM
        5 K = K + 1
          IF(S1(K).LT.0.) GO TO 5
          SID(I) = S1(K)
          DO 10 J = 1,NALTC
       10 RT(I,J) = 0.
          V(6) = 0.
```

```
      V(7) = 1.
      V(8) = 1.
      V(9) = M
      READ(MED3)NQ,NALT,(X,I=1,17)
      DO 20 I = 1,NQ
   20 READ(MED3) (X,J=1,19),(X,J=1,NALT),NX,X,X
      I = 50
   30 CALL MEDIAT(M,NP,NP,M,D,XX,NQ,SCON,NCON)
      IF(V(8).EQ.2.) GO TO 40
      CALL CLSAM(XX,NQ,SACON,NACON,NIN,NSAM)
      IF(NIN.EQ.0) GO TO 30
      IF(ITCR.LE.3) CALL CLASIF(D(NCR),DMAXC,DMINC,ITCR,NCL(NCR),JR)
      IF(ITCR.GE.4) JR = 1
      RT(NIN,JR) = RT(NIN,JR) + 1.
      IF(ITCR.LE.3) GO TO 35
      DX = D(NCR)
      RT(NIN,2) =RT(NIN,2) + DX
      RT(NIN,3) = RT(NIN,3) + DX*DX
   35 IF(NOP.LE.7.OR.LC.LE.1) GO TO 30
      I = I+1
      IF(I.GT.50) WRITE(MED2,900)TT,TTC
      IF(I.GT.50) I = 1
      WRITE(MED2,908) V(6),SID(NIN)
      GO TO 30
   40 V(10) = V10
      REWIND MED3
C FIND MOST SIMILAR PAIR OF SAMPLES - CONDENSE TABLE BY COMBINING THEM
      IF(ITCR.LT.3) CALL CHISQD(RT,NSAM,NALTC,CX,RX,KC,KR,2,ITCR,
     1SID,TRTC,DMINR,DMINC,DMAXR,DMAXC,V,MED2)
      IF(ITCR.EQ.3) CALL KW1W(RT,SID,NSAM,NALTC,V,MED2)
      IF(ITCR.GT.3) CALL PAR1W(RT,SID,NSAM,V,DMAXC,DMINC,2,MED2)
      IF(ITCR.GT.3) V(11) =V(12)
      IF(ITCR.GT.3) V(12) =V(14)
      PB = V(11)
      PBS = PB
      SB = V(12)
      SBS = SB
      NSIZ = NSAM
      DO 500 II =2,NSIZ
      NSAMB = NSIZ+2 - II
C EN-ROUTE CANNOT RE-COMBINE LAST TWO SAMPLES
      IF(NSAMB.EQ.2.AND.LC.LE.1) GO TO 550
      IF(NOP.EQ.0) GO TO 150
      IF(NOP.LE.1.AND.LC.LE.1) GO TO 150
      IF(NOP.LE.3.AND.NSAMB.LT.NSAM) GO TO 150
      WRITE(MED2,900)TT,TTC
      WRITE(MED2,901) (SID(I),I=1,NSAMB)
      IF(ITCR.LE.3) GO TO 120
      DO 100 I = 1,NSAMB
      RT(I,2) = RT(I,2)/RT(I,1)
      IF(RT(I,1).GT.1.5) RT(I,3) =
     1 SQRT(ABS(RT(I,3)-RT(I,2)*RT(I,2)*RT(I,1))/(RT(I,1)-1.))
  100 IF(RT(I,1).LT.1.5) RT(I,3) = 0.
      WRITE(MED2,902)XN,(RT(I,1),I=1,NSAMB)
      WRITE(MED2,902)AM,(RT(I,2),I=1,NSAMB)
      WRITE(MED2,902)SD,(RT(I,3),I=1,NSAMB)
      DO 110 I = 1,NSAMB
      RT(I,3) = RT(I,3)*RT(I,3)*(RT(I,1)-1.) + RT(I,2)*RT(I,2)*RT(I,1)
  110 RT(I,2) = RT(I,2)*RT(I,1)
      GO TO 140
  120 DO 130 JJ = 1,NALTC
      J = NALTC - JJ + 1
      WRITE(MED2,903) (RT(I,J),I=1,NSAMB)
```

```
      130 CALL PRTCLS(DMAXC,DMINC,J,TRTC(J),NALTC,ITCR,MED2)
      140 IF(NSAMB.LT.NSIZ) GO TO 150
          WRITE(MED2,912)
          WRITE(MED2,911) PB,SB
          IF(ITCR.LE.3) WRITE(MED2,913)
          IF(ITCR.GE.4) WRITE(MED2,914)
      150 IA = 1
          IB = 2
          IF(LC.GE.2) PB = 1.5
          IF(NSAMB.EQ.2) GO TO 411
          IA = 0
          NL = NALTC + 3
          DO 400 I1 = 1,NSAMB
          IF(I1.EQ.NSAMB) GO TO 400
          DO 200 J = 1,NALTC
          ST(1,J) = RT(I1,J)
      200 ST(2,J) = RT(I1+1,J)
          TS1 =SID(I1)
          TS2 =SID(I1+1)
          DO 220 I2 = I1,NSAMB
          IF(I2.EQ.NSAMB) GO TO 220
          DO 210 J = 1,NALTC
      210 RT(I2,J) = RT(I2+1,J)
          SID(I2) =SID(I2+1)
      220 CONTINUE
          DO 300 I2 = I1,NSAMB
          IF(I2.EQ.I1) GO TO 300
          IF(LC.GE.2) GO TO 235
C EN-ROUTE CANNOT RECOMBINE UNCHANGED SAMPLES (TO AVOID LOOPING)
          J = 0
          DO 230 I = 1,NC
          S2X = ABS(S2(I))
          S3X = ABS(S3(I))
          IF( J.EQ.0) GO TO 225
          IF(TS1.EQ.S2X.AND.TS2.NE.S3X) J = 2
          IF(TS1.EQ.S3X.AND.TS2.NE.S2X) J = 3
          IF(TS2.EQ.S2X.AND.TS1.NE.S3X) J = 2
          IF(TS2.EQ.S3X.AND.TS1.NE.S2X) J = 3
          IF(J.EQ.2.AND.NOP.GE.6) WRITE(MED2,921) S3X,S2X
          IF(J.EQ.3.AND.NOP.GE.6) WRITE(MED2,921) S2X,S3X
          IF(J.GT.1) GO TO 235
          GO TO 230
      225 IF(TS1.EQ.S2X.AND.TS2.EQ.S3X) J = 1
          IF(TS1.EQ.S3X.AND.TS2.EQ.S2X) J = 1
          IF(J.EQ.0.OR.NOP.LE.5) GO TO 230
          NL = NL + 2
          IF(NL.GT.50)WRITE(MED2,900) TT,TTC
          IF(NL.GT.50) NL = 2
          WRITE(MED2,920)S3X,S2X
      230 CONTINUE
          IF(J.EQ.1.AND.NOP.GE.6) WRITE(MED2,922)
          IF(J.EQ.1) GO TO 280
      235 DO 240 J =1,NALTC
      240 RT(I1,J) = ST(1,J) + ST(2,J)
          SID(I1) = TS1*100. + TS2
          IC = 0
          JC = 1
          DO 250 J = 1,NALTC
          DO 250 I = 1,NSAMB
          IF(I.EQ.NSAMB) GO TO 250
          IC = IC + 1
          IF(IC.GT.NSIZ) JC = JC + 1
          IF(IC.GT.NSIZ) IC = 1
```

```
            RT(IC,JC) = RT(I,J)
250     CONTINUE
        IF(ITCR.LT.3) CALL CHISQD(RT,NSAMB-1,NALTC,CX,BX,KC,KR,2,ITCR,
       1SID,TRTC,DMINR,DMINC,DMAXR,DMAXC,V,MED2)
        IF(ITCR.EQ.3) CALL KW1W(RT,SID,NSAMB-1,NALTC,V,MED2)
        IF(ITCR.GT.3) CALL PAR1W(RT,SID,NSAMB-1,V,DMAXC,DMINC,2,MED2)
        I = NSAMB - 1
        J = NALTC
260     RT(I,J) = RT(IC,JC)
        IC = IC - 1
        IF(IC.EQ.0) JC = JC - 1
        IF(IC.EQ.0) IC = NSIZ
        I = I - 1
        IF(I.EQ.0) J = J-1
        IF(I.EQ.0) I = NSAMB - 1
        IF(J.GE.1) GO TO 260
        IF(ITCR.GT.3) V(11) =V(12)
        IF(ITCR.GT.3) V(12)=V(14)
        IGO = 0
        IF(V(11).GT.PB.OR.V(11).EQ.PB.AND.V(12).LE.SB) IGO = 1
        IF(NOP.GE.6.OR.NOP.GE.4.AND.IGO.EQ.0) NL = NL + 2
        IF(NL.GT.50) WRITE(MED2,900) TT,TTC
        IF(NL.GT.50) NL = 0
        IF(NOP.GE.6.OR.NOP.GE.4.AND.IGO.EQ.0) WRITE(MED2,910) TS1,TS2
        IF(NOP.GE.6.OR.NOP.GE.4.AND.IGO.EQ.0) WRITE(MED2,911) V(11),V(12)
        IF(NOP.GE.6.AND.ITCR.LE.3.OR.NOP.GE.4.AND.IGO.EQ.0.AND.ITCR.LE.3)
       1 WRITE(MED2,913)
        IF(NOP.GE.6.AND.ITCR.GE.4.OR.NOP.GE.4.AND.IGO.EQ.0.AND.ITCR.GE.4)
       1 WRITE(MED2,914)
        IF(NOP.GE.6.AND.IGO.EQ.1) WRITE(MED2,905)
        IF(IGO.EQ.1) GO TO 280
        IF(NOP.GE.4) WRITE(MED2,906)
        SB = V(12)
        PB = V(11)
        IA = I1
        IB = I2
        IF(ITCR.GT.3) PX = RT(IA,2)/RT(IA,1)
280     DO 290 J =1,NALTC
        X = ST(2,J)
        ST(2,J) = RT(I2,J)
290     RT(I2,J) = X
        X = TS2
        TS2 = SID(I2)
        SID(I2) = X
300     CONTINUE
        DO 310 J = 1,NALTC
310     RT(I1,J) = ST(1,J)
        SID(I1) = TS1
400     CONTINUE
410     IF(IA.EQ.0.AND.NOP.GE.4) WRITE(MED2,909)
        IF(IA.EQ.0) GO TO 550
411     IF(NOP.GE.4) WRITE(MED2,910) SID(IA),SID(IB)
        IF(NSAMB.GT.2.AND.NOP.GE.4) WRITE(MED2,911) PB,SB
        IF(NSAMB.GT.2.AND.ITCR.LE.3.AND.NOP.GE.4) WRITE(MED2,913)
        IF(NSAMB.GT.2.AND.ITCR.GE.4.AND.NOP.GE.4) WRITE(MED2,914)
        IF(PB.LT.PBS.OR.PB.EQ.PBS.AND.SB.GT.SBS.OR.LC.GE.2) GO TO 414
        IF(NOP.GE.4) WRITE(MED2,905)
        GO TO 550
414     IF(NOP.GE.4) WRITE(MED2,907)
        NC = NC + 1
        IF(SID(IA).GT.SID(IB)) S2(NC) = ABS(SID(IB))
        IF(SID(IA).GT.SID(IB)) S3(NC) =-ABS(SID(IA))
        IF(SID(IA).LT.SID(IB)) S2(NC) = ABS(SID(IA))
```

```
            IF(SID(IA).LT.SID(IB))S3(NC) =-ABS(SID(IB))
C FIND PX = COMMON MEAN/MEDIAN/MODE FOR IA AND IB - MEAN FIRST
            IF(ITCR.GT.3)  PX = (RT(IA,2)+RT(IB,2))/(RT(IA,1)+RT(IB,1))
            IF(ITCR.GT.3)  GO TO 418
            IF(ITCR.LT.3)  GO TO 416
C MEDIAN CALCULATED HERE
            TY = 0.
            DO 412 J = 1,NALTC
    412 TY = TY+RT(IA,J)+RT(IB,J)
            TX = 0
            DO 413 J = 1,NALTC
            B = RT(IA,J) + RT(IB,J)
            IF(TX+B+B.LT.TY) GO TO 413
            PX = J
            IF(J.EQ.1)  A = 0.
            IF(J.GT.1)  A = RT(IA,J-1)+RT(IB,J-1)
            IF(J.EQ.NALTC) C = 0.
            IF(J.LT.NALTC) C = RT(IA,J+1)+RT(IB,J+1)
            PX = PX + (B-A)/(B+B-A-C)
            GO TO 418
    413 TX = TX + B + B
C MODE CALCULATED HERE
    416 B = RT(IA,1)+RT(IB,1)
            JM = 1
            DO 417 J = 1,NALTC
            C = RT(IA,J) + RT(IB,J)
            IF(C.GT.B) JM = J
    417 IF(C.GT.B) B = C
            IF(JM.EQ.1)  A = 0.
            IF(JM.GT.1)  A = RT(IA,JM-1) + RT(IB,JM-1)
            IF(JM.EQ.NALTC) C = 0.
            IF(JM.LT.NALTC) C = RT(IA,J+1) + RT(IB,J+1)
            PX = JM
            PX = PX + (A-C)/B*0.5
    418 IF(SID(IA).GT.SID(IB)) SID(IA) = SID(IB)
            DO 420 J = 1,NALTC
    420 RT(IA,J) =RT(IA,J) + RT(IB,J)
            DO 440 I = IB,NSAMB
            IF(IB.EQ.NSAMB) GO TO 440
            SID(I) =SID(I+1)
            DO 430 J = 1,NALTC
    430 RT(I,J) = RT(I+1,J)
    440 CONTINUE
            CALL IJOIN(SN,SP,S1,SACON,IA,IB,PX,NSAM,NALL,NACON)
            PBS = PB
            SBS = SB
    500 CONTINUE
    550 V(1) = V1
            V(2) = V2
            V(8) = V8
            RETURN
    900 FORMAT(23H1SPATCAT PROGRAM STAIAD,7X,1H-,4X,35HAUTOMATIC INTERACTI
          1ON DETECTOR      /16H DATA BANK TITLE,14X,1H-,4X,10A4/23H DATA BANK
          2 SUBSET TITLE,7X,1H-,4X,10A4/10H RUN TITLE,20X,1H-,4X,10A4/
          313H CRITERION - ,A4,4H OF ,A4,1H=,F4.0,1H-,4X,A2,18A4)
    901 FORMAT(1H0,7X,13HSAMPLE NUMBER,10(F6.0,4X)/(21X,10(F6.0,4X)))
    902 FORMAT(11X,A4,6X,10F10.4/(21X,10F10.4))
    903 FORMAT(21X,10(F6.0,4X))
    905 FORMAT(1H+,100X,14HNO IMPROVEMENT)
    906 FORMAT(1H+,100X,11HBEST SO FAR)
    907 FORMAT(1H+,100X, 7HADOPTED)
    908 FORMAT(6H ENTRY,F8.0,19H ASSIGNED TO SAMPLE,F6.0)
    909 FORMAT(40H0 NO IMPROVEMENT FROM COMBINING SAMPLES )
```

```
      910 FORMAT(7H0SAMPLE,F4.0,21H COMBINED WITH SAMPLE,F4.0)
      911 FORMAT(1H+,36X,25HASSOCIATED PROBABILITY = ,F12.8,13X,F12.4)
      912 FORMAT(27H0 WITHOUT COMBINING SAMPLES )
      913 FORMAT(1H+,74X,12HCHISQUARED =)
      914 FORMAT(1H+,74X,12H"F" VALUE   =)
      920 FORMAT(7H0SAMPLE,F4.0,19H WAS SEPARATED FROM,F4.0)
      921 FORMAT(1H+,34X,3HBUT,F4.0,25H WAS LATER SEPARATED FROM,F4.0)
      922 FORMAT(1H+,34X,34HAND CANNOT THEREFORE BE RECOMBINED)
          END


          SUBROUTINE ISPLIT(SN,SP,SID,SACON,MAXSAC,NSMAX,PY,PZ,TB,VB,CB,PB,
         1PN,IS,NSAM,NALL,NACON,IFAULT)
C ISPLIT (SEE  8.2 ) SYSTEM        SPLITS SAMPLE INTO TWO
          DIMENSION SN(NSMAX),SP(NSMAX),SID(NSMAX),SACON(5,MAXSAC)
          NSAM = NSAM + 1
          NALL = NALL + 1
C IS IS THE SET OF CONDITIONS - JS IS THE SAMPLE ID CORRESPONDING
          JS = 0
          DO 12 I = 1,IS
       13 JS = JS + 1
          IF(SID(JS).LT.0.) GO TO 13
       12 CONTINUE
          DO 1 I = 1,NALL
          J = NALL + 1 -I
          IF(J.LT.JS) GO TO 2
          IF(J.GT.JS) SN(J) = SN(J-1)
          IF(J.EQ.JS+1) SN(J) = SN(J)-TB
          IF(J.GT.JS)SP(J) = SP(J-1)
          IF(J.EQ.JS+1)  SP(J) = PZ
          IF(J.GT.JS)SID(J) = SID(J-1)
          IF(J.EQ.JS)SID(J) = NALL
          IF(J.EQ.JS) SP(J) = PY
        1 IF(J.EQ.JS)SN(J) = TB
C START=N1S/END=N1F/NOMT=NO OF MINTERMS IN IS BEING SPLIT
        2 I = 0
          NOMT = 1
          IF(IS.EQ.1) N1S = 1
          DO 3 J = 1,NACON
          IF(SACON(1,J).EQ.3.) NOMT = NOMT + 1
          IF(SACON(1,J).LE.3.) GO TO 3
          I = I + 1
          IF(I.EQ.IS-1) N1S = J+1
          IF(I.LT.IS)   NOMT= 1
          IF(I.EQ.IS)   N1F = J
          IF(I.EQ.IS)   GO TO 4
        3 CONTINUE
        4 NEWL = N1F-N1S + 2*NOMT + 1
C NO MORE STORAGE AVAILABLE FOR CONDITIONS
          IF(NACON+NEWL.GT.MAXSAC) IFAULT = 1
          IF(NACON+NEWL.GT.MAXSAC) RETURN
C SHIFT DOWN FOLLOWING SAMPLES
          DO 5 JX = 1,NACON
          J = NACON + 1 -JX
          K = J + NEWL
          IF(J.LE.N1F)GO TO 6
          DO 5 I = 1,5
        5 SACON(I,K) = SACON(I,J)
        6 NOM = NOMT
          NACON = NACON + NEWL
C INSERT NEW CONDITION AT END OF EACH MIN-TERM, MOVING UP ACCORDINGLY
          DO 8 JX = N1S,N1F
          J = N1S + N1F - JX
```

```
          K = J + NOM
          DO 7 I = 1,5
        7 SACON(I,K) = SACON(I,J)
          IF(SACON(1,J).LT.2.5) GO TO 8
          NOM = NOM - 1
          K = J + NOM
          SACON(1,K) = 7.
          SACON(2,K) = VB
          SACON(3,K) = CB
          SACON(4,K) = PN
          SACON(5,K) = PB
          IF(NOM.EQ.0) GO TO 9
        8 CONTINUE
        9 N1F = N1F + NOMT
          NDIS = N1F -N1S + 1
          DO 11 J = N1S,N1F
          K = J + NDIS
          DO 10 I = 1,5
       10 SACON(I,K) = SACON(I,J)
          IF(SACON(1,J).LT.6.) GO TO 11
          IF(J.EQ.N1S) SACON(1,J) = 1.
          IF(J.GT.N1S) SACON(1,J) = 2.
          SACON(1,K) = SACON(1,J)
          IF(CB.LT.3.)SACON(3,K) = 2.
          IF(CB.GT.3.)SACON(3,K) = 4.
       11 CONTINUE
          RETURN
          END


          SUBROUTINE IJOIN (SN,SP,SID,SACON,I1,I2,PX,NSAP,NALL,NACON)
    C IJOIN   (SEE 8.2 ) SYSTEM       COMBINES SAMPLES
          DIMENSION SN(NALL),SP(NALL),SID(NALL),SACON(5,NACON)
    C I1, I2 ARE ACTUAL SAMPLE POSITIONS - FIND N1,N2 = INCLUDING STUBS
          I = 0
          DO 1 J = 1,NALL
          IF(SID(J).GT.0.) I = I + 1
          IF(SID(J).LE.0.) GO TO 1
          IF(I.EQ.I1) N1 = J
          IF(I.EQ.I2) N2 = J
        1 CONTINUE
    C LOWER BECOMES COMBINED/ HIGHER BECOMES STUB
          IF(SID(N1).GT.SID(N2)) M1 = N2
          IF(SID(N1).LT.SID(N2)) M1 = N1
          IF(SID(N1).GT.SID(N2)) M2 = N1
          IF(SID(N1).LT.SID(N2)) M2 = N2
          SN(M1)= ABS(SN(M1))+ ABS(SN(M2))
          SP(M1)= PX
          SN(M2)=-SID(M1)
          SID(M2)=-SID(N2)
    C COMBINE SAMPLES - FIRST FIND LIMITS - N2 IS TO BE ADDED TO N1
          IF(I1.LT.I2) GO TO 2
          I = I1
          I1= I2
          I2= I
        2 IF(I1.EQ.1) N1S = 1
          I = 0
          DO 3 J = 1,NACON
          IF(SACON(1,J).NE.4.) GO TO 3
          I = I + 1
          IF(I.EQ.I1-1) N1S = J+1
          IF(I.EQ.I1)   N1F = J
          IF(I.EQ.I2-1) N2S = J+1
```

```
      IF(I.EQ.I2)    N2F = J
    3 CONTINUE
C MOVE SAMPLES BETWEN 1 AND 2 BEHIND SAMPLE 2
      DO 6 J = N1F,N2S
      IF(J.EQ.N2S) GO TO 6
      DO 4 K = N1F,N2F
      DO 4 I = 1,5
    4 SACON(I,K)= SACON(I,K+1)
      DO 5 I = 1,5
    5 SACON(I,N2F) = SACON(I,N1F)
    6 CONTINUE
      SACON(1,N1F) = 3.
C MOVE UP ALL AFTER ORIGINAL N2F TO REMOVE EXTRA END
      NACON = NACON - 1
      NSAM = NSAM - 1
      DO 8 J = N2F,NACON
      DO 8 I = 1,5
    8 SACON (I,J) = SACON(I,J+1)
      RETURN
      END


      SUBROUTINE ITIDY(SN,SP,SID,SACON,NSMAX,NSAM,NAIL,NACON,MAXSAC)
C ITIDY   (SEE  8.2 ) SYSTEM      ARRANGES SAMPLES IN ORDER OF PARAMETER
      DIMENSION SN(NSMAX),SP(NSMAX),SID(NSMAX),SACON(5,MAXSAC)
C SORT TERMS + MARK REDUNDANT LINES
      N1 = 1
      J = 0
      DO 5 I = 1,NSAM
    1 J = J + 1
      IF(SACON(1,J).LT.2.5) GO TO 1
      N2 = J - 1
      DO 3 K = N1,N2
      DO 3 L = K,N2
      IF(K.EQ.L) GO TO 3
      IF(SACON(2,K).LT.SACON(2,L)) GO TO 3
      IF(SACON(2,K).EQ.SACON(2,L).AND.SACON(3,K).LT.SACON(3,L))GO TO 3
      IF(SACON(2,K).EQ.SACON(2,L).AND.SACON(3,K).EQ.SACON(3,L)
     1 .AND.SACON(5,K).LE.SACON(5,L))GO TO 3
      DO 2 M = 1,5
      X = SACON (M,L)
      SACON(M,L) = SACON(M,K)
    2 SACON(M,K) = X
    3 CONTINUE
      DO 4 K = N1,N2
      DO 4 L = K,N2
      IF(K.EQ.L) GO TO 4
      IF(SACON(2,K).NE.SACON(2,L)) GO TO 4
      IF(SACON(3,K).EQ.1..AND.SACON(3,L).EQ.2.)SACON(1,L) = 7.
      IF(SACON(3,K).EQ.4..AND.SACON(3,L).EQ.4.)SACON(1,K) = 7.
      IF(SACON(3,K).EQ.5..AND.SACON(3,L).EQ.5.)SACON(1,L) = 7.
    4 CONTINUE
      N1 = J + 1
      IF(SACON(1,J).LT.3.5) GO TO 1
    5 CONTINUE
C DELETE ALL MARKED LINES
      NOUT = 0
      DO 14 J = 1,NACON
   11 IF(J+NOUT.GT.NACON) GO TO 15
      IF(SACON(1,J+NOUT).LT.4.5) GO TO 12
      NOUT = NOUT + 1
      GO TO 11
   12 DO 13 I = 1,5
```

```
   13 SACON(I,J) = SACON(I,J+NOUT)
   14 CONTINUE
   15 NACON = NACON - NOUT
C 'IF' FOR FIRST LINE ONLY
      SACON(1,1) = 1.
      DO 16 J = 2,NACON
      IF(SACON(1,J-1).EQ.4.) SACON(1,J) = 1.
   16 IF(SACON(1,J-1).NE.4..AND.SACON(1,J).EQ.1.) SACON(1,J) = 2.
C ORDER SAMPLES (ACCORDING TO SAMPLE PARAMETER)
      DO 100 N1 = 1,NALL
      IF(N1.EQ.NALL) GO TO 100
      DO 90 N2 = N1,NALL
      IF(SP(N1).LE.SP(N2)) GO TO 90
      IF(SID(N1).LT.0..OR.SID(N2).LE.0.) GO TO 85
C SWAP N1 AND N2 - FIRST FIND LIMITS
      IF(N1.EQ.1) N1S = 1
      I = 0
      DO 17 J = 1,NACON
      IF(SACON(1,J).NE.4.) GO TO 17
      I = I + 1
      IF(I.EQ.N1-1) N1S = J+1
      IF(I.EQ.N1)    N1F = J
      IF(I.EQ.N2-1) N2S = J+1
      IF(I.EQ.N2)    N2F = J
      IF(I.EQ.N2) GO TO 20
   17 CONTINUE
C N1 FROM N1S TO N1F/ N2 FROM N2S TO N2F
   20 CONTINUE
      IF (N1F+1.EQ.N2S) GO TO 50
      N1L = N1F-N1S+1
      DO 45 K = 1,N1L
      DO 25 I = 1,5
   25 SACON(I,MAXSAC) = SACON(I,N1S)
      DO 35 J = N1S,N2S
      IF(J.GE.N2S-1) GO TO 35
      DO 30 I = 1,5
   30 SACON(I,J) = SACON(I,J+1)
   35 CONTINUE
      DO 40 I = 1,5
   40 SACON(I,N2S-1)=SACON(I,MAXSAC)
   45 CONTINUE
   50 CONTINUE
C MOVE N2 TO POSITION OF N1S
      DO 80 J = N1S,N2S
      IF(J.EQ.N2S) GO TO 80
      DO 55 I = 1,5
   55 SACON (I,MAXSAC)=SACON(I,N1S)
      DO 65 K = N1S,N2F
      IF(K.EQ.N2F) GO TO 65
      DO 60 I = 1,5
   60 SACON (I,K) = SACON(I,K+1)
   65 CONTINUE
      DO 70 I = 1,5
   70 SACON(I,N2F)= SACON(I,MAXSAC)
   80 CONTINUE
   85 X = SID(N1)
      SID(N1) = SID(N2)
      SID(N2) = X
      X = SP(N1)
      SP(N1) = SP(N2)
      SP(N2) = X
      X = SN(N1)
      SN(N1) = SN(N2)
```

```
      SN(N2) = X
   90 CONTINUE
  100 CONTINUE
      RETURN
      END


      SUBROUTINE WSPLIT(S1,Y,Z,NS,S2,S3,NC,MED2)
C WSPLIT (SEE  8.2 ) SYSTEM      PRODUCES DIAGRAM OF SPLITTING RECORD
C S1 = SAMPLE NUMBERS IN ORDER (MEAN/MEDIAN/MODE)
C S2 = LOWER NUMBERED SAMPLE (ORIGINAL/KEPT)
C S3 = HIGHER NUMBERED SAMPLE (+ = NEW / - = DESTROYED)
      DIMENSION S1(NS),S2(NC),S3(NC),Y(NS),Z(NS),V3(30),V4(4)
      DATA V4/4H(1H+,4H,       ,4H       ,4H,I3)/
      DATA V3/4H  1X,4H  5X,4H  9X,4H 13X,4H 17X,4H 21X,4H 25X,4H 29X,
     1 4H 33X,4H 37X,4H 41X,4H 45X,4H 49X,4H 53X,4H 57X,4H 61X,4H 65X,
     2 4H 69X,4H 73X,4H 77X,4H 81X,4H 85X,4H 89X,4H 93X,4H 97X,4H101X,
     3 4H105X,4H109X,4H113X,4H117X/
      DATA C4/4H    |/,H4/4H----/,B4/4H    /,SB/4H   ,/,SD/4H   '/
      DATA EB/4H---,/,EC/4H--- /,ED/4H---'/
      DO 20 NA = 1,NS,30
      NB= NA + 29
      IF(NB.GT.NS)NB = NS
      ND = NB-NA+1
      DO 5 K = 1,ND
    5 CALL COPYA(Z(K),B4)
      NL = 50
      DO 15 M = 1,NC
      IF(NL.GE.50)WRITE(MED2,902)
      IF(NL.GE.50)NL = 0
      NL = NL + 2
      IB = 0
      N2 = S2(M)
      N3 = S3(M)
      IF(N3.LT.0) IA = -1
      IF(N3.GT.0) IA = 1
      N3 = N3*IA
      K = 0
      DO 10 J = 1,NB
      I = J - NA + 1
      N1 = ABS(S1(J))
      IF(I.LT.1) GO TO 8
      IF(N1.EQ.N3)CALL COPYA(V4(3),V3(I))
      IF(N1.EQ.N3)K = I
      IF(IB.EQ.0) CALL COPYA(Y(I),B4)
      IF(IB.EQ.1) CALL COPYA(Y(I),H4)
      IF(N1.EQ.N3.AND.IB.EQ.0.AND.IA.EQ. 1) CALL COPYA(Y(I),SB)
      IF(N1.EQ.N3.AND.IB.EQ.0.AND.IA.EQ.-1) CALL COPYA(Y(I),SD)
      IF(N1.EQ.N3.AND.IB.EQ.1.AND.IA.EQ. 1) CALL COPYA(Y(I),EB)
      IF(N1.EQ.N3.AND.IB.EQ.1.AND.IA.EQ.-1) CALL COPYA(Y(I),ED)
      IF(N1.EQ.N2.AND.IB.EQ.1) CALL COPYA(Y(I),EC)
    8 IF(N1.EQ.N2)IB = 1 - IB
   10 IF(N1.EQ.N3)IB = 1 - IB
      IF(IA.EQ.-1.AND.K.GT.0) CALL COPYA(Z(K),B4)
      WRITE(MED2,900) (Z(L),L=1,ND)
      IF(IA.EQ.-1.AND.K.GT.0)WRITE(MED2,V4) N3
      IF(IA.EQ. 1)WRITE(MED2,901) (Y(L),L=1,ND)
      WRITE(MED2,900) (Z(L),L=1,ND)
      IF(IA.EQ. 1.AND.K.GT.0)WRITE(MED2,V4) N3
      IF(IA.EQ.-1)WRITE(MED2,901) (Y(L),L=1,ND)
   15 IF(IA.EQ. 1.AND.K.GT.0) CALL COPYA(Z(K),C4)
   20 CONTINUE
      RETURN
```

```
    900 FORMAT(1H ,30A4)
    901 FORMAT(1H+,30A4)
    902 FORMAT(1H1,10X,84HSPLITTING LARGEST UNTESTED SAMPLE - COMBINING TO
   1 MAXIMISE SIGNIFICANCE OF DIFFERENCE)
        RETURN
        END


        SUBROUTINE WSAMP(SACON,SID,SN,SP,TRTC,TTC,SH,NSAM,NALTC,MAXSAC,NQ
   1,ITCR)
C WSAMP   (SEE  8.2 ) SYSTEM      WRITES SAMPLE DEFINITION
C NSAM=TOTAL SAMPS/SN=NO. IN SS/SP=PARAM OF SS/SID=IDENTITY OF SS (NO.)
        DIMENSION SACON(5,MAXSAC),C1(4),C3(6),SH(NQ),TRTC(NALTC)
        DIMENSION SN(NSAM),SP(NSAM),SID(NSAM),TTC(21)
        DATA C1/4H.IF.,4HAND.,4H.OR.,4H       /
        DATA C3/4H.EQ.,4H.NE.,4H.GT.,4H.GE.,4H.LT.,4H.LE./
        COMMON /STCT/MED1,MED2,MED3,MED4,MED5,MED6,MED13,Q,V(20),TT(30)
        J = 0
        NL=15
        IF(SACON(1,1).LT.3.5) SACON(1,1) = 1.
        DO 3 I = 1,NSAM
        NL = NL + 4
        IF(NL.GT.50)WRITE(MED2,900) TT,TTC
        IF(NL.GT.50)NL = 13
        N1= ABS(SID(I))
        K1= ABS(SN(I))
        IF(SID(I).LT.0.) WRITE(MED2,907) N1,K1
        IF(SID(I).LT.0.) GO TO 3
        WRITE(MED2,901) N1,K1
        IF(ITCR.LE.3) N2 = SP(I)
        IF(ITCR.LT.3) WRITE(MED2,902) TRTC(N2)
        IF(ITCR.EQ.3) WRITE(MED2,903) TRTC(N2)
        IF(ITCR.GT.3) WRITE(MED2,904) SP(I)
      1 J = J + 1
        N = SACON(1,J)
        IF(N.EQ.4) GO TO 2
        K1= SACON(2,J)
        K2= SACON(3,J)
        NL = NL + 1
        CALL COMPA(C1(4),SACON(4,J),L)
        IF(L.EQ.1)WRITE(MED2,905)C1(N),SH(K1),C3(K2),SACON(4,J),SACON(5,J)
        IF(L.EQ.2)WRITE(MED2,905)C1(N),SH(K1),C3(K2),SACON(4,J)
        GO TO 1
      2 WRITE(MED2,906) N1
      3 CONTINUE
        RETURN
    900 FORMAT(23H1STATCAT PROGRAM STAIAD,7X,1H-,4X,35HAUTOMATIC INTERACTI
   1ON DETECTOR      /16H DATA BANK TITLE,14X,1H-,4X,10A4/23H DATA BANK
   2 SUBSET TITLE,7X,1H-,4X,10A4/10H RUN TITLE,20X,1H-,4X,10A4/
   313H CRITERION - ,A4,4H OF ,A4,1H=,F4.0,1H-,4X,A2,18A4)
    901 FORMAT(14H0SAMPLE NUMBER,I3,11H CONTAINING,I6 ,8H ENTRIES)
    902 FORMAT (1H+,45X,7HMODE = ,A4/)
    903 FORMAT(1H+,45X,9HMEDIAN = ,A4/)
    904 FORMAT(1H+,45X,7HMEAN = ,F22.6/)
    905 FORMAT(11X,4A4,F20.6)
    906 FORMAT(11X,20HEND OF SAMPLE NUMBER,I3)
    907 FORMAT(14H0SAMPLE NUMBER,I3,19H ABSORBED BY SAMPLE,I4)
        END
```

8.3   PROGRAM STCLUS - CLUSTERING CORRELATION MATRIX

8.3.1   Purpose

This program re-arranges a correlation matrix to bring the most closely related variates closest to each other. The program begins by constructing a correlation matrix for a set of variates drawn from a STATCAT data bank subset, which may be transformed or delayed. It then takes a selection of these variates, and re-arranges them until the total of the correlation coefficients multiplied by their square distance from the diagonal of the matrix is minimised. Because the number of possible arrangements increases sharply with the number of variates selected, the program adopts a 'hill climbing' strategy if the number of variates exceeds a threshold value. This value will normally be seven variates, unless changed by the user. For details of the 'hill climbing' strategy see 8.3.5.

The user may specify that the signs of the correlation coefficients are to be ignored, or that the signs of variates are to be inverted as necessary to maximise the positive correlations.

Figure 8.31a contains a simplified flow-chart of the main program STCLUS, and Figure 8.31b contains a simplified flow-chart of the executive subroutine CLUST.

8.3.2   Input

Summary

Item	Level	Format	Function	Section
1	0	A	File Control Card	3.2.
2	1	E	Subset Specification	3.6.
3	2	F	Set of Variates	3.7.
4	3	F	Selected Variates	3.7.
5	4	G	Data Handling Instruction	below+3.8.

3 - Set of Variates

This is a standard set of variates, as defined in 3.7. Only the transform code, the data column name or number and the number of entries delay are employed by this program, although any comment provided will be printed when the card is read. If delays are employed, the first variate specified here (which must not be delayed itself) will be taken as the time scale. If this variate is less than its previous value, all 'delayed' values will be lost, and the 'time' sequence will be considered to re-start. If several analyses are to be carried out, it will be more economic in time to specify all variates at this stage, but if only one analysis or group of analyses is planned, it is equally efficient to specify the variates as they are required, specifying only the 'time variate' at this stage.

4 - Selected Variates

This is a standard set of variates, as defined in 3.7. Only the transform code, the data column name or number and the number of entries delay are used, although the comment given on the card will be printed when the card is read.

The variates specified should preferably be part of the set specified at the previous level, unless this is the first run with that set of variates, to avoid unnecessary data sweeps. If variates are specified which are not part of the original set of variates, they will be added to the set of variates, but a new sweep will be required.

5 - Data Handling Instruction

This is a standard data handling instruction of the type specified in 3.8. It is used to specify the amount of detail to be output and the way in which the signs of the correlation matrix are to be treated.

Card Layout - Data Handling Instruction - STCLUS

```
ABCCCDDDEEEEEEEEFFFFFFGGGGGGGGGGGGHHHHHHHHHHH........
```

Columns on Card	Type Code	Function	See
1	A	Output Control Index	Below
2	B	Analysis Control Index	Below
3 - 5	C	Acceptable Number Of 'Non-Values'	Below
6 - 8	D	Revised Permutation Limit	Below
9 - 16	E	Maximum Trials for 'Hill Climbing'	Below
17 - 24	F	Percentage Improvement	Below
25 - 40	G	Comment (printed with line)	-
41 - 80	H	Run Title	-

A - Output Control Index

This index controls the amount of detail output by the system. <u>Unless otherwise specified</u>, only the re-arranged correlation matrix is printed.

Alternatives

A = 0 or blank : Only the re-arranged correlation matrix is printed.

A = 1 : In addition, the correlation matrix for the selected variates as specified, with the number of readings, arithmetic mean and standard deviation of each variate is printed out.

A = 2 : In addition, the correlation matrix for the set of variates, with the complete set of numbers of readings, arithmetic means and standard deviations is printed.

A = 3 : Each re-arrangement adopted as an improvement is listed, with the total correlation-square-distance.

A = 4 : Each re-arrangement tested is listed, with the total correlation-square-distance.

A = 5 - 9 : As for A = 0

B - Analysis Control Index

This index controls the way in which the signs of correlation coefficients are treated. _Unless otherwise specified_ they will be used as calculated.

Alternatives

B = 0 or blank : Signs used as calculated.

B = 1   : Absolute values used - i.e. negative signs ignored.

B = 2   : Signs inverted for variates to maximise total correlation.

B = 3 - 9   : As for B = 0

C - Acceptable Number of 'Non-Values'

This index specifies the number of 'non-values' which will be accepted in a set of transformed variates derived from an entry. (Non-values may occur because a value is not present in the entry, because the transform specified has no value for the given data item, or because not enough entries have been read for 'delayed' values to have been sufficiently delayed.)

If this number of non-values is exceeded, the set of values will not be included in the analysis, but will count towards any required delays. _Unless otherwise specified_ this value will be taken as zero. If this value is left blank or set to zero for a run which is not the first with a given set of variates and requires no new variates, the previously specified value of this parameter will be retained. If this value is a non-zero value different from that for the previous data sweep a new data sweep will be carried out.

D - Revised Permutation Limit

This number specifies the maximum number of variates for which the program will carry out a complete permutation of the selected variates. If this index is blank or zero, the system will retain the previous value of this index. If the first value read is blank or zero, the value 7 will be taken.

E - Maximum Trials for 'Hill Climbing'

If the number of variates selected exceeds D, the program will operate by 'hill climbing', as described in 8.3.5. Because this process may be extremely time consuming, a limit to the number of trials may be imposed. If the program is still 'hill climbing' after E trials, the process will be terminated, and the best arrangement so far found will be printed, with an appropriate heading.

If the value is not specified, or is left blank or zero, the value 1000 will be taken for E. If a negative value for E is inserted, the process will run indefinitely until a local minimum is found. (For a large number of variates with no marked structure, this may take a very long time.)

F - <u>Percentage Improvement</u>

When a large correlation matrix is to be clustered by 'hill climbing' starting from a completely un-ordered matrix, time and effort are saved if a minimum improvement is required before a changed order is accepted. This improvement is specified as a percentage of the correlation-square-distance. When an arrangement is reached from which no further improvement of this magnitude can be found, the system accepts any improvement, and resets the percentage to the specified level if an improvement is found, until a final arrangement (from which no improvement of any size can be made) is reached, or the limit to the number of trials (E) is reached.

8.3.3   <u>Input Example</u>

Figure 8.32 is a summary of the input structure for three runs of STCLUS, using first the default value, then a re-arrangement of the selected variates, then a complete permutation of those variates. The whole STATCAT data bank is included in the sample employed and the values of all the data columns are specified. From these variates, the same eight are selected to be included in the clustering process as were used for factor analysis (See 7.3.).

Figure 8.33 is a listing of the input cards required to carry out these analyses.

8.3.4   <u>Output Example</u>

Figure 8.34 is a general summary of the output produced by this program, indented according to the program structure. Figure 8.35 is a page-by-page summary of the output corresponding to the specific input of Figure 8.33. The input checking information is essentially standard and therefore not given here.

Figure 8.36 gives the default output - consisting only of the re-arranged correlation matrix. Figure 8.37 gives part of the record of successive improved arrangements and the final arrangement for the second run employing the same variates, in a different initial order, with an increased percentage improvement threshold. Figure 8.38 gives the re-arranged correlation matrix for the same variates when all possible permutations are evaluated.

8.3.5   <u>"Hill Climbing"</u>

'Hill Climbing' is a general term applied to any mathematical method of finding the 'best' value of some criterion by taking an initial setting of the parameters used, finding how they can be varied to improve the criterion, modifying the values accordingly and repeating the routine until no change can be found which produces an improvement on the best so far.

In the subroutine CLUST, the system begins by calculating the total of the squares of the diagonal distances times the correlation coefficients for the matrix in its original order. It then exchanges pairs of variates systematically, starting with the first and second, and ending with the last-but-one and last. If, at this stage, it encounters an arrangement which improves on the current one by more than the limit set by E, it accepts this arrangement and starts again by exchanging the first and second columns and so on. If it finds no improvement better than the limit (E), it repeats the process accepting any improvement. If it finds no improvement, it prints the re-arranged matrix as the 'local minimum'. If it finds any improvement, it accepts it, and returns to the original exchange process, with the limit (E).

The process terminates either by arriving at an arrangement from which no improvement can be found, or by reaching the limit to the number of trials (P).

Where a large matrix is being clustered, it is wise to specify the variates at least twice, interchanging blocks of correlated variates, to avoid accepting a local minimum which is not the best of all possible arrangements. For large matrices with a few large correlation coefficients, a large value of E should be used (5 to 10), while for matrices that are relatively uniform, a smaller value (1) may be better.

The decision whether to employ 'hill climbing' or to try all possible permutations will depend largely on the speed of the available computer and the extent of variation among the correlation coefficients. As a guide, it may be noted that the number of permutations of seven variates is 5,040 and of ten variates is 3,628,800.

8.3.6 Clustering

Clustering, in general, is a term currently applied to various techniques for forming clusters of variables or of entries. There is some disagreement about the best, most efficient or most justifiable methods of defining and forming clusters. A complete session of COMPSTAT 80 was concerned with this topic, and the published record forms a useful introduction to the subject.

REFERENCE : COMPSTAT 80

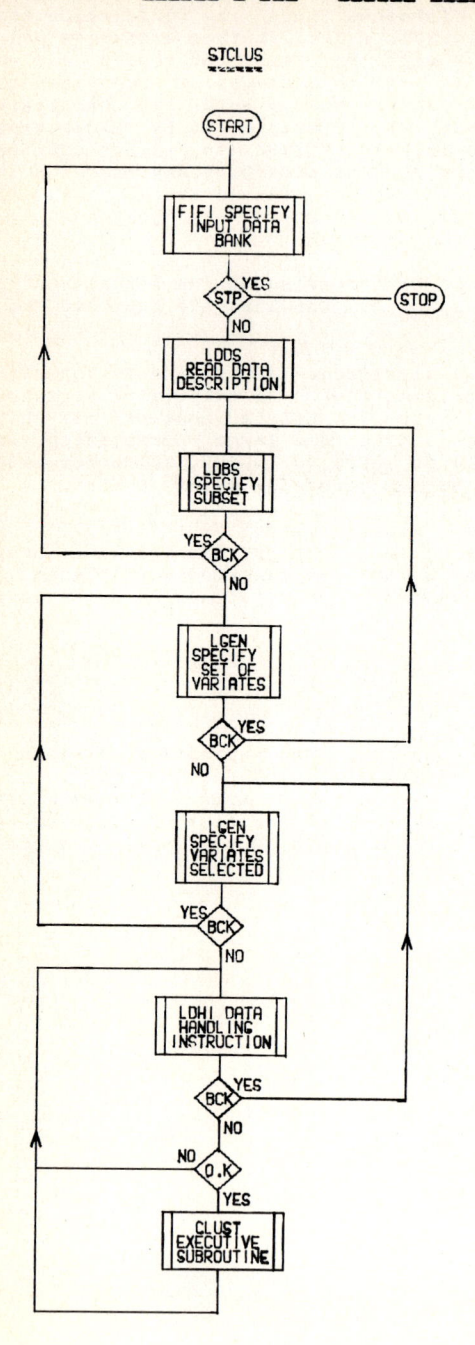

Figure 8.31a - System Flow-Chart - STCLUS

Figure 8.31b - System Flow-Chart - CLUST

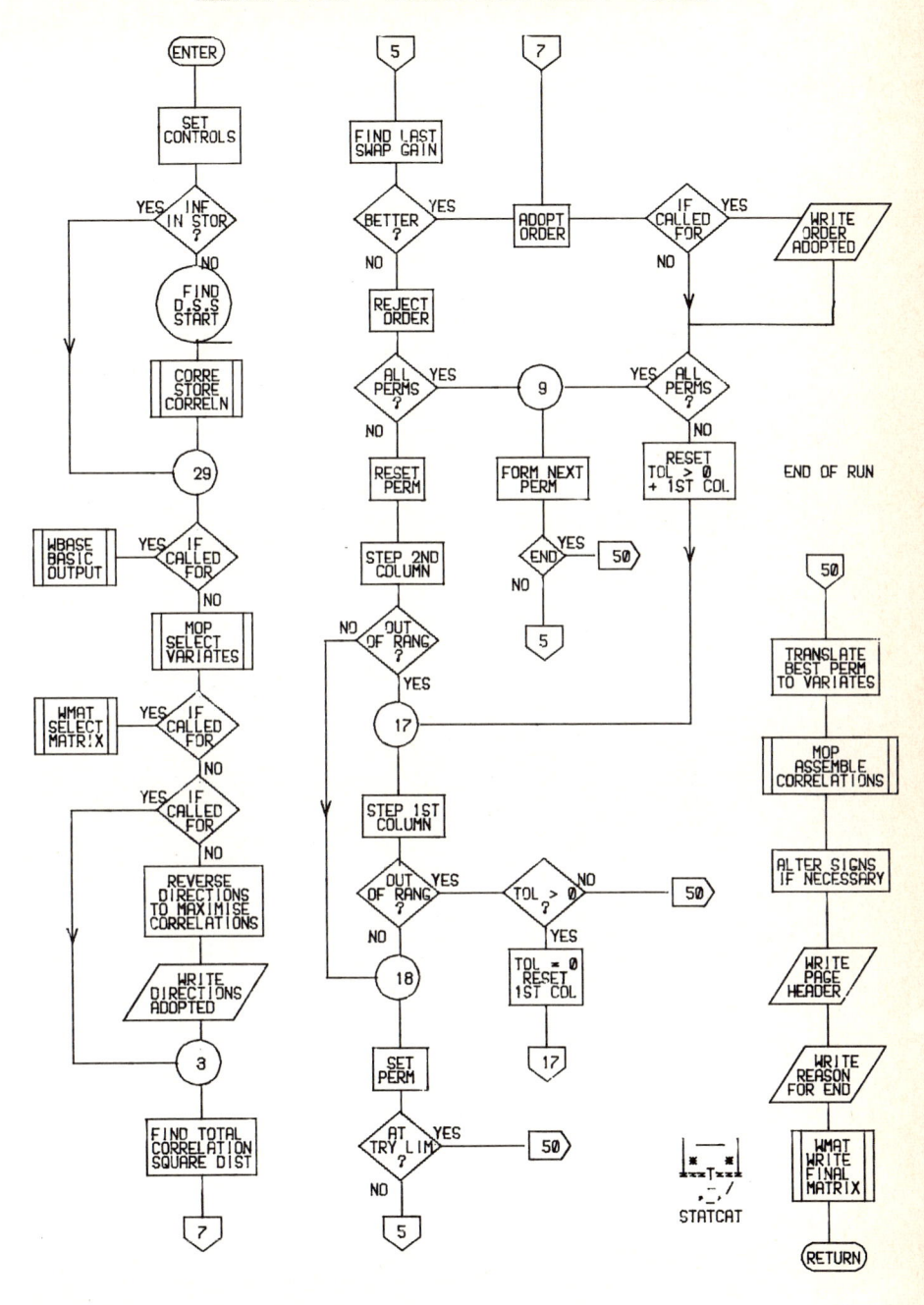

530

Figure 8.32 - STCLUS - Input Structure

```
        Level
 0   1   2   3   4   5   6   7   8   9
FILE CONTROL CARD
    SUBSET SPECIFICATION
        VARIATE SPECIFICATION
            SELECTED VARIATES
                DATA HANDLING INSTRUCTION
                BACK TO READ SELECTED VARIATES
            SELECTED VARIATES
                DATA HANDLING INSTRUCTION
                DATA HANDLING INSTRUCTION
            STOP
```

Figure 8.33 - STCLUS - Input Example

```
---------1----------2----------3----------4---------5---------6---------7--
**STCLUSDEMO                             DEMONSTRATION STATCAT DATA BANK
ALL DATA                                 WHOLE DATA BANK TO BE INCLUDED
END OF SUBSET DEFINITION
VAL.NTRY
END OF SET OF VARIATES
VAL.OPER
VAL.W.P.
VAL.STRS
VAL.TASK
VAL.DIFF
VAL.EFOP
VAL.H.R.
VAL.EFOB
END OF SELECTED VARIATES                 FOR CLUSTER ANALYSIS
GO                                       DEFAULT OUTPUT
BACK TO READ NEW SELECTED VARIATES       SAME VARIATES IN DIFFERENT ORDER
VAL.STRS
VAL.TASK
VAL.OPER
VAL.W.P.
VAL.H.R.
VAL.EFOB
VAL.DIFF
VAL.EFOP
END OF SELECTED VARIATES                 FOR CLUSTER ANALYSIS
GO                                       DEFAULT OUTPUT
32      8                                DIRECTION ADJUSTED - ALL PERMUTA
STOP
---------1----------2----------3----------4---------5---------6---------7--
```

Figure 8.34 - STCLUS - Output Structure

```
For each      ) : File Control Record
output file   )   File Parameters
                  Data Description
                  For each) :  Subset Input Record
                  Subset )     For each Set  ) Input Record
                               of Variates   )   For Each    ) Input
                                             )   Selection   ) Record
                                             )   of Variates ) See Left
For each     ) <Number, mean and s.d. for selected variates >
Selection    ) <Number, mean and s.d. for all variates >
of variates  ) <Correlation Matrix - All Variates >
               <Correlation Matrix - Selected Variates >
               <Sign Change Record>
               For Each trial) : < Score and ordering >< If improvement >
               permutation   )
               Re-arranged Correlation matrix
```

Carated(<>) items are optional.

Figure 8.35 - STCLUS - Page-by-page output summary

Page	Contents	Origin
1-2	File Control Record	FIFI
	Program Title	STCLUS
	File Parameters	LDAP
	Data Description record	LDDS
3	Subset record	LDBS
4-5	Set of Variates	LGEN
6	Selected Variates	LGEN
7	Data Handling Instruction	LDHI
8	Clustered Matrix	CLUST/WMAT
9	Data Handling Instruction (BACK)	LDHI
10	Selected Variates	LGEN
11	Data Handling Instruction	LDHI
12	Clustered Matrix	CLUST/WMAT
13	Data Handling Instruction	LDHI
14	Number, a.m. and s.d. (for this selection)	WBASE
15	Number, a.m. and s.d. (all variates)	WBASE
16	Correlation Matrix (all variates)	WBASE
17	Correlation Matrix (for this selection)	WBASE
18	Choice of Directions	CLUST
19-21	Successive Improvements	CLUST
22	Clustered Matrix	CLUST/WMAT
23	Data Handling Instruction (STOP)	LDHI

Figure 8.36 - STCLUS - Output Example - Default Output

```
STATCAT PROGRAM STCLUS        -    CORRELATION MATRIX CLUSTERING
DATA BANK TITLE               -    DEMONSTRATION STATCAT DATA BANK
DATA BANK SUBSET TITLE        -    ALL DATA
RUN TITLE                     -    DEFAULT OUTPUT

         CLUSTERED CORRELATION MATRIX

BY 'HILL-CLIMBING' ACCEPTING   1. PER CENT IMPROVEMENT

HALTED AFTER       2. TRIALS AT PRE-SET LIMIT

   TRANSFORM         VAL. OF    VAL. OF    VAL. OF    VAL. OF    VAL. OF    VAL. OF    VAL. OF    VAL. OF
   COLUMN (NAME)     4.=OPER    5.=W.P.    6.=STRS    9.=TASK   10.=DIFF   13.=EFOP   15.=H.R.   14.=EFOB
TRANSFORM COLUMN
VAL. OF   4(OPER)    1.0000     0.0        0.0805     0.0        0.8550     0.8987     0.4419    -0.4207
VAL. OF   5(W.P.)    0.0        1.0000    -0.1744     0.0        0.1644     0.1395     0.4228     0.1076
VAL. OF   6(STRS)    0.0805    -0.1744     1.0000     0.1476     0.2885     0.2195     0.0421    -0.3387
VAL. OF   9(TASK)    0.0        0.0        0.1476     1.0000     0.2795     0.2349     0.6165     0.0214
VAL. OF  10(DIFF)    0.8550     0.1644     0.2885     0.2795     1.0000     0.9856     0.7407    -0.3900
VAL. OF  13(EFOP)    0.8987     0.1395     0.2195     0.2349     0.9856     1.0000     0.6976    -0.3598
VAL. OF  15(H.R.)    0.4419     0.4228     0.0421     0.6165     0.7407     0.6976     1.0000    -0.1197
VAL. OF  14(EFOB)   -0.4207     0.1076    -0.3387     0.0214    -0.3900    -0.3598    -0.1197     1.0000
```

Figure 8.37 - STCLUS - Output Example - Revision Record

```
STATCAT PROGRAM STCLUS        -    CORRELATION MATRIX CLUSTERING
DATA BANK TITLE               -    DEMONSTRATION STATCAT DATA BANK
DATA BANK SUBSET TITLE        -    ALL DATA
RUN TITLE                     -    DEFAULT OUTPUT

         CLUSTERED CORRELATION MATRIX

BY 'HILL-CLIMBING' ACCEPTING   1. PER CENT IMPROVEMENT

HALTED AFTER     236. TRIALS AT LOCAL MINIMUM

   TRANSFORM         VAL. OF    VAL. OF    VAL. OF    VAL. OF    VAL. OF    VAL. OF    VAL. OF    VAL. OF
   COLUMN (NAME)    14.=EFOB    5.=W.P.    9.=TASK   15.=H.R.   10.=DIFF   13.=EFOP    4.=OPER    6.=STRS
TRANSFORM COLUMN
VAL. OF  14(EFOB)    1.0000     0.1076     0.0214    -0.1197    -0.3900    -0.3598    -0.4207    -0.3387
VAL. OF   5(W.P.)    0.1076     1.0000     0.0        0.4228     0.1644     0.1395     0.0       -0.1744
VAL. OF   9(TASK)    0.0214     0.0        1.0000     0.6165     0.2795     0.2349     0.0        0.1476
VAL. OF  15(H.R.)   -0.1197     0.4228     0.6165     1.0000     0.7407     0.6976     0.4419     0.0421
VAL. OF  10(DIFF)   -0.3900     0.1644     0.2795     0.7407     1.0000     0.9856     0.8550     0.2885
VAL. OF  13(EFOP)   -0.3598     0.1395     0.2349     0.6976     0.9856     1.0000     0.8987     0.2195
VAL. OF   4(OPER)   -0.4207     0.0        0.0        0.4419     0.8550     0.8987     1.0000     0.0805
VAL. OF   6(STRS)   -0.3387    -0.1744     0.1476     0.0421     0.2885     0.2195     0.0805     1.0000
```

Figure 8.38 - STCLUS - Output Example - Final Ordering

```
STATCAT PROGRAM STCLUS      -    CORRELATION MATRIX CLUSTERING
DATA BANK TITLE             -    DEMONSTRATION STATCAT DATA BANK
DATA BANK SUBSET TITLE      -    ALL DATA
RUN TITLE                   -    DIRECTION ADJUSTED - ALL PERMUTATIONS

            TRIALS

                    VAL. OF   VAL. OF   VAL. OF   VAL. OF   VAL. OF   VAL. OF   VAL. OF   VAL. OF
SCORE =    86.41326904 FOR COLUMN ORDER    1    6    2    7    3    5    4           BEST SO FAR
                    6 =STRS  14 =EFOB   5 =TASK  10 =DIFF   4 =OPER  13 =EFOP  15 =H.R.   5 =W.P.

                    VAL. OF   VAL. OF   VAL. OF   VAL. OF   VAL. OF   VAL. OF   VAL. OF   VAL. OF
SCORE =    80.87660217 FOR COLUMN ORDER    1    6    8    3    7    5    4    2      BEST SO FAR
                    6 =STRS  14 =EFOB   9 =TASK  10 =DIFF  13 =EFOP   4 =OPER  15 =H.R.   5 =W.P.

                    VAL. OF   VAL. OF   VAL. OF   VAL. OF   VAL. OF   VAL. OF   VAL. OF   VAL. OF
SCORE =    72.37303162 FOR COLUMN ORDER    1    6    3    8    7    5    4    2      BEST SO FAR
                    6 =STRS  14 =EFOB  13 =EFOP   4 =OPER  10 =DIFF  15 =H.R.   5 =W.P.   9 =TASK

                    VAL. OF   VAL. OF   VAL. OF   VAL. OF   VAL. OF   VAL. OF   VAL. OF   VAL. OF
SCORE =    71.45939636 FOR COLUMN ORDER    6    1    3    7    5    2    4           BEST SO FAR
                    6 =STRS  14 =EFOB   4 =OPER  13 =EFOP  10 =DIFF  15 =H.R.   5 =W.P.   9 =TASK

                    VAL. OF   VAL. OF   VAL. OF   VAL. OF   VAL. OF   VAL. OF   VAL. OF   VAL. OF
SCORE =    62.53331343 FOR COLUMN ORDER    6    1    3    8    7    5    2    4      BEST SO FAR
                   14 =EFOB   6 =STRS  13 =EFOP   4 =OPER  10 =DIFF  15 =H.R.   9 =TASK   5 =W.P.

                    VAL. OF   VAL. OF   VAL. OF   VAL. OF   VAL. OF   VAL. OF   VAL. OF   VAL. OF
SCORE =    59.29934692 FOR COLUMN ORDER    1    6    3    7    3    5    2    4      BEST SO FAR
                   14 =EFOB   6 =STRS   4 =OPER  13 =EFOP  10 =DIFF  15 =H.R.   9 =TASK   5 =W.P.

                    VAL. OF   VAL. OF   VAL. OF   VAL. OF   VAL. OF   VAL. OF   VAL. OF   VAL. OF
SCORE =    58.26116943 FOR COLUMN ORDER    1    6    3    8    7    5    2    4      BEST SO FAR
                    6 =STRS  14 =EFOB   4 =OPER  13 =EFOP  10 =DIFF  15 =H.R.   9 =TASK   5 =W.P.

                    VAL. OF   VAL. OF   VAL. OF   VAL. OF   VAL. OF   VAL. OF   VAL. OF   VAL. OF
SCORE =    55.50300171 FOR COLUMN ORDER    4    2    5    8    7    3    6    1      BEST SO FAR
                    5 =W.P.   9 =TASK  15 =H.R.  13 =EFOP  10 =DIFF   4 =OPER  14 =EFOB   6 =STRS

                    VAL. OF   VAL. OF   VAL. OF   VAL. OF   VAL. OF   VAL. OF   VAL. OF   VAL. OF
SCORE =    55.36982422 FOR COLUMN ORDER    4    2    5    7    8    3    6    1      BEST SO FAR
                    5 =W.P.   9 =TASK  15 =H.R.  10 =DIFF  13 =EFOP   4 =OPER  14 =EFOB   6 =STRS


STATCAT PROGRAM STCLUS      -    CORRELATION MATRIX CLUSTERING
DATA BANK TITLE             -    DEMONSTRATION STATCAT DATA BANK
DATA BANK SUBSET TITLE      -    ALL DATA
RUN TITLE                   -    DIRECTION ADJUSTED - ALL PERMUTATIONS


    CLUSTERED CORRELATION MATRIX

ALL POSSIBLE ARRANGEMENTS CONSIDERED

DIRECTIONS CHOSEN TO MAXIMISE CORRELATION
```

TRANSFORM COLUMN (NAME)	VAL. OF 5.=W.P.	VAL. OF 9.=TASK	VAL. OF 15.=H.R.	VAL. OF 10.=DIFF	VAL. OF 13.=EFOP	VAL. OF 4.=OPER	VAL. OF 14.=EFOB	VAL. OF 6.=STRS
VAL. OF 5(W.P.)	1.0000	0.0	0.4228	0.1644	0.1395	0.0	-0.1076	-0.1744
VAL. OF 9(TASK)	0.0	1.0000	0.6165	0.2795	0.2349	0.0	-0.0214	0.1476
VAL. OF 15(H.R.)	0.4228	0.6165	1.0000	0.7407	0.6976	0.4419	0.1197	0.0421
VAL. OF 10(DIFF)	0.1644	0.2795	0.7407	1.0000	0.9856	0.8550	0.3900	0.2885
VAL. OF 13(EFOP)	0.1395	0.2349	0.6976	0.9856	1.0000	0.8987	0.3588	0.2195
VAL. OF 4(OPER)	0.0	0.0	0.4419	0.8550	0.8987	1.0000	0.4207	0.0805
VAL. OF 14(EFOB)	-0.1076	-0.0214	0.1197	0.3900	0.3588	0.4207	1.0000	0.3387
VAL. OF 6(STRS)	-0.1744	0.1476	0.0421	0.2885	0.2195	0.0805	0.3387	1.0000

```
C MASTER STCLUS - CLUSTERS CORRELATION MATRIX
C         SUBROUTINES AND FUNCTIONS REQUIRED
C NAME         TYPE              COMMENT
C AN       (SEE  3.1 ) SERVICE     ALPHA - TO NUMERIC VALUE
C CLUST    (SEE  8.3 ) EXECUTIVE   CLUSTERS CORRELATION MATRIX
C CHIKEN   (SEE 11.9 ) SERVICE     WARNS OF MISMATCHED DATA LEVEL
C CLSAM    (SEE  3.5 ) SERVICE     ALLOTS ENTRY TO SAMPLE/SUBSET
C COMPA    (SEE  3.1 ) SERVICE     COMPARES ALPHAMERIC VALUES
C COPYA    (SEE  3.1 ) SERVICE     COPIES ALPHAMERIC VALUE
C CORRE    (SEE  7.2 ) SYSTEM      MULTIPLE CORRELATION DATA
C FIFI     (SEE  3.2 ) SYSTEM      ALLOCATES PERIPHERALS
C GAUS     (SEE 11.8 ) STATISTICAL FINDS ASS. PROB. OF N VALUE
C IBL      (SEE  3.1 ) SERVICE     DETECTS BLANK,END AND STOP CARDS
C ICH      (SEE  3.1 ) SERVICE     IDENTIFIES ALPHAMERIC CODES
C LCOM     (SEE  3.4 ) SERVICE     LOADS COMPLEMENTARY INFORMATION
C LDAP     (SEE  3.3 ) SYSTEM      LOADS/CHECKS DATA BANK PARAMETERS
C LDBS     (SEE  3.6 ) SYSTEM      LOADS SUBSET DEFINITION
C LDDS     (SEE  3.4 ) SYSTEM      LOADS DATA DESCRIPTION SEGMENT
C LDHI     (SEE  3.8 ) SYSTEM      LOADS/CHECKS DATA HANDLING INSTN
C LGEN     (SEE  3.7 ) SYSTEM      LOADS GENERALISED VARIATES
C LSET     (SEE  3.5 ) SYSTEM      LOADS DEFINING CONDITIONS
C MEDIAT   (SEE  3.7 ) SERVICE     FETCHES NEXT VARIATE SET
C MOP      (SEE 11.3 ) SERVICE     SELECTS/CONVERTS STORED MATRIX
C PRBF     (SEE 11.8 ) STATISTICAL FINDS PROBABILITY OF F-RATIO
C TRANS    (SEE  3.7 ) SERVICE     CARRIES OUT REQUIRED TRANSFORM
C WBASE    (SEE  7.5 ) SYSTEM      WRITE CORRELATION MATRIX ETC.
C WDCD     (SEE  3.4 ) SERVICE     WRITES DATA COLUMN DESCRIPTION
C WMAT     (SEE 11.3 ) SERVICE     WRITE MATRIX WITH VARIATE TITLES
C SETTING OF ARRAY DIMENSIONS
C THE FOLLOWING DIMENSIONS MUST BE AT LEAST AS BIG AS THOSE
C SPECIFIED BY THE DATA TAPE,SAMPLE SPECIFICATIONS, ETC.
C NQMAX = MAXIMUM NUMBER OF DATA COLUMNS
C DIMENSION X(NQMAX),ST(NQMAX) ,IT(NQMAX),CN(NQMAX)
      NQMAX = 100
      DIMENSION X(100),ST(100),IT(100),CN(100)
      DATA  CN/4HCOL1,4HCOL2,4HCOL3,4HCOL4,4HCOL5,4HCOL6,4HCOL7,4HCOL8,4
     1HCOL9,4HCL10,4HCL11,4HCL12,4HCL13,4HCL14,4HCL15,4HCL16,4HCL17,4HCL
     218,4HCL19,4HCL20,4HCL21,4HCL22,4HCL23,4HCL24,4HCL25,4HCL26,4HCL27,
     34HCL28,4HCL29,4HCL30,4HCL31,4HCL32,4HCL33,4HCL34,4HCL35,4HCL36,4HC
     4L37,4HCL38,4HCL39,4HCL40,4HCL41,4HCL42,4HCL43,4HCL44,4HCL45,4HCL46
     5,4HCL47,4HCL48,4HCL49,4HCL50,4HCL51,4HCL52,4HCL53,4HCL54,4HCL55,4H
     6CL56,4HCL57,4HCL58,4HCL59,4HCL60,4HCL61,4HCL62,4HCL63,4HCL64,4HCL6
     75,4HCL66,4HCL67,4HCL68,4HCL69,4HCL70,4HCL71,4HCL72,4HCL73,4HCL74,4
     8HCL75,4HCL76,4HCL77,4HCL78,4HCL79,4HCL80,4HCL81,4HCL82,4HCL83,4HCL
     984,4HCL85,4HCL86,4HCL87,4HCL88,4HCL89,4HCL90,4HCL91,4HCL92,4HCL93,
     94HCL94,4HCL95,4HCL96,4HCL97,4HCL98,4HCL99,4HC100/
C MI = MAXIMUM NUMBER OF DIFFERENT VARIATES
C DIMENSION ISAVE(MI),NP(MI),NDP(MI),IX(MI),IY(MI),LX(MI),LY(MI)
      MI = 50
      DIMENSION ISAVE(50),NP(50),NDP(50),IX(50),IY(50),LX(50),LY(50)
C MAXAV = GENERAL STORE FOR CORRELATION AND ANALYSIS MATRICES
C MAXAV MUST BE AT LEAST MDIAG + 4*M + K*K
C WHERE MDIAG = M*(M+1)/2 IF NO MISSING VALUES
C             = M*(M+1)*3 IF MISSING VALUES ALLOWED
C       M = NUMBER OF DIFFERENT VARIATES IN STORE
C       K = NUMBER OF VARIATES SELECTED FOR THIS ANALYSIS
C   DIMENSION R(MAXAV)
      MAXAV = 3775
      DIMENSION R(3775)
C MAXD = STORAGE AVAILABLE FOR DELAYED ENTRIES
C (MAXIMUM DELAY + 3.) * M MUST NOT EXCEED MAXD
C DIMENSION D(MAXD) IF MAXD NOT ZERO
C DIMENSION D(MAXD)
```

```
      MAXD = 500
      DIMENSION D(500)
C IF ALL 50 VARIATES ARE USED MAXIMUM DELAY = 8
C IF ONLY 2 ARE USED MAXIMUM DELAY = 248
C FIRST VARIATE MUST BE TIME VARIATE
C NALTMX = MAXIMUM NUMBER OF CLASSES ON TAPE
C DIMENSION      TRT(NALTMX)
      NALTMX = 50
      DIMENSION TRT(50)
C MAXDBC = MAXIMUM NUMBER OF DATA BANK SUBSET CONDITIONS
C DIMENSION SCON(5,MAXDBC)
      MAXDBC = 50
      DIMENSION SCON(5,50)
C THE FOLLOWING DIMENSION STORES THE NAMES OF THE DATA TRANSFORMS
C AND THE ACCEPTABLE LEVELS FOR TRANSFORMATIONS
      DIMENSION U(60),LU(60)
      NU = 60
C TRANSFORMATION CODES
C UNITS                       BLOCKS
C       0 - 9  10 - 19   20 - 29   30 - 39   40 - 49   50 - 59
C       POWERS TRIG      TRIG      STATIST   MATHS     TEST
C              RADIANS   DEGREES   TRANSF    FUNCTS    FUNCTIONS
C  0     -              H.MS       -          -         RM10
C  1    VAL.   SINR     SIND      PSNA       RECP      +/-1
C  2    SQAR   COSR     COSD      PSNB       SQRT      ADD1
C  3    CUBE   TANR     TAND      BINO       ABSV      SUB1
C  4    4PWR   ASIR     ASID      LG+1       SIGN      NOB1
C  5    5PWR   ACOR     ACOD      LOGE       INTG      +/-P
C  6    6PWR   ATAR     ATAD      LG10       FRAC      ADDP
C  7    7PWR   SINH     DTOR      AL10       EXPT      SUBP
C  8    8PWR   COSH     RTOD       -         PRES      NOBP
C  9    9PWR   TANH     H.HH       -         NEG.      +100
      DATA U/4HVAL.,4HSQAR,4HCUBE,4H4PWR,4H5PWR,4H6PWR,4H7PWR,4H8PWR,4H9
     1PWR,4HVAL ,4HSINR,4HCOSR,4HTANR,4HASIR,4HACOR,4HATAR,4HSINH,4HCOSH
     2,4HTANH,4HH.MS,4HSIND,4HCOSD,4HTAND,4HASID,4HACOD,4HATAD,4HDTOR,4H
     3RTOD,4HH.HH,4H VAL,4HPSNA,4HPSNB,4HBINO,4HLG+1,4HLOGE,4HLG10,4HAL1
     40,4H    ,4H    ,4H    ,4HRECP,4HSQRT,4HABSV,4HSIGN,4HINTG,4HFRAC,4
     5HEXPT,4HPRES,4HNEG.,4HRM10,4H+/-1,4HADD1,4HSUB1,4HNOB1,4H+/-P,4HAD
     6DP,4HSUBP,4HNORP,4H+100,4H    /
C ACCEPTABLE CODE LEVELS
      DATA LU/60*4/
C DUMMY ARRAYS USED IN LGEN + D.H.I INPUT ARRAY
      DIMENSION IH(1),H(1),FORM(40)
      COMMON /STCT/MED1,MED2,MED3,MED4,MED5,MED6,MED13,Q,V(20),TT(30)
      DATA PROG/4HCLUS/
      MED1 = -1
C SETTING UP * LEVEL 0
C VLIM DETERMINES PERMUTATION MAXIMUM - UNLESS SPECIFIED
C CLIM DETERMINES HILL-CLIMBING TRIALS - UNLESS SPECIFIED
      VLIM = 7.
      CLIM = 1000.
    1 CALL COPYA(TT(1),PROG)
      CALL FIFI
      WRITE(MED2,901)
      CALL LDAP(MED2,MED3,V,TT,Q,MQ,NALT,NCMAX,NALTMX,IGO)
      IF(IGO.GT.0) GO TO 1
      LI = 18
      CALL LDDS(TRT,NALT,D,NQ,ST,MQ,IT,MQ,H,0,H,H,0,LI,0,Q,VX,
     1 0,MED2,MED3,0,IGO)
      IF(IGO.GT.0) GO TO 1
C LEVEL 2 - READ DATA BANK SUBSET DEFINITION
   21 IF(V(10).GE.20.) V(10) = 0.
      CALL LDBS(SCON,NCON,MAXDBC,CN,ST,IT,MQ,TRT,NALT,IGO)
```

```
      IF(IGO.GT.0) GO TO 1
      DO 22 I = 11,20
   22 CALL COPYA(TT(I),TT(I+10))
      ARAN = 5236.
C LEVEL 4 - READ SET OF VARIATES FOR DATA SWEEP
   41 IF(V(10).GE.40.) V(10) = 0.
      M = 0
      C = 2*MAXAV - 2
      MAXM = SQRT(C) - 5.
      IF(MAXM.GT.MI) MAXM = MI
      WRITE(MED6,941)
      WRITE(MED6,944)
      CALL LGEN(U,NU,LU,NU,ST,IT,CN,NQ,IH,0,H,H,0,H,H,0,MAXD,NALT,NDP,NP
     1,MAXM,M,MAXM,1,NALT)
      IF(V(11).LT.0.5.AND.V(20).LT.0.5)GO TO 21
      BRAN = ARAN
C READ PREDICTED VARIATES - LEVEL 5
   51 IF(V(10).GT.50.) V(10) = 0.
      WRITE(MED6,951)
      WRITE(MED6,944)
      NPV = 0
      C = MAXAV - M*(M+9)/2
      MX = SQRT(C)
      IF(MX.GT.MI) MX = MI
      CALL LGEN(U,NU,LU,NU,ST,IT,CN,NQ,IH,0,H,H,0,H,H,0,MAXD,0,IX,IY,MX,
     1NPV,MX,1,NALT)
      IF(V(11).LT.0.5.AND.V(20).LT.0.5)GO TO 41
      IF(V(10).LT.0.5.AND.V(20).GT.0.5) V(10) = 55.
      IF(NPV.LT.1) GO TO 54
C STORE AS NUMBERS IN VARIATE SET - ADD IF MISSING
      C = MAXAV - NPV*NPV
      MAXM = SQRT(2.*C) - 5.
      IF(MAXM.GT.MI) MAXM = MI
      KM = 0
      DO 53 J = 1,NPV
      DO 52 L = 1,M
      IF(IX(J).NE.NDP(L).OR.IY(J).NE.NP(L)) GO TO 52
      ISAVE(J) = L
      GO TO 53
   52 CONTINUE
      V(19) = V(19) + 2.
      IF(V(19).GT.50.) WRITE(MED2,950)
      IF(V(19).GT.50.) V(19) = 2.
      WRITE(MED2,952) J
      IF(MAXM.EQ.M) WRITE(MED6,954)
      IF(MAXM.EQ.M) KM = KM + 1
      IF(MAXM.EQ.M) GO TO 53
      WRITE(MED2,953)
      M = M + 1
      NDP(M) = IX(J)
      NP(M) = IY(J)
      ISAVE(J) = M
      V(6) = 0.
      BRAN = ARAN
   53 CONTINUE
      NPV = NPV - KM
   54 IF(NPV.LT.3.AND.V(10).LT.0.5) V(10) = 56.
      IF(NPV.GT.0.AND.NPV.LT.3) WRITE(MED6,955) NPV
      IF(NPV.LE.0) WRITE(MED6,956)
      IF(NPV.GE.7) WRITE(MED6,901)
C LEVEL 9 - DATA HANDLING INSTRUCTION
   91 IF(V(10).GT.90.) V(10) = 0.
      CALL LDHI(V(1),1,V(2),2,VX,7,VY,12,V(8),14,V(3),17,V7,V(10),
```

```
      1   TT(21),FORM,MED1,MED2,MED4,Q,NQ,NWARN,1,IGO)
          IF(IGO.GT.0) GO TO 51
C STANDARDISATION
          NWARN = 0
          IF(V(2).GT.2.) NWARN = NWARN + 1
          IF(V(2).GT.2.) V(2) = 0.
          IF(V(1).GT.6.) NWARN = NWARN + 1
          IF(V(1).GT.6.) V(1) = 0.
          IF(VY.LT.0.5) NWARN = NWARN + 1
          IF(VY.LT.0.5) V(7) = V7
          IF(VY.GT.0.5) V(7) = VY
          IF(V(7).LT.0.5) V(7) = VLIM
          V7 = V(7)
          J = V7
          IF(V(8).LT.0.5.AND.NPV.GT.J) NWARN = NWARN + 1
          IF(V(8).LT.0.5.AND.NPV.GT.J) V(8) = CLIM
          IF(V(3).LT.0.5.AND.NPV.GT.J) NWARN = NWARN + 1
          IF(V(3).LT.0.5.AND.NPV.GT.J) V(3) = 1.
C MAXIMUM NUMBER OF MISSING VALUES
          IF(V(6).EQ.0.) V(9) = VX
          IF(VX.NE.V(9).AND.VX.NE.0.) V(6) = 0.
          IF(VX.NE.V(9).AND.VX.NE.0.) V(9) = VX
          MXM = 4*M + NPV*NPV
          MDIAG = M*(M+1)/2
          IF(V(9).GT.0.5) MDIAG = MDIAG*6
          IF(MXM+MDIAG.LE.MAXAV) GO TO 97
          IF(V(9).LT.0.5) GO TO 96
          WRITE(MED6,980)
          V(9) = 0.
          MDIAG = M*(M+1)/2
   96     IF(MXM+MDIAG.LE.MAXAV) GO TO 97
          IF(V(10).LT.0.5) V(10) = 91.
          WRITE(MED2,992) MDIAG,MXM,MAXAV
   97     CALL LDHI(V(1),1,V(2),2,VX,7,VY,12,V(8),14,V(3),17,V7,V(10),
      1   TT(21),FORM,MED1,MED2,MED4,Q,NQ,NWARN,2,IGO)
          IF(IGO.GT.0) GO TO 91
          IF(NPV.LE.J) WRITE(MED6,981) NPV
          IF(NPV.GT.J) WRITE(MED2,982) NPV,V(8),V(3)
  101     WRITE(MED6,998)
          KXK = NPV*NPV
          IXB = MDIAG + 1
          IST = IXB + M
          IB = IST + M
          JT = IB + M
          IS = JT + M
          V(10) = BRAN
          CALL CLUST(M,R(IB),ISAVE,IX,IY,LX,LY,NP,NDP,R(IST),R(JT),R(IXB),MD
      1IAG,R,MAXD,D,NPV,KXK,R(IS),NQ,X,ST,U,NU,NCON,SCON)
          ARAN = V(10)
          V(10) = 0.
          WRITE(MED6,999)
          GO TO 91
  901 FORMAT (1H0,20X,31HSTATCAT CLUSTERING CORRELATIONS)
  941 FORMAT (1H1,10X,30HSET OF VARIATES FOR DATA SWEEP/)
  944 FORMAT(7H0NUMBER,6X,19HTRANS    DATA   CYCLES/5H CODE,8X,18H-FORM COL
     1UMN DELAY,66X,7HCOMMENT)
  950 FORMAT (41H1SELECTED VARIATES NOT IN SET OF VARIATES)
  951 FORMAT (1H1,10X,18H SELECTED VARIATES/)
  952 FORMAT (15H0VARIATE NUMBER,I4,30H IS NOT IN THE SET OF VARIATES)
  953 FORMAT(1H+,50X,33H- ADDED (NEW DATA SWEEP REQUIRED))
  954 FORMAT (1H+,50X,26H-NOT ADDED - NO MORE SPACE)
  955 FORMAT(38H0AT LEAST THREE VARIATES NEEDED - ONLY,I2,9H ACCEPTED)
  956 FORMAT (47H0AT LEAST THREE VARIATES NEEDED - NONE ACCEPTED)
```

```
      980 FORMAT(46H0 NOT ENOUGH STORAGE TO INCLUDE MISSING VALUES)
      981 FORMAT (1H0,10X,32HALL POSSIBLE ARRANGEMENTS OF THE,I4,23H VARIATE
     1S WILL BE TRIED)
      982 FORMAT (1H0,10X,47HHILL-CLIMBING APPROACH WILL BE ADOPTED FOR THE
     1,I4,19H VARIATES SPECIFIED/1H0,10X,F10.0,36H POSSIBLE ARRANGEMENTS
     2 WILL BE TRIED/11X,37H (UNLESS A MINIMUM IS REACHED EARLIER)/1H0,10
     3X,32HMINIMUM PERCENTAGE IMPROVEMENT - ,F8.2)
      992 FORMAT(29H0 CORRELATION MATRIX REQUIRES,I6,6H CELLS/21H       ANALYSI
     1S REQUIRES,I6,6H CELLS/6H0 ONLY,I6,27H AVAILABLE - INCREASE MAXAV)
      998 FORMAT (36H0INPUT ACCEPTED - ANALYSIS COMMENCES)
      999 FORMAT (36H1ANALYSIS COMPLETED - READ NEW INPUT)
          END


          SUBROUTINE CLUST (M,B,ISAVE,KX,LX,MX,NX,NP,NDP,STD,T,XBAR,MDIAG,R
         1,MN,D,K,KXK,RS,NQ,X,ST,U,NU,NCON,SCON)
    C CLUST    (SEE  8.3 ) EXECUTIVE   CLUSTERS CORRELATION MATRIX
          DIMENSION B(M),STD(M),T(M),XBAR(M),D(MN)
          DIMENSION NP(M),NDP(M),ISAVE(K),KX(K),LX(K),MX(K),NX(K)
          DIMENSION X(NQ),ST(NQ),SCON(5,NCON),U(NU),R(MDIAG),RS(KXK)
          COMMON /STCT/MED1,MED2,MED3,MED4,MED5,MED6,MED13,Q,V(20),TT(30)
    C V(2) = ANALYSIS CONTROL INDEX
    C V(1) = OUTPUT CONTROL INDEX
          NDEL = 0
          DO 26 L = 1,M
       26 IF(NDP(L).GT.0) NDEL = 1
          IC2 = V(2) + 1.01
          IC3 = V(7)
          IF(K.LE.IC3) IC3 = 1
          IF(IC3.GT.1)IC3 = 2
          ND = V(1) + .01
          VX = 1. - V(3)*.01
          IF(IC3.EQ.1)VX = 1.
          IF(V(6).GT.0.5) GO TO 27
          REWIND MED3
          READ(MED3) NQ,NALT,Q,(TT(J),J=1,10),(P,J=1,6)
          DO 29 I = 1,NQ
       29 READ(MED3) (P,J=1,19),(P,J=1,NALT),J,P,P
          V(6) = 0.
          V(7) = 3.
          CALL CORRE(M,XBAR,STD,R,B,D,T,MDIAG,NP,NDP,X,NQ,SCON,NCON,MN)
          IF(V(6).GT.0.5) GO TO 27
          WRITE(MED2,902) TT
          WRITE(MED2,946)
       27 N= V(6)
          IF(ND.GT.0) CALL WBASE(ISAVE,NP,NDP,T,XBAR,STD,U,NU,ST,NQ,R,MDIAG,
         1 M,NDEL,K,ND)
          CALL MOP(R,3,M,M,MDIAG,RS,2,K,K,KXK,ISAVE,3,K,ISAVE,3,K,2 ,MED2)
          IF(ND.LE.0) GO TO 39
          WRITE(MED2,902) TT
          WRITE(MED2,910)
          CALL WHAT(RS,K,K,KXK,NP,NDP,M,ST,NQ,ISAVE,ISAVE,U,NU,MED2)
       39 V10 = V(10)
    C SETTING-UP
          ILS = 0
          INDX = 0
          DO 1 L = 1,K
          MX(L) = L
          NX(L) = -1
          D(L) = 1.
        1 KX(L) = 1
          NX(1) = 0
          V(10) = 1.
```

```
      IF(IC2.LT.3) GO TO 3
C BEST CHOICE OF DIRECTIONS
   20 INDX = 0
      IMIN = 0
      DO 22 I = 1,K
      D(I) = -1.
      DO 21 J = 1,K
      INDX = INDX+1
      IF(KX(I).NE.KX(J)) D(I) = D(I) - RS(INDX)
   21 IF(KX(I).EQ.KX(J)) D(I) = D(I) + RS(INDX)
      IF(D(I).GE.0.) GO TO 22
      IF(IMIN.EQ.0) IMIN = I
      IF(D(I).LT.D(IMIN))IMIN = I
   22 CONTINUE
      IF(IMIN.NE.0) KX(IMIN) = -KX(IMIN)
      IF(IMIN.NE.0) GO TO 20
      WRITE(MED2,902) TT
      WRITE(MED2,949)
      IF(NDEL.GT.0) WRITE(MED2,943)
      DO 23 L = 1,K
      I = ISAVE(L)
      JT=NP(I)/1000
      JC=NP(I)-1000*JT
      WRITE(MED2,944) U(JT),JC,ST(JC)
      IF(NDEL.GT.0) WRITE(MED2,945) NDP(I)
      IF(KX(L).GT.0) WRITE(MED2,947)
      IF(KX(L).LT.0) WRITE(MED2,948)
   23 D(L) = KX(L)
    3 CONTINUE
C INITIAL VALUE OF CORRELATION-SQUARE DISTANCE
      TX = 0.
      DO 2 I = 1,K
      DO 2 J = 1,K
      XX = I-J
      IJ = I + (J-1)*K
      Y = RS(IJ)
      IF(IC2.EQ.3.AND.KX(I).NE.KX(J)) Y = -Y
      IF(IC2.EQ.2.AND.Y.LT.0.) Y = -Y
    2 TX = TX + XX*XX*Y
      NSF = 0
      IF(ND.LT.3) GO TO 7
      WRITE(MED2,902) TT
      WRITE(MED2,950)
      IF(ND.EQ.4) WRITE(MED2,951) TX,MX
      GO TO 7
C CALCULATE IMPROVEMENT DUE TO LAST CHANGE
    5 TX = TMIN
      DO 6 K1 = 1,K
      IF(K1.EQ.I.OR.K1.EQ.J) GO TO 6
      KX1 = MX(K1)
      KK = (KX1-1)*K
      IK = IX+KK
      JK = JX+KK
      XX = (I-J)*(2*K1-I-J)
      Y = RS(IK)
      Z = RS(JK)
      IF(IC2.EQ.3.AND.KX(IX).NE.KX(KX1)) Y = -Y
      IF(IC2.EQ.3.AND.KX(JX).NE.KX(KX1)) Z = -Z
      IF(IC2.EQ.2.AND.Y.LT.0.) Y = -Y
      IF(IC2.EQ.2.AND.Z.LT.0.) Z = -Z
      TX = TX + XX*(Y-Z)*2.
    6 CONTINUE
      IF(ND.GE.4) NSF = NSF + 1
```

```
      IF(NSF.LE.50) GO TO 19
      NSF = 0
      WRITE(MED2,902) TT
      WRITE(MED2,950)
   19 CONTINUE
      IF(TX.LT.TMIN)ILS = 1
      IF(ND.GE.4) WRITE(MED2,951)TX,MX
      IF(TX.GE.TL.AND.IC3.EQ.2) GO TO 15
      IF(TX.GE.TL.AND.IC3.EQ.1) GO TO 9
C ADOPT BEST SO FAR
    7 TMIN = TX
      IF(ND.EQ.3) WRITE(MED2,951)TX,MX
      IF(ND.EQ.3) NSF = NSF + 1
      IF(ND.GE.3) WRITE(MED2,952)
      IF(ND.LT.3) GO TO 45
      IF(NSF+(K+9)/10*3.LE.49) GO TO 46
      NSF = 0
      WRITE(MED2,902) TT
      WRITE(MED2,950)
   46 DO 43 IS = 1,K,10
      NIL = K-IS+1
      IF(NIL.GT.10) NIL = 10
      DO 40 L = 1,NIL
      LL = IS+L-1
      JC = MX(LL)
      JC = ISAVE(JC)
      LX(L) = JC
      JC = NP(JC)/1000
   40 CALL COPYA(D(L),U(JC))
      WRITE(MED2,911) (D(L),L=1,NIL)
      DO 41 L = 1,NIL
      JC = LX(L)
      JC = NP(JC)-NP(JC)/1000*1000
      CALL COPYA(D(L),ST(JC))
   41 LX(L) = JC
      WRITE(MED2,912) (LX(L),D(L),L=1,NIL)
      NSF = NSF + 3
      IF(NDEL.EQ.0) GO TO 43
      DO 42 L = 1,NIL
      LL = IS+L-1
      JC = MX(LL)
      JC = ISAVE(JC)
   42 LX(L) = NDP(JC)
      WRITE(MED2,913) (LX(L),L=1,NIL)
      NSF = NSF + 1
   43 CONTINUE
      NSF = NSF + 1
      WRITE(MED2,912)
   45 TL = VX*TX
C TX MAY BE NEGATIVE
      IF(TX.LT.0.) TL = TX*(2.-VX)
      DO 44 L = 1,K
   44 LX(L) = MX(L)
      IF(IC3.EQ.2) GO TO 14
C NEXT PERMUTATION
    9 I = 0
      DO 11 L = 1,K
   10 IF(MX(L).EQ.0) GO TO 11
      IF(I.EQ.0) I = L
      IF(MX(L).GT.MX(I))I = L
   11 CONTINUE
      IF(I.EQ.0) GO TO 50
      TMIN = TX
```

```
      J = I + NX(I)
      IX = MX(I)
      JX = MX(J)
      MX(I) = JX
      MX(J) = IX
      L = NX(I)
      NX(I) = NX(J)
      NX(J) = L
      L = J + L
      IF(L.LT.1.OR.L.GT.K) NX(J) = 0
      IF(L.LT.1.OR.L.GT.K) GO TO 12
      IF(MX(L).GT.MX(J)) NX(J) = 0
   12 DO 13 L = 1,K
      IF(MX(L).GT.MX(J).AND.L.LT.J) NX(L) = 1
   13 IF(MX(L).GT.MX(J).AND.L.GT.J) NX(L) = -1
      GO TO 5
C NEXT EXCHANGE - LAST WAS ACCEPTED
   14 J = 0
      ILS = 0
      IF(VX.NE.1..OR.V(3).EQ.0.) GO TO 17
      VX = 1. - V(3)*0.01
      IF(ND.LT.3) GO TO 17
      NSF = NSF + 3
      WRITE(MED2,916) V(3)
      GO TO 17
C NEXT EXCHANGE - LAST REJECTED
   15 MX(I) = IX
      MX(J) = JX
      I = I + 1
      IF(I.LE.K) GO TO 18
   17 J = J+1
      JX = MX(J)
      I = J+1
      IF(I.LE.K) GO TO 18
      IF(ILS.EQ.0.OR.VX.EQ.1.)GO TO 49
      TL = TMIN
      VX = 1.
      J = 0
      IF(ND.LT.3) GO TO 17
      WRITE(MED2,915) V(3)
      NSF = NSF + 3
      GO TO 17
   18 IX = MX(I)
      V(10) = V(10) + 1.
      MX(J) = IX
      MX(I) = JX
      IF(V(10).LT.V(8))GO TO 5
   49 IF(ND.GE.3)WRITE(MED2,917)
   50 DO 51 I = 1,K
      J = LX(I)
   51 MX(I) = ISAVE(J)
      CALL MOP (R,3,M,M,MDIAG,RS,2,K,K,KXK,MX,3,K,MX,3,K,2,MED2)
      IF(IC2.EQ.1) GO TO 54
      INDX = 0
      DO 53 I = 1,K
      IX = LX(I)
      DO 53 J = 1,K
      JX = LX(J)
      INDX = INDX + 1
      IF(IC2.EQ.2.AND.RS(INDX).LT.0.) RS(INDX) = -RS(INDX)
   53 IF(IC2.EQ.3.AND.KX(IX).NE.KX(JX)) RS(INDX) = -RS(INDX)
   54 CONTINUE
      WRITE(MED2,902) TT
```

```
      WRITE(MED2,920)
      IF(IC3.EQ.1) WRITE(MED2,921)
      IF(IC3.EQ.1) GO TO 52
      WRITE(MED2,922)
      IF(V(3).EQ.0.) WRITE(MED2,923)
      IF(V(3).GT.0.) WRITE(MED2,924) V(3)
      IF(V(10).NE.V(8)) WRITE(MED2,927) V(10)
      IF(V(10).EQ.V(8)) WRITE(MED2,928) V(10)
   52 IF(IC2.EQ.2)WRITE(MED2,919)
      IF(IC2.EQ.3) WRITE(MED2,918)
      CALL WHAT (RS,K,K,KXK,NP,NDP,M,ST,NQ,MX,MX,U,NU,MED2)
      V(10) = V10
      RETURN
  901 FORMAT (1H+,60X,I4,25H MISSING VALUES ESTIMATED)
  902 FORMAT(23H1STATCAT PROGRAM STCLUS,7X,1H-,4X,29HCORRELATION MATRIX
     1CLUSTERING/16H DATA BANK TITLE,14X,1H-,4X,10A4/23H DATA BANK SUBSE
     1T TITLE,7X,1H-,4X,10A4/10H RUN TITLE,20X,1H-,4X,10A4/)
  910 FORMAT(1H0,5X,48HCORRELATION MATRIX FOR THIS ANALYSIS              )
  911 FORMAT(1H0,20X,10(A4,3H OF,3X))
  912 FORMAT(19X,10(I4,2H =,A4))
  913 FORMAT(12X,9HDELAY =   ,10(I5,3X))
  915 FORMAT(30H0         NO IMPROVEMENT EXCEEDING,F7.4,35H PER CENT CHECK F
     1OR ANY IMPROVEMENT/)
  916 FORMAT(23H0         IMPROVEMENT BELOW ,F7.4,17H PER CENT ADOPTED/)
  917 FORMAT (28H0         NO FURTHER IMPROVEMENT)
  918 FORMAT(42H0DIRECTIONS CHOSEN TO MAXIMISE CORRELATION)
  919 FORMAT(43H0IGNORING SIGNS OF CORRELATION COEFFICIENTS)
  920 FORMAT(1H0,5X,30HCLUSTERED CORRELATION MATRIX              )
  921 FORMAT (37H0ALL POSSIBLE ARRANGEMENTS CONSIDERED      )
  922 FORMAT (19H0BY 'HILL-CLIMBING'      )
  923 FORMAT (1H+,24X,25HACCEPTING ANY IMPROVEMENT      )
  924 FORMAT (1H+,19X,9HACCEPTING,F4.0,21H PER CENT IMPROVEMENT)
  927 FORMAT(13H0HALTED AFTER,F7.0,24H TRIALS AT LOCAL MINIMUM)
  928 FORMAT(13H0HALTED AFTER,F7.0,24H TRIALS AT PRE-SET LIMIT)
  943 FORMAT(1H+,17X,5HDELAY)
  944 FORMAT(1H ,A4,3H OF,I3,1H(,A4,1H),9X,3F20.8)
  945 FORMAT(1H+,16X,I4)
  946 FORMAT(///19H0 NO DATA IN SAMPLE)
  947 FORMAT(1H+,21X,18H  NORMAL DIRECTION   )
  948 FORMAT(1H+,21X,18HREVERSED DIRECTION   )
  949 FORMAT(1H0,10X,45HCHOICE OF DIRECTIONS FOR MAXIMUM CORRELATION   /
     117H0TRANSFORM COLUMN)
  950 FORMAT(1H0,10X,6HTRIALS/)
  951 FORMAT(8H SCORE =,F20.8,17H FOR COLUMN ORDER,10I4/(45X,10I4))
  952 FORMAT(1H+,91X,11HBEST SO FAR)
      END
```

Chapter IX

STATCAT PLAIN-LANGUAGE DATA BANKS

Although most users of statistics are primarily concerned with the analysis of numerical data, it is often useful to be able to store and treat non-numeric data. FORTRAN is not well adapted for this purpose, but it can be used for the treatment of plain-language data, although in a rather indirect and inefficient way. Serious users will find other languages (PL/I, BASIC or even ALGOL) more efficient than the techniques given in this chapter. For relatively small files, and where there is no time or effort for programming, the techniques provided in this chapter allow some basic word-oriented processing.

The chapter begins by showing how a special-purpose input subroutine may be incorporated to read and store information from punched cards. A minimum of structure is imposed on the data as they are loaded. (9.1)

The second section (9.2) shows how a special-purpose output subroutine WOWN can be used to provide a variety of word-oriented output forms.

The third section (9.3) provides an example of another special-purpose subroutine DATA used to perform a cross-indexing task.

The fourth section of the chapter describes a specialised program (9.4 - STWORD) designed to search for entries containing particular words, combinations of words, or names - recognising some mis-spellings.

The final section of this chapter (9.5) discusses how other STATCAT programs may be used in combination with these special adaptations, to combine, update, or copy plain language STATCAT data banks.

9.1   PROGRAM STLOAD - PLAIN-LANGUAGE INPUT

9.1.1   Purpose

The purpose of program STLOAD, as laid down in 4.2, is to load and check STATCAT data banks from outside media. If the special subroutine DATA (PLAN) is used as explained here, the STATCAT data bank so produced will be suitable for use with the output subroutine WOWN(PLAN) described in 9.2, with the subroutine DATA(XREF) described in 9.3 and with the special program STWORD, described in 9.4.

The main program STLOAD and the executive subroutine CLOAD are exactly those described in 4.2. The subroutine DATA described there is replaced by the subroutine DATA described here, with the auxiliary function NPACK. System flow-charts for DATA(PLAN) (see 9.1.5) and for NPACK (see 9.1.6) are provided in Figure 9.11. The input data follow the same pattern as given in 4.2, but with some constraints.

Figure 4.21 contains system flow-charts for the main program STLOAD and the executive subroutine CLOAD

9.1.2   Input Data

Item	Level	Format	Function	See
1	0	A	File control	3.2
2	0	B	Data starter	3.3
3	0	C	Data description segment	9.1.3 + 3.4
4	1	-	Entries	Below

Data Starter

Card Layout - Data Starter - STLOAD

ABCCCDDDEEEEEEEEF..COLS 17-56..FG..COLS 57-72..GHHHHIIII

Columns	Item	Function	See
1	A	Output control index (Set to 4)	4.2
2	B	Data checking control index (Set to 5)	4.3
3 - 5	C	Number of data columns (Set to 21)	4.2
6 - 8	D	Default value for number of classes (Set to 10)	4.2
9 - 16	E	Non-value (Set to -1)	4.2
17 - 56	F	Title of STATCAT data bank	4.2
57 - 72	G	Not defined (used for auxiliary security key)	-
73 - 76	H	Security key	4.2
77 - 80	I	Data bank name	4.2

9.1.3   Input Example

Figure 9.12 is a summary of the input data for a demonstration STATCAT plain-language data bank, showing the general structure of the input data modules, including the arrangement of entries within a record. This is, in fact, the data bank containing the bibliography appearing at the end of this book.

Figure 9.13a lists the file control card, data starter card and data description segment. (The data description segment should be the same for any plain-language STATCAT data bank.) Figure 9.13b lists the start and end of the data storage segment. Note that the last card of this is an END card.

9.1.4 Output Example

Figure 9.14 is a summary of the output structure corresponding to the input structure of 9.12. Figure 9.15 is a page-by-page summary of the output corresponding to the specific example given in 9.1.3. Figure 9.17 shows part of the listing produced during the construction of the data storage segment.

9.1.5 Subroutine DATA(PLAN)

The special-purpose subroutine DATA(PLAN) is used to read plain language data card-by-card and to produce the data storage segment of a plain-language STATCAT data bank. A simplified flow-chart is given in Figure 9.11. Apart from start and end effects, the subroutine works by reading each card into an 80-word array as single characters, verifying that the first four characters are compatible with the existing record number, converting the eighty characters into twenty integer values using the function NPACK, and storing them in the real array D for output to tape by the main program.

If the input card is the start of a new record (See 9.1.7) this subroutine will return to the main program with an 'end-of-record' for the previous record, and derive a new record number on its return, so there will be one extra entry per record.

If the input is an END or STOP card, the system stops reading data, and inserts a data terminator.

9.1.6 Subroutine NPACK

The function NPACK (Figure 9.11) takes ND alphanumeric codes and packs them into a single integer value. The function has been designed to accept a variable number of characters, although four are used in this chapter, and a variable number of different characters, including blank, although fifty are always used in this program. This facilitates the use of this function with fewer than four letters, or less than 50 characters.

9.1.7 Special conventions for Plain-language storage

Plain-language input data are read from 80-column cards, or equivalent media, initially as single characters. These characters should be ASA FORTRAN characters, and will be converted to the numerical values given in Figure 9.16. The character having the numerical equivalent 49 is the "currency symbol" and may have different representations on machines of different national origin. Any symbol not on the list will be converted to this symbol.

The bracketed symbols (&, ! and ?) given for codes 27-29 are not ASA FORTRAN and should not normally be used. They are provided for use in the unpacking of numbers not derived from the compacted form described below.

For compact storage, these numbers are combined so that four characters form one number - essentially a four-digit modulo 50 number. For example, the four character sequence A:B:C:D is converted to the digits 1:2:3:4 and combined to form

$$((50 \times 1 + 2) \times 50 + 3) \times 50 + 4 = 130134.$$

Numeric values for sets of four characters range from four blanks (=0) to four currency symbols (= 6249999).

The first four characters on each card are assumed to carry the identifying number for the record involved. In order to have the possibility of multiple card records, certain four-character codes are reserved. Four blanks implies that this is a continuation of the previous card. REFR implies that the remainder of the card will contain the four-character codes of records referring to this one. REFT implies that the card contains four-character codes of records that this one refers to. The code TEXT implies that the entry contains more plain-language information to supplement that already given. REFR, REFT or TEXT cards may be followed by more cards with blanks in the first four columns, and with extra text or reference codes as appropriate. To allow subsequent programs to know when a record ends, an 'END OF RECORD' entry is added at the end of each record. This is done automatically by the subroutine DATA, as soon as the first card of the new record is read in. This 'END OF RECORD' entry has non-values in each of the first twenty columns, and the record number in the last.

Figure 9.11 - System Flow-Charts - DATA(PLAN) and NPACK

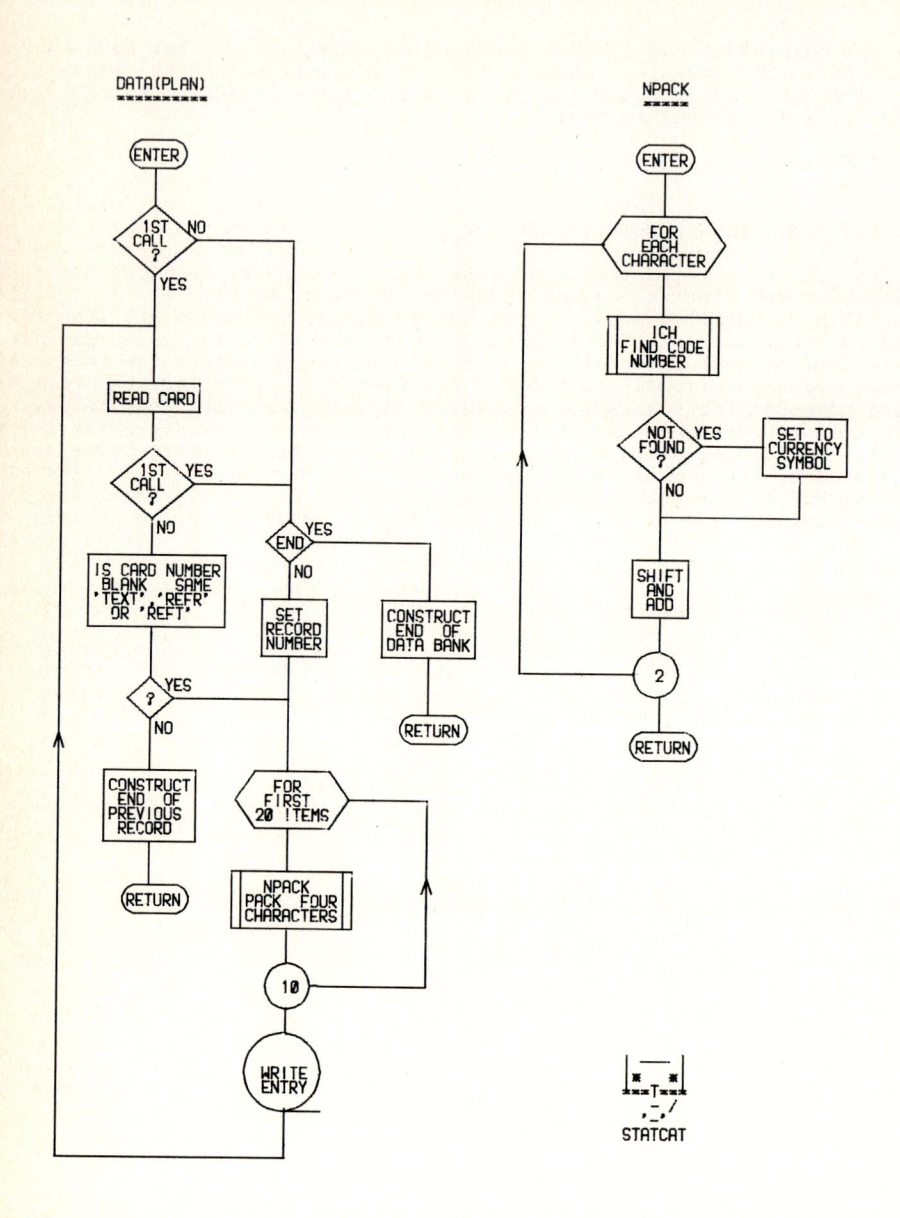

Figure 9.12 - STLOAD - Input Structure

```
        Level
0   1   2   3   4   5   6   7   8   9
FILE CONTROL CARD
DATA DESCRIPTION SEGMENT
DATA STORAGE SEGMENT
    RECORDS
        PRIMARY ENTRY
            SECONDARY ENTRIES
    END CARD
STOP
```

Figure 9.13a - STLOAD - Input Example - Header to DDS

```
---------1---------2---------3---------4---------5----///--7---------8
**STLOAD       PLAN
40 21  5 -1.0  PLAIN LANGUAGE STATCAT DEMONSTRATION              PLAN
     1 1 4DATA COLUMNS  1 -  4 (COMPRESSED)                      DUMMY
     2 5 8DATA COLUMNS  5 -  8 (COMPRESSED)                      DUMMY
     3 912DATA COLUMNS  9 - 12 (COMPRESSED)                      DUMMY
     41316DATA COLUMNS 13 - 16 (COMPRESSED)                      DUMMY
     51720DATA COLUMNS 17 - 20 (COMPRESSED)                      DUMMY
     62124DATA COLUMNS 21 - 24 (COMPRESSED)                      DUMMY
     72528DATA COLUMNS 25 - 28 (COMPRESSED)                      DUMMY
     82932DATA COLUMNS 29 - 32 (COMPRESSED)                      DUMMY
     93336DATA COLUMNS 33 - 36 (COMPRESSED)                      DUMMY
    103740DATA COLUMNS 37 - 40 (COMPRESSED)                      DUMMY
    114144DATA COLUMNS 41 - 44 (COMPRESSED)                      DUMMY
    124548DATA COLUMNS 45 - 48 (COMPRESSED)                      DUMMY
    134952DATA COLUMNS 49 - 52 (COMPRESSED)                      DUMMY
    145356DATA COLUMNS 53 - 56 (COMPRESSED)                      DUMMY
    155760DATA COLUMNS 57 - 60 (COMPRESSED)                      DUMMY
    166164DATA COLUMNS 61 - 64 (COMPRESSED)                      DUMMY
    176568DATA COLUMNS 65 - 68 (COMPRESSED)                      DUMMY
    186972DATA COLUMNS 69 - 72 (COMPRESSED)                      DUMMY
    197376DATA COLUMNS 73 - 76 (COMPRESSED)                      DUMMY
    207780DATA COLUMNS 77 - 80 (COMPRESSED)                      DUMMY
    21RCRDRECORD NUMBER        (COMPRESSED)                      DUMMY
END OF DATA DESCRIPTION SEGMENT
---------1---------2---------3---------4---------5----///--7---------8
```

Figure 9.13b - STLOAD - Input Example - Data Storage Segment

```
---------1---------2---------3---------4---------5---------6---------7--
   1ADAMS D,HITCHHIKERS GUIDE TO THE GALAXY
     PAN BOOKS 1980
TEXTA STRIKING EXAMPLE OF THE IMPORTANCE OF CONTEXT.
     (MORE ACCURATE THAN TRUE)
REFTCNTX
   2ASA,USA STANDARD FORTRAN
     AMERICAN NATIONAL STANDARDS INSTITUTE,NEW YORK 1966
TEXTTHE OFFICIAL STANDARD FOR FORTRAN IV. DEVELOPED BY COMMITTEE
     (USAS=ANS=ASA X3.9-1966).  THERE IS ALSO A BASIC FORTRAN ALIAS
     FORTRAN II - THIS HAS NOTHING TO DO WITH THE
     COMPUTER LANGUAGE BASIC. A REVISED STANDARD (FORTRAN 77) IS NOW
     COMING INTO USE, BUT THERE IS AN ENORMOUS INVESTMENT IN PROGRAMS
     CONFORMING TO THE FORTRAN IV (FORTRAN 66) STANDARD.
REFTFORT
   3BARRITT M M + WISHART D (EDS), COMPSTAT 80
     PHYSICA-VERLAG WUERZBURG 1980
     ISBN 3 7908 0229 8
TEXTPROCEEDINGS OF BI-ANNUAL CONFERENCE ON COMPUTER STATISTICS.
     PREVIOUS ISSUES COMPSTAT 76, COMPSTAT 78 ARE ALSO RELEVAnt.
     COMPSTAT 82 WILL BE PUBLISHED AUGUST 1982.
REFTBKGDPKGS
===================================================================
( some data omitted)
===================================================================
MANWMANN_WHITNEY TEST
MATRMATRIX ALGEBRA
MEDTMEDIAN TEST
MUCAMULTIPLE CANONICAL CORRELATION
MUDIMULTIPLE DISCRIMINANT ANALYSIS
MUREMULTIPLE REGRESSION ANALYSIS
ORTHORTHOGONALITY
PKGSPACKAGES
PROBPROBABILITY
RANDRANDOMNESS
REGNREGRESSION
RESIRESIDUALS
SIGNSIGN TEST
SNDFSNEDECOR F TEST
SNDXSOUNDEX CODE
STUTSTUDENT T TEST
TIMSTIME SERIES
TRELT FOR RELATED SAMPLES
WLCXWILCOXON TEST
END OF DATA STORAGE SEGMENT
STOP
---------1---------2---------3---------4---------5---------6---------7--
```

Figure 9.14 - STLOAD - Output Structure

```
For each    )      : File Control Record output file )      Data Star-
ter Record
                    Data Description Record
                    for each   )  : Data Column Title
                    data column)    Complementary Information
                    Data Storage Record
                    for each record : standard listing
                    Data Terminator Record
                    <Data Bank Checks: not recommended>
```

Carated(<>) items are optional.

Figure 9.15 - STLOAD - Output Example page-by-page Listing

Page	Contents	Origin
1-2	File Control/Program Title	FIFI/LDAP/STLOAD
	Data Description record	LDDS
3-5	Data Storage Segment	CLOAD
6	Data Handling Instruction (STOP)	LDHI

Figure 9.16 - Conversion of Plain-language characters

No.	Char--acter	No.	Char--acter	No.	Char--acter	No.	Char--acter	No.	Char--acter
0	blank	10	J	20	T	30	0	40	+
1	A	11	K	21	U	31	1	41	-
2	B	12	L	22	V	32	2	42	*
3	C	13	M	23	W	33	3	43	/
4	D	14	N	24	X	34	4	44	(
5	E	15	O	25	Y	35	5	45	)
6	F	16	P	26	Z	36	6	46	.
7	G	17	Q	27	(&)	37	7	47	,
8	H	18	R	28	(!)	38	8	48	=
9	I	19	S	29	(?)	39	9	49	F

Figure 9.17 - Data Storage Segment - Checking output

```
                         DATA INPUT RECORD


CARD -     1ADAMS D,HITCHHIKERS GUIDE TO THE GALAXY
CARD -        PAN BOOKS 1980
CARD -  TEXTA STRIKING EXAMPLE OF THE IMPORTANCE OF CONTEXT.
CARD -        (MORE ACCURATE THAN TRUE)
CARD -  REFTCNTX
*********************************************************************
CARD -     2ASA,USA STANDARD FORTRAN
CARD -        AMERICAN NATIONAL STANDARDS INSTITUTE,NEW YORK 1966
CARD -  TEXTTHE OFFICIAL STANDARD FOR FORTRAN IV. DEVELOPED BY COMMITTEE
CARD -        (USAS=ANS=ASA X3.9-1966) THERE IS ALSO A BASIC FORTRAN ALIAS
CARD -        FORTRAN II - THIS HAS NOTHING TO DO WITH THE
CARD -        COMPUTER LANGUAGE BASIC. A REVISED STANDARD (FORTRAN 77) IS NOW
CARD -        COMING INTO USE, BUT THERE IS AN ENORMOUS INVESTMENT IN PROGRAMS
CARD -        CONFORMING TO THE FORTRAN IV (FORTRAN 66) STANDARD.
CARD -  REFTFORT
*********************************************************************
CARD -     3BARRITT M M + WISHART D (EDS), COMPSTAT 80
CARD -        PHYSICA-VERLAG WUERZBURG  1980
CARD -        ISBN 3 7908 0229 8
CARD -  TEXTPROCEEDINGS OF BI-ANNUAL CONFERENCE ON COMPUTER STATISTICS.
CARD -        PREVIOUS ISSUES COMPSTAT 76, COMPSTAT 78 ARE ALSO RELEVANT.
CARD -        COMPSTAT 82 WILL BE PUBLISHED AUGUST 1982.
CARD -  REFTBKGDPKGS
*********************************************************************
CARD -     4BOURNE C P + FORD D F,METHODS FOR SYSTEMATICALLY ABBREVIATING
CARD -        ENGLISH WORDS AND NAMES
CARD -        JOURNAL OF THE ASSOCIATION FOR COMPUTING MACHINERY,OCT 1961
CARD -  TEXTTHE BEST AVAILABLE REFERENCE FOR SOUNDEX CODING IN THE COMPUTING
CARD -        LITERATURE.
CARD -  REFTSNDX
*********************************************************************
CARD -     5BOX G E P + JENKINS G M, TIME SERIES ANALYSIS FORECASTING AND
CARD -        CONTROL
CARD -        HOLDEN-DAY,SAN FRANCISCO,1976
CARD -  REFTTIMS
*********************************************************************
CARD -     6BRIGHT H + ENISON R J,QUASI-RANDOM NUMBER SEQUENCES
CARD -        ACM COMPUTING SURVEYS VOL 11 NO 4, DC 1979
CARD -  REFTRAND
*********************************************************************
CARD -     7DIXON W J + MASSEY F J,INTRODUCTION TO STATISTICAL ANALYSIS
CARD -        MCGRAW-HILL,NEW YORK 1957, LOC 56-9605
CARD -  TEXTA DETAILED INTRODUCTION TO CLASSICAL PARAMETRIC STATISTICAL TESTS,
CARD -        WIDELY USED AS A REFERENCE FOR T AND F TESTS (CH 9).
CARD -        TREATS PROBABILITY ONLY AS AN AFTERTHOUGHT.
CARD -  REFTANOVBKGDDESCCHISSTUTSNDFBRTTTRELREGN
*********************************************************************
CARD -     8DRAPER N R + SMITH H,APPLIED REGRESSION ANALYSIS
CARD -        WILEY,NEW YORK 1966
CARD -  TEXTAN EXTREMELY VALUABLE GENERAL TEXT ON MULTIPLE LINEAR REGRESSION,


                         DATA INPUT RECORD


CARD - MUDIMULTIPLE DISCRIMINANT ANALYSIS
*********************************************************************
CARD - MUREMULTIPLE REGRESSION ANALYSIS
*********************************************************************
CARD - ORTHORTHOGONALITY
*********************************************************************
CARD - PKGSPACKAGES
*********************************************************************
CARD - PROBPROBABILITY
*********************************************************************
CARD - RANDRANDOMNESS
*********************************************************************
CARD - REGNREGRESSION
*********************************************************************
CARD - RESIRESIDUALS
*********************************************************************
CARD - SIGNSIGN TEST
*********************************************************************
CARD - SNDFSNEDECOR F TEST
*********************************************************************
CARD - SNDXSOUNDEX CODE
*********************************************************************
CARD - STUTSTUDENT T TEST
*********************************************************************
CARD - TIMSTIME SERIES
*********************************************************************
CARD - TRELT FOR RELATED SAMPLES
*********************************************************************
CARD - WLCXWILCOXON TEST
*********************************************************************

NULL ENTRY FOUND
TOTAL OF     70 ENTRIES (CALLS OF DATA SUBROUTINE)

LOADING COMPLETED - CHECKING SUPPRESSED
```

```
      SUBROUTINE DATA(D,NQ,FORM)
C DATA        (SEE  9.1 ) SERVICE      USER INPUT - PLAIN LANGUAGE RECORD
      DIMENSION D(NQ),FORM(80),C(50)
      DATA C/1H ,1HA,1HB,1HC,1HD,1HE,1HF,1HG,1HH,1HI,1HJ,1HK,1HL,1HM,1HN
     1,1HO,1HP,1HQ,1HR,1HS,1HT,1HU,1HV,1HW,1HX,1HY,1HZ,1H ,1H ,1H ,1HO,1
     2H1,1H2,1H3,1H4,1H5,1H6,1H7,1H8,1H9,1H+,1H-,1H/,1H*,1H(,1H),1H,,1H.
     3,1H=,1HF/
      COMMON /STCT/MED1,MED2,MED3,MED4,MED5,MED6,MED13,Q,V(20),TT(30)
C IF RECORD NO. EXISTS THIS IS NOT START - BEGIN NEW RECORD
      IF(D(NQ).NE.Q)GO TO 7
      V(10) = 0.
C START OR NEW CARD REQUIRED - DISCARD BLANKS
    2 READ(MED1,900)FORM
      IF(IBL(FORM,80,1).LT.0)GO TO 2
C IF START BEGIN NEW RECORD - END OF RECORD NOT NEEDED
      IF(D(NQ).EQ.Q) GO TO 7
C TEST IF CARD IS PART OF SAME RECORD
    3 N=NPACK(FORM,4,C,50)
      NX= D(NQ)+.1
C IS FIRST WORD BLANK,SAME,TEXT,REFR OR REPT
      IF(N.EQ.0.OR.N.EQ.NX.OR.N.EQ.2513720) GO TO 9
      IF(N.EQ.2262818.OR.N.EQ.2262820) GO TO 9
C CARD IS NEW RECORD - INSERT END OF RECORD
      WRITE(MED2,903)
      V(10) = V(10) + 1.
    5 DO 6 I=2,NQ
    6 D(I-1)=Q
      RETURN
C NEW RECORD - PREVIOUS END OF RECORD IS INSERTED -        TEST FOR END
    7 IF(IBL(FORM,80,1).LT.1) GO TO 8
      D(NQ)=Q
      GO TO 5
    8 D(NQ)=NPACK(FORM,4,C,50)
C PACK WHOLE OF CARD - NEW OR OLD
    9 J=1
      DO 10 I=2,NQ
      D(I-1)=NPACK(FORM(J),4,C,50)
   10 J=J+4
      V(10) = V(10) + 1.
      IF(V(10).GT.50.) WRITE(MED2,901)
      IF(V(10).GT.50.) V(10) = 1.
      WRITE(MED2,902) FORM
      WRITE(MED4) D
      GO TO 2
  900 FORMAT(80A1)
  901 FORMAT (1H1,20X,17HDATA INPUT RECORD//)
  902 FORMAT(8H CARD - ,80A1)
  903 FORMAT(1H ,87(1H*))
      END


      FUNCTION NPACK(D,ND,C,NC)
C NPACK    (SEE  9.1 ) SERVICE      PACKS CODE DIGITS INTO INTEGER
      DIMENSION D(ND),C(NC)
      NPACK=0
      DO 2 I=1,ND
      K=ICH(D(I),C,NC)
      IF(K.EQ.0)K=NC
    2 NPACK=NPACK*NC+K-1
      RETURN
      END
```

9.2 PROGRAM STLIST - PLAIN-LANGUAGE OUTPUT

9.2.1 Purpose

The purpose of program STLIST is to list entries in a STATCAT data bank, or a subset thereof. If the special-purpose subroutine WOWN (PLAN) is used with a STATCAT plain-language data bank (See 9.1) several specially adapted forms of listing may be obtained.

The main program STLIST and the executive subroutine CLIST are as defined in 5.1. The default subroutine WOWN is replaced by the subroutine WOWN (PLAN) (See 9.2.5) and the auxiliary subroutine UNPACK (see 9.2.6), of which simplified flow-charts are given in Figure 9.21. The input data are in the same form as for 5.1, except that some input values are fixed, and some control options should be avoided.

9.2.2 Input Data

Item	Level	Format	Function	See
1	0	A	File control	3.2
2	4	E	Subset specification	3.6
3	9	H	Data handling instruction	Below, 5.1 + 3.8

Data Handling Instruction

Card Layout - Data Handling Instruction - STLIST

ABCCCDDDEEEEEEEEFFFFFFFFGGGGGGGGGGGGGGGGHHHHHHHH.....etc

Columns	Item	Function	See
1	A	Output control index (set to 6)	5.1
2	B	Auxiliary control index	Below
3 - 5	C	First data column output (not used by WOWN(PLAN))	5.1
6 - 8	D	Last data column output (not used by WOWN(PLAN))	5.1
9 - 16	E	Output Device (not used by WOWN(PLAN))	5.1
17 - 24	F	Not used	-
25 - 40	G	Auxiliary Security Key	Below
41 - 80	H	Run Title (KEPT)	-

B - Auxiliary Control Index

This index controls the amount of detail included in an output listing. Its exact meaning depends on the value of the Output control index A.

If A is set to 6, the following alternatives apply : -

ALTERNATIVES

B = 0 , blank   : For the first entry in each record, the record number or non-numeric   and the rest of the first entry (on one line)

B = 1   : As for B = 0, plus secondary records

B = 2   : As for B = 1, plus cross-references

B = 3   : As for B = 2, plus any text.

B = 4   : As for B = 0 - starting a new line at each comma.

B = 5   : As for B = 1 - starting a new line at each comma.

B = 6   : As for B = 5, but with cross-references (not stepped)

B = 7   : As for B = 6, but with text (not stepped)

B = 8   : Special index format; As for B = 2 plus 'referred
                   to by' codes following, separated by commas.
B = 9   : Special checking output - Each entry, including
                   'end-of-record' entries printed as stored, with its
                   unpacked equivalent.

DEFAULT value = 0 (0, blank or non-numeric character)

G - Auxiliary Security Key

This value is an optional extra for the system, designed to prevent casual snooping. The user should make his own arrangements for its use, the adaptation here being used only as an example.

In the main program STLOAD, the unused, unprinted part of the data starter card is treated as a number, and its value stored in the thirteenth word of the data starter recorded on tape. In STLIST this value is placed in auxiliary storage, as is the auxiliary security key read from this card. The special output subroutine will only produce decoded plain-language information if the two are IDENTICAL.

Users who wish to take advantage of this feature should modify the way in which checking is carried out, allow the users access to compiled programs only, and treat source material (cards and listings alike) as confidential. The auxiliary security key is never printed by the program STLIST, whatever subroutine is actually used for output.

9.2.3   Input Example

Figure 9.22 is a summary of the input structure for three runs of STLIST, in which a selected record in the demonstration STATCAT data bank is listed in its basic minimum form, in complete form and in checking form.

Figure 9.23 is a listing of the input cards required to carry out these three runs.

9.2.4   Output Example

Figure 9.24 is a general summary of the output for this program, indented to correspond to the overall program structure. Figure 9.25 is a page-by-page summary of the output corresponding to the specific example given in 9.2.3. Figure 9.26 shows the output of the first two runs, and Figure 9.27 shows that produced by the third run.

9.2.5   Subroutine WOWN (PLAN)

This subroutine is a special-purpose subroutine used to produce outputs in convenient form from STATCAT plain-language data banks (see 9.1.7). The subroutine WOWN(PLAN) operates on a record-by-record basis, except in the special checking mode.

When the system enters this subroutine it will have the first entry of a record in the array D. This entry is 'unpacked' into single characters in the array FORM, and printed in plain or stepped form as required, making due allowance for paging etc. The program then reads supplementary entries from the STATCAT data bank, printing them if required, until an END-OF-RECORD entry is read, and the program returns to the main program. When the special 'index' output is used, only the first card, and any supplementary cards (recognised by blanks in the first four card columns) are printed normally, text and 'refers to' information being suppressed, and 'is referred to' information being printed immediately following the entry, overflowing to later lines if necessary.

In the special checking mode, the subroutine simply lists each entry, returning immediately to the main program. Only in this mode will END-OF-RECORD entries be listed.

WOWN(PLAN) includes dummy orders using MED7, SCON and NCON to justify the appearance of these variates in the subroutine title. (Some FORTRAN IV compilers treat the presence of unused variates in a subroutine title as a fatal error).

9.2.6   Subroutine UNPACK

The subroutine UNPACK performs essentially the opposite of the function NPACK. It breaks down the compressed code D into the single character codes in the array FORM. The characters are right-justified, and leading cells are blanked. Thus if the compressed code is 1580 and four cells are available, these will be set to blank, blank, one and zero respectively. (See Figure 9.17)

557

Figure 9.21 - System Flow-Charts - WOWN(PLAN) and UNPACK

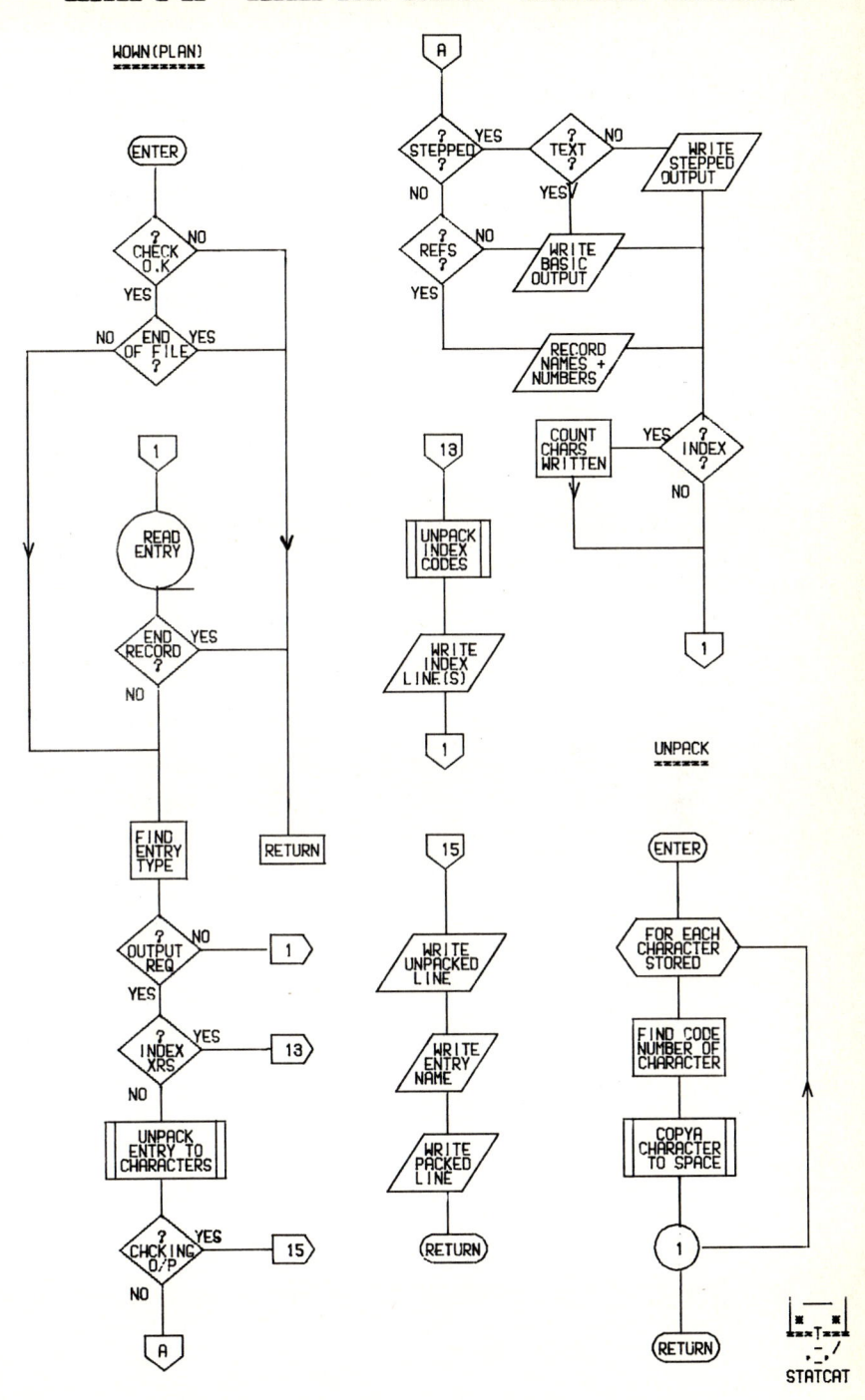

Figure 9.22 - STLIST - Input Structure

```
        Level
0   1   2   3   4   5   6   7   8   9
FILE CONTROL CARD
    SUBSET SPECIFICATION
        DATA HANDLING INSTRUCTION
        DATA HANDLING INSTRUCTION
        DATA HANDLING INSTRUCTION
        DATA HANDLING INSTRUCTION
        DATA HANDLING INSTRUCTION
        STOP
```

Figure 9.23 - STLIST - Input Example

```
---------1---------2---------3---------4---------5---------6---------7--
**STLISTPLAN
ALL DATA
END OF SUBSET
60                                  BASIC OUTPUT - PRIMARY
67                                  FULL OUTPUT
69                                  SPECIAL CHECKING OUTPUT
STOP
---------1---------2---------3---------4---------5---------6---------7--
```

Figure 9.24 - STLIST - Output Structure

```
For each  ) : File Control Record
output file )   File Parameters
                Data Description
                For each)  :  Subset Input Record
                Subset )      For each    ) Input Record
                              Data Handling ) For each) Listing
                              Instruction   ) entry in) as
                                            ) subset  ) specified
```

Figure 9.25 - STLIST - Output Example - Page-by-Page Listing

Page	Contents	Origin
1- 2	File Control Record	FIFI
	Program Title	STLIST
	File Parameters	LDAP
	Data Description record	LDDS
3	Subset record	LSAMP
	Data Handling Instruction	LDHI
4	Listing of entries (Basic output)	CLIST/WOWN
5	End of Run Message	CLIST
9	Data Handling Instruction	LDHI
6	Listing of Entries (Full output)	CLIST/WOWN
7	End of Run Message	CLIST
	Data Handling Instruction	LDHI
8	Listing of Entries (Checking format)	CLIST/WOWN
9	End of Run Message	CLIST
	Data Handling Instruction (STOP)	LDHI

Figure 9.26 - STLIST - Basic Plain Language format

```
     DATA BANK SUBSET TITLE - ONE RECORD ONLY                    COMMENT
.IF.  RCRD  .EQ.       1586.000000                               COMMENT
DATA USED ARE ON A DUMMY SCALE     THEY SHOULD BE ON A NOMINAL SCALE    ARE EXTRA ASUMPTIONS VALID
END OF INPUT SPECIFICATION                                       COMMENT

                              DATA HANDLING INSTRUCTION - ECHO PRINT

   ABCCCODDEEEEEEEEFFFFFFFGGGGGGGGGGGGGGGGHHHHHHHHHHHHHHHHHHHHHHHHHHHHHH
   60                       XXXXXXXXXXXXXXXXBASIC OUTPUT - PRIMARY



USER-WRITTEN SUBROUTINE CALLED FOR
               NO STANDARDISATION OF INPUT VALUES
               V(1) =    6.
               V(2) =    0.0
               V(7) =    0.0
               V(8) =              0.0
               V(9) =              0.0


INPUT ACCEPTED - LISTING COMMENCES




PLAIN LANGUAGE OUTPUT        -   LISTING OF ENTRIES
DATA BANK TITLE              -   PLAIN LANGUAGE STATCAT DEMONSTRATION
DATA BANK SUBSET TITLE       -   ONE RECORD ONLY
RUN TITLE                    -   BASIC OUTPUT - PRIMARY

    1586( 16)    KENDALL M G + STUART A,THE ADVANCED THEORY OF STATISTICS
```

Figure 9.27 - STLIST - Basic Plain Language format

```
LISTING COMPLETED - READ NEW INPUT

                              DATA HANDLING INSTRUCTION - ECHO PRINT

   ABCCCODDEEEEEEEEFFFFFFFFGGGGGGGGGGGGGGGGGHHHHHHHHHHHHHHHHHHHHHHHHHHHHHHH
   67                       XXXXXXXXXXXXXXXXFULL OUTPUT



USER-WRITTEN SUBROUTINE CALLED FOR
               NO STANDARDISATION OF INPUT VALUES
               V(1) =    6.
               V(2) =    7.0
               V(7) =    0.0
               V(8) =              0.0
               V(9) =              0.0


INPUT ACCEPTED - LISTING COMMENCES

PLAIN LANGUAGE OUTPUT        -   LISTING OF ENTRIES
DATA BANK TITLE              -   PLAIN LANGUAGE STATCAT DEMONSTRATION
DATA BANK SUBSET TITLE       -   ONE RECORD ONLY
RUN TITLE                    -   FULL OUTPUT

    1586( 16)        KENDALL M G + STUART A
                     THE ADVANCED THEORY OF STATISTICS
                     GRIFFIN
                     LONDON
                     3VOLS 1958-66

                     VOL 1  1963 DISTRIBUTION THEORY
                     VOL 2  1961 INFERENCE AND RELATIONSHIP
                     VOL 3  1966 DESIGN OF EXPERIMENTS, ANALYSIS AND TIME SERIES
                     THE BIBLE OF CLASSICAL STATISTICAL METHODS AND THEORY. COMPREHENSIVE
                     BUT DIFFICULT.
       REFERS TO        ANOV      BKGD      DESC     CRTH      CHIS      KS2S      MANW      BRTT      SIGN      WLCX
                        160772.   277854.   513453.  1921008.  395469.   1424119.  1628223.  296020.   2397864.  2905174.
       REFERS TO        CORR      REGN      MURE     FACT
                        413418.   2262864.  1678405. 752670.
```

Figure 9.28 - STLIST - Plain Language Checking Format

LISTING COMPLETED - READ NEW INPUT

```
                    DATA HANDLING INSTRUCTION - ECHO PRINT

 ABCCCDDDEEEEEEEEFFFFFFFGGGGGGGGGGGGGGGGHHHHHHHHHHHHHHHHHHHHHHHHHHHHHHHHHHH
 69                         XXXXXXXXXXXXXXXXCHECK OUTPUT
```

USER-WRITTEN SUBROUTINE CALLED FOR
        NO STANDARDISATION OF INPUT VALUES
        V(1) =   6.
        V(2) =   9.0
        V(7) =   0.0
        V(8) =   0.0
        V(9) =   0.0

INPUT ACCEPTED - LISTING COMMENCES

```
PLAIN LANGUAGE OUTPUT      -   LISTING OF ENTRIES
DATA BANK TITLE            -   PLAIN LANGUAGE STATCAT DEMONSTRATION
DATA BANK SUBSET TITLE     -   ONE RECORD ONLY
RUN TITLE                  -   CHECK OUTPUT
       1586.       16KENDALL M G + STUART A,THE ADVANCED THEORY OF STATISTICS            16
       1586.   1388204.    155600.    162535C.    5000970.   2628420.      4820.   1012501.    555064.    387700.
    2520265.   2312515.    750970.    175469.    2522669.         0.         0.         0.         0.         0.
       1586.
       1586.       GRIFFIN,LONDON,3VOLS 1958-66                                          16
          0.    920456.    773246.   1538204.    1912333.   2788119.     79485.   4854336.         0.         0.
          0.         0.         0.         0.         0.         0.         0.         0.         0.         0.
       1586.
       1586.       TEXT VOL 1  1963 DISTRIBUTION THEORY                                  16
    2513720.     55762.     77500.   3974333.      10469.   2545452.   2675463.   1751008.    663425.         0.
          0.         0.         0.         0.         0.         0.         0.         0.         0.         0.
       1586.
       1586.       VOL 2  1961 INFERENCE AND RELATIONSHIP                                16
          0.     55762.     80000.   3974331.      23206.    670264.    387501.   1760018.    655070.   1163219.
    1023300.         0.         0.         0.         0.         0.         0.         0.         0.         0.
       1586.
       1586.       VOL 3  1966 DESIGN OF EXPERIMENTS, ANALYSIS AND TIME SERIES           16
          0.     55762.     82500.   3974336.      10269.   1143200.   1890005.   3040268.   1157764.   2545800.
     160062.   3172969.      3204.     50403.    625955.   2272769.         0.         0.         0.         0.
       1586.
       1586.       THE BIBLE OF CLASSICAL STATISTICAL METHODS AND THEORY. COMPREHENSIVE
          0.   2520250.    272612.    625756.       8101.   2422953.    155019.   2503509.   2425453.    155013.
     675415.    547501.   1760020.   1013268.   3242503.   1508318.    645264.   2398605.         0.         0.
       1586.
       1586.       BUT DIFFICULT.
          0.    303500.    522806.   1133562.    2617500.         0.         0.         0.         0.         0.
          0.         0.         0.         0.         0.         0.         0.         0.         0.         0.
       1586.
       1586.       REFTANOVBKGODESCORTHCHISKS2SMANWBRTTSIGNWLCXCORRREGNMUREFACT
    2262820.    160772.    277854.    513453.    1921008.    395469.   1424119.   1628223.    296020.   2397864.
    2905174.    413418.   2262864.   1678405.      75267C.        0.         0.         0.         0.         0.
       1586.
       1586.                                                                             16
         -1.        -1.        -1.        -1.         -1.        -1.        -1.        -1.        -1.        -1.
         -1.        -1.        -1.        -1.         -1.        -1.        -1.        -1.        -1.        -1.
       1586.
```

```
      SUBROUTINE WOWN(D,NQ,FORM,SCON,NCON,MED7)
C WOWN    (SEE  9.2 ) SERVICE      USER OUTPUT - PLAIN LANGUAGE
      DIMENSION D(NQ),FORM(80),SCON(5,NCON),C(50)
      COMMON /STCT/MED1,MED2,MED3,MED4,MED5,MED6,MED13,Q,V(20),TT(30)
      DATA C/1H ,1HA,1HB,1HC,1HD,1HE,1HF,1HG,1HH,1HI,1HJ,1HK,1HL,1HM,1HN
     1,1HO,1HP,1HQ,1HR,1HS,1HT,1HU,1HV,1HW,1HX,1HY,1HZ,1H&,1H?,1H#,1HO,1
     2H1,1H2,1H3,1H4,1H5,1H6,1H7,1H8,1H9,1H+,1H-,1H/,1H*,1H(,1H),1H,,1H.
     3,1H=,1HF/
C V(2)           OUTPUT PRODUCED
C  0             FIRST ENTRY         BASIC FORMAT
C  1             + SUPPLEMENTS       BASIC FORMAT
C  2             + REFERENCES        BASIC FORMAT
C  3             + TEXT              BASIC FORMAT
C  4             FIRST ENTRY         STEPPED AT COMMA
C  5             +SUPPLEMENTS        STEPPED AT COMMA
C  6             +REFERENCES         BASIC FORMAT
C  7             TEXT                BASIC FORMAT
C  8             SPECIAL INDEX FORMAT
C  9             SPECIAL CHECK OUTPUT
      IF(V(13).NE.V(14)) RETURN
C FINAL CALL NOT REQUIRED
      IF(D(NQ).EQ.Q) RETURN
      MED7 = MED7
      LT = 1
      NP = V(2) + .1
      GO TO 5
    1 READ(MED3) D
    2 DO 3 I = 2,NQ
      IF(D(I-1).NE.Q) GO TO 4
    3 CONTINUE
C END OF RECORD
      RETURN
C SET LT - INDICATES TYPE OF DATA IN         D
    4 N = D(1) + 0.01
      IF(N.EQ.2262818) LT = 3
      IF(N.EQ.2262820) LT = 5
      IF(N.EQ.2513720) LT = 7
      IF(N.EQ.0) LT = (LT+1)/2*2
C DISCARD ENTRY IF NOT REQUIRED
      IF(NP.EQ.0.AND.LT.GT.1) GO TO 1
      IF(NP.EQ.1.AND.LT.GT.2) GO TO 1
      IF(NP.EQ.2.AND.LT.GT.6) GO TO 1
      IF(NP.EQ.4.AND.LT.GT.1) GO TO 1
      IF(NP.EQ.5.AND.LT.GT.2) GO TO 1
      IF(NP.EQ.6.AND.LT.GT.6) GO TO 1
      IF(NP.EQ.8.AND.LT.GT.4) GO TO 1
C UNPACK,EXCEPT SPECIAL FORMATS
    5 IF(NP.EQ.8.AND.LT.GT.2) GO TO 13
      N = D(1)
      I = 1
      DO 6 J = 2,NQ
      CALL UNPACK(D(J-1),FORM(I),4,C,50)
      IF(D(J-1).GT.0.5) NW=J-1
    6 I = I+4
      IF(NP.EQ.9) GO TO 15
      IF(LT.LE.2.AND.NP.GE.4.AND.NP.NE.8) GO TO 7
C BASIC OUTPUT FORMAT
      V(10) = V(10) + 1.
      IF(LT.EQ.1.AND.NP.NE.8.OR.LT.EQ.7)V(10)=V(10)+1.
      IF(V(10).GT.50.)WRITE(MED2,901)TT
      IF(V(10).GT.50.) V(10) = 0.
      IF(LT.EQ.1.AND.NP.NE.8)WRITE(MED2,907)   N,FORM
      IF(LT.EQ.1.AND.NP.EQ.8) WRITE(MED2,904)(FORM(I),I=5,80)
```

```
      IF(LT.EQ.7) WRITE(MED2,900)
      IF(LT.EQ.2.OR.LT.GT.6)   WRITE(MED2,904) (FORM(I),I=5,80)
C WRITE CROSS-REFS NAME + NUMBER    (NW IS POSITION OF LAST ONE)
      IF(LT.LT.3.OR.LT.GT.6) GO TO 69
      V(10)=V(10)-1.
      DO 61 ISN=2,NW,10
      IFN=ISN+9
      IF(IFN.GT.NW) IFN = NW
      ISA=ISN*4-3
      IFA=IFN*4
      V(10)=V(10)+3.
      IF(V(10).GT.50.)WRITE(MED2,901)TT
      IF(V(10).GT.50.)V(10)=0.
      IF(LT.LE.4) WRITE(MED2,905) (FORM(I),I=ISA,IFA)
      IF(LT.GE.5) WRITE(MED2,906) (FORM(I),I=ISA,IFA)
   61 WRITE(MED2,909) (D(I),I=ISN,IFN)
   69 IF(NP-8)1,11,1
C STEPPED OUTPUT
    7 XL = 3
      DO 8 I = 5,80
      CALL COMPA(FORM(I),C(47),L)
    8 IF(L.EQ.1) XL = XL + 1.
      V(10) = V(10) + XL
      IF(V(10).GT.50.) WRITE(MED2,901) TT
      IF(V(10).GT.50.) V(10) = XL
      IF(LT.EQ.1) WRITE(MED2,907) N, (FORM(I),I=1,4)
      NF = 4
    9 NS = NF + 1
   10 NF = NF + 1
      CALL COMPA(FORM(NF),C(47),L)
      IF(L.NE.1.AND.NF.NE.80) GO TO 10
      IF(NF.NE.80) NF = NF-1
      WRITE(MED2,904) (FORM(I),I=NS,NF)
      NF = NF + 1
      IF(NF-80) 9,1,1
C SPECIAL INDEX OUTPUT - INDEX ENTRY - NC IS LAST OUTPUT COLUMN+1
   11 DO 12 I = 5,80
      CALL COMPA(FORM(I),C(1),L)
   12 IF(L.NE.1)NC = I-4
      LK = 1
      GO TO 1
C SPECIAL INDEX OUTPUT - REFERRED-TO-BY CODES IN D(2) TO D(NQ-1)
   13 DO 14 IP = 3,NQ
      DX = D(IP-1)
      IF(DX.LT.0.5) GO TO 14
      L = 2
      IF(DX.GT.49.5)       L = L+1
      IF(DX.GT.2499.5)     L = L+1
      IF(DX.GT.124999.5) L = L+1
      CALL UNPACK(DX,FORM,L,C,50)
      IF(IP.GT.3.OR.LT.EQ.4) CALL COPYA(FORM(1),C(47))
      IF(NC+L.LT.80) WRITE(MED2,910) (C(1),K=1,NC),(FORM(K),K=LK,L)
      NC = NC + L -LK+1
      LK = 1
      IF(FORM(L).EQ.C(42)) LK = 2
      IF(NC.LT.80) GO TO 14
      V(10) = V(10) + 1.
      IF(V(10).GT.50.)WRITE(MED2,901)TT
      IF(V(10).GT.50.)V(10) = 0.
      WRITE(MED2,900)
      NC = L
      WRITE(MED2,910) (FORM(K),K=2,L)
   14 CONTINUE
```

```
      GO TO 1
C SPECIAL CHECKING OUTPUT
   15 IF(V(10).GT.50.)WRITE(MED2,901) TT
      IF(V(10).GT.50.) V(10) = 0.
      V(10) = V(10) + 4.
      WRITE(MED2,904) FORM
      CALL UNPACK(D(NQ),FORM,4,C,50)
      WRITE(MED2,911) D(NQ),(FORM(I),I=1,4)
      WRITE(MED2,912) D
      RETURN
  900 FORMAT(1H )
  901 FORMAT(23H1PLAIN LANGUAGE OUTPUT ,7X,1H-,4X,18HLISTING OF ENTRIES/
     1        16H DATA BANK TITLE,14X,1H-,4X,10A4/23H DATA BANK SUBSET TI
     2TLE,7X,1H-,4X,10A4/10H RUN TITLE,20X,1H-,4X,10A4)
  902 FORMAT(1H ,4X,4A1,10X,80A1)
  903 FORMAT(1H ,4X,4A1,10X,20(4A1,1X))
  904 FORMAT(1H ,18X,80A1)
  905 FORMAT(18H0IS REFERRED TO BY,10(5X,4A1))
  906 FORMAT(18H0    REFERS TO     ,10(5X,4A1))
  907 FORMAT(1H0,I8,1H(,4A1,1H),4X,76A1)
  908 FORMAT(1H0,17X,10(5X,4A1))
  909 FORMAT(19X,10F9.0)
  910 FORMAT(1H+,18X,80A1)
  911 FORMAT(1H+,F12.0,86X,4A1)
  912 FORMAT(10F12.0)
      END


      SUBROUTINE UNPACK(X,D,ND,C,NC)
C UNPACK (SEE      9.2 ) SERVICE     EXPANDS NUMBER TO CHARACTERS
      DIMENSION D(ND),C(NC)
      M=X+.1
      DO 1 J=1,ND
      I=ND+1-J
      N=M/NC
      K=M-N*NC+1
      CALL COPYA(D(I),C(K))
    1 M=N
      RETURN
      END
```

9.3 PROGRAM STLOAD - PLAIN-LANGUAGE CROSS-REFERENCING

9.3.1 Purpose

This program loads STATCAT data banks. If the special-purpose subroutine DATA(XREF) is used, a plain-language data bank can be cross-referenced.

Figure 9.31 contains a system flow-chart for the subroutine DATA(XREF). The main program STLOAD and executive subroutine CLOAD are exactly as defined in 4.2, although some items are fixed.

9.3.2 Input Data

Item	Level	Type	Function	See
1	0	A	File control card (Input + Output)	Below + 3.2
2	0	B	Data Starter	Below, 9.1 + 3.3
3	0	C	Data Description Segment (Identical to 9.1)	9.1 + 3.4

1 - File Control Card

The input file must be a STATCAT plain-language data file. The output will be the same file, with full cross-references.

Data Starter

Card Layout - Data Starter - STLOAD

ABCCCDDDEEEEEEEEF..COLS 17-56..FG..COLS 57-72..GHHHHIIII

Columns	Item	Function	See
1	A	Output control index	Below
2	B	Data Checking Control Index	4.3 + Below
3 - 5	C	Number of data columns (Set to 21)	9.1
6 - 8	D	Value for number of classes (Set to 10)	9.1
9 - 16	E	Non-value (Set to -1.)	9.1
17 - 56	F	Title of STATCAT Data Bank output	9.1
57 - 72	G	Auxiliary security Key	9.1
73 - 76	H	Security Key	4.2 + 3.2
77 - 80	I	Data Bank Name	4.2 + 3.2

A - Output Control Index

This index specifies the output produced during the running of the executive subroutine.

ALTERNATIVES

A = 0, blank, or   ; All entries referred to printed, with names of
    non-numeric   records providing the cross-reference.

A = 1 - 9   ; No output.

DEFAULT value ; As for A = 0.

9.3.3 Input Example

Figure 9.32 is a summary of the input structure for one run of STLOAD using DATA(XREF). Figure 9.33 lists the necessary input cards.

9.3.4 Output Example

Figure 9.34 is a summary of the output structure corresponding to the input structure of 9.32. Figure 9.35 is a page-by-page summary of the output corresponding to the specific example given in 9.3.3. The listing produced during construction of the new data storage segment is in the standard index format. (In fact, it forms the Subject/Reference index following the bibliography.)

9.3.5 Subroutine DATA (XREF)

Subroutine DATA(XREF) differs from the previously described DATA subroutines in that, instead of reading one entry at each call, and returning to the main program, it constructs a complete data storage segment, and stores it, returning to the main program only to load the data terminator, check the data bank if required, and re-start or stop as required.

DATA(XREF) operates in several distinct phases. First, it sweeps through the input STATCAT data bank, collecting all cross-references to or from records. It stores these in an array, record numbers for records referred to in ascending numerical order, with the numbers of records referring to each, following, also in ascending numerical order. (But tagged with a negative sign to distinguish them).

After a complete sweep through the input STATCAT data bank, it establishes the highest record number for which it knows that it has full information, and, in a second sweep, transfers all records, up to and including that record into the output file, deleting all original 'is-referred-to-by' entries and replacing them with similar entries placed immediately before the 'END-OF-RECORD' marker, containing all records referring to the current record, from whatever source they were obtained. When the sweep is completed, a check is made for any records referred to but not included in the STATCAT input data bank. These are added to the output STATCAT data bank, with an appropriate warning message. If there are any further cross-references a new data sweep is carried out, and the process continued until a sweep is made in which the storage for cross-references is not completely filled.

As listed here, the subroutine is limited to 499 references to any one record. Consult the comments in the listing if this limit must be increased. (If more records than 499 refer to a single other record, a warning message will be produced, and excess references will be dropped from the output STATCAT data bank)

After writing the last record to the output medium, the subroutine returns to the main program with the array D completely filled with non-values, signalling the end of the data bank. Because there have been no previous calls of the data subroutine, the program will print the message '0 ENTRIES (CALLS OF SUBROUTINE DATA)'. Disregard this message.

Figure 9.31 - System Flow-Chart - DATA(XREF)

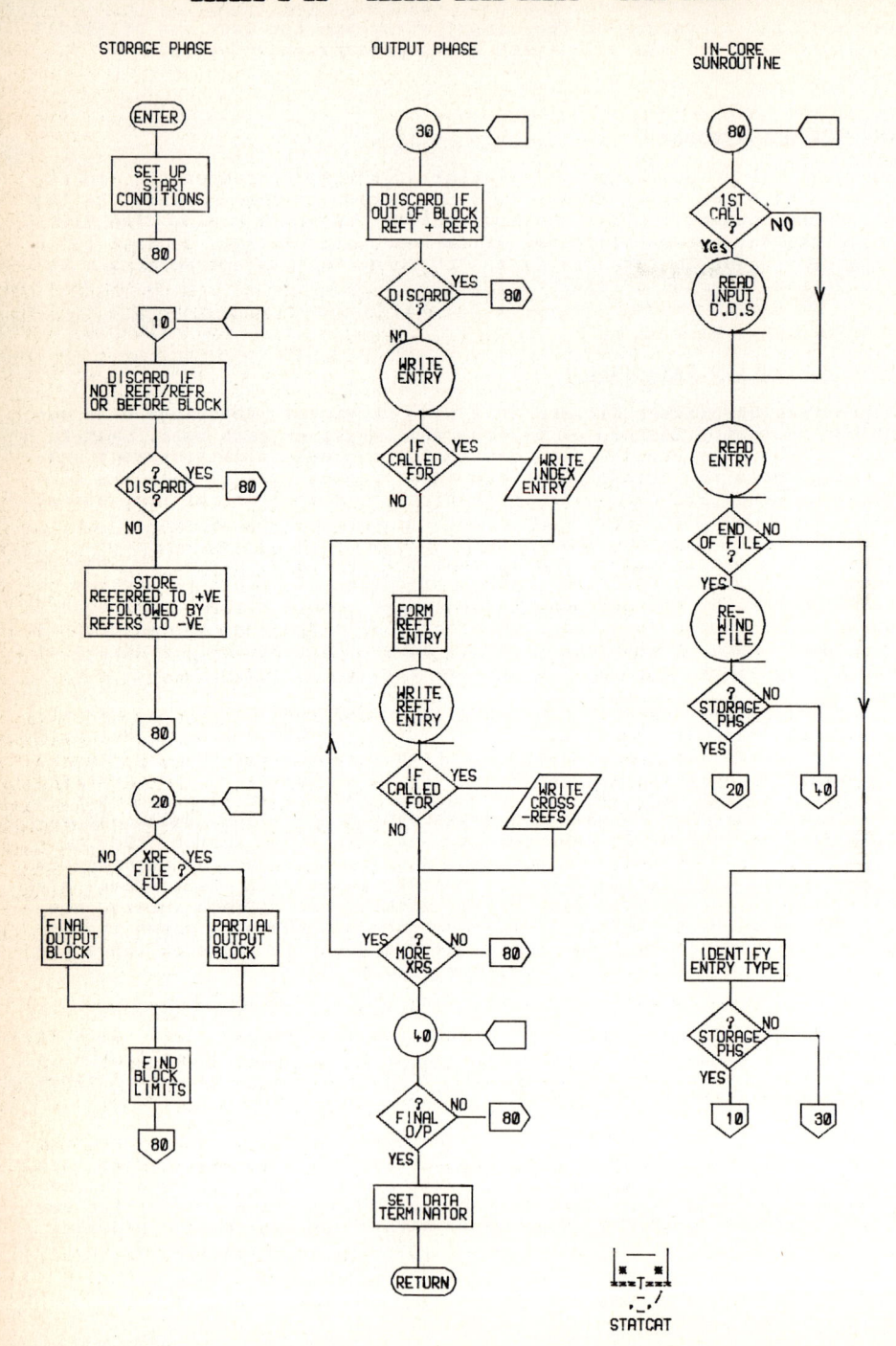

STORAGE PHASE / OUTPUT PHASE / IN-CORE SUBROUTINE

STATCAT

Figure 9.32 - STLOAD - Input Structure

```
        Level
  0     1     2     3     4     5     6     7     8     9
FILE CONTROL CARD
DATA STARTER
DATA DESCRIPTION SEGMENT
STOP
```


Figure 9.33 - STLOAD - Input Example using DATA (XREF)

```
---------1---------2---------3---------4---------5----///--7---------8
**STLOADPLAN      DUFF
40 21  5 -1.0     PLAIN LANGUAGE STATCAT DEMONSTRATION            DUFF
       1 1 4DATA COLUMNS  1 -  4 (COMPRESSED)                     DUMMY
       2 5 8DATA COLUMNS  5 -  8 (COMPRESSED)                     DUMMY
       3 912DATA COLUMNS  9 - 12 (COMPRESSED)                     DUMMY
       41316DATA COLUMNS 13 - 16 (COMPRESSED)                     DUMMY
       51720DATA COLUMNS 17 - 20 (COMPRESSED)                     DUMMY
       62124DATA COLUMNS 21 - 24 (COMPRESSED)                     DUMMY
       72528DATA COLUMNS 25 - 28 (COMPRESSED)                     DUMMY
       82932DATA COLUMNS 29 - 32 (COMPRESSED)                     DUMMY
       93336DATA COLUMNS 33 - 36 (COMPRESSED)                     DUMMY
      103740DATA COLUMNS 37 - 40 (COMPRESSED)                     DUMMY
      114144DATA COLUMNS 41 - 44 (COMPRESSED)                     DUMMY
      124548DATA COLUMNS 45 - 48 (COMPRESSED)                     DUMMY
      134952DATA COLUMNS 49 - 52 (COMPRESSED)                     DUMMY
      145356DATA COLUMNS 53 - 56 (COMPRESSED)                     DUMMY
      155760DATA COLUMNS 57 - 60 (COMPRESSED)                     DUMMY
      166164DATA COLUMNS 61 - 64 (COMPRESSED)                     DUMMY
      176568DATA COLUMNS 65 - 68 (COMPRESSED)                     DUMMY
      186972DATA COLUMNS 69 - 72 (COMPRESSED)                     DUMMY
      197376DATA COLUMNS 73 - 76 (COMPRESSED)                     DUMMY
      207780DATA COLUMNS 77 - 80 (COMPRESSED)                     DUMMY
       21RCRDRECORD NUMBER         (COMPRESSED)                   DUMMY
END OF DATA DESCRIPTION SEGMENT
STOP
---------1---------2---------3---------4---------5----///--7---------8
```

Figure 9.34 - STLOAD - Output Structure

```
For each     )     : File Control Record
output file  )       Data Starter Record
                     Data Description Record
                      for each   )  : Data Column Title
                      data column)    Complementary Information
                     Data Storage Record
                      for each entry : index listing
                     Data Terminator Record
```

Figure 9.35 - STLOAD - Output Example page-by-page Listing

Page	Contents	Origin
1-2	File Control/Program Title	FIFI/LDAP/STLOAD
	Data Description record	LDDS
3	Data Storage Segment	WOWN/CLOAD
4	Data Handling Instruction (STOP)	LDHI

```
      SUBROUTINE DATA (D,NQ,FORM)
C DATA    (SEE  9.3 ) SERVICE       USER INPUT - CROSS-REFERENCING
      DIMENSION D(NQ),FORM(80),NS(500),C(50)
      COMMON /STCT/MED1,MED2,MED3,MED4,MED5,MED6,MED13,Q,V(20),TT(30)
C NIS = NO. IN STORE                 MIS = MAXIMUM IN STORE
C XOP = LAST RECORD OUTPUT(VALUE)    XCR = LAST COMPLETE XREF
C NS STORES +VE RECORD WITH - RECORDS REFERRING TO IT
C IGO = PHASE OF SUBROUTINE          LT = ENTRY TYPE
C  0 START UP                         -
C  1 COLLECTION OF X-REFS            PRIMARY RECORD
C  2 END OF COLLECTION               SECONDARY
C  3 PARTIAL OUTPUT                  REFERRED TO BY   (REFR)
C  4 END OF PARTIAL OUTPUT           REFERED TO BY - OTHERS
C  5 FINAL OUTPUT                    REFERS TO        (REFT)
C  6 END OF FINAL OUTPUT             REFERS TO        OTHERS
C  7                                 TEXT             (TEXT)
C  8                                 TEXT             OTHERS
C  9                                 END OF RECORD
      DATA C/1H ,1HA,1HB,1HC,1HD,1HE,1HF,1HG,1HH,1HI,1HJ,1HK,1HL,1HM,1HN
     1,1HO,1HP,1HQ,1HR,1HS,1HT,1HU,1HV,1HW,1HX,1HY,1HZ,1H ,1H ,1H ,1HO,1
     2H1,1H2,1H3,1H4,1H5,1H6,1H7,1H8,1H9,1H+,1H-,1H/,1H*,1H(,1H),1H,,1H.
     3,1H=,1HF/
      XOP = 0.1
      MIS = 500
      IGO = 1
      NIS = 0
      XCR = XOP
      WRITE(MED2,900)
      GO TO 80
C COLLECTION PHASE        (NB REFERS TO NA)
   10 IF(D(NQ).LE.XOP.OR.LT.LE.2.OR.LT.GE.7) GO TO 80
      I1 = NQ
      I2 = NQ
      J1 = 2
      J2 = NQ - 1
      IF(LT.LT.4) GO TO 111
      I1 = 2
      I2 = NQ - 1
      J1 = NQ
      J2 = NQ
  111 DO 19 IX = I1,I2
      NA = D(IX)+0.1
      IF(NA.EQ.0) GO TO 19
      DO 18 JX = J1,J2
      NB = D(JX) + 0.1
      IF(NB.EQ.0) GO TO 18
      ISP = 0
   11 ISP = ISP + 1
      IF(ISP.GT.MIS)GO TO 18
      IF(ISP.GT.NIS) NS(ISP) = NA
      IF(ISP.GT.NIS) NIS = NIS + 1
      IF(NS(ISP).LT.0) GO TO 11
C NA IS BEFORE/AT/AFTER NS(ISP)
      IF(NA-NS(ISP)) 12,14,11
   12 NIS = NIS + 1
      IF(NIS.GT.MIS) NIS = MIS
      K = NIS + 1
   13 K = K - 1
      IF(K.EQ.ISP)NS(K) = NA
      IF(K.GT.ISP)NS(K) = NS(K-1)
      IF(K.GT.ISP) GO TO 13
   14 JSP = ISP
   15 JSP = JSP + 1
```

```
      IF(JSF.GT.MIS) GO TO 18
      IF(JSF.GT.NIS)NS(JSF) = -NB
      IF(JSF.GT.NIS) NIS = NIS + 1
      IF(NS(JSF).GT.0) GO TO 16
C NB BEF/AT/AFTER NS(ISF)
      IF(NB+NS(JSF))16,18,15
   16 NIS = NIS + 1
      IF(NIS.GT.MIS)NIS = MIS
      K = NIS + 1
   17 K = K - 1
      IF(K.EQ.JSF) NS(JSF) = -NB
      IF(K.GT.JSF) NS(K) = NS(K-1)
      IF(K.GT.JSF) GO TO 17
   18 CONTINUE
   19 CONTINUE
      GO TO 80
C END OF COLLECTION PHASE
   20 IF(NIS.EQ.MIS) GO TO 25
      IGO = 5
      K = NIS
   21 K = K-1
      IF(K.EQ.0) GO TO 27
      IF(NS(K).LT.0) GO TO 21
      XCR = NS(K)
      XCR = XCR + 0.1
      NA = 1
      GO TO 80
   25 IGO = 3
      K = NIS
   26 K = K - 1
      IF(NS(K).LT.0) GO TO 26
      NIS = K
      GO TO 21
   27 WRITE(MED2,902) NS(1),MIS
      K = 2
      NIS = MIS
      GO TO 21
C OUTPUT PHASE
C DISCARD OUT OF RANGE(EXCEPT LAST RUN) + PRESENT REFR ENTRIES
   30 IF(D(NQ).GT.XCR.AND.IGO.EQ.5) GO TO 32
      IF(D(NQ).GT.XCR.OR.D(NQ).LT.XOP) GO TO 80
      IF(LT.EQ.3.OR.LT.EQ.4) GO TO 80
      NB = D(NQ) + 0.1
      NA = 1
   31 IF(NB-NS(NA))32,134,33
C NORMAL OUTPUT
   32 WRITE(MED4) D
      GO TO (80,80,80,40,80,40),IGO
C STORED CROSS-REFERENCE BEFORE CURRENT
   33 NA = NA + 1
      IF(NS(NA)) 33,33,31
  134 IF(V(1).GT.0.5.OR.LT.GT.1) GO TO   35
C     OUTPUT INDEX ENTRY
      I = 1
      DO 34 J = 3,NQ
      CALL UNPACK(D(J-1),FORM(I),4,C,50)
      K = I
      M = I + 3
      I = I + 4
      DO 34 L = K,M
      CALL COMPA(FORM(L),C(1),LL)
      IF(LL.NE.1) NC = L
   34 CONTINUE
```

```
      IF(V(10).GT.50.) WRITE(MED2,900)
      IF(V(10).GT.50.) V(10) = 0.
      V(10) = V(10) + 1.
      WRITE(MED2,903)
      WRITE(MED2,910) (FORM(I),I=1,NC)
      LOP = 1
      LK = 51
   35 IF(LT.LT.9) GO TO 32
      FORM(1) = 2262818
      FORM(NQ) = NS(NA)
      NS(NA) = 0
   36 DO 37 I = 3,NQ
      FORM(I-1) = 0.
      IF(NA.EQ.NIS) GO TO 37
      IF(NS(NA+1).GE.0) GO TO 37
      NA = NA + 1
      FORM(I-1) = -NS(NA)
   37 CONTINUE
      WRITE(MED4) (FORM(I),I=1,NQ)
      IF(V(1).GT.0.5) GO TO 39
      DO 38 I = 3,NQ
      DX = FORM(I-1)
      IF(DX.LT.0.5) GO TO 38
      L = 2
      IF(DX.GT.49.5) L = L + 1
      IF(DX.GT.2499.5) L = L + 1
      IF(DX.GT.124999.5) L = L + 1
      L50 = L + 50
      CALL UNPACK(DX,FORM(51),L,C,50)
      IF(I.GT.3.OR.LOP.GT.1) CALL COPYA(FORM(51),C(47))
      IF(NC+L.LT.80) WRITE(MED2,910) (C(1),K=1,NC),(FORM(K),K=LK,L50)
      NC = NC + L50-LK + 1
      LK = 51
      LOP = LOP + 1
      IF(FORM(L50).EQ.C(42)) LK = 52
      IF(NC.LT.80) GO TO 38
      V(10) = V(10) + 1.
      WRITE(MED2,903)
      NC = L
      WRITE(MED2,910) (FORM(K),K=52,L50)
   38 CONTINUE
   39 FORM(1) = 0
      IF(NA+1.GT.NIS) GO TO 32
      IF(NS(NA+1).LT.0) GO TO 36
      NA = NA + 1
      GO TO 31
C END OF OUTPUT - INTRODUCE ANY RECORDS REFERRED TO BUT NOT PRESENT
   40 XOP = XCR
      LOP = 1
      DO 41 NA = 1,NIS
      N = NS(NA)
      IF(N.LE.0) GO TO 41
      IF(V(1).LT.0.5) WRITE(MED2,901) N
      D(NQ) = N
      FORM(1) = N
      FORM(2) = N
      DO 42 I = 3,NQ
   42 FORM(I) = 0
      FORM(NQ) = N
      NS(NA) = 0
      WRITE(MED4) (FORM(I),I=1,NQ)
      FORM(1) = 2262818
      IF(LL.NE.1) NC = I
```

```
      IF(V(1).GT.0.5) GO TO 36
      CALL UNPACK(FORM(2),FORM(51),4,C,50)
      WRITE(MED2,903)
      WRITE(MED2,910) (FORM(I),I=51,54)
      NC = 4
      LK = 51
      LOP = 1
      GO TO 36
   41 CONTINUE
C IF FINAL OUTPUT TERMINATE,OTHERWISE NEW INPUT SWEEP
      IF(IGO.EQ.6) GO TO 60
      IGO = 1
      NIS = 0
      GO TO 80
C END OF FINAL OUTPUT
   60 D(NQ) = Q
      WRITE(MED2,900)
      RETURN
C INTERNAL SUBROUTINE TO FIND AND CLASSIFY NEXT ENTRY
   80 DO 81 I = 1,NQ
      IF(D(I).NE.Q) GO TO 83
   81 CONTINUE
      REWIND MED3
      READ(MED3) NQ,NALT,Q,(X,I=1,16)
      DO 82 J = 1,NQ
   82 READ(MED3) (X,I=1,19),(X,I=1,NALT),NX,NX,X
      LT = 1
   83 READ(MED3) D
      IF(LT.EQ.9) LT = 1
      DO 84 I = 2,NQ
      IF(D(I-1).NE.Q) GO TO 85
   84 CONTINUE
      LT = 9
      IF(D(NQ).NE.Q) GO TO 85
C END OF DATA BANK
      REWIND MED3
      IGO = IGO + 1
      IF(IGO-3) 20,40,40
   85 NN = D(1) + 0.1
      IF(NN.EQ.2262820) LT = 5
      IF(NN.EQ.2262818) LT = 3
      IF(NN.EQ.2513720) LT = 7
      IF(NN.EQ.0.AND.LT.LT.9) LT = (LT+1)/2*2
      IF(IGO-3) 10,30,30
  900 FORMAT(1H1)
  901 FORMAT(15H MISSING RECORD ,I10,14H ADDED TO FILE)
  902 FORMAT (8H RECORD , I10,5H HAS ,I4,70H OR MORE CROSS-REFERENCES -
     1  SOME WILL BE LOST IF NS IS NOT INCREASED                      )
  903 FORMAT(1H )
  910 FORMAT(1H+,18X,80A1)
      END
```

9.4 PROGRAM STWORD - KEYWORDS AND SOUNDEX CODES

9.4.1 Purpose

This program selects and prints records from STATCAT plain-language data banks. It can be used to print (or punch) all records containing certain words, or particular combinations of words, certain specified records or records referred to by or referring to other records.

Figure 9.41a contains system flow-charts for the main program STWORD and the executive subroutine CWORD. Figure 9.41b contains system flow-charts for the subroutines LWORD, which loads the keyword definition, CLWORD, which determines whether a record is to be output (see 9.4.5) and the function SNDX, which generates a 'Soundex code' from a name (See 9.4.6)

9.4.2 Input Data

Item	Level	Format	Function	See
1	0	A	File control	3.2
2	4	Special	Record specification	Below
3	9	H	Data handling instruction	Below + 3.8

2 - Record Specification

The record specification is a module which specifies which keywords or proper names should be searched for, which records, by name or number should be output, etc. The module contains a title card, record specification cards and an END card.

MODULE STRUCTURE

```
TITLE CARD
RECORD SPECIFICATION CARD
RECORD SPECIFICATION CARD
RECORD SPECIFICATION CARD
RECORD SPECIFICATION CARD
RECORD SPECIFICATION CARD
RECORD SPECIFICATION CARD
etc....
END of module card
```

Title Card

This is a standard title card, the first 40 characters being retained as the module title. If this is an END card, the system will step back to read a new file control card.

Record Specification card

These cards specify the groups of conditions which must be satisfied if the record is to be printed.

Card Layout - Record Specification - STWORD

AAAABBBBCCCCDDDDDDDDDDDDDDDDDDDDDDDDDDDDDDDDDD........

Columns on card	Item Code	FORTRAN Type	Function	See

1- 4	A	A	Logical Connector	Below
5 - 8	B	A	Specification Code	Below
9 - 12	C	A	Condition Code	Below
13 - 80	D	A	Complementary Inofrmation	Below

A - Logical Connector

This is a four-character code, defining how the condition specified on this card is connected with the previous conditions. It may be : -
".IF." "AND." ".OR."

The code ".IF." means that the condition defined on the card must be satisfied for the record to be included in the specification.

The code "AND." has the same significance, but is used for the second and following cards.

The code ".OR." is followed by the first of a new set of conditions. If, at the time an ".OR." or an END card is found, all conditions have been satisfied the record is accepted. Once a record has been accepted no further logical conditions are tested.

B - Specification Code

This is a four character code which defines the type of specification being applied by the card. Eight possible types are available.

- RCNA and RCNO specify the current records by their names or numbers (9.1.7) respectively.

- RFNA and RFNO specify all records referring to the current records specified by their names or numbers respectively.

- RTNA and RTNO specify all records referred to by the current records specified by their names or numbers respectively.

- SNDX indicates that the complementary information contains up to seventeen proper names of which the "Soundex codes" (9.4.6) are to be matched with the "Soundex Code" for the record.

- WORD indicates that the complementary information is a keyword to be matched with the record (see 9.4.7)

C - Condition Code

This is a four-character code specifying the logical condition to be applied to the item specified by the specification B. The usual six codes are available : -

".GE." ".EQ." ".LE." ".GT." ".NE." ".LT."

These have their usual meanings. (For the codes SNDX or WORD, the conditions "Greater than" and "Less than" are undefined, because the complementary information is not numeric. For SNDX or WORD the codes ".GE." and ".LE." are equivalent to ".EQ." and ".GT." and ".LT." are are equivalent to ".NE.".

For all specification codes for which the complementary information may specify several possibilities (all except WORD) the conditions ".GE.", ".EQ.", ".LE.", ".GT." and ".LT." are considered to be satisfied they if they hold for any of the possibilities, but the condition ".NE." is satisfied only if it holds for all the possibilities specified in the complementary information.

D - Complementary Information

The way in which the complementary information is used depends on the specification code; -

RCNA, RFNA, RTNA

Up to seventeen four-character record names - with no separators - to be compared as laid down in the specification code.

RCNO, RFNO, RFNA

Up to seventeen numerical values, separated by at least one blank - to be converted to names and compared as laid down in the specification code.

SNDX

Up to seventeen names, separated by at least one blank, which are converted to Soundex codes as described in 9.4.6 and compared with the Soundex code derived from the present record, according to the condition code.

WORD

A single string of up to 68 characters, which is matched to the record according to the rules for keyword comparison, given in 9.4.7. following. The system will normally search the primary entry, all secondary entries and all text, but the data handling instruction may be used to restrict the search.

Data Handling Instruction

Card Layout - Data Handling Instruction - STWORD

A BCCCDDDEEEEEEEE EFFFFFFFFFGGGGGGGGGGGGGGGGGGHHHHHHH.....etc

Columns	Item	Function	See
1	A	Output control index	Below
2	B	Auxiliary control index	Below
3 - 5	C	First card column searched	Below
6 - 8	D	Last card column searched	Below
9 - 16	E	Output Device	Below
17 - 24	F	Not used	-
25 - 40	G	Auxiliary Security Key	9.2
41 - 80	H	Run Title (KEPT)	-

A - Output Control Index

This index controls the choice of the type of listing that will be produced, and the extent of the search for key-words.

ALTERNATIVES

A = 0, blank : All entries searched for key-words.
(DEFAULT)   Output by WOWN (PLAN)
A = 1   : Primary entry only searched for keywords.
                Output by WOWN (PLAN)
A = 2   : Primary and secondary entries searched for key-words.
                Output by WOWN (PLAN)

A = 3   : Primary, secondary and text extries searched for key-words.
              Output by WOWN(PLAN)
A = 4   : Text entries only searched for keywords.
              Output by WOWN(PLAN)
A = 5   : Primary entry only searched for keywords.
              Output by WCAR
A = 6   : Primary and secondary entries searched for key-words.
              Output by WCAR
A = 7   : Primary, secondary and text extries searched for key-words.
              Output by WCAR
A = 8   : Text entries only searched for keywords.
              Output by WCAR
A = 9   : As for A = 0

DEFAULT value = 0 (0, blank or non-numeric characters)

B - Auxiliary Control Index

This index controls the amount of detail included in an output listing, Its exact meaning depends on the value of the Output control index A.

If A is non-numeric, blank 0 to 4 or 9 see 9.1.4 for the use of B with WOWN(PLAN)

If A = 5 to 8 the following alternatives apply : -

ALTERNATIVES

B = 0 , blank   : Records specified are listed.
or non-numeric
B = 1   : Records specified are output on medium E.
B = 2   : Records specified listed and output on medium E.
B = 3   : Records not specified listed.
B = 4   : Records not specified output on medium E
B = 5   : Records not specified listed and output on medium E.
B = 6 - 9   : As for 0

DEFAULT value = 0 (0, 6-9, blank or non-numeric character)

C - First Card Column to be Listed

This is the number of the card column at which the key-word search routine will start looking for matching.

DEFAULT value = 5

D - Last Card Column Listed

This is the number of the last column which will be included in the search for key-words.

DEFAULT value = 80

E - Output Device

This value gives the numerical code for the peripheral used by WCAR. Normally this will be a card punch, but other devices capable of handling eighty-character records without line controls may be used. This value is available to the user-written subroutine WOWN (9.4.5).

DEFAULT value :

If set to blank, zero, or a non-numeric value the value of MEDP set in the main program STWORD will be used.

9.4.3 Input Example

Figure 9.42 is a summary of the input structure for three runs of STWORD. Figure 9.43 is a listing of the input cards required to carry out these three runs.

9.4.4 Output Example

Figure 9.44 is a general summary of the output for this program, indented to correspond to the overall program structure. Figure 9.45 is a page-by-page listing for the example output. Figure 9.46 shows the record definition, data handling instruction and complete listing for the first run. Figure 9.47 shows the output for the second run: - record specification, data handling instruction and partial listing. Figure 9.48 shows the complete output for the third run.

9.4.5 Keywords

If a specification code WORD is used the complementary information will be a string of characters, which will be matched to the current record at all possible positions in the primary, secondary and text entries stored, subject to the restrictions imposed by the data handling instruction.

The following conventions apply within the string : -

- Except as specified below each character in the string must match the corresponding character in the STATCAT data bank.

- The character . in the string must correspond to a blank in the entry, or to the end of the entry. Other blanks in the string and in the entry are ignored.

- The character + in the string may match any letter (A - Z) in the entry.

- The character - in the string may match any digit (0 - 9) in the entry.

- The character * in the string may match any letter or digit in the entry.

- The character = in the string may match any special character (+ - * / ( ) = . , F) in the entry.

- The character / in the string may match any character in the entry, except a blank.

- The character , in the string represents a suspension of the matching process until the first occurrence of a character matching the next character in the string. (The suspension may be of nil length e.g. A,B in the string will match AB in the entry.) Several commas may occur in one string.

- A string may carry over from one entry onto a second, but not onto a third. A string may not carry over from one record to the next.

9.4.6 Soundex Codes

The function SNDX, for which a system flow-chart is given in Figure 9.41, provides a 'Soundex code' from a string of characters. It is used by LWORD to convert a series of names for which it is desired to search in the data bank, and by CLWORD to convert the first word, apart from the record name, in a record, under the hypothesis that this represents a proper name.

A Soundex code is a number derived from a name, in such a fashion that the most frequently confused names may have the greatest probability of having the same code. This allows the system to retrieve misspelt names (authors, clients or other individuals) at the price of a certain number of 'false drops'. In general, users prefer to retrieve a few extra unwanted records rather than to fail to find records they want.

The rules for constructing a Soundex code (slightly modified for computer use) are as follows:

- Code the initial letter of the word (1-26).

- To obtain the first following digit:-

    1 - Discard A, E, I, O, U, Y, W, H and all letters identical to the preceding letter.

    2 - Code B, P, F, V = 1

    3 - Code C, G, J, K, Q, S, X, Z = 2

    4 - Code T, D = 3

    5 - Code L = 4

    6 - Code M, N = 5

    7 - Code R = 6

- Repeat for three more digits. (Code consists of initial character plus four digits) If end of word is reached before four digits have been generated fill the unallocated spaces with zeros. (e.g. BROWN = 26500)

Figure 9.41a - System Flow-Charts - STWORD and CWORD

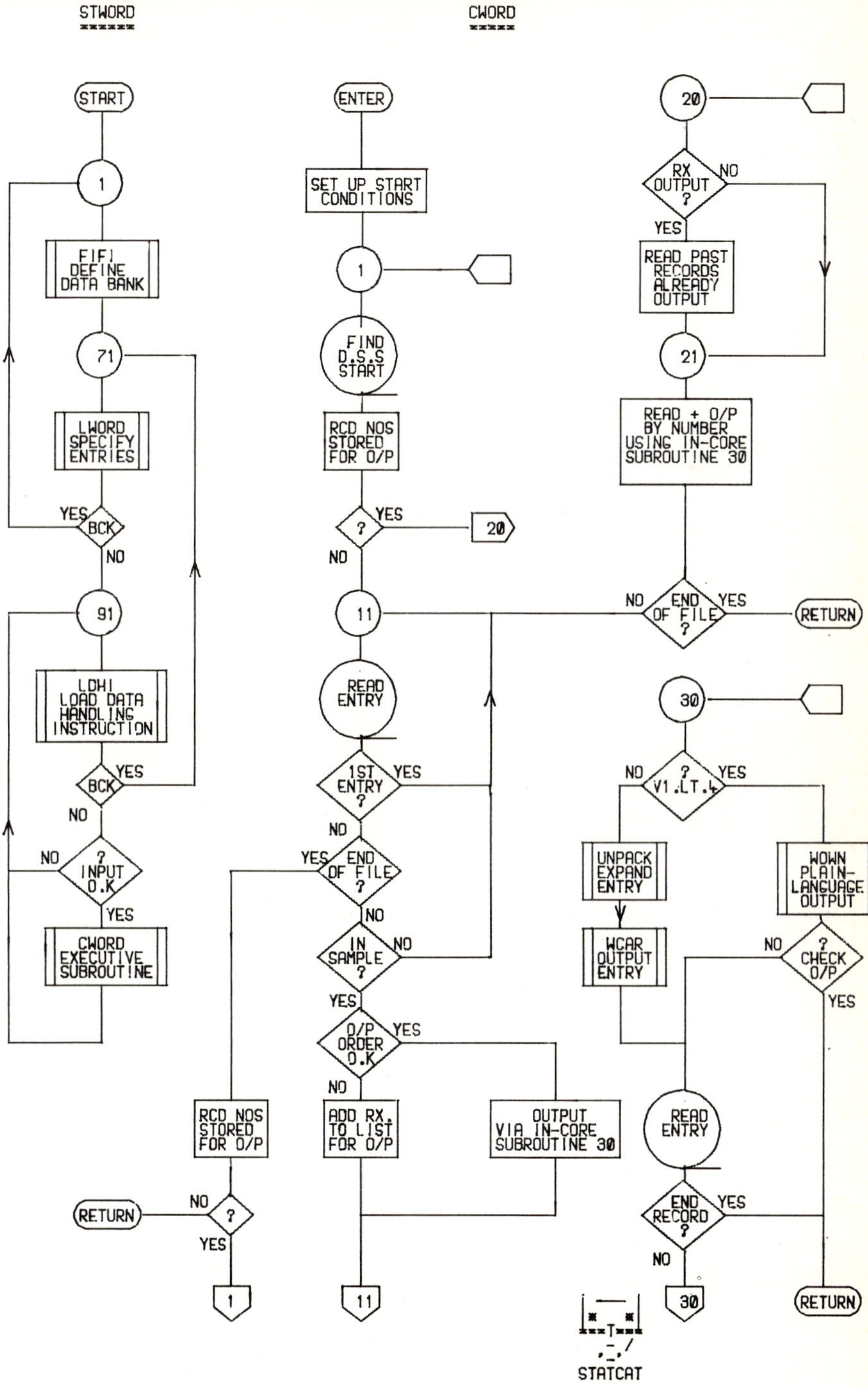

Figure 9.41b - System Flow-Charts - LWORD, CLWORD and SNDX

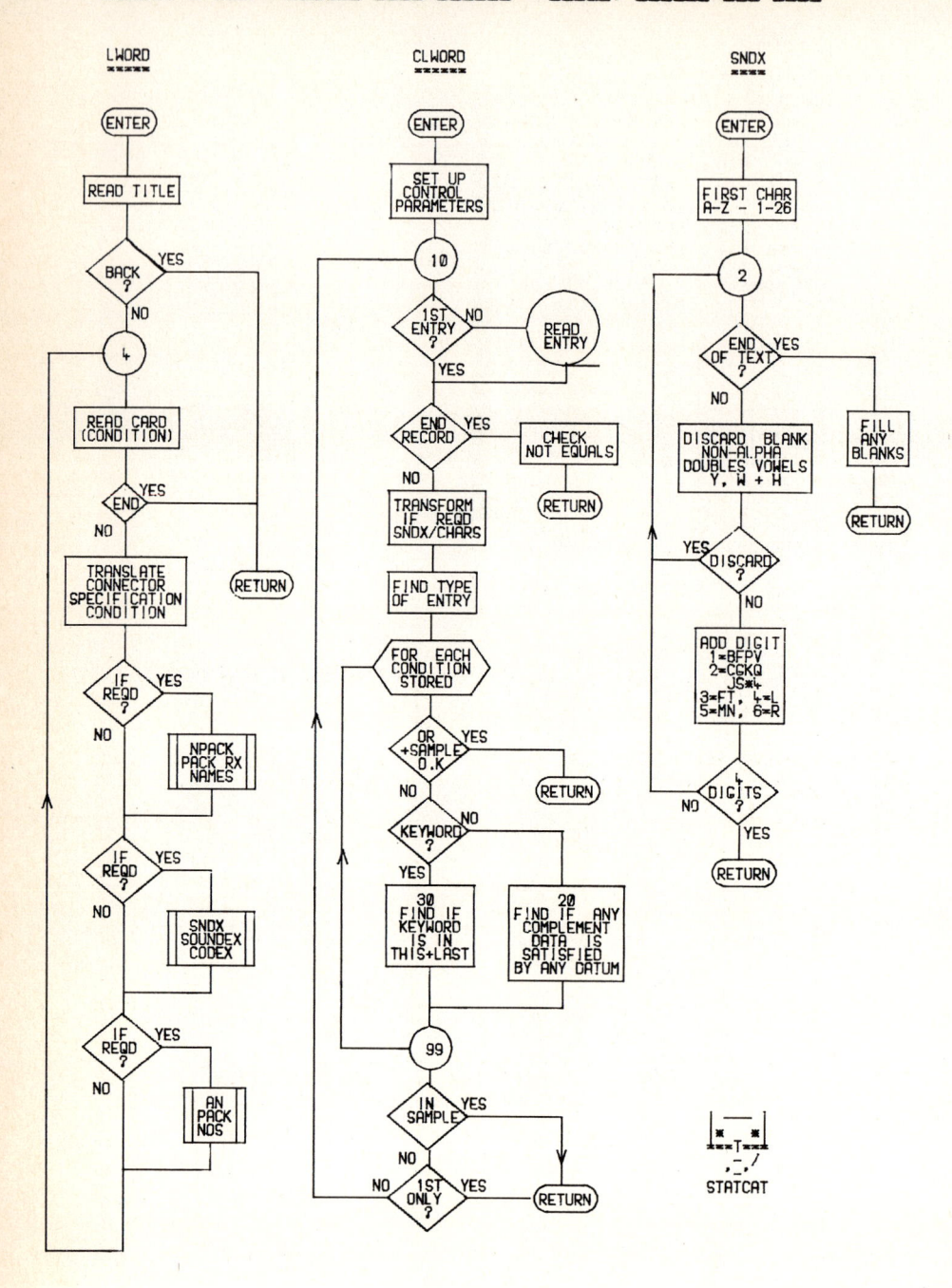

Figure 9.42 - STWORD - Input Structure

```
        Level
0    1    2    3    4    5    6    7    8    9
FILE CONTROL CARD
    KEYWORD SPECIFICATION
        DATA HANDLING INSTRUCTION
        BACK TO READ NEW KEYWORD SPECIFICATION
    KEYWORD SPECIFICATION
        DATA HANDLING INSTRUCTION
        BACK TO READ NEW KEYWORD SPECIFICATION
    KEYWORD SPECIFICATION
        DATA HANDLING INSTRUCTION
        STOP
```

Figure 9.43 - STWORD - Input Example

```
---------1---------2---------3---------4---------5---------6---------7--
**STWORDPLAN
LOOKING FOR KENDALL - MIS-SPELT
.IF.SNDX.EQ.KENDAL
END OF RECORD SPECIFICATION
17                              IN FIRST ENTRY BUT PRINTING ALL
BACK TO READ NEW RECORD SPECIFICATION
ANY REFERENCE TO REGRESSION IN TEXT
.IF.WORD.EQ.REGRESSION
END OF RECORD SPECIFICATION
40                              ANYWHERE, PRINTING TITLE ONLY
BACK TO READ NEW RECORD SPECIFICATION
ANY USE OF KEYWORD REGN
.IF.RTNA.EQ.REGN
END OF RECORD SPECIFICATION
02                              REDUCED FORMAT - LESS TEXT
STOP
---------1---------2---------3---------4---------5---------6---------7--
```

Figure 9.44 - STWORD - Output Structure

```
For each   ) : File Control Record output file )   File Parameters
               Data Description
               For each) : Keyword Input Record
               Subset  )   For each      ) Input Record
                           Data Handling ) For each) Listing
                           Instruction   ) entry in) as
                                         subset   ) specified
```

Figure 9.45 - STWORD - Output Example page-by-page Listing

Page	Contents	Origin
1-2	File Control Record	FIFI
	Program Title	STWORD
	File Parameters	LDAP
2	Record Specification	LWORD
	Data Handling Instruction	LDHI
3- 4	Record Listing	CWORD/WOWN
5	End of Run Message	CWORD
	Data Handling Instruction (BACK)	LDHI
6	Record Specification	LWORD
	Data Handling Instruction	LDHI
7	Record Listing	CWORD/WOWN
8	End of Run Message	CWORD
	Data Handling Instruction (BACK)	LDHI
9	Record Specification	LWORD
	Data Handling Instruction	LDHI
10	Record Listing	CWORD/WOWN
11	End of Run Message	CWORD
	Data Handling Instruction (STOP)	LDHI

Figure 9.46 - STWORD - Output Example - First Run

```
RECORD SPECIFICATION - LOOKING FOR KENDALL - MIS-SPELT        COMMENT
  .IF.SNDX.EQ.KENDLE
  END OF RECORD SPECIFICATION

              DATA HANDLING INSTRUCTION - ECHO PRINT

ABCCCDDDEEEEEEEEFFFFFFFGGGGGGGGGGGGGGGHHHHHHHHHHHHHHHHHHHHHHHHHHHHHHHHH
  17                   XXXXXXXXXXXXXXXIN FIRST ENTRY BUT PRINTING ALL

              OUTPUT CONTROL INDEX  =      1
              GENERAL CONTROL INDEX =      7
         NUMBER OF FIRST COLUMN OUTPUT =   5
         NUMBER OF LAST COLUMN OUTPUT. =   80
         NUMBER OF OUTPUT DEVICE ...... =   0

   THE SYSTEM HAS STANDARDISED  2 CONTROL VALUES FROM THE DATA HANDLING INSTRUCTION          ** WARNING **

   PLEASE VERIFY THAT THE ASSUMPTIONS IT HAS MADE ARE CORRECT AND ADJUST STORAGE IF NECESSARY

INPUT ACCEPTED - LISTING COMMENCES


PLAIN LANGUAGE OUTPUT      -     LISTING OF ENTRIES
DATA BANK TITLE            -     PLAIN LANGUAGE STATCAT DEMONSTRATION
DATA BANK SUBSET TITLE     -     LOOKING FOR KENDALL - MIS-SPELT
RUN TITLE                  -     IN FIRST ENTRY BUT PRINTING ALL

   1588(  18)
                    KENDALL M G
                    MULTIVARIATE ANALYSIS
                    GRIFFIN
                    LONDON
                    1975
                    ISBN 0 85264 234 4

                    AN EXCELLENT REVIEW OF THE CURRENT STATE OF OPINION ON MULTIVARIATE
                    METHODS. DISCUSSES OBJECTIONS TO MAHALONOBIS DISTANCE IN
                    DISCRIMINANT ANALYSIS. NOT EXCESSIVELY MATHEMATICAL TREATMENT.
                    THE AUTHORS INFORMAL COMMENTS AT THE END OF EACH CHAPTER ARE
                    PARTICULARLY VALUABLE.

   REFERS TO          MUCA      MUDI     MURE
                    1677651. 1677709. 1678405.

   1388220(KENT)
                    KENDALL TAU STATISTIC
```

Figure 9.47 - STWORD - Output Example - Second Run

```
RECORD SPECIFICATION - ANY REFERENCE TO REGRESSION IN TEXT        COMMENT
   .IF.WORD.EQ.REGRESSION
   END OF RECORD SPECIFICATION

                       DATA HANDLING INSTRUCTION - ECHO PRINT

ABCCCDDDEEEEEEEEFFFFFFGGGGGGGGGGGGGGGHHHHHHHHHHHHHHHHHHHHHHHHHHHHHHHHHH
40                      XXXXXXXXXXXXXXXXANYWHERE, PRINTING TITLE ONLY


               OUTPUT CONTROL INDEX  =    4
               GENERAL CONTROL INDEX =    0
         NUMBER OF FIRST COLUMN OUTPUT =    5
         NUMBER OF LAST COLUMN OUTPUT. =   80
         NUMBER OF OUTPUT DEVICE ......=    0

      THE SYSTEM HAS STANDARDISED  2 CONTROL VALUES FROM THE DATA HANDLING INSTRUCTION      ** WARNING **
      PLEASE VERIFY THAT THE ASSUMPTIONS IT HAS MADE ARE CORRECT AND ADJUST STORAGE IF NECESSARY
INPUT ACCEPTED - LISTING COMMENCES



   BDRAPER N R + SMITH H,APPLIED REGRESSION ANALYSIS
      WILEY,NEW YORK 1966
   TEXTAN EXTREMELY VALUABLE GENERAL TEXT ON MULTIPLE LINEAR REGRESSION,
      COMPUTER-ORIENTED BUT GIVING A THOROUGH DISCUSSION OF MANUAL METHODS
      CONTAINS A VALUABLE DISCUSSION OF ALTERNATIVE VARIATE SELECTION
      METHODS, AND OF THE USE OF TRANSFORMS TO REDUCE NON-LINEARITY.
      PARTICULARLY STRONG ON THE ANALYSIS OF RESIDUALS.
   REFT BKGD MURER REGN RESI
```

Figure 9.48 - STWORD - Output Example - Third Run

```
RECORD SPECIFICATION - ANY USE OF KEYWORD REGN        COMMENT
   .IF.RTNA.EQ.REGN
   END OF RECORD SPECIFICATION

                       DATA HANDLING INSTRUCTION - ECHO PRINT

ABCCCDDDEEEEEEEEFFFFFFGGGGGGGGGGGGGGGHHHHHHHHHHHHHHHHHHHHHHHHHHHHHHHH
02                      XXXXXXXXXXXXXXXXREDUCED FORMAT - LESS TEXT


               OUTPUT CONTROL INDEX  =    0
               GENERAL CONTROL INDEX =    2
         NUMBER OF FIRST COLUMN OUTPUT =    5
         NUMBER OF LAST COLUMN OUTPUT. =   80
         NUMBER OF OUTPUT DEVICE ......=    0

      THE SYSTEM HAS STANDARDISED  2 CONTROL VALUES FROM THE DATA HANDLING INSTRUCTION      ** WARNING **
      PLEASE VERIFY THAT THE ASSUMPTIONS IT HAS MADE ARE CORRECT AND ADJUST STORAGE IF NECESSARY
INPUT ACCEPTED - LISTING COMMENCES


PLAIN LANGUAGE OUTPUT       -   LISTING OF ENTRIES
DATA BANK TITLE             -   PLAIN LANGUAGE STATCAT DEMONSTRATION
DATA BANK SUBSET TITLE      -   ANY USE OF KEYWORD REGN
RUN TITLE                   -   REDUCED FORMAT - LESS TEXT

    34(   4)   DIXON W J + MASSEY F J,INTRODUCTION TO STATISTICAL ANALYSIS
               MCGRAW-HILL,NEW YORK 1957, LOC 56-9805
     REFERS TO       ANOV     BKGD      FTES      PAST     REGN
                   160772.  277854.   800269.  2003470. 2262864.

    35(   5)   DRAPER N R + SMITH H,APPLIED REGRESSION ANALYSIS
               WILEY,NEW YORK 1966
     REFERS TO       BKGD     MLRG      PAST      REGN     RESI
                   277854. 1655907.  2003470. 2262864. 2263459.

   1580(  10)  KENDALL M G + STUART A,THE ADVANCED THEORY OF STATISTICS
               GRIFFIN,LONDON,3VOLS 1958-66
     REFERS TO       ANOV     BKGD      DESC      FTES     ORTH     PAST     REGN     XDES
                   160772.  277854.   513453.   800269. 1921008. 2003470. 2262864. 3010259.
```

```
C MASTER STWORD - LISTS RECORDS/ENTRIES SATISFYING KEYWORD SPECIFICATION
C   SUBROUTINES AND FUNCTIONS REQUIRED
C   NAME            TYPE              COMMENT
C   AN      (SEE 3.1 ) SERVICE    ALPHA - TO NUMERIC VALUE
C   COMPA   (SEE 3.1 ) SERVICE    COMPARES ALPHAMERIC VALUES
C   COPYA   (SEE 3.1 ) SERVICE    COPIES ALPHAMERIC VALUE
C   CLWORD  (SEE 9.4 ) SYSTEM     SELECT PLAIN-LANGUAGE RECORDS
C   CWORD   (SEE 9.4 ) EXECUTIVE  FIND+LIST PLAIN-LANGUAGE RECORDS
C   FIFI    (SEE 3.2 ) SYSTEM     ALLOCATES PERIPHERALS
C   IBL     (SEE 3.1 ) SERVICE    DETECTS BLANK,END AND STOP CARDS
C   ICH     (SEE 3.1 ) SERVICE    IDENTIFIES ALPHAMERIC CODES
C   LDAP    (SEE 3.3 ) SYSTEM     LOADS/CHECKS DATA BANK PARAMETERS
C   LDHI    (SEE 3.8 ) SYSTEM     LOADS/CHECKS DATA HANDLING INSTN
C   LWORD   (SEE 9.4 ) SYSTEM     SPECIAL PLAIN-LANGUAGE SPECIFICN
C   NPACK   (SEE 9.1 ) SERVICE    PACKS CODE DIGITS INTO INTEGER
C   SNDX    (SEE 9.4 ) SERVICE    PRODUCES SOUNDEX CODE
C   UNPACK  (SEE 9.2 ) SERVICE    UNPACKS DIGIT CODES FROM VALUE
C   WCAR    (SEE 5.1 ) SERVICE    OUTPUT PUNCHED CARDS
C SETTING OF ARRAY DIMENSIONS
C DIMENSIONS SPECIFIC TO PLAIN-LANGUAGE DATA BANKS
C COMMON VARIABLE STORAGE - REQUIRES AT LEAST 21*NF + 100 CELLS
C WHERE NF IS THE NUMBER OF CONDITIONS READ IN
C 20 PER CONDITION TO STORE IT + 1 TRUE/FALSE
C AT LEAST 100 FOR RECORD NUMBERS FOR OUTPUT
C DIMENSION A(NCAV)
      NCAV = 5000
      DIMENSION A(5000)
C THE FOLLOWING DIMENSIONS ARE FIXED
      DIMENSION D(21),TRT(10),FORM(80),C(50)
      DATA C/1H ,1HA,1HB,1HC,1HD,1HE,1HF,1HG,1HH,1HI,1HJ,1HK,1HL,1HM,1HN
     1,1HO,1HP,1HQ,1HR,1HS,1HT,1HU,1HV,1HW,1HX,1HY,1HZ,1H ,1H ,1H ,1HO,1
     2H1,1H2,1H3,1H4,1H5,1H6,1H7,1H8,1H9,1H+,1H-,1H/,1H*,1H(,1H),1H,,1H.
     3,1H=,1HF/
      COMMON /STCT/MED1,MED2,MED3,MED4,MED5,MED6,MED13,Q,V(20),TT(30)
      DATA PROG/4HWORD/
      MED1 = -1
C LEVEL 0 - SETTING UP
    1 CALL COPYA(TT(1),PROG)
      CALL FIFI
      IF(MED3.GT.0) WRITE(MED2,901)
      CALL LDAP(MED2,MED3,V,TT,Q,NQ,NALT,NQMAX,NALTMX,IGO)
      IF(IGO.GT.0) GO TO 1
      IF(NQ.NE.21)  V(10) = 7.
      IF(NQ.NE.21)  WRITE(MED2,902) NQ
C LEVEL 7 - LOAD PLAIN-LANGUAGE SPECIFICATION
   71 IF(V(10).GT.70.) V(10) = 0.
      NFMAX = (NCAV-100)/21
      CALL LWORD(A,NFMAX,NF,FORM,C,IGO)
      IF(IGO.GT.0) GO TO 1
      IF(V(20).GT.0.5.AND.V(10).LT.0.5) V(10) = 71.
      IB = NF*20+1
      IC = IB + NF
      IS = NCAV-NF*21
C LEVEL 9 - READ DATA HANDLING INSTRUCTION
   91 IF(V(10).GT.90.) V(10) = 0.
      CALL LDHI(V(1),1,V(2),4,V(7),1,V(8),2,V(9),3,H,0,V(13),V(10),
     1 TT(21),FORM,MED1,MED2,0,Q,NQ,NWARN,1,IGO)
      IF(IGO.GT.0) GO TO 71
C STANDARDISATION
      IF(V(1).GT.7.5)  NWARN = NWARN + 1
      IF(V(1).GT.7.5)  V(1) = 0.
      IF(V(1).GT.3.5.AND.V(2).GT.5.5)  NWARN = NWARN + 1
      IF(V(1).GT.3.5.AND.V(2).GT.5.5)  V(2) = 0.
```

```
      IF(V(7).LT.0.5) NWARN = NWARN + 1
      IF(V(7).LT.0.5) V(7) = 5.
      IF(V(8).LT.0.5.OR.V(8).GT.80.5)    NWARN = NWARN + 1
      IF(V(8).LT.0.5.OR.V(8).GT.80.5)    V(8) = 80.
      IF(V(8).LT.V(7)) V(8) = V(7)
      CALL LDHI(V(1),1,V(2),4,V(7),1,V(8),2,V(9),3,H,0,V(13),V(10),
     1 TT(21),FORM,MED1,MED2,0,Q,NQ,NWARN,2,IGO)
      IF(IGO.GT.0) GO TO 91
  101 WRITE(MED6,998)
      V(10) = 100.
      CALL CWORD(A,NF,A(IC),IS,C,D,NQ,A(IB),FORM)
      V(10) = 0.
      WRITE(MED6,999)
      GO TO 91
  901 FORMAT(1H0,20X,27HSTATCAT SEARCH FOR KEYWORDS )
  902 FORMAT(67H0PLAIN-LANGUAGE STATCAT DATA BANK SHOULD HAVE 21 COLUMNS
     1 - THIS HAS,I4,18H PROGRAM WILL FAIL/)
  998 FORMAT(35H0INPUT ACCEPTED - LISTING COMMENCES)
  999 FORMAT(35H1LISTING COMPLETED - READ NEW INPUT)
      END


      SUBROUTINE CWORD(A,NF,B,NAV,C,D,NQ,E,FORM)
C CWORD    (SEE  9.4 ) EXECUTIVE    FIND+LIST PLAIN-LANGUAGE RECORDS
      DIMENSION A(20,NF),B(NAV),C(50),D(NQ),E(NF),FORM(80),SCON(5,1)
      COMMON /STCT/MED1,MED2,MED3,MED4,MED5,MED6,MED13,Q,V(20),TT(30)
C STARTING CONDITIONS
      REWIND MED3
      V7 = V(7)
      V8 = V(8)
      MED7 = V(9)
      NOP = 0
      NSF = 0
      NIL = 0
      NCH = 1
      IF(V(1).GT.3.5.AND.V(2).GT.2.5) NCH = -1
      IGO = 0
C FIND DATA START
    1 READ(MED3) NQ,NALT,Q,(X,I=1,16)
      DO 2 J = 1,NQ
    2 READ(MED3) (X,I=1,19),(X,I=1,NALT),NX,X,X
      ISF = 1
      IF(IGO.GT.0.AND.NOP.EQ.0) GO TO 21
      IF(IGO.GT.0) GO TO 20
C IDENTIFY RECORDS REQUIRED
   11 READ(MED3) D
      IF(D(1).NE.D(NQ)) GO TO 11
      IF(D(NQ).NE.Q) GO TO 13
      IF(NSF.EQ.0) RETURN
      IGO = 2
      GO TO 15
   13 CALL CLWORD(A,NF,C,D,NQ,E,FORM,MIN)
      IF(MIN*NCH.LT.0) GO TO 11
      INK = 1
      IF(D(1).EQ.D(NQ).AND.NSF.EQ.0) NOP = NOP + 1
      IF(D(1).EQ.D(NQ).AND.NSF.EQ.0) GO TO 30
      NSF = NSF + 1
      IF(NSF.GT.NAV) GO TO 14
      B(NSF) = D(NQ)
      GO TO 11
   14 NSF = NAV
      IGO = 1
   15 REWIND MED3
```

```
          GO TO 1
C READ UP TO START OF OUTPUT
   20 READ(MED3) D
      IF(D(1).NE.D(NQ)) GO TO 20
      CALL CLWORD(A,NF,C,D,NQ,E,FORM,NIN)
      IF(NIN*NCH.LT.0) GO TO 20
      ISF = ISF + 1
      IF(ISF.LE.NOP) GO TO 20
      ISF = 1
C RUNNING OUTPUT
   21 READ(MED3) D
      IF(D(NQ).EQ.Q) RETURN
      IF(D(1).NE.D(NQ)) GO TO 21
      IF(D(NQ).NE.B(ISF)) GO TO 21
      INK = 2
      GO TO 30
   24 ISF = ISF + 1
      IF(ISF.LE.NSF) GO TO 21
      NOP = NOP + NSF
      NSF = 0
      IF(IGO.EQ.1) GO TO 11
      REWIND MED3
      RETURN
C IN-CORE OUTPUT FOR RECORDS
   30 IF(V(1).LT.3.5) CALL WOWN(D,NQ,FORM,SCON,NIL,MED7)
      IF(V(1).LT.3.5.AND.V(2).LT.8.5) GO TO 34
      IF(V(1).LT.3.5) GO TO 32
      I = 1
      DO 31 J = 1,20
      CALL UNPACK(D(J),FORM(I),4,C,50)
   31 I = I + 4
      V(7) = 1.
      V(8) = 80.
      CALL WCAR(FORM,80,V,MED2,MED7)
      V(8) = V8
      V(7) = V7
   32 READ(MED3) D
      DO 33 I = 2,NQ
      IF(D(I-1).NE.Q) GO TO 30
   33 CONTINUE
   34 GO TO (11,24),INK
      END


      SUBROUTINE CLWORD(A,NF,C,D,NQ,E,FORM,NIN)
C CLWORD (SEE  9.4 ) SYSTEM        SELECT PLAIN-LANGUAGE RECORDS
      DIMENSION A(20,NF),C(50),D(NQ),E(NF),FORM(80),GORM(80),WORD(68)
C KEY SYMBOLS   .  =  -  +  *  /  (  )   F (, = SKIP TILL NEXT MATCH)
C LETTERS       N  N  N  Y  Y  Y  Y  N  Y
C DIGITS        N  N  Y  N  Y  Y  N  Y  Y
C SYMBOLS       N  Y  N  N  N  Y  Y  Y  Y
C BLANKS        Y  N  N  N  N  N  N  N  Y
      COMMON /STCT/MED1,MED2,MED3,MED4,MED5,MED6,MED13,Q,V(20),TT(30)
      NIN = 1
      IF(NF.LE.0) RETURN
      JJ = V(1) + 0.1
      JS = V(7) + 0.1
      JF = V(8) + 0.1
      JT = JF-JS+1
      IF(JJ.GE.4) JJ = JJ - 4
      IF(JJ.GE.4) JJ = 0
C NOW=1 UNPACK CARD - NFIR=1 EXAMINE MORE THAN FIRST ENTRY
      NOW = 0
```

```
      NFIR = 0
       DO 3 J = 1,NF
      K = A(2,J)
      IF(K.EQ.1.OR.K.EQ.5) NOW = 1
      IF(K.NE.2.AND.K.NE.5.AND.K.NE.6) NFIR = 1
    3 E(J) = -0.5
      LT = 0
   10 IF(LT.GT.0) READ(MED3) D
      IF(LT.EQ.0) LT = 1
      IF(LT.EQ.1) RCN = D(NQ)
      DO 6 I = 2,NQ
      IF(D(I-1).NE.Q) GO TO 7
    6 CONTINUE
      IF(NIN.NE.1)  GO TO 100
      RETURN
    7 CONTINUE
      IF(NOW.EQ.0) GO TO 9
      J = 1
      DO 8 I = 1,20
      CALL UNPACK(D(I),FORM(J),4,C,50)
    8 J = J + 4
      IF(LT.EQ.1) SND = SNDX(FORM(JS),JT,C(2))
      LTX = 1
      DO 88 J = 1,80
      FORM(J) = ICH(FORM(J),C,50)
   88 IF(FORM(J).GT.1.5) LTX = J
    9 K = D(1)
      IF(K.EQ.2262818) LT =  4
      IF(K.EQ.2262820) LT =  6
      IF(K.EQ.2513720) LT =  8
      IF(K.EQ.0) LT= (LT+1)/2*2
      DO 99 J = 1,NF
      LC = A(1,J) + 0.1
      IF(LC.EQ.2.AND.NIN.EQ.1) RETURN
      IF(LC.EQ.2) NIN = 1
      LS = A(2,J) + 0.1
      LS1 = LS - LS/4*4
      LD = A(3,J) + 0.1
C DISCARD UNWANTED ENTRIES
      IF(LS.EQ.1) GO TO 30
      IF(LS1.EQ.0.AND.LT.NE.6) GO TO 90
      IF(LS1.EQ.1.AND.LT.NE.1) GO TO 90
      IF(LS1.EQ.2.AND.LT.NE.1) GO TO 90
      IF(LS1.EQ.3.AND.LT.NE.4) GO TO 90
      IF(LS.EQ.5)LD = (LD-1)/3*3 + 1
      NIS = 0
      NX = 20
      IF(LS1.EQ.2.OR.LS.EQ.5) NX = 2
      DO 20 K = 2,NX
      NR = D(K) +0.1
      IF(LS1.EQ.2) NR = RCN +0.1
      IF(LS.EQ.5) NR = SND + 0.1
      IF(NR.EQ.0) GO TO 20
      DO 18 I = 4,20
      NT = A(I,J) + 0.1
      IF(NT.EQ.0) GO TO 18
      NT = NR-NT
      GO TO (11,12,13,14,15,16),LD
   11 IF(NT)  18,17,18
   12 IF(NT)  17,17,18
   13 IF(NT)  18,17,17
   14 IF(NT)  18,17,18
   15 IF(NT)  17,18,18
```

```
      16 IF(NT) 18,18,17
      17 NIS = 1
      18 CONTINUE
      19 IF(LD.NE.4.AND.NIS.EQ.1) E(J) = 1.
         IF(LD.EQ.4.AND.NIS.EQ.1) E(J) = 0.
      20 CONTINUE
         GO TO 90
C TEST KEYWORD
      30 IF(E(J).GT.-0.25) GO TO 90
         IF(E(J).GT.-0.75) E(J) = -80.
C REJECT IRRELEVANT CARDS - CONDITION NOT SATISFIED
         IF(LT.EQ.4.OR.LT.EQ.6) GO TO 90
         IF(JJ.EQ.1.AND.LT.GT.1) GO TO 90
         IF(JJ.EQ.2.AND.LT.GT.2) GO TO 90
         IF(JJ.EQ.3.AND.LT.LT.8) GO TO 90
         K = 1
         DO 31 I = 4,20
         CALL UNPACK(A(I,J),WORD(K),4,C,50)
      31 K = K + 4
         LK = 1
         DO 311 K = 1,68
         WORD(K) = ICH(WORD(K),C,50)
         IF(WORD(K).GT.1.5) LK = K
     311 CONTINUE
C START COMPARISON
      40 NK = 0
         NT = E(J)-1.1
         IC = 0
      42 NK = NK + 1
         IF(NK.GT.LK) GO TO 50
         IK = WORD(NK) + 0.1
         IF(IK.EQ.1) GO TO 42
         IF(IK.EQ.47) IC = 1
         IF(IK.EQ.47) GO TO 42
      43 NT = NT + 1
         IF(NT.GT.0) GO TO 60
         IF(IK.EQ.50) GO TO 45
         IT = 1
         IF(NT.LE.-JS.AND.NT.GE.-JF) IT = FORM(81+NT)
         IF(NT.LE.-81-JS.AND.NT.GE.-81-JF) IT = GORM(162+NT)
C DISCARD LEADING,SKIP UNWANTED INTERNAL BLANKS IN TEXT
         IF(IT.EQ.1.AND.IK.NE.48.AND.NK.EQ.1) GO TO 46
         IF(IT.EQ.1.AND.IK.NE.48) GO TO 43
         IF(IT.EQ.1) GO TO 45
         IF(IK.EQ.41.AND.IT.LE.27) GO TO 45
         IF(IK.EQ.42.AND.IT.LE.40.AND.IT.GE.31) GO TO 45
         IF(IK.EQ.43) GO TO 45
         IF(IK.EQ.44.AND.IT.LE.40) GO TO 45
         IF(IK.EQ.45.AND.IT.LE.27) GO TO 45
         IF(IK.EQ.45.AND.IT.GE.41) GO TO 45
         IF(IK.EQ.46.AND.IT.GE.28) GO TO 45
         IF(IK.EQ.49.AND.IT.GE.41) GO TO 45
         IF(IK.GE.41) GO TO 46
         IF(IK-IT) 46,45,46
      45 IC = 0
         GO TO 42
      46 IF(IC.EQ.1) GO TO 43
         E(J) = E(J) + 1.
         GO TO 40
C KEYWORD FOUND   REJECT CONDITION IF NE,LT OR GT ACCEPT IF EQ GE LE
      50 IF(LD.LE.3) E(J) = 1.
         IF(LD.GE.4) E(J) = 0.
         GO TO 90
```

```
      60 E(J) = E(J) - 81.
         IF(NK.EQ.1) E(J) = -0.5
      90 IF(E(J).LT.0.8) NIN = -1
      99 CONTINUE
         IF(NFIR.EQ.0.OR.NIN.EQ.1) RETURN
         DO 102 I = 1,80
     102 GORM(I) = FORM(I)
         GO TO 10
C FINAL CHECK - UNSATISFIED NOT EQUALS CONDITIONS
     100 NIN = 1
         DO 101 J=1,NF
         LC = A(1,J)
         IF(LC.EQ.2.AND.NIN.EQ.1) RETURN
         IF(LC.EQ.2) NIN = 1
         LD = A(3,J)
         IF(LD.NE.4.AND.E(J).LE.0.5) NIN =-1
         IF(LD.EQ.4.AND.E(J).LT.0.5.AND.E(J).GT.-0.5) NIN = -1
     101 CONTINUE
         RETURN
         END


         SUBROUTINE LWORD(A,NFMAX,NF,FORM,C,IGO)
C LWORD    (SEE   9.4 ) SERVICE      DEFINES PLAIN LANGUAGE RECORDS
         DIMENSION A(20,NFMAX),FORM(71),C1(3),C2(8),C3(6),C(50)
         COMMON /STCT/MED1,MED2,MED3,MED4,MED5,MED6,MED13,Q,V(20),TT(30)
         DATA C1/4H.IF.,4HAND.,4H.OR./
         DATA C2/4HWORD,4HRCNA,4HRFNA,4HRTNA,4HSNDX,4HRCNO,4HRFNO,4HRTNO/
         DATA C3/4H.EQ.,4H.GE.,4H.LE.,4H.NE.,4H.GT.,4H.LT./
C LOAD TITLE - IF END RETURN
       1 READ(MED1,900)(TT(I),I=11,20),(FORM(I),I=1,10)
         IGO = IBL(TT(11),10,4)
         IF(IGO) 1,3,2
       2 WRITE(MED2,901)(TT(I),I=11,20),(FORM(I),I=1,10)
         RETURN
       3 NF = 0
       3 NF = 0
         WRITE(MED2,902)(TT(I),I=11,20),(FORM(I),I=1,10)
         V(20) = 0.
C LOAD CONDITION - REJECT BLANK - PRINT
       4 NF = NF + 1
         IF(NF.GT.NFMAX)WRITE(MED2,903) NFMAX
         IF(NF.GT.NFMAX) NF = NFMAX
       5 READ(MED1,904)FORM
         IF(IBL(FORM,3,4).LT.0) GO TO 5
         WRITE(MED2,905) FORM
         IF(IBL(FORM,3,4).GT.0) GO TO 20
C TRANSLATE AND CHECK
         V20 = 0.
         K = ICH(FORM(1),C1,3)
         A(1,NF) = K
         IF(K.GT.0) GO TO 6
         WRITE(MED2,906)
         IF(V20.LT.0.5) V20 = 1.
       6 A(2,NF) = ICH(FORM(2),C2,6)
         IF(A(2,NF).GT.0.5)GO TO 7
         IF(V20.LT.0.5) V20 = 2.
         WRITE(MED2,907)
       7 A(3,NF) = ICH(FORM(3),C3,6)
         IF(A(3,NF).GT.0.5) GO TO 8
         IF(V20.LT.0.5) V20 = 3.
         WRITE(MED2,908)
       8 IF(V(20).LT.0.5) V(20) = V20
```

```
      IF(V20.GT.0.5) WRITE(MED2,909)
      IF(V20.GT.0.5) GO TO 5
      IF(A(2,NF).GT.4.5) GO TO 10
C STORE RECORDS GIVEN IN NAME FORM.
      J = 4
      DO 9 I = 4,20
      A(I,NF) = NPACK(FORM(J),4,C,50)
    9 J = J + 4
      GO TO 4
C STORE FREE-FORMAT RECORDS NUMBERS OR SOUNDEX CODED NAMES
   10 NB = 3
      DO 12 I = 4,20
      A(I,NF) = 0.
      NA = NB + 1
      NX = 0
      IF(NA.GT.71) GO TO 12
      NB = NA
   11 NB = NB + 1
      L = ICH(FORM(NB),C(2),39)
      IF(L.NE.0) NX = 1
      IF(L.NE.0.AND.NB.LT.71.OR.NX.EQ.0.AND.NB.LT.71) GO TO 11
      NX = NB+1-NA
      IF(A(2,NF).LT.5.5) A(I,NF) = SNDX(FORM(NA),NX,C(2) )
      IF(A(2,NF).GT.5.5) A(I,NF) = AN(FORM,NB,NA,NB)
   12 CONTINUE
      GO TO 4
   20 NF = NF - 1
      IF(NF.EQ.0) WRITE(MED2,910)
      RETURN
  900 FORMAT(20A4)
  901 FORMAT(1H0,10X,20A4)
  902 FORMAT(1H1,7X,23HRECORD SPECIFICATION - ,10A4,10H  COMMENT ,10A4)
  903 FORMAT(43H0INSUFFICIENT STORAGE - INCREASE NFMAX FROM, I6)
  904 FORMAT(3A4,68A1)
  905 FORMAT(10X,3A4,68A1)
  906 FORMAT(10X,30HUNIDENTIFIED LOGICAL CONNECTOR)
  907 FORMAT(14X,22HUNIDENTIFIED PROCEDURE)
  908 FORMAT(18X,22HUNIDENTIFIED CONDITION)
  909 FORMAT(1H+,40X,12H - DISCARDED)
  910 FORMAT(1H0,65X,48HSYSTEM COMMENT - SUBSET WILL CONTAIN ALL ENTRIES
     1)
      END


      FUNCTION SNDX(A,NQ,B)
C SNDX     (SEE  9.4 ) SERVICE      PRODUCES SOUNDEX CODE
C FIRST LETTER = 1 - 26
C NEXT FOUR DIFFERENT LETTERS IN WORD
C DUPLICATES DISCARDED
C A E I O U Y W H DISCARDED
C 1 = B F P V
C 2 = C G J K Q S X Y
C 3 = D T
C 4 = L
C 5 = M N
C 6 = R
C IF END OF WORD IS REACHED FILL UP WITH BLANKS
C I.E. BROWN = 26500
      DIMENSION  A(NQ),B(26),C(18)
      DATA C/1HB,1HP,1HV,1HF,1HG,1HJ,1HK,1HQ,1HS,1HX,1HZ,1HC,1HT,1HD,1HL
     1,1HN,1HM,1HR/
      DATA BL/1H /
      I = 0
```

```
1 I = I + 1
  IF(I.GT.NQ) RETURN
  SNDX = ICH(A(I),B,26)
  IF(SNDX.LT.0.5) GO TO 1
  J = 1
2 I = I + 1
  IF(I.GT.NQ) GO TO 3
  IF(ICH(A(I),BL,1).EQ.1) GO TO 3
  IF(ICH(A(I),B,26).LT.1)GO TO 2
  IF(A(I).EQ.A(I-1)) GO TO 2
  X = ICH(A(I),C,18)
  IF(X.LT.0.5) GO TO 2
  J = J+1
  SNDX = SNDX*10. + 1.
  IF(X.GT.4.5)SNDX = SNDX + 1.
  IF(X.GT.12.5)SNDX= SNDX + 1.
  IF(X.GT.14.5)SNDX= SNDX + 1.
  IF(X.GT.15.5)SNDX= SNDX + 1.
  IF(X.GT.17.5)SNDX= SNDX + 1.
  IF(J.LT.4) GO TO 2
3 IF(J.EQ.3) SNDX = SNDX*10.
  IF(J.EQ.2) SNDX = SNDX*100.
  IF(J.EQ.1) SNDX = SNDX*1000.
  RETURN
  END
```

Chapter X

DATA MANIPULATION

When a computer program is produced for general release, one of the most difficult problems facing the writer is to decide how much to leave to the user. The simplest answer, which is often perfectly adequate, is to adopt a simple and completely rigid format for input data. This makes for ease of programming, but for any statistical program (which is more than a toy) may require much unnecessary effort from the user, who must laboriously insert thousands of values, or write his own special programs to force his data into the mould. At the other extreme the program or system may be reduced to a skeleton of functional units forming a higher-order language, which the user must master before he can write his own program to carry out the analysis he requires. This approach, provided it is sufficiently disciplined, and the users are sufficiently motivated (or sufficiently docile) is equally practical, but it requires considerable system analysis insight, and involves extraordinary programming efforts. It reduces the data handling effort from the user, but replaces it by the requirement that he learns what is virtually a new language.

This system represents a compromise between the extreme approaches. As such, it will not satisfy enthusiasts for either, but it may be useful to the less committed. Most of the programs described so far contain facilities for the transformation of individual data before they are analysed. The range of transformations is relatively limited, because too many options make programs too difficult to explain, and because such manipulations eat up time and storage space. Many users will find that the limited possibilities so far provided do not cover all their requirements. To assist users in the manipulation of their STATCAT data banks, five programs (described in this chapter) have been developed. These programs are not, except incidentally, statistical in intent. They operate on STATCAT data banks to produce other STATCAT data banks. Entries may be selected, synchronised, transformed, combined with other entries, ordered and otherwise treated to prepare them for analysis.

The programs described in this chapter normally require two STATCAT data banks. One of these is the input STATCAT data bank, and the other the output STATCAT data bank under construction. The program STMERG, which is used to combine STATCAT data banks, can be operated with a secondary STATCAT input data bank as the source of one input data stream, but this is not strictly necessary, since the second input stream may be taken directly from the input medium.

The program STCORR(4.4) is normally used to correct errors and to add entries to an existing STATCAT data bank. It can also be used as a data handling program, to provide a specified subset of an original STATCAT data bank, or to eliminate or insert entries into a STATCAT data bank. It does not allow the user to eliminate data columns except those at the end of the data description segment. It does not allow the user to manipulate or transform data within an entry, and or to discard data columns in the centre of the data description segment.

The program STMANI(10.1) the first described in this chapter, enables the user to extract and manipulate items from individual entries. It handles the entries one-by-one transforming and combining data according to the instructions given by the user in a special data manipulation specification. An intermediate storage area is provided, so that data may be held in store from one entry to the next. Non-values are recognised, and treated appropriately, and logical tests may be applied to control the transformation process.

The program STSORT(10.2) is a general-purpose entry sorting program. It sorts the entries in a STATCAT data bank into order on successive data columns, each of which may be in increasing or decreasing order, with or without including non-values. This program is most used in preparing STATCAT data banks for other data manipulation programs, or for analyses in which sequential effects are expected to be important.

The program STMERG(10.3) is used to combine entries from an input STATCAT data bank with other data from another STATCAT data bank, from store or from an input device. This program may be used to merge existing STATCAT data banks, or to add data items required for multiple regression analyses, or to protect confidentiality by allowing confidential items to be included in a data bank without their being physically identified to a recognisable individual.

The program STSYNC(10.3) is a general data synchroniser. It takes an initial STATCAT data bank containing time-linked records at irregular intervals, and produces data interpolated by an appropriate algorithm at regular time intervals.

The program STCOMB(10.5) is a general data reducer. It produces (for all observed combinations of a specified set of variates) such parameters as the number of observations falling into the group, their arithmetic or geometric mean, standard deviation, variance, maximum, minimum and other potentially useful statistics. The program may be used to tabulate the values, or to store them in a STATCAT data bank for further analysis. This program is particularly useful where it is necessary to produce analyses which do not depend on the amount of data in each cell, where individual information must not be released because it is confidential, or where the initial number of entries is very large, and the data must be reduced before more sophisticated analysis.

These relatively simple programs cannot, of course, cover all eventualities. Many users will find it easier to construct a special input subroutine DATA to read data from the original STATCAT data bank, and carry out the transformation required. Chapter 9.3 gives an example of such a subroutine, and 4.2.5 contains some points to be born in mind while writing it. The user should specify his original STATCAT data bank as the first (input) STATCAT data bank, and his revised STATCAT data bank as the second (output) STATCAT data bank. He should make sure that his subroutine will at the first call (when D is full of non-values) read the data starter and data description segment for the input STATCAT data bank so as to reach the data storage segment of that data bank.

10.1 PROGRAM STMANI - MANIPULATING SINGLE ENTRIES

10.1.1 Purpose

This program manipulates the data within each entry for a subset, or a series of subsets of a STATCAT data bank, or a series of data banks, to produce a new STATCAT data bank. The way in which the data are manipulated is determined by a data manipulation specification, which is virtually a FORTRAN program provided by the user at run-time. It may involve arithmetic operations on data, or any of the transforms given in Figure 3.71 and logical conditions may be used to control the sequence of manipulations The data manipulation specification module LMAN is written in ASA FORTRAN IV, and is therefore rather clumsy and restricted in its possibilities. As has been mentioned earlier, some users may find it easier to write a special DATA subroutine for STLOAD rather than use this program.

This program may operate on several different subsets of data from the input STATCAT data bank, applying a different manipulation specification to each, and can be applied to several successive input STATCAT data banks to form a single output STATCAT data bank. The amount of information output during the construction of the output STATCAT data bank, and the amount of data checking may be varied at the user's discretion.

Figure 10.11a contains a system flow-chart for the main program STMANI. (There is no executive subroutine for this program.) Figure 10.11b contains system flow-charts for the data manipulation specification subroutine LMAN and the data manipulation subroutine MANIP.

10.1.2 Input Data

Summary

Item	Level	Format	Function	See
1	0	A	File control card (First input+output)	3.2
2	0	B	Data starter card	3.3
3	0	C	Data description module	Below + 3.4
(4	1	A	File control card (later input)	3.2)
5	2	-	Data manipulation Specification	Below
6	3	E	Subset specification	3.6
7	4	G	Data handling instruction	3.8

2 - Data Starter Card

Standard - Indices A and B not used.

3 - Data Description module.

This is a standard data description module, as described in 3.4. It appears on the output STATCAT data bank, so must contain the information necessary for the use of the data bank being constructed. It need not necessarily contain descriptions of how the items are derived, but should contain a description of what they represent. Because the column titles are in plain language, the system cannot check them. The user must therefore take great care to verify that the data items and their descriptions correspond and are correct, either by working through examples, or by use of STDESC, STCHEK, STLIST and STBANK as convenient.

(4 - File Control Card - Later input)

This file control card is employed only when a second STATCAT input is to be used to in place of that specified at the start of the program. The code SAME must be given for the output STATCAT data bank - to avoid rewinding and over-writing.

5 - Manipulation Specification

This is essentially a simplified run-time FORTRAN program, specifying the data manipulations to be carried out. It consists of a series of manipulation cards, terminated by an END card. These specify a series of arithmetic operations and transforms, with some logical operations and tests which may be used to alter the sequence of manipulations. General principles, use of storage and error messages are described in 10.1.5.

Card Layout - Manipulation Card - STMANI

```
AAAABBBBCCCCDDDDEEEEFFFFFFFFFFFFGGGGGGGGGGGGGGGGGGGGGGGGGGGGGGGG....
```

Columns on card	Item code	FORTRAN type	Function	See
1 - 4	A	I	Card number	Below
5 - 8	B	A	Manipulation Code or Transform code	Below
9 - 12	C	A	First data column name (Column A)	Below
13 - 16	D	A	Logical condition	Below
17 - 20	E	A	Second data column name (Column B)	Below
21 - 32	F	F	Numerical value (V)	Below
33 - 80	G	A	Comment (not kept)	Below

A - Card Number

This is a four digit number, commencing with 1 and continuing in ascending consecutive order, on the following manipulation cards. It is checked to ensure that all cards are present and in the correct order.

B - Manipulation Code

This is a four-character code which may be any of the codes given in Figure 10.18, or any of the transform codes given in Figure 3.71. This code determines what action will be carried out. Any code not in Figure 3.71 or Figure 10.18 will produce an error message, and lead to a fatal error.

C - First Data Column Name (Column A)

This is a four-character code, which may be any data column name or number from the current input STATCAT data bank (not the output STATCAT data bank), or a code S followed by a right justified number from 1 to 100 -referring to a storage location with that number. (i.e. Sbb1, Sb10, S100, where b indicates a blank)

D - Logical Condition

This is a four-character code, drawn from those in Figure 10.19. If the manipulation code A was .IF. then an error message will be generated if any other code is encountered. If the manipulation code is not .IF. any code in this field will be ignored. The codes .TO. , .FROM, or .BY. may be inserted to make the output record easier to read.

E - Second Data Column Name (Column B)

This is a four-character code which, like the first data column A, may be any column name or number from the Input STATCAT data bank. It may also be a completely blank field (see below).

F - Numerical value

This is a twelve-digit number, which may be used in place of the second data column if the latter is left blank.

G - Comment

This comment is printed when the card is read, but is not retained.

Data Handling Instruction

This is a standard data handling instruction. It is used to specify the amount of information printed during entry manipulation, to indicate whether to close the output STATCAT data bank, and what checking procedures are to be used.

Card Layout - Data Handling Instruction - STMANI

```
ABCCCDDDEEEEEEEEFFFFFFFFFFFFFFFFFFFFFFFFGGGGGGGGGGGGGGGG.....
```

Columns on Card	Item code	FORTRAN Type	Function	See
1	A	I	Data Output Control Index	Below
2	B	I	Data Checking Control Index	4.3
3 - 5	C	I	Maximum number of non-values	Below
6 - 8	D	I	Maximum number of s.d. from the mean	4.3
9 - 16	E	F	Minimum percentage in class	4.3
17 - 40	F	A	Comment (printed with line)	Below
41 - 80	G	A	Comment (printed separately)	Below

A - Data Output Control Index

This index controls the amount of description output during the construction of the revised data storage segment. Unless otherwise specified only entry numbers of original and manipulated entries are output.

ALTERNATIVES

A = 0 or blank: Only the number of the entry in the input STATCAT data bank, with the corresponding entry number for the output STATCAT data bank are printed.

A = 1 : In addition, the manipulated (output) entry is printed

A = 2 : In addition, the original (input) entry is printed

A = 3 : In addition, the current (stored) data are printed

A = 4 : Values generated during the construction of the entry are printed

A = 5-9 : No output during data manipulation.

C - Maximum Number of Non-values

This is the maximum number of non-values that will be accepted in a manipulated entry being written to the output STATCAT data bank.

DEFAULT value = N-1 where N is the number of data columns in the output STATCAT data bank. (A completely blank record would terminate the data bank - rendering any subsequent entries inaccessible.)

10.1.3   Input Example

Figure 10.12 is a summary of the input structure for two runs of STMANI, using the vector score weightings derived by STFACT to derive factor scores for each of the 64 original entries, printing the first entry in full detail, and summarising the rest. Figure 10.13 lists the corresponding input cards.

10.1.4   Output Example

Figure 10.14 is a general summary of the output produced by this program, indented according to the program structure. Figure 10.15 is a page-by-page summary of the output corresponding to the specific input of 10.1.3. Figure 10.16 shows the output for the first entry in full detail. Figure 10.17 shows part of the output for the remaining entries. Figure 10.18 lists the acceptable manipulation codes, with their effects, and Figure 10.19 lists the logical conditions and their interpretation.

10.1.5   Subroutine MANIP

Subroutine MANIP, of which a system flow-chart is provided in Figure 10.11b, carries out the manipulations of data within an entry according to the instructions provided by the Manipulation Specification.

At the first call to MANIP for a given STATCAT output data bank, the array S will contain only 'non-values'. S is re-set to non-values whenever a new output STATCAT data bank is started, but not when a new data manipulation specification, subset or entry is read in. Cells must be tested and set to zero if they are to be used for accumulation of totals or cross-products.

The result of any arithmetic operation in which one quantity is a non-value will be a non-value. Logical conditions do not make any special distinction for the non-value, treating it like any other number. If special procedures are required for treating non-values, they must be programmed explicitly in the manipulation specification. Within MANIP, the non-value used is that from the original input STATCAT data bank. These non-values are converted to the numerical value specified for the output STATCAT data bank and the total number counted just before output. If at this point, there are too many non-values, as defined by field C of the data handling instruction, the output does not take place, but no other manipulation is omitted.

Certain types of errors in the manipulation specification cards can be detected by the system, and will produce error messages:-

- 1 - DATA MANIPULATION CARDS OUT OF ORDER

This means that the cards are not in regular ascending consecutive order, so that at least one card is missing or misplaced. This is a fatal error, but the program will continue to read and test cards for other errors.

- 2 - UNRECOGNISABLE ORDER CODE

The code in columns 5-8 is not in Figure 10.18 or Figure 3.71. Again a fatal error.

- 3 - FIRST DATA COLUMN IS NOT RECOGNISED

- 4 - SECOND DATA COLUMN IS NOT RECOGNISED

The code in columns 9-12 or 17-20 is not a data column name or number from the input STATCAT data bank. (Both fatal errors.)

- 5 - COLUMN AFTER GOTO OUT OF RANGE

the GOTO transfers control to a point outside the set of manipulation instructions. This is not a fatal error, because the user may use this as a means of stopping the manipulation. When the program is running, an attempt to go to an instruction out of the range will cause the subroutine to return to the main program.

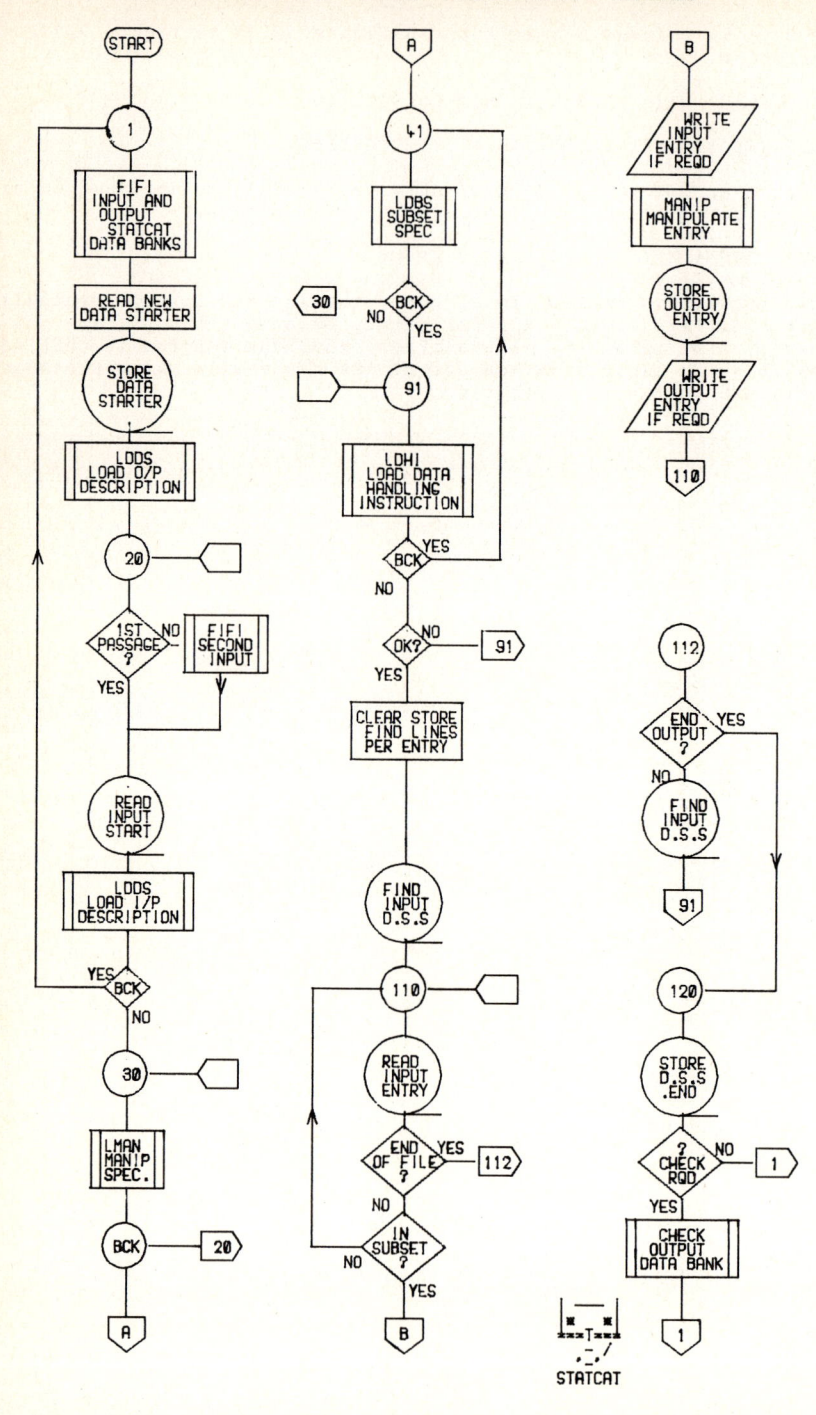

Figure 10.11a - System Flow-Chart - STMANI

601

Figure 10.11b - System Flow-Charts - LMAN and MANIP

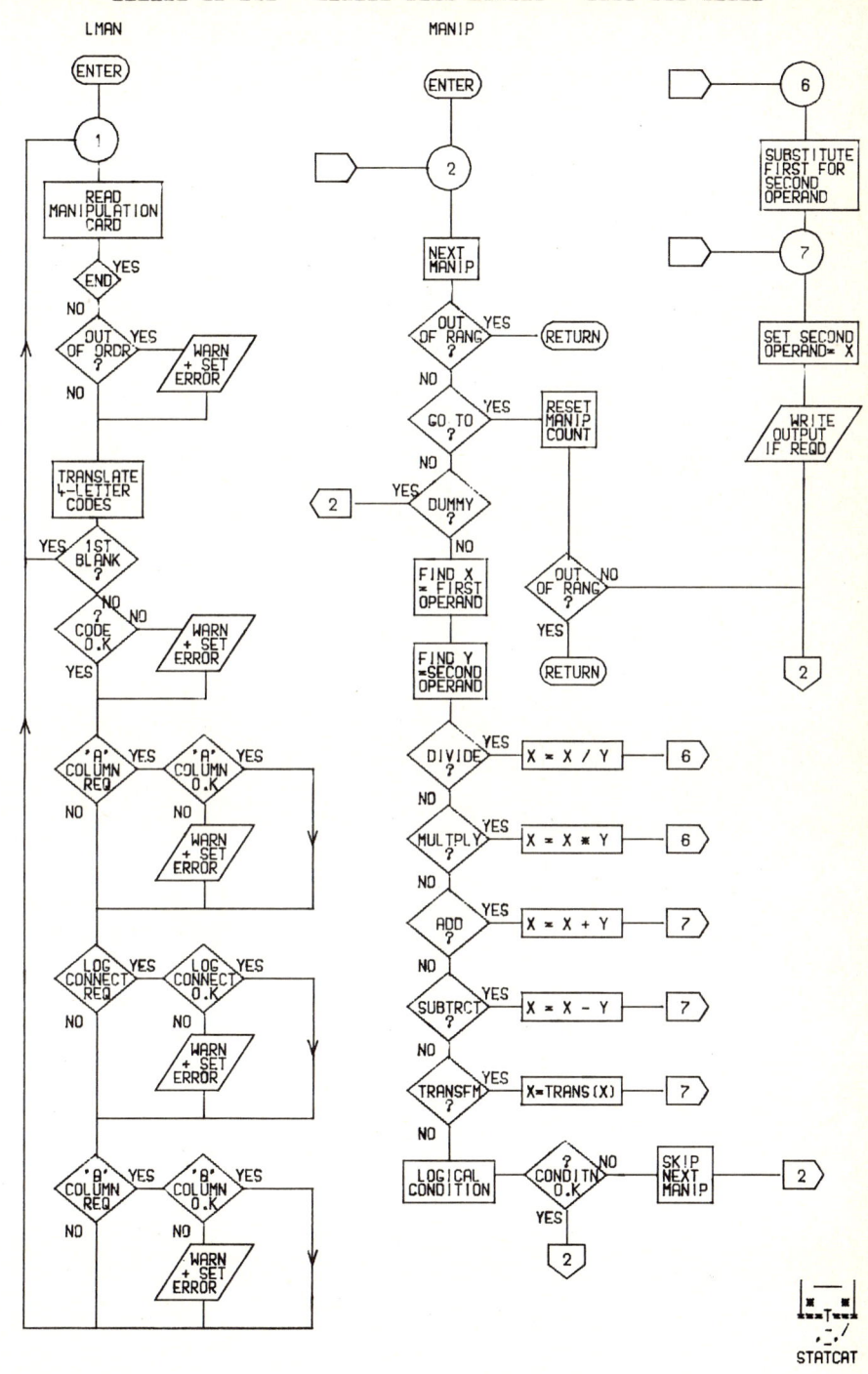

Figure 10.12 - STMANI - Input Structure

```
          Level
  0    1    2    3    4    5    6    7    8    9
FILE CONTROL CARD
DATA STARTER CARD
DATA DESCRIPTION SEGMENT
     MANIPULATION SPECIFICATION
          SUBSET SPECIFICATION
               DATA HANDLING INSTRUCTION
               DATA HANDLING INSTRUCTION (BACK)
          SUBSET SPECIFICATION
               DATA HANDLING INSTRUCTION
  STANDARD CHECKING OUTPUT
STOP
```

Figure 10.13 - STMANI - Input Example

```
---------1---------2---------3---------4---------5---------6-//------8
**STMANIDEMO     DUFF
     2 22    -1.0   TRANSFORMATION - FACTOR WEIGHTS TEST            DUFF
       1NTRY             ENTRY NUMBER- FACTOR WEIGHTS TEST          DUMMY
       2PCOM             PRINCIPAL COMPONENT - EIGHT PREDICTORS     INTERVAL
           1.0       1.0
END OF DDS
     1SET.S     1.TO.        -2.5                       SUBTRACT MEAN
     2SET.S     2.TO.        -2.5
     3SET.S     3.TO.        -2.59375
     4SET.S     4.TO.        -2.5
     5SET.S     5.TO.        -3.71875
     6SET.S     6.TO.       -56.72595215
     7SET.S     7.TO.       -47.53305054
     8SET.S     8.TO.       -79.64724731
     9ADD.OPER.TO.S   1                                 ADD VALUE
    10ADD.W.P..TO.S   2
    11ADD.STRS.TO.S   3
    12ADD.TASK.TO.S   4
    13ADD.DIFF.TO.S   5
    14ADD.EFOP.TO.S   6
    15ADD.H.R..TO.S   7
    16ADD.EFOB.TO.S   8
    17MULTS    1.BY.         0.2263
    18MULTS    2.BY.         0.0530
    19MULTS    3.BY.         0.0769
    20MULTS    4.BY.         0.1019
    21MULTS    5.BY.         0.2645
    22MULTS    6.BY.         0.2606
    23MULTS    7.BY.         0.2144
    24MULTS    8.BY.        -0.1239
    25PUT.S    1.IN.COL2                                CUMULATE
    26ADD.S    2.TO.COL2
    27ADD.S    3.TO.COL2
    28ADD.S    4.TO.COL2
    29ADD.S    5.TO.COL2
    30ADD.S    6.TO.COL2
    31ADD.S    7.TO.COL2
    32ADD.S    8.TO.COL2
    33PUT.NTRY.IN.COL1
END                                     OF MANIPULATION SPECIFICATION
FIRST ENTRY ONLY
.IF.NTRY.LT.        1.5
END OF SUBSET
4                                       FULL OUTPUT - NO CHECKING
BACK
REST OF INPUT FILE
.IF.NTRY.GT.        1.5
END OF SUBSET
GO                                      STANDARD O/P AND CHECKING
STOP
---------1---------2---------3---------4---------5---------6-//------8
```

Figure 10.14 - STMANI - Output Structure

```
For each  ) : Output File Control   Record output     )     Output File Par-
ameters data bank )    Output Data Description Record
                For each  )  Input File Parameters
                Input     )  Input Data Description
                data bank )  For each       )  Manipulation Record
                   .            Manipulation  )  For each ) Subset Record
                   .            Specification )  Subset   ) See below left
                   .
                   .        <For each ) <Entry Number Original/Revised>
                   .        <  Entry  ) <Output Entry>
                   .                    <Input Entry>
                   .                    <Stored Data>
                   .                    <Intermediate values>
                   . <Standard Data Bank Checking>
```

Carated(<>) items are optional.

Figure 10.15 - STMANI - Page-by-page output summary

Page	Contents	Origin
1	File Control Record	FIFI
2	Output Data Header Output File Parameters Output Data Description record	STMANI STMANI LDDS
3- 4	Input Data Header Input File Parameters Input Data Description record	STMANI STMANI LDDS
5	Data Manipulation Specification	LDBS/LSET
6	Subset Specification Data Handling Instruction	LDBS LDHI
7- 8	Entry Record	MANIP
9	End of Transformation Data Handling Instruction(BACK)	STMANI LDHI
10	Subset Specification Data Handling Instruction	LDBS LDHI
11-12	Entry Records	MANIP
13	End of Transformation Data Handling Instruction(BACK)	STMANI LDHI
14-26	Standard Data Checking	CHECK
27	Data Handling Instruction (STOP)	LDHI

Figure 10.16 - STMANI - Output Example - Detailed Output

```
STATCAT PROGRAM STMANI       -   MANIPULATION OF ENTRIES
OUTPUT DATA BANK TITLE       -   TRANSFORMATION - FACTOR WEIGHTS TEST
 INPUT DATA BANK TITLE       -   DEMONSTRATION STATCAT DATA BANK
DATA BANK SUBSET TITLE       -   FIRST ENTRY ONLY

                   DATA STORAGE SEGMENT

 ENTRY     1. ON ORIGINAL BECOMES      1. ON TRANSFORMED TAPE

 ORIGINAL ENTRY   -
              1.0000     1.0000    1.0000    1.0000    1.0000    1.0000    1.0000    1.0000    1.0000    1.0000
             22.0000     0.6200   13.3100   91.5900   35.5200   48.3000   48.0000    0.5000

 MANIPULATIONS IN ORDER

 MANIPULATION    1  - STORE    1 BECOMES     -2.500000
 MANIPULATION    2  - STORE    2 BECOMES      2.500000
 MANIPULATION    3  - STORE    3 BECOMES     -2.593750
 MANIPULATION    4  - STORE    4 BECOMES      2.500000
 MANIPULATION    5  - STORE    5 BECOMES     -3.718750
 MANIPULATION    6  - STORE    6 BECOMES     36.725906
 MANIPULATION    7  - STORE    7 BECOMES    -47.533005
 MANIPULATION    8  - STORE    3 BECOMES     19.647202
 MANIPULATION    9  - STORE    1 BECOMES     -1.500000
 MANIPULATION   10  - STORE    2 BECOMES      1.500000
 MANIPULATION   11  - STORE    3 BECOMES     -1.593750
 MANIPULATION   12  - STORE    4 BECOMES      1.500000
 MANIPULATION   13  - STORE    5 BECOMES     -2.718750
 MANIPULATION   14  - STORE    6 BECOMES     43.415854
 MANIPULATION   15  - STORE    7 BECOMES    -12.013016
 MANIPULATION   16  - STORE    8 BECOMES     11.942795
 MANIPULATION   17  - STORE    1 BECOMES     -0.339450
 MANIPULATION   18  - STORE    2 BECOMES      0.079500
 MANIPULATION   19  - STORE    3 BECOMES     -0.122559
 MANIPULATION   20  - STORE    4 BECOMES      0.152850
 MANIPULATION   21  - STORE    5 BECOMES     -0.719109
 MANIPULATION   22  - STORE    6 BECOMES     11.314160
 MANIPULATION   23  - STORE    7 BECOMES     -2.575590
 MANIPULATION   24  - STORE    8 BECOMES      1.479712
 MANIPULATION   25  - ITEM     2 BECOMES     -0.339450
 MANIPULATION   26  - ITEM     2 BECOMES      0.418950
 MANIPULATION   27  - ITEM     2 BECOMES     -0.854309
 MANIPULATION   28  - ITEM     2 BECOMES      0.694359
 MANIPULATION   29  - ITEM     2 BECOMES     -1.152667
 MANIPULATION   30  - ITEM     2 BECOMES    -12.727042
 MANIPULATION   31  - ITEM     2 BECOMES     -5.303238
 MANIPULATION   32  - ITEM     2 BECOMES    -16.732344
 MANIPULATION   33  - ITEM     2 BECOMES       .000000


STATCAT PROGRAM STMANI       -   MANIPULATION OF ENTRIES
OUTPUT DATA BANK TITLE       -   TRANSFORMATION - FACTOR WEIGHTS TEST
 INPUT DATA BANK TITLE       -   DEMONSTRATION STATCAT DATA BANK
DATA BANK SUBSET TITLE       -   FIRST ENTRY ONLY

                   DATA STORAGE SEGMENT

 MANIPULATED ENTRY  -
              1.0000    -16.7825

 STORED DATA
             -0.3394    -0.3795    -0.1226    -0.1528    -0.7191   -11.3142    -2.5756    -1.4797    -.0000    -1.0000
             -1.0000    -1.0000    -1.0000    -1.0000     1.0000    -1.0000     1.0000     1.0000     1.0000    -1.0000
             -1.0000    -1.0000    -1.0000    -1.0000    -1.0000    -1.0000    -1.0000    -1.0000    -.0000    -1.0000
             -1.0000    -1.0000    -1.0000    -1.0000    -1.0000    -1.0000    -1.0000    -1.0000    -.0000    -1.0000
             -1.0000    -1.0000    -1.0000    -1.0000    -1.0000    -1.0000    -1.0000    -1.0000     1.0000    -1.0000
             -1.0000    -1.0000    -1.0000    -1.0000    -1.0000    -1.0000    -1.0000    -1.0000    -1.0000    -1.0000
             -1.0000    -1.0000     1.0000     1.0000     1.0000     1.0000    -1.0000     1.0000    -1.0000

                   DATA HANDLING INSTRUCTION - ECHO PRINT

ABCCCDDDEEEEEEEFFFFFFFGGGGGGGGGGGGHHHHHHHHHHHHHHHHHHHHHHHHHHHHHHHH
BACK               XXXXXXXXXXXXXXX
```

Figure 10.17 - STMANI - Output Example - Default Output

```
STATCAT PROGRAM STMANI        -    MANIPULATION OF ENTRIES
OUTPUT DATA BANK TITLE        -    TRANSFORMATION - FACTOR WEIGHTS TEST
 INPUT DATA BANK TITLE        -    DEMONSTRATION STATCAT DATA BANK
DATA BANK SUBSET TITLE        -    REST OF INPUT FILE

                     DATA STORAGE SEGMENT

ENTRY     44. ON ORIGINAL BECOMES      44. ON TRANSFORMED TAPE
ENTRY     45. ON ORIGINAL BECOMES      45. ON TRANSFORMED TAPE
ENTRY     46. ON ORIGINAL BECOMES      46. ON TRANSFORMED TAPE
ENTRY     47. ON ORIGINAL BECOMES      47. ON TRANSFORMED TAPE
ENTRY     48. ON ORIGINAL BECOMES      48. ON TRANSFORMED TAPE
ENTRY     49. ON ORIGINAL BECOMES      49. ON TRANSFORMED TAPE
ENTRY     50. ON ORIGINAL BECOMES      50. ON TRANSFORMED TAPE
ENTRY     51. ON ORIGINAL BECOMES      51. ON TRANSFORMED TAPE
ENTRY     52. ON ORIGINAL BECOMES      52. ON TRANSFORMED TAPE
ENTRY     53. ON ORIGINAL BECOMES      53. ON TRANSFORMED TAPE
ENTRY     54. ON ORIGINAL BECOMES      54. ON TRANSFORMED TAPE
ENTRY     55. ON ORIGINAL BECOMES      55. ON TRANSFORMED TAPE
ENTRY     56. ON ORIGINAL BECOMES      56. ON TRANSFORMED TAPE
ENTRY     57. ON ORIGINAL BECOMES      57. ON TRANSFORMED TAPE
ENTRY     58. ON ORIGINAL BECOMES      58. ON TRANSFORMED TAPE
ENTRY     59. ON ORIGINAL BECOMES      59. ON TRANSFORMED TAPE
ENTRY     60. ON ORIGINAL BECOMES      60. ON TRANSFORMED TAPE
ENTRY     61. ON ORIGINAL BECOMES      61. ON TRANSFORMED TAPE
ENTRY     62. ON ORIGINAL BECOMES      62. ON TRANSFORMED TAPE
ENTRY     63. ON ORIGINAL BECOMES      63. ON TRANSFORMED TAPE
ENTRY     64. ON ORIGINAL BECOMES      64. ON TRANSFORMED TAPE




TRANSFORMATION COMPLETED   CHECKING COMMENCES
```

Figure 10.18 - STMANI - Manipulation Codes

Code	Operation	Logical Condition
ADD.	Add value in column A to Column B	TO (optional)
DIVD	Divide Col A value by Col B value or by V if Col B is blank	BY (optional)
MULT	Multiply Col A value by Col B value or by V if Col B is blank	BY (optional)
PUT.	Put Col A value in Col B	IN (optional)
SET.	Set col A value to Col B value or to V if Col B is blank	TO (optional)
.IF.	Carry out the next order if the given logical condition holds between the values in Col A and Col B (or V if Col B is blank)	Logical Condition from Figure 10.19 (Required)
GOTO	Skip to the card numbered V	leave blank
Any Transform From Figure 3.71	Carry out the specified transform on the value from Col A, placing the result in Col B.	IN (optional)

Figure 10.19

Logical Conditions

.EQ. Value in Col A equals value in Col B
        (or to V if Col B is blank)

.GE. Value in Col A greater than or equal to Col B
        (or to V if Col B is blank)

.GT. Value in Col A greater than Col B
        (or to V if Col B is blank)

.LE. Value in Col A less than or equal to Col B
        (or to V if Col B is blank)

.LT. Value in Col A less than Col B
        (or to V if Col B is blank)

.NE. Value in Col A not equal to Col B
        (or to V if Col B is blank)

```
C     MASTER STMANI - MANIPULATES ENTRIES ACCORDING TO RUN-TIME INSTRUCTIONS
C     SUBROUTINES AND FUNCTIONS REQUIRED
C     NAME                    TYPE              COMMENT
C     CHECK     (SEE  4.2 )   EXECUTIVE         CHECKS DATA BANK OR SUBSET
C     CLSAM     (SEE  3.5 )   SERVICE           ALLOTS ENTRY TO SAMPLE/SUBSET
C     COMPA     (SEE  3.1 )   SERVICE           COMPARES ALPHAMERIC VALUES
C     COPYA     (SEE  3.1 )   SERVICE           COPIES ALPHAMERIC VALUE
C     FIFI      (SEE  3.2 )   SYSTEM            ALLOCATES PERIPHERALS
C     IBL       (SEE  3.1 )   SERVICE           DETECTS BLANK,END AND STOP CARDS
C     ICH       (SEE  3.1 )   SERVICE           IDENTIFIES ALPHAMERIC CODES
C     LCOM      (SEE  3.4 )   SYSTEM            LOADS COMPLEMENTARY INFORMATION
C     LDBS      (SEE  3.6 )   SYSTEM            LOADS SUBSET DEFINITION
C     LDDS      (SEE  3.4 )   SYSTEM            LOADS DATA DESCRIPTION SEGMENT
C     LDHI      (SEE  3.8 )   SYSTEM            LOADS/CHECKS DATA HANDLING INSTN
C     LMAN      (SEE 10.1 )   SYSTEM            LOADS MANIPULATION INSTRUCTIONS
C     LSET      (SEE  3.5 )   SYSTEM            LOADS DEFINING CONDITIONS
C     MANIP     (SEE 10.1 )   SYSTEM            MANIPULATES DATA
C     TRANS     (SEE  3.7 )   SERVICE           CARRIES OUT REQUIRED TRANSFORM
C     WDCD      (SEE  3.4 )   SERVICE           WRITE DATA COLUMN DESCRIPTION
C     SETTING OF ARRAY DIMENSIONS
C     THE FOLLOWING DIMENSIONS MUST BE AT LEAST AS BIG AS THOSE
C     SPECIFIED BY THE DATA TAPE,SAMPLE SPECIFICATIONS,ETC.
C     NQMAX = MAXIMUM NUMBER OF DATA COLUMNS
C     DIMENSION D(NQMAX),DMAX(NQMAX),DMIN(NQMAX),IT(NQMAX),ST(NQMAX)
C     DIMENSION NP(NQMAX),NDP(NQMAX),IY(NQMAX),CN(NQMAX),XX(NQMAX)
      NQMAX = 100
      DIMENSION D(100  ),DMAX(100  ),DMIN(100  ),IT(100  ),ST(100   )
      DIMENSION NP(  100),NDP(  100),IY(  100),CN(   100),XX(   100)
C     DATA BANK COLUMN NUMBERS - MAY BE USED IN PLACE OF NAMES
C     IF THE DIMENSION OF NQMAX IS INCREASED,THE EXTRA CODES MUST BE
C     INCLUDED IN THIS DATA STATEMENT
      DATA  CN/4HCOL1,4HCOL2,4HCOL3,4HCOL4,4HCOL5,4HCOL6,4HCOL7,4HCOL8,4
     1HCOL9,4HCL10,4HCL11,4HCL12,4HCL13,4HCL14,4HCL15,4HCL16,4HCL17,4HCL
     218,4HCL19,4HCL20,4HCL21,4HCL22,4HCL23,4HCL24,4HCL25,4HCL26,4HCL27,
     34HCL28,4HCL29,4HCL30,4HCL31,4HCL32,4HCL33,4HCL34,4HCL35,4HCL36,4HC
     4L37,4HCL38,4HCL39,4HCL40,4HCL41,4HCL42,4HCL43,4HCL44,4HCL45,4HCL46
     5,4HCL47,4HCL48,4HCL49,4HCL50,4HCL51,4HCL52,4HCL53,4HCL54,4HCL55,4H
     6CL56,4HCL57,4HCL58,4HCL59,4HCL60,4HCL61,4HCL62,4HCL63,4HCL64,4HCL6
     75,4HCL66,4HCL67,4HCL68,4HCL69,4HCL70,4HCL71,4HCL72,4HCL73,4HCL74,4
     8HCL75,4HCL76,4HCL77,4HCL78,4HCL79,4HCL80,4HCL81,4HCL82,4HCL83,4HCL
     984,4HCL85,4HCL86,4HCL87,4HCL88,4HCL89,4HCL90,4HCL91,4HCL92,4HCL93,
     94HCL94,4HCL95,4HCL96,4HCL97,4HCL98,4HCL99,4HC100/
C     NORD = NUMBER OF MANIPULATION ORDERS AVAILABLE
C     DIMENSION ORD(4,NORD)
      NORD = 100
      DIMENSION ORD(4,100)
C     NALTMX = MAXIMUM NUMBER OF CLASSES ON TAPE
C     DIMENSION RT(NQMAX,NALTMX),TRT(NALTMX)
      NALTMX = 50
      DIMENSION RT(  100,   50 ),TRT(    50)
C     MAXDBC = MAXIMUM NUMBER OF DATA BANK SUBSET CONDITIONS
C     DIMENSION SCON(5,MAXDBC)
      MAXDBC = 50
      DIMENSION SCON(5,   50)
C     THE FOLLOWING DIMENSIONS ARE FIXED
C     NAMES FOR STORAGE CELLS OF MANIP,TRANSFORMS,TITLES,ETC
      DIMENSION STN(100),STORE(100),U(60),TTA(16),FORM(50)
      DATA STN/4HS  1,4HS  2,4HS  3,4HS  4,4HS  5,4HS  6,4HS  7,4HS  8,4
     1HS  9,4HS 10,4HS 11,4HS 12,4HS 13,4HS 14,4HS 15,4HS 16,4HS 17,4HS
     218,4HS 19,4HS 20,4HS 21,4HS 22,4HS 23,4HS 24,4HS 25,4HS 26,4HS 27,
     34HS 28,4HS 29,4HS 30,4HS 31,4HS 32,4HS 33,4HS 34,4HS 35,4HS 36,4HS
     4 37,4HS 38,4HS 39,4HS 40,4HS 41,4HS 42,4HS 43,4HS 44,4HS 45,4HS 46
     5,4HS 47,4HS 48,4HS 49,4HS 50,4HS 51,4HS 52,4HS 53,4HS 54,4HS 55,4H
```

```
                  6S 56,4HS 57,4HS 58,4HS 59,4HS 60,4HS 61,4HS 62,4HS 63,4HS 64,4HS 6
                 75,4HS 66,4HS 67,4HS 68,4HS 69,4HS 70,4HS 71,4HS 72,4HS 73,4HS 74,4
                 8HS 75,4HS 76,4HS 77,4HS 78,4HS 79,4HS 80,4HS 81,4HS 82,4HS 83,4HS
                 984,4HS 85,4HS 86,4HS 87,4HS 88,4HS 89,4HS 90,4HS 91,4HS 92,4HS 93,
                 94HS 94,4HS 95,4HS 96,4HS 97,4HS 98,4HS 99,4HS100/
C TRANSFORMATION CODES
C UNITS                          BLOCKS
C           0 - 9   10 - 19   20 - 29   30 - 39   40 - 49    50 - 59
C           POWERS  TRIG       TRIG     STATIST    MATHS      TEST
C                   RADIANS    DEGREES  TRANSF    FUNCTS     FUNCTIONS
C   0        -       -         H.MS      -         -         RM10
C   1        VAL.    SINR      SIND      PSNA      RECP      +/-1
C   2        SQAR    COSR      COSD      PSNB      SQRT      ADD1
C   3        CUBE    TANR      TAND      BINO      ABSV      SUB1
C   4        4PWR    ASIR      ASID      LG+1      SIGN      NOB1
C   5        5PWR    ACOR      ACOD      LOGE      INTG      +/-P
C   6        6PWR    ATAR      ATAD      LG10.     FRAC      ADDP
C   7        7PWR    SINH      DTOR      AL10      EXPT      SUBP
C   8        8PWR    COSH      RTOD      -         PRES      NOBP
C   9        9PWR    TANH      H.HH      -         NEG.      +100
      DATA 0/4HVAL.,4HSQAR,4HCUBE,4H4PWR,4H5PWR,4H6PWR,4H7PWR,4H8PWR,4H9
     1PWR,4HVAL ,4HSINR,4HCOSR,4HTANR,4HASIR,4HACOR,4HATAR,4HSINH,4HCOSH
     2,4HTANH,4HH.MS,4HSIND,4HCOSD,4HTAND,4HASID,4HACOD,4HATAD,4HDTOR,4H
     3RTOD,4HH.HH,4H VAL,4HPSNA,4HPSNB,4HBINO,4HLG+1,4HLOGE,4HLG10,4HAL1
     40,4H    ,4H    ,4H    ,4HRECP,4HSQRT,4HABSV,4HSIGN,4HINTG,4HFRAC,4
     5HEXPT,4HPRES,4HNEG.,4HRM10,4H+/-1,4HADD1,4HSUB1,4HNOR1,4H+/-P,4HAD
     6DP,4HSUBP,4HNORP,4H+100,4H    /
      COMMON /STCT/MED1,MED2,MED3,MED4,MED5,MED6,MED13,Q,V(20),TT(30)
      DATA PROG/4HMANI/
      MED1 = -1
C LEVEL 0 - ASSIGN PERIPHERALS
    1 CALL COPYA(TT(1),PROG)
      CALL FIFI
      ARAN = 5236.
C LEVEL 1 - READ,CHECK AND LOAD STARTER AND DDS OUTPUT
      READ(MED1,900) (FORM(J),J=1,16),(TT(J),J=1,16)
      DO 15 I = 1,10
   15 CALL COPYA(TTA(I),TT(I))
      NQ = AN(FORM,5,3,5)
      NALT=AN(FORM,8,6,8)
      Q  = AN(FORM,16,9,16)
      WRITE(MED6,906)
      WRITE(MED6,901) NQ,NALT,Q,(TT(J),J=1,10),TT(16)
C CHECK SIZE OF STORAGE
      IF(NQ.LE.NQMAX) GO TO 2
      WRITE(MED6,902) NQ,NQMAX
      IF(V(10).LT.0.5) V(10) = 1.
      NQ = NQMAX
    2 IF(NALT.LE.NALTMX) GO TO 3
      WRITE(MED6,903) NALT,NALTMX
      NALT = NALTMX
      IF(V(10).LT.0.5) V(10) = 2.
C LOAD DATA COLUMN DESCRIPTIONS
    3 IF(MED4.LT.1) WRITE(MED6,909)
      IF(MED4.LT.1) GO TO 1
      WRITE(MED4) NQ,NALT,Q,(TT(J),J=1,16)
      V(3) = Q
      V(4) = NQ
      NUSED = 1
      LI = 18
      CALL LDDS(TRT,NALT,D,NQ,ST,NQ,IT,NQ,H,0,H,H,0,LI,0,Q,VX,
     1 MED1,MED2,0,MED4,IGO)
      IF(IGO.GT.0.AND.V(10).LT.0.5) V(10) =  4 + IGO
```

```
C LEVEL 1 - DATA MANIPULATION SPECIFICATION - REPEAT INPUT SPEC
   20 IF(V(10).GT.20.) V(10) = 0.
   18 IF(NUSED.EQ.0) CALL FIFI
      IF(MED3.LT.1) WRITE(MED6,910)
      IF(MED3.LT.1) GO TO 1
      REWIND MED3
      DO 16 I = 1,10
   16 CALL COPYA(TT(I),TTA(I))
      READ(MED3)NQ1,NALT1,Q1,(TT(J),J=11,20),(FORM(J),J=1,6)
C LOAD ORIGINAL DATA COLUMN DESCRIPTIONS
      WRITE(MED6,904)
      WRITE(MED6,901)NQ1,NALT1,Q1,(TT(J),J=11,20),FORM(6)
      IF(NQ1.LE.NQMAX) GO TO 22
      WRITE(MED6,902) NQ1,NQMAX
      IF(V(10).LT.0.5) V(10) = 28.
   22 IF(NALT1.LE.NALTMX) GO TO 23
      WRITE(MED6,903) NALT1,NALTMX
      NALT1 = NALTMX
      IF(V(10).LT.0.5) V(10) = 28.
   23 LI = 18
C READ FROM TAPE TO STORE - LISTING
      CALL LDDS(TRT,NALT1,D,NQ1,ST,NQ1,IT,NQ1,H,0,DMIN,DMAX,NQ,LI,1,Q
     1,VX,0,MED2,MED3,0,IGO)
      IF(IGO.GT.0) GO TO 1
      IF(IGO.GT.0.AND.V(10).LT.0.5) V(10) = 22 + IGO
C REVISED MANIPULATION SPECIFICATION
   30 IF(V(10).GT.30.) V(10) = 0.
      CALL LMAN(ORD,NORD,NUSED,ST,CN ,STN,NQ1,U,60)
      X3 = 0.
      IF(NUSED.EQ.0) GO TO 20
      DO 82 J = 1,NUSED
      IF(ORD(2,J).LT.X3) X3 = ORD(2,J)
   82 IF(ORD(4,J).LT.X3) X3 = ORD(4,J)
   83 NSTU = -X3 + 0.01
      BRAN = ARAN
C LEVEL 2 - DATA BANK SUBSET SPECIFICATION
   41 IF(V(10).GT.40.) V(10) = 0.
      CALL LDBS(SCON,NCON,MAXDBC,CN,ST,IT,NQ1,TRT,NALT1,IGO)
      IF(IGO.LT.0) GO TO 30
C LEVEL 9 - DATA HANDLING INSTRUCTION
   91 IF(V(10).GT.90.) V(10) = 0.
      CALL LDHI(V(1),1,V(2),3,V(9),7,ASDL,18,APT,15,H,0,H,V(10),
     1FORM(41),FORM,MED1,MED2,MED4,Q,NQ,NWARN,1,IGO)
      IF(IGO.GT.0) GO TO 41
      IF(V(1).GT.4.5) NWARN = NWARN + 1
      IF(V(1).GT.4.5) V(1) = -1.
      NX = V(9)
      IF(NX.LE.0.OR.NX.GE.NQ) NWARN = NWARN + 1
      IF(NX.LE.0.OR.NX.GE.NQ) V(9) = NQ-1
      IF(IBL(FORM(2),1,1).LT.0.AND.IBL(FORM(6),11,1).LT.0) NX = 0
      IF(IBL(FORM(2),1,1).GE.0.OR .IBL(FORM(6),11,1).GE.0) NX = 1
      IF(NX.EQ.0)CALL LDHI(V(1),1,H,0,V(9),7,H,0,H,0,H,0,H,V(10),
     1FORM(41),FORM,MED1,MED2,MED4,Q,NQ,NWARN,2,IGO)
      IF(NX.EQ.0) GO TO 92
      IF(ASDL.LE.0.) NWARN = NWARN + 1
      IF(ASDL.EQ.0.) ASDL = 5.
      IF(ASDL.LT.0.) ASDL = 9999.
      IF(APT.LE.0.) NWARN = NWARN + 1
      IF(APT.EQ.0.) APT = 1.
      IF(APT.LT.0.) APT = 0.
      CALL LDHI(V(1),1,V(2),3,V(9),7,ASDL,18,APT,15,H,0,H,V(10),
     1FORM(41),FORM,MED1,MED2,MED4,Q,NQ,NWARN,2,IGO)
   92 IF(IGO.GT.0) GO TO 91
```

```
      WRITE(MED6,990)
C   LOAD DATA STORAGE SEGMENT
      REWIND MED3
      V(10) = BRAN
      NQ2 = NQ
      IF(NQ2.LT.NQ1) NQ2 = NQ1
      XQ1 = NQ1
      DO 105 I = 1,100
  105 STORE(I) = Q
      V(6) = 0.
      V(8) = 50.
      X1 = (NQ+29)/10
      X2 = (NQ1+29)/10
      X3 = (NSTU+29)/10
      US = NUSED + 3
      VT = 0.
      IF(V(1).GT.-0.5) VT = VT + 2.
      IF(V(1).GT. 0.5) VT = VT + X1
      IF(V(1).GT. 1.5) VT = VT + X2
      IF(V(1).GT. 2.5) VT = VT + X3
      IF(V(1).GT. 3.5) VT = VT + US
      READ(MED3) NQ1,NALT1,Q1,(X,I=1,16)
      DO 107 J = 1,NQ1
  107 READ(MED3) (X,I=1,19),(X,I=1,NALT1),NY,X,X
  110 READ(MED3) (D(I),I=1,NQ1)
      V(6) = V(6) + 1.
      DUDS = 0.
      DO 111 I = 1,NQ1
      IF(D(I).EQ.Q1) D(I) = Q
  111 IF(D(I).EQ.Q) DUDS = DUDS + 1.
      IF(DUDS.EQ.XQ1) GO TO 112
      IF(DUDS.GT.V(9)) GO TO 110
      CALL CLSAM(D,NQ1,SCON,NCON,NIN,1)
      IF(NIN.NE.1) GO TO 110
      V(7) = V(7) + 1.
      IF(V(1).LT.-0.5) GO TO 113
      IF(V(8)+VT.GT.50.) WRITE(MED6,918) TT
      IF(V(8)+VT.GT.50.) V(8) = 7.
      WRITE(MED2,982) V(6),V(7)
      V(8) = V(8) + 2.
      IF(V(1).LT.1.5) GO TO 113
      IF(V(8)+X2.GT.50.) WRITE(MED6,918) TT
      IF(V(8)+X2.GT.50.) V(8) = 7.
      WRITE(MED6,983) (D(I),I=1,NQ1)
      V(8) = V(8) + X2
      IF(V(1).LT.3.5) GO TO 113
      IF(V(8)+US.GT.50.) WRITE(MED6,918) TT
      IF(V(8)+US.GT.50.) V(8) = 7.
  113 CALL MANIP(ORD,NUSED,D,NQ2,STORE)
      WRITE(MED4) (D(I),I=1,NQ)
      IF(V(1).LT.0.5) GO TO 110
      IF(V(8)+X1.GT.50.) WRITE(MED6,918) TT
      IF(V(8)+X1.GT.50.) V(8) = 7.
      WRITE(MED6,984) (D(I),I=1,NQ)
      V(8) = V(8) + X1
      IF(V(1).LT.2.5) GO TO 110
      IF(V(8)+X3.GT.50.) WRITE(MED6,918) TT
      IF(V(8)+X3.GT.50.) V(8) = 7.
      V(8) = V(8) + X3
      IF(NSTU.GT.0) WRITE(MED6,985) (STORE(I),I=1,NSTU)
      IF(NSTU.EQ.0) WRITE(MED6,986)
      GO TO 110
  112 IF(NX.GT.0) GO TO 120
```

```
C PREPARE FOR NEW DHI/SUBSET SPEC
      REWIND MED3
      READ(MED3)NX,NX,(X,I=1,17)
      DO 115 J = 1,NQ1
  115 READ(MED3) (X,I=1,19),(X,I=1,NALT1),NX,X,X
      BRAN = V(10)
      V(10) = 0.
      GO TO 91
C END TAPE - TEST IF REQUIRED
  120 WRITE(MED4) (Q,I=1,NQ)
      REWIND MED4
      IF(V(2).LT.0.) WRITE(MED2,995)
      IF(V(2).LT.0.) GO TO 1
C CARRY OUT PRELIMINARY CHECK OF DATA TAPE
      WRITE(MED2,996)
      APT = APT*.01
      NCON=0
      CALL CHECK (D,DMAX,DMIN,RT,IT,TRT,NQ,NALT,ASDL,APT,SCON,NCON,ST)
      WRITE(MED6,999)
      GO TO 1
  900 FORMAT(16A1,16A4)
  901 FORMAT(1H0,20X,31HSTATCAT MANIPULATION OF ENTRIES
     1                             /16H0FILE PARAMETER
     2S/29H0NUMBER OF DATA COLUMNS IS - ,I6/29H0STORED NUMBER OF CLASSES
     3 IS ,I6/34H0VALUE USED FOR MISSING DATA IS - ,F20.8/13H0FILE TITLE
     4 ,10A4,10X,15HFILE REFERENCE ,A4)
  902 FORMAT (4H0THE,I6,   37H ITEMS PER ENTRY EXCEED THE AVAILABLE,I6,1
     16H STORAGE COLUMNS)
  903 FORMAT (4H0THE,I6,40H CLASSES PER COLUMN EXCEED THE AVAILABLE,I6,1
     13H STORAGE ROWS)
  904 FORMAT (24H1 FOR ORIGINAL DATA BANK   )
  906 FORMAT (27H1 FOR MANIPULATED DATA BANK)
  909 FORMAT(41H0NO OUTPUT FILE - PROGRAM CANNOT CONTINUE)
  910 FORMAT(41H0 NO INPUT FILE - PROGRAM CANNOT CONTINUE)
  918 FORMAT(23H1STATCAT PROGRAM STMANI,7X,1H-,4X,23HMANIPULATION OF ENT
     1RIES/23H OUTPUT DATA BANK TITLE,7X,1H-,4X,10A4/23H  INPUT DATA BAN
     2K TITLE,7X,1H-,4X,10A4/23H DATA BANK SUBSET TITLE,7X,1H-,4X,10A4/
     31H0,20X,20HDATA STORAGE SEGMENT/)
  982 FORMAT(6H0ENTRY,F7.0,20H ON ORIGINAL BECOMES,F7.0,20H ON TRANSFORM
     1ED TAPE   )
  983 FORMAT (20H0ORIGINAL ENTRY       -  /(10X,10F11.4))
  984 FORMAT (23H0 MANIPULATED ENTRY    -  /(10X,10F11.4))
  985 FORMAT(13H0 STORED DATA/(10X,10F11.4))
  986 FORMAT(22H0STORED ITEMS NOT USED)
  990 FORMAT(42H0INPUT ACCEPTED - TRANSFORMATION COMMENCES)
  995 FORMAT(47H0TRANSFORMATION COMPLETED - CHECKING SUPPRESSED)
  996 FORMAT(46H1TRANSFORMATION COMPLETED - CHECKING COMMENCES)
  998 FORMAT(41H1TRANSFORMATION COMPLETED - PROGRAM HALTS)
  999 FORMAT(36H1CHECKING COMPLETED - READ NEW FILES)
      END


      SUBROUTINE LMAN(ORD,NMAX,ISF,CNAM,CNO,ST,NQ,TR,NR)
C LMAN     (SEE 10.1 ) SYSTEM        LOADS MANIPULATION INSTRUCTIONS
C CARD FIELDS
C  1-4 5-8   9-12    13-16    17-20 21-40 41-80            RESULT
C NO. CODE COL.A CONNECTOR COL.B VALUE COMMENT             IN COL.
C ADD. C OR S  .TO.   C OR S N.U.    N.U.= NOT USED        B
C SUBT C OR S  FROM   C OR S N.U.                          B
C MULT C OR S  .BY.   C OR S USED   (USED = VALUE USED)    A
C DIVD C OR S  .BY.   C OR S USED   (IF COL B IS BLANK)    A
C TRAN C OR S  .IN.   C OR S N.U.   TRAN IS ANY TRANSFORM  B
C PUT. C OR S  .IN.   C OR S N.U.                          B
```

```
C SET.   C OR S   .EQ.     N.U.      USED                                        A
C GOTO   C OR S   N.U.     N.U.      USED    GO TO ORDER WITH SAME NUMBER
C                                            IF OUT OF RANGE END OF MANIPULN.
C .IF.   C OR S   .LC.     C OR S    USED    LC=LOGICAL CONDITION - MAY BE
C                                            .EQ./.NE./.GT./.LT./.GE./.LE.
C                                    NEXT ORDER EXECUTED IF LC IS TRUE
C C=COLUMN NUMBER/NAME    S = STORE NUMBER   V = NUMERICAL VALUE(REAL)
C BLANK CODE - NO OPERATION -GO TO NEXT MANIPULATION
C COMPLETELY BLANK CARD - IGNORED
C 'END' CARD - END OF LOADING MODULE
      DIMENSION ORD(4,NMAX),CNAM(NQ),CNO(NQ),TR(NR)
      DIMENSION CODE(17),ST(100),C(38)
      COMMON /STCT/MED1,MED2,MED3,MED4,MED5,MED6,MED13,Q,V(20),TT(30)
      DATA CODE/4H    ,4HADD.,4HDIVD,4H.EQ.,4H.GE.,4HGOTO,4H.GT.,4H.IF.,
     14H.LE.,4H.LT.,4HMULT,4H.NE.,4HNORM,4HPUT.,4HSTAN,4HSET.,4HSUBT/
      NOK = 0
      ISF = 0
      WRITE(MED2,900)
    1 ISF = ISF + 1
    2 READ(MED1,901) C
      IF(IBL(C,4,1).LT.0.AND.IBL(C(5),4,4).LT.0
     1.AND.IBL(C(9),20,1).LT.0.AND.IBL(C(29),10,4).LT.0) GO TO 2
      WRITE(MED2,902) C
      IF(IBL(C,4,1)-1) 4,4,3
    3 ISF = ISF - 1
      RETURN
    4 IN = AN(C,4,1,4)
      IF(IN.NE.ISF.AND.NOK.EQ.0) GO TO 30
    5 Y = AN(C,28,9,28)
      ORD(1,ISF) = ICH(C(5),CODE,17)
      ORD(2,ISF) = ICH(C(6),CNAM ,NQ)+ICH(C(6),CNO,NQ)-ICH(C(6),ST,100)
      ORD(3,ISF) = ICH(C(7),CODE,17)
      ORD(4,ISF) = ICH(C(8),CNAM ,NQ)+ICH(C(8),CNO,NQ)-ICH(C(8),ST,100)
      IF(ORD(1,ISF).EQ.0.)ORD(1,ISF) = ICH(C(5),TR,60)+20
      IF(ORD(1,ISF).EQ.6.)ORD(2,ISF) = Y
      I = ORD(1,ISF)
      J = ORD(2,ISF)
      K = ORD(3,ISF)
      L = ORD(4,ISF)
      M = 0
      IF(I.GT.20) I = 2
      IF(I.GT.17) GO TO 31
    6 GO TO (1,11,11,31,31,13,31,11,31,31,11,31,11,11,11,11,11),I
C TEST IF COLUMN A IS IN RANGE
   11 IF(J.LT.-100.OR.J.EQ.0.OR.J.GT.NQ) GO TO 33
      GO TO (1,15,15,1,1,1,1,14,1,1,15,1,1,15,1,15,15),I
C TEST IF SECOND COLUMN IS IN RANGE 1 TO NMAX   (WARNING ONLY)
   13 IF(J.LT.1.OR.J.GT.NMAX) GO TO 35
      GO TO 1
C TEST IF THIRD COLUMN IS A LOGICAL CONDITION
   14 IF(K.EQ.0) GO TO 36
      GO TO (36,36,36,15,15,36,15,36,15,15,36,15,36,36,36,36,36),K
   15 GO TO (36,18,16,36,36,36,36,16,36,36,16,36,36,18,36,17,18),I
C IF FOURTH COLUMN IS BLANK SUBSTITUTE NUMERIC VALUE
   16 IF(L.NE.0) GO TO 18
      IF(IBL(C(8),1,4).GT.0) GO TO 37
   17 ORD(4,ISF) = Y
      IF(I.EQ.3)ORD(1,ISF) = 18
      IF(I.EQ.8)ORD(1,ISF) = 19
      IF(I.EQ.11)ORD(1,ISF) = 20
      GO TO 1
C TEST IF FOURTH COLUMN IS IN RANGE -100 TO -1,1 TO NQ
   18 IF(L.LT.-100.OR.L.EQ.0.OR.L.GT.NQ) GO TO 37
```

```
      GO TO 1
   30 WRITE(MED2,930)
      IF(V(10).LT.0.5) V(10) = 14.
      NOK = 1
      GO TO 5
   31 WRITE(MED2,931)
      IF(V(10).LT.0.5) V(10) = 15.
      I = 2
      GO TO 6
   33 WRITE(MED2,933)
      IF(V(10).LT.0.5) V(10) = 15.
      GO TO 15
   35 WRITE(MED2,935)
      GO TO 15
   36 WRITE(MED2,936)
      IF(V(10).LT.0.5) V(10) = 15.
      GO TO 16
   37 WRITE(MED2,937)
      IF(V(10).LT.0.5) V(10) = 15.
      GO TO 1
  900 FORMAT(1H1,20X,31HDATA MANIPULATION SPECIFICATION/1H0,12X,30HCARD
     1    MANIP-    FIRST     SECOND/12X,41HNUMBER  ULATION   COLUMN    COLUMN
     2CONSTANT   ,20X,7HCOMMENT/)
  901 FORMAT(4A1,4A4,20A1,10A4)
  902 FORMAT(13X,4A1,2(4X,A4),2A4,4X,20A1,5X,10A4)
  930 FORMAT(13X,40HDATA MANIPULATION CARDS ARE OUT OF ORDER)
  931 FORMAT(21X,22HUNRECOGNISABLE MANIPULATION CODE)
  933 FORMAT(29X,28HUNRECOGNISABLE DATA COLUMN A)
  935 FORMAT(29X,39HGO TO ORDER OUT OF RANGE (WARNING ONLY))
  936 FORMAT(33X,45HINADMISSIBLE LOGICAL CONDITION - WRONG CODING)
  937 FORMAT(29X,28HUNRECOGNISABLE DATA COLUMN B)
      END


      SUBROUTINE MANIP(ORD,NMAX,D,NQ,ST)
C MANIP (SEE 10.1 ) SYSTEM       MANIPULATES DATA
      DIMENSION D(NQ),ORD(4,NMAX),ST(100)
      COMMON /STCT/MED1,MED2,MED3,MED4,MED5,MED6,MED13,Q,V(20),TT(30)
      IBASE = V(10)
      IF(V(1).GT.3.5) WRITE(MED2,903)
      IF(V(1).GT.3.5) V(8) = V(8) + 3.
      ISP = -1
    1 ISP = ISP + 1
    2 ISP = ISP + 1
      IF(ISP.GT.NMAX) RETURN
    3 I = ORD(1,ISP)
      IF(I.EQ.1) GO TO 2
      IF(I.EQ.6) GO TO 10
      J = ORD(2,ISP)
      K = ORD(3,ISP)
      L = ORD(4,ISP)
C FIRST OPERAND
      JS = 0
      IF(J.LT.1)JS = 1
      IF(J.LT.1) J = -J
      IF(JS.EQ.0) X = D(J)
      IF(JS.EQ.1) X = ST(J)
C SECOND OPERAND
      IF(I.EQ.16.OR.I.GE.18.AND.I.LE.20) Y = ORD(4,ISP)
      IF(I.EQ.16.OR.I.GE.18.AND.I.LE.20) GO TO 4
      LS = 0
      IF(L.LT.1)LS = 1
      IF(L.LT.1) L = -L
```

```
      IF(LS.EQ.0) Y = D(L)
      IF(LS.EQ.1) Y = ST(L)
    4 CONTINUE
      IF(I.GT.20) X = TRANS(X,Q,I-20,IBASE)
      V(10) = IBASE
      IF(I.GT.20) GO TO 7
C CHOICE OF OPERATION
    5 GO TO (2,8,9,2,2,10,2,11,2,2,12,2,7,7,7,16,17,9,11,12),I
    6 L = J
      LS = JS
    7 IF(LS.EQ.0) D(L) = X
      IF(LS.EQ.1) ST(L) = X
      IF(V(1).LT.3.5) GO TO 2
      V(8) = V(8) + 1.
      IF(V(8).GT.50.) WRITE(MED2,918) TT
      IF(V(8).GT.50.) WRITE(MED2,903)
      IF(V(8).GT.50.) WRITE(MED2,904)
      IF(V(8).GT.50.) V(8) = 10.
      WRITE(MED2,900) ISP,L,X
      IF(LS.EQ.0) WRITE(MED2,901)
      IF(LS.EQ.1) WRITE(MED2,902)
      GO TO 2
    8 IF(X.NE.Q.AND.Y.NE.Q) X = X + Y
      IF(Y.EQ.Q) X = Q
      GO TO 7
    9 IF(X.NE.Q.AND.Y.NE.Q.AND.Y.NE.0.) X = X/Y
      IF(Y.EQ.Q .OR.Y.EQ.0.) X = Q
      GO TO 6
   10 ISP = ORD(2,ISP)
      IF(ISP.LT.1.OR.ISP.GT.NMAX) RETURN
      GO TO 3
C CHOICE OF LOGICAL OPERATION
   11 GO TO (2,2,2,18,19,2,20,2,21,22,2,23,2,2,2,2,2),K
   12 IF(X.NE.Q.AND.Y.NE.Q) X = X * Y
      IF(Y.EQ.Q) X = Q
      GO TO 6
   16 X = ORD(4,ISP)
      GO TO 6
   17 IF(X.NE.Q.AND.Y.NE.Q) X = Y - X
      IF(Y.EQ.Q) X = Q
      GO TO 7
   18 IF(X.EQ.Y) GO TO 2
      GO TO 1
   19 IF(X.GE.Y) GO TO 2
      GO TO 1
   20 IF(X.GT.Y) GO TO 2
      GO TO 1
   21 IF(X.LE.Y) GO TO 2
      GO TO 1
   22 IF(X.LT.Y) GO TO 2
      GO TO 1
   23 IF(X.NE.Y) GO TO 2
      GO TO 1
  900 FORMAT(14H  MANIPULATION,I6,2H -,6X,I4,8H BECOMES,F20.6)
  901 FORMAT(1H+,22X,4HITEM)
  902 FORMAT(1H+,22X,5HSTORE)
  903 FORMAT(23H0MANIPULATIONS IN ORDER/)
  904 FORMAT(12H+(CONTINUED)/)
  918 FORMAT(23H1STATCAT PROGRAM STMANI,7X,1H-,4X,23HMANIPULATION OF ENT
     1RIES/23H OUTPUT DATA BANK TITLE,7X,1H-,4X,10A4/23H  INPUT DATA BAN
     2K TITLE,7X,1H-,4X,10A4/23H DATA BANK SUBSET TITLE,7X,1H-,4X,10A4/
     3 1H0,20X,20HDATA STORAGE SEGMENT )
      END
```

10.2 PROGRAM STSORT - SORTING ENTRIES INTO ORDER

10.2.1 Purpose

This program sorts the entries in specified subsets of a STATCAT data bank into specified order, and produces an output STATCAT data bank. The subsets of the original STATCAT data bank need not be mutually exclusive or exhaustive, and need not be ordered in the same way. The amount of information output during sorting and checking may be controlled by the user.

Figure 10.21a contains a system flow-chart for the main program STSORT. Figure 10.21b contains a system flow-chart for the executive subroutine CSORT.

10.2.2 Input Data

Summary

Item	Level	Format	Function	See
1	0	A	File control card (First input+output)	3.2
2	0	B	Data starter card	Below + 3.3
(3	1	A	File control card (later input)	Below + 3.2)
4	2	F	Priority specification	Below
5	3	E	Subset specification	3.6
6	4	G	Data handling instruction	Below + 3.8

2 - Data Starter Card

Standard - Fields A to E not used. Only revised STATCAT data bank title, name and key used. Number of data columns, number of classes and non-value taken from input STATCAT data bank.

(3 - File Control Card - Later input)

This file control card is employed only when a second STATCAT input is to be used to in place of that specified at the start of the program. The code SAME must be given for the output STATCAT data bank - to avoid rewinding and over-writing.

4 - Priority Specification

This has the same format as the variate specification described in 3.7. Only the first two four-character fields are used. The first must contain a priority code, as specified in Figure 11.42, and the second the name or number of a data column in the current input STATCAT data bank. The priority conditions are applied in the order specified to the data specified until a decision on priority can be reached. If two entries have equal priority, they are maintained in their original order on the input STATCAT data bank.

Data Handling Instruction

This is a standard data handling instruction. It is used to specify the amount of information printed during entry manipulation, to indicate whether to close the output STATCAT data bank, and what checking procedures are to be used.

Card Layout - Data Handling Instruction - STSORT

```
ABCCCDDDEEEEEEEEFFFFFFFFFFFFFFFFFFFFFFFFFGGGGGGGGGGGGGGGG.....
Columns     Item    FORTRAN         Function                        See
on Card     code    Type
    1         A       I      Data Output Control Index              Below
    2         B       I      Data Checking Control Index             4.3
  3 -  5     C       I      Maximum number of non-values           Below
  6 -  8     D       I      Maximum number of s.d. from the mean    4.3
  9 - 16     E       F      Minimum percentage in class             4.3
 17 - 40     F       A      Comment (printed with line)              -
 41 - 80     G       A      Comment (printed separately)             -
```

A - Data Output Control Index

This index controls the amount of description output during the construction of the revised data storage segment. Unless otherwise specified only indications of the progress of the sorting procedure are output.

ALTERNATIVES

A = 0 or blank: Only indications of the progress of sorting are
(default)   output.

A = 1   :   In addition, messages tracing the allocation of input
                  entries to stores, tentative output of entries,
                  confirmation of tentative output and confirmed output
                  are also produced.

A = 2   :   In addition, completed output subsets are printed
                  as they are completed.

A = 3   :   In addition, original (input) entries are printed
                  as they are read.

A = 4   :   In addition, each output entry is printed as it is
                  stored.

A = 5-9   :   No output during combining

C - Maximum Number of Non-values

This is the maximum number of non-values that will be accepted in an ordered entry being written to the output STATCAT data bank.

DEFAULT value = N-1 where N is the number of data columns in the output STATCAT data bank. (A completely blank record would terminate the data bank - rendering any subsequent entries inaccessible.)

10.2.3   Input Example

Figure 10.22 is a summary of the input structure for two runs of STSORT, using a subset specification to divide the STATCAT data bank into two subsets which are then ordered and placed in the same output STATCAT data bank, which is then checked by CHECK. The output STATCAT data bank is re-ordered so that the entries appear in order for each observer, rather than in day-by-day order. Figure 10.23 lists the input cards corresponding to the summary of Figure 10.22.

10.2.4 Output Example

Figure 10.24 is a general summary of the output produced by this program, indented according to the program structure. Figure 10.25 is a page-by-page summary of the output corresponding to the specific input of 10.2.3. (For demonstration purposes, the number of words of storage available in the main program was deliberately reduced to 2,000 words, to demonstrate sorting where the storage capacity is exceeded.)

Figure 10.26 shows part of the output of the first sweep through the data, in which only the entries relating to the observer Eric were selected. It will be observed that, where the capacity of the store is not exceeded, input, sorting and output require only one sweep through the data bank. Figures 10.27 and 10.28 show the start and end of the output for the sorting of the remaining entries. The span of entries now required in store at any time exceeds the storage available, so the subroutine CSORT now adopts a different strategy, involving repeated sweeps through the input STATCAT data bank.

The checking output (not shown) is identical with that produced in 4.2 - no entries having been duplicated, omitted or altered.

10.2.5 Sorting Logic

Although a simplified flow-chart of the executive subroutine CSORT is provided in Figure 10.21a, and detailed comments are provided in the listing of this subroutine, a more general description may assist users to follow the strategy of the system.

Each time the subroutine CSORT is called it sorts the entries in a subset of the input STATCAT data bank into the specified order, and adds them to the output STATCAT data bank. Wherever possible, the subroutine sorts the data in internal storage - not by physically moving them, but by maintaining a list of pointers to the array of stored entries. If the data are completely dis-ordered, the system may not have enough room to store enough entries in core. If this is so, the system searches the input data bank for as many entries as it can store in order, writes these in one block to the output data bank and repeats the process, reverting to continuous sorting until it again encounters an excessive span of entries to be sorted.

Because several subsets of data banks may be included with the same or different priority orderings, the system maintains a note of the number of entries correctly loaded to the STATCAT output data bank, and skips these before accepting the output of the current stage of sorting.

If 'underflow' (see below) has occurred, then a number of entries in the output STATCAT data bank will have been confirmed in their places in the output STATCAT data bank. The index of correct output will have been updated accordingly, and the last entry known to be in its correct place will also be in store.

The sorting proper begins by loading entries in the subset from the input medium to core storage, discarding those which have been correctly output. The subroutine keeps track of the positions of stored entries in the input STATCAT data bank, and of their correct priority order. When the store is completely filled, the subroutine puts the first two entries (in priority order) to the output STATCAT data bank. These are tentative outputs, since it is possible that some entries not yet read into store may have a higher priority. The store which contained the first entry is now liberated to accept a new entry from the input, and the second entry output becomes the 'last entry output'.

The next entry on the input is now read into the freed line, entries already output correctly and entries not in the subset being dropped automatically. The position of the new entry in priority order is determined. If the entry does not come before the 'last entry output' the highest priority entry in store is output, becoming the new 'last entry output' and the previous 'last entry output' is freed to accept a new input entry. This cycle is repeated until either the data terminator is reached, or an entry is found which should come before the 'last entry output'. (This is the condition called 'underflow', and indicates that there is not enough storage to complete the sorting in one sweep through the input STATCAT data bank.)

When underflow has occurred the program continues to read and store entries in priority order, discarding those not in the sample, or already output in their correct place, but puts no more entries into the output STATCAT data bank. Space is found for new entries by discarding the lowest priority entry. This process is continued until the end of the subset is reached. At this point, the highest priority entries in store are the highest priority entries not yet output. The output STATCAT data bank is now re-read, noting the position of the last entry before the highest priority entry in store, discarding all entries before this entry, re-loading all entries following it into store (finding space by discarding the current lowest priority entry) until the point of previous failure is reached. The store now contains the entries immediately following the first entry not in the output STATCAT data bank, including those from the rest of the input STATCAT data bank, and those already output tentatively to the output STATCAT data bank. The output STATCAT data bank is now re-positioned after the last confirmed entry, and all the entries in store are output, in priority order. The number of confirmed entries is increased accordingly, the last priority entry becomes the last entry known to be correctly output (last confirmed entry) and the subroutine re-starts itself.

When the data terminator is reached without an 'underflow' having occured, the store contains all remaining entries in their correct order. These entries are transferred to the output STATCAT data bank, the number of confirmed entries is increased accordingly, and the subroutine returns to the main program.

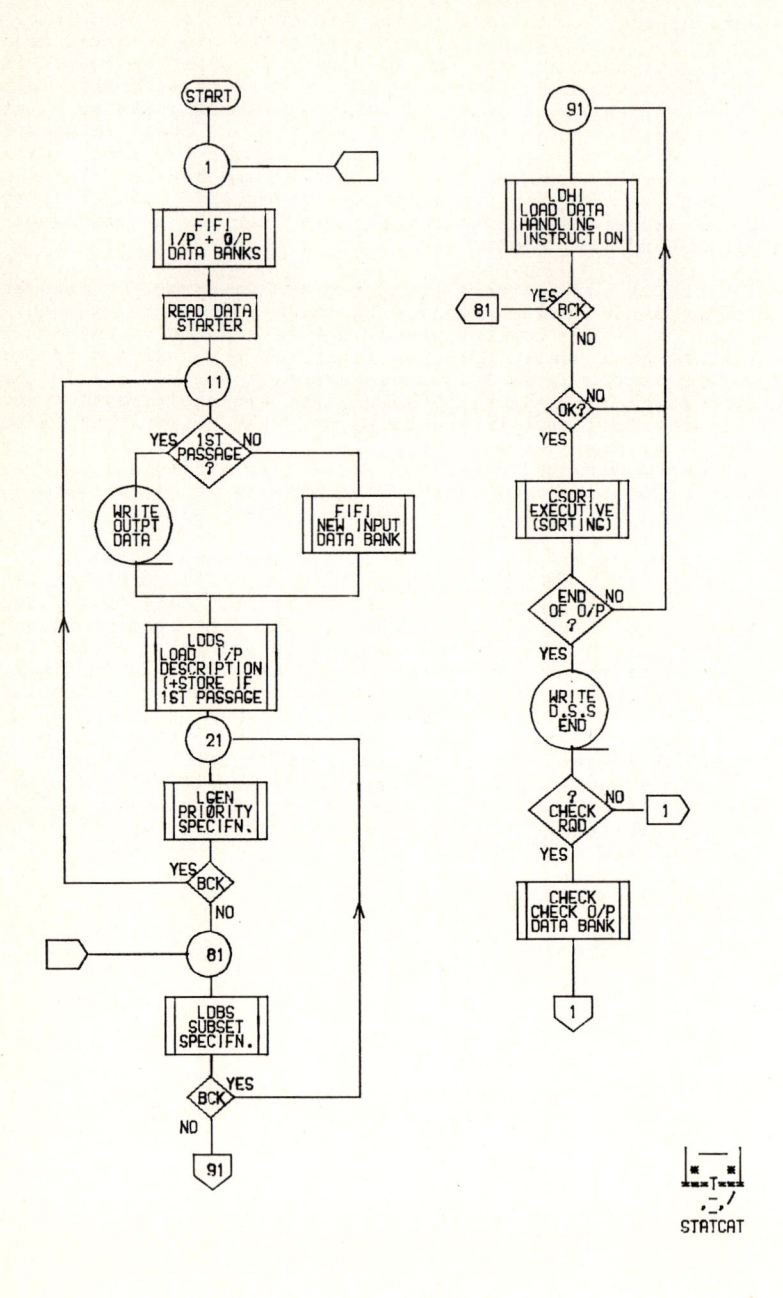

Figure 10.21a - System Flow-Chart - S1SORT

621

Figure 10.21b - System Flow-Chart - CSORT

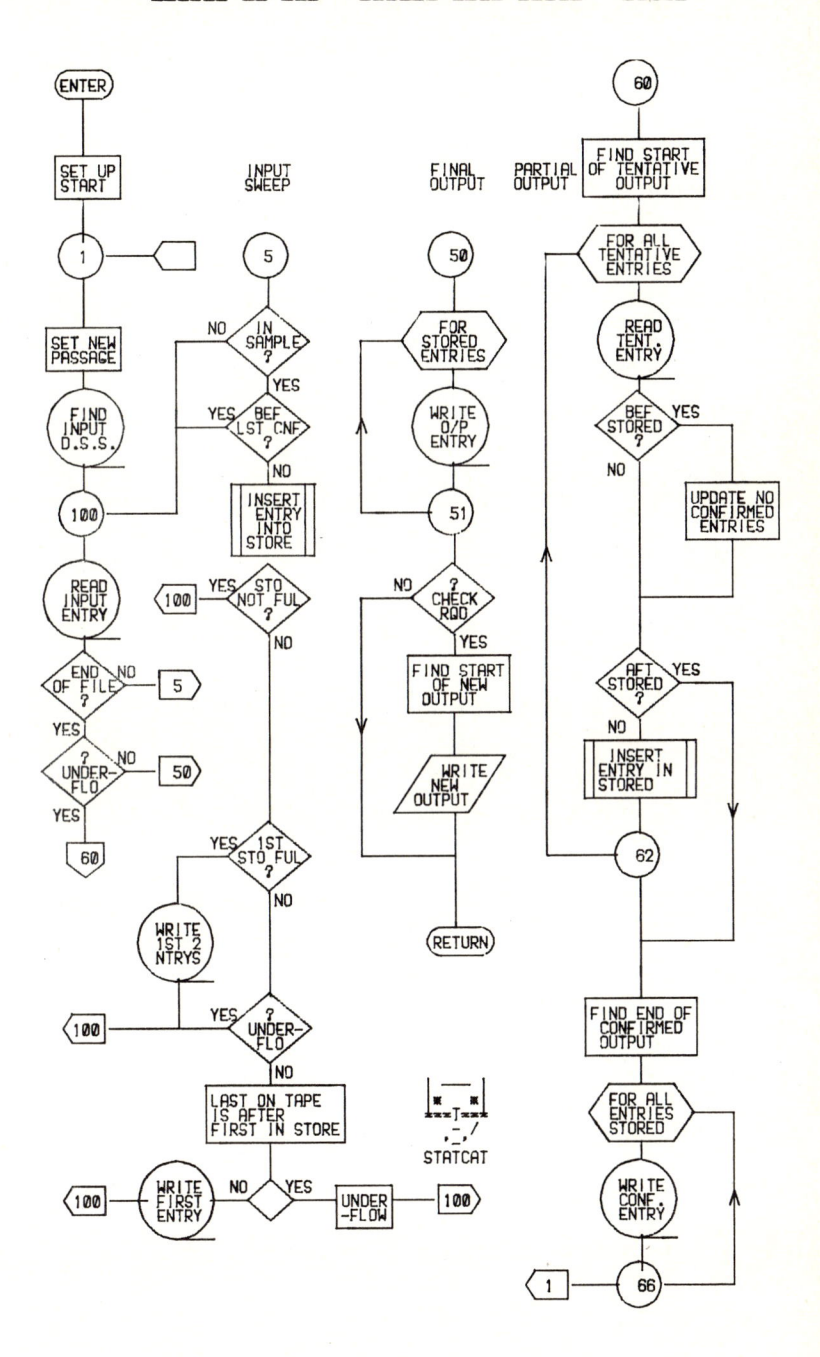

Figure 10.22 - STSORT - Input Structure

```
         Level
  0   1   2   3   4   5   6   7   8   9
FILE CONTROL CARD
    DATA STARTER CARD
        PRIORITY SPECIFICATION
            SUBSET SPECIFICATION
                DATA HANDLING INSTRUCTION
                BACK TO READ NEW SUBSET
            SUBSET SPECIFICATION
                DATA HANDLING INSTRUCTION
                STOP
```

Figure 10.23 - STSORT - Input Example

```
---------1---------2---------3---------4---------5---------6---------7--
**STSORTDEMO   DUFF                    INPUT=DEMONSTRATION OUTPUT=DUMMY
               RE-ORDERED STATCAT DEMONSTRATION
1Q2.OPER
END OF PRIORITY SPECIFICATION
ERIC ONLY
.IF.OPER.EQ.ERIC
END OF SUBSET DEFINITION
1                              ERIC ONLY - ALL EQUAL PRIORITY
BACK TO READ NEW SUBSET
ALL EXCEPT ERIC
.IF.OPER.NE.ERIC
END OF SUBSET DEFINITION
GO
STOP
---------1---------2---------3---------4---------5---------6---------7--
```

Figure 10.24 - STSORT - Output Structure

```
For each  ) : Output File Control Record
output    )   Output File Parameters
data bank )   Output Data Description Record (= first input)
              For each  ) Input File Parameters
              Input     ) For each  ) Priority Record
              Data Bank ) Priority  ) For each ) Subset Record
              .           Specification ) Subset ) See below left
              .
              .
                  For each ) Event Records
                  Sweep    ) <Allocation of Entries>
              .                  <Output Subsets>
              .                  <Entries Input>
              .                  <Entries Stored>
              .<Standard Data Bank Checking>
```

Carated(<>) items are optional.

Figure 10.25 - STSORT - Page-by-page output summary

Page	Contents	Origin
1	File Control Record	FIFI
2- 3	Output Data Header Output File Parameters Output Data Description record	STSORT STSORT LDDS
4	Priority Specification	LDBS/LSET
5	Subset Specification Data Handling Instruction	LDBS LDHI
6	Sorting Record (one sweep) Data Handling Instruction	CSORT LDHI
7	Subset Specification Data Handling Instruction	LDBS LDHI
8-12	Sorting Records	CSORT
13-23	Standard Data Checking	CHECK
24	End of Sorting Message	STSORT
25	Data Handling Instruction (STOP)	LDHI

Figure 10.26 - STSORT - Output Example - Single sweep

```
STATCAT PROGRAM STSORT        -     ORDERING OF ENTRIES
OUTPUT DATA BANK TITLE        -     RE-ORDERED STATCAT DEMONSTRATION
INPUT DATA BANK TITLE         -     DEMONSTRATION STATCAT DATA BANK
DATA BANK SUBSET TITLE        -     ERIC ONLY

ENTRY    1 FROM ORIGINAL  INPUT PLACED IN STORE    1
ENTRY    8 FROM ORIGINAL  INPUT PLACED IN STORE    2
ENTRY   10 FROM ORIGINAL  INPUT PLACED IN STORE    3
ENTRY   15 FROM ORIGINAL  INPUT PLACED IN STORE    4
ENTRY   18 FROM ORIGINAL  INPUT PLACED IN STORE    5
ENTRY   23 FROM ORIGINAL  INPUT PLACED IN STORE    6
ENTRY   25 FROM ORIGINAL  INPUT PLACED IN STORE    7
ENTRY   32 FROM ORIGINAL  INPUT PLACED IN STORE    8
ENTRY   35 FROM ORIGINAL  INPUT PLACED IN STORE    9
ENTRY   38 FROM ORIGINAL  INPUT PLACED IN STORE   10
ENTRY   44 FROM ORIGINAL  INPUT PLACED IN STORE   11
ENTRY   45 FROM ORIGINAL  INPUT PLACED IN STORE   12

                          STORE IS NOW FULL

ENTRY    1 FROM ORIGINAL  INPUT PLACED IN TENTATIVE OUTPUT    1 FROM STORE   1
ENTRY    8 FROM ORIGINAL  INPUT PLACED IN TENTATIVE OUTPUT    2 FROM STORE   2
ENTRY   52 FROM ORIGINAL  INPUT PLACED IN STORE    1
ENTRY   10 FROM ORIGINAL  INPUT PLACED IN TENTATIVE OUTPUT    3 FROM STORE   3
ENTRY   53 FROM ORIGINAL  INPUT PLACED IN STORE    2
ENTRY   15 FROM ORIGINAL  INPUT PLACED IN TENTATIVE OUTPUT    4 FROM STORE   4
ENTRY   59 FROM ORIGINAL  INPUT PLACED IN STORE    3
ENTRY   18 FROM ORIGINAL  INPUT PLACED IN TENTATIVE OUTPUT    5 FROM STORE   5
ENTRY   62 FROM ORIGINAL  INPUT PLACED IN STORE    4
ENTRY   23 FROM ORIGINAL  INPUT PLACED IN TENTATIVE OUTPUT    6 FROM STORE   6

                          END OF INPUT WITHOUT OVERFLOW

ENTRY    1 FROM TENTATIVE OUTPUT IS CONFIRMED - WITHOUT RELOADING TO STORE
ENTRY    2 FROM TENTATIVE OUTPUT IS CONFIRMED - WITHOUT RELOADING TO STORE
ENTRY    3 FROM TENTATIVE OUTPUT IS CONFIRMED - WITHOUT RELOADING TO STORE
ENTRY    4 FROM TENTATIVE OUTPUT IS CONFIRMED - WITHOUT RELOADING TO STORE
ENTRY    5 FROM TENTATIVE OUTPUT IS CONFIRMED - WITHOUT RELOADING TO STORE
ENTRY    6 FROM TENTATIVE OUTPUT IS CONFIRMED - WITHOUT RELOADING TO STORE
ENTRY   25 FROM ORIGINAL  INPUT PLACED IN CONFIRMED OUTPUT    7 FROM STORE   7
ENTRY   32 FROM ORIGINAL  INPUT PLACED IN CONFIRMED OUTPUT    8 FROM STORE   8
ENTRY   35 FROM ORIGINAL  INPUT PLACED IN CONFIRMED OUTPUT    9 FROM STORE   9
ENTRY   38 FROM ORIGINAL  INPUT PLACED IN CONFIRMED OUTPUT   10 FROM STORE  10
ENTRY   44 FROM ORIGINAL  INPUT PLACED IN CONFIRMED OUTPUT   11 FROM STORE  11
ENTRY   45 FROM ORIGINAL  INPUT PLACED IN CONFIRMED OUTPUT   12 FROM STORE  12
ENTRY   52 FROM ORIGINAL  INPUT PLACED IN CONFIRMED OUTPUT   13 FROM STORE   1
ENTRY   53 FROM ORIGINAL  INPUT PLACED IN CONFIRMED OUTPUT   14 FROM STORE   2
ENTRY   59 FROM ORIGINAL  INPUT PLACED IN CONFIRMED OUTPUT   15 FROM STORE   3
ENTRY   62 FROM ORIGINAL  INPUT PLACED IN CONFIRMED OUTPUT   16 FROM STORE   4

                SORTING OF SUBSET COMPLETED

                      DATA HANDLING INSTRUCTION - ECHO PRINT

ABCCCDDUEEEEEEFEFFFFFFFGGGGGGGGGGGGGGGGHHHHHHHHHHHHHHHHHHHHHHHHHHHHHHHHHHHHH
BACK TO READ NEW SUBSET XXXXXXXXXXXXXXX
```

Figure 10.27 - STSORT - Output Example - Multiple Sweep - Start

```
STATCAT PROGRAM STSORT        -      ORDERING OF ENTRIES
OUTPUT DATA BANK TITLE        -      RE-ORDERED STATCAT DEMONSTRATION
INPUT DATA BANK TITLE         -      DEMONSTRATION STATCAT DATA BANK
DATA BANK SUBSET TITLE        -      ALL EXCEPT ERIC

ENTRY     2 FROM ORIGINAL     INPUT PLACED IN STORE         1
ENTRY     3 FROM ORIGINAL     INPUT PLACED IN STORE         2
ENTRY     4 FROM ORIGINAL     INPUT PLACED IN STORE         3
ENTRY     5 FROM ORIGINAL     INPUT PLACED IN STORE         4
ENTRY     6 FROM ORIGINAL     INPUT PLACED IN STORE         5
ENTRY     7 FROM ORIGINAL     INPUT PLACED IN STORE         6
ENTRY     9 FROM ORIGINAL     INPUT PLACED IN STORE         7
ENTRY    11 FROM ORIGINAL     INPUT PLACED IN STORE         8
ENTRY    12 FROM ORIGINAL     INPUT PLACED IN STORE         9
ENTRY    13 FROM ORIGINAL     INPUT PLACED IN STORE        10
ENTRY    14 FROM ORIGINAL     INPUT PLACED IN STORE        11
ENTRY    16 FROM ORIGINAL     INPUT PLACED IN STORE        12

                              STORE IS NOW FULL

ENTRY     3 FROM ORIGINAL     INPUT PLACED IN TENTATIVE OUTPUT   17 FROM STORE    2
ENTRY     6 FROM ORIGINAL     INPUT PLACED IN TENTATIVE OUTPUT   18 FROM STORE    5
ENTRY    17 FROM ORIGINAL     INPUT PLACED IN STORE         2
ENTRY    12 FROM ORIGINAL     INPUT PLACED IN TENTATIVE OUTPUT   19 FROM STORE    9
ENTRY    19 FROM ORIGINAL     INPUT PLACED IN STORE         5
ENTRY    13 FROM ORIGINAL     INPUT PLACED IN TENTATIVE OUTPUT   20 FROM STORE   10
ENTRY    20 FROM ORIGINAL     INPUT PLACED IN STORE         9
ENTRY    20 FROM ORIGINAL     INPUT PLACED IN TENTATIVE OUTPUT   21 FROM STORE    6
ENTRY    21 FROM ORIGINAL     INPUT PLACED IN STORE        10
ENTRY    21 FROM ORIGINAL     INPUT PLACED IN TENTATIVE OUTPUT   22 FROM STORE   10
ENTRY    22 FROM ORIGINAL     INPUT PLACED IN STORE         6
ENTRY     4 FROM ORIGINAL     INPUT PLACED IN TENTATIVE OUTPUT   23 FROM STORE    3
ENTRY    24 FROM ORIGINAL     INPUT PLACED IN STORE        10
ENTRY     5 FROM ORIGINAL     INPUT PLACED IN TENTATIVE OUTPUT   24 FROM STORE    4
ENTRY    26 FROM ORIGINAL     INPUT PLACED IN STORE         3
ENTRY    11 FROM ORIGINAL     INPUT PLACED IN TENTATIVE OUTPUT   25 FROM STORE    8
ENTRY    27 FROM ORIGINAL     INPUT PLACED IN STORE         4

              STORE IS NOT BIG ENOUGH - PRIORITY ENTRIES TO BE FOUND

ENTRY    28 FROM ORIGINAL     INPUT PLACED IN STORE         3
ENTRY    29 FROM ORIGINAL     INPUT PLACED IN STORE        10
ENTRY    30 FROM ORIGINAL     INPUT PLACED IN STORE         2
ENTRY    31 FROM ORIGINAL     INPUT PLACED IN STORE        12
ENTRY    33 FROM ORIGINAL     INPUT PLACED IN STORE        12
ENTRY    34 FROM ORIGINAL     INPUT PLACED IN STORE         7
```

Figure 10.28 - STSORT - Output Example - Multiple Sweep - End

```
STATCAT PROGRAM STSORT        -      ORDERING OF ENTRIES
OUTPUT DATA BANK TITLE        -      RE-ORDERED STATCAT DEMONSTRATION
INPUT DATA BANK TITLE         -      DEMONSTRATION STATCAT DATA BANK
DATA BANK SUBSET TITLE        -      ALL EXCEPT ERIC

ENTRY    16 FROM ORIGINAL     INPUT PLACED IN STORE         1
ENTRY    17 FROM ORIGINAL     INPUT PLACED IN STORE         2
ENTRY    24 FROM ORIGINAL     INPUT PLACED IN STORE         3
ENTRY    26 FROM ORIGINAL     INPUT PLACED IN STORE         5
ENTRY    31 FROM ORIGINAL     INPUT PLACED IN STORE         6
ENTRY    36 FROM ORIGINAL     INPUT PLACED IN STORE         7
ENTRY    37 FROM ORIGINAL     INPUT PLACED IN STORE         8
ENTRY    43 FROM ORIGINAL     INPUT PLACED IN STORE         9
ENTRY    46 FROM ORIGINAL     INPUT PLACED IN STORE        10
ENTRY    51 FROM ORIGINAL     INPUT PLACED IN STORE        11
ENTRY    54 FROM ORIGINAL     INPUT PLACED IN STORE        12

                              STORE IS NOW FULL

ENTRY    16 FROM ORIGINAL     INPUT PLACED IN TENTATIVE OUTPUT   52 FROM STORE    1
ENTRY    17 FROM ORIGINAL     INPUT PLACED IN TENTATIVE OUTPUT   53 FROM STORE    2
ENTRY    60 FROM ORIGINAL     INPUT PLACED IN STORE         1
ENTRY    24 FROM ORIGINAL     INPUT PLACED IN TENTATIVE OUTPUT   54 FROM STORE    3
ENTRY    61 FROM ORIGINAL     INPUT PLACED IN STORE         2
ENTRY    26 FROM ORIGINAL     INPUT PLACED IN TENTATIVE OUTPUT   55 FROM STORE    5

                          END OF INPUT WITHOUT OVERFLOW

ENTRY    52 FROM TENTATIVE OUTPUT IS CONFIRMED - WITHOUT RELOADING TO STORE
ENTRY    53 FROM TENTATIVE OUTPUT IS CONFIRMED - WITHOUT RELOADING TO STORE
ENTRY    54 FROM TENTATIVE OUTPUT IS CONFIRMED - WITHOUT RELOADING TO STORE
ENTRY    55 FROM TENTATIVE OUTPUT IS CONFIRMED - WITHOUT RELOADING TO STORE
ENTRY    31 FROM ORIGINAL     INPUT PLACED IN CONFIRMED OUTPUT   56 FROM STORE    6
ENTRY    36 FROM ORIGINAL     INPUT PLACED IN CONFIRMED OUTPUT   57 FROM STORE    7
ENTRY    37 FROM ORIGINAL     INPUT PLACED IN CONFIRMED OUTPUT   58 FROM STORE    8
ENTRY    43 FROM ORIGINAL     INPUT PLACED IN CONFIRMED OUTPUT   59 FROM STORE    9
ENTRY    46 FROM ORIGINAL     INPUT PLACED IN CONFIRMED OUTPUT   60 FROM STORE   10
ENTRY    51 FROM ORIGINAL     INPUT PLACED IN CONFIRMED OUTPUT   61 FROM STORE   11
ENTRY    54 FROM ORIGINAL     INPUT PLACED IN CONFIRMED OUTPUT   62 FROM STORE   12
ENTRY    60 FROM ORIGINAL     INPUT PLACED IN CONFIRMED OUTPUT   63 FROM STORE    1
ENTRY    61 FROM ORIGINAL     INPUT PLACED IN CONFIRMED OUTPUT   64 FROM STORE    2

                          SORTING OF SUBSET COMPLETED

NO MORE INPUT DATA - CHECKING STARTS
```

Figure 10.29 - STSORT - Priority Codes

Priority Code	Ordering	Non-values
1Q2.	Low value first	Included
2Q1.	High value first	Included
12Q.	Low value first	Following
21Q.	High value first	Following
Q12.	Low value first	Leading
Q21.	High value first	Leading
12-.	Low value first	Ignored
21-.	High value first	Ignored

Included - When non-values are included in the ordering, they are treated as normal numbers and ordered accordingly.

Following- When non-values are placed following, they are given lower priority than any value and ordered accordingly.

Leading - When non-values are placed leading, they are given higher priority than any value and ordered accordingly.

Ignored - When non-values are ignored, the ordering process skips the data columns where either entry has a non-value, and continues with the next priority specification, if any.

```
C MASTER STSORT - PLACES SUBSETS OF STATCAT DATA BANKS IN PRIORITY ORDER
C   SUBROUTINES AND FUNCTIONS REQUIRED
C   NAME                 TYPE             COMMENT
C   AN       (SEE  3.1 ) SERVICE    ALPHA - TO NUMERIC VALUE
C   CHECK    (SEE  4.2 ) EXECUTIVE  CHECKS DATA BANK OR SUBSET
C   CHIKEN   (SEE 11.9 ) SERVICE    WARNS OF MISMATCHED DATA LEVEL
C   CLSAM    (SEE  3.5 ) SERVICE    ALLOTS ENTRY TO SAMPLE/SUBSET
C   COMPA    (SEE  3.1 ) SERVICE    COMPARES ALPHAMERIC VALUES
C   COPYA    (SEE  3.1 ) SERVICE    COPIES ALPHAMERIC VALUE
C   CSORT    (SEE 10.2 ) EXECUTIVE  SORTS SUBSET INTO ORDER
C   FIFI     (SEE  3.2 ) SYSTEM     ALLOCATES PERIPHERALS
C   IBL      (SEE  3.1 ) SERVICE    DETECTS BLANK,END AND STOP CARDS
C   ICH      (SEE  3.1 ) SERVICE    IDENTIFIES ALPHAMERIC CODES
C   INSERT   (SEE 11.4 ) SERVICE    INSERTS ENTRY INTO ARRAY
C   LCOM     (SEE  3.4 ) SYSTEM     LOADS COMPLEMENTARY INFORMATION
C   LDBS     (SEE  3.6 ) SYSTEM     LOADS SUBSET DEFINITION .
C   LDDS     (SEE  3.4 ) SYSTEM     LOADS DATA DESCRIPTION SEGMENT
C   LDHI     (SEE  3.8 ) SYSTEM     LOADS/CHECKS DATA HANDLING INSTN
C   LGEN     (SEE  3.7 ) SYSTEM     LOADS GENERALISED VARIATES
C   LSET     (SEE  3.5 ) SYSTEM     LOADS DEFINING CONDITIONS
C   POSN     (SEE 11.4 ) SERVICE    FINDS POSITION OF ENTRY IN ORDER
C   PR       (SEE 10.2 ) SERVICE    DETERMINES PRIORITY IN SORTING
C   WDCD     (SEE  3.4 ) SERVICE    WRITE DATA COLUMN DESCRIPTION
C SETTING OF ARRAY DIMENSIONS
C THE FOLLOWING DIMENSIONS MUST BE AT LEAST AS BIG AS THOSE
C SPECIFIED BY THE DATA TAPE,SAMPLE SPECIFICATIONS,ETC.
C NQMAX = MAXIMUM NUMBER OF DATA COLUMNS
C DIMENSION D(NQMAX),RX(NQMAX),DMIN(NQMAX),IT(NQMAX),CN(NQMAX)
C DIMENSION RX(NQMAX),DMIN(NQMAX),IT(NQMAX),CN(NQMAX)
C DIMENSION NP(NQMAX),NDP(NQMAX),ST(NQMAX)
      NQMAX=100
      DIMENSION D(100),RX(100),DMIN(100),IT(100),CN(100)
      DIMENSION NP( 100),NDP( 100),ST( 100)
C DATA BANK COLUMN NUMBERS - MAY BE USED IN PLACE OF NAMES
C IF THE DIMENSION OF NQMAX IS INCREASED,THE EXTRA CODES MUST BE
C INCLUDED IN THIS DATA STATEMENT
      DATA   CN/4HCOL1,4HCOL2,4HCOL3,4HCOL4,4HCOL5,4HCOL6,4HCOL7,4HCOL8,4
     1HCOL9,4HCL10,4HCL11,4HCL12,4HCL13,4HCL14,4HCL15,4HCL16,4HCL17,4HCL
     218,4HCL19,4HCL20,4HCL21,4HCL22,4HCL23,4HCL24,4HCL25,4HCL26,4HCL27,
     34HCL28,4HCL29,4HCL30,4HCL31,4HCL32,4HCL33,4HCL34,4HCL35,4HCL36,4HC
     4L37,4HCL38,4HCL39,4HCL40,4HCL41,4HCL42,4HCL43,4HCL44,4HCL45,4HCL46
     5,4HCL47,4HCL48,4HCL49,4HCL50,4HCL51,4HCL52,4HCL53,4HCL54,4HCL55,4H
     6CL56,4HCL57,4HCL58,4HCL59,4HCL60,4HCL61,4HCL62,4HCL63,4HCL64,4HCL6
     75,4HCL66,4HCL67,4HCL68,4HCL69,4HCL70,4HCL71,4HCL72,4HCL73,4HCL74,4
     8HCL75,4HCL76,4HCL77,4HCL78,4HCL79,4HCL80,4HCL81,4HCL82,4HCL83,4HCL
     984,4HCL85,4HCL86,4HCL87,4HCL88,4HCL89,4HCL90,4HCL91,4HCL92,4HCL93,
     94HCL94,4HCL95,4HCL96,4HCL97,4HCL98,4HCL99,4HC100/
C NALTMX = MAXIMUM NUMBER OF CLASSES ON TAPE
C DIMENSION       TRT(NALTMX)
      NALTMX = 50
      DIMENSION  TRT(50)
C NCMAX = NUMBER OF STORES AVAILABLE 2500 REDUCED TO 250 FOR DEMO
C DIMENSION RT(NCMAX),ID(NCMAX)
      NCMAX=250
      DIMENSION RT(2500),ID(2500)
      EQUIVALENCE (RT(1),ID(1))
C MAXDBC = MAXIMUM NUMBER OF DATA BANK SUBSET CONDITIONS
C DIMENSION SCON(5,MAXDBC)
      MAXDBC = 50
      DIMENSION SCON(5,   50)
C THE FOLLOWING DIMENSIONS ARE FIXED
      DIMENSION  U(8),LU(8),FORM(50)
C THE FOLLOWING DIMENSION STORES THE NAMES OF THE PRIORITY RULES
```

```
C     RULES       1       2       3       4       5       6       7       8
      DATA U/4H1Q2.,4H2Q1.,4HQ12.,4HQ21.,4H12Q.,4H21Q.,4H12-.,4H21-./
      DATA LU/8*3/
      COMMON /STCT/MED1,MED2,MED3,MED4,MED5,MED6,MED13,Q,V(20),TT(30)
      DATA PROG/4HSORT/
      MED1 = -1
C ASSIGN PERIPHERALS
      MED1 = -1
    1 CALL COPYA(TT(1),PROG)
      CALL FIFI
C READ REVISED TITLE,KEY AND NAME
    2 READ(MED1,900) (TT(J),J=1,10),(FORM(J),J=1,6)
      IF(IBL(TT,10,4).LT.0.AND.IBL(FORM,6,4).LT.0) GO TO 2
      IF(MED4.LT.1) WRITE(MED6,909)
      IF(MED4.LT.1) GO TO 1
      ISF = -1
C LEVEL 1 - LOAD DATA DESCRIPTION OF INPUT FILE
   11 IF(V(10).GT.10.) V(10) = 0.
      IF(ISF.GE.0) CALL FIFI
      IF(MED3.LT.1) WRITE(MED6,910)
      IF(MED3.LT.1) GO TO 1
      REWIND MED3
      READ(MED3) NQ1,NALT1,Q1,(TT(J),J=11,26)
      IF(ISF.LT.0) NQ = NQ1
      IF(ISF.LT.0) NALT = NALT1
      IF(ISF.LT.0) Q = Q1
      WRITE(MED2,901) NQ,NALT,Q,(TT(J),J=1,10),FORM(6)
      WRITE(MED2,904) (TT(J),J=11,20),TT(26)
      V(3) = NCMAX
      V(4) = NQ
      NCAV = V(3)/(V(4)+2.)
      WRITE(MED6,907) NCAV
      ID1 = NCAV*NQ + 1
      IO1 = ID1 + NCAV
      V(3) = Q
      IF(NQ.LE.NQMAX) GO TO 12
      WRITE(MED6,902) NQ,NQMAX
      V(10) = 1.
      NQ = NQMAX
   12 IF(NQ1.NE.NQ) WRITE(MED6,911) NQ,NQ1
      IF(NQ1.NE.NQ.AND.V(10).LT.0.5) V(10) = 13.
      IF(NALT1.LE.NALTMX) GO TO 13
      WRITE(MED2,903) NALT1,NALTMX
      IF(V(10).LT.0.5) V(10) = 17.
   13 IF(NALT1.NE.NALT) WRITE(MED6,912) NALT,NALT1
      NALT = NALT1
      IF(ISF.LT.0.AND.V(10).LT.0.5)
     1WRITE(MED4) NQ,NALT,Q,(TT(J),J=1,10),(FORM(J),J=1,6)
      MED = 0
      IF(ISF.LT.0) MED = MED4
      LI = 18
      CALL LDDS(TRF,NALT1,D,NQ1,ST,MQ1,IT,NQ1,H,0,H,H,0,LI,0,Q,VX,
     1 0,MED2,MED3,MED,IGO)
      IF(IGO.GT.0) GO TO 1
C LEVEL 3 - LOAD PRIORITY SPECIFICATION
   31 IF(V(10).GT.20.) V(10) = 0.
      ISF = 0
      IFIN = NQ
      M = IFIN
      WRITE(MED2,930) (TT(J),J=1,20)
      CALL LGEN(U,8 ,LU,0,ST,IT,CN ,NQ1,NCL,0,DMIN,DMAX,0,TMIN,TMAX,0,0,
     1 10,NDP,NP,NQMAX,ISF,IFIN,1,0)
      IF(ISF.EQ.0) GO TO 11
```

```
      IF(V(20).NE.0..AND.V(10).EQ.0.)V(10) = 39.
      IF(ISF.LT.NQ) NP(ISF+1) = 0
      DO 32 I = 1,ISF
      NDP(I) = NP(I)/1000
   32 NP(I) = NP(I) - NDP(I)*1000
C LEVEL 4 - DATA BANK SUBSET SPECIFICATION
   41 IF(V(10).GT.80.) V(10) = 0.
      CALL LDBS(SCON,NCON,MAXDBC,CN ,ST,IT,NQ1,TRT,NALT1,IGO)
      IF(IGO.GT.0) GO TO 31
C LEVEL 9 - DATA HANDLING INSTRUCTION
   91 IF(V(10).GT.90.) V(10) = 0.
      CALL LDHI(V(1),1,V(2),3,V(9),7,ASDL,18,APT,15,H,0,H,V(10),
     1FORM(41),FORM,MED1,MED2,MED4,Q,NQ,NWARN,1,IGO)
      IF(IGO.GT.0) GO TO 41
      IF(V(1).GT.4.5) NWARN = NWARN + 1
      IF(V(1).GT.4.5) V(1) = -1.
      NX = V(9)
      IF(NX.LE.0.OR.NX.GE.NQ)   NWARN = NWARN + 1
      IF(NX.LE.0.OR.NX.GE.NQ)   V(9) = NQ-1
      IF(IBL(FORM(2),1,1).LT.0.AND.IBL(FORM(6),11,1).LT.0) NX = 0
      IF(IBL(FORM(2),1,1).GE.0.OR .IBL(FORM(6),11,1).GE.0) NX = 1
      IF(NX.EQ.0)CALL LDHI(V(1),1,H,0,V(9),7,H,0,H,0,H,0,H,V(10),
     1FORM(41),FORM,MED1,MED2,MED4,Q,NQ,NWARN,2,IGO)
      IF(NX.EQ.0) GO TO 92
      IF(ASDL.LE.0.) NWARN = NWARN + 1
      IF(ASDL.EQ.0.) ASDL = 5.
      IF(ASDL.LT.0.) ASDL = 9999.
      IF(APT.LE.0.) NWARN = NWARN + 1
      IF(APT.EQ.0.) APT = 1.
      IF(APT.LT.0.) APT = 0.
      CALL LDHI(V(1),1,V(2),3,V(9),7,ASDL,18,APT,15,H,0,H,V(10),
     1FORM(41),FORM,MED1,MED2,MED4,Q,NQ,NWARN,2,IGO)
   92 IF(IGO.GT.0) GO TO 91
  101 WRITE(MED6,998)
C  LOAD DATA STORAGE SEGMENT
      CALL CSORT (RT,ID(ID1),ID(IO1),NP,NDP,NQ,NCAV,SCON,NCON)
  112 IF(NX.EQ.0) GO TO 91
C END TAPE - TEST IF REQUIRED
  120 WRITE(MED4) (V(3),I=1,NQ)
      REWIND MED4
      IF(V(2).GE.0.) GO TO 150
      WRITE(MED6,955)
      GO TO 1
C CARRY OUT PRELIMINARY CHECK OF DATA TAPE
  150 WRITE(MED6,956)
      APT = APT*.01
      NCON=0
      Q = V(3)
      CALL CHECK (D,RX,DMIN,RT,IT,TRT,NQ,NALT,ASDL,APT,SCON,NCON,ST)
      WRITE(MED6,999)
      GO TO 1
  900 FORMAT(16X,16A4)
  901 FORMAT (1H1,20X,40HSTATCAT ORDERING DATA BANK SUBSET(S)
     1                                           /16H0FILE PARAMETER
     2S/29H0NUMBER OF DATA COLUMNS IS - ,I6/29H0STORED NUMBER OF CLASSES
     3 IS ,I6/34H0VALUE USED FOR MISSING DATA IS - ,F20.8/
     4            28H0OUTPUT STATCAT DATA BANK - ,10A4,10X,10HFILE NAME ,A4/)
  902 FORMAT (4H0THE,I6,    37H ITEMS PER ENTRY EXCEED THE AVAILABLE,I6,1
     16H STORAGE COLUMNS)
  903 FORMAT (4H0THE,I6,40H CLASSES PER COLUMN EXCEED THE AVAILABLE,I6,1
     13H STORAGE ROWS)
  904 FORMAT(28H0 INPUT STATCAT DATA BANK - ,10A4,10X,10HFILE NAME ,A4/)
  907 FORMAT(1H0,20X,17HPROGRAM CAN STORE,I5,8H ENTRIES/)
```

```
      909 FORMAT(41HONO OUTPUT FILE - PROGRAM CANNOT CONTINUE)
      910 FORMAT(41H0 NO INPUT FILE - PROGRAM CANNOT CONTINUE)
      911 FORMAT(29HOOUTPUT STATCAT DATA BANK HAS,I4,20H COLUMNS - INPUT HAS
     1,I4,17H MUST BE THE SAME)
      912 FORMAT(29HOOUTPUT STATCAT DATA BANK HAS,I4,20H CLASSES - INPUT HAS
     1,I4,19H SHOULD BE THE SAME,34X,11H**WARNING**)
      930 FORMAT(23H1STATCAT PROGRAM STSORT,7X,1H-,4X,23H   ORDERING OF ENT
     1RIES/23H OUTPUT DATA BANK TITLE,7X,1H-,4X,10A4/23H  INPUT DATA BAN
     2K TITLE,7X,1H-,4X,10A4/18HOPRIORITY ORDERING/6H ORDER,5X,14HPRIORI
     3TY   DATA/7H OF USE,8X,12HRULE   COLUMN)
      955 FORMAT (54HONO MORE INPUT DATA - NO CHECKING - PROGRAM STOPS      )
      956 FORMAT (54HONO MORE INPUT DATA - CHECKING STARTS                  )
      958 FORMAT (54HOCHECKING COMPLETED - PROGRAM STOPS                    )
      998 FORMAT (35HOINPUT ACCEPTED - SORTING COMMENCES )
      999 FORMAT (36H1 SORTING COMPLETED - READ NEW INPUT)
          END


          SUBROUTINE CSORT(RT,IL,ID,NP,NDP,NQ,NC,SCON,NCON)
C CSORT    (SEE 10.2 ) EXECUTIVE  SORTS SUBSET INTO ORDER
          DIMENSION RT(NQ,NC),ID(NC),IL(NC),NP(NQ),NDP(NQ),SCON(5,NCON)
          COMMON /STCT/MED1,MED2,MED3,MED4,MED5,MED6,MED13,Q,V(20),TT(30)
          NL = 60
          NO = V(1)
          LOKT = 0
          NM = (NQ + 29)/10
          REWIND MED3
          NOKT = V(6)+.001
          NOLD = NOKT
          NEQOP = 0
C INITIAL SETTINGS
        1 LONT = 0
          NONT = NOKT
          A = 1.001
          IF(LOKT.NE.0)A = 2.001
          K = 0
          DO 2 J = 1,NC
          IF(J.EQ.1.AND.LOKT.NE.0) GO TO 2
          K = K + 1
          IF(K.EQ.LOKT)  K = K+1
          IL(J) = K
        2 CONTINUE
          NIP = 0
          LIN = A-1.
          IST = 1
          NEXT = A
          LEXT = A
          IF (NO.GT.0) NL = 60
          NEQIP = 0
          READ(MED3) NQ,NALT,Q,(X,I=1,16)
          DO 3 I = 1,NQ
        3 READ(MED3) (X,K=1,19),(X,K=1,NALT),NX,X,X
C READ INPUT ENTRY
      100 NEXT = IL(LEXT)
          READ(MED3) (RT(I,NEXT),I = 1,NQ)
          NIP = NIP + 1
          DO 4 I = 1,NQ
          IF (RT(I,NEXT).NE.Q) GO TO 5
        4 CONTINUE
          REWIND MED3
          GO TO (50,50,60,60),IST
        5 CALL CLSAM(RT(1,NEXT),NQ,SCON,NCON,NIN,1)
          IF(NIN.NE.1) GO TO 100
```

```
      DO 6 I = 1,NQ
    6 IF(RT(I,NEXT).EQ.Q) RT(I,NEXT) = V(3)
      POS = POSN(RT,NQ,NC,IL,NDP,NP,LEXT,LIN,V(3))
      ID(NEXT) = NIP
C ACCEPT IF THERE IS NO LAST CONFIRMED OR ENTRY FOLLOWS IT
      IF(LOKT.LE.0.OR.POS.GT.1.3) GO TO 7
C DISCARD IF ENTRY IS BEFORE LAST CONFIRMED
      IF(POS.LT.0.9) GO TO 100
      NEQIP = NEQIP + 1
C DISCARD EQUAL PRIORITY TO LAST CONFIRMED IF ALREADY OUTPUT
      IF(NEQIP.LE.NEQOP) GO TO 100
    7 IF(NO.LT.1) GO TO 8
C LIST INPUT IF NO GT OR EQ 3
      NL = NL + 1
      IF(NO.GE.3) NL = NL + NM
      IF(NL.GT.50) WRITE(MED2,900) TT
      IF(NL.GT.50.AND.NO.GE.3) NL = NM + 6
      IF(NL.GT.50) NL = 6
      IF(NO.GE.3) WRITE(MED2,901)
      WRITE(MED2,902) NIP,NEXT
      IF(NO.GE.3) WRITE(MED2,907) (RT(I,NEXT),I=1,NQ)
    8 CALL INSERT(RT,NQ,NC,IL,NDP,NP,LEXT,LIN,V(3),0,0,POS)
C ACTION DEPENDS ON STATE
      IF(LIN.EQ.0) GO TO 10
      LIN1 = LIN + 1
      GO TO (10,20,30),IST
C STORE NOT FULL - NO UNDERFLOW
   10 LIN = LIN + 1
      LEXT = LIN + 1
      IF(LEXT.GT.NC) GO TO 15
      GO TO 100
C STORE IS NOW FULL - SET STATE = 2 - FIRST ENTRY TO TAPE
   15 J = A
      IST = 2
      LEXT = NC
      LIN = NC-1
      NEXT = IL(J)
      NONT = NONT + 1
      WRITE(MED4) (RT(I,NEXT),I=1,NQ)
      IF(NO.LT.0) GO TO 21
      NL = NL + 4
      IF(NO.GE.4) NL = NL + NM
      IF(NL.GT.50) WRITE(MED2,900) TT
      IF(NL.GT.50.AND.NO.GE.4) NL = NM + 6
      IF(NL.GT.50) NL = 6
      WRITE(MED2,908)
      IF(NO.LT.1) GO TO 21
      WRITE(MED2,903) ID(NEXT),NONT,NEXT
      IF(NO.GE.4) WRITE(MED2,907) (RT(I,NEXT),I=1,NQ)
      GO TO 21
C STORE IS FULL - TEST FOR UNDERFLOW (POS BEFORE LAST ON TAPE)
   20 IF(POS.LT.A) GO TO 25
      J = A
      NEXT = IL(J)
C WRITE SECOND ENTRY TO TAPE (BECOMES LONT) SHIFT UP IL CODES
   21 LONT = IL(J+1)
      WRITE(MED4) (RT(I,LONT),I=1,NQ)
      NONT = NONT + 1
      DO 22 L = J,LIN
   22 IL(L) = IL(L+1)
      LEXT = NC
      IL(NC) = NEXT
      IF(NO.LT.1) GO TO 100
```

```
      NL = NL + 1
      IF(NO.GE.4) NL = NL + NM
      IF(NL.GT.50) WRITE(MED2,900) TT
      IF(NL.GT.50.AND.NO.GE.4) NL = NM + 6
      IF(NL.GT.50) NL = 6
      IF(NO.GE.4) WRITE(MED2,901)
      WRITE(MED2,903) ID(LONT),NONT,LONT
      IF(NO.GE.4) WRITE(MED2,907) (RT(I,NEXT),I=1,NQ)
      GO TO 100
C UNDERFLOW FOUND - STATE = 3  REWIND OUTPUT/NEXT FROM END
   25 IST = 3
      REWIND MED4
      NOFL = NIP
      IF(NO.LT.0) GO TO 30
      NL = NL + 3
      IF(NL.GT.50) WRITE(MED2,900) TT
      IF(NL.GT.50) NL = 6
      WRITE(MED2,909)
C UNDERFLOW FOUND - CONTINUING TO TAPE END
   30 CONTINUE
      LEXT = NC
      GO TO 100
C END WITHOUT UNDERFLOW - OUTPUT STORED ENTRIES
   50 K = A
      IF(LONT.NE.0) K = K + 1
      IF(NO.GE.0) WRITE(MED2,916)
      IF(NO.GE.0) NL = NL + 3
      IF(LIN.EQ.0) GO TO 52
   56 IF(NOKT.EQ.NONT.OR.NO.LT.1) GO TO 57
      NOKT = NOKT + 1
      NL = NL + 1
      WRITE(MED2,913) NOKT
      IF(NOKT.LT.NONT) GO TO 56
   57 DO 51 J = K,LIN
      NONT = NONT + 1
      NEXT = IL(J)
      IF(NO.LT.1) GO TO 51
      IF(NO.GE.4) NL = NL + NM
      IF(NL.GT.50) WRITE(MED2,900) TT
      IF(NL.GT.50.AND.NO.GE.4) NL = NM + 6
      IF(NL.GT.50) NL = 6
      IF(NL.GT.50) NL = 6
      IF(NO.GE.3) WRITE(MED2,901)
      WRITE(MED2,904) ID(NEXT),NONT,NEXT
      IF(NO.GE.3) WRITE(MED2,907) (RT(I,NEXT),I=1,NQ)
   51 WRITE(MED4) (RT(I,NEXT),I=1,NQ)
   52 V(6) = NONT
      J = NONT - NOLD
      IF(NO.LT.0) RETURN
      IF(NO.GE.2) WRITE(MED2,900) TT
      WRITE(MED2,910)
      IF(J.EQ.0) WRITE(MED2,911)
      IF(NO.LT.2.OR.J.EQ.0) RETURN
C CHECK NEW SECTION OF OUTPUT TAPE
      NL = 7
      REWIND MED4
      READ(MED4) NQ,NALT,(X,I=1,17)
      DO 53 I = 1,NQ
   53 READ(MED4) (X,K=1,19),(X,K=1,NALT),NX,X,X
      DO 55 I = 1,NONT
      READ(MED4) (RT(K,NEXT),K=1,NQ)
      IF(I.LE.NOLD) GO TO 55
      NL = NL + NM + 1
```

```
      IF(NL.LT.50) GO TO 54
      WRITE(MED2,900) TT
      WRITE(MED2,912)
      NL = 8 + NM
   54 WRITE(MED2,905) I
      WRITE(MED2,907) (RT(K,NEXT),K=1,NQ)
   55 CONTINUE
      RETURN
C END - WITH UNDERFLOW - RE-POSITION OUTPUT TAPE
   60 READ(MED4) NQ,NALT,(X,I=1,17)
      DO 61 I = 1,NQ
   61 READ(MED4) (X,K=1,19),(X,K=1,NALT),NX,X,X
C RETURN REMAINING TENTATIVE OUTPUT TO STORE
      DO 62 K = 1,NONT
      LEXT = NC
      NEXT = IL(LEXT)
      READ(MED4) (RT(I,NEXT),I=1,NQ)
      IF(K.LE.NOKT.OR.K.EQ.NONT) GO TO 62
      IF(NO.GE.1) NL = NL + 1
      IF(NO.GE.3) NL = NL + NM
      IF(NL.GT.50) WRITE(MED2,900) TT
      IF(NL.GT.50.AND.NO.GE.3) NL = NM + 6
      IF(NL.GT.50) NL = 6
      IF(NO.GE.3) WRITE(MED2,901)
      POS = POSN(RT,NQ,NC,IL,NDP,NP,LEXT,LIN,V(3))
      IF(POS.LT.A+0.2) GO TO 73
C CONFIRM TENTATIVE OUTPUT AS FAR AS POSSIBLE
C EQUAL PRIORITY FROM OUTPUT TAPE PRECEDE THOSE FROM INPUT
      ID(NEXT) = -K
C CALL TO PR REQUIRED TO PLACE NEXT BEFORE EQUAL PRICIRTIES
      LEXQ = POS
      X = LEXQ
      X = POS-X
      IF(X.GT.0.3) GO TO 69
   68 NEXQ = IL(LEXQ)
      IF(ID(NEXQ).LT.0) GO TO 70
      CALL PR(NEXT,NEXQ,I,RT,NP,NDP,NQ,NC,V(3))
      IF(I.EQ.2) GO TO 70
      IF(I.EQ.0.AND.ID(NEXQ).LT.0) GO TO 70
      LEXQ = LEXQ - 1
      IF(LEXQ.GE.1) GO TO 68
   70 POS = LEXQ
      POS = POS + 0.5
      IF(POS.LT.A+0.2) GO TO 73
   69 CALL INSERT(RT,NQ,NC,IL,NDP,NP,LEXT,LIN,V(3),0,0,POS)
      IF(NO.GE.1) WRITE(MED2,915) K,NEXT
      IF(NO.GE.3) WRITE(MED2,907) (RT(I,NEXT),I=1,NQ)
      LEXT = NC
      NEXT = IL(LEXT)
C STOP RETURNING TENTATIVE OUTPUT IF STORE IS FULL
      IF(ID(NEXT).LT.NOFL) GO TO 63
      GO TO 62
   73 NOKT = NOKT + 1
      IF(NO.GE.1) WRITE(MED2,914) NOKT,NEXT
      IF(NO.GE.3) WRITE(MED2,907) (RT(I,NEXT),I=1,NQ)
   62 CONTINUE
   63 REWIND MED4
      READ(MED4) NQ,NALT,(X,I=1,17)
      DO 64 I = 1,NQ
   64 READ(MED4) (X,K=1,19),(X,K=1,NALT),NX,X,X
C RUN FORWARD, COUNT NUMBER EQUAL TO NEW LAST CONFIRMED
C LAST ENTRY IN STORE IS NEW LAST CONFIRMED
      NEQOP = 0
```

```
      LOKT = IL(LIN)
      IF(NOLD.EQ.0) GO TO 71
      DO 72 K = 1,NOLD
   72 READ(MED4)  (RT(I,NEXT),I = 1,NQ)
   71 IF(NOKT.EQ.NOLD) GO TO 67
      K1 = NOLD+1
      DO 65 K=K1,NOKT
      READ(MED4)  (RT(I,NEXT),I = 1,NQ)
      CALL PR (NEXT,LOKT,I,RT,NP,NDP,NQ,NC,Q)
   65 IF(I.EQ.0) NEQOP = NEQOP + 1
   67 J = A
C OUTPUT STORED ENTRIES - KNOWN TO BE IN CORRECT ORDER
      DO 66 K1 = J,LIN
      NEXT = IL(K1)
      CALL PR(NEXT,LOKT,I,RT,NP,NDP,NQ,NC,Q)
      IF(I.EQ.0) NEQOP = NEQOP + 1
      NOKT = NOKT + 1
      IF(NO.LT.1) GO TO 66
      NL = NL + 1
      IF(NO.GE.4) NL = NL + NM
      IF(NL.GT.50) WRITE(MED2,900) TT
      IF(NL.GT.50.AND.NO.GE.4) NL = NM + 6
      IF(NL.GT.50) NL = 6
      IF(NO.GE.4) WRITE(MED2,901)
      K = ID(NEXT)
      IF(K.LT.0) K = -K
      IF(ID(NEXT).GT.0)   WRITE(MED2,904) K,NOKT,NEXT
      IF(ID(NEXT).LT.0)   WRITE(MED2,906) K,NOKT,NEXT
      IF(NO.GE.4) WRITE(MED2,907) (RT(I,NEXT),I=1,NQ)
   66 WRITE(MED4)  (RT(I,NEXT),I = 1,NQ)
      IL(1) = LOKT
      GO TO 1
  900 FORMAT(23H1STATCAT PROGRAM STSORT,7X,1H-,4X,23H      ORDERING OF ENT
     1RIES/23H OUTPUT DATA BANK TITLE,7X,1H-,4X,10A4/23H   INPUT DATA BAN
     2K TITLE,7X,1H-,4X,10A4/23H DATA BANK SUBSET TITLE,7X,1H-,4X,10A4/)
  901 FORMAT(1H )
  902 FORMAT(7H ENTRY ,I6,38H FROM    ORIGINAL   INPUT PLACED IN STORE,I6)
  903 FORMAT(7H ENTRY ,I6,49H FROM    ORIGINAL   INPUT PLACED IN TENTATIVE
     1OUTPUT,I6,11H FROM STORE,I6)
  904 FORMAT(7H ENTRY ,I6,49H FROM    ORIGINAL   INPUT PLACED IN CONFIRMED
     1OUTPUT,I6,11H FROM STORE,I6)
  905 FORMAT(7H0ENTRY ,I6,41H ON OUTPUT STATCAT DATA BANK (CONFIRMED) /)
  906 FORMAT(7H ENTRY ,I6,49H FROM TENTATIVE OUTPUT PLACED IN CONFIRMED
     1OUTPUT,I6,11H FROM STORE,I6)
  907 FORMAT(1H0,10X,10F11.4/(11X,10F11.4))
  908 FORMAT(1H0,40X,17HSTORE IS NOW FULL/)
  909 FORMAT(1H0,20X,54HSTORE IS NOT BIG ENOUGH - PRIORITY ENTRIES TO BE
     1 FOUND/)
  910 FORMAT(1H0,20X,27HSORTING OF SUBSET COMPLETED)
  911 FORMAT(1H0,20X,28HSUBSET IS EMPTY - NO ENTRIES)
  912 FORMAT(1H0,20X,26HCONFIRMED ENTRIES IN ORDER)
  913 FORMAT(7H ENTRY ,I6,64H FROM TENTATIVE OUTPUT IS CONFIRMED - WITHO
     1UT RELOADING TO STORE)
  914 FORMAT(7H ENTRY ,I6,55H FROM TENTATIVE OUTPUT IS CONFIRMED BY LOAD
     1ING TO STORE,I6)
  915 FORMAT(7H ENTRY ,I6,43H FROM TENTATIVE OUTPUT IS RELOADED TO STORE
     1,I6)
  916 FORMAT(1H0,20X,29HEND OF INPUT WITHOUT OVERFLOW/)
      END
```

10.3   PROGRAM STMERG - MERGING/MATCHING STATCAT DATA BANKS

10.3.1   Purpose

This program combines two STATCAT data banks to form a single standard STATCAT data bank. The first input and the output are always standard STATCAT data banks, but the second input may be a STATCAT data bank, a stream of entries from an input device (read by a DATA subroutine) or a set of entries held in direct-access storage.

The program may be used to perform two different functions.

If the two data banks are to be "merged" then complete entries are taken from the two STATCAT data banks, and selected items are placed together to form an entry in the output STATCAT data bank. This function can be particularly useful for the combination of two STATCAT data banks with identical data description segments, derived from successive experiments or plain-language reference files subject to periodic updating.

If the two data banks are to be "matched", entries taken from the first input STATCAT data bank are matched to corresponding entries in the other data bank, and selected items from the matched entries are placed together to form an entry in the output STATCAT data bank. This process is particularly useful when many of the data required in a data bank do not change rapidly, or when information is to be added to a data bank that cannot be included in the original STATCAT data bank for mechanical, ethical or other reasons.

The user may vary the amount of information produced during the checking process, and the amount of checking carried out on the output STATCAT data bank when completed.

Figure 10.31a is a simplified flow-chart for the main program STMERG, and Figure 10.31b is a simplified flow-chart for CMERG, the executive subroutine.

10.3.2   Input Data

Summary

Item	Level	Function	See	
1	0	File control card (Input-Output-?Input)	Below +	3.2
2	0	Data Starter (Output)		3.3
(3	1	File control card (Second Input)		3.2)
(4	1	Data starter (Second Input)		3.3)
5	2	Priority specification (Second Input)	10.2 +	3.7
6	3	Subset specification (Second Input)		3.5
(7	4	File control card (First Input)		3.2)
8	5	Merging Specification	Below +	3.7
9	6	Priority specification (First Input)	10.2 +	3.7
10	7	Subset specification (First Input)		3.5
11	8	Data Handling Instruction		3.8
(12	9	Data column descriptions	Below +	3.4)
(13	9	Entries	Below	)

Bracketed items are not called for for the first passage.

1 - File Control Card (Input-Output-?Input)

The file control card specifies the file name and security key of the first input STATCAT data bank, the output STATCAT data bank, and the second input STATCAT data bank (if it is used). If either the first input or the output STATCAT data bank is not specified, or if any specified data bank is not available, the program will continue to read data until a valid file control card is read, or a 'STOP' card is found.

2 - Data Starter (Output)

This is a standard data starter, except that the first index (A) is differently defined, and the second (B) is not used.

Card layout - Data Starter - STMERG

A BCCCDDDEEEEEEEEFFFFFFFFFFFFFFFFFFFFFFFFFFFFFF.........GGGGHHHH

Columns On Card	Item Code	FORTRAN Type	Function	see
1	A	-	Not Used	-
2	B	I	Secondary input type	below
3 - 5	C	I	Number of data columns	4.2
6 - 8	D	I	Number of alternative classes	4.2
9 - 16	E	F	'Non-Value'	4.2
17 - 56	F	A	Title of STATCAT data bank	4.2
57 - 72	.	-	Not Used	-
73 - 76	G	A	Security Key	4.2
77 - 80	H	A	File Name	4.2

B - Secondary Input Type

This index specifies the type of secondary input which will be employed during the construction of this output STATCAT data bank. Unless otherwise specified, it will be assumed to be a standard STATCAT data bank.

ALTERNATIVES

B = 0,blank : Secondary input from a standard STATCAT data bank.
 (DEFAULT)   If no third STATCAT data bank was specified on the file control card, the program will fail.

B = 1   : Secondary input from input device - read as a stream but not stored.

B = 2   : Secondary input from input device - read and stored at the start of the output phase.

B = 3 - 9 : As for A = 0

DEFAULT value = 0 (0 blank or non-numeric)

(3 - File Control Card - Secondary Input)

If the secondary input is to be read from a standard STATCAT data bank, not from cards, and the program is stepping back to read instruction instructions for a repeat run, a new secondary input must be specified at this point. This card is required for the second and later STATCAT secondary data banks - not for the first run, where the secondary input is specified on the initial file control card.

(4 - Data Starter - Secondary Input)

If the secondary input is to be read from cards, not from a standard STATCAT data bank, the system must have the necessary information for the card file. This information is provided by a standard data starter card, as given in 3.2 and above. Only items C, D, E and F are needed. (number of columns, number of alternative classes, non-value and title.)

6 - Subset Specification - Secondary Input

If the secondary input is from cards, it should not be necessary to specify subset conditions (although this can be done if it should be useful) so that a title card and an END card will suffice. If conditions are applied to a card input file, they must be given in terms of column numbers, because no column names are available.

(7 - File Control Card - Primary Input)

If the program is stepping back for a repeat run, a new primary input STATCAT data bank must be supplied at this point, using a standard file control card. This card is not required for the first call of the program.

8 - Merging Specification

The merging specification is of the standard form described in 3.7. Only the first two four-character fields are used. The first specifies the data bank from which the datum is to be taken. This code may be FIRS, in which case the datum is taken from the primary input STATCAT data bank, or SECO, in which case it will be taken from the second input data bank (standard STATCAT or cards), or BOTH, in which case it will be taken from the primary data bank, unless this is a non-value, when it will be taken from the second data bank. The second code specifies the column number in the input (Column names are not available)

If there are no occurrences of the code 'BOTH' in the merging specification, the program will carry out a matching operation. One entry will be produced in the output STATCAT data bank for each entry in the primary input STATCAT data bank (included in the subset). Data specified as FIRS will be taken from the appropriate column in the primary input STATCAT data bank. Data columns specified as SECO will be taken from the first entry in the second input STATCAT data bank which has the same priority as the entry from the first input STATCAT data bank. If there is no entry with the same priority, then these columns will be filled with non-values. Entries in the second input data bank which do not have the same priority as an entry in the first input STATCAT data bank, or which follow an entry with the same priority will not contribute to the output STATCAT data bank.

If the code BOTH appears for any data column, then entries in the second input data bank which do not correspond to entries in the primary STATCAT data bank will appear as entries in the output STATCAT data bank, items coded FIRS being, in this case, replaced by non-values. Entries with the same priority as the preceding entry in either input data bank will be matched with entries having the same priority in the other data bank, until the last of either is reached. Data columns coded BOTH are filled by values from the primary data bank, except that non-values are replaced by the corresponding values from the second input data bank.

If all the columns are specified by the code BOTH a simple merging operation is carried out. Entries from the second input data bank will be interpolated between those in the primary STATCAT data bank if they do not have the same priority. If they do have the same priority, they will be used to fill in non-values, but otherwise ignored.

If the merging specification consists of one card containing in the first two fields (the first eight card columns) the codes BOTH and .ALL, followed by an END card, then the program will merge the entries, taking data in order from each data bank, until the required number of data columns has been found. Surplus columns will be discarded and unfilled output cells filled with non-values.

9 - Priority Specification - Primary Input

This is a standard priority specification, as described in 10.1. It is only important when the secondary input is from a card input stream, which is read in as necessary. It must have the same priority codes as the secondary input priority specification, although they need not refer to the same data column numbers. If the priority specification is not observed in one or other input data bank, the system will endeavour to find the correct matching item, printing a warning message, although for an input card stream this will not be possible.

11 - Data Handling Instruction

This is a standard data handling instruction as described in 3.8. It is used here to specify what information is to be printed during the construction of the output STATCAT data bank, and to control the amount of checking undertaken (when an output data bank is completed).

Card layout - Data Handling Instruction - STMERG

```
A BCCCDDDEEEEEEE EFFFFFFFFFFFFFFFFFFFFF............GGGGGGGGGG
```

Columns on Card	Item Code	FORTRAN Type	Function	See
1	A	I	Output Control Index	Below
2	B	I	Checking Control Index	4.3
3 - 5	C	I	Maximum number of non-values	Below
6 - 8	D	F	Number of s.d.s from the mean	4.3
9 - 16	E	F	Minimum percentage in class	4.3
17 - 40	F	A	Comment (not kept)	-
41 - 80	G	A	Comment (not kept)	-

A - Output Control Index

This index controls the amount of descriptive output produced during the construction of the data storage segment. (The data description segment is constructed by selecting the relevant data column descriptions from the primary and secondary input data banks on the first run of the executive subroutine. It is always listed in full.)

ALTERNATIVES

A = 0, blank or non-numeric	: Number of output entry and numbers of input entries of which it is composed are printed.
A = 1	: In addition, the first datum of the entry is printed
A = 2	: In addition, the complete output entry is printed.
A = 3	: In addition, the complete input entries are printed.
A = 4	: In addition, secondary input entries are printed, as they are read in.
A = 5 to 9	: No output

DEFAULT value = 0 (blank or non-numeric characters)

C - <u>Maximum Number of Non=values</u>

This is the maximum number of non-values that will be accepted in an output entry.

DEFAULT value (blank or non-numeric characters) = number of data columns less one. (A completely blank entry is a data terminator.)

SPECIAL CASE

If the data handling instruction is completely blank, except for the value of A, then the system will read a new data handling instruction after completing the current sweep. If it is not, the program will write a data terminator to the output STATCAT data bank, and procede to the CHECK subroutine.

(<u>12</u> - <u>Data Column Descriptions</u> - <u>if second input from cards</u>)

If the second input is not a STATCAT data bank, but is read from cards, the system will not have data column descriptions to be placed on the output tape. Descriptions, of the type described in 3.4, with the necessary complementary information, must be supplied in order for each SECO card in the merging specification. The order of these descriptions must be that of the column numbers on the SECO cards, which need not be numeric or ascending. These data descriptions are read and stored on the first pass through the input STATCAT data bank, and are not needed on second and subsequent passes while constructing the same output STATCAT data bank.

(<u>13</u> - <u>Entries</u> - <u>if second input is from cards</u>)

If the second input medium is not a STATCAT data bank the data storage segment should consist of entries to be read by the subroutine DATA, which may be a version of DATA given here or a user-written version. The last entry returned by DATA must consist of non-entries throughout.

If the secondary data are to be read as required, the **entries must be in an order consistent with the priority specifications.**

If the secondary input is to be stored in an array, there must be enough storage available to accommodate all entries, including a final entry consisting of non-values exclusively.

10.3.3 Input Example

Figure 10.32 is a summary of the input structure for one run of STMERG, in which the age of the operator is added to each entry. This is an example of the 'matching' mode. Figure 10.33 lists the input cards corresponding to the summary given in Figure 10.32.

10.3.4 Output Example

Figure 10.34 is a general summary of the output produced by this program, indented according to the program structure. Figure 10.35 is a page-by-page summary of the output corresponding to the specific input of Figure 10.33. Figure 10.36 shows the checking information corresponding to the first part of Figure 10.33, (output and secondary input) and Figure 10.37 shows the merging and primary input specifications. Figure 10.38 shows part of the output produced during the running of the program.

10.3.5 Commentary

Figure 10.39 illustrates the difference between the merging and matching processes. In the first case illustrated, a matching operation has been specified, items being drawn from one input or the other, but not both. In the second, some items are coded BOTH, so that a merging operation is carried out. In the third all items are coded BOTH, but their order is not the same, and some items are not used. In the last case, the code BOTH.ALL is used, and a direct merging operation is carried out.

The input to this program being both specific and complex, the user is advised to consider only his particular case, ignoring all items not needed by that case. Figure 10.39 also presents input sequences for two common types of merging and matching operations.

Figure 10.31a - System Flow-Chart - STMERG

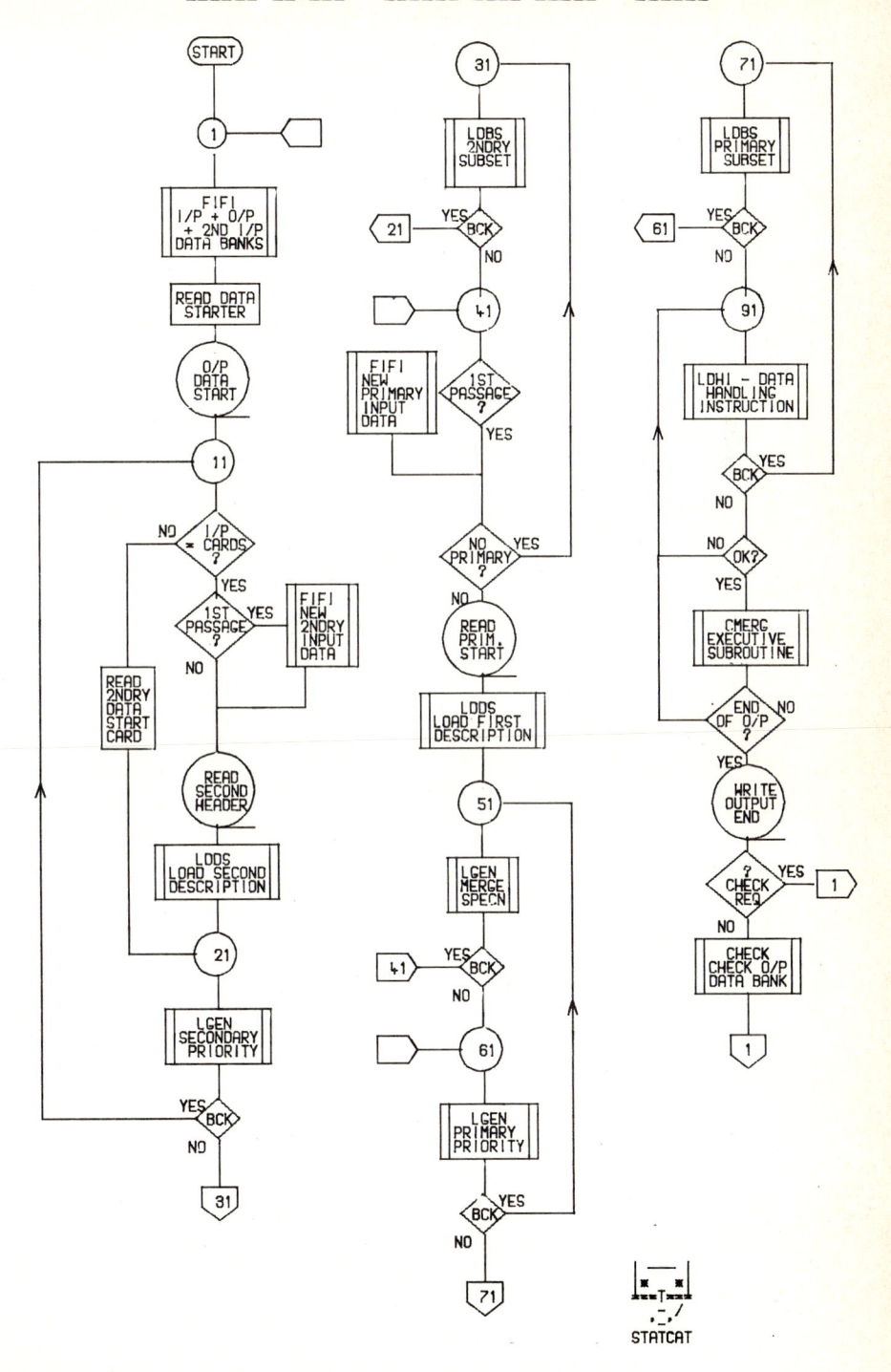

Figure 10.31b - System Flow-Chart - CMERG

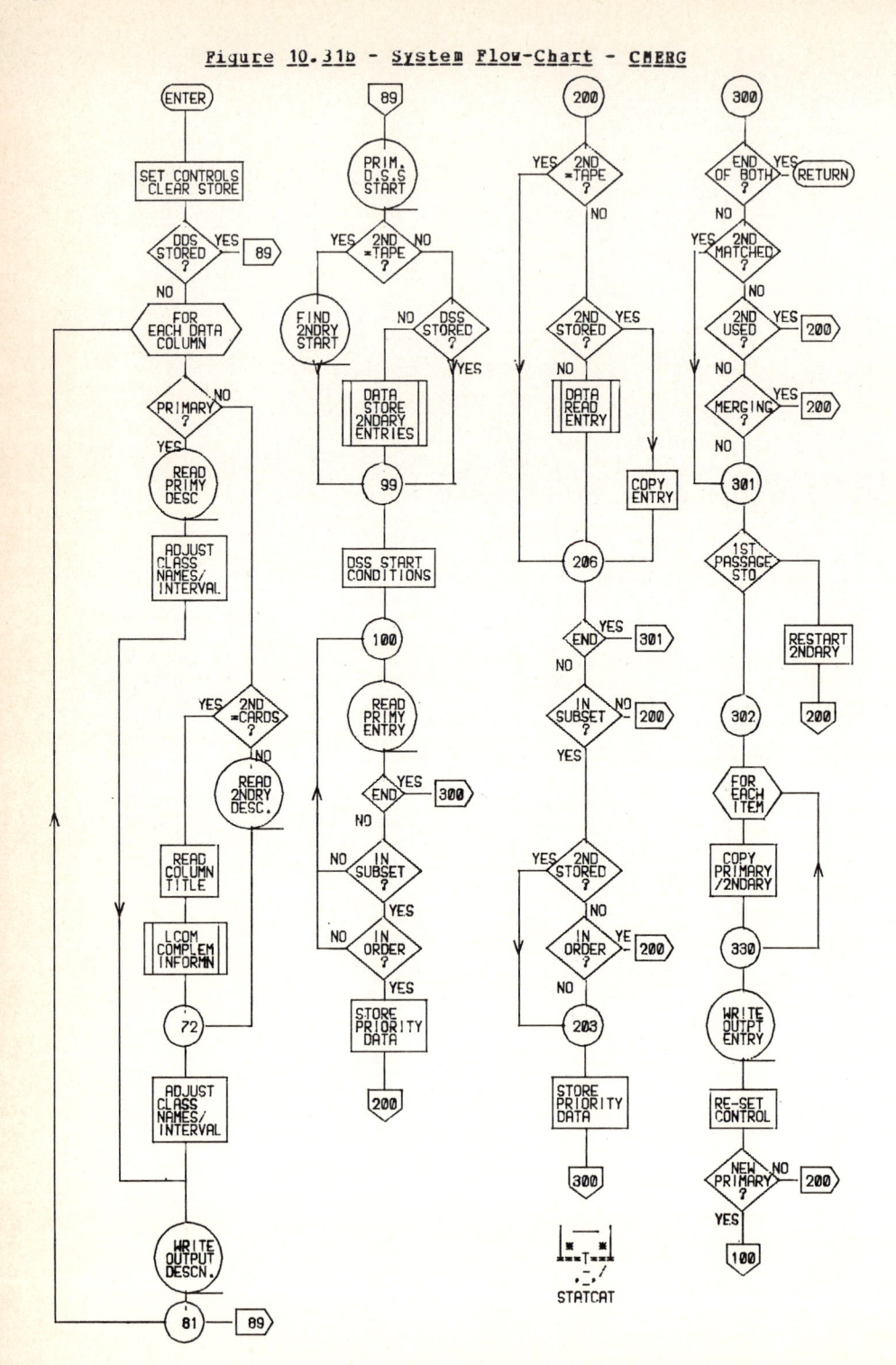

Figure 10.32 - STMERG - Input Structure

```
            Level
  0    1    2    3    4    5    6    7    8    9
FILE CONTROL CARD
DATA STARTER
     SECONDARY FILE STARTER FROM CARD
          SECONDARY PRIORITY SPEC
               SECONDARY SUBSET SPECIFICATION
                    MERGING SPECIFICATION
                         PRIMARY PRIORITY SPECIFICATION
                              PRIMARY SUBSET SPECIFICATION
                                   DATA HANDLING INSTRUCTION
                                        DATA COLUMN DESCRIPTION FROM CARD
                                        ENTRIES FROM CARDS
                                        NULL ENTRY FROM CARD
STOP
```

Figure 10.33 - STMERG - Input Example

```
---------1---------2---------3---------4---------5---------6---------7--
**STMERGDEMO    DUFF
  2  3 10  -1.0  ADDING AGE TO OPERATOR
     2 10  -1.0  AGE OF OPERATOR
1Q2.COL1
END OF SECONDARY PRIORITY SPECIFICATION
ALL DATA
END OF SECONDARY SUBSET    SPECIFICATION
PRIMNTRY
PRIMOPER
SECOCOL2
END OF MATCHING SPECIFICATION
1Q2.OPER
END OF    PRIMARY PRIORITY SPECIFICATION
ALL DATA
END OF    PRIMARY SUBSET    SPECIFICATION
GO
      3AGE.          AGE OF OPERATOR
        10.      10.
        1.       17.
        2.       32.
        3.       36.
        4.       45.
 -1.     -1.
STOP
---------1---------2---------3---------4---------5---------6---------7--
```

Figure 10.34 - STMERG - Output Structure

```
For each   ) : Output File Control Record
output     )   Output File Parameters
data bank  )   Output Data Description Record (= first input)
               For each  ) Input File Parameters
               Input     ) For each   ) Priority Record
               Data Bank ) Priority   ) For each ) Subset Record
             .            Specification ) Subset   ) See below left
             .
             .
             .     For each ) Event Records
             .     Sweep    )<Allocation of Entries>
             .              <Output Subsets>
             .              <Entries Input>
             .              <Entries Stored>
             .<Standard Data Bank Checking>
```

Carated(<>) items are optional.

Figure 10.35 - STMERG - Page-by-page output summary

Page	Contents	Origin
1	File Control Record	FIFI
2- 3	Output Data Header	STSORT
	Output File Parameters	STSORT
	Output Data Description record	LDDS
4	Priority Specification	LDBS/LSET
5	Subset Specification	LDBS
	Data Handling Instruction	LDHI
6	Sorting Record (one sweep)	CSORT
	Data Handling Instruction	LDHI
7	Subset Specification	LDBS
	Data Handling Instruction	LDHI
8-12	Sorting Records	CSORT
13-23	Standard Data Checking	CHECK
24	End of Sorting Message	STSORT
25	Data Handling Instruction (STOP)	LDHI

Figure 10.36 - STMERG - Output Example - Output + 2ndary

```
                    STATCAT DATA BANK MERGING OR MATCHING
            OUTPUT FILE PARAMETERS
NUMBER OF DATA COLUMNS IS -     3
STORED NUMBER OF CLASSES IS    10
VALUE USED FOR MISSING DATA IS -       -1.00000000
        OUTPUT STATCAT DATA BANK - ADDING AGE TO OPERATOR                FILE NAME DUFF
                    STATCAT DATA BANK MERGING OR MATCHING
 SECONDARY INPUT FILE PARAMETERS
NUMBER OF DATA COLUMNS IS -     2
STORED NUMBER OF CLASSES IS    10
VALUE USED FOR MISSING DATA IS -       -1.00000000
 SECONDARY INPUT STATCAT DATA BANK - AGE OF OPERATOR                     FILE NAME CARD

                    PROGRAM CAN STORE 2500 ENTRIES

STATCAT PROGRAM STMERG          -     MERGING OR MATCHING OF ENTRIES
        OUTPUT DATA BANK TITLE -    ADDING AGE TO OPERATOR
 SECONDARY INPUT DATA BANK TITLE -  AGE OF OPERATOR
PRIORITY ORDERING

ORDER    PRIORITY   DATA
OF USE     RULE    COLUMN

  1 ORIGINAL 1Q2.   COL1
  A STANDARD 1Q2.   COL1
END OF SECONDARY PRIORITY SPECIFICATION

        DATA BANK SUBSET TITLE - ALL DATA            COMMENT
END OF SECONDARY SUBSET    SPECIFICATION             COMMENT
                                                     SYSTEM COMMENT - SUBSET WILL CONTAIN ALL ENTRIES
```

Figure 10.37 - STMERG - Output Example - Merging and Primary

```
                    STATCAT DATA BANK MERGING OR MATCHING

  PRIMARY INPUT FILE PARAMETERS

NUMBER OF DATA COLUMNS IS -      18
STORED NUMBER OF CLASSES IS      10
VALUE USED FOR MISSING DATA IS           -1.00000000
     PRIMARY INPUT STATCAT DATA BANK - DEMONSTRATION STATCAT DATA BANK                  FILE NAME DEMO

                    DATA DESCRIPTION SEGMENT

COLUMN  SCALE   SHORT       FULL TITLE
NUMBER  CODE    TITLE                                                                   LEVEL

   1      1     NTRY        ENTRY NUMBER                                                DUMMY

   2      1     SESS        NUMBER OF TEST SESSION                                      DUMMY

   3      2     OBSR        OBSERVER                                                    NOMINAL
                MIKE-NOEL-JOCK-PETE-      -      -      -      -      -      -

   4      2     OPER        OPERATOR                                                    NOMINAL
                ERIC-FRED-GINA-HUGH-      -      -      -      -      -      -

STATCAT PROGRAM STMERG          -    MERGING OR MATCHING OF ENTRIES

          OUTPUT DATA BANK   TITLE -   ADDING AGE TO OPERATOR
  SECONDARY INPUT DATA BANK  TITLE -   AGE OF OPERATOR
  SECONDARY INPUT    SUBSET  TITLE -   ALL DATA
    PRIMARY INPUT DATA BANK  TITLE -   DEMONSTRATION STATCAT DATA BANK

MERGING OR MATCHING SPECIFICATION

OUTPUT    INPUT DATA BANK
COLUMN    IDENTITY  COLUMN

  1 ORIGINAL PRIM   NTRY
  A STANDARD PRIM   COL3

  2 ORIGINAL PRIM   OPER
  B STANDARD PRIM   COL6

  3 ORIGINAL SECO   COL2
  C STANDARD SECO   COL2

END OF MATCHING SPECIFICATION

THIS IS A MATCHING OPERATION


STATCAT PROGRAM STMERG          -    MERGING OR MATCHING OF ENTRIES

          OUTPUT DATA BANK   TITLE -   ADDING AGE TO OPERATOR
  SECONDARY INPUT DATA BANK  TITLE -   AGE OF OPERATOR
  SECONDARY INPUT    SUBSET  TITLE -   ALL DATA
    PRIMARY INPUT DATA BANK  TITLE -   DEMONSTRATION STATCAT DATA BANK

  1 ORIGINAL 1Q2.   OPER
  A STANDARD 1Q2.   COL4

DATA USED ARE ON A NOMINAL SCALE    THEY SHOULD BE ON AN ORDINAL SCALE      ARE EXTRA ASUMPTIONS VALID       **WA
END OF    PRIMARY PRIORITY SPECIFICATION



      DATA BANK SUBSET TITLE - ALL DATA                                COMMENT
END OF    PRIMARY SUBSET   SPECIFICATION                               COMMENT
                                                            SYSTEM COMMENT - SUBSET WILL CONTAIN ALL ENTRIES

                    DATA HANDLING INSTRUCTION - ECHO PRINT

ABCCCDDDEEEEEEEEEEFFFFFFFFGGGGGGGGGGGGGGGHHHHHHHHHHHHHHHHHHHHHHHHHHHHHHHHHHHHHH
49                      XXXXXXXXXXXXXXXX

                    OUTPUT CONTROL INDEX =     +
                    CHECKING CONTROL INDEX =    Y
MAXIMUM NUMBER OF NON-VALUES (MISSING) =       2
MAXIMUM NUMBER OF STD. DEVN. FROM A.M. =     5.0000
MINIMUM PERCENTAGE OF ITEMS IN CLASS  . =    1.0000

          THE SYSTEM HAS STANDARDISED  3 CONTROL VALUES FROM THE DATA HANDLING INSTRUCTION       ** WAR
          PLEASE VERIFY THAT THE ASSUMPTIONS IT HAS MADE ARE CORRECT AND ADJUST STORAGE IF NECESSARY
INPUT ACCEPTED - MATCHING BEGINS
```

Figure 10.38 - **STMERG** - **Output Example** - **O/P DSS and Merging**

```
STATCAT PROGRAM STMERG        - MATCHING OF ENTRIES
         OUTPUT DATA BANK TITLE -    ADDING AGE TO OPERATOR
  PRIMARY INPUT DATA BANK TITLE -    DEMONSTRATION STATCAT DATA BANK
SECONDARY INPUT DATA BANK TITLE -    AGE OF OPERATOR
                    DATA DESCRIPTION SEGMENT

COLUMN  SCALE   SHORT           FULL TITLE                              DATA       WAS ORIGINALLY
NUMBER  CODE    TITLE                                                   LEVEL      COLUMN OF BANK

  1       1     NTRY            ENTRY NUMBER                            DUMMY           1       PRIM

  2       2     OPER            OPERATOR                                NOMINAL         4       PRIM
                ERIC-FRED-GINA-HUGH-   -    -    -    -    -


  3       6     AGE.            AGE OF OPERATOR                         INTERVAL        2       SECO
                     CLASSES FROM BELOW    10.0000 BY CLASSES OF    10.000000 TO    90.0000 AND OVER



STATCAT PROGRAM STMERG        - MATCHING OF ENTRIES
         OUTPUT DATA BANK TITLE -    ADDING AGE TO OPERATOR
  PRIMARY INPUT DATA BANK TITLE -    DEMONSTRATION STATCAT DATA BANK
  PRIMARY INPUT     SUBSET TITLE -   ALL DATA
SECONDARY INPUT DATA BANK TITLE -    AGE OF OPERATOR
SECONDARY INPUT   SUBSET TITLE -     ALL DATA

            SECONDARY INPUT ENTRY      1 INTO INTERNAL STORE

    1.000000    17.000000

            SECONDARY INPUT ENTRY      2 INTO INTERNAL STORE

    2.000000    32.000000

            SECONDARY INPUT ENTRY      3 INTO INTERNAL STORE

    3.000000    36.000000

            SECONDARY INPUT ENTRY      4 INTO INTERNAL STORE

    4.000000    45.000000



STATCAT PROGRAM STMERG        - MATCHING OF ENTRIES
         OUTPUT DATA BANK TITLE -    ADDING AGE TO OPERATOR
  PRIMARY INPUT DATA BANK TITLE -    DEMONSTRATION STATCAT DATA BANK
  PRIMARY INPUT     SUBSET TITLE -   ALL DATA
SECONDARY INPUT DATA BANK TITLE -    AGE OF OPERATOR
SECONDARY INPUT   SUBSET TITLE -     ALL DATA

ENTRY     1                   PRIMARY INPUT ENTRY        1              SECONDARY INPUT ENTRY        1

    1.000000    1.000000    17.000000
            PRIMARY INPUT ENTRY

    1.000000    1.000000    1.000000    1.000000    1.000000    1.000000    1.000000    1.000000    1.000000    1.000000
   22.000000    0.620000   13.309999   91.589996   35.519989   48.299988   48.000000    0.500000
            SECONDARY INPUT ENTRY

    1.000000   17.000000

ENTRY     2                   PRIMARY INPUT ENTRY        2              SECONDARY INPUT ENTRY        4

    2.000000    4.000000    45.000000
            PRIMARY INPUT ENTRY

    2.000000    1.000000    3.000000    4.000000    2.000000    3.000000    1.000000    1.000000    4.000000    6.000000
   25.000000  -12.500000   95.989990   84.129990   54.449997   63.000000   72.000000    1.299999
            SECONDARY INPUT ENTRY

    4.000000   45.000000

ENTRY     3                   PRIMARY INPUT ENTRY        3              SECONDARY INPUT ENTRY        2

    3.000000    2.000000    32.000000
            PRIMARY INPUT ENTRY

    3.000000    1.000000    4.000000    2.000000    3.000000    3.000000    1.000000    1.000000    2.000000    2.000000
   27.000000   -5.959999   27.239990   78.819992   40.069992   43.259995   46.000000    1.299999
            SECONDARY INPUT ENTRY

    2.000000   32.000000
```

Figure 10.39 - STMERG - Merging vs Matching

MERGING

```
FIRST INPUT                OUTPUT                        SECOND INPUT
Priority    Values         Priority    Values            Priority    Values

   1         3  2   ----->    1         3  2                1          2  4
                              2         3  3  <----------   2          3  3
   3         3  ?   ----->    3         3  5  <----------   3          2  5
   5         3  ?   ----->    5         3  ?
   6         7  1   ----->    6         7  1                6          6  3
   8         5  ?   ----->    8         5  3                8          ?  3
   9         4  ?   ----->    9         4  ?                9          6  ?
```

MATCHING

```
FIRST INPUT                OUTPUT                        SECOND INPUT
Priority    Values         Priority    Values            Priority    Values
COL7        COL8                       FIRS  SECO        COL2        COL2
                                       COL8  COL2

   1         1     ----->    1          1    15   <--,-,----1          15
   1         1     ----->    1          1    15   <-' / /--2           17
   1         2     ----->    1          2    17   <--/-'       3       19
   1         1     ----->    1          1    15   <-'   /  4            21
   1         4     ----->    1          4    21   <------'  4           25*
   1         5     ----->    1          5    ?               6          29*
```

(? = non-value)   * = Not used

STMERG - Input Sequences

```
Matching an Input STATCAT            Merging two input STATCAT data
Data Bank to a card input            banks with identical data
held in direct store                 description segments

File Control (Input/Output)          File Control (Input/Output/2nd Input)
Data Starter for Output (A=2)        Data Starter for Output (A = 0)
Priority Specification (Card I/P)    Priority Specification (2nd Input)
Subset Specification (Card I/P)      Subset Specification (2nd Input)
Matching Specification (No BOTHs)    Merging Specification (BOTH.ALL)
Priority Specification (Tape I/P)    Priority Specification (1st Input)
Subset Specification   (Tape Input)  Subset specificantion  (1st Input)
Data Handling Instruction.           Data Handling Instruction
Data Column Descriptions (Card)
Entries (Card)
```

```
C MASTER STMERG - MERGES TWO (OR MORE) STATCAT DATA BANKS
C SUBROUTINES AND FUNCTIONS REQUIRED
C SETTING OF ARRAY DIMENSIONS
C AN       (SEE  3.1 ) SERVICE    ALPHA - TO NUMERIC VALUE
C CHECK    (SEE  4.2 ) EXECUTIVE  CHECKS DATA BANK OR SUBSET
C CHIKEN   (SEE 11.9 ) SERVICE    WARNS OF MISMATCHED DATA LEVEL
C CLSAM    (SEE  3.5 ) SERVICE    ALLOTS ENTRY TO SAMPLE/SUBSET
C CMERG    (SEE 10.3 ) EXECUTIVE  MERGES/MATCHES STATCAT DATA BANKS
C COMPA    (SEE  3.1 ) SERVICE    COMPARES ALPHAMERIC VALUES
C COPYA    (SEE  3.1 ) SERVICE    COPIES ALPHAMERIC VALUE
C FIFI     (SEE  3.2 ) SYSTEM     ALLOCATES PERIPHERALS
C IBL      (SEE  3.1 ) SERVICE    DETECTS BLANK,END AND STOP CARDS
C ICH      (SEE  3.1 ) SERVICE    IDENTIFIES ALPHAMERIC CODES
C LCOM     (SEE  3.4 ) SYSTEM     LOADS COMPLEMENTARY INFORMATION
C LDBS     (SEE  3.6 ) SYSTEM     LOADS SUBSET DEFINITION
C LDDS     (SEE  3.4 ) SYSTEM     LOADS DATA DESCRIPTION SEGMENT
C LDHI     (SEE  3.8 ) SYSTEM     LOADS/CHECKS DATA HANDLING INSTN
C LGEN     (SEE  3.7 ) SYSTEM     LOADS GENERALISED VARIATES
C LSET     (SEE  3.5 ) SYSTEM     LOADS DEFINING CONDITIONS
C PR       (SEE 10.2 ) SERVICE    DETERMINES PRIORITY IN SORTING
C WDCD     (SEE  3.4 ) SERVICE    WRITE DATA COLUMN DESCRIPTION
C NQ1M = MAXIMUM NUMBER OF DATA COLUMNS ON PRIMARY TAPE
C DIMENSION D1(NQ1M),IDP1(NQ1M),IP1(NQ1M),RT1(NQ1M,2),RT3(NQ1M,2)
      NQ1M = 100
      DIMENSION D1(100),IDP1(100),IP1(100),RT1(100,2),RT3(100)
C NQ2M = MAXIMUM NUMBER OF DATA COLUMNS ON SECONDARY INPUT
C DIMENSION D2(NQ2M),IDP2(NQ2M),IP2(NQ2M),RT2(NQ2M,2)
      NQ2M = 100
      DIMENSION D2(100),IDP2(100),IP2(100),RT2(100)
C NQMAX = MAXIMUM NUMBER OF DATA COLUMNS ON MERGED TAPE
C DIMENSION D(NQMAX),DMAX(NQMAX),DMIN(NQMAX),IT(NQMAX)
C DIMENSION IP(NQMAX),IDP(NQMAX),ST(NQMAX),CN(NQMAX)
      NQMAX = 100
      DIMENSION D(100 ),DMAX(100 ),DMIN(100 ),IT(100 )
      DIMENSION IP(100  ),IDP(100  ),ST(100  ),CN(100  )
C DATA BANK COLUMN NUMBERS - MAY BE USED IN PLACE OF NAMES
C IF THE DIMENSION OF NQMAX IS INCREASED,THE EXTRA CODES MUST BE
C INCLUDED IN THIS DATA STATEMENT
      DATA  CN/4HCOL1,4HCOL2,4HCOL3,4HCOL4,4HCOL5,4HCOL6,4HCOL7,4HCOL8,4
     1HCOL9,4HCL10,4HCL11,4HCL12,4HCL13,4HCL14,4HCL15,4HCL16,4HCL17,4HCL
     218,4HCL19,4HCL20,4HCL21,4HCL22,4HCL23,4HCL24,4HCL25,4HCL26,4HCL27,
     34HCL28,4HCL29,4HCL30,4HCL31,4HCL32,4HCL33,4HCL34,4HCL35,4HCL36,4HC
     4L37,4HCL38,4HCL39,4HCL40,4HCL41,4HCL42,4HCL43,4HCL44,4HCL45,4HCL46
     5,4HCL47,4HCL48,4HCL49,4HCL50,4HCL51,4HCL52,4HCL53,4HCL54,4HCL55,4H
     6CL56,4HCL57,4HCL58,4HCL59,4HCL60,4HCL61,4HCL62,4HCL63,4HCL64,4HCL6
     75,4HCL66,4HCL67,4HCL68,4HCL69,4HCL70,4HCL71,4HCL72,4HCL73,4HCL74,4
     8HCL75,4HCL76,4HCL77,4HCL78,4HCL79,4HCL80,4HCL81,4HCL82,4HCL83,4HCL
     984,4HCL85,4HCL86,4HCL87,4HCL88,4HCL89,4HCL90,4HCL91,4HCL92,4HCL93,
     94HCL94,4HCL95,4HCL96,4HCL97,4HCL98,4HCL99,4HC100/
C NALTMX = MAXIMUM NUMBER OF ALTERNATIVE CLASSES ON ANY TAPE
C DIMENSION RT(NQMAX,NALTMX),TRT(NALTMX)
      NALTMX = 50
      DIMENSION RT(100,50),TRT(50)
C MAXDBC = MAXIMUM NUMBER OF DATA BANK SUBSET CONDITIONS
C DIMENSION SCON(5,MAXDBC)
      MAXDBC = 50
      DIMENSION SCON(5,    50)
C THE FOLLOWING DIMENSIONS ARE FIXED
      DIMENSION TTB(20),U(8),LU(8),UU(3),H(1),IH(1),REAS1(3),REAS2(3)
      DIMENSION FORM(80),TIN(4),TOUT(4),THIRD(4),TYPE(2,2),DB(3),SS(3)
C NAMES AND REQUIRED LEVELS FOR PRIORITY RULES
C     RULES       1      2      3      4      5      6      7      8
      DATA U/4H1Q2.,4H2Q1.,4HQ12.,4HQ21.,4H12Q.,4H21Q.,4H12-.,4H21-./
```

```
      DATA LU/8*3/,BL/4H    /,UU/4HPRIM,4HSECO,4HBOTH/,CARD/4HCARD/
      DATA TIN/4H   P,4HRIMA,4HRY I,4HNPUT/
      DATA TOUT/4H    ,4H    ,4H  OU,4HTPUT/
      DATA THIRD/4H SEC,4HONDA,4HRY I,4HNPUT/
      DATA REAS1/4HNOT ,4HAVAI,4HLABL/,DB/4H DAT,4HA BA,4HNK   /
      DATA REAS2/4HEXCE,4HEDS ,4HSTOR/,SS/4H    ,4HSUBS,4HET   /
      DATA TYPE/3H  M,3HERG,3H MA,3HTCH/,ALL/4H.ALL/
      DATA PROG/4HMERG/
      COMMON /STCT/MED1,MED2,MED3,MED4,MED5,MED6,MED13,Q,V(20),TT(30)
      MED1 = -1
C LEVEL 0 - ALLOCATE PERIPHERALS - DEFINE OUTPUT TAPE
    1 CALL COPYA(TT(1),PROG)
      CALL FIFI
      M2 = -1
      V(6) = -1
C READ REVISED TITLE,KEY AND NAME
    2 READ(MED1,900) (FORM(J),J=1,16),(TT(J),J=1,10),(FORM(J),J=17,34)
      IF(IBL(TT,10,4).LT.0.AND.IBL(FORM,32,1).LT.0) GO TO 2
      IF(MED4.LT.1) WRITE(MED6,910) TOUT,REAS1
      IF(MED4.LT.1) GO TO 1
      V(2) = AN(FORM,2,2,2)
      IF(V(2).GT.2.5) V(2) = 0.
      V2 = V(2)
      NQ = AN(FORM,5,3,5)
      NALT = AN(FORM,8,6,8)
      Q = AN(FORM,16,9,16)
      FORM(32) = AN(FORM,32,17,32)
      WRITE(MED6,901) TOUT,NQ,NALT,Q,TOUT,(TT(J),J=1,10),FORM(34)
      REWIND MED4
      IF(NQ.EQ.0) WRITE(MED6,908)
      IF(NQ.EQ.0) V(10) = 1.
      IF(NQ.GT.NQMAX) WRITE(MED6,902) NQ,NQMAX
      IF(NQ.GT.NQMAX.AND.V(10).LT.0.5) V(10) = 1.
      IF(NALT.GT.NALTMX) WRITE(MED6,903) NALT,NALTMX
      IF(NALT.GT.NALTMX)V(10) = V(10) + 2.
      IF(V(10).GT.0.5)WRITE(MED6,910) TOUT,REAS2
      IF(V(10).GT.0.5) GO TO 1
      WRITE(MED4) NQ,NALT,Q,(TT(J),J=1,10),BL,BL,BL,(FORM(J),J=32,34)
C LEVEL 1 - DEFINE SECONDARY INPUT - ALLOCATE TAPE IF ANY
   11 IF(V(10).GT.10.) V(10) = 0.
      IF(V(2).GT.0.5) GO TO 12
C HEADER FROM TAPE
      V10 = V(10)
      V6 = V(6)
      IF(M2.GE.0)CALL FIFI
      V(6) = V6
      V(10) = V10
      IF(MED13.LT.0) WRITE(MED6,910) THIRD,REAS1
      IF(MED13.LT.0) GO TO 11
      REWIND MED13
      READ(MED13) NQ2,NALT2,Q2,(TTB(J),J=1,16)
      GO TO 13
C HEADER FROM CARDS
   12 READ(MED1,900) (FORM(J),J=1,16),(TTB(J),J=1,16)
      IF(IBL(TTB,10,4).LT.0.AND.IBL(FORM,16,1).LT.0) GO TO 12
      NQ2 = AN(FORM,5,3,5)
      NALT2 = AN(FORM,8,6,8)
      V(7) = NALT2
      Q2 = AN(FORM,16,9,16)
      CALL COPYA(TTB(16),CARD)
C CHECK SIZES
   13 WRITE(MED2,901) THIRD,NQ2,NALT2,Q2,THIRD,(TTB(J),J=1,10),TTB(16)
      IF(NQ2.GT.NQMAX) WRITE(MED6,902) NQ2,NQMAX
```

```
      IF(NQ2.GT.NQMAX.AND.V(10).LT.0.5) V(10) = 16.
      IF(NALT2.GT.NALTMX)WRITE(MED6,903)NALT2,NALTMX
      IF(NALT2.GT.NALTMX.AND.V(10).LT.0.5) V(10) = 17.
      IF(V(10).GT.0.5)WRITE(MED2,910) THIRD,REAS2
      IF(V(10).GT.0.5) GO TO 11
      LI = 18
      IF(V(2).LT.0.5) CALL LDDS(TRT,NALT2,D,NQ2,ST,NQ2,IT,NQ2,H,O,H,H,O,
     1LI,O,Q,VX,O,MED2,MED13,IGO)
      DO 14 J = 1,NQ
      IF(V(2).GT.0.5) IT(J) = 3
   14 IF(V(2).GT.0.5) CALL COPYA(ST(J),CN(J))
C CALCULATE STORAGE ROWS AVAILABLE
      X = NALTMX
      Y = NQMAX
      X= X*Y
      Y = NQ2
      NCAV = X/Y
      WRITE(MED6,907) NCAV
C LEVEL 2 - DEFINE SECONDARY PRIORITY
   21 IF(V(10).GT.20.) V(10) = 0.
      WRITE(MED2,920)TOUT,DB,(TT(I),I=1,10),THIRD,DB,(TTB(I),I=1,10)
      WRITE(MED2,931)
      M2 = 0
      CALL LGEN(U,8,LU,8,ST,IT,CN,NQ2,IH,O,H,H,O,H,H,O,O,NALT2,IH,IP2,NQ
     12M,M2,NQ2M,1,NALT2)
      IF(V(11).EQ.0.) GO TO 11
      IF(V(20).GT.0.5.AND.V(10).LT.0.5) V(10) = 24.
C LEVEL 3 - DEFINE SECONDARY SUBSET
   31 IF(V(10).GT.30.) V(10) = 0.
      CALL LDBS(SCON,NCON,MAXDBC,CN,ST,IT,NQ2,TRT,NALT2,IGO)
      IF(IGO.GT.0) GO TO 21
      DO 32 I = 11,20
   32 CALL COPYA(TTB(I),TT(I+10))
      M1 = -1
C LEVEL 4 - DEFINE PRIMARY INPUT - ALLOCATE TAPE
   41 IF(V(10).GT.40.) V(10) = 0.
      V6 = V(6)
      V10 = V(10)
      IF(M1.GE.0) CALL FIFI
      IF(MED3.LT.0) WRITE(MED6,910) TIN,REAS1
      IF(MED3.LT.0) GO TO 11
      REWIND MED3
      READ(MED3) NQ1,NALT1,Q1,(TT(J),J=11,26)
      WRITE(MED6,901)TIN,NQ1,NALT1,Q1,TIN,(TT(J),J=11,20),TT(26)
      V(3) = Q
      V(4) = NQ
      V(6) = V6
      V(8) = NALT1
      V(10) = V10
      IF(NQ1.GT.NQMAX)WRITE(MED6,902) NQ1,NQMAX
      IF(NQ1.GT.NQMAX.AND.V(10).LT.0.5) V(10) =42.
      IF(NALT1.GT.NALTMX)WRITE(MED6,903)NALT1,NALTMX
      IF(NALT1.GT.NALTMX.AND.V(10).LT.0.5)V(10) = 43.
      IF(V(10).GT.0.5)WRITE(MED6,910) TIN,REAS2
      IF(V(10).GT.0.5) GO TO 41
      N1 = NQ2+1
      LI = 10
      CALL LDDS(TRT,NALT1,D,NQ1,ST(N1),NQ1,IT(N1),NQ1,H,O,H,H,O,LI,O,Q
     1,VX,O,MED2,MED3,O,IGO)
C LOAD MERGING SPECIFICATION
   51 IF(V(10).GE.50.) V(10) = 0.
      WRITE(MED2,920)TOUT,DB,(TT(I),I=1,10),THIRD,DB,(TTB(I),I=1,10),
     1THIRD,SS,(TTB(I),I=11,20),TIN,DB,(TT(I),I=11,20)
```

```
      WRITE(MED6,916)
      NQ3 = NQ1+NQ2+1
      CALL COPYA(ST(NQ3),ALL)
      M3 = 0.
      CALL LGEN(UU,3,IH,0,ST,IT,CN,NQ3,IH,0,H,H,0,H,H,0,0,NALT,IH,IP,NQ,
     1M3,NQ,0,NALT)
      IF(V(11).LT.0.5) GO TO 41
      IF(V(20).GT.0.5.AND.V(10).LT.0.5)V(10) = 57.
      IMERG = 0
      IF(IP(1).EQ.3000+NQ3) IMERG = 1
      IF(IMERG.EQ.1)M3 = NQ
      IF(M3.NE.NQ) WRITE(MED6,919) NQ
      IF(M3.NE.NQ.AND.V(10).LT.0.5)  V(10) = 58.
      DO 65 I = 1,M3
      IF(IMERG.EQ.1) IP(I) = 3000+I
      IDP(I) = IP(I)/1000
      IP(I)  = IP(I) - IDP(I)*1000
      IF(IDP(I).NE.3)IMERG = IMERG -1
      IF(IP(I).GT.NQ1.AND.IDP(I).EQ.1)WRITE(MED2,960) I,TIN,DB
      IF(IP(I).GT.NQ2.AND.IDP(I).EQ.2)WRITE(MED2,960) I,THIRD,DB
   65 CONTINUE
      IF(IMERG.NE.1) IMERG = 2
      WRITE(MED2,962)TYPE(1,IMERG),TYPE(2,IMERG)
C LEVEL 5 - DEFINE PRIMARY PRIORITY
   61 IF(V(10).GT.60.) V(10) = 0.
      WRITE(MED2,920)TOUT,DB,(TT(I),I=1,10),THIRD,DB,(TTB(I),I=1,10),
     1THIRD,SS,(TTB(I),I=11,20),TIN,DB,(TT(I),I=11,20)
      M1 = 0
      CALL LGEN(U,8,LU,8,ST(N1),IT(N1),CN,NQ1,IH,0,H,H,0,H,H,0,0,NALT1,I
     1H,IP1,NQ1M,M1,NQ1M,1,0)
      IF(V(11).LT.0.5) GO TO 51
      IF(V(20).GT.0.5.AND.V(10).LT.0.5) V(10) = 64.
C CHECK THAT PRIORITY ORDERINGS ARE COMPATIBLE
      IF(M1.EQ.M2)GO TO 55
      IF(V(10).LT.0.5) V(10) = 65.
      WRITE(MED6,917)M1,M2
   55 DO 57 I = 1,M1
      IF(I.GT.M2) GO TO 57
      IDP1(I) = IP1(I)/1000
      IDP2(I) = IP2(I)/1000
      IP1(I) = IP1(I) - IDP1(I)*1000
      IP2(I) = IP2(I) - IDP2(I)*1000
      IF(IDP1(I).EQ.IDP2(I))GO TO 56
      IF(V(10).LT.0.5) V(10) = 66.
      WRITE(MED6,918)I,IDP1(I),IDP2(I)
   56 IDP2(I) = I
   57 CONTINUE
C LEVEL 6 - DEFINE PRIMARY SUBSET
   71 IF(V(10).GT.70.) V(10) = 0.
      IC2 = NCON+1
      MAXDBD = MAXDBC-NCON
      CALL LDBS(SCON(1,IC2),NCONB,MAXDBD,CN,ST(N1),IT(N1),NQ1,TRT,NALT1,
     1IGO)
      IF(IGO.GT.0) GO TO 61
C LEVEL 9 - DATA HANDLING INSTRUCTION
   91 IF(V(10).GT.90.) V(10) = 0.
      CALL LDHI(V(1),1,VCH,3,V(9),7,ASDL,18,APT,15,H,0,H,V(10),
     1FORM(41),FORM,MED1,MED2,MED4,Q,NQ,NWARN,1,IGO)
      IF(IGO.GT.0) GO TO 61
      IF(V(1).GT.4.5) NWARN = NWARN + 1
      IF(V(1).GT.4.5) V(1) = -1.
      NX = V(9)
      IF(NX.LE.0.OR.NX.GE.NQ)  NWARN = NWARN + 1
```

```
      IF(NX.LE.0.OR.NX.GE.NQ)  V(9) = NQ-1
      IF(IBL(FORM(2),1,1).LT.0.AND.IBL(FORM(6),11,1).LT.0) NX = 0
      IF(IBL(FORM(2),1,1).GE.0.OR .IBL(FORM(6),11,1).GE.0) NX = 1
      IF(NX.EQ.0)CALL LDHI(V(1),1,H,0,V(9),7,H,0,H,0,H,0,H,V(10),
     1FORM(41),FORM,MED1,MED2,MED4,Q,NQ,NWARN,2,IGO)
      IF(NX.EQ.0) GO TO 92
      IF(ASDL.LE.0.) NWARN = NWARN + 1
      IF(ASDL.EQ.0.)  ASDL = 5.
      IF(ASDL.LT.0.)  ASDL = 9999.
      IF(APT.LE.0.) NWARN = NWARN + 1
      IF(APT.EQ.0.)  APT = 1.
      IF(APT.LT.0.)  APT = 0.
      CALL LDHI(V(1),1,VCH,3,V(9),7,ASDL,18,APT,15,H,0,H,V(10),
     1FORM(41),FORM,MED1,MED2,MED4,Q,NQ,NWARN,2,IGO)
   92 IF(IGO.GT.0) GO TO 91
  101 WRITE(MED2,998)TYPE(1,IMERG),TYPE(2,IMERG)
C LOAD DATA STORAGE SEGMENT
      CALL CMERG(D1,IDP1,IP1,RT1,RT3,D2,IDP2,IP2,RT2,D,IP,IDP,TRT,SCON
     1(1,IC2),SCON,NQ1,M1,NQ2,NQ,NALT,NCONB,NCON,Q1,Q2,RT,NCAV,NALTMX,
     2TTB,UU,DB,SS,TIN,TOUT,THIRD,TYPE(1,IMERG))
      WRITE(MED2,999)TYPE(1,IMERG),TYPE(2,IMERG)
  112 IF(NX.GT.0.5) GO TO 120
      WRITE(MED6,991)
      GO TO 91
C END TAPE - TEST IF REQUIRED
  120 WRITE(MED4) (V(3),I=1,NQ)
      V(2) = VCH
      REWIND MED4
      IF(V(2).GE.0.) GO TO 150
      WRITE(MED6,992)
      WRITE(MED6,995)TIN,THIRD,TOUT(3),TOUT(4)
      GO TO 1
C CARRY OUT PRELIMINARY CHECK OF DATA TAPE
  150 WRITE(MED6,993)
      APT = APT*.01
      NCON=0
      Q = V(3)
      CALL CHECK (D,DMIN,DMAX,RT,IT,TRT,NQ,NALT,ASDL,APT,SCON,NCON,ST)
      WRITE(MED6,994)
      WRITE(MED6,995)TIN,THIRD,TOUT(3),TOUT(4)
      GO TO 1
  900 FORMAT(16A1,10A4,16A1,2A4)
  901 FORMAT(1H1,20X,37HSTATCAT DATA BANK MERGING OR MATCHING
     1                        /1H0,4A4,16H FILE PARAMETER
     2S/29H0NUMBER OF DATA COLUMNS IS - ,I6/29H0STORED NUMBER OF CLASSES
     3 IS ,I6/34H0VALUE USED FOR MISSING DATA IS - ,F20.8/
     4          1H0,4A4,21H STATCAT DATA BANK - ,10A4,10X,10HFILE NAME ,A4/)
  902 FORMAT (4H0THE,I6,   37H ITEMS PER ENTRY EXCEED THE AVAILABLE,I6,1
     16H STORAGE COLUMNS)
  903 FORMAT (4H0THE,I6,40H CLASSES PER COLUMN EXCEED THE AVAILABLE,I6,1
     13H STORAGE ROWS)
  907 FORMAT(1H0,20X,17HPROGRAM CAN STORE,I5,8H ENTRIES/)
  908 FORMAT(26H0NO DATA COLUMNS SPECIFIED)
  910 FORMAT(1H0,4A4,11H DATA BANK ,3A4,35HE - PROGRAM TRIES TO FIND NEX
     1T FILE  )
  916 FORMAT(34H0MERGING OR MATCHING SPECIFICATION/25H0OUTPUT    INPUT DA
     1TA BANK/26H COLUMN    IDENTITY    COLUMN)
  917 FORMAT (30H0NUMBER OF MATCHING COLUMNS IS,I6,20H IN PRIMARY BANK A
     1ND,I6,18H IN SECONDARY BANK)
  918 FORMAT (23H0RANKING ORDER FOR ITEM,I4,14H ON PRIMARY IS,I4,19H.ON
     1SECONDARY IT IS,I4)
  919 FORMAT (4H0ALL,I4,21HCOLUMNS NOT SPECIFIED)
  920 FORMAT(23H1STATCAT PROGRAM STMERG,7X,1H-,4X,30HMERGING OR MATCHING
```

```
      1 OF ENTRIES //(1H ,7A4,7HTITLE -,4X,10A4))
  921 FORMAT(24H0PARAMETER SPECIFICATION/25H0OUTPUT   PARAMETER   INPUT/
     1 17H COLUMN,7X,12HCODE   COLUMN)
  922 FORMAT( 5H0ONLY,I4,23H PARAMETERS - SHOULD BE,I4)
  931 FORMAT(18H0PRIORITY ORDERING/6H0ORDER,4X,14HPRIORITY   DATA/
     1 17H OF USE,7X,12HRULE   COLUMN )
  932 FORMAT(64H0TOTAL INTERMEDIATE ITEMS EXCEEDS STORAGE LIMIT - INCREA
     1SE NQMAX)
  960 FORMAT(12H0DATA COLUMN,I4,53H REFERS TO A DATA COLUMN WHICH DOES N
     1OT EXIST IN THE ,7A4/)
  962 FORMAT(10H0THIS IS A,2A3,13HING OPERATION)
  991 FORMAT(1H+,20X,35H-READ NEW DATA HANDLING INSTRUCTION)
  992 FORMAT(1H+,20X,13H- NO CHECKING)
  993 FORMAT(1H+,20X,7H- CHECK,7A4)
  994 FORMAT(19H0CHECKING COMPLETED )
  995 FORMAT(1H+,35X,10H- READ NEW,4A4,1H,,4A4,4H AND,6A4)
  998 FORMAT(17H0INPUT ACCEPTED -,2A3,10HING BEGINS)
  999 FORMAT(1H0,2A3,13HING COMPLETED)
      END
```

655

```
      SUBROUTINE CMERG(D1,IDP1,IP1,RT1,RT3,D2,IDP2,IP2,RT2,D,IP,IDP,TRT,
     1 SCONA,SCONB,NQ1,M1,NQ2,NQ,NALT,NCONA,NCONB,Q1,Q2,RT,NCAV,NALTMX,T
     2TB,UU,DB,SS,TIN,TOUT,THIRD,TYPE)
C CMERG   (SEE 10.3 ) EXECUTIVE    MERGES/MATCHES STATCAT DATA BANKS
      DIMENSION D1(NQ1),RT1(NQ1,2),D2(NQ2),RT2(NQ2,2),RT(NQ2,NCAV)
      DIMENSION D(NQ),IP(NQ),IDP(NQ),TRT(NALTMX),TTB(20),TX(19)
      DIMENSION IDP1(M1),IP1(M1),IDP2(M1),IP2(M1), RT3(M1,2)
      DIMENSION DB(3),SS(3),TIN(4),TOUT(4),THIRD(4),TYPE(2),EN(2)
      DIMENSION SCONA(5,NCONA),SCONB(5,NCONB),FORM(80),UU(3)
      DATA BL/4H    /,AB/4H NO /,EN/4H ENT,4HRY /
      COMMON /STCT/MED1,MED2,MED3,MED4,MED5,MED6,MED13,Q,V(20),TT(30)
      REWIND MED3
      IF(V(2).LT.0.5) REWIND MED13
      NOP = 0
      NIP2 = 0
      IF(V(1).GT.-0.5) NOP = 1
      IF(V(1).GT.1.5) NOP = (NQ+39)/10
      IF(V(1).GT.2.5) NOP = NOP + (NQ1+39)/10 + (NQ2+39)/10
      IF(V(1).GT.3.5) NIP2 = (NQ2+39)/10
      NALT1 = V(8)
      NALT2 = V(7)
      A = NALT1
      B = NALT2
      C = NALT
      A = (C-2.)/(A-2.)
      B = (C-2.)/(B-2.)
      JSF = 0
      ISF = 0
      IBOTH = 0
C PREPARE INTERNAL STORE - FIRST NULL TO SIGNAL START
      IF(V(2)-1.)54,50,52
   50 DO 51 I = 1,NQ2
   51 D2(I) = Q
      GO TO 54
   52 DO 53 I = 1,NQ2
      RT(I,1) = Q
      D2(I) = Q + 1.
      DO 53 J = 2,NCAV
   53 RT(I,J) = Q + 1.
   54 DO 55 I = 1,NQ
   55 IF(IDP(I).EQ.3) IBOTH = 1
      READ(MED3) NX,NX,(X,I=1,17)
      IF(V(2).LT.0.5) READ(MED13) NX,NX,(X,I=1,17)
      IF(V(6).GT.-0.5) GO TO 89
      V(6) = 0.
C ASSEMBLE DATA DESCRIPTION SEGMENT
      NLIN = 49
      DO 81 K = 1,NQ
      L = IDP(K)
      M = IP(K)
      IF(L.EQ.2) GO TO 70
   60 IF(ISF.EQ.M) GO TO 62
      IF(ISF.GT.M) GO TO 61
      READ (MED3 ) TX,(TRT(J),J=1,NALT1),NX,DMINX,DMAXX
      ISF = ISF + 1
      GO TO 60
   61 REWIND MED3
      READ(MED3) NX,NX,X,(X,J = 1,16)
      ISF = 0
      GO TO 60
   62 IF(NALT.LE.NALT1) GO TO 64
      I = NALT1+1
      DO 63 J = I,NALT
```

```
   63 CALL COPYA(TRT(J),BL)
   64 IF(ITX.LE.5) GO TO 80
      DMAXX = DMINX + (DMAXX-DMINX)*A
      GO TO 80
   70 IF(JSF.EQ.M) GO TO 72
      IF(JSF.GT.M) GO TO 71
      IF(V(2).LT.0.5) READ(MED13)TX,(TRT(J),J=1,NALT2),NX,DMINX,DMAXX
      JSF = JSF + 1
      IF(JSF.NE.M.OR.V(2).LT.0.5) GO TO 70
      READ(MED1,930) (FORM(J),J=1,6),TX
      CALL LCOM(TX,TRT,NALT,NX,DMINX,DMAXX,MED1,MED2)
      GO TO 70
   71 IF(V(2).EQ.0.) REWIND MED13
      IF(V(2).EQ.0.) READ (MED13) NX,NX,X,(X,J=1,16)
      JSF = 0
      GO TO 70
   72 IF(NALT.LE.NALT2) GO TO 74
      I = NALT2 + 1
      DO 73 J = I,NALT
   73 CALL COPYA(TRT(J),BL)
   74 IF(ITX.LE.5) GO TO 80
      DMAXX = DMINX + (DMAXX-DMINX)*B
   80 IF(NX.LE.1) NL = 2
      IF(NX.EQ.2.OR.NX.EQ.3) NL = (39+NQ)/10
      IF(NX.GE.4) NL = 4
      NLIN = NLIN + NL
      IF(NLIN.GT.50) WRITE(MED2,901)TYPE,TOUT,DB,(TT(I),I=1,10),
     1 TIN,DB,(TT(I),I=11,20),THIRD,DB,(TTB(I),I=1,10)
      IF(NLIN.GT.50) WRITE(MED2,900)
      IF(NLIN.GT.50) NLIN = 6 + NL
      WRITE(MED2,904)K,NX,TX,M,UU(L)
      DEL = (DMAXX-DMINX)/(C-2.)
      IF(NX.EQ.2.OR.NX.EQ.3) WRITE(MED2,990) (TRT(J),J = 1,NALT)
      IF(NX.EQ.4.OR.NX.EQ.5) WRITE(MED2,995)
      IF(NX.EQ.6.OR.NX.EQ.7) WRITE(MED2,996)DMINX,DEL,DMAXX
   81 WRITE (MED4) TX,(TRT(J),J=1,NALT ),NX,DMINX,DMAXX
C SET TAPES TO START OF DATA STORAGE SEGMENT
   89 IF(ISF.EQ.NQ1) GO TO 91
      ISF = ISF + 1
      DO 90 I = ISF,NQ1
   90 READ (MED3 ) TX,(TRT(J),J=1,NALT1),NX,DMINX,DMAXX
   91 IF(JSF.EQ.NQ2.OR.V(2).GT.0.5) GO TO 93
      JSF = JSF + 1
      DO 92 I = JSF,NQ2
   92 READ (MED13) TX,(TRT(J),J=1,NALT2),NX,DMINX,DMAXX
   93 IF(V(2).LT.1.5) GO TO 99
C LOAD DATA TO INTERNAL STORAGE - WARN IF OVERFLOW
      ISF = NCAV
      NLIN = 50
      DO 95 J = 1,NCAV
      CALL DATA(RT(1,J),NQ2,FORM)
      DO 94 I = 1,NQ2
      IF(RT(I,J).NE.Q2) GO TO 85
   94 CONTINUE
      ISF = J-1
      GO TO 99
   85 NLIN = NLIN + NIP2
      IF(NLIN.GT.50) WRITE(MED2,901)TYPE,TOUT,DB,(TT(I),I=1,10),
     1 TIN,DB,(TT(I),I=11,20),TIN,SS,(TT(I),I=21,30),
     2 THIRD,DB,(TTB(I),I=1,10),THIRD,SS,(TTB(I),I=11,20)
      IF(NLIN.GT.50) NLIN = 6 + NIP2
   95 IF(V(1).GT.3.5) WRITE(MED2,940)THIRD,EN,J,(RT(I,J),I=1,NQ2)
      J=NCAV
```

```
   96 J = J+1
      CALL DATA(D2,NQ2,FORM)
      DO 97 I = 1,NQ2
      IF(D2(I).NE.Q2) GO TO 98
   97 CONTINUE
      GO TO 99
   98 WRITE(MED2,941)THIRD,EN,J,D2
      GO TO 96
   99 NCAV = ISF
C DATA STORAGE SEGMENT
      IEND1 = 0
      IEND2 = 0
      ISF = V(6)
      JSF = 0
      KSF = 0
      JLAST = 0
      NP = 0
      NEW1 = 1
      NEW2 = 1
      NLIN = 50
C FIND NEXT ITEM IN PRIMARY INPUT FILE
  100 IF(IEND1.NE.2.AND.NEW1.EQ.1)READ(MED3)(D1(I),I=1,NQ1)
      KSF = KSF + 1
      IF(IEND1.NE.0)IEND1 = 2
      DO 101 I = 1,NQ1
  101 IF(D1(I).NE.Q1.AND.IEND1.NE.0)IEND1 = 1
      IF(IEND1.EQ.2) GO TO 300
      CALL CLSAM(D1,NQ1,SCONA,NCONA,NIN,1)
      IF(NIN.EQ.0) GO TO 100
      DO 102 I = 1,NQ1
  102 RT1(I,1) = D1(I)
      IF(IEND1.EQ.0) GO TO 103
      CALL PR(2,1,NP,RT1,IP1,IDP1,NQ1,2,Q)
      IF(NP.NE.2) GO TO 103
      IF(V(2).LT.1.5) WRITE(MED2,991) TIN,DB,ORD
      IF(V(2).LT.1.5) GO TO 100
      NEW2 = 1
      IEND2 = 0
      JSF = 0
  103 DO 104 I = 1,NQ1
      IF(I.GT.M1) GO TO 104
      J = IP1(I)
      RT3(I,1)=RT1(J,1)
      IF(RT1(J,1).EQ.Q1)RT3(I,1) = Q
  104 RT1(I,2) = RT1(I,1)
      IEND1 = 1
      NEW1 = 0
      IF(IEND2.NE.0) GO TO 300
C FIND NEXT ITEM ON SECONDARY INPUT
  200 IF(NEW2.NE.1) GO TO 300
  207 IF(IEND2.EQ.2) GO TO 300
      IF(V(2).EQ.0.) READ(MED13)(D2(I),I=1,NQ2)
      IF(V(2).EQ.1.) CALL DATA (D2,NQ2,FORM)
      JSF = JSF + 1
      IF(V(2).LT.1.5) GO TO 206
      DO 205 I = 1,NQ2
      IF(JSF.LE.NCAV)D2(I) = RT(I,JSF)
  205 IF(JSF.GT.NCAV) D2(I) = Q2
  206 CONTINUE
      IF(IEND2.NE.0) IEND2 = 2
      DO 201 I = 1,NQ2
  201 IF(D2(I).NE.Q2.AND.IEND2.NE.0)IEND2 = 1
      IF(IEND2.EQ.2) GO TO 301
```

```
      CALL CLSAM(D2,NQ2,SCOMB,NCOMB,NIN,1)
      IF(NIN.EQ.0) GO TO 200
      DO 202 I = 1,NQ2
  202 RT2(I,1) = D2(I)
C IF SECONDARY DATA IN CORE STORE, IT NEED NOT BE IN ORDER
      IF(V(2).EQ.2.) GO TO 203
      NLIN = NLIN + NIP2
      IF(NLIN.GT.50) WRITE(MED2,901)TYPE,TOUT,DB,(TT(I),I=1,10),
     1 TIN,DB,(TT(I),I=11,20),TIN,SS,(TT(I),I=21,30),
     2 THIRD,DB,(TTB(I),I=1,10),THIRD,SS,(TTB(I),I=11,20)
      IF(NLIN.GT.50) NLIN = 8 + NIP2
      IF(NIP2.GT.0) WRITE(MED2,940)THIRD,EN,JSF,D2
      IF(IEND2.EQ.0) GO TO 203
      CALL PR(2,1,NP,RT2,IP2,IDP1,NQ1,2,Q)
      IF(NP.NE.2)GO TO 203
      WRITE(MED2,991)THIRD,DB,ORD
      GO TO 200
  203 DO 204 I = 1,NQ2
      IF(I.GT.M1) GO TO 204
      J = IP2(I)
      RT3(I,2) = RT2(J,1)
      IF(RT2(J,1).EQ.Q2)RT3(I,2) = Q
  204 RT2 (I,2) = RT2(I,1)
      IEND2 = 1
      NEW2 = 0
  300 NP = 0
C RETURN WHEN BOTH INPUT DATA BANKS EXHAUSTED
      IF(IEND1.EQ.2.AND.IEND2.EQ.2) V(6) = ISF
      IF(IEND1.EQ.2.AND.IEND2.EQ.2) RETURN
      IF(IEND1.EQ.2) NP = 2
      IF(IEND2.EQ.2) NP = 1
      IF(NP.EQ.0)CALL PR(1,2,NP,RT3,IDP2,IDP1,M1,2,Q)
C DISCARD ALL USED UNMATCHED SECONDARIES
      IF(NP.EQ.2.AND.NEW2.EQ.2) GO TO 207
C DISCARD ALL UNMATCHED SECONDARIES IF MATCHING
      IF(IBOTH.EQ.0.AND.NP.EQ.2) GO TO 207
C NO EQUIVALENT ON SECOND INPUT CHANNEL
  301 IF(JLAST.NE.0.OR.V(2).NE.2.) GO TO 302
C RE-RUN IF SECONDARY DATA IN CORE STORE
      JLAST = 1
      NEW2 = 1
      IEND2 = 0
      JSF = 0
      GO TO 200
C ASSEMBLE MERGED ENTRY
  302 IF(IEND2.EQ.2.AND.NEW1.EQ.1) GO TO 100
      IF(IEND2.EQ.2) NP = 1
      VMIS = -0.5
      DO 330 I = 1,NQ
      J = IP(I)
      D(I) = Q
      IF(NP.EQ.1.OR.IDP(I).EQ.1) GO TO 320
      IF(D2(J).NE.Q2) D(I) = D2(J)
  320 IF(NP.EQ.2.OR.IDP(I).EQ.2) GO TO 330
      IF(D1(J).NE.Q1) D(I) = D1(J)
  330 IF(D(I).EQ.Q) VMIS = VMIS + 1.
      IF(VMIS.LT.V(9)) WRITE(MED4) (D(I),I = 1,NQ)
      ISF = ISF + 1
      IF(V(1).LT.0.) GO TO 331
      NLIN = NLIN + NOP
      IF(NLIN.GT.50) WRITE(MED2,901)TYPE,TOUT,DB,(TT(I),I=1,10),
     1 TIN,DB,(TT(I),I=11,20),TIN,SS,(TT(I),I=21,30),
     2 THIRD,DB,(TTB(I),I=1,10),THIRD,SS,(TTB(I),I=11,20)
```

```
      IF(NLIN.GT.50) NLIN = 8 + NOP
      IF(NP.EQ.1.AND.V(1).GT.2.5) NLIN = NLIN -(NQ2+39)/10
      IF(NP.EQ.2.AND.V(1).GT.2.5) NLIN = NLIN -(NQ1+39)/10
      IF(V(1).GT.1.) WRITE(MED2,903)
      WRITE(MED2,902) EN,ISF
      IF(NP.EQ.1)     WRITE(MED2,905)  AB,THIRD,EN
      IF(NP.NE.1)     WRITE(MED2,905)  BL,THIRD,EN,JSF
      IF(NP.EQ.2)     WRITE(MED2,906)  AB,TIN,EN
      IF(NP.NE.2)     WRITE(MED2,906)  BL,TIN,EN,KSF
      IF(V(1).EQ.1.)  WRITE(MED2,907)  D(1)
      IF(V(1).GT.1.)  WRITE(MED2,908)  D
      IF(NP.NE.2.AND.V(1).GT.2.) WRITE(MED2,915)TIN,EN,D1
      IF(NP.NE.1.AND.V(1).GT.2.) WRITE(MED2,915)THIRD,EN,D2
C IF NOT UNMATCHED SECONDARY READ NEW PRIMARY
  331 IF(NP.NE.2) NEW1 = 1
C IF SECONDARY WAS MATCHED NOTE IT HAS BEEN USED
      IF(NP.EQ.0) NEW2 = 2
C IF SECONDARY WAS UNMATCHED READ NEW SECONDARY
      IF(NP.EQ.2) NEW2 = 1
      IF(NP.EQ.2) GO TO 200
  333 CONTINUE
      GO TO 100
  900 FORMAT (1H0,20X,25HDATA DESCRIPTION SEGMENT    /
     121H0COLUMN SCALE    SHORT,10X,10HFULL TITLE,45X,4HDATA,6X,14HWAS OR
     2IGINALLY     /
     321H NUMBER CODE     TITLE,65X,5HLEVEL,5X,14HCOLUMN OF BANK)
  901 FORMAT(23H1SFATCAT PROGRAM STMERG,7X,1H-,2A3,14HING OF ENTRIES//
     1 (1H ,7A4,7HTITLE -,4X,10A4))
  902 FORMAT(2A4,I6)
  903 FORMAT(1H0)
  904 FORMAT(1H0,I3,I6,6X,A4,4X,A2,17A4,I6,6X,A4)
  905 FORMAT(1H+,78X,7A4,I6)
  906 FORMAT(1H+,28X,7A4,I6)
  907 FORMAT (1H+,70X,18HFIRST DATA ITEM = ,F20.8)
  908 FORMAT(1H0,10F12.6/(1H ,10F12.6))
  915 FORMAT(1H0,10X,6A4/1H0,10F12.6/(1H ,10F12.6))
  930 FORMAT(6A1,A4,A2,17A4)
  940 FORMAT(1H0,10X,6A4,I4,20H INTO INTERNAL STORE/
     1 1H0,10F12.6/(1H ,10F12.6))
  941 FORMAT(1H0,10X,6A4,I4,21H NOT STORED - NO ROOM /
     1 1H0,10F12.6/(1H ,10F12.6))
  990 FORMAT(1H0,20X,10(A4,1H-)/(21X,10(A4,1H-)))
  991 FORMAT (20A4)
  995 FORMAT(21X,77HLOWEST CLASS LIMIT = OBSERVED MINIMUM, HIGHEST CLASS
     1 LIMIT = OBSERVED MAXIMUM        )
  996 FORMAT (21X,18HCLASSES FROM BELOW,F12.4,14H BY CLASSES OF,F12.6,3H
     1 TO,F12.4,9H AND OVER  )
      END
```

10.4 PROGRAM STSYNC - SYNCHRONISING STATCAT DATA

10.4.1 Purpose

This program allows the user to synchronise continuous sampled information. It assumes that the input STATCAT data bank contains information in time order from a number of sources, (having been loaded directly in this form, or produced by merging several separate original STATCAT data banks). The different time streams may involve different sampling rates or different times of sampling. The user can specify which data columns are linked to which "time scales" and how the interpolation function is to be performed. He may also specify the time period(s) over which they are to be synchronised, and the sampling rate to be employed.

Figure 10.41a contains system flow-charts for the main program STSYNC and the interpolation function VNOW, and Figure 10.41b contains a system flow-chart for CSYNC, the executive subroutine.

10.4.2 Input Data

Summary

Item	Level	Function	See
1	0	File control card (Input-Output)	3.2
2	0	Data Starter (Output) (A and B not used)	3.3
3	0	Data Description Segment (Output)	Below + 3.4
(4	1	File control card (Later Input)	3.2)
5	2	Synchronisation Specification	Below + 3.7
6	3	Time Interval Specification	Below + 3.7
7	4	Subset specification (First Input)	3.5
8	5	Data Handling Instruction	3.8

Bracketed items are not called for for the first passage.

3 - Data Description Segment (Output)

This is a standard data description segment, for the output STATCAT data bank. It should contain information on what the output columns contain, not necessarily what they were derived from. The system has no way of checking that these columns correspond to what has been calculated and stored, so that great care must be taken to ensure that the data description is in agreement with the data stored. The first datum, and first column must be the 'true-time variate' (see item 6)

5 Synchronisation Specification.

This is a standard variate specification, as described in 3.7, with some additional restrictions.

Only the first two four-character codes are used on each card.

Two cards are used to define each datum in the output STATCAT data bank, with the exception of the first. The first card of each pair in the synchronisation specification defines the interpolation method (by one of the codes given in Figure 10.49 and explained in 10.4.5) and the time variate for an output data column. The second card of the pair must have a standard transform name (from Figure 3.71) as the first code, and the name or number of a data column in the input STATCAT data bank as the second code.

Each pair of cards defines a datum in the output STATCAT data bank, starting with the second. The output data are constructed by storing the values of the data column specified by the second card, transformed according to the transform from the second card, and interpolating values according to the method given on the first card, the times of the observations being taken from the column specified by the first card.

The synchronisation specification ends with a standard 'END' card.

For a data bank of NQ data columns, the synchronisation specification should contain 2*NQ-2 cards, plus the END card.

6 - Time Interval Specification

The time interval specification is of the standard form given in 3.7. It is used to specify the 'true-time variate' which is used during an interpolation. Several successive time intervals may be specified at the same time if required. These may overlap, leave gaps, or use different variates, as may be necessary. The use of the fields on the input is different from that of 3.7, so the whole card is given here as a memory aid.

Card Layout - Time Interval Specification - STSYNC

AAAABBBBCCCCDDDDEEEEEEEEFFFFFFFFGGGGGGGGHHHHHHHHHHHHHHHH.....

Columns on Card	Item Code	FORTRAN Type	Function	See
1 - 4	A	A	Transform Name	3.7
5 - 8	B	A	Data Column Name or Number	3.7
9 - 12	C	A	Not used	-
13 - 16	D	A	Not used	-
17 - 24	E	F	Start time for interpolation	Below
25 - 32	F	F	Sampling interval	Below
33 - 40	G	F	End time for interpolation	Below
41 - 80	H	A	Comment (not kept)	

E - Start Time for Interpolation

This is the time, in terms of the variate specified by B, transformed according to A, at which the first interpolated entry is to be produced.

F - Sampling Interval

This is the time interval between successive synchronised entries.

G - End Time for Interpolation

This is the time at or before which the last interpolated entry will be produced.

8 - Data Handling Instruction

This is a standard data handling instruction as described in 3.8. It is used here to specify what information is to be printed during the construction of the output STATCAT data bank, and to control the amount of checking undertaken (when an output data bank is completed).

Card layout - Data Handling Instruction - STSYNC

ABCCCDDDEEEEEEEEFFFFFFFFFFFFFFFFFFFFFFFF............GGGGGGGGGG

Columns on Card	Item Code	FORTRAN Type	Function	See
1	A	I	Output Control Index	Below
2	B	I	Checking Control Index	4.3
3 - 5	C	I	Maximum number of non-values	10.3
6 - 8	D	F	Number of s.d.s from the mean	4.3
9 - 16	E	F	Minimum percentage in class	4.3
17 - 40	F	A	Comment (not kept)	-
41 - 80	G	A	Comment (not kept)	-

A - Output Control Index

This index controls the amount of descriptive output produced during the construction of the data storage segment.

ALTERNATIVES

A = 0, blank or : Number of synchronised entry and time listed.
non-numeric

A = 1   : In addition, the complete output entry is printed.

A = 2   : In addition, the complete input entries are printed.

A = 3   : In addition, the full stored data is output whenever more is added. (for checking and error detection)

A = 3 to 9   : No output

DEFAULT value = 0 (blank or non-numeric characters)

C - Maximum Number of Non=values

This is the maximum number of non-values that will be accepted in an output entry.

DEFAULT value (blank or non-numeric characters) = number of data columns less one. (A completely blank entry is a data terminator.)

SPECIAL CASE

If the data handling instruction is completely blank, except for the value of A, then the system will read a new data handling instruction after completing the current sweep. If it is not, the program will write a data terminator to the output STATCAT data bank, and procede to the CHECK routine.

10.4.3   Input Example

Figure 10.42 is a summary of the input structure for one run of STSYNC. The 'true-time variate' used is the session number, and the three variates for which interpolation is undertaken are the temperature at the working position, the difficulty as assessed by the operator, and the heart rate. Only the data for the operator FRED are used. (If such interpolation was required for each operator, either four subsets could be specified in succession, or the input STATCAT data bank could be sorted into operator order by STSORT before running this program.) Figure 10.43 lists the input cards corresponding to the summary given in Figure 10.42.

10.4.4   Output Example

Figure 10.44 is a general summary of the output produced by this program, indented according to the program structure. Figure 10.45 is a page-by-page summary of the output corresponding to the specific input of Figure 10.43. Figure 10.46 shows the data description segment of the output STATCAT data bank, and Figure 10.47 shows the echo-check information for the synchronisation and time variate specifications. Figure 10.48 shows part of the output produced during the construction of the data storage segment.

10.4.5   Interpolation Modes

Figure 10.49 lists the possible modes of interpolation. Most of these are practically self-explanatory, but some may not be immediately obvious.

AVE2 and AVE4 provide the arithmetic mean of the nearest one or two points on each side - irrespective of the distance involved.

SMCU and OGIV both fit smooth curves through the points. OGIV fits a curve which is flat at the two adjacent points. SMCU fits a smooth curve which passes through each point, and at the two adjacent points is parallel to a line drawn through the other adjacent point and the next point on the other side. (This provides a better fit where the data are subject to a systematic trend.) These two types of interpolation are best employed when the data from which the interpolation is being made are known to be precise, with little random error. The nine methods EXP1 to EXP9 may be employed where there is known to be some noise present. They operate by calculating a running exponential smoothing point-by-point for each observation - for instance for EXP1, each point is calculated as 0.1 of the present value plus 0.9 of the previous one. The actual value is obtained by finding the inverse of the linearly interpolated value of the inverses of these values.

LINE provides a simple linear interpolation between the adjacent data. AVEW provides a weighted average for the closest two points on each side, weighted according to their distance, slightly more stable in the presence of noise. The remaining 'interpolation' techniques are mainly useful as means transferring constant values from the original STATCAT data bank to the standardised one.

A convention is adopted that, although there is no requirement that the original time variate should advance regularly (there may be gaps due to failure of recording equipment etc.), it must not reverse itself. If a value of 'true-time' is found which is less than the previous one, it is assumed that a new run is commencing, all cumulated values are cleared and the system re-starts. Thus, if we have data for 0900-1700 each day, we can interpolate at, say, half-hourly intervals by setting our start and end times at 0800 and 1800 and using a single time interval specification card, rather than setting a new time interval for each day. A similar method can be employed with virtually any cyclic phenomenon.

It may be worth adding that the 'true time' variate, and its equivalents need not necessarily be in units of time. Analyses may be made in terms of the distance travelled by a vehicle, a cost-of-living index (considered as a constantly increasing variable), or the distance between two ships, as examples.

Figure 10.41a - System Flow-Charts - STSYNC and VNOW

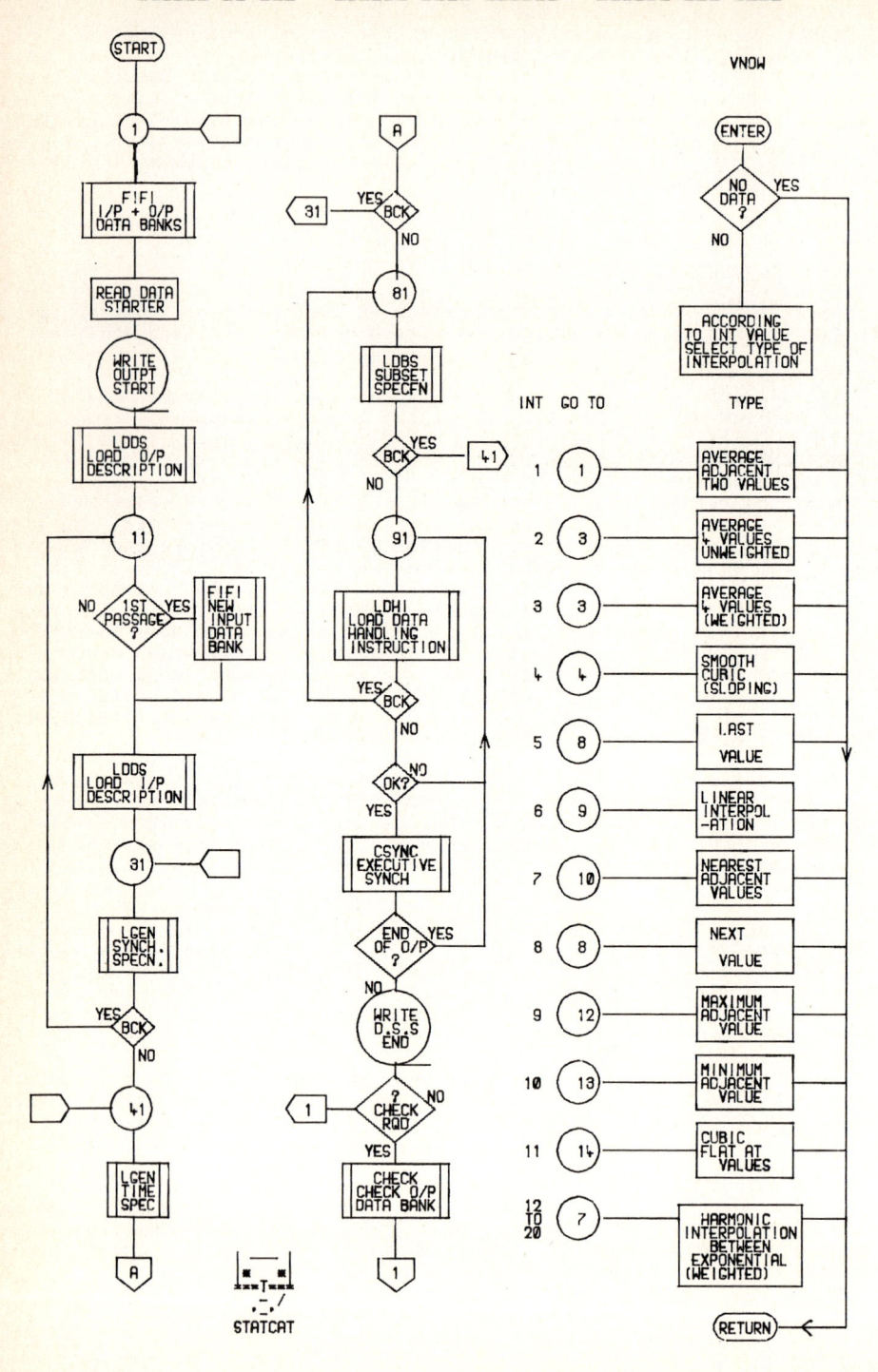

STSYNC

START → (1)
- FIFI I/P + O/P DATA BANKS
- READ DATA STARTER
- WRITE OUTPT START
- LDDS LOAD O/P DESCRIPTION
- (11)
- 1ST PASSAGE?
  - YES → FIFI NEW INPUT DATA BANK
  - NO → LDDS LOAD I/P DESCRIPTION
- (31)
- LGEN SYNCH SPECN.
- BCK?
  - YES → (back)
  - NO → (41)
- LGEN TIME SPEC
- A

From A:
- BCK? YES → (31)
- NO → (81)
- LDBS SUBSET SPECFN
- BCK? YES → (41)
- NO → (91)
- LDHI LOAD DATA HANDLING INSTRUCTION
- BCK? YES → (back)
- NO → OK?
  - NO → (back)
  - YES → CSYNC EXECUTIVE SYNCH
- END OF O/P?
  - YES → WRITE D.S.S END
  - NO → (back)
- CHECK RQD?
  - NO → (1)
  - YES → CHECK CHECK O/P DATA BANK → (1)

STATCAT

VNOW

ENTER
- NO DATA?
  - YES → RETURN
  - NO → ACCORDING TO INT VALUE SELECT TYPE OF INTERPOLATION

INT	GO TO	TYPE
1	1	AVERAGE ADJACENT TWO VALUES
2	3	AVERAGE 4 VALUES UNWEIGHTED
3	3	AVERAGE 4 VALUES (WEIGHTED)
4	4	SMOOTH CUBIC (SLOPING)
5	8	LAST VALUE
6	9	LINEAR INTERPOLATION
7	10	NEAREST ADJACENT VALUES
8	8	NEXT VALUE
9	12	MAXIMUM ADJACENT VALUE
10	13	MINIMUM ADJACENT VALUE
11	14	CUBIC FLAT AT VALUES
12 TO 20	7	HARMONIC INTERPOLATION BETWEEN EXPONENTIAL (WEIGHTED)

RETURN

Figure 10.41b - System Flow-Chart - CSYNC

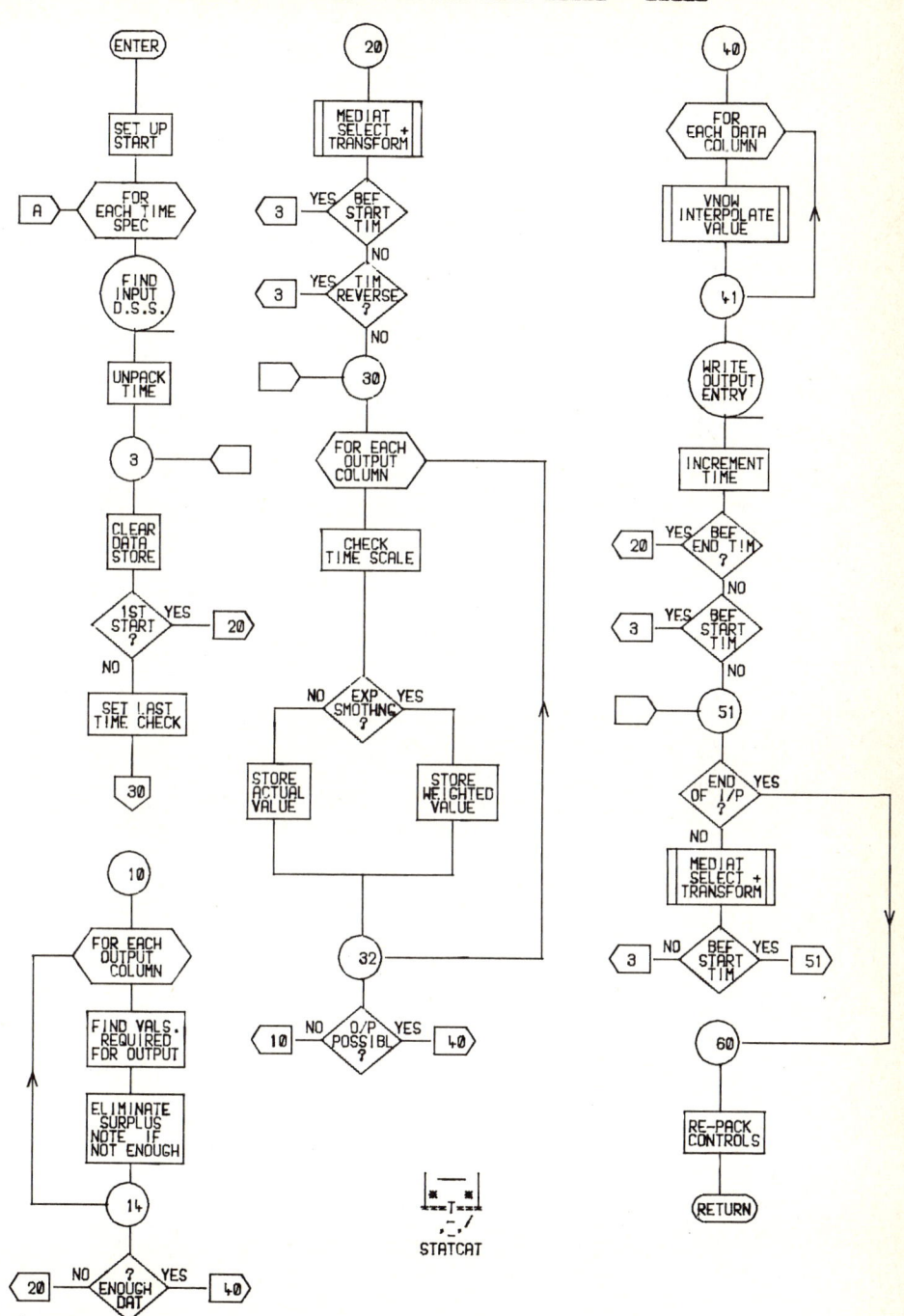

Figure 10.42 - STSYNC - Input Structure

```
        Level
0    1    2    3    4    5    6    7    8    9
FILE CONTROL CARD
DATA STARTER
DATA DESCRIPTION SEGMENT
     SYNCHRONISATION SEGMENT
          TIME VARIATE SPECIFICATION
               SUBSET SPECIFICATION
                    DATA HANDLING INSTRUCTION
                    STOP
```

Figure 10.43 - STSYNC - Input Example

```
---------1---------2---------3---------4---------5---------6---------7--
**STSYNCDEMO    DUFF                      INPUT = DEMO    OUTPUT = DUFF
     4 20  -1.0  SYNCHRONISED STATCAT DATA BANK
     1SIMTSIMULATED TIME (INTERPOLATED FROM SESSION NUMBER)
     0.0      1.0
     2TEMPTEMPERATURE AT WORKING POSITION (ESTIMATED)
    24.0      1.0
     3DIFFDIFFICULTY AS ASSESSED BY OPERATOR
VEASEASYREASNULLRHARHARDVHAR
     4H.R.HEART RATE (BEATS/MINUTE)
    25.0      5.0
END OF DATA DESCRIPTION SEGMENT
LINESESS
VAL.TEMP
NEARSESS
VAL.DIFF
OGIVSESS
VAL.H.R.
END OF SYNCHRONISATION SEGMENT
VAL.SESS          1.0       0.1      16.0
END OF TIME VARIATE
FRED ONLY
.IF.OPER.EQ.FRED
END OF SUBSET
1                                NORMAL CHECKING
STOP
---------1---------2---------3---------4---------5---------6---------7--
```

Figure 10.44 - STSYNC - Output Structure

```
For each    ) : File Control Record
input file  )   File Parameters
                Data Description
                For each    )  : Data Starter
                output file    Data Description Segment (Input Record)
                               For each            ) : Input Record
                               Synchronisation )      For each       ) Input
                               Specification   )      Time Variate   ) Record
For each) : Subset Input Record
Subset    )   For each               ) : Input Record
              Data Handling  )         For Each           ) : <For each> )<No+Time>
              Instruction    )         Data Sweep         )   <Output>)<Entry>
                                                              <Entry> )

                                                              <For each> )  <Entry>
                                                              <Input>)<Complete
                                                              <Entry>    )  <Current>
Carated (<>) items are optional.                                             <Data>
```

Figure 10.45 - STSYNC - Output Example - Page-by-Page Listing

Page	Contents	Origin
1	File Control Record	FIFI
2	Program Title	STSYNC
	File Parameters (Output)	STSYNC
	Data Description record (Output)	LDDS
3- 4	File Parameters (Output)	LDAP
	Data Description record (Output)	LDDS
5	Synchronisation Specification	LGEN
	Time Variate Specification	LGEN
6	Subset record	LSAMP
	Data Handling Instruction	LDHI
7-15	En-route Checks	CSYNC
16	Limit Check	CHECK
17-25	Distribution Check	CHECK
26	Abnormal Entries	CHECK
27	Data Handling Instruction (STOP)	LDHI

Figure 10.46 - STSYNC - Output Example - Data Description

```
FOR SYNCHRONISED DATA BANK
                    STATCAT SYNCHRONISATION OF ASYNCHRONOUS TIME DATA
FILE PARAMETERS
NUMBER OF DATA COLUMNS IS -      4
STORED NUMBER OF CLASSES IS     20
VALUE USED FOR MISSING DATA IS -         -1.00000000
FILE TITLE  SYNCHRONISED DATA BANK - DUMMY                FILE REFERENCE DUFF
                    DATA DESCRIPTION SEGMENT
COLUMN SCALE   SHORT         FULL TITLE
NUMBER CODE    TITLE                                                   LEVEL
   1     6     SIMT          SIMULATED TIME - FROM SESSION NUMBER       INTERVAL
                   CLASSES FROM BELOW    0.0    BY CLASSES OF    1.000000 TO    18.0000 AND OVER
   2     4     TEMP          TEMPERATURE AT WORKING POSITION            INTERVAL
                   LOWEST CLASS LIMIT = OBSERVED MINIMUM, HIGHEST CLASS LIMIT = OBSERVED MAXIMUM
   3     3     DIFF          DIFFICULTY EXPERIENCED BY OPERATOR         ORDINAL
                   VEAS-EASY-REAS-NULL-RHAR-HARD-VHAR-  -   -
                                          -   -   -   -   -
   4     4     H.R.          HEART RATE (BEATS/MINUTE) INTERPOLATED     INTERVAL
                   LOWEST CLASS LIMIT = OBSERVED MINIMUM, HIGHEST CLASS LIMIT = OBSERVED MAXIMUM
```

Figure 10.47 - STSYNC - Output - Synchronisation and Timing

```
1 INTERPOLATION IN TIME COLUMN       EACH SYNCHRONISED VARIATE IS SPECIFIED
2    TRANSFORM OF VALUE COLUMN       AS A PAIR OF CARDS OF THIS TYPE

  2 ORIGINAL LINE   SESS
  B STANDARD LINE   COL2

  3 ORIGINAL VAL.   TEMP
  C STANDARD VAL.   CL11

  4 ORIGINAL NEAR   SESS
  D STANDARD NEAR   COL2

  5 ORIGINAL VAL.   DIFF
  E STANDARD VAL.   CL10

  6 ORIGINAL OGIV   SESS
  F STANDARD OGIV   COL2

  7 ORIGINAL VAL.   H.R.
  G STANDARD VAL.   CL15
END OF SYNCHRONISATION SPECIFICATION

  TIME BASE IS DERIVED FROM
     TRANSFORM  OF DATA COLUMN       START - SAMPLE EVERY - UNTIL -

  8 ORIGINAL VAL.   SESS                    1.0         0.1        16.0
  H STANDARD VAL.   COL2          152       1.0000      0.1000     16.0000
END OF TIME VARIATE
```

Figure 10.48 - STSYNC - Output Example - Data Storage (Part)

```
STATCAT PROGRAM STSYNC      -   SYNCHRONISATION OF DATA
OUTPUT DATA BANK TITLE      -   SYNCHRONISED DATA BANK - DUMMY
 INPUT DATA BANK TITLE      -   DEMONSTRATION STATCAT DATA BANK
DATA BANK SUBSET TITLE      -   FRED ONLY
```

DATA STORAGE SEGMENT

STANDARDISED ENTRY				ORIGINAL ENTRY				
				3.0000	1.0000	4.0000	2.0000	3.0000
				3.0000	1.0000	1.0000	2.0000	2.0000
				27.0000	-5.9600	27.2400	78.8200	40.0700
				43.2600	46.0000	1.3000		
				6.0000	2.0000	2.0000	2.0000	2.0000
				2.0000	1.0000	2.0000	1.0000	2.0000
				26.0000	-1.2900	26.1300	77.8900	41.2800
				47.3800	48.0000	1.4000		
1.0000	27.0000	2.0000	40.0700					
1.1000	26.9000	2.0000	40.1039					
1.2000	26.8000	2.0000	40.1958					
1.3000	26.7000	2.0000	40.3313					
1.4000	26.6000	2.0000	40.4959					
1.5000	26.5000	2.0000	40.6750					
1.6000	26.4000	2.0000	40.8540					
1.7000	26.3000	2.0000	41.0186					
1.8000	26.2000	2.0000	41.1541					
1.9000	26.1000	2.0000	41.2461					
2.0000	26.0000	2.0000	41.2800					
				12.0000	3.0000	1.0000	2.0000	4.0000
				2.0000	1.0000	3.0000	4.0000	4.0000
				28.0000	0.1400	51.2200	75.1100	60.3800
				72.1000	72.0000	2.1000		
2.1000	26.2000	2.0000	41.8147					
2.2000	26.4000	2.0000	43.2663					
2.3000	26.6000	2.0000	45.4054					
2.4000	26.8000	2.0000	48.0030					
2.5000	27.0000	2.0000	50.8297					
2.6000	27.2000	4.0000	53.6565					

Figure 10.49 - STSYNC - Synchronisation codes

Code	Type of Interpolation
AVE2	Mean of two adjacent points
AVE4	Mean of four adjacent points (two before, two after)
AVEW	Weighted average of two closest points
EXP1	Exponential smoothing:0.1 of next point plus 0.9 of last value
EXP2	Exponential smoothing:0.2 of next point plus 0.8 of last value
EXP3	Exponential smoothing:0.3 of next point plus 0.7 of last value
EXP4	Exponential smoothing:0.4 of next point plus 0.6 of last value
EXP5	Exponential smoothing:0.5 of next point plus 0.5 of last value
EXP6	Exponential smoothing:0.6 of next point plus 0.4 of last value
EXP7	Exponential smoothing:0.7 of next point plus 0.3 of last value
EXP8	Exponential smoothing:0.8 of next point plus 0.2 of last value
EXP9	Exponential smoothing:0.9 of next point plus 0.1 of last value
LAST	Previous value of variate
LINE	Linear interpolation between adjacent points
NEAR	Nearest adjacent value
NEXT	Next value of variate
MAXI	Maximum adjacent value
MINI	Minimum adjacent value
OGIV	Smooth cubic - flat at adjacent points (parallel to axis)
SMCU	Smooth cubic - parallel to line joining neighbouring points at adjacent points.

```
C MASTER STSYNC - SYNCHRONISES AND INTERPOLATES AT REGULAR INTERVALS
C   SUBROUTINES AND FUNCTIONS REQUIRED
C   NAME                TYPE            COMMENT
C   CHECK    (SEE  4.2 ) EXECUTIVE   CHECKS DATA BANK OR SUBSET
C   CHIKEN   (SEE 11.9 ) SERVICE     WARNS OF MISMATCHED DATA LEVEL
C   CLSAM    (SEE  3.5 ) SERVICE     ALLOTS ENTRY TO SAMPLE/SUBSET
C   COMPA    (SEE  3.1 ) SERVICE     COMPARES ALPHAMERIC VALUES
C   COPYA    (SEE  3.1 ) SERVICE     COPIES ALPHAMERIC VALUE
C   CSYNC    (SEE 10.4 ) EXECUTIVE   INTERPOLATES TIME DEPENDENT ITEMS
C   FIFI     (SEE  3.2 ) SYSTEM      ALLOCATES PERIPHERALS
C   ICH      (SEE  3.1 ) SERVICE     IDENTIFIES ALPHAMERIC CODES
C   LCOM     (SEE  3.4 ) SYSTEM      LOADS COMPLEMENTARY INFORMATION
C   LDAP     (SEE  3.3 ) SERVICE     LOAD/CHECK DATA BASE PARAMETERS
C   LDBS     (SEE  3.6 ) SYSTEM      LOADS SUBSET DEFINITION
C   LDDS     (SEE  3.4 ) SYSTEM      LOADS DATA DESCRIPTION SEGMENT
C   LDHI     (SEE  3.8 ) SYSTEM      LOADS/CHECKS DATA HANDLING INSTN
C   LGEN     (SEE  3.7 ) SYSTEM      LOADS GENERALISED VARIATES
C   MEDIAT   (SEE  3.7 ) SERVICE     FETCHES NEXT VARIATE SET
C   TRANS    (SEE  3.7 ) SERVICE     CARRIES OUT REQUIRED TRANSFORM
C   VNOW     (SEE 10.4 ) SERVICE     GIVES VALUES AT CURRENT TIME
C   WDCD     (SEE  3.4 ) SERVICE     WRITE DATA COLUMN DESCRIPTION
C   SETTING OF ARRAY DIMENSIONS
C   THE FOLLOWING DIMENSIONS MUST BE AT LEAST AS BIG AS THOSE
C   SPECIFIED BY THE DATA TAPE,SAMPLE SPECIFICATIONS,ETC.
C   NQMAX = MAXIMUM NUMBER OF DATA COLUMNS
C   DIMENSION D(NQMAX),DMAX(NQMAX),DMIN(NQMAX),IT(NQMAX),ST(NQMAX)
C   DIMENSION NP(NQMAX),NDP(NQMAX),IY(NQMAX),CN(NQMAX),XX(NQMAX)
C   DIMENSION TMAX(NQMAX),TMIN(NQMAX),NCL(NQMAX)
      NQMAX = 100
      DIMENSION D(100  ),DMAX(100  ),DMIN(100  ),IT(100  ),ST(100  )
      DIMENSION NP( 100),NDP( 100),IY( 100),CN(  100),XX( 100)
      DIMENSION TMAX(100),TMIN(100),NCL(100)
C   DATA BANK COLUMN NUMBERS - MAY BE USED IN PLACE OF NAMES
C   IF THE DIMENSION OF NQMAX IS INCREASED,THE EXTRA CODES MUST BE
C   INCLUDED IN THIS DATA STATEMENT
      DATA  CN/4HCOL1,4HCOL2,4HCOL3,4HCOL4,4HCOL5,4HCOL6,4HCOL7,4HCOL8,4
     1HCOL9,4HCL10,4HCL11,4HCL12,4HCL13,4HCL14,4HCL15,4HCL16,4HCL17,4HCL
     218,4HCL19,4HCL20,4HCL21,4HCL22,4HCL23,4HCL24,4HCL25,4HCL26,4HCL27,
     34HCL28,4HCL29,4HCL30,4HCL31,4HCL32,4HCL33,4HCL34,4HCL35,4HCL36,4HC
     4L37,4HCL38,4HCL39,4HCL40,4HCL41,4HCL42,4HCL43,4HCL44,4HCL45,4HCL46
     5,4HCL47,4HCL48,4HCL49,4HCL50,4HCL51,4HCL52,4HCL53,4HCL54,4HCL55,4H
     6CL56,4HCL57,4HCL58,4HCL59,4HCL60,4HCL61,4HCL62,4HCL63,4HCL64,4HCL6
     75,4HCL66,4HCL67,4HCL68,4HCL69,4HCL70,4HCL71,4HCL72,4HCL73,4HCL74,4
     8HCL75,4HCL76,4HCL77,4HCL78,4HCL79,4HCL80,4HCL81,4HCL82,4HCL83,4HCL
     984,4HCL85,4HCL86,4HCL87,4HCL88,4HCL89,4HCL90,4HCL91,4HCL92,4HCL93,
     94HCL94,4HCL95,4HCL96,4HCL97,4HCL98,4HCL99,4HCL100/
C   DIMENSION TRT(NALTMX),RT(NQMAX,NALTMX) = MAX NO OF CLASSES ON TAPE
      NALTMX = 50
      DIMENSION  TRT(50),RT(100,50)
C   DIMENSION SCON(5,MAXDBC)= MAX NO OF DATA BANK SUBSET CONDITIONS
      MAXDBC = 50
      DIMENSION SCON(5,50)
C   THE FOLLOWING DIMENSIONS ARE FIXED
      DIMENSION U(80),FORM(50)
      DATA U/4HVAL.,4HSQAR,4HCUBE,4H4PWR,4H5PWR,4H6PWR,4H7PWR,4H8PWR,4H9
     1PWR,4HVAL ,4HSINR,4HCOSR,4HTANR,4HASIR,4HACOR,4HATAR,4HSINH,4HCOSH
     2,4HTANH,4H VAL,4HSIND,4HCOSD,4HTAND,4HASID,4HACOD,4HATAD,4HDTOR,4H
     3RTOD,4H    ,4H    ,4H    ,4HPSNA,4HPSNB,4HBINO,4HLG+1,4HLOGE,4HLG10,4H
     4    ,4H    ,4H    ,4H    ,4HRECP,4HSQRT,4HABSV,4HSIGN,4HINTG,4HFRAC,4
     5HEXPT,4HPRES,4HNEG.,4H    ,4H+/-1,4HADD1,4HSUB1,4HNOR1,4H+/-P,4HAD
     6DP,4HSUBP,4HNORP,4H+100,4H    ,4HAVE2,4HAVE4,4HAVEW,4HSMCU,4HLAST,
     74HLINE,4HNEAR,4HNEXT,4HMAXI,4HMINI,4HOGIV,4HEXP1,4HEXP2,4HEXP3,4HE
     8XP4,4HEXP5,4HEXP6,4HEXP7,4HEXP8,4HEXP9/
```

```
      COMMON /STCT/MED1,MED2,MED3,MED4,MED5,MED6,MED13,Q,V(20),TT(30)
      DATA PROG/4HSYNC/
C ASSIGN PERIPHERALS
      MED1 = -1
    1 CALL COPYA(TT(1),PROG)
      CALL FIFI
      ARAN = 5236.
C READ,CHECK AND LOAD STARTER AND DESCRIPTION FOR TRANSFORMED TAPE
      READ(MED1,900) (FORM(J) ,J=1,16), (TT(J) ,J=1,16)
      NQ = AN(FORM,5,3,5)
      NALT=AN(FORM,8,6,8)
      Q  = AN(FORM,16,9,16)
      WRITE(MED6,906)
      WRITE(MED6,901) NQ,NALT,Q,(TT(J),J=1,10),TT(16)
C CHECK SIZE OF STORAGE
      IF(NQ.LE.NQMAX) GO TO 2
      WRITE(MED6,902) NQ,NQMAX
      V(10) = 1.
      NQ = NQMAX
    2 IF(NALT.LE.NALTMX) GO TO 3
      WRITE(MED6,903) NALT,NALTMX
      NALT = NALTMX
      V(10) = V(10) + 2.
C LOAD DATA COLUMN DESCRIPTIONS
    3 IF(MED4.LT.1) WRITE(MED6,909)
      IF(MED4.LT.1) GO TO 1
      WRITE(MED4) NQ,NALT,Q,(TT(J),J=1,16)
      V(3) = Q
      V(4) = NQ
      LI = 18
      CALL LDDS(TRT,NALT,D,NQ,ST,0,IT,0,H,0,H,H,0,LI,0,Q,VX,
     1 MED1,MED2,0,MED4,IGO)
      IF(IGO.GT.0) GO TO 1
      ISF = 0
C LEVEL 1 - LOAD DATA DESCRIPTION OF INPUT FILE
   11 IF(V(10).GE.10.) V(10) = 0.
      IF(ISF.EQ.1) CALL FIFI
      IF(MED3.LT.1) WRITE(MED6,910)
      IF(MED3.LT.1) GO TO 1
      WRITE(MED6,904)
      CALL LDAP(MED2,MED3,V,TT(11),Q1,NQ1,NALT1,NQMAX,NALTMX,IGO)
      IF (IGO.GT.0) GO TO 11
      LI = 18
      CALL LDDS(TRT,NALT1,D,NQ1,ST,NQ1,IT,NQ1,H,0,H,H,0,LI,0,Q,VX,
     1 0,MED2,MED3,0,IGO)
      IF(IGO.GT.0.AND.V(10).LT.0.5) V(10) = 27.
      DO 24 I = 1,NQ1
      DMIN(I) = 0.
   24 DMAX(I) = NALT1-2
C LEVEL 3 - LOAD TIME/VARIATE PAIRS
   31 IF(V(10).GT.30.) V(10) = 0.
      ISF = 1
      IFIN = 2*NQ - 1
      M = IFIN
      WRITE(MED6,931)
      CALL LGEN(U,80,LU,0,ST,IT,CN ,NQ1,NCL,0,DMIN,DMAX,0,TMIN,TMAX,0,0,
     1 10,NDP,NP,NQMAX,ISF,IFIN,1,0)
      IF(ISF.EQ.1) GO TO 11
      IF(ISF.NE.IFIN) WRITE(MED6,932)
      IF(ISF.NE.IFIN.AND.V(10).EQ.0.) V(10) = 33.
C LEVEL 4 - LOAD TIME COLUMN - LIMITS - STEP INTERVAL
   41 IF(V(10).GT.40.) V(10) = 0.
      ISF = IFIN
```

```
      WRITE(MED6,941)
      CALL LGEN(U,60,LU,O,ST,IT,CN ,NQ1,NCL,NQMAX,DMIN,DMAX,NQMAX,TMIN,T
     1MAX,NQMAX,0,99999,NDP,NP,NQMAX,ISF,NQMAX,1,1)
      IF(ISF.EQ.IFIN.AND.V(20).LT.0.5) GO TO 31
      IF(ISF.EQ.IFIN.AND.V(10).LT.0.5) V(10) = 49.
      ITOT = ISF
      BRAN = ARAN
C LEVEL 8 - DATA BANK SUBSET SPECIFICATION
   81 IF(V(10).GT.80.) V(10) = 0.
      CALL LDBS(SCON,NCON,MAXDBC,CN ,ST,IT,NQ1,TRT,NALT1,IGO)
      IF(IGO.GT.0) GO TO 41
C LEVEL 9 - DATA HANDLING INSTRUCTION
   91 IF(V(10).GT.90.) V(10) = 0.
      CALL LDHI(V(1),1,V(2),3,V(9),7,ASDL,18,APT,15,H,0,H,V(10),
     1FORM(41),FORM,MED1,MED2,MED4,Q,NQ,NWARN,1,IGO)
      IF(IGO.GT.0) GO TO 81
      IF(V(1).GT.4.5) NWARN = NWARN + 1
      IF(V(1).GT.4.5) V(1) = -1.
      NX = V(9)
      IF(NX.LE.0.OR.NX.GE.NQ)  NWARN = NWARN + 1
      IF(NX.LE.0.OR.NX.GE.NQ)  V(9) = NQ-1
      IF(IBL(FORM(2),1,1).LT.0.AND.IBL(FORM(6),11,1).LT.0) NX = 0
      IF(IBL(FORM(2),1,1).GE.0.OR. IBL(FORM(6),11,1).GE.0) NX = 1
      IF(NX.EQ.0)CALL LDHI(V(1),1,H,0,V(9),7,H,0,H,0,H,0,H,V(10),
     1FORM(41),FORM,MED1,MED2,MED4,Q,NQ,NWARN,2,IGO)
      IF(NX.EQ.0) GO TO 92
      IF(ASDL.LE.0.) NWARN = NWARN + 1
      IF(ASDL.EQ.0.) ASDL = 5.
      IF(ASDL.LT.0.) ASDL = 9999.
      IF(APT.LE.0.) NWARN = NWARN + 1
      IF(APT.EQ.0.) APT = 1.
      IF(APT.LT.0.) APT = 0.
      CALL LDHI(V(1),1,V(2),3,V(9),7,ASDL,18,APT,15,H,0,H,V(10),
     1FORM(41),FORM,MED1,MED2,MED4,Q,NQ,NWARN,2,IGO)
   92 IF(IGO.GT.0) GO TO 91
  101 WRITE(MED6,998)
C  LOAD DATA STORAGE SEGMENT
      V(10) = BRAN
      Q = Q1
      X = NQMAX
      Y = NALTMX
      X = X*Y
      Y = M
      NR = X/Y
      CALL CSYNC(D,DMAX,M,MP,NDP,IY,NCL,TMAX,TMIN,ITOT,XX,ST,NQ1,SCON,NC
     1ON,RT,NR)
  112 IF(NX.GT.0) GO TO 120
      BRAN = V(10)
      V(10) = 0.
      GO TO 91
C END TAPE - TEST IF REQUIRED
  120 WRITE(MED4) (Q,I=1,NQ)
      REWIND MED4
      IF(V(2).GE.0.) GO TO 150
      WRITE(MED6,995)
      GO TO 1
C CARRY OUT PRELIMINARY CHECK OF DATA TAPE
  150 WRITE(MED6,996)
      APT = APT*.01
      NCON=0
      Q = V(3)
      CALL CHECK (D,DMAX,DMIN,RT,IT,TRT,NQ,NALT,ASDL,APT,SCON,NCON,ST)
      WRITE(MED6,999)
```

```
      GO TO 1
  900 FORMAT(16A1,16A4)
  901 FORMAT (1H0,20X,80HSTATCAT SYNCHRONISATION OF ASYNCHRONOUS TIME DA
     1TA                                            /16HOFILE PARAMETER
     2S/29H0NUMBER OF DATA COLUMNS IS - ,I6/29H0STORED NUMBER OF CLASSES
     3 IS ,I6/34H0VALUE USED FOR MISSING DATA IS - ,F20.8/13H0FILE TITLE
     4 ,10A4,10X,15HFILE REFERENCE ,A4)
  902 FORMAT (4H0THE,I6,     37H ITEMS PER ENTRY EXCEED THE AVAILABLE,I6,1
     16H STORAGE COLUMNS)
  903 FORMAT (4H0THE,I6,40H CLASSES PER COLUMN EXCEED THE AVAILABLE,I6,1
     13H STORAGE ROWS)
  904 FORMAT (24H1 FOR ORIGINAL DATA BANK    )
  905 FORMAT(1H0,10X,8HTOTAL OF,F4.0,28H SUCCESSIVE INPUT DATA BANKS )
  906 FORMAT(30H1  FOR SYNCHRONISED DATA BANK  )
  908 FORMAT (1H0,20X,25H DATA DESCRIPTION SEGMENT /
     121H0COLUMN SCALE    SHORT,10X,10HFULL TITLE/
     221H NUMBER  CODE    TITLE,5X,21HCLASS NAMES OR LIMITS)
  909 FORMAT(41H0NO OUTPUT FILE - PROGRAM CANNOT CONTINUE)
  910 FORMAT(41H0 NO INPUT FILE - PROGRAM CANNOT CONTINUE)
  911 FORMAT (1H0,I4,I6,6X,A4,4X,A2,17A4)
  912 FORMAT (26H0DATA BANK SUBSET TITLE - ,10A4)
  915 FORMAT((21X,10(A4,1H-)))
  916 FORMAT(21X,77HLOWEST CLASS LIMIT = OBSERVED MINIMUM, HIGHEST CLASS
     1 LIMIT = OBSERVED MAXIMUM     )
  917 FORMAT (21X,18HCLASSES FROM BELOW,F12.4,14H BY CLASSES OF,F12.6,3H
     1 TO,F12.4,9H AND OVER   )
  918 FORMAT(1H1,20X,20HDATA STORAGE SEGMENT    )
  931 FORMAT (31H11 INTERPOLATION IN TIME COLUMN,10X,38HEACH SYNCHRONISE
     1D VARIATE IS SPECIFIED  /31H 2        TRANSFORM OF VALUE COLUMN,10X,31
     2HAS A PAIR OF CARDS OF THIS TYPE    )
  932 FORMAT (77H0NUMBER OF VARIATES DOES NOT AGREE WITH NUMBER OF COLUM
     1NS IN DATA DESCRIPTION )
  941 FORMAT (28H0   TIME BASE IS DERIVED FROM /5X,25HTRANSFORM  OF DATA
     1 COLUMN,7X,30HSTART - SAMPLE EVERY - UNTIL -    )
  995 FORMAT (48H0SYNCHRONISATION COMPLETED - CHECKING SUPPRESSED)
  996 FORMAT (47H1SYNCHRONISATION COMPLETED - CHECKING COMMENCES)
  998 FORMAT (43H0INPUT ACCEPTED - SYNCHRONISATION COMMENCES)
  999 FORMAT (43H1SYNCHRONISATION COMPLETED - READ NEW INPUT)
      END


      SUBROUTINE CSYNC(D,E,M,NP,NDP,JPR,NCL,TMAX,TMIN,ITOT,XX,ST,NQ,SCON
     1,NCON,RT,NR)
C CSYNC   (SEE 10.4 ) EXECUTIVE   INTERPOLATES TIME DEPENDENT ITEMS
      DIMENSION NP(ITOT),NDP(ITOT),JPR(M),D(M),XX(NQ),ST(NQ),ITYP(20)
      DIMENSION SCON(5,NCON),RT(NR,M),NCL(ITOT),TMAX(ITOT),TMIN(ITOT)
      DIMENSION E(M)
C NP CONTAINS THE NUMBERS OF M SELECTED COLUMNS
C NDP CONTAINS   M/2 PAIRS OF  VALUE CODE AND INTERP METHOD
C JPR CONTAINS NUMBER OF DATA IN STORE FOR A PAIR
C ITYP CONTAINS THE NUMBER OF CELLS REQUIRED FOR A GIVEN METHOD
      DATA ITYP/3,3*4,2,3,3,1,12*3/
      COMMON /STCT/MED1,MED2,MED3,MED4,MED5,MED6,MED13,Q,V(20),TT(30)
C SORT INTERPOLATION DEFINITION INTO NDP,SET COUNTERS TO 0,SET CONTROLS
      L = M/2
      V(7) = 1.
      KL = L/10 + 2
      NQL = (NQ+19)/10
      IDATA = -1
      JSTORE = -1
      DO 1 I = 2,M,2
      J = NP(I)/1000 - 60
      NDP(I) = ITYP(J)
```

```
      NDP(I+1) = J
    1 NP(I) = NP(I) - 1000*(J+60)
      M1 = M + 1
      DO 60 IBASE = M1,ITOT
      V(6) = 0.
      V(8) = 1.
C V(9) = NUMBER OF MISSING VALUES ACCEPTABLE IN  ENTRIES
      V(11) = 1.
      REWIND MED3
      READ(MED3) NQ,NALT,Q,(X   ,J=1,16)
      DO 5 J = 1,NQ
    5 READ(MED3) (X,I=1,19),(X,I=1,NALT),NX,X,X
      TBASE = TMIN(IBASE)
      TSTEP = NCL(IBASE)
      TEND = TMAX(IBASE)
      TSTEP = (TEND-TBASE)/(TSTEP-2.)
      NP(1) = NP(IBASE)
      IDATA = 0
      NLIN = 60
    3 DO 2 J = 1,M
      N = NR
      IF(JSTORE.GE.0) N = JPR(J) + 1
      JPR(J) = 0
      DO 2 I = 1,N
    2 RT(I,J) = Q
      TNOW = TBASE
      IF(IDATA.EQ.0) GO TO 20
      DLAST = D(1)
      IDATA = 2
      GO TO 30
C ELIMINATE UNNEEDED VALUES + CHECK IF MORE NEEDED
   10 JSTORE = 0
   11 DO 14 I = 2,M,2
      KTYP = NDP(I)
      JTYP = KTYP/2 + 1
      IF(KTYP.EQ.2.OR.KTYP.EQ.3) KTYP = KTYP - 1
C IS ELIMINATION NOT REQUIRED
   12 IF(JTYP.EQ.1.AND.RT(2,I).EQ.Q) GO TO 14
      IF(JTYP.EQ.1.AND.RT(2,I).GT.TNOW) GO TO 14
      IF(JTYP.NE.1.AND.RT(JTYP,I).GT.TNOW.AND.RT(JTYP,I).NE.Q) GO TO 14
      IF(JTYP.NE.1.AND.RT(JTYP,I).EQ.Q) GO TO 14
      I2 = JPR(I) - 1
      IF(I2.GE.0) JPR(I) = I2
      IF(I2.EQ.0) GO TO 15
      IF(I2.LT.1) GO TO 14
      DO 13 I1 = 1,I2
      RT(I1,I) = RT(I1+1,I)
   13 RT(I1,I+1) = RT(I1+1,I+1)
   15 RT(I2+1,I) = Q
      RT(I2+1,I+1) = Q
      IF(I2.GT.0) GO TO 12
   14 IF(KTYP.GT.JPR(I))JSTORE = 1
C IS ENOUGH DATA PRESENT FOR OUTPUT
      IF(JSTORE.EQ.0) GO TO 40
C READ NEW DATA IF POSSIBLE AND REQUIRED
      IF(IDATA.GE.3) GO TO 40
      IF(IDATA.GT.0) DLAST = D(1)
   20 CONTINUE
      CALL MEDIAT(M,NDP,NP,M,D,XX,NQ,SCON,NCON)
      IF(IDATA.EQ.0) DLAST = D(1)
      IDATA = 2
      IF(D(1).GT.TEND) IDATA = 4
      IF(D(1).LT.DLAST) IDATA = 3
```

```
      IF(D(1).LT.TBASE) IDATA = 7
      IF(V(8).GT.1.5) IDATA = 6
      IF(V(1).LT.0.5) GO TO 21
      NLIN = NLIN + NQL
      IF(D(1).LT.DLAST.AND.D(1).GE.TBASE) NLIN = 60
      IF(NLIN.GT.50) WRITE(MED2,982) TT
      IF(NLIN.GT.50) WRITE(MED2,985)
      IF(NLIN.GT.50) WRITE(MED2,980)
      IF(NLIN.GT.50) NLIN = NQL + 7
      IF(V(8).LT.1.5) WRITE(MED2,983) XX
      IF(V(8).GT.1.5) WRITE(MED2,981)
   21 CONTINUE
      IF(IDATA.EQ.7) GO TO 3
      IF (IDATA.GE.5) GO TO 40
      IF (IDATA.EQ.4) IDATA = 5
C LOAD NEW DATA TO STORE
   30 CONTINUE
      DO 32 I = 2,M,2
      IF(D(I).EQ.Q.OR.D(I+1).EQ.Q) GO TO 32
      IF(JPR(I).EQ.NR) WRITE(MED2,933)
      IF(JPR(I).EQ.NR) GO TO 32
      J = JPR(I)+1
      IF(J.EQ.1) GO TO 31
      IF(D(I).GT.RT(J-1,I)) GO TO 31
      NLIN = NLIN + 1
      IF(NLIN.GT.50) WRITE(MED2,982) TT
      IF(NLIN.GT.50.AND.V(1).GT.0.5) WRITE(MED2,985)
      IF(NLIN.GT.50.AND.V(1).GT.1.5) WRITE(MED2,980)
      IF(NLIN.GT.50) NLIN = 8
      K = I/2 + 1
      IF(D(I).LT.RT(J-1,I)) WRITE(MED2,932) K,D(I),RT(J-1,I)
      IF(D(I).LT.RT(J-1,I)) GO TO 32
      J = J-1
      WRITE(MED2,931) K,D(I)
      IF(NDP(I).LT.12) RT(J,I+1) = (RT(J,I+1)+D(I))*0.5
      IF(NDP(I).GE.12) X = NDP(I)-11
      IF(NDP(I).GE.12) RT(J,I+1) = RT(J,I+1)*(1.-0.1*X)+D(I+1)*0.1*X
      GO TO 32
   31 RT(J,I) = D(I)
      JPR(I) = J
      IF(NDP(I).LT.12.OR.J.EQ.1) RT(J,I+1) = D(I+1)
      IF(NDP(I).GT.11.AND.J.GT.1) X = NDP(I)-11
      IF(NDP(I).GE.12.AND.J.GT.1)
    1 RT(J,I+1) = RT(J-1,I+1)*(1.-0.1*X) + D(I+1)*0.1*X
   32 CONTINUE
      IF(IDATA.LE.2) GO TO 10
C CALCULATE + LOAD OUTPUT FOR TNOW
   40 DO 41 I = 2,M,2
      K = I/2 + 1
      E(K) = VNOW(TNOW,RT(1,I),RT(1,I+1),Q,NDP(I+1))
   41 IF(E(K).EQ.Q) E(K) = V(3)
      E(1) = TNOW
C WRITE TO OUTPUT TAPE
      K = L + 1
      WRITE(MED4) (E(I),I = 1,K )
      IF(V(1).LT.1.) GO TO 50
      NLIN = NLIN + KL
      IF(NLIN.GT.50) WRITE(MED2,982) TT
      IF(NLIN.GT.50) WRITE(MED2,985)
      IF(NLIN.GT.50.AND.V(1).GT.1.5) WRITE(MED2,980)
      IF(NLIN.GT.50) NLIN = KL + 7
      WRITE(MED2,984) (E(I),I=1,K)
   50 TNOW = TNOW + TSTEP
```

```
      IF(TNOW.LE.TEND+.0001) GO TO 10
      IF(IDATA.EQ.7) GO TO 3
   51 IF(V(8).GT.1.5) GO TO 60
      CALL MEDIAT(M,NDP,NP,M,D,XX,NQ,SCON,NCON)
      IF(V(1).LT.0.5) GO TO 52
      NLIN = NLIN + NQL
      IF(D(1).LE.TBASE) NLIN = 60
      IF(NLIN.GT.50) WRITE(MED2,982) TT
      IF(NLIN.GT.50) WRITE(MED2,985)
      IF(NLIN.GT.50) WRITE(MED2,980)
      IF(NLIN.GT.50) NLIN = NQL + 7
      IF(V(8).GT.1.5) WRITE(MED2,981)
      IF(V(8).LT.1.5) WRITE(MED2,983) XX
   52 IF(D(1).GT.TBASE) GO TO 51
      GO TO 3
   60 CONTINUE
C RECONSTRUCT ORIGINAL VALUES OF NP FOR NEXT PASSAGE
      DO 4 I = 2,M,2
    4 NP(I) = NP(I) + 1000*(NDP(I+1)+60)
      RETURN
  931 FORMAT (18H FOR OUTPUT COLUMN,I4,17H TIME-SCALE VALUE,F12.4,35H IS
     1 REPEATED IN THE INPUT DATA BANK)
  932 FORMAT (18H FOR OUTPUT COLUMN,I4,17H TIME-SCALE VALUE,F12.4, 8H FO
     1LLOWS,F12.4,23H IN THE INPUT DATA BANK)
  933 FORMAT(1H0,60X,28HSAMPLING RATES TOO DIFFERENT )
  980 FORMAT(1H+,83X,14HORIGINAL ENTRY)
  981 FORMAT(1H0,43X,25HEND OF ORIGINAL DATA BANK   )
  982 FORMAT(23H1STATCAT PROGRAM STSYNC,7X,1H-,4X,23HSYNCHRONISATION OF
     1DATA/23H OUTPUT DATA BANK TITLE,7X,1H-,4X,10A4/23H   INPUT DATA BAN
     2K TITLE,7X,1H-,4X,10A4/23H DATA BANK SUBSET TITLE,7X,1H-,4X,10A4/
     31H0,50X,20HDATA STORAGE SEGMENT/)
  983 FORMAT (1H0,60X,5F12.4/(61X,5F12.4))
  984 FORMAT(1H0,5F12.4/(1X,5F12.4))
  985 FORMAT(22X,18HSTANDARDISED ENTRY)
      ST(1) = ST(1)
      END



      FUNCTION VNOW (TNOW,T,V,Q,INT)
C VNOW     (SEE 10.4 ) SERVICE     GIVES VALUES AT CURRENT TIME
C INTERPOLATES VALUES ACCORDING TO CODE INT (U-20)
C TNOW IS CURRENT TIME
C T IS TWO/FOUR TIMES BEFORE AND AFTER NOW
C V IS TWO/FOUR VALUES AT THESE TIMES
C IF INT IS BETWEEN 2 AND 4 FOUR VALUES ARE REQUIRED
C OTHERWISE FIRST TWO VALUES ONLY ARE REQUIRED
C IF INT IS GREATER THAN 11 VALUES ARE EXPONENTIALLY SMOOTHED
C Q IS MISSING VALUE
      DIMENSION T(4),V(4)
      VNOW = Q
      IF(INT.LE.0.OR.INT.GT.20) RETURN
      IF(V(1).EQ.Q.OR.V(2).EQ.Q) RETURN
      IF(INT.GT.11) GO TO 7
      GO TO (1,3,3,4,8,9,10,8,12,13,14),INT
C AVERAGE OF TWO NEAREST READINGS
    1 VNOW = (V(1)+V(2))*.5
      RETURN
C (WEIGHTED IF INT=3/UNWEIGHTED IF INT=2) AVERAGE OF 4 READINGS
    3 D1 = 0.
      D2 = 0.
      DT = 1.
      DO 31 I = 1,4
      IF(T(I).EQ.Q) GO TO 31
```

```
      IF(INT.EQ.2) GO TO 30
      DT = T(I) - TNOW
      IF(DT.EQ.0.) VNOW = V(I)
      IF(DT.EQ.0.) RETURN
      DT = DT*DT
   30 D1 = D1 + V(I)/DT
      D2 = D2 + 1./DT
   31 CONTINUE
      IF(D2.GT.0.) VNOW = D1/D2
      RETURN
C CUBIC FIT WITH SMOOTH SLOPE AT POINTS
    4 IF(V(3).EQ.Q) RETURN
      TA = T(3)-T(2)
      IF(TA.EQ.0.) VNOW = (V(2)+V(3))*.5
      IF(TA.EQ.0.) RETURN
      S1 =(V(3)-V(1))/(T(3)-T(1))
      S2 = (V(4)-V(2))/(T(4)-T(2))
      IF(V(4).EQ.Q) S2 = (V(3)-V(2))/(T(3)-T(2))
      TB = TNOW - T(2)
      VA = V(3) - V(2)
      VNOW = V(2) + S1*TB +(3.*VA-S2*TA-2.*S1*TA)/TA/TA*TB*TB
    1       +(S1*TA + S2*TA - 2.*VA)/TA/TA/TA*TB*TB*TB
      RETURN
C HARMONIC INTERPOLATION BETWEEN EXPONENTIALLY WEIGHTED VARIATES
    7 VNOW = (T(2)-T(1))/(1./V(2)*(TNOW -T(1))+ 1./V(1)*(T(2)-TNOW))
      RETURN
C LAST VALUE
    8 VNOW = V(1)
      RETURN
C LINEAR INTERPOLATION
    9 VNOW = V(1)
      IF(T(2).EQ.T(1)) GO TO 1
      VNOW = (V(2)*(TNOW-T(1))+V(1)*(T(2)-TNOW))/(T(2)-T(1))
      RETURN
C NEAREST VALUE
   10 VNOW = V(1)
      IF((TNOW-T(1)).GT.(T(2)-TNOW)) VNOW = V(2)
      RETURN
C MAXIMUM VALUE
   12 VNOW = V(1)
      IF(VNOW.LT.V(2)) VNOW = V(2)
      RETURN
C MINIMUM VALUE
   13 VNOW = V(1)
      IF(VNOW.GT.V(2)) VNOW = V(2)
      RETURN
C OGIVAL FIT - CUBIC ALWAYS FLAT AT DATA POINTS
   14 TA = T(2) - T(1)
      IF(TA.EQ.0.) GO TO 1
      TB = TNOW-T(1)
      VA = V(2) - V(1)
      VNOW = V(1) + 3.*VA/TA*TB/TA*TB-2.*VA/TA*TB/TA*TB/TA*TB
      RETURN
      END
```

10.5 PROGRAM STCOMB - COMBINING ENTRIES

10.5.1 Purpose

This program combines entries in specified subsets of a STATCAT data bank to produce an output STATCAT data bank containing one entry for each combination of values of specified variates. In addition to the values of the specified variates, the entries in the output STATCAT data bank may contain the maximum, minimum, arithmetic, geometric or harmonic means, the standard deviation, variance, skewness, kurtosis or number of data items present for any specified columns in the input STATCAT data bank(s). The subsets of the original STATCAT data bank need not be mutually exclusive or exhaustive, and need not be ordered in the same way. The amount of information output during sorting and checking may be controlled by the user.

Figure 10.51a contains system flow-charts for the main program STCOMB, the subroutine OPST, which determines what information must be stored and the function STAT, which combines this information to provide the values required. Figure 10.51b contains a system flow-chart for the executivesubroutine CCOMB.

10.5.2 Input Data

Summary

Item	Level	Format	Function	See
1	0	A	File control card (First input+output)	3.2
2	0	B	Data starter card	Below + 3.3
3	0	C	Data Description Segment	3.4
(4	1	A	File control card (later input)	Below + 3.2)
5	2	F	Parameter specification	Below + 3.7
6	3	F	Priority specification	Below + 3.7
7	4	E	Subset specification	3.6
8	5	G	Data handling instruction	Below + 3.8

2 - Data Starter Card

Standard - Fields A and B not used. Number of data columns, number of classes, non-value, file title, security key and file name accepted normally.

(4 - File Control Card - Later input)

This file control card is employed only when a second STATCAT input is to be used to in place of that specified at the start of the program. The code SAME must be given for the output STATCAT data bank - to avoid rewinding and over-writing.

5 - Parameter Specification

This is a variate specification of the form described in 3.7. Only the first two four-character codes are employed. The first is used to specify a parameter code, which may be any of those given in Figure 5.39 and discussed in 5.3.5. The second four-character code may be either a data column name from the input STATCAT data bank, or a column number. The number of parameters specified must equal the number of columns in the output STATCAT data bank. They define the data stored in these columns, and the user must ensure that the content of the column is compatible with its description in the data description segment.

6 - Priority Specification

This has the same format as the variate specification described in 3.7. Only the first two four-character fields are used. the first must contain a priority code, as specified in Figure 11.42, and the second the name or number of a data column in the current input STATCAT data bank. The priority conditions are applied in the order specified to the data specified until a decision on priority can be reached. Entries having equal priority will be combined to form an entry in the output STATCAT data bank.(Each entry in that data bank is made up of the parameters defined in the parameter specification in the order there defined. Data that cannot be derived, because no entries contained data, or because they have become undefined - for example, the geometric mean where negative values are encountered, or IDEN where the data are not identical - are replaced by non-values)

8 - Data Handling Instruction

This is a standard data handling instruction. It is used to specify the amount of information printed during entry manipulation, to indicate whether to close the output STATCAT data bank, and what checking procedures are to be used.

Card Layout - Data Handling Instruction - STCOMB

```
ABCCCDDDEEEEEEEEFFFFFFFFFFFFFFFFFFFFFFFFGGGGGGGGGGGGGGGG.....
```

Columns on Card	Item code	FORTRAN Type	Function	See
1	A	I	Output Control Index	Below
2	B	I	Checking Control Index	4.3
3 - 5	C	I	Maximum number of non-values	10.1
6 - 8	D	I	Maximum number of s.d. from the mean	4.3
9 - 16	E	F	Minimum percentage in class	4.3
17 - 40	F	A	Comment (printed with line)	-
41 - 80	G	A	Comment (printed separately)	-

A - Output Control Index

This index controls the amount of description output during the construction of the revised data storage segment. Unless otherwise specified only indications of the progress of the combining operation are output.

ALTERNATIVES

A = 0 or blank: Only indications of the progress of combining are
(default)   output.

A = 1   : In addition, messages tracing the allocation of input entries to stores, combined stored entries to temporary output, temporary output back to store and confirmed output to permanent output are also produced.

A = 2   : In addition, completed output subsets are printed as they are completed.

A = 3   : In addition, original (input) entries are printed as they are read.

A = 4   : In addition, each output entry is printed as it is stored.

A = 5-9   : No output during combining

10.5.3   Input Example

Figure 10.52 is a summary of the input structure for three runs of STCOMB, producing tabulations of the minimum and maximum subjective difficulty, and the minimum, mean and maximum efficiency as assessed by observer and operator, for each observer, for each operator and for each observer-operator pair. Each entry stored in the temporary form (see below) requires 15 words of storage, so that the 2500 words reserved in the listing would allow 166 entries to be accumulated in store. To demonstrate the multiple-pass operation of the program this was reduced to 100 words, allowing only six lines to be held. This is sufficient for the first two runs, but not for the third, where sixteen operator-observer pairs are stored. Figures 10.53 lists the input cards corresponding to the summary of Figure 10.52.

10.5.4   Output Example

Figure 10.54 is a general summary of the output produced by this program, indented according to the program structure. Figure 10.55 is a page-by-page summary of the output corresponding to the specific input of 10.53.

Figure 10.56 shows part of the output for the third of four sweeps through the data needed to combine operator-observer pairs. At this point the last pair known to have been correctly stored was (3, 1) - using the first digit for operator number, and the second for observer number. This last correctly stored entry is at present in store #2 - which does not therefore appear in the records of storage allocated during this sweep. All entries coming at or before this entry will be discarded immediately on entry. The first five entries retained in store are, in priority order no. 4 (3, 2) 5(3, 4) 7 (4, 1) 9 (4, 2) and 2 (4, 3). To make room for the next entry, entries 4 and 5 are tentatively output. Entry 11(3, 3) is then written over entry 4. This is compared with entry 5, still in store representing the last output to file, and found to come before it. We have therefore more entries to combine than we can hold in store, and must find the highest priority entries not yet stored. We must keep entry 11, so we sacrifice the lowest priority line 2, and start reading entries into store 1. Entries 16 and 17 come after entry 9 and are therefore discarded. Entries 22, 24, 26 and 28 have the same priorities as 11, 9, 7 and 5 respectively, and are therefore combined with these entries. Entry 29 (3, 2) has a higher priority than anything in store, and therefore becomes the head of the priority list. Entry 9 has lowest priority, and is therefore overwritten by entry 31. The remaining entries fall after all entries in store or are combined with one of these.

At the end of the data sweep we have two tentative output entries. The second of these was never in fact removed from store (entry 5), so is not considered further. The first is read into the spare storage line, then combined with entry 29, which has equal priority. Entries 29 (3, 2) 11 (3, 3) 5 (3, 4) and 7 (4, 1) are now known to be complete, and can be written as confirmed output. Entry 7, in store 5, becomes the last known line correctly output - replacing store 2 which is now used as the input line.

Note that the four combinations output at the third sweep are the tenth to thirteenth, not the ninth to twelfth. This is because the first sweep needed no space for the last correct output, and could therefore store five complete entries not four. In the fourth and final sweep only three entries are completed, there is no overflow, no temporary output is made, and the output file need not be re-positioned.

10.5.5   Combining and Sorting Logic

Although a simplified flow-chart for the executive subroutine CCOMB is provided in Figure 10.51a, and detail comments appear in the listing of that subroutine, a more general verbal description of the program's operation may make it clearer to the user.

CCOMB is generally similar to CSORT, with several important differences reflecting the different task carried out. Because entries may be combined with entries already in store, it is not necessary to provide a fresh storage line for each entry. Because the output entries are not identical with input entries, it may be necessary to store several values to generate one output datum. (For example, the standard deviation requires the number of values, their sum and the sum of their squares). This tends to require more storage for any one line in store, but the possibility of sharing parameters (if the standard deviation is being calculated, the arithmetic mean can be calculated without further storage.) and the reduction in the number of different lines counteract this tendency. Because all entries of equal priority are combined, it is not necessary to search for the last entry with a given priority, nor to maintain a count of the number of lines of identical priority. On the other hand, it is possible to have temporarily output lines which have the same priority as entries in store, and must be combined with them. This requires that temporary output lines should contain the information necessary for combining to make an entry, rather than the entry itself, so that they cannot be confirmed without being read into store and converted to the proper output form.

Each time the subroutine CCOMB is called, it sorts the entries in a specified subset of the input STATCAT data bank into the required order, and stores the specified descriptive parameters for each set of entries of the same priority, loading these to the output file in priority order. It does not disturb output entries already on the output medium at the time it starts. Wherever possible, the subroutine carries out its sorting in internal storage, but it occasionally encounters data bank subsets which contain too many disordered entries to allow it a sufficient span of combinations in store. In this case, it searches the input data bank for as many combinations as it can store in order, writes the corresponding entries to the output STATCAT data bank, and returns to continuous sorting and storage until it again encounters an excessive span of entries.

Because several subsets of several different data banks may be included in the same or different priority orderings, there may be entries in the output STATCAT data bank when CCOMB starts work. An index is therefore maintained of the number of entries known to be correctly placed in the output STATCAT data bank.

If 'underflow' or 'overflow' has occurred (see below), a number of entries in the current subset will also have been confirmed in their corect output positions. The index of correct entries is updated accordingly, and the last output entry known to have been in its correct place will also be in store. In addition - and in contrast to CSORT - it may be known that a certain number of tentative output records were in the correct order, but could not be returned to store in the previous sweep. (These become the first output records for the present sweep.)

The subroutine actually begins by reading entries, converting them to the necessary storage values in a line of the storage array, rejecting entries not in the subset, or which have already been output correctly, and combining entries having the same priority. A new storage line is required only when the current input line cannot be combined with an existing storage line. (Entries are physically added, but are not actually moved physically when placed in order.)

When the store is completely filled (overflow), the first two stored lines are output. If it is known that these lines were in the correct order from a previous passage, they will be output as confirmed entries, and the number of confirmed output entries increased accordingly. If it is not known that they are in the correct order, then they will be temporarily output in their storage line form. The line which contained the first output entry is now free to be overwritten, and the second entry is the 'last entry output'.

The next entry is then read, converted to storage form, and placed in the free line. If it is added to the table, the line following the 'last entry output' is output, in temporary or confirmed form as before, and becomes the 'last entry output'. The previous location of the 'last entry output' is freed and becomes the free line, and the process continues. (If the line entered is rejected, or combined with another line of equal priority, there is no need for any output, since the free line is again freed.)

This process is continued until either the data terminator is reached on the input STATCAT data bank, or an entry is found which should come before the last entry output, or be combined with it. (Underflow). The occurrence of underflow means that there is insufficient storage to complete the combining operation in one sweep through the input STATCAT data bank.

If underflow occurs, the program continues to read and store entries in priority order, discarding those not in the sample, or already output, combining those with equal priority to existing lines in store, and inserting lines with higher priority than the last of those in store. Space for new storage lines is found by discarding those with the lowest priority, if necessary. No more lines are written to the output STATCAT data bank, and the process is continued until the end of the subset is reached.

When the end of the input STATCAT data bank is found, if there have been any temporary outputs, with or without underflow, the output STATCAT data bank is re-read, and the temporary outputs are re-loaded into the internal store, combining with existing lines as necessary. The last line in the store is used as input until a line containing a temporary output is the last-but-one in store. At this point, the store contains the next output lines in order, but cannot write them to the output STATCAT data bank because the previous output is still being read. The remaining temporary outputs are read into the last line in store, and counted -forming the number that could not be returned to store. (The last temporary output in the output STATCAT data bank is discarded, since it was never over-written in store and is still there somewhere.)

If there were any temporary outputs, the output STATCAT data bank is positioned at the end of the confirmed output entries, and the correctly ordered stored lines are output as confirmed entries. The number of confirmed entries is increased, and the line corresponding to the last output becomes the last entry known to be correct. The subroutine then takes a deep breath and carries out an "internal re-start".

If there were no temporary outputs, then there was no underflow, and no overflow, and the store must contain all remaining output entries in their correct order. These entries are output to the output STATCAT data bank, the number of confirmed entries increased accordingly, and the subroutine CCOMB ends by returning to the main program.

Figure 10.51a - System Flow-Charts - STCOMB, STAT and OPST

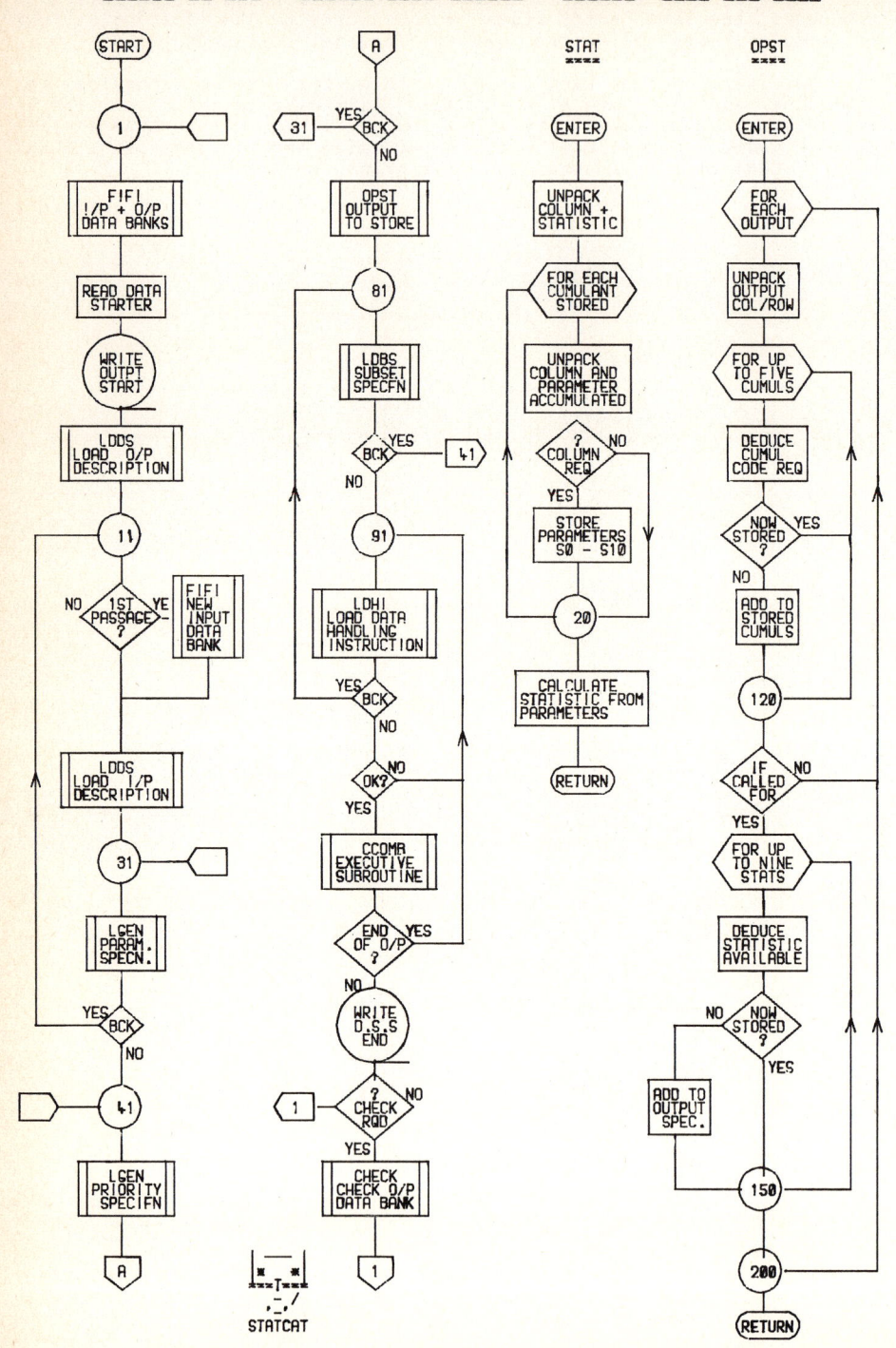

Figure 10.51b - System Flow-Chart - CCOMB

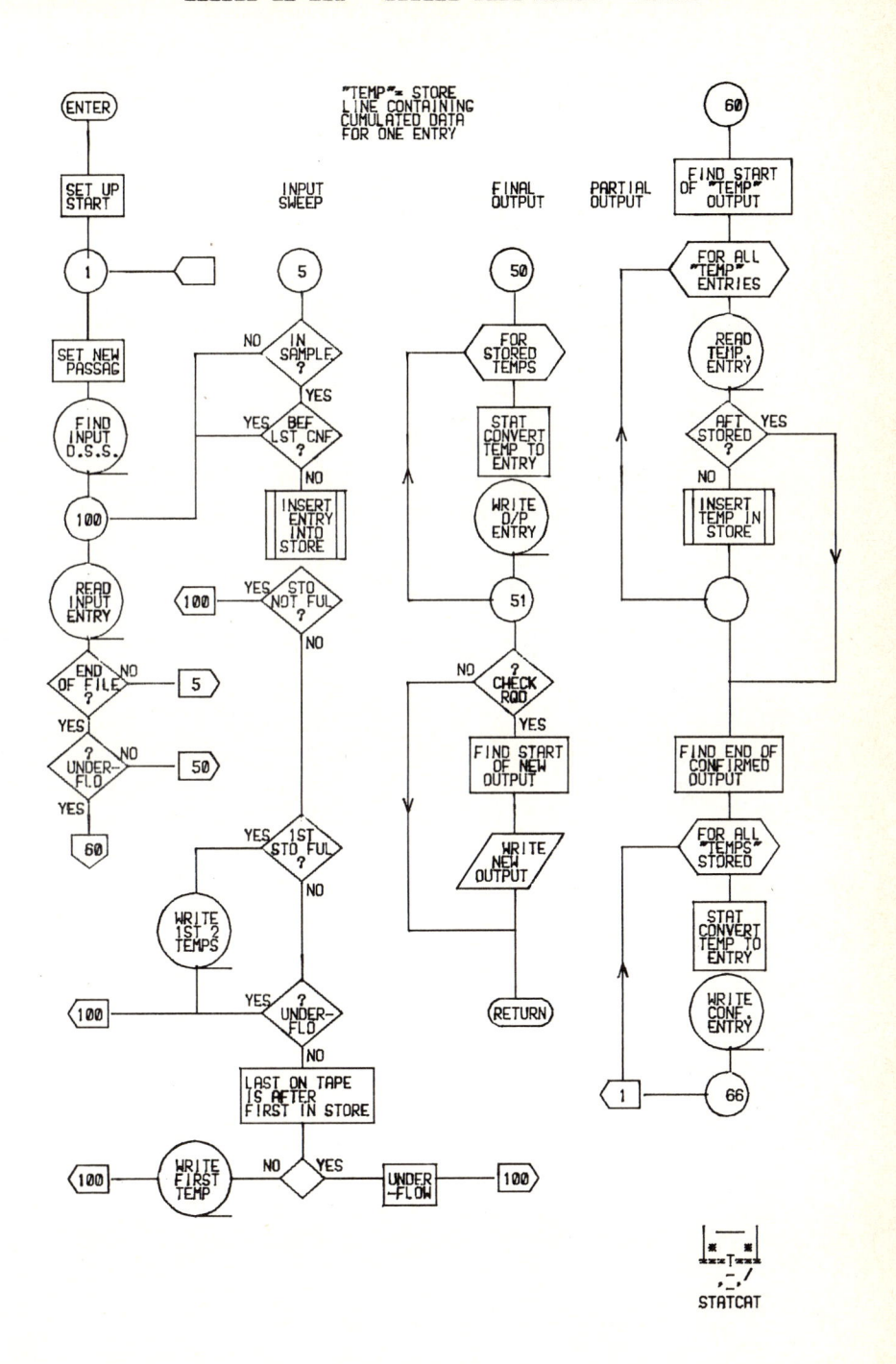

Figure 10.52 - STCOMB - Input Structure

```
        Level
0   1   2   3   4   5   6   7   8   9
FILE CONTROL CARD
DATA STARTER CARD
DATA DESCRIPTION SEGMENT
     (FILE CONTROL CARD - SECOND OR LATER INPUT)
          PARAMETER SPECIFICATION
               PRIORITY SPECIFICATION
                    SUBSET SPECIFICATION
                         DATA HANDLING INSTRUCTION
                         BACK TO READ NEW SUBSET
                    BACK TO READ NEW PRIORITY SPECIFICATION
               PRIORITY SPECIFICATION
                    SUBSET SPECIFICATION
                         DATA HANDLING INSTRUCTION
                         BACK TO READ NEW SUBSET
                    BACK TO READ NEW PRIORITY SPECIFICATION
               PRIORITY SPECIFICATION
                    SUBSET SPECIFICATION
                         DATA HANDLING INSTRUCTION
                              STOP
```

Figure 10.54 - STCOMB - Output Structure

```
For each  ) : Output File Control Record
output    )   Output File Parameters
data bank )   Output Data Description Record
              For each  ) Input File Parameters
              Input     ) Input Data Description
              Data Bank ) Parameter Record
                  .          for each ) Priority Record
                  .          Priority ) for each ) Subset Record
                  .     Specification ) Subset    ) see left
                  .          Sweep    )<Allocation of Entries>
                  .                    <Output Subsets>
                  .                    <Entries Input>
                  .                    <Entries Stored>
              .<Standard Data Bank Checking>
```

Carated(<>) items are optional.

Figure 10.53 - STCOMB - Input Example

```
---------1---------2---------3---------4---------5--------///7---------8
**STCOMBDEMO      DUFF                       INPUT=DEMO OUTPUT=DUMMY
   11 10  -1.0  DIFFICULTY+EFFICIENCY (STCOMB)
     1NUMB            NUMBER OF ENTRIES COMBINED                     INTERVAL
   1.5         1.0
     2OPER            OPERATOR                                        NOMINAL
ERICFREDGINOHUGH
     3OBSR            OBSERVER                                        NOMINAL
MIKENOELOSCRPETE
     4MIND            MINIMUM ASSESSED DIFFICULTY BY OPERATOR         ORDINAL
VEASEASYREASNULLRHARHARDVHAR
     5MAXD            MAXIMUM ASSESSED DIFFICULTY BY OPERATOR         ORDINAL
VEASEASYREASNULLRHARHARDVHAR
     6MIOP            MINIMUM EFFICIENCY RATING BY OPERATOR          INTERVAL
     30.         10.
     7AMOP            MEAN EFFICIENCY RATING BY OPERATOR             INTERVAL
     30.         10.
     8MAOP            MAXIMUM EFFICIENCY RATING BY OPERATOR          INTERVAL
     30.         10.
     9MIOB            MINIMUM EFFICIENCY RATING BY OBSERVER          INTERVAL
     30.         10.
    10AMOB            MEAN EFFICIENCY RATING BY OBSERVER             INTERVAL
     30.         10.
    11MAOB            MAXIMUM EFFICIENCY RATING BY OBSERVER          INTERVAL
     30.         10.
END OF DATA DESCRIPTION SEGMENT
NUMBNTRY
IDENOPER
IDENOBSR
MINIDIFF
MAXIDIFF
MINIEFOP
A.M.EFOP
MAXIEFOP
MINIEFOB
A.M.EFOB
MAXIEFOB
END OF PARAMETER SPECIFICATION
1Q2.OBSR
END OF PRIORITY SPECIFICATION
ALL DATA
END OF SUBSET
2
BACK TO READ NEW SUBSET
BACK TO READ NEW PRIORITY SPECIFICATION
1Q2.OPER
END OF PRIORITY SPECIFICATION
ALL DATA
END OF SUBSET
2
BACK TO READ NEW SUBSET
BACK TO READ NEW PRIORITY SPECIFICATION
1Q2.OPER
1Q2.OBSR
END OF PRIORITY SPECIFICATION
ALL DATA
END OF SUBSET
20
STOP
---------1---------2---------3---------4---------5---------6---------7--
```

Figure 10.55 - STCOMB - Page-by-page output summary

Page	Contents	Origin
1	File Control Record	FIFI
2-3	Program Title	STCOMB
	Output File Parameters	STCOMB
	Output Data Description record	LDDS
4-5	Input File Parameters	STCOMB
	Input Data Description record	LDDS
6	Parameter Specification	LGEN
7	Priority Specification	LGEN
8	Subset Specification	LDBS
	Data Handling Instruction	LDHI
9-10	Input Record (first sweep)	CCOMB
11	Output Record (first sweep)	CCOMB
12	Output Subset listing (first sweep)	CCOMB
	Data Handling Instruction	LDHI
	Back to read priority	LGEN
13	Priority Specification	LGEN
14	Subset Specification	LDBS
	Data Handling Instruction	LDHI
15-18	Second Sweep records	CCOMB
	Data Handling Instruction	LDHI
	Back to read priority	LGEN
19	Priority Specification	LGEN
20	Subset Specification	LDBS
	Data Handling Instruction	LDHI
21-32	Third to sixth sweep records	CCOMB
33-34	Output Subset listing	CCOMB
35-41	Standard Data Checking	CHECK
42	End of Combining record	STCOMB
43	Data Handling Instruction (STOP)	LDHI

Figure 10.56 - STCOMB - Output Example - Third Subset - Third Sweep

```
STATCAT PROGRAM STCOMB      -    COMBINATION OF ENTRIES
OUTPUT DATA BANK TITLE      -    DIFFICULTY+EFFICIENCY (STCOMB)
 INPUT DATA BANK TITLE      -    DEMONSTRATION STATCAT DATA BANK
DATA BANK SUBSET TITLE      -    ALL DATA

                    START OF INPUT SWEEP

ENTRY       2          FROM ORIGINAL   INPUT PLACED IN STORE      1
ENTRY       4          FROM ORIGINAL   INPUT PLACED IN STORE      3
ENTRY       5          FROM ORIGINAL   INPUT PLACED IN STORE      4
ENTRY       7          FROM ORIGINAL   INPUT PLACED IN STORE      5
ENTRY       9          FROM ORIGINAL   INPUT PLACED IN STORE      6

                    STORE IS NOW FULL

ENTRY       4 (ALONE) FROM ORIGINAL   INPUT PLACED IN TENTATIVE OUTPUT    1 FROM STORE   3
ENTRY       5 (ALONE) FROM ORIGINAL   INPUT PLACED IN TENTATIVE OUTPUT    2 FROM STORE   4
ENTRY      11          FROM ORIGINAL   INPUT PLACED IN STORE      3

            STORE IS NOT BIG ENOUGH - PRIORITY ENTRIES TO BE FOUND

ENTRY      16          FROM ORIGINAL   INPUT PLACED IN STORE      1
ENTRY      17          FROM ORIGINAL   INPUT PLACED IN STORE      1
ENTRY      22          FROM ORIGINAL   INPUT PLACED IN STORE      1    THEN ADDED TO STORE   3
ENTRY      24          FROM ORIGINAL   INPUT PLACED IN STORE      1    THEN ADDED TO STORE   6
ENTRY      26          FROM ORIGINAL   INPUT PLACED IN STORE      1    THEN ADDED TO STORE   5
ENTRY      28          FROM ORIGINAL   INPUT PLACED IN STORE      1    THEN ADDED TO STORE   4
ENTRY      29          FROM ORIGINAL   INPUT PLACED IN STORE      1
ENTRY      31          FROM ORIGINAL   INPUT PLACED IN STORE      6
ENTRY      34          FROM ORIGINAL   INPUT PLACED IN STORE      6    THEN ADDED TO STORE   4
ENTRY      36          FROM ORIGINAL   INPUT PLACED IN STORE      6    THEN ADDED TO STORE   5
ENTRY      37          FROM ORIGINAL   INPUT PLACED IN STORE      6
ENTRY      39          FROM ORIGINAL   INPUT PLACED IN STORE      6    THEN ADDED TO STORE   1
ENTRY      43          FROM ORIGINAL   INPUT PLACED IN STORE      6
ENTRY      46          FROM ORIGINAL   INPUT PLACED IN STORE      6
ENTRY      48          FROM ORIGINAL   INPUT PLACED IN STORE      6    THEN ADDED TO STORE   3
ENTRY      49          FROM ORIGINAL   INPUT PLACED IN STORE      6    THEN ADDED TO STORE   3
ENTRY      51          FROM ORIGINAL   INPUT PLACED IN STORE      6
ENTRY      54          FROM ORIGINAL   INPUT PLACED IN STORE      6
ENTRY      58          FROM ORIGINAL   INPUT PLACED IN STORE      6    THEN ADDED TO STORE   1
ENTRY      60          FROM ORIGINAL   INPUT PLACED IN STORE      6
ENTRY      61          FROM ORIGINAL   INPUT PLACED IN STORE      6    THEN ADDED TO STORE   5
ENTRY      63          FROM ORIGINAL   INPUT PLACED IN STORE      6    THEN ADDED TO STORE   4

                    END OF INPUT SWEEP



STATCAT PROGRAM STCOMB      -    COMBINATION OF ENTRIES
OUTPUT DATA BANK TITLE      -    DIFFICULTY+EFFICIENCY (STCOMB)
 INPUT DATA BANK TITLE      -    DEMONSTRATION STATCAT DATA BANK
DATA BANK SUBSET TITLE      -    ALL DATA

ENTRY       1 FROM TENTATIVE OUTPUT IS RELOADED TO STORE    6     THEN ADDED TO STORE    1
ENTRY      29 (ET AL) FROM ORIGINAL   INPUT PLACED IN CONFIRMED OUTPUT   18 FROM STORE   1
ENTRY      11 (ET AL) FROM ORIGINAL   INPUT PLACED IN CONFIRMED OUTPUT   19 FROM STORE   3
ENTRY       5 (ET AL) FROM ORIGINAL   INPUT PLACED IN CONFIRMED OUTPUT   20 FROM STORE   4
ENTRY       7 (ET AL) FROM ORIGINAL   INPUT PLACED IN CONFIRMED OUTPUT   21 FROM STORE   5

            END OF PARTIAL OUTPUT - MORE INPUT SWEEPS
```

Figure 10.57 - STCOMB - Output Example - Third Subset - Last Sweep

```
STATCAT PROGRAM STCOMB       -     COMBINATION OF ENTRIES
OUTPUT DATA BANK TITLE       -     DIFFICULTY+EFFICIENCY (STCCMB)
INPUT DATA BANK TITLE        -     DEMONSTRATION STATCAT DATA BANK
DATA BANK SUBSET TITLE       -     ALL DATA

                    START OF INPUT SWEEP

ENTRY      2      FROM  ORIGINAL   INPUT PLACED IN STORE   1
ENTRY      9      FROM  ORIGINAL   INPUT PLACED IN STORE   2
ENTRY     16      FROM  ORIGINAL   INPUT PLACED IN STORE   3
ENTRY     17      FROM  ORIGINAL   INPUT PLACED IN STORE   4    THEN ADDED TO STORE   3
ENTRY     24      FROM  ORIGINAL   INPUT PLACED IN STORE   4    THEN ADDED TO STORE   2
ENTRY     31      FROM  ORIGINAL   INPUT PLACED IN STORE   4    THEN ADDED TO STORE   1
ENTRY     37      FROM  ORIGINAL   INPUT PLACED IN STORE   4    THEN ADDED TO STORE   1
ENTRY     43      FROM  ORIGINAL   INPUT PLACED IN STORE   4    THEN ADDED TO STORE   3
ENTRY     46      FROM  ORIGINAL   INPUT PLACED IN STORE   4    THEN ADDED TO STORE   2
ENTRY     51      FROM  ORIGINAL   INPUT PLACED IN STORE   4    THEN ADDED TO STORE   2
ENTRY     54      FROM  ORIGINAL   INPUT PLACED IN STORE   4    THEN ADDED TO STORE   3
ENTRY     60      FROM  ORIGINAL   INPUT PLACED IN STORE   4    THEN ADDED TO STORE   1

                    END OF INPUT SWEEP


STATCAT PROGRAM STCOMB       -     COMBINATION OF ENTRIES
OUTPUT DATA BANK TITLE       -     DIFFICULTY+EFFICIENCY (STCCMB)
INPUT DATA BANK TITLE        -     DEMONSTRATION STATCAT DATA BANK
DATA BANK SUBSET TITLE       -     ALL DATA

ENTRY      9 (ET AL) FROM ORIGINAL  INPUT PLACED IN CONFIRMED OUTPUT   22 FROM STORE   2
ENTRY      2 (ET AL) FROM ORIGINAL  INPUT PLACED IN CONFIRMED OUTPUT   23 FROM STORE   1
ENTRY     16 (ET AL) FROM ORIGINAL  INPUT PLACED IN CONFIRMED OUTPUT   24 FROM STORE   3

              END OF FINAL OUTPUT - NO MORE INPUT SWEEPS
```

```
C MASTER STCOMB - COMBINES ENTRIES TO FORM CONDENSED STATCAT DATA BANK
C    SUBROUTINES AND FUNCTIONS REQUIRED
C    NAME              TYPE            COMMENT
C    AN     (SEE  3.1 ) SERVICE        ALPHA - TO NUMERIC VALUE
C    CCOMB  (SEE 10.5 ) EXECUTIVE      COMBINES ENTRIES
C    CHECK  (SEE  4.2 ) EXECUTIVE      CHECKS DATA BANK OR SUBSET
C    CHIKEN (SEE 11.9 ) SERVICE        WARNS OF MISMATCHED DATA LEVEL
C    CLSAM  (SEE  3.5 ) SERVICE        ALLOTS ENTRY TO SAMPLE/SUBSET
C    COMPA  (SEE  3.1 ) SERVICE        COMPARES ALPHAMERIC VALUES
C    COPYA  (SEE  3.1 ) SERVICE        COPIES ALPHAMERIC VALUE
C    FIFI   (SEE  3.2 ) SYSTEM         ALLOCATES PERIPHERALS
C    IBL    (SEE  3.1 ) SERVICE        DETECTS BLANK,END AND STOP CARDS
C    ICH    (SEE  3.1 ) SERVICE        IDENTIFIES ALPHAMERIC CODES
C    INSERT (SEE 11.4 ) SERVICE        INSERTS ENTRY INTO ARRAY
C    LCOM   (SEE  3.4 ) SYSTEM         LOADS COMPLEMENTARY INFORMATION
C    LDBS   (SEE  3.6 ) SYSTEM         LOADS SUBSET DEFINITION
C    LDDS   (SEE  3.4 ) SYSTEM         LOADS DATA DESCRIPTION SEGMENT
C    LDHI   (SEE  3.8 ) SYSTEM         LOADS/CHECKS DATA HANDLING INSTN
C    LGEN   (SEE  3.7 ) SYSTEM         LOADS GENERALISED VARIATES
C    LSET   (SEE  3.5 ) SYSTEM         LOADS DEFINING CONDITIONS
C    POSN   (SEE 11.4 ) SERVICE        FINDS POSITION OF ENTRY IN ORDER
C    PR     (SEE 10.2 ) SERVICE        DETERMINES PRIORITY IN SORTING
C    WDCD   (SEE  3.4 ) SERVICE        WRITE DATA COLUMN DESCRIPTION
C    SETTING OF ARRAY DIMENSIONS
C    THE FOLLOWING DIMENSIONS MUST BE AT LEAST AS BIG AS THOSE
C    SPECIFIED BY THE DATA TAPE,SAMPLE SPECIFICATIONS,ETC.
C    NQMAX = MAXIMUM NUMBER OF DATA COLUMNS (INPUT OR OUTPUT)
C    DIMENSION D(NQMAX),RX(NQMAX),DMIN(NQMAX),IT(NQMAX),CN(NQMAX)
C    DIMENSION IX(NQMAX),IY(NQMAX),IPQ(NQMAX)
C    DIMENSION NP(NQMAX),NDP(NQMAX),ST(NCMAX)
      NQMAX = 100
      DIMENSION D(100),RX(100),DMIN(100),IT(100),CN(100)
      DIMENSION NP(  100),NDP(  100),ST(  100)
      DIMENSION IX(100),IY(100),IPQ(100)
C    MAXM = MAXIMUM STORAGE AVAILABLE FOR ACCUMULATED TOTALS
      MAXM = 2*NQMAX
C    DIMENSION IDP(MAXM),IP(MAXM)
      DIMENSION IDP(200),IP(200)
C    DATA BANK COLUMN NUMBERS - MAY BE USED IN PLACE OF NAMES
C    IF THE DIMENSION OF NQMAX IS INCREASED,THE EXTRA CODES MUST BE
C    INCLUDED IN THIS DATA STATEMENT
      DATA   CN/4HCOL1,4HCOL2,4HCOL3,4HCOL4,4HCOL5,4HCOL6,4HCOL7,4HCOL8,4
     1HCOL9,4HCL10,4HCL11,4HCL12,4HCL13,4HCL14,4HCL15,4HCL16,4HCL17,4HCL
     218,4HCL19,4HCL20,4HCL21,4HCL22,4HCL23,4HCL24,4HCL25,4HCL26,4HCL27,
     34HCL28,4HCL29,4HCL30,4HCL31,4HCL32,4HCL33,4HCL34,4HCL35,4HCL36,4HC
     4L37,4HCL38,4HCL39,4HCL40,4HCL41,4HCL42,4HCL43,4HCL44,4HCL45,4HCL46
     5,4HCL47,4HCL48,4HCL49,4HCL50,4HCL51,4HCL52,4HCL53,4HCL54,4HCL55,4H
     6CL56,4HCL57,4HCL58,4HCL59,4HCL60,4HCL61,4HCL62,4HCL63,4HCL64,4HCL6
     75,4HCL66,4HCL67,4HCL68,4HCL69,4HCL70,4HCL71,4HCL72,4HCL73,4HCL74,4
     8HCL75,4HCL76,4HCL77,4HCL78,4HCL79,4HCL80,4HCL81,4HCL82,4HCL83,4HCL
     984,4HCL85,4HCL86,4HCL87,4HCL88,4HCL89,4HCL90,4HCL91,4HCL92,4HCL93,
     94HCL94,4HCL95,4HCL96,4HCL97,4HCL98,4HCL99,4HC100/
C    NALTMX = MAXIMUM NUMBER OF CLASSES ON TAPE
C    DIMENSION       TRT(NALTMX)
      NALTMX = 50
      DIMENSION  TRT(50)
C    NCMAX = NUMBER OF STORES AVAILABLE
C    (NCMAX WAS REDUCED TO 100 FOR DEMONSTRATION OF OVERFLOW)
C    DIMENSION RT(NCMAX),ID(NCMAX)
      NCMAX = 100
      DIMENSION RT(2500),ID(2500)
      EQUIVALENCE (RT(1),ID(1))
C    MAXDBC = MAXIMUM NUMBER OF DATA BANK SUBSET CONDITIONS
```

```
C DIMENSION SCON(5,MAXDBC)
      MAXDBC = 50
      DIMENSION SCON(5,   50)
C THE FOLLOWING DIMENSIONS ARE FIXED
      DIMENSION U(8),LU(8),PC(17),LC(17),FORM(50)
C NAMES AND REQUIRED LEVELS FOR PRIORITY RULES
C     RULES     1      2       3       4       5       6       7       8
      DATA U/4H1Q2.,4H2Q1.,4HQ12.,4HQ21.,4H12Q.,4H21Q.,4H12-.,4H21-./
      DATA LU/8*3/
C NAMES AND REQUIRED LEVELS FOR DESCRIPTIVE PARAMETERS
      DATA PC/4HA.M.,4HS.D.,4HVAR.,4HSKEW,4HKURT,4HG.M.,4HH.M.,4HMINI,4H
     1MAXI,4HNUMB,4HTOT.,4HSSQ.,4HSCUB,4HS4TH,4HSLOG,4HSREC,4HIDEN/
      DATA LC/5*4,2*5,2*3,1,4*4,2*5,1/
      DATA TIN/3H IN/,TOUT/3HOUT/
      NPC = 17
      COMMON /STCT/MED1,MED2,MED3,MED4,MED5,MED6,MED13,Q,V(20),TT(30)
      DATA PROG/4HCOMB/
      MED1 = -1
C ASSIGN PERIPHERALS
    1 CALL COPYA(TT(1),PROG)
      CALL FIFI
      ISF = -1
C READ REVISED TITLE,KEY AND NAME
    2 READ(MED1,900) (FORM(J),J=1,16),(TT(J),J=1,10),(FORM(J),J=17,34)
      IF(IBL(TT,10,4).LT.0.AND.IBL(FORM,32,1).LT.0) GO TO 2
      IF(MED4.LT.1) WRITE(MED6,909)
      IF(MED4.LT.1) GO TO 1
      NQ = AN(FORM,5,3,5)
      NALT = AN(FORM,8,6,8)
      Q = AN(FORM,16,9,16)
      FORM(32) = AN(FORM,32,17,32)
      WRITE(MED6,901)TOUT,NQ,NALT,Q,TOUT,(TT(J),J=1,10),FORM(34)
      IF(MED4.LT.0) WRITE(MED6,909)
      IF(MED4.LT.0) GO TO 1
      REWIND MED4
      IF(NQ.EQ.0) WRITE(MED6,908)
      IF(NQ.EQ.0) V(10) = 1.
      IF(NQ.GT.NQMAX) WRITE(MED6,902) NQ,NQMAX
      IF(NQ.GT.NQMAX.AND.V(10).LT.0.5) V(10) = 2.
      IF(NALT.GT.NALTMX)WRITE(MED6,903) NALT,NALTMX
      IF(NALT.GT.NALTMX.AND.V(10).LT.0.5)V(10) = 3.
      IF(V(10).GT.0.5)WRITE(MED6,997)V(10)
      IF(V(10).GT.0.5) GO TO 1
      WRITE(MED4)NQ,NALT,Q,(TT(J),J=1,10),BL,BL,BL,(FORM(J),J=32,34)
      LI = 18
C LOAD DATA DESCRIPTION SEGMENT FROM CARDS TO MED4
      CALL LDDS(TRT,NALT,D,NQ,ST,NQ,IT,NQ,H,0,H,H,0,LI,0,Q,VX,
     1 MED1,MED2,0,MED4,IGO)
      IF(IGO.NE.0) GO TO 1
C LEVEL 1 - LOAD INPUT STATCAT DATA BANK
   11 IF(V(10).GT.10.) V(10) = 0.
      V6 = V(6)
      V10 = V(10)
      IF(ISF.GE.0) CALL FIFI
      IF(MED3.LT.0) WRITE(MED6,910)
      IF(MED3.LT.0) GO TO 11
      REWIND MED3
      READ(MED3) NQ1,NALT1,Q1,(TT(J),J=11,26)
      WRITE(MED6,901) TIN,NQ1,NALT1,Q1,TIN,(TT(J),J=11,20),TT(26)
      V(3) = Q
      V(4) = NQ
      V(5) = NALT
      V(6) = V6
```

```
          V(10) = V10
          IF(NQ1.GT.NQMAX) WRITE(MED6,902) NQ1,NQMAX
          IF(NQ1.GT.NQMAX.AND.V(10).LT.0.5) V(10) =16.
          IF(NALT1.GT.NALTMX) WRITE(MED6,903) NALT1,NALTMX
          IF(NALT1.GT.NALTMX.AND.V(10).LT.0.5)V(10) = 17.
          IF(V(10).GT.0.5)WRITE(MED6,997)V(10)
          IF(V(10).GT.0.5) GO TO 11
          CALL LDDS(TRF,NALT1,D,NQ1,ST,NQ1,IT,NQ1,H,0,DMIN,DMAX,NQ,LI,0,Q
         1,VX,0,MED2,MED3,0,IGO)
          IF(IGO.GT.0) GO TO 11
C LEVEL 2 - LOAD PARAMETER SPECIFICATION FOR OUTPUT+CONVERT
       21 IF(V(10).GT.20.) V(10) = 0.
          WRITE(MED2,920) (TT(I),I=1,20)
          WRITE(MED2,921)
          ISP = 0
          CALL LGEN(PC,NPC,LC,NPC,ST,IT,CN,NQ1,IH,0,H,H,0,H,H,0,0,0,IH,IPQ,N
         1Q,ISP,NQ,1,NALT1)
          IF(V(11).LT.0.5) GO TO 11
          IF(ISP.NE.NQ) WRITE(MED6,922) ISP,NQ
          IF(V(20).GT.0.5.AND.V(10).LT.0.5)V(10) = 25.
          IF(ISP.NE.NQ.AND.V(10).LT.0.5) V(10) = 26.
C CONVERT PARAMETER SPEC TO STORE SPEC
          V(1) = 0.
          CALL OPST(IP,IDP,MAXM,0,NQS,IPQ,NQ,NQ,NQ)
C LEVEL 4 - LOAD PRIORITY SPECIFICATION
       41 IF(V(10).GT.30.) V(10) = 0.
          WRITE(MED2,920) (TT(I),I=1,20)
          WRITE(MED2,931)
          IPR = 0.
          CALL LGEN(U,8,LU,8,ST,IT,CN,NQ1,IH,0,H,H,0,H,H,0,0,0,IH,IX,NQ1,IPR
         1,NQ1,1,NALT1)
          IF(V(11).EQ.0.) GO TO 21
          IF(V(20).GT.0.5.AND.V(10).LT.0.5) V(10) = 4.
C CONVERT PRIORITY SPEC FROM INPUT TO OUTPUT - ADDING COLS REQD.
          NQST = NQS
          DO 45 I = 1,IPR
          IY(I) = IX(I)/1000
          IXT = IX(I) + (30-IY(I))*1000
          DO 43 J = 1,NQST
          IF(IP(J).NE.IXT.OR.IDP(J).NE.0) GO TO 43
          IX(I) = J
          GO TO 45
       43 CONTINUE
          IF(NQST.EQ.MAXM) GO TO 44
          NQST = NQST + 1
          IDP(NQST) = 0
          IP(NQST) = IXT
          IX(I) = NQST
          GO TO 45
       44 WRITE(MED6,932)
          IF(V(10).LT.0.5)V(10) = 45.
       45 CONTINUE
C COMPLETE VECTORS WITH REMAINING STORE COLUMNS
          NQST1 = NQST-1
          DO 47 I = IPR,NQST1
          DO 47 J = 1,NQST
          DO 46 K = 1,I
          IF(IX(K).EQ.J) GO TO 47
       46 CONTINUE
          IX(I+1) = J
          IY(I+1) = IDP(J)
       47 CONTINUE
C CALCULATE STORAGE ROWS AVAILABLE
```

```
        NCAV = NCMAX/(NQST+2)
        WRITE(MED6,907) NCAV
        IL1 = NQST*NCAV+1
        ID1 = IL1 + NCAV
C LEVEL 8 - DATA BANK SUBSET SPECIFICATION
   81 IF(V(10).GT.80.) V(10) = 0.
        CALL LDBS (SCON,NCON,MAXDBC,CN,ST,IT,NQ1,TRT,NALT1,IGO)
        IF(IGO.GT.0) GO TO 41
C LEVEL 9 - DATA HANDLING INSTRUCTION
   91 IF(V(10).GT.90.) V(10) = 0.
        CALL LDHI(V(1),1,V(2),3,V(9),7,ASDL,18,APT,15,H,0,H,V(10),
       1FORM(41),FORM,MED1,MED2,MED4,Q,NQ,NWARN,1,IGO)
        IF(IGO.GT.0) GO TO 81
        IF(V(1).GT.4.5) NWARN = NWARN + 1
        IF(V(1).GT.4.5) V(1) = -1.
        NX = V(9)
        IF(NX.LE.0.OR.NX.GE.NQ) NWARN = NWARN + 1
        IF(NX.LE.0.OR.NX.GE.NQ) V(9) = NQ-1
        IF(IBL(FORM(2),1,1).LT.0.AND.IBL(FORM(6),11,1).LT.0) NX = 0
        IF(IBL(FORM(2),1,1).GE.0.OR .IBL(FORM(6),11,1).GE.0) NX = 1
        IF(NX.EQ.0)CALL LDHI(V(1),1,H,0,V(9),7,H,0,H,0,H,0,H,V(10),
       1FORM(41),FORM,MED1,MED2,MED4,Q,NQ,NWARN,2,IGO)
        IF(NX.EQ.0) GO TO 92
        IF(ASDL.LE.0.) NWARN = NWARN + 1
        IF(ASDL.EQ.0.) ASDL = 5.
        IF(ASDL.LT.0.) ASDL = 9999.
        IF(APT.LE.0.) NWARN = NWARN + 1
        IF(APT.EQ.0.) APT = 1.
        IF(APT.LT.0.) APT = 0.
        CALL LDHI(V(1),1,V(2),3,V(9),7,ASDL,18,APT,15,H,0,H,V(10),
       1FORM(41),FORM,MED1,MED2,MED4,Q,NQ,NWARN,2,IGO)
   92 IF(IGO.GT.0) GO TO 91
  101 WRITE(MED6,998)
C LOAD DATA STORAGE SEGMENT
        CALL CCOMB(RF,ID(IL1),ID(ID1),IP,IX,IY,NQST,NCAV,SCON,NCON,D,NQMAX
       1,IPQ,NQ)
  112 IF(NX.EQ.0) GO TO 91
C END TAPE - TEST IF REQUIRED
  120 WRITE(MED4) (V(3),I=1,NQ)
        REWIND MED4
        IF(V(2).GE.0.) GO TO 150
        WRITE(MED6,995)
        GO TO 1
C CARRY OUT PRELIMINARY CHECK OF DATA TAPE
  150 WRITE(MED6,996)
        APT = APT*.01
        NCON=0
        Q = V(3)
        CALL CHECK (D,RX,DMIN,RT,IT,TRT,NQ,NALT,ASDL,APT,SCON,NCON,ST)
        WRITE(MED6,999)
        GO TO 1
  900 FORMAT(16A1,10A4,16A1,2A4)
  901 FORMAT(1H1,20X,25HSTATCAT COMBINING ENTRIES        /
       1                                    1H0,A3,19HPUT FILE PARAMETER
       2S/29H0NUMBER OF DATA COLUMNS IS - ,I6/29H0STORED NUMBER OF CLASSES
       3 IS ,I6/34H0VALUE USED FOR MISSING DATA IS - ,F20.8/
       4          1H0,A3,24HPUT STATCAT DATA BANK - ,10A4,10X,10HFILE NAME ,A4/)
  902 FORMAT (4H0THE,I6,    37H ITEMS PER ENTRY EXCEED THE AVAILABLE,I6,1
       16H STORAGE COLUMNS)
  903 FORMAT (4H0THE,I6,40H CLASSES PER COLUMN EXCEED THE AVAILABLE,I6,1
       13H STORAGE ROWS)
  907 FORMAT(1H0,20X,17HPROGRAM CAN STORE,I5,8H ENTRIES/)
  908 FORMAT(26H0NO DATA COLUMNS SPECIFIED)
```

```
      909 FORMAT(41H0NO OUTPUT FILE - PROGRAM CANNOT CONTINUE)
      910 FORMAT(41H0 NO INPUT FILE - PROGRAM CANNOT CONTINUE)
      912 FORMAT(29H0OUTPUT STATCAT DATA BANK HAS,I4,20H CLASSES - INPUT HAS
     1,I4,19H SHOULD BE THE SAME,34X,11H**WARNING**)
      920 FORMAT(23H1STATCAT PROGRAM STCOMB,7X,1H-,4X,23H COMBINATION OF ENT
     1RIES/23H OUTPUT DATA BANK TITLE,7X,1H-,4X,10A4/23H   INPUT DATA BAN
     2K TITLE,7X,1H-,4X,10A4)
      921 FORMAT(24H0PARAMETER SPECIFICATION/25H0OUTPUT   PARAMETER   INPUT/
     17H COLUMN,7X,12HCODE   COLUMN)
      922 FORMAT( 5H0ONLY,I4,23H PARAMETERS - SHOULD BE,I4)
      931 FORMAT(18H0PRIORITY ORDERING/6H0ORDER,4X,14HPRIORITY   DATA/
     17H OF USE,7X,12HRULE   COLUMN )
      932 FORMAT(64H0TOTAL INTERMEDIATE ITEMS EXCEEDS STORAGE LIMIT - INCREA
     1SE NQMAX)
      995 FORMAT (54H0NO MORE INPUT DATA - NO CHECKING - PROGRAM STOPS        )
      996 FORMAT (54H0NO MORE INPUT DATA - CHECKING STARTS                    )
      997 FORMAT (54H0CHECKING COMPLETED - PROGRAM STOPS                      )
      998 FORMAT(39H0INPUT ACCEPTED - COMBINATION COMMENCES )
      999 FORMAT(40H1 COMBINATION COMPLETED - READ NEW INPUT)
          END


          SUBROUTINE CCOMB(RT,IL,ID,NP,IP,IDP,NQST,NC,SCON,NCON,D,NQIO,IPQ,N
         1QOP)
C CCOMB   (SEE 10.5 ) EXECUTIVE   COMBINES ENTRIES
C NQIO = MAXIMUM NUMBER OF ITEMS INPUT/OUTPUT
C NQST = NUMBER OF ITEMS STORED AND ACCUMULATED
C NPR = NUMBER OF PRIORITY DETERMINING COMPARISONS
          DIMENSION RT(NQST,NC),ID(NC),IL(NC),NP(NQST),IP(NQST),IDP(NQST)
          DIMENSION SCON(5,NCON),D(NQIO),IPQ(NQOP)
          COMMON /STCT/MED1,MED2,MED3,MED4,MED5,MED6,MED13,Q,V(20),TT(30)
          NL = 60
          NO = V(1)
          LOKT = 0
          NM = (NQOP+29)/10
          REWIND MED3
          NOKT = V(6)+.001
          NOLD = NOKT
          NTEMP = 0
C INITIAL SETTINGS
        1 LONT = 0
          A = 1.001
          IF(LOKT.NE.0) A = 2.001
          K = 0
          DO 2 J = 1,NC
          IF(J.EQ.1.AND.LOKT.NE.0) GO TO 2
          K = K + 1
          IF(K.EQ.LOKT) K = K+1
          IL(J) = K
        2 CONTINUE
          NIP = 0
          LIN = A-1.
          IST = 1
          NEXT = A
          LEXT = A
          NL = NL + 3
          IF (NO.GT.0) NL = 60
          IF(NL.GT.50.AND.NO.GE.0) WRITE(MED2,900) TT
          IF(NL.GT.50) NL = 9
          IF(NO.GE.0) WRITE(MED2,922)
          READ(MED3) NQ,NALT,Q,(X,I=1,16)
          DO 3 I = 1,NQ
        3 READ(MED3) (X,K=1,19),(X,K=1,NALT),NX,X,X
```

```
C READ INPUT ENTRY
  100 NEXT = IL(LEXT)
      READ(MED3) (D(I),I=1,NQ)
      NIP = NIP + 1
      DO 4 I = 1,NQ
      IF(D(I).NE.Q) GO TO 5
    4 CONTINUE
      IF(NO.GE.0) WRITE(MED2,910)
      IF(NO.GT.0) NL = 60
      REWIND MED3
      IF(IST.EQ.1) GO TO 50
      IF(IST.EQ.2) REWIND MED4
      GO TO 60
    5 CALL CLSAM(D,NQ,SCON,NCON,NIN,1)
      IF(NIN.NE.1) GO TO 100
      DO 6 I = 1,NQST
      RT(I,NEXT) = V(3)
      NTR = NP(I)/1000
      NCOL=NP(I)-NTR*1000
      X = TRANS(D(NCOL),Q,NTR,J)
    6 IF(X.NE.Q)RT(I,NEXT) = X
      POS = POSN(RT,NQST,NC,IL,IDP,IP,LEXT,LIN,V(3))
      ID(NEXT) = NIP
C DISCARD IF AT OR BEFORE LAST CONFIRMED
      IF(POS.LT.1.3.AND.LOKT.GT.0) GO TO 100
    7 IF(NO.LT.1) GO TO 8
C LIST INPUT IF NO GT OR EQ 3
      NL = NL + 1
      IF(NO.GE.3) NL = NL + (NQ+29)/10
      IF(NL.GT.50) WRITE(MED2,900) TT
      IF(NO.GE.3.AND.NL.GT.50) NL = (NQ+89)/10
      IF(NL.GT.50) NL = 6
      IF(NO.GE.3) WRITE(MED2,901)
      I = POS
      X = I
      X = POS-X
      IF(I.EQ.0) I = 1
      ILX = IL(I)
      IF(X.LT.0.3.AND.ID(ILX).GT.0) ID(ILX) = - ID(ILX)
      WRITE(MED2,902) NIP,NEXT
      IF(X.LT.0.3) WRITE(MED2,917) ILX
      IF(NO.GE.3) WRITE(MED2,907) (D(I),I=1,NQ)
    8 LEST = LEXT
      CALL INSERT(RT,NQST,NC,IL,IDP,IP,LEXT,LIN,V(3),1,0,POS)
C ROW IS COMBINED WITH ONE IN STORE
      IF(LEXT.NE.0) GO TO 100
    9 IF(LIN.EQ.0) GO TO 10
      LIN1 = LIN + 1
      GO TO (10,20,30),IST
C STORE NOT FULL - NO UNDERFLOW
   10 LIN = LIN + 1
      LEXT = LIN + 1
      IF(LEXT.GT.NC) GO TO 15
      GO TO 100
C STORE IS NOW FULL - SET STATE = 2 - FIRST ENTRY TO TAPE
   15 J = A
      IST = 2
      LEXT = NC
      LIN = NC-1
      NEXT = IL(J)
      DO 16 I = 1,NQOP
   16 D(I) = STAT(IPQ(I),RT(1,NEXT),NP,NQST)
      NTEMP = NTEMP + 1
```

```
      IF(NTEMP.LE.0)NOKT = NOKT + 1
      IF(NTEMP.LE.0) WRITE(MED4) (D(I),I=1,NQOP)
      IF(NTEMP.GT.0) WRITE(MED4) (RT(I,NEXT),I=1,NQST)
      IF(NO.LT.0) GO TO 21
      NL = NL + 4
      IF(NO.GE.4) NL = NL + NM
      IF(NL.GT.50) WRITE(MED2,900) TT
      IF(NL.GT.50.AND.NO.GE.4) NL = NM + 6
      IF(NL.GT.50) NL = 6
      WRITE(MED2,908)
      IF(NO.LT.1) GO TO 21
      IDX = ID(NEXT)
      IF(IDX.LT.0) IDX = - IDX
      IF(NTEMP.GE.1) WRITE(MED2,903) IDX,NTEMP,NEXT
      IF(NTEMP.LE.0) WRITE(MED2,904) IDX,NOKT,NEXT
      IF(ID(NEXT).GT.0) WRITE(MED6,920)
      IF(ID(NEXT).LT.0) WRITE(MED6,921)
      IF(NO.GE.4)WRITE(MED2,907) (D(I),I=1,NQOP)
      GO TO 21
C STORE IS FULL - TEST FOR UNDERFLOW (POS BEFORE LAST ON TAPE)
   20 IF(POS.LT.A) GO TO 25
      J = A
      NEXT = IL(J)
C WRITE SECOND ENTRY TO TAPE (BECOMES LONT) SHIFT UP IL CODES
   21 LONT = IL(J+1)
      NOPT = 0
      DO 23 I = 1,NQOP
   23 D(I) = STAT(IPQ(I),RT(1,LONT),NP,NQST)
      NTEMP = NTEMP + 1
      IF(NTEMP.LE.0)NOKT = NOKT + 1
      IF(NTEMP.LE.0) WRITE(MED4) (D(I),I=1,NQOP)
      IF(NTEMP.GT.0) WRITE(MED4) (RT(I,LONT),I=1,NQST)
      DO 22 L = J,LIN
   22 IL(L) = IL(L+1)
      LEXT = NC
      IL(NC) = NEXT
      IF(NO.LT.1) GO TO 100
      NL = NL + 1
      IF(NO.GE.4) NL = NL + NM
      IF(NL.GT.50) WRITE(MED2,900) TT
      IF(NL.GT.50.AND.NO.GE.4) NL = NM + 6
      IF(NL.GT.50) NL = 6
      IF(NO.GE.4) WRITE(MED2,901)
      IDX = ID(LONT)
      IF(IDX.LT.0) IDX = - IDX
      IF(NTEMP.LE.0) WRITE(MED2,904) IDX,NOKT,LONT
      IF(NTEMP.GE.1) WRITE(MED2,903) IDX,NTEMP,LONT
      IF(ID(LONT).LT.0) WRITE(MED6,921)
      IF(ID(LONT).GT.0) WRITE(MED6,920)
      IF(NO.GE.4)WRITE(MED2,907) (D(I),I=1,NQOP)
      GO TO 100
C UNDERFLOW FOUND - STATE = 3  REWIND OUTPUT/NEXT FROM END
   25 IST = 3
      REWIND MED4
      NOFL = NIP
      IF(NO.LT.0) GO TO 30
      NL = NL + 3
      IF(NL.GT.50) WRITE(MED2,900) TT
      IF(NL.GT.50) NL = 6
      WRITE(MED2,909)
C UNDERFLOW FOUND - CONTINUING TO TAPE END
   30 CONTINUE
      LEXT = NC
```

```
          GO TO 100
C END WITHOUT OVERFLOW OR UNDERFLOW
   50 K = A
      IF(LONT.NE.0) K = K + 1
      IF(NO.GE.0) NL = NL + 3
      IF(LIN.EQ.0) GO TO 52
   57 DO 51 J = K,LIN
      NOKT = NOKT + 1
      NEXT = IL(J)
      DO 59 I = 1,NQOP
   59 D(I) = STAT(IPQ(I),RT(1,NEXT),NP,NQST)
      IF(NO.LT.1) GO TO 51
      NL = NL + 1
      IF(NO.GE.4) NL = NL + NM
      IF(NL.GT.50) WRITE(MED2,900) TT
      IF(NL.GT.50.AND.NO.GE.4) NL = NM + 6
      IF(NL.GT.50) NL = 6
      IF(NO.GE.4) WRITE(MED2,901)
      IDX = ID(NEXT)
      IF(IDX.LT.0) IDX = -IDX
      WRITE(MED2,904)IDX,NOKT,NEXT
      IF(ID(NEXT).LT.0) WRITE(MED2,921)
      IF(ID(NEXT).GT.0) WRITE(MED2,920)
      IF(NO.GE.4) WRITE(MED2,907) (D(I),I=1,NQOP)
   51 WRITE(MED4) (D(I),I=1,NQOP)
   52 V(6) = NOKT
      J = NOKT - NOLD
      IF(NO.LT.0) RETURN
      WRITE(MED2,916)
      IF(NO.GE.2) WRITE(MED2,900) TT
      IF(J.EQ.0) WRITE(MED2,911)
      IF(NO.LT.2.OR.J.EQ.0) RETURN
C CHECK NEW SECTION OF OUTPUT TAPE
      NL = 7
      REWIND MED4
      READ(MED4) NQ, NALT, (X,I=1,17)
      DO 53 I = 1,NQ
   53 READ(MED4) (X,K=1,19),(X,K=1,NALT),NX,X,X
      DO 55 I = 1,NOKT
      READ(MED4) (RT(K,NEXT),K=1,NQ)
      IF(I.LE.NOLD) GO TO 55
      NL = NL + NM + 1
      IF(NL.LT.50) GO TO 54
      WRITE(MED2,900) TT
      WRITE(MED2,912)
      NL = 8 + NM
   54 WRITE(MED2,905) I
      WRITE(MED2,907) (RT(K,NEXT),K=1,NQ)
   55 CONTINUE
      RETURN
C END WITH OVERFLOW (AND POSSIBLY UNDERFLOW)
   60 READ(MED4) NQ, NALT, (X,I=1,17)
      DO 61 I = 1,NQ
   61 READ(MED4) (X,K=1,19),(X,K=1,NALT),NX,X,X
C RETURN REMAINING TENTATIVE OUTPUT TO STORE
      IF(NOKT.EQ.0) GO TO 63
      DO 62 K = 1,NOKT
   62 READ(MED4) (D(I),I=1,NQOP)
C COMBINE TEMPORARIES WITH INPUT SO FAR     COUNT NUMBER LEFT
   63 KTEMP = NTEMP - 1
      DO 64 I = 1,NC
   64 IF(ID(I).LT.0) ID(I) = ID(I)-KTEMP
      NTEMP = 0
```

```
      LEXT = NC
      NEXT = IL(LEXT)
      LIN = NC - 1
      IF(KTEMP.LE.0) GO TO 73
      DO 66 K = 1,KTEMP
      READ(MED4) (RT(I,NEXT),I=1,NQST)
      IF(LIN.LT.NC-1) GO TO 65
      IF(NO.GE.1) NL = NL + 1
      IF(NL.GT.50.AND.NO.GE.0) WRITE(MED2,900) TT
      IF(NO.GE.4) NL = NL + (NQST+29)/10
      IF(NL.GT.50.AND.NO.GE.4) NL = (NQST+89)/10
      IF(NL.GT.50) NL = 6
      POS = POSN(RT,NQST,NC,IL,IDP,IP,LEXT,LIN,V(3))
      LEXQ = POS
      X = LEXQ
      X = POS-X
      ID(NEXT) = -K
      IF(LEXQ.EQ.0) LEXQ = 1
      ILX = IL(LEXQ)
      IF(X.LT.0.3.AND.ID(ILX).GT.0) ID(ILX) = - ID(ILX) - KTEMP
      IF(NO.GE.1) WRITE(MED2,915)K,NEXT
      IF(NO.GE.1.AND.X.LT.0.3) WRITE(MED2,917) ILX
      IF(NO.GE.4) WRITE(MED2,901)
      IF(NO.GE.4) WRITE(MED2,907) (RT(I,NEXT),I=1,NQST)
      CALL INSERT(RT,NQST,NC,IL,IDP,IP,LEXT,LIN,V(3),1,0,POS)
      IF(LEXT.NE.0) GO TO 66
      IST = 3
      NEXT = IL(LEXT)
C TEST IF STORE IS FULL - MUST KEEP LOWEST FOUND
      NEXQ = IL(NC-1)
      IF(ID(NEXQ).GT.-KTEMP.AND.ID(NEXQ).LT.0) LIN = NC - 2
      GO TO 66
   65 CALL PR(NEXQ,NEXT,I,RT,IP,IDP,NQST,NC,V(3))
      IF(I.NE.1) GO TO 70
      NTEMP = NTEMP - 1
   66 CONTINUE
C REWIND MED4 - OUTPUT STORED VALUES OVER TEMPORARIES
   70 REWIND MED4
      READ(MED4)NQ,NALT,(X,I=1,17)
      DO 71 I = 1,NQ
   71 READ(MED4) (X,K=1,19),(X,K=1,NALT),NX,X,X
      IF(NOKT.EQ.0) GO TO 73
      DO 72 K = 1,NOKT
   72 READ(MED4)(D(I),I=1,NQOP)
   73 J = A
      DO 76 K1 = J,LIN
      NEXT = IL(K1)
      NOKT = NOKT + 1
      DO 75 I = 1,NQOP
   75 D(I) = STAT(IPQ(I),RT(1,NEXT),NP,NQST)
      IF(NO.LT.1) GO TO 76
      NL = NL + 1
      IF(NO.GE.4) NL = NL + NM
      IF(NL.GT.50) WRITE(MED2,900) TT
      IF(NL.GT.50.AND.NO.GE.4) NL = NM + 6
      IF(NL.GT.50) NL = 6
      IF(NO.GE.4) WRITE(MED2,901)
      K = ID(NEXT)
      IF(K.LT.-KTEMP) K = -KTEMP - K
      IF(K.LT.0) K = -K
      IF(ID(NEXT).LT.-KTEMP.OR.ID(NEXT).GT.0) WRITE(MED2,904)K,NOKT,NEXT
      IF(ID(NEXT).GE.-KTEMP.AND.ID(NEXT).LT.0) WRITE(MED2,906)K,NOKT,NEXT
      IF(ID(NEXT).GE.-KTEMP) WRITE(MED2,920)
```

```
      IF(ID(NEXT).LT.-KTEMP) WRITE(MED2,921)
      IF(NO.GE.4) WRITE(MED2,907) (D(I),I=1,NQOP)
   76 WRITE(MED4) (D(I),I=1,NQOP)
      IF(NO.GE.0.AND.IST.EQ.3) WRITE(MED2,919)
      IF(IST.EQ.2.AND.NTEMP.EQ.0) GO TO 52
      IF(NO.GE.0.AND.IST.EQ.2) WRITE(MED2,918)
      IF(IST.EQ.2) NTEMP = NTEMP - 2
      LOKT = IL(LIN)
      IL(1) = LOKT
      GO TO 1
  900 FORMAT(23H1STATCAT PROGRAM STCOMB,7X,1H-,4X,23H COMBINATION OF ENT
     1RIES/23H OUTPUT DATA BANK TITLE,7X,1H-,4X,10A4/23H  INPUT DATA BAN
     2K TITLE,7X,1H-,4X,10A4/23H DATA BANK SUBSET TITLE,7X,1H-,4X,10A4/)
  901 FORMAT(1H )
  902 FORMAT(6H ENTRY,I7,9X,37HFROM    ORIGINAL   INPUT PLACED IN STORE,I6)
  903 FORMAT(6H ENTRY,I7,9X,48HFROM    ORIGINAL   INPUT PLACED IN TENTATIVE
     1 OUTPUT,I6,11H FROM STORE,I6)
  904 FORMAT(6H ENTRY,I7,9X,48HFROM    ORIGINAL   INPUT PLACED IN CONFIRMED
     1 OUTPUT,I6,11H FROM STORE,I6)
  905 FORMAT(7H0ENTRY ,I6,41H ON OUTPUT STATCAT DATA BANK (CONFIRMED) /)
  906 FORMAT(6H ENTRY,I7,9X,48HFROM TENTATIVE OUTPUT PLACED IN CONFIRMED
     1 OUTPUT,I6,11H FROM STORE,I6)
  907 FORMAT(1H0,10X,10F11.4/(11X,10F11.4))
  908 FORMAT(1H0,20X,17HSTORE IS NOW FULL/)
  909 FORMAT(1H0,20X,54HSTORE IS NOT BIG ENOUGH - PRIORITY ENTRIES TO BE
     1 FOUND/)
  910 FORMAT(1H0,20X,18HEND OF INPUT SWEEP/)
  911 FORMAT(1H0,20X,28HSUBSET IS EMPTY - NO ENTRIES)
  912 FORMAT(1H0,20X,26HCONFIRMED ENTRIES IN ORDER)
  914 FORMAT(7H ENTRY ,I6,55H FROM TENTATIVE OUTPUT IS CONFIRMED BY LOAD
     1ING TO STORE,I6)
  915 FORMAT(7H ENTRY ,I6,43H FROM TENTATIVE OUTPUT IS RELOADED TO STORE
     1,I6)
  916 FORMAT(1H0,20X,42HEND OF FINAL OUTPUT - NO MORE INPUT SWEEPS/)
  917 FORMAT(1H+,70X,19HTHEN ADDED TO STORE,I5)
  918 FORMAT(1H0,20X,44HEND OF PARTIAL OUTPUT - ONE MORE INPUT SWEEP/)
  919 FORMAT(1H0,20X,42HEND OF PARTIAL OUTPUT - MORE INPUT SWEEPS /)
  920 FORMAT(1H+,13X,7H(ALONE))
  921 FORMAT(1H+,13X,7H(ET AL))
  922 FORMAT(1H0,20X,20HSTART OF INPUT SWEEP/)
      END



      SUBROUTINE OPST(IP,IDP,MAXM,IS1,IS2,IQ,NPMAX,NP1,NP2)
C OPST    (SEE 10.5 ) SERVICE      DEDUCES SUMS REQUIRED FOR STATISTIC
C CONVERSION OF OUTPUT REQUIREMENT CODES TO STORAGE CODES
C AT ENTRY FIRST IS1 CODES OF ID,IDP CONTAIN ROW+COLUMN VALUES
C AT EXIT THESE ARE FOLLOWED BY REQUIRED PARAMETER CODES FOR DATA
C AT EXIT THESE ARE FOLLOWED BY REQUIRED PARAMETER CODES
C THESE CODES DEFINE THE DATA TO BE CUMULATED
C CODES 10 AND 20 CONTAIN VALUES,FROM WHICH MAXIMA+MINIMA CAN BE
C DERIVED IF REQUIRED WITHIN PROGRAM
C AT ENTRY IQ CONTAINS PARAMETER NAMES FOR OUTPUT - UP TO NP1
C AT EXIT IQ ALSO CONTAINS IMPLIED AND TOTAL NAMES IF REQUIRED
C IMPLIED CODES ARE ADDED IF V(1) GT 3 - TOTALS IF V(1) GT 7
      DIMENSION IP(MAXM),IDP(MAXM),IQ(NPMAX)
      COMMON /STCT/MED1,MED2,MED3,MED4,MED5,MED6,MED13,Q,V(20),TT(30)
      IS2 = IS1
      NP2 = NP1
      ISF = IS1
      IST = ISF+1
      DO 200 I = 1,NP1
      NCOL = IQ(I)-IQ(I)/1000*1000
```

```
      DO 120 J = 1,5
      NPAR = IQ(I)/1000
      IF(NPAR.GT.7.AND.J.GE.2) GO TO 125
      IPX = NCOL + 1000
      IF(NPAR.EQ.11)NPAR = 1
      IF(NPAR.EQ.17) NPAR = 20
      IF(NPAR.GT.11)NPAR = NPAR-9
      GO TO (101,102,103,104,105),J
  101 GO TO (114,113,113,112,111,108,107,109,110,106,117),NPAR
  102 GO TO (106,114,114,113,112,106,106),NPAR
  103 GO TO (125,106,106,114,113,125,125),NPAR
  104 GO TO (125,125,125,106,114,125,125),NPAR
  105 GO TO (125,125,125,125,106,125,125),NPAR
  106 IPX = IPX +   7000
  107 IPX = IPX +   6000
  108 IPX = IPX +   5000
  117 IPX = IPX + 10000
  109 IPX = IPX + 10000
  110 IPX = IPX +   6000
  111 IPX = IPX +   1000
  112 IPX = IPX +   1000
  113 IPX = IPX +   1000
  114 IF(IST.GT.ISF) GO TO 116
      DO 115 IX = IST,ISF
      IF(NPAR.EQ.11.AND.IDP(IX).NE.0) GO TO 115
      IF(NPAR.EQ.8.AND.IDP(IX).NE.-2) GO TO 115
      IF(NPAR.EQ.9.AND.IDP(IX).NE.-3) GO TO 115
      IF(IPX.EQ.IP(IX))GO TO 120
  115 CONTINUE
  116 IF(ISF.EQ.MAXM) WRITE(MED2,900) MAXM
      ISF = ISF + 1
      IF(ISF.GT.MAXM) GO TO 120
      IP(ISF) = IPX
      IDP(ISF)= -1
      IF(NPAR.EQ.8) IDP(ISF) = -2
      IF(NPAR.EQ.9) IDP(ISF) = -3
      IF(NPAR.EQ.11)IDP(ISF) = 0
  120 CONTINUE
  125 IF(ISF.GT.MAXM) WRITE(MED2,901) MAXM,ISF
      IF(V(1).LT.4.) GO TO 200
      NPAR = IQ(I)/1000
      IF(NPAR.GT.7) GO TO 200
C IMPLIED PARAMETERS AND TOTALS
      DO 150 J = 1,9
      IPX = 1000+NCOL
      IF(J.GT.5.AND.V(1).LT.8.) GO TO 200
      GO TO (210,132,133,134,135,136,137,138,139),J
  132 GO TO (150,201,201,201,201,150,150),NPAR
  133 GO TO (150,203,202,202,202,150,150),NPAR
  134 GO TO (150,150,150,203,203,150,150),NPAR
  135 GO TO (150,150,150,150,204,150,150),NPAR
  136 GO TO (211,211,211,211,211,215,216),NPAR
  137 GO TO (200,212,212,212,212,200,200),NPAR
  138 GO TO (200,200,200,213,213,200,200),NPAR
  139 GO TO (200,200,200,200,214,200,200),NPAR
  216 IPX = IPX + 1000
  215 IPX = IPX + 1000
  214 IPX = IPX + 1000
  213 IPX = IPX + 1000
  212 IPX = IPX + 1000
  211 IPX = IPX + 1000
  210 IPX = IPX + 6000
  204 IPX = IPX + 1000
```

```
    203 IPX = IPX + 1000
    202 IPX = IPX + 1000
    201 DO 131 K = 1,NP2
        IF(IPX.EQ.IQ(K)) GO TO 150
    131 CONTINUE
        IF(NP2.EQ.NPMAX) WRITE(MED2,912)
        IF(NP2.EQ.NPMAX) GO TO 150
        NP2 = NP2 + 1
        IQ(NP2) = IPX
    150 CONTINUE
    200 CONTINUE
        IS2 = ISF
        RETURN
    900 FORMAT(61H STORAGE FOR SIGMA TERMS IS INSUFFICIENT - INCREASE MNPQ
       1 FROM,I4)
    901 FORMAT(61H STORAGE FOR SIGMA TERMS IS INSUFFICIENT - INCREASE MNPQ
       1 FROM,I4,13H TO AT LEAST ,I4)
    912 FORMAT(62H STORAGE FOR PARAMETERS IS INSUFFICIENT - INCREASE NPMAX
       1 FROM ,I4)
        END


        FUNCTION STAT(IPQ,R,IX,NPAR)
C STAT    (SEE 10.5 ) SERVICE      CONVERTS SUMS TO STATISTICS
C CALCULATES STATISTIC DEFINED BY IPQ - CODES GIVEN IN STASTA - 5.3
        DIMENSION R(NPAR),IX(NPAR)
C NULL VALUE
        STAT = -999.99
        IP = IPQ/1000
        IQ = IPQ - IP*1000
        S0 = 0.
        DO 20 I = 1,NPAR
        JP = IX(I)/1000
        JQ = IX(I) - JP*1000
        IF(JQ.NE.IQ) GO TO 20
        IF(JP.EQ.48) S0 = R(I)
        IF(JP.EQ. 1) S1 = R(I)
        IF(JP.EQ. 2) S2 = R(I)
        IF(JP.EQ. 3) S3 = R(I)
        IF(JP.EQ. 4) S4 = R(I)
        IF(JP.EQ. 5) S5 = R(I)
        IF(JP.EQ.10) S6 = R(I)
        IF(JP.EQ.20) S7 = R(I)
        IF(JP.EQ.30) S10= R(I)
        IF(JP.EQ.35) S8 = R(I)
        IF(JP.EQ.41) S9 = R(I)
     20 CONTINUE
        GO TO (1,2,2,4,4,6,7,8,9,10,11,12,13,14,15,16,17),IP
      1 IF(S0.GT.0.) STAT = S1/S0
        RETURN
      2 IF(S0.LE.1.) RETURN
        STAT = (S2-S1/S0*S1)/(S0-1.)
        IF(IP.EQ.2) STAT = SQRT(ABS(STAT))
        RETURN
      4 IF(S0.LE.1.) RETURN
        AM = S1/S0
        V = (S2-AM*S1)/(S0-1.)
        IF(IP.EQ.4)STAT =(S3/S0-3.*S2/S0*AM+2.*AM*AM*AM)/V/SQRT(ABS(V))
        IF(IP.EQ.5)STAT=(S4/S0-4.*S3/S0*AM+6.*S2/S0*AM*AM-3.*AM*AM*AM*AM)
       1/V/V
        RETURN
      6 IF(S0.LE.0.) RETURN
        STAT = EXP(S8/S0)
```

```
      RETURN
    7 IF(S0.LE.0..OR.S9.LE.0.) RETURN
      STAT = S0/S9
      RETURN
    8 STAT = S6
      RETURN
    9 STAT = S7
      RETURN
   10 STAT = S0
      RETURN
   11 STAT = S1
      RETURN
   12 STAT = S2
      RETURN
   13 STAT = S3
      RETURN
   14 STAT = S4
      RETURN
   15 STAT = S8
      RETURN
   16 STAT = S9
      RETURN
   17 STAT = S10
      RETURN
      END
```

Chapter XI

AUXILIARY PROGRAMS AND SUBROUTINES

This chapter describes two short programs and a number of auxiliary subroutines and functions not described elsewhere.

STCOPY provides a duplicate of a STATCAT data bank, with only the possibility of changing the data starter. This facility is useful for the provision of a back-up tape or disc file to protect against damage to (or loss of) the original.

STBANK provides a listing of the data starter, data description segment and the first ten entries of the data storage segment. This provides a quick check on the current contents of a STATCAT data bank. (It is surprisingly easy to forget what has been stored in a data bank, and the cost of confusion can be enormous.)

Section 11.3 describes subroutines for handling matrices. As well as mathematical manipulations, such as extracting eigenroots and eigen vectors, subroutines are provided for extracting matrices by selecting rows or columns, producing suitably labelled outputs or changing the way in which the matrix is stored.

Section 11.4 describes subroutines and functions used in ordering entries, matching entries, combining entries and determining priority.

Section 11.5 describes subroutines used in determining values for the chi-squared statistic, respecting conventions on the minimum expected values, and determining which rows or columns should be combined to minimise information loss.

Section 11.6 describes three small subprograms used to control the choice of tests and outputs in sample testing, to determine the start position of two-dimensional arrays using dynamic allocation, and to determine the next combination of variates to be used.

Section 11.7 describes subroutines which allocate data to classes, determine convenient class-intervals where these are not given, and output class descriptions when required.

Section 11.8 describes a particularly useful function for the derivation of the associated probability of various statistics.

Finally Section 11.9 describes two minor but ubiquitous subroutines which warn of mismatching of data and technique and find particular data column descriptions.

11.1 PROGRAM STCOPY - COPYING ENTIRE STATCAT DATA BANK

11.1.1 Purpose

This program makes an exact copy of a STATCAT data bank. The file name and security key of the input and output STATCAT data banks must be given, although the output file name and security key can be changed if required. Figure 11.11 is a system flow-chart for this program. There is no executive subroutine.

11.1.2 Input Data

Summary

Item	Level	Format	Function	See
1	0	A	File Control Card (Input and Output)	3.2
2	0	B	Data Starter	Below + 3.3

2 - Data Starter

This is a standard data starter, as described in 3.3, but only the items shown below are used.

Card Layout - Data Starter - STCOPY

```
ABCCCDDDEEEEEEEEFFFFFFFFFFFFFFFFFFFFFFFFFFFFFFFFFFFFFFFFGG...HHHHIIII
```

Columns on card	Item Code	FORTRAN Type	Function	See
1	A	I	Not used	-
2	B	I	Not used	-
3 - 5	C	F	Not used	-
6 - 8	D	F	Not used	-
9 - 16	E	F	Not used	-
17 - 56	F	A	STATCAT Data bank title	Below + 3.3
57 - 72	G	A	Auxiliary Security key	9.2
73 - 76	H	A	Security Key	3.3
77 - 80	I	A	File Name	3.3

STATCAT Data bank title

If this title is blank throughout the original title will be copied in its place.

11.1.3 Input Example

Figure 11.12 is a listing of input modules, indented according to the program structure, for copying a STATCAT data bank. Figure 11.13 lists the input cards required. The demonstration STATCAT data bank is copied onto another STATCAT data bank. The title of the copy is modified.

11.1.4 Output Example

Figure 11.14 gives the general structure of the output of STCOPY. Figure 11.15 gives a page-by-page summary of the output corresponding to the input example of Figure 11.13. Figure 11.16 gives the complete output for the copying operation. Note that the tape title has been changed from the original to that given on the data starter card, and that the tape name has also been changed from the original (specified on the file control card), to that specified on the data starter card. (In fact, the security key has also been changed, but this will not appear on the output for obvious reasons.)

11.1.5 Commentary

This program can only copy complete correct STATCAT data banks onto output STATCAT data banks which have already a correct readable data starter ready to be read by FIFI. Virgin tapes must be given a name by the use of STHEAD.

707

Figure 11.11 - System Flow-Chart - STCOPY

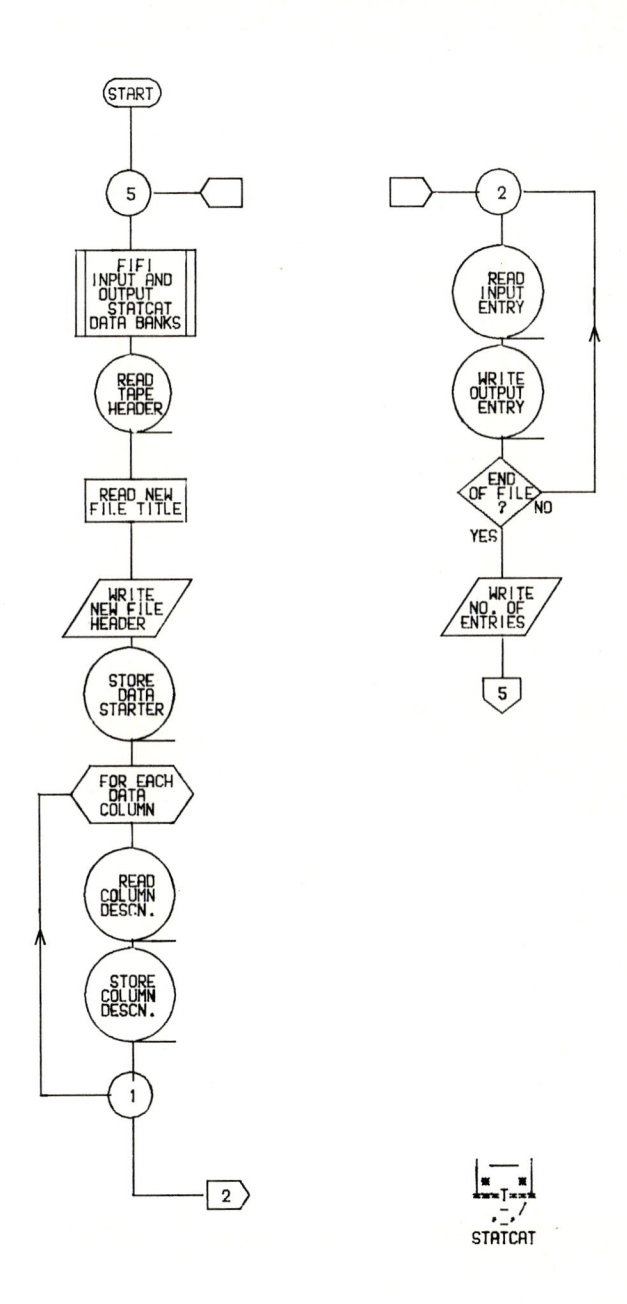

Figure 11.12 - STCOPY - Input Structure

```
        Level
 0    1   2   3   4   5   6   7   8   9
FILE CONTROL CARD
DATA STARTER CARD
STOP
```

Figure 11.13 - STCOPY - Input Example

```
---------1---------2---------3---------4---------5-----///-7---------8
**STCOPYDEMO    COPY
                DUPLICATE STATCAT DATA BANK                       COPY
STOP
---------1---------2---------3---------4---------5-----///-7---------8
```

Figure 11.14 - STCOPY - Output Structure

```
For each    ) : File Control Record
input and   )   Original File Parameters
output file     Revised File title
                Completion Message
                Entry Count
```

Figure 11.15 - STCOPY - Output Example - Page-by-Page Listing

Page	Contents	Origin
1	File Control Record	FIFI
4	Subset record Completion Record Entry Count	LSAMP
3	File Control Record (STOP)	FIFI

Figure 11.16 - STCOPY - Output Example - listing

```
RECORD OF FILE CONTROL OPERATIONS - PROGRAM STCOPY

LOAD FILE DEMO ON UNIT  17 READ ONLY
LOAD FILE COPY ON UNIT  18 READ/WRITE
                                                              - COMMENT
FILE ON UNIT  17 IS DEMO (FREE)
FILE ON UNIT  18 IS COPY (FREE)
SYSTEM RETURNS TO MAIN PROGRAM



            STATCAT COPY COMPLETE DATA BANK
```

FILE PARAMETERS

NUMBER OF DATA COLUMNS IS -   18

STORED NUMBER OF CLASSES IS   10

VALUE USED FOR MISSING DATA IS -   -1.00000000

FILE TITLE ON ORIGINAL TAPE WAS - DEMONSTRATION STATCAT DATA BANK   TAPE NAME DEMO

    FILE TITLE ON COPY TAPE IS - DUPLICATE STATCAT DATA BANK   TAPE NAME COPY

       COPYING COMPLETED

          64 ENTRIES ON NEW TAPE


```
        RECORD OF FILE CONTROL OPERATIONS - PROGRAM STCOPY
        STOP
```

```
C    MASTER STCOPY - COPIES STATCAT DATA BANK
C         SUBROUTINES AND FUNCTIONS EMPLOYED
C    NAME            TYPE                COMMENT
C    COMPA   (SEE  3.1 ) SERVICE    COMPARES ALPHAMERIC VALUES
C    COPYA   (SEE  3.1 ) SERVICE    COPIES ALPHAMERIC VALUE
C    FIFI    (SEE  3.2 ) SYSTEM     ALLOCATES PERIPHERALS
      DIMENSION TRT(1000),D(1000)
      COMMON /STCT/MED1,MED2,MED3,MED4,MED5,MED6,MED13,Q,V(20),TT(30)
      DATA PROG/4HCOPY/
      MED1 = -1
    5 CALL COPYA(TT(1),PROG)
      CALL FIFI
      REWIND MED3
      REWIND MED4
      READ (MED3) NQ,NALT,Q,(TT(J),J = 1,16)
      WRITE(MED2,901) NQ,NALT,Q,(TT(J),J = 1,10),TT(16)
      READ(MED1,900) (TT(J),J=1,16)
      WRITE(MED2,903) (TT(J),J=1,10),TT(16)
      WRITE(MED4    ) NQ,NALT,Q,(TT(J),J = 1,16)
      DO 1 I = 1,NQ
      READ (MED3) (TT(J),J =1,19),(TRT(J),J =1,NALT),IT,DMIN,DMAX
    1 WRITE(MED4) (TT(J),J =1,19),(TRT(J),J =1,NALT),IT,DMIN,DMAX
      ND = 0
    2 READ(MED3) (D(J),J =1,NQ)
      WRITE(MED4) (D(J),J =1,NQ)
      ND = ND + 1
      DO 3 J = 1,NQ
      IF(D(J).NE.Q) GO TO 2
    3 CONTINUE
      ND = ND - 1
    4 WRITE(MED4) (Q,J=1,NQ)
      WRITE(MED2,902)  ND
      REWIND MED3
      REWIND MED4
      GO TO 5
  900 FORMAT (16X,16A4)
  901 FORMAT (1H1,20X,46HSTATCAT COPY COMPLETE DATA BANK
     1                              /16H0FILE PARAMETER
     2S/29H0NUMBER OF DATA COLUMNS IS - ,I6/29H0STORED NUMBER OF CLASSES
     3 IS ,I6/34H0VALUE USED FOR MISSING DATA IS - ,F20.8/35H0FILE TITLE
     4 ON ORIGINAL TAPE WAS - ,10A4,10X,11H TAPE NAME ,A4)
  902 FORMAT (1H0,20X,17HCOPYING COMPLETED/1H0,20X,I6,20H ENTRIES ON NEW
     1 TAPE     )
  903 FORMAT (1H0, 6X,29HFILE TITLE ON COPY TAPE IS - ,10A4,10X,11H TAPE
     1 NAME ,A4)
      END
```

11.2 PROGRAM STBANK - VERIFYING STATCAT DATA BANK CONTENTS

11.2.1 Purpose

This program provides a rapid check on the contents of existing STATCAT data banks. It lists the data starter, data description segment, and the first ten entries (if there are that many). Figure 11.21 is a system flow-chart of the program. There is no executive subroutine.

11.2.2 Input Data

Summary

Item	Level	Format	Function	See
1	1	A	File Control Card (Input Only)	Below + 3.2

(Program will continue to read file control cards until it encounters a STOP card.)

11.2.3 Input Example

Figure 11.22 is a listing of the input modules indented according to the program structure . (In this case the program structure is as simple as it could be, so that this Figure is practically redundant.) Figure 11.23 lists the corresponding input cards for examining one STATCAT data bank.

11.2.4 Output Example

Figure 11.24 gives the general structure of the output of STBANK. Figure 11.25 gives a page-by-page summary of the output corresponding to the input example. Figure 11.26 lists the complete output for an empty STATCAT data bank (created by STHEAD - 4.1).

11.2.5 Commentary

This program produces a fixed format output. It assumes that numbers are within a reasonable range, and prints out the data in alphabetic form as well as in numeric.

Figure 11.21 - System Flow-Chart - STBANK

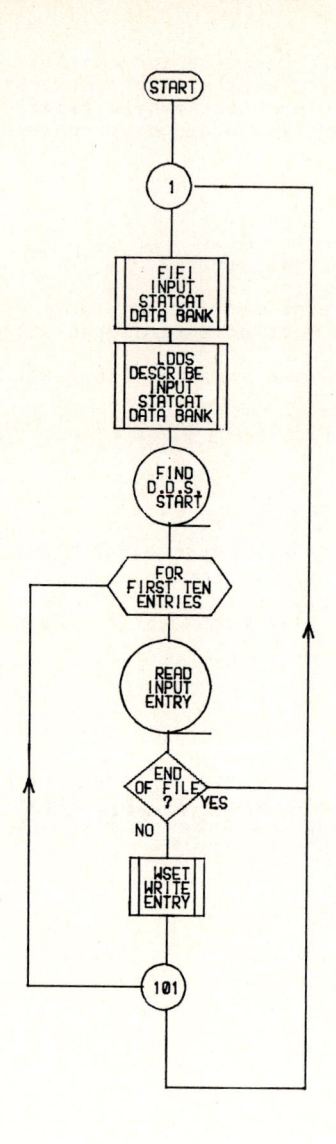

Figure 11.22 - STBANK - Input Structure

```
            Level
   0     1     2     3     4     5     6     7     8     9
FILE CONTROL CARD
STOP
```

Figure 11.23 - STBANK - Input Example

```
---------1----------2----------3----------4---------5---------6---------7--
**STBANKDUFF                             GENERAL OUTPUT DATA BANK
STOP
---------1----------2----------3----------4---------5---------6---------7--
```

Figure 11.24 - STBANK - Output Structure

```
For each    ) : File Control Record
input file  )   File Parameters
                Data Description
                For first ) : Entry Listing
                ten entries)
```

Figure 11.25 - STBANK - Output summary - Page-by-Page

Page	Contents	Origin
1	File Control Record	FIFI
	Program Title	STBANK
	File Parameters	LDAP
	Data Description record	LDDS
2 - 3	Entries	WSET
4	File Control Record (STOP)	FIFI

Figure 11.26 - STBANK - Output Example - Partial Output

```
                    RECORD OF FILE CONTROL OPERATIONS - PROGRAM STBANK

                    LOAD FILE DUFF ON UNIT  17 READ ONLY
                                 GENERAL OUTPUT DATA BANK               - COMMENT
                    FILE ON UNIT  17 IS DUFF (FREE)
                    SYSTEM RETURNS TO MAIN PROGRAM

                    STATCAT CHECKING TAPE DESCRIPTION

                    DATA BANK PARAMETERS FOR DUFF
                    ( EMPTY STATCAT DATA BANK - READY FOR USE  )

                       1 DATA COLUMNS (=ITEMS PER ENTRY)
                       1 CLASSES UNLESS OTHERWISE SPECIFIED
                      -1.0000 = NON-VALUE (MISSING DATUM)


                         DATA DESCRIPTION SEGMENT

COLUMN SCALE    SHORT           FULL TITLE
NUMBER CODE     TITLE                                                           LEVEL

  1     1       NULL        EMPTY STATCAT DATA BANK - READY FOR USE             DUMMY



          DATA BANK TITLE - EMPTY STATCAT DATA BANK - READY FOR USE
          DATA BANK SUBSET TITLE - FIRST TEN ENTRIES
                LISTED FROM COLUMN   1 TO COLUMN   1

          ENTRY NUMBER       1    FIRST DATA ITEM        0.0

              1
            NULL
            0.0


          ENTRY NUMBER       2    FIRST DATA ITEM        0.0

              1
            NULL
            0.0


          ENTRY NUMBER       3    FIRST DATA ITEM        0.0

              1
            NULL
            0.0


          ENTRY NUMBER       4    FIRST DATA ITEM        0.0

              1
            NULL
            0.0


          ENTRY NUMBER       5    FIRST DATA ITEM        0.0

              1
            NULL
            0.0


          ENTRY NUMBER       6    FIRST DATA ITEM        0.0

              1
            NULL
            0.0
```

```
C MASTER STBANK - CHECKS DATA DESCRIPTIONS OF DATA BANKS
C SUBROUTINES AND FUNCTIONS REQUIRED
C NAME          TYPE                   COMMENT
C COMPA   (SEE  3.1 ) SERVICE   COMPARES ALPHAMERIC VALUES
C COPYA   (SEE  3.1 ) SERVICE   COPIES ALPHAMERIC VALUE
C FIFI    (SEE  3.2 ) SYSTEM    ALLOCATES PERIPHERALS
C IBL     (SEE  3.1 ) SERVICE   DETECTS BLANK,END AND STOP CARDS
C LCOM    (SEE  3.4 ) SERVICE   LOADS COMPLEMENTARY INFORMATION
C LDAP    (SEE  3.3 ) SERVICE   LOAD/CHECK DATA BASE PARAMETERS
C LDDS    (SEE  3.4 ) SYSTEM    LOADS DATA DESCRIPTION SEGMENT
C WDCD    (SEE  3.4 ) SERVICE   WRITES DATA COLUMN DESCRIPTION
C WSET    (SEE  5.1 ) SERVICE   WRITE ENTRY - STANDARD FORM
C NQMAX = MAXIMUM NUMBER OF DATA COLUMNS
C DIMENSION D(NQMAX),DMAX(NQMAX),DMIN(NQMAX),IT(NQMAX),ST(NQMAX)
      NQMAX = 200
      DIMENSION D(200),DMAX(200),DMIN(200),IT(200),ST(200)
C DIMENSION  TRT(NALTMX) = NO. OF CLASSES ON FILE
      NALTMX = 100
      DIMENSION TRT(50)
C DIMENSION RT(NCAV) = REMAINING STORE : S = SUBSET TITLE
      NCAV = 5000
      DIMENSION RT(5000),S(5)
      COMMON /STCT/MED1,MED2,MED3,MED4,MED5,MED6,MED13,Q,V(20),TT(30)
      DATA PROG/4HBANK/,S/4HFIRS,4HT TE,4HN EN,4HTRIE,4HS    /
      MED1 = -1
C SETTING UP * LEVEL 0
    1 CALL COPYA(TT(1),PROG)
      CALL FIFI
      IF(MED2.GT.0) WRITE(MED2,901)
      CALL LDAP(MED2,MED3,V,TT,Q,NQ,NALT,NQMAX,NALTMX,IGO)
      NQALT = NQ*NALT
      IF(NQALT.GT.NCAV) NQR = 0
      IF(NQALT.LE.NCAV) NQR = NQ
      LI = 18
      CALL LDDS(TRT,NALT,D,NQ,ST,NQ,IT,NQ,RT,NQR,DMIN,DMAX,NQ,LI,0,Q,VX,
     1 0,MED2,MED3,0,IGO)
      IF(IGO.GT.0) GO TO 1
      REWIND MED3
C SET CONTROLS FOR WSET
      IF(NQALT.GT.NCAV) V(2) = 1.
      IF(NQALT.LE.NCAV) V(2) = 0.
      V(7) = 1.
      V(8) = NQ
      V(10) = 60.
      DO 98 I = 1,5
   98 CALL COPYA(TT(I+20),S(I))
      READ(MED3) NQ,NALT,Q,(TT(J),J=1,16)
      DO 99 I = 1,NQ
   99 READ(MED3) (X,J=1,19),(X,J=1,NALT),NX,X,X
      DO 101 NR = 1,10
      READ(MED3) (D(J),J=1,NQ)
      DO 100 J = 1,NQ
      IF(D(J).NE.Q) GO TO 101
  100 CONTINUE
      WRITE(MED2,902)
      REWIND MED3
      GO TO 1
  101 CALL WSET(D,NQ,RT,NQ,NALT,IT,ST,NR,TT,V,MED2)
      GO TO 1
  901 FORMAT (1H0,20X,33HSTATCAT CHECKING TAPE DESCRIPTION)
  902 FORMAT (1H0,20X,33HEND OF DATA STORAGE SEGMENT FOUND)
      END
```

11.3 MATRIX OPERATIONS MINV, MOP, WMAT, MATM AND ASEV

11.3.1 Purpose

These subroutines are employed by multivariate (and other) analysis programs to carry out matrix operations and to present matrices to the user in readable form.

Figure 11.31a contains system flow-charts for the subroutines MINV which inverts a matrix, MOP which moves matrices from store to store with a basic output in the process, and WMAT which provides a more elaborate output format. Figure 11.31b provides system flow-charts for the subroutines MATM which multiplies two matrices to form a third, and ASEV which finds the eigen-values and eigen-roots of a matrix - symmetrical or non-symmetrical. Brief descriptions of each subroutine follow, but space does not allow a detailed explanation of matrix algebra - the user should consult a reference text, or an expert.

It should be noted that all these subroutines employ arrays with single subscripts, and that the sizes of arrays are defined in the headings of the subroutines. This apparently clumsy technique has practical advantages - it improves the use of storage and allows more flexibility in defining arrays.

These subroutines are not necessarily the most efficient for all purposes, but they perform adequately in the context. (Faster versions can no doubt be derived by better mathematicians.)

11.3.2 Subroutine MINV

The subroutine MINV inverts a square matrix (which need not be symmetrical) using the Gauss-Jordan method. In principle, this subroutine operates by finding successive 'pivot' elements, swapping rows to place the pivot on the diagonal, dividing the pivot row by the pivot element, subtracting this row from the others and finding the next pivot element. When all rows have been treated, it returns the columns to their original order and returns to the calling program.

11.3.3 Subroutine MOP

The subroutine MOP is essentially a utility subroutine for moving matrices and changing their form. It can be used to select data stored in one matrix form, (square, rectangular, triangular) and store it in another form, with a print-out of the matrix on the way, if required.

11.3.4 Subroutine WMAT

The subroutine WMAT provides an annotated output of a matrix, with row and column identifications as required. It is limited to rectangular matrices.

11.3.5 Subroutine MATM

The subroutine MATM simply cross-multiplies two stored rectangular matrices to form a third matrix. The matrices are stored as single dimensioned arrays (vectors), but treated as being two-dimensional.

11.3.6 Subroutine ASEV

The subroutine ASEV extracts the roots and 'eigenvectors' from a square matrix. It can be used on either symmetric or non-symmetric matrices. This subroutine is based on the version provided by Veldmann (1967).

REFERENCES : Morrison (Ch 2), Searle (1966), Veldmann (Ch 7)

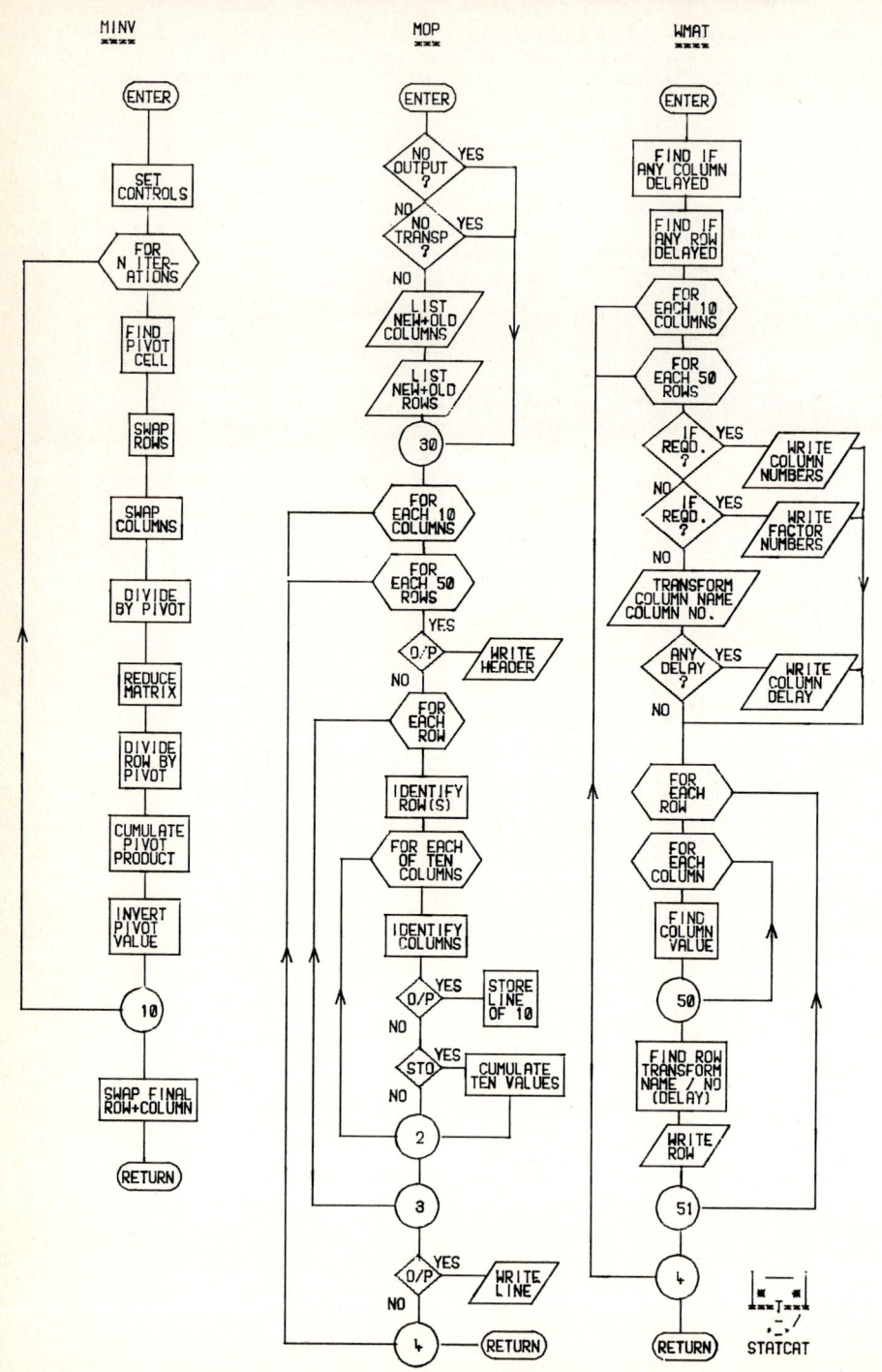

Figure 11.31a - System Flow-Charts - MINV, MOP and MOP

Figure 11.31b - System Flow-Charts - **MATM** and **ASEV**

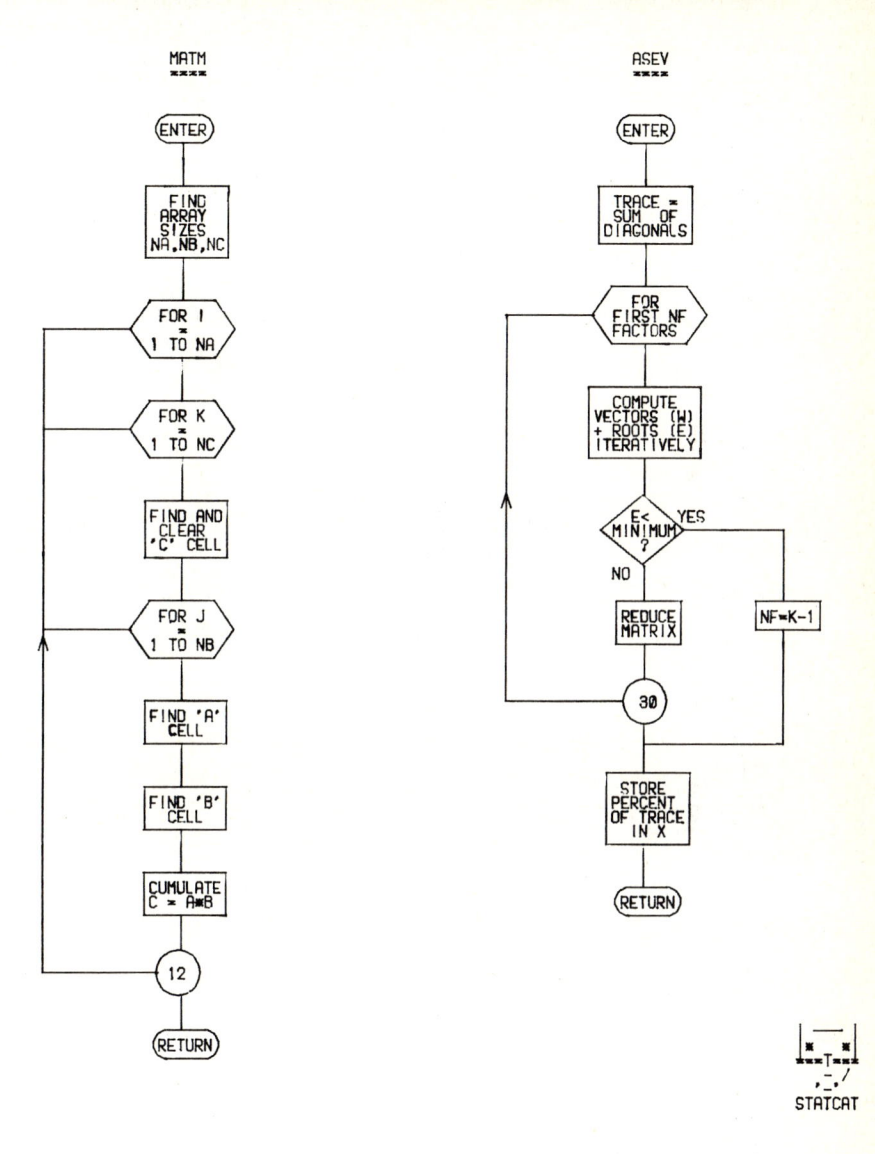

MATM

ENTER
↓
FIND ARRAY SIZES NA,NB,NC
↓
FOR I = 1 TO NA
↓
FOR K = 1 TO NC
↓
FIND AND CLEAR 'C' CELL
↓
FOR J = 1 TO NB
↓
FIND 'A' CELL
↓
FIND 'B' CELL
↓
CUMULATE C = A*B
↓
(12)
↓
RETURN

ASEV

ENTER
↓
TRACE = SUM OF DIAGONALS
↓
FOR FIRST NF FACTORS
↓
COMPUTE VECTORS (W) + ROOTS (E) ITERATIVELY
↓
E < MINIMUM? — YES → NF=K-1
↓ NO   ↓
REDUCE MATRIX
↓
(30) ←──────────────────┘
↓
STORE PERCENT OF TRACE IN X
↓
RETURN

STATCAT

```
      SUBROUTINE ASEV(A,C,E,M,MK,MXM,NF,W,X,Y,Z)
C ASEV    (SEE  7.5 ) SERVICE     EIGEN ROOTS ETC ASYMMETRIC MATRIX
C ROOTS AND DENORMALISED EIGENVECTORS FROM NON-SYMMETRIC SQUARE MATRIX
C A=SQUARE INPUT MATRIX (DESTROYED) C=SMALLEST EIGENVALUE TO BE EXTRACTD
C E = OUTPUT VECTOR OF ROOTS M=ORDER OF MATRIX MXM = M SQUARED
      DO 5 I = 1,M
      II = II + M + 1
    5 T = T + A(II)
C EXTRACT SUCCESSIVE ROOTS
      KBASE = -M
      DO 30 K = 1,NF
C ROOTS IN E(K) AND EK, VECTORS IN W(K) AND Z
      KBASE = KBASE + M
      DO 10 I = 1,M
      X(I) = 1.
   10 Y(I) = 1.
      EK = 1.
      E(K) = 1.
      DO 25 MM = 1,25
      DO 15 I = 1,M
      IK = I + KBASE
      W(IK) = X(I)/E(K)
   15 Z(I)  = Y(I)/EK
      LI = 0
      DO 20 I = 1,M
      X(I) = 0.
      Y(I) = 0.
      IL = I-M
      DO 20 L = 1,M
      IL = IL + M
      LK = L + KBASE
      LI = LI + 1
      X(I) = X(I) + A(IL)*W(LK)
   20 Y(I) = Y(I) + A(LI)*Z(L)
      EK = 0.
      E2 = 0.
      DO 21 L = 1,M
      EK = EK + Y(L)*Z(L)
      LK = L + KBASE
   21 E2 = E2 + X(L)*W(LK)
      E(K) = SQRT(ABS(E2))
   25 EK   = SQRT(ABS(EK))
      IF(E2.LT.C*C) GO TO 35
C DEFLATE R MATRIX
      D = 0.
      DO 26 L = 1,M
      LK = L + KBASE
   26 D = D + W(LK)*Z(L)
      D = E(K)/D
      DO 30 I = 1,M
      IJ = I - M
      IK = I + KBASE
      DO 30 J = 1,M
      IJ = IJ + M
   30 A(IJ) = A(IJ) - W(IK)*Z(J)*D
      GO TO 40
   35 NF = K-1
C PERCENTAGES OF TRACE
   40 DO 45 I = 1,NF
   45 X(I) = E(I)/T*100.0
      RETURN
      END
```

```
      SUBROUTINE MATM(A,B,C,KA,KB,KC,NAB,NBC,NAC)
C MATM    (SEE  7.5 ) SERVICE     MULTIPLIES MATRICES
C MULTIPLIES MATRIX A BY MATRIX B TO FORM MATRIX C
C A IS A KA BY KB MATRIX - IF KA IS NEGATIVE IT IS STORED TRANSPOSED
C B IS A KB BY KC MATRIX - IF KB IS NEGATIVE IT IS STORED TRANSPOSED
C C IS A KA BY KC MATRIX - IF KC IS NEGATIVE IT IS STORED TRANSPOSED
      DIMENSION A(NAB),B(NBC),C(NAC)
      NA = KA
      IF(NA) 1,13, 2
    1 NA = 0 - NA
    2 NB = KB
      IF(NB) 3,13,4
    3 NB = 0 - NB
    4 NC = KC
      IF(NC) 5,13, 6
    5 NC = 0 - NC
    6 DO 12 I = 1,NA
      DO 12 K = 1,NC
      INDC = I + (K - 1)*NA
      IF(KC) 7,13, 8
    7 INDC = K + (I - 1)*NC
    8 C(INDC) = 0.
      DO 12 J = 1,NB
      INDA = I + (J - 1)*NA
      IF(KA)9 ,13,10
    9 INDA = J + (I - 1)*NB
   10 INDB = J + (K - 1)*NB
      IF(KB)11,13,12
   11 INDB = K + (J - 1)*NC
   12 C(INDC) = C(INDC) + A(INDA)*B(INDB)
   13 RETURN
      END


      SUBROUTINE MINV(A,N,D,L,M,NXN)
C MINV    (SEE  7.3 ) SERVICE     GAUSS-JORDAN MATRIX INVERSION
      DIMENSION A(NXN),L(N),M(N)
C FIND LARGEST ELEMENT
      D=1.0
      NK=-N
      DO 10 K=1,N
      NK=NK+N
      L(K)=K
      M(K)=K
      KK=NK+K
      PV=A(KK)
      DO 2 J=K,N
      IZ=N*(J-1)
      DO 2 I=K,N
      IJ=IZ+I
      IF(ABS(PV).GE.ABS(A(IJ)))GO TO 2
      PV=A(IJ)
      L(K)=I
      M(K)=J
    2 CONTINUE
C SWAP ROWS
      J=L(K)
      IF(J.LE.K) GO TO 4
      KI=K-N
      DO 3 I=1,N
      KI=KI+N
      X=-A(KI)
      JI=KI-K+J
```

```
          A(KI)=A(JI)
        3 A(JI)=X
C SWAP COLUMNS
        4 I=M(K)
          IF(I.LE.K) GO TO 6
          JP=N*(I-1)
          DO 5 J=1,N
          JK=NK+J
          JI=JP+J
          X=-A(JK)
          A(JK)=A(JI)
        5 A(JI) =X
C SCALE DOWN BY -PV (RETURN IF PV IS ZERO WITH ZERO DETERMINANT)
        6 IF(PV.EQ.0.) D = 0.
          IF(PV.EQ.0.) RETURN
          VP = 1./PV
          DO 7 I=1,N
          IF(I.EQ.K) GO TO 7
          IK=NK+I
          A(IK)=-A(IK)*VP
        7 CONTINUE
C     REDUCE MATRIX
          DO 8 I=1,N
          IK=NK+I
          IJ=I-N
          DO 8 J=1,N
          IJ=IJ+N
          IF(I.EQ.K.OR.J.EQ.K) GO TO 8
          KJ=IJ-I+K
          A(IJ)=A(IK)*A(KJ)+A(IJ)
        8 CONTINUE
C     DIVIDE ROW BY PIVOT
          KJ=K-N
          DO 9 J=1,N
          KJ=KJ+N
        9 IF(J.NE.K) A(KJ) = A(KJ)*VP
C     PRODUCT OF PIVOTS
          D=D*PV
C     REPLACE PIVOT BY RECIPROCAL
          A(KK)= VP
       10 CONTINUE
C SWAP FINAL ROW AND COLUMN
          DO 14 KK = 1,N
          K= N - KK
          IF(K.EQ.0) RETURN
          I=L(K)
          IF(I.LE.K) GO TO 12
          JQ=N*(K-1)
          JR=N*(I-1)
          DO 11 J=1,N
          JQ=JQ+1
          X=A(JQ)
          JR=JR+1
          A(JQ)=-A(JR)
       11 A(JR)=X
       12 J=M(K)
          IF(J.LE.K) GO TO 14
          KI=K-N
          DO 13 I=1,N
          KI=KI+N
          X=A(KI)
          JI=KI-K+J
          A(KI)=-A(JI)
```

```
   13 A(JI)=X
   14 CONTINUE
      END


      SUBROUTINE MOP (A,MA,NCA,MRA,NSA,B,MB,NCB,MRB,NSB,NC,MC,NSC,NR,MR,M
     1NSR,NT,MED2)
C MOP      (SEE  7.4 ) SERVICE       SELECTS/CONVERTS STORED MATRIX
C TRANSFORMS SQUARE OR TRIANGULAR MATRICES + WRITES MATRIX
C MATRIX A IN MODE MA HAS NCA BY NRA = NSA CELLS INPUT
C MATRIX B IN MODE MB HAS NCB BY NRB = NSB CELLS OUTPUT
C VECTOR NC HAS NSC CELLS - CONTROL MODE MC    COLUMNS
C VECTOR NR HAS NSR CELLS - CONTROL MODE MR        ROWS
C NT IS STRATEGIC CONTROL
C MED2 IS OUTPUT MEDIUM
C VALUE     MA,MB              MC,MR                   NT
C   1       RECTANGULAR        PRESENT ORDER       WRITE ONLY
C   2       SQUARE             I IN A= NC(I) IN B LOAD TO B
C   3       UPPER TRIANGULAR   NC(I) IN A = I IN B WRITE + LOAD
C   4       LOWER TRIANGULAR
      DIMENSION A(NSA),B(NSB),NC(NSC),NR(NSR),X(10)
      NRA = MRA
      NRB = MRB
      IF(MA.GT.1) NRA = NCA
      IF(MB.GT.1) NRB = NCB
      IF(NT.EQ.1) GO TO 50
      DO 1 I = 1,NSB
    1 B(I) = 0.
   50 IF(NT.EQ.2) GO TO 30
      IF(MC.EQ.1.AND.MR.EQ.1) GO TO 30
      WRITE(MED2,902)
      DO 55 I = 1,NCB
      IF(MC-2)51,53,52
   51 WRITE(MED2,904)I,I
      GO TO 55
   52 WRITE(MED2,904)I,NC(I)
      GO TO 55
   53 WRITE(MED2,904)I
      DO 54 J = 1,NCA
      IF(NC(J).NE.I) GO TO 54
      WRITE(MED2,905) J
   54 CONTINUE
   55 CONTINUE
      WRITE(MED2,906)
      DO 60 I = 1,NRB
      IF(MR-2)56,58,57
   56 WRITE(MED2,904)I,I
      GO TO 60
   57 WRITE(MED2,904)I,NC(I)
      GO TO 60
   58 WRITE(MED2,904)I
      DO 59 J = 1,NRA
      IF(NR(J).NE.I) GO TO 59
      WRITE(MED2,905) J
   59 CONTINUE
   60 CONTINUE
   30 DO 4 IST = 1,NCB,10
      IFIN = IST + 9
      IF(IFIN.GT.NCB) IFIN = NCB
      DO 4 JST = 1,NRB,50
      JFIN = JST + 49
      IF(JFIN.GT.NRB) JFIN = NRB
      IF(NT.NE.2) WRITE(MED2,901) (I,I=IST,IFIN)
```

```
      DO 4 J = JST,JFIN
      DO 3 I = IST,IFIN
      K = I - IST + 1
      IF(NT.NE.2)X(K) = 0.
      DO 3 IA = 1,NCA
      IF(MC.EQ.1.AND.IA.NE.I)        GO TO 3
      IF(MC.NE.2) GO TO 31
      IF(IA.GT.NSC  ) GO TO 3
      IF(NC(IA).NE.I) GO TO 3
   31 IF(MC.NE.3) GO TO 32
      IF(I.GT.NSC   ) GO TO 3
      IF(IA.NE.NC(I)) GO TO 3
   32 DO 2 JA = 1,NRA
      IF(MR.EQ.1.AND.JA.NE.J)        GO TO 2
      IF(MR.NE.2) GO TO 33
      IF(JA.GT.NSR  ) GO TO 2
      IF(NR(JA).NE.J) GO TO 2
   33 IF(MR.NE.3) GO TO 34
      IF(J.GT.NSR   ) GO TO 2
      IF(JA.NE.NR(J)) GO TO 2
   34 IJ = IA + (JA-1)*NCA
      IF(MA.EQ.3) IJ = IA +(JA-1)*(2*NCA - JA)/2
      IF(MA.EQ.3.AND.IA.LT.JA)IJ = JA + (IA-1)*(2*NCA-IA)/2
      IF(MA.EQ.4) IJ = IA +(JA-1)*JA/2
      IF(MA.EQ.4.AND.IA.GT.JA) IJ = JA + (IA-1)*(IA)/2
      IF(NT.NE.2)X(K) = X(K) + A(IJ)
      IF(NT.EQ.1) GO TO 2
      IF(MB.EQ.3.AND.I.LT.J) GO TO 2
      IF(MB.EQ.4.AND.I.GT.J) GO TO 2
      IJB = I + (J-1)*NCB
      IF(MB.EQ.3)IJB = I + (J-1)*(2*NCB-J)/2
      IF(MB.EQ.4) IJB = I +(J-1)*J/2
      B(IJB) = B(IJB) + A(IJ)
    2 CONTINUE
    3 CONTINUE
      IF(NT.EQ.2) GO TO 4
      IJ = IFIN - IST + 1
      WRITE(MED2,903)(J,(X(K),K = 1,IJ))
    4 CONTINUE
      RETURN
  901 FORMAT(10(6X,I4))
  902 FORMAT (19HONUMBERS OF COLUMNS/1H ,5X,13HNEW    ORIGINAL)
  903 FORMAT(I4,10F10.4)
  904 FORMAT (1H ,2(4X,I4))
  905 FORMAT (1H+,12X,I4/)
  906 FORMAT (19HONUMBERS OF ROWS   /1H ,5X,13HNEW    ORIGINAL)
      END


      SUBROUTINE WMAT (A,NC,NR,NCR,NP,NDP,M,ST,MQ,ISAVE,JSAVE,U,NU,MED2)
C WMAT    (SEE 7.4 ) SERVICE     WRITE MATRIX WITH VARIATE TITLES
      DIMENSION A(NCR),NP(M),NDP(M),ST(NQ),ISAVE(NC),JSAVE(NR)
      DIMENSION X(10),U(NU)
      DATA EQ/1H=/
      KC = 1
      IF(JSAVE(1).LT.0) KC = -1
      IF(JSAVE(1).LT.0) JSAVE(1) = - JSAVE(1)
      JDEL = 0
      DO 52 J = 1,NR
      INDX = JSAVE(J)
   52 IF(NDP(INDX).NE.0) JDEL = 1
      IDEL = 0
      IF(ISAVE(1).LE.0) GO TO 54
```

```
      DO 53 I = 1,NC
      INDX = ISAVE(I)
   53 IF(NDP(INDX).NE.0) IDEL = 1
   54 DO 50 IST = 1,NC,10
      NLIN = 0
      IFIN = IST + 9
      IF(IFIN.GT.NC)IFIN = NC
      IMAX = IFIN-IST + 1
      DO 50 JST = 1,NR,50
      JFIN = JST + 49
      IF(JFIN.GT.NR) JFIN = NR
      NLIN = NLIN + 6 + JFIN - JST
      IF(NLIN.GT.55)WRITE(MED2,900)
      IF(NLIN.GT.55)NLIN = 0
C     PRINT COLUMN TITLES - STARTING WITH COLUMN NUMBER IN ARRAY
      IF(ISAVE(1).EQ.0) WRITE(MED2,901) (I,I=IST,IFIN)
      IF(ISAVE(1).EQ.-1)WRITE(MED2,910) (I,I=IST,IFIN)
      IF(ISAVE(1).LE.0) GO TO 49
C     TRANSFORM NAME
      DO 1 I = 1,IMAX
      INDX = I+IST-1
      INDX = ISAVE(INDX)
      INDX = NP(INDX)/1000
    1 CALL COPYA(X(I),U(INDX))
      WRITE(MED2,902) (X(I),I = 1,IMAX)
C     ORIGINAL DATA COLUMN SHORT NAME
      DO 2 I = 1,IMAX
      INDX = I+IST-1
      INDX = ISAVE(INDX)
      INDX = NP(INDX)
      INDX = INDX- INDX/1000*1000
    2 CALL COPYA(X(I),ST(INDX))
      WRITE(MED2,903) (EQ,X(I),I=1,IMAX)
C     ORIGINAL DATA COLUMN NUMBER
      DO 4 I = 1,IMAX
      INDX = I + IST - 1
      INDX = ISAVE(INDX)
    4 X(I) = NP(INDX)-NP(INDX)/1000*1000
      WRITE(MED2,907) (X(I),I=1,IMAX)
C     DELAY IF ANY
      IF(IDEL.EQ.0) GO TO 49
      DO 3 I = 1,IMAX
      INDX = I+IST-1
      INDX = ISAVE(INDX)
    3 X(I) = NDP(INDX) -NDP(INDX)/1000*1000
      WRITE(MED2,906) (X(I),I=1,IMAX)
C     ROW  TITLE HEADER
   49 WRITE (MED2,904)
      IF(JDEL.NE.0) WRITE(MED2,909)
C     WRITE MATRIX WITH ROW TITLES - LINE BY LINE
      DO 50 J = JST,JFIN
      DO 51 I = 1,IMAX
      IF(KC.LT.0) INDX = J + (I+IST-2)*NR
      IF(KC.GT.0)INDX = I + IST - 1 + (J-1) * NC
   51 X(I) = A(INDX)
      INDX = JSAVE(J)
      INDA = NP(INDX)
      INDB = INDA/1000
      INDA = INDA - INDB*1000
      INDX = NDP(INDX)
      INDX = INDX- INDX/1000*1000
      WRITE(MED2,905)U(INDB),INDA,ST(INDA),      (X(I),I = 1,IMAX)
   50 IF(INDX.NE.0) WRITE(MED2,908)   INDX
```

```
      JSAVE(1) = JSAVE(1) * KC
      RETURN
  900 FORMAT (1H1)
  901 FORMAT(17X                , 10(6X,I4))
  902 FORMAT(15H0   TRANSFORM    ,5X,10(2X,A4,4H OF ))
  903 FORMAT (3X,13HCOLUMN (NAME),4X,10(5X,A1,A4))
  904 FORMAT(17H TRANSFORM COLUMN      )
  905 FORMAT(1H ,A4,3H OF,I3,1H(,A4,1H),4X,10F10.4)
  906 FORMAT(14H ENTRIES DELAY,6X,10(F5.0,5X))
  907 FORMAT(1H+,14X,10(5X,F5.0))
  908 FORMAT (1H+,16X,I4)
  909 FORMAT(1H+,17X,5HDELAY)
  910 FORMAT (14H FACTOR NUMBER,3X,10(6X,I4))
      END
```

11.4 ORDERING SUBROUTINES - PR, INSERT, POSN AND POSCL

11.4.1 Purpose

These subroutines are used to sort and order entries from a STATCAT data bank into a specified order, to provide ordered or synchronised outputs, directly to the user or for incorporation in an output STATCAT data bank.

Figure 11.41a contains a system flow-charts for the subroutine INSERT which inserts an entry into a stored array and the function PR which determines priority. Figure 11.41b contains system flow-charts for the functions POSN which finds the position of an entry in an array and POSCL which operates similarly where entries are in classes). entries are in classes).

The two subroutines INSERT and PR and the function POSN are used to perform the tactical operations of ordering entries in direct access storage in a specified priority order.

The array RT is used to store the entries being sorted in successive rows. The vector IL contains the numbers of the rows in priority order, the value in IL(1) being the row in which the first priority entry is stored.

11.4.2 Subroutine INSERT

The subroutine INSERT adds the line ILX in the position given by the parameter POS, finding a value for POS if it is not given, and updating the priority list RL accordingly. It can also be used (in STASTA - 5.3) to combine entries having equal priority according to specified combination codes. The subroutine INSERT may be arranged to reject values coming before or after the block already arranged in order.

11.4.3 Function PR

The subroutine PR determines which of the two lines in RT specified its two first parameters is first in priority order. If they are of equal priority, it returns with the value 0 in NP, otherwise with the number 1 or 2. It uses the priority codes and variates specified in the priority specification, in the order specified. It tests each specified data column according to the priority rule specified, until it reaches a decision or it has no more columns to test and assumes a tie.

11.4.4 Function POSN

The function POSN determines the correct position of a specified line of RT (ILX) in the priority order. It does not insert the entry, because intervening logic may require the entry to be rejected in some circumstances. POSN operates in principle by testing whether the entry is in front of, or behind, the block of entries represented by existing lines in RT, then by carrying out a binary search of the entries until either a pair of entries is found between which this entry should be placed, or an entry is found with the same priority, in which case succeeding entries are examined to find the last in order with the same priority. The value of POSN is increased by 0.5 in the first and by 0.1 in the second case.

11.4.5 Function POSCL

The function POSCL carries out essentially the same task as POSN, except that, where required, it classifies the data in the original line (replacing values by their class numbers) before finding its place in the array.

729

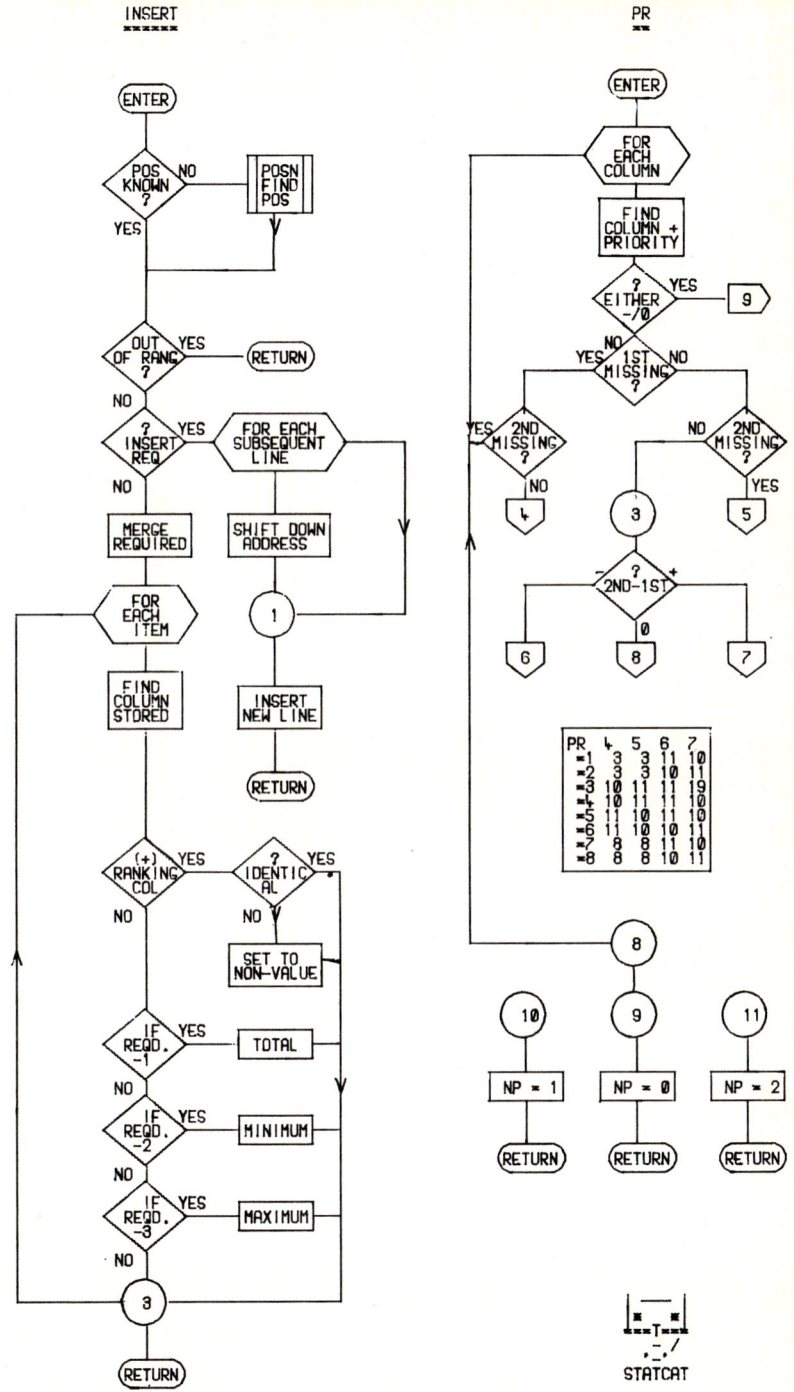

Figure 11.41a - System Flow-Charts - INSERT and PR

Figure 11.41b - System Flow-Charts - POSN and POSCL

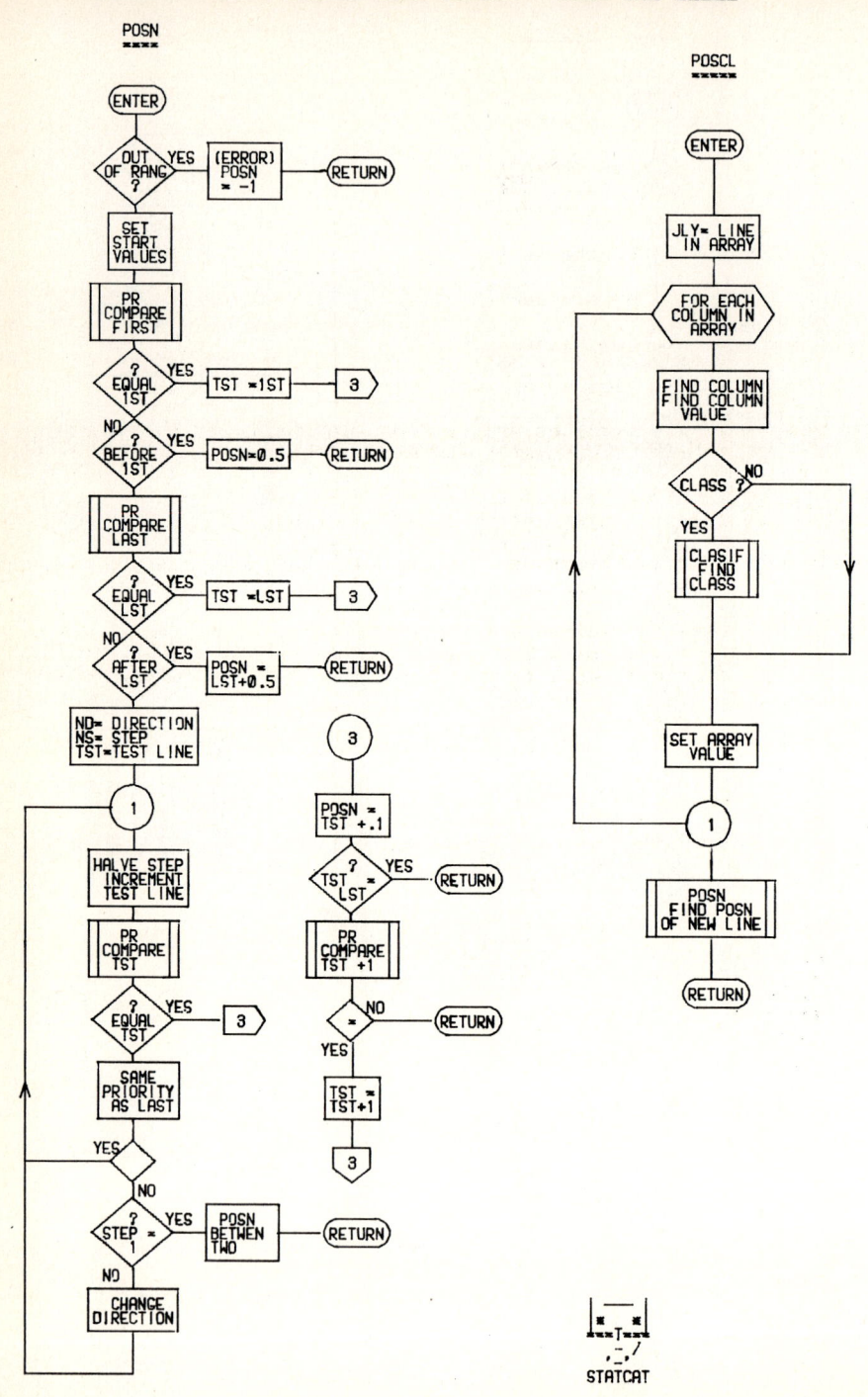

Figure 11.42 - Priority Codes

Priority Code	Ordering	Non-values
1Q2.	Low value first	Included
2Q1.	High value first	Included
12Q.	Low value first	Following
21Q.	High value first	Following
Q12.	Low value first	Leading
Q21.	High value first	Leading
12-.	Low value first	Ignored
21-.	High value first	Ignored

Included - When non-values are included in the ordering, they are treated as normal numbers and ordered accordingly.

Following- When non-values are placed following, they are given lower priority than any value and ordered accordingly.

Leading   - When non-values are placed leading, they are given higher priority than any value and ordered accordingly.

Ignored   - When non-values are ignored, the ordering process skips the data columns where either entry has a non-value, and continues with the next priority specification, if any.

```
      SUBROUTINE INSERT(RT,IMAX,NLMAX,IL,IDP,IP,ILX,NL,Q,IC,ID,POS)
C INSERT (SEE 11.4 ) SERVICE     INSERTS ENTRY INTO ARRAY
C INSERTS ( + IF IC=1 MERGES) LINE ILX(LE.NLMAX) IN ARRAY IL
C LINES ARE IMAX LONG, ORDERING GIVEN BY IP/IDP
C ID =      0         1          2          3        OTHER
C ACCEPT BEFORE                 BEFORE                BEFORE
C         WITHIN    WITHIN      WITHIN     WITHIN     WITHIN
C         AFTER     AFTER                             AFTER
C IP(N) = NTH COLUMN IN ORDER
C IDP(N) = ORDERING/MERGING CONTROL FOR NTH COLUMN IN ORDER
C IDP = -3    -2    -1    0    1    2    3    4    5    6    7    8
C  MINI MAXI     SUM   KEEP  1Q2  2Q1  Q12  Q21  12Q  21Q  12   21
C IF IDP = 0 VALUE IS KEPT IF EQUAL TO VALUE SO FAR - IE COMMON
C IF IDP LE 0 RANKING STOPS
      DIMENSION RT(IMAX,NLMAX),IDP(IMAX),IP(IMAX),IL(NLMAX)
      IF(POS.LT.0.) POS=POSN(RT,IMAX,NLMAX,IL,IDP,IP,ILX,NL,Q)
      IX = POS
      IF(IX.EQ.0.AND.ID.EQ.1.OR.IX.EQ.0.AND.ID.EQ.3) RETURN
      POSX = IX
      IF(POS-POSX.LT..3.AND.IC.EQ.1) GO TO 2
C INSERT LINE IN SEQUENCE
      ILX = IL(ILX)
      ILN = POS + 1.0
      IF(ILN.GT.NL.AND.ID.EQ.2.OR.ILN.GT.NL.AND.ID.EQ.3) RETURN
      IF(NL.EQ.0) GO TO 4
      DO 1 I = 1,NL
      J = NL + 1 - I
      IF(J.GE.ILN.AND.J.LT.NLMAX) IL(J+1) = IL(J)
      IF(J.LT.ILN) GO TO 4
    1 CONTINUE
    4 IL(ILN) = ILX
      ILX = 0
      RETURN
C ADD TO EXISTING LINE
    2 IX = IL(IX)
      ILY = IL(ILX)
      DO 3 I = 1,IMAX
      J = IP(I)-IP(I)/1000*1000
      IF(IDP(I).LT.0.AND.RT(J,IX).EQ.Q) GO TO 3
      IF(IDP(I).GE.0.AND.RT(J,IX).NE.RT(J,ILY)) RT(J,IX) = Q
      IF(IDP(I).EQ.-1.AND.RT(J,ILY).NE.Q)RT(J,IX) = RT(J,IX) + RT(J,ILY)
      IF(IDP(I).EQ.-2.AND.RT(J,IX).LT.RT(J,ILY)) RT(J,IX) = RT(J,ILY)
      IF(IDP(I).EQ.-3.AND.RT(J,IX).GT.RT(J,ILY)) RT(J,IX) = RT(J,ILY)
    3 IF(IDP(I).LT.0.AND.RT(J,IX).EQ.Q)            RT(J,IX) = RT(J,ILY)
      RETURN
      END


      FUNCTION POSCL(RT,NC,NRAV,IL,D,DMAX,DMIN,NCL,IT,M,IC,IP,IE,IG,NL,I
     1LX)
C POSCL  (SEE 11.4 ) SERVICE     FINDS POSITION - CLASSIFIED IF REQD
C PUTS SET,CLASSIFIED IF NECESSARY,INTO ILX - RETURNS WITH POSN OF ILX
C NC = NUMBER OF COLUMNS IN ARRAY    IC=0;VALUE  IC=1;CLASS
C IP=COLUMNS SELECTED FROM D IN ORDER IE=ORDER IN WHICH COLS ARE TESTED
C IG = PRIORITY RULES FOR COLUMNS UP TO NC IN ORDER
      DIMENSION RT(NC,NRAV),IL(NRAV),D(M),DMAX(M),DMIN(M),NCL(M),IT(M)
      DIMENSION IC(NC),IE(NC),IG(NC),IP(NC)
      COMMON /STCT/MED1,MED2,MED3,MED4,MED5,MED6,MED13,Q,V(20),TT(30)
      JLY = IL(ILX)
      DO 1 I = 1,NC
      ILY = IP(I) - IP(I)/1000*1000
      X = D(ILY)
      IF(IC(I).EQ.0) GO TO 1
```

```
      CALL CLASIF(X,DMAX(ILY),DMIN(ILY),IT(ILY),NCL(ILY),J)
      X = J
    1 RT(I,JLY) = X
      POSCL = POSN(RT,NC,NRAV,IL,IG,IE,ILX,NL,Q)
      RETURN
      END


      FUNCTION POSN (RT,IMAX,NLMAX,IL,IDP,IP,ILX,NL,Q)
C POSN    (SEE 11.4 ) SERVICE       FINDS POSITION OF ENTRY IN ORDER
C FINDS CORRECT POSITION FOR LINE IN ARRAY
C   ILX IS POSITION OF LINE IN ARRAY      MUST EXCEED NL,BUT NOT NLMAX
C POSN = I+ .1 WHERE I IS LAST ITEM EQUAL TO ILX
C I = I + .5 IF ILX COMES BETWEEN I AND I+1
      DIMENSION RT(IMAX,NLMAX),IDP(IMAX),IP(IMAX),IL(NLMAX)
      POSN = -1.
      IF(ILX.LE.NL.OR.ILX.GT.NLMAX) RETURN
      POSN = 0.5
      IF(NL.EQ.0) RETURN
      IQ = IL(ILX)
      IT = IL(1)
      NT = 1
      CALL PR(IQ,IT,NP,RT,IP,IDP,IMAX,NLMAX,Q)
      IF(NP.EQ.0) GO TO 3
C BEFORE FIRST ITEM IN PRIORITY ORDER
      IF(NP.NE.2) RETURN
      POSN = FLOAT(NL) + 0.5
      IT = IL(NL)
      NT = NL
      CALL PR(IQ,IT,NP,RT,IP,IDP,IMAX,NLMAX,Q)
      IF(NP.EQ.0) GO TO 3
C AFTER LAST ITEM IN PRIORITY ORDER
      IF(NP.NE.1) RETURN
      ND = -1
      NS = NL
      NT = NL
      NPL = 1
    1 NS = NS/2
      IF(NS.LE.0) NS = 1
      NT = NT + ND*NS
      IF(NT.LT.1) NT = 1
      IF(NT.GT.NL) NT = NL
      IT = IL(NT)
      CALL PR(IQ,IT,NP,RT,IP,IDP,IMAX,NLMAX,Q)
      IF(NP.EQ.0) GO TO 3
      IF(NP.EQ.NPL) GO TO 1
      IF(NS.LE.1) GO TO 2
      ND = -ND
      NPL = NP
      GO TO 1
C BETWEEN VALUES
    2 POSN =FLOAT(NT*2 - ND*NS) + 0.5
      RETURN
C FIND LAST VALUE EQUAL TO ITEM GIVEN
    3 POSN = FLOAT(NT) + 0.1
      IF(NT.EQ.NL) RETURN
      IT = IL(NT+1)
      CALL PR(IQ,IT,NP,RT,IP,IDP,IMAX,NLMAX,Q)
      IF(NP.NE.0) RETURN
      NT = NT + 1
      GO TO 3
      END
```

```
      SUBROUTINE PR (NA,NB,NP,RT,IP,IDP,NQ,NCAV,Q)
C PR     (SEE 11.4 ) SERVICE      DETERMINES PRIORITY IN SORTING
      DIMENSION RT(NQ,NCAV),IP(NQ),IDP(NQ)
C IDP
C  1   LOW VALUE FIRST     (MISSING VALUES INCLUDED)
C  2   HIGH VALUE FIRST    (MISSING VALUES INCLUDED)
C  3   LOW VALUE FIRST     (MISSING VALUES FIRST   )
C  4   HIGH VALUE FIRST    (MISSING VALUES FIRST   )
C  5   LOW VALUE FIRST     (MISSING VALUES LAST    )
C  6   HIGH VALUE FIRST    (MISSING VALUES LAST    )
C  7   LOW VALUE FIRST     (MISSING VALUES IGNORED )
C  8   HIGH VALUE FIRST    (MISSING VALUES IGNORED )
      NP = 0
      IPR = 0
      DO 8 I = 1,NQ
      ICH = IP(I)
      IF(IDP(I).LE.0) RETURN
      IF(IDP(I).NE.0) IPR = IDP(I)
      IF(ICH.EQ.0) GO TO 9
      IF(IPR.EQ.0) GO TO 8
      IF(RT(ICH,NA)-Q) 1,2,1
    1 IF(RT(ICH,NB)-Q) 3,5,3
    2 IF(RT(ICH,NB)-Q) 4,8,4
    3 IF(RT(ICH,NB)-RT(ICH,NA))6,8,7
    4 GO TO (3,3,10,10,11,11,8,8),IPR
    5 GO TO (3,3,11,11,10,10,8,8),IPR
    6 GO TO (11,10,11,10,11,10,11,10),IPR
    7 GO TO (10,11,10,11,10,11,10,11),IPR
    8 CONTINUE
    9 RETURN
   10 NP = 1
      RETURN
   11 NP = 2
      RETURN
      END
```

11.5   CHI-SQUARED AUXILIARIES - REDROW, DICOLA AND CHISQ

11.5.1   Purpose

These subroutines are employed by several statistical tests - CHISQD, MEDEX and QAREX - to ensure that the frequency tables on which the chi-squared test is carried out conforms to the conventional requirements - that not more than 20 per cent of expected values should be less than five, and that none should be less than one.

Figure 11.51 provides system flow-charts for the subroutines REDROW which finds the preferred combination of rows (or columns), DICOLA (which reports the choices to the user) and CHISQ (which evaluates the actual chi-squared value).

11.5.2   Subroutine REDROW

The subroutine REDROW operates on the row and column totals for a two-way table, and a pair of vectors storing the numbers of the combined rows or columns to which the totals are currently allocated. For each combined row, the total numbers of cells with expected frequencies under five and under one are calculated, the totals are cumulated, and the row with the largest number of expectations below five is noted. If after cumulating for all rows, the total of cells below five is greater than one-fifth of the number of separate cells, or if any cell has an expectation below one, then the noted row is combined with its neighbour, and the total cells below one and below five recalculated.

Note that only one row is eliminated at each call to REDROW. This allows it to be used more flexibly, by - for example - CHISQD, in which it may be called as described here, or (with rows and columns reversed) to reduce the number of columns, depending on the number of separate rows and columns remaining and their data levels.

11.5.3   Subroutine DICOLA

The subroutine DICOLA reports which rows and/or columns have been combined when a chi-squared statistic is obtained from a two-way table where rows or columns have been combined - to respect frequency minima or to perform a Median test.

11.5.4   Subroutine CHISQ

The subroutine CHISQ is the basic work-horse for chi-squared tests. Working from a two-way table, and index vectors specifying how rows and columns should be combined, it returns with the resultant associated probability, chi-squared value, remaining degrees of freedom, and number of cells with expected values remaining below one and below five.

With an appropriate setting for the output control index, this subroutine will also tabulate cell values (observed and expected), with their contribution to the total chi-squared value, printing warnings if the frequency minima are not respected.

Figure 11.51 - System Flow-Charts - REDROW, DICOLA and CHISQ

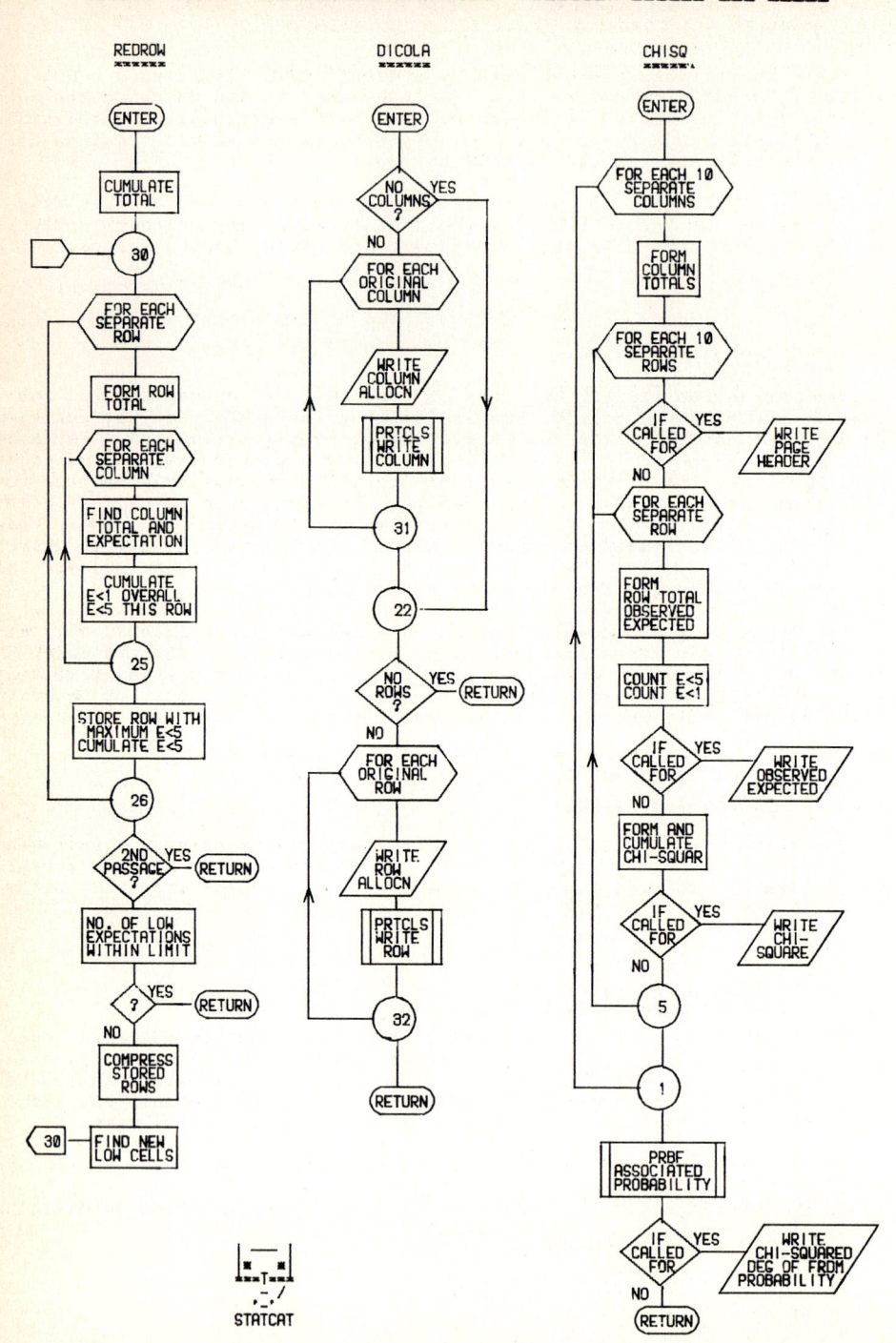

```
      SUBROUTINE CHISQ (RT,NC,NR,KC,KR,NSC,NSR,NUND5,NUND1,V,MED2)
C CHISQ  (SEE 11.5 ) STATISTICAL BASIC CHI-SQUARED CALCULATION
C CHI-SQUARED FOR COMBINED TABLE-NOT SELF ADJUSTING
C USED BY CHISQD, MEDEX AND QAREX
      DIMENSION RT(NC,NR),KR(NR),KC(NC),CT(10),COB(10),CEX(10)
      DIMENSION V(20)
      CHI=0.
      NUND1=0
      NUND5=0
      DO 1 ISF=1,NSC,10
      IFIN=ISF+9
      IF(IFIN.GT.NSC) IFIN=NSC
    2 NUSED=IFIN-ISF+1
      GT=0.
      DO 3 L=1,NUSED
    3 CT(L)=0.
      DO 4 J=1,NR
      DO 4 I=1,NC
      IQ=KC(I)-ISF+1
      IF(IQ.LT.1.OR.IQ.GT.NUSED) GO TO 4
      CT(IQ)=CT(IQ)+RT(I,J)
    4 GT=GT+RT(I,J)
      DO 5 JST=1,NSR,10
      IF(V(1).GT.1..AND.ISF.NE.1.OR.V(1).GT.1..AND.JST.NE.1) WRITE(MED2,9
     189)
      JFIN = JST + 9
      IF(JFIN.GT.NSR) JFIN = NSR
      DO 5 JSF = JST,JFIN
      DO 6 L=1,NUSED
    6 COB(L)=0.
      RRT=0.
      DO 7 I=1,NC
      DO 7 J=1,NR
      IF(KR(J).NE.JSF) GO TO 7
      RRT=RRT+RT(I,J)
      IQ=KC(I)-ISF+1
      IF(IQ.LT.1.OR.IQ.GT.NUSED) GO TO 7
      COB(IQ)=COB(IQ)+RT(I,J)
    7 CONTINUE
      DO 8 L=1,NUSED
      CEX(L)=CT(L)*RRT/GT
      IF(CEX(L).GE.5.) GO TO 8
      NUND5=NUND5+1
      IF(CEX(L).GE.1.) GO TO 8
      NUND1=NUND1+1
    8 CONTINUE
      IF(V(1).LE.1.) GO TO 11
      WRITE (MED2,991) JSF,(COB(L),L=1,NUSED)
      WRITE (MED2,992) (CEX(L),L=1,NUSED)
   11 CONTINUE
      DO 9 L=1,NUSED
      IF(CEX(L).EQ.0.) GO TO 9
      COB(L)=(COB(L)-CEX(L))*(COB(L)-CEX(L))/CEX(L)
      CHI=CHI+COB(L)
    9 CONTINUE
    5 IF(V(1).GT.1.) WRITE(MED2,993) (COB(L),L=1,NUSED)
    1 CONTINUE
      NDF=(NSR-1)*(NSC-1)
      DF=NDF
      P=PRBF(DF,1000.,CHI/DF)
      IF(V(1).LT.0.) GO TO 12
      IF(V(1).EQ.0..AND.V(2).LT.P) GO TO 12
      WRITE(MED2,995) CHI,NDF,P
```

```
      NDP=NSR*NSC
      IF(NUND5*5.GE.NDF.OR.NUND1.GE.1)   WRITE(MED2,998)
      WRITE(MED2,996)NUND1
      WRITE(MED2,997)NUND5
   12 V(11)=P
      V(12)=CHI
      V(13)=NDF
      RETURN
  989 FORMAT(1H1)
  990 FORMAT(11H0 COLUMN (-,10(2X,I4,4X))
  991 FORMAT (4H0ROW,I4/11H OBSERVED   ,10(F10.4))
  992 FORMAT (11H EXPECTED   ,10(F10.4))
  993 FORMAT (11H CHI-SQUARE,10(F10.4))
  995 FORMAT (20H0      CHI-SQUARED IS ,F10.2,6H WITH ,I4,35H DEGREES OF F
     1REEDOM PROBABILITY OF ,F10.8)
  996 FORMAT (31H0NUMBER OF CELLS LESS THAN ONE ,I4)
  997 FORMAT (31H NUMBER OF CELLS LESS THAN FIVE,I4)
  998 FORMAT (1H+,88X,32HTHIS CHI-SQUARED IS NOT RELIABLE      )
      END


      SUBROUTINE DICOLA(TRTC,TRTR,KC,KR,NC,NR,ITC,ITR,DMINC,DMINR,DMAXC,
     1DMAXR,NSC,NSR,MED2)
C DICOLA (SEE 11.5 ) STATISTICAL DESCRIBES ROW/COLUMN COMBINATION
C PRINTS OUT WHICH ROWS AND COLUMNS HAVE BEEN COMBINED IN CHISQUARED
      DIMENSION TRTC(NC),TRTR(NR),KC(NC),KR(NR)
      NL = 0
      IF(NSC.EQ.0) GO TO 22
      WRITE(MED2,98)
      NL = NL + 10
      DO 31 I = 1,NSC
      IF(NL.EQ.0) WRITE(MED2,98)
      NL = NL + 1
      IF(NL.EQ.50) NL = 0
      WRITE(MED2,90)I,KC(I)
      CALL PRTCLS(DMAXC,DMINC,I,TRTC(I),NC,ITC,MED2)
   31 IF(NL.EQ.0) WRITE(MED2,91)
   22 IF(NSR.EQ.0) RETURN
      IF(NL+NSR+5.GT.50) WRITE(MED2,91)
      IF(NL+NSR+5.GT.50) NL = 5
      WRITE(MED2,99)
      DO 32 J = 1,NSR
      IF(NL.EQ.0) WRITE(MED2,99)
      NL = NL + 1
      IF(NL.EQ.50) NL = 0
      WRITE(MED2,90)J,KR(J)
      CALL PRTCLS(DMAXR,DMINR,J,TRTR(J),NR,ITR,MED2)
   32 IF(NL.EQ.0) WRITE(MED2,91)
      RETURN
   90 FORMAT(1H ,20X,I6,4X,I6)
   91 FORMAT(1H1)
   98 FORMAT(24H0COMBINATIONS OF COLUMNS/13H0COLUMN TITLE,7X,18H ORIGINA
     1L COMBINED/)
   99 FORMAT(21H0COMBINATIONS OF ROWS/10H0ROW TITLE,10X,18H ORIGINAL COM
     1BINED/)
      END


      SUBROUTINE REDROW(RT,KR,NR,NSR,CT,KC,NC,NSC,NUND5,NUND1)
C REDROW (SEE A2.4 ) STATISTICAL CHOOSES ROW/COLUMN FOR COMBINATION
      DIMENSION RT(NR),KR(NR),CT(NC),KC(NC)
      TT=0.
      DO 20 I=1,NC
```

```
   20 TT=TT+CT(I)
      NREP=0
   30 NREP=NREP+1
      KWSF=1
      NWSF=0
      NUND1=0
      NUND5=0
      DO 26 JSR=1,NSR
      RSF=0.
      J=0
      DO 21 J=1,NR
   21 IF(KR(J).EQ.JSR) RSF = RSF + RT(J)
   22 I=0
      NUNC=0
      DO 25 ISC=1,NSC
      CSF=0.
      DO 23 I=1,NC
   23 IF(KC(I).EQ.ISC) CSF = CSF + CT(I)
   24 E=RSF*CSF/TT
      IF(E.LT.5.) NUNC = NUNC + 1
      IF(E.LT.1.) NUND1= NUND1+ 1
   25 CONTINUE
      IF(NUNC.GT.NWSF) KWSF = JSR
      IF(NUNC.GT.NWSF) NWSF = NUNC
   26 NUND5 = NUND5 + NUNC*5
      IF(NREP.GT.1) RETURN
      N=NSR*NSC
      IF(NUND1.LT.1.AND.NUND5.LT.N)GO TO 30
      DO 27 J=1,NR
   27 IF(KR(J).GT.KWSF)KR(J) = KR(J) - 1
      IF(NSR.NE.KWSF)GO TO 29
      DO 28 J=1,NR
   28 IF(KR(J).EQ.NSR) KR(J) = NSR - 1
   29 NSR=NSR-1
      GO TO 30
      END
```

11.6 SWITCHING AUXILIARIES - ISW, NEXY AND NEXC

11.6.1 Purpose

Figure 11.61 provides system flow-charts for the function ISW which determines whether a statistical test or description should be carried out, and with what detail of output), and the subroutines NEXY which finds the coordinates for the start of an array in dynamic allocation, and NEXC which finds the next combination of predictors in multiple regression.

11.6.2 Function ISW

The function ISW is a specialised switching function. It is used to determine whether a test or block of description should be carried out or not. (It returns +1 for YES, -1 for NO and 0 for "run the test without output to see if it is significant")

Codes LT=6, 7 and 8 refer to frequency tables, descriptive statistics and summary tabulations. Here the decision depends only on the output control index to form a YES/NO response.

Codes LT=2, 3, 4 or 5 refer to tests on NOMINAL, ORDINAL, INTERVAL or RATIO scales. Here the logic is more complex since the stored data level given by LDA may be over-ridden by the value of LCA. In addition, tests may be required only at the exact level of the data, or for all levels up to that of the data. Finally, significant tests only may be required. (Figure 11.61a illustrates how ISW is used in the last instance - all statistical tests in the system can be carried out in a 'switched-off' mode, so that the apparently paradoxical requirement that the result should be known before the calculation is carried out is resolved.)

11.6.3 Subroutine NEXY

The subroutine NEXY simplifies the allocation of space by dynamic allocation. (See particularly CAIAD). It assumes that there exists a FORTRAN two-dimensional array with IMAX columns width. The first free cell in this array is at IA, JA and an array of K cells must be allocated. The subroutine calculates the position of the next free cell after the allocation (IB, JB). In addition to simplifying the allocation of arrays, it can be used to verify that enough space is available for all arrays, if it is called again after finding the start of the last array to find the first free cell following the last array, and this position compared with the number of rows in the common array.

11.6.4 Subroutine NEXC

The subroutine NEXC is used to form combinations of predictors from a set specified in IV. NREQ out of the NPOS available are selected, under the control of the index NC. If NC is zero when the subroutine is called then it arranges the numbers in IV in ascending order, and the first NREQ of these form the first combination. On subsequent calls, it forms the next combination in order from the one existing at the time it was called, until it is called with the final combination - it then returns with NC equal to zero to indicate the end of the sequence.

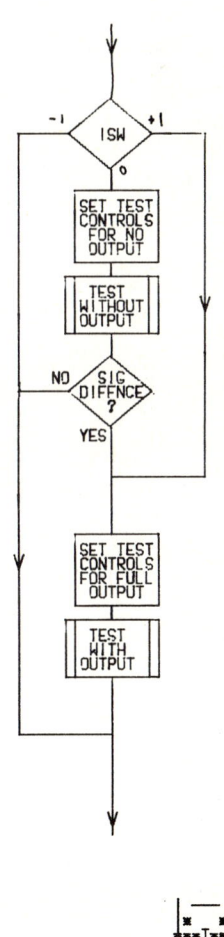

Figure 11.61a - System Flow-Chart - ISW

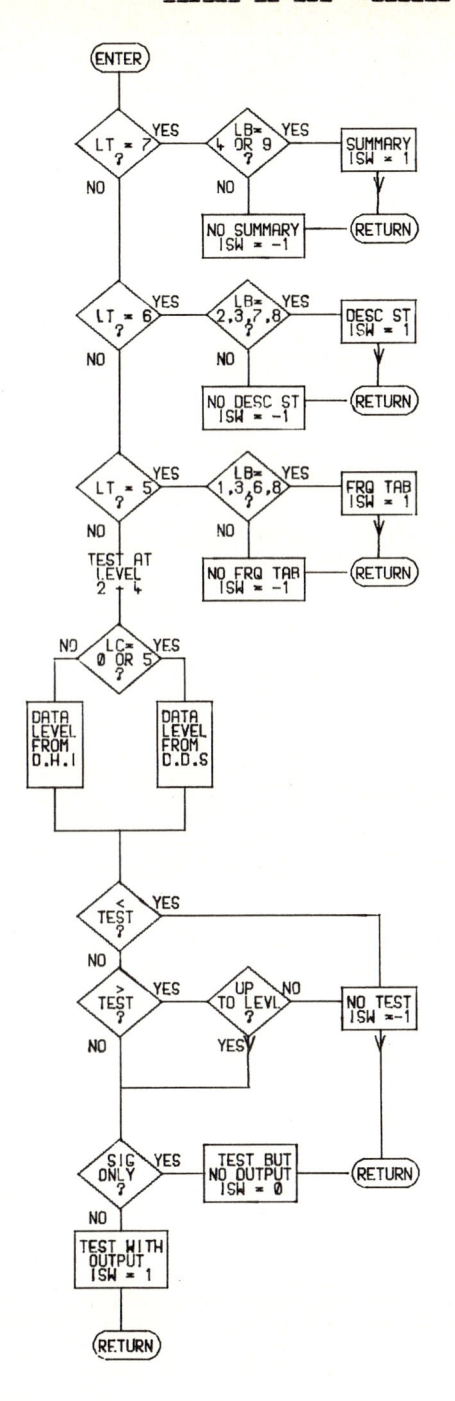

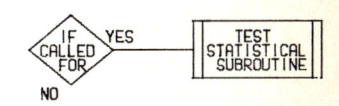

Figure 11.61b - System Flow-Charts - NEXY and NEXC

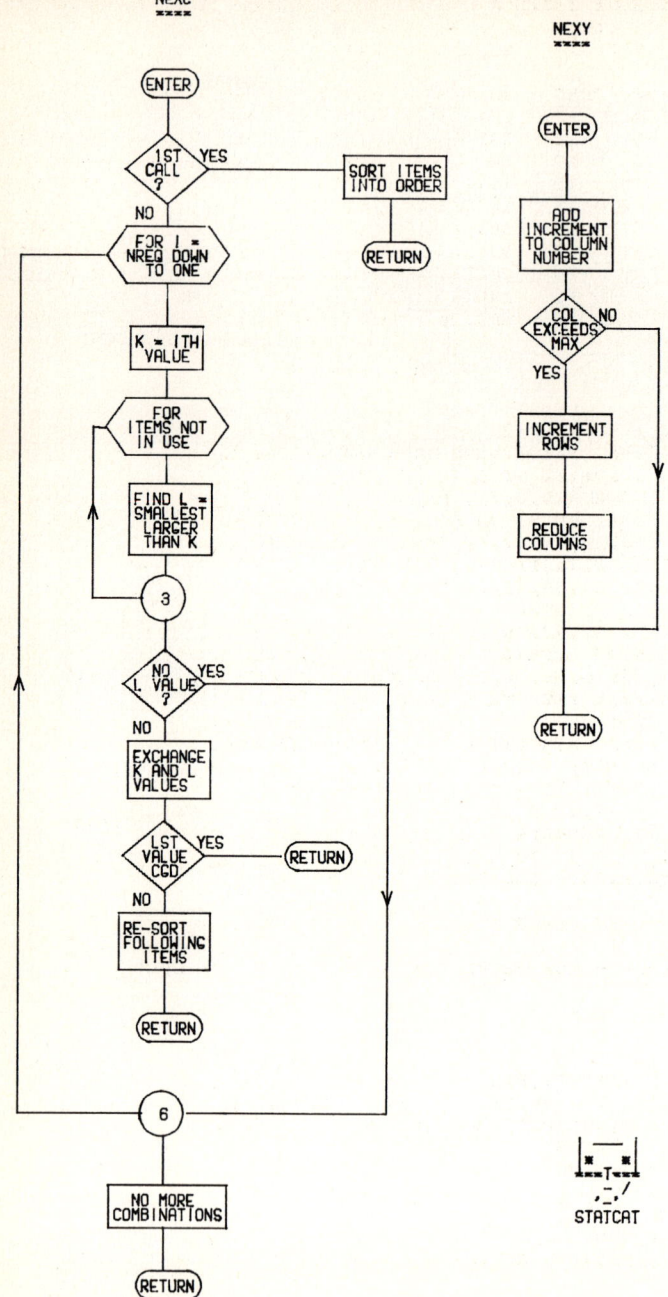

```
      FUNCTION ISW(LBA,LCA,LDA,LT)
C ISW    (SEE 11.6 ) SERVICE      CHOOSES TEST/DESCRIPTION REQUIRED
C CONTROLS CHOICE OF TESTS AND OUTPUTS IN LEVEL-SENSITIVE ANALYSES
C VARIABLE        LBA         LCA         LDA         LT          ISW
C PURPOSE        OUTPUT      TEST        DATA        TYPE OF     COMMAND
C VALUE
C  NEG           NO DESC     NO TEST     NOT USED    NOT USED    SKIP TEST
C  0             NIL   AT    LDA SIG     NOT USED    NOT USED    TRIAL
C  1             FT    AT    NOM SIG     DUMMY       NOT USED    RUN DIRECT
C  2             DS    AT    ORD SIG     NOMINAL     NOM TEST    NOT USED
C  3             FTDS  AT    INT SIG     ORDINAL     ORD TEST    NOT USED
C  4             SUMM  AT    RAT SIG     INTERVAL    INT TEST    NOT USED
C  5             NIL   TO    LDA ALL     RATIO       RAT TEST    NOT USED
C  6             FT    TO    NOM ALL     F.INT=4     FREQ TAB    NOT USED
C  7             DS    TO    ORD ALL     F.RAT=5     DESC STS    NOT USED
C  8             FTDS  TO    INT ALL     NOT USED    SUMMARY     NOT USED
C  9             SUMM  TO    RAT ALL     NOT USED    NOT USED    NOT USED
      ISW = -1
      LB = LBA+1
      LC = LCA+1
      LD = LDA
      IF(LD.GT.5) LD = LD-2
      IF(LB.LT.1.AND.LT.GT.5.OR.LC.LT.1.AND.LT.LT.6.OR.LD.LT.1.OR.LD.GT.
     15.OR.LT.LT.1.OR.LT.GT.8) GO TO 12
      GO TO  (12,4,4,4,4,1,2,3),LT
C IS FREQUENCY TABLE TO BE OUTPUT
    1 GO TO (12,10,12,10,12,12,10,12,10,12),LB
C ARE DESCRIPTIVE STATISTICS TO BE OUTPUT
    2 GO TO (12,12,10,10,12,12,12,10,10,12),LB
C IS SUMMARY TO BE PRINTED
    3 GO TO (12,12,12,12,10,12,12,12,12,10),LB
C DOES TEST DECISION DEPEND ON ABSOLUTE OR DATA LEVEL
    4 GO TO ( 5, 6, 6, 6, 6, 5, 6, 6, 6, 6),LC
C COMPARE DATA LEVEL WITH TEST LEVEL
    5 IF(LD - LT) 12,8,7
C COMPARE SPECIFIED ABSOLUTE LEVEL WITH TEST LEVEL
    6 IF(LC-LC/6*5-LT)    12,8,7
C HIGHER THAN TEST LEVEL - TEST IF REQUIRED
    7 IF(LB - 5 ) 12,12,8
C ONLY SIGNIFICANT RESULTS
    8 IF(LC - 5 ) 11,11,10
C DIRECT RUN REQUIRED - ISW RETURNS AS +1
   10 ISW = ISW + 1
C PRELIMINARY SIGNIFICANCE TEST - ISW RETURNS AS 0
   11 ISW = ISW + 1
C NO TEST REQUIRED - ISW RETURNS AS -1
   12 RETURN
      END


      SUBROUTINE NEXC(IV,NPOS,NREQ,NC)
C NEXC    (SEE 7.2 ) SERVICE      NEXT COMBINATION OF PREDICTORS
C NC= 0 INPUT=START OUTPUT=NO MORE COMBS    NC=1 IN=CONTINUE OUT=O.K.
      DIMENSION IV(NPOS)
      IF(NC.EQ.1) GO TO 2
C SORT INTO ORDER
      DO 1 I = 1,NPOS
      DO 1 J = I,NPOS
      IF(IV(I).LE.IV(J)) GO TO 1
      K= IV(I)
      IV(I) = IV(J)
      IV(J) = K
    1 CONTINUE
```

```
      NC = 1
      RETURN
C FIND FIRST FROM END TO STEP UP-REARRANGE FOLLOWING
    2 IF (NPOS.LE.NREQ) GO TO 7
      NRQ1= NREQ + 1
      DO 6 I1 = 1,NREQ
      I = NRQ1-I1
      K = IV(I)
      L = 0
      DO 3 J = NRQ1,NPOS
      IF(IV(J).LT.K) GO TO 3
      IF(L.EQ.0) L = J
      IF(IV(J).LT.IV(L)) L=J
    3 CONTINUE
C L= 0 MEANS NO HIGHER THAN IV(I) NOT IN USE
      IF(L.EQ.0) GO TO 6
      IV(I) = IV(L)
      IV(L) = K
C I1 = 1 MEANS LAST VALUE CHANGED- NO REARRANGEMENTS NEEDED
      IF(I1.EQ.1) RETURN
      DO 5 I2 = I,NREQ
      IF(I2.EQ.I) GO TO 5
      DO 4 I3 = I2,NPOS
      IF(IV(I3).GE.IV(I2).OR.IV(I3).LE.IV(I2-1)) GO TO 4
      K =IV(I3)
      IV(I3) =IV(I2)
      IV(I2) = K
    4 CONTINUE
    5 CONTINUE
      RETURN
    6 CONTINUE
C NO FURTHER COMBINATION POSSIBLE
    7 NC = 0
      RETURN
      END


      SUBROUTINE NEXY(IA,IB,IMAX,JA,JB,K)
C NEXY   (SEE  6.3 ) SERVICE      FINDS NEXT ARRAY COORDS
C STEPS INDICES ON K STEPS IN IMAX COLUMN MATRIX
      I = IA + K
      JB= JA + (I-1)/IMAX
      IB= I - (I-1)/IMAX*IMAX
      RETURN
      END
```

11.7 CLASS AUXILIARIES - CLASIF, CLIMS AND PRTCLS

11.7.1 Purpose

These subroutines are employed by many system subroutines to treat data assigned to classes.

Figure 11.71 provides system flow-charts for the subroutine CLASIF which determines into which class a datum should be placed, the subroutine CLIMS which produces convenient class intervals where these have not been specified by the user, and the subroutine PRTCLS, which prints the class name, number or limits, depending on the actual or imposed data level.

11.7.2 Subroutine CLASIF

The subroutine CLASIF determines to which class a datum belongs. It begins by determining whether the data is already a valid class number (level NOMINAL or ORDINAL with class limits unchanged.) If this is not so, it calculates the appropriate class on the basis of the upper and lower class limits and number of classes, taking account of the two-class cases, with or without zero class interval. Finally, it checks that the class number is within the range defined, allocating it to the highest or lowest class if necessary.

11.7.3 Subroutine CLIMS

The subroutine CLIMS rounds off the irregular minima and maxima found by LDDS or CHECK from the data. It is called with a minimum, a maximum and a number of classes. It begins by assuming that two classes will be reserved for the extremes, and determining the interval resulting. It then takes the logarithm of this to the base ten, and rounds up the fractional part of the logarithm so that the interval becomes one, two or five to a power of ten. This interval is returned to natural form. The mid-range is found from the maximum and minimum, and rounded down to an exact number of class intervals. The lower limit is then redefined as half the number of classes below this, and the upper limit as the full number of classes above the lower limit. (Some difficulty may occur with rounding errors when large numbers of classes are involved - they may be resolved by adjusting the constants used in logarithm form.)

11.7.4   Subroutine PRTCLS

The subroutine PRTCLS is used to print out the appropriate class name or number, depending on the data level employed.

DUMMY data are given as class number and a warning (DUMMY).

NOMINAL or ORDINAL data are given as the class number and class name (or an 'OUT OF RANGE' message.)

INTERVAL or RATIO level classes are given as a class number, upper and lower class limit. The extremes are given by "UNDER(lower limit)" and "(upper limit)+OVER". (Data on the exact edge of a class are allocated to the class above - but remember that the precision with which limits is specified may exceed that shown. To minimise the possible consequences, CLIMS normally underestimates very slightly - a nominal 2.00 unit class limit may be 1.999998, but an input datum will be correctly classified.)

Figure 11.71 - System Flow-Charts - CLASIF, CLIMS and PRTCLS

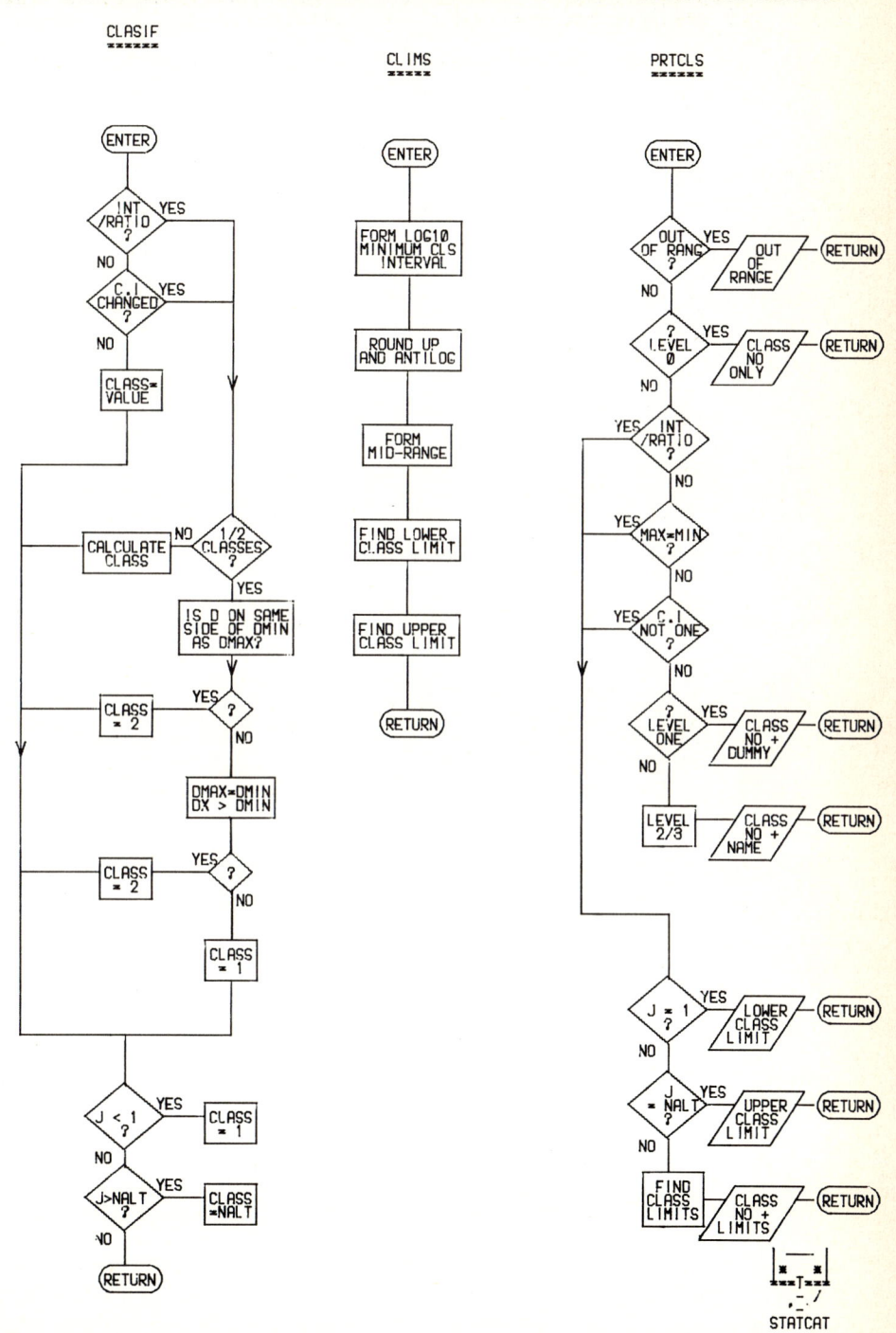

```
      SUBROUTINE CLASIF(D,DMAX,DMIN,NX,NALT,J)
C CLASIF (SEE 11.7 ) SERVICE      CLASSIFIES DATA ITEM
C REJECT MISSING VALUES BEFORE CALLING THIS SUBROUTINE
      J = 1
      DX = NALT-2
      IF(NX.GE.4.OR.DMIN.NE.1.5) GO TO 1
      IF(DMAX-DMIN-DX.GT.0.1.OR.DMAX-DMIN-DX.LT.-0.1) GO TO 1
      J = D
      GO TO 3
    1 IF(DX.LE.0.) GO TO 2
      J = (D-DMIN)/(DMAX-DMIN)*DX + 2.
      GO TO 3
    2 IF((D-DMIN)*(DMAX-DMIN).GT.0.) J = 2
      IF(DMAX.EQ.DMIN.AND.D.GT.DMIN) J = 2
    3 IF(J.LT.1) J = 1
      IF(J.GT.NALT) J = NALT
      RETURN
      END


      SUBROUTINE CLIMS(DL,DH,N)
C CLIMS  (SEE 11.5 ) SERVICE      ROUNDS CLASS LIMITS FROM DATA
      A = N - 2
      B = N/2 - 1
      IF(B.LT.0.) B = 0.
      DT = ALOG10((DH-DL)/A)
      DF = AMOD(DT,1.)
      IF(DF.LE.0.30103) DT = 10.**(DT-DF+0.30103)
      IF(DF.GT.0.30103.AND.DF.LT.0.69897)DT= 10.**(DT-DF+0.69897)
      IF(DF.GT.0.69897) DT = 10.**(DT-DF+1.0)
      DF = (DL+DH)*0.5
      DL = DF - AMOD(DF,DT) - B*DT
      IF(DF.LT.0.)DL = DL - DT
      DH = DL + A*DT
      RETURN
      END
```

```
      SUBROUTINE PRTCLS(DMAX,DMIN,J,TRT,NALT,NX,MED2)
C PRTCLS (SEE 11.7 ) SERVICE      PRINTS CLASS NAME/LIMITS
C THIS SUBROUTINE PRINTS APPROPRIATE CLASS TITLES
      IF(J.GT.0.AND.J.LE.NALT) GO TO 1
      WRITE(MED2,994) J
      RETURN
    1 IF(NX.EQ.0) GO TO 7
      AJ = NALT -2
      IF(NX.NE.2.AND.NX.NE.3) GO TO 4
      CI = DMAX - DMIN - AJ
      IF(DMAX.EQ.DMIN)CI=0.
      IF(CI.GT.0.1.OR.CI.LT.-0.1) GO TO 4
      IF(NX.NE.1) GO TO 3
    2 WRITE(MED2,995)J
      RETURN
    3 WRITE(MED2,996)J,TRT
      RETURN
    4 IF(J.NE.1) GO TO 5
      WRITE(MED2,997)J,DMIN
      RETURN
    5 IF(J.NE.NALT) GO TO 6
      WRITE(MED2,998)J,DMAX
      RETURN
    6 AJ = NALT - 2
      DEL=(DMAX-DMIN)/AJ
      AJ = J - 2
      AX=DMIN+AJ*DEL
      BX=DMIN+(AJ+1.)*DEL
      WRITE(MED2,999)J,AX,BX
      RETURN
    7 WRITE(MED2,996) J
      RETURN
  994 FORMAT(1H+,I2,13H OUT OF RANGE)
  995 FORMAT(1H+,I2,8H (DUMMY))
  996 FORMAT (1H+,I2,6X,A4)
  997 FORMAT (1H+,I2,3X,6HUNDER ,F8.2)
  998 FORMAT (1H+,I2,F8.2,6H +OVER)
  999 FORMAT (1H+,I2,F7.2,3H TO,F7.2)
      END
```

11.8   PROBABILITY EVALUATION - PRBF AND GAUS

11.8.1   Purpose

The function PRBF is employed by many subroutines to evaluate the associated probability of parametric statistics. By judicious selection of the calling parameters, the same function may be used to evaluate Student 't', Snedecor's 'F' and the normal statistic 'Z'.

Figure 11.81 provides a system flow-chart for the function PRBF.

11.8.2   Function PRBF

The function PRBF is based on the function of the same name by Veldmann(1967), although the internal operations of the subroutine have been revised to use more modern approximations. The general principles have been taken from Morris(1969), except that the evaluation for a single degree of freedom above and a large number below is carried out directly by the function GAUS.

In general, if either the upper or lower degrees of freedom are even, an iterative evaluation can be carried out. Similarly if both are odd and their total is less than 500, a double iteration can be used. If both are odd or exceed the iteration limit an approximation to the normal distribution is derived and evaluated using the function GAUS.

11.8.3   Evaluation of "F" ratio using PRBF

To evaluate an "F" ratio, or a statistic distributed in the same way, PRBF is called with the the value of the "F" ratio, the degrees of freedom in the numerator (upper), and the degrees of freedom in the denominator (lower).

11.8.4   Evaluation of Chi-squared using PRBF

To evaluate a Chi-squared value PRBF is called using the value of chi-squared divided by the degrees of freedom, the number of degrees of freedom and a sufficiently large value (say 1000). The last parameter represents infinity - since chi-squared divided by its degrees of freedom is distributed like a "F" ratio with its degrees of freedom in the numerator and infinity as the denominator.

11.8.5   Evaluation of Student "t" using PRBF

To evaluate a "t" value, PRBF is called using the square of the "t" value, the value one, and the degrees of freedom of "t". (Because the square of "t" is distributed like "F" with one degree of freedom in the numerator, and the degrees of freedom for "t" in the denominator.

11.8.6 Evaluation of the Normal variate "Z" using PRBF

To evaluate a normal variate, PRBF can be called using the square of the "Z" value, one and a sufficiently large value (say 1000). (Z can be thought of as "t" with an infinite number of degrees of freedom.) In practice, since the subroutine in any case transforms its "F" value to a "Z" value a short cut is taken directly to the evaluation of "Z" within the subroutine.

11.8.7 Evaluation of the Normal variate "Z" using GAUS

The associated probability of a Normal variate can be found using the function GAUS. This is based on the Algol procedure 'gauss' by Ibbotson, modified to reduce rounding errors.

REFERENCES : Veldman (Ch 6), Morris (1969), Ibbotson (1963), NBS (1965)

Figure 11.81 - System Flow-Chart - PRBF + GAUS

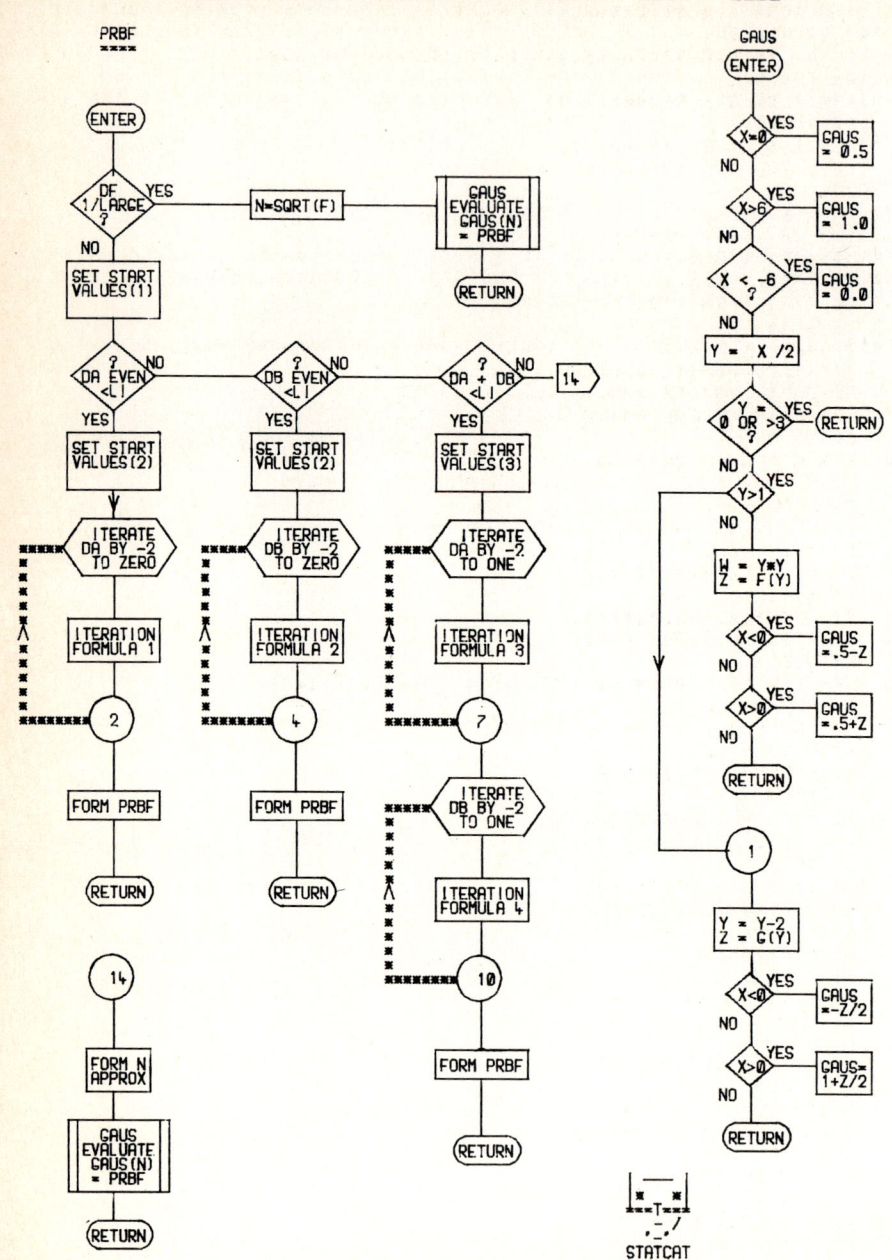

```
      FUNCTION PRBF(DA,DB,FR)
C PRBF    (SEE 11.8) STATISTICAL FINDS PROBABILITY OF F-RATIO
C DA = DF ABOVE,DB=DF BELOW,FR=F RATIO - PRBF=-999 =OUT OF RANGE
      PRBF = -999.
      IF(DA.LE.0.0.OR.DB.LE.0.0.OR.FR.LT.0.0) RETURN
      PRBF = 1.
      IF(FR.EQ.0.) RETURN
      LI = 500
      IF(DA.EQ.1.0.AND.DB.GT.LI) X = SQRT(FR)
      IF(DA.EQ.1.0.AND.DB.GT.LI) GO TO 15
      FT = 0.
      PRBF = 0.
      X = DB/(DB + DA*FR)
      NA = DA + 0.5
      NB = DB + 0.5
      VP = NA + NB - 2
      FA = NA
      FB = NB
      IF(NA.EQ.NA/2*2.AND.NA.LT.LI) GO TO 1
      IF(NB.EQ.NB/2*2.AND.NB.LT.LI) GO TO 4
      IF(NA+NB.LT.LI) GO TO 6
      GO TO 14
C FA EVEN AND LESS THAN LI (THE LIMIT FOR ITERATION)
    1 XX = 1.-X
    2 FA = FA - 2.
      IF(FA.LT.1.) GO TO 3
      VP = VP - 2.
      FT = XX*VP/FA*(FT+1.)
      GO TO 2
    3 FT = X**(.5*FB)*(FT+1.)
      IF(FT.GT.0.)PRBF = FT
      RETURN
C FB EVEN AND LESS THAN LI (THE LIMIT FOR ITERATION)
    4 FB = FB - 2.
      IF(FB.LT.1.) GO TO 5
      VP = VP - 2.
      FT = X*VP/FB*(FT+1.)
      GO TO 4
    5 FT = 1. - (1.-X)**(0.5*FA)*(FT+1.)
      IF(FT.GT.0.)PRBF = FT
      RETURN
C FA AND FB ODD - FA+FB LESS THAN LIMIT FOR ITERATION
    6 TH = ATAN(SQRT(FA*FR/FB))
      ST = SIN(TH)
      CT = COS(TH)
      C2 = CT*CT
      S2 = ST*ST
      A = 0
      B = 0
      IF(DB.LE.1.) GO TO 9
    7 FB = FB - 2.
      IF(FB.LT.2.) GO TO 8
      A = C2*(FB-1.)/FB*(1.+A)
      GO TO 7
    8 A = ST*CT*(1.+A)
    9 A = TH + A
      IF (DA.LE.1.) GO TO 13
   10 FA = FA - 2.
      IF (FA.LT.2.) GO TO 11
      VP = VP - 2.
      B = S2*VP/FA*(1.+B)
      GO TO 10
   11 GF = 1.
```

```
      K = DB*0.5
      DO 12 I = 1,K
      X1 = I
   12 GP = X1*GP/(X1-0.5)
      B = GP*ST*CT**DB*(1.+B)
   13 FT = 1. + 0.636619772368*(B-A)
      IF(FT.GT.0.)PRBF = FT
      RETURN
C FA AND/OR FB EXCEED LIMITS
   14 FA = 2./9./FA
      FB = 2./9./FB
      CR =FR**0.333333333333
      X = (1.-FA +(FB-1.)*CR )/SQRT(FB*CR*CR + FA)
   15 FT = GAUS(X)
      IF(FT.GT.0.) PRBF = FT
      RETURN
      END

      FUNCTION GAUS(X)
C GAUS    (SEE 11.8 ) STATISTICAL FINDS ASS. PROB. OF N VALUE
      IF(X.EQ.0.) GAUS = 0.5
      IF(X.LT.-6.)GAUS = 0.0
      IF(X.GT.6.) GAUS = 1.0
      Y =ABS(X)*0.5
      IF(X.EQ.0..OR.Y.GT.3.)RETURN
      IF(Y.GT.1.) GO TO 15
      W = Y*Y
      Z =((((((((0.000124818987 *W - 0.001075204047)*W + 0.005198775019)
     1 * W      - 0.0191982914)*W + 0.059054035642)*W - 0.151968751364)
     2 * W      + 0.319152932694)*W - 0.53192171)*W + 0.797884560593)
     3 * Y
      IF(X.LE.0.) GAUS = 0.5 - Z
      IF(X.GT.0.) GAUS = 0.5 + Z
      RETURN
   15 Y = Y - 2.
      Z = ((((((((((((((-0.000045255659*Y + 0.000152529290)*Y
     1 - 0.000019538132)*Y - 0.000676904986)*Y + 0.001390604284)*Y
     2 - 0.0007948820)*Y - 0.002034254874)*Y + 0.006549791214)*Y
     3 - 0.010557625006)*Y + 0.0119447319)*Y - 0.009279453341)*Y
     4 + 0.005353579108)*Y - 0.002141268741)*Y + 0.0005353849)*Y
     5 - 0.000063342476
      IF(X.LE.0.) GAUS = - Z * 0.5
      IF(X.GT.0.) GAUS = 1.+ Z*0.5
      RETURN
      END
```

11.9 MISCELLANEOUS AUXILIARIES - CHIKEN AND FITIT

11.9.1 Purpose

These two subroutines are used for different purposes, but by most programs in the STATCAT system.

Figure 11.91 provides system flow-charts for the subroutine CHIKEN and the subroutine FITIT.

11.9.2 Subroutine CHIKEN

CHIKEN is used to give a specific warning whenever a statistical test transform or statistic is used which may not be appropriate to the level of data defined in the Data Description segment. (In many cases the warning will be redundant, but it is nevertheless retained in case it is not.) The name was originally chosen with the phrase "playing chicken" in mind, but has been overtaken by the image of an agitated mother hen clucking over its errant chicks.

11.9.3 Subroutine FITIT

The subroutine FITIT simply positions the serial input file where neccessary to read a column description - or at the start of the STATCAT data bank, of the Data Description segment, or the Data Storage segment.

Figure 11.91 - System Flow-Charts - CHIKEN and FITIT

FIGURE 11.91 - SYSTEM FLOW-CHARTS - FITIT AND CHIKEN

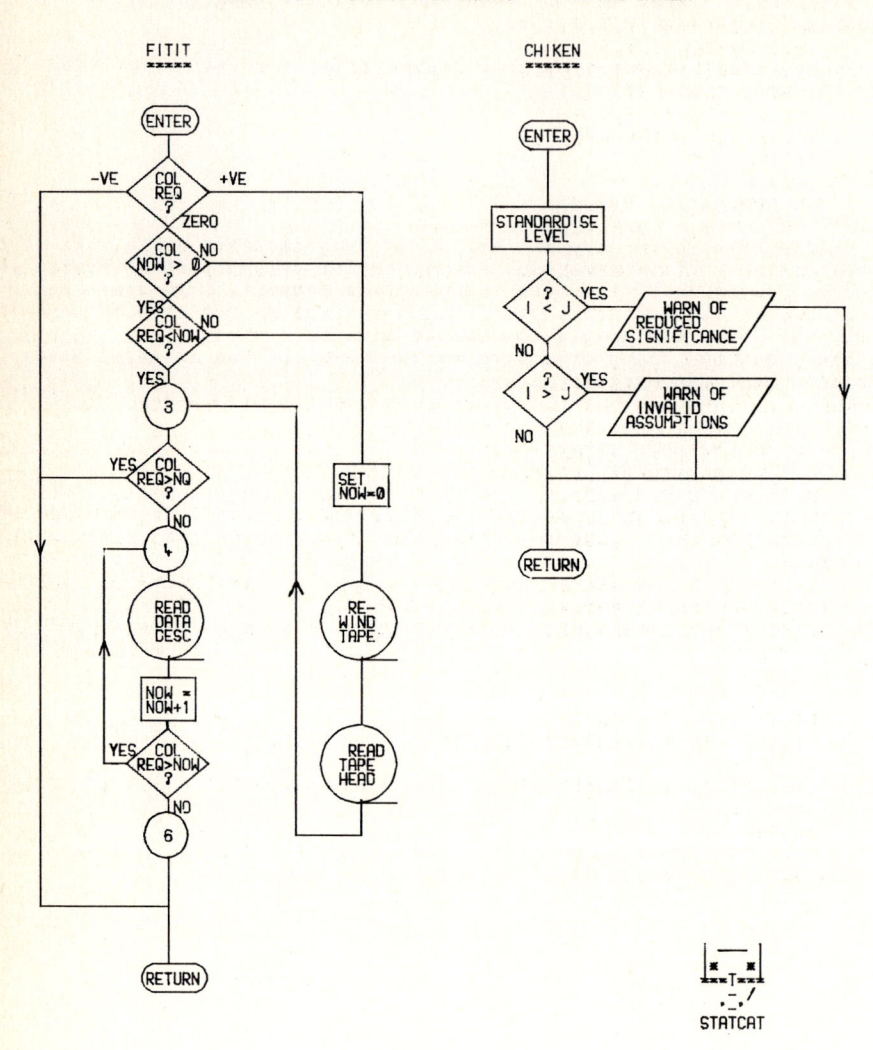

```
      SUBROUTINE FITIT(INOW,IREQ,NQ,NALT)
C FITIT   (SEE 11.9 ) SERVICE      FINDS COLUMN TITLE + DESCRIPTION
      COMMON /STCT/MED1,MED2,MED3,MED4,MED5,MED6,MED13,Q,V(20),TT(30)
      IF(IREQ)5,7,1
    1 IF(INOW)7,7,2
    2 IF(IREQ-INOW) 7,7,3
    3 IF(IREQ-NQ) 4,4,5
    4 READ(MED3) (X,J=1,19),(X,J=1,NALT),IT,X,X
      INOW = INOW + 1
      IF(IREQ-INOW) 7,6,4
    5 WRITE(MED2,900)IREQ,NQ
    6 RETURN
    7 INOW = 0
      REWIND MED3
      READ (MED3) NQ,NALT,Q,(X,J=1,16)
      IF(IREQ - INOW) 5,6,3
  900 FORMAT ( 7H COLUMN,I6,43H OUT OF RANGE - DATA BANK HAS COLUMNS 1 T
     10 ,I4)
      END


      SUBROUTINE CHIKEN(II,JJ)
C CHIKEN (SEE 11.9 ) SERVICE     WARNS OF MISMATCHED DATA LEVEL
C II = DATA LEVEL REQUIRED FOR ACTIVITY
C JJ = DATA LEVEL OF ACTUAL DATA
      DIMENSION SN(4,7),TN(7,2)
      DATA SN/4H DUM,4HMY S,4HCALE,4H    ,4H NOM,4HINAL,4H SCA,4HLE  ,4H
     1N OR,4HDINA,4HL SC,4HALE ,4HN IN,4HTERV,4HAL S,4HCALE,4H RAT,4HIO
     2S,4HCALE,4H    ,4HN IN,4HTERV,4HAL S,4HCALE,4H RAT,4HIO S,4HCALE,4
     3H    /
      DATA TN/4HSIGN,4HIFIC,4HANCE,4H MAY,4H BE ,4HREDU,4HCED ,4HARE ,4H
     1EXTR,4HA AS,4HUMPT,4HIONS,4H VAL,4HID  /
      COMMON /STCT/MED1,MED2,MED3,MED4,MED5,MED6,MED13,Q,V(20),TT(30)
      I = II
      J = JJ
      IF(II.GT.5) I = II - 2
      IF(JJ.GT.5) J = JJ-2
      IF(I.LT.J) WRITE(MED2,900) (SN(K,J),K=1,4),(SN(K,I),K=1,4),(TN(K,1)
     1,K=1,7)
      IF(I.GT.J) WRITE(MED2,900) (SN(K,J),K=1,4),(SN(K,I),K=1,4),(TN(K,2)
     1,K=1,7)
      RETURN
  900 FORMAT(19HODATA USED ARE ON A,4A4,20H THEY SHOULD BE ON A,4A4,4X,7
     1A4,7X,11H**WARNING**)
      END
```

Chapter XII

STATISTICAL DIFFICULTIES AND DANGERS

This chapter differs in form from the main bulk of this book. It is a sort of scrap-book of points that are not easily attached to any one statistical technique, because they are difficult to express concisely, because they apply to many techniques, or because they are fundamental to the science, art or mystery of statistics.

The sections of this chapter are arranged in alphabetical order, in default of any systematic structure, for simple ease of reference.

12.1 CONSTRUCTED SIGNIFICANCE

If we carry out a statistical test, we usually end with an 'associated probability'. This is an estimate of the probability of obtaining the results we have observed (or more extreme results) if there is in fact no difference in the populations from which our samples are drawn.

The user should always remember that a probability exists only in a context - it is not valid except when the conditions of the context have been met. One of the most important conditions in the calculation of probabilities, generally speaking, is that the test is of a hypothesis that was stated before the data were collected - or at least before they were inspected by the person generating the hypothesis. (If we make use of information gathered from the data in the course of the experiment we must make allowances for this - for example by adjusting the 'degrees of freedom' involved.)

If we have no definite hypothesis in mind, but we feel sure that there is some sort of relation between some measurements and others, we may be tempted to form our hypothesis after we have seen what the data look like.

The computer is particularly well adapted to such techniques, not so much because of its speed, as because of its ability to make logical choices. The techniques illustrated in Chapters 7 and , even more, in Chapter 8, show how the computer can be given a general technique and a bunch of potentially important variates, and asked to derive an explanation for the mutual dependencies observed. In principle, in most of these techniques, many hypotheses are generated and the most effective in accounting for the observations are retained.

The statistical purist simply forbids this practice, calling such results 'Constructed Significance' and refusing to accept any analysis for which the hypothesis was not formally stated before the experiment. Where experiments may be repeated economically, it is possible to carry out initial experiments to explore the field, followed by formal experiments for scientific publication. Often, however, it is financially or physically impossible to adopt this practice, which seems intuitively wasteful of effort, so that exploratory techniques may be used by themselves, without formal confirmatory experiments.

The pragmatist allows this procedure with some reservations, trying to form an estimate of the number of hypotheses that have been considered, and of the effect of selecting the most striking difference and treating it as if it was the sole effect for which he has been testing. The techniques for doing this are by no means standardised, and the underlying theory is even less developed. Some general methods for assessing the sensitivity of the resultant hypotheses to particularities in the data have been mentioned in various program descriptions. (For example, dividing the data into two samples by some criterion known to be irrelevant, and comparing the results of analysing these two samples separately - or adding small amounts of random noise to the data, and observing the deterioration in significance observed.)

It is an observation of human nature, (and statistical writers, except the best, are prone to forget that they are human) that the originator of an hypothesis or a theory is liable to become emotionally attached to it. This applies not only to the great hypotheses that shake the world, but even to minor studies in marginal fields of learning, and outside. It seems that the predisposition to impose regularity on the random is inherent in the very physiology of the human frame. Part of the value of statistics is its disciplined protection against wishful thinking. Purism should not therefore be too hastily discarded, simply because it may appear uncreative.

The 'fishing expedition' is a search for 'any sort of significant effect', without any reasoned basis. It tends to occur where the user is under pressure to justify a data gathering exercise by showing a 'practical value'. Many more-or-less innumerate managers tend to feel that a study which produces no statistically significant differences is in some way a failure. Given sufficient special pleading, and enough computer time some form of 'constructed significance' will almost always be found. It is a part of the professional responsibility of the statistician to dissuade his clients from leading themselves astray in this way. Reference to a suitably primed consultant, or demonstration of 'constructed significance' using deliberately random data is advised.

12.2   ERROR - ROUNDING AND RESIDUAL

Most of the mathematical operations involved in statistical calculation are carried out in 'real numbers'. In terms of Chapter 2 these are on at least an INTERVAL level. These numbers therefore represent physical quantities on continuous scales. Because they must be expressed as a finite number of digits, there must always be a certain lack of absolute precision. Within a computer numbers are expressed as a mantissa linked to an exponent. (The non-mathematical reader should think of this as a decimal fraction, multiplied by a power of ten - although in practice a binary fraction is multiplied by a power of two in most modern machines.) The precision with which a number can be specified depends on the size of the mantissa (the fraction) available, and the range of values that can be stored on the size of the exponent permitted. These features depend largely on the machine architecture, although there exist some systems which permit the user to control the size of the fractional part, and hence the precision, at least. No formal limits are laid down in the ASA FORTRAN IV definition, but it is reasonable to expect values in the range from 10 to the 64th to 10 to the -64th, and with a precision of at least five decimal places. The user should be aware of the precision and range of the machine on which his work is carried out. This is the ultimate limiting precision of the system, and it is relatively rare for it to affect statistical calculations. Limitations of input and output precision are much more likely to affect accuracy.

(ASA FORTRAN IV allows for the specification of some values as 'double precision' - in which case they are allotted extra space, and calculations carried out to twice the normal number of digits (or more). The STATCAT system does not make use of this facility for a number of reasons, among which are the additional cost in specialised subroutines, the slight differences between realisations of ASA FORTRAN IV, and the the extra storage required. See below in addition.)

Numbers are usually input with a fixed number of decimal places, which in itself involves an inherent rounding error. To elaborate on a very old joke, when a statistician says 4 he means 3.5 to 4.5 ; when he says 4.0 he means between 3.95 and 4.05 and when he says 4.00 he means 3.995 to 4.005. For reasonably precise measurements, the distribution within the interval of true values will be nearly uniform, with a variance of one twelfth of the least significant digit. Similar considerations apply to output expressions, where the number of places is determined in advance.

Rounding errors at input are the responsibility of the user. It is up to him to ensure that the data are expressed to sufficient decimal places to reflect the precision of the data. In most statistical applications, the precision of the measurement is greatly in excess of the precision of the data - rounding errors are negligible. Similarly he should be aware that the output is expressed to a pre-determined number of decimal places, which does not reflect the true precision of the result.

Considerations of internal word length and of input/output precision apart, there are certain internal operations which may magnify errors.

Exponentiation or the use of high powers of values may lead to approximation, particularly if it is combined with its inverse operation. There is little that the user can do to minimise this effect, apart from attempting to ensure that the range of the variate is as restricted as possible. Numbers to be raised to exact powers are so raised by successive multiplication to avoid the use of the logarithmic conversion and its inverse.

Errors are liable to occur during the calculation of correlation coefficients or in the accumulation of sums of squares for analysis of variance because totals, especially totals of squares, may become very large if there are many entries involved. Where the coefficient of variation is small (standard deviation small in comparison with mean) analysis of variance in particular finds itself concerned with small differences between large numbers. Ideally, sums of squares should be calculated around the arithmetic mean of the data, but this would often require a second sweep through the entire STATCAT data bank. A simpler and faster technique is to use the first datum encountered as a working mean, subtracting it from all following values. In analysis of variance in particular, the traditional method involves the cumulation of data, its squaring and subsequent division by the number of data. If the cumulated data is first divided by the number of readings (forming the group mean, which is of interest in itself), squared and multiplied by the number of data, the same answer is reached without any number being generated that exceeds the total sum of squares, and so without loss of significant figures.

A major problem in multivariate statistics is the inversion of matrices. This operation is equivalent to the solving of a set of simultaneous equations. If some of the equations turn out to be linear combinations of others, the problem becomes insoluble, because there are more unknowns than equations. (This is known as 'singularity' in mathematical jargon.) The system can detect exact combinations of variates, but when variates are nearly but not quite identical the system may produce erratic results without detecting any abnormality. Some writers suggest that double precision should be used at this point for some or all of the data involved, but this merely postpones the problem. In statistical analysis any process which is so sensitive to rounding error in the internal representation of data as to require double precision must be equally sensitive to the truncation error when the original values were expressed as finite decimal numbers, and to the true errors of measurement when the data were collected. Rather than attempt to enforce a spurious precision of output, it appears wiser to make an assessment of the nearness to singularity by injecting known 'random noise' into the system by a suitable transform, as described above, and to apply appropriate manipulations to the data to form the differences of near-identical variates for example. For the statistician, neither number-crunching nor mathematical acrobatics, however interesting in themselves, are valid substitutes for clear and coherent thought applied to the actual problem.

The subroutines employed for matrix inversion, for the extraction of eigenroots and eigenvectors and for Varimax rotation are not necessarily the most efficient, fastest, or most precise, they are merely the best available to the author at this time. Better algorithms and tighter codings are constantly appearing, and may be adapted or adopted as the user wishes - at his own risk.

12.3 ESTIMATION OF MISSING VALUES

All the programs in this system make some form of provision for accomodating 'non-values'. These are in fact numeric codes used to indicate that a datum is simply not available. Sometimes these are simply a convenience, corresponding to details that do not exist for certain groups, and allowing simpler or more economic coding of data. (For example, it is convenient to code 'number of children' and 'age of eldest child' as two data, although the second of these data does not exist for the childless.) In other cases, they correspond to data that should exist but have been lost or found to be invalidated. (For example, growth rate for an experimental animal that died during the experiment.)

Most programs can cope with such data without difficulty - for example the programs in Chapters 4 to 6. The programs in Chapter 7, particularly STANOV, are more sensitive. Approximations are available for patching up these techniques, but they can be seriously in error, and it may be necessary in extreme cases to resort to the construction of dummy data, estimated from those remaining. The methods available have been mentioned where appropriate, but they have not been incorporated in the system because they tend to be specialised, controversial, and very time consuming. In addition, there is a fundamental objection to the estimation of missing data, which is that even the best estimate gives what might be expected, not what would actually have been observed.

12.4 FREEDOM OF INFORMATION, PRIVACY AND SECURITY

It may well escape the notice of some users of these programs that they are constructing Computer Data Banks, and, in some countries, may be subject to legislation accordingly.

The scope and effects of data control legislation vary greatly from country to country, and in many countries are in the course of change. Only the most general comments can therefore be made here. In some jurisdictions, the user may be obliged to supply data on any named individual to that individual (subject to a reasonable fee.) This implies that the information is supplied in a form suitable for a human reader - (see 5.1 or 9.2). The present author can only add that it is well to verify the identity of the individual requesting the information on himself - see below. In other circumstances, the user may be at fault if he allows his data to be accessed by others without the express permission of the subjects of his research, while elsewhere, he may be required to retain the data in accessible form for inspection or verification by supervisor or professional ethics committee. The author can only suggest that the user make sure that the subjects are aware that their data will be "stored in a computer", and are told how it will be used.

The elementary precautions described in 3.1, 5.1 and 9.2 are designed more to avoid accidental erasure and casual snooping than to resist determined attack. For software protection of data, the (U.S.) Standard Data Encryption algorithm is recommended. (NBS 1977) Two points should be kept in mind when attempts to protect data are made: -

- There can be no guarantee that a coded storage system will not be (sooner or later) broken into - usually sooner rather than later.

- If there is any link between the computer using to data and a network system, or (worse) if the system is in fact a remote one, it is always possible for some ingenious individual to find a way of tapping the system, before coding or after de-coding.

If strict security is imperative, ensure that the system is physically and electrically isolated and that all output (printed and magnetic media) is physically destroyed (not merely shredded or erased) and consult a trustworthy security specialist regularly.

REFERENCES Goldberg (1979) is a survey of computer cryptography, as far as it is in the public domain.

12.5 NON-ORTHOGONALITY

Many analytic techniques are much simplified if it can be assumed that the factors whose effects are being considered are 'orthogonal'. This term, of geometrical origin, originally meant 'mutually at right angles'. In practice, this means that varying one factor should have no effect on the levels of the other(s). Factor analysis, for example, is a method for the derivation of mutually independent, orthogonal factors from data which are not originally orthogonal.

The most common occurrence of 'non-orthogonality' is in analysis of variance, where the numbers of items in the cells of a multi-way analysis of variance may not be proportional.

It is not easy to explain the phenomenon in non-mathematical language, but what happens in practice is that some of the individual variation may be ascribed to two factors at the same time. In some extreme cases, the quantity of variation double-charged may exceed the total, producing obviously wrong negative sums of squares. Equally frequent, less obvious and hence more dangerous are instances where the double-charged variation is less than the true residual. In this case, the residual will be under-estimated, and hence the statistical significance of the factors will be over-estimated. For example, if the data given in Figure 12.51 are analysed for the effects of Factors A and B by the simple method which assumes the data to be orthogonally disposed, we obtain the alarming results given in Figure 12.52.

Obviously something is wrong. We can cut the Gordian knot by analysing only the arithmetic means of readings in each cell, but in doing so we lose our residual and most of our degrees of freedom, as in Figure 12.53. We can estimate the residual from the within cells variation, giving the same result as line 2 in Figure 12.52, but, because the cell means for factor A have been treated as if they were from single values, we obtain a smaller sum-of-squares term (line 1). Winer(1970) suggests treating each cell as if it were based on the harmonic mean of the number of readings in all cells, which would in this case multiply the sums of squares by 16/13 - although the true ratio is in fact 16/7.

This method gives equal weight to all cells of the analysis - an advantage when the losses of values are purely accidental, but a defect if the proportions in the samples reflect the frequency of occurrence in nature.

Alternative methods do exist, mostly based on the conversion of analysis of variance to multiple regression. Such methods require that the factors be on INTERVAL rather than NOMINAL or ORDINAL level, or require that each class become a binary choice, and require the solution of enormous matrices of simultaneous equations. Even with the aid of the digital computer they can become extremely cumbersome, particularly if interaction terms must also be isolated.

Figure 12.51 - **Non-orthogonally partitioned data**

Factor A	Factor B	Factor C	Value(s)
Level 1	Level 1	Level 1	35, 35, 35, 35
Level 2	Level 2	Level 1	0
Level 3	Level 1	Level 2	0
Level 4	Level 2	Level 2	0

Figure 12.52 - **Analysis of Variance**

Source of Variation	Total sum of Squares	Degrees of Freedom	Mean Sum of Squares
Factor A	2100	3	700
Factor B	1120	1	1120
Factor C	1120	1	1120
B/C Interaction	-140	1	-140
Residual	0	3	0
TOTAL	2100	6	

Figure 12.53 - **Analysis of Variance (unweighted means)**

Source of Variation	Total sum of Squares	Degrees of Freedom	Mean Sum of Squares
Factor A	918.75	3	306.25
Factor B	306.25	1	306.25
Factor C	306.25	1	306.25
B/C Interaction	306.25	1	306.25
Residual	0	0	does not exist
TOTAL	918.75	3	

12.6 PROVING A NEGATIVE

In general, a statistical test produces an 'associated probability'. This is NOT the probability of the result. (Since the result is usually a value on a continuous scale, strictly speaking its probability is always zero.) It is the probability of observing a value as extreme as, or more extreme than, the value observed, if the assumptions made in calculation are justified.

Traditionally, it has been the practice to define a 'null hypothesis' (Samples A and B do not differ significantly in mean value) and to define a 'rejection region' (Associated probability less than a certain value - usually 0.05, 0.01 or 0.001). If the associated probability falls into the rejection region, we reject the null hypothesis and state that it is not true that the two samples do not differ significantly in mean value. If however the associated probability does not fall into the rejection region we CANNOT say that we have 'proved the null hypothesis'. All that we can say is that we have not yet rejected it.

Usually when we reject a null hypothesis, we accept an 'alternative hypothesis'. This is usually of the same form as the null hypothesis, but in exactly the opposite sense. If our null hypothesis is that samples A and B do not differ significantly in mean value, then our alternative hypothesis is that samples A and B do differ in mean value. It is often tempting, when considering the meaning of a statistical analysis to simplify or mis-state the alternative hypothesis. For example, if we reject our null hypothesis given above, it is not true that we can accept the hypothesis that 'Sample A has a significantly larger mean than sample B'. To be able to do this, we would have to test the null hypothesis that 'Sample A is not significantly larger than sample B'.

Similarly, if we find that the correlation coefficient for two variates is statistically significant, it may not necessarily be true that the two variates are linearly related. It may be that a more complex formulation describes their relationship more closely.

12.7 RANDOMNESS

The concept of 'randomness' is closely linked with the fundamental notion of probability, and is almost as elusive to formal analysis.

Tremendous efforts have been devoted in recent years to the elaboration of methods for the generation of random or 'quasi-random' numbers by digital computer.

True random numbers are usually generated by some form of hardware device, or by the reading of a prepared table of such numbers. True random numbers are most useful for gambling machines or computer games, where unpredictability is of the essence. In many computer applications, it is important to be able to reconstruct the stream of random numbers employed. ASA FORTRAN IV has no formal provision for the generation of true random numbers.

Pseudo-random numbers are generated by a mathematical algorithm starting from a definite 'seed'. If the 'seed' is stored, the stream can be repeated from the start. They are called 'quasi-random' because it is possible to determine the numbers in advance, by running the generating algorithm, and because they are in fact determinate. The use of a quasi-random number generator enables analyses to be repeated, allows the use of a sequence containing no spontaneous regularities (which cannot be guaranteed for a true random number generator) and can be carried out in ASA FORTRAN IV.

The pseudo-random number generator here employed is the FORTRAN realisation of a shift register with feed-back of the most significant digit to a lower position. The initial state of the generator can be considered to be a string of sixteen binary bits. The most-significant bit is taken as the first random binary bit, removed when the register shifts upward, and compared with the value in the seventh place. If they differ a 1 is generated, if they are identical a 0 is generated. The bit so generated becomes the least significant of the register. It can be shown that the original value of the generator will be reproduced after 32767 bits have been generated. (These represent all possible values from 1-32767 for the string expressed in decimal terms. The value 0 is not part of the sequence.) Random choices are made by cycling the generator eleven times before taking a value. Approximately normal distributions can be obtained by summing sixteen successive values from the binary generator and adjusting the arithmetic mean and standard deviation to provide a normalised distribution. This is a deliberately crude generator, used to emphasise the artificial nature of this sort of randomisation. (It is for this reason that the suggestion that these numbers should be called 'quasi-random' on linguistic grounds has not been adopted. These numbers are 'pseudo-random' in the full pejorative sense of the prefix.)

Within the STATCAT system, a single random-number seed is used to generate a single stream of random numbers, for all purposes. For purely private reasons the number 5326 is used. eleven bits are used for each unit random transform (+/-1 or +/-P) and sixteen for each approximately normal transform (NOR1 or NORP). Thus the generation of a set of transformed variates including two +/-1 transforms, one +/-P and three NORP transforms will require eighty-one random bits for each entry generated.

The starting value of the generator is preserved, and is re-set for a re-run with the same sample and subset. When running, for example, STKIND to compare several independent samples, runs with different data handling instructions, but unchanged subset and samples, will use the same random disturbances. If the set of variates is re-read, even if identical variates are used, different random disturbances will be applied, unless the sample specification is also re-read, in which case the original sequence will be re-started. (If different variates are introduced, requiring a different number of random bits per entry, the sequence will rapidly become de-synchronised.)

The theory of random and pseudo-random numbers bristles with philosophical problems. Bright and Enison (1979) provide an up-to-date survey of quasi-random number generation and testing, and the references provided with that paper should give the ordinary user more than he has ever wished to know on the subject.

12.8 SAMPLES, POPULATIONS AND GENERALISATION

The data in a STATCAT data bank are usually a sample from an population (known, for no clear reason as an 'underlying' population). They may be, as examples, the responses of a number of individuals (taken to represent the population as a whole), the readings of instruments while an experiment is performed (supposed to isolate a generally occurring process) or selected economic statistics for areas held to represent different types of economic structure. We are not, as a general rule, particularly concerned with the actual measured differences, but with what we can reasonably deduce about the underlying population, or similar populations.

There do exist nevertheless some occasions where we have data on the whole population. A well-known example is an investigation of economic statistics for all towns in the United Kingdom with a population exceeding a million at a given census. There is a finite, known number of these, and it is possible to be sure that none has been omitted. If we were to ask whether the alcohol consumption per head (ethyl alcohol internally applied) was higher in Scots than in English towns of this size, it would not be necessary to carry out a statistical test to determine if the difference was statistically significant since a simple comparison of the means would provide a precise reply. There is no underlying population of Englands or Scotlands about which we wish to make deductions.

It should be noted that certain procedures in statistics do not strictly speaking apply to samples. Factor analysis is an example, being essentially a descriptive technique, intended for the simplification of large quantities of data, rather than as an analytic technique.

A major part of scientific endeavour, and one in which statistical methods are frequently employed, is the derivation of general 'laws' relating observable phenomena. It is often possible to derive from experimental observations some form of relation between variates. This relation, being derived by what are basically mathematical methods, usually takes the form of a mathematical equation. It is an unfortunate characteristic of mathematical notation that such equations do not indicate the range of values over which they are applicable.

The user should take care to define the circumstances under which the equations he has derived can be applied. Where the equations are simple, involving fewer than four variates, this task may not be difficult, but where they are complex, involving more than eight variates, it may be practically impossible.

As a general rule equations ought not to be 'extrapolated' - taken beyond the range of the variates they are based on. This rule is a generalisation, and like all generalisations, except the present one, has exceptions. When the user is in doubt, he should consult a professional statistician. Empirical tests may be made by applying the prediction equations to data from extreme situations, and comparing the results with actual information.

12.9   WEIGHTING, SCALING AND NORMALISATION

It is not always possible to attach equal significance to all entries in a data bank used for an analysis. Where some data are more reliable than others, some form of weighting is required. Because the form of weighting used depends intimately on the circumstances, no general methods for weighting data have been included in this book. It should be noted, however, that most multivariate techniques imply some form of weighting, using, for example, weights derived from the data to produce predicted scores in multiple regression, or factor scores in factor analysis. It is important to remember that these weights are dependent on the data gathered, both in terms of the variates selected for analysis and of the distribution of the data themselves.

To illustrate the first point, consider a factor analysis of data from our STATCAT demonstration data bank in which only entries having a low percentage of errors are included. If the percentage of errors is correlated with other variates, clipping the most extreme values will reduce the correlation coefficient, and cause the relationship to be under-estimated. Conversely, suppose that the variate 'TASK' were included in our set of variates. This is an ORDINAL level variate, designed to occur at four levels of difficulty, coded 1-4, with equal frequency. If we correlate these data with the corresponding values of assessed difficulty, we will obtain an exaggerated correlation, because we have deliberately spaced out our values, obtaining more extreme values than would normally occur - this point is dealt with in more detail in 6.3.7. The user should be aware that a departure from the underlying assumptions - in this case that the data are normally distributed - can distort the conclusions.

To illustrate the second point, that the choice of variates may affect the results of a factor analysis, consider an analysis in which one factor is almost identical with one of the original variates, which had little relation to the other variates. If this variate were to be removed, the factor would probably disappear, and would certainly be greatly reduced in importance. If, on the other hand, the same variate appeared twice (Say as a value and its absolute value, when the value never becomes negative - camouflaged by some noise.) it might well make the factor appear much more important. This point is discussed in more detail elsewhere, but the user should remember that the results of a factor analysis may be biased by measurements concentrated on a particular aspect of a more general problem. He should also remember that there may be factors in the underlying data structure which have been omitted from the analysis because no relevant measures were available (for example the age of the operator), because they were held constant during the data collection (for example the season of the year) or simply because no-one thought of them at the time (for example atmospheric ionisation).

Scaling problems are less immediately visible in statistical processing by computer, because they can be handled for the most part by routine pre-processing operations. Indeed most multivariate testing and modelling techniques tend to begin by reducing the data to an arbitrary unit scale for ease of computation. It is sometimes, as in cluster analysis, not possible to do this, with the consequent possibility of obtaining different results if different scales of measurement are employed for some variates. Scaling usually involves the addition of a constant and multiplication by a constant, so that NOMINAL and ORDINAL level measures are unchanged. This type of scaling is sometimes called 'normalisation'. If data are transformed to have 100 as mean and 10 as standard deviation, this is known as 'standardisation' (Different values are sometimes employed in educational studies.)

REFERENCES : NBS (1978)

INDEX

A

Analysis control
   Automatic Interaction
      Detector ... 489
   Canonical Analysis ... 442
   Clustering Correlation
      Matrix ... 524
   Data checking ... 115
   Factor Analysis ... 392
   Multiple discriminant
      analysis ... 419
   Multiple regression ... 364
   Samples
      several independent ... 252
      several related ... 301
      two independent ... 228
      two related ... 276
   Semi-automatic Grouping ... 468
Analysis of variance
   general ... 324
      dependent variates ... 328
      Error messages ... 326
      independent variates ... 324
      model specification ... 324
   non-orthogonality ... 332
   one-way ... 255
   two-way
      related samples ... 303
Auto-correlation ... 362
Automatic Interaction
   Detector ... 488
Auxiliary Control
   listing ... 155
   plain-language
      retrieval ... 576

B

Bar charts ... 179
Bartlett Test
   independent samples ... 256
   related samples ... 304
blank
   cards ... 21
   data bank key ... 28, 102
   data bank name ... 28, 103

C

Canonical Analysis ... 441
Chi-squared test
   independent samples ... 229
   several related samples ... 303
   two related samples ... 278
Class
   Allocation ... 745
   interval
      modified ... 67
      original ... 43
   limits
      modified ... 67
      original ... 43
   Operations ... 745
   printing ... 746
   rounding ... 745
Classification Code ... 66
Clustering Correlation
   Matrix ... 523
Code
   classification ... 66
   correction ... 135
   Data Column
      name ... 41, 66
      number ... 66
   delay ... 66
   manipulation ... 607
   Parameter ... 210
   Priority ... 731
   transform ... 73
Constructed Significance ... 758
   Automatic Interaction
      Detector ... 492
   Multiple Regression ... 370
Context ... 6
Correction
   Card ... 135
Correlated predictors
   Automatic Interaction
      Detector ... 492
Correlation Coefficient
   two related samples ... 280
Cross-Tabulations ... 201
Cumulative frequency curves ... 179

D

Data
   defined ... 5
Data bank
   correction ... 133
   creation ... 96
   explained ... 19
   key ... 28
      input ... 102
      revised ... 134
   loading ... 101
   Name ... 27
      input ... 103
      revised ... 134
   title
      input ... 102
      revised ... 134

Data checking ... 115
  Control Index ... 115
  Special methods ... 117
Data Column
  Complementary Information
    Card ... 42
  revised ... 135
  Title card ... 41
Data Column Description ... 8
Data Description
  module ... 41
Data Description Segment
  described ... 8
  explained ... 19
  justified ... 7
Data Handling Instruction ... 85
  card ... 85
Data Level ... 11
  choice ... 17
  mis-match
    consequences ... 17
    warnings ... 755
Data Manipulation ... 593
  Combining Entries ... 678
  Combining Logic ... 681
  Copying Entire STATCAT Data
    Bank ... 705
  Correction ... 133
  Individual Entries ... 595
  Manipulation code ... 596, 607
  Matching ... 635
  Merging ... 635
  sorting entries ... 616
  sorting logic ... 618
  Synchronisation ... 660
  Verifying STATCAT data Bank
    contents ... 711
Data Starter ... 8
  card ... 35
  explained ... 19
Data Storage Segment ... 7
  explained ... 19
  input ... 103
Data Terminator ... 8
  explained ... 20
Decision Making ... 5
Delay code ... 66
Demonstration data
  explained ... 10
  listed ... 107
Descriptive Statistics ... 177
DUMMY data level ... 11

E
Empirical methods ... 5
Entries
  listing ... 154
  revised ... 136
entry
  Canonical Analysis ... 444
  defined ... 7
  Multiple Discriminant ... 422
  Regression ... 368

equipment required ... 3
Error
  in matrix inversion ... 760
  residual ... 303, 759
    abnormal ... 370
    test for systematic
      trends ... 369
  Rounding ... 759
Error Messages
  analysis of variance
    model ... 326
  Data Manipulation
    Individual Entries ... 598
  earliest uncorrected
    retained ... 92
  Sample/Subset ... 59
  summary ... 93
  variate ... 67
Extrapolation
  undesirable ... 767

F
Factor Analysis ... 391
File Control Card ... 27
Fishing expeditions ... 226, 759
FORTRAN
  double precision - not
    used ... 760
  reasons for choice ... 2
  Standard characters ... 23
  type ... 22
  version employed ... 2
FORTRAN source modules ... see
  following index
Freidmann Two-way A.o.V. by Ranks
  several related samples ... 303
Frequency Tabulation
  multi-way ... 201
  one-way ... 176
  two-way ... 304

G
Generalisation ... 766
Guttman Image Analysis ... 395

H
Hill Climbing
  Clustering Correlation
    Matrix ... 525, 526

I
independent samples ... see
  samples,independent
Input Conventions ... 21
Input modules
  combination ... 92
Interpolation modes
  Data Manipulation
    Synchronisation ... 663

K
Kendall Tau Statistic
  two related samples ... 279
Keywords ... 573
  Conventions ... 577
Kolmogorov-Smirnov Test
  two independent samples ... 230
Kruskall-Wallis A.o.V. by Ranks
  several independent
    samples ... 255

L
Lag-correlation ... 362
Listing
  entries ... 154

M
Mann-Whitney "U" Test
  two independent samples ... 230
Matrix
  Eigen-Values ... 717
  Inversion ... 716
  Movement ... 716
  Multiplication ... 717
  Operations ... 716
Median Test
  independent samples ... 254
merging ... 3
Merging Specification ... 637
Minterms ... 60
Multiple Discriminant
  Analysis ... 418
Multiple Regression ... 362

N
NOMINAL data level ... 11
Non-orthogonality ... 762
  analysis of variance ... 332
  Example ... 764
non-value
  defined ... 102
  in specification ... 60
  revised ... 134
Non-values
  Estimation ... 761
Normalisation ... 768
Number of Alternative Classes
  modified ... 66
  original ... 102
  revised ... 134
Number of data columns
  original ... 102
  revised ... 134

O
Ordering ... 727
ORDINAL data level ... 13
Output Control
  analysis of variance ... 329
  Automatic Interaction
    Detector ... 489
  Canonical Analysis ... 441
  Clustering Correlation
    Matrix ... 524
  Cross-referencing ... 564
  Data Manipulation
    Combining Entries ... 679
    Individual Entries ... 597
    Merging/Matching ... 638
    sorting entries ... 617
    Synchronisation ... 662
  Factor Analysis ... 391
  Multiple discriminant
    analysis ... 418
  Multiple regression ... 363
  plain-language
    retrieval ... 575
  Samples ... 227
  Semi-automatic Grouping ... 467

P
Parameter Codes ... 210
Parametric variate card ... 65
permission to use STATCAT ... 3
Pinned Predictors ... 365
Plain-language ... 544
  character codes ... 551
  conventions ... 546
  Cross-referencing ... 564
  input ... 545
  Output ... 554
    Auxiliary control ... 554
  packing ... 546
  unpacking ... 556
Polynomial Regression ... 362
Principal Components ... 393
Priority Codes ... 626, 731
Probability
  Evaluation ... 750
    F ratio ... 750
    Normal Variate ... 751
Programming note
  Character strings ... 58
  input ... 22
  output subroutine ... 157
  Run-time Format
    input ... 138
    output ... 158
  Special input subroutine ... 104, 105, 565
    example - XREF ... 565

Q
Quartile Test
  independent samples ... 254

R
Random Number
  Control ... 71
  Generation ... 765, 766
  Theory ... 766
RATIO data level ... 16
Record Specification ... 573
  card ... 573
  title ... 573

Regression
    Multiple ... 362
Regression equations
    two related samples ... 281
related samples ... see
    samples, related
Residual Analysis
    Regression ... 369
Restrictions and Reservations
    Analysis of variance ... 331
    Automatic Interaction
        Detector ... 491
    Canonical Analysis ... 445
    Factor Analysis ... 395
    Multiple discriminant
        analysis ... 422
    Multiple Regression ... 370
    Non-orthogonality ... 332
    Semi-automatic Grouping ... 470
Robot Data Analyser ... see
    Automatic Interaction Detector
Run-time Format
    input ... 138
    output ... 158

S
Samples
    independent
        defined ... 225
        described ... 225
    related
        defined ... 225
        described ... 225
    Set Title Card ... 49
    several independent ... 252
    several related ... 301
    Specification ... 49
    Specification Card ... 57
    Specification Module
        minterm form ... 60
    Title card ... 49
    two independent ... 227
    two related ... 276
Samples and Populations ... 766
Scale of measurement ... see Data
    Level
Scaling ... 768
Security ... 28, 35, 96, 762
    Auxiliary key ... 156
Semi-Automatic Grouping of
    Entries ... 467
Sign Test
    two related samples ... 278
Significance Level ... 229
Snedecor "F" Test
    two independent samples ... 231
Soundex Codes ... 573
    Conventions ... 578
source
    modules' ... 4
special cards ... 21
Standardisation ... 768
STATCAT

    defined ... 1
STATCAT data bank ... see Data bank
Student "t" Test
    "t-like" test ... 231
    two independent samples ... 231
    two related samples
        means ... 280
        variances ... 280
Subset
    Specification Card ... 57
    Specification Module ... 57
        minterm form ... 60
    title card ... 57
Switching ... 740

T
Transform ... 66
    Codes ... 69
    NAME ... 159

V
Variate
    Specification ... 65
Varimax Rotation ... 395

W
Weighting ... 767
Wilcoxon Matched-pairs Signed-ranks
    Test
    two related samples ... 279

INDEX OF SOURCE MODULES

A
AN ... 25
AOVOUT ... 358
ASEV ... 720

B
BSPLIT ... 508

C
CAIAD ... 505
CANON ... 459
CANOV ... 348
CASIGS ... 353
CASTA ... 217
CCOMB ... 695
CDESC ... 191
CFACT ... 409
CGRPS ... 482
CHECK ... 127
CHIKEN ... 757
CHISQ ... 737
CHISQD ... 246
CHISQ1 ... 317
CKIND ... 267
CKREL ... 314
CLASIF ... 748
CLENT ... 487
CLIMS ... 748
CLIST ... 169
CLOAD ... 113
CLSAM ... 64
CLUST ... 539
CLWORD ... 587
CMDIS ... 435
CMERG ... 655
CMULT ... 384
COMPA ... 25
COPYA ... 26
COREG ... 298
CORRE ... 463
CRECT ... 148
CSORT ... 630
CSYNC ... 673
CWORD ... 586
C2IND ... 242
C2REL ... 290

D
DATA
   CROSS-REFERENCING ... 569
   FREE-FORMAT(DEFAULT) ... 114
   PLAIN-LANGUAGE ... 553
   RUN-TIME FORMAT ... 152
DCBC ... 194
DCDS ... 197
DCFT ... 195
DCPS ... 199
DFADJ ... 360
DFSET ... 360
DICOLA ... 738

F
FIFI ... 32
FITIT ... 757
FORMAS ... 219
FORMTI ... 218
FREID2 ... 318

G
GAUS ... 754

I
IBL ... 26
ICH ... 26
IJOIN ... 518
INSERT ... 732
ISPLIT ... 517
ISW ... 743
ITIDY ... 519

K
KENTAU ... 296
KS2SA ... 248
KW1W ... 273

L
LANOV ... 349
LCOM ... 47
LDAP ... 40
LDBS ... 64
LDDS ... 45
LDHI ... 90
LGEN ... 78
LMAN ... 612
LSAMP ... 54
LSET ... 54
LWORD ... 590

M
MANIP ... 614
MANWIT ... 249
MATM ... 721
MDISC ... 435
MDSWE ... 483
MEDEX ... 271
MEDIAT ... 81
MINV ... 721
MOP ... 723
MULTR ... 388

N
NEXC ... 743
NEXY ... 744
NPACK ... 553

O
OPST ... 700

P
PAR1W ... 274
PAR2W ... 320
POSCL ... 732
POSN ... 733
PR ... 734
PRBF ... 753
PRTCLS ... 749

Q
QAREX ... 272

R
RECOMB ... 512
REDROW ... 738
RESID ... 414

S
SIGN ... 295
SIGSUM ... 351
SNDX ... 591
STAIAD ... 502
STANOV ... 344
STASTA ... 214
STAT ... 702
STBANK ... 715
STCANO ... 455
STCHEK ... 126
STCLUS ... 535
STCOMB ... 691
STCOPY ... 710
STCORR ... 146
STDESC ... 189
STFACT ... 405
STGRPS ... 479
STHEAD ... 100
STKIND ... 265
STKREL ... 311
STLIST ... 166
STLOAD ... 112
STMANI ... 608
STMDIS ... 431
STMERG ... 649
STMULT ... 380
STSORT ... 627
STSYNC ... 670
STWORD ... 585
ST2IND ... 240
ST2REL ... 288

T
TAB2W ... 319
TFIND ... 250
TFREL ... 299
TRANS ... 82

U
UNPACK ... 563

V
VARMX ... 412
VNOW ... 676

W
WASTA ... 221
WBASE ... 464
WDCD ... 48
WFLEX ... 171
WILCOX ... 296
WMAT ... 724
WMULT ... 389
WOWN
    DEFAULT ... 173
    PLAIN-LANGUAGE ... 561
WSAMP ... 522
WSET ... 169
WSPLIT ... 521

BIBLIOGRAPHY

31(1)   ADAMS D,HITCHHIKERS GUIDE TO THE GALAXY
         PAN BOOKS 1980

         A STRIKING EXAMPLE OF THE IMPORTANCE OF CONTEXT.
         (MORE ACCURATE THAN TRUE)

REFERS TO   CNTX
                 411024.

32(2)   ASA,USA STANDARD FORTRAN
         AMERICAN NATIONAL STANDARDS INSTITUTE,NEW YORK 1966

         THE OFFICIAL STANDARD FOR FORTRAN IV. DEVELOPED BY COMMITTEE
         (USAS=ANS=ASA X3.9-1966) THERE IS ALSO A BASIC FORTRAN ALIAS
         FORTRAN II - THIS HAS NOTHING TO DO WITH THE
         COMPUTER LANGUAGE BASIC. A REVISED STANDARD (FORTRAN 77) IS NOW
         COMING INTO USE, BUT THERE IS AN ENORMOUS INVESTMENT IN PROGRAMS
         CONFORMING TO THE FORTRAN IV (FORTRAN 66) STANDARD.

REFERS TO   FORT
                 788420.

33(3)   BARRITT M M + WISHART D (EDS), COMPSTAT 80
         PHYSICA-VERLAG WUERZBURG 1980
         ISBN 3 7908 0229 8

         PROCEEDINGS OF BI-ANNUAL CONFERENCE ON COMPUTER STATISTICS.
         PREVIOUS ISSUES COMPSTAT 76, COMPSTAT 78 ARE ALSO RELEVANT.
         COMPSTAT 82 WILL BE PUBLISHED AUGUST 1982.

REFERS TO   BKGD   PKGS
                 277854.   2027369.

34(4)   BOURNE C P + FORD D F,METHODS FOR SYSTEMATICALLY ABBREVIATING
         ENGLISH WORDS AND NAMES
         JOURNAL OF THE ASSOCIATION FOR COMPUTING MACHINERY,OCT 1961

         THE BEST AVAILABLE REFERENCE FOR SOUNDEX CODING IN THE COMPUTING
         LITERATURE.

REFERS TO   SNDX
                 2410224.

35(5)   BOX G E P + JENKINS G M, TIME SERIES ANALYSIS FORECASTING AND
         CONTROL
         HOLDEN-DAY,SAN FRANCISCO,1976

REFERS TO   TIMS
                 2523169.

36(6)   BRIGHT H + ENISON R J,QUASI-RANDOM NUMBER SEQUENCES
         ACM COMPUTING SURVEYS VOL 11 NO 4, DC 1979

REFERS TO   RAND
                 2253204.

37(7)   DIXON W J + MASSEY F J,INTRODUCTION TO STATISTICAL ANALYSIS
         MCGRAW-HILL,NEW YORK 1957, LOC 56-9805

         A DETAILED INTRODUCTION TO CLASSICAL PARAMETRIC STATISTICAL TESTS,
         WIDELY USED AS A REFERENCE FOR T AND F TESTS (CH 9).
         TREATS PROBABILITY ONLY AS AN AFTERTHOUGHT.

REFERS TO   ANOV   BKGD   DESC   CHIS   STUT   SNDF   BRTT
                 160772.   277854.   513453.   395469.   2426070. 2410206. 296020.

REFERS TO   TREL   REGN
                 2545262. 2262804.

775

38(8)   DRAPER N R + SMITH H,APPLIED REGRESSION ANALYSIS
         WILEY,NEW YORK 1966

         AN EXTREMELY VALUABLE GENERAL TEXT ON MULTIPLE LINEAR REGRESSION,
         COMPUTER-ORIENTED BUT GIVING A THOROUGH DISCUSSION OF MANUAL METHODS
         CONTAINS A VALUABLE DISCUSSION OF ALTERNATIVE VARIATE SELECTION
         METHODS, AND OF THE USE OF TRANSFORMS TO REDUCE NON-LINEARITY.
         PARTICULARLY STRONG ON THE ANALYSIS OF RESIDUALS.

REFERS TO   BKGD   MJRE   REGN   REST
                277854.   1678405. 2262864. 2263459.

39(9)   FRANCIS I, STATISTICAL SOFTWARE
         NORTH HOLLAND, AMSTERDAM 1981, ISBN 0 444 00658 3

REFERS TO   PKGS
                2027869.

         A SYSTEMATIC REVIEW OF THE MAJOR COMMERCIALLY AVAILABLE PACKAGES
         FOR COMPUTER STATISTICS BASED ON A USER SURVEY.

1580(10) GOLDBERG A J (ED), CRYPTOGRAPHY
          ACM COMPUTING SURVEYS, VOL 11 NO 4, DEC 1979

          AN UP-TO-DATE SURVEY OF MODERN CRYPTOGRAPHIC METHODS,WITH
          COMMENT ON THE NBS STANDARD, AND A DETAILED DISCUSSION OF
          QUASI-RANDOM NUMBER GENERATION.

REFERS TO   CRYP   RAND
                421266.   2253204.

1581(11) HASTINGS N A J + PEACOCK J B, STATISTICAL DISTRIBUTIONS,
          BUTTERWORTHS, LONDON 1975, ISBN 0 408 70568 X

          A USEFUL COMPENDIUM OF STATISTICAL DISTRIBUTIONS WITH THEIR
          PARAMETERS - WELL LAID OUT FOR REFERENCE

REFERS TO   DESC   DIST
                513453.   523470.

1582(12) HOLLANDER M + WOLFE D A, NON-PARAMETRIC STATISTICAL METHODS
          WILEY, NEW YORK 1973, ISBN 0 471 40635 X

          A MODERN, MORE THEORETICALLY ORIENTED WORK THAN SIEGEL,
          WRITTEN WITH THE NON-COMPUTER USER IN MIND - MANY TABULATIONS.

REFERS TO   KENT   KS2S   MANW   WLCX
                1388220. 1424119. 1628223. 2905174.

1583(13) IBBOTSON D,GAUSS
          ACM COLLECTED ALGORITHMS , NO. 209 ,1963

          AN ACCURATE APPROXIMATION FOR THE ASSOCIATED PROBABILITY OF THE
          NORMAL DISTRIBUTION.

REFERS TO   PROB
                2045752.

1584(14) KEMENY J G SNELL J L + THOMPSON G L,INTRO TO FINITE MATHEMATICS
          PRENTICE-HALL, ENGLEWOOD CLIFFS NEW JERSEY USA, 1957

          GOOD BASIC TEXT ON LOGIC

REFERS TO   LOGI
                1537859.

1585(15) KENDALL M G,RANK CORRELATION METHODS
          GRIFFIN 1955 (2ND ED.)

          THE SOURCE OF KENDALLS TAU TEST

REFERS TO   KENT
                1388220.

1586(16)   KENDALL M G + STUART A,THE ADVANCED THEORY OF STATISTICS
            GRIFFIN,LONDON,3VOLS 1958-66

            VOL 1   1963 DISTRIBUTION THEORY
            VOL 2   1961 INFERENCE AND RELATIONSHIP
            VOL 3   1966 DESIGN OF EXPERIMENTS, ANALYSIS AND TIME SERIES
            THE BIBLE OF CLASSICAL STATISTICAL METHODS AND THEORY. COMPREHENSIVE
            BUT DIFFICULT.

REFERS TO   ANOV   BKGD   DESC   ORTH   CHIS   KS2S   MANW
                160772. 277854. 513453. 1921008. 355469. 1424119. 1623223.

REFERS TO   BRTT   SIGN   WLCX   CORR   REGN   MURE   FACT
                296020. 2397364. 2905174. 413418. 2262864. 1678405. 752670.

1587(17)   KENDALL M G,TIME SERIES
            GRIFFIN, LONDON, 1973

            SIMPLER THAN BOX+JENKINS - EASIER TO READ

REFERS TO   TIMS
                2523169.

1588(18)   KENDALL M G,MULTIVARIATE ANALYSIS
            GRIFFIN,LONDON,1975,ISBN 0 85264 234 4

            AN EXCELLENT REVIEW OF THE CURRENT STATE OF OPINION ON MULTIVARIATE
            METHODS. DISCUSSES OBJECTIONS TO MAHALONOBIS DISTANCE IN
            DISCRIMINANT ANALYSIS. NOT EXCESSIVELY MATHEMATICAL TREATMENT.
            THE AUTHORS INFORMAL COMMENTS AT THE END OF EACH CHAPTER ARE
            PARTICULARLY VALUABLE.

REFERS TO   MUCA   MUDI   MURE
                1677651. 1677709. 1678405.

1589(19)   LI C C,INTRODUCTION TO EXPERIMENTAL STATISTICS
            MCGRAW-HILL,NEW YORK,1964

            THE MOST DETAILED AND CONVINCING EXPLANATION FOR NON-MATHEMATICIANS
            OF WHAT ANALYSIS OF VARIANCE ACTUALLY DOES.

REFERS TO   ANOV   BKGD
                160772. 277854.

1630(20)   MCCRACKEN D D,A GUIDE TO FORTRAN IV PROGRAMMING
            WILEY,NEW YORK 1972, 2ND EDITION ISBN 0 471 58281 6

            THE BEST AVAILABLE GUIDE TO FORTRAN PROGRAMMING,
            BY THE DOYEN OF COMPUTER PROGRAMMERS.

REFERS TO   FORT
                788420.

1631(21)   MORRIS J, FTEST
            ACM COLLECTED ALGORITHMS, NO 346, 1969

REFERS TO   PROB   SNDF
                2045752. 2410206.

1632(22)   MORRISON D F, MULTIVARIATE STATISTICAL METHODS
            MCGRAW-HILL NY 1967

            MODERATELY MATHEMATICAL - MODERATELY DETAILED TEXT

REFERS TO   MUCA   MUDI   MURE
                1677651. 1677709. 1678405.

1633(23)   MOSTELLER F + ROURKE R E K + THOMAS J R,PROBABILITY WITH STATISTICAL
            APPLICATIONS
            ADDISON-WESLEY,NEW YORK 1974, LCC 74-87039

A THROUGH DISCUSSION OF CLASSICAL PROBABILITY THEORY.
(DOES NOT COVER THE BAYESIAN APPROACH.)

REFERS TO   LOGI   PROB   RAND
           1537859. 2045752. 2253204.

1634(24)   NBS,HANDBOOK OF MATHEMATICAL FUNCTIONS,
            NATIONAL BUREAU OF STANDARDS,WASHINGTON,1965
            (VOLUME 55)

            SOURCE FOR ITERATIVE CALCULATION OF ASSOCIATED PROBABILITY
            OF SNEDECOR F STATISTIC.

REFERS TO   PROB   SNDF
           2045752. 2410206.

1635(25)   NBS,STANDARD DATA ENCRYPTION ALGORITHM
            NATIONAL BUREAU OF STANDARDS, WASHINGTON ,1977
            (FIPS PUBLICATION NO 46 U.S. DEPT OF COMMERCE)

            A STANDARD BIT-WISE DATA ENCRYPTION - ORIGINALLY DESIGNED FOR
            HARDWARE BUT ALSO USABLE FOR SOFTWARE

REFERS TO   CRYP
            421266.

1636(26)   SEARLE S R,MATRIX ALGEBRA FOR THE BIOLOGICAL SCIENCES
            WILEY,NEW YORK 1966   LOC 66-11528

            A GOOD NOT TOO MATHEMATICAL INTRODUCTION TO MATRIX ALGEBRA - WITH
            EMPHASIS ON THE STATISTICAL AND BIOLOGICAL APPLICATIONS.

REFERS TO   ANOV   MATR   MORE
           160772. 1628518. 1678405.

1637(27)   SEARLE S R,LINEAR MODELS
            WILEY,NEW YORK 1971

            A DEFINITIVE STUDY OF NON-ORTHOGONAL DATA ANALYSIS - PESSIMISTIC
            ABOUT ESTIMATION OF MISSING CELLS - DISCUSSES ALTERNATIVE METHODS

REFERS TO   ANOV   BKGD   ORTH   MORE
           160772. 277854. 1921008. 1678405.

1638(28)   SELBY S + SWEET L,SETS RELATIONS AND FUNCTIONS
            MCGRAW-HILL 1963

            CLEAR TEACHING TEXT ON BASIC LOGIC

REFERS TO   LOGI
           1537859.

1639(29)   SIEGEL S,NON-PARAMETRIC STATISTICS
            MCGRAW-HILL, NEW YORK 1956

            A SYSTEMATICALLY-ORGANISED, USER-ORIENTED TEXT. VERY WIDELY USED,
            BUT NOW APPROACHING OBSOLESCENCE. (THE CC-3 OF NON-PARAMETRIC
            STATISTICS.) THE BASIS FOR MOST NON-PARAMETRIC STATISTICS IN THIS
            SYSTEM. (TREATMENT OF MULTIPLE TIES IS NOT ALWAYS CORRECT.)

REFERS TO   CHIN   CHIS   KENT   KS2S   KW1W   MANW   MEDT
           395464. 395464. 1588220. 1424119. 1434073. 1628223. 1637720.
REFERS TO   SIGN   WLCX
           2397864. 2905174.

1680(30)   STILSON D W,PROBABILITY + STATISTICS IN PSYCHOLOGICAL RESEARCH +
            THEORY,HOLDEN-DAY,SAN FRANCISCO,1966,LOC 66-11141

            GOOD NON-TECHNICAL DISCUSSION OF ORIGINS OF PROBABILITY AND OF
            LOGIC

```
REFERS TO          LOGI      PROB      RAND
                   1537859.  2045757.  2253204.

1681(  31)   SPIEGEL M R, THEORY AND PROBLEMS OF STATISTICS
             SCHAUM (OUTLINE SERIES) N Y USA, 1961

             A GOOD CHEAP GUIDE TO DESCRIPTIVE STATISTICS + BASIC ANALYSIS

REFERS TO          CHIS      DESC.     DIST      REGN      CORR
                   395469.   513453.   523470.   2262864.  413418.

1682(  32)   VELDMANN D J, FORTRAN PROGRAMMING FOR THE BEHAVIOURAL SCIENCES
             HOLT RINEHART AND WINSTON, NEW YORK 1967 , LOC 67-11808

             CLEAR BEGINNERS GUIDE TO STATISTICAL PROGRAMMING - FORTRAN USES
             NON-STANDARD AND OBSOLESCENT FEATURES.

REFERS TO          DESC      FORT      SNDF      MURE      FACT      MUDI      MUCA
                   513453.   788420.   2410206.  1678405.  752670.   1677709.  1677651.

REFERS TO          MATR
                   1628518.

1683(  33)   WINER B J, STATISTICAL PRINCIPLES IN EXPERIMENTAL DESIGN
             MCGRAW-HILL, NEW YORK 1970

             A VALUABLE TEXTBOOK FOR EXPERIMENTAL DESIGN AND FOR THE ANALYSIS OF
             VARIANCE WITH PROPORTIONAL NUMBERS OF CELLS.

REFERS TO          ANOV      BRTT      ORTH      RESI
                   160772.   296020.   1921008.  2263459.
```

SUBJECT / REFERENCE INDEX

ANALYSIS OF VARIANCE 7,16,19,26,27,33
BACKGROUND READING 3,7,8,16,19,27
BARTLETT TEST 7,16,33
CHI-SQUARED TEST FOR INDEPENDENCE 29
                  FOR SAMPLE DIFFERENCES 7,16,29,31
CONTEXT 1
CORRELATION 16,31
CRYPTOGRAPHY FOR DATA PROTECTION 10,25
DESCRIPTIVE STATISTICS 7,11,16,31,32
DISTRIBUTIONS 11,31
FACTOR ANALYSIS 16,32
FORTRAN 2,20,32
KENDALL TAU STATISTIC 12,15,29
KOLMOGOROV-SMIRNOV TWO SAMPLE TEST 12,16,29
KRUSKALL-WALLIS ONE-WAY ANALYSIS OF VARIANCE BY RANK 29
LOGIC 14,23,28,30
MANN-WHITNEY TEST 12,16,29
MATRIX ALGEBRA 26,32
MEDIAN TEST 29
MULTIPLE CANONICAL CORRELATION 18,22,32
MULTIPLE DISCRIMINANT ANALYSIS 18,22,32
MULTIPLE REGRESSION ANALYSIS 8,16,18,22,26,27,32
ORTHOGONALITY 16,27,33
PACKAGES 3,9
PROBABILITY 13,21,23,24,30
RANDOMNESS 6,10,23,30
REGRESSION 7,8,16,31
RESIDUALS 8,33
SIGN TEST 16,29
SNEDECOR F TEST 7,21,24,32
SOUNDEX CODE 4
STUDENT T TEST 7
TIME SERIES 5,17
T FOR RELATED SAMPLES 7
WILCOXON TEST 12,16,29